# North Carolina Real Estate

## Principles & Practices

Sixth Edition

Nancy F. Keck

Anne Rasheed

THOMSON
SOUTH-WESTERN

Australia · Canada · Mexico · Singapore · Spain · United Kingdom · United States

THOMSON
SOUTH-WESTERN™

**North Carolina Real Estate: Principles and Practices, Sixth Edition**
Nancy F. Keck and Anne Rasheed

**VP/Editorial Director:**
Jack W. Calhoun

**VP/Editor-in-Chief:**
Dave Shaut

**Executive Editor:**
Scott Person

**Associate Acquisitions Editor:**
Sara Glassmeyer

**Developmental Editor:**
Arlin Kauffman, LEAP

**Sr. Marketing Manager:**
Mark Linton

**Content Project Manager:**
Diane Bowdler

**Marketing Communications Manager:**
Jim Overly

**Sr. Technology Project Editor:**
Matt McKinney

**Sr. Manufacturing Coordinator:**
Charlene Taylor

**Production House:**
International Typesetting and Composition

**Art Director:**
Linda Helcher

**Internal Designer:**
Patti Hudepohl

**Cover Designer:**
Grannan Graphic Design

**Printer:**
West Group
Eagan, MN



Printed in the United States of America
2 3 4 5 09 08 07

Student Edition ISBN 13:
978-0-324-40091-5

Student Edition ISBN 10:
0-324-40091-8



For more information about our products, contact us at:

Thomson Learning Academic Resource Center
1-800-423-0563

**Thomson Higher Education**
5191 Natorp Boulevard
Mason, OH 45040
USA

# Brief Contents



FOR A COMPLETE TABLE OF CONTENTS, SEE PAGE IV.

# Contents

# Preface

*North Carolina Real Estate: Principles & Practices,* Sixth Edition, provides the knowledge that is fundamental to a successful career in real estate. This text blends information regarding national laws and concepts with information specific to North Carolina statutes, principles, and practices. The subject matter and study materials are based on the North Carolina Real Estate Pre-license Course Syllabus.

We have made every effort to present step-by-step explanations and to offer guidance regarding the most effective use of this material. Each chapter begins with *key terms* and *learning objectives* and concludes with a *summary of important points,* which reviews the chapter's key ideas in a succinct list that facilitates review. Most chapters also include *review questions* to allow students to self-test and a useful section of *items to consider for the state exam*, designed to focus students' *preparation for the North Carolina State Licensing Exam.* Finally, a complete *diagnostic test* and a sample *pactice exam* in the appendixes will furnish students with the opportunity to practice for a successful outcome on the licensing exam.

Although this text prepares students for licensing, passing the licensing exam is only the first step in a career in real estate. A central theme in this text is the need for a high degree of competence and responsibility in those practicing in all fields of the profession.

## ABOUT THE AUTHORS

**Nancy Keck.** Nancy Keck has been a real estate broker for 23 years; she is the Owner/Broker-in-Charge of Houser Associates Real Estate, Inc. in Goldsboro, NC. Nancy received an Associate Degree in Nursing from Sacred Heart College, a BSPA from St. Joseph's College and an M.A. from Central Michigan University. She taught real estate part-time for over fifteen years while managing her real estate company and listing and selling real estate. Nancy holds CRB, CRS, CRP and GRI designations. Nancy has served on the North Carolina Real Estate Commission's Exam Review Committee. She has previously served as president of the Goldsboro/Wayne County Association of REALTORS® and been selected REALTOR® of the year by the Association.

**Anne Rasheed.** Anne Rasheed is a Broker/Partner at Lenmark Properties Inc. located in Boone, North Carolina. Anne received her BSBA in Real Estate from Appalachian State University. She has been an approved real estate instructor since 1989. In 2003 she received the NCREEA Instructor of the Year Award and was also the recipient of the first ever Billie J. Mercer Excellence in Education Award. She has developed and taught continuing education electives throughout North Carolina and has also served on the North Carolina Real Estate Commission's Exam Review Committee. Anne would like to express her deep appreciation to Kimberly A. Cornell for her assistance in proofing and updating the entire textbook. Ms. Cornell is an honors graduate of the University of Florida. She is a North Carolina Broker and a licensed CPA.

## ACKNOWLEDGMENTS

I would like to express my sincere appreciation to Larry Outlaw, Patricia Moylan, and the North Carolina Real Estate Commission staff who reviewed this text and offered suggestions toward its improvement.

Many other individuals contributed to this new edition of the text. I am deeply indebted to the following people for their review of or assistance with sections of the text corresponding to their areas of expertise: Jack Edwards (law), Elaine Wilcox (finance), Walter J. Pikul (tax), and David Littleton (valuation). I would also like to thank Oscar Agurs for his insightful review of this edition. Their work and time are much appreciated.

This edition would not have been possible without the professional guidance and expertise of Sara Glassmeyer, Associate Acquisitions Editor for Thomson South-Western, and Arlin Kauffman. My heartfelt thanks to my husband Hal and my family; my office staff, Martha Pate, Deane Bernel, Laurie Keck: and my sister and business partner, Mary Sullivan. I am deeply grateful for their patience, support, and assistance throughout this project. Finally, for your continued support, my sincere thanks to each of you who uses this text.

*Nancy F. Keck*

# Preparing for the Real Estate Licensing Exam

North Carolina prepares its own examination for the licensing of real estate agents. This is good news for students in this state because the Real Estate Commission publishes a booklet that provides exact details of the examination process. Additionally, only topics relevant to North Carolina are tested on the examination. Therefore, applicants do not need to be concerned with practices and procedures in other states that may be different from theirs.

## COMMISSION LICENSE INFORMATION BOOKLET

The information booklet of the North Carolina Real Estate Commission, entitled "Real Estate Licensing in North Carolina," is referred to in this text as the Booklet. The Booklet has all the relevant information for the state exam, including an outline of the application process, a format of exam questions, an outline of the exam topics, and the exam application form.

The Booklet is updated frequently to reflect changes in the statutes and Commission Rules. The most current copy at time of publication is printed in its entirety in Appendix A of this text. To obtain the latest information contained in the Booklet, go to **www.ncrec. state. nc.us** and click on "Apply for License" to only order the booklet with application form. Click on "Publications" to read and/or order the booklet. There you can view the Booklet as well as request the necessary application form. You can also request a copy of the Booklet from the Commission at the following address:

North Carolina Real Estate Commission
P. O. Box 17100
Raleigh, N.C. 27619–7100
919/875-3700

# QUESTION FORMAT

The questions on the state exam are multiple choice. There are several basic formats, as illustrated in the following examples. An asterisk (*) indicates the correct answer.

1. *Direct question.*
   Real property includes which of the following?
   A. automobiles
   B. land*
   C. contracts
   D. notes

2. *Exception.*
   All of the following are physical characteristics of land EXCEPT:
   A. mobility*
   B. permanence
   C. indestructibility
   D. nonhomogeneity

3. *Roman numeral format with two numerals.*
   Which of the following statements is (are) correct?
   I. The listing broker is the agent of the seller.
   II. The listing broker may not misrepresent the property to the buyer.
   A. I only
   B. II only
   C. both I and II*
   D. neither I nor II

# EXAMINATION CONTENT, PREREQUISITES, AND TESTING INFORMATION

The North Carolina Real Estate Commission Booklet, "Licensing in North Carolina," provides comprehensive information to guide you through the licensing process from qualification, application, examination, to issuance of licenses and requirements for maintaining or reinstating your license. You should be thoroughly familiar with the booklet before applying for a license.

Before you can apply to take the state licensing examination, North Carolina requires the completion of a 75-hour broker pre-licensing course including passing the course examination. The passing requirement for the 110 questions state examination is 75 percent. There are 5 additional unscored test questions interspersed with the scored questions. North Carolina is a single license state; that is, it has only one category of license and one type of license exam. Although only broker exams are given and only broker licenses are issued, a newly licensed broker has a provisional status on his or her license until he or she successfully completes the three 30-hour broker post-licensing courses and passes the course exams. See "Continuing Education" for post-licensing education requirements.

The real estate examination is administered via computer at several sites in North Carolina. In addition to the license application fee, you pay an examination fee directly to the company contracted by the Commission to administer the exam. If you pass the licensing examination, you are not allowed a review. If you fail the examination, you may immediately review the examination at the testing center.

## TEST REGULATIONS

To ensure fair and equitable testing conditions, the Commission requires observance of the following regulations at the test center.

1. In the testing area, applicants may bring only the following: a wallet, two forms of identification (one of which is a photo ID) bearing the applicant's signature, eyeglasses, medications, personal hygiene products, a coat or sweater, and a calculator.
2. The exam proctor will provide all applicants with scratch paper and pencils before the exam.
3. Applicants may take breaks of 10 minutes or less *in the designated break areas or in the restroom*. Only one male and one female applicant are permitted to take a restroom break at a time.
4. All applicants have a maximum of four hours to complete the test.
5. No telephones, PDAs, computers, or other communication devices are allowed in the testing area.
6. All calculators must be silent and handheld, must not be programmable, and must not allow entry of words. Applicants may not share calculators.
7. Applicants must arrive on time at the testing center. Late applicants will forfeit their application and examination fees.

## TAKING THE EXAMINATION

The following suggestions should prove beneficial when you take the licensing examination.

1. Continue to study after you have completed your prelicensing course until you take the examination.
2. Take the following items to the test:
   a. calculator with an extra set of fresh batteries (calculators must not be programmable or permit the entry or retrieval of words)
   b. two forms of identification with signature. One must be a photo ID (review Commission booklet for specific requirements).
   c. a watch
3. Read each question and all answer choices carefully before selecting an answer. Be sure you know what the question is asking.
4. Skip questions that are long and involved, as well as questions you do not know the answer to, and come back to them later. The computer allows you to skip a question by going to the next item or marking the question for later review. Review the test to make sure you answered all the questions. Remember, a blank answer is a wrong answer.
5. Be alert to certain words that may determine the correct answer, for example, *must* and *may*, *always* and *never*, *can* and *cannot*, *not* and *except*.
6. Be alert for the suffixes *or* and *ee*. The *or* (as in *grantor*) gives the paper; the *ee* (as in *grantee*) receives it.
7. Avoid jumping to conclusions; study all of the given information to see what information is relevant and what is not.
8. Do not make hasty or snap decisions on an item. You may miss a key term or a piece of information by scanning the item too quickly.
9. Do not change an answer you have selected unless you are positive your first selection was incorrect.
10. After you have answered all questions that you are sure of, go back over the examination and answer questions that you skipped. Questions not answered will be considered incorrect. Therefore, you should make an educated guess after eliminating the choices you are certain are incorrect.

## CONTINUING EDUCATION

To renew licenses on active status, 8 hours of real estate continuing education is required annually for all real estate licensees. Of those, 4 hours must be a "mandatory update course." The additional 4 hours are chosen from a variety of elective courses. The elective, but not the update, courses may be taken online. If more than 4 hours of electives are earned, up to 4 hours of electives can be carried over to the following year. Continuing education is not required to renew on inactive status; however, certain continuing education requirements must be met before the license is placed back on active status.

A newly licensed broker with provisional status must complete three 30-hour broker post-licensing courses. (These courses do not substitute for continuing education requirements; therefore, 8 hours of continuing education is required annually after the first license renewal in addition to the required post-licensing courses.) At least one course must be completed by the first anniversary of licensing. At least two courses must be completed by the second anniversary and all three by the third anniversary. All three courses may be completed in the first or second year; however, at least one must be completed in each of the first two years in order to maintain the license on active status. Failure to complete one course during the first year or two courses by the end of two years will cause the license to be placed on inactive status until the deficiencies are corrected. Failure to complete all three courses before the third anniversary will cause the license to be cancelled.

The unlicensed former broker may be required to re-take the pre-licensing course and repeat the entire licensing procedure if he wishes to obtain another N.C. Real Estate Broker License. A provisional broker cannot be a broker-in-charge. Even if a new broker completes all three courses in the first or second year, thereby removing the provisional status, he cannot become a BIC until he has the requisite two years of experience under the supervision of a BIC. See the Booklet for other BIC requirements including specific BIC continuing education.

## LEARNING TOOLS: THE COMPLETE PROGRAM

### *The Text*

This easy-to-read text offers all the information you need to prepare for your licensing exam and a successful career in real estate, including a **chapter-by-chapter diagnostic exam (Appendix D) and a 107-question practice exam (Appendix E).**

### *The Interactive Software Tutorial*

*Preparing for the State Real Estate Licensing Examination* Provided are 600-plus questions cross-referenced to this text by chapter and page number; you will know exactly where to check to restudy an incorrect answer. The tutorial includes explanations of correct and incorrect responses for each question. You can take chapter quizzes and practice for your North Carolina licensing test with a timed comprehensive exam.

# North Carolina Real Estate

## Principles & Practices

# Chapter 1

## KEY TERMS

bill of sale
chattel
closing
free market
highest and best use
immobility
improvements
indestructibility
land use controls
listing contract
nonhomogeneity
offer to purchase and contract
personal property
personalty
real estate
real property
REALTOR®
realty
scarcity
situs
specific performance

## LEARNING OBJECTIVES

At the conclusion of this chapter, you should be able to:

1. Describe the characteristics of real estate, including classes of property, physical characteristics of land, and economic characteristics of land.
2. Describe the concepts of land use and investment, including highest and best use, land use controls, investment objectives, scope of the real estate business, and the real estate market.

# Basic Real Estate Concepts

## IN THIS CHAPTER

This text is designed to help you master the fundamentals of real estate by introducing information in a step-by-step format that requires no real estate background. This chapter is an overview of the entire real estate business. Each topic introduced here is discussed in more detail in the following chapters.

You should use this chapter to become familiar with the format of the book, including objectives, summary of important points, and questions. Each of these sections is designed to help you study the material efficiently in order to master the information. Finally, we offer advice on preparation for the North Carolina Real Estate Licensing Examination.

## GENERAL CHARACTERISTICS OF REAL ESTATE

Real property has certain physical and economic characteristics that set it apart from other marketable commodities. These characteristics are so interrelated that they have a definite effect on one another and are sometimes difficult to separate in a practical sense. This chapter discusses these characteristics and their effects on real property value.

### Classes of Property

**Real estate** or **real property** or **realty** (these terms are, for most purposes, interchangeable) consists of *land and everything that is permanently attached to land.* Land is but one component of these terms. *Land* is, therefore, less inclusive and should not be used interchangeably with the other terms. Ownership in land includes not only the surface of the earth but also the area below the surface to the center of the earth and the area above the surface, theoretically, to the highest heavens. These three aspects of ownership in any specific tract or parcel of land—surface, subsurface, and air rights—are separable. The owner of the land may retain the ownership of the surface but may sell or lease the mineral rights below the surface and/or the air rights above the surface. All structures and other **improvements,** such as *fences, swimming pools, flagpoles, driveways,* and *walkways,* as well as things growing naturally in the soil without cultivation, are included in the definition of real estate. The property owner, when conveying the title to the property, conveys all aspects of real estate unless there is a prior agreement to exempt some portion of the real estate from the conveyance. Title to real property is evidenced by deed.

The only category of property defined in law other than real property is **personal property,** also called **chattel** or **personalty.** From the definition of real property, you can see that personal property *is everything that is not land or that is not permanently attached to land. Personal property is readily movable.* A **bill of sale** is an *instrument that may be used to transfer ownership of personal property.* Property can begin as personal property and become real property when attached to the land. For example, a gas grill that begins as a separate item of personal property may then be affixed to the property and later sold as part of the real property. The test used to determine if an item is real or personal property is discussed in Chapter 2.

## Physical Characteristics of Land

### *Immobility*

An essential physical characteristic of land (Figure 1.1) is its **immobility.** That *land cannot be relocated from one place to another* is an obvious feature of land as a commodity and is the primary distinguishing feature between land and personal property. The physical characteristic of immobility is the reason the economic characteristic of location significantly affects land value, making the market for land a strictly local market. This local aspect of the real estate market requires brokers and agents to have specific knowledge of their local real estate market to serve buyers and sellers in their respective market areas.

### *Permanence (Indestructibility)*

Another unique feature of land is its physical characteristic of **indestructibility.** *Land is a permanent commodity, and it cannot be destroyed.* It may be altered substantially in its topography or other aspects of its appearance, but its geographic coordinates remain. Land values can change positively or negatively as a result of changing conditions in the surrounding area and are said to suffer from *economic obsolescence* when such changes adversely affect the value of land. For example, the construction of an interstate highway can radically affect land values. Do not confuse economic obsolescence with physical depreciation, which is a loss in value from deterioration of the improvements on the property itself (see Chapter 9).

The permanence or indestructibility of land makes it attractive as a long-term investment, but an investor should be alert to changing conditions that can affect the value of the investment.

### *Uniqueness (Nonhomogeneity)*

An important feature of the land is that no two parcels are identical, in either a physical or a legal sense. For example, land is very different from two cars that come off an assembly line. Two cars may be nearly identical, and one could be substituted for the other; this is clearly not the case with real estate. Even two apparently identical adjoining parcels differ in aspects such as soil, drainage, view, and vegetation, to name just a few.

This *uniqueness,* or **nonhomogeneity,** of each parcel of land gives rise to the concept of **specific performance.** *If a seller contracts to sell her real property, the law does not consider money a substitute for this duty.* Thus, if a seller tried to breach the contract and pay financial damages instead, *the buyer could refuse to accept the money and insist on taking title to the land as the only acceptable performance of the contract.* For example, one might sign a purchase agreement for a home in a particular neighborhood because it was next to friends, family, or schools. If the seller changed her mind and offered another, better home on the other side of town, the buyer could hold the seller to specific performance of the original contract for the unique advantages of that property.

**FIGURE 1.1**
Physical characteristics of land

1. Immobility
2. Permanence
3. Uniqueness

## Economic Characteristics of Land

### *Scarcity*

An important economic characteristic of real property (Figure 1.2) is its availability or **scarcity.** Land is a commodity that has a fixed supply base. No additional physical supply of land is being produced to keep pace with the ever-increasing population. However, the problems created by an ever-increasing demand for the limited supply of land have been substantially eased by the increase in the economic supply of land. This increase has come about as a result of the greater utilization of the existing physical supply of land. Farmers are continuing to increase the use of land in the agricultural area. Greater crop yields per acre are being achieved as a result of scientific and technological advances. Today the agricultural industry is producing more cattle per acre and more bushels of crops per acre than it did just a few years ago.

In urban areas, land is being utilized to a greater extent through high-density development. Advances in science and technology result in the creation of high-rise office buildings, apartment complexes, and multilevel shopping centers. Consequently, one acre of land serves many times the number of people who could use the land in the absence of these improvements.

**Modification by improvement.** Another factor that has increased the *economic supply* of land has been the construction of highways, bridges, water reservoirs, purification plants, and public utilities. The improvements and expansions of public air and land transportation systems also make a significant contribution in this regard. These accomplishments in the fields of construction and transportation have converted land that had not been accessible and useful in a practical sense into land that can now be used. A substantial increase in the economic supply of land has resulted from these improvements *to* the land (rather than improvements *on* the land).

### *Permanence of Investment*

Because of the physical characteristics of immobility and indestructibility of land, the investment of capital and labor to create improvements to the land and improvements on the land is a long-term investment. Many years are required to recoup the investment made to improve the value and quality of land. If a developer misjudges the demand for land-specific improvements or if economic conditions, including real estate market conditions, change dramatically, the developer may never recoup his full investment.

### *Location (Situs)*

The *location of land,* or **situs,** is an extremely important economic (or more precisely, socioeconomic) characteristic of land, and it is the characteristic that has the greatest effect on property value. The physical characteristic of immobility dictates that the location of a parcel of land is permanent. Therefore, if the land is located in an area where demand is high, the land will have a substantially increasing value. Conversely, if the land is inaccessible from a practical standpoint or is located in an area with little or no demand, its economic value will be depressed.

Although the location of land cannot be changed, the value of the location (and consequently, the value of the land) can be increased by improvements to access and other modifications. Additionally, the value of the location can change as the result of the changes in preferences of people. In the 1950s there was a great flight from the urban centers to the suburbs. This resulted in property value reductions in urban areas. This trend has moderated in recent years. People are rediscovering the inner cities, rehabilitating older properties, and restoring lost urban property values.

1. Scarcity
2. Permanence of investment
3. Location

**FIGURE 1.2**
Economic characteristics of real property.

# GENERAL CONCEPTS OF LAND USE AND INVESTMENT

## The Highest and Best Use Concept

The concept of **highest and best use** is of extreme importance and considers all the physical and economic factors affecting the land. The highest and best use of land is *that use which will provide the property owner the best possible return on an investment over a specified time period, resulting in the highest possible present value of land. Present value* is defined as the value at the time of the appraisal; therefore, highest and best use can and does change with time. The use must be legal and must comply with zoning ordinances, government regulations, legally enforceable private deed restrictions, and restrictive covenants. The highest and best use of land is attained by the intelligent use of capital, labor, and other resources to improve the land and its productivity.

The task of coordinating and combining capital, labor, and resources to create an improvement is performed by an expert in real estate. The expert may be an individual developer or may be a general partner in a limited partnership with the other investors providing the capital as limited partners. The expert must determine the use of the land that will provide the necessary income from the land after labor and capital have been paid. For example, the expert will establish the optimum size of a building to be constructed on a particular site. The space should not be overimproved or underimproved. The building must not contain more space than can be rented in the market, nor should it fail to provide the space that the market demands. An overimprovement or an underimprovement does not provide the optimum income to the land, and as a result, the land is not put to its highest and best possible use.

There is only one highest and best use for a particular parcel of land at any particular time. The loss of residual income to the land resulting from failure to employ the land to its highest and best use causes the value of the property to diminish.

## Public and Private Land Use Restrictions

Even though most land in the United States is privately owned, there is a vested public interest in land because the type of property use affects surrounding property owners and the general public. Because of this interest of the general public and of other property owners, the use of land requires regulation for the benefit of all. The need for **land use controls** has existed since the country's founding. This is especially true in areas of very dense population, where land uses radically affect a great number of people.

*Public land use controls exist in the form of city planning and zoning, state and regional planning, building codes, suitability for occupancy requirements, and environmental control laws.* Additionally, there is substantial public control of land use as a result of government ownership. Examples of government ownership include public buildings, public parks, watersheds, streets, and highways.

Regulation of land use in the private sector exists in the form of *protective* or *restrictive covenants* established by developers, restrictions in individual deeds (private deed restrictions) requiring the continuation of a specified land use or prohibiting a specified land use, and use restrictions imposed on a lessee in a lease contract.

## Real Estate Investment Objectives

Real estate investors come in many varieties, ranging from the individual who buys one rundown property and fixes it up for resale or rental to the individuals or corporations who buy large commercial complexes such as shopping centers and factories.

The primary purpose of any investment is to produce income or profit, balancing the profit the investor desires against the risk he is willing to take. Real estate offers the opportunity to make a profit in three ways: appreciation, positive cash flow, and tax advantage.

*Appreciation* is the increase in market value during the time the investor holds the property. If an investor buys a property for $100,000 and it increases 3 percent in value annually and he holds the property for ten years, the property will have appreciated to a value of $134,391.46.

A *positive cash flow* exists when the gross effective income produced by the property exceeds the total expense. (See Chapter 9, Property Valuation, for the discussion of gross effective income and expense.)

*Tax advantages* may result from appreciation or gains being taxed at a capital gain rate lower than the investor's marginal tax rate when the property is sold and from deductions of property taxes, insurance, and other expenses during the time the investor owns the property. Depreciation may provide an annual tax reduction, postponing the tax on the depreciated amount until the property is sold.

While appreciation, positive cash flow, and tax advantage are ways to make money on real estate investments, leverage allows more money to be made on less investment. For a simplified example, suppose an investor buys a $100,000 property with an initial investment of $10,000 for down payment and closing costs. The property appreciates $3,000 the first year, has a positive before-tax cash flow of $50 a month, and produces a tax savings of $400 for the year. This $4,000 is only 4 percent of $100,000, which is not a very good return on an investment. However, it is 40 percent of $10,000, which is an excellent return on an investment.

An investment analysis to determine the return on investment can be relatively simple, such as the gross rent multiplier or capitalization rate discussed in Chapter 9. It can also be a highly sophisticated internal rate of return, considering virtually all factors involved in the investment. Some of the factors, which are beyond the scope of this text, are the time value of money, the investor's marginal tax rate, the costs of acquiring and disposing of the property, and debt service.

Real estate, like any investment, has risks. The real estate's market value can decline, the property can deteriorate, or the area surrounding the property can change, adversely affecting the property value. Rent or income may not meet expectations. Plants or military installations nearby can close. An "oil glut" can change to an "oil bust," leaving an overabundance of office space, homes, and so on. Environmental problems may adversely affect the property. If any of these things occurs, the effect may be compounded by the real estate's lack of liquidity. The investor most likely cannot sell the property instantly for its full value.

Real estate practitioners, in order to serve their clients and themselves well, may further their real estate investment knowledge through the REALTORS® Institute, the REALTORS® National Marketing Institute (RNMI), and Commercial-Investment Real Estate Institute (CIREI). See Figure 1.3 for designations offered through these organizations. Although these programs teach the practitioner to gather and analyze market data using a form, such as the annual property operating data form or a computer program, the practitioner should refer the investor to competent legal and accounting advisors.

## SCOPE OF THE REAL ESTATE BUSINESS

The real estate business is extensive in scope and is a complex industry. Usually, when people think of the real estate business, they think only of residential brokerage. This is just one of several specializations within the real estate business, however. In fact, within the field of brokerage, there are several specializations, including farm and land brokerage, residential property brokerage, and commercial and investment property brokerage. In addition to brokerage, other specializations in real estate include property management, appraising, financing, construction, property development, real estate education, and government service.

Real estate transactions can be traced to early written records from biblical times, but those transactions were between seller and buyer directly, without the participation of a real estate broker. The business of real estate brokerage is a product of the twentieth century. In the early 1900s, states began enacting licensing law legislation, and today all states in the nation require real estate brokers and/or salespeople to be licensed. North Carolina adopted its Real Estate License Law statute in 1957.

The establishment of the National Association of Real Estate Boards in 1908 was a major factor in the development of real estate brokerage. During the 1970s, the name of this trade group was changed to the National Association of REALTORS® (NAR). The

**FIGURE 1.3**

Some of the many real estate institutes, societies, and councils, together with their related designations.

**NATIONAL ASSOCIATION OF REALTORS®**

REALTOR® Institute
- —Graduate, REALTOR® Institute (GRI)
- —Certified International Property Specialist (CIPS)

The Counselors of Real Estate
- —Counselor of Real Estate (CRE®)

Commercial-Investment Real Estate Institute (CIREI)
- —Certified Commercial-Investment Member (CCIM)

Institute of Real Estate Management (IREM)
- —Accredited Management Organization® (AMO®)
- —Accredited Residential Manager® (ARM®)
- —Certified Property Manager® (CPM®)

REALTORS® Land Institute (RLI)
- —Accredited Land Consultant (ALC®)

REALTORS® NATIONAL MARKETING INSTITUTE (RNMI®)
- —Real Estate Brokerage Council: Certified Real Estate Brokerage Manager (CRB®)
- —Residential Sales Council: Certified Residential Specialist (CRS®)

Society of Industrial and Office REALTORS® (SIOR®)
- —Professional Real Estate Executive (P.R.E.)

Women's Council of REALTORS® (WCR)
- —Leadership Training Graduate (LTG)

Real Estate BUYER'S AGENT Council (REBAC)
- —Accredited Buyer Representative (ABR®)

REAL ESTATE APPRAISAL
- —General Accredited Appraiser (GAA)
- —Residential Accredited Appraiser (RAA)

**NATIONAL ASSOCIATION OF RESIDENTIAL PROPERTY MANAGERS**

Residential Property Managers (RPM)

Master Property Managers (MPM)

Certified Residential Management Company (CRMC)

**APPRAISAL INSTITUTE®**

MAI—Appraisers experienced in commercial and industrial properties

SRA—Appraisers experienced in residential income properties

term **REALTOR®** *is a registered trademark of NAR, and it identifies licensees who are also members of the local, the state, and the national association.*

It is important to remember that all licensees are not REALTORS® and that only the active members of these associations may use the term REALTOR® or REALTOR ASSOCIATE®. One of the most important accomplishments of the National Association of REALTORS® and its predecessor organization was the creation of a Code of Ethics in

1913. This code has contributed significantly to the professional stature of real estate brokerage. There are strong parallels between the licensing laws and this original Code of Ethics.

Other significant contributions of the National Association of REALTORS® include efforts that have resulted in licensing laws being enacted in all states, legislative activity on the federal level to prevent unnecessary and harmful legislation from diminishing rights of private ownership in real property, and excellent programs of continuing education for members and nonmembers through NAR and its affiliated organizations.

Relocation is a growing part of the real estate business. A vast relocation network exists. Many corporations offer transferring employees generous relocation packages, including paying the closing costs for selling old homes and purchasing new homes. Some corporations have in-house relocation departments to assist employees with every aspect of their move. Others contract with third-party relocation companies to provide these services. Many corporations, relocation companies, real estate brokerage firms, appraisers, attorneys, and others who work with relocation belong to the Employees Relocation Council (ERC), which provides networking, research, education, and so on, to its members. In-depth coverage of relocation is beyond the scope of the text, however, new agents are advised to become familiar with the wants, needs, and expectations of relocating individuals, families, and employers, as well as relocation companies.

Real estate brokerage is the bringing together of buyers and sellers or landlords and tenants for the temporary or permanent transfer of an interest in real property owned by others through purchase, sale, lease, or rental by a real estate broker for compensation. In North Carolina, such brokerage activities require a North Carolina broker's license.

The fact that real estate represents a growing percentage of the wealth in the United States illustrates the extremely broad scope and importance of the real estate business. The complexity of this business requires that agents have continual interaction with people in a variety of other professions. Today's real estate practitioner needs a basic knowledge of the many functions performed by other members of the real estate and allied professions.

Real estate professionals must work with mortgage bankers or brokers to secure financing for their clients; appraisers to validate the value of the property; home inspectors and wood-destroying insect inspectors to determine the condition of the property; developers and contractors when selling new construction; attorneys, surveyors, and insurance agents when closing properties; and governmental officials such as tax assessors, environmental health specialists, and city and county planners when necessary.

Successful real estate practitioners are also counselors and educators who must recognize the limits of their knowledge and guard against giving legal, accounting, or tax advice.

## The Real Estate Market

A **free market** is *one in which the buyer and seller negotiate a purchase and sale without undue pressure, urgency, or outside influence other than the principle of supply and demand.* Although government regulations may indirectly affect the price of real estate or the costs of borrowing money to buy real estate, the government does not set real estate prices. The principle of supply and demand determines real estate prices; thus, the real estate market is an excellent example of the free market concept. Market value, which is discussed in Chapter 9, depends on the free market concept.

### *Special Characteristics*

The physical characteristics of land create special characteristics of the real estate market that do not exist in other markets. As noted previously, the immobility of real estate causes the market to be local in character, requiring local specialists who are currently familiar with local market conditions, property values, and availability. The nonhomogeneity, or uniqueness, of each parcel of real estate also requires that the market be local. Each parcel of real estate is unique, primarily because of its location.

The physical characteristic of immobility also results in a market that is slow to react to changes in supply and demand. When supply substantially exceeds demand, existing properties cannot be withdrawn from a local market area and relocated to an area in which there is a higher demand. Conversely, when the demand exceeds supply, new supplies of housing and business properties cannot be constructed quickly. Therefore, after a recession, it takes many months for the supply to equal or exceed demand in the real estate market.

### *Factors Affecting Supply and Demand*

Several factors affect supply and demand in the real estate market, on both the local and national levels. Examples of these factors include interest rates; availability of financing for purchase and construction; population migrations; variations in population trends and family formations; government regulations; local and national economic conditions; and the availability and cost of building sites, construction materials, and labor.

### *Historical Trends*

Just as the economy as a whole is subject to peaks and valleys of activity that have recurred over the years with fairly reasonable regularity, the real estate industry, as a part of this economy, is also subjected to recurring periods of recession and prosperity.

The real estate industry is often the first industry to feel the adverse effects of depressed conditions in the national and local economies. It may also take the real estate industry longer than the economy as a whole to climb out of a recession because of the inability of the real estate industry to react quickly to radical changes in supply and demand. But that is not always the case. In recent times, real estate has sometimes remained strong during a recession or led the recovery from an economic downturn.

Another characteristic of the real estate cycle is that the real estate industry usually attains a much higher level of activity in prosperous times than does the economy in general.

## The Real Estate Practitioner

North Carolina defines only one real estate license category, broker, since it became an all-broker state on April 1, 2006. All individuals or entities who want to engage in real estate brokerage activities in North Carolina must first be licensed as a broker. Many current brokers have received their licenses under previous criteria of either education and experience and the passing of a state examination. Some have been licensed based on education and experience in other states. Those who met the criteria for and were licensed as brokers before April 1, 2006, can remain brokers with no provisional status attached to their licenses. Those who were licensed as salespersons as of that date were automatically licensed as brokers at that time, although with provisional status. Several options are available to these former salespersons to remove the provisional status from their licenses, based on the time of licensure and education and experience. The only option for brokers licensed after April 1, 2006, who have not been granted a broker's license without provisional status by education and experience in another state, is to complete the three thirty-hour post-licensing courses and pass the course exams.

A broker without provisional status is able to practice independently. A broker with attached provisional status is not. He or she must work under the supervision of a broker who is a broker-in-charge (BIC) until he or she has completed all post-licensing requirements to remove the provisional status and to practice independently. A provisional broker cannot become a BIC. A BIC must have a minimum of two years full-time real estate experience which may be met as a broker regardless of provisional status or lack thereof; however, provisional status must be removed prior to becoming a BIC. Although the broker-in-charge is ultimately responsible for all actions of the brokers (agents) he or she supervises, the individual agent cannot escape responsibility for his or her duties and actions.

Real estate brokers, whether provisional or not, are commonly referred to as brokers or agents. The real estate broker-in-charge is the agent of his or her principal. Any brokers under a BIC's supervision, regardless of provisional status or lack thereof, are agents of the BIC and subagents of the broker's principal.

These relationships are discussed extensively in Chapter 5. They are mentioned here only to clarify the terminology used in this text. The word *broker* or *agent* is used when the text is referring to a broker or a provisional broker when differentiation between the two is not required. The terms *broker* and *provisional broker* are used to differentiate the two categories of licensees, when necessary.

The successful real estate practitioner is not engaged in applying techniques of the "hard sell." Rather, she is a counselor or an adviser working diligently to solve the problems of buyers, sellers, and renters of real estate. Everyone who contacts a real estate office has a problem. The problem involves real property—the need to buy, sell, or lease. The real estate practitioner's ability to solve these problems for the benefit of others results in a successful career. Like any good counselor, the real estate practitioner provides information to, but does not make decisions for, the clients and customers. What information can and cannot be provided depends on several factors, but especially on the law of agency, which is discussed in Chapter 5.

A career in real estate can provide the practitioner with satisfaction from serving the needs of people and with accompanying financial rewards. Success in the real estate business is built on knowledge, service to others, and ethical conduct in all dealings.

## Agency Contracts

A **listing contract** is *a contract wherein a property owner employs a real estate broker to market his or her property.* The listing contract is, therefore, an employment contract under which the real estate firm becomes the *agent* of the property owner. Listings are the inventory of a real estate office and are the lifeblood of the business.

Many people misunderstand the relationships defined by the listing contract. An agent and/or a subagent of the seller are employees of the seller. The listing contract does not authorize the agent(s) to bind the seller in a contract to sell the property. The agent's purpose is to find qualified prospective buyers for the property, to present offers from these buyers to the property owner for consideration, and to offer advice. Rules of the Real Estate Commission make it absolutely clear that agents must immediately present all offers to purchase and contract to the seller for a decision. The ability to match qualified buyers with suitable properties enables the real estate agent to solve buyers' and sellers' problems and provide commission income to the firm and to its agents.

Another type of employment contract is a *buyer's brokerage* or *buyer's agency agreement,* in which the real estate broker contracts with the buyer to act as the buyer's agent. If a buyer client wishes to purchase a property listed by a seller client of the same firm, a potential conflict of interest arises. One solution is that the firm become a *disclosed* dual agent.

The buyer's agent and the seller's agent owe all the duties of agency (see Chapter 5) to their respective clients before, during, and after the preparation and acceptance of the offer to purchase. It is imperative that each agent have a thorough understanding of these duties, including what information should and should not be disclosed.

## Offer to Purchase and Contract

*A binding contract to buy and sell real property* results from the communication of a seller's written acceptance of a valid written **offer to purchase and contract** from the buyer or the buyer's written acceptance of a new offer (counteroffer) made by the seller. Real estate practitioners can assist buyers and sellers in the process of making offers and counteroffers by filling in the blanks of an approved preprinted contract form; however, they *cannot* draft a contract.

## Financing

One of the most important aspects of real estate transactions is financing. If the property cannot be financed, it usually cannot be sold. Occasionally a broker will have the good fortune of obtaining a prospective buyer who is able to pay cash for the full purchase price and who does not wish to finance the transaction. This is the exception in the real estate business. The real estate practitioner needs to have a day-to-day working knowledge of the loan programs available from local lending institutions, and he must continually keep in touch with these local lenders and develop a cordial working relationship with them. A new real estate professional should make a point of calling on local mortgage lenders personally to start this mutually supportive relationship. The lender is interested in making loans and in working to make the sales transaction possible, but the real estate agent must know the lender's guidelines to prequalify the transaction. No agent can ever hope to know all of the details of every program in the area, but she does need to know the fundamental guidelines of each program to match these programs to the buyer's needs and to get the financing process started. A broker's knowledge of financing and the use of modern techniques in this area are essential to conclude the sale of a property successfully.

In times of high interest rates, the broker may need to look to the seller for financing because the latter's equity in the property can be a primary source of funds. The broker needs to know when this technique is possible with existing financing, and he needs to have an appreciation of the liabilities this arrangement may place on the seller.

## Final Settlement

The *completion of the real estate transaction occurs at* **closing,** *or final settlement.* This is the time when the buyer receives a deed conveying title to the property, when the seller receives compensation for the sale of the property, and when the real estate practitioner receives a well-earned commission. The real estate professional—along with an attorney, the buyer, the seller, and sometimes a loan officer of a lending institution—is usually present at the closing and is responsible for coordinating the various activities preliminary to closing.

## Other Aspects

In addition to the activities involved in the real estate brokerage business discussed previously, the real estate practitioner must be knowledgeable in a variety of other subjects necessary for satisfactorily performing one's obligations in real estate transactions. These other subjects, which are discussed in depth in later chapters of this text, include property ownership and interests, transfer of title to real property, fundamentals of residential construction, valuation of real estate, land use controls, fair housing laws, property management, insurance, and federal income tax implications of real estate ownership and sale. The real estate practitioner also must understand the meaning of the various real estate and legal terms used in real estate transactions. Finally, the practitioner must have a basic understanding of the various arithmetic problems that are common in the activities of real estate brokerage.

# SUMMARY OF IMPORTANT POINTS

1. Real property includes the surface of the land, all improvements that are attached to the property, the things beneath the surface, and the airspace above the land.
2. Personal property (also called personalty or chattel) is the opposite of real property; that is, everything that is not real property is considered personal property. Things that are readily movable (that is, not attached to the land) are personal property.
3. Real property has the physical characteristics of immobility, permanence, and uniqueness.
4. Real property has unique economic characteristics based on its physical location (situs).
5. The principle of highest and best use of land is an all-important concept in land use. Failure to make the highest and best use of land results in a lower value.
6. Controls of land use are necessary to protect the vested interests of the general public as well as the interests of surrounding landowners. Land use controls can be private,

such as private deed restrictions and restrictive covenants, or public, such as zoning ordinances.

7. The real estate business involves many specialties besides residential brokerage and requires knowledge of many fields, including finance, housing codes, government regulations, contract law, and appraisal.

8. A real estate market is local and is an example of the free market concept wherein buyers and sellers have adequate time and information to reach a purchase and sale agreement without undue pressure and with factual knowledge of all important aspects of the transaction. The physical and economic characteristics of land create a market that is local and slow to react to fluctuations in supply and demand.

9. The effects of depressed economic conditions are sometimes felt by the real estate industry before other segments of the economy. The real estate industry has traditionally been slower to pull out of depressed economic periods, but typically reaches higher peaks of activity and prosperity during prosperous times than many other segments of the economy. In recent times, however, the real estate market has remained strong during a recession and has sometimes led the recovery from an economic downturn.

10. The real estate agent acts as an advisor or problem solver for the benefit of one's clients and customers. Since the purchase of a home involves the seller's most important financial asset and creates long-term financial obligations for the buyer, the agent must be thoroughly knowledgeable, competent, and responsible.

11. Real estate investment offers the opportunity to earn profits through appreciation of the property value, tax advantages, and positive cash flow. Leverage allows an investor to earn a greater return on a smaller initial investment. Some of the risks involved in real estate investments are market value declines, property deterioration, and adverse changes in the surrounding area.

## ITEMS TO CONSIDER FOR THE STATE EXAM

### Defining Broker and REALTOR®

The general public has a poor understanding of the distinction between a broker and a REALTOR®.

North Carolina, through the North Carolina Real Estate Commission, issues only broker licenses, initially with a provisional status until a broker completes the education or experience required to remove the provisional status. A broker without provisional status does not need to be associated with another real estate broker and can practice independently. The provisional broker cannot. He or she must be supervised by a sponsoring broker known as a broker-in-charge (BIC). All brokers, with or without provisional status, may be referred to as brokers. The term REALTOR® designates a licensee who is also a member of the local association of REALTORS® at the city or county level, a state association of REALTORS®, such as the North Carolina Association of REALTORS® (NCAR), and the National Association of REALTORS® (NAR).The REALTOR® association is in no way associated with or regulated by the Real Estate Commission, although the two groups work together for advancement of professionalism in the real estate business.

Not all licensees are REALTORS®. North Carolina has approximately 94,500 active licensees, of whom almost 64,000 are on active status, while the North Carolina Association of REALTORS® (NCAR) has approximately 29,000 members. In addition to being answerable to the Real Estate Commission and to the civil and criminal courts for wrongdoing or failure of duty, the REALTOR® is also accountable under the Code of Ethics to the local association of REALTORS®.

## REVIEW QUESTIONS

Answers to the review questions are in the Answer Key at the back of the book.

1. All of the following are separable ownerships in land EXCEPT:
   A. surface of the land
   B. area below the surface
   C. nonhomogeneity
   D. air rights

2. The characteristic of land that causes the real estate market to be essentially a local market is the physical characteristic of:
   A. indestructibility
   B. immobility
   C. availability
   D. natural features

3. The nonhomogeneity of land:
   A. is the basis for the legal remedy of specific performance
   B. results from the uniqueness of every parcel of real estate
   C. is a physical characteristic of land
   D. all of the above

4. An increase in the economic supply of land has resulted from:
   A. increased utilization of the physical supply of land
   B. modification by improvements to the land
   C. high-density development
   D. all of the above

5. The quality of the location of land and consequently the value of the land can be changed by:
   A. the principle of nonhomogeneity
   B. relocation of the land
   C. changes in the national scope of the real estate business
   D. improvements to the land that result in accessibility not previously available

6. The employment of the concept of highest and best use:
   A. includes consideration of the physical and economic factors affecting land use
   B. results in the greatest present value of the land
   C. must be a use feasible in the near future
   D. all of the above

7. An example of public land use controls is:
   A. restrictive covenants
   B. zoning laws
   C. deed restrictions
   D. protective covenants

8. Real estate investment offers the opportunity to produce a profit in the following ways EXCEPT:
   A. appreciation
   B. positive cash flow
   C. specific performance
   D. tax advantages

9. The physical characteristics of land create a real estate market that has special features not inherent in other markets, including:
   I. the characteristic that the real estate market is slow to react to changes in the supply and demand for real estate
   II. the characteristic of the necessity for local specialists to adequately serve the buying and selling public
   A. I only
   B. II only
   C. both I and II
   D. neither I nor II

10. The real estate market may be described in all the following ways EXCEPT:
    A. free market
    B. local market
    C. movable market
    D. market that is slow to react to changes in supply and demand

11. The function of a real estate agent in dealings with buyers and sellers in the real estate market may best be described as which of the following?
    A. financier
    B. counselor or adviser
    C. contractor
    D. salesperson

12. A real estate firm becomes an agent of a property owner as a result of which of the following?
    A. contract of sale
    B. final settlement
    C. specialized knowledge
    D. listing contract

13. The real estate agent must have specialized knowledge of a variety of subjects that include the following EXCEPT:
    A. financing
    B. contracts
    C. legal advice
    D. valuation of property

14. Which of the following is (are) accurate regarding a successful career in real estate?
    I. A successful career in real estate is based on ethical conduct and service to others.
    II. A successful career in real estate is based on knowledge of a great variety of subjects.
    A. I only
    B. II only
    C. both I and II
    D. neither I nor II

15. All of the following are real property EXCEPT:
    A. standing timber
    B. underground minerals
    C. readily movable items
    D. naturally growing vegetation

16. Economic characteristics of real property include which of the following?
    A. situs
    B. immobility
    C. indestructibility
    D. nonhomogeneity

17. Which of the following has the greatest effect on real property value?
    A. tax rates
    B. location/situs
    C. availability
    D. indestructibility

18. Which of the following is an example of the private control of land use?
    A. zoning
    B. restrictive covenants
    C. building codes
    D. environmental controls

19. The real estate market is:
    I. an example of the free market concept.
    II. local in character.
    A. I only
    B. II only
    C. both I and II
    D. neither I nor II

20. The term REALTOR® designates:
    A. any real estate licensee
    B. a real estate licensee who is a member of the national, state, and local association of REALTORS®
    C. only licensees who hold broker's licenses
    D. all of the above

21. The real estate market is subject to:
    I. the cyclic changes in the national economy.
    II. the law of supply and demand.
    A. I only
    B. II only
    C. both I and II
    D. neither I nor II

22. Which of the following statements regarding the real estate business is (are) correct?
    I. Real estate transactions can be traced to biblical times.
    II. The business of real estate brokerage is a product of the twentieth century.
    A. I only
    B. II only
    C. both I and II
    D. neither I nor II

23. Physical characteristics of land include all of the following EXCEPT:
    A. situs
    B. nonhomogeneity
    C. permanence
    D. immobility

24. The National Association of REALTORS® is:
    A. a government organization
    B. a trade group
    C. an organization for buyers and sellers of commercial real estate
    D. all of the above

25. Which of the following is a contract in which a buyer employs a real estate broker to assist him in finding and purchasing a property and to look out solely for his (the buyer's) interest?
    A. a listing agreement
    B. a dual agency agreement
    C. a buyer agency agreement
    D. none of the above

26. Factors affecting supply and demand in real estate include all of these items EXCEPT:
    A. government regulations
    B. interest rates
    C. local economic conditions
    D. real estate investment trusts

27. A REALTOR® must be:
    I. a licensee.
    II. a broker.
    A. I only
    B. II only
    C. both I and II
    D. neither I nor II

28. The item(s) included as real estate is (are):
A. trees
B. fences
C. a built-in microwave
D. all of the above

29. Scarcity and situs are examples of:
A. physical characteristics of the land
B. highest and best use
C. permanence of investment
D. economic characteristics of the land

30. All of the following are public land use restrictions EXCEPT:
A. building codes
B. protective covenants
C. zoning
D. regional planning

# Chapter 2

## KEY TERMS

air rights
alienation
allodial system
appurtenance
appurtenant easement
bundle of rights
condemnation
condominium
cooperative
co-ownership
curtesy
declaration of restrictions
defeasible fee
dower
easement
easements in gross
emblements
eminent domain
encroachment
encumbrance
escheats
estate
estovers
fee simple absolute
fixture
foreshore
freehold estate
fruits of industry (fructus industriales)
fruits of the soil (fructus naturales)
hereditament
intestate succession
joint tenancy
judgment lien
land
lateral support
leasehold estates
levy
lien
life estate
life tenant
lis pendens
Littoral rights
marital life estates
mineral lease
nonfreehold estate
North Carolina Condominium Act
partition
party wall
police power
prescription
profit or profit à prendre
pur autre vie
remainderman
reversionary interest
riparian rights
severalty
subjacent support
survivorship
tenancy by the entirety
tenancy in common
tenements
time sharing
townhouse
Uniform Commercial Code (UCC)

# Property Ownership and Interests

## LEARNING OBJECTIVES

At the conclusion of this chapter, you should be able to:

1. Define and give examples of real property and personal property.
2. Define and give examples of fixtures, as well as describe tests for determining if an item is a fixture.
3. Define and list the freehold estates.
4. Define severalty and concurrent property ownership, including condominiums, townhouses, cooperatives, PUDs, and time-share property.
5. List and define types of lien.
6. List and define types of easement.
7. Define encroachments and appurtenances such as water, air, and subsurface rights.
8. Describe real property taxation and special assessment systems in North Carolina.

## IN THIS CHAPTER

This chapter begins the discussion of the various forms of real property ownership. Real estate is defined by (and is subject to) a complex and unique body of laws. Although you will be exploring a variety of legal terms, you should not give legal advice. Providing legal advice or opinions is defined as the practice of law, which only attorneys are authorized to do. It is, however, the duty of real estate agents to recognize basic concepts of law as they affect clients and customers and to see that they are properly informed of their rights and obligations through appropriate legal counsel.

## THE CONCEPT OF PROPERTY

Property is an all-inclusive term encompassing an individual's, group's, or entity's ownership rights, interest, and legal relationship to some thing, tangible or intangible, to the exclusion of other individuals, groups, and entities. Property may, therefore, be considered a legally created and protected "bundle of rights," which an individual, a group, or an entity has in a tangible item and/or an intangible concept. This bundle includes the rights of ownership, possession, use, and disposal of the property as well as the right to profits generated by the property. The components of the bundle can belong to one owner or can be separated with rights or groups of rights belonging to different owners. Examples of separate ownership of various rights in the bundle abound. For example, Hertz, a corporate entity, owns cars (tangible property) but rents the right to use those cars (intangible property) to individuals; an owner of an office building leases office space (right to possess and use) to a corporation; and a landowner sells the mineral rights to his property while retaining all other rights.

Property is divided into real property and personal property. Real estate practitioners must have a thorough understanding of the differences between real and personal property. Different laws apply to each type of property. Most items of personal property do not require written documentation of transfer of ownership, but all transfers of ownership of an interest in real property must be in writing. Personal and real property are taxed differently. Owners' and creditors' rights differ depending on whether the property is real or personal.

## Real Property

In Chapter 1, real property, also called real estate and realty, was defined as **land** and everything permanently attached to the land. A concept of the law of real property is that real property consists of lands, tenements, and hereditaments; therefore, everything included in the following definitions of these terms is a component of the property owner's bundle of rights.

*Land is the surface of the earth; the area below the surface to the center of the earth; and the area above the surface, theoretically, to the highest heavens.*

Land includes structures and other improvements (such as fences, swimming pools, flagpoles, and retaining walls) that have been placed there with the intention that they be a permanent part of the land.

### Tenements and Hereditaments

**Tenements** *include all those things that are included in the definition of land and include both corporeal and incorporeal rights in land.* Corporeal rights are tangible things—things that can be touched and seen. *Incorporeal* rights are things that are intangible. Tenements include buildings (corporeal). Tenements also include rights in the property of another, such as an easement (incorporeal). In addition, tenements include *intangible rights in the land of another, such as the right to take minerals, soils, timber, fish, or game from that land.* This right is called **profit à prendre,** or simply **profit.**

**Hereditament** is a term that *includes everything in the term* land *and everything in the term* tenements *that is capable of being inherited.* The land and buildings are capable of being inherited and are therefore hereditaments. Some personal rights in land, such as the right to fish and some easements, may not be inheritable. If these rights are not inheritable, they are not hereditaments.

Things that grow in the soil may be included in the definition of real property. *Growing things that do not require planting or cultivation but that grow naturally and are perennial are* **fruits of the soil (fructus naturales)** and are designated in law as real property. Examples include forest trees, native shrubs, and wild berries. *Growing things that require planting and cultivation are* **fruits of industry (fructus industriales)** or **emblements** and are defined as *personal property.* These are usually annual crops, and examples include corn, wheat, melons, and soybeans. The term *emblements* is also used to denote the right of a tenant to reenter the property and harvest the emblements after the termination of the tenancy.

## Appurtenances

An **appurtenance** is something that cannot exist by itself but depends on a principal item to which it appends or attaches. Therefore, it transfers with title to the land. Several of the items discussed next are examples of common appurtenances, such as subsurface, air, and riparian (water) rights. These three examples illustrate that an appurtenance cannot exist by itself; that is, the easement must attach to the primary item, the land that it affects. Other examples of appurtenances include appurtenant easements and the benefits of restrictive (protective) covenants (discussed later in this chapter).

## Subsurface Rights

A subsurface right, or mineral right, is an interest in real property that allows the owner to take minerals from the earth. The owner may conduct mining operations or drilling operations personally or may sell or lease these rights to others on a royalty basis. A **mineral lease** *permits the use of land for mineral exploration and mining operations.* (The Statute of Frauds, discussed in Chapter 3, requires that such a lease be in writing to be enforceable.) The lease may be for a definite term or for a period as long as the land is productive. A mineral royalty is income received from leases of mineral land.

## Air Rights

Ownership of land includes *ownership of and the rights to the area above the surface of the earth* **(air rights).** The right of ownership of the airspace enables the landowner to use that space to construct improvements, to lease, or to sell to others.

The right of ownership and control of the airspace is limited, however, by zoning ordinances and federal laws. Zoning ordinances often restrict the height of improvements constructed on the land, and federal laws permit the use of the airspace by air traffic flying at an altitude specified by the government.

## Riparian Rights

The *appurtenant rights of an owner of property bordering a flowing body of water* are **riparian rights.** Riparian rights attach to the land but cannot exist by themselves. Generally, property adjacent to a river or watercourse affords the landowner the right to access and use the water for purposes such as drawing water for personal use and entering the water via a boat pier. Actual ownership of the water depends on a number of factors. North Carolina recognizes the distinction between a *navigable* and a nonnavigable watercourse. In the former, adjacent owners are limited to the banks of the watercourse, while the state owns the body of water and the right to use it. If one owner owns all of the land surrounding a nonnavigable body of water, that owner owns all of the land under the water. If more than one owner owns property surrounding a nonnavigable body of water, ownership extends to the center of the water, unless the deed states otherwise.

**Littoral rights** are *the rights of landowners whose property borders an ocean or a lake.* If the water levels fluctuate, as with ocean tides, the landowner owns to the mean high watermark. The state owns the **foreshore,** which is *the land between the mean high watermark and low watermark.*

An owner's riparian property and property rights can be affected by changes in boundaries caused by the natural forces interacting with land and water. Although the geographic coordinates of land do not change, the part of the surface covered by the land and water can and do change over time.

The real estate practitioner should understand the following four natural processes that affect riparian boundaries.

1. Accretion is a gradual process in which the boundary of riparian land is extended by natural forces, usually water from a river, a lake, or an ocean depositing soil, sand, or rock onto areas previously covered by water. This acquired land becomes the property of the riparian property owner.
2. Reliction is also a gradual process; however, the boundary of riparian land is extended as a body of water gradually and permanently recedes, leaving the ground under it dry and exposed. This acquired land becomes the property of the riparian property owner.

3. Erosion, the reverse of accretion, is a natural process in which the flow or movement of water gradually produces a loss of riparian land; for example, beach erosion. The riparian property owner loses title to the land.
4. Avulsion, unlike accretion, reliction, and erosion, is not a gradual process. It is a rapid or sudden change in riparian land, either loss or gain, resulting from violent natural forces. There is no legal boundary change for land affected by avulsion. The owner can reclaim the lost land. Theoretically, an owner retains title to and can reclaim land lost through avulsion; however, environmental laws may limit or void his right to do so.

## *Lateral and Subjacent Support*

Land was previously defined as the surface of the earth; the area below the surface to the center of the earth; the air above the earth, theoretically, to the highest heavens; and everything permanently attached to the earth. For purposes of understanding lateral and subjacent support, consider only the solid surface of the earth. The ground is surrounded by more ground or by water. Riparian rights, the rights of landowners whose property borders water, are well defined in law. The solid surface of land can be gained or lost by forces of nature or by man's activity. What would happen if your neighbor decided to excavate the dirt from her land bordering your property for a project elsewhere? Unless your land is solid rock, the solid surface could shift, perhaps destroying or undermining the support of improvements on your land. Your neighbor cannot remove the dirt because you have a right of **lateral support,** which means the right of land to be supported in its natural state by adjacent land.

Now consider the part of the land that is below the surface of the earth. Suppose you sell the mineral rights. The owner of those subsurface rights can mine beneath your surface, but he must support your surface rights from below. He cannot cause the surface of your land to collapse. **Subjacent support** is the right to have one's land supported from below.

## Personal Property

Personal property is anything that is not real property; therefore, it is not land or anything permanently attached to land. Unlike real property, it is readily, although not necessarily easily, movable. Its "bundle of rights" is not identical to that of real property. Some property can be classified as real or personal property, depending on circumstances.

## *Fixtures*

A **fixture** is an item of personal property that is attached to the land or a permanent improvement on the land in such a manner that the law deems it to be part of the real property to which it is attached. Fixtures cause many problems due to misunderstandings by the parties involved. Real estate practitioners can avoid problems by thoroughly understanding the criteria for a fixture and paying careful attention to detail when listing and selling property.

**Total circumstance test.** This test, composed of four criteria or factors, may be used to determine an item's identification as a fixture *in the absence of a contractual agreement by the parties.*

1. *Intention:* Did the person making the attachment intend to make a permanent improvement? Would it be evident to a reasonable, rational person that the annexor's intention was that the improvement be permanent? For example, the owner of a property installs a ceiling fan in the family room. This criterion should be used in conjunction with the other criteria. If the owner expressly states his intention that the attachment is permanent and all parties involved are aware of the express intention, the express intention will rule without regard to the other three criteria.
2. *Relation of the attacher:* An owner is presumed to make a permanent improvement, whereas a renter may be presumed to make a temporary attachment. However, the real

estate agent should not presume anything about the annexor's ownership but should ask questions if a tenant is involved. If the real property owner has permanently attached personal property to his real property during his ownership, the attached property is usually considered real property. (See "Effects of the Uniform Commercial Code" later in this chapter for an exception.) Once the item becomes real property, its ownership passes to the new owner when the present owner sells or otherwise disposes of the property, absent a contract or an agreement to the contrary. Take the example regarding the ceiling fan. If a tenant instead of the owner of the property were to install the fan, would his intention be that the ceiling fan remain with the property or would he plan to take down the ceiling fan he had purchased and replace it with the original fixture?

3. *Method:* Does the method of attachment mean that removal of the item will damage the property? This is a bit tricky. What constitutes damage? Is a small nail or screw hole damage? Define "permanently attached." It may not actually need to be attached. This criterion absolutely must be used in conjunction with the other circumstances. A small picture hanger on a wall probably does not constitute substantial or permanent attachment, but a pair of thousand-pound statues sitting on custom-made concrete pillars may.
4. *Adaptation:* How is the item being used? Is the item adapted to the real property to which it is attached? An example would be blinds custom made to fit nonstandard windows.

Courts have not been consistent in their application of the total circumstance test. If the courts cannot agree, buyers, sellers, and real estate agents are unlikely to always agree. Remember that while real estate agents must understand these criteria, they should not give legal advice as to what is or is not a fixture in a given circumstance. That would be practicing law without a license. They can, however, avoid most problems in this area by using and understanding the North Carolina Bar Association/ North Carolina Association of REALTORS® (NCBA/NCAR) Standard Form No. 2-T, Offer to Purchase and Contract, found in Chapter 6, page 163. Paragraph 2 of this form itemizes fixtures and asks that personal property that conveys be identified in paragraph 3. Familiarizing the seller with these items at the time of listing and the buyer at the initial buyer interview, or at least by the time of the offer, is an excellent way to prevent misunderstandings.

The practitioner must ensure that all parties understand all contracts. This can be accomplished by clearly identifying fixtures and personal property in both the listing and the sales contracts. Real property can become personal property by contract. For example, a chandelier is personal property until it is installed in the house, and becomes a fixture upon installation. If the contract provides for the chandelier to be replaced with a less expensive one, the original chandelier again becomes personal property upon removal according to the contract, and the new, less expensive chandelier, which is personal property when it is purchased, becomes real property when it is installed according to the contract. If the contract were silent about the chandelier, the buyers could reasonably expect the chandelier to be a fixture and to convey as real property.

**Trade fixtures.** A special category of fixtures is recognized for the items of personal property that are used in the course of a business operating in a leased property. For example, a merchant may rent a store and install shelves to display merchandise. These shelves are a temporary attachment necessary for the operation of the business. A more complex situation would arise in the operation of a restaurant in a rented space. Consider all the items required in this operation, including stoves, ovens, grills, chairs, tables, and so on. Such attachments are recognized as trade fixtures, and they retain their personal property classification such that the restaurant tenant can remove them at the termination of the lease.

**Agricultural fixtures.** A special category of fixtures exists in North Carolina that results from common law interpretation in the state. Whereas statutory law is based on the written statutes (laws) of the state, common law comes from precedent or court decisions. Although there is no specific court decision in this area, the general interpretation is that fixtures used in a leased farm operation differ from trade fixtures, described above, in that agricultural fixtures are presumed to be classified as real property.

Therefore, if a tenant farmer installed items such as a corncrib or a feeder silo, the general interpretation is that these items become the property of the landowner and are not ordinarily removable by the tenant at the end of the lease.

Again, the agent must ensure that all understandings of the parties are supported by terms of a rental contract. Recall, however, that only attorneys can draft contracts. Real estate practitioners would exceed their authority and be entering the prohibited practice of law if they attempted to write legal clauses in a contract.

**Effect of the Uniform Commercial Code.** A special situation occurs when an owner has financed the purchase of an item installed in her property. The **Uniform Commercial Code (UCC)** *provides for the lender to retain a security interest in a chattel (personal property) until the lender is paid in full.* The security interest is created by an instrument called a security agreement, which is put on the public record by the filing of a notice called a financing statement. This notice is filed in the office of the Register of Deeds. The filing of the financing statement provides constructive notice to all the world that a security interest exists in the item. As a result, the attached item is not legally classified as a fixture, or a part of the real property, until the security agreement has been satisfied by full payment.

Consequently, the lender can remove the item in the event the buyer/borrower defaults in payment, even though the item has been attached to real property. Subsequent purchasers, as well as a subsequent lender, are bound by the filing of the financing statement. Therefore, a purchaser of the home or a lender accepting the property as security for a mortgage must complete the payments or permit the removal of the item by the lender in the event the property owner does not satisfy the debt.

## *Improvements*

Numerous improvements must be made to and on raw land to make it accessible and suitable for the various uses people have for it. An improvement is anything of value that is added to real property or anything that alters real property in such a way as to increase its utility or value; however, these do not include repairs and replacements. The definition has two parts: (1) private improvements, usually done *on the land* by the property owner and (2) public improvements such as streets, sewers, water, and sidewalks done *to the land* by government or quasi-government organizations. From a practical point of view, the agent should make certain that all parties understand the meaning each party intends to convey when using the terms *improvements, improvements to the land, improvements on the land, improved land,* or *improved lot.*

Improvements on the land done by property owners include buildings, paved driveways and walkways, tennis courts, fences, walls, and swimming pools. They do not include routine maintenance, repairs, or replacements.

Improvements to the land done by government or quasi-government entities may include the following:

1. Roads, highways, and bridges built to make the land accessible.
2. Utilities such as electric power, water, sewer, gas lines, and phone lines brought to the site.
3. Modifications or improvements such as clearing, grading, and draining to make it suitable for its intended use.

"Improved land" or "improved lot" could mean the land or lot has had improvements to it to prepare it for a building, or it could mean that improvements such as buildings have already been constructed on it. The important thing is for the agent to make certain that the meaning is clear when listing, advertising, and negotiating offers to purchase and in all other aspects of the transaction.

# ESTATES IN REAL PROPERTY

## Systems of Property Ownership

The *feudal system* of land ownership originated in British law almost a thousand years ago. Under the feudal system, only the king could hold title to real property; however, he offered the use of certain lands to loyal subjects. These lands were called feuds or fees. These feudal arrangements did not provide ownership of land; they were simply a right of use and possession of land as long as the holder provided certain services to the king. The feuds were approximately equivalent to the modern concept of leasehold estates or rental interests in a property. Under the feudal system, outright ownership could not be obtained. Feudal rights could continue only as long as the holder provided services to the king.

One of the fundamental issues of the American Revolution was the colonists' insistence on outright and absolute ownership of land in this country. As a result, the *system of land ownership in the United States* is the **allodial system** and not the feudal system. In this country, *title to real property may be held absolutely by individuals*. However, even the allodial system of property ownership is subject to four very important powers of federal and local governments. These powers are eminent domain, police, taxation, and escheat.

### *Eminent Domain*

The power of **eminent domain** is the *government's power to take private property for public use.* Governments exercise this power themselves and also delegate it to public utility companies. The *taking of property under the power of eminent domain is called* **condemnation.**

There are two limitations on the power of eminent domain: (1) The property condemned must be for the use and benefit of the general public, and (2) the property owner must be paid the fair market value of the property lost through condemnation. The property owner has the right to go to court if she is not satisfied with the compensation offered by the condemning authority.

### *Police Power*

**Police power** is the *power a government has to enable it to fulfill its responsibility to provide for the health, safety, and welfare of the public.* Examples of the exercise of police power affecting property use are zoning ordinances, subdivision ordinances, building codes, and environmental protection laws. Property owners affected by the exercise of police power are not compensated for the restrictions on their use of property.

### *Taxation*

The government's power of taxation is well known. Taxes are imposed upon real property *ad valorem,* that is, according to value. Real property taxes are by far the largest source of income for local governments (see "Property Taxation in North Carolina" later in this chapter).

### *Escheat*

If a property owner dies and leaves a valid will (i.e., dies "testate"), the individual's property is distributed to the heirs as specified in the will. If an owner dies without a valid will (i.e., "intestate"), however, the *deceased's property is distributed according to statutes* of **intestate succession.** In the event there are no heirs to receive property left by the deceased, the property **escheats** to the state. In other words, *if there is no one legally eligible as designated by statute to receive the property, it goes to the state.*

## Definition of Estate

An **estate** in real property is *an interest in the property sufficient to give the owner of the estate the right to possession of the property.* Here you must understand the difference between the *right of possession* and the *right of use.* The owner of an estate in land has the right of possession of the land in addition to the right to use it. An easement owner, in contrast, has the use of the land but not the right to possess it; therefore, the easement is a nonpossessory interest in land. The Latin translation for the word *estate* is "status." This indicates the relationship in which the estate owner stands with reference to rights in the property, and it establishes the degree, quantity, nature, and extent of interest a person has in real property.

## Types of Estate in Land

Estates in land are divided into two groups: estates of freehold and estates of less than freehold (also called leasehold estates and nonfreehold estates). Two estates can exist simultaneously in land. The owner (lessor) of a property has a freehold estate. If he leases the property, the tenant (lessee) has a leasehold estate. Each of these two major divisions contains various groupings or subheadings.

### *Freehold Estates*

**Freehold** is defined as *an interest in land of at least a lifetime and is therefore generally identified with the concept of title or ownership.* Freehold estates may be fee simple estates or life estates (see Figure 2.1). Fee simple estates are inheritable; most life estates are not.

Freehold estates are divided into two categories: estates of inheritance and estates not of inheritance.

I. *ESTATES OF INHERITANCE*

These estates last a lifetime and continue after the death of the titleholder as they are passed on to one's heirs.

A. Fee simple estates

1. *Fee simple absolute.* The estate of **fee simple absolute** *provides the greatest form of ownership available in real property.* This estate may be described as fee simple absolute, fee simple, or ownership in fee. Ownership in fee simple absolute provides certain legal rights usually described as a **bundle of rights.** This bundle includes the *right to possession of the property; the right of quiet enjoyment of the property; the right to dispose of the property by gift, by sale, or by will; and the right to control the use of the property within the limits of the law.* The owner in fee simple absolute may convey a life estate to another, may pledge the property

**FIGURE 2.1**

Estates and rights in real estate property (in descending order of importance).

| FREEHOLD ESTATES | NONFREEHOLD ESTATES (LEASEHOLD ESTATES) | RIGHTS IN THE LAND OF ANOTHER |
|---|---|---|
| I. Inheritable<br>A. Fee simple estates<br>1. Absolute<br>2. Determinable<br>3. Conditional<br>B. Life estate pur autre vie (inheritable during measuring lifetime)<br>II. Not inheritable<br>A. Conventional life estate<br>B. Marital life estate<br>Note: Freehold estates provide title. | A. Estate for years<br>B. Estate from year to year<br>C. Estate at will<br>D. Estate at sufferance<br>Note: Provide possession and control, but not title. | A. Easements<br>B. Profits<br>Note: Provide a right, but not title or possession. |

as security for a mortgage debt, may convey a leasehold estate to another, may grant an easement in the land to another, or may give a license to conduct some activity on the property to another. Some of these rights may be removed from the bundle, leaving the other rights intact. For example, if the owner conveyed a lease or an easement to another, the owner's remaining rights would be a fee simple subject to the lease or easement.

2. *Fee simple determinable.* This **defeasible fee or qualified fee** estate is also an inheritable freehold estate in the form of a fee simple estate; however, the title can be terminated by the grantor under certain conditions. An example of a fee simple determinable is a situation in which a grantor conveys title to a college and in the conveyance stipulates that the title is good as long as the property is used for scholastic purposes. Title received by the college can be for an infinite period of time. If the property is not used for the purpose specified in the conveyance, however, the title will automatically terminate and revert to the original grantor or the grantor's heirs.
3. *Fee simple subject to a condition subsequent.* The fee simple subject to a condition subsequent can continue for an infinite period, as is the case with the fee simple absolute. The fee simple subject to a condition subsequent also can be defeated, and is, therefore, a defeasible title. The fee simple subject to a condition subsequent is created by the grantor (the one conveying title), who restricts the future use of the property in some way. For example, a grantor may convey property with the condition that it can never be used as a landfill. As long as the property is never used for this purpose, the title will continue indefinitely in the name of the initial grantee or any subsequent grantee. Any use of the property for a landfill will violate the covenant in the deed and the original grantor and/or her heirs may reenter the property and take possession or go to court and sue to regain possession. By doing so, the titleholder's estate is terminated.

   A grantor may want to convey a title this way for several reasons. In the case of the landfill, the owner may be protecting the property he owns that is close to the landfill. In the case of the college, the grantor may be highly committed to education but may not want to give up ownership of the property for any other reason. Notice that in the case of a fee simple determinable, the estate in the grantee automatically terminates in the event the designated use of the property is not continued or a prohibited use is undertaken. This is contrasted with the fee simple subject to a condition subsequent, in which the termination is not automatic. In the latter case, the grantor and/or the heirs must either reenter the property or go to court to obtain possession of the property and to terminate the estate in the grantee. It should be noted that qualified fee or use conditions based on race, color, sex, national origin, familial status, handicap, or religion are void since they are against public policy; therefore, if a qualified fee or use condition based on any of these factors appears as a condition of title, the title is really a fee simple absolute.

B. *Estates* ***pur autre vie*** *(for the life of another).* These estates are *measured by the lifetime of a person other than the person receiving the title.* They may be willed or inherited by heirs of the life estate grantee if the grantee dies before the person who is the measuring life.

For example, Dad may grant title to his son for as long as Mom (his widow) is still alive. If the son dies before Mom, the title to the life estate pur autre vie would pass to the son's heirs, such as a grandson or a granddaughter. Therefore, the life estate is not only for the duration of the son's life, but will last until Mom's death, as hers is still the measuring life. At Mom's death, the life estate terminates.

II. *ESTATES NOT OF INHERITANCE*

These estates are good only for the life of the tenant (freehold) and do not pass on to his or her heirs, but are disposed of by some other route.

In addition to being created by an intentional conveyance, life estates can also be created by operation of law. Life estates created by act of the parties are called

**FIGURE 2.2**
Life estate in reversion.

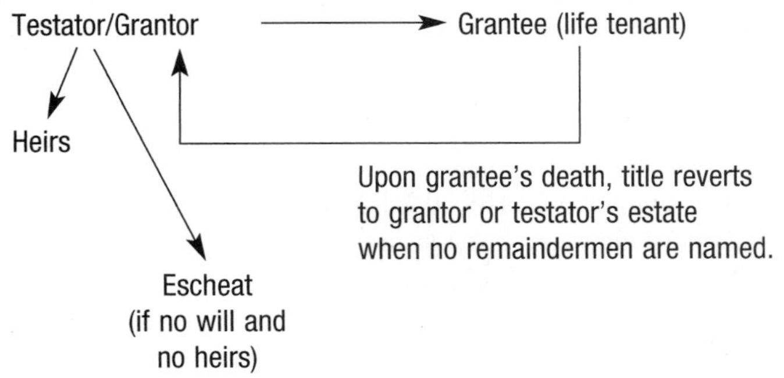


conventional life estates, whereas life estates created by operation of law are called **marital life estates.**

A. *Conventional life estates (estate for tenant's own life).* A **life estate** is a noninheritable **freehold estate.** It is created only for the life of the named **life tenant;** that is, *one who holds a life estate.* The question arises as to what will happen to the estate at the death of the life tenant. *If nothing else is specified in the conveyance of the life estate, it will revert to the grantor or to his heirs at the death of the life tenant.* The grantor or his heirs thus would have a **reversionary interest** in this case (see Figure 2.2). Alternatively, the conveyance of the life estate could specify that the estate pass on to someone other than the grantor or his heirs. This person would be called a **remainderman** and has a *remainder, or future, interest in the property.* After the death of the life tenant, the remainderman would then have title in fee simple absolute (see Figure 2.3).

B. *Marital life estates.* A marital life estate is created in North Carolina by the intestate succession statutes governing the distribution of property of one who dies intestate, that is, dies without leaving a valid will. This statute allows the surviving spouse to choose a life estate in one-third of the real property owned in severalty (sole ownership) by the deceased spouse at any time during the marriage under certain conditions. If the surviving spouse is entitled to any property of the deceased spouse through a will or intestate succession statues and the surviving spouse has not joined in the transfer of such property by signing the deed, the surviving spouse must forfeit any interest in the deceased spouse's property resulting from a will or an inheritance in order to claim his

**FIGURE 2.3**
Life estate in remainder.

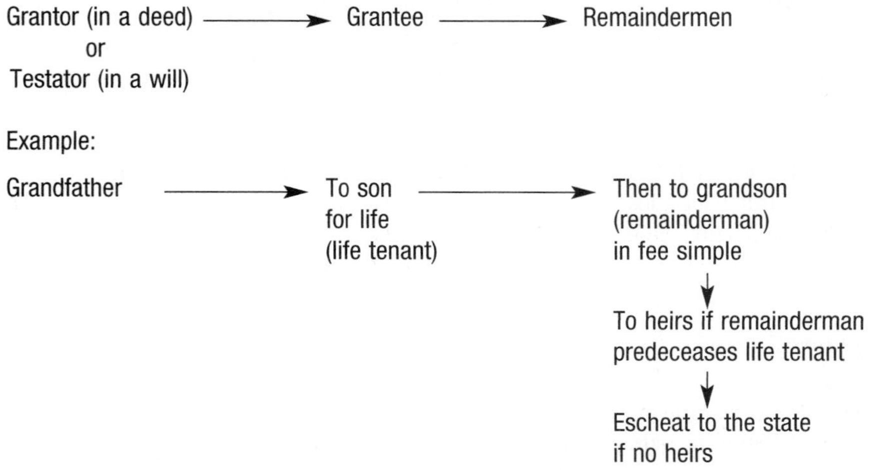

or her marital estate. Few surviving spouses elect the marital life estate option because it is seldom advantageous for them to do so.

Several important points to remember about marital life estates:

- A will cannot defeat the marital interest of a surviving spouse.
- Statute does not apply to property owned as tenants by the entirety.
- Surviving spouse has a choice of either marital life estate or property of the deceased spouse willed to the surviving spouse.

From these requirements, you can see that it is extremely important for both husband and wife to join in the conveyance of any property owned by either of them while they are married. Otherwise, the grantee's title could be affected by a marital interest of the surviving spouse.

Some states still provide dower and curtesy rights to a surviving spouse. **Dower** is *the wife's right* and **curtesy** is *the husband's right to a life estate in the property owned by a deceased spouse* during the marriage. North Carolina's intestate succession statutes abolished dower and curtesy rights and provided a substitute, which sets forth the manner in which the property of an intestate (one who has died without leaving a valid will) is distributed to the heirs.

**Rights and responsibilities of life tenants.** A life tenant has the right of **alienation.** That is, the life tenant can *transfer his or her title to another person or pledge the title as security for a debt.* Of course, the individual cannot give a title for a duration longer than his life or the life of the person named in the creation of a life estate to establish its duration. The life tenant also has the right to the net income produced by the property, if any. The life tenant can legally mortgage the life estate. It is unlikely that a lending institution would accept a life estate as security for a mortgage, however, since the estate terminates on the death of the life tenant. If the life tenant were able to do this, however, she would be responsible for the principal and interest on that mortgage note. An outstanding mortgage on the property is the responsibility of the grantor or the remainderman, the life tenant must pay the interest, but not the principal.

A life tenant has certain responsibilities. He or she must not commit waste and must preserve the estate for the benefit of the remainderman or for the person who holds the reversionary interest. Otherwise, the life tenant is not answerable to the future holder of the estate. The life tenant has a legal right called the right to **estovers** which allows him or her *to cut and use a reasonable amount of timber from the land to repair buildings or to use for fuel, but does not allow the tenant to cut and sell the timber for profit.* A violation of the right of estovers is called an *act of waste.*

A life tenant has an obligation to pay the real property taxes on the property in which he has a life estate. The tenant also has the duty to pay any assessments levied against the property by a county or municipality for improvements to the property. Assessments are levied against land for improvements made to the land, such as paving streets and laying water and sewer lines.

The life tenant also has a duty to make repairs to the improvements on the land. He cannot permit the property to deteriorate because of lack of repairs and thus cause depreciation to existing improvements.

## Nonfreehold Estates

The **nonfreehold estates,** also known as less-than-freehold or **leasehold estates,** *confer a rental interest in real property.* Four estates are recognized:

1. *Estate for years* is for any fixed period of time and automatically terminates at the end of that period.
2. *Estate from year to year* is a periodic estate that automatically renews at the end of its period if the parties do not provide otherwise.

3. An *estate at will* is for an indefinite time and may be terminated by either party instantaneously by giving notice to the other party.
4. An *estate at sufferance* is not truly an estate but rather a holdover situation created when the tenant's lease has expired and she fails to vacate the premises.

These nonfreehold estates are described in more detail in Chapter 10.

# OWNERSHIP OF REAL PROPERTY

## Ownership in Severalty

When *title to real property is held in the name of only one person,* it is called ownership in **severalty.** The person holding title is the sole or only owner.

## Concurrent (Joint) Ownership

*Simultaneous ownership of real property by two or more people* is called concurrent ownership or **co-ownership.** There are various types of co-ownership, and the rights of the owners depend on the type of ownership they have. The types of co-ownership are tenancy in common, joint tenancy, tenancy by the entirety, and community property. North Carolina is not a community property state; therefore, this type of co-ownership is not discussed here.

The co-owners may hold title in the same manner as owners in severalty—for example, fee simple absolute, fee simple subject to a condition subsequent and fee simple determinable.

### *Tenancy in Common*

**Tenancy in common** is characterized by *two or more persons holding title to a property at the same time, with no right of survivorship.* Anyone can hold title as a tenant in common. Each owner holds an undivided interest in the entire property, rather than one specific part of it. Upon the death of a tenant in common, the deceased's share goes to his heirs.

A tenant in common may sell his share to anybody without destroying the tenancy relationship. Each tenant in common may also pledge his or her share of the property as security for a loan. This creates an encumbrance against that share only, not against the entire property. Tenants in common do not need to have the same amount of interest in the property. For example, one tenant may hold a 50 percent interest, with two other tenants holding 25 percent each. If the deed does not specify the interest each holds, their interest will be considered equal.

A tenant in common may bring legal action to have the property **partitioned** so *each tenant has a specific portion of the property exclusively.* If this can be done fairly with a piece of land, each tenant receives title to a tract according to his share of interest. If the land cannot be divided to the satisfaction of the co-owners, the court may order its sale, with appropriate shares of the proceeds distributed to the tenants.

### *Joint Tenancy*

This form of co-ownership requires the four unities of time, title, interest, and possession. People with **joint tenancy** *must have the same interest in the property, must receive their title at the same time from the same source, and must have the same degree of undivided ownership and right to possession in the property.* For example, if there are three joint tenants, each must own an undivided one-third interest in the property, they must all receive their title from the same source at the same time, and they must continue to hold possession concurrently.

If a joint tenant sells her share of ownership, the sale violates the requirement of unity of time, title, interest, and possession as far as the new buyer is concerned. Upon the sale of an interest by a joint tenant, the person buying this share does not become a joint tenant with the other tenants, but joins them as a tenant in common.

Some states, but not North Carolina, provide the concept of **survivorship** in joint tenancies, wherein *the surviving partners automatically take over the share of a deceased partner.* The right of survivorship is not favored in law today except in joint ownership by husband and wife as tenants by the entirety. Therefore, a North Carolina court does not recognize a joint tenancy unless the deed of conveyance makes it absolutely clear that the right of survivorship is intended by the parties. The granting clause must contain wording such as "to A, B, and C as joint tenants, to their survivors, and to the survivors' heirs and assigns forever." Other attempts by deed or will to create a joint tenancy in North Carolina are treated as tenancies in common.

### Tenancy by the Entirety

*Ownership through* **tenancy by the entirety** *is limited to husband and wife.* To receive title as tenants by the entirety, *there must be a legal marriage at the time that the husband and wife receive title to the property.* It is not necessary for the deed to read "to husband and wife as tenants by the entirety" to create a tenancy by the entirety. The deed only needs to convey the property "to John A. Jones and Mary A. Jones, who are husband and wife," and a tenancy by the entirety is automatically created. Tenancy by the entirety does contain the right of survivorship. The surviving spouse receives title to the property automatically by operation of law. Creation of tenancy by the entirety requires the five unities of time, title, interest, possession, and marriage.

A husband or wife owning land as tenants by the entirety may not legally convey property to a third party without the other spouse joining in the deed. There can be no partition of real property held by tenants by the entirety.

Tenancy by the entirety exists as long as the tenants hold title to the property and are legally married. Tenancy by the entirety is abolished by decree of divorce. A mere legal separation is not sufficient. When a final decree of absolute divorce is obtained, however, the ownership is automatically changed to tenancy in common by operation of law, eliminating the right of survivorship.

Married people may, if they elect to do so, own property as tenants in common. It is not necessary for them to take title as tenants by the entirety.

In North Carolina, one spouse can purchase a property, but it usually takes the signature of the husband and the wife to convey and give a clear title to a grantee, regardless of how the property is held. If a mortgage or deed of trust is given to secure a note for a property being purchased by one spouse, the lender usually requires the other spouse to sign the deed of trust or mortgage but does not require the nonpurchasing spouse to sign the note unless that spouse's income is used to qualify for the loan.

## Combination (Hybrid) Forms of Ownership

### Condominiums

Condominium ownership is a form of ownership in real estate that is now recognized in all states. North Carolina statutes define this type of ownership, set forth the requirements for the creation of a condominium, and set special restrictions on the offering of a condominium for sale.

A condominium purchaser receives a fee simple title to an apartment. Condominium unit owners can hold ownership of their units in the same ways owners of any freehold estate hold ownership; that is, in severalty, as tenants in common, as joint tenants, or as tenants by the entirety. Individuals, groups, and business entities can hold ownership in condominium units in the same ways they can hold ownership in other freehold estates, providing they meet the criteria for the specific type of ownership. For example, only a married couple can own real estate as tenants by the entirety. The owner can convey title by deed or leave it to an heir by will. **Condominium** ownership includes *ownership of the airspace of the individual unit, as well as co-ownership in the common areas* of the condominium along with the other unit owners. This co-ownership is as a tenant in common in the common areas—the corridors, grounds, parking areas, and recreational facilities, among others.

**FIGURE 2.4**
Condominium ownership.

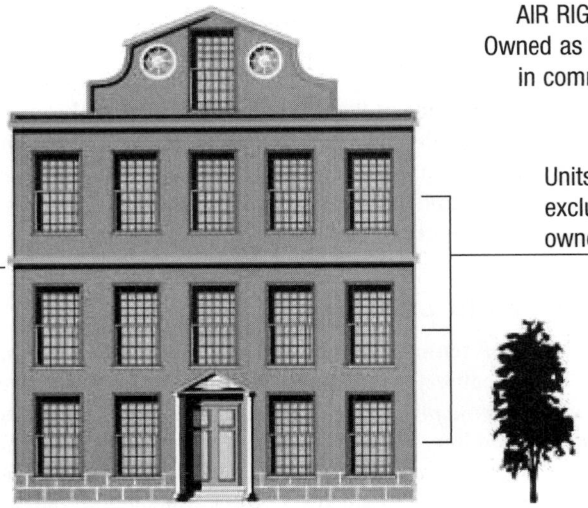


Condominiums can also be one-story, attached, or detached units, but the individual owner still owns only the airspace that constitutes his unit. All ground and common areas are still owned as tenants in common.

The right to partition is waived in this tenancy in common ownership of common areas. (See Figure 2.4.)

North Carolina statutes prescribe the manner in which a condominium is to be created. This includes a declaration, by-laws, and a copy of the construction plans. In order to be valid, the declaration, articles, and by-laws must be recorded on the public record in the Register of Deeds office in the county where the property is located.

The declaration includes a legal description of the property; a plat of the property with the location of the buildings, plans, and specifications for the buildings and the various units; a description of the common areas; and the degree of ownership in the common areas available to each unit owner. It also includes covenants, conditions, and restrictions affecting the property. It may also include a "right of first refusal" clause, giving the association the first opportunity to purchase a unit if the owner wishes to sell.

The articles of association establish an association to provide for the maintenance and management of the common areas and other services for the owner-members. Owners, as members of the association, are assessed to pay for these necessary services. Such assessments are usually in the form of monthly dues, but periodic special assessments can also be levied. The by-laws set forth the various officers in the association and the way they are elected, and they set forth the requirements for amending the by-laws.

The creation of a condominium is not limited to residential purposes. Other purposes may be office space, parking space, an industrial park, and so on. The purpose of the condominium must be set forth in the declaration as required by state statute.

A condominium unit can be mortgaged just as any other property. Federal Housing Administration (FHA) financing has been available for condominiums since 1961, and the Department of Veterans Affairs (VA) guarantees mortgage loans for the purchase of condominiums. A condominium project must have FHA or VA approval before FHA will make loans on any of the units. FHA further requires that condominium projects have a specified percentage of owner-occupancy before FHA will make a loan on any of the units. The occupancy rate is monitored. That percentage can vary by region.

The **North Carolina Condominium Act** (1986) sets specific requirements on offering for sale or resale a condominium created on or after October 1, 1986. Essentially the act offers the following consumer protections (these protections apply only to condominiums, not to townhouses or planned unit developments [PUDs]).

1. *Public offering statement:* A public offering statement must be provided by the developer to the prospective buyer of a new condominium before the contract is signed. The North Carolina Condominium Act requires that the developer disclose certain information pertaining to the condominium project, including the purchaser's right to cancel. The public offering statement is not required for resale of units.
2. *Purchaser's right to cancel:* A purchaser has the right to cancel, absolutely and without penalty, the purchase of a new condominium unit from the developer for any reason during the first seven days after signing the contract. Title cannot pass during this seven-day period. Like the public offering statement, the purchaser's right to cancel does not apply to resale units.
3. *Escrow of deposit:* Any deposits made by the purchaser must remain in the developer's or his agent's escrow account the full seven days, unless the purchaser cancels the contract earlier. In that case, the money is to be refunded to the purchaser. All escrow accounts must be held in an insured bank or savings and loan in North Carolina.
4. *Resale certificates:* When reselling a condominium built on or after October 1, 1986 the unit's owner or owner's agent must provide a resale certificate to the purchasers that discloses monthly assessment for the common areas and other fees for which unit owners are responsible. A public offering statement and/or right to cancel are *not* required for resale of a unit.
5. *Warranties:* There is an implied warranty that the unit is constructed in an acceptable manner, free from defects, and suitable for the purpose intended unless there is an agreement to the contrary or the warranty has been disclaimed in such a manner as to make it void.

The agent must provide his client with a public offering statement if the client is purchasing a new condominium or a resale certificate if reselling a unit subject to this statute. Failure to do so violates the agency relationship and, therefore, the Real Estate License Law. It also leaves the agent potentially liable to the purchaser in civil court.

## Townhouse Ownership

The **townhouse** form of ownership is somewhat different from the condominium form in that the townhouse *provides for the ownership of the unit as well as the specific portion of land upon which the individual unit is located.* Because each unit rests on its own foundation and its own piece of land, it cannot have another unit above it. A townhouse is, therefore, a vertical structure that is attached horizontally to other units, which also rest on their own foundations. The townhouse may be two or three stories, but all the stories are part of one unit. This is in contrast to condominium units, which are attached vertically but whose horizontal stacks of units share a foundation and ground.

There is another significant difference in the ownership of the common grounds. Because the townhouse owner owns the land of his specific unit, the owners' association owns the remainder of the common areas, such as the walks and swimming pool. This is different from condominium ownership, in which the owners' association owns nothing itself because the owners own the common elements together as tenants in common.

## Cooperatives

Ownership in a **cooperative** results from *ownership of shares of stock in a corporation that owns a building containing cooperative apartments.* The right of stockholders to occupy an apartment is provided by a proprietary lease. The only real property interest of the stockholders is a leasehold estate providing the right to possession of an apartment. The stockholders, as lessees, pay no rent but do pay an assessment to cover the cost of maintaining and operating the building, real property taxes, and debt service if there is a mortgage against the building. The owners' rights and obligations are specified in the lease and the stock certificate. Proprietary lease tenants do not "own" real property.

### Time Sharing

Time sharing is a fairly recent innovation. North Carolina has very specific statutes defining and regulating time-shares. **Time sharing** is defined *as any right to occupy a property for five or more separated time periods over a span of five or more years.* Any interest meeting this definition is classified as real property, and the laws pertaining to real estate transactions apply. Article IV of the Real Estate License Law sets specific regulations on the sale of time-share property. The developer must obtain a registration certificate from the Real Estate Commission before offering the units for sale to the public, and all persons selling an interest in a time-share must have a real estate license. Additionally, purchasers must be given a public offering statement meeting North Carolina Real Estate Commission guidelines before a contract is signed and must have a five-day right of rescission after executing such a contract. See Appendix A for rules and regulations for time shares and real estate laws.

### Planned Unit Developments

A planned unit development (PUD) is really a small community that includes some form of cluster housing as well as recreational areas and supporting commercial activities such as retail shops. Any form of residential ownership may be present, such as single-family homes, condominiums, or townhouses. Therefore, the concept is not so much a form of ownership as it is a concept of land development that combines mixed uses and mixed densities. The owner usually receives title to the residential unit and, at the same time, becomes a member of the association that owns the other elements of the development.

## ENCUMBRANCES TO REAL PROPERTY

An **encumbrance** is *anything that diminishes the bundle of rights of real property.* As such, it is usually considered a burden on the property. Charges, claims, restrictions, or infringements on a property reduce its overall value in some manner. In some instances, however, an encumbrance has a positive effect on the value of the property; an example might be restrictive covenants, discussed later in this chapter. Therefore, an encumbrance can affect value either positively or negatively.

This section discusses liens, easements, and encroachments. Chapter 4 discusses other land use controls, such as zoning ordinances and deed restrictions.

### Liens

A **lien** is *a claim or a charge against the property that can result from a contractual agreement or from the operation of law.* For example, a lien can result from an owner's contracting to have work done on property and not fulfilling part of the contract, from the owner's failure to pay taxes, or as a result of a lawsuit. A lien creates a cloud on the title. If this claim is not satisfied in the required time, the lien holder may execute the lien by process of foreclosure, which forces the property to be sold at public auction. Proceeds of the foreclosure sale are applied to outstanding liens in the order of priority of the liens, which is discussed later in this chapter.

Liens fall into two groups, which are shown in Figure 2.5:

1. *Specific liens* are claims against a specific property, such as mortgages, property taxes, and mechanics' liens.
2. *General liens* are claims against a person or that person's property, such as judgment liens, personal property tax liens, income tax liens, and estate and inheritance tax liens.

1. Specific Liens: Claims against a particular property
   a. Mortgage
   b. Real property tax and special assessment
   c. Mechanic's
2. General Liens: Claims against all assets of a person
   a. Judgment
   b. Personal property tax
   c. Income tax
   d. Estate and inheritance tax

**FIGURE 2.5**
Classification of liens.

## Specific Liens

***Mortgage liens.*** A mortgage or deed of trust pledges a specific property, such as a home, as security for a debt. If the borrower does not pay the debt as promised (defaults), the lender can foreclose the mortgage by having the property sold at public auction and applying the proceeds of the sale to the debt.

**Real property (ad valorem) tax and special assessment liens.** The taxes levied by a local government constitute a specific lien against the real estate. State laws provide that real property tax liens have priority over all other liens. An assessment is a **levy,** or *tax, against a property for payment of a share of the cost of improvements made to areas adjoining the property.* Examples of these improvements are paving streets, installing sewer or water lines, and constructing sidewalks. Special assessments constitute a specific lien against the property until paid. Ad valorem and special tax liens are valid for ten years.

**Mechanics' liens.** In North Carolina, the term *mechanic's lien* includes a lien filed by anyone (such as carpenters, lumber companies, appraisers, and surveyors) who provides labor or material to a property or property improvement. If these people are not paid according to the terms of their contract, they can file a lien against the property to which they provided work or materials any time up to 120 days after the last day that any labor or material was furnished to the property. The mechanic's lien is unique in that when it is filed, it becomes effective as of the first day any labor or material was furnished rather than on the day the lien is recorded. The mechanic's lien holder has up to 180 days after the last labor or materials were furnished to take court action to enforce her lien, provided she filed the lien within the 120-day filing period. The Statute of Limitations sets the time limit for the filing of lawsuits in various situations. If a lawsuit is not filed within the statutory time period, the injured party loses the right of legal remedy by operation of law. Therefore, the mechanic's lien must be filed within the statutory period. The special treatment the mechanic's lien receives as to effective date makes it necessary to verify that all work done on a property within 120 days before closing has been paid for.

## General Liens

**Judgment liens.** A judgment is a court decree establishing that one person is indebted to another and establishing the amount of that indebtedness. A **judgment lien** constitutes *a general lien against all real and personal property the judgment debtor owns* in the county in which the judgment is recorded. The lien takes effect from the time the judgment is recorded. A judgment creditor may record a judgment in any county in the state, and it will constitute a general lien against all of the judgment debtor's property in that county. The judgment also creates a lien against any property the judgment debtor acquires subsequent to the judgment during the existence of the judgment.

A general lien does not apply to real property owned by husband and wife by the entirety or as joint tenants if the judgment is against only one of them. For the lien to attach to property in such cases, the judgment must be obtained against husband and wife on a debt they both incurred. A judgment lien remains in effect for ten years in North Carolina unless the judgment is paid. Judgments may be renewed and kept in force for an additional period if the creditor brings another action on the original judgment before the original period has elapsed. Judgment liens have a priority relationship based on the time of recording. The creditor who records a lien before another creditor records a lien against the same judgment debtor has a higher priority claim. The judgment debtor's obligation to the creditor who has priority must be satisfied before creditors with a lower priority. Judgment liens are enforced by an order called an execution. This is an order signed by the clerk of court that instructs the sheriff to sell the property of the judgment debtor and apply the proceeds of the sale to the satisfaction of the judgment.

**Personal property tax liens.** Personal property taxes are assessed on certain personal property owned as of January 1 of the tax year. If these taxes are not paid, they become a general lien against all of the property the individual owns. Like the real property tax lien, this lien takes priority over other liens. The tax on licensed motor vehicles no longer constitutes a lien on real property.

**Federal tax liens.** The Internal Revenue Service of the United States can create a general lien against all of a taxpayer's property for overdue federal taxes. This lien is created by obtaining a judgment in a federal court against the taxpayer and by filing a certificate of lien against the landowner in the office of the clerk of the superior court in the county in which the taxpayer's land is located. A federal tax lien does not have a special priority. Its priority is established by time of recording, and its validity extends for ten years. The federal government imposes a tax on the estate of deceased persons, which is called the federal estate tax. This tax creates a lien that attaches to all property, both real and personal, in the estate and continues until the tax is paid.

**State tax liens.** The North Carolina Commissioner of Revenue can create a general lien against all of a taxpayer's property for overdue state taxes. This lien becomes effective from the time of docketing in the office of the clerk of the superior court in the county in which the delinquent taxpayer's property is located and remains effective for ten years.

All states impose a state inheritance tax upon the inheritance of real and personal property. This tax is paid by the heirs to the estate and remains a lien on the property until it is paid. The estate can sell sufficient property to satisfy the tax bill.

### *Priority of Liens*

The priority of most liens in relation to other liens is based on the time (day and hour) they were recorded. North Carolina practices this system, which is known as the *pure race system.* This system provides that liens are established in priority by the time they are recorded; that is, the person who wins the race to the courthouse is at the head of the list. When the proceeds from the foreclosure sale are distributed, the lien holder with the highest priority gets paid first. With the exception of lien holders with special priority, the first to record is the first to be paid. However, certain liens have special priority by North Carolina statute, as is the case with mechanics' liens, where lien priority relates to the first day of work on the job rather than to the date of recordation. The highest priority of all liens is given to liens for real property taxes.

## Restrictive (Protective) Covenants

Restrictive (protective) covenants are private restrictions that limit the way land may be used. They attach to the land, and they pass with title to successive purchasers. Often a developer defines such covenants to establish characteristics of a new residential subdivision. They may limit construction to single-family homes on a specific lot size, or they may require a given size or type of architecture. The covenants can address anything that is legal. Careful consideration should go into establishing restrictive covenants because property becomes more difficult to sell as the number of restrictions increases. The *restrictions may be written in the individual deed or recorded as a master instrument,* a **declaration of restrictions.**

## Lis Pendens

This *notice of pending litigation* indicates existence of an unresolved lawsuit that affects title to all or part of the property of the defendant. Recording of the **lis pendens** *(lawsuit pending)* provides constructive notice of the forthcoming legal action and its possible outcome. As a result, if the property is transferred to a new owner after the notice of lis pendens is placed on the public record in the county where the property is located, any court order or lien resulting from the lawsuit will affect the new owner's title to the property. Notices of lis pendens are routinely filed in boundary dispute cases.

## Easements

An **easement** is a *nonpossessory interest in land owned by another.* It provides a right of use in land and not a right of possession.

### General Classification of Easements

Easements can exist for a variety of legal uses, such as right-of-way for ingress and egress; a party wall; the right to take water from the land of another; the right to receive air, light, or heat from above the land of another; the right to obtain water from a well or spring on the land of another; and a right-of-way for the purpose of putting utility lines under and above the surface of the land.

### Appurtenant Easement

An **appurtenance** is *something that has been added to something else and, as a result, becomes an inherent part of that to which it has been added.* In real property law, an appurtenance is the right that one property owner has in the property of another as a result of the first property owner's ownership in a particular parcel of real estate. For example, if a purchaser receives a title to a tract of land and included in this title is an easement in the form of a right-of-way across the adjoining land of another, this easement is an appurtenance to that title. *Whenever the titleholder conveys that title to another, the conveyance includes the easement since the easement is appurtenant to the title.* Since an **appurtenant easement** moves with a title, it is said to *run with the land.* The land that is benefited by the easement is described as the *dominant tenement,* dominant land, or dominant estate, and the land encumbered by the easement (the land on which the easement exists) is described as the *servient tenement,* servient land, or servient estate. (See Figure 2.6.)

**FIGURE 2.6** An example of an appurtenant easement.

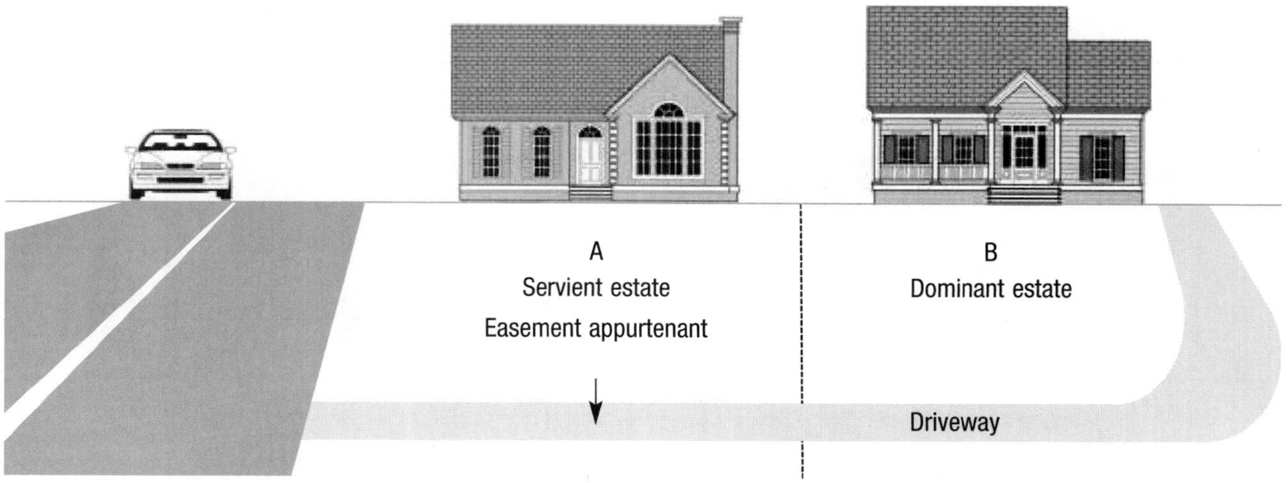

## Easements in Gross

Unlike appurtenant easements, **easements in gross** *are not dependent upon ownership of an adjoining property.* Easements in gross have no dominant tenement, only a servient one. Typically, the owner of an easement in gross does not necessarily own property in the area of the property in which the easement exists. The owner of an easement in gross usually receives an easement by contract.

The most prevalent use of easements in gross is in the form of commercial easements. Commercial easements are common throughout the United States and are typically held by utility companies for the purpose of installing power lines, telephone lines, and gas lines above the surface of the earth, on the earth itself, or underground. Railroad rights-of-way are another prominent example of a commercial easement.

Commercial easements in gross are assignable and can be conveyed. Personal easements in gross (easements in gross held by an individual) are not assignable, cannot be conveyed, and are not inheritable. Personal easements in gross are rare today.

## Creation of Easements

Easements may be created by the use of an express written agreement, may be implied by the actions of a person, or may be created by the operation of law. (See Figure 2.8.) The Statute of Frauds requires that all transfers of interest in real property be in writing; therefore, an express easement cannot be created orally.

## Express Easements

Express easements have written documentation and should be recorded. An owner selling his land can expressly grant an easement to a buyer by using the appropriate language in the deed. In Figure 2.6, if A sold the land to B, A could grant the easement to B to cross A's land. If the situation were the other way around and B sold the land to A, B would reserve the easement. The party walls illustrated in Figure 2.7 are a second example of express written easements. A **party wall** *is used by two adjoining neighbors to support the side wall of each unit.* If the property line ran down the middle of the wall, each party would have a cross easement in the other or would have a tenancy in common. If the wall were entirely within the property of one party, however, the other would have an easement in the use of the wall. Easements may be created by express dedication, in which a portion of a property is set aside for use by the public. For example, a developer who is building a residential subdivision may dedicate a portion of the land for use by the public, such as roadways or recreational parks.

**FIGURE 2.7** Party wall.

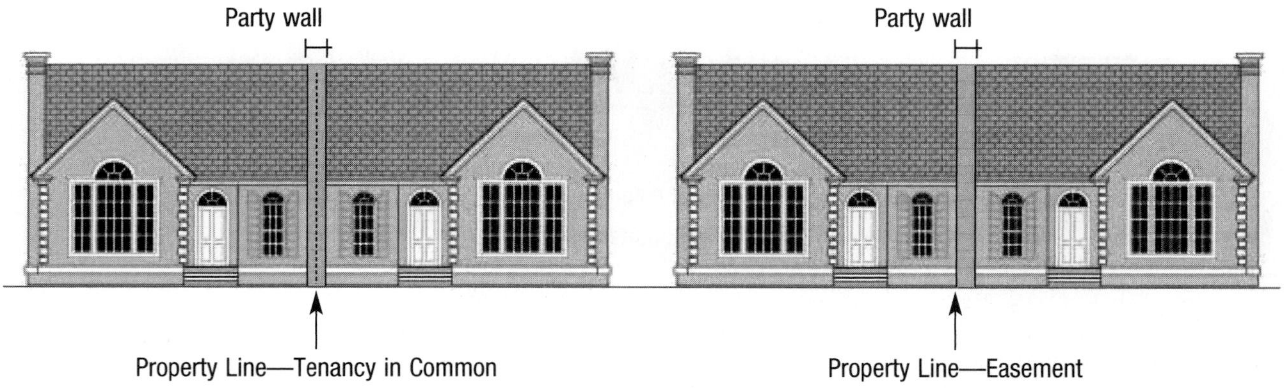

1. Express (words are used to spell out the agreement)
   a. Grant or reserve
   b. Party walls
   c. Dedication
2. Implied (actions of the parties)
   a. Necessity
   b. Reference to a recorded plat
3. Operation of law (court order)
   a. Prescription
   b. Condemnation

**FIGURE 2.8**

The way easements arise.

## Implied Easements

In contrast to express easements, implied easements have no documentation. In certain cases, the actions of a party create an easement when these actions demonstrate an intent to create an easement. An *easement by necessity* is implied if a seller conveys title to a buyer who would be landlocked without access to a road. In Figure 2.6, if A sold the property to B and did not grant B the easement shown, B would have the right to claim such an easement by reason of the necessity to get to the public road. An *easement by dedication* may be implied as well as express. If the developer described in the preceding section had not expressly granted the roadways in the new subdivision but had described the property by referring to a map showing the existence of such streets, the easement would be implied.

## Easements by Operation of Law

An easement may be obtained by **prescription,** that is, by *using another's land for a prescribed period of time.* The use must be open and well known to others (notorious) and must be continued and uninterrupted for the period of time required by laws of the state. Users must prove in court that they have satisfied all the requirements for the intended use. An easement can also be created by condemnation under the power of eminent domain of the government. This power enables the government to take private land for the benefit of the general public. In all cases, the property owner must be compensated for differences in value before and after the action by the government. Usually, condemnations for rights-of-way for various public uses are for the purpose of obtaining an easement rather than for acquiring title.

A statutory cartway proceeding is another easement that can arise by operation of law. The owner of a landlocked parcel of property can petition to have a cartway sectioned off over someone else's property. A three-person jury decides where the cartway is to be and what damages the owner of the landlocked property must pay the owners of the land where the cartway is located. Specific statutes govern this proceeding. A cartway of at least 18 feet in width may be obtained to connect the landlocked property to a public highway if the cartway is for the purpose of cultivation or for using the land for one of the purposes listed in the statute.

## Termination of Easements

Easements may be terminated as follows: by the release of the easement by the dominant owner to the servient owner, by combining the dominant and servient lands into one tract of land, by abandonment of the easement by the dominant owner, by the cessation of the purpose for which an easement was created, and by the expiration of a specified period of time for which the easement was created.

## Encroachments

An **encroachment** is a *trespass on the land of another as a result of an intrusion or invasion by some structure or other object,* such as a wall, fence, overhanging balcony, or driveway. The encroaching owner may obtain title to the area of the land upon which the encroachment exists by adverse possession (discussed in Chapter 3) or may obtain an easement by prescription in the case of the encroaching driveway if the owner of the land subject to the encroachment does not take appropriate legal action. Since encroachments are illegal, the owner who is being encroached upon can sue for damages (a judgment by the court requiring the encroacher to compensate the owner for the encroachment) or petition the court for a decree ordering the encroachment to be removed.

Encroachments caused by building improvements straddling property boundaries are a major reason why lending institutions require surveys that specify the location of all improvements on the property.

# PROPERTY TAXATION IN NORTH CAROLINA

The taxation on real property is the major source of revenue for the local units of government, including both the county and the city or township. Taxes are imposed upon real property ad valorem, that is, according to value. North Carolina's statute, known as the Machinery Act, sets forth the details of property taxation. A key point of the act is that it requires the assessed value (AV) to be set at full market value (MV), a 100 percent assessment, at least once every eight years. This reappraisal of property every eight years is called an *octennial reappraisal.* A horizontal adjustment upward or downward may be made at the four-year interval between the eight-year adjustments.

An official called a tax assessor is responsible for the valuation of property for tax purposes. Property values must be reasonably uniform to provide equal taxation of property owners. Many property owners take advantage of an appeal process when they believe their property has been overvalued. As a practical matter, a real estate agent can expect numerous phone calls from past clients asking for information to support a value of their property that is less than the new assessment if they believe assessment is higher than the actual market value. Often all they need is information on the selling prices of similar homes in their neighborhood. If they need an appraisal, the agent should refer them to a licensed appraiser.

## Tax Rate and Calculations

Each local government sets a tax rate annually to meet the needs of its budget. It does this by dividing the total assessed value of all the property subject to taxation by the amount of money needed for the budget. The rate is then applied to the assessed value of the individual properties subject to taxation. The rate must be sufficient to provide the revenue for the local government's budget and may be changed every year. North Carolina uses the formula of a tax rate per $100 of assessed valuation. Given the assessed value of the property and the current tax rate, you can easily calculate the annual property taxes. For example, if the AV is $48,000 and the tax rate is $0.50, the annual tax is calculated as ($48,000 ÷ $100) × $.50 = 480 units of $100 × $.50 = $240.

## Property Subject to Taxation

Generally, at some point, all real and personal property is subject to taxation in North Carolina. Most people know of several exceptions to this generalization, however, such as property owned by churches and nonprofit charities. According to new tax laws, licensed personal property (such as automobiles) is now taxed upon relicensing. The legislature has also exempted household goods from personal property taxation and eliminated the intangibles tax on funds in the bank. Additionally, special cases exist for historic and certain types of agricultural property and for the property of elderly and disabled people.

## Listing Property for Taxation

All property subject to taxation must be listed with the local tax office. Real property is listed in the county where the property is located; personal property is listed in the county where the owner has her permanent residence if this is different. The Machinery Act requires property to be listed during January, even though the localities operate on a July 1 fiscal year. In certain circumstances where the taxing authority considers it necessary, it has a local option to extend the listing period for another month.

## Appraisal and Assessment

The distinction between appraisal and assessment often confuses people. *Appraisal* is the process of determining a market value; it is discussed in detail in Chapter 9. *Assessment* is the determination of a value of the property for taxation purposes. As noted previously, real property must be revalued at least every eight years, at which time the assessed value is set at the appraised or market value. As a practical matter, however, one would not expect the two values to be identical at times other than this revaluation, as the property usually appreciates in value over the course of the eight years.

## Timetable for Listing and Tax Collection

Real and personal property taxes attach to the property on January 1 when the property is due for listing. The property owner has until January 31 to list the property. Property taxes are due September 1 and are paid in arrears. Penalties are assessed at the beginning of January if taxes are not paid at that time. Many property owners think the taxes are due January 1 of the year after they are billed in September because they do not have to pay a penalty for late payment until then. All real estate agents should be aware that this is not the case; the taxes are due September 1.

## Property Tax Lien

As noted in the discussion of liens, the real property tax lien takes the first priority. As such, it is an exception to North Carolina's pure race system since, in essence, the tax collector has already won the race to the courthouse, even before the others start.

### *Special Priority of the Tax Lien*

Even though a lien is recorded against a property in one year, a subsequent default in the payment of property taxes years later will take precedence over the earlier recorded lien. As a practical matter, most creditors understand this situation and see to the payment of taxes so their lien priority is not disturbed. For example, mortgage lenders prefer to collect monthly tax escrow payments from the borrower so the lender has the funds to pay the taxes on time to protect the mortgage lien.

## Special Assessments

In addition to the ordinary property taxes that are collected by the local government for normal operating expenses, taxes may be levied for special county, city, or town projects (such as paving streets, building sidewalks, or installing sewer or water lines) that benefit certain properties. The statutes allow a number of ways to determine the amount of these assessments. A common way is to base the assessments on the number of feet a property has that borders on the improvement.

### *By County*

Counties have the authority to establish special assessments for new utilities to the area, such as a new water reservoir or sewage treatment facility, that benefit all properties within the jurisdiction. The statutes specify a detailed process of determining the cost of the project, publishing a notice of the intended assessment, and setting a schedule for the payment of the tax by the individual property owners.

### By City and Town

Procedures are also established for cities and towns to levy and collect special assessments that are similar to those established for the counties.

### Special Assessment Liens

As a real property tax lien, the special assessment attaches to the land and enjoys a high, although unique, priority. This lien is behind the real and personal property tax liens, but takes priority over other liens.

## SUMMARY OF IMPORTANT POINTS

1. Real property consists of land and everything attached to the land, including things that grow naturally without requiring planting and cultivation. Real property ownership is often described as a bundle of rights because it involves many attributes.
2. Annual crops that require planting and cultivation are personal property and are called emblements or *fructus industriales.*
3. Ownership in land includes the surface of the earth and the areas above and below the surface.
4. A fixture begins as personal property and becomes real property when attached to land improvements or the land. Since fixtures create many practical problems in real estate transactions, practitioners need to pay careful attention to this concept.
5. The allodial system of real property ownership used in the United States provides for private ownership of real estate.
6. Private ownership of property is subject to four powers of government: eminent domain, police power, taxation, and escheat.
7. Estates involve the definition of the scope of one's interest in real property. Estates in land are divided into two groups: freehold and estates of less than freehold (leasehold). In freehold estates, one has an ownership interest in realty that lasts at least a lifetime. The nonfreehold, or rental, interests last less than a lifetime.
8. The freehold estates are the fee simple estates, which are inheritable, and life estates, which are not inheritable unless the life estate is for the life of another (pur autre vie).
9. The most comprehensive form of ownership in real property is fee simple absolute.
10. Life estates revert to the grantor or pass on to a remainderman.
11. The duration of a life estate is measured by the life of the life tenant.
12. Conventional life estates are created by someone's intentional act. Legal life estates, such as marital life estates, are created by operation of law.
13. A life tenant has the right of alienation, the right of encumbrance, the right of estovers, and the rights of possession and enjoyment of the property and of deriving certain income from it.

14. A life tenant is obligated to preserve and maintain the property for the benefit of the future interest.

15. Title held in the name of one person only is called ownership in severalty.

16. When title is held concurrently by two or more persons or organizations, it is called co-ownership (also, concurrent, or joint ownership). The forms of co-ownership are tenancy in common, joint tenancy, tenancy by the entirety, and certain aspects of condominiums and cooperatives.

17. Joint tenancy and tenancy by the entirety require the four unities of time, title, interest, and possession. Tenancy by the entirety is limited to husband and wife and requires a fifth unity, marriage (or unity of person) and includes the right of survivorship.

18. The owner of a condominium unit holds title to the unit either in severalty or as a co-owner with another, and she and any co-owners of the individual unit hold title to the common areas as a tenant in common with the owners of the other units.

19. The creation of a condominium requires the recording of a declaration, articles of association, by-laws, and construction plans.

20. The North Carolina Condominium Act applies to the sale or resale of condominiums created on or after October 1, 1986. This act provides consumer protection by requiring a developer to disclose certain information on new condominiums before a contract is signed, allowing the purchaser of a new condominium a seven-day right to cancel the purchase, requiring owners of resale units to disclose monthly assessments and other fees, and providing an implied warranty that the unit is constructed in an acceptable manner.

21. Ownership in a cooperative results from stock ownership in a corporation that owns a building containing cooperative apartments. Stockholders occupy apartments under a lease.

22. Business organizations may receive, hold, and convey title to real property.

23. Less-than-freehold estates are also called leasehold estates and are estates of limited duration, providing possession and control but not title (as in the case of freehold estates).

24. The leasehold estates are estate for years, estate from year to year, estate at will, and estate at sufferance.

25. Encumbrances are things that diminish the bundle of rights. They may take the form of a claim, lien, charge, or liability attached to and binding upon real property. Examples are encroachments, liens, restrictive (protective) covenants, easements, marital life estates, and deed restrictions. A lien is a claim or charge against property that may result in the loss of title through foreclosure. Restrictive covenants, lis pendens, easements, and encroachments also encumber, or diminish, the full interest in title.

26. An appurtenance is a right or privilege that results from ownership of a particular property and moves with the title. An appurtenance depends on a principal item or the real estate. It belongs to that to which it is attached. It cannot stand alone.

27. Property taxation in North Carolina is governed by the Machinery Act. This act requires that the assessed value (AV) be set at the market value (MV) at least every eight years (octennial reappraisal). Essentially, all real and some personal property is subject to ad valorem taxation.

28. The tax rate can change annually.

## ITEMS TO CONSIDER FOR THE STATE EXAM

An analysis of performance by exam category on the state licensing examination indicates that the following points are often confused.

1. Definitions of encumbrance and appurtenance.
2. The test to determine whether an item is a fixture.
3. The interaction between a fee simple absolute title and encumbrances. The title is freely transferable by the owner since she has the highest rights in the property, but the title may not always be free of encumbrances. Fee simple titles often have encumbrances, which pass with the title. To be effective, however, such encumbrances need to be recorded where they are easily discoverable (with certain exceptions, such as the potential for a mechanic's lien).
4. A freehold and a nonfreehold estate can exist at the same time in a rental property. The landlord retains the title (freehold) but has handed over the right of possession (nonfreehold) for a period of time.
5. Riparian rights are the rights of property owners adjoining a watercourse, such as a river. Such owners have the right to draw reasonable amounts of water from and enjoy access to the watercourse.

   Boundary lines of property bordering water include:

   a. Navigable waterway: Adjacent landowners own to banks.
   b. Nonnavigable waterway:
      - One owner owning all the land surrounding water also owns the land under water.
      - If more than one owner owns surrounding land, each owns land to center of water.
   c. Oceans or lakes where water levels fluctuate: Adjacent owners own to mean high water mark.
   d. State owns land under navigable waterway and the foreshore (land between high and low watermarks) of oceans and lakes.

The tax rate may be changed *annually.* Do not confuse this with the requirement for revaluation on an eight-year (octennial) basis.

## REVIEW QUESTIONS

Answers to the review questions are in the Answer Key at the back of the book.

1. Personal property attached to real property is prevented from becoming real property by which of the following?
   A. value
   B. an appurtenance
   C. security agreement and financing statement
   D. mineral rights

2. Which of the following is a right in the property of another that results from ownership in a particular parcel of real estate?
   A. easement in gross
   B. appurtenant easement
   C. license - unwrttn. permission
   D. condemnation

3. Which of the following is (are) correct?
   A. an easement provides a nonpossessory interest in land
   B. the land on which an easement exists is the dominant tenement → Servient
   C. the land that benefits from an easement is the servient tenement → dominant
   D. all of the above

4. Easements may be created in all of the following ways EXCEPT:
   A. condemnation
   B. dedication
   C. prescription
   D. assessment

5. An easement is terminated:
   A. when the purpose for which the easement was created ceases to exist
   B. when the adjoining dominant and servient tenements are combined into one tract of land
   C. by abandonment of the easement by the dominant owner
   D. all of the above

6. If a property owner gives a specific person permission to cross his property, this is a(n):
   A. easement in gross
   B. easement appurtenant
   C. lease
   D. encroachment

7. The creation of an easement by condemnation results from the exercise of which of the following?
   A. prescription
   B. eminent domain
   C. dedication
   D. implication

8. A fee simple determinable is an example of:
   I. nonfreehold estate.
   II. defeasible estate.
   A. I only
   B. II only
   C. both I and II
   D. neither I nor II

9. If a widow inherits an estate by will granting her the right of use and possession of a parcel of land for the rest of her life, with the provision that the estate will go to her children in fee simple upon her death, she has received:
   A. an inheritable freehold estate
   B. a life estate with remainder
   C. a life estate pur autre vie
   D. none of the above

10. The highest and best form of estate in real property is which of the following?
   A. appurtenant easement
   B. defeasible fee
   C. life estate in reversion
   D. fee simple absolute

11. Estate for years, estates from year to year, estates at will, and estates by sufferance:
   A. are leasehold estates
   B. create a legal relationship between the parties of landlord and tenant
   C. are nonfreehold estates
   D. all of the above

12. When title to real property is held in the name of one person only:
   I. it is called ownership in severalty.
   II. if the owner is a married person, it is called tenancy by the entirety.
   A. I only
   B. II only
   C. both I and II
   D. neither I nor II

13. Which of the following types of ownership requires unity of interest, title, time, and possession?
   A. cooperative
   B. tenancy in common
   C. joint tenancy
   D. condominium

14. None of the following includes the right of survivorship in North Carolina EXCEPT:
   A. tenancy in common
   B. tenancy by the entirety
   C. life estate
   D. joint tenancy

15. The purchaser of a condominium unit receives title to the land on which the condominium is situated as a:
   A. tenant by the entirety
   B. tenant in common
   C. joint tenant
   D. tenant at sufferance

16. The purchaser of a condominium time-share:
   A. takes title for a specified time period (or periods) each calendar year
   B. may not convey title to anyone else
   C. has a 30-day right to rescind the purchase contract
   D. all of the above

17. In the cooperative form of ownership:
   A. the owner owns his unit in severalty
   B. each owner owns an interest in the common areas
   C. the owners own the building as tenants in common
   D. none of the above

18. A tenant in common:
   A. may sell her interest in the property
   B. may pledge the entire property as security for a mortgaged loan
   C. may not bring legal action to partition the property
   D. has the right of survivorship in the property

19. Ownership as tenants by the entirety includes which of the following?
   A. the right of one owner to convey title to his share of ownership without the participation of the other owner
   B. the right of survivorship
   C. ownership of an unequal interest in the property with another
   D. conversion to ownership as joint tenants if the owners are divorced

20. The tax levy against real property to provide the funds to pay all or part of the cost of an improvement to the property is which of the following?
   A. mechanic's lien
   B. special assessment
   C. general lien
   D. judgment lien

21. All of the following are examples of specific liens EXCEPT:
   A. income tax liens
   B. mortgage liens
   C. mechanics' liens
   D. real property tax liens

22. Which of the following statements regarding judgment liens is correct?
   A. judgment liens will not attach to property to which title is held by a husband and wife as tenants by the entirety unless both participated in the creation of the debt and are both named as defendants in the judgment
   B. judgment liens have a priority over the real property tax assessment
   C. judgment liens have a priority over all liens other than property tax liens
   D. none of the above

23. Liens, easements, encroachments, and restrictive covenants are examples of which of the following?
   A. emblements
   B. estovers
   C. estates
   D. encumbrances

24. Which of the following is an estate that automatically renews itself for consecutive periods?
   A. estate at will
   B. life estate
   C. estate from year to year
   D. estate for years

25. After the termination of a lease, the tenant continued in possession of the property without permission of the property owner. The tenant's status is:
   A. tenant at will
   B. lessee
   C. trespasser
   D. tenancy at sufferance

26. Time-share property in North Carolina requires:
   I. the developer to have a real estate license.
   II. project registration with the commission before marketing.
   III. all time-share salespersons to have a real estate license.
   A. I and II only
   B. II and III only
   C. I and III only
   D. I, II, and III

27. Time-share property in North Carolina is:
    I. deemed real property.
    II. defined as the right to occupy a property during separated time periods over five years or more.
    A. I only
    B. II only
    C. both I and II
    D. neither I nor II

28. Real property taxation in North Carolina:
    A. requires listing the property by December 30
    B. makes September 1 the due date of the tax
    C. requires penalties for paying after September 1
    D. none of the above

29. How often may the North Carolina property tax rate be changed?
    A. every eight years
    B. every four years
    C. every two years
    D. each year

30. The Jones's home has an assessed value of $100,000 in a locality where the tax rate is $1.45. What is their monthly payment for tax escrow?
    A. $83
    B. $100
    C. $121
    D. $1,450

31. The tax rate is calculated on every $100 of the:
    A. sales price
    B. appraised value
    C. listing price
    D. assessed value

32. Real estate property taxes are due and payable:
    A. January 1
    B. July 1
    C. September 1
    D. December 31

33. An appurtenant easement must:
    I. involve a servient and dominant estate.
    II. run with the land.
    III. be obtained by condemnation.
    A. I only
    B. III only
    C. I and II
    D. I, II, and III

34. All of the following involve ownership of real property EXCEPT:
    A. cooperatives
    B. condominiums
    C. townhouses
    D. time-shares

35. An encumbrance always:
    A. has a positive effect on property value
    B. has a negative effect on property value
    C. is a lien
    D. none of the above

# Chapter 3

**KEY TERMS**

acknowledgment
adverse possession
beneficiary
bequest
chain of title
cloud on a title
color of title
Conner Act
constructive notice
covenant against encumbrances
covenant of quiet enjoyment
covenant of right to convey
covenant of seisin
covenant of warranty
deed
descent
devise
devisee
excise tax
executor
executrix
foreclosure
grantee
grantor
intestate
judicial deed
legal description
lien foreclosure sale
Marketable Title Act
metes and bounds
plat
point of beginning
probate
quitclaim deed
recording
special warranty deed
Statute of Frauds
suit to quiet title
testate
testator
testatrix
title examination
title insurance
will
words of conveyance

# Transfer of Title to Real Property

## LEARNING OBJECTIVES

At the conclusion of this chapter, you should be able to:

1. List the methods of transferring title by the four categories of alienation—voluntary, involuntary, during life, and at death.
2. List and describe the essential elements of deeds in North Carolina.
3. Describe the three primary types of deed in North Carolina.
4. List the miscellaneous types of special purpose deed in North Carolina.
5. Describe excise tax, defining the rate and calculating the cost.
6. Describe the process of title examination.
7. Describe title insurance and the types of coverage.
8. Describe the importance and process of title recordation.
9. Explain the system of property description used in North Carolina.

## IN THIS CHAPTER

The transfer of a title to real property is described in law as alienation. The property owner is alienated, or separated, from the title by transfer of the title to another. The alienation may be voluntary or involuntary and may occur during life or after death.

## PROPERTY DESCRIPTION

### Adequacy of Description

Any method that enables a surveyor or civil engineer to locate property with certainty is an acceptable legal method; however, the three most acceptable types of property description are metes and bounds, the governmental rectangular survey system, and description by reference. One should avoid using a simple street address, a tax description, or any ambiguous description. Although a description containing a latent ambiguity (one in which the property can be identified by extrinsic information) is legally sufficient, it is not professionally acceptable. A description containing a patent ambiguity (one in which the property cannot be identified with any certainty) is neither legally nor professionally acceptable.

Contracts should include an adequate legal description. If none exists, an attorney should be consulted. Real Estate brokers are not allowed to write legal descriptions.

## Methods of Describing Real Property

### Metes and Bounds

The property description primarily used in North Carolina (and commonly used in the states that were part of the original 13 colonies) is the metes and bounds description. In the metes and bounds description, the **metes** are the *distances from point to point in the description* and the **bounds** are the *directions from one point to another in the description.*

A metes and bounds description is made from a survey performed by a licensed, registered land surveyor. One of the most important aspects of the metes and bounds description is the selection of the **point of beginning.** This point should be *one that is reasonably easy to locate and tied to a reference point that is well established.* After selecting the point of beginning, the surveyor identifies the boundaries of the property by a series of "calls" that consist of distances (metes) and directions (bounds) between natural or artificial markers called landmarks or monuments. After all the calls have been made, the description must close; that is, the last call must end at the point of beginning. The directions in the metes and bounds description might read "N-45° E." There may be a further refinement of the direction. Degrees (°) are divided into minutes (′), with 1 degree containing 60 minutes, and each minute is divided into 60 seconds (″). A description then might read "N-45°, 30′,10″E." These bearings are illustrated in Figure 3.1.

Often a description also contains a statement as to the number of acres or quantity of land being conveyed. In the event this quantity is inconsistent with the description by metes and bounds, the quantity of land yields to the number of acres as actually established by the metes and bounds description.

### Government Rectangular Survey System

This system is not used as a practical matter in North Carolina and is mentioned here only to describe systems of other states. This system is not tested on the North Carolina real estate licensing exam.

In the government rectangular survey system, the country is divided by north-south lines called principal meridians and by east-west lines called base lines. The areas between the base lines and north-south meridians are called ranges. Within the ranges are townships. Each township is a square, 6 miles by 6 miles, and is, therefore, 36 square miles in area. Each township is divided into 36 sections. Each section is 1 mile square, or 1 square mile. A section is divided into quarter sections and may be subdivided into areas smaller than one-quarter sections. Each section contains 640 acres; therefore, a quarter section is 160 acres. Here is an example of a legal description using the government rectangular survey: "All of the southwest quarter of the northwest quarter of section 25, range 1 east, township 1 north, Huntsville meridian and base line."

Examination of these sections as a measurement of land area can provide an introduction to the simple arithmetic of real estate. You can calculate the number of acres in a section by recalling the one familiar number of 5,280 feet per mile and by learning the new number of 43,560 square feet per acre. The number of acres in a square mile is figured by calculating the total square feet and dividing by the number of square feet per acre; that is:

$$\text{Acres} = \frac{5,280 \times 5,280}{43,560} = 640$$

Furthermore, you can divide a section into quarter sections by dividing by four; that is, 160 acres per quarter section, and so on.

**FIGURE 3.1** A sample metes and bounds description in conjunction with a description by reference.

An example of a typical metes and bounds description and the plat resulting from that description follow.

*Being all of Lot No. 20 of the subdivision of a portion of the property of Mortgage Heights Land Company, Inc., Centre County, as shown by plat thereof prepared by Worley and Gray, Consulting Engineers, dated October 1, 1995, and recorded in Book 5, page 40, Records of Plats for Centre County, and more particularly bounded and described as follows:

**BEGINNING on a stake in the northeast margin of Amortization Drive, south corner of Lot No. 20 of the subdivision or a portion of the property of Mortgage Heights Land Company, Inc., and running thence North 6° 18' East 215.2 feet to a stake; thence North 8° 49' West 241.0 feet to a stake, common corner of Lot Nos. 20 and 19 of said subdivision; thence with the dividing line between said Lot Nos. 19 and 20, South 87° 50' West 138.5 feet to a stake in the east margin of a cul-de-sac; thence with the east margin of said cul-de-sac in a southwesterly direction along a curve with the radius of 50.0 feet, 61.2 feet to a stake in said margin; thence with the east margin of a drive leading to Amortization Drive, South 5° 19' West 132.8 feet to a stake in the point of intersection of said margin of said drive with Amortization Drive; thence with the northeast margin of said Amortization Drive, South 51° 17' East 84.7 feet to a stake in said margin; thence still with said margin of said drive, South 42° 27' East 47.2 feet to a stake in said margin; thence still said margin of said drive, South 29° 36' East 199.9 feet to the BEGINNING.

*Description by reference
**Description by metes and bounds

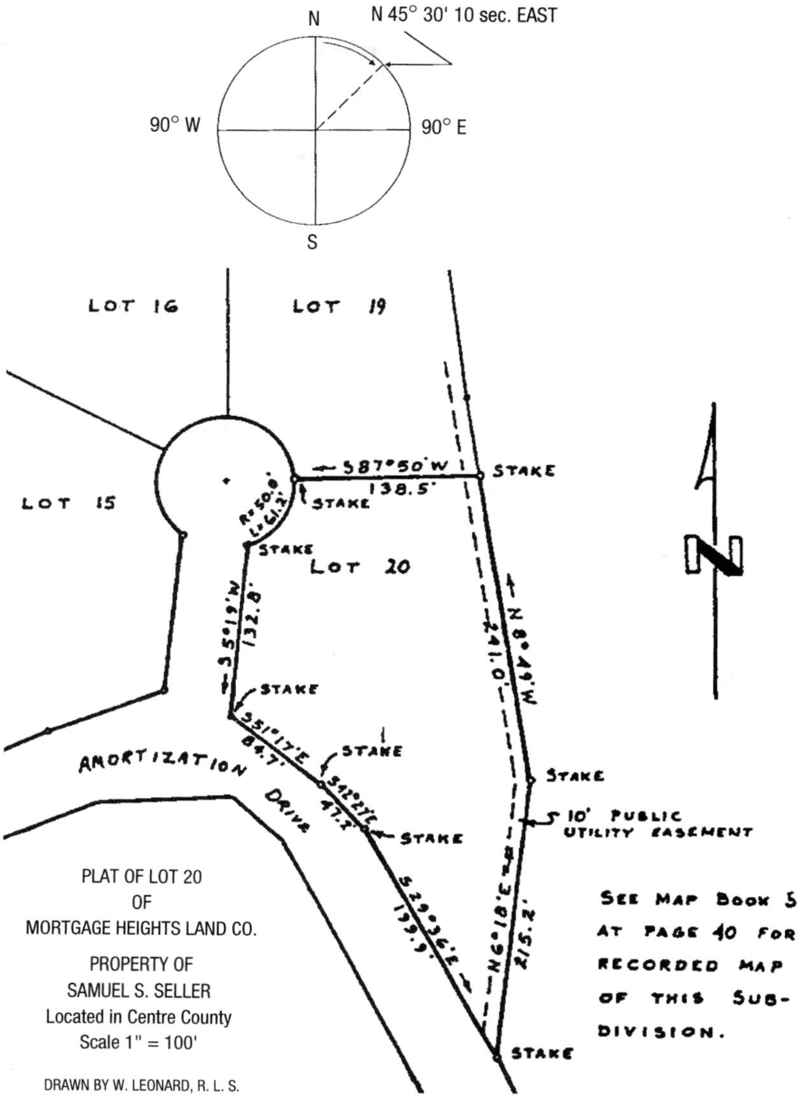


## Description by Reference

A description by reference is a valid legal description. Sometimes an attorney incorporates into the deed a description by reference in addition to a metes and bounds description. Sometimes the description by reference is the only description in the deed.

**Reference to recorded plat (lot and book).** A description by reference is one in which a reference is made to a **plat,** or a *property map,* and a lot number that has been recorded. The description states the plat book number and page number in which the plat is recorded. The reader can refer to the plat and determine the exact location and dimensions of the property. An example of description by reference to a subdivision plat is shown in Figure 3.1. A sample subdivision plat map is shown in Figure 3.2.

**Reference to publicly recorded documents.** Sometimes a property is described by reference to a previous deed that conveyed the same property. This reference incorporates the description in the previous deed by reference into the deed being prepared. If the description in

**FIGURE 3.2** A sample subdivision plat map.

the previous deed is accurate, all is well and good. If the description in the previous deed is faulty, the subsequent deed is still bound by that description.

**Informal reference.** An informal reference such as a street address, a tax parcel number, or a word picture describing the property is a legally acceptable method if such a description identifies the property to the exclusion of all other properties. However, there is a huge potential for error. Street names can change. Streets can have similar names; for example, Plantation Place and Plantation Road. An individual can own several adjoining lots that are not part of the property identified by the street address. Mr. Jones, the owner of several farms, can convey his farm described only as adjacent to widow Smith's property, unaware that another widow named Smith recently purchased property adjoining another of his farms. This description does not adequately describe the property, although it may have before the second widow Smith purchased her farm.

## Property Survey

A property survey is a determination of the boundaries of a specific tract of land that is done by a licensed surveyor or civil engineer. After determining the boundaries of a tract, the surveyor or engineer prepares a map or plat of the parcel of land. In addition to the boundaries of a property, a survey includes such important information as the location of buildings, fences, and other structures and the location of easements and rights-of-way.

It is not uncommon for survey markers (monuments or landmarks) to become lost over time and for boundaries to become indistinct. Additionally, encroachments on another's property may have occurred. When a garage was built, it may have violated setback requirements or encroached upon a neighbor's property. A survey prior to closing on a property will identify problems while they can still be corrected by the seller. Real estate practitioners should not venture opinions as to this information; instead, they should refer their clients to a licensed surveyor or engineer.

# METHODS OF TRANSFERRING TITLE

## By Descent (Intestate Succession)

If *a person dies without leaving a valid will* (**intestate**), *property is distributed to the heirs* by **descent** according to laws called intestate succession statutes. The person appointed by a court to distribute the property of an intestate according to the provisions of the statute is called an *administrator* if a man or *administratrix* if a woman.

## By Will

A **will** is *a legal instrument designed to dispose of a decedent's property according to her instructions.* If *a person dies and leaves a valid will,* he is said to have died **testate.** *The deceased is the* **testator** or **testatrix.** A *person appointed in a will to carry out the provisions of that will* is an **executor** or **executrix.** **Probate** is the *judicial determination of the validity of a will by the courts. A gift of real property by will* is a **devise,** and the *recipient of real property* is a **devisee.** A *gift of personal property by will* is a **bequest,** and the *recipient of personal property* is the **beneficiary.**

## By Deed (Voluntary Alienation)

This type of alienation is of primary importance to the real estate business. Voluntary alienation during life is accomplished by the delivery of a valid deed by the grantor to the grantee during the life of both of them. A **deed** is a *written instrument that transfers an interest in real property when delivered to and voluntarily accepted by the grantee.* The contract of sale for real property is consummated by this delivery as required in the contract.

## By Involuntary Alienation

*Title to real property may be transferred during life by involuntary alienation (against the owner's wishes)* as a result of a **lien foreclosure sale,** adverse possession, or condemnation under the power of eminent domain. Title may be transferred by involuntary alienation after death as a result of escheat.

### *Lien Foreclosure Sale*

Chapter 2 notes that real property can be sold at public auction to satisfy a specific or a general lien against the property. These lien **foreclosure** sales are *conducted without the consent of the property owner who incurred the debt that resulted in a lien.* Foreclosure sales are either ordered by a court or conducted under a *power of sale* clause of a deed of trust, and title is conveyed to a purchaser at the sale by a judicial deed or a trustee's deed. A **judicial deed** is *executed by the official authorized by the court to conduct the sale and transfer the title.* In these cases, titles are typically conveyed by a sheriff's deed or trustee's deed, generally without the participation of the property owner who lost the title as the result of the foreclosure.

### *Adverse Possession*

**Adverse possession** is a *method of acquiring title to real property by conforming to statutory requirement.* Title to real property can be claimed by a person other than the owner if the other person takes use of the land under the following conditions:

1. The possession or occupation must be open and well known to others (notorious).
2. The possession must be without the permission of the true owner (hostile) and must be exclusive (not shared with the true owner).

3. The possession must be available to view by the public (open and notorious) and must not be hidden or secret so all can see that the use or claim is being made.
4. The possession must be continuous and uninterrupted for a period specified by statute. The state provides by statute a shorter period of time if possession is under **color of title.** Color of title exists when someone has *a document (such as a will, a deed, or a divorce decree) that appears to give him or her title to the property but actually does not.* For example, the document may be defective or the person who created the document may not have owned the property or may not have had the authority to convey it. In North Carolina, the period is as short as 7 years when claiming individual land and 21 years when claiming state land under color of title and is as long as 20 years when claiming individual land and 30 years when claiming state land without color of title.

The adverse possessor does not automatically acquire title to the property by merely meeting the requirements just listed. To obtain marketable title to the property, the claimant must satisfy the court that she has *fulfilled the requirements of the adverse possession statute in the particular state* by **suit to quiet title.** If the court is satisfied that the statutory requirements have been met, the court will award the title by court order to the claimant under adverse possession.

## Escheat

Escheat occurs when no one is eligible to receive the property of the intestate. If no heirs can be found as specified by the statute, the property escheats (falls back) to the state. This means that in the absence of heirs, the state takes title to the property of the deceased. The deceased has no control over the transfer of title to the state, resulting in an involuntary alienation at death.

## Condemnation under Eminent Domain

The federal government, states and their agencies, counties, cities, and towns have the power of eminent domain. This power provides the right to take private property for public use and benefit. The taking of the property under the power of eminent domain is called condemnation. The property owner must be compensated for the fair market value of the property lost through condemnation. The condemning authority must use due process of law, and the property owner must have the right to appeal the value of the property as established by the condemning authority through the court system. The property owner cannot prevent the condemnation; therefore, the loss of title is involuntary.

# Deeds

## Essential Elements of a Valid Deed

The following is a discussion of the requirements for the creation of a valid deed and the conveyance of title.

*Writing:* The **Statute of Frauds** is *a law in effect in all states requiring that every deed must be written to be valid.* An oral conveyance is ineffective. The written form of the deed must meet the legal requirements of the state.

*Grantor:* The **grantor** *(the one conveying the title)* must be legally competent; that is, the individual must have the capacity to contract. This requirement exists for all parties to a valid contract. The grantor must have reached the age of majority and must be mentally competent at the time of deed execution. Also, the grantor must be named with a certainty (see *Execution,* below, for grantee requirements). It must be possible to positively identify the grantor. A corporation may be a grantor. Although title may be held and transferred in an assumed name, title may not be held or transferred in the name of a fictitious person or organization. The person or organization must exist. If a corporation is a grantor, it must be legally incorporated, the person signing for the corporation must be authorized to do so, and the corporate seal must be on the deed.

*Property Description:* The deed must contain an adequate **legal description,** or a *description of land recognized by law.* The three most acceptable methods of providing such a description are discussed at the beginning of this chapter (see "Property Description").

*Words of Conveyance:* The deed must contain *words demonstrating that it is the grantor's intention to transfer the title to the named* **grantee,** or the *one receiving title to the real property.* These **words of conveyance** are contained in the granting clause. Typical wording is "has given, granted, bargained, sold, and conveyed" in the case of warranty deeds. If the property is being sold subject to specific encumbrances of record, such as easements or a mortgage lien, the deed should recite these encumbrances. Please note two items in regard to encumbrances: The transfer of a fee simple absolute title does not mean there are no encumbrances, and the **covenant against encumbrances** in a deed (discussed below) is only a covenant against encumbrances that have not been disclosed.

*Execution:* The deed must be executed (signed) by each grantor conveying an interest in the property. Only the grantors execute the deed, and they must be competent to do so. The grantee does not need to sign the deed or pass the test of competency; however, the grantee must be named with a certainty. A minor could be a valid grantee, but not a grantor.

*Delivery and Acceptance:* To effect a transfer of title by deed, there must be a delivery of a valid deed by the grantor to the grantee and the deed must be voluntarily accepted by the grantee. Delivery is made directly to the grantee or to an agent of the grantee. Typically, the agent for this purpose is the grantee's attorney, his or her real estate broker, or the lending institution providing the mortgage loan to finance the purchase of the property. If delivery is made to a real estate broker or to an agent, that person must be an agent of the grantee, not an agent of the grantor. In almost every case, acceptance by the grantee is presumed. This presumption is especially strong if the deed has been recorded and the conveyance is beneficial to the grantee.

## Nonessential Elements of a Deed

The following items, although usually found in a deed, are not required to create a valid deed.

*Acknowledgment:* For a deed to be eligible for recording, it must be acknowledged. The grantor must appear before a public officer, such as a notary public, who is eligible to take an **acknowledgment** and state that *the signing of the deed was done by the grantor and was a voluntary act.* A deed is perfectly valid and enforceable between the grantor and grantee without an acknowledgment, but without the acknowledgment, the deed cannot be recorded by the grantee. Therefore, it will not provide the grantee protection of title against subsequent creditors or purchasers of the same property from the same grantor if the subsequent creditors or purchasers record their lien or deed before the original grantee records his deed. Therefore, the grantee should insist upon receiving a deed that has been acknowledged and then promptly record it.

*Consideration:* A deed does not need to recite the actual amount of consideration (money) involved. However, it must provide evidence that consideration (something of value, such as money) is present. A phrase such as "ten dollars, and other consideration" is sufficient to accomplish this purpose.

*Seal:* In North Carolina, deeds do not have to be sealed in order to be valid even if the deed form has the word "seal" after the signature.

*Recording:* The purpose of **recording** the deed, or *registering the document on public record,* is to protect the grantee's title. This protection is provided by **constructive notice,** meaning that *all the world is bound by knowledge of the existence of the conveyance of*

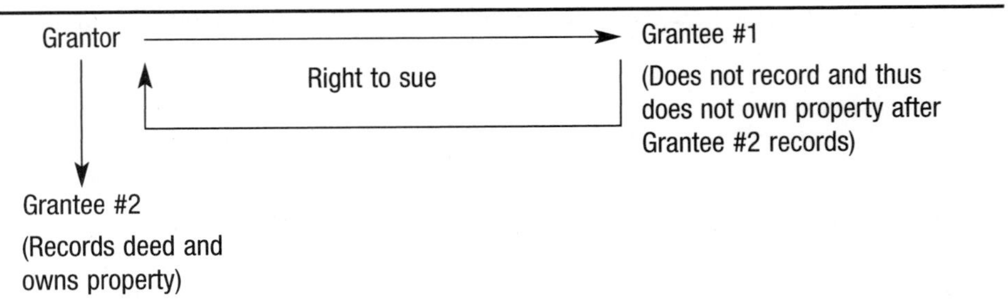


**FIGURE 3.3**
The possible effects of failure of grantee to record a deed.

*title* and the fact that the title is now vested in the grantee. This protection is against everyone, including subsequent purchasers of the same property from the same grantor.

Constructive notice is binding on everyone, even those who have not actually read the deed (actual notice) as recorded. Figure 3.3 illustrates the possible effect of the failure of the grantee to record a deed and the protection provided to a grantee who does record a deed.

As seen in Figure 3.3, there was an effective transfer of title from Grantor to Grantee 1, but the title in Grantee 1 was defeated by his failure to record the deed and the subsequent conveyance of the same title by Grantor to Grantee 2, who did record the deed. Grantee 2 now holds the title, and Grantee 1 has a right to sue Grantor to get his money back. This right may be worthwhile, provided Grantor can be found and has money or property.

In summary, Figure 3.3 illustrates that a valid conveyance of title can exist between grantor and grantee without the deed's being recorded. The deed must be recorded, however, to protect grantee's title from third parties, such as subsequent purchasers from the grantor, subsequent creditors, or other lien holders of the grantor.

*Witnessing:* North Carolina is not one of the few states that require that the grantor's signature be *witnessed* on the deed by one or more witnesses for the deed to be valid.

*Date:* A deed does not need to be dated to be valid between the parties. If the grantee wants to record the deed to protect his interest against future claims on the property, he must have it acknowledged. The acknowledgment will provide a date. Because a gift deed must be recorded within two years, a date is needed to establish the time of the gift, and acknowledgment is needed to allow the deed to be recorded so it remains valid after the two-year period.

## Types of Deed

Variations in types of deed result from the forms of warranty of title contained in the deed and from a special purpose for which the deed is drawn. Warranties, or covenants, in a deed are promises or guarantees made by the grantor to the grantee to protect the grantee against specific defects in the title. The following is a discussion of the various types of deed, by type of warranty and special purpose, that are common in North Carolina.

### *General Warranty Deed*

The general warranty deed contains the strongest and broadest form of guarantee of title of any type of deed; therefore, it provides the greatest protection to the grantee and the greatest liability to the grantor. The general warranty deed usually contains the following covenants (see Figure 3.4):

**Covenant of seisin.** The typical wording of a covenant of seisin (pronounced like "season") is "grantor covenants that he or she is seised of said premises in fee." This covenant *provides an assurance to the grantees that the grantors hold the title that they specify in the deed that they are conveying to the grantees.* The grantors promise the grantees that they have fee simple title to the property.

**FIGURE 3.4** North Carolina warranty deed.

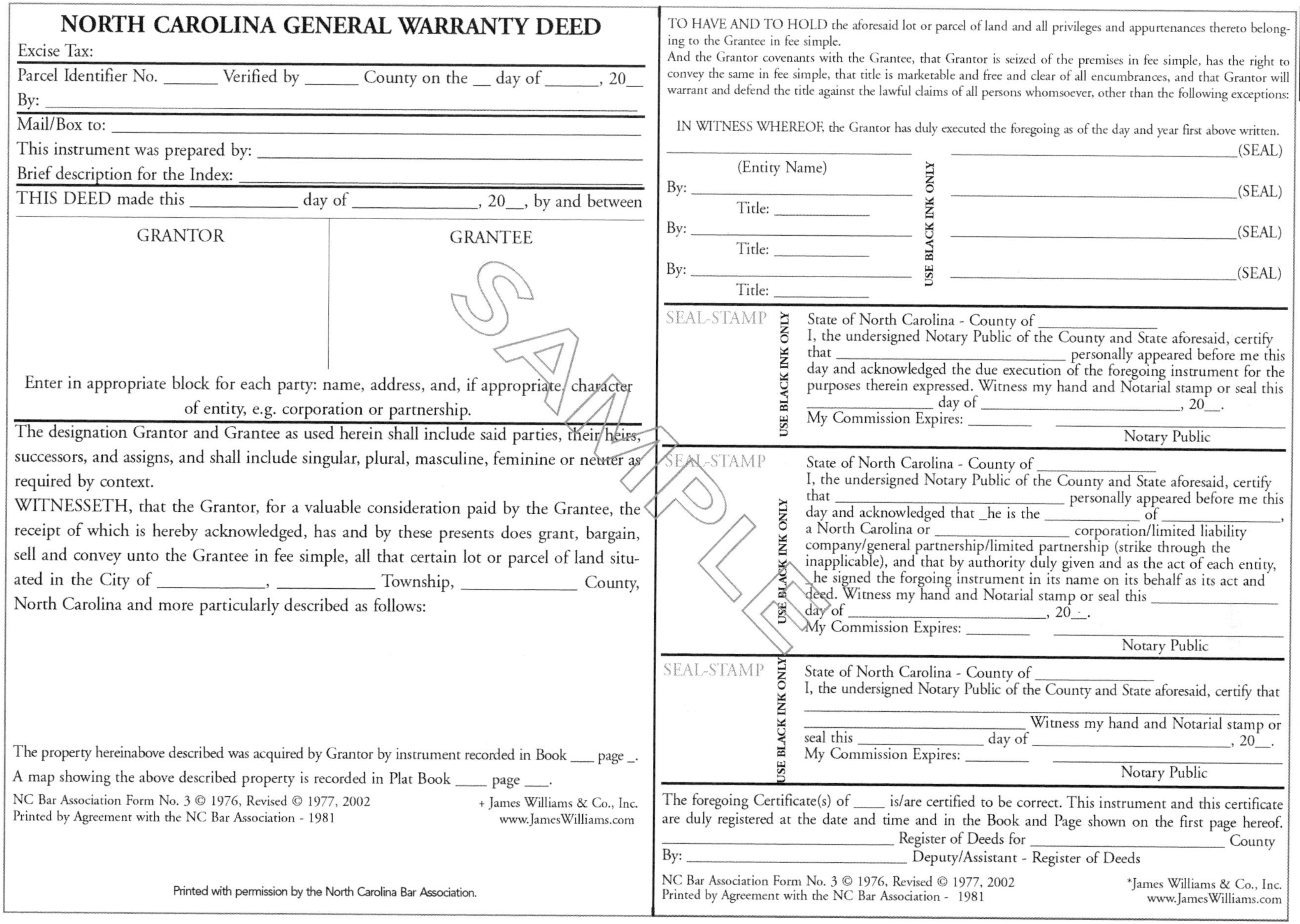

NORTH CAROLINA GENERAL WARRANTY DEED

Excise Tax:

Parcel Identifier No. ______ Verified by ______ County on the __ day of ______, 20__

By: ______

Mail/Box to: ______

This instrument was prepared by: ______

Brief description for the Index: ______

THIS DEED made this ______ day of ______, 20__, by and between

| GRANTOR | GRANTEE |
| --- | --- |
| | |

Enter in appropriate block for each party: name, address, and, if appropriate, character of entity, e.g. corporation or partnership.

The designation Grantor and Grantee as used herein shall include said parties, their heirs, successors, and assigns, and shall include singular, plural, masculine, feminine or neuter as required by context.

WITNESSETH, that the Grantor, for a valuable consideration paid by the Grantee, the receipt of which is hereby acknowledged, has and by these presents does grant, bargain, sell and convey unto the Grantee in fee simple, all that certain lot or parcel of land situated in the City of ______, ______ Township, ______ County, North Carolina and more particularly described as follows:

The property hereinabove described was acquired by Grantor by instrument recorded in Book ___ page _.

A map showing the above described property is recorded in Plat Book ____ page ___.

NC Bar Association Form No. 3 © 1976, Revised © 1977, 2002
Printed by Agreement with the NC Bar Association - 1981

+ James Williams & Co., Inc.
www.JamesWilliams.com

Printed with permission by the North Carolina Bar Association.

TO HAVE AND TO HOLD the aforesaid lot or parcel of land and all privileges and appurtenances thereto belonging to the Grantee in fee simple.

And the Grantor covenants with the Grantee, that Grantor is seized of the premises in fee simple, has the right to convey the same in fee simple, that title is marketable and free and clear of all encumbrances, and that Grantor will warrant and defend the title against the lawful claims of all persons whomsoever, other than the following exceptions:

IN WITNESS WHEREOF, the Grantor has duly executed the foregoing as of the day and year first above written.

______ (Entity Name)

By: ______ Title: ______

By: ______ Title: ______

By: ______ Title: ______

USE BLACK INK ONLY

______(SEAL)

______(SEAL)

______(SEAL)

______(SEAL)

SEAL-STAMP | USE BLACK INK ONLY

State of North Carolina - County of ______
I, the undersigned Notary Public of the County and State aforesaid, certify that ______ personally appeared before me this day and acknowledged the due execution of the foregoing instrument for the purposes therein expressed. Witness my hand and Notarial stamp or seal this ______ day of ______, 20__.
My Commission Expires: ______ ______ Notary Public

SEAL-STAMP | USE BLACK INK ONLY

State of North Carolina - County of ______
I, the undersigned Notary Public of the County and State aforesaid, certify that ______ personally appeared before me this day and acknowledged that _he is the ______ of ______, a North Carolina or ______ corporation/limited liability company/general partnership/limited partnership (strike through the inapplicable), and that by authority duly given and as the act of each entity, _he signed the forgoing instrument in its name on its behalf as its act and deed. Witness my hand and Notarial stamp or seal this ______ day of ______, 20_.
My Commission Expires: ______ ______ Notary Public

SEAL-STAMP | USE BLACK INK ONLY

State of North Carolina - County of ______
I, the undersigned Notary Public of the County and State aforesaid, certify that ______ ______ Witness my hand and Notarial stamp or seal this ______ day of ______, 20__.
My Commission Expires: ______ ______ Notary Public

The foregoing Certificate(s) of ____ is/are certified to be correct. This instrument and this certificate are duly registered at the date and time and in the Book and Page shown on the first page hereof.
______ Register of Deeds for ______ County
By: ______ Deputy/Assistant - Register of Deeds

NC Bar Association Form No. 3 © 1976, Revised © 1977, 2002
Printed by Agreement with the NC Bar Association - 1981

*James Williams & Co., Inc.
www.JamesWilliams.com

SAMPLE

**Covenant of right to convey.** This covenant usually follows the covenant of seisin in the general warranty deed and typically reads, "and has the right to convey the same in fee simple." By this covenant, the grantor *provides an assurance to the grantee that the grantor has legal capacity to convey the title* and also has the title to convey.

**Covenant against encumbrances.** This covenant typically states "that said premises are free from encumbrances (with the exceptions below stated, if any)." The grantor is *assuring the grantee that there are no encumbrances against the title except those of record.* Typical encumbrances that are acceptable to grantees are the encumbrances of a mortgage lien when grantee is assuming grantor's existing mortgage, of recorded easements, and of restrictive covenants. As noted previously, this does *not* mean there are no encumbrances, only that there are none other than those of public record, such as easements, restrictive covenants, or zoning regulations.

**Covenant of quiet enjoyment.** This covenant typically reads, "the grantee, his or her heirs and assigns, shall quietly and peaceably have, hold, use, possess, and enjoy the premises." This covenant is an *assurance by the grantor to the grantee that the grantee shall have a quiet possession and enjoyment of the property being conveyed and that the grantee will not be disturbed in the use and enjoyment of the property because of a defect in the title being conveyed by the grantor.* In warranty deeds that do not contain this specific covenant, such as the North Carolina Warranty Deed shown in Figure 3.4, the covenant of warranty assures the grantee of quiet enjoyment of the property.

**Covenant of warranty.** The warranty of title in the general warranty deed provides that *the grantor "will warrant and defend the title to the grantee against the lawful claims of all persons whomsoever"* This is the best form of warranty for the protection of the grantee and contains no limitations as to possible claimants protected against, because the grantor specifies that he will defend the title against "the lawful claims of all persons whomsoever." The covenant of warranty is the most important of all the covenants.

Note: The covenants of seisin and the right to convey are often considered one covenant, as are the covenants of warranty and quiet enjoyment.

**Grantee's rights to recovery.** If the covenant of seisin or the covenant of warranty is broken, a grantee may recover from the seller any financial loss up to the price paid for the property. If the covenant against encumbrances is broken, the grantee may recover from the grantor any expense incurred to pay off the encumbrance. The amount the grantee may recover in this case is also limited to the price paid for the property.

## Special Warranty Deed

In the **special warranty deed,** the *warranty is limited to claims against the title arising out of the period of ownership of the grantor.* Therefore, the warranty goes back in time only to the date when the grantor acquired the title, as contrasted with the general warranty deed, in which the warranty is against defects in the title going back for an unlimited period of time.

## Quitclaim Deed

The **quitclaim deed** *contains no warranties whatsoever but is simply a deed of release.* It releases or conveys to the grantee any interest, including title, that the grantor may have. Even fee simple absolute title can be passed by a quitclaim deed if the grantor holds fee simple absolute title. However, the grantor does not state in the deed that she has any title or interest in the property. Execution of the quitclaim deed by the grantor prevents the grantor from asserting any claim against the title at any time in the future.

Quitclaim deeds may be used to clear a **cloud on a title,** a situation that occurs when someone has *a possible claim against a title.* As long as this possibility exists, the title is cloudy and therefore is not a good and marketable title. To remove this cloud and create a good and marketable title, the possible claimant must execute a quitclaim deed as grantor to the true titleholder as grantee. The granting clause in a quitclaim deed contains the words "remise, release, and quitclaim" instead of "grant, bargain, sell, and convey," as used in warranty deeds.

## Special Purpose Deeds

**Deed of confirmation.** This deed is also called a *deed of correction* and is used when a deed contains an error that requires correction. Examples of the errors that are corrected by this type of deed are errors in the names of the parties, errors in the property description, and mistakes made in execution of the deed.

**Deed of release.** The primary use of a deed of release is to release a property from the lien of a mortgage when the debt secured by the mortgage has been paid in full or, in the case of a blanket mortgage, to release individual parcels of land from the lien of the blanket mortgage.

**Deed of surrender.** The deed of surrender is used by a life tenant to convey his or her estate to the reversionary interest or to the remainder interest, depending on the form of the life estate. This same result is accomplished by the use of a quitclaim deed.

**Deed of gift.** A gift of real property may be made by general warranty deed, by special warranty deed, or by quitclaim deed. If the warranty deed is used, however, the warranties cannot be enforced against the grantor by the grantee. This is because the grantor received no compensation for conveying the title to the grantee since the conveyance was a gift. Any type of deed will convey the property, provided the grantor has title to convey. In North Carolina, a deed of gift must be recorded within two years to remain valid. Two other important points about a gift deed are these: It requires no excise tax, and it is fraudulent to convey property with a gift deed to defeat a creditor's rights.

## Judicial Deeds

Authority for execution of these deeds results from a court order to the official executing the deed. The various types of judicial deed are named according to the title of the official who executes the deed. The various names of these deeds include sheriff's deed, tax deed, guardian's deed, commissioner's deed, executor's deed, and administrator's deed.

## Excise Tax

North Carolina statutes require an **excise tax** to be paid by the seller. The amount of tax is *based on the consideration received by the seller in the sale of the real property by deed.* The statute requires the amount of the excise tax *to be $1 per $500,* or a fraction thereof, *based on the full purchase price.*

Excise tax is assessed only in multiples of $1. There are no fractional prices, only a $1 increment for each portion of $500 of sales price. An easy way to calculate the excise tax is to round the sales price up to the next $500 and divide that number by 500. The answer is the amount of excise tax required; for example,

$74,000 cash sale, no rounding required; $74,000 ÷ 500 = $148 tax

$74,100 cash sale, round up to $74,500; $74,500 ÷ 500 = $149 tax

$74,700 cash sale, round up to $75,000; $75,000 ÷ 500 = $150 tax

The excise tax on deeds is often used as a rough indication of value paid for the property. The state has a statute requiring the amount of the tax to properly reflect the sales price. Since this information is a part of the public record, brokers draw information from these data for their comparable property sales files.

## County Transfer Tax

A few counties in North Carolina impose a transfer tax on the sale of real property. These taxes require approval on a county-by-county basis from the North Carolina General Assembly. Fourteen such bills have been introduced and defeated by the General Assembly since 1991. The North Carolina Association of REALTORS® opposes the land transfer tax because it affects housing affordability. Passage of such bills would diminish the effects of federal and state programs designed to make home ownership more affordable.

# TITLE ASSURANCE

## Covenants of Title in Deeds

*Covenants of title in deeds* is a method of title assurance. In addition to other methods of protecting the purchaser with regard to the quality of title, *covenants of title in deeds* provides the grantee with the added assurance that the grantor can be sued if a covenant is breached. See the discussion of the various covenants of title on page 56.

## Title Examination Procedures

Regardless of the warranties in a deed, the grantee should retain the services of an attorney to conduct an examination of the public record to verify if, in fact, the grantee is receiving a good and marketable title free from encumbrances, except those he has agreed to accept. The purpose of a **title examination** is *to determine the quality of a title.* Anyone can do a title search; however, only an attorney can give a legal opinion as to the quality of a title.

The title search consists of an examination of all public records that possibly affect a title to real estate. The examiner uses the grantor and grantee indexes maintained by the Register of Deeds office to trace the successive conveyance of title from the present to an appropriate time in the past, typically 40 to 60 years. The examiner must be able to show a consecutive and unbroken **chain of title** for the statutory time period (see "Marketable Title Act," page 62, for statutory time period). A chain of title refers to *successive conveyances of title to a piece of land.* If links are missing in the grantor and grantee indexes, the examiner must check other recorded documents, such as wills, to establish the required unbroken chain of title. A missing link could be the result of such things as failure to record a deed, a name change during ownership of the property whereby a person takes title under one name and grants that title to someone else under another name, or fraud. The sale should not close until proper documents are found to clear the title. If the missing link cannot be found, ownership may need to be established by a suit to quiet title. Additionally, the examiner searches all other public records, such as records of judgments, special proceedings, liens, restrictive covenants, easements, and any other recordings or documents that could affect the title.

This search is done by name. For example, Jim Jones contracts to sell a property to John Smith. Jim is the grantor and John is the grantee when the property is conveyed. A title examination is done before this conveyance occurs. Jim, the grantor, was the grantee when he received the title to the property; therefore, the title examiner begins his search by finding Jim Jones in the grantee index. The grantee index also identifies the grantor, Jeff Best, and the book and page number for the deed. The examiner determines the time period in which Jim Jones owned the property and searches the public records for anything Jim may have done to affect the title during his ownership.

Since Jeff Best was the grantor to Jim Jones, Jeff was the grantee when he acquired title. The examiner finds Jeff Best in the grantee index, identifies the grantor in the transaction as Ann Todd, and determines Jeff's period of ownership. The examiner then searches the public records under Jeff's name for anything Jeff may have done to affect the title.

The title examiner follows the same procedure for Ann Todd and other previous owners until the appropriate time period has been searched.

## Attorney's Opinion of Title

Upon completion of the title examination, the examining attorney provides an opinion of title, which sets forth the legal description of the property, a statement that the records have been carefully examined, the period of time covered by the examination, specific information about any liens or other encumbrances against the title, and the examiner's opinion of the quality of the title.

A title examination is only concerned with *recorded documents* on the public record. Circumstances affecting the property that are not a part of the public record are not covered. For example, the record may not reflect a missing heir, a mentally incapacitated grantor, or a forgery.

Therefore, even though a title examination indicates that a title is good and marketable, this may not actually be the case. The attorney may make a mistake, or the defect may be one not evident in the public record. An example is a forgery. The warranties in the deed and the attorney's opinion of title may be adequate protection provided the grantor and attorney are alive, available, and financially solvent. A lawsuit may become necessary should the grantor or attorney refuse to fulfill their responsibilities voluntarily.

## Title Insurance

For maximum protection against a financial loss, the grantee should take advantage of the protection afforded by a **title insurance** policy. A title insurance policy is *an indemnity contract that protects the purchaser or mortgagee against loss resulting from a defect in title that is covered in the policy and is in existence when the policy becomes effective.* Conversely, it does not cover defects that are listed as exceptions in the policy or defects arising after the effective date of the policy. A one-time premium provides coverage for as long as the insured or his heirs have an interest in the property.

A rule of thumb for calculating title insurance is to estimate $2 per thousand. For example, insuring a $100,000 property requires a one-time premium of $200. The rate per thousand decreases for amounts over $100,000. Each $1,000 of value over $100,000 is typically charged at $1.50 per thousand. For example, the premium for a $200,000 property could be $350, $200 for the first $100,000 and $150 for the second $100,000. Rates for values over $500,000 can be even lower. Rates are significantly lower when the new buyer purchases the new policy from the company that issued the seller's policy. Considering the substantial financial loss that may occur as a result of a defective title, this cost is quite reasonable. A purchaser may save money on the policy by purchasing it from the company holding the seller's policy, thus *tacking on* to the previous policy.

Although title insurance companies perform their own title searches in many states, they rely on approved attorneys to do the searches in North Carolina. An attorney searches the title, submits a preliminary title opinion to the insurance company, and receives a preliminary title commitment.

After closing but before recording closing documents such as the deed and deed of trust, the attorney does a final search to ensure that nothing affecting title has been recorded since the initial search. He then records the documents and issues a final title opinion to the title insurance company, which issues the title policy to the insured owner and/or mortgagee.

Although a title insurance policy is usually the best form of insurance, it has limitations. Ordinarily, it limits coverage to the purchase price of the property, not covering future improvements or increased values due to appreciation. There are usually exceptions to the policy. Major commercial real estate purchases may exceed the title company's ability or willingness to insure. Title insurance companies are often easier to find and more financially solvent than many grantors or attorneys, however, these companies can become insolvent and dissolve if claims exceed their assets.

The major advantage of a title insurance policy is the title company's responsibility to defend the title against defects not evident in the public record and errors made in the title search.

### *Owner's Policy*

The owner's policy is for the protection of the owner and is written for the amount that the owner paid for the property. The amount of coverage remains the same for the life of the policy. The policy remains in effect for the duration of the insured's ownership of the property and continues in effect after the owner's death to benefit heirs who receive an interest in the property. Although the owner's title policy is optional, real estate agents should advise buyers of the advantages of purchasing this policy.

### *Mortgagee's Policy*

This policy protects only the mortgagee (lender). Under the terms of the policy, the mortgagee is insured against defects in the title pledged as security in the mortgage. The mortgagee's insurable interest is only to the extent of the outstanding loan balance at any given time. Therefore, the mortgagee's policy is one of diminishing liability; it provides coverage equivalent to the amount of the loan balance, which decreases as the loan principal decreases. Since most lenders require a mortgagee's policy and there is little or no increase in premium to the buyer to purchase a mortgagee's policy and an owner's policy (typically, these policies together are referred to as a simultaneous policy), it is prudent and cost-effective for the buyer to purchase both.

### *Leasehold Policy*

The leasehold policy is written to protect a lessee (leaseholder) and/or a mortgagee against defects in the lessor's title. This policy is issued to a mortgagee if the mortgagor has pledged a leasehold interest instead of a fee simple title as security for the mortgage debt.

## Title Recordation

Although the recording of title is not required in North Carolina, it should be considered essential by all persons. By recording the title, constructive notice is established that puts all the world on notice as to the claim in title. North Carolina has two statutes that make the recording of title extremely important.

### *The Conner Act*

The North Carolina **Conner Act** provides that certain real estate documents *are not valid against third parties until recorded.* This act places a great potential burden on the grantee. If the grantee does not record the document and a subsequent purchaser does, the latter would take priority. Therefore, it is important to know which documents must be recorded. The Conner Act requires that the following documents be recorded: purchase and option contracts, deeds, mortgage instruments (deeds of trust and mortgages), assignments of interest in real property, leases of more than three years, easements, and restrictive covenants.

**Recording contracts.** In theory, any real estate contract that grants the purchaser the right to receive title at some future time should be recorded. This way, a purchaser is protected against the owner's reselling the property to another party. This is especially important in the case of contracts in which there is much time before title is to be conveyed, such as option and installment land contracts. However, most standard offers to purchase and contract call for closing to take place within a relatively short time. In actual practice, these contracts are rarely recorded due to the short duration (usually less than 60 days) and the fact that problems arising from lack of recordation are rare. Should a purchaser raise the question of recording a standard residential offer to purchase and contract, the purchaser should be advised to consult an attorney.

**Recording procedures.** Document recordation is done at the Register of Deeds office in the county where the property is located. Copies of each instrument are placed in a book in the chronological order in which they are received. The documents are then recorded in the grantor and grantee indexes. After recordation, the original document is returned to the owners or the owner's designee.

## Marketable Title Act

The North Carolina **Marketable Title Act** aims to *extinguish old defects in the title by providing that if a chain of title can be established for 30 years without conflicts, claims outside* *this chain are extinguished.* Paired with the Conner Act, this act emphasizes the importance of recording instruments and upholds the value of examining the record.

## The Torrens System

North Carolina is one of about a dozen states that has a statute providing for title registration under the Torrens System. Essentially, land under this system is registered in a way similar to motor vehicles registration. A change in the status of the property, such as a transfer of ownership or placement of a lien on the property, requires that the old registration certificate be destroyed and replaced with a new one. The single registration certificate on the property at a particular time reflects the current status of the property. Anything not on the certificate does affect the title.

One advantage of the Torrens System is that it does not allow property to be taken by adverse possession. This feature may make it attractive to an owner of thousands of acres of mountain property who does not want to be bothered with policing his land to prevent adverse possession. However, there are major disadvantages. The process of initially registering property under the system is lengthy and costly. Each issuance of a new registration certificate is time-consuming.

## SUMMARY OF IMPORTANT POINTS

1. The three methods of property description in use in the United States are metes and bounds, reference, and rectangular survey. A complete legal description of a property is essential for proper conveyance of title. A simple street address will not do.
2. The primary method of property description in the original 13 colonies is metes and bounds.
3. Transfer of title is known as alienation. Involuntary alienation occurs during life as a result of adverse possession, lien foreclosure sale, and condemnation under the power of eminent domain. Involuntary alienation at death is escheat. Voluntary alienation during life can occur only by delivery of a valid deed.
4. The requirements for deed validity are (1) the deed must be written, (2) the grantor must be competent, (3) the grantor and grantee must be named with a certainty, (4) there must be an adequate property description, (5) there must be words of conveyance, (6) the deed must be properly executed by the grantor, and (7) delivery and acceptance must occur to convey title. Real estate practitioners have no authority to prepare wills or deeds for others, but they should be familiar with the essential elements of the common forms of deeds used in the state.
5. To be eligible for recording on the public record, a deed must be acknowledged. Recording protects the grantee's title against creditors of the grantor and subsequent conveyances by the grantor.
6. A general warranty deed is the strongest and broadest form of title guarantee. The general warranty deed typically contains five covenants: seisin, right to convey, against encumbrances, quiet enjoyment, and warranty. It provides the most protection for the grantee and the most liability for the grantor.
7. A quitclaim deed is a deed of release and contains no warranties. It conveys any interest, including fee simple absolute, the grantor may have. The primary use of the quitclaim deed is to remove a cloud from a title.
8. Other types of deed are special warranty, confirmation, release, surrender, gift, and judicial.

9. North Carolina state law requires the grantor to affix an excise tax to the deed. Because the tax is accrued in multiples of $500 of purchase price, examination of the tax provides a rough indication of purchase price and is a valuable data source for the broker's office records.

10. The purpose of a title examination is to determine the quality of a title. Only an attorney can legally give an opinion as to quality of title. The Conner Act and the Marketable Title Act lend significance to the value of a record.

11. A title insurance policy protects the insured against a financial loss caused by a title defect. The three types of policy are owner's, mortgagee's, and leasehold. A title insurance policy is the best form of title assurance.

## ITEMS TO CONSIDER FOR THE STATE EXAM

1. *Characteristics of a special warranty deed.* The promises or warranties from the grantor apply only to the time during which she held the title. These assurances do not, therefore, apply to any problems or defects in the title prior to the present owner's period of ownership. Therefore, the grantor is only promising that no claims arose against the property while it was in her hands.

2. *Fee simple absolute title versus encumbrances.* A possible exam question might be similar to the following:

   A conveyed title to B, giving B title in a fee simple absolute using a general warranty deed. Therefore, B is assured that:

   A. the title is freely transferable
   B. there are no encumbrances against the property
   C. the seller is warranting the title only from the time she purchased the property
   D. all of the above

In analyzing the question, you might quickly accept A as correct. The problem arises in evaluating B. In your analysis, you recall that a general warranty deed includes the warranties of seisin and conveyance, against encumbrances, and of warranty. You might be tempted to focus on the warranty against encumbrances and jump to the conclusion that B is also correct. However, this covenant against encumbrances applies to all claims that are not exempted on the deed, such as a mechanic's potential claim to a lien for work done 60 days ago. Encumbrances on the record (such as easements, restrictive covenants, and so on) may be numerous, but they are easily discoverable by examining the record. If you mistakenly assume B also to be correct, you might make a premature conclusion that D is the correct answer and not read C carefully. Choice C is not true because there are no exceptions limiting the warranty to the seller's ownership period in a general warranty deed. Choice C would be true for a special warranty deed. Thus, the answer is A. This question illustrates the necessity of carefully reading and evaluating all of the answers before choosing one.

3. *Reading plats.* A significant problem on the exam may arise from the interpretation of plats. There is a simple three-step process to help you master this area:

   a. Study Figure 3.1 and take time to grasp the significance of how metes and bounds descriptions are constructed. Recall that a circle has 360 degrees. Thus, a quadrant (quarter circle) has 90 degrees. Metes are described as a compass direction starting from north or south and moving into the east or west quadrant. Thus, a call starts with a north or south direction and has a number of degrees, minutes, and seconds into an east or west quadrant (that is, N/S, number of degrees, E/W). Thus, Figure 3.1 indicates a direction 45° 30'10" off north to the east, or N-45° 30'10"E.

   b. Now using Figure 3.1, apply this understanding of directions. Start in the lower right corner of the plat at the stake on Amortization Drive. Look at the direction up the page. It is 6 degrees, 18 minutes, to the east of north; that is, N-6 degrees, 18 minutes-E. Add the distance (metes), which is measured in feet and decimal fractions (not inches). In this case, it is 215.20 feet. Look at the next call; it is 8 degrees, 49 minutes west of north (or N-8 degrees, 49 minutes-W) for a distance of 241.00 feet. Now study the line between lots 19 and 20. It appears to be almost directly east-west, but study the call and notice that it is essentially 2 degrees less than 90 degree from south into the west quadrant—here a label of S-87 degrees, 50 minutes-W. Work around the rest of the plat back to the beginning. Compare the plat with the written description of Figure 3.1—at the "BEGINNING on a stake. . . ."

   c. Now go over questions 21 and 22 at the end of the chapter. Once you understand these questions, you are well prepared to answer questions about interpreting plats on the state exam. Congratulations!

## REVIEW QUESTIONS

Answers to the review questions are in the Answer Key at the back of the book.

1. All of the following are methods of title assurance EXCEPT:
   A. color of title
   B. title insurance
   C. covenants of title in the deed
   D. title examination by an attorney

2. Voluntary alienation during life occurs only in which of the following ways?
   A. will
   B. foreclosure sale
   C. deed delivery
   D. devise

3. Essential elements of a valid deed include all of the following EXCEPT:
   A. acknowledgment
   B. writing
   C. competent grantor
   D. execution by grantor

4. The purpose of a deed's being acknowledged is to:
   A. make the deed valid
   B. make the deed eligible for delivery
   C. make the deed eligible for recording
   D. identify the grantee with certainty

5. Which of the following is the type of notice provided by recording?
   A. actual
   B. reasonable
   C. protective
   D. constructive

6. Of the following types of deed, which provides the grantee with the greatest assurance of title?
   A. special warranty
   B. deed of confirmation
   C. grant deed
   D. general warranty

7. Which of the following covenants assures the grantee that the grantor has the legal capacity to transfer title?
   A. covenant of quiet enjoyment
   B. covenant of right to convey
   C. covenant of seisin
   D. covenant of warranty

8. A deed in which the wording in the granting clause is "remise and release" is which of the following?
   A. quitclaim deed
   B. special warranty
   C. grant deed
   D. general warranty

9. A general warranty deed and a quitclaim deed are equally suitable for which of the following?
   A. judicial deed
   B. deed of confirmation
   C. official deed
   D. deed of gift

10. A grantor left a deed for the grantee to find after the grantor's death. The result was to:
    A. convey the title during the grantor's life
    B. convey the title after the grantor's death
    C. have the title automatically escheat to the state
    D. none of the above

11. The type of deed used to remove a mortgage lien when the debt is satisfied is a:
    A. deed of surrender
    B. grant deed
    C. deed of release
    D. special warranty deed

12. If the covenants in a general warranty deed are broken, the grantee's remedy is to:
    I. sue the grantor for damages in the amount of the loss up to the amount of the purchase price.
    II. require the grantor to execute a deed of confirmation.
    A. I only
    B. II only
    C. both I and II
    D. neither I nor II

13. A claim of title by adverse possession may be defeated by the property owner by which of the following?
    A. permission
    B. confirmation
    C. will
    D. condemnation

14. The type of deed that guarantees the title only against defects that were created during the grantor's ownership is which of the following?
A. general warranty
B. special warranty
C. surrender
D. release

15. Which of the following statements regarding a title examination is (are) correct?
I. The purpose of a title examination is to determine the quality of a title.
II. A title opinion can be given only by an attorney.
A. I only
B. II only
C. both I and II
D. neither I nor II

16. The successive conveyances of a title are called:
A. releases
B. remises
C. links in the chain of title
D. abstracts of title

17. A title insurance policy can be written to protect all of the following EXCEPT:
A. owner
B. grantor
C. lessee
D. mortgagee

18. A title insurance policy protects the insured against loss caused by:
A. defects in the title existing at the time the insured acquired title
B. defects in the title created during the insured's ownership
C. defects in the title created after the insured's ownership
D. all of the above

19. With reference to the metes and bounds property description, which of the following is correct?
A. it is a description by distances and directions
B. it is the primary method of description used in the original 13 colonies
C. it must have a point of beginning
D. all of the above

20. A description by reference may refer to:
I. a prior deed.
II. a recorded plat.
A. I only
B. II only
C. both I and II
D. neither I nor II

Interpreting Plats ?

21. In reference to the plat of Lot 20 in Mortgage Heights, Figure 3.1, all of the statements about this lot are correct EXCEPT:
A. Lot 20 has a radius of 50 feet on the cul-de-sac
B. Lot 16 is an adjoining lot
C. there is a 10-foot public utility easement along the eastern boundary of Lot 20
D. the plat of the Mortgage Heights subdivision is recorded in Map Book 5 on page 40

22. In reference to the sample subdivision plat in Figure 3.2, which of the following statements is true?
A. the Southern Pacific Railroad borders Block "F"
B. Lot 33 of Block "A" is 2.005 acres
C. there are ten lots in Block "C"
D. Lot 34 of Block "A" is on a cul-de-sac

23. Of the following types of deed, which provides the grantor with the greatest liability?
A. special warranty
B. deed of confirmation
C. grant deed
D. general warranty deed

24. In a metes and bounds description, the description must close; that is, it must do the following:
A. end at the northeast corner of property
B. end at the point of beginning
C. end at a known government marker
D. none of the above

25. Lucy Landlord owns a house that she leases to Tim Tenant. Which of the following estates in real property exists during the time of Tim Tenant's lease?
A. leasehold estate
B. freehold estate
C. neither a leasehold nor a freehold
D. both a leasehold and a freehold

26. Which of the following is an adequate property description?
A. 123 Smith Road, North Carolina
B. the old Martin place
C. Book 1968, page 924, Halifax County, North Carolina
D. none of the above

27. A _____ property description has a point of beginning.
A. government rectangular system
B. legal
C. points and calls
D. metes and bounds

28. If a person dies intestate and has no heirs, his property will _____ to the state.
A. devise
B. escheat
C. demise
D. grant

29. Essential elements of a deed include all of the following EXCEPT:
A. a legal description
B. delivery and acceptance
C. words of conveyance
D. recording

30. A home is sold for $103,250. What is the amount of excise tax to be paid by the seller?
A. $206
B. $207
C. $103
D. $104

# Chapter 4

## KEY TERMS

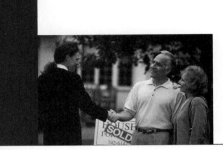

amendment
building codes
Certificate of Occupancy
conditions
covenant
deed restrictions
enabling acts
Environmental Policy Act
Environmental Protection Agency (EPA)
highway access controls
injunction
Interstate Land Sales Full Disclosure Act
master plan
negative easement
nonconforming use
overlay district
planned unit developments (PUDs)
private land use controls
property report
public land use controls
restrictive/protective covenants
run with the land
setback
special use
spot zoning
statement of record
subdivision regulations (ordinances)
variance
zoning ordinance

## LEARNING OBJECTIVES

At the conclusion of this chapter, you should be able to:

1. Describe the general methods of creating land use controls and give examples of public land use controls and private restrictions.
2. Describe zoning concepts, including terminology, authority, purposes, and procedures.

# Land Use Controls

## IN THIS CHAPTER

Land use controls are very important to the real estate agent. Almost every property is subject to some form of control, whether it is the zoning ordinance of a city, subdivision ordinances, or restrictive (protective) covenants, the general restrictions of a subdivision plan, the unique deed restrictions of one parcel of land, or the impact of federal legislation. Any of these can have a major impact on the owner's rights.

## HISTORICAL DEVELOPMENT OF LAND USE CONTROLS

Private control of land use was the forerunner of public controls. In 1848 the United States Supreme Court first recognized and enforced restrictive covenants regulating land use in residential subdivisions, but it was not until 1926, when the Court upheld the validity of zoning ordinances, that **public land use controls** became legally reliable. This refers to *the government regulation of land use through zoning laws, building codes, subdivision ordinances, and environmental protection laws.* Before these two important legal events, a developer or governmental unit had no way to regulate land use, even though the need for such controls was apparent.

The increase in population density dictates the necessity for land use controls. The abuses of a few property owners in the use of their land can have a substantial adverse effect on the rights of other property owners and can cause the property value of those other owners to depreciate.

## IMPORTANCE TO REAL ESTATE PRACTITIONERS AND BUYERS

Real estate practitioners must realize that all land is subject to restrictive controls, whether they be public laws or privately imposed restrictions. Rather than ask if restrictions apply to a given property, a safer approach is to assume that many restrictions do apply and then seek to identify which controls affect the given property. We recommend giving a potential buyer a copy of subdivision covenants and any deed restrictions before he makes an offer. An agent should be aware of zoning issues in his area, but should avoid giving advice about the suitability of zoning for an intended use. The buyer may check with the zoning board or an attorney to ascertain how zoning will affect his intended use of a property. This is best done before making an offer or by making an offer contingent upon proper zoning for his intended use. Additionally, it is not appropriate to assume that an existing use by the present owner is in compliance with regulations. In documented cases, such unfortunate assumptions have worked adversely against the unwary buyer.

In some instances, a purchaser's intended use of property may be contrary to that allowed by the present regulations. Of course, the agent should not make representations as to the likelihood of obtaining approval for a different use. One should never make assumptions about the legality of a particular use, especially if that use is different from the present one. Rather, one should urge appropriate investigation before any purchase contract is signed. Although it is one thing to provide for a specific contingency approval in a purchase offer, it is quite another to make any such promises or representations.

The duty of real estate professionals is to be knowledgeable about the types of restriction that can affect property they are representing and to ensure that appropriate disclosures are made to the parties.

# PUBLIC LAND USE CONTROLS

**Private land use controls** (see Figure 4.1) are *limited in scope, and only a specific area can be subject to private use controls in the form of restrictive covenants.* The owners of property in subdivisions in which restrictive covenants exist have no control over surrounding land uses. Therefore, a subdivision may be affected adversely by an uncontrolled use of an adjoining property outside the subdivision. As a result, people became aware of the need for planning and land use controls for large areas.

Zoning starts with city or county planning, which is implemented and enforced by zoning laws. Violations of zoning laws can be corrected by a court **injunction,** an *action of the court that requires the violation to be discontinued,* even to the extent of ordering an unlawful structure removed.

## Planning and Zoning

The purpose of planning is to provide for the orderly growth of a community that will result in the greatest social and economic benefits to the people in the community. The North Carolina General Assembly has passed **enabling acts** that *provide the legal basis for the local cities and counties to develop long-range plans for growth.* Therefore, the state delegates authority to the local government to develop its own plan. An example of this delegation of authority was seen in Asheville some years ago, when the city wanted to develop comprehensive regulation of the cutting of trees in the front **setback** area of private property. A setback refers to the *distance from a front or interior property line to the point where a structure can be located.* The city realized that this type of ordinance was not within its current authority and that it had to go to the state legislature for additional enabling legislation for the proposed regulation of trees. Zoning ordinances must adhere to federal and state due process provisions and provide for the health, safety, and general welfare of the public as required by the concept of police power. Ordinances must be reasonable, clear, precise, nondiscriminatory, and fairly applied; otherwise, they may not be valid.

The first step in developing a **master plan** is to determine what the city, municipality, or county contains by making a survey of the community's physical and economic assets.

**FIGURE 4.1** Public land use controls.

1. Zoning
2. Urban and regional planning
3. Subdivision regulations
4. Building codes
5. Highway access controls
6. Federal legislation
   A. Interstate land sales
   B. Environmental laws

With this information as a basis, a master plan for orderly growth can be created. As a result of the plan, the various uses to which property may be put in specific areas are designated. The plan addresses such issues as land use, public resources and facilities, and transportation, as well as environmental concerns such as noise and air pollution. The zoning ordinances implement the plan by controlling population density and traffic congestion and promoting health and general welfare by providing water, sewer, adequate light, clean air, fire and environmental protection, schools, parks, and recreational facilities.

Zoning divides land within a county or municipality into areas, districts, or zones and specifies how the land within the zones may or may not be used. Zoning classifications usually include residential, commercial, industrial, and agricultural, which are then subclassified. For example, residential may be divided into single family or multifamily and industrial may be divided into light industry and heavy industry. In actuality, each classification can be subdivided into numerous subclasses. Zoning classifications vary by locality. A zoning classification in Raleigh may not have the same regulations as a classification with the same name in Charlotte.

A **zoning ordinance** consists of two parts: the *zoning map, which divides the community into various designated districts, and the text of the ordinance, which sets forth the type of use permitted under each zoning classification and specific requirements for compliance.* The extent of authority for zoning ordinances is prescribed by the enabling acts passed by the state legislatures. These acts specify the types of use subject to regulation and limit the geographic area subject to the ordinances to the boundaries of the government unit enacting the zoning laws and to certain authorized extraterritorial areas outside a municipality's border. For example, city zoning may extend for some specified distance into the county.

Several types of zone are established by local ordinances: residential (which can be subdivided into single-family and various levels of multifamily dwellings), commercial, light manufacturing, heavy industrial, and multiple use or cluster zoning. The last category provides for **planned unit developments (PUDs),** which *create a neighborhood of cluster housing and supporting business establishments.*

Zoning ordinances provide for either exclusive-use zoning or cumulative-use zoning. In exclusive-use zoning, only the specific uses specified for a particular zone may be made of property in that zone. For example, if a zone is commercial, residential uses will not be permitted. In contrast, under cumulative-use zoning, more protected or higher category uses that are not designated are permitted in the zone. For instance, if an area is zoned for commercial use, a residential use could be made of the property. In cumulative-use zoning, uses are placed in an order of priority; therefore, a use of a higher priority may be made in an area where the zoned use has a lower priority. The priorities are in the following order: residential, commercial, and industrial. In addition to simply specifying the permitted use or uses in a zone, zoning laws define certain standards and requirements that must be met for each permitted type of use. These requirements include such things as minimum setbacks from front property lines to the building line as well as setbacks from the interior property lines, lot size on which a structure may be placed, height restrictions to prevent interference with the reception of sunlight and air to other properties, regulations against building on flood plains, and requirements for off-street parking.

A property owner is not reimbursed for loss of property value caused by a zoning change; however, the government must compensate a property owner whose land it takes under the power of eminent domain. These two very different powers of the government have different purposes, methods of implementation, and results. A municipality cannot "take" land without compensation by downzoning it to the point of making it unusable to avoid acquiring it by paying fair market value under eminent domain.

Zoning concepts and regulations undergo change as society's demographics, lifestyles, needs, and desires change.

## *Zoning Concepts and Terms*

Nonconforming use. A legal **nonconforming use** occurs when the *use of property in a zoned area is different from that specified by the zoning code for the area.* When zoning is first imposed on an area or when property is rezoned, the zoning authority cannot require the

**FIGURE 4.2**
Zoning concepts.

1. Nonconforming use
2. Illegal use
3. Zoning amendments
4. Variance
5. Special use (exception)
6. Overlay districts
7. Historic preservation zoning
8. Aesthetic zoning
9. Spot zoning

property owners to immediately discontinue an existing use that does not conform to the new zoning ordinance. See Figure 4.2 for all zoning concepts. The nonconforming use must be permitted because it may be unconstitutional to require the property owners to terminate the nonconforming use. Therefore, in these cases, the property owner is permitted to continue a nonconforming use, which is lawful. However, the nonconforming user is subject to certain requirements that exist to make everything conform eventually by gradually eliminating the nonconforming use. Examples of these requirements are as follows:

1. If the property owner abandons the nonconforming use, the owner cannot resume that type of use at a later date but may use the property only in a manner that conforms to the zoning ordinance.
2. The property owner cannot make structural changes to the property to expand the nonconforming use or to change the use to a different nonconforming use. The owner is permitted to make only normal necessary repairs to the structure.
3. The nonconforming use cannot be changed from one type of nonconforming use to another type of nonconforming use.
4. If a nonconforming structure is destroyed by fire or another disaster, it often cannot be replaced by another nonconforming structure. Some zoning ordinances, however, do allow for a nonconforming structure that has been destroyed to be replaced by one of the same type and size if done within a reasonable time period, such as one year.
5. Some ordinances provide for a long-term amortization period during which the nonconforming owner is permitted to continue the nonconforming use. At the end of this period, the owner must change the use to conform to the zoning ordinance, rebuilding the structure if necessary.

Despite these restrictions, however, nonconforming uses may be sold with full rights to continue the nonconforming use.

**Illegal use.** An illegal use is one that is contrary to the existing ordinance at the time the use is instituted. The difference between this concept and that of the nonconforming use is that the latter was preexisting (existed at the time the zoning regulation was instituted). Note that the illegal use and the nonconforming use give rise to apparently the same situation, namely a violation of the current code. Since the illegal use is a violation of the present law, however, it may be stopped or removed by an injunction, which is the exercise of the police power of the government.

Attempting to convert a single-family home into a business activity in an area that is zoned for residential use is an illegal use that can be prevented by enforcement of the code.

**Zoning amendments.** An actual *change in the zoning code* itself is known as an **amendment.** It is often difficult for individuals to persuade the city to amend its current regulations to allow a use of their property that is prevented by the code. A formal process is necessary to obtain a zoning change. The process usually includes such things as applications, fees, postings of intent to rezone, and public hearings before the zoning authority rules on the request. The real estate agent is cautioned not to promise or imply to a buyer that she can obtain such a change but to point out the difficulty of obtaining this result if it is essential to the purchaser's intended use.

**Variance.** A **variance** is a *permitted deviation from specific requirements of the existing zoning ordinance.* For example, if an owner's lot is slightly smaller than the requirements of the zoning ordinance as to the minimum lot size upon which a structure may be built, the owner can be granted a variance by petitioning the appropriate authorities.

Variances are permitted if the deviation is not substantial and if strict compliance would impose an undue hardship on the property owner. The hardship must be applicable to one property only and must be a peculiar or special hardship for that property under the zoning law. The special hardship does not exist if all property owners in the zoned area have the same difficulty.

**Special use (exception).** In contrast to the difficult and unpredictable process of obtaining a variance for a specific use for a property, the application of **special use** is essentially automatic in that the use is already provided for in the code. One of the pitfalls in just looking at the symbols on a zoning map to infer what uses may be made of the respective land is that underlying provisions of the text of the code in the given area may have provided for an unexpected application.

Although an area may be generally zoned for residential use, the planners could have provided for the location of a medical office building in the area for the benefit of the local owners. Thus, one wishing to establish such a use need only conform to the provisions established for the special use or exception. Note the difference between the process of obtaining a special use and obtaining a variance. Whereas in the latter, there is no requirement for the authority to grant the petition, in the former, there is no basis to deny the application.

**Overlay districts.** An **overlay district** is a *zoning device that superimposes one zoning area over another.* Visualize a plastic transparency placed on top of a map that shows further restricted areas of the map. Suppose a river runs through the middle of a town, establishing the northern part of the town as residential and the southern half as commercial. As indicated by the general map, landowners south of the river could engage in the permitted commercial uses anywhere along the southern banks of the river. If an overlay transparency restricted the high-water flood plain of the river, however, only certain uses would be permitted. Instead of establishing a building close to the river, the owners may be able to use the land only for something such as a parking lot.

A special application of a flood plain ordinance created a landmark Supreme Court decision in 1987. In the particular instance, the California courts had ruled that the danger of the flood plain prevented all use of the land. The Supreme Court subsequently ruled that this action constituted the "taking" of land and required compensation to the owners as provided by the Constitution. Many people then tried, to no avail, to interpret this decision as requiring compensation to owners for any diminution of property by zoning. Thus, zoning or downgrading still is not considered taking of land requiring compensation to the owner.

**Historic preservation zoning.** Many cities have established specific zoning regulations to preserve the irreplaceable historic legacies of its architecture. In areas where such regulations have been established, one must obtain required approvals before materially modifying the exterior of a structure. This can cause significant problems for the owners or purchasers of property in the affected area if they want to remove existing structures to make way for modern improvements. Several areas have historic resource commissions that seek to provide comprehensive protection of existing buildings. Agents need to stay informed about current and proposed regulations that preserve the heritage of their area.

**Aesthetic zoning.** North Carolina also has specific interpretations providing that an area can be regulated for essentially aesthetic considerations. This can be viewed as an application of the historic preservation areas, designed to achieve a specific impact on a given property or area.

**Spot zoning.** Spot zoning occurs when a *certain property within a zoned area is rezoned to permit a use that is different from the zoning requirements for that zoned area.* If the rezoning of a particular property is simply for the benefit of the property owner and has the effect of increasing the land value, the spot zoning is illegal and invalid. It also is illegal to single out one person's property for spot zoning that will place a burden on that property and not on surrounding properties. North Carolina courts have ruled spot zoning to be legal in some cases where a reasonable basis for it can be clearly demonstrated.

## Urban and Regional Planning

This form of long-range planning takes into account wide areas or multicounty regions and uses zoning as a local method to implement the overall plan. Topics addressed in the wide-region plan include the development of water resources and the placement of major utilities such as power plants, airports, and sanitary landfills.

## Subdivision Regulations

There is no national planning or land development legislation; rather, the state empowers *local governments, cities, and counties to regulate the creation of subdivisions within their particular jurisdictions.* North Carolina General Statute (N.C.G.S.) 153A-335 defines subdivision as "all divisions of a tract or parcel of land into two or more lots, building sites or other divisions for the purpose of sale or building development (whether immediate or future) and includes all divisions of land involving the dedication of a new street or a change in an existing street."

Some exemptions apply when parts of previously subdivided and recorded lots are combined or recombined, when the government purchases land to develop or widen streets, and when land is subdivided into plots of more than 10 acres or a 2-acre or smaller tract is subdivided into three or fewer lots without street right-of-way dedication.

The purpose of **subdivision regulations** is to protect purchasers of property within the subdivisions and to protect the taxpayers in the city or county from significantly increased tax burdens resulting from the demands for services generated by a new subdivision.

Subdivision ordinances typically address the following requirements:

1. Streets must be of a specified width, be curbed, have storm drains, and not exceed certain maximum grade specifications.
2. Lots may not be smaller than a specified minimum size.
3. Dwellings in certain areas must be for single-family occupancy only. Specific areas may be set aside for multifamily dwellings.
4. Utilities, including water, sewer, electric, and telephone, must be available to each lot.
5. All houses must be placed on lots to meet specified minimum standards for setbacks from the front property line as well as from interior property lines.
6. Adequate area drainage must provide for satisfactory runoff of rainfall to avoid damage to properties.

Once a subdivision ordinance has been adopted, subdivision developers must obtain the approval of the appropriate officials; then the final subdivision plat is recorded on the public record, and development can begin. The State of North Carolina changed the law regulating the sale or lease of subdivision lots effective January 1, 2006. Owners, developers, or their agents may offer to sell or lease lots in a subdivision after obtaining preliminary approval of the subdivision plat provided all required statutory provisions are included in the contracts.

These required statutory provisions are as follows:

1. A copy of preliminary map must be attached to the contract and language in the contract must require delivery of a copy of the final recorded plat to the buyer before closing and conveyance.
2. Notifies buyer or lessee of the following in a plain and conspicuous manner.
   - Final plat is not yet recorded.
   - No obligation by any government body to buyer or lessee exists as to final plat approval.
   - Final recorded plat may differ from preliminary plat.
   - Buyer or lessee has right to terminate contract without penalty if there is a material difference between the preliminary and final recorded plats.

3. The buyer or lessee has at least five days to close after receiving from the seller or lessor a copy of a final recorded plat provided the preliminary and final plats have no material difference.
4. The buyer has fifteen days after receiving the final recorded plat to terminate the contract without penalty provided the preliminary and final plats have material differences.

These statutory provisions do not apply to anyone contracting to purchase or lease land to construct any type of building on the land or to resell or lease the land to anyone whose purpose it is to construct any type of building on the land.

Real estate licensees must be careful in offering lots for sale or lease between approval of the preliminary plat and approval and recording of the final plat. Violation of the statutes is a misdemeanor and can subject the licensee to both criminal prosecution in the courts and disciplinary action by the Real Estate Commission.

In no circumstance can conveyance or lease become effective until final plat is recorded. A careful and prudent licensee will verify the approval of the preliminary plat and the approval and recording of the final plat before taking any action requiring these approvals.

Licensees are advised to use a contract form that meets the statutory requirements and that was drafted by an attorney because there is currently no standard form for the purpose. As always, the licensee must never draft a contract or improvise one from existing standard forms as that would be an unauthorized practice of law.

## Disclosure Requirements

Before a developer or seller of a property in a (new) subdivision contracts to sell or convey a property, she must furnish a *subdivision street disclosure statement* to the purchaser and receive a signed acknowledgment by the purchaser that he has received it. This disclosure statement must indicate whether the street in front of the property is public or private. If public, the seller must certify that the Division of Highways has approved the design and right-of-way and that the street meets or will meet, upon completion, the Board of Transportation's criteria for acceptance into the system. If private, the developer or seller must disclose who will be responsible for the construction and maintenance of the street, explain the consequences involved in maintaining the street, and disclose that the street does not meet the minimum criteria for state maintenance (see N.C.G.S. 136-102.6).

Private roads can present practical problems. If the road maintenance agreement provides that responsibility for road maintenance be turned over to the property owners whose property fronts the road, the property owners must have some organizational structure for implementing the agreement.

Sometimes a problem arises in an older subdivision with private streets and no recorded private road maintenance agreement. In such cases, a street maintenance agreement may need to be signed by the property owners, notarized, and recorded before the lender will approve a buyer's loan for a property on the street.

## Building Codes

**Building codes** provide another form of *control of land use for the protection of the public.* These codes regulate such things as materials used in construction, electrical wiring, fire and safety standards, and sanitary equipment facilities. The codes require that a permit be obtained from the appropriate local government authority before the construction or renovation of any property is begun. While construction is in progress, frequent inspections are performed by local government inspectors to make certain that the code requirements are being met.

After a satisfactory final inspection, a **Certificate of Occupancy** is issued. This *permits the occupation of the structure by tenants or the owner.* Some cities today require that a Certificate of Occupancy, *based upon a satisfactory inspection of the property,* be issued prior to occupancy by a new owner or tenant of any structure even though it is not new construction and/or has not been renovated. Inspection is required to reveal deficiencies in the structure that require correction before the city will issue a Certificate of Occupancy for the protection of the new purchaser or tenant.

## Highway Access Controls

A major danger could exist to the public if unlimited access were permitted to high-speed roads with significant traffic. Therefore, the local government may use **highway access controls** to *condemn areas of a property for connection to the highway.* This requires compensation to the present owner but could well provide problems for a future owner. For example, a developer may want to purchase a tract of land for the construction of single-family homes. If the land use has been restricted, she may not be able to connect individual driveways to the highway and would need to construct a single-access road.

## Interstate Land Sales Full Disclosure Act

The **Interstate Land Sales Full Disclosure Act** is a *federal regulation of the interstate (across state lines) sale of unimproved lots* that became effective in 1969 and was made more restrictive by an amendment in 1980. The Act is administered by the secretary of Housing and Urban Development (HUD) through the office of Interstate Land Sales Registration.

The purpose of the Act is to prevent fraudulent marketing schemes when land is sold by misleading sales practices on a sight-unseen basis. The Act requires that a developer file a **statement of record** with HUD before offering unimproved lots in interstate commerce by telephone or through the mail. The statement of record *requires disclosure of information about the property as specified by HUD.*

The developer is also required to provide each purchaser or lessee of property with a printed **property report,** which *discloses specific information about the land before a purchase contract or lease is signed by the purchaser or lessee.* The property report contains specific information about the land for the protection of the purchaser or lessee. Required information includes such things as the type of title a buyer will receive, the number of homes currently occupied, availability of recreation facilities, distance to nearby communities, utility services and charges, and soil or other foundation problems in construction. If the purchaser or lessee is not supplied with a copy of the property report prior to signing a purchase contract or lease, the purchaser or lessee can void the contract.

The Act provides for several exemptions, the most important of which are:

1. Subdivisions in which the lots are of five acres or more.
2. Subdivisions that consist of fewer than 100 lots are exempt from the registration requirements of the Act. Subdivisions of fewer than 25 lots are exempt from the Act, including both the registration and antifraud provisions.
3. Lots that are offered for sale exclusively to building contractors.
4. Lots on which a building exists or where a contract obligates the lot seller to construct a building within two years.

If a developer offered only part of the total tract owned and thereby limited the subdivision to fewer than 100 lots to acquire an exemption, the developer could not then sell additional lots within the tract. HUD considers these additional lots part of a common plan for development and marketing, thereby eliminating the developer's opportunity for several exemptions as a result of a piecemeal development of a large tract in sections of fewer than 100 lots at a time.

The Act provides severe penalties for violation by a developer or a real estate agent participating in marketing the property. The developer and/or the real estate agent can be sued for damages by a purchaser or lessee and is potentially subject to a criminal penalty by fine of up to $5,000 or imprisonment for up to five years or both. Therefore, before acting as an agent for a developer in marketing property, real estate agents must ascertain that a developer has complied with the law or is exempt.

## Environmental Protection Legislation

The national **Environmental Policy Act** of 1969 *requires filing an environmental impact statement with the* **Environmental Protection Agency (EPA)** *prior to changing or initiating a land use or development in public trust areas under federal jurisdiction* to ensure that the use will not adversely affect the environment. Typical subject areas regulated by the Act include air, noise, and water pollution, as well as chemical and solid waste disposal.

Since 1969, several amendments and companion legislation have been passed to more clearly define the EPA's role in land use. The Resource Conservation and Recovery Act (RCRA), passed in 1976, defined hazardous substances. In 1980 Congress passed the Comprehensive Environmental Response, Compensation and Liability Act (CERCLA) to provide solutions to the environmental problems created over the years by uncontrolled disposal of wastes. Under CERCLA, a program was created to identify sites containing hazardous substances, to ensure that those sites were cleaned up by the parties responsible or by the government, and to establish a procedure to seek reimbursement for cleanup from the party responsible for placing the hazardous substance.

In 1986 CERCLA was amended by the Superfund Amendments and Reauthorization Act (SARA). The amendments imposed stringent cleanup standards and expanded the definition of persons liable for the cost of cleanup. Under CERCLA and SARA, every landowner is potentially affected.

In addition to federal legislation, some states now require full disclosure, prior to title transfer by deed, if real estate is listed by a federal or state agency as contaminated by hazardous substance.

More recent environmental issues include protection of habitats for wildlife, wetlands, shorelines, and endangered species, as well as issues such as lead-based paint, radon, and asbestos.

## *Residential Lead-Based Paint Hazard Reduction Act of 1992*

For more than two decades, the threat of hazards posed by lead-based products has been an environmental concern. Lead is a highly toxic metal that can be ingested or inhaled. Lead levels can build up in the body and attack the central nervous system, causing damage ranging from mild to severe. The ingestion or inhalation of lead is of particular concern for young children, women of child-bearing age, and unborn babies. The use of lead in gasoline and food products has been restricted for many years, and the use of lead-based paint in residential properties was banned in 1978. However, a large percentage of occupied homes in this country were built prior to 1978; therefore, the risk of exposure to lead in residential properties continues to be a concern. To address this concern, Congress passed the Housing and Community Development Act of 1992. Title X of this Act is entitled the *Residential Lead-Based Paint Hazard Reduction Act of 1992.* This Act authorized HUD to develop a set of rules to address this concern. In conjunction with the EPA, a set of rules was developed; they were published in 1996.

As a result of these rules, the following activities must be completed before a purchaser or renter is obligated under a contract to purchase or lease most residential properties built before 1978:

1. A purchaser or lessee must be provided with the EPA pamphlet "Protect Your Family From Lead in Your Home" (EPA #747-K-94-001) or an equivalent EPA approved state publication.
2. The seller or lessor must disclose to the purchaser, lessee, or his agent the presence of any known lead-based paint and provide any available records or reports pertaining to lead-based paint or hazards.

If any of the required disclosures occurs after the purchaser or lessee has made an offer, the purchaser or lessee has the right to amend the offer after the disclosure is made.

In addition to the preceding requirements, a seller must permit the purchaser an amount of time mutually agreed upon by purchaser and seller to conduct a risk assessment or inspection for lead-based paint or related hazards. This evaluation period does not apply to rentals.

**Certification and acknowledgment of disclosure.** Each sales contract or lease for a residential property built prior to 1978 must have an addendum containing the specified "Lead Warning Statement" and signed statements from all parties and agents of the seller or lessor certifying that all requirements were completed (see NCBA/NCAR Standard Form No. 2A9-T, Figure 4.3). A copy of this addendum must be retained by the seller or lessor and any agent for three years.

**FIGURE 4.3** Lead-based paint addendum.

## LEAD-BASED PAINT OR LEAD-BASED PAINT HAZARD ADDENDUM

Property Address: ______________________________

It is a condition of this contract that, until ______________________ or the Option Termination Date, whichever occurs first, Buyer shall have the right to obtain a risk assessment or inspection of the Property for the presence of lead-based paint and/or lead-based paint hazards* at Buyer's expense. This contingency will terminate at that time unless Buyer or Buyer's agent delivers to the Seller or Seller's agent a written inspection and/or risk assessment report listing the specific existing deficiencies and corrections needed, if any. If any corrections are necessary, Seller shall have the option of completing them or refusing to complete them. If Seller elects not to complete the corrections, then Buyer shall have the option of accepting the Property in its present condition or terminating this contract, in which case all earnest monies shall be refunded to Buyer. Buyer may waive the right to obtain a risk assessment or inspection of the Property for the presence of lead-based paint and/or lead-based paint hazards at any time without cause.

***Intact lead-based paint that is in good condition is not necessarily a hazard. See EPA pamphlet "Protect Your Family From Lead in Your Home" for more information.**

### Disclosure of Information on Lead-Based Paint and Lead-Based Paint Hazards

**Lead Warning Statement**
*Every Buyer of any interest in residential real property on which a residential dwelling was built prior to 1978 is notified that such property may present exposure to lead from lead-based paint that may place young children at risk of developing lead poisoning. Lead poisoning in young children may produce permanent neurological damage, including learning disabilities, reduced intelligence quotient, behavioral problems, and impaired memory. Lead poisoning also poses a particular risk to pregnant women. The Seller of any interest in residential real property is required to provide the Buyer with any information on lead-based paint hazards from risk assessments or inspections in the Seller's possession and notify the Buyer of any known lead-based paint hazards. A risk assessment or inspection for possible lead-based hazards is recommended prior to purchase.*

**Seller's Disclosure (initial)**

_______ (a) Presence of lead-based paint and/or lead-based paint hazards (check one below):
- ❑ Known lead-based paint and/or lead-based paint hazards are present in the housing (explain).
  ______________________________
  ______________________________
- ❑ Seller has no knowledge of lead-based paint and/or lead-based paint hazards in the housing.

_______ (b) Records and reports available to the Seller (check one)
- ❑ Seller has provided the Buyer with all available records and reports pertaining to lead-based paint and/or lead-based paint hazards in the housing (list documents below).
  ______________________________
  ______________________________
- ❑ Seller has no reports or records pertaining to lead-based paint and/or lead-based paint hazards in the housing.

**Buyer's Acknowledgement (initial)**

_______ (c) Buyer has received copies of all information listed above.
_______ (d) Buyer has received the pamphlet *Protect Your Family from Lead in Your Home.*
_______ (e) Buyer has (check one below):
- ❑ Received a 10-day opportunity (or mutually agreed upon period) to conduct a risk assessment or inspection for the presence of lead-based paint and/or lead-based paint hazards; or
- ❑ Waived the opportunity to conduct a risk assessment or inspection for the presence of lead-based paint and/or lead-based paint hazards.



REALTOR®

**This form jointly approved by:**
**North Carolina Bar Association**
**North Carolina Association of REALTORS®, Inc.**

EQUAL HOUSING OPPORTUNITY

**STANDARD FORM 2A9 - T**


Buyer Initials _______ _______ Seller Initials _______ _______

**FIGURE 4.3** Continued.

**Agent's Acknowledgment (initial)**

______ (f) Agent has informed the Seller of the Seller's obligations under 42 U.S.C. 4852d and is aware of his/her responsibility to ensure compliance.

**Certification of Accuracy**

The following parties have reviewed the information above and certify, to the best of their knowledge, that the information provided by the signatory is true and accurate.

THE NORTH CAROLINA ASSOCIATION OF REALTORS®, INC. AND THE NORTH CAROLINA BAR ASSOCIATION MAKE NO REPRESENTATION AS TO THE LEGAL VALIDITY OR ADEQUACY OF ANY PROVISION OF THIS FORM IN ANY SPECIFIC TRANSACTION. IF YOU DO NOT UNDERSTAND THIS FORM OR FEEL THAT IT DOES NOT PROVIDE FOR YOUR LEGAL NEEDS, YOU SHOULD CONSULT A NORTH CAROLINA REAL ESTATE ATTORNEY BEFORE YOU SIGN IT.

Buyer:________________________________(SEAL) Date________________

Buyer:________________________________(SEAL) Date________________

Agent:________________________________ Date________________

Seller:________________________________(SEAL) Date________________

Seller:________________________________(SEAL) Date________________

Agent:________________________________ Date________________

Page 2 of 2

STANDARD FORM 2A9 - T

**Agent's responsibilities.** Agents must ensure compliance with all requirements of the rules. This includes seller's agents, seller's subagents, and buyer's agents if paid by the seller or through a cooperative brokerage agreement with the listing agent. A buyer's agent is specifically excluded only if compensated by the buyer. The agent must inform the seller or lessor of his obligations under the rules and ensure that the seller or lessor has performed all activities required or personally ensure compliance. Note that the agent shares legal responsibility with the seller or lessor. If the agent has ensured compliance, she shall not be liable for failure to disclose the presence of lead-based hazards known to the seller but not disclosed to the agent. Sellers, lessors, and agents who fail to comply with the federal rules are subject to civil monetary penalties, civil suits, and criminal prosecution.

**Exceptions to the federal rules.** The lead-based paint disclosure rules apply to housing constructed prior to 1978 and includes the "common area" in multifamily structures. The exceptions to this rule include housing for the elderly (unless a child under 6 years of age resides in such housing) and no-bedroom dwellings (those with no separate sleeping area, such as studio apartments, and rentals of individual rooms in a home). Other exemptions include sales at foreclosure, houses certified as *lead-free* by a certified inspector, leases of 100 days or less with no option to renew or extend the lease, and renewals of leases if the disclosure requirements were previously satisfied.

## Asbestos

Asbestos is a fibrous material that has been used in building products such as flooring, ceiling tiles, insulation, and exterior shingles. Asbestos has been found to cause cancer in the lungs and stomach of workers who inhale or ingest the fibers over a prolonged period of time. The federal government regulates asbestos under several acts, including the Clean Air Act and the Occupational Safety and Health Act. The presence of asbestos in residential property is addressed on the Residential Property Disclosure Statement. While the statement asks about the presence of asbestos, the fact that asbestos is present is not necessarily a cause for concern. Since it is the fibers that are a cause for concern, intact asbestos is not a health hazard. It is asbestos that has become friable (crumbling or easily crumbled) that creates the risk of inhalation of fibers. Paragraph 13 Alt 1(a) (Property Inspection, Appraisal, Investigation) of the NCBA/NCAR Offer to Purchase and Contract form states that "there shall be no friable asbestos." For additional information on asbestos, see Appendix C.

## Radon

Radon is a chemically inert gas that occurs naturally in the decay process of uranium. Radon seeps from the ground and enters buildings through cracks and other openings in foundations. In the open air, radon dissipates harmlessly. However, in enclosed spaces, the chemical can damage lungs when inhaled. This damage can lead to cancer of the lungs. Many states, including North Carolina, now require disclosure of radon. This hazard is addressed on the Residential Property Disclosure Statement and the NCBA/NCAR Offer to Purchase and Contact form, Paragraph 13 under Alternative 1d. As of January 1, 1997, EPA guidelines define an "acceptable" level of radon as anything less than 4.0 pico curies/liter of air. For additional information regarding radon, see Appendix C.

## Mold

Mold is an old problem currently getting a lot of attention. It can be found anywhere that appropriate nutrients, temperature, and moisture allow its growth. Mold reproduces by releasing tiny spores into the air, where people are exposed to them. Some of these spores produce powerful microtoxins that can be harmful in large amounts; however, there is no proof that a person can inhale enough of these to cause serious damage.

There are thousands of species of mold, including common household mildew. People exhibit varying degrees of sensitivity to the different types of mold spores. Some people have no reaction; others have mild irritation of the skin and mucous membranes or infection of the respiratory tract and eyes. A small percentage of the population suffers severe allergic reactions, such as asthma.

Agents should not create unnecessary problems about mold since it is a common occurrence. If there is evidence of mold (such as discolored growth or staining on walls, floors, ceilings, or bathroom and kitchen fixtures; an allergic reaction in a mold-sensitive person; or an indication of past or present excess water), the property owner should take appropriate steps to remove the mold and eliminate the underlying conditions causing it. If the mold is not eliminated and the excess moisture is not corrected, the mold will recur. Known mold problems that adversely affect people or the property must be disclosed on the seller's property disclosure sheet.

Agents are advised to neither offer advice about mold and mildew nor recommend specific experts to evaluate or remedy mold. Agents may suggest to clients that they contact a federal or state agency or the agency's web site for assistance in choosing a consultant to determine the presence, absence, or extent of a mold problem and the proper remedy for any problem found.

## *The North Carolina Coastal Area Management System*

Through the Coastal Zone Management Act, the federal government assists states in establishing management programs for coastal areas and water resources. North Carolina's management program, the North Carolina Coastal Area Management Act of 1974 (CAMA), is of prime importance to real estate practitioners and developers in the coastal areas; therefore, they should be familiar with the goals of the Act, which are reproduced in the feature box. If an area of "environmental concern" is designated under CAMA, a prospective developer must obtain a permit before development. The approval process can be relatively simple or more extensive, depending on the nature of the proposed development.

## *N.C. Leaking Petroleum Underground Storage Tank Cleanup Act*

The *N.C. Leaking Petroleum Underground Storage Tank Cleanup Act* addresses the problem of contamination caused by discharge of oil and other hazardous substances

**The goals of the coastal area management system to be created pursuant to this Article are as follows:**

1. To provide a management system capable of preserving and managing the natural ecological conditions of the estuarine system, the barrier dune system, and the beaches, so as to safeguard and perpetuate their natural productivity and their biological, economic, and esthetic values;
2. To insure that the development or preservation of the land and water resources of the coastal area proceeds in a manner consistent with the capability of the land and water for development, use, or preservation based on ecological considerations;
3. To insure the orderly and balanced use and preservation of our coastal resources on behalf of the people of North Carolina and the nation;
4. To establish policies, guidelines, and standards for:
   a. Protection, preservation, and conservation of natural resources, including but not limited to water use, scenic vistas, and fish and wildlife; and management of transitional or intensely developed areas and areas especially suited to intensive use or development, as well as areas of significant natural value;
   b. The economic development of the coastal area, including but not limited to construction, location, and design of industries, port facilities, commercial establishments, and other developments;
   c. Recreation and tourist facilities and parklands;
   d. Transportation and circulation patterns for the coastal area, including major thoroughfares, transportation routes, navigation channels and harbors, and other public utilities and facilities;
   e. Preservation and enhancement of the historic, cultural, and scientific aspects of the coastal area;
   f. Protection of present common-law and statutory public rights in the lands and waters of the coastal area;
   g. Any other purposes deemed necessary or appropriate to effectuate the policy of this Article.

from underground storage tanks. Commercial tanks are subject to technical regulations, but home-heating oil tanks are not regulated. This means that home tanks are exempt from closure requirements (closure means removing tanks or filling them with solid inert material, such as sand, and analyzing for possible contamination). However, some groundwater regulations apply if there is a leak or spill. For this reason, homeowners should empty a tank that is no longer in use. North Carolina has established a cleanup fund that pays for reasonable and necessary costs related to the cleanup of spills from home storage tanks.

### *Clean Water Acts*

Federal and state Clean Water Acts protect waters by making it illegal to deposit dredged or fill materials into wetlands and other waters unless a permit is obtained. The U.S. Army Corp of Engineers administers the dredge and fill permit program. The *North Carolina Dredge and Fill Act* also requires that a permit be obtained before dredging or filling in North Carolina's waters. The Coastal Resources Commission issues this permit.

### *N.C. Sediment Pollution Control Act*

The *N.C. Sediment Pollution Control Act* addresses the problem of sedimentation of waters in North Carolina. Sedimentation is the result of erosion or the depositing of soil into waters. Sedimentation can result from such activities as mining, farming, and land development and can have adverse effects on the waters and aquatic plants and animals. Any activity that disturbs vegetation or topography in such a way as to create sedimentation is subject to this act. The North Carolina Department of Environment, Health, and Natural Resources regulates these activities.

### *Flood Hazard Area Regulations and Insurance*

Real estate that is designated as being in a *flood hazard area* is subject to certain federal laws and regulations. The Federal Emergency Management Agency (FEMA) issues maps that designate flood hazard areas. All real estate in flood hazard areas that is mortgaged through any federally related loan program (FHA, VA, and most secondary mortgage market loans) must be covered by flood insurance (see Chapter 14) under the *National Flood Insurance Program.*

### The North Carolina Planned Community Act

The definition of a planned community is "real estate with respect to which any person, by virtue of that person's ownership of a lot, is expressly obligated by a declaration to pay real property taxes, insurance premiums, or other expenses to maintain, improve, or benefit other lots or other real estate described in the declaration." Very simply put, a planned community is one where each lot owner is subject to a fee for the maintenance of the common areas. An owner may not simply ignore the fee because the Planned Community Act makes the owner legally obligated to pay. The main difference between a traditional subdivision and a planned community is that the government has now granted certain statutory powers to the homeowner's association or developer to enforce rules, regulations, and procedures.

The Planned Community Act is a relatively new creature to real estate in North Carolina, having been created in 1999. The items an agent needs to be aware of in the protection of a buyer are the new legal obligations set forth in this Act. For example, the buyer must adhere to the restrictive covenants as a matter of statutory law as opposed to civil law.

## PRIVATE LAND USE CONTROLS

### Individual Deed Restrictions

Individual **deed restrictions,** or *limits on land use,* exist in the form of covenants or in the form of conditions. A **covenant,** or a *promise in writing,* exists in a deed to benefit property that is sold or to benefit a property that is retained, as in the case of a sale of adjoining

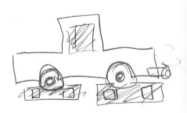

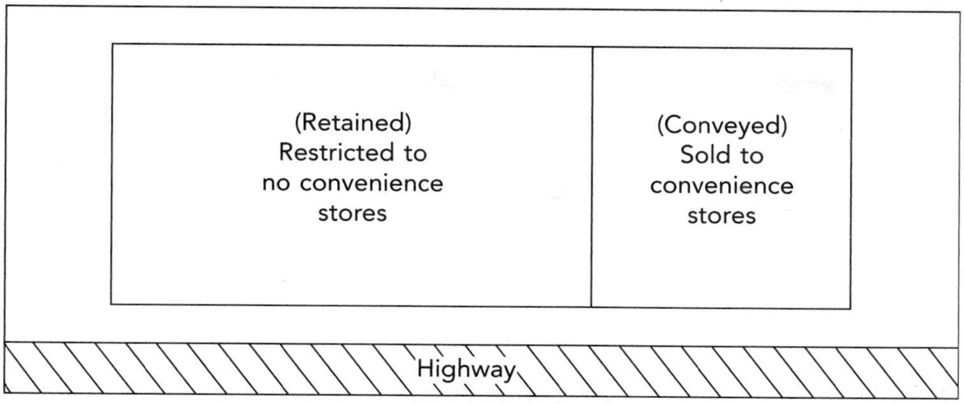


**FIGURE 4.4**
Restrictions applied to land retained.

property. For example, an owner selling an adjoining property provides in the deed that a structure may not be erected in a certain area of the property sold to protect the view from the property retained or to prevent the loss of reception of light and air to the property retained. Conversely, the purchaser of a property may require as part of the purchase that the owner restrict the part of the property he is retaining. For example, a buyer purchases a piece of property to use as a convenience store and requires the owner to restrict the remaining property to prohibit convenience stores (see Figure 4.4). These restrictions are covenants that **run with the land,** meaning that they *move with the title in any subsequent conveyance.* Covenants are enforced by a suit for damages or by injunction. *Restrictions that provide for a reversion of title if they are violated* are called **conditions.** If a condition is violated, ownership reverts to the grantor, his heirs or assigns.

## Restrictive/Protective Covenants

**Restrictive/protective covenants** are *restrictions placed on the use of land by the developer of a residential subdivision.* Historically these covenants have been called restrictive covenants, but current usage favors protective covenants to emphasize their positive aspects. The purpose of these covenants is to preserve and protect the quality of land in subdivisions and to maximize land values by requiring the homogeneous or compatible use of land by purchasers of property in a subdivision The covenants are *promises on the part of the purchasers of property in the subdivision to limit their use of their property to comply with the requirements of the restrictive/protective covenants* and are therefore **negative easements.** The deed conveying title to property in the subdivision contains a reference to a recorded plat of the subdivision and a reference to the recording of the restrictive/protective covenants, or the restrictions may be recited in each deed of conveyance. Restrictions must be reasonable, and they must be beneficial to all property owners alike.

If the subdivision is in a zoned area, the restrictive/protective covenants have priority over the zoning ordinance, to the extent that the covenants are more restrictive than the zoning requirements. For example, if the zoning permits multifamily dwellings and the restrictive/protective covenants limit land use to single-family dwellings, the restrictive/protective covenants will be enforced. Covenants contrary to public law and public policy will not be enforced. For example, a restrictive/protective covenant requiring discrimination on the basis of race, color, religion, sex, national origin, disability, or familial status is invalid. Also, restrictive/protective covenants are not binding on the general public unless they are recorded on the public record in the county where the land is located (Conner Act).

Restrictive/protective covenants are land use limitations that provide a general plan for development of a subdivision. Prior to the start of development, the developer establishes a list of rules each lot purchaser is required to adhere to in the use of the property. These rules controlling the use of land are then recorded in an instrument called the declaration of restrictions. The declaration is recorded simultaneously with the plat and includes a reference to the plat. Typical restrictive/protective covenants are as follows:

1. Only single-family dwellings may be constructed in the subdivision.
2. Dwellings must contain a specified minimum number of square feet of living area.
3. Only one single-family dwelling may be constructed on a lot.
4. No lot may be subdivided.
5. Dwellings must be of a harmonious architectural style. To ensure this, a site plan and plans and specifications for the structure must be submitted to and approved by a committee prior to the start of construction.
6. Structures must be set back a specified distance from the front property line and a specified distance from interior property lines.
7. Temporary structures may not be placed on any lot.
8. Covenants may be enforced by any one property owner or several property owners of land within the subdivision by taking appropriate court actions.
9. The covenants will remain in effect for a specified time period and may be changed by a vote of the property owners. There may be specified automatic renewal periods.

Real estate practitioners are expected to be aware of the existence of restrictive/protective covenants in subdivisions, condominiums, townhouses, and multifamily developments where they are selling property. NCBA/NCAR Standard Form No. 2T, Offer to Purchase and Contract, contains a note advising the buyer to review restrictive covenants and other documents pertaining to the property prior to making his offer. The broker may assist the prospective buyer in locating a copy of the protective/restrictive covenants if the buyer requests one. Copies may be obtained from the Register of Deeds Office in the County where the property is located or from the developer if he is still on site. When providing the buyer a copy of the protective/restrictive covenants, check to make sure the ones given are for the right phase of the subdivision, as covenants sometimes differ from phase to phase.

## Termination of Covenants

Covenants are terminated in the following ways:

1. Expiration of the time period for which the covenants were created.
2. Unanimous vote of the property owners to terminate the covenants, unless the covenants provide for termination by vote of a smaller number of landowners.
3. Changes in the character of the subdivision that make it unsatisfactory for the type of use specified by the covenants to continue. For example, as a result of the failure of property owners in a subdivision restricted to single-family residential use to enforce that restriction, the area gradually changes to commercial use. Consequently, the subdivision is no longer suitable for limitation to residential use.
4. The right to enforce particular restriction in the protective covenants may be lost by abandonment, which occurs when the property owners have violated their covenants and many of them have participated in the violations. As a result, a court may rule that there has been an abandonment of the original general plan by the property owners; therefore, the court will not enforce the covenants.
5. Failure to enforce restrictions on a timely basis. An owner or owners cannot sit idly by and watch someone complete a structure in a subdivision in violation of the protective covenants and then attempt to enforce the restriction by court action. The court will not apply the restriction against the violator. Therefore, the restriction is terminated by the failure of action on a timely basis by the property owners to enforce protective covenants.

## *Enforcement of Covenants*

Private land use controls are enforced by public law but not by public officials or agencies. This is accomplished by the action of a court, known as an injunction. An injunction prevents a use contrary to the restrictions of record or orders the removal of any such uses that have been implemented. In a practical sense, the individuals who bear the primary responsibility for seeing that the restrictions are enforced are the developer or other owners of property in the affected area. Any property owner within the subdivision can enforce the covenants. If property owners do not enforce the subdivision covenants within the period of time required by the Statute of Limitations, they can lose their right to enforce.

Enforcement of the covenants is not limited to the original purchasers of property in the subdivision. Subsequent purchasers must abide by and can enforce the protective covenants until such time as the covenants are terminated, as previously discussed; that is, the restrictions run with the land.

## Responsibility of Real Estate Agents

Real estate agents must be knowledgeable of existing public and private land use controls within their market area and must keep abreast of changes in the requirements as they occur. This knowledge is necessary to enable real estate agents to fulfill their obligations to their principals as well as to the buying public. Lack of knowledge in these areas may subject real estate agents to civil liability to injured parties and possible criminal liability under certain federal laws.

## SUMMARY OF IMPORTANT POINTS

1. The purpose of planning is to provide for the orderly growth of a community that will result in the greatest social and economic benefits to the people. Therefore, a real estate practitioner has a clear duty to identify and disclose which controls affect any given property.
2. Controls are grouped in two general categories. Public land use controls are best recognized in the form of zoning ordinances. Although zoning is strictly a local regulation, other public controls such as building codes and environmental protection legislation add a state and federal level of regulation to property. Private land use controls arise from a grantor of title who wishes to restrict the way a property is used by successive grantees. Often this is done to maintain the essential residential character of a new development. Once restrictions are properly developed and recorded, they pass with the title; that is, run with the land.
3. The plan for development is enforced by zoning ordinances. Planning and zoning are exercises of police power.
4. Typical zones include residential, commercial, planned unit developments (PUDs), industrial, and agricultural. Zoning may be either exclusive-use or cumulative-use.
5. In addition to specifying permitted uses, zoning ordinances define standards and requirements that must be met for each type of use.
6. A nonconforming use is one that is different from the type of use permitted in a particular zone but that is allowed to continue because it existed before the zoning prohibiting it was enacted.
7. An illegal use is one that is contrary to the existing ordinance at the time the use is established.

8. A zoning amendment is a change or modification of the existing ordinance by the local governing body.

9. A variance is a permitted deviation from specific requirements of a zoning ordinance because a special hardship would be imposed on a property owner by strict enforcement.

10. A special use or special exception is already provided for in the code. There is no basis for the authority to deny the application if the described conditions are met.

11. Overlay districts can be seen as a transparency that is placed on top of a zoning map to show further restricted areas of the map. The area identified by the overlay transparency may cover all or parts of one or more zoning districts.

12. Historic preservation zoning preserves the architectural legacies of an area by preventing the modification or removal of buildings.

13. North Carolina provides for aesthetic zoning.

14. Spot zoning occurs when a certain property within a zoned area is rezoned to permit a use that is different from the zoning requirements for that area. Spot zoning is invalid unless a reasonable basis for it can be clearly demonstrated.

15. Urban and regional planning provide for long-term planning in a wide area that may affect several counties.

16. Subdivision ordinances regulate the development of residential subdivisions to protect property purchasers as well as to protect area taxpayers from increased tax burdens resulting from the demand for services generated by the subdivisions.

17. Building codes require that certain standards of construction be met. The codes are primarily concerned with electrical systems, fire and safety standards, and sanitary systems and equipment.

18. Highway access controls represent condemnation of areas of a property for connection to areas of major highways.

19. The Interstate Land Sales Full Disclosure Act is a federal law that regulates the sale of unimproved lots in interstate commerce to prevent fraudulent schemes that may occur when land is sold on a sight-unseen basis.

20. Environmental protection laws are a form of land use control to protect the public against abuses of the environment.

21. Private land use controls are in the form of deed restrictions and restrictive/protective covenants.

22. Restrictive/protective covenants must be reasonable and must be equally beneficial to all property owners.

23. Restrictive/protective covenants are recorded on the public record in an instrument called a declaration of restrictions. They are not enforceable unless recorded.

24. Restrictive/protective covenants are enforced by court injunction upon a petition by one or more property owners on a timely basis.

## ITEMS TO CONSIDER FOR THE STATE EXAM

A common area of trouble on the exam is confusion of terminology. Applicants often have only a cursory knowledge of the distinction between the terms *nonconforming use, variance, special use,* and *illegal use.* The terms are not interchangeable, and one should have a concise picture of what each means. Refer to the text and the following capsule definitions.

1. *Nonconforming use.* This use was already in effect before the conflicting ordinance was passed. It is allowed to continue but not be expanded, and it can be freely marketed with the same reservation. If abandoned, it cannot be reinstituted. If destroyed, local zoning ordinances may or may not allow it to be reinstituted within a short period of time.
2. *Illegal use.* This use is contrary to the existing law at the time the use was instituted and may be prevented or removed by an exercise of the state's police power through an injunction. Prolonged illegal use does not mature into a legal one.
3. *Amendment.* City hall may change its mind about a given regulation and change or amend the code. Some cities maintain their code in a loose-leaf notebook so new amendments can be easily substituted.
4. *Variance.* If owners can establish that a given law works an undue hardship on their property that prevents a fair return on their ownership, they can seek approval for a variance that is a permitted violation of the ordinance. There is no requirement for the city to approve the petition.
5. *Special use permit.* The special use, or special exception, is provided for in the code itself. No appeal process is necessary if the requested use complies with the established provisions of the special exception. The opposite of a variance, there is no authority for the city to deny this request.
6. *Spot zoning.* The rezoning of one person's property solely for personal benefit is illegal. Spot zoning must have a clear, reasonable basis in order to be legal.

## REVIEW QUESTIONS

Answers to the review questions are in the Answer Key at the back of the book.

1. Which of the following statements about land use controls is NOT correct?
   A. deed restrictions are a form of private land use control
   B. public land use controls are an exercise of police power
   C. subdivision covenants are a form of public and use controls
   D. localities receive their power to develop long-range plans for growth and the power to zone from the North Carolina General Assembly

2. Deed restrictions that run with the land are which of the following?
   A. ordinances
   B. variances
   C. declarations
   D. covenants

3. All of the following statements about restrictive/protective covenants are correct EXCEPT:
   A. they must be reasonable
   B. they are enforceable even though not recorded
   C. they are not enforceable if contrary to law
   D. they provide for a general plan for development

4. The instrument used for recording restrictive/protective covenants is a:
   A. plat
   B. master deed
   C. covenant
   D. declaration of restrictions

5. Restrictive/protective covenants are terminated in all of the following ways EXCEPT:
   A. expiration
   B. transfer of title
   C. failure to enforce on a timely basis
   D. abandonment

6. Restrictive/protective covenants are enforced by which of the following?
   A. zoning
   B. injunction
   C. police power
   D. condemnation

7. The type of zoning that permits a higher priority use in a lower priority zone is called:
   A. exclusive use
   B. nonconforming use
   C. amortizing use
   D. cumulative use

8. Which of the following is a permitted deviation from the standards of a zoning ordinance?
   A. variance
   B. nonconforming use
   C. spot zoning
   D. special use

9. Which of the following is an illegal rezoning of a particular property solely for the benefit of the owner?
   A. variance
   B. nonconforming use
   C. spot zoning
   D. special use

10. Which of the following statements about subdivision ordinances is (are) correct?
    A. the purpose is to protect taxpayers from increased taxes caused by increased demand for services to subdivisions
    B. the purpose is to protect developers during the development period from excessive costs and thereby to encourage residential development
    C. the purpose is to provide uniformity of structures within the subdivision
    D. all of the above

11. Which of the following powers gives the government the right to zone?
    A. power of eminent domain
    B. police power
    C. power of escheat
    D. power of taxation

12. Building codes require which of the following?
    A. property report
    B. PUDs
    C. certificate of occupancy
    D. statement of record

13. Which of the following statements concerning the Interstate Land Sales Full Disclosure Act is correct?
    A. the Act regulates sales of large parcels of unimproved land (over five acres) across state lines
    B. the Act is administered by the Environmental Protection Agency
    C. the Act is administered by HUD
    D. the Act only covers land with buildings on it

14. Exemptions to the registration requirements of the Interstate Land Sales Full Disclosure Act include all of the following EXCEPT:
    A. subdivisions of fewer than 100 lots
    B. lots offered only to building contractors
    C. lots on which there is a building
    D. subdivisions in which the lots are four acres or more

15. John starts operating a five-unit apartment building in an area that has been zoned for a duplex only. John lists the property with Larry Listing Agent who eventually sells the property to Bob Buyer. Bob continues to operate the five-unit building for the next 20 years. Which of the following statements is (are) correct?
    I. John had a legal nonconforming use.
    II. Larry was responsible for discovering and disclosing the situation to Bob.
    III. Bob has obtained a legal nonconforming use.
    A. I only
    B. II only
    C. I and III only
    D. I, II, and III

16. The Residential Lead-Based Paint Hazard Reduction Act of 1992 requires that a buyer or lessee of a residential property built prior to 1978 be provided with all of the following EXCEPT:
    A. the EPA pamphlet entitled "Protect Your Family from Lead in Your Home"
    B. certification by HUD that the home is "lead free"
    C. disclosure of known lead-based paint
    D. a period of time agreed upon by purchaser and seller in which to conduct a risk assessment or inspection for lead-based paint.

17. Which of the following statements concerning flood hazard areas is correct?
    A. real estate designated as being in a flood hazard area cannot be financed through any federally related loan program
    B. the Department of Housing and Urban Development issues maps that designate flood hazard areas
    C. there are currently no federal laws or regulations concerning flood hazard areas
    D. flood insurance is available under the National Flood Insurance Program

18. A property owner is reimbursed for loss when:
    A. a loss of property value is caused by a zoning change
    B. a property is taken under the power of eminent domain
    C. aesthetic zoning causes an undue hardship
    D. all of the above

19. The goals of the North Carolina Coastal Area Management Act include which of the following?
    A. to insure the orderly and balanced use and preservation of our coastal resources
    B. to insure that developers can obtain permits with relative ease
    C. to provide disclosure to purchasers in areas of environmental concern
    D. all of the above

20. Which of the following statements concerning zoning ordinances is/are true?
    A. zoning ordinances must adhere to federal and state due process provisions
    B. zoning ordinances must be reasonable and nondiscriminatory
    C. zoning ordinances must provide for the health and safety of the general public
    D. all of the above

21. Clark has operated a small convenience store in a rural area for 20 years. Recent development has changed the rural area into a thriving residential area. The property the convenience store is located on is now zoned for residential only. Which of the following statements is true?
    I. This is an illegal use and must be stopped.
    II. Clark can expand the convenience store to sell gasoline.
    III. Clark can continue operating the store due to spot zoning.
    IV. Clark must petition for a variance to continue doing business as a convenience store.
    A. I and IV
    B. II and III
    C. I, II, III, and IV
    D. none is true

22. Private land controls are enforced by:
    A. deed restrictions
    B. the Interstate Land Sales Full Disclosure Act
    C. the Conner Act
    D. court injunction

23. A variance can be obtained in which of the following scenarios?
    A. placing a factory in an area zoned for residential only
    B. placing a daycare in an area zoned for residential only
    C. changing the setback lines for an entire subdivision
    D. none of the above

24. The government regulates all of the following EXCEPT:
    A. creation of subdivisions
    B. building codes
    C. subdivision regulations
    D. protective covenants

25. Which of the following requires a property owner to go before the planning commission?
    A. a variance
    B. an illegal use
    C. a nonconforming use
    D. all of the above

# Chapter 5

## KEY TERMS

agent
apparent authority
breach of duty
buyer agency agreement
caveat emptor
civil penalty
client
customer
disclosure of information
dual agency agreement
employment authority
estoppel
express agency
express authority
fiduciary
first substantial contact
general agency
implied authority
listing agreement
loyalty
misdemeanor
negligent misrepresentation
negligent omission
omission
principal
special agency
subagent
tenant agency
third party
universal agency
willful misrepresentation
willful omission

## LEARNING OBJECTIVES

At the conclusion of this chapter, you should be able to:

1. Define the basic concepts of agency.
2. Define three types of agency.
3. Define the employment authority of real estate agents.
4. Describe agency and subagency relationships in real estate contracts.
5. Define duties and liabilities of principals and real estate agents.
6. Describe examples of willful misrepresentation and negligent misrepresentation.

# Laws and Regulations Governing Brokerage Relationships

## IN THIS CHAPTER

The body of laws and regulations that govern the relationship of agents to their principals and to one another is known as the law of agency. Inasmuch as most brokerage relationships are based on contractual agreements, contract law also governs real estate transactions. In addition, the conduct of real estate agents is governed by the North Carolina Real Estate License Law and the Rules and Regulations of the Real Estate Commission. Real estate agents are also responsible for complying with federal and state statutes that address consumer protection and unfair trade or business practices, as well as the common law of fraud and tort law.

## GENERAL AGENCY CONCEPTS AND DEFINITIONS

An **agent** is a person authorized by another to act on the latter's behalf or, in a legal concept, to stand in the place of the other person. Another term for an agent is trustee; the agent has been entrusted with something for another. Considering an individual's home is probably the largest financial asset that person will ever own, you can appreciate how important trust and duty are when hiring a real estate agent. Agency is a **fiduciary** (trust) relationship between a **principal** (also referred to as a **client**) and an agent in which both agree that the agent will act under the direction and control of the principal, in the principal's behalf, and for the principal's best interest. Thus, agency is a relationship that places great responsibility and substantial duties on the agent. Any licensee working through the agent is considered a **subagent** of the principal and owes the same duties that the agent owes to the principal, unless that person discloses at the beginning of the relationship that he is not acting as a subagent. Agency relationships must be disclosed in writing in North Carolina. Although an agent may be compensated for services by his principal, by a third party, or from the proceeds of a transaction, the source of compensation does not determine the agency relationship. The agency agreement and the behaviors of the parties are the important determinants of the agency relationship.

## CLASSIFICATION OF AGENCY RELATIONSHIPS

Three general classifications of agency are recognized: universal, general, and special. The first two are included for background material only and do not represent the typical real estate transaction.

### Universal Agency

A **universal agency** provides for an agent to have all-encompassing powers to make decisions and act on behalf of the principal. Such a situation might arise under a power of attorney signed by parents entrusting all their property and assets to their adult children for the general welfare and benefit of the parents. In this case, the children could be authorized to sell the parents' home and automobile and to make investment decisions with the proceeds to provide the best income for the parents. Essentially, the children have been authorized to manage all the affairs of their parents. Universal agency rarely occurs in real estate relationships.

### General Agency

**General agency** confers a broad scope of authority on the agent, but the authority is not as broad as the universal agency and is limited to some particular field. When a real estate licensee becomes associated with a brokerage firm, the licensee becomes a general agent of the broker/principal. As a sales associate, the licensee is permitted to solicit real estate business from the public on behalf of the broker, to place advertising in various publications, to place real estate signs on listed properties, and so on. The sales associate represents the broker in the field of real estate. However, the sales associate is not given the authority to hire or fire the broker's secretary, to make deposits or withdrawals from the trust account, or to otherwise make decisions regarding management of the broker's business. Sales associates are given a broad range of duties limited to real estate brokerage, not duties related to the management of a real estate office.

### Special Agency

A **special agency** is limited to one well-defined task. In this situation, the agent is not authorized to make decisions on the part of the principal but only to stand in the principal's place to receive information and to bring this information to the principal for a decision. The agent is not empowered to evaluate offers but is required to transmit such information to the principal immediately for an evaluation and a decision. A real estate agency contract, such as a listing agreement, buyer agency agreement, or property management agreement, creates a special agency.

## CREATION OF AGENCY

### Express Agency

The common law of agency defines any oral or written agreement as an **express agency.** North Carolina Real Estate License Law dictates that all agency relationships must be express, oral or written, from the beginning of the relationship. Agency agreements with property owners selling or leasing their property must be in writing from the creation of the agency relationship. Agency agreements with buyers or tenants may be oral in the beginning, but they must be reduced to writing prior to submitting an offer to purchase, rent, or exchange real estate. More details about types of agency are discussed later in this chapter.

### Implied Agency

When the actions of the principal and agent indicate that they have an agency agreement, this is called an implied agency or ostensible agency. For example, a broker who puts herself in the position in which she appears to be an agent of the buyer (that is, showing homes, gathering information on properties, referring to herself as the buyer's real estate agent) is, in fact, the implied agent of the prospective purchaser. The duties and responsibilities created by an implied agency are the same as those created by an express agency. Implied agency is unacceptable in real estate brokerage practice because NCREC Rule 58A, section A.0104 requires all agency relationships to be in writing. Providing the "Working with Real Estate Agents" publication, reviewing it with clients, and determining whether the agent will work for the buyer or seller in the transaction at first substantial contact, as required by A.0104, substantially reduces the possibility of an inadvertent dual agency. The agent, when dealing with a third party, must continue to avoid acting in such a way as to imply an agency relationship.

### Estoppel

An agency relationship also can be created by **estoppel.** This occurs when an individual claims incorrectly that a person is his agent and a third party relies on the incorrect representation. In these cases, the person making the incorrect statement is estopped and prohibited from later claiming that the agency relationship does not exist. For example, Broker A states to Mr. and Mrs. R that Betty is an **agent** in Broker A's office, when he knows this is not true. If Mr. and Mrs. R rely on this incorrect statement, Broker A cannot later claim that Betty is not an agent, and Broker A is liable for Betty's actions.

## EMPLOYMENT AND AUTHORITY OF REAL ESTATE AGENTS

Before a real estate broker goes to work for a principal, there must be complete **employment authority**: a written agreement specifying the authority given to the agent and the compensation of the agent.

### Brokerage Contracts (Agency Agreements)

Real estate agency relationships are created by a variety of agency agreements. An owner of a property may engage a real estate broker to locate a purchaser **(listing agreement).** In this relationship, the owner is the principal and the broker is the owner's agent. A prospective buyer may engage the services of a broker to locate a property **(buyer agency agreement).** In this relationship, the buyer is the principal and the broker is the buyer's agent. A broker may represent two parties with informed consent of both parties **(dual agency agreement).** Under dual agency, the seller and buyer are principals and the broker is the agent of both. If the owner of a rental property engages a broker to manage the property **(property management agreement),** the owner is the principal and the broker is the owner's agent. A prospective tenant may hire a real estate broker to locate a rental property **(tenant agency agreement).** This is more often done in commercial transactions. The tenant is the principal, and the broker is the agent. Every real estate company has a broker-in-charge, and all agents employed by the firm are agents of the BIC. In-house brokerage employment contracts between a brokerage firm and a real estate licensee affiliated with that firm define the legal and agency relationships between the firm and the licensee.

### Extent (Scope) of Agent's Authority

The real estate agency agreement (employment contract) defines a special agency situation in which the agent's authority is usually limited to a single charge. In the listing agreement, that charge is, "Go find a buyer for the property." In the buyer's agency agreement, it is, "Find a property for the buyer." In the property management agreement, it is, "Manage the property to gain the maximum advantage of the property for the owner." In a tenant agency agreement, it is, "Find a suitable rental property." In an in-house brokerage employment contract, it may be, "Generate listings, sales, and rentals for the firm." The duties of the agent to the principals and third parties under these agreements are discussed later in this chapter.

### Source of Agent's Authority

The source of an agent's authority is an important aspect of the agency relationship. Three important legal sources of an agent's authority are **express authority, implied authority,** and **apparent authority.** While express authority is that authority specifically granted in the contract, implied authority arises from custom. For example, an exclusive right-to-sell contract does not authorize the agent to sell the owner's property. Custom dictates that the agent's authority is limited to advertising the property and presenting offers to the owner. Apparent authority arises when a party allows a situation to exist that creates the *appearance* of an agent's authority. For example, a broker who is an exclusive rental agent for only *some* of an owner's properties advertises that he is an exclusive rental agent for *all* of this owner's properties. If the owner is aware of this advertising and allows it to continue, the broker would have the apparent authority to rent all of this owner's properties.

### Agency and Agent Compensation

Historically, it was believed that the agent worked for the person who paid her commission. With the evolution of buyer agency, agency representation is no longer determined solely by who compensates the agent. Today, an agent may be compensated by the buyer, the seller, or even a third party whose interest actually conflicts with that of the agent's principal. Regardless of who is compensating the agent, the agent still owes her fiduciary duty to her principal. For example, a buyer's agent may be paid from the seller's proceeds at closing, but nonetheless, the agent still represents the buyer, not the seller.

## AGENCY AND SUBAGENCY RELATIONSHIPS

### Exclusive Seller Agency

#### *Listing with an Independent Broker*

The simplest and clearest relationship between principal and agent is that of a one-person brokerage firm. In the case of a one-person office, there is a very close one-to-one relationship between the principal and the broker. There is relatively little opportunity for confusion in the fulfillment of the broker's role to the principal as long as the broker represents only one principal.

#### *Listing with a Multiagent Firm*

A brokerage firm consists of two or more licensed individuals working in the same office and sharing information. The agency agreement is between the principal and the brokerage firm. When an agent affiliated with a real estate firm enters into an agency contract with a buyer or seller, the *firm* owns the agency agreement and is the agent for that buyer or seller. All agents affiliated with the firm automatically become subagents for the buyer or seller.

This presents an interesting situation in regard to communication of the acceptance, rejection, or withdrawal of an offer. Communication to any agent within the firm fulfills the communication requirement; therefore, agents should note the date and time of any such communication. This will prevent conflicts when an acceptance has been communicated to one agent and a withdrawal has been communicated to another agent in the same firm. The existence of a contract depends on which communication came first.

#### *Subagency*

The sales associates affiliated with the brokerage firm are agents of the broker and subagents of the brokerage firm's principals (clients). The fiduciary duty of sales associates thus extends both to their employing brokerage firm and to the firm's principals.

In this situation, the broker is in two separate agency relationships. The broker is the agent of the principal under the agency agreement; the broker is also the principal of the sales associates under an agency agreement in the brokerage firm. Therefore, the broker is responsible for the actions of the sales associates even though in almost all cases the sales associates are independent contractors. As general agents of the broker and subagents of the seller in reference to the listing agreements, the sales associates are required to comply with the terms of all the firm's agency agreements and with all rules of the brokerage firm.

## Cooperating with Other Brokers

When a cooperating broker associated with another firm accepts the offer of subagency associated with a listing, she and her firm work through the listing broker; therefore, she and her firm are the principal's subagent, just as the sales associates in the listing agency's office are. The listing agent and the subagent work with—not for—the buyer; therefore, the buyer is a customer. The cooperating broker acting as a subagent has the same responsibility as the listing broker does—to work for the best interest of the seller.

## Cooperating Firm Acting as Seller's Agent

Agency is a legal relationship that considers agents, subagents, and principals as the same legal entity. Figure 5.1 illustrates a cooperating broker relationship in which listing and selling brokers work exclusively for the seller. The buyer should acknowledge in writing that he has been informed that the agent is working for the seller. This can be accomplished when reviewing the pamphlet "Working With Real Estate Agents" (see Figure 5.5 later in this chapter). A buyer who will be a customer (not a client) should check the box and initial the section of the signature panel entitled Disclosure of Seller Subagency. Everyone above the line of separation is, therefore, the same legal entity and is presumed to share all information. The agent has a duty to transmit all information about the transaction to the principal to ensure that the principal has all the information the agent knows. In this case, the buyer is alone on the other side of the line of separation. The agent must inform the buyer of the agent's duty to transmit all information to the seller or listing agent. This lets the buyer know he should not tell the agent any confidential information he does not want the seller to know.

Note: Both agent and subagent owe to the buyer certain duties, which are discussed in the section "Agent's Duties to Third Parties."

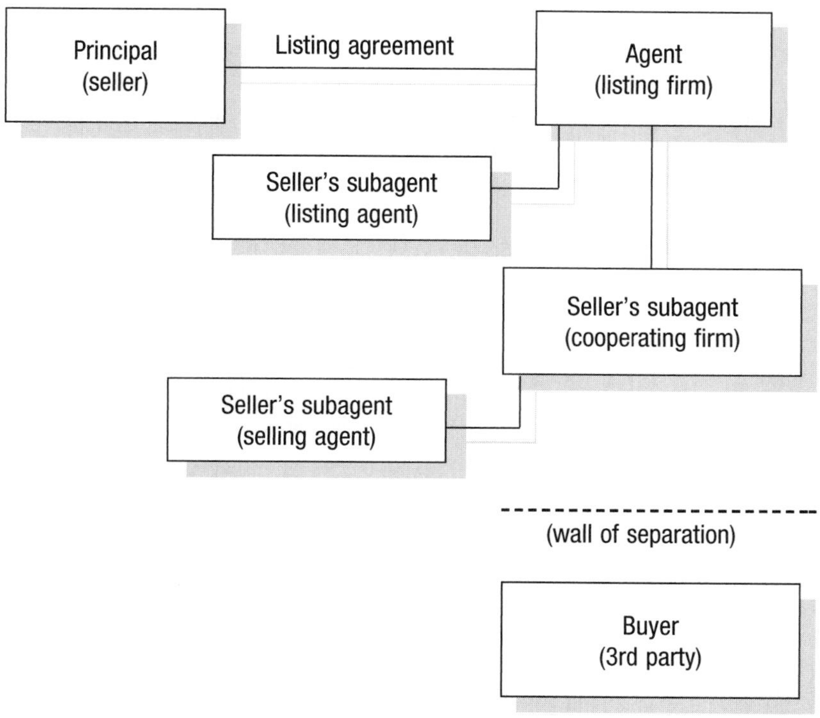


**FIGURE 5.1**

Agency relationships when seller is principal. Both listing and selling agents represent the seller.

## Exclusive Buyer Agency

Many real estate buyers now hire brokers to represent them. Under an exclusive buyer agency agreement (see Chapter 6, Figure 6.5) the buyer is the broker's principal (client), and the agency relationship is between the buyer and the broker. As a principal of the brokerage firm, buyers also are due the fiduciary duties of agency from the firm's sales associates.

## Buyer as Principal

Figure 5.1 illustrates the fact that the buyer is alone when all agents are working for the seller. She has no one to help her negotiate, to advise her on value, or to look out primarily for her interest. It is not difficult to understand why buyers are increasingly demanding their own advocate, their own agent, and a level playing field. Figure 5.2 shows the buyer with her agent on her side of the line of separation. The definition of appraised value assumes a knowledgeable buyer and a knowledgeable seller. The buyer's agent can now provide the same level of knowledge to the buyer that the seller has always had. She knows that when she has a confidential discussion with her agent, the information will not cross the line of separation.

Note: The buyer's agent owes to the seller the duties that will be discussed in "Agent's Duties to Third Parties." Also note that in Figure 5.1 and 5.2, confidential information does not cross the wall of separation.

## Dual Agency

A dual agency exists when a real estate firm attempts to represent the buyer and the seller in the same transaction. Dual agency is now quite common in the state of North Carolina, and many firms practice dual agency. The practice of dual agency, however, is more complicated than an agency relationship in which an agent represents only one party in a transaction. It is more difficult to fulfill the duties an agent owes to a principal when the agent represents two parties with conflicting interests. The nature of the dual agency relationship requires

**FIGURE 5.2**

Agency relationships when both seller and buyer have their own agents.

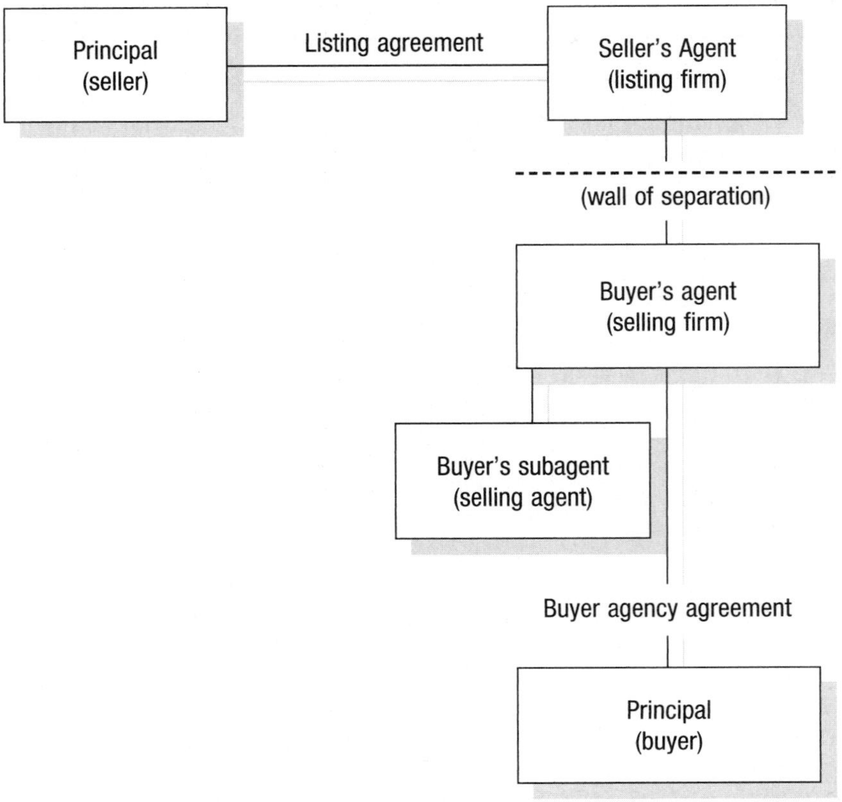

thoroughly understanding the duties and responsibilities to both parties. An agent owes both principals a wide range of duties, including loyalty, skill, care, diligence, disclosure of material facts, and accounting. The agent's duties to principals are more inclusive than an agent's duties to third parties, which are fairness and honesty, avoiding misrepresentation, and disclosing material facts. This makes dual agency a difficult situation that requires good judgment and strict impartiality.

The North Carolina Real Estate License Law requires *informed consent* of the principals in a dual agency situation. The agent should review and discuss with the potential client the pamphlet "Working With Real Estate Agents" (see Figure 5.5) and the company's policy on dual agency to obtain informed consent. Dual agency must be disclosed to both buyer and seller, and both must agree to that dual relationship in writing.

This may be accomplished by having the seller-client and the buyer-client sign a Dual Agency Addendum (see Figure 5.3) when they sign their respective agency agreements. If these addenda are signed at the time the seller signs the Exclusive Right to Sell Listing Agreement (see Chapter 6, Figure 6.1) and the buyer signs a Buyer Agency Agreement (see Chapter 6, Figure 6.5), the agent only needs to mark the dual agency blocks on the Offer to Purchase and Contract (see Chapter 6, Figure 6.7). If a buyer has agreed orally to buyer agency and dual agency, the buyer agency agreement with the dual agency addendum can be used for reducing the oral agreement to writing. If dual agency has not been expressly agreed to by both parties (the seller in writing and the buyer orally or in writing) by the time an offer is to be made, a dual agency agreement must be signed by the buyer and the seller, according to the following guidelines.

The seller must authorize seller agency in writing from the outset and should also specify whether he is or is not permitting dual agency. Consider that the seller has authorized seller agency, but not dual agency, unless indicated in writing for the following scenarios:

- If seller authorizes dual agency in writing when he authorizes seller agency, no further written authorization from him is necessary.
- If seller does not authorize dual agency in writing at the outset and a situation arises where dual agency is needed, the method and time of the seller's authorization of dual agency depend upon whether the buyer agency agreement is oral or in writing.
- If both buyer agency and dual agency are authorized in writing at the outset, no further authorization of dual agency is necessary by the buyer.
- If buyer has previously authorized buyer agency, but not dual agency in writing, buyer must authorize dual agency in writing before any action which would constitute dual agency is taken. Seller must also authorize dual agency in writing before the property is shown, if he has not already done so.
- Buyer may orally authorize both buyer agency and dual agency, but must commit these agency agreements to writing before making an offer. Only when both the buyer agency and dual agency are oral may a seller who has authorized seller agency, but not dual agency in writing orally authorize dual agency; however, that dual agency must be committed to writing before the offer is presented to him. The ideal procedure in this situation is to have both parties, especially the seller, authorize dual agency in writing before entering into a dual agency situation. Undisclosed dual agency is a breach of a broker's fiduciary duty and is a violation of North Carolina Real Estate Licensing Law.

When a dual agency situation arises where there has been no previous agency agreements with either buyer or seller, as sometimes happens in a commercial transaction, a dual agency agreement will have to be committed to writing before an agent may render services to either client. This dual agency situation, of course, must be authorized into writing as soon as the dual agency situation becomes evident.

As might be expected, maintaining this balance of neutrality is difficult because the simultaneous responsibilities to both buyer and seller are difficult to define in practice. Brokers who choose to engage in dual agency may find that when the transaction has ended, one of the clients may think the other received more effective representation and may challenge the broker's actions in court. Because of the difficulties of achieving

**FIGURE 5.3** Dual Agency Addendum

## DUAL AGENCY ADDENDUM

This DUAL AGENCY ADDENDUM hereby modifies the attached: ***(Instructions: Initial applicable agreement)***

| | | |
|---|---|---|
| ________ | NCAR Form #101 (Exclusive Right to Sell Listing Agreement) | dated________________ |
| ________ | NCAR Form #103 (Exclusive Right to Sell Listing Agreement (Vacant Land)) | dated________________ |
| ________ | NCAR Form #201 (Exclusive Right to Represent Buyer) | dated________________ |
| ________ | NCAR Form #203 (Agency Disclosure & Non-Exclusive Buyer Agency Agreement) | dated________________ |
| ________ | NCAR Form #601 (Exclusive Right to Sell Listing Agreement – Auction Sales) | dated________________ |

employing ________________________________________________________________
(hereinafter referred to as "Broker"). The term "Broker" shall sometimes hereinafter include Broker and its individual sales associates, as the sense requires.

The potential for Dual Agency arises if a Buyer who has an agency relationship with the Broker becomes interested in viewing a property listed with the Broker. A Broker may represent more than one party in the same transaction only with the knowledge and informed consent of all parties for whom the Broker acts.

1. **DUAL AGENCY:** It is agreed that Broker, acting by and through its individual sales associates, may serve as both Seller's Agent and Buyer's Agent in the representation of Seller's property to Buyer should circumstances creating Dual Agency arise. In the event Broker serves as a Dual Agent, the parties agree that without permission from the party about whom the information pertains, Broker shall not disclose to the other party the following information:

(a) that a party may agree to a price, terms, or any conditions of sale other than those offered;
(b) the motivation of a party for engaging in the transaction, unless disclosure is otherwise required by statute or rule; and
(c) any information about a party which that party has identified as confidential unless disclosure is otherwise required by statute or rule.

2. **BROKER'S DUAL AGENT ROLE:** If Broker serves as Agent for both Seller and Buyer in a transaction, Broker shall make every reasonable effort to represent Seller and Buyer in a balanced and fair manner. Broker shall also make every reasonable effort to encourage and effect communication and negotiation between Seller and Buyer. Seller and/or Buyer understand and acknowledge that:

(a) Prior to the time Dual Agency occurs, Broker will act as the exclusive Agent of Seller and/or Buyer;
(b) In those separate roles Broker may obtain information which, if disclosed, could harm the bargaining position of the party providing such information to Broker;
(c) Broker is required by law to disclose to Buyer and Seller any known or reasonably ascertainable material facts.

Seller and/or Buyer agree Broker shall not be liable to either party for (1) disclosing material facts required by law to be disclosed; and (2) refusing or failing to disclose other information the law does not require to be disclosed which could harm or compromise one party's bargaining position but could benefit the other party.

3. **SELLER'S AND BUYER'S ROLES:** Should Broker become a Dual Agent, Seller and/or Buyer understand and acknowledge that:

(a) They have the responsibility of making their own decisions as to what terms are to be included in any purchase and sale agreement between them;
(b) They are fully aware of and understand the implications and consequences of Broker's dual agency role as expressed herein to provide balanced and fair representation of Seller and Buyer and to encourage and effect communication between them rather than as an advocate or exclusive agent or representative;
(c) They have determined that the benefits of entering into this Dual Agency relationship with Broker, acting as Agent for them both, outweigh any disadvantages or adverse consequences;
(d) They may seek independent legal counsel to assist them with the negotiation and preparation of a purchase and sale agreement or with any matter relating to the transaction which is the subject matter of a purchase and sale agreement.

Page 1 of 2

REALTOR®

**North Carolina Association of REALTORS®, Inc.**

Client Initials _______ _______ Broker Initials _______

EQUAL HOUSING OPPORTUNITY

**STANDARD FORM 901**
**© 7/2006**

**FIGURE 5.3** Continued.

Seller and/or Buyer agree to indemnify and hold Broker harmless against all claims, damages, losses, expenses or liabilities, other than violations of the North Carolina Real Estate License Law and intentional wrongful acts, arising from Broker's role as a Dual Agent. Seller and Buyer shall have a duty to protect their own interests and should read this agreement and any purchase and sale agreement carefully to ensure that they accurately set forth the terms which they want included in said agreements.

4. **DESIGNATED AGENT OPTION (initial only if applicable):**

______ Buyer hereby authorizes the Broker (Firm) to designate an agent(s) to represent the Buyer, to the exclusion of any other licensees associated with the Broker. The agent(s) shall not be so designated and shall not undertake to represent only the interests of the Buyer if the agent(s) has actually received confidential information concerning the Seller in connection with the transaction. The designated agent(s) shall represent only the interests of the Buyer to the extent permitted by law.

______ Seller hereby authorizes the Broker (Firm) to designate an agent(s) to represent the Seller, to the exclusion of any other licensees associated with the Broker. The agent(s) shall not be so designated and shall not undertake to represent only the interests of the Seller if the agent(s) has actually received confidential information concerning the Buyer in connection with the transaction. The designated agent(s) shall represent only the interests of the Seller to the extent permitted by law.

THIS IS INTENDED TO BE A LEGALLY BINDING DUAL AGENCY ADDENDUM THAT MAY ULTIMATELY RESTRICT YOUR LEGAL RIGHTS OR REMEDIES. IF YOU DO NOT UNDERSTAND THIS ADDENDUM OR FEEL THAT IT DOES NOT PROVIDE FOR YOUR LEGAL NEEDS, YOU SHOULD CONSULT AN ATTORNEY BEFORE YOU SIGN IT.

**Buyer or Seller and Broker each hereby acknowledge receipt of a signed copy of this Dual Agency Addendum.**

THE NORTH CAROLINA ASSOCIATION OF REALTORS®, INC. MAKES NO REPRESENTATION AS TO THE LEGAL VALIDITY OR ADEQUACY OF ANY PROVISION OF THIS FORM IN ANY SPECIFIC TRANSACTION.

| | | | |
|---|---|---|---|
| Buyer | Date | Seller | Date |
| Buyer | Date | Seller | Date |
| Broker (Firm) | Date | Broker ( Firm) | Date |
| By: Sales Associate | Date | By: Sales Associate | Date |



**STANDARD FORM 901**
**© 7/2006**

successful dual agency, this agency relationship is discouraged and is prohibited without full disclosure and informed consent of both buyer and seller.

## Dual Agency with Designated Agents

When a firm represents both buyer and seller in a dual agency role, the firm may—with written approval of both buyer and seller—designate an agent to represent only the interests of the seller and another agent to represent only the interests of the buyer. In this agency relationship, the firm acts as the dual agent.

The broker-in-charge cannot act as a designated agent for one party when a provisional broker under his supervision will act as a designated agent for another party in the transaction. The BIC can be a designated agent if the other designated agent within the company is a broker without provisional status, since this broker is not considered to be under the supervision of the broker-in-charge. No agent with prior confidential information about the other party can be appointed a designated agent. But what happens when a designated agent obtains confidential information after being appointed? This can happen easily in an office through overheard phone conversations, incoming faxes, and company files. What the designated agent is to do with such information is not clear on the dual agency addendum. Company security policies should minimize opportunities for such information dispersal, and policy manuals and training programs should spell out what happens when security is compromised. Last, the clients should understand thoroughly what they can and cannot expect of their designated agent and how they can communicate confidential information to their designated agent.

In agency relationships, perception is as important as reality. In typical dual agency, both parties understand that the NCAR Dual Agency Addendum modifies agency duties so that even if every agent in the office knows confidential information, no agent is going to disclose such information to either party. Dual agency with a designated agency option has a different agent representing the buyer's and the seller's interests with the firm still acting as a dual agent. Informed consent in designated agency, as in all other types of agency, is essential to avoiding the perception or reality of agency violations.

## Both Buyer and Seller as Principal

Theoretically, there is no line of separation in dual agency. If the seller and agent are considered the same person and the buyer and agent are considered the same person, it would appear that seller, buyer, and agent are considered the same person. Without modifying agency duties and responsibilities, dual agency would never work. The NCAR Dual Agency Addendum (Figure 5.3) modifies agency duties sufficiently to allow dual agency to be practiced by agents with good judgment and a thorough understanding of agency, encountering only occasional difficulties.

Figure 5.4 illustrates the modified lines of separation in dual agency. Disclosure of material fact must still cross these lines just as it does in other agency situations. If an

**FIGURE 5.4** Agency relationship when both seller and buyer have same agent (dual agent).

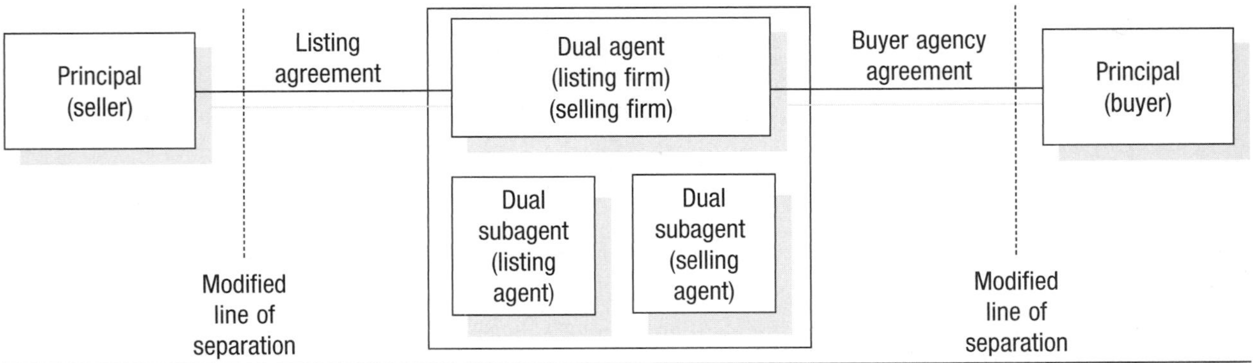

NCAR Dual Agency Addendum has been signed by both parties, disclosure of confidential information does not pass across these lines from the agent to either principal. The agent is not obligated to inform one principal of confidential information he knows about the other principal. In order to avoid even the perception that confidential information is crossing the line, an agent must educate her potential client at the initial agency discussion to limit the confidential information told to the agent to essential information that the agent needs to know to better assist the client. The agency discussion should also contain instructions for the principal to obtain independent outside professional advice should it become necessary.

## Dual Agency Addendum

The following is a summary of the key points on NCAR's Dual Agency Addendum (Figure 5.3). This addendum can be attached to either a listing or a buyer agency agreement. If this addendum is not attached to both the listing and buyer agency agreement, the buyer needs to sign the addendum before an offer is made and the seller must sign before the offer is presented.

1. When a firm represents both buyer and seller in a dual agency situation, the agent should not disclose certain information to either party without express, written permission from the other party. This information includes a party's motivation, willingness to pay a price and terms other than those offered, and any information identified as confidential by the party to whom the information pertains. It never includes material fact that must always be disclosed.
2. The broker's role is to encourage and effect communication, represent buyer and seller in a fair and balanced manner, and disclose material facts to both parties.
3. The seller and buyer are responsible for making their own decisions regarding purchase terms, must understand and agree to the dual agent's role as an advocate rather than an exclusive agent, and have the right to seek independent counsel for assistance with negotiation or preparation of contracts.
4. Designated agency option: Buyer and seller authorize the broker to designate an agent to represent only the interests of the seller and an agent to represent only the interest of the buyer.

## Agency Relationships in Real Estate Rentals

Agency law also applies to real estate agents and firms who act as property managers. When a landlord contracts with a broker to manage properties on his behalf, the landlord is the agent's principal. It is important that the broker disclose to prospective tenants her representation of the landlord. Likewise, a prospective tenant may hire a broker to find a suitable rental property. In this case, the tenant is the broker's principal. In the unlikely event an agent finds herself in the potential position of representing a tenant and a landlord in the same transaction, all the rules and duties of dual agency apply. See Chapter 11 for further discussion of agency relationships with landlords and tenants.

## Agency's Effect on Communication Requirements for Contracts

Agency status is often an important determinant of when the communication of the acceptance, rejection, or withdrawal of an offer has occurred. The following example illustrates how agency status affects the communication requirement in the acceptance of a contract.

*Seller signs and accepts offer to purchase and contract in listing agent's presence, thus notifying listing agent of acceptance:*

- If listing agent is an exclusive seller's agent and the buyer has no agent or has an exclusive buyer's agent, communication has not occurred.
- If listing agent is an exclusive seller's agent and buyer is working with a subagent, communication has not occurred.

- If listing agent or subagent notifies either buyer or buyer's agent, communication has occurred.
- If listing agent is also the buyer's agent (consequently, a dual agent), communication has occurred as soon as listing/dual agent knows of acceptance.

The following examples illustrate how communication requirements are met in a counteroffer situation.

*Seller receives an offer from buyer and makes a counteroffer. (Seller thus rejects the offer and makes a new offer.) The rejection is considered communicated according to the same rules as listed previously. Acceptance or rejection by the buyer of the new offer from the seller is considered to be officially communicated as follows:*

- If the buyer has no agent, communication occurs when she communicates her acceptance or rejection to the seller, his agent, or subagent.
- If the buyer has a buyer's agent, communication does not occur when she notifies her buyer's agent. It occurs only when she or her agent notifies the seller, his agent, or a seller's subagent.
- If the buyer's agent is the same agent as the seller's agent (dual agent), communication occurs as soon as the dual agent is notified.

Note: An agent should never make a judgment call as to whether there is a contract. An attorney should be consulted immediately in any situation that requires such a judgment.

## Agency's Effect on Disclosure of Material Facts

In an agency relationship with a single principal (buyer or seller), material facts that an agent would present to his principal include *any* fact that might influence the principal's decisions in the transaction. This includes any confidential information that an agent is privy to regarding a third party in the transaction. For example, if a buyer's agent knows that a seller is in the midst of a divorce and believes that this personal financial situation may lead the seller to negotiate a lower sales price, the agent can and should make his buyer aware of this situation.

In the practice of dual agency, contractual agreements such as those in the dual agency addendum and a dual agency agreement, alter agent's duties to disclose. These duties to both parties become, in effect, those duties owed to a third party in a transaction rather than those disclosure duties of an agent to a principal. In a dual agency situation, material facts are limited to facts about the property itself (e.g., defects), matters affecting the property and/or property value (e.g., pending zoning changes), and facts relating to a principal's ability to complete the transaction. Matters not directly related to the property, such as a seller's personal financial situation, are not material facts.

## Termination of Agency

An agency relationship ends in accordance with the terms of the agency contract. All agency contracts must have an expiration date with no provision for automatic renewal. When the contract expires, the agency relationship terminates and so does any authority of the agent to act on behalf of the principal. An agency relationship is also terminated by completion of the terms of the agency; that is, completion of the sale of the listed real estate and the payment of commission. Agency agreements are personal service contracts that are not assignable; therefore, the death or insanity of a broker in a single-broker firm would terminate the contract. In some cases, operation of law may terminate the agency relationship. For instance, a power of attorney terminates automatically at the death of either principal or agent. Another example is the termination of a listing agreement held by a broker whose license is revoked or by a brokerage firm that closes or dissolves. If a listed property is totally destroyed, the listing contract terminates. If the property is partially destroyed, the listing contract would likely be voidable by either party. The listing contract can be terminated by the injured party if either agent or principal breaches agency duties.

## Disclosure of Agency Relationships

The Real Estate License Law carefully regulates agency agreements and disclosures. All agency agreements, including listing agreements, exclusive buyer agency agreements, property management agreements, and any other real estate brokerage service agreements other than oral buyer agency agreements that do not bind the buyer to an agent or a time period must be in writing and provide for a definitive period of time, at the end of which the agreement automatically terminates with no prior notice required. All such agreements must conspicuously incorporate the nondiscrimination language (Rule A.0104) as follows: **"The broker shall conduct all his or her brokerage activities in regard to this agreement without respect to the race, color, religion, sex, national origin, handicap, or familial status of any buyer, prospective buyer, seller or prospective seller."**

All preprinted offers or sales contracts must provide for the identification of each real estate agent and firm involved and for the disclosure of whom each agent and firm represents (see Chapter 6, Figure 6.6). Because no agency contract transfers an interest in land, the Statute of Frauds does not require agency contracts to be in writing. Rather, it is the North Carolina Real Estate Commission Rule (Rule 58A.0104) that specifically requires all real estate agency contracts to be in writing.

The same rule (58A.0104e) requires an agent to review the Commission's brochure "Working With Real Estate Agents" (see Figure 5.5) with a potential client or customer, whether buyer or seller, at **first substantial contact** and have the client or customer sign that she received the brochure and that it was reviewed with her. Written disclosure by seller's agent to buyer at first substantial contact is also required. The agent and potential client or customer can then agree upon the desired agency relationship, if any.

If the agent will be working as an agent or a subagent of the seller and working directly with the buyer (customer), when reviewing the brochure the agent must disclose to the buyer that he or she works in the seller's interest and have the buyer acknowledge disclosure by initialing "Disclosure of seller subagency" on the acknowledgment panel.

If a buyer wants buyer agency but does not want to sign an exclusive buyer agency agreement for a specific period of time, the agent can work as a buyer agent and/or a dual agent on a verbal agreement under certain conditions. The buyer must sign the acknowledgment panel on the "Working With Real Estate Agents" brochure, and the buyer and/or dual agency agreement must be committed to writing before an offer on a property is made. The oral agreement cannot bind the buyer to work exclusively with the agent or be for a specific period of time. An agent working as a buyer's agent should disclose this relationship to the seller's agent at first substantial contact and follow the oral disclosure with the written disclosure to the seller or the seller's agent before or with the delivery of the offer to purchase (see Figure 6.7).

An agent selling a buyer (client) a property offered directly by the seller must review the brochure with the seller at first substantial contact and have the seller sign the acknowledgment of receipt. He must notify the seller that he is acting as a buyer's agent, just as he would notify the seller's agent (if the seller had one) of that fact. NCAR Form 150 (not shown) may be used to notify a For Sale by Owner of agency status. NCAR Form 220, Confirmation of Agency, Relationship Appointment, and Compensation (see Figure 5.6) may be used to notify a seller's agent of the status of the agent working with or for the buyer. If the seller wants dual agency, both buyer and seller must agree to that arrangement and the appropriate dual agency documents must be signed.

A listing agent must review with a potential seller the "Working With Real Estate Agents" brochure and have him sign it at first substantial contact. If the seller lists his property, the listing agent will become a seller's agent with or without the potential of being a dual agent, depending on the agreement between the agent and the seller.

If after presentation of the "Working With Real Estate Agents" brochure the customer does not wish to sign the acknowledgment, the agent is required to indicate this fact on the brochure acknowledgment panel. This does not alleviate the requirement that the acknowledgment be retained by the agent.

## First Substantial Contact

Real Estate Commission Rule A.0104(e) requires a broker who is the agent or subagent of a seller and who is working directly with a buyer to disclose to that buyer in writing at first

**FIGURE 5.5** Working With Real Estate Agents.

# WORKING WITH REAL ESTATE AGENTS

*NOTE: Effective July 1, 2001, in every real estate sales transaction, a real estate agent shall, at first substantial contact directly with a prospective buyer or seller, provide the prospective buyer or seller with the following information [NC Real Estate Commission Rule 21 NCAC 58A.0104(c)].*

When buying or selling real estate, you may find it helpful to have a real estate agent assist you. Real estate agents can provide many useful services and work with you in different ways. In some real estate transactions, the agents work for the seller. In others, the seller and buyer may each have agents. And sometimes the same agents work for both the buyer and the seller. It is important for you to know whether an agent is working for you as **your** agent or simply working **with** you while acting as an agent of the other party.

This brochure addresses the various types of working relationships that may be available to you. It should help you decide which relationship you want to have with a real estate agent. It will also give you useful information about the various services real estate agents can provide buyers and sellers, and it will help explain how real estate agents are paid.

## SELLERS

***Seller's Agent***

If you are selling real estate, you may want to "list" your property for sale with a real estate firm. If so, you will sign a "listing agreement" authorizing the firm and its agents to represent you in your dealings with buyers as your *seller's agent*. You may also be asked to allow agents from other firms to help find a buyer for your property.

Be sure to read and understand the listing agreement before you sign it.

*Duties to Seller*: The listing firm and its agents must • promote your best interests • be loyal to you • follow your lawful instructions • provide you with all material facts that could influence your decisions • use reasonable skill, care and diligence, and • account for all monies they handle for you. Once you have signed the listing agreement, the firm and its agents may not give any confidential information about you to prospective buyers or their agents without your permission so long as they represent you. But **until you sign the listing agreement, you should avoid telling the listing agent anything you would *not* want a buyer to know.**

*Services and Compensation*: To help you sell your property, the listing firm and its agents will offer to perform a number of services for you. These may include • helping you price your property • advertising and marketing your property • giving you all required property disclosure forms for you to complete • negotiating for you the best possible price and terms • reviewing all written offers with you and • otherwise promoting your interests.

For representing you and helping you sell your property, you will pay the listing firm a sales commission or fee. The listing agreement must state the amount or method for determining the commission or fee and whether you will allow the firm to share its commission with agents representing the buyer.

***Dual Agent***

You may even permit the listing firm and its agents to represent you **and** a buyer at the same time. This "dual agency relationship" is most likely to happen if an agent with your listing firm is working as a *buyer's agent* with someone who wants to purchase your property. If this occurs and you have not already agreed to a dual agency relationship in your listing agreement, your listing agent will ask you to sign a separate agreement or document permitting the agent to act as agent for both you and the buyer.

It may be difficult for a *dual agent* to advance the interests of both the buyer and seller. Nevertheless, a *dual agent* must treat buyers and sellers fairly and equally. Although the *dual agent* owes them the same duties, buyers and sellers can prohibit *dual agents* from divulging **certain** confidential information about them to the other party.

Some firms also offer a form of dual agency called "designated agency" where one agent in the firm represents the seller and another agent represents the buyer. This option (when available) may allow each "designated agent" to more fully represent each party.

If you choose the "dual agency" option, remember that since a dual agent's loyalty is divided between parties with competing interests, it is especially important that you have a clear understanding of • what your relationship is with the *dual agent* and • what the agent will be doing for you in the transaction.



REALTOR®

North Carolina Association of REALTORS®, Inc.

EQUAL HOUSING OPPORTUNITY

STANDARD FORM 520
REC 8/1/2005

**FIGURE 5.5** Continued.

## BUYERS

When buying real estate, you may have several choices as to how you want a real estate firm and its agents to work with you. For example, you may want them to represent only you (as a **buyer's agent**). You may be willing for them to represent both you and the seller at the same time (as a **dual agent**). Or you may agree to let them represent only the seller (**seller's agent** or **subagent**). Some agents will offer you a choice of these services. Others may not.

***Buyer's Agent***

*Duties to Buyer*: If the real estate firm and its agents represent you, they must • promote your best interests • be loyal to you • follow your lawful instructions • provide you with all material facts that could influence your decisions • use reasonable skill, care and diligence, and • account for all monies they handle for you. Once you have agreed (either orally or in writing) for the firm and its agents to be your *buyer's agent*, they may not give any confidential information about you to sellers or their agents without your permission so long as they represent you. But **until you make this agreement with your buyer's agent, you should avoid telling the agent anything you would *not* want a seller to know.**

*Unwritten Agreements*: To make sure that you and the real estate firm have a clear understanding of what your relationship will be and what the firm will do for you, you may want to have a written agreement. However, some firms may be willing to represent and assist you for a time as a *buyer's agent* without a written agreement. But if you decide to make an offer to purchase a particular property, the agent must obtain a written agency agreement. If you do not sign it, the agent can no longer represent and assist you and is no longer required to keep information about you confidential. Furthermore, if you later purchase the property through an agent with another firm, the agent who first showed you the property may seek compensation from the other firm.

Be sure to read and understand any agency agreement before you sign it.

*Services and Compensation*: Whether you have a written or unwritten agreement, a *buyer's agent* will perform a number of services for you. These may include helping you • find a suitable property • arrange financing • learn more about the property and • otherwise promote your best interests. If you have a **written** agency agreement, the agent can also help you prepare and submit a written offer to the seller.

A *buyer's agent* can be compensated in different ways. For example, you can pay the agent out of your own pocket. Or the agent may seek compensation from the seller or listing agent first, but require you to pay if the listing agent refuses. Whatever the case, be sure your compensation arrangement with your *buyer's agent* is spelled out in a buyer agency agreement before you make an offer to purchase property and that you carefully read and understand the compensation provision.

***Dual Agent***

You may permit an agent or firm to represent you **and** the seller at the same time. This "dual agency relationship" is most likely to happen if you become interested in a property listed with your *buyer's agent* or the agent's firm. If this occurs and you have not already agreed to a dual agency relationship in your (written or oral) buyer agency agreement, your *buyer's agent* will ask you to sign a separate agreement or document permitting him or her to act as agent for both you and the seller. It may be difficult for a *dual agent* to advance the interests of both the buyer and seller. Nevertheless, a *dual agent* must treat buyers and sellers fairly and equally. Although the *dual agent* owes them the same duties, buyers and sellers can prohibit *dual agents* from divulging **certain** confidential information about them to the other party.

Some firms also offer a form of dual agency called "designated agency" where one agent in the firm represents the seller and another agent represents the buyer. This option (when available) may allow each "designated agent" to more fully represent each party.

If you choose the "dual agency" option, remember that since a *dual agent's* loyalty is divided between parties with competing interests, it is especially important that you have a clear understanding of • what your relationship is with the *dual agent* and • what the agent will be doing for you in the transaction. This can best be accomplished by putting the agreement in writing at the earliest possible time.

***Seller's Agent Working with a Buyer***

If the real estate agent or firm that you contact does not offer *buyer agency* or you do not want them to act as your *buyer agent*, you can still work with the firm and its agents. However, they will be acting as the *seller's agent* (or "subagent"). The agent can still help you find and purchase property and provide many of the same services as a *buyer's agent*. The agent must be fair with you and provide you with any "material facts" (such as a leaky roof) about properties.

But remember, the agent represents the seller – not you – and therefore must try to obtain for the seller the best possible price and terms for the seller's property. Furthermore, a *seller's agent* is required to give the seller any information about you (even personal, financial or confidential information) that would help the seller in the sale of his or her property. Agents must tell you *in writing* if they are *sellers' agents* before you say anything that can help the seller. But **until you are sure that an agent is not a *seller's agent*, you should avoid saying anything you do *not* want a seller to know.**

*Sellers' agents* are compensated by the sellers.

Page 2 of 3

**STANDARD FORM 520**
**REC 8/1/2005**

**FIGURE 5.5** Continued.

**WORKING WITH REAL ESTATE AGENTS**

***This is not a contract***

By signing, I acknowledge that the agent named below furnished a copy of this brochure and reviewed it with me.

| | |
|---|---|
| ______________________ | ______________________ |
| *Buyer or Seller Name (Print or Type)* | *Buyer or Seller Name (Print or Type)* |
| ______________________ | ______________________ |
| *Buyer or Seller Signature* | *Buyer or Seller Signature* |
| ______________________ | ______________________ |
| *Date* | *Date* |

______________________
*Firm Name*

______________________
*Agent Name and License Number*

***Disclosure of Seller Subagency***

☐ *When showing you property and assisting you in the purchase of a property, the above agent and firm will represent the SELLER. For more information, see "Seller's Agent Working with a Buyer" in the brochure.*

*Buyer's Initials Acknowledging Disclosure:* ____________

***Agents must retain this acknowledgment for their files.***

Page 3 of 3

**STANDARD FORM 520**
**REC 8/1/2005**

**FIGURE 5.6** Confirmation of Agency Relationship, Appointment & Compensation.

**CONFIRMATION OF AGENCY RELATIONSHIP, APPOINTMENT & COMPENSATION**

***NOTE:*** *When working with a For Sale By Owner you should use Form 150*
*See Guidelines (Standard Form 220G) on proper use of this form.*

TO LISTING AGENT:______________________________

FIRM NAME:______________________________ FAX#:______________

FROM:______________________________

FIRM NAME:______________________________ FAX#:______________

Thank you for checking with your seller and permitting me to show your listing as a ☐ buyer agent ☐ subagent.

PROPERTY DESCRIPTION:______________________________

NAME OF BUYER:______________________________

APPOINTMENT DATE:______________________ TIME:______________

FEE ARRANGEMENT:

(a) You hereby confirm that your offer of compensation to my firm regarding any sale of the Property to Buyer shall be as follows: ______________________________

______________________________

I understand that my firm's entitlement to the compensation set forth above will be determined by my performance as the procuring cause of any sale of the Property to Buyer. **Your signature on this document does not constitute an acknowledgment that I am the procuring cause of any such sale.**

(b) If I have received or am to receive any other fee(s) in connection with the sale of the Property, I hereby confirm that such fee(s) are as follows:______________________________

______________________________

Please sign below and fax this Confirmation back to me at your earliest convenience at the fax # listed above. Please call me at my office:______________________ or at :______________________ if there are any further instructions or communications prior to the showing. Thank you for your cooperation.

THE NORTH CAROLINA ASSOCIATION OF REALTORS®, INC. MAKES NO REPRESENTATION AS TO THE LEGAL VALIDITY OR ADEQUACY OF ANY PROVISION OF THIS FORM IN ANY SPECIFIC TRANSACTION.

______________________________ ______________________________
Selling Agent Date

______________________________ ______________________________
Listing Agent Date

**ACKNOWLEDGEMENT BY BUYER AND/OR SELLER (*Optional*—see Guidelines)**

Seller hereby acknowledges receipt of a copy of this form and consents to the fee arrangements set forth herein.

Seller: ______________________ Seller: ______________________
Date: ______________________ Date: ______________________

Buyer hereby acknowledges receipt of a copy of this form and consents to the fee arrangements set forth herein.

Buyer: ______________________ Buyer: ______________________
Date:______________________ Date: ______________________

Page 1 of 1

REALTOR®

North Carolina Association of REALTORS®, Inc.

EQUAL HOUSING OPPORTUNITY

STANDARD FORM 220
© 7/2004

substantial contact that he is working for the seller. This does not mean the agent must disclose his status immediately after he says hello. The North Carolina Real Estate Commission realizes that it is not always necessary or appropriate to make this disclosure at the very "first" contact. The standard is flexible, but agency status of a seller's agent or subagent working with a "customer" (not a "client") must be disclosed in writing prior to obtaining any confidential information. Once the discussion centers on properties or financing, the buyer is likely to volunteer confidential information; therefore, one should disclose before such a discussion begins.

Although the best approach is to disclose agency status as soon as possible, this is not always practical (at an open house or on the phone, for example). Only when a prospect visiting an open house shows a sincere interest in the property would the agent need to provide and review the Commission's pamphlet "Working With Real Estate Agents" before the buyer volunteers any confidential information.

It is best to keep the conversation with a phone prospect brief and general by making an appointment to discuss the firm's agency policies and disclosure requirements. Rule A.0104(e) states: "If the first substantial contact occurs by telephone or by means of other electronic communication where it not practical to provide written disclosure, the broker or salesperson shall immediately disclose by similar means whom he represents and shall immediately, but in no event later than three days from the date of first substantial contact, mail or otherwise transmit a copy of the written disclosure to the buyer."

Certain exemptions apply to auction sale situations (Rule A.0104). The seller's agent is exempt from the agency disclosure requirement; the buyer's agent must disclose verbally to the seller or seller's agent at initial contact but has until the time the written contract confirming his purchase is executed to put the disclosure in writing.

# DUTIES AND LIABILITIES OF AGENTS

## Agent's Duties to Principal

The broker is in a fiduciary relationship to the principal. It is a position of trust. The broker's principal may be a buyer, seller, landlord, or tenant. A firm's broker is also the principal of the agents who work for the firm. The firm's agents are agents of the broker and subagents of the principal whether the principal is buyer, seller, landlord, or tenant. Brokers and agents of firms cobrokering with a listing firm are subagents of the listing firm and the seller if they are not buyer's agents. The broker has certain obligations to the principal as required of every agent by law. The agent's duties and responsibilities are the same whether his principal is buyer, seller, landlord, tenant, or broker; these duties are described next.

## Loyalty

The real estate broker must be **loyal** to the principal (her client) and must work diligently to serve the best interests of the principal under the terms of the employment contract creating the agency. The agent cannot work for personal interests or the interests of others to the adverse interests of the principal. The real estate broker cannot legally represent any other person in the activities of his agency without disclosing this fact to the principal and obtaining the principal's consent. Therefore, a real estate broker cannot represent buyer and seller in the same transaction and receive a commission from both without the knowledge and informed consent of both buyer and seller. It is a violation of the requirement of loyalty for a broker to purchase the listed property without knowledge by the principal that the broker is, in fact, the purchaser. It is also a violation of agency for a buyer's agent to sell a client a property in which the buyer's agent has an interest without disclosing that interest.

Loyalty requires that the agent put the client's interest above his own. For example, suppose a listing agent receives two offers on a property he has listed: one from another company and one from his customer. The agent gets the whole commission if his customer's offer is accepted. However, the offer from the other company is better. The agent's customer will not pay more than she has offered. Loyalty to the principal (and other laws, rules, and regulations) prohibits the agent from not disclosing the offer from the other company. If the agent did not actually have the offer in hand but knew the offer was coming, loyalty (and other laws, rules, and regulations) would still require him to disclose this to the seller.

Loyalty to a buyer/principal requires the agent to help the buyer find a property that best suits the buyer's need rather than show only the agent's listings or properties that pay the highest commission. When a buyer signs a dual agency addendum, he is not authorizing the agent to show him only the agent's company listings. If the buyer is paying his agent a flat commission, the commission will not be a significant factor. If the buyer is paying a commission based on a percentage of the sales price or the buyer's agent is being paid by the seller as offered through the listing agreement or multiple listing service (MLS), the commission could become a significant factor. Agents should be very careful not to let the amount of commission influence the advice and professional services they give to their buyer/clients.

L.oyalty
O.bedience
A.ccounting
D.isclosure
S.kill

## Obedience

The duty of the agent is to obey all reasonable and legal instructions from his seller/principal. For example, the seller may specify that the property be shown only during certain times of the day or that it not be shown on days of religious observance. Or the seller might instruct the agent not to place the listing in the MLS or place signs on the property. However, if the seller were to instruct the agent to do an illegal act, such as promoting the property in violation of the fair housing laws, the agent could not comply. Because the agent cannot disobey, he must withdraw from the agency relationship, if the seller insists. For example, a buyer/principal may specify that she does not want certain facts about her identity or planned use of the property disclosed. The agent must obey these directives. However, a buyer/principal may want to make an offer on a property for which he obviously does not qualify. He may instruct his agent not to inform the seller of this. The agent cannot obey this request; therefore, he must withdraw from the agency relationship if the buyer will not reconsider his instructions. While it may seem incomprehensible that anyone would want to make an offer for which they do not qualify, it happens occasionally. Some buyers are eternal optimists, always hoping for a miracle.

## Skill, Care, and Diligence

In offering services as a real estate broker to the public, the broker is asserting that she possesses the necessary skill and training to perform the employment requirements. In performing duties as an agent, the broker must exercise the degree of skill, care, and diligence the public is entitled to expect of real estate brokers. If a broker's principal incurs a financial loss as a result of the broker's negligence and failure to meet these standards of skill, care, and diligence, the broker is liable for any loss incurred by the principal. Additionally, the principal would not be required to pay compensation to the broker as agreed in the employment contract.

A real estate agent is expected to perform with a degree of care and skill that is common to other reasonable prudent professionals engaged in similar undertakings. For example, if an agent listed a property several months ago and property values increased or decreased since the time the agent did the market analysis for the seller, the agent has the responsibility to advise the seller of the change in the property's value. A seller relies on an agent's knowledge of the market in setting a list price and has a right to expect his agent to be knowledgeable about the value of his property. Real estate agents have the responsibility to ascertain all material facts concerning a property they are listing, and a buyer's agent also has a responsibility to verify information about a property for a prospective buyer. A *material fact* is any fact about a property that is important to a party in making decisions about a transaction. A material fact can be information about a property's features, defects, condition, or value. The agent should investigate the property for defects as well as all matters relating to the property. She should not, however, offer opinions or give advice outside or beyond her area of expertise. Rather, she should suggest that clients and customers seek competent professional advice when necessary. Matters relating to the property include any public or private restrictions, as well as public policies and proposed legislation affecting the property. For example, if a proposed highway will cut across a property, this becomes a material fact affecting the property, which the agent should disclose. An agent is responsible not only for *known* facts relating to a property but also for facts that the agent *reasonably should have known.* This means that if an agent is unaware of the proposed highway but this highway's location has been well publicized in local newspapers, the agent could be held to the *reasonably should have known* doctrine. That is, if a prudent agent using reasonable skill and care would have known about this proposed highway, the agent could be held responsible for having known and disclosed this information.

An agent's duty to perform with care and skill does not end with the signing of a contract. An agent has the duty to perform any tasks required to get the contract to closing. If a buyer is represented by a buyer's agent, the buyer's and seller's agents have the responsibility of working together to ensure that all preparations for closing are completed. If the buyer is not represented by a buyer's agent, the seller's agent may need to perform such tasks as assisting the buyer in obtaining financing. It is in the seller's best interest that the buyer be able to consummate the transaction.

An agent's failure to exercise skill, care, and diligence is not only a breach of duties under agency law, it is also grounds for disciplinary action by the North Carolina Real Estate Commission. Brokers and agents should constantly strive to improve their knowledge and skill, considering their real estate license as a license to continue learning. The required eight hours of continuing education is just a beginning; all the knowledge in the world will not help if the agent does not take the time and effort to apply it. This may mean limiting the number of clients to ensure sufficient time to perform all the duties required to bring each transaction to a successful conclusion.

## Disclosure of Information

A real estate broker is required to keep the principal fully informed of all important matters involved with the purpose of the broker's employment. Any information that is material to the transaction for which the broker is employed must be communicated promptly and totally to the principal. This requirement for **disclosure of information** is first discussed from the perspective of the seller/listing broker relationship. It includes the requirement that the broker present all offers to the seller. It is the seller's prerogative to decide whether to reject or accept an offer for the purchase of the property. In presenting the offer, the broker should provide the principal with knowledge of all circumstances surrounding the offer. An offer must be presented even though the seller may have several offers under consideration at the time an additional offer is made. The broker must continue to present offers during the term of the listing contract until the property sale is closed. Thus, even if an offer has been accepted, all subsequent offers must be presented until the sale is completed, unless the seller has instructed the broker otherwise.

A broker and any subagents of the seller working through him also have an obligation to the principal not to disclose certain information to third parties. A **third party** is the person in a transaction other than the principal and her agent. In this case, the third party is the buyer. When a buyer's agent is involved, however, the seller becomes the third party to the buyer's agent and any subagents. For example, if a listing broker knows that a seller will actually accept a price for the property lower than the listed price, the broker is obligated not to disclose this information to others. The listing broker and any subagents may offer the property only at the listed price. It is a violation of the broker's fiduciary obligation to the seller to offer the property at any price other than the listed price.

Even though one of the broker's obligations to the seller includes the requirement not to disclose certain confidential information to third parties that would be injurious to the seller, the broker cannot misrepresent the property in any way to the buyer. The law provides that liability may be imposed upon a broker for the misrepresentation of the existence of a defect in the real estate, for concealing defects in the property, or for failing to disclose the existence of defects (omission). This liability may be imposed for both willful (intentional) and negligent (unintentional) misrepresentation or omission by the broker (see the section "Agent's Duties to Third Parties").

## Accounting

A real estate broker must account for and promptly remit as required all money or property entrusted to the broker for the benefit of others. The broker is required to keep adequate and accurate records of all receipts and expenditures of other people's money so a complete accounting can be provided. A real estate broker must maintain a special account for the deposit of other people's money. This account must be entitled either "trust account" or "escrow account" and must be maintained in a North Carolina or federally insured bank or savings and loan association. It is a violation of the law of agency and the Real Estate Licensing Law for a broker to commingle funds or property she is holding in trust for others with personal money or property or with the operating account of her business. A broker is required to deliver immediately to the employing broker all monies received. This is essentially the only duty a broker other than the BIC has regarding accounting for funds and record keeping. See Appendix A for the North Carolina Real Estate Commission's rules regarding accounting.

## Agent's Duties to Third Parties

The agent's primary duty to the principal does not excuse the agent from his duty to make complete, honest representations to the third party, who is also referred to as the **customer.** The agent must inform the third party of all information about the property that the agent knows or should reasonably have known by making a prudent and diligent investigation. The North Carolina Real Estate Commission, agency 1aw, and other laws, rules and regulations require that any disclosure or representation be accurate; that is, any assertions, disclosures, or representation an agent chooses to make must be true. This duty cannot be avoided by a statement in an *agency* agreement, an advertisement, or MLS disclaiming liability. The affirmative duty to disclose material fact applies to any party whether they are clients (principals) or customers (third parties). It also applies to others involved in the transaction, such as attorneys, lenders, home inspectors, etc. An agent may not disregard information from a reputable source, such as a home inspector and engage another professional to give them a report without the material fact in it while hiding the original defect from the second inspector or the original report from the buyer.

The duty to disclose material fact may be breached by willful or negligent misrepresentation, as well as by willful or negligent omission. An agent's duty to disclose is closely related to duties of honesty, skill, care, and diligence. If an agent performs due diligence to discover problems and honestly communicates these problems to the proper parties, she should have no problems with her duty to disclose.

The agent cannot escape this duty simply by representing a property "as is." Rather, the agent needs to document that she disclosed to the customer what the "as is" conditions really are. Is the agent responsible for information published in the local newspaper relating to conditions that would adversely affect the property, such as a zoning change or annexation to the city? The answer is clearly yes, in that the agent must disclose all pertinent material facts to the third party.

Specifically, Chapter 93A-6 of the North Carolina General Statutes prohibits the following acts in regard to the agent's duty to the third party:

1. Willful misrepresentation, which is intentionally informing the third party of something the agent knows to be false, or without regard for its truth, such as telling the third party that the property is subject only to county taxes when he knows the property is within the jurisdiction of the city or when he does not know, and answers anyway.
2. Negligent misrepresentation, which is unintentionally informing the third party of something that is false but that the agent does not know to be false because she did not exercise proper skill, care, or diligence
3. Willful omission, which is deliberately failing to inform the third party of a known defect in the property
4. Negligent omission, which is unintentionally failing to inform the third party of something that the agent should have known but did not know because he did not exercise proper skill, care, or diligence

An understanding of the meaning of "material fact" is necessary to understand what should and should not be disclosed. Material facts which would impact a buyer's decision to buy or a seller's decision to accept an offer must be revealed to all parties to a transaction, whether they are a buyer, seller, or other agent. Material facts relate to the property itself, such as specified defects, and to external factors outside of the property which may impact the property such as new roads, airplane flight patterns, zoning changes, and commercial development. Agency status does not determine disclosure of these material facts.

Facts relating to a buyer's or seller's ability to complete the transaction also must be disclosed as material fact. The seller's inability to give clear title due to foreclosure proceedings or a buyer's inability to qualify for a loan are both examples of facts affecting a party's ability to complete a transaction. A third type of material fact is one that is known to be important to a party. This type of material fact must be disclosed to that party. For example, a truck driver wants to park his 18 wheeler on his property. The agent knows that restrictive (protective) covenants forbid this. It becomes a material fact. Other facts that only have to be disclosed to the agent's principal are the third party's motivation for entering the transaction and the third party's willingness to pay more or accept less for the property. These are not material facts.

An agent must disclose any interest he has in the property to the third party. Any funds the agent is furnishing to the buyer must be disclosed to the seller. Other offers and the potential for other offers must be disclosed to the seller. The duty to submit all offers to the principal remains until the transaction is closed. Conversely, there is an obligation not to disclose certain things to third parties. Non-material facts include confidential information about an agent's principal which might compromise the principal's bargaining position, such as the principal's motivation for selling or buying or that the principal is willing to pay more or accept less for the property. When the buyer is the principal (client), the agent may not disclose his client's planned use of the property or motivation for purchasing it to the seller (third party) without authorization from the principal to do so. If asked directly, however, the buyer's agent must decline to answer, or answer honestly.

## Misrepresentation

The communication of false or incorrect information is a *misrepresentation.* **Willful misrepresentation** occurs when an agent knowingly communicates information she knows to be false or when an agent provides false information with no regard for the truth of such a statement. For example, an agent who tells a prospective buyer that he can place a mobile home on a vacant lot when she knows the restrictive covenants prohibit mobile homes is guilty of willful misrepresentation. She knows that statement of material fact is wrong and lies about it. Likewise, an agent who assures a prospective buyer that a mobile home can be placed on this same lot without knowing whether this is true and without checking to verify the truth of this statement is also considered to have made a willful misrepresentation. In the first example, the agent clearly made a willful misrepresentation by communicating information the agent knew to be false. In the second example, the agent still made a willful misrepresentation (even though the agent did not know the statement to be false) because the agent made the false statement intentionally and without regard for the truth of the statement. That is, she knew she did not know, made no effort to find out, and made the statement anyway. She may try to justify this action by the thought process "If I do not know the answer, it is not a lie," but she would be absolutely wrong. "I don't know, but I'll find out" is a much better answer than lying. Willful misrepresentation is fraud.

While willful misrepresentation involves an intentional act, **negligent misrepresentation** involves an unintentional act. Negligent misrepresentation results from the failure to exercise reasonable care. If an agent does not know the information she is conveying is false, she is guilty of negligent misrepresentation. She thought it was true; therefore, she saw no need to check it out, and she acted in good faith. It doesn't matter. She is guilty anyway, but not of fraud.

If an agent misinforms a party regarding a material fact about a property and the agent *reasonably should have known* the truth, the agent is guilty of negligent misrepresentation. Remember that an agent is held to a standard based on what a reasonably prudent agent could have been expected to know. Suppose an agent advertises a home and incorrectly states the home's heated square footage based on information on a tax sheet without actually measuring the home personally. If the standard of practice in the local market is for agents to measure a home when they list it, the agent is guilty of negligent misrepresentation.

Agents cannot avoid responsibility for negligent misrepresentation because information was obtained from a seller/principal, another agent, the MLS, or another source. An agent bears the responsibility of investigating facts whenever a reasonably prudent agent should have suspected that the information was incorrect.

A listing agent is held accountable for the accuracy of information placed in an MLS or on a listing information sheet. Because the seller's agent is responsible for compiling this information, the listing agent is held to a high standard regarding accuracy of information on a property. However, the selling agent will still be held to the "reasonableness" standard and should not rely solely on information provided by the listing agent. For example, if a home is advertised as containing 1,500 square feet of heated living space and it actually contains only 1,483 square feet, the selling agent would probably not be considered negligent. However, if the home actually contained only 1,300 square feet, the selling agent would probably be considered negligent in not verifying that the stated square footage was accurate, the premise being that a reasonably careful agent would have noticed that the house appeared smaller than the advertised size.

The basis for the imposition of liability in misrepresentation consists of a false representation of a material fact; that is, the fact that the person making the false representation knew or should have known it to be false, the fact that the misrepresentation was made with an intent to induce the party to act or refrain from acting in reliance upon the misrepresentation, the fact that the party relied on the misrepresentation in acting or failing to act, and the fact that there was damage to the party who relied upon the misrepresentation in acting or not acting. The agent cannot disclaim liability for misrepresentation by using a liability disclaimer in the MLS and in advertising.

Puffing differs from material fact in that it is a statement of opinion, often exaggerated, which should be recognized as an opinion. For example, an agent may describe a property as the most beautiful setting in Wayne County. It may or may not be, but that is only one person's opinion. It is not a representation of material fact.

## Omission

Unlike misrepresentation, which is the communication of false or incorrect information, **omission** is the failure to disclose information. Omission may be willful or negligent.

**Willful omission** is the *deliberate failure to disclose material facts known to the agent.* **Negligent omission** *is the unintentional failure to disclose material facts that should have been but are not known to the agent.* When an agent knows a material fact and unintentionally rather than deliberately neglects to disclose it, the agent is guilty of negligent omission. The two facts could be the same. The classification of willful or negligent hinges upon whether the agent knew the facts and whether he deliberately chose not to reveal the material facts he did know. An agent has a duty to disclose material facts to third parties in a transaction, limited to facts about the property or to matters relating directly to the property and a party's ability to complete the transaction. This duty does not include the obligation to disclose facts not directly related to the property, such as a seller's motivation for selling (unless that motivation is the result of a defect or another fact affecting the property).

North Carolina has several exceptions to the duty to disclose. The fact that a person died or was seriously ill in a house listed for sale or in a residential rental unit is not deemed a material fact that an agent must disclose. However, an agent may not make a false statement about past occupancy. Therefore, the agent must answer truthfully about a past occupant if asked by a prospective purchaser. A special rule applies to deaths due to acquired immune deficiency syndrome (AIDS). Persons with AIDS are considered legally handicapped and are, therefore, a protected class under the federal fair housing laws. If a real estate agent is asked by a prospective purchaser whether the previous occupant had AIDS, she should treat the question as impermissible.

The buyer's agent has a duty to disclose to the seller when the agent is aware of a financial problem that might affect the buyer's ability to close the transaction. This seems to be in conflict with the agent's duty to his principal, the buyer; however, an agent's duty to his principal does not relieve the agent of the duty to disclose material facts and to deal with third parties in a fair and honest manner. A seller's agent is obligated to disclose known material facts about the property to third parties, such as prospective buyers or tenants. Deliberate failure to disclose such known facts constitutes willful omission.

Negligent omission is perhaps the most likely way a real estate practitioner can inadvertently violate her duties to her principals and to third parties, consequently violating the law of agency and the Real Estate Licensing Law. When the agent knowingly misrepresents or omits something, she knows she is doing wrong. When she negligently misrepresents a fact, she does not know the correct answer, but believes the answer she gives to be correct. With negligent omission, the agent may not have a clue she is doing anything wrong. She either does not know the facts or knows the facts but negligently, rather than deliberately, does not reveal them. This act arises from not taking the necessary precautions to stay informed about properties, external factors affecting properties, and issues that would affect a client's or customer's decision to buy or sell. For example, the agent may not make a visual inspection of a property she lists, thereby missing defects that a reasonable, prudent agent would have known and disclosed. An agent may be oblivious to what is going on in her area, such as proposed new roads, zoning changes, or emerging environmental issues. When this knowledge is readily available to the public, the agent has a duty to know and disclose. Some agents may consider themselves too busy to keep up with the current environment or to visually inspect houses they list or sell, but ignorance is no excuse. The only way to avoid negligent omission is to constantly practice due diligence.

## Consumer Legislation

The North Carolina Unfair and Deceptive Trade Practices Act prohibits the use of unfair or deceptive practices in commerce. Essentially, the conduct and practices prohibited under this Act are also prohibited by the North Carolina Real Estate License Law and case law. Unfair and deceptive acts include the offering of a misleading opinion, failure to disclose a material fact, misleading advertising, misrepresentation, and false inducement.

## "As Is" Sale

The listing of a property "as is" or an "as is" provision in the contract does *not* relieve the agent of the responsibility to reveal material facts, including defects, to a prospective purchaser.

## Purchaser's Responsibilities

A purchaser bears certain responsibilities for investigating a property before entering into a contract. Under the doctrine of **caveat emptor** (let the buyer beware), the seller has no obligation to the buyer beyond avoiding intentionally fraudulent acts, including misrepresentation.

While the doctrine of caveat emptor may be the acceptable legal standard between buyer and seller, "Let the agent take care" is the acceptable practical standard for the relationship between real estate agent and his clients and/or third parties.

While real estate agents are held accountable to buyers for negligent as well as willful misrepresentations and omissions, this fact does not relieve the buyer of all responsibility for verifying easily verifiable information and examining the property. If a defect or misinformation regarding the property is so obvious that a buyer acting in a reasonable manner should have discovered the inaccuracy, the courts may find that the agent did not behave in an unlawful manner under the common law.

Even though the agent may be relieved of civil liability for misrepresentation or failure to disclose a material fact in this situation, it *will not* relieve the agent of responsibility for his actions under the North Carolina Real Estate License Law. When representing a purchaser as a buyer's agent, the agent has the duty to assist the buyer in verifying information and adequately inspecting the property.

### Liabilities for Breach of Duty

There are two major areas of accountability of an agent's failure to fulfill her duty, that is, **breach of duty** of agency.

1. *Accountability to the North Carolina Real Estate Commission for disciplinary action against a licensee.* The Commission is the only regulatory body that can take action against an agent's license. The actions include, in order of severity, reprimand, censure, suspension, and revocation.
2. *Accountability through the court system.* A **civil penalty** may result from a suit for monetary damages or injunctive relief. Thus, if an agent's action costs a client or prospect any financial loss, the injured party may sue to recover damages.

In addition, violation of the real estate law is a criminal violation (a **misdemeanor**) and is punishable by fine and/or imprisonment.

## DUTIES AND LIABILITIES OF PRINCIPALS

### Principal's Duties to Agent

The principal has definite duties to the agent. The principal must cooperate with the broker; that is, act in good faith. Therefore, a seller must cooperate with the listing broker in making the property available for inspection by prospective buyers at reasonable times. The principal is required to compensate the agent at the time when the agent accomplishes what she contracted to do. When the seller is the principal, the agent's duty is to find a buyer who is ready, willing, and able to purchase the property at terms acceptable to the seller. When the agent brings an offer from a buyer for the full terms of the listing contract, does the owner have to sell the property? No, but the agent has earned a commission. Compensation or the source of compensation alone does not determine the agency relationship. A seller/principal can pay the buyer's agent or provide for the buyer's agent to be paid out of the transaction's proceeds without creating any agency relationship with the buyer's agent.

### Principal's Duties to Third Parties

*Caveat emptor* is a legal maxim that means "let the buyer beware." In the context of a real estate transaction, this doctrine places the burden on the buyer to inspect the property and absolves the seller of responsibility for any defects that should have been discovered during a reasonable inspection. The law places no duty on the seller to disclose a defect. The only duties owed by a seller are a duty not to conceal defects (such as painting over a water stain to conceal evidence of a leak) and a duty to be truthful in the disclosures a seller *chooses* to make. The consumer protection concept of implied warranty—that the property is as it is represented—is the current prevailing force in legal actions.

### North Carolina Residential Property Disclosure Act

The Residential Property Disclosure Act applies to residential real estate contracts and requires sellers (including owners selling their own property and relocation companies) to furnish purchasers with a statutorily prescribed Residential Property Disclosure Statement (see Appendix A, page 483). The seller must answer questions regarding the property with one of three answers: yes, none known, or no representations. If the seller chooses to make no representation as to the condition of the property, the seller is relieved of the obligation to disclose any condition even if the seller knew or should have known it.

Certain properties are exempt from the Residential Property Act. These include properties that have never been occupied; transfers by lease with an option to purchase, where the purchaser will occupy the property prior to purchase; transfers between co-owners, spouses, or heirs; and transfers by fiduciaries or pursuant to legal proceedings.

The statement must be provided to a buyer no later than the time at which the Offer to Purchase and Contract is signed by the buyer. Note that this statement is a two-sided form. Both sides must be delivered to a buyer. If the disclosure statement is *not* delivered prior to the time a buyer makes an offer, the buyer has the right to cancel any resulting contract within these limitations:

1. If the disclosure statement is delivered after an offer is made but *before acceptance,* the purchaser has three days after receipt of disclosure to cancel the contract.
2. If the disclosure statement is delivered *after acceptance* (or never delivered), the purchaser has three days after date of acceptance of contract to cancel.

The buyer's right to cancel expires when settlement takes place or the buyer occupies the property.

The Act also requires that the seller amend the statement if the seller discovers a material inaccuracy in the statement or if events change so as to render the statement inaccurate at any time up until the time of closing.

The Residential Property Disclosure Act provides that *any* agent involved in an affected residential transaction has a duty to inform her client of the client's rights and obligations under the Act. This duty falls upon seller's agents and buyer's agents. The Act does *not* relieve an agent of responsibility to discover and disclose material facts under the Real Estate License Law.

## Lead-Based Paint Disclosure

For properties built before 1978, the seller or lessor of a property and any agents representing sellers or lessors must provide to the buyers or lessees the EPA pamphlet "Protect Your Family From Lead in Your Home," must disclose the presence of any known lead-based paint, and must provide any available records or reports pertaining to lead-based paint or hazards. The agent has a duty to his principal, whether his principal is a seller/lessor or buyer/lessee, to make her aware of rights and responsibilities under the Residential Lead-Based Paint Hazard Reduction Act of 1992 (see Chapter 4 for a full discussion of the Act).

## Synthetic Stucco Disclosure

"Synthetic stucco" (Figure 5.7) is a term commonly used to describe the exterior finish product that is properly known as exterior insulating and finishing system (EIFS). This so-called synthetic stucco differs from real stucco in several ways. The most important is that unlike real stucco, synthetic stucco, or EIFS, is impervious to water. This means that no water is absorbed by the EIFS. Unfortunately, it also means that any water that enters through a seam or break in the finish becomes trapped in the wall. This trapped water can cause significant damage to wall framing due to excess moisture. For this reason, the North Carolina Real Estate Commission considers the existence of synthetic stucco to be a *material fact* that should be discovered and disclosed to prospective buyers.

If siding material looks like stucco, the agent has a duty to investigate and ascertain whether the material is real or synthetic stucco. If an agent knows or "reasonably should have known" that a structure was *formerly* sided with synthetic stucco, this is also considered a material fact, which the agent has a duty to disclose. An example of a situation where it might be determined that an agent "reasonably should have known" that a structure was formerly sided with synthetic stucco is if all homes in a subdivision were sided with this product. The former existence of synthetic stucco must be disclosed even if the agent has reliable information that all moisture damage was corrected, although the agent can provide this repair information to the prospective buyer.

If a structure has or formerly had synthetic stucco, the agent has a duty to *disclose* its existence, *explain* the fact that there have been numerous instances of moisture damage to structures sided with this product, and recommend that the buyer have the property inspected by a qualified inspector for excess moisture and moisture damage.

**FIGURE 5.7** Synthetic Stucco: The Straight Facts.

# synthetic stucco

THE STRAIGHT FACTS

Information provided by NCAR INC. NORTH CAROLINA ASSOCIATION OF REALTORS®, INC.

During the latter half of the 1990s, "synthetic stucco," or EIFS (Exterior Insulation and Finish Systems, pronounced "eefs"), became a hot-button consumer issue. EIFS are multi-layered exterior wall systems used on both homes and commercial buildings. Moisture intrusion and retention problems with the product first surfaced in 1996 in Wilmington, N.C., where 90 percent of the homes clad in synthetic stucco tested by local architects and building inspectors were found to have high moisture levels in the wood components of the wall cavities. Resulting litigation led to settlements with and verdicts against manufacturers and builders. (For more information about the North Carolina Synthetic Stucco Class Action and the National Synthetic Stucco Class Action, visit www.ncstucco.com and www.kinsella.com/eifs.)

## What Is Synthetic Stucco?

Conventional EIFS is a multi-layered system of styrofoam panels adhered to wood or gypsum sheathing and finished with a waterproof resin. This application process is less expensive than applying real or traditional stucco (made with cement) to masonry or wire mesh subsurfaces. While conventional EIFS resists water penetration at its surface, it is not designed to drain water that gets behind it. It is also known as non-drainable EIFS and was effectively banned in new home construction in North Carolina in March 1996.

This information sheet focuses on conventional, non-drainable EIFS, but there are other types of synthetic stucco, such as DEFS or EFS ("Direct-applied Exterior Finish Systems") and drainable EIFS. DEFS is a system that involves the use of cement board panels rather than styrofoam panels. Drainable EIFS systems incorporate drainage channels behind the styrofoam panels. Discussion about these other types of synthetic stucco is beyond the scope of this information sheet.

## How Can I Tell If the Structure Has Synthetic Stucco?

There are many types of cladding that look like stucco. One simple way to check is to tap the exterior of the structure. Synthetic stucco is relatively light and sounds hollow when tapped, while real stucco is heavy and sounds solid when tapped. Real stucco is much harder than EIFS. With drainable EIFS, the drainage channels might be visible at the bottom of the exterior synthetic stucco wall. Sources such as warranties or bills of sale might be helpful in determining which product is on a property. The builder, contractor or synthetic stucco applicator also can be of assistance. Property owners or prospective purchasers who are unsure what type of product is on a property should have it inspected, perhaps by a structural engineer.

## What Problems Have Been Observed In Structures Clad with Conventional EIFS?

High moisture levels often lead to damage of structural features behind conventional EIFS, including wood rot and delamination and deterioration of plywood or other sheathing. Often, termites are the first visible clue that there is a problem, because in some instances, excess moisture can contribute to infestation.

Water intrusion most frequently occurs around windows, when water enters either through the joint around the window's perimeter or through seams and joints in the window itself. Water also can enter at roof-to-wall intersections; large quantities of water resulting in some of the most severe damage frequently get in this way. Other potential water-entry points include chimneys, decks and any other penetration of the conventional EIFS layer.

## What Is Causing the Problems?

Some builders and inspection officials contend that water entering the wall cavities of an EIFS-clad structure cannot easily escape to the outside, unlike water entering other finishing systems, like brick veneer and wood siding. EIFS manufacturers, however, defend their product, blaming the problems on improper application, use of poor quality windows and inadequate flashing and sealing.

**FIGURE 5.7** Continued.

## What Are My Responsibilities As a Seller Or Buyer?

Sellers may make a disclosure on the North Carolina Residential Property Disclosure Statement that the siding is synthetic stucco. Real estate licensees, if they know or reasonably should know that a structure is clad or was previously clad in EIFS, must disclose it as a material fact to prospective purchasers.

Prior to listing a property or making an offer, it is recommended that the seller or buyer:

- Have the structure thoroughly examined.

(Homeowner guidelines are available from the North Carolina Department of Insurance Office of the State Fire Marshal. See the "For More Information" section below for details on how to obtain them.)

- Discuss the product and recommended methods of application and maintenance with the builder.

- Consult the resources listed below.

A REALTOR® will be able to assist you in obtaining professional guidance.

## For More Information

North Carolina Department of Insurance
Office of State Fire Marshal (OSFM)
Engineering and Codes Division
www.ncdoi.com/OSFM *
(919) 661-5880 or (800) 634-7854

* For Homeowner Maintenance Guidelines and Inspection Guidelines published by the North Carolina Department of Insurance, click on the OSFM Divisions tab, select "Engineering and Codes," then "NC Building Code Council," then "Exterior Insulation Finish System."

**Your Local Building Inspector**

For a directory, go to www.ncdoi.com/OSFM, click on the OSFM Divisions tab, select "Engineering and Codes," then "Inspection Department Directories."

North Carolina Department of Justice
Consumer Protection Section
www.ncdoj.com
(919) 716-6000

National Association of Home Builders
www.nahb.org
(800) 368-5242

EIFS Industry Members Association
www.eima.com
(800) 294-3462

**Other Online EIFS Resources**
www.stuccolaw.com
www.eifsalliance.com

By signing, I acknowledge that the agent named below furnished a copy of this brochure and disclosed to me that the property described below is or may be clad in or has previously been clad in synthetic stucco.

______________________________
Property

| | |
|---|---|
| Buyer Name (Print or Type) | Buyer Name (Print or Type) |
| Buyer Signature | Buyer Signature |
| Date | Date |

______________________________
Firm Name

______________________________
Agent Name

## Liabilities of Principals

Since the principal is not likely to have a real estate license, he would not be accountable to the Real Estate Commission for disciplinary action as the agent would be, but the principal is fully responsible to the public—through the courts—for both civil and criminal wrongdoings. He is further responsible to the agent if he withholds information or gives false information that causes the agent relying on the information to be liable for misrepresentation to a third party. The principal must indemnify the agent for any legal action brought against the agent by an innocent third party by repaying the agent's losses.

The principal is also responsible to third parties for the actions of the agent. For example, if the principal properly discloses material facts to his agent, who then willfully misrepresents or neglects to disclose to the third party, the principal may be civilly liable for the wrongful actions of his agent. However, he may have some legal recourse against the agent for his losses.

## SUMMARY OF IMPORTANT POINTS

1. An agent is a fiduciary and therefore has the following obligations to the principal: loyalty; obedience; skill, care, and diligence; accounting; and disclosure of all material facts. The broker becomes an agent by the employment authority of the listing agreement, the property management agreement, the buyer agency agreement, or the tenant agency agreement. The principal and the agent have duties to each other under the contract.
2. All agents have the affirmative duty to represent the property honestly, fairly, and accurately to all prospective purchasers, making full disclosure of any facts that would adversely affect the property.
3. Subagency relationships are viewed in two contexts. First is the in-house situation, in which a sales associate works for a broker. The sales associate is simultaneously an agent for the broker and a subagent of all the principals who have employed the broker as their agent. The second subagency situation occurs in the listing/selling context with the cooperating broker of another firm. All cooperating selling brokers and their sales associates are presumed to be subagents of the seller/principal unless a buyer has employed the cooperating broker through the use of a written buyer agency agreement and that fact is disclosed at first contact between the firms. In both subagency situations, the subagent has the same duties to the principal as the primary agent has.
4. A buyer agency relationship is created when a broker is hired under a buyer agency agreement to represent the buyer. The buyer's agent owes the duties of agency to the buyer.
5. Disclosed dual agency exists when a real estate firm attempts to represent the buyer and the seller in the same transaction with the full knowledge and consent of both. Undisclosed dual agency is a violation of North Carolina Real Estate Law. A designated agency is a type of dual agency in which the firm acts as a dual agent, but one agent in the firm represents only the seller's interest and another only the buyer's interest.
6. The National Association of REALTORS® requires all multiple listing services owned by boards/associations to allow participants to offer subagency, buyer's agency, or both at the discretion of the listing broker.
7. The North Carolina General Statutes specifically prohibit willful misrepresentation, negligent misrepresentation, willful omission, and negligent omission. The agent is accountable not only to the North Carolina Real Estate Commission, but also to the civil and criminal courts.

8. The pamphlet "Working With Real Estate Agents" is a document created and published by the North Carolina Real Estate Commission. All agents must review this document with sellers, potential sellers, buyers, and potential buyers at first substantial contact. Sellers, potential sellers, buyers, and potential buyers must sign the acknowledgment panel. The agent retains this panel for three years from the time it is signed or three years after the finalization of the transaction, whichever comes later.

## REVIEW QUESTIONS

Answers to the review questions are in the Answer Key at the back of the book.

1. A real estate listing agent advised a buyer (customer) that a property was zoned for the type of commercial use for which the buyer intended to use the property. Relying on the agent's advice, the buyer contracted to purchase the property. In making the statement regarding the zoning, the agent did not know what zoning applied to the property. The buyer subsequently learned that the zoning was such that he could not use the property as he intended. Which of the following is (are) correct?
   A. the agent committed an act of misrepresentation and is liable to the buyer for any loss the buyer suffered as a consequence
   B. since the agent did not know the true facts regarding the zoning, no misrepresentation of the property to the buyer took place; therefore, the agent is not liable
   C. the seller is not liable to the buyer for the agent's misrepresentation
   D. all of the above

2. Misrepresentation occurs when:
   A. the party making a false representation knows it to be false
   B. the party making a false representation does not know if the statement is true or false, but should have known
   C. the party making the false representation makes no effort to determine if it is true
   D. all of the above

3. A contract in which a property owner employs a broker to market her property creates an agency relationship between which of the following?
   A. buyer and seller
   B. buyer and broker
   C. broker and seller
   D. broker, seller, and buyer

4. An agent's duties to the principal include all of the following EXCEPT:
   A. loyalty
   B. accountability
   C. obedience
   D. legal advice

5. Which of the following is NOT an agency relationship?
   A. the relationship between a sales associate and the broker with whom the associate is associated
   B. the relationship between a listing broker and a cooperating broker acting as a subagent of the seller
   C. the relationship between a seller's agent and a buyer's agent
   D. the relationship between a seller and the listing agent

6. A real estate broker presented an offer to the property owner during the listing term for the listed price payable in cash with no contingencies and a 10 percent deposit. This offer met all the terms of the listing agreement. In this situation, which of the following is correct?
   A. the property owner is required to accept the offer
   B. the listing brokerage company is legally entitled to the commission agreed upon in the listing contract only if the property owner accepts the offer
   C. the property owner is not required to accept the offer but is legally obligated to pay the listing company the commission agreed upon in the listing agreement
   D. the buyer can sue the property owner for damages if the owner refuses to accept the buyer's offer

7. A broker should present:
   I. offers generated by a cooperating (subagent) office.
   II. only those offers that appear to be in the seller's best interest.
   A. I only
   B. II only
   C. both I and II
   D. neither I nor II

8. The employment authority of the listing agreement:
   I. binds the agent to the best interests of the seller.
   II. gives the agent authority to screen offers for the seller.
   A. I only
   B. II only
   C. both I and II
   D. neither I nor II

9. A listing broker has the duty to disclose to the buyer (customer):
   A. the amount of the commission
   B. the seller's financial status
   C. the seller's reason for selling
   D. structural defects

10. Working for Beth Buyer under an exclusive buyer agency agreement, Babs Broker of ABC Realty sells Beth a house listed by XYZ Realty. Sabrina Seller pays Babs Broker's commission through Sabrina's listing agent at XYZ Realty, Lois Lister. Which one of the following statements is TRUE?
    A. Beth Buyer is Babs Broker's customer
    B. Beth Buyer is Lois Lister's client
    C. Sabrina Seller is Lois Lister's customer
    D. Beth Buyer is Babs Broker's client

11. Brokerage relationships are governed by which of the following?
    A. the law of agency
    B. contract law
    C. North Carolina Real Estate License Law
    D. all of the above

12. Which of the following statements is true regarding the Residential Property Disclosure Act?
    A. the Act relieves agents of the responsibility to discover and disclose material facts regarding a property
    B. once a seller has completed the disclosure statement, he is under no obligation to amend the statement if the condition of the property changes
    C. a seller of residential property who does not complete the Residential Property Disclosure Statement may be fined $500
    D. a disclosure statement should be provided to the buyer no later than the time at which an offer to purchase and contract is signed by the buyer

13. Sally Smith, an agent at ABC Realty, presented an offer to Bob Broker of XYZ Realty. Sally is a buyer's agent, and Bob is the listing agent. Bob presents a counteroffer from his seller to Sally, who contacts her buyer. At 11:30 a.m., the buyer accepts the counteroffer in Sally's presence. Meanwhile, at 11:45 a.m. on the same day, Bob's seller receives a better offer, which he wants to accept, and tells Bob to withdraw the counteroffer. Bob immediately communicates this to Sally before Sally can tell him of her buyer's acceptance. Which of the following is (are) true?
    A. Bob's seller cannot withdraw the counteroffer since Sally has been notified of the acceptance of the counteroffer
    B. Bob's seller can withdraw the counteroffer since neither Bob nor his seller has been notified of acceptance
    C. Bob's seller cannot withdraw the counteroffer because it was accepted before the seller received the new offer
    D. none of the above

Dual Agency

14. Sally Smith and Bob Broker are agents at XYZ Realty. Sally presented an offer to Bob on one of his listings. Bob presents a counteroffer from the seller to Sally, who contacts her buyer/client. At 11:30 a.m., the buyer accepts the counteroffer in Sally's presence. Meanwhile, at 11:45 a.m. on the same day, the seller receives a better offer, which he wants to accept, and tells Bob to withdraw the counteroffer. Bob immediately communicates this to Sally before Sally can tell him of the buyer's acceptance. Which of the following is true?
    A. Bob's seller cannot withdraw the counteroffer because acceptance in Sally's presence provides notification to the seller
    B. Bob's seller can withdraw the counteroffer because the new offer is a better offer
    C. Bob's seller can withdraw the counteroffer because Sally did not notify Bob of the acceptance before the seller asked Bob to withdraw the counteroffer
    D. none of the above

15. Which of the following statements is (are) true concerning designated dual agency?
    A. a broker-in-charge cannot be a designated dual agent if the other agent is a provisional broker
    B. an agent cannot be appointed as a designated dual agent if the agent has prior knowledge of confidential information about the other party to the transaction
    C. only the broker-in-charge can serve as a designated agent for both parties in a transaction
    D. both a and b

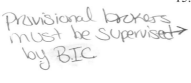

Provisional brokers must be supervised by B.I.C.

Designated Agency - 2 rules

16. Oral buyer agency is:
   I. no longer permitted in North Carolina.
   II. permitted in North Carolina.
   III. must be converted to writing after the offer is accepted.
   A. I only
   B. II only
   C. III only
   D. II and III

17. The "Working With Real Estate Agents" pamphlet:
   A. must be presented at first substantial contact
   B. has the same legal weight as the listing or buyer's agency contract
   C. should not be used if the customer desires oral buyer agency
   D. should be presented at the same time as the Offer to Purchase

18. Designated agency is permitted:
   A. if the parties agree to do it in advance
   B. if the designated agent does not have confidential information about the other agent's principal
   C. if the designated agent is not directly supervised by the other designated agent
   D. all of the above

19. Which type(s) of agency agreement must be in writing from the time of its (their) inception?
   I. Exclusive Right to Sell
   II. Exclusive Right to Represent Buyer
   III. Oral Dual Agency
   A. I only
   B. II only
   C. I and II
   D. I, II, and III

20. For a violation of licensing laws, the Commission can:
   A. bring about criminal charges
   B. reprimand the licensee
   C. fine the licensee
   D. all of the above

21. Which of the following must be disclosed to a buyer-customer by the listing agent?
   A. the reason the seller needs to sell quickly
   B. the death of the previous occupant from AIDS
   C. only the material facts the seller has authorized the agent to disclose
   D. none of the above

22. Which of the following constitutes a material fact?
   A. a readily noticeable crack in the foundation
   B. a broken heat pump
   C. pending zoning changes
   D. all of the above

23. An agent may not accept an Offer to Purchase for her principal because the typical listing contract is a form of
   A. universal agency
   B. general agency
   C. special agency
   D. free agency

24. An agent meets prospective buyers at an open house he is holding. The buyers disclose their combined salary and ask if the agent can prequalify them to purchase the home. Which of the following is a true statement?
   I. The buyers have created an oral buyer agency by their actions.
   II. The agent is now an undisclosed dual agent.
   A. I only
   B. II only
   C. both I and II
   D. neither I nor II

25. Allen Agent of ABC Realty is working with Betty Buyer under an oral buyer agency agreement. He shows her a house listed by Beatrice Broker of XYZ Realty. Betty wants to buy the home. Which contract does Allen prepare first?
   A. the Residential Property Disclosure
   B. the Oral Agency Conversion
   C. the Exclusive Right to Represent Buyer
   D. the Offer to Purchase

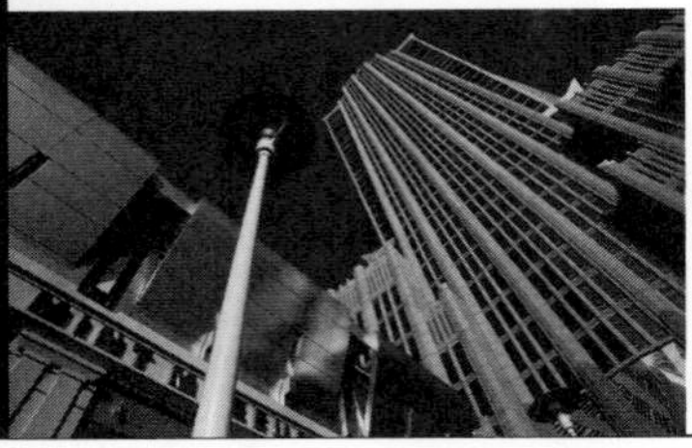

# Chapter 6

## KEY TERMS

accord and satisfaction
alienation clause
assignment
bilateral contract
breach of contract
consideration
contract for deed
contractual capacity
counteroffer
damages
due-on-sale clause
duress
earnest money
equitable title
exclusive agency
exclusive right to sell
executed contract
extender clause
executory contracts
express contract
flat fee
full performance
illusory offer
implied contract
land contracts
multiple listing service (MLS)
mutual assent
negligent misrepresentation
net listing
novation
offeree
offeror
open listing
option
override clause
Parol Evidence Rule
ready, willing, and able
right of first refusal
Sherman Antitrust Act
success fee
unilateral contract
valid contract
void contract
voidable contract

# *Real Estate Contracts

level 3

## LEARNING OBJECTIVES

At the conclusion of this chapter, you should be able to:

1. Define basic contract terms, including express, implied, bilateral, unilateral, executed, executory, valid, void, and voidable contracts.
2. Define the essential elements of a contract, including mutual assent, consideration, capacity of the parties, and lawful objective.
3. Define the requirements for reality of consent to a contract.
4. Describe the contract law of auction sales.
5. Describe how contracts are discharged.
6. Describe the assignment of contracts.
7. List the rules for interpretation of contracts.
8. Describe contract remedies.
9. Define the types and characteristics of listing contracts.
10. Describe the function and agency characteristics of the multiple listing service.
11. Define the essential and common provisions of the listing contract.
12. Define the broker's entitlement to commission.
13. Describe various commission arrangements.
14. Describe the termination of listing contracts.
15. Describe the property data sheet.
16. Describe the essential and common provisions of the purchase contract.
17. Describe the rights and obligations of the parties to a purchase contract.
18. Describe the characteristics and requirements of the offer.
19. Define the characteristics and requirements of the counteroffer.
20. Describe the requirements for handling earnest money.

# STANDARD CONTRACT FORMS

Contracts used for illustration in this text are the North Carolina Association of REALTORS®, Inc. (NCAR) Standard Forms, which have been revised to incorporate changes in real estate law through July 1, 2006. The following is a partial list of forms available from NCAR for use by its members:

Exclusive Right to Sell Listing Contract

Agency Agreement Renewal and/or Amendment Form

Exclusive Right to Represent Buyer

Agency Disclosure and Non-Exclusive Buyer Agency Agreement

Dual Agency Addendum

Offer to Purchase and Contract

Additional Provisions Addendum

Guidelines for Completing the Offer to Purchase and Contract

For Sale by Owner Disclosure and Fee Agreement

Agency Forms Checklist

Back-Up Contract Addendum

Although these forms meet statutory requirements, using them is not mandatory. Any real estate firm or broker can have an attorney draft a form that meets the statutory requirements and the firm's or broker's own needs. The only form mandated by the General Assembly is the Residential Property Disclosure Statement. (See Appendix A, page 483). Please note that this is not an NCAR form.

# BASIC CONTRACT LAW

## Basic Contract Terms and Classifications

A *contract* is an agreement between properly identified, legally competent parties to do some legal act in exchange for **consideration.** A contract establishes the rights as well as the duties, or responsibilities, of the parties. Care should be taken to see that all contracts are valid and that no errors are introduced that make them voidable or void. Consideration refers to *anything of value offered as an inducement to contract, such as money, action, or forbearance, under the law.*

### *Express Contracts*

An **express contract** is one in which the parties to the contract have definitely expressed *all the terms and conditions as agreed upon between them.* For most purposes, an express contract *can be either oral or written.* As you will see subsequently, however, certain types of contract must be in writing to be enforceable. A real estate listing contract and a real estate sales contract are examples of express contracts. All the terms and conditions of the contractual agreement are set forth in each of these contracts. The contracts are entered into expressly by the parties.

### *Implied Contracts*

An **implied contract** is a contract that is implied from the *conduct and actions* of the parties. Implied contracts are enforced when the conduct of the parties clearly illustrates their intention to contract. A court implies a contract when a benefit has been received by one party at the expense of the other party. A court will require the recipient of the benefit to pay a reasonable compensation to the party rendering the benefit unless the benefit was actually a gift.

An implied contract is created, for example, when one party orders merchandise from another party without stipulating the price to be paid for the merchandise. An implied contract to pay the reasonable value of the merchandise when delivered is created.

## Bilateral and Unilateral Contracts

A **bilateral contract** is one that is *based on mutual exchange of promises or acts between the parties* at the time the contract is signed. The contract to purchase a home is bilateral in that the seller is promising to convey title to the buyer at the same time the buyer is promising to pay a certain price.

Most listing contracts are bilateral in that the seller and the broker both promise something. The seller gives the broker the right to market the property during the listing period and promises a commission if the broker provides a **ready, willing, and able** buyer; that is, a buyer who is *ready to buy, willing to buy, and financially able to pay the asking price.* The broker promises to spend time and money marketing the property.

In contrast, a **unilateral contract** arises when *one party makes a promise to the other and the second party returns an action in response to the promise* although he or she is not legally obligated to do so. For example, your promise to a woodcutter to pay him a certain price for a cord of wood is a unilateral contract in that the woodcutter is not obligated to deliver the wood. If he does deliver, you are obligated to pay him the money. Unlike other listing contracts, the open listing contract is unilateral; the seller makes a promise to pay the broker if the broker sells the property, but the broker makes no promises. If the broker sells the property according to the terms offered in the open listing, the seller owes the broker a commission.

## Executed and Executory Contracts

*A contract that has been fully performed* by the parties is called an **executed contract.** *All contracts that have not been fully performed* (because things still need *to be done* as required by the contract) *are* **executory contracts.**

## Valid Contracts

A **valid contract** is a contract that is *binding and enforceable.* The parties to a valid contract are legally obligated to abide by the terms and conditions of the contract. If a party to a valid contract defaults in the performance of obligations under the contract, the individual is subject to legal action by the other party or parties to the contract. In creating contracts, every effort should be made to ensure that a contract is valid.

## Voidable Contracts

A **voidable contract** *results from failure to meet some legal requirement* in negotiating the agreement. One of the parties may elect to avoid (or make void) the contract by stating this intention, or he may go ahead and consummate the agreement. For example, if a buyer contracted to purchase a house that was represented to be 2,000 square feet and later found that the actual size was only 1,800 square feet, the buyer could elect to avoid the contract or take the house anyway.

The parties to a voidable contract are not required to set aside or avoid the contract, but may voluntarily choose to fulfill their obligations under the contract and receive their benefits. At any time prior to complete performance of the contract, however, the disadvantaged party can elect to discontinue. Examples of conditions that result in the creation of voidable contracts appear in the subsequent discussion of requirements for contract validity.

## Void Contracts

A **void contract** is one that is *absolutely unenforceable and has no legal force or effect,* such as a contract to perform an unlawful act. Another example of a void contract is an oral contract for the transfer of an interest in real property because such transfer is required to be in writing by the Statute of Frauds. If a contract is void, it is void to all the parties to the contract. By comparison, a voidable contract is one that can be avoided by one or more parties to the contract. A void contract has no legal force or effect from its inception, whereas a voidable contract is not voided until some party to the contract takes action to create this result.

## Essential Elements of a Valid Contract

The objective in drawing up a contract is to create an agreement that is binding and enforceable. The essential elements required to create a valid, enforceable contract follow.

### *Mutual Assent*

To create a valid contract, the parties must enter into it voluntarily. The parties must be in **mutual assent** *(agree) to the terms and conditions in the contract.* If a person has entered into a written contract as evidenced by her signature on the contract, the individual is presumed to have assented to the terms and conditions of the contract.

The consent of the parties to enter into a contractual agreement must be a real consent. This is a consent that is based on the parties having an accurate knowledge of the terms and conditions of the contract. The failure of contract validity because of the lack of real and mutual consent by the parties results from the presence of mutual mistake, misrepresentation, fraud, undue influence, or duress (see the section "Requirements for Reality of Consent").

### *Offer and Acceptance*

Each contract must contain an *offer* and an unconditional *acceptance* of the offer. The *party making an offer* is the **offeror,** and the *party to whom the offer is made* is the **offeree.** Since an offer may be withdrawn any time prior to acceptance, it is very important that an offer be expeditiously presented. The contract is created at the time the unconditional acceptance of the offer is communicated to the offeror. The requirement of mutual assent, necessary for contract validity, is evidenced in the contract by the *unconditional* acceptance of an offer.

The offer must be definite and specific in its terms. If the offer is vague and indefinite and, therefore, subject to various interpretations, its acceptance will not result in the creation of a valid contract. For example, if an offer is made to a seller to purchase a house in the Executive Heights Subdivision without a specific property description and the seller actually owns three houses in that subdivision, the *offer is vague and an acceptance will not result in the creation of a valid contract.* The offer must not be illusory and therefore not binding upon the offeror if accepted. For example, a person cannot offer to buy the seller's home in Security Estates only if the offeror decides to move to Security Estates. Here the offer is not binding upon the offeror; therefore, it is illusory, since the offeror has complete control over whether to move to Security Estates. The acceptance of an illusory offer does not result in the creation of a valid contract.

A unilateral offer is accepted only by the performance of the action specified in the offer, such as a promise to pay money upon the delivery of goods. The acceptance of this unilateral offer is made by the delivery of the goods. A bilateral offer is accepted by a promise to do the things requested in the offer. For a contract to be created, the acceptance of a bilateral offer must be communicated to the offeror. The acceptance must be absolutely unconditional in the case of either a bilateral offer or a unilateral offer. If the acceptance varies in any way from the offer as presented, it will not qualify as an acceptance and, instead, is actually a rejection of the offer. Sometimes an offer specifies the manner in which the acceptance of the offer must be communicated to the offeror by the offeree. In the absence of any specific provision in this regard, the communication of acceptance should be made by the offeree in the same manner as the offer was made or in a customary manner. In the event that acceptance is by mail, the communication is effective and a contract is created at the time the acceptance is mailed by the offeree to the offeror or to the offeror's agent. This is known as the mailbox rule. Mailing it from the offeree to the offeree's agent does not constitute acceptance.

A contract for the sale of real property is a bilateral contract because it is based on the mutual promises of the seller to sell and of the buyer to buy. Therefore, the acceptance of the offer must be communicated to the offeror to create the contract. In presenting an offer to purchase real property, the broker should counsel the seller regarding all aspects of the offer. If the broker believes acceptance of a particular offer is not in the best interests of the seller, the broker should so advise the seller. However, if the broker believes the offer is probably the best that can be obtained, the broker should urge the seller to accept. In any case, it is the seller's prerogative to accept or reject any offer.

## 3. Counteroffer

In the event a seller rejects an offer, the broker should encourage the seller to make a **counteroffer.** A counteroffer is actually a *new offer wherein the seller becomes the offeror and the prospective purchaser the offeree.*

Three aspects are key to a counteroffer. First, the parties must understand that the original offer has been rejected, or killed, and therefore cannot be reinstituted by the rejecting party. Thus, if a seller rejects an offer, he or she has terminated this proposal, relieving the buyer from any further obligation at this point. Second, if the party who has rejected the original offer (seller) has proposed a new offer in its place, he has reversed the roles of the offeror and the offeree. Finally, the party rejecting the offer must restore the offeror to his original position; that is, tender the return of any earnest money. The counteroffer then must be presented by the broker to the prospective buyer for acceptance or rejection. In some real estate transactions, there are several offers and counteroffers before the buyer and seller reach an acceptable agreement.

## 4. Termination of Offers

Offers are terminated in the following ways: (1) by the expiration of a time limit specified by the offeror prior to acceptance, (2) by the death or insanity of the offeror or the offeree prior to acceptance, (3) by the revocation of the offer by the offeror prior to acceptance, (4) by the expiration of a "reasonable" period of time after the offer is made and prior to acceptance, (5) by the failure of the offeree to comply with the terms of the offer as to the specific manner in which the acceptance must be communicated, (6) by the expiration of a power of attorney when the offeror or the offeree is acting as attorney-in-fact under a power of attorney, and (7) by acceptance of the offer by the offeree. When the offer is accepted, a contract is created.

## 5. Consideration

Consideration must be present in every contract for the contract to be valid and enforceable. Consideration is *anything of value,* such as money, or it consists of a promise in return for the performance of a specified act, as is the case in unilateral contracts. Unless there are mutual promises in a bilateral contract, the contract is not valid. For example, if one party promises to make a gift to another party, the contract will not be enforced because the one to receive the gift has furnished no consideration. There must be mutuality. Each party to the contract must do something or promise to do something. There are two exceptions to the general rule that mutual promises constitute consideration: a promise to fulfill a moral obligation and a promise to fulfill a legal obligation.

Consideration is not the same thing as earnest money. **Earnest money** is *money the buyer deposits with the offer to purchase to show that the buyer is earnest, or sincere, in intent to purchase the property.* Many buyers, sellers, real estate students, and new agents confuse these terms. An important difference is that consideration is necessary for contract validity; earnest money is not. It is simply good business practice to collect earnest money with an offer to purchase.

## 6. Capacity of the Parties

The parties to a contract must have **contractual capacity.** They must be *legally competent* to contract. Most people possess contractual capacity; therefore, this subject is discussed by pointing out the few conditions resulting in incompetency, which are age (minors) and mental competency. Minors are those who have not reached the age of majority as established by statutory law in each particular state. North Carolina specifies this age to be 18 years.

If either party to a contract is mentally incompetent, the contract is voidable by the incompetent party and unenforceable against that party. In the case of minors, the contract is voidable at the option of the minor. The minor can hold an adult to a contract, but an adult cannot legally hold a minor to the contract. The contract is not legally enforceable against the minor. A minor may fulfill the terms of a contract. If he does (and does not take steps to terminate the contract after reaching the age of majority), the individual is said to have ratified the contract as an adult, and the contract will be binding. If a party to a contract is intoxicated or under the influence of drugs at the time of entering into the contract so that the person does not understand what is happening, the individual is considered temporarily mentally incompetent to contract; therefore, the contract will be unenforceable against that person.

### Lawful Objective

The contract must be for a *legal purpose.* A contract for an illegal purpose is void. Examples of illegal contracts include contracts to sell a public office, contracts in restraint of trade, contracts to promote litigation or stifle prosecution, and contracts that restrain freedom to marry.

## Requirements for Reality of Consent

A valid contract is based on the voluntary meeting of the minds, or mutual assent. Several factors can defeat this voluntary assent and therefore invalidate the contract.

### Mutual Mistake

A mistake of a material fact can constitute grounds to nullify (rescind) a contract. This does not cover a misunderstanding of the law by one party or the other. However, if an incorrect property description has been used that identifies a property other than the one intended, the contract may be rescinded.

### Willful Misrepresentation/Fraud

Fraud is a willful misrepresentation of a material fact or the willful omission of a material fact that effectively constitutes a false misrepresentation made for the purpose of inducing someone to enter into a contract. If a party enters into a contract because of fraud, the defrauded party can avoid the contract. A false representation is deemed to be fraudulent when the party making the representation knows it to be false or when the person making the false representation does not know whether the statement is true or untrue but without regard for its truth makes the statement anyway.

If a real estate broker, as agent of an owner of real property, commits an act of fraud, the injured party may rescind any contract entered into with the seller. Also, the agent is liable to the buyer and the seller for damages incurred. See Chapter 5 for complete coverage of misrepresentation and fraud.

### Negligent Misrepresentation

A **negligent misrepresentation** occurs as a result of *misconception as to the facts* on the part of the person making the unintentional misrepresentation. The person making the representation believes it to be true; however, a reasonable person in the same situation should have known it was not true. That the party making the representation was acting in good faith is not a defense. A contracting party who has entered a contract in reliance upon a negligent misrepresentation of a material fact (important fact) is legally entitled to rescind the contract. The contract is voidable by any party who relied upon the negligent misrepresentation as a basis for entering the contract.

## Unfair and Deceptive Trade Practices

North Carolina General Statute 75-1.1 covers real estate agents and sellers who sell real estate on a regular basis. This statute, sometimes called the Unfair and Deceptive Trade Practices Act (see Chapter 5), can invalidate a contract if the seller or his agent violates it. Proven fraud is an unfair and deceptive trade practice; however, it is not necessary to prove fraud to obtain legal relief under this Act. The seller or his agent could find their contract invalidated and/or be liable for treble damages if they violate this statute.

This statute does not prevent a party to a real estate contract injured by unfair and deceptive trade practices from taking additional legal actions under other laws.

## Duress

The essential element of **duress** is that of *fear or threat*. One cannot be forced to sign a contract at gunpoint because this defeats the requirement for a voluntary meeting of the minds or reality of consent. Duress introduced in the negotiation of a contract renders it voidable, thereby allowing the threatened person to escape the contract if she takes a positive action to do so.

## Undue Influence

Undue influence is any improper or wrongful influence by one person over another whereby the will of a person is overpowered so that she is induced to act or is prevented from acting of free will. Undue influence occurs when one person takes advantage of another person's lack of mental ability or when a person takes advantage of a special relationship that enables him to have an unusual influence over another person. Examples of such relationships are those between legal advisor and client or between employer and employee. If a person is induced to enter a contract because undue influence is exerted, the individual can avoid the contract.

## Contract Law and Auction Sales

A special case in real estate is the transaction of a real estate auction. The auctioneer differs from the typical real estate agent in that the auctioneer has the capacity to bind the seller to the transaction. Although the real estate listing contract gives the agent strictly a limited or special agency and, therefore, empowers the agent to act only as a negotiator on behalf of the seller, an auctioneer actually accepts a bid (offer), something the agent should never consider doing.

Two types of auction represent two types of agreement between the auctioneer and the seller. In the first arrangement, the seller reserves the right to halt the bidding if the results do not appear to be satisfactory to her terms. This situation is known as an auction "With Reserve"; that is, the seller has reserved the right to reject all incoming bids. The seller should do so before the auction is completed and before the auctioneer has indicated an acceptance that would bind the seller anyway.

The second type of auction arrangement is "Without Reserve" or "Absolute"; that is, the seller holds no reservations and has indicated her acceptance of whatever bids are obtained. In either type of auction, "With Reserve" or "Without Reserve," the auctioneer binds the seller when he says "sold."

Even though the auctioneer has bound the seller to acceptance of a contract at the conclusion of the bidding, it is still necessary to formalize this agreement with a written document to comply with the Statute of Frauds. An auction is an example of a circumstance in which two or more documents may be used together to satisfy the Statute of Frauds requirement that all real estate contracts be in writing.

## Statute of Frauds

For most purposes, an oral contract is just as valid and enforceable as a written contract. The difficulty with oral contracts, however, lies in their leading to misunderstandings of the rights and obligations of the parties, and they may be extremely difficult to prove in a court proceeding if that should become necessary. A primary purpose of the Statute of Frauds is to "prevent fraudulent proof of an oral contract."

Contracts involving the creation or conveyance of an interest in real property must be written to be enforceable. This requirement is created by the Statute of Frauds. This statute was derived from an English statute by the same name. To prevent fraud in real estate contracts, this statute requires that they be written and contain all the elements essential for contract validity. Oral testimony does not suffice to create obligations under a contract involving transfer of title to real property. The statute does not require any particular form of writing. To be sufficient to satisfy the requirements of the statute, the writing can be a formal contract, a short memorandum, a receipt, and so on. The contract need not be in one document. Several documents can be put together to create the contract. The best form, however, is to have the entire contract in one document and signed by the parties.

Examples of real estate contracts falling under the Statute of Frauds are contracts to buy and sell real estate, options, **land contracts** (also called *contracts for deed, installment contracts,* and *conditional sale contracts*), and contracts for the exchange of real estate. Lease contracts fall under the Statute of Frauds in North Carolina when the lease term exceeds three years. Note that listing and other agency contracts do not convey an interest in real estate and are not required by the Statute of Frauds to be in writing. However, the Real Estate Commission rules require those contracts to be in writing.

## Discharge of Contracts

Contracts are terminated by agreement of the parties, full performance, impossibility of performance, and operation of law.

### Agreement of the Parties

Executory contracts are terminated by the mutual agreement of all parties to the contract. The release of each party by the other supplies the consideration.

An **accord and satisfaction** is a *new agreement between the parties, often in the form of some compromise,* that replaces the original agreement. A situation may arise in which the buyer wants to get out of a purchase agreement, that is, default on the contract. A compromise is reached when the seller agrees to accept an amount of money as substitution for full performance of the buyer. This can be the earnest money or some other negotiable amount of money. If the contract specifies the amount of damages, the specified amount is called *liquidated damages.* The agent should not presume such an agreement unless clear, written intention of the parties is obtained, which would best be done in consultation with their respective attorneys. The North Carolina Real Estate license laws put a clear burden on the agent to make certain all requirements are met before disbursing trust or escrow funds.

A **novation** is *the substitution of a new contract for a prior contract.* There are two ways to create a novation. First, the parties to the original contract are changed. A new party to the contract agrees to satisfy a former contracting party's obligation to the second party in the previous contract. When the novation (new contract) is created, the old contract is discharged. Second, a novation is created when the same parties change the terms of the contract and void the old contract.

### Full Performance

The usual manner of terminating contracts is by **full performance.** When *all the terms of the contract have been fully performed by all parties,* the contract is executed and terminated.

### Impossibility of Performance

The general rule is that even if a party to a contract is not able to perform obligations under the contract, the party is still not relieved of liability. The reasoning behind this is that the one who cannot perform should have provided for this possibility by a provision or contingency in the contract relieving him from liability.

There are exceptions to the general rule, however. One exception is in the case of a personal service contract. If a person contracts to render services to another person and those services cannot be rendered by someone else, the person obligated to render the service is relieved from liability in the event she dies or becomes incapacitated so that she cannot render the service. For example, the listing contract is a service contract. If the listing is with a one-broker firm and that broker dies, the listing contract is terminated. This is the only case in which contractual obligations are terminated by death or incapacity. In other words, death or incapacity of a seller or a buyer prior to closing does not terminate the contract; contracts survive death. Heirs can carry out the terms of the contract. A contingency in the contract could possibly terminate it, however. For example, the income of the one who died could be necessary to fulfill a loan contingency in the contract. In that case, the inability of the heirs to obtain the loan would terminate the contract. Another exception to the general rule occurs when the performance of an obligation under a contract becomes illegal as a result of a change in law after the contract was created. As a result, the obligated parties are relieved of responsibility.

## Operation of Law

The term *operation of law* describes the manner in which the rights and/or liabilities of parties may be changed by the application of law without the act or cooperation of the parties affected. The following are examples of discharge of contracts by operation of law.

The time within which a legal action may be brought against a party to a contract by another party to the contract is limited by statute in every state. The statutes are called Statutes of Limitations. If a party to a contract fails to bring a lawsuit against a defaulting party to a contract within the statutory time period, the right of legal remedy is lost to the injured party by operation of law.

The bankruptcy of a party to a contract as established by the Federal Bankruptcy Act has the effect of terminating contracts because the bankruptcy law relieves the bankrupt party from liability under contracts to which he or she is a party as of the date of filing the bankruptcy petition with the federal court.

## Assignment of Contracts

A contract is assignable provided no prohibition against assignment is spelled out in the contract itself. **Assignment** refers to *the transfer of legal rights and obligations by one party to another.* The assignment of the contract, however, does not relieve the assignor of the responsibility for performance in the event the assignee fails to perform. An exception would be if the assignor has been specifically released by the other contracting party who accepts the assignee in place of the assignor. If that is not the case, the assignee is in the first position of responsibility and the assignor is in the second position of liability. A novation removes the liability of the assignor.

## Rules for Interpretation of Contracts

There are several rules and conventions for the interpretation of contracts in the event the writing of the contract is not sufficiently clear to all parties. The first convention involves the **Parol Evidence Rule.** This assumes that *the written words reflect the entire agreement and that oral statements that do not agree with the written words in the document are to be disregarded.* This rule enforces the concept that the written document embodies the entire agreement.

Contracts are assumed to be reasonable versus unreasonable. Therefore, a discrepancy of interpretation is resolved in favor of the most reasonable meaning. Words are to be construed in their ordinary sense, in place of connoting any unusual meaning in a given word or phrase. Although linguists would argue that meaning is in persons rather than words, ordinary meanings are given to words in their everyday context. It is this ordinary meaning that should be used in the interpretation of contracts.

If there is still ambiguity in the meaning of the document in the words that are chosen or in the way in which they are put together, the burden will fall on the person who constructed the document. It is assumed that when someone put the document together, he or she should have taken care to make the meaning clear to all parties and, therefore, should have the document interpreted most seriously against himself rather than the other party in the event the meaning is ambiguous. Remember that real estate agents must not "construct/draft" contracts, which is the practice of law limited to attorneys. Therefore, agents should take care not to draft complex statements, but rather simply "fill in blanks" on standard forms, such as names, price, description of the property, and so on.

A final rule on the written word revolves around whether the words were printed on a form or written in by hand, such as in the margins of a standard contract form. In this case, the handwritten words are intended to modify the meaning of the printed form and, therefore, take precedence.

## Contract Remedies

**Breach of contract** is defined as *failure, without legal excuse, to perform any promise that forms the whole or part of a contract.* The effect of the breach of contractual obligations by a party to a contract is to terminate the contract. The breach does not terminate the right to legal remedies against the defaulting party by the injured party, however.

### Money Damages

The injured party is entitled to receive *compensation for any financial loss caused by the breach as may be awarded by a court.* This is called *compensatory* **damages.** Additionally, the court can award punitive damages if the breach of contract was willful, malicious, and committed intentionally to do harm to the plaintiff. In actuality, courts seldom award punitive damages in breach of contract cases. If the amount of money for damages is agreed upon in the contract, this sum is referred to as *liquidated damages.* This amount does not need to be the same amount as the earnest money.

### Specific Performance

A second remedy is that of specific performance. As you learned in Chapter 1, every parcel of land has a unique value that cannot be substituted for by any other commodity. Therefore, if one signals an intention to breach the contract to convey title to real property under a valid written contract, the legal remedy enforced by the courts will probably be to require the consummation of the specific contract as agreed. Monetary damages cannot substitute for the unique value of land in a given location. Therefore, the prospective purchaser may insist on title to the property in place of any other remedy. If factors such as the amount of land and the quality of title are misrepresented to the buyer to the extent that the value is affected, the buyer may sue for specific performance in addition to abatement. If the buyer wins, she may be able to enforce specific performance of the contract in addition to an abatement of the purchase price attributable to the difference between actual property value and the value of the misrepresented property.

### Rescission

A final remedy is that of rescission of the contract by the injured party. In essence, a rescission renders the contract null and void, returning the parties to their original positions. The buyer's original position would be to have the refund of any money she advanced on behalf of the transaction. A buyer might request such a remedy in the event that the property proved to be different from what was represented, such as the size of a home, the number of acres in a tract of land, or a given zoning classification.

# BROKER'S ENTITLEMENT TO A COMMISSION

Three primary elements govern a broker's right to claim a commission. First, the broker must have a valid real estate license. Unlicensed persons are not entitled to claim a commission in any negotiation of real estate and would be in violation of the real estate licensing statutes if they did so. Second, there must be a valid written contract of employment (listing) between the principal and the agent. Whereas there is no particular form this employment authority must take, there must be a definite promise to pay a commission or fee to the broker. Finally, depending on the form of the listing arrangement, the broker may need to demonstrate that he was the procuring cause of the sale. This is especially true of the open listing, but it is not a requirement of the **exclusive right to sell** listing (see the section "Exclusive Right to Sell Listing"). The exclusive agency listing falls somewhere in between. It entitles the broker to a commission if he or another broker is the procuring cause of sale but not if the owner sells the property himself. The exclusive right to sell listing contract *entitles the broker to a commission if the property is sold during the listing term,* even though the broker may not have been the procuring cause of the sale.

Under the listing contract, the broker's entitlement to commission is determined by two tests. The first is the ready, willing, and able test. If the broker brings a buyer to the seller who is ready to buy, is willing to buy, and is able (financially) to buy under the terms and conditions of the listing contract, the broker is legally entitled to the commission. The broker has done the job she was hired to do in the listing contract, that is, find a buyer who will pay the listed price in cash under all terms of the listing agreement. When the broker does this, the commission has been earned under the ready, willing, and able test. It does not matter whether the owner actually agrees to sell the property to the prospective buyer. Remember, the seller can reject any offer.

Note that price is not the only term of the listing contract. For example, the listing contract may require that the sale be closed within 60 days after the contract date, and the buyer may want a delayed closing date six months from the contract. Also note that contracts that contain financing or other contingencies do not qualify the buyer as able until the contingency is met. For example, if a buyer cannot close because he cannot obtain the contingent financing, the agent is not due a commission.

The next test, and the more usual way in which a broker becomes legally entitled to a commission, is on the basis of acceptance. When a broker brings a buyer who is accepted by the seller, the broker is legally entitled to the commission. This acceptance could be on some price or terms other than the listed price in cash. For example, the listing contract may have specified $80,000 to be payable in cash. A broker may bring an offer to the seller of $78,500, and the offer may not be for payment in cash but may be subject to the assumption of seller's existing mortgage by the buyer. If the seller accepts this offer, the broker is legally entitled to the commission on the basis of acceptance. The broker has brought the seller a buyer who is acceptable to the seller. Both tests are not required. This is an either/or situation. The broker earns a commission either on the basis of having brought a ready, willing, and able buyer or on the basis of having brought a buyer who is accepted by the seller.

## Commission Sharing

### *Cobrokered Sales*

When a property is sold as the result of cooperating efforts of two real estate firms, one of which is the listing firm and the other the selling firm, the commission agreed upon in the listing contract is paid to the listing broker by the property owner. This commission is shared by the listing broker with the selling broker on a predetermined basis. The division of the commission to be received by the listing broker should be determined by agreement between the two cooperating brokers prior to the participation of the selling broker in the transaction.

The National Association of REALTORS® requires Board/Association multiple listing service (MLS) participants to offer cooperation as follows:

MLS Participants will be required to offer cooperation with accompanying compensation to other Participants. This cooperation can take the form of offers to subagents, buyer agents or to both, at the listing broker's discretion. Listing brokers will still have the choice of offering subagency, of offering cooperation to buyer agents, or of making both offers. While all offers of cooperation must be accompanied by an offer of compensation, the listing broker may offer differing amounts to subagents and to buyer agents. As before, offers to particular brokers may be modified by advance, written communication to the other broker.

Now that MLS arrangements allow listing brokers to offer both subagency and buyer's agency, it is very important that the position of the selling agent as agent for seller or agent for buyer be disclosed when the selling agent first contacts the listing agent for information and/or an appointment.

## *In-House Sales*

Commissions to be paid to sales associates in a real estate office are established by an agreement between the real estate firm and the associates. This is true whether the brokers are licensed with or without provisional status attached to their license. Under the usual agreement, two commissions can be earned by sales associates. One is a commission for listing the property. When a sales associate sells a property she has listed, the sales associate receives both the listing and the selling commission. At closing, the seller's commission is paid in full to the listing firm, which subsequently splits the fee among the respective parties. For example, assume a $6,000 total fee paid by a seller. A possible split of this might be as follows: Company A lists the property, and Company B finds a buyer. Company A gets $3,000, half of which goes to the brokerage firm and half to the listing agent; Company B receives the other half and gives 60 percent to the selling agent and retains 40 percent for the brokerage firm. If, however, Agent A with Company A lists and sells the property, Company A gets both parts of the commission, which is then split with Agent A according to Company A's commission split agreement. The listing company decides what split to offer to cobrokering companies. Each company determines what split it offers its agents. Commission splits cannot be set by MLS, NAR, or any group of people such as firm principals. To do so constitutes an antitrust violation.

## Cobrokerage with an Out-of-State Broker

It is permissible for a broker to share a commission with a broker who is licensed in another state, as long as the out-of-state broker does *not* engage in activity that requires a real estate license while in North Carolina. For example, an out-of-state broker can refer a prospective buyer to a North Carolina broker and the North Carolina broker can pay a referral fee to the out-of-state broker if a sale results. The Real Estate License Law provides that an out-of-state broker cannot come into North Carolina and show the property, participate in negotiations, or conduct other activities that require a license. A nonresident may obtain a nonresident license in North Carolina by meeting the requirements set out in 93A-9(a) of the General Statutes of North Carolina. (See Appendix A.)

A limited broker's license (for commercial transactions only) may be issued to a nonresident who is licensed in another state or territory and who affiliates with a resident North Carolina broker. The North Carolina broker cannot be a provisional broker and must personally and actively supervise the nonresident broker to assure compliance with North Carolina real estate law and rules. See 93A-9(b) of the General Statutes of North Carolina in Appendix A.

## Earning Commission as a Buyer's Broker

Historically, the brokerage fee has been paid to the listing broker by the seller, who then splits the fee with the agent who actually listed the property and with the cooperating broker if another company was involved in the sale. With the advent of buyer brokerage, however, the issue of a buyer's broker's compensation becomes a little more complex. A buyer's agent must have a buyer agency agreement, and this agreement controls how the buyer's agent is compensated.

The North Carolina Buyer Agency Agreement (Figure 6.5, Exclusive Right to Represent Buyer) allows the agent to receive a **retainer fee.** This is usually a small monetary compensation paid by the buyer up front for an agent's services. A **success fee** or buyer's agent's compensation may be received from the seller if the seller or seller's agent has offered compensation to the buyer's agent(s). This agreement also provides for the buyer to directly compensate the buyer's broker.

# LISTING CONTRACTS AND PRACTICES

## Definition and Purpose of Listing Contracts

A listing contract is a contract whereby the owner of property *employs* a real estate broker to find a buyer for his property. This contract creates an agency relationship in which the seller is the principal and the broker is the seller's special agent for this particular purpose.

No transfer of interest in real property occurs under this contract. No title passes between the seller and the broker. Therefore, this contract does *not* fall under the Statute of Frauds in North Carolina. However, the Real Estate Commission requires it to be in writing to be enforceable and requires it to specify a time period. The written contract clearly spells out that the broker has been hired by the seller and sets forth all the terms and conditions of employment. The written listing contract substantially reduces lawsuits between brokers and property owners concerning matters of the broker's employment.

3 ## Types of Listing Contract

Three types of listing contract are in general use: the open listing, the exclusive agency listing, and the exclusive right to sell listing. Each of these contracts gives different rights to the broker and seller. A brief description of each type of listing contract follows.

### 1. *Open Listing*

Under an **open listing,** *the seller lists a property with the assistance of one or more brokers. The broker effecting the sale is entitled to the commission. If, however, the owner sells the property (not to a prospect generated by the broker), the owner owes no commission.*

This type of listing is not beneficial to the owner or the broker. Usually a broker cannot afford to spend advertising dollars and sales staff time on an open listing. The broker is competing with the owner and with every other broker who has an open listing on the property or who learns about the availability of the property and obtains an open listing. This type of listing also can lead to disputes among brokers about commissions and can present legal problems for the owner.

### 2. *Exclusive Agency Listing*

In an **exclusive agency** listing, *the property is listed exclusively with one broker.* This is the basis for the name "exclusive" listing. If the broker effects a sale of the property, he is legally entitled to the commission agreed upon. Under this type of listing, however, *if the owner sells the property, the broker earns no commission.* If this type of listing is entered into the MLS, it must be identified as an exclusive agency listing.

This type of listing is somewhat better than the open listing in that only one broker is involved, but that broker is still competing with the owner. The broker's advertising programs, including the office's "For Sale" sign on the property, may generate prospects for the owner.

### 3. *Exclusive Right to Sell Listing* * Best

This is the best type of listing contract from the standpoint of both the broker and the seller. Under this listing contract, the property is listed with only one broker (exclusive). If the property is sold by anyone during the term of the listing contract, the broker is legally entitled to the commission. The seller is legally obligated to pay the broker's commission if the broker, the seller or some third party effects a sale of the property during the term of the listing contract.

The exclusive right to sell listing contract benefits the owner because the broker is secure enough in the opportunity to earn a commission that she can afford to spend time and advertising dollars to effect a quick and satisfactory sale of the listed property. Also, with the agreement of the seller, the broker can put the listing in a multiple listing service (see later discussion), providing significantly increased market exposure for the property.

### *Protection Agreement*

In this arrangement, a seller agrees to pay a fee to a broker for the sale to a specific buyer but does not list the property for sale to the general public. For example, a broker may have a client who is particularly interested in a specific type of home in Mortgage Heights Subdivision, even though no such homes are currently on the market. A given owner may consent to have his property shown to this specific buyer, but only under established terms.

## Listing Contract Provisions

NR

Figure 6.1 shows an Exclusive Right to Sell Listing Agreement. In this contract, the broker is promising to do certain things: to use her best efforts to procure a buyer; to take all actions considered appropriate to effect a satisfactory sale of the property, including advertising the property; and to provide the owner the benefit of the office staff's knowledge of financing, and other real estate matters. Additionally, the broker promises to enter the listing in the multiple listing service. The illustrated Exclusive Right to Sell Listing Agreement is broken down into numbered sections for reference to the discussion of the contract that follows.

The parties are identified at the top of the form, as is the date the contract was executed.

*Section 1* contains the property description. The street address and subdivision are included primarily for the purpose of enabling agents of the listing company to locate the property and to provide the same information to cooperating brokers acting as agents of the listing company. The additional descriptions identify the property by reference to recorded documents. These references eliminate any doubt as to the specific property listed.

*Section 2* lists fixtures included in the transaction that will convey free of liens. Examples of fixtures that convey unless excluded are ceiling fans, drapery and curtain rods, outdoor plants and trees, and any object attached or affixed to the property. The "total circumstances test" in Chapter 2 explains how to determine whether an item is a fixture. When the seller wishes to exclude a listed item or any item meeting the definition of a fixture, it must be entered as an exception in the space provided. The agent should assure that the exclusion is also entered in the appropriate space in the Offer to Purchase and Contract at the time the contract is executed.

*Section 3* provides for the inclusion of any personal property in the sale of the real property. Since personal/real property definitions are the cause of many misunderstandings that arise in the world of practice, it is important to pay special attention to this section. Note: Freestanding appliances and draperies are examples of personal property often included here and in the contract. Other large expensive items of personal property, such as a riding lawn mower, may cause problems with the appraisal and are best handled through a separate sales agreement.

*Section 4* establishes whether or not the seller will provide a one-year home warranty for the property.

*Section 5* establishes the list price of the property and the type of financing the sellers will accept. Since few buyers have all the cash to purchase a home without a mortgage loan, most sellers need to allow for some type of loan contingency in the contract. Sellers need to understand that certain costs, conditions, and risks apply to some types of loan before they accept an Offer to Purchase and Contract with a loan contingency. For example, there are certain VA and FHA fees a buyer cannot pay and the seller will be asked to pay. A second example is that stringent condition and thermal standard requirements of RD may add

**FIGURE 6.1** Exclusive Right to Sell Listing Agreement.

Level 3

## EXCLUSIVE RIGHT TO SELL LISTING AGREEMENT

This EXCLUSIVE RIGHT TO SELL LISTING AGREEMENT ("Agreement") is entered into (Date)____________________, between__________________________________________________________ as Seller(s) ("Seller") of the property described below (the "Property"), and____________________________________________ as Listing Firm ("Agent").

1. **REAL PROPERTY**. The real property that is the subject of this Agreement is located in the City of____________________, County of________________________________, State of North Carolina, and is known more particularly and described as: Street Address______________________________________________________________________
Zip__________________ Legal Description________________________________________________________________
(❑ All ❑ A portion of the property in Deed Reference: Book ______ Page No. ______, ______________________________County.)

2. **FIXTURES.** The following items, if any, are included free of liens: any built-in appliances, light fixtures, ceiling fans, attached floor coverings, blinds, shades, drapery rods and curtain rods, brackets and all related hardware, window and door screens, storm windows, combination doors, awnings, antennas, satellite dishes and receivers, burglar/fire/smoke alarms, pool and spa equipment, solar energy systems, attached fireplace screens, gas logs, fireplace inserts, electric garage door openers with controls, outdoor plants and trees (other than in movable containers), basketball goals, storage sheds, mailboxes, wall and/or door mirrors, and any other items attached or affixed to the Property, EXCEPT the following items:____________________________________________________________________________________________________________________________.

3. **PERSONAL PROPERTY.** The following personal property is included in the listing price:_______________________________________________________________________________________________________________________________________________________________________________.

4. **HOME WARRANTY.** Seller ❑ agrees ❑ does not agree to obtain and pay for at closing a one year home warranty for the Property at a cost not to exceed $___________.

5. **LISTING PRICE**. Seller lists the Property at a price of $_________________________________________on the following terms:
( ) Cash ( ) Loan Assumption ( ) Conventional ( ) FHA ( ) VA ( ) Seller Financing ( ) Other ______________________. Seller agrees to sell the Property for the Listing Price or for any other price or on any other terms acceptable to Seller.

6. **TERM.** In consideration of the Seller agreeing to list the Property for sale and in further consideration of Agent's services and efforts to find a buyer, Agent is hereby granted the exclusive right to sell the Property from (Date) _________________________ until midnight, (Date) ______________________.

7. **AGENCY RELATIONSHIPS.** Seller has received a copy of the "Working With Real Estate Agents" brochure and has reviewed it with Agent. With respect to dual agency ***(Check only ONE)***:
   - ❑ Seller authorizes the Agent to act as a Dual Agent, representing both the Seller and the Buyer, subject to the terms and conditions of the attached Dual Agency Addendum.
   - ❑ Seller desires exclusive representation at all times during this agreement and does NOT authorize Agent to act in the capacity of Dual Agent.

*8. **AGENT'S COMPENSATION.** Seller agrees to pay Agent a total fee of ____________ % of the gross sales price of the Property, OR__________________________________________________________________________________, which shall include the amount of any compensation paid by Agent to a cooperating agent as set forth in paragraph 9 below. Such fee shall be deemed earned under any of the following circumstances:

(a) If a ready, willing and able buyer is procured by Agent, the Seller, or anyone else during the Term of this Agreement at the price and on the terms set forth herein, or at any price and upon any terms acceptable to the Seller;
(b) If the Property is sold, exchanged, conveyed or transferred, or the Seller agrees to sell, exchange, convey or transfer the Property at any price and upon any terms whatsoever, during the Term of this Agreement or any renewal hereof;

– Net listing + NOT Reccommended in residential

**FIGURE 6.1** Continued.

(c) If, within ________ days after expiration of the Term of this Agreement (the "Protection Period"), Seller either directly or indirectly sells, exchanges, conveys or transfers, or agrees to sell, exchange, convey or transfer the Property upon any terms whatsoever, to any person with whom Seller, Agent, or any real estate licensee communicated regarding the Property during the Term of this Agreement or any renewal hereof, provided the names of such persons are delivered or postmarked to the Seller within 15 days from date of expiration. HOWEVER, Seller shall NOT be obligated to pay such fee if a valid listing agreement is entered into between Seller and another real estate broker and the Property is sold, exchanged, conveyed or transferred during such Protection Period.

Once earned as set forth above, Agent compensation will be due and payable at the earlier of: (i) closing on the Property; (ii) the Seller's failure to sell the Property (including but not limited to the Seller's refusal to sign an offer to purchase the Property at the price and terms stated herein or on other terms acceptable to the Seller, the Seller's default on an executed sales contract for the Property, or the Seller's agreement with a buyer to unreasonably modify or cancel an executed sales contract for the Property); or (iii) Seller's breach of this Agreement.

9. **COOPERATION WITH/COMPENSATION TO OTHER AGENTS.** Agent has advised Seller of Agent's company policies regarding cooperation and the amount(s) of any compensation that will be offered to subagents, buyer agents or both. Seller authorizes Agent to (*Check ALL applicable authorizations*):

- ☐ Cooperate with subagents representing only the Seller and offer them the following compensation:__________% of the gross sales price or $________________.
- ☐ Cooperate with buyer agents representing only the buyer and offer them the following compensation:__________ % of the gross sales price or $________________.
- ☐ Cooperate with and compensate agents from other firms according to the attached company policy.

Agent will promptly notify Seller if Agent offers compensation to a cooperating agent(s) that is different from that set forth above. Cooperating agents must orally disclose the nature of their relationship with a buyer (subagent or buyer agent) to Agent at the time of initial contact with Agent, and confirm that relationship in writing no later than the time an offer to purchase is submitted for the Seller's consideration. Seller should be careful about disclosing confidential information because agents representing buyers must disclose all relevant information to their clients.

10. **AGENT'S DUTIES.** Agent agrees to provide Seller the benefit of Agent's knowledge, experience and advice in the marketing and sale of the Property. Seller understands that Agent makes no representation or guarantee as to the sale of the Property, but Agent agrees to use his best efforts in good faith to find a buyer who is ready, willing and able to purchase the property. Seller acknowledges that Agent is required by law to disclose to potential purchasers of the Property all material facts pertaining to the Property about which the Agent knows or reasonably should know, and that REALTORS® have an ethical responsibility to treat all parties to the transaction honestly. Seller further acknowledges that Agent is being retained solely as a real estate professional, and understands that other professional service providers are available to render advice or services to Seller, including but not limited to an attorney, insurance agent, tax advisor, surveyor, structural engineer, home inspector, environmental consultant, architect, or contractor. Although Agent may provide Seller the names of providers who claim to perform such services, Seller understands that Agent cannot guarantee the quality of service or level of expertise of any such provider. Seller agrees to pay the full amount due for all services directly to the service provider whether or not the transaction closes. Seller also agrees to indemnify and hold Agent harmless from and against any and all liability, claim, loss, damage, suit, or expense that Agent may incur either as a result of Seller's selection and use of any such provider or Seller's election not to have one or more of such services performed.

In connection with the marketing and sale of the Property, Seller authorizes and directs Agent: ***(Check ALL applicable sections)***

- ☐ to place "For Sale," "Under Contract," "Sale Pending," or other similar signs on the Property (where permitted by law and relevant covenants) and to remove other such signs.
- ☐ to place a lock box on the Property.
- ☐ to advertise the Property, including, but not limited to, placing information about the Property on the Internet either directly or through a program of any listing service of which the Agent is a member or in which any of Agent's sales associates participates.
- ☐ to permit other firms who belong to any listing service of which the Agent is a member to advertise the Property on the Internet in accordance with the listing service rules and regulations.
- ☐ to submit pertinent information concerning the Property to any listing service of which Agent is a member or in which any of Agent's sales associates participates and to furnish to such listing service notice of all changes of information concerning the Property authorized in writing by Seller. Seller authorizes Agent, upon execution of a sales contract for the Property, to notify the listing service of the pending sale, and upon closing of the sale, to disseminate sales information, including sales price, to the listing service, appraisers and real estate brokers.



Agent Initials _______ Seller Initials _______ _______

**FIGURE 6.1** Continued.

NOTE: Once information about the Property has been placed on the Internet or furnished to any listing service in which any of Agent's sales associates participates, Agent cannot control access to or uses of the information.

**THE AGENT SHALL CONDUCT ALL BROKERAGE ACTIVITIES IN REGARD TO THIS AGREEMENT WITHOUT RESPECT TO THE RACE, COLOR, RELIGION, SEX, NATIONAL ORIGIN, HANDICAP OR FAMILIAL STATUS OF ANY PARTY OR PROSPECTIVE PARTY TO THE AGREEMENT.**

11. **SELLER'S DUTIES.** Seller agrees to cooperate with Agent in the marketing and sale of the Property, including but not limited to:

(a) providing to Agent, in a timely manner, accurate information including but not limited to the Residential Property Disclosure Statement (unless exempt), and the Lead-Based Paint or Lead-Based Paint Hazard Addendum with respect to any residential dwelling built prior to 1978;
(b) making the Property available for showing (including working, existing utilities) at reasonable times and upon reasonable notice;
(c) providing Agent as soon as reasonably possible after the execution of this Agreement copies of restrictive covenants, if any, and copies of the bylaws, articles of incorporation, rules and regulations, and other governing documents of the owners' association and/or the subdivision, if applicable;
(d) immediately referring to Agent all inquiries or offers it may receive regarding the Property; showing the Property only by appointment made by or through Agent; and conducting all negotiations through Agent.

If the Property is sold during the period set forth herein, the Seller agrees to execute and deliver a GENERAL WARRANTY DEED conveying fee simple marketable title to the Property, including legal access to a public right of way, free of all encumbrances except ad valorem taxes for the current year, utility easements, rights-of-way, and unviolated restrictive covenants, if any, and those encumbrances that the buyer agrees to assume in the sales contract. Seller represents that the Seller has the right to convey the Property, and that there are currently no circumstances that would prohibit the Seller from conveying fee simple marketable title as set forth in the preceding sentence.

❑ Seller acknowledges receipt of a sample copy of an Offer to Purchase And Contract for review purposes.
❑ Seller acknowledges receipt of a copy of the brochure *Questions and Answers on: Home Inspections.*

12. **FLOOD HAZARD INSURANCE.** The Seller ❑ does ❑ does not currently maintain flood hazard insurance on the Property.

13. **SYNTHETIC STUCCO.** To the best of Seller's knowledge, the Property has not been clad previously (either in whole or in part) with an "exterior insulating and finishing system," commonly known as "EIFS" or "synthetic stucco", unless disclosed as follows: *(If the Seller does not wish to disclose, put "No Representation")*: ______________________________
______________________________________________________________________________.

14. **EARNEST MONEY.** Unless otherwise provided in the sales contract, earnest money deposits paid toward the purchase price shall be held by the Agent, in escrow, until the consummation or termination of the transaction. Any earnest money forfeited by reason of the Buyer's default under a sales contract shall be divided equally between the Agent and Seller. In no event shall the sum paid to the Agent because of a Buyer's default be in excess of the fee that would have been due if the sale had closed as contemplated in the sales contract.

15. **MEDIATION.** If a dispute arises out of or related to this Agreement or the breach thereof, and if the dispute cannot be settled through negotiation, the parties agree first to try in good faith to settle the dispute by mediation before resorting to arbitration, litigation, or some other dispute resolution procedure. If the need for mediation arises, the parties will choose a mutually acceptable mediator and will share the cost of mediation equally.

16. **ADDITIONAL TERMS AND CONDITIONS.** The following additional terms and conditions shall also be a part of this Agreement:______________________________________________________________________
______________________________________________________________________________
______________________________________________________________________________
______________________________________________________________________________

17. **ENTIRE AGREEMENT/CHANGES.** This Agreement constitutes the entire agreement between Seller and Agent and there are no representations, inducements, or other provisions other than those expressed herein. All changes, additions, or deletions to this Agreement must be in writing and signed by both Seller and Agent.

Page 3 of 4

Agent Initials _______ Seller Initials _______ _______

**STANDARD FORM 101**
**© 7/2006**

**FIGURE 6.1** Continued.

**Seller and Agent each acknowledge receipt of a signed copy of this Agreement.**

THE NORTH CAROLINA ASSOCIATION OF REALTORS®, INC. MAKES NO REPRESENTATION AS TO THE LEGAL VALIDITY OR ADEQUACY OF ANY PROVISION OF THIS FORM IN ANY SPECIFIC TRANSACTION.

Seller_______________________________________________

Seller_______________________________________________

Mailing Address _______________________________________

Home Phone__________ Work Phone __________ Work Phone __________

Fax __________ E-mail Address __________________________

Agent (Firm) __________________________ Office Phone__________

By: __________________________ Individual license #__________

Fax __________ E-mail Address __________________________

Office Address_________________________________________



STANDARD FORM 101

expense or prevent the contract from closing. Still another example is the risks of owner financing due to the seller's inability to get a deficiency judgment in case of foreclosure.

*Section 6* establishes the term of the contract, which provides for automatic termination of the contract on a given date without notice by the principal to the agent.

*Section 7* sets forth the firm's policy on agency. It requires the seller to receive the "Working With Real Estate Agents" pamphlet and to authorize the listing firm to act as a dual agent (subject to the terms and conditions set forth in the Dual Agency Addendum) or authorizes the firm to provide only exclusive representation, disallowing the firm to act as a dual agent.

*Section 8* is the essential part of the employment contract that spells out the compensation to the agent and the fact that the commission includes any compensation paid to a cooperating agent as well as the conditions under which the commission is earned. The meaning of the exclusive right to sell arrangement is reinforced in paragraph (a), which indicates that a sale or an exchange effected by any person during the term of the listing entitles the agent to the full commission. Paragraph (c) is known as the extender clause (or carry-over or override clause) that provides for the full commission for any sale or exchange to registered prospects within the specified period after the termination of the contract.

*Section 9* establishes the firm's ability to cooperate with other agents. The sellers can authorize the firm to cooperate and compensate subagents of the seller or exclusive buyer agents. One or both options can be selected.

*Section 10* establishes the promises of the agent to use her best efforts and expertise to market the property, but it does not guarantee the sale. It also clearly states to the sellers that the agent is required to disclose all material facts that she knows or reasonably should know regarding the property. The section also outlines other professional services the seller may need to retain regarding the transaction (i.e., surveyor, attorney, or insurance agent). The language stipulated by fair housing rules is also presented in Section 10. It itemizes the agent's authority in marketing the property, such as being able to place a sign in the yard or enter the new listing in a listing service.

*Section 11* establishes the good faith of the owners to work toward effecting the sale, which is in their mutual interest. This arrangement can work properly only in the exclusive right to sell form of listing contract. The sellers agree to provide the following documents to the agent in a timely manner, when applicable: Residential Property Disclosure Statement, Lead-Based Paint or Lead-Based Paint Hazard Addendum, Restrictive Covenants, copies of bylaws, articles of incorporation, rules and regulations, and other documents of the owners' association. They further agree in this section that they will be able to execute and deliver a General Warranty Deed conveying fee simple title with the usual covenants of warranty, with certain exceptions, including taxes, recorded easements, zoning regulations, and restrictive covenants (if any). The sellers also agree to work directly through the agent on all inquiries, appointments, offers, negotiations and to check and acknowledge that they received a sample copy of the Offer to Purchase and Contract as well as the pamphlet "Questions and Answers on: Home Inspections."

*Section 12* establishes whether the sellers currently maintain flood insurance on the property.

*Section 13* establishes whether, to the sellers' best knowledge, the property is currently or ever has been clad in synthetic stucco. The sellers are able to list "No Representation" in this section. Sections 12 (Flood Insurance) and 13 (Synthetic Stucco) are also referenced on the Seller's Disclosure form that is mandated by state statutes.

*Section 14* specifies that the agent will receive and hold in trust for the benefit of the principals all earnest money paid toward the purchase price of the property until final settlement or other termination of the contract. The listing office usually holds the earnest money. This section also provides for the division of the earnest money between the seller and the broker in the event the buyer defaults on a contract of sale with the seller and forfeits the earnest money as specified in the contract. The broker's share of the forfeited deposit cannot be in excess of the amount of commission the broker would have earned had the transaction been consummated.

*Section 15* explains that if a dispute arises out of the agreement or the breach of the agreement, the sellers and the agents will seek a settlement through mediation. The parties

NR

can proceed to other dispute resolution options, such as arbitration or litigation, if the dispute is not settled in mediation. The cost of the mutually acceptable mediator will be split equally.

*Section 16* lists additional conditions, such as possession dates, financing, and seller concessions on closing costs or discount points. This section also may be used to detail consequences or procedures of early termination of the agreement.

*Section 17* indicates that this instrument contains the entire substance of the employment agreement between the owner and the agent.

The individual agent's license number is required below the signature line. The listing contract must be prepared with enough copies to provide each party with a copy. Commission rules mandate a specific expiration date. As a separate form (See Figure 6.2), the NCAR Exclusive Agency Agreement Renewal and/or Amendment provides for a renewal by the parties if they mutually agree and the property is not sold at the end of the initial listing period. This form also provides an easy way to amend the contract for price adjustments or other changes.

## Brokerage Fee

### *Percentage of Final Sales Price*

The most common commission arrangement found in listing contracts is for the commission to be a specified percentage of the final sales price of the property. Notice that this is not a percentage of the listed price (unless the listed price and final sales price are identical), but it is the price for which the property sells.

### *Flat Fee and Limited Service Agreements*

Another form of commission arrangement is the **flat fee.** *The broker takes the listing based on a specified payment of money by the seller to the broker at the time of listing.* The broker is entitled to retain this fee for his marketing efforts. The broker's compensation, in this case, does not depend on the sale of the property. The amount of the flat fee is often substantially less than the broker would normally receive had the compensation been based on a percentage of the selling price. These contracts often are limited service contracts. The broker may contract to only advertise the property and put together a sales contract when buyer and seller agree on the terms. There may be several plans to choose from, each with specified services and fees. The seller has the sole responsibility for all aspects of the transaction other than those he contracted with the broker to do. In this type of arrangement, the agency is paid only for efforts and not for results, as is the case in the typical brokerage listing. In similar arrangements, however, the agency is paid the flat fee only at the conclusion of the sale. While a broker may limit services by using a carefully worded listing contract, he/she cannot limit his/her duties under agency law and North Carolina Real Estate Law, Rules, and Regulations as they apply to the contracted services.

### *Net Listing*

Another type of commission arrangement is the **net listing.** This is a situation in which *the seller, when listing the property, specifies a net amount of money she must receive from the sale.* All money received that is above the net amount the seller specified is designated as the broker's commission in effecting the sale. This type of commission arrangement is not recommended but is legal in North Carolina. The net listing is, at best, a very poor arrangement of commission schedule. It can lead to a great deal of dissatisfaction on the part of the owner if the property sells for substantially more than the owner anticipated, resulting in a disproportionate share of the proceeds for the broker. At the other extreme, sellers can request a net listing at a price that does not allow the broker to make any money.

When you consider the broker's responsibility to his principal, the owner, and look at the situation in light of the fact that one of the broker's responsibilities is to establish a fair market price for the property, it would seem the broker is fulfilling the responsibility in a much better and more professional manner by recommending a fair market price that

**FIGURE 6.2** Agency Agreement Renewal and/or Amendment.

## AGENCY AGREEMENT RENEWAL AND/OR AMENDMENT

This AGENCY AGREEMENT RENEWAL AND/OR AMENDMENT renews and/or amends the following agency agreement (referred to hereafter as the "Agency Agreement"):

_______ NCAR Form #101 (Exclusive Right to Sell Listing Agreement) dated_______________
_______ NCAR Form #201 (Exclusive Right to Represent Buyer) dated_______________
_______ NCAR Form #203 (Agency Disclosure & Non-Exclusive Buyer Agency Agreement) dated_______________
_______ NCAR Form #601 (Exclusive Right to Sell Listing Agreement – Auction Sales) dated_______________

entered into by and between_______________________________________________("Client")
and_______________________________________________Real Estate Firm ("Agent").

Property Address/MLS# (if applicable): _______________________________________________

Client and Agent agree that the Agency Agreement is hereby renewed and/or amended in the manner indicated below ***(Fill in applicable blanks; enter "N/A" in any blank not used)***:

Renewed and extended until midnight, ______________________________, 20_________. In the event that the term of the Agency Agreement has expired, Client and Agent specifically agree that this Agency Agreement Amendment And/Or Renewal shall operate to revive the Agency Agreement for the agreed-upon period of time.

Other amendments :_______________________________________________

_______________________________________________

_______________________________________________

_______________________________________________

_______________________________________________

_______________________________________________

All terms and conditions of the Agency Agreement not specifically amended herein shall remain the same.

**Client and Agent each hereby acknowledges receipt of a signed copy of this document.**

THE NORTH CAROLINA ASSOCIATION OF REALTORS®, INC. MAKES NO REPRESENTATION AS TO THE LEGAL VALIDITY OR ADEQUACY OF ANY PROVISION OF THIS FORM IN ANY SPECIFIC TRANSACTION.

Client_______________________________________________ Date_______________

Client_______________________________________________ Date_______________

Agent (Firm Name)_______________________________________________

By_______________________________________________ Date_______________

Page 1 of 1

REALTOR®

**North Carolina Association of REALTORS®, Inc.**

EQUAL HOUSING OPPORTUNITY

**STANDARD FORM 710**
**© 7/2005**

would include a reasonable rate of commission established as a percentage of the sales price or at a reasonable flat fee.

## *Referral Fees*

Brokers often pay a referral fee to other licensed brokers outside their locality when the other broker refers prospective buyers and sellers. Since real estate is a highly local market, the area of referral may be a nearby town or the other side of the country. A broker from another state may make a referral to a North Carolina broker. All that is necessary is that both brokers be duly licensed in their own states.

## Duration of the Listing

North Carolina License Law Rule A.0104 specifies that all agency contracts, including the listing contract, be in writing and that they specify an automatic termination date. This means that the principal (owner) is not required to take any positive action to terminate the listing. Therefore, the agent is employed for a specific period of time unless the owner authorizes an extension. No automatic renewals are allowed.

## *Override or Extender Clause*

Another negotiable item in the listing contract, the **override clause,** *protects the agent for a period of time after expiration of the listing from sales to prospects the agent recruited.* A typical clause might specify that at the termination of the listing period, the agent will register with the seller prospects who were shown the property. A subsequent sale to any of these prospects within a specified period of time would require payment of the commission to the agent. This clause, also called a *carry-over clause,* protects the agent from the seller's trying to strike a private deal with a buyer recruited by the agent's efforts in order to avoid payment of a commission.

## Property Data Sheet

When the listing agent collects data on the subject property for dissemination to prospective buyers or other brokers through a multiple listing service, she must take care to ensure that the data are complete and accurate. The agent has an affirmative duty to "discover and disclose" all material facts about the property. Although no specific format is required, the agent is responsible for proper disclosure. Furthermore, a subagent or a buyer's agent is not entitled to rely blindly on these data but has an affirmative duty to verify the information in making representations to his prospects. A disclaimer does not relieve an agent of responsibility or possible disciplinary action by the Real Estate Commission for failure to disclose.

## Termination of Listing Contracts

Two factors have an influence on the termination of the listing contract. The first significant factor is Rule A.0104, which requires that all written listing contracts have an automatic termination date, with no action required by the seller. Any failure to abide by this provision, such as leaving the contract duration indefinite, would subject the agent to disciplinary action by the Real Estate Commission.

Unfortunately, some brokers have a mistaken concept on a second factor influencing the duration of a listing contract. Just as when one is hired by any other employer, one is subject to being discharged or fired ("dehired" in a modern euphemism), and so it is with the listing contract. As you know, the listing contract is nothing more than an employment arrangement. Just as your present boss can fire you at almost any time, the seller-principal can terminate the listing contract at any time, regardless of how much time is left to run on the original agreement. If the sellers withdraw the agency authorization, the agent has no further right to proceed in representing them. The principal may, however, be liable to the agent for damages, which are up to the agent to prove. The seller cannot use this strategy to circumvent the agent's commission when the agent has done what he or she contracted to do, namely, find a ready, willing, and able buyer.

## MULTIPLE LISTING SERVICE ARRANGEMENTS

The term *multiple listing* refers to an *organized method of placing listings in a pool of listings by member brokers;* it is not a type of listing. Multiple listing provides substantially increased market exposure for the listings placed in the pool. For this reason, a **multiple listing service (MLS)** is of significant benefit to brokers and sellers.

The listing broker is the agent of the property owner. The other member brokers participating to effect a sale of another broker's listing are either subagents of the listing broker or agents of the buyer.

A listing firm may offer cooperation and compensation to other MLS members who sell their properties. This offer may be made to subagents, buyer's agents, or both. Compensation may differ for subagents and buyer's agents. A cooperating broker acting as a subagent owes the same duties of agency to the seller as the listing firm does. A cooperating buyer's agent owes the duties of agency to the buyer. All agents should be especially careful to understand and adhere to the law of agency, since a violation of agency is a violation of the Real Estate License Law.

## NEGOTIABILITY OF COMMISSION

The amount or rate of commission to be charged by or paid to a real estate broker is strictly a negotiable matter between the broker and the listing seller. It is a violation of federal law for any person or organization—either governmental or private—even to recommend a commission schedule to a broker or group of brokers. It is also illegal for two or more brokers to agree to charge certain rates of commission to listing sellers. These activities are "price fixing" and are acts in the restraint of trade in violation of the **Sherman Antitrust Act.**

Competing brokers cannot even be a party to a discussion of commission rates or the boycott of a competitor on the basis of his rates. Agents who are present in a room where such illegal activities are discussed might be held to be parties to a price-fixing conspiracy unless they take specific steps to disavow themselves from the discussion. For example, if an agent at a meeting, such as that of an MLS committee, were to say, "I think we ought to charge 10 percent," other members have a duty to protest that statement, leave the meeting, and report the discussion to the proper authorities to absolve themselves of complicity to the discussion.

## LISTING PROCEDURES

Impeccable listing procedures are essential to a successful real estate transaction. Major problems result from an improperly or sloppily listed property. The listing agent's fiduciary duty to his seller requires the agent to use due diligence in listing, pricing, and marketing the property to achieve an optimum outcome for the seller with the fewest possible risks or problems. An agent's duties to third parties require an accurate representation of the property being sold, including material facts. Since these duties are discussed in detail elsewhere, they are not presented here.

An agent with a firm that practices dual agency may find that he is also responsible to a buyer client of his firm who may want to purchase his listing. He may find himself in practical and public relations trouble in a dual agency situation, even if he has not actually violated any laws or commission rules. The agent, therefore, needs to think ahead to a possible dual agency situation and thoroughly educate the seller-client at the time of listing about how to protect her own interest in a dual agency situation, including how to obtain information from outside professionals, if necessary. The seller should understand that any of the firm's buyer-clients will receive the buyer's version of the same briefing when the buyer signs a buyer agency agreement.

## Preliminary Listing Procedures

1. At first substantial contact with seller, the agent must review with the seller the brochure "Working With Real Estate Agents" to make sure the seller adequately understands agency. The agent must see that the seller signs the perforated panel attached to the brochure to acknowledge explanation and receipt of the brochure. This acknowledgment is kept on file whether or not the seller lists the property with the agent. When and if the seller signs the listing contract, she should do so with informed consent.
2. The agent must educate the seller (client), as follows:
   - Discuss listing contract provisions and seller's and agent's duties and responsibilities under contract.
   - Explain duties of seller and agent to third-party buyers and buyer-clients of the listing firm to disclose material fact and to provide a Property Disclosure Statement as well as a Lead-Based Paint or a Synthetic Stucco Disclosures when applicable.
   - Discuss company's generic marketing plan, including frequency and types of advertising, such as Internet, newspapers, brochures, television, and radio, as applicable. Customize a plan for seller's property at some point during the listing process.
   - Provide the seller with company's commission policy and additional fees, if any. Avoid suggesting that there are set commissions other than what each company sets for itself independently of all other companies.
   - Explain the importance of proper pricing and how you will arrive at a suggested price range through a carefully prepared comparative market analysis (CMA). If property is unique and has few, if any, recent comparables, you may suggest an appraisal. Discuss CMAs and appraisals as a reflection of market value, not a setting of market value. Suggest that whatever the listing price, it should be reevaluated every four to six weeks until the property is sold.
   - Give seller a sample copy of the NCAR Offer to Purchase and Contract. Review provisions with seller and answer any questions.
3. The agent must sell himself and his company. If he cannot inspire confidence in this prelisting phase, he may not get the listing. If he does, he can proceed to the actual listing procedures. Educating the seller and selling himself and his company are usually accomplished at the same time. Properly educating the seller contributes greatly to the company's and the agent's image.

## Final Listing Procedures

The following listing procedures may be followed by the agent as the individual situation requires:

1. The agent should inspect the property with the seller, referring to paragraph 13 of NCBA/NCAR Offer to Purchase and Contract, and should accurately complete a property data sheet and a "red flag" checklist of the property. He should note any physical defects and discuss repairs with the seller. The seller must decide what she is willing to repair and when. Ideally, repairs should be made before the property is marketed to help maximize the sales price. If the seller is unwilling to repair anything that will be required to be repaired by an appraisal, especially an FHA or VA or RD appraisal, she needs to understand that the buyer may not be able to get a loan on a property with problems such as peeling paint, a leaking roof, rotten wood, broken glass, or safety hazards. Failure to do repairs may diminish her pool of buyers. The agent should determine what, if any, fixtures do not convey and what items of personal property, if any, do convey and should include this information in the listing contract. The agent may assist the seller in completing the Seller Property Disclosure Statement, but not do it for her. The agent should explain the difference between the seller's duties and the agent's duties. Although the seller can check "No Representation," the agent has a legal obligation to disclose all material facts to buyers. The agent may explain the practical considerations of "No Representation" to the seller and refer the seller to an attorney if she wants legal advice. Failure to fill out

the form is not illegal, but it gives the buyer a three-day right of limited rescission. The agent should assist the seller in completing the Lead-Based Paint Disclosure, if applicable. This is a joint responsibility. The agent and the seller are legally liable for compliance. Note: Inspection and completion of these forms at this time identify factors that may affect the sale price of the property and, therefore, should be considered in the CMA.

2. The agent should carefully measure all structures according to Real Estate Commission Square Foot guidelines (see Appendix B). Accuracy and adherence to guidelines are imperative. Note: The agent may compare his measurements with the appraiser's measurements when the appraisal is done for the buyer before closing. It is preferable to find mistakes before, rather than after, closing. The agent cannot rely on tax data, building plans, seller, or previous MLS listing information.
3. The broker can avoid many problems from the time of the listing through contract and closing if he gathers the following documents at the time of the listing.
   - Copies of deeds and title policies
   - Zoning restrictions
   - Restrictive/protective covenants
   - Transferable warranties

   From these documents, the broker can verify information such as the dimensions and size of the lot, the legal description and the seller's interest in the property. The local planning board should be able to answer questions about zoning and designated flood plains.

   The agent should gently question the seller. Occasionally, a seller forgets to tell the agent that she sold an interest in the property to her brother or sold a half-acre section off the back corner or gave an easement to a neighbor after purchasing the property. The seller may also conveniently forget to mention a second mortgage, lien, or home equity line, which, when combined with the first mortgage balance, total more than the property is worth. In this case, the sale may fall through if the seller has no money to pay the difference and a compromise cannot be reached with the mortgage companies. If the agent is unaware of this fact until the closing attorney for the new "almost" buyer discovers it in the title search; agents, mortgage companies, attorneys, and other professionals may have expended a lot of effort for nothing. If any doubt exists about the seller's ability to convey clear title, and the agent should consider obtaining a preliminary title search.
4. The agent can prepare and present a CMA. After obtaining and verifying all of the information on the seller's property, the listing agent can carefully prepare a CMA on the seller's property and an estimate of the seller's closing costs. The agent can also discuss with the seller any local market trends, such as sellers paying buyers' closing costs. With this information in hand, the agent is ready to advise the seller on an appropriate listing price and on the amount the seller can expect in terms of proceeds from the sale of the property.
5. The agent can assist the seller in determining the listing price, preferably within the range determined by the market analysis. Should the seller want to list at an unrealistically high price, the agent must decide whether to take the listing. Pricing objections can usually be overcome if the agent educates the seller about the disadvantages of listing too high.
6. The agent may prepare an estimated net proceeds sheet based on the listing price at the time of listing. See Figure 6.3 for a sample form designed for an area where it is customary for the seller to pay some or all of a buyer's closing costs. Any firm may design its own estimated net proceeds sheet reflecting general terms, conditions, and cost in its area. This sample form may be used for estimating either the seller's or buyer's cost or both if the seller is paying the buyer's closing costs. The agent would be wise to prepare a net proceeds estimate before presenting an offer and to emphasize that it is estimated. The estimate should be adjusted with each counteroffer.
7. A prudent broker will review the accuracy of the property data sheet completed at the inspection of the property with the seller. The broker will also check the MLS computer printout with the property data sheet after information is entered into the computer.

NR

**FIGURE 6.3** Net Proceeds Sheet.

## SELLER'S ESTIMATED NET PROCEEDS

DATE ________________

SELLERS ____________________________________

ADDRESS ____________________________________

SALES PRICE ________________

**SELLER'S CLOSING COSTS**

$________________ DEED PREPARATION
$________________ EXCISE TAX
$________________ VA MANDATORY SELLER PAID CLOSING COSTS*
$________________ BROKERAGE SERVICES
$________________ 20___ REAL ESTATE TAXES
$________________ 1ST MORTGAGE PAYOFF
$________________ 2ND MORTGAGE PAYOFF
$________________ ADDITIONAL LIENS
$________________ INTEREST IN ARREARS
$________________ ONE-YEAR WARRANTY
$________________ LENDER'S INSPECTION FEE

$________________ TOTAL

**BUYER'S CLOSING COSTS**

$________________ SURVEY
$________________ TITLE INSURANCE
$________________ ATTORNEY'S FEES
$________________ RECORDING FEES
$________________ LOAN ORIGINATION FEE
$________________ APPRAISAL FEE
$________________ CREDIT REPORT
$________________ LENDER FEES*
$________________ TERMITE INSPECTION*

$________________ TOTAL

**BUYER'S PREPAIDS**

$______________ INTERIM INTEREST
@ $ ______ PER DAY
$______________ 14-MO. HAZARD INS.
$______________ ___-MO. TAX ESCROW

$______________ TOTAL

TOTAL BUYER CLOSING COSTS $ ______________

*NOTE: ON VA LOANS, THE TERMITE INSPECTION AND CERTAIN LENDER FEES ARE PAID BY SELLER.

$________________ SALES PRICE
–________________ SELLER'S CLOSING COSTS
–________________ BUYER'S CLOSING COSTS AND/OR REPAIRS PAID BY SELLER (PUT -0- IF NOT APPLICABLE)
$________________ SELLER'S ESTIMATED NET PROCEEDS (THIS AMOUNT WILL BE REDUCED BY THE COSTS OF ANY REPAIRS SELLER MAKES PER REPAIR PROVISIONS OF THE CONTRACT, APPRAISAL, OR WDI REPORT.)

THE SELLER ACKNOWLEDGES THAT THIS IS ONLY AN ESTIMATE AND FINAL FIGURES MAY VARY.

SELLER ____________________ DATE __________ SELLER ____________________ DATE __________

8. The agent needs to use a well-drafted listing contract form, such as the Exclusive Right to Sell Listing Agreement in Figure 6.1 and a Dual Agency Addendum, if applicable. Other forms are acceptable as long as they meet the requirements of the Real Estate Commission. After all of these steps are complete and the agent is reasonably sure the seller understands what she is signing, the agent should have the seller sign the listing contract and any applicable addenda and disclosures. The agent should give the seller a copy of everything she signs.
9. The agent should process the listing according to office procedures (see sample listing folder checklist in Figure 6.4). The listing checklist is not all-inclusive, and not all items are necessary for every listing. For example, some sellers may choose not to offer a homeowner's warranty. The agent must include all items required by Real Estate law, rules, and regulations, such as listing contracts and dual agency addendum, if applicable, and signed acknowledgment from the working with Real Estate Agents brochure.
10. The agent must implement the panel agreed-upon marketing plan.
11. The agent must maintain communication with the seller throughout the listing period. The agent should set appointments, offer feedback, discuss changes with the seller in price or market strategy, maintain a communication log, get any changes to the listing contract in writing, and refer to the listing contract when an offer to purchase is received. Items in the listing contract may be negotiated in or out of a sales contract, but reviewing the listing contract at this time prevents oversights.

# BUYER AGENCY CONTRACTS

A buyer agency contract is an agreement between a prospective buyer and a broker in which the broker is contracted to act as the buyer's agent in the purchase of real estate.

## Agency Disclosure and Nonexclusive Buyer Agency Agreement

A nonexclusive buyer agency agreement is one that retains a broker to act as the buyer's agent in the purchase of real estate but leaves the buyer free to enter into additional nonexclusive relationships with other brokers, to purchase real estate through a broker acting as a seller's agent or subagent, or to purchase real estate directly from an owner. Under this type of agreement, the broker is entitled to a commission or success fee when the broker is the procuring cause of the purchase. Oral nonexclusive buyer agency is now allowed, provided it does not bind the buyer-client to a specific agent or company or to a definite period of time.

## Exclusive Buyer Agency Agreement

An exclusive buyer agency contract is one in which the prospective buyer retains a broker as her *exclusive* agent. Under this type of contract, the broker who is a party to the contract is the only real estate agent with whom the buyer can work in the purchase of a property as described in the agreement. Depending on the wording of the contract, the buyer may also be obligated to pay the broker compensation even if the buyer purchases a property from an owner without the assistance of a real estate agent.

## Typical Provisions of a Buyer Agency Contract

When entering into a buyer agency agreement, all parties should be named on the contract and all parties should sign the contract. This includes *all* persons who will be purchasing the property. The following list is a brief discussion of the typical provisions of a buyer agency contract. Reference is made to NCAR Standard Form 201, Exclusive Right to Represent Buyer; see Figure 6.5.

1. The type and general location of the property is described.
2. A specific duration for the contract must be stated.
3. The effect of the agreement is to employ the broker as the buyer's exclusive agent, but buyer may choose to allow or disallow dual agency.

**FIGURE 6.4** Listing Folder Checklist.

LISTING FOLDER CHECKLIST

PROPERTY ADDRESS________________________________________________

THE FOLLOWING ITEMS MUST BE IN THE OFFICE LISTING FOLDER BEFORE A LISTING WILL BE ENTERED INTO MLS.

***THE PERSON ENTERING THIS INFORMATION INTO MLS SHOULD INITIAL THE ITEMS ON THIS LIST. ONCE ALL ITEMS HAVE BEEN COMPLETED AND AGENT HAS CHECKED AND INITIALED THE MLS PRINTOUT, THIS FORM WILL BE PLACED INTO OFFICE LISTING FILE.***

_____WORKING WITH REAL ESTATE AGENTS BROCHURE

_____LISTING FOLDER CHECKLIST WITH PROPERTY ADDRESS ENTERED

_____LISTING CONTRACT

_____PROPERTY DISCLOSURE

_____LEAD-BASED PAINT ADDENDUM—ENTER N/A IF NEWER THAN 1978

_____DUAL AGENCY ADDENDUM

_____MLS SHEET

_____LOAN RELEASE FORM

_____MEASUREMENT SHEET or SOURCE OF SQUARE FOOTAGE QUOTED

_____DEED (48 HOUR HOLD)

_____PLAT MAP (48 HOUR HOLD)

_____RESTRICTIVE COVENANTS

_____CMA or APPRAISAL

_____TAX SHEET

_____INSPECTION (OPTIONAL)

_____SIGNED WARRANTY AGREEMENT

_____SHOWING INSTRUCTIONS

HOLD AFTER ENTERED IN MLS UNTIL:

_____A COPY OF THE MLS PRINTOUT HAS BEEN CHECKED AND INITIALED BY AGENT AND PLACED IN OFFICE FILE

**FIGURE 6.5** Exclusive Right to Represent Buyer.

**EXCLUSIVE RIGHT TO REPRESENT BUYER**
**Buyer Agency Agreement**
[Consult "Guidelines" (Form 201G) for guidance in completing this form]

STATE OF NORTH CAROLINA, County of ______________________, Date ______________________,
______________________________________________ ("Buyer"),
hereby employs ______________________________________ [Firm Name] as the Buyer's exclusive agent ("Agent") to assist the Buyer in the acquisition of real property which may include any purchase, option and/or exchange on terms and conditions acceptable to Buyer.

**Buyer represents that, as of the commencement date of this Agreement, the Buyer is not a party to a buyer representation agreement with any other Agent. Buyer has received a copy of the "Working with Real Estate Agents" brochure and has reviewed it with Agent. Buyer further represents that Buyer has disclosed to Agent information about any properties of the type described in paragraph 1 below that Buyer has visited at any open houses or that Buyer has been shown by any other real estate agent.**

1. **TYPE OF PROPERTY:** ☐ Residential (improved and unimproved) ☐ Commercial (improved and unimproved) ☐ Other ______________________

(a) General Location: ______________________
(b) Other: ______________________

2. **DURATION OF AGENCY:** Agent's authority as Buyer's exclusive Agent shall begin ______________________, and subject to paragraph 4, shall expire at midnight, ______________________, or when Buyer acquires real property of the type described in paragraph 1, whichever occurs sooner.

3. **EFFECT OF AGREEMENT:** Buyer intends to acquire real property of the type described in paragraph 1. *By employing Agent as Buyer's exclusive Agent, Buyer agrees to conduct all negotiations for such property through Agent, and to refer to Agent all inquiries received in any form from other agents, salespersons, prospective sellers or any other source, during the time this Agreement is in effect.*

**[Instructions: Initial only ONE]**

________ In the event Buyer wishes to consider a property listed with the Agent's firm, Buyer authorizes Agent to act as a dual agent, representing both Buyer and Seller, subject to the terms and conditions of the attached Dual Agency Addendum.

________ Buyer does NOT authorize Agent to act in the capacity of dual agent.

4. **COMPENSATION OF AGENT:**

(a) Agent acknowledges receipt of a non-refundable retainer fee in the amount of $______________ which ☐shall ☐ shall not be credited toward any compensation due Agent under this Agreement.

(b) Except as otherwise provided below, Agent shall seek compensation from a cooperating listing firm (through the listing firm's offer of compensation in MLS or otherwise) or from the seller if there is no listing firm, and Buyer agrees that Agent shall be entitled to receive same in consideration for Agent's services hereunder. If Buyer purchases property where no compensation is offered by either the listing firm or the seller, then Buyer agrees to pay Agent a fee of ______________________
______________________________________________
***(insert dollar amount, percentage of purchase price, or other method of determining Agent's compensation for each type of property the Buyer may purchase).*** If the compensation offered by the listing firm or seller is less than the compensation inserted above, Buyer agrees to pay Agent the difference. **If additional compensation and/or a selling incentive (bonus, trip, money, etc.) is offered through the MLS or otherwise, Buyer will permit the Agent to receive it in addition to the compensation set forth above.**

**FIGURE 6.5** Continued.

4. **COMPENSATION OF AGENT (continued):**

(c) The compensation shall be deemed earned under any of the following circumstances:

i. If, during the term of this Agreement, Buyer, any assignee of Buyer or any person/legal entity acting on behalf of Buyer directly or indirectly enters into an agreement to purchase, option, and/or exchange any property of the type described above regardless of the manner in which Buyer was introduced to the property; or

ii. If, within _________ days after expiration of this Agreement, Buyer enters into a contract to acquire property introduced to Buyer during the term of this Agreement by Agent or any third party, unless Buyer has entered into a valid buyer agency agreement with another real estate agent; or

iii. If, having entered into an enforceable contract to acquire property during the term of this Agreement, Buyer defaults under the terms of that contract.

(d) The compensation will be due and payable at closing or upon Buyer's default of any purchase agreement. If Buyer defaults, the total compensation that would have been due the Agent will be due and payable immediately in cash from the Buyer. No assignment of rights in real property obtained for Buyer or any assignee of Buyer or any person/legal entity acting on behalf of Buyer pursuant to this Agreement shall operate to defeat any of Agent's rights under this Agreement.

Notice: Buyer understands and acknowledges that there is the potential for a conflict of interest generated by a percentage of price based fee for representing Buyer. The amount, format or rate of real estate commission is not fixed by law, but is set by each broker individually, and may be negotiable between Buyer and Agent.

5. **DISCLOSURE OF BUYER'S IDENTITY:** Unless otherwise stated in Paragraph 12 below, Agent has Buyer's permission to disclose Buyer's identity.

6. **OTHER POTENTIAL BUYERS:** Buyer understands that other prospective purchasers represented by Agent may seek property, submit offers, and contract to purchase property through Agent, including the same or similar property as Buyer seeks to purchase. Buyer acknowledges, understands and consents to such representation of other prospective purchasers by Agent through its sales associates.

7. **AGENT'S DUTIES:** During the term of this Agreement, Agent shall promote the interests of Buyer by: (a) performing the terms of this Agreement; (b) seeking property at a price and terms acceptable to Buyer; (c) presenting in a timely manner all written offers or counteroffers to and from Buyer; (d) disclosing to Buyer all material facts related to the property or concerning the transaction of which Agent has actual knowledge; and (e) accounting for in a timely manner all money and property received in which Buyer has or may have an interest. Unless otherwise provided by law or Buyer consents in writing to the release of the information, Agent shall maintain the confidentiality of all personal and financial information and other matters identified as confidential by Buyer, if that information is received from Buyer during the brokerage relationship. In satisfying these duties, Agent shall exercise ordinary care, comply with all applicable laws and regulations, and treat all prospective sellers honestly and not knowingly give them false information. In addition, Agent may show the same property to other buyers, represent other buyers, represent sellers relative to other properties, or provide assistance to a seller or prospective seller by performing ministerial acts that are not inconsistent with Agent's duties under this Agreement.

Upon closing of any sale of property not entered in a listing service of which Agent is a member, Buyer authorizes Agent to submit pertinent information concerning the property, including sales price, to such listing service.

8. **BUYER'S DUTIES:** Buyer shall: (a) work exclusively with Agent during the term of this Agreement; (b) pay Agent, directly or indirectly, the compensation set forth above; (c) comply with the reasonable requests of Agent to supply any pertinent financial or personal data needed to fulfill the terms of this Agreement; (d) be available for reasonable periods of time to examine properties; and (e) pay for all products and/or services required in the examination and evaluation of properties (examples: surveys, water/soil tests, title reports, property inspections, etc.).

9. **NON-DISCRIMINATION: THE AGENT SHALL CONDUCT ALL BROKERAGE ACTIVITIES IN REGARD TO THIS AGREEMENT WITHOUT RESPECT TO THE RACE, COLOR, RELIGION, SEX, NATIONAL ORIGIN, HANDICAP OR FAMILIAL STATUS OF ANY PARTY OR PROSPECTIVE PARTY TO THE AGREEMENT.**



Buyer Initials _______ _______ Agent Initial _______

**FIGURE 6.5** Continued.

10. **OTHER PROFESSIONAL ADVICE:** In addition to the services rendered to Buyer by the Agent under the terms of this Agreement, Buyer is advised to seek other professional advice in matters of law, taxation, financing, insurance, surveying, wood-destroying insect infestation, structural soundness, engineering, and other matters pertaining to any proposed transaction. Although Agent may provide Buyer the names of providers who claim to perform such services, Buyer understands that Agent cannot guarantee the quality of service or level of expertise of any such provider. Buyer agrees to pay the full amount due for all services directly to the service provider whether or not the transaction closes. Buyer also agrees to indemnify and hold Agent harmless from and against any and all liability, claim, loss, damage, suit, or expense that Agent may incur either as a result of Buyer's selection and use of any such provider or Buyer's election not to have one or more of such services performed.

☐ Buyer acknowledges receipt of a sample copy of an Offer to Purchase And Contract for review purposes.
☐ Buyer acknowledges receipt of a copy of the brochure *Questions and Answers on: Home Inspections*.

11. **HOME WARRANTY:** The seller of any property Buyer may be interested in buying may or may not provide a home warranty as a part of any sale. If the seller does not provide a home warranty, Buyer may elect to purchase one. Buyer understands that although Agent will assist Buyer in identifying available home warranty products, Buyer must refer specific questions regarding coverage afforded by any such product to the provider thereof.

12. **ADDITIONAL PROVISIONS:** ______________________________
______________________________________________
______________________________________________.

13. **ENTIRE AGREEMENT:** This Agreement constitutes the entire agreement between the parties relating to the subject thereof, and any prior agreements pertaining thereto, whether oral or written, have been merged and integrated into this Agreement. No modification of any of the terms of this Agreement shall be valid, binding upon the parties, or entitled to enforcement unless such modification has first been reduced to writing and signed by the parties.

14. **MEDIATION:** If a dispute arises out of or related to this Agreement or the breach thereof, and if the dispute cannot be settled through negotiation, the parties agree first to try in good faith to settle the dispute by mediation before resorting to arbitration, litigation, or some other dispute resolution procedure. If the need for mediation arises, the parties will choose a mutually acceptable mediator and will share the cost of mediation equally.

15. **CONFIDENTIALITY OF OFFERS:** Agent hereby advises Buyer of the possibility that sellers or sellers' representatives may not treat the existence, terms, or conditions of any offers Buyer may make as confidential.

**(NOTE: Buyer should consult with Agent before visiting any resale or new homes or contacting any other real estate agent representing sellers, to avoid the possibility of confusion over the brokerage relationship and misunderstandings about liability for compensation.)**

**Buyer and Agent each hereby acknowledge receipt of a signed copy of this Agreement.**

THE NORTH CAROLINA ASSOCIATION OF REALTORS®, INC. MAKES NO REPRESENTATION AS TO THE LEGAL VALIDITY OR ADEQUACY OF ANY PROVISION OF THIS FORM IN ANY SPECIFIC TRANSACTION.

Buyer ______________________________

Buyer ______________________________

Mailing Address ______________________________

Phone: Home ______________ Work ______________ Fax ______________

E-mail ______________________________

Agent (Firm) ______________________________ Phone ______________

By: ______________________________ Individual license #______________

Office Address: ______________________________

Phone ______________ Fax ______________ E-mail______________

Page 3 of 3

STANDARD FORM 201
© 7/2006

4. The amount and method of compensation are defined.
5. Agent is given permission to disclose buyer's identity.
6. Buyer is informed of and consents to agent's representation of other prospective buyers.
7. Agent's duties are described.
8. Buyer's duties are described.
9. Standard nondiscrimination language is included.
10. Buyer is advised agent cannot give professional advice outside of his field of expertise and cannot guarantee quality of service from any provider whose name the agent may provide to buyer. Buyer further agrees to pay for any authorized services and to hold agents harmless in regard to acts of contractors and quality of services provided by them. Buyer acknowledges that he or she received a sample copy of an Offer to Purchase and Contract and a copy of the pamphlet "Questions and Answers on: Home Inspections."
11. The buyer has the right to purchase a home warranty if one is not provided by the seller.
12. Additional provisions that may be negotiated between buyer and agent.
13. Entire agreement is contained herein.
14. Parties agree to mediation first if a dispute arises.
15. Confidentiality of offers is addressed.
    - Individual's license number is required below signature line.

The Agency Disclosure and Non-Exclusive Buyer Agency Agreement (see Figure 6.6) is much less comprehensive than the Exclusive Right to Represent Buyer. It establishes a buyer agency relationship but does not require the buyer to pay or assume the payment of a brokerage fee. The broker is compensated through the cooperating seller or listing firm. In the absence of a cooperating seller or listing firm, buyer and agent may enter into a separate agreement regarding compensation. Both the Exclusive Right to Represent Buyer and the Agency Disclosure and Non-Exclusive Buyer Agency Agreement require the individual agent's license number below the signature line.

## PROCEDURES FOR BUYERS' AGENTS

Before entering into an exclusive or a non-exclusive buyer agency agreement (written or oral) with a prospective buyer, the agent must carefully explain to the buyer the agency options, duties and relationships involved in each type of agency. North Carolina Real Estate Commission Rule A.0104(c) requires that all potential and actual clients and customers receive and the agent review with them the Commission pamphlet "Working With Real Estate Agents" (see Figure 5.5).

Rule A.0104 also requires that every agreement for brokerage services in a transaction be in writing, provide for its existence for a definite period of time, and provide for termination without prior notice at the expiration of that time period. This rule applies to all agency agreements resulting in a real estate transaction. The oral buyer and dual agency may be express and non-exclusive until such time as the buyer or tenant wishes to contract for sale or lease of a property (i.e., a real estate transaction). Rule A.0104 applies to buyer agency agreements that seek to bind the buyer to exclusive representation or for a specific time period even if the agreement does not culminate in a transaction. It also requires that all brokerage service agreements contain the following provision: **"The broker shall conduct all his brokerage activities in regard to this agreement without respect to the race, color, religion, sex, national origin, handicap or familial status of any buyer, prospective buyer, seller or prospective seller."** This provision must be set forth in a clear and conspicuous manner that distinguishes it from other provisions in the contract.

The first step in any brokerage situation is explaining agency and having the prospect choose the type of agency he wants. If an agent subsequently is hired as a buyer's agent using a buyer agent agreement, the next step is to assist the buyer (client) to qualify for a loan, if financing is necessary. The agent should not only assist the buyer in determining

**FIGURE 6.6** Agency Disclosure and Non-Exclusive Buyer Agency Agreement.

**AGENCY DISCLOSURE AND NON-EXCLUSIVE BUYER AGENCY AGREEMENT**

Buyer:_______________________________________________ (referred to below as "you")

Firm:_______________________________________________ (referred to below as "Firm")

The purpose of this form is to properly establish a buyer agency relationship. Historically, in a real estate transaction, the listing and selling firms have been paid by and were the agents of the seller. Today, many firms represent the buyer. When entering into a discussion with a real estate agent regarding a real estate transaction, you should understand what type of agency relationship or representation you have with the agent's firm. The various forms of agency relationships are discussed in the "Working with Real Estate Agents" brochure, a copy of which you have received and reviewed with the agent. In North Carolina the existence of a buyer agency relationship with a real estate agent for a period of time **must be in writing** to be recognized as valid. Your execution of this form confirms that you have read and understand the contents of that brochure, and are making a decision to request buyer agency for the period of time set forth below.

Firm agrees to act as a non-exclusive buyer's agent representing you in the acquisition of real property by **[check all that apply]**:

❑ locating suitable real estate ❑ showing the following specific property_______________________________

_______________________________ for the period from ____________________ to ____________________.

If you are interested in property listed with Firm **[check only one]**: ❑ you authorize Firm to act as a dual agent, representing both the seller and you, subject to the terms and conditions of the attached Dual Agency Addendum ❑ you do not authorize Firm to act as a dual agent.

This agreement does **not** obligate you to pay a brokerage fee or assure the payment of a brokerage fee to Firm, which will be compensated under an offer of compensation from a cooperating seller/listing firm. In the event you wish to consider the purchase of a property offered for sale privately, or through sources other than a cooperating seller/listing firm, you and Firm may enter into an agreement establishing the details of, and your liability for, compensating Firm in the transaction.

**DO NOT SIGN THIS FORM UNTIL YOU HAVE RECEIVED AND READ THE "WORKING WITH REAL ESTATE AGENTS" BROCHURE**

❑ Buyer acknowledges receipt of a copy of the brochure *Questions and Answers on: Home Inspections*

**THE AGENT SHALL CONDUCT ALL BROKERAGE ACTIVITIES IN REGARD TO THIS AGREEMENT WITHOUT RESPECT TO THE RACE, COLOR, RELIGION, SEX, NATIONAL ORIGIN, HANDICAP OR FAMILIAL STATUS OF ANY PARTY OR PROSPECTIVE PARTY TO THE AGREEMENT.**

THE NORTH CAROLINA ASSOCIATION OF REALTORS®, INC. MAKES NO REPRESENTATION AS TO THE LEGAL VALIDITY OR ADEQUACY OF ANY PROVISION OF THIS FORM IN ANY SPECIFIC TRANSACTION.

BUYER:

| ____________________ | ____________________ | ____________________ |
|---|---|---|
| Print or type name | Signature | Date |
| ____________________ | ____________________ | ____________________ |
| Print or type name | Signature | Date |
| ____________________ | ____________________ | ____________________ |
| Address | City, State | Phone number |

FIRM:

| ____________________ | ____________________ | ____________________ |
|---|---|---|
| Print or type firm name | Agent Signature and individual license # | Date |

Page 1 of 1

**North Carolina Association of REALTORS®, Inc.**

REALTOR®

EQUAL HOUSING OPPORTUNITY

**STANDARD FORM 203**

the amount a buyer is qualified for, but she should also help the buyer secure the best possible terms and conditions for a loan.

The successful buyer's agent will develop a thorough understanding of the buyer's needs and preferences in order to facilitate the buyer's search for a property. The agent's job entails much more than just showing properties. While the listing agent may be held to a higher standard about material facts relating to the property, the buyer's agent also has the responsibility to discover and disclose material facts regarding a property and to verify information regarding the property. Before making an offer to purchase, the buyer's agent is expected to see that the buyer receives the North Carolina Residential Property Disclosure Statement as well as any other relevant disclosures concerning such issues as lead-based paint and synthetic stucco. The buyer's agent may help the buyer obtain copies of any documents that restrict or limit the use of the property, such as restrictive/protective covenants and homeowners' association bylaws. NCAR's Offer to Purchase and Contract (Standard Form No. 2T) advises the buyer to review these documents prior to signing an offer to purchase.

Once a property has been identified, the buyer's agent has the responsibility of preparing, presenting, and negotiating the offer to purchase. Part of this preparation may be to perform a CMA for the buyer. When conducting negotiations, the buyer's agent must remember her obligation to obtain the best price and terms possible for her buyer and not to disclose confidential information relating to the buyer.

Once an accepted contract is in place, the buyer's agent is expected to assist the buyer with preparations for the closing. This includes such activities as getting inspections performed, coordinating the closing with the attorney and the lender, performing a final walk-through inspection before closing, notifying the buyer of the amount of certified funds needed for closing, and confirming the accuracy of the closing statement.

## DUAL AGENCY AGREEMENTS

Permission for agency with the seller, whether exclusive or dual, must be in writing from the outset. The listing agreement should clearly indicate whether dual agency is authorized. Oral dual agency in conjunction with oral buyer agency is permissible, but must be reduced to writing before an offer is made, provided that neither the oral buyer nor dual agency seeks to bind a buyer to a specific agent for any definite period of time.

Firms that represent both buyers and sellers encounter situations where an existing listing or buyer agency contract needs to be modified. Before showing a property listed with a firm to a buyer client of this same firm, the firm must have the "informed consent" of the buyer and the seller to act as a dual agent. If written consent is obtained from both parties at the time the listing contract or buyer agency agreement is signed, NCAR's Dual Agency Addendum (Standard Form 901) may be used for this purpose. In this case, all that has to be done at the time of the offer is to indicate the dual agency status on the Offer to Purchase and Contract.

If both the buyer's and seller's agency agreements are written and have no dual agency addenda attached, both parties must agree in writing to dual agency before the property can be shown. The simplest way is to have both parties sign the Dual Agency Addendum to their respective agency contracts as soon as dual agency becomes a possibility. They may, instead, sign the same dual agency agreement. The Dual Agency Addendum form may be used for this. The important thing to remember is that they must both authorize dual agency in writing prior to showing the property. This is mandatory if the agent has a written buyer agency agreement with the buyer.

If the buyer agency agreement is oral, then the buyer can orally authorize dual agency; however, both the Buyer Agent Agreement and Dual Agency Agreement must be in writing before making any offer. The situation with the seller is a little more complicated. Ideally, the seller should authorize the dual agency agreement in writing before the agent shows the property to the buyer client. The agent may, however, explain dual agency and get oral dual agency authorization from the seller which must be committed to writing before the buyer extends his offer to the seller. The latter is only allowed if the buyer agency agreement is orally authorized from the beginning. The NCAR Dual Agency Addendum or a dual agency agreement drafted by an attorney may be used to commit the oral agreements to writing.

It is also possible to enter into a dual agency agreement with a buyer and seller where no previous agency relationships exist. This is more likely to occur in a commercial transaction. When there is no existing agency contract with either party, a dual agency agreement must contain all the provisions of the employment arrangement; that is, what the agent will do for each party, what each party will do for the agent, and what information will or will not be kept confidential. This dual agency situation, of course, must be put into writing as soon as the dual agency situation becomes evident.

# SALES CONTRACTS AND PRACTICES

## Offer to Purchase and Contract

Once a real estate licensee has obtained an employment authority by the execution of a listing, her efforts are directed toward finding a buyer for the listed property. That buyer must be ready and willing to buy the property and able to obtain the necessary financing. The agent may produce the buyer herself, or a selling agent from the same or another company may produce the buyer. The selling agent may be a subagent, a buyer's agent, or a dual agent, depending on the circumstances and agency agreements. Once a buyer is found, the agent working with or for the buyer helps the buyer complete the offer to purchase. (Remember that real estate practitioners can fill in the blanks on a standard offer to purchase but cannot draft a contract.) The selling agent then presents the offer to purchase to the listing agent, who presents the offer to the seller.

North Carolina Real Estate Commission Rule A.0112 requires that specific provisions be included in any preprinted offer or sales contract (see Appendix A). NCBA/NCAR Offer to Purchase and Contract (Standard Form 2-T) meets these requirements. Real estate agents who are not REALTORS®, and therefore cannot use this form, must contact an attorney about acquiring proper contract forms.

Figure 6.7 is a copy of the NCBA/NCAR's Standard Form 2-T, Offer to Purchase and Contract. This contract provides for the use of addenda, which greatly enhances the contract's value to real estate agents because it allows a standard addendum for situations that would otherwise require the services of an attorney. See Figure 6.8 for the "additional provisions addendum." The guidelines for completing this contract (see Figure 6.9) are excellent and should be understood thoroughly by all real estate agents. The following is a list of items and features covered by the contract.

- Defines and lists fixtures.
- Suggests buyer obtain and read restrictive covenants before making offer.
- Allows additional earnest money deposit to be easily indicated.
- Makes available financing addenda for FHA/VA loans, loan assumptions, and seller financing.
- Gives seller the right to ask for evidence of loan commitment and to terminate the contract if such evidence is not provided in the specified time.
- Includes a statement that property must have legal access to public right-of-way.
- Addresses both pending and confirmed assessments.
- Includes disclosure provisions for homeowners' association dues and prorations.
- Acknowledges the receipt or nonreceipt of the Residential Property Disclosure Statement or the exempt status of the property.
- Provides a place for acknowledging that property was built before 1978 and identifies need to attach lead-based paint disclosure, if required.
- Requires the buyer to choose one of the following alternatives:
- *Alternative 1.* Prior to a stated date, the buyer has the option of having the property inspected to determine the proper functioning of certain major systems; tested for the presence of radon; appraised to ensure that the property's value is at least equal to the

**FIGURE 6.7** Offer to Purchase and Contract.

# OFFER TO PURCHASE AND CONTRACT

______________________________________________________________________________, as Buyer, hereby offers to purchase and _______________________________________________________, as Seller, upon acceptance of said offer, agrees to sell and convey, all of that plot, piece or parcel of land described below, together with all improvements located thereon and such fixtures and personal property as are listed below (collectively referred to as the "Property"), upon the following terms and conditions:

1. **REAL PROPERTY:** Located in the City of ______________________________________________,
County of ______________________________, State of North Carolina, being known as and more particularly described as:
Street Address____________________________________________________________ Zip________
Legal Description:__________________________________________________________________
( ❑ All ❑ A portion of the property in Deed Reference: Book________, Page No.________, _______________ County. )
**NOTE:** Prior to signing this Offer to Purchase and Contract, Buyer is advised to review Restrictive Covenants, if any, which may limit the use of the Property, and to read the Declaration of Restrictive Covenants, By-Laws, Articles of Incorporation, Rules and Regulations, and other governing documents of the owners' association and/or the subdivision, if applicable.

2. **FIXTURES:** The following items, if any, are included in the purchase price free of liens: any built-in appliances, light fixtures, ceiling fans, attached floor coverings, blinds, shades, drapery rods and curtain rods, brackets and all related hardware, window and door screens, storm windows, combination doors, awnings, antennas, satellite dishes and receivers, burglar/fire/smoke alarms, pool and spa equipment, solar energy systems, attached fireplace screens, gas logs, fireplace inserts, electric garage door openers with controls, outdoor plants and trees (other than in movable containers), basketball goals, storage sheds, mailboxes, wall and/or door mirrors, and any other items attached or affixed to the Property, EXCEPT the following items:
____________________________________________________________________________________
___________________________________________________________________________________.

3. **PERSONAL PROPERTY:** The following personal property is included in the purchase price:__________________
___________________________________________________________________________________.

4. **PURCHASE PRICE:** The purchase price is $_________________________________ and shall be paid as follows:
(a) $____________________, EARNEST MONEY DEPOSIT with this offer by ❑ cash ❑ personal check ❑ bank check ❑ certified check ❑ other: __________________________________________ to be deposited and held in escrow by _________________________________________________ ("Escrow Agent") until the sale is closed, at which time it will be credited to Buyer, or until this contract is otherwise terminated. In the event: (1) this offer is not accepted; or (2) any of the conditions hereto are not satisfied, then all earnest monies shall be refunded to Buyer. In the event of breach of this contract by Seller, all earnest monies shall be refunded to Buyer upon Buyer's request, but such return shall not affect any other remedies available to Buyer for such breach. In the event of breach of this contract by Buyer, then all earnest monies shall be forfeited to Seller upon Seller's request, but such forfeiture shall not affect any other remedies available to Seller for such breach. **NOTE:** In the event of a dispute between Seller and Buyer over the return or forfeiture of earnest money held in escrow by a broker, the broker is required by state law to retain said earnest money in the broker's trust or escrow account until a written release from the parties consenting to its disposition has been obtained or until disbursement is ordered by a court of competent jurisdiction.
(b) $____________________, ADDITIONAL EARNEST MONEY DEPOSIT to be paid to Escrow Agent no later than ______________________, TIME BEING OF THE ESSENCE WITH REGARD TO SAID DATE.
(c) $____________________, OPTION FEE in accordance with paragraph 13, Alternative 2, to be paid to Seller on the Effective Date as set forth in paragraph 23. (NOTE: If Alternative 2 applies, then do not insert $0, N/A, or leave blank).
(d) $____________________, BY ASSUMPTION of the unpaid principal balance and all obligations of Seller on the existing loan(s) secured by a deed of trust on the Property in accordance with the attached Loan Assumption Addendum.
(e) $____________________, BY SELLER FINANCING in accordance with the attached Seller Financing Addendum.
(f) $____________________, BALANCE of the purchase price in cash at Closing.



REALTOR®

**This form jointly approved by:**
**North Carolina Bar Association**
**North Carolina Association of REALTORS®, Inc.**

EQUAL HOUSING OPPORTUNITY

**STANDARD FORM 2 - T**
**© 7/2005**

Buyer Initials ______ ______ Seller Initials ______ ______

**FIGURE 6.7** Continued.

**5. CONDITIONS:** (State N/A in each blank that is not a condition to this contract.)

(a) Buyer must be able to obtain a ❑ FHA ❑ VA (attach FHA/VA Financing Addendum) ❑ Conventional ❑ Other: ____________________ loan at a ❑ Fixed Rate ❑ Adjustable Rate in the principal amount of ____________________ (plus any financed VA Funding Fee or FHA MIP) for a term of __________ year(s), at an initial interest rate not to exceed __________ % per annum, with mortgage loan discount points not to exceed ______ % of the loan amount. Buyer shall apply for said loan within ________ days of the Effective Date of this contract. Buyer shall use Buyer's best efforts to secure the lender's customary loan commitment letter on or before ____________________ and to satisfy all terms and conditions of the loan commitment letter by Closing. After the above letter date, Seller may request in writing from Buyer a copy of the loan commitment letter. If Buyer fails to provide Seller a copy of the loan commitment letter or a written waiver of this loan condition within five days of receipt of Seller's request, Seller may terminate this contract by written notice to Buyer at any time thereafter, provided Seller has not then received a copy of the letter or the waiver.

(b) There must be no restriction, easement, zoning or other governmental regulation that would prevent the reasonable use of the Property for ________________________________________ purposes.

(c) The Property must be in substantially the same or better condition at Closing as on the date of this offer, reasonable wear and tear excepted.

(d) All deeds of trust, liens and other charges against the Property, not assumed by Buyer, must be paid and satisfied by Seller prior to or at Closing such that cancellation may be promptly obtained following Closing. Seller shall remain obligated to obtain any such cancellations following Closing.

(e) Title must be delivered at Closing by GENERAL WARRANTY DEED unless otherwise stated herein, and must be fee simple marketable and insurable title, free of all encumbrances except: ad valorem taxes for the current year (prorated through the date of Closing); utility easements and unviolated restrictive covenants that do not materially affect the value of the Property; and such other encumbrances as may be assumed or specifically approved by Buyer. The Property must have legal access to a public right of way.

**6. SPECIAL ASSESSMENTS:** Seller warrants that there are no pending or confirmed governmental special assessments for sidewalk, paving, water, sewer, or other improvements on or adjoining the Property, and no pending or confirmed owners' association special assessments, except as follows: ________________________________________
________________________________________.
(Insert "None" or the identification of such assessments, if any.) Seller shall pay all owners' association assessments and all governmental assessments confirmed through the time of Closing, if any, and Buyer shall take title subject to all pending assessments, if any, unless otherwise agreed as follows: ________________________________________
________________________________________.

**7. PRORATIONS AND ADJUSTMENTS:** Unless otherwise provided, the following items shall be prorated and either adjusted between the parties or paid at Closing: (a) Ad valorem taxes on real property shall be prorated on a calendar year basis through the date of Closing; (b) Ad valorem taxes on personal property for the entire year shall be paid by the Seller unless the personal property is conveyed to the Buyer, in which case, the personal property taxes shall be prorated on a calendar year basis through the date of Closing; (c) All late listing penalties, if any, shall be paid by Seller; (d) Rents, if any, for the Property shall be prorated through the date of Closing; (e) Owners' association dues and other like charges shall be prorated through the date of Closing. Seller represents that the regular owners' association dues, if any, are $______________ per _________________.

**8. EXPENSES:** Unless otherwise agreed, Buyer shall be responsible for all costs with respect to any loan obtained by Buyer, title search, title insurance, recording the deed and for preparation and recording of all instruments required to secure the balance of the purchase price unpaid at Closing. Seller shall pay for preparation of a deed and all other documents necessary to perform Seller's obligations under this agreement, and for excise tax (revenue stamps) required by law. Seller shall pay at Closing $______________________ toward any of Buyer's expenses associated with the purchase of the Property, including any FHA/VA lender and inspection costs that Buyer is not permitted to pay, but excluding any portion disapproved by Buyer's lender.

**9. FUEL:** Buyer agrees to purchase from Seller the fuel, if any, situated in any tank on the Property at the prevailing rate with the cost of measurement thereof, if any, being paid by Seller.

**10. EVIDENCE OF TITLE:** Seller agrees to use his best efforts to deliver to Buyer as soon as reasonably possible after the Effective Date of this contract, copies of all title information in possession of or available to Seller, including but not limited to: title insurance policies, attorney's opinions on title, surveys, covenants, deeds, notes and deeds of trust and easements relating to the Property. Seller authorizes (1) any attorney presently or previously representing Seller to release and disclose any title insurance policy in such



Buyer Initials _______ _______ Seller Initials _______ ______

**FIGURE 6.7** Continued.

attorney's file to Buyer and both Buyer's and Seller's agents and attorneys; and (2) the Property's title insurer or its agent to release and disclose all materials in the Property's title insurer's (or title insurer's agent's) file to Buyer and both Buyer's and Seller's agents and attorneys.

**11. LABOR AND MATERIAL:** Seller shall furnish at Closing an affidavit and indemnification agreement in form satisfactory to Buyer showing that all labor and materials, if any, furnished to the Property within 120 days prior to the date of Closing have been paid for and agreeing to indemnify Buyer against all loss from any cause or claim arising therefrom.

**12. PROPERTY DISCLOSURE:**

- ☐ Buyer has received a signed copy of the N.C. Residential Property Disclosure Statement prior to the signing of this Offer to Purchase and Contract.
- ☐ Buyer has NOT received a signed copy of the N.C. Residential Property Disclosure Statement prior to the signing of this Offer to Purchase and Contract and shall have the right to terminate or withdraw this contract without penalty prior to WHICHEVER OF THE FOLLOWING EVENTS OCCURS FIRST: (1) the end of the third calendar day following receipt of the Disclosure Statement; (2) the end of the third calendar day following the date the contract was made; or (3) Closing or occupancy by the Buyer in the case of a sale or exchange.
- ☐ Exempt from N.C. Residential Property Disclosure Statement because (SEE GUIDELINES) ______________________________.
- ☐ The Property is residential and was built prior to 1978 (Attach Lead-Based Paint or Lead-Based Paint Hazards Disclosure Addendum.)

**13. PROPERTY INSPECTION, APPRAISAL, INVESTIGATION (Choose ONLY ONE of the following Alternatives):**

**☐ ALTERNATIVE 1:**

**(a) Property Inspection:** Unless otherwise stated herein, Buyer shall have the option of inspecting, or obtaining at Buyer's expense inspections, to determine the condition of the Property. Unless otherwise stated herein, it is a condition of this contract that: (i) the built-in appliances, electrical system, plumbing system, heating and cooling systems, roof coverings (including flashing and gutters), doors and windows, exterior surfaces, structural components (including foundations, columns, chimneys, floors, walls, ceilings and roofs), porches and decks, fireplaces and flues, crawl space and attic ventilation systems (if any), water and sewer systems (public and private), shall be performing the function for which intended and shall not be in need of immediate repair; (ii) there shall be no unusual drainage conditions or evidence of excessive moisture adversely affecting the structure(s); and (iii) there shall be no friable asbestos or existing environmental contamination. Any inspections shall be completed and written notice of necessary repairs shall be given to Seller on or before ______________ (the "Inspection Date"). Seller shall provide written notice to Buyer of Seller's response within ________ days of Buyer's notice. Buyer is advised to have any inspections made prior to incurring expenses for Closing and in sufficient time to permit any required repairs to be completed by Closing.

**(b) Wood-Destroying Insects:** Unless otherwise stated herein, Buyer shall have the option of obtaining, at Buyer's expense, a report from a licensed pest control operator on a standard form in accordance with the regulations of the North Carolina Structural Pest Control Committee, stating that as to all structures, except ______________________________, there was no visible evidence of wood-destroying insects and containing no indication of visible damage therefrom. The report must be obtained in sufficient time so as to permit treatment, if any, and repairs, if any, to be completed prior to Closing. All treatment required shall be paid for by Seller and completed prior to Closing, unless otherwise agreed upon in writing by the parties. The Buyer is advised that the inspection report described in this paragraph may not always reveal either structural damage or damage caused by agents or organisms other than wood-destroying insects. If new construction, Seller shall provide a standard warranty of termite soil treatment.

**(c) Repairs:** Pursuant to any inspections in (a) and/or (b) above, if any repairs are necessary, Seller shall have the option of completing them or refusing to complete them. If Seller elects not to complete the repairs, then Buyer shall have the option of accepting the Property in its present condition or terminating this contract, in which case all earnest monies shall be refunded. Unless otherwise stated herein, any items not covered by (a)(i), (a)(ii), (a)(iii) and (b) above are excluded from repair negotiations under this contract.

**(d) Radon Inspection**: Buyer shall have the option, at Buyer's expense, to have the Property tested for radon on or before the date for completion of inspections as set forth in paragraph 13 (a) above. The test result shall be deemed satisfactory to Buyer if it indicates a radon level of less than 4.0 pico curies per liter of air **(as of January 1, 1997, EPA guidelines reflect an "acceptable" level as anything less than 4.0 pico curies per liter of air).** If the test result exceeds the above-mentioned level, Seller shall have the option of: a) remediating to bring the radon level within the satisfactory range; or b) refusing to remediate. Upon the completion of remediation, Buyer may have a radon test performed at Seller's expense, and if the test result indicates a radon level less than 4.0 pico curies per liter of air, it shall be deemed satisfactory to the Buyer. If Seller elects not to remediate, or if remediation is attempted but fails to bring the radon level within the satisfactory range, Buyer shall have the option of: a) accepting the Property with its then current radon level; or b) terminating the contract, in which case all earnest monies shall be refunded.



Buyer Initials _______ _______ Seller Initials _______ _______

**STANDARD FORM 2 - T**

**FIGURE 6.7** Continued.

**(e) Cost Of Repair Contingency:** Notwithstanding the above and as an additional remedy of Buyer, if a reasonable estimate obtained by Buyer of the total cost of repairs required by (a) and (b) and/or remediation required by (d) above equals or exceeds $_______________, then Buyer shall have the option to terminate this contract pursuant to this Cost of Repair Contingency no later than seven (7) days following the Inspection Date and all earnest monies shall be refunded to Buyer.
**(f) Appraisal Contingency**: The Property must appraise at a value equal to or exceeding the purchase price or, at the option of Buyer, this contract may be terminated and all earnest monies shall be refunded to Buyer. If this contract is not subject to a financing contingency requiring an appraisal, Buyer shall arrange to have the appraisal completed on or before _________________________. The cost of the appraisal shall be borne by Buyer.
**(g) CLOSING SHALL CONSTITUTE ACCEPTANCE OF THE PROPERTY IN ITS THEN EXISTING CONDITION UNLESS PROVISION IS OTHERWISE MADE IN WRITING.**

☐ **ALTERNATIVE 2:** ***(This Alternative applies ONLY if Alternative 2 is checked AND Buyer has paid the Option Fee.)***
**(a) Property Investigation with Option to Terminate:** In consideration of the sum set forth in paragraph 4(c) paid by Buyer to Seller (not Escrow Agent) and other valuable consideration, the sufficiency of which is hereby acknowledged (the "Option Fee"), Buyer shall have the right to terminate this contract **for any reason or no reason, whether related to the physical condition of the Property or otherwise,** by delivering to Seller written notice of termination (the "Termination Notice") by 5:00 p.m. on ____________________________, 20____, ***time being of the essence*** (the "Option Termination Date"). At any time prior to Closing, Buyer shall have the right to inspect the Property at Buyer's expense (Buyer is advised to have all inspections and appraisals of the Property, including but not limited to those matters set forth in Alternative 1, performed prior to the Option Termination Date).
**(b) Exercise of Option:** If Buyer delivers the Termination Notice prior to the Option Termination Date, ***time being of the essence***, this contract shall become null and void and all earnest monies received in connection herewith shall be refunded to Buyer; however, the Option Fee will not be refunded and shall be retained by Seller. If Buyer fails to deliver the Termination Notice to Seller prior to the Option Termination Date, then Buyer will be deemed to have accepted the Property in its physical condition existing as of the Option Termination Date; provided such acceptance shall not constitute a waiver of any rights Buyer has under paragraph 5. The Option Fee is not refundable, is not a part of any earnest monies, and will be credited to the purchase price at Closing.
(c) **CLOSING SHALL CONSTITUTE ACCEPTANCE OF THE PROPERTY IN ITS THEN EXISTING CONDITION UNLESS PROVISION IS OTHERWISE MADE IN WRITING.**

**14. REASONABLE ACCESS:** Seller will provide reasonable access to the Property (including working, existing utilities) through the earlier of Closing or possession by Buyer, to Buyer or Buyer's representatives for the purposes of appraisal, inspection, and/or evaluation. Buyer may conduct a walk-through inspection of the Property prior to Closing.

**15. CLOSING:** Closing shall be defined as the date and time of recording of the deed. All parties agree to execute any and all documents and papers necessary in connection with Closing and transfer of title on or before ____________________________, at a place designated by Buyer. The deed is to be made to ________________________________________________.

**16. POSSESSION:** Unless otherwise provided herein, possession shall be delivered at Closing. In the event possession is NOT to be delivered at Closing: ☐ a Buyer Possession Before Closing Agreement is attached. OR, ☐ a Seller Possession After Closing Agreement is attached.

**17. OTHER PROVISIONS AND CONDITIONS:** (ITEMIZE ALL ADDENDA TO THIS CONTRACT AND ATTACH HERETO.)

**18. RISK OF LOSS:** The risk of loss or damage by fire or other casualty prior to Closing shall be upon Seller. If the improvements on the Property are destroyed or materially damaged prior to Closing, Buyer may terminate this contract by written notice delivered to Seller or Seller's agent and all deposits shall be refunded to Buyer. In the event Buyer does NOT elect to terminate this contract, Buyer shall be entitled to receive, in addition to the Property, any of the Seller's insurance proceeds payable on account of the damage or destruction applicable to the Property being purchased.

**19. ASSIGNMENTS:** This contract may not be assigned without the written consent of all parties, but if assigned by agreement, then this contract shall be binding on the assignee and his heirs and successors.

Page 4 of 5

Buyer Initials _______ _______ Seller Initials _______ ______

**STANDARD FORM 2 - T**
**© 7/2005**

**FIGURE 6.7** Continued.

**20. PARTIES:** This contract shall be binding upon and shall inure to the benefit of the parties, i.e., Buyer and Seller and their heirs, successors and assigns. As used herein, words in the singular include the plural and the masculine includes the feminine and neuter genders, as appropriate.

**21. SURVIVAL:** If any provision herein contained which by its nature and effect is required to be observed, kept or performed after the Closing, it shall survive the Closing and remain binding upon and for the benefit of the parties hereto until fully observed, kept or performed.

**22. ENTIRE AGREEMENT:** This contract contains the entire agreement of the parties and there are no representations, inducements or other provisions other than those expressed herein. All changes, additions or deletions hereto must be in writing and signed by all parties. Nothing contained herein shall alter any agreement between a REALTOR® or broker and Seller or Buyer as contained in any listing agreement, buyer agency agreement, or any other agency agreement between them.

**23. NOTICE AND EXECUTION:** Any notice or communication to be given to a party herein may be given to the party or to such party's agent. This offer shall become a binding contract (the "Effective Date") when signed by both Buyer and Seller and such signing is communicated to the offering party. This contract is executed under seal in signed multiple originals, all of which together constitute one and the same instrument, with a signed original being retained by each party and each REALTOR® or broker hereto, and the parties adopt the word "SEAL" beside their signatures below.

**Buyer acknowledges having made an on-site personal examination of the Property prior to the making of this offer.**

THE NORTH CAROLINA ASSOCIATION OF REALTORS®, INC. AND THE NORTH CAROLINA BAR ASSOCIATION MAKE NO REPRESENTATION AS TO THE LEGAL VALIDITY OR ADEQUACY OF ANY PROVISION OF THIS FORM IN ANY SPECIFIC TRANSACTION. IF YOU DO NOT UNDERSTAND THIS FORM OR FEEL THAT IT DOES NOT PROVIDE FOR YOUR LEGAL NEEDS, YOU SHOULD CONSULT A NORTH CAROLINA REAL ESTATE ATTORNEY BEFORE YOU SIGN IT.

Date: ______________________ Date: ______________________

Buyer ______________________ (SEAL) Seller ______________________ (SEAL)

Date: ______________________ Date: ______________________

Buyer ______________________ (SEAL) Seller ______________________ (SEAL)

**Escrow Agent acknowledges receipt of the earnest money and agrees to hold and disburse the same in accordance with the terms hereof.**

Date ______________________ Firm: ______________________

By: ______________________
(Signature)

Selling Agent/Firm/Phone ______________________
Acting as ❑ Buyer's Agent ❑ Seller's (sub)Agent ❑ Dual Agent

Listing Agent/Firm/Phone ______________________
Acting as ❑ Seller's (sub)Agent ❑ Dual Agent

Page 5 of 5

**STANDARD FORM 2 - T**
**© 7/2005**

**FIGURE 6.8** Additional Provisions Addendum.

## ADDITIONAL PROVISIONS ADDENDUM

Property Address: ______________________________

**NOTE:** All of the following provisions which are marked with an "X" shall apply to the attached Offer to Purchase and Contract or Offer to Purchase and Contract – Vacant Lot/Land ("Contract"). Those provisions marked "N/A" shall not apply.

1. ________ **EXPIRATION OF OFFER:** This offer shall expire unless acceptance is delivered to Buyer or to ____________ ______________________________, on or before ______________ ❑ AM ❑ PM, on ______________________, or until withdrawn by Buyer, whichever occurs first.

2. ________ **INTEREST BEARING TRUST ACCOUNT: Any earnest monies deposited by Buyer may be placed in the interest bearing trust account of the Escrow Agent named in the Contract. Any interest earned thereon shall belong to the Escrow Agent in consideration of the expenses incurred by maintaining such account and records associated therewith.**

3. ________ ***(To be used with Alternative 1 only)*** **SEWER SYSTEM:** This Contract is contingent upon ❑ Buyer ❑ Seller ("Responsible Party") obtaining an Improvement Permit or written evaluation from the County Health Department ("County") for a (check only ONE) ❑ conventional or ❑ other ______________________ ground absorption sewage system for a ______ bedroom home. All costs and expenses of obtaining such Permit or written evaluation shall be borne by Responsible Party unless otherwise agreed. In any event Seller, by no later than ________________, shall be responsible for clearing that portion of the Property required by the County to perform its tests and/or inspections. Responsible Party shall use best efforts to obtain such Permit or written evaluation. If the Improvement Permit or written evaluation from the County cannot be obtained by ______________(date), either party may terminate this Contract and the Earnest Money Deposit shall be refunded to Buyer.

4. ________ **FLOOD HAZARD ZONE:** Buyer has been advised that the Property is located in an area which the Secretary of HUD has found to have special flood hazards and that it may be necessary to purchase flood insurance in order to obtain any loan secured by the Property from any federally regulated institution or a loan insured or guaranteed by an agency of the U.S. Government.

5. ________ **CLOSING OF EXISTING CONTRACT CONTINGENCY:** This Contract is contingent upon closing of an existing contract on Buyer's real property located at: ______________________________ ______________________________ on or before ____________________. If this contingency is not removed on or before midnight of ______________________, Seller may terminate this Contract and all earnest monies shall be returned to Buyer.

6. ________ **RENTAL/INCOME/INVESTMENT PROPERTY:** The Property is subject to existing leases and/or rights of tenants in possession under month-to-month tenancies. Seller agrees to deliver to Buyer on or before ______________________, true and complete copies of all existing leases, rental agreements, outstanding tenant notices, written statements of all oral tenant agreements, statement of all tenant's deposits, uncured defaults by Seller or tenants, and claims made by or to tenants, if any. This Contract is contingent upon Buyer's approval of said documents. Buyer shall be deemed to have approved said documents unless written notice to the contrary is delivered to Seller or Seller's agent within seven (7) days of receipt of same. If Buyer does not approve said documents and delivers written notice of rejection within the seven day period, this Contract shall be terminated and all earnest monies shall be returned to Buyer. NOTE: DO NOT USE THIS PROVISION FOR PROPERTY SUBJECT TO THE NORTH CAROLINA VACATION RENTAL ACT. A VACATION RENTAL ADDENDUM SHOULD BE USED IN SUCH CASES.

7. ________ **HOME WARRANTY** (select only one of the following): ❑ Buyer may obtain a one-year home warranty at a cost not to exceed $________ and Seller agrees to pay for it at Closing. ❑ Seller has obtained and will provide a one-year home warranty from ______________________________ at a cost of $ ________ and will pay for it at Closing.





Buyer Initials ______ ______ Seller Initials ______ ______

**FIGURE 6.8** Continued.

8. ____________ **REMOVAL OF PERSONAL PROPERTY AND DEBRIS:** Seller shall remove, by the date possession is made available to the Buyer, all personal property which is not a part of the purchase and all garbage and debris from the Property.

9. ____________ **TAX-DEFERRED EXCHANGE:** In the event Buyer or Seller desires to effect a tax-deferred exchange in connection with the conveyance of the Property, Buyer and Seller agree to cooperate in effecting such exchange; provided, however, that the exchanging party shall be responsible for all additional costs associated with such exchange, and provided further, that a non-exchanging party shall not assume any additional liability with respect to such tax-deferred exchange. Seller and Buyer shall execute such additional documents, at no cost to the non-exchanging party, as shall be required to give effect to this provision. (NOTE: If Alternative 2 under paragraph 13 of this Contract will apply, Seller should seek advice concerning the taxation of the Option Fee.)

10. ____________ **BUYER'S RESPONSE TIME PROVISION (to be used in lieu of paragraph 13(a) of Alternative 1):**
(a) Property Inspection: Unless otherwise stated herein, Buyer shall have the option of inspecting, or obtaining at Buyer's expense inspections, to determine the condition of the Property. Unless otherwise stated herein, it is a condition of this contract that: (i) the built-in appliances, electrical system, plumbing system, heating and cooling systems, roof coverings (including flashing and gutters), doors and windows, exterior surfaces, structural components (including foundations, columns, chimneys, floors, walls, ceilings and roofs), porches and decks, fireplaces and flues, crawl space and attic ventilation systems (if any), water and sewer systems (public and private), shall be performing the function for which intended and shall not be in need of immediate repair; (ii) there shall be no unusual drainage conditions or evidence of excessive moisture adversely affecting the structure(s); and (iii) there shall be no friable asbestos or existing environmental contamination. Any inspections shall be completed and written notice of necessary repairs shall be given to Seller on or before ________________________ (the "Inspection Date"). Seller shall provide written notice to Buyer of Seller's response within _______ days of Buyer's notice. The Buyer shall deliver to Seller within five (5) days after receiving the Seller's written response the Buyer's written decision either (a) accepting the Property in its present condition, (b) accepting Seller's offer to make repairs to the extent and as described in the Seller's response, or (c) terminating this contract, ***time being of the essence***. Failure of Buyer to provide this written decision by the time stated herein shall constitute acceptance of Seller's agreement to make repairs to the extent and as described in the Seller's response.
<u>Buyer is advised to have any inspections made prior to incurring expenses for Closing and in sufficient time to permit any required repairs to be completed by Closing</u>.

IN THE EVENT OF A CONFLICT BETWEEN THIS ADDENDUM AND THE OFFER TO PURCHASE AND CONTRACT OR THE OFFER TO PURCHASE AND CONTRACT—VACANT LOT/LAND, THIS ADDENDUM SHALL CONTROL.

THE NORTH CAROLINA ASSOCIATION OF REALTORS®, INC. AND THE NORTH CAROLINA BAR ASSOCIATION MAKE NO REPRESENTATION AS TO THE LEGAL VALIDITY OR ADEQUACY OF ANY PROVISION OF THIS FORM IN ANY SPECIFIC TRANSACTION. IF YOU DO NOT UNDERSTAND THIS FORM OR FEEL THAT IT DOES NOT PROVIDE FOR YOUR LEGAL NEEDS, YOU SHOULD CONSULT A NORTH CAROLINA REAL ESTATE ATTORNEY BEFORE YOU SIGN IT.

Buyer: ________________________________________(SEAL) Date:________________________

Buyer: ________________________________________(SEAL) Date:________________________

Seller: ________________________________________(SEAL) Date:________________________

Seller: ________________________________________(SEAL) Date:________________________

Page 2 of 2

STANDARD FORM 2A11 - T

**FIGURE 6.9** Guidelines for Completing the Offer to Purchase and Contract Form.

## GUIDELINES FOR COMPLETING THE OFFER TO PURCHASE AND CONTRACT
**(Standard Form No. 2 - T; Copyright 7/2004)**

**INTRODUCTION:** These guidelines are provided to assist agents and attorneys who are completing the Offer to Purchase and Contract form on behalf of Buyers and Sellers. The Offer to Purchase and Contract is the most important document in any real estate sale and it is imperative that it accurately reflects the entire agreement of the Buyer and Seller. An improper contract may have substantial adverse effects on the rights and interests of the parties. These guidelines include general comments about contract completion as well as suggestions and explanations regarding selected contract provisions with which agents often have difficulty. However, situations will frequently arise that are not covered by these guidelines. Agents should always remember that an attorney should be consulted any time there is uncertainty regarding the proper completion of this important form.

**USE OF FORM:** The Offer to Purchase and Contract form, Copyright 7/2004, is jointly approved by the NORTH CAROLINA ASSOCIATION OF REALTORS®, INC. and the NORTH CAROLINA BAR ASSOCIATION, as Standard Form No. 2 - T. The version of this form with the REALTOR® logo is produced by NCAR for use by its members, only as printed. The version of this form without the REALTOR® logo is produced for the NORTH CAROLINA BAR ASSOCIATION and may be used, only as printed, by attorneys and any real estate agent.

This form may be used in a variety of real estate sales transactions, but it was developed primarily for use in the sale of existing single-family residential properties. Do not use this form as a substitute for a lease-option agreement, lease-purchase agreement or installment land contract. Also, if the sale involves the construction (or completion of construction) of a new single-family dwelling, use the current standard New Construction Addendum (NCAR/NCBA Form 2A3) or consult a NC real estate attorney for an appropriate form.

**GENERAL INSTRUCTIONS:**

1. Type this form if possible; otherwise print or write legibly in ink.
2. Fill in all blank spaces. If any space is not used, enter "N/A" or "None" as appropriate.
3. Be precise. Avoid the use of abbreviations, acronyms, jargon, and other terminology that may not be clearly understood.
4. Every change, addition or deletion to an offer or contract must be initialed and should be dated by both Buyer and Seller.
5. If numerous changes are made or if the same item (such as the purchase price) is changed more than once, complete a new contract form to avoid possible confusion or disputes between the parties. If, *after the parties have entered into a valid contract,* you prepare a new form for the parties to sign because the existing contract contains so many changes that it is difficult to read, then do not discard the existing contract. Keep it with the new form.
6. Review with the parties all contract provisions. Advise the parties to consult their attorney if they have any questions about the legal consequences of the contract or any particular provision.

---

**NAMES OF BUYER AND SELLER:** Fill in the complete name of each Buyer. If husband and wife, show the names of both (John A. Doe and wife, Mary B. Doe). Do not use "Mr. and Mrs. John A. Doe." Fill in the complete name of each Seller. If husband and wife, show the names of both (John A. Doe and wife, Mary B. Doe). Do not use "Mr. and Mrs. John A. Doe," "Owner of Record," or last name only.

**1. REAL PROPERTY:** Fill in City, County and Street Address. If any are not applicable, indicate by "None." CAUTION: A street address alone is generally not an adequate legal description.

**Legal Description:** Even if the Property has a street address, include a legal description sufficient to identify and distinguish the Property from all other property. An adequate legal description includes any of the following:

**(1) Reference to a recorded plat (map):** Include the lot #, block #, name of subdivision, and recording reference for the plat as recorded in the Register of Deeds office and fill in the county (or counties). CAUTION: A reference to a tax map alone is generally not an adequate legal description.

**(2) Reference to a recorded deed:** Determine whether the Property is all or a portion of the land described in the deed. Check the applicable box. Insert the book # and page # of the Deed Book as recorded in the Register of Deeds office and fill in the county (or counties).

**(3) Metes and bounds description:** Do not attempt to complete a metes and bounds exhibit. An attorney should be consulted prior to completing the Offer to Purchase and Contract if a metes and bounds description is necessary or if any of the above legal descriptions is not available.

**FIGURE 6.9** Continued.

**Covenants:** Purchasers take title to property subject to the restrictive covenants and are bound to follow them, even if they did not actually know the property was subject to restrictive covenants. Once restrictions are properly imposed upon a property, they "run with the land" and are binding on the owner and all subsequent purchasers. No owner or purchaser can use the property for any purpose that violates the restrictions. Therefore, before the Buyer signs an offer to purchase for property which is located in a subdivision or development, the Buyer should review any document that may limit the use of the Property or govern the Property owner or obligate the Property owner to a financial payment other than the purchase price, taxes, and governmental assessments. If such documents are not available from either the listing agent or the seller, then an attorney should be consulted prior to completing the form.

If the Property is subject to an owners' association, it is recommended that the current standard Owners' Association Addendum (NCAR/NCBA Form 2A12) be attached.

2. **FIXTURES:** If the Seller wishes to ***exclude*** from the sale any items that are presently on the Property and are listed in the fixtures clause, or to ***exclude*** any items that are presently on the Property that may usually be considered to be real property ("fixtures") and are NOT listed in the fixtures clause, list such items. (EXAMPLES: Storage shed; mailboxes; wall/door mirrors; etc.) It is not necessary to cross out items that are listed in the fixtures clause but are not present on the Property. *NOTE: Care should be taken to ascertain that any fixtures* ***included*** *in the sale are owned by the Seller and are not merely rented or leased.* (EXAMPLE: Water treatment/conditioner equipment; gas tank) It is advisable to list any excluded item about which a dispute may arise.

3. **PERSONAL PROPERTY:** List all items of personal property that are to be included in the sale. (EXAMPLES: Curtains, draperies, etc.; free standing appliances such as a refrigerator or range; fireplace tools; window air conditioner; etc.) It is advisable to list any item included in the sale about which some dispute may arise. *NOTE: Care should be taken to ascertain that any personal property* ***included*** *in the sale is owned by the Seller and is not merely rented or leased.*

4. **PURCHASE PRICE:** Insert the amount of the purchase price in dollars.
**Subparagraph (a):** Insert the amount of the earnest money deposit in dollars, check the appropriate box for method of payment, and insert the name of the Escrow Agent designated to hold the earnest money (usually the listing firm), not the name of an individual agent (unless it is to be held by a broker who is a sole practitioner). Note that the name indicated here should also be indicated on the "Firm" line at the bottom of the form under the acknowledgment of receipt of the earnest money. NOTE: Any earnest money check should be made payable to the designated Escrow Agent.
**Subparagraph (b):** If an additional earnest money deposit is to be given at a later date, insert the amount of the additional deposit in dollars and insert the due date. **NOTE: Time is "of the essence" with respect to the payment of any additional earnest money deposit.**
**Subparagraph (c):** Insert the dollar amount of the existing loan on the Property; complete and attach the current standard Loan Assumption Addendum (NCBA/NCAR Form 2A6).
**Subparagraph (d):** Insert the dollar amount of the financing from the Seller; complete and attach the current standard Seller Financing Addendum (NCAR/NCBA Form 2A5).
**Subparagraph (e):** Insert the dollar amount of the balance due from the Buyer. NOTE: This amount should equal the purchase price minus any dollar amounts inserted in subparagraphs (a), (b), (c), or (d). In the case of a counteroffer, which alters any figure in Paragraph 4, all altered figures must be initialed and dated by all parties. Care should be taken to be certain that the figures in subparagraphs (a) through (e), when added, always equal the purchase price.

5. **CONDITIONS:**
**Subparagraph (a):** When this financing contingency provision is used, remember the following points:
(1) Check off or insert the type of loan the Buyer will be obtaining. If FHA or VA financing is being used, attach the current standard FHA/VA Financing Addendum (NCAR/NCBA Form 2A4).
(2) The principal amount may be either a specific loan amount expressed as a dollar figure or as a percentage of the purchase price (EXAMPLE: 95% of purchase price).
(3) Insert the specific term of the desired loan.
(4) Insert a specific maximum interest rate and a specific maximum percentage for discount points. ***Do NOT use "market" or "prevailing."***
(5) Insert the number of days the Buyer has to apply for the loan. Insert the date by which the Buyer is to obtain the loan commitment letter. Allow for sufficient time. Remember, when that date passes, if the Seller wants a copy of the commitment letter, then the Seller must request it in writing.

**Subparagraph (b):** Insert the ***intended*** use of the Property by the Buyer. Be specific. (EXAMPLES: Single-family residential; two-family residential; three-family residential; type of business or office use; type of commercial use.) If the intended use is unusual or different from the current allowable use, the Buyer should make an inquiry ***prior to completing the Offer to Purchase and Contract*** to determine if there are any zoning ordinances, governmental regulations or restrictive covenants that would prohibit such intended use. If the Buyer indicates that there is more than one intended use of the Property, consult an attorney prior to completing the Offer to Purchase and Contract.

**FIGURE 6.9** Continued.

6. <u>SPECIAL ASSESSMENTS:</u> This paragraph deals only with ***special*** assessments levied by a governmental agency or an owners' association for the purpose(s) stated. A "Confirmed" assessment is defined as an assessment that has been imposed by a governing body. A "Pending" assessment is defined as an assessment that is under consideration by a governing body. ***Regular owners' association dues are covered in Paragraph 7.***

7. <u>PRORATIONS AND ADJUSTMENTS:</u> Insert the dollar amount and time period covered by payment of the regular owners' association dues. In the case of a condominium or townhouse resale, it is recommended that the current standard Owners' Association Addendum (NCAR/NCBA Form 2A12) be attached.

8. <u>CLOSING EXPENSES:</u> Insert the **fixed** dollar amount the Seller will pay. This amount may also be expressed as a percentage of the purchase price. **Include in this amount any FHA/VA lender and inspection costs (seller mandated fees) to be paid by Seller**. ***Do NOT use "expenses not to exceed" or "a maximum of" or similar language.*** Examples of Buyer's expenses associated with closing may include, but are not necessarily limited to, discount points, loan origination fees, appraisal fees, attorney's fees, inspection fees and loan "pre-paids" (taxes, insurance, etc.).

12. <u>PROPERTY DISCLOSURE:</u> Indicate the status of the Buyer's receipt of the required N.C. Residential Property Disclosure Statement by checking the appropriate box. If the transaction is exempt from the N. C. Residential Property Disclosure Act, then enter one of the following: (1) Court Ordered Transfer; (2) Borrower to Lender Transfer; (3) Fiduciary Transfer; (4) Co-owner to Co-owner Transfer; (5) Within Family Transfer; (6) Spouse to Spouse Divorce Decree Transfer; (7) Tax Sale; (8) Governmental Transfer; (9) First Sale of Dwelling Never Inhabited; (10) Lease with Option to Purchase (where lessee occupies or intends to occupy the dwelling) **(Caution: See warning under "Use of Form")**; (11) Buyer and Seller Agreement; or (12) Property to be transferred consists of less than 1 or more than 4 residential units. ***See North Carolina General Statutes Section 47E-2 for a complete description of exemptions.***

If the Property is residential property built prior to 1978, the current standard Lead-Based Paint or Lead-Based Paint Hazard Addendum (NCAR/NCBA Form 2A9) must be attached.

13. <u>PROPERTY INSPECTION, APPRAISAL, INVESTIGATION:</u> Check *either* ALTERNATIVE 1 *or* ALTERNATIVE 2.

**ALTERNATIVE 1:**
**Subparagraph (a), Property Inspection:** Insert the date by which all Property inspections will be completed by the Buyer *and* written notice of necessary repairs given to Seller. Also insert the number of days Seller has to provide Buyer a written response to Buyer's notice of necessary repairs. It is strongly recommended that the Property inspections be completed within 14 days of formation of the contract unless there are extenuating circumstances that would prohibit such inspections being completed by such time. ***In all cases, the inspections should be performed as soon as possible.***
**Subparagraph (b), Wood-Destroying Insects:** Insert any structures on the Property that are not subject to a wood-destroying insect inspection. NOTE: Lender may not permit exclusions.
**Subparagraph (f), Appraisal Contingency:** If the contract is *not* subject to a financing contingency requiring an appraisal, then insert the date for completion of the appraisal. If the contract *is* subject to a financing contingency requiring an appraisal, then insert N/A in the blank.

**ALTERNATIVE 2:**
**Subparagraph (a), Property Investigation with Option to Terminate:** Insert the amount of the Option Fee. You must insert an amount greater than zero in the blank. It represents the money paid by Buyer for the exclusive right to purchase the Property during the option period. Upon acceptance of the offer, the Option Fee must be paid directly to Seller. Insert the date for termination of the option. During this time, Seller may entertain other offers only in a back-up position. ***Time is of the essence with regard to the Option Termination Date.***
**Subparagraph (b), Exercise of Option:** The Option Fee cannot be refundable. Do *not* alter this provision to make the Option Fee refundable.

15. <u>CLOSING:</u> Insert the desired closing date. The closing date established should provide a reasonable period of time for obtaining inspections, obtaining loan approval, satisfying contract conditions, and preparing closing documents. Also, provide the full name of each grantee in the deed.

16. <u>POSSESSION:</u> The contract assumes possession will be delivered at closing. "Closing" is defined in Paragraph 15 as the date and time of recording of the deed. If the parties agree to transfer possession to Buyer prior to recording of the deed, then attach a Buyer Possession Before Closing Agreement (NCAR/NCBA Form 2A7) or consult a NC real estate attorney for an appropriate agreement. If the parties agree to permit Seller to remain in possession after recording of the deed, then attach a Seller Possession After Closing Agreement (NCAR/NBCA Form 2A8) or consult a NC real estate attorney for an appropriate agreement.

**FIGURE 6.9** Continued.

17. <u>OTHER PROVISIONS AND CONDITIONS:</u> Indicate by name any attached Addenda. Any Addenda referred to here should be properly identified, signed under seal by the parties, and attached to each original of the contract. Any copy of the contract must always have all Addenda attached. Additional provisions or conditions may be added in this space if necessary. Identify each such provision or condition as (a), (b), etc. If any added provision conflicts with another provision of the contract, clarify which provision is to govern. ***CAUTION: Agents must be extremely careful when adding contract provisions. The drafting of such provisions could constitute the unauthorized practice of law and could result in disciplinary action against an agent by the North Carolina Real Estate Commission, as could the inclusion of an inadequate or improper provision.***

23. <u>NOTICE AND EXECUTION:</u> Usually, at least six originals of the completed and signed contract are needed: one each for Buyer and Seller, the real estate firms involved, the closing attorney and the lender. When using one original contract and making copies for the parties to sign, original signatures should be affixed to each copy as well as the original.

**<u>Buyer acknowledges having made an on-site personal examination of the Property prior to the making of this offer:</u>** If Buyer is purchasing the Property *without* personally having examined it, this sentence should be deleted by marking through it and having the parties both initial and date the deletion.

<u>SIGNATURES AND DATES:</u> All parties with an ownership interest must sign as Seller and all parties named as Buyer must sign as Buyer.

(1) If a married Buyer is taking title as sole owner, and if the contract contains a financing contingency provision, it is advisable to have the Buyer's spouse join in signing the contract so that the spouse will be obligated to join in signing any deed of trust that may be required by the lender to secure the Buyer's loan. Otherwise, the Buyer may be able to avoid performance of the contract if the spouse refuses to sign the deed of trust.

(2) ***If the Seller(s) is married, both the husband and wife always must sign the contract.*** This is true even if the Property is owned by only one spouse. The non-owner spouse holds a potential "marital life estate" under North Carolina law and must sign the deed in order for the other spouse to convey clear title. The signature of the non-owner spouse on the contract will obligate that spouse to join in signing the deed. Note, however, that the non-owner spouse cannot legally be forced to sign the contract.

(3) Indicate the dates that the parties actually sign the Offer to Purchase and Contract.

<u>EARNEST MONEY ACKNOWLEDGEMENT:</u> The "Firm" should be the same as the firm indicated as Escrow Agent (usually the listing firm) in Paragraph 4(a). The agent signing for the firm serving as Escrow Agent on the "By:" line must be associated with that firm. Usually, this will be the individual listing agent.

<u>AGENT/FIRM NAMES AND CONFIRMATION OF AGENCY RELATIONSHIP:</u> Enter the name of the individual selling agent and his or her firm and phone number, and the name of the individual listing agent and his or her firm and phone number, and check the appropriate agency representation box for each. Note that this procedure is ***confirmation*** of a prior disclosure of the agency relationship and in no way should be considered as an initial disclosure of agency relationship. Signatures are not necessary.



**STANDARD FORM 2G**

purchase price; and inspected for the presence of or damage from wood-destroying insects. The buyer may request that the seller make any "eligible" repairs discovered by these inspections or to "cure" a radon problem. If the seller refuses to make these repairs, the buyer's only options are to accept the property "as is" or terminate the contract.

- Cautions buyer that termite inspection may not discover structural damage and damage from sources other than wood-destroying insects.
- *Alternative 2.* The buyer pays a non-refundable option fee directly to the seller. Rule A.0107 was amended July 1, 2005, and now allows a licensee to hold the option fee made payable to the seller; however, the licensee must deliver the option fee to the seller within three days after acceptance of the contract. As always, an offer to purchase real estate becomes a contract when all parties have agreed to all terms of the offer, have indicated their acceptance by signing the Offer to Purchase and Contract and initialing changes, if any, made during any counteroffer negotiations and the last offeree has indicated his acceptance to the last offeror . It is important to date signatures and initialed changes in order to be able to determine the time of contract formation, which begins a three-day period for the delivery of option money.
- For this fee, the buyer is given the right to cancel the contract *at will anytime prior to the option termination date.* The buyer may cancel the contract for any reason or for no reason at all, as long as written notice is provided to the seller before 5:00 p.m. on the option termination date. The amount of this option fee is entered into Offer to Purchase and Contract, paragraph 4(c).
- Defines closing as the time of the recording of the deed.
- Requires the seller to provide reasonable access for inspections.
- Provides addenda for early or late occupancy.
- Requires all addenda to be listed on and attached to all counterparts of the offer to purchase and contract.
- Buyer acknowledges an on-site examination of property before making offer to purchase.
- Features in bold print above the signature lines a clause advising buyers and sellers who do not understand the contract to consult a North Carolina real estate attorney.

Keep these features in mind as you study the Offer to Purchase and Contract and the guidelines for completing it. Practice completing the Offer to Purchase and Contract, following the guidelines, until you are proficient.

## Property Inspections, Repairs, and Buyer's Right to Terminate Offer to Purchase and Contract

Disputes between buyers and sellers regarding repairs to a property under contract have been far too common. Even worse, the arguments have often continued right up to the closing date, adding unwanted stress to an already stressful event. The most current Offer to Purchase and Contract, NCBA/NCAR Form 2T, Paragraph 13, Property Inspection, Appraisal, and Investigation, require the buyer to choose only one of the two alternatives.

## Alternative 1

### *Property Inspection, Appraisal, Investigation*

This alternative most closely resembles the practice licensees are accustomed to regarding property inspections. If the buyer chooses this alternative, she may obtain, at her expense,an inspection of the property to ensure that certain specified "systems" are performing the function for which they were intended and need no immediate repair. Inspections may also be undertaken to determine whether there are drainage issues affecting the structure or whether there is friable asbestos or other environmental contamination.

The date by which the buyer should inform the seller in writing of necessary repairs uncovered from the inspections must be written into the contract in Paragraph 13, Alternative 1(a). The North Carolina Association of REALTORS® has devised a Repair Agreement (Standard Form 310-T) to aid the buyer in notifying the seller of requested repairs. The guidelines recommend that all inspections be completed within 14 days of contract acceptance, but there is no requirement to do so. The key is that the buyer is making an earnest attempt to complete the inspections in a timely manner and that the seller is aiding in this endeavor. Factors outside of both the buyer's and the seller's influence may not make a 14-day window feasible, so there is some flexibility in this date.

The report prepared by the inspector(s) will likely contain repairs that may be necessary but that are not covered by the Offer to Purchase and Contract. Remember, only eligible repairs are subject to negotiation once the offer has been accepted. Eligible repairs are those repairs that must be made to bring specific "systems" listed in Paragraph 13 up to good working order; that is, to the condition where systems are performing the intended function and do not need immediate repair. Malfunctions or deficiencies in "systems" not listed in Paragraph 13 are not subject to negotiation after the Offer to Purchase and Contract has been accepted and they must be accepted "as is." Licensees should be sure to educate their clients on this difference between eligible repairs and the matters noted in an inspector's report. Such communication between licensees and their clients early in the relationship will minimize disputes over repairs.

Once the seller receives the Repair Agreement Form, she has the number of days written into the contract in Paragraph 13, Alternative 1(a) in which to respond to the buyer. It is up to the seller to decide whether to make the eligible repairs listed on the inspection report. She cannot be forced to complete them. If the seller refuses to make legitimate, material repairs of items listed in Paragraph 13, the buyer is left with two options. She can accept the property in its present condition or she may terminate the contract. Once again, the seller's refusal to make noneligible repairs to the property, even those uncovered in the property inspections, does not constitute grounds for the buyer to terminate the contract.

## Wood-Destroying Insects

Alternative 1 also gives the buyer the option of obtaining, at the buyer's expense, a report from the licensed pest control operator stating that there was no "visible evidence of wood-destroying insects" and no indication of "visible damage therefrom." If the pest control inspector notes evidence of wood-destroying insects, the buyer can actually force the seller to pay for the *treatment* (but not the damage therefrom) to rid the property of the insects. This is the one exception to the general rule that the seller can not be forced to make the repairs listed on the inspection report. The seller retains the option of deciding whether he wants to fix the *damage* caused by the insects.

## Radon Inspection

The buyer may pay to have property tested for radon. The test should be completed prior to the date written into the contract in Paragraph 13(a), Alternative 1. The maximum level determined by the Environmental Protection Agency to be acceptable is anything less than 4.0 pico curies per liter of air. If the radon test reveals a level of 4.0 or more, the seller may try to "cure" the problem by taking corrective measures to reduce the radon level. If the seller takes corrective measures, the buyer is entitled to another radon test, for which the seller pays. If the seller is unable to bring the radon levels down to less than 4.0 pico curies per liter or if the seller simply refuses to cure the radon problem, the buyer may terminate the contract and have earnest money returned or accept the property with the existing radon levels.

## Cost of Repair Contingency

This contingency allows the buyer to write in a maximum acceptable dollar amount of eligible repairs discovered in the Paragraph 13, Alternative 1 inspections. This maximum includes repairs necessary as a result of the home inspection, the radon inspection, and the wood-destroying insect inspection. If the dollar amount of all of these repairs exceeds the dollar amount written into this section, the buyer may terminate the contract *even if the seller agrees to make and pay for all necessary repairs.* The buyer is responsible for getting an estimate.

### *Appraisal Contingency*

If the property does not appraise at a value equal to or greater than the purchase price, the buyer may terminate the contract. For sales in which the buyer is not seeking a loan, the buyer must pay for the appraisal and must ensure that the appraisal is completed prior to the date written into the contract in Paragraph 13(f).

## Alternative 2

### *General*

Buyers who choose this alternative elect to pay a specified sum of money, the "Option Fee," directly to the seller for the right to terminate the contract for any reason as long as the "Option Termination Date" has not passed. Both the Option Fee and the Option Termination Date are determined by negotiation between the buyer and the seller and are written into the contract.

### *Buyer's Right to Terminate Prior to the Option Termination Date*

The ease with which a buyer wishing to terminate the Offer to Purchase and Contract may do so varies depending on whether the Option Termination Date has passed. Prior to the Option Termination Date, the buyer may terminate the contract for any reason whatsoever or for no reason at all. As long as the buyer provides the seller (or the seller's agent) with written notice of her intention to terminate the contract before 5:00 p.m. on the Option Termination Date, she is entitled to a full return of her earnest money. Note that time is always "of the essence" in regard to the Option Termination Date. There is simply no flexibility. If the seller does not receive written notice of the buyer's intention to terminate the contract in a timely manner, both parties are bound to move forward with the transaction. The North Carolina Association of REALTORS® has created Standard Form 350-T, Notice of Termination of Contract, for its members to use in giving sellers the requisite notice. (See Figure 6.10.)

If the buyer decides to exercise the right to terminate the contract and does so in writing in a timely manner, the seller keeps the Option Fee. The Option Fee belongs to the seller and is not refundable to the buyer. The language of the contract is very clear on this point. Even if the contract fails to close because of a defect in the seller's title or through some other fault of the seller, the seller keeps the Option Fee. The rationale behind this seemingly harsh treatment of the buyer is that the buyer has already received that for which he/she paid the Option Fee—time. The potential buyer has been allowed to hold the property under contract for the option period and that is in essence what he paid for. A buyer in this situation may consult a real estate attorney to determine whether he has a claim against the seller for breach of contract; however, the agent should never give legal advice.

### *Buyer's Right to Terminate Subsequent to the Option Termination Date*

If the Option Termination Date has passed, it is considerably more difficult for a buyer to terminate the contract without forfeiting her right to a refund of her earnest money, in addition to other remedies sought by the seller. If any of the conditions set forth in Paragraph 5 of the Offer to Purchase and Contract are not satisfied, the transaction still may fail. As discussed in the preceding paragraph, the seller retains the Option Fee.

**FIGURE 6.10** Notice of Termination of Contract.

**NOTICE TO SELLER THAT BUYER IS EXERCISING THEIR RIGHT TO TERMINATE THE OFFER TO PURCHASE AND CONTRACT (FORM 2-T)**

Buyer:________________________________________("Buyer")

Seller:________________________________________("Seller")

Property Address:________________________________("Property")

1. **Contract**. Buyer and Seller entered into a contract for the purchase and sale of the Property on the Offer to Purchase and Contract (form 2-T) ("Contract"). The Effective Date of the Contract is ____________________.

2. **Termination by Buyer**. Buyer hereby terminates the contract between Buyer and Seller for the Property for the following reason(s) (check all applicable boxes):

- ❑ Non-receipt of a signed copy of the N.C. Residential Property Disclosure Statement prior to the signing of this Offer to Purchase and Contract (see paragraph 12 of Contract)
- ❑ Seller's election not to complete necessary repairs requested by Buyer (see Subsections (a) and (c) of Alternative 1 of paragraph 13 of Contract)
- ❑ Seller's election not to remediate or failure of attempted remediation to bring radon level within satisfactory range (see Subsection (d) of Alternative 1 of paragraph 13 of the Contract)
- ❑ Reasonable estimate of total cost of repairs required by (a) and (b) and/or remediation required by (d) of Alternative 1 equals or exceeds agreed-upon amount (see Subsection (e) of Alternative 1 of paragraph 13 of the Contract)
- ❑ Property does not appraise at a value equal to or exceeding the purchase price (see Subsection (f) of Alternative 1 of paragraph 13 of the Contract)
- ❑ Exercise by Buyer of option to terminate under Alternative 2 of the Contract (see Subsections (a) and (b) of Alternative 2 of paragraph 13 of the Contract)
- ❑ Inability of Buyer to obtain the loan as set forth in Paragraph 5(a) of the Contract

THE NORTH CAROLINA ASSOCIATION OF REALTORS®, INC. MAKES NO REPRESENTATION AS TO THE LEGAL VALIDITY OR ADEQUACY OF ANY PROVISION OF THIS FORM IN ANY SPECIFIC TRANSACTION.

________________________ __________ __________
Buyer Date Time

________________________ __________ __________
Buyer Date Time

**RELEASE OF EARNEST MONEY BY SELLER***

Seller acknowledges that Buyer is entitled to a refund of any earnest monies received in connection with the contract as a result of Buyer's termination of the contract for the reason(s) set forth above, and hereby agrees that Escrow Agent may disburse any such earnest monies to Buyer.

________________________ __________
Seller Date

________________________ __________
Seller Date

*Seller's written release is not required before Escrow Agent may lawfully disburse any earnest money deposit to Buyer. However, as set forth in paragraph 4(a) of the Contract, in the event of a dispute between Seller and Buyer over the return or forfeiture of earnest money held in escrow by a broker, the broker is required by state law to retain said earnest money in the broker's trust or escrow account until a written release from the parties consenting to its disposition has been obtained or until disbursement is ordered by a court of competent jurisdiction.

Page 1 of 1

REALTOR® North Carolina Association of REALTORS®, Inc. EQUAL HOUSING OPPORTUNITY

STANDARD FORM 350 - T

## Payment of Option Fee to the Seller

It is specifically stated in the Offer to Purchase and in the Guidelines that the Option Fee should be paid directly by the buyer to the seller, not to the Escrow Agent.

Although typically option money is given directly to the seller (optionor) when the seller gives an option contract to the optionee, this practice has some practical drawbacks in regard to the option created by Paragraph 13 Alternative 2. NCREC rule 58A, 0107 now allows some leeway in this situation. The option fee check is payable directly to the seller, but the buyer's agent can hold the check in safe keeping for up to three business days after the option contract is finalized or fully accepted. The buyer's agent must deliver the check to the seller's agent or the seller within that three-day period. The option check cannot and should not be deposited into the agent's excrow account but must be adequately safeguarded while in the broker's possession.

## Buyer's Right to Inspect the Property

A buyer using Alternative 2 retains the right to complete any inspections on the property he wants to do, but the Offer to Purchase expressly advises the buyer to complete all inspections before the Option Termination Date. The buyer should consider the number and timing of the property inspections before writing the Option Termination Date into the contract. Thus, if the buyer intends to have many inspections done on the property, he should attempt to secure a longer option period.

Unlike Alternative 1, Alternative 2 does not restrict negotiable repairs on the property to "eligible repairs." An Alternative 2 buyer can request that the seller make any repairs the buyer desires, as long as the Option Termination Date has not been passed. As with Alternative 1, the seller cannot be forced to make any repairs. The seller is free to agree to complete some, all, or none of them. As long as the Option Termination Date has not passed, the buyer is free to walk away from the transaction if the seller refuses to make requested repairs. The buyer who walks away would forfeit only the Option Fee but would be entitled to a return of earnest money. If the Option Termination Date has passed and the buyer failed to give the seller written notice of intention to terminate the contract, the buyer will be considered to have accepted the property "as is" as of the Option Termination Date. After the Option Termination Date, a buyer's bargaining power regarding repairs diminishes significantly or disappears. The buyer is truly at the mercy of a seller who no longer has much incentive to complete the repairs.

Once the repairs are negotiated between the buyer and seller, it is particularly important that buyers who choose Alternative 2 have the seller commit to the agreed-upon repairs to writing before the Option expires. The North Carolina Association of REALTORS® has created a Repair Agreement Form, Standard Form 310-T (Figure 6.11). This form may be used only by its members; it is not a joint form with the North Carolina Bar Association. Once form 310-T (or similar form) is signed, the buyer waives the right to terminate the contract for the remaining option period, *for repair issues*. The buyer may still terminate the contract later on under Paragraph 5 (financing, zoning, condition of the property, etc.) of the Offer to Purchase and Contract.

## Appraisal Contingencies and Alternative 2

Since the appraisal contingency is found only under Alternative 1, a buyer who wishes to use Alternative 2, and who wishes to determine whether the property's value is at least equal to the sales price, should have the appraisal completed before the option period has expired. If the property fails to appraise at a value suitable to the buyer, the buyer may simply send notice to the seller of her intention to terminate the contract prior to the option period.

## The Option Fee in a Closed Transaction

While the Option Fee is never refundable to the buyer if a proposed transaction fails to make it to closing, the buyer is allowed a credit for the Option Fee if the transaction actually closes. The credit will go toward the purchase price of the property at closing.

**FIGURE 6.11** Repair Request and Agreement Form.

**REPAIR REQUEST AND AGREEMENT**
**[See Guidelines for completing this form (Standard form # 310G)]**

______________________________________________________________, as Buyer,

and ___________________________________________________________, as Seller,

have entered into an Offer to Purchase and Contract ("Contract") regarding the purchase and sale of the following property (insert property address): ______________________________________________

_________________________________________________________ ("Property").

1. **Requested Repairs.** Buyer hereby requests Seller to complete the following repairs to the Property, including but not limited to radon remediation (*attach additional page(s) if needed*):

_____________________________________________________________________

_____________________________________________________________________

_____________________________________________________________________

_____________________________________________________________________

_____________________________________________________________________

_____________________________________________________________________

_____________________________________________________________________

_____________________________________________________________________

_____________________________________________________________________

_____________________________________________________________________

_____________________________________________________________________

_____________________________________________________________________

_____________________________________________________________________

_____________________________________________________________________

_____________________________________________________________________

2. **Agreement**. At such time as Buyer and Seller agree which of the repairs set forth in paragraph 1 above will be completed, Seller shall complete, prior to Closing, the agreed-upon repairs (the "Repairs") at Seller's expense and in a good and workmanlike manner.

3. **Notification, Verification.** Seller shall notify Buyer upon completion of the Repairs and provide Buyer with documentation thereof. Buyer shall have the right to verify that the Repairs have been completed in a good and workmanlike manner. Unless otherwise indicated in the Contract or this Agreement, such verification shall be at Buyer's expense.

4. **Additional Inspections.** (*applicable only if Alternative 1 of paragraph 13 of the Contract is in effect*) Buyer reserves the right to obtain the following additional inspections:

(i) A wood-destroying insect report permitted under Alternative 1, subsection (b) of the Contract;

(ii) Inspections of any hidden defects covered under subsection (a) of Alternative 1 that may be revealed by the performance of the Repairs; and

(iii) _____________________________________________________________

_____________________________________________________________

_____________________________________________________________

Any additional repairs that Buyer may request and Seller may agree to complete as a result of any such additional inspections will be added to paragraph 1 above and shall become a part of this Agreement.

5. **Release of Inspection Reports.** Buyer ❑ does ❑ does not agree to release any inspection reports to Seller.



REALTOR®

**North Carolina Association of REALTORS®, Inc.**

Buyer Initials ______ ______ Seller Initials ______ ______

EQUAL HOUSING OPPORTUNITY

**STANDARD FORM 310 - T**
**© 7/2005**

**FIGURE 6.11** Continued.

6. **Agreement not to terminate Contract.**

IF ALTERNATIVE 1 OF PARAGRAPH 13 OF THE CONTRACT IS IN EFFECT: In consideration for Seller's agreement to make the Repairs, Buyer agrees to otherwise accept the Property in its current condition and without regard to the estimated cost of any repairs and/or radon remediation, provided that the Repairs are made as agreed. This agreement is subject to buyer's rights under paragraph 4 above as well as any rights Buyer may have under paragraph 5(c) of the Contract.

IF ALTERNATIVE 2 OF PARAGRAPH 13 OF THE CONTRACT IS IN EFFECT: In consideration for Seller's agreement to make the Repairs, Buyer agrees not to terminate the contract under subsection (a) of Alternative 2. This agreement is subject to any rights Buyer may have under paragraph 5(c) of the Contract.

7. **Effective Date; Entire Agreement.** This Agreement shall become effective on the date it has been signed by both parties. Prior to the effective date, a party's signature hereunder shall not constitute a waiver of any right or option that such party may have under paragraph 13 of the Contract. This Agreement contains the entire agreement of the parties regarding Repairs and there are no representations, inducements or other provisions other than those expressed herein. All changes, additions or deletions hereto must be in writing and signed by all parties.

THE NORTH CAROLINA ASSOCIATION OF REALTORS®, INC. MAKES NO REPRESENTATION AS TO THE LEGAL VALIDITY OR ADEQUACY OF ANY PROVISION OF THIS FORM IN ANY SPECIFIC TRANSACTION.

Buyer: ____________________ Date ________ Seller: ____________________ Date ________

Buyer: ____________________ Date ________ Seller: ____________________ Date ________



**STANDARD FORM 310 - T**

## Vacant Lot Offer to Purchase and Contract

The Vacant Lot Offer to Purchase and Contract (NCAR Standard Form 12-T) (see Figure 6.12) was developed specifically to address the purchase of a vacant lot. This form is very similar to the Offer to Purchase and Contract (NCAR Standard Form 2-T), with the following noted exceptions and explanations:

- The contract states that the form is to be used only for vacant lots and that if the buyer's builder is selling the lot, Standard Form 2-T should be used. The contract also notes that the lot must be developed per the presiding locality's subdivision ordinances.
- No fixtures or personal property section is included because a vacant lot typically does not have these items.
- Fuel section found in Standard Form 2-T is omitted.
- There is no Property Disclosure section. Section 11, Alternative 1(a), gives the buyer the right to obtain reports to ascertain whether the property is suitable for her intended use as regards to utilities, water, environmental hazards, flooding, laws, rules and regulations. If reports are unsatisfactory or cannot be obtained, the buyer may avoid contract without penalty by giving the seller written notice by the specified date, time being of the essence.

  Section 11, Alternative 1(b) requires the buyer to check one of the three following options regarding the sewer system.

  1. The buyer has investigated the costs and expenses of installing the sewer system.
  2. The seller represents that the sewer system has been installed. The seller does not make further representations regarding the system. The buyer has the option, at his expense, of obtaining an inspection of the system to determine its condition. If the system is not performing adequately, the buyer has the right to terminate the contract. The buyer must notify the seller of this fact in writing, time being of the essence.
  3. The contract is contingent upon the buyer being able to obtain an Improvement Permit or like from the County Health Department for the type of structure specified in the paragraph. If the desired ground adsorption system is not allowed, the buyer may terminate the contract if the buyer notifies the seller in writing, time being of the essence.
  4. The buyer has accepted the availability and cost of connecting to a public or community sewer system.
- Section 11, Alternative 1(c) gives the buyer the right to cancel the contract if the vacant lot does not appraise at a value greater than or equal to the purchase price.
- Section 12, Right of Entry, Restoration and Indemnity.
- The buyer, and his agents and contractors, may enter the property for any required examination of the property. The buyer agrees to restore the property to its original condition should the contract be terminated. The buyer also agrees to hold the seller harmless for any losses or damages arising from this section.
- The risk of loss falls upon the seller.

The remaining provisions of this contract are the same as the Offer to Purchase and Contract, Standard Form 2-T.

## Guidelines for Preparation of Purchase Contracts

The preparation of a purchase contract places a serious responsibility on the real estate agent. This is such an important transaction that several states do not allow the agent to perform this act and require that an attorney prepare the contract. North Carolina allows real estate agents to "prepare" contracts as long as this practice is limited to "filling in the blanks"; that is, the agent can write in the names and numbers. North Carolina licensees are specifically prohibited from "drafting" contracts; that is, it is illegal for them to write legal clauses or construct a contract for others. Note that Real Estate Commission rules specifically prohibit any provision in the Offer to Purchase and Contract that concerns the payment of commission or compensation to a broker or any clause that attempts to disclaim liability of a broker for his representations in connection with the transaction.

**FIGURE 6.12** North Carolina Offer to Purchase Contract.

**OFFER TO PURCHASE AND CONTRACT - VACANT LOT/LAND**

**NOTE:** This contract is intended for unimproved real property that Buyer will purchase only for personal use and will not subdivide. It should not be used to sell subdivided property that has not been platted, properly approved and recorded with the register of deeds as of the date of the contract. If Seller is Buyer's builder and the sale involves the construction of a new single family dwelling prior to closing, use the standard Offer to Purchase and Contract (Form 2-T) with the New Construction Addendum (Form 2A3-T).

______________________________________________________, as Buyer, hereby offers to purchase and ____________________________________________, as Seller, upon acceptance of said offer, agrees to sell and convey, all of that plot, piece or parcel of land described below (hereafter referred to as the "Property"), upon the following terms and conditions:

**1. REAL PROPERTY:** Located in the City of ________________________________________, County of ________________________________, State of North Carolina, being known as and more particularly described as:
Street Address__________________________________________________ Zip__________
Subdivision Name________________________________________________________
Plat Reference: Lot________________, Block or Section ________________________________ as shown on Plat Book or Slide ____________ at Page(s) ____________(Property acquired by Seller in Deed Book ____________ at Page ____________).
❑ All ❑ A portion of the property in Deed Reference: Book _________ Page No. _________, __________________County

**NOTE:** Prior to signing this Offer to Purchase and Contract - Vacant Lot/Land, Buyer is advised to review Restrictive Covenants, if any, which may limit the use of the Property, and to read the Declaration of Restrictive Covenants, By-Laws, Articles of Incorporation, Rules and Regulations, and other governing documents of the owners' association and/or the subdivision, if applicable.

**2. PURCHASE PRICE:** The purchase price is $________________________________ and shall be paid as follows:

**(a)** $______________________, EARNEST MONEY DEPOSIT with this offer by ❑ cash ❑ personal check ❑ bank check ❑ certified check ❑ other: ________________________________________ to be deposited and held in escrow by ________________________________________ ("Escrow Agent"); until the sale is closed, at which time it will be credited to Buyer, or until this contract is otherwise terminated. In the event: (1) this offer is not accepted; or (2) any of the conditions hereto are not satisfied, then all earnest monies shall be refunded to Buyer. In the event of breach of this contract by Seller, all earnest monies shall be refunded to Buyer upon Buyer's request, but such return shall not affect any other remedies available to Buyer for such breach. In the event of breach of this contract by Buyer, then all earnest monies shall be forfeited to Seller upon Seller's request, but such forfeiture shall not affect any other remedies available to Seller for such breach.
**NOTE:** In the event of a dispute between Seller and Buyer over the return or forfeiture of earnest money held in escrow by a broker, the broker is required by state law to retain said earnest money in the broker's trust or escrow account until a written release from the parties consenting to its disposition has been obtained or until disbursement is ordered by a court of competent jurisdiction.

**(b)** $________________, ADDITIONAL EARNEST MONEY DEPOSIT to be paid to Escrow Agent no later than __________________________, TIME BEING OF THE ESSENCE WITH REGARD TO SAID DATE.

**(c)** $______________________, OPTION FEE in accordance with paragraph 11, Alternative 2, to be paid to Seller on the Effective Date as set forth in paragraph 19. (NOTE: If Alternative 2 applies, then do not insert $0, N/A, or leave blank).

**(d)** $______________________, BY ASSUMPTION of the unpaid principal balance and all obligations of Seller on the existing loan(s) secured by a deed of trust on the Property in accordance with the attached Loan Assumption Addendum.

**(e)** $______________________, BY SELLER FINANCING in accordance with the attached Seller Financing Addendum.

**(f)** $______________________, BALANCE of the purchase price in cash at Closing.

**3. CONDITIONS:** (State N/A in each blank that is not a condition to this contract.)

**(a)** Buyer must be able to obtain a ❑ Conventional ❑ Other:____________________ loan at a ❑ Fixed Rate ❑ Adjustable Rate in the principal amount of __________________________ for a term of _____ year(s), at an initial interest rate not to exceed ______% per annum, with mortgage loan discount points not to exceed ______ % of the loan amount. Buyer shall apply for said loan within _______ days of the Effective Date of this contract. Buyer shall use Buyer's best efforts to secure the lender's customary loan commitment letter on or before __________________________ and to satisfy all terms and conditions of the loan commitment letter by Closing. After the above letter date, Seller may request in writing from Buyer a copy of the loan commitment letter. If Buyer fails to provide Seller a copy of the loan commitment letter or a written waiver of this loan condition within five days of receipt of Seller's request, Seller may terminate this contract by written notice to Buyer at any time thereafter, provided Seller has not then received a copy of the letter or the waiver.





Buyer Initials ______ ______ Seller Initials ______ ______

**FIGURE 6.12** Continued.

(b) There must be no restriction, easement, zoning or other governmental regulation that would prevent the reasonable use of the Property for ______________________________ purposes ("Intended Use").

(c) The Property must be in substantially the same or better condition at Closing as on the date of this offer, reasonable wear and tear excepted.

(d) All deeds of trust, liens and other charges against the Property, not assumed by Buyer, must be paid and satisfied by Seller prior to or at Closing such that cancellation may be promptly obtained following Closing. Seller shall remain obligated to obtain any such cancellations following Closing.

(e) Title must be delivered at Closing by GENERAL WARRANTY DEED unless otherwise stated herein, and must be fee simple marketable and insurable title, free of all encumbrances except: ad valorem taxes for the current year (prorated through the date of Closing); utility easements and unviolated restrictive covenants that do not materially affect the value of the Property; and such other encumbrances as may be assumed or specifically approved by Buyer. The Property must have legal access to a public right of way.

**4. SPECIAL ASSESSMENTS:** Seller warrants that there are no pending or confirmed governmental special assessments for sidewalk, paving, water, sewer, or other improvements on or adjoining the Property, and no pending or confirmed owners' association special assessments, except as follows: ______________________________

______________________________.

(Insert "None" or the identification of such assessments, if any.) Seller shall pay all owners' association assessments and all governmental assessments confirmed through the time of Closing, if any, and Buyer shall take title subject to all pending assessments, if any, unless otherwise agreed as follows: ______________________________

______________________________.

**5. PRORATIONS AND ADJUSTMENTS:** Unless otherwise provided, the following items shall be prorated and either adjusted between the parties or paid at Closing: (a) Ad valorem taxes on real property shall be prorated on a calendar year basis through the date of Closing; (b) All late listing penalties, if any, shall be paid by Seller; (c) Rents, if any, for the Property shall be prorated through the date of Closing; (d) Owners' association dues and other like charges shall be prorated through the date of Closing. Seller represents that the regular owners' association dues, if any, are $____________ per ______________.

**6. EXPENSES:** Unless otherwise agreed, Buyer shall be responsible for all costs with respect to any loan obtained by Buyer, title search, title insurance, recording the deed and for preparation and recording of all instruments required to secure the balance of the purchase price unpaid at Closing. Seller shall pay for preparation of a deed and all other documents necessary to perform Seller's obligations under this agreement, and for excise tax (revenue stamps) required by law. Seller shall pay at Closing $____________________ toward any of Buyer's expenses associated with the purchase of the Property, including any FHA/VA lender and inspection costs that Buyer is not permitted to pay, but excluding any portion disapproved by Buyer's lender.

**7. EVIDENCE OF TITLE:** Seller agrees to use his best efforts to deliver to Buyer as soon as reasonably possible after the Effective Date of this contract, copies of all title information in possession of or available to Seller, including but not limited to: title insurance policies, attorney's opinions on title, surveys, covenants, deeds, notes and deeds of trust and easements relating to the Property. Seller authorizes (1) any attorney presently or previously representing Seller to release and disclose any title insurance policy in such attorney's file to Buyer and both Buyer's and Seller's agents and attorneys; and (2) the Property's title insurer or its agent to release and disclose all materials in the Property's title insurer's (or title insurer's agent's) file to Buyer and both Buyer's and Seller's agents and attorneys.

**8. LABOR AND MATERIAL:** Seller shall furnish at Closing an affidavit and indemnification agreement in form satisfactory to Buyer showing that all labor and materials, if any, furnished to the Property within 120 days prior to the date of Closing have been paid for and agreeing to indemnify Buyer against all loss from any cause or claim arising therefrom.

**9. CLOSING:** Closing shall be defined as the date and time of recording of the deed. All parties agree to execute any and all documents and papers necessary in connection with Closing and transfer of title on or before ______________________, at a place designated by Buyer. The deed is to be made to ______________________________.

**CLOSING SHALL CONSTITUTE ACCEPTANCE OF THE PROPERTY IN ITS THEN EXISTING CONDITION UNLESS PROVISION IS OTHERWISE MADE IN WRITING.**

**10. POSSESSION:** Unless otherwise provided herein, possession shall be delivered at Closing. No alterations, excavations, tree removal or other such activities may be done before possession is delivered.



Buyer Initials _______ _______ Seller Initials _______ _______

**FIGURE 6.12** Continued.

**11. PROPERTY INSPECTION, APPRAISAL, INVESTIGATION (Choose ONLY ONE of the following Alternatives):**

❑ **ALTERNATIVE 1:**

**(a) Soil, Water, Utilities And Environmental Contingency:** This contract is contingent upon Buyer obtaining report(s) that (i) the soil is suitable for Buyer's Intended Use, (ii) utilities and water are available to the Property, (iii) there is no environmental contamination, law, rule or regulation that prohibits, restricts or limits Buyer's Intended Use, and (iv) there is no flood hazard that prohibits, restricts or limits Buyer's Intended Use (collectively the "Reports"). All costs and expenses of obtaining the Reports shall be borne by Buyer. Buyer shall use Buyer's best efforts to obtain such Reports. If the Reports cannot be obtained, Buyer may terminate this contract and the Earnest Money Deposit shall be refunded to Buyer. Buyer waives this condition unless Buyer provides written notice to Seller by ______________________________ that this condition cannot be satisfied, **time being of the essence.**

**(b) Sewer System** (check only **ONE**):

❑ Buyer has investigated the costs and expenses to install the sewer system approved by the Improvement Permit attached hereto as Exhibit A and hereby approves and accepts said Improvement Permit.

❑ Seller represents that the system has been installed, which representation survives Closing, but makes no further representations as to the system. Buyer acknowledges receipt of the Improvement Permit attached hereto as Exhibit A. Buyer shall have the option of inspecting or obtaining, at Buyer's expense, inspection(s) to determine the condition of the system. If the system is not performing the function for which intended and is in need of immediate repair, Buyer may terminate this Contract and the Earnest Money Deposit shall be refunded to Buyer. Buyer waives this condition unless Buyer provides written notice to Seller by ______________________ that this condition cannot be satisfied, **time being of the essence.**

❑ This Contract is contingent upon ❑ Buyer ❑ Seller ("Responsible Party") obtaining an Improvement Permit or written evaluation from the County Health Department ("County") for a (check only ONE) ❑ conventional or ❑ other ______________________________________ ground absorption sewage system for a _______ bedroom home. All costs and expenses of obtaining such Permit or written evaluation shall be borne by Responsible Party unless otherwise agreed. In any event Seller, by no later than ______________________, shall be responsible for clearing that portion of the Property required by the County to perform its tests and/or inspections. Responsible Party shall use best efforts to obtain such Permit or written evaluation. If the Improvement Permit or written evaluation from the County cannot be obtained by __________________(date), either party may terminate this Contract and the Earnest Money Deposit shall be refunded to Buyer.

❑ Buyer has investigated and approved the availability, costs and expenses to connect to a ❑ public or ❑ community sewer system.

**(c) Appraisal Contingency**: The Property must appraise at a value equal to or exceeding the purchase price or, at the option of Buyer, this contract may be terminated and all earnest monies shall be refunded to Buyer. If this contract is not subject to a financing contingency requiring an appraisal, Buyer shall arrange to have the appraisal completed on or before _________________________. The cost of the appraisal shall be borne by Buyer.

**(d) CLOSING SHALL CONSTITUTE ACCEPTANCE OF THE PROPERTY IN ITS THEN EXISTING CONDITION UNLESS PROVISION IS OTHERWISE MADE IN WRITING.**

❑ **ALTERNATIVE 2**: *(This Alternative applies ONLY if Alternative 2 is checked AND Buyer has paid the Option Fee.)*

**(a) Property Investigation with Option to Terminate:** In consideration of the sum set forth in paragraph 2(c) paid by Buyer to Seller (not Escrow Agent) and other valuable consideration, the sufficiency of which is hereby acknowledged (the "Option Fee"), Buyer shall have the right to terminate this contract for any reason or no reason, whether related to the physical condition of the Property or otherwise, by delivering to Seller written notice of termination (the "Termination Notice") by 5:00 p.m. on ______________________________, 20____, *time being of the essence* (the "Option Termination Date"). At any time prior to Closing, Buyer shall have the right to inspect the Property at Buyer's expense (Buyer is advised to have all inspections and appraisals of the Property, including but not limited to those matters set forth in Alternative 1, performed prior to the Option Termination Date).

**(b) Exercise of Option**: If Buyer delivers the Termination Notice prior to the Option Termination Date, *time being of the essence*, this contract shall become null and void and all earnest monies received in connection herewith shall be refunded to Buyer; however, the Option Fee will not be refunded and shall be retained by Seller. If Buyer fails to deliver the Termination Notice to Seller prior to the Option Termination Date, then Buyer will be deemed to have accepted the Property in its physical condition existing as of the Option Termination Date; provided such acceptance shall not constitute a waiver of any rights Buyer has under paragraph 3. The Option Fee is not refundable, is not a part of any earnest monies, and will be credited to the purchase price at Closing.

**(c) CLOSING SHALL CONSTITUTE ACCEPTANCE OF THE PROPERTY IN ITS THEN EXISTING CONDITION UNLESS PROVISION IS OTHERWISE MADE IN WRITING.**



Buyer Initials _______ _______ Seller Initials _______ _______

**FIGURE 6.12** Continued.

**12. RIGHT OF ENTRY, RESTORATION AND INDEMNITY:** Buyer and Buyer's agents and contractors shall have the right to enter upon the Property for the purpose of appraising the Property, and performing the tests and inspections permitted in this contract. If Buyer terminates this contract as provided herein, Buyer shall, at Buyer's expense, restore the Property to substantially its pre-entry condition within thirty days of contract termination. Buyer will indemnify and hold Seller harmless from all loss, damage, claims, suits or costs, which shall arise out of any contract, agreement, or injury to any person or property as a result of any activities of Buyer and Buyer's agents and contractors relating to the Property. This indemnity shall survive this contract and any termination hereof. Notwithstanding the foregoing, Seller shall be responsible for any loss, damage, claim, suit or cost arising out of pre-existing conditions of the Property and/or out of Seller's negligence or willful acts or omissions.

**13. OTHER PROVISIONS AND CONDITIONS:** (ITEMIZE ALL ADDENDA TO THIS CONTRACT AND ATTACH HERETO.)

**14. RISK OF LOSS:** The risk of loss or damage by fire or other casualty prior to Closing shall be upon Seller.

**15. ASSIGNMENTS:** This contract may not be assigned without the written consent of all parties, but if assigned by agreement, then this contract shall be binding on the assignee and his heirs and successors.

**16. PARTIES:** This contract shall be binding upon and shall inure to the benefit of the parties, i.e., Buyer and Seller and their heirs, successors and assigns. As used herein, words in the singular include the plural and the masculine includes the feminine and neuter genders, as appropriate.

**17. SURVIVAL:** If any provision herein contained which by its nature and effect is required to be observed, kept or performed after the Closing, it shall survive the Closing and remain binding upon and for the benefit of the parties hereto until fully observed, kept or performed.

**18. ENTIRE AGREEMENT:** This contract contains the entire agreement of the parties and there are no representations, inducements or other provisions other than those expressed herein. All changes, additions or deletions hereto must be in writing and signed by all parties. Nothing contained herein shall alter any agreement between a REALTOR® or broker and Seller or Buyer as contained in any listing agreement, buyer agency agreement, or any other agency agreement between them.

**19. NOTICE AND EXECUTION:** Any notice or communication to be given to a party herein may be given to the party or to such party's agent. This offer shall become a binding contract (the "Effective Date") when signed by both Buyer and Seller and such signing is communicated to the offering party. This contract is executed under seal in signed multiple originals, all of which together constitute one and the same instrument, with a signed original being retained by each party and each REALTOR® or broker hereto, and the parties adopt the word "SEAL" beside their signatures below.

**Buyer acknowledges having made an on-site personal examination of the Property prior to the making of this offer.**

THE NORTH CAROLINA ASSOCIATION OF REALTORS®, INC. AND THE NORTH CAROLINA BAR ASSOCIATION MAKE NO REPRESENTATION AS TO THE LEGAL VALIDITY OR ADEQUACY OF ANY PROVISION OF THIS FORM IN ANY SPECIFIC TRANSACTION. IF YOU DO NOT UNDERSTAND THIS FORM OR FEEL THAT IT DOES NOT PROVIDE FOR YOUR LEGAL NEEDS, YOU SHOULD CONSULT A NORTH CAROLINA REAL ESTATE ATTORNEY BEFORE YOU SIGN IT.

Date: ______________________ Date: ______________________

Buyer ______________________(SEAL) Seller ______________________(SEAL)

Date: ______________________ Date: ______________________

Buyer ______________________(SEAL) Seller ______________________(SEAL)

**Escrow Agent acknowledges receipt of the earnest money and agrees to hold and disburse the same in accordance with the terms hereof.**

Date______________________ Firm:______________________

By:______________________
(Signature)

Selling Agent/Firm/Phone______________________
Acting as ❑ Buyer's Agent ❑ Seller's (sub)Agent ❑ Dual Agent
Individual license #:______________________

Listing Agent/Firm/Phone______________________
Acting as ❑ Seller's (sub)Agent ❑ Dual Agent
Individual license #:______________________

Page 4 of 4

**STANDARD FORM 12 - T**
**© 7/2006**

When the buyer and seller enter into this binding agreement, the seller obligates his most important financial assets, and the buyer enters into a long-term financial obligation. Therefore, the agent must exercise due care to see that the preparation of this agreement represents the complete understanding of the parties. Practitioners should previously have given the buyer and seller a blank copy with the word "SAMPLE" overlaid on the Offer to Purchase and Contract at the time the agency agreements were signed. This gives both parties time to become familiar with the form and to ask questions of the licensee or an attorney. The licensee should be careful to refer legal questions to an attorney. The Real Estate Commission will hold the agent responsible for mistakes made in preparation of the contract.

Guidelines on the NCBA/NCAR Standard Form 2G, Guidelines for Completing the Offer to Purchase and Contract Form (see Figure 6.9) are comprehensive and do not need to be reiterated here; however, here are a few comments and caveats to note.

1. If in doubt about the suitability of this document for a particular transaction, consult an attorney.
2. The offer is created when the buyer signs the offer to purchase, and it becomes a contract when the seller accepts it and that acceptance is communicated to the buyer or her agent.
3. The broker collects earnest money to protect the seller's interest. The seller decides how much earnest money he will accept; however, earnest money is not necessary for the contract to be valid.
4. The three purposes of earnest money are to demonstrate the buyer's sincerity, to demonstrate the buyer's financial capability to raise the money called for in the agreement, and to serve as compensation to the seller in the event of default by the buyer.
5. For the protection of the broker, it is important to list the method of payment of the earnest money in the offer to purchase and contract. If the payment by personal check is not specified in the contract and the buyer defaults, the seller would be entitled to rely on the fact that the broker is holding the earnest money in cash. If the buyer's personal check fails to clear the bank, the seller could hold the broker responsible for the earnest money.
6. The financing contingency is important. Before showing the property and writing the offer, the licensee should have prequalified the buyer and should be reasonably certain the buyer is financially able to buy, based on the information provided to her by the buyer. The terms of the financing contingency must be specified.
7. The agent should provide a reasonable time for loan processing and closing. The closing can take place before the closing date or within a reasonable time afterward if everyone involved is making a diligent effort to close. Failure to close on time does not nullify the contract unless there is a "time is of the essence" clause. It is usually not a good idea to include a time is of the essence clause because this clause can work against the agent and often creates problems between the buyer and seller.
8. The offer to purchase and contract should specify the type of property use. For example, residential property should be specified as single-family, multifamily, and so on. Real Estate practitioners should be aware of any anticipated changes from the current use.
9. Personal property may, and often should, be handled outside the contract with a bill of sale.
10. A commission amount or a disclaimer of responsibility should not be included in an offer to purchase and contract.
11. NCAR Standard Forms are available from several vendors. They allow for perfectly keyed contracts and simplify changes in offers and counteroffers because only the changes must be inserted. NCAR provides its forms online to members.

## Forms Accompanying an Offer to Purchase and Contract

The Residential Property Disclosure Statement must be presented to the buyer before he makes the offer. Sellers of residential units built before 1978 must provide lead-based paint disclosure statement (see Chapter 4, Figure 4.3).

Agency status of both the listing and *sales agents* must be indicated on the Offer to Purchase and Contract. Agency status should have been disclosed to the listing agent before showing the property. That notification can be documented through the use of NCAR Standard Form 220, Confirmation of Agency Relationships, Appointment and Compensation (see chapters 5 and 6). Agency contracts and verbal notifications should have been accomplished earlier.

If dual agency addenda have not been signed and the firm finds itself in a position where it needs to act as a dual agent, the situation may be handled by having the buyer and seller sign a dual agency addendum to their respective agency contracts or obtaining a dual agency agreement signed by both parties. (See pages 5-97 and 6-162 for a more complete discussion of methods, times, and forms for authorizing dual agency in differing situations.)

## Submitting Offers to Sellers

Licensing regulations, Rule A.0106, make it absolutely clear that the agent is to submit all instruments to the principal immediately. This regulation specifically addresses offers as an important instrument. Therefore, the agent has no latitude in screening offers for the seller but must deliver all offers for the seller's decision. It is not the agent's prerogative to decide what constitutes a reasonable offer. As a function of the limited agency relationship, the agent is not empowered to make decisions for her employer but must pass on all information for the latter's decision.

## Back-up Offers

There are cases in which an offer is accepted by the seller and another buyer wants to submit an offer. Agents should be clear about their duty in this event. The agent's duty to the seller is not discharged until the final sale and conveyance of the title has been consummated. Thus, there is a decided difference between "sold" and "contract pending." Although there is no clear rule in North Carolina regarding this point in the display of yard signs, it is becoming the standard practice to use the "pending" designation until the closing has been accomplished.

Until closing, then, it is the duty of the agent to transmit immediately all offers to the seller for a decision. If the seller wants to consider the subsequent offer as a backup to the current contract, NCBA/NCAR Standard Form 2A1-T, Back-Up Contract Addendum (see Figure 6.13) may be used for this purpose. This form addresses the following points:

1. Provides that primary contract shall be terminated and specified evidence of termination shall be provided before parties to back-up contract are obligated to perform.
2. Specifies effects of modification of primary contract or terms.
3. Limits buyer's access to primary contract.
4. Specifies how earnest money will be handled.
5. Provides for termination of back-up contract upon closing of primary contract.
6. Defines notification of termination of primary contract and specifies number of days after termination of primary contract in which back-up offer must close.
7. Specifies time in which back-up contract becomes null and void if buyer or buyer's agent has not been notified of termination of primary contract.

An agent may only fill in the blanks on this or another attorney-generated back-up contract addenda. If no satisfactory form exists for the specific circumstances, the seller should consult an attorney.

## Acceptance of Offers

An offer is just an offer until it is accepted and the acceptance is communicated to the offeror or his agent. Then it is a contract. It is accepted when the offeree has agreed to all terms of

**FIGURE 6.13** Back-Up Contract Addendum.

## BACK-UP CONTRACT ADDENDUM

Property Address: ______________________________

The additional provisions set forth below are hereby made a part of the Offer to Purchase and Contract or the Vacant Lot Offer to Purchase and Contract (the "Back-up Contract") for the Property located at ______________________________

______________________________
between Buyer: ______________________________
and Seller: ______________________________.

Buyer and Seller acknowledge that Seller has previously entered into an Offer to Purchase and Contract or a Vacant Lot Offer to Purchase and Contract (the "Primary Contract") with ______________________ [insert last name only](the "Primary Buyer" under the Primary Contract), that the Primary Contract is currently pending, and that this Back-up Contract is accepted in a secondary or back-up position to the Primary Contract under the following terms and conditions:

(1) It is a condition of this Back-up Contract that the Primary Contract is terminated as described below before the Buyer and Seller shall be obligated to perform under this Back-up Contract. Termination of the Primary Contract shall be evidenced by:

(a) a written release signed by all parties thereto;
(b) a Termination Notice pursuant to Alternative 2 of paragraph 13 of the Primary Contract; or
(c) a final judgment of a court of competent jurisdiction that the Primary Contract is invalid, illegal, unenforceable, or is otherwise terminated thereby.

(2) Modification of the terms or conditions of the Primary Contract by the parties thereto, including extensions of time, shall not constitute a termination of the Primary Contract as contemplated herein, and shall not cause this Back-up Contract to move into a primary position.

(3) Buyer and Seller agree that Buyer may not examine or otherwise have access to the Primary Contract absent written permission from the Seller and the Primary Buyer. Nevertheless, Seller represents that the Primary Contract calls for loan commitment by ______________________ (date) and closing by ______________________ (date).

(4) Buyer and Seller agree that the earnest money paid by Buyer in connection with this Back-up Contract shall be deposited within three (3) banking days following acceptance of this offer and in accordance with the terms of the contract, even while it is in secondary position.

(5) In the event the Primary Contract closes, then this Back-up Contract shall become null and void, and all earnest monies received in connection herewith shall be returned to the Buyer.

(6) In the event the Primary Contract is terminated, Seller shall promptly provide Buyer or Buyer's agent:

(a) written Notice thereof (the "Notice") which Notice shall state that this Back-up Contract has become primary and that its terms and conditions are in effect; and
(b) written evidence that the Primary Contract has been terminated as provided in paragraph 1 above.

Buyer shall close within __________ days from receipt of the written Notice or by the dates specified in the Back-up Contract, whichever occurs later.

(7) In any event, Buyer or Buyer's agent must receive notification from the Seller on or before ____________________, *time being of the essence*, that the Primary Contract has been terminated or this Back-up Contract shall become null and void and all earnest monies received in connection herewith shall be refunded to Buyer. Buyer may terminate this Back-up Contract before said date without liability by giving written notice of termination to Seller or Seller's agent at any time prior to receipt by Buyer or Buyer's agent of written Notice from Seller that this Back-up Contract has become primary.

IN THE EVENT OF A CONFLICT BETWEEN THIS ADDENDUM AND THE OFFER TO PURCHASE AND CONTRACT OR THE VACANT LOT OFFER TO PURCHASE AND CONTRACT, THIS ADDENDUM SHALL CONTROL.

Page 1 of 2

REALTOR®

**This form jointly approved by:**
**North Carolina Bar Association**
**North Carolina Association of REALTORS®, Inc.**

EQUAL HOUSING OPPORTUNITY

**STANDARD FORM 2A1 - T**
**© 7/2004**

Buyer Initials _______ _______ Seller Initials _______ _______

**FIGURE 6.13** Continued.

THE NORTH CAROLINA ASSOCIATION OF REALTORS®, INC. AND THE NORTH CAROLINA BAR ASSOCIATION MAKE NO REPRESENTATION AS TO THE LEGAL VALIDITY OR ADEQUACY OF ANY PROVISION OF THIS FORM IN ANY SPECIFIC TRANSACTION. IF YOU DO NOT UNDERSTAND THIS FORM OR FEEL THAT IT DOES NOT PROVIDE FOR YOUR LEGAL NEEDS, YOU SHOULD CONSULT A NORTH CAROLINA REAL ESTATE ATTORNEY BEFORE YOU SIGN IT.

Buyer: ______________________________(SEAL) Seller: ______________________________(SEAL)

Date: ______________ Date: ______________

Buyer: ______________________________(SEAL) Seller: ______________________________(SEAL)

Date: ______________ Date: ______________

[NOTE: The following are suggested notices that may be copied for the purpose of complying with the notice provisions contained in paragraphs (6) and (7) of the Back-Up Contract Addendum. DO NOT DETACH THE ORIGINAL OF THIS FORM FROM THE BACK-UP CONTRACT.]

**NOTICE TO BUYER THAT BACK-UP CONTRACT IS NOW IN EFFECT**

NOTICE is hereby given to ______________________________(insert name of Buyer) from Seller under the Back-up Contract between them dated ______________ that Seller has terminated the Primary Contract with ______________________________(Primary Buyer), as evidenced by the **ATTACHED**:

(a) _____ written release of the parties;

(b) _____ Termination Notice pursuant to Alternative 2 of paragraph 13 of the Primary Contract; or

(c) _____ final judgment of a court of competent jurisdiction that the Primary Contract is invalid, illegal, unenforceable or otherwise terminated thereby;

and that the Back-up Contract entered into between Seller and Buyer has become primary and its terms and conditions are now in effect.

Seller: ______________________________

Date: ______________________________

Seller: ______________________________

Date: ______________________________

**NOTICE TO SELLER THAT BACK-UP CONTRACT IS NOW TERMINATED**

NOTICE is hereby given to ______________________________(insert name of Seller) from Buyer under the Back-Up Contract between them dated ______________ that Buyer has terminated the Back-Up Contract.

Buyer: ______________________________

Date: ______________________________

Buyer: ______________________________

Date: ______________________________

Page 2 of 2

**STANDARD FORM 2A1 – T**
**© 7/2004**

the offer exactly as it is written by signing the Offer to Purchase and Contract. To help understand when acceptance is communicated, see the line of separation as illustrated earlier in Figures 5.1 and 5.2. Consider the following situation in which buyer is offeror and seller is offeree. Remember, the firm is the agent and when any licensed member of a firm is notified of acceptance, the communication requirement has been met.

- If the agent working with buyer is a subagent of seller, communication of acceptance is accomplished only when buyer is notified.
- If the agent working with buyer is a buyer's agent, communication of acceptance is accomplished when either buyer or buyer's agent is notified.
- If the agent working with a buyer is a dual agent, notification is accomplished when the seller accepts the contract in the presence of the dual agent or communicates acceptance to the dual agent if the contract is not accepted in his presence.

If an offeree accepts all terms of an offer and communicates the acceptance to offeror in an appropriate manner, the offer becomes a contract and there is no need for contract modification or a counteroffer.

## *Contract Modifications and Counteroffers*

An original offer is often modified several times before the parties reach agreement. The agent should be careful in handling these counterproposals. A primary consideration to keep in mind is that once an offer has been changed in any manner, the offeror is relieved of obligation since the offer has been rejected (killed).

There are two primary methods of handling modifications or counteroffers. First, since the modification killed the original offer, an agent could use a new clean offer at any time in the process of negotiation. Whereas this would be the preferable format for clarity, it is often not practical. Therefore, brokers usually resort to the more common technique of striking out terms on the original document and inserting new terms in their place. When using this method of modification, certain standards of practice apply. All changes should be initialed and dated by all parties to the contract. Only one set of modifications should be included on a form. If a second or subsequent set of changes are to be proposed, a new form should be used. If extensive changes are made, an agent should consider starting with a new form.

## Acceptance of Counteroffers

If a seller rejects a contract by making a counteroffer, the seller becomes the offeror and the buyer becomes the offeree; therefore, communication of the acceptance of a counteroffer is accomplished when:

- The offeree (buyer) communicates acceptance of the offer to the agent or subagent of the offeror (seller) working with the buyer.
- The offeree (buyer) or buyer's agent communicates acceptance of the offer to the offeror (seller) or seller's agent or subagent.
- The offeree (buyer) accepts and signs the offer in the presence of a dual agent or communicates acceptance to a dual agent if the offer is not accepted in the dual agent's presence.

Multiple offers on one property can pose a dilemma for buyers, sellers, and agents. While the seller's agent must present all offers, the seller himself must decide how to deal with the offers. The sellers may accept any one of the offers even if it is not the best offer. He should not counter more than one offer at the same time.

Each counteroffer must be rejected by the buyer or withdrawn by the seller before moving on to another counteroffer. Another way the seller can handle multiple offers is by rejecting all offers and issuing a Memo to Buyer to all offerors stating the terms he would consider accepting. This leaves him free to accept a new offer from either an original offeror or a new offeror without having to withdraw a counter offer, since an offer was not made.

Negotiating multiple offers is a risk for both buyers and sellers. A seller's strategy may result in a higher price or in losing all the buyers. A buyer may end up paying too much for the property or being unable to obtain a loan because the property does not appraise for the contract price.

It is wise to deal with the potential of multiple offers before they materialize by educating buyers and sellers about multiple offers, the practical and ethical methods of handling them, and the advantages and risks to both parties.

The National Association of REALTORS® publishes an excellent consumer brochure called "A Buyers' and Sellers' Guide to Multiple Offer Negotiations," which can be downloaded by REALTORS® from the NAR web site for use in informing their buyer and seller clients about multiple offers.

The agent, buyer, and seller must understand when an offer becomes an accepted contract and that an offer or a counteroffer can be withdrawn at any time before acceptance and communication of acceptance to the offeror or her agent. If the offeree (seller) receives a better offer after he has signed an offer—but before acceptance has been communicated to the buyer—the seller may be able to void his acceptance and accept the better offer. The agent should advise the seller to consult an attorney before accepting any other offer. Even though the agent may think there is no contract, he cannot give legal advice. Suppose the agent is a dual agent who does not fully understand dual agency (a horrible thought!). He may not realize that acceptance in his presence constitutes communication. If the seller accepts the second offer in this case, he could have two contracts to sell one property to two people.

Agents should document the time of revocation or acceptance of an offer. Otherwise, there may be cases where it is difficult to determine which came first, the revocation or apparent acceptance. Consider an example of a dual agency situation. Laurie and Austin both work for ABC Realty, a firm that practices dual agency. Laurie lists a property at Park Place. Austin brings her an offer from a buyer-client on Friday evening. The sellers are out of town and cannot be reached until Sunday night. Laurie meets with the sellers at 6 p.m. to present the offer, and they accept at 6:30 p.m. Meanwhile, the buyers have found the home of their dreams while visiting open houses on Sunday afternoon. They rush home, contact Austin immediately by phone, and revoke the offer at 5:45 p.m. Austin is unable to contact Laurie before she presents the offer. Since the offer was revoked before the apparent acceptance, there is no contract.

Counteroffers can present an even more difficult situation. The agent should deal with outstanding counteroffers before allowing the seller to accept an offer from another party. The agent must be sure the outstanding counteroffer has not been accepted and communicated to another agent in the firm or to a subagent from another company working with the buyer. If it has not been accepted, it can and should be withdrawn before accepting another offer.

A memo to buyer is preferable to a counteroffer. This is a rejection along with an offer to consider another offer from the offeror with suggested terms. It does not need to be withdrawn before accepting an offer from another party. The memo to buyer is especially useful for handling multiple offers. The seller cannot make a counteroffer to more than one person at a time; however, he can give a memo to as many potential buyers as necessary. The seller can then choose from all offers that result from the memo.

All agents should understand the following facts about offers:

- An expiration date in an offer does not preclude the offeror from withdrawing the offer before the expiration date. It means only that if the offer is not accepted or rejected by that time, it is automatically terminated.
- Changing any term in an offer is a rejection of the offer and thus makes a counteroffer.
- Once the offeree rejects an offer, he cannot change his mind and accept it later. The offeror, however, can resubmit the same offer if he chooses.
- An offer with no specified expiration date terminates after a reasonable time period. It is best not to depend on this and to specifically terminate all offers which are not accepted within a reasonable time.

- An offer is terminated by the death or insanity of the offeror before the offer is accepted.
- An offer cannot be withdrawn after the communication of its acceptance. The parties can, however, terminate the resulting contract by mutual agreement.

## Electronically Submitted Offer and Acceptance

Offers can be made and transmitted by facsimile devices (fax). The acceptance can also be transmitted by fax. The faxed offer to purchase must be signed before faxing. The faxed copy of the signed offer the offeree receives is an indication that there is an original signature on an original document. If the offeree signs the faxed copy and faxes it back to the offeror, the signed faxed copy also indicates the presence of an original signature. Although the original signatures are on two different copies of the document, it still creates a valid contract. Since a copy with original signatures is needed for each company, the buyer, the seller, the mortgage company, and closing attorney, the agent should follow up a faxed acceptance by obtaining original signatures on multiple copies of the contract. Each copy should be signed by the offeror and the offeree in a timely fashion. This is easily accomplished using express mail or delivery services.

The original signed offer can be scanned into a computer and sent via electronic mail (e-mail). The e-mail can be printed, signed, scanned, and e-mailed back. This often makes a clearer copy than a copy that has been faxed to and from a buyer or seller. The important thing to remember is that original signatures must exist. E-mailing an unsigned offer back and forth is like a verbal agreement. If nothing is signed, it is not enforceable. With the advent and proliferation of e-signature programs whereby a document can be e-mailed, e-signed, and e-mailed back to the original source without downloading, signing and scanning it, agents should assure that any methods used to obtain signatures are secure and are legally acceptable.

### *Furnishing Copies to Buyer and Seller*

At the time of execution, all parties must be provided with a copy of any instrument they signed. Thus, it is common practice for the offer to be prepared in six copies—one for the prospective buyer, one for the selling agent, one for the listing agent, one for the seller, one for the mortgage company, and one for the closing attorney. Brokers are required to keep all instruments on file for three years for inspection by the Real Estate Commission at any time. This regulation applies to offers that are rejected or withdrawn even if there is no further action on the offer. The practice by some agents of not getting rejected offers and counteroffers signed by the appropriate parties is not acceptable. Rejected offers should be signed as rejected and kept on file for three years.

## Installment Land Contracts (Contract for Deed)

This type of agreement for the purchase and sale of real property is known as a **contract for deed,** conditional sales contract, installment sales contract, and installment or land contract. The essence of this contract is that *the purchaser is contracting to obtain title to the property by paying the purchase price in installments and the seller is agreeing to transfer the title to the purchaser* by the delivery of a deed upon payment of the purchase price or an agreed-upon part of the purchase price by the purchaser. The seller's obligation under the contract is to deliver a deed and thereby convey a marketable title to the purchaser when the purchaser fulfills his obligations under the contract. The contract for deed must be in writing to be enforceable, as required by the Statute of Frauds.

This type of contract was originally used to purchase relatively inexpensive pieces of land, but there is no reason why it cannot be used for any type of property. It offers major advantages to the buyer in times of tight credit (high-interest) markets, or when the buyer has credit problems, such that commercial lenders may not provide the required financing. Since this form of contract puts the seller in a particularly strong position, the seller may be more willing to provide the financing through this type of agreement than through a sale, in which the title is passed and the seller holds the mortgage.

Caution should be observed in instances where the mortgage contains a **due-on-sale clause,** also called an **alienation clause.** This clause *specifies that the entire principal balance due on the mortgage must be paid if a sale of the property is effected.* In these situations, the lending institution holding the mortgage can declare the contract for deed to be a sale of property and thereby require the mortgage to be paid off by the seller.

North Carolina has no standard form for this contract. Consultation with legal counsel prior to the creation of the contract for deed is necessary for the protection of all parties. This is especially important if the property is encumbered by a mortgage containing a due-on-sale clause. *In all cases where the property being purchased under a contract for deed is encumbered by a mortgage, the contract must specify that the seller is to pay off the remaining principal balance due at the time of conveyance of title or to provide for the assumption of the mortgage balance at that time by the purchaser.*

## Advantages and Disadvantages

A land contract is strongly weighted in favor of the seller. The seller holds title to the property during the contract period. In the event the buyer were to default in his obligation to make the payments as specified in the contract, the seller would need to evict the buyer (tenant) and could incur significant legal expenses and time delays in clearing the title. In this case, all the payments that had been made would be considered rent instead of payment toward purchase of title. For this reason, the contract should clearly set forth the understandings of the parties in the event of default.

The buyer has a substantial right in the property, known as **equitable title.** This is *the right to claim title from the seller upon completion of payment of the obligation to the seller.* The purchaser can strengthen the right by recordation of the contract. This protects the purchaser's interests against further action by the seller during the period of the contract. Unfortunately, recordation of contracts for deed are often prohibited in the terms of the agreement and may be the source of a dispute between the parties.

# Option to Purchase

An **option** is *a contract wherein a property owner (optionor) sells a right to purchase his or her property to a prospective buyer (optionee).* The price paid for the option is not escrow money or earnest money or binder; it is money paid for the right to purchase the property at the price specified in the option contract, provided the optionee exercises his right within the time period set forth in the option. Therefore, the option money is paid directly to the property owner and is retained by that individual as agreed upon in the option contract.

The optionor is obligated to convey the title to the property if the option is exercised and the purchase price paid as agreed upon in the contract. Once the option is exercised, it becomes a contract of sale and is binding on both buyer and seller. With the inclusion of Alternative 2 in the Offer to Purchase and Contract, the separate form for a traditional option to purchase was eliminated. If the parties want a traditional option, they should consult a qualified attorney to draft the contract. The critical difference between a traditional option and Alternative 2 is the way in which they are exercised. A traditional option is exercised by the buyer giving the seller written notice of intent to complete the transaction. With an Alternative 2 option, the buyer must give written notice if he or she elects not to complete the transaction. If the buyer neglects to give such notice to the seller by the option termination date, the buyer is obligated under the terms of the contract to continue with the transaction.

## Rights of the Parties

An option is the payment of consideration to acquire the right to purchase property during a specified time period rather than the outright purchase of the property itself. The optionee has purchased a period of time in which she can execute the right to purchase the property. The optionor (seller) has sold this period of time and is compensated for this sale by receiving the option price at the time the option is executed. Whereas the buyer (optionee) has no further duties under the contract, she may elect to execute the option and contract for the property. At the same time, the seller (optionor) is bound to abide by the terms of the option for the time period he has sold and for which he has been compensated.

## Requirements of Options

Since an option is the right to purchase title to real property, it falls under the Statute of Frauds and therefore must be in writing. Additionally, the Conner Act specifies that the contract must be recorded to be enforceable against claims of third parties.

All options should be clear and definite in their terms, to the extent that provisions can be specified at the time of execution. Thus, a specific sale price and terms should be set forth rather than left to negotiation at some later time. If the period for consummation of the transaction is in the reasonably near future, a definite price should be specified rather than leaving this to be a "fair market value." If the option provides for an execution date at some considerably later time, however, the specification of a market value at that time may be fairer to the parties.

Disposition of the option money should also be addressed. It should be clear whether the purchase price is in addition to the option price or whether these funds are to be applied to the purchase price.

In sum, all terms of the option should be specified as clearly as possible, including terms of financing, payment of expenses on the property during the option period, type of conveyance, and method of notification between the parties.

## Right of First Refusal versus Option

A **right of first refusal** is distinguished from an option in that the former is usually a preexisting agreement in some contract, whereas the latter arises independently at some later time. For example, a lease can provide a right of first refusal to the tenant. This right provides that *if an offer to purchase the leased premises is received during the period of the lease, the lessee (tenant) has the right to protect leasehold interests by purchasing the property at the same terms of the other offer.* This takes precedence over that other offer. Another example is neighbors in a subdivision having the right to purchase adjoining properties if these are ever exposed for sale.

In contrast, an option arises at some future time independent of the existing rights of others in the property. If one offers to option, or purchase, a property where there is a right of first refusal by others, this prospective purchaser cannot consummate the transaction until the others have waived their right of first refusal. In an option, the optionor is bound to sell the property to the optionee if the optionee exercises his option within the stated time period. In a right of first refusal, the property owner is not obligated to sell his property. He is only obligated to give the holder of the right of first refusal the first opportunity to buy the property if he decides to sell and actually receives another offer on the property.

# SUMMARY OF IMPORTANT POINTS

1. A contract is an agreement between competent parties, upon legal consideration, to do or abstain from doing some legal act and which is enforceable by law.
2. Bilateral contracts are based on mutual promises. Unilateral contracts are based on a promise by one party and an act by another party.
3. The requirements for contract validity are (1) competent parties, (2) mutual assent, (3) offer and acceptance, (4) consideration, and (5) legality of object.
4. Even though real estate agents are not legally authorized to "draft" contracts, they are permitted to use contract forms drawn by attorneys. In using these prepared forms, the

real estate agent is restricted to filling in the blank spaces but must understand the meaning of all contract clauses in the form. He cannot give legal advice.

5. An offer must not be indefinite or illusory.

6. An offer can be revoked by an offeror at any time prior to acceptance.

7. A contract is created by the unconditional acceptance of a valid offer. Acceptance of bilateral offers must be communicated. Communication of the acceptance of unilateral offers results from the performance of an act by the promisee.

8. Mutual assent is defeated and a contract made voidable by (1) misrepresentation, (2) fraud, (3) undue influence, or (4) duress.

9. Contracts are assignable in the absence of a specific prohibition against assignment in the contract.

10. A contract that transfers an interest in real property, including but not limited to sales contracts, must be in writing per the Statute of Frauds. The Real Estate Commission, not the Statute of Frauds, requires real estate agency contracts to be in writing. The only exception to this law is temporary oral buyer or oral dual agency. Even this type of agency agreement must be committed to paper prior to submission of an Offer to Purchase and Contract.

11. A listing contract is one in which a property owner employs a broker to find a buyer for her property. The contract creates an agency relationship wherein the seller is the principal and the broker is the special or limited agent of the seller.

12. Even though the listing agent does not represent the buyer, the real estate agent must represent the property honestly, fairly, and accurately to all prospective buyers.

13. The primary types of listing contract are (1) open listing, (2) exclusive agency, and (3) exclusive right to sell.

14. If a contracting party defaults in the performance of contractual obligations, the injured party can sue for damages in a suit for breach of contract. If the contract is one for the purchase and sale of real property, an alternative remedy in the form of a suit for specific performance is available to the injured party.

15. A contract for deed is also called an installment land contract, conditional sale contract, or land contract. It is a contract of sale and a method of financing by the seller for the buyer. Title does not pass until all or some specified part of the purchase price is paid by the buyer.

16. An option provides a right to purchase property under specified terms and conditions. During the option term, the contract is binding on the optionor (seller) but not the optionee (buyer). When an option is exercised, it becomes a contract of sale and is, therefore, binding on both parties.

17. A right of first refusal differs from an option in that it usually is a part of a preexisting agreement that gives the holder of the right the first opportunity to purchase a property according to the same terms and conditions as the seller will accept from another bona fide purchaser, when and if the seller decides to sell.

## ITEMS TO CONSIDER FOR THE STATE EXAM

1. Four points about contracts are important to remember for the exam:
   a. Contracts play an extremely important part in everyday real estate practice.
   b. The exam emphasizes practical application of real estate knowledge.
   c. The Real Estate Commission, which took an active part in the preparation of the standard Offer to Purchase and Contract form, expects you to be familiar with all parts of this form. Your best preparation for this challenge is to practice completing the form and applying it to various standard situations. You should have done this in class as required by the state syllabus. Be certain you understand how each paragraph applies to the data for a given situation because this is the type of question you will face on the exam.
   d. All of the following dates should be included in an Offer to Purchase and Contract: date of offer, date of acceptance, date of closing, and date of possession; if Alternative 2 of Paragraph 13 is used, the Option Termination Date must also be specified.
2. Additionally, the following points and definitions may help you avoid common exam problems:
   a. The primary purpose of the Statute of Frauds is "to prevent fraudulent proof on an oral contract."
   b. Be certain you understand the distinction between the primary forms of listing contract and how/when the broker is entitled to a commission under each form—open listing, exclusive agency, and exclusive right to sell. *Note:* An agent can be "fired" during the listing period; that is, the seller can terminate the contract at any time before the agreed-to expiration date. Although the agent would have no authority to continue, the seller may be liable to the agent for damages.
   c. The listing contract is simply an employment authority (not an interest in land) and therefore is *not* regulated by the Statute of Frauds. Real estate laws require that the listing and all agency contracts be in writing.
   d. At what point is the buyer actually "ready, willing, and able"? If a condition of the purchase offer is that the buyer obtain a certain loan (make sure the loan terms are precise), she is not "able" until the lender approves her for the specified loan.
   e. A counteroffer is made by (1) making changes on the original offer form or (2) creating a new offer from scratch. Recall that a change of a material fact to an offer is a *rejection* of the offer that kills this proposal beyond the ability of the offeree to retrieve it (once the rejection has been communicated to the offeror). If the first method is used, as is the common practice, remember that the following points apply:
      - All parties must initial and date a legible change.
      - Only one set of changes should be made on the original form; if the other party wants to make a second set of changes, use a new original. The crux of this discussion is that for the exam, you must (a) have your facts together and (b) be prepared to *think.*
   f. Students err in calculating the square footage of a single-family house. The convention used is to take the *external* dimensions of the heated living area of the home, that is, only those portions you would live in during the winter. Exclude porch, garage, or unfinished basement. The only time you need to deal with the thickness of the walls is when you are forced to take the inside dimensions of an area and calculate the external dimensions. See Chapter 9 and Appendix B for in-depth discussion of calculating square footage.
   g. Date of closing. As a general rule, there is moderate leeway in the actual day of closing of a few days or so. A buyer is not in default if he cannot meet the exact closing date, for example, if the loan processing is slightly delayed. Therefore, if a purchase contract called for closing by the 15th of the month but the loan was not ready until the 17th, the seller would have no choice but to wait. The major exception to this rule is when the contract contains the clause "time is of the essence," which means the exact date must be observed. As a practical matter, it is poor business to put this clause in the contract. It would be foolish to throw away the whole deal just because the lender needed another day to complete the loan processing.
   h. Broker dispute with the seller. If a seller refused to pay the full commission to the broker when due and the broker were holding earnest money for the seller, the broker cannot keep those funds. The broker must

*immediately remit* all trust funds in full when due. He can then pursue a lawsuit for compensation if desired.

i. Land contracts. In a contract for deed (land contract, installment contract), the seller is holding actual title to the property until the buyer performs her duty of payment. However, the buyer has acquired what is known as equitable title, essentially a claim on the actual title.

j. Liquidated damages are the amount of money for damages agreed upon in the contract.

k. Compensatory damages are the compensation awarded by the court to the injured party for financial loss caused by a breach of contract by the defaulting party.

l. The Statute of Frauds requires the following types of contract to be in writing: contract to buy and sell real estate, options, land contracts, contracts for the exchange of real estate, and lease contracts exceeding three years.

m. The Statute of Frauds does *not* require the following types of contract to be in writing: agency contracts (listing, buyer agency, dual agency) and leases for three years or less.

n. Real estate rules require agency contracts to be in writing. Exception: Temporary oral buyer agency, exclusive or dual, can be authorized but must be written before submission of an Offer to Purchase.

o. Open listing. Agent gets nothing if property is sold by anyone else, such as the owner or another broker.

p. A net listing is one where all the money above the amount specified by the seller that she wants to net, if any, goes to the broker.

q. Exclusive agency listing and open listing. Owner does not pay a commission if he sells the property himself.

r. In an exclusive agency listing, the agency gets commission if another broker sells the property.

s. Exclusive right to sell listing agreement. Broker gets paid even if the owner sells the property himself.

t. Earnest money and consideration are not the same thing.

u. The three main purposes of earnest money are to demonstrate the buyer's sincerity, to demonstrate his financial capacity to fulfill the agreement, and to compensate the seller in the event of default by the buyer. It *is not* necessary to the validity of the contract. Consideration is anything of value, such as money or a promise. It *is* necessary for the validity of the contract.

## REVIEW QUESTIONS

Answers to the review questions are in the Answer Key at the back of the book.

1. A contract in which mutual promises are exchanged at the time of signing (execution) is termed:
   A. multilateral
   B. unilateral
   C. bilateral
   D. promissory

2. Of the following statements regarding voidable contracts, which is NOT correct?
   A. a voidable contract can be avoided by one or more parties
   B. a voidable contract can be legally consummated by the parties
   C. a voidable contract can never be consummated
   D. a voidable contract results from failure to meet some legal requirement in negotiating the agreement

3. For contracts in general, except for those of the sale of real property, the essential elements include all of the following EXCEPT:
   A. competent parties
   B. offer and acceptance
   C. legality of object
   D. writing

4. A false representation is deemed to be fraudulent when:
   I. the party making a false representation knows it to be false.
   II. the party making a false representation does not know if the statement is true or false, but he should have known.
   A. I only
   B. II only
   C. both I and II
   D. neither I nor II

5. Which of the following is the basis of duress?
   A. fear
   B. mistake
   C. indefiniteness
   D. illusion

6. A contract to sell real property may be terminated by each of the following EXCEPT:
   A. full performance
   B. breach of contract
   C. mutual agreement
   D. death

7. Which of the following has the effect of terminating contracts?
   A. consideration
   B. bankruptcy
   C. exercise
   D. assignment

8. The clause in a listing contract that protects the broker's commission entitlement beyond the listing term in the event of a sale of the property by the owner to a prospect who was shown the property by the listing firm or its agents is called a(n):
   A. forfeiture clause
   B. extender clause
   C. settlement clause
   D. exclusive right clause

9. When an offer is contingent upon the buyer obtaining a new first mortgage loan, which of the following provisions is (are) necessary for the protection of the parties?
   A. a requirement that the buyer make diligent efforts to obtain a loan commitment
   B. detailed specifications regarding the loan upon which the contract is contingent
   C. length of time the buyer has to obtain the loan
   D. all of the above

10. Each of the following should be present in offers and contracts of sale EXCEPT:
    A. date of final settlement
    B. date possession will be given to the purchaser
    C. date of commission payment
    D. date of contract inception

11. In the event a seller defaults in his obligation to convey title to the property as agreed upon in a contract sale, which of the following remedies is available to the purchaser?
    A. suit for breach of contract
    B. suit for specific performance
    C. suit for compensatory damages
    D. all of the above

12. Which of the following most accurately describes an agreement wherein a property owner agrees to convey title to the property when another party satisfies all obligations agreed to in the contract?
    A. lease contract
    B. listing contract
    C. legal contract
    D. land contract

13. During the term of an option, which of the following is correct?
   A. the option is binding upon the optionee
   B. the option is not binding upon the optionor
   C. the optionor can sell the property to anyone he chooses during the option period
   D. time is of the essence; the option can only be exercised up to the exact expiration date and time

14. When a party purchases an option, the optionee is purchasing which of the following?
   A. right
   B. title
   C. land
   D. exercise

15. Which of the following describes the situation existing after an option is exercised?
   A. the option is converted into a contract of sale
   B. the contract is now binding upon all parties to the contract
   C. the optionor must convey title to the property when the purchase price is paid as agreed upon in the contract
   D. all of the above

16. All of the following are requirements of options EXCEPT:
   A. options must be in writing to be enforceable
   B. options must contain a description of the property
   C. options must be exercised
   D. options must contain a recital of consideration

17. Upon the receipt of a buyer's offer, the seller accepted all of the terms of the offer except the amount of earnest money. Instead, the seller agreed to accept an amount that was 50 percent higher than the buyer had offered. This fact was promptly communicated to the offeree by the real estate agent. Which of the following most accurately describes these events?
   A. the communication created a bilateral contract
   B. the seller accepted the buyer's offer
   C. the seller conditionally rejected the buyer's offer
   D. the seller rejected the buyer's offer and made a new offer, or counteroffer, to the buyer

18. The only form mandated for use by the General Assembly in the residential real estate (properties with 1 to 4 units) sales process is:
   1. Offer to Purchase and Contract
   2. Residential Property Disclosure Statement
   3. Dual Agency Agreement
   4. none of the above

19. All of the following contracts are unilateral EXCEPT a(n):
   A. contract for the sale of real estate
   B. open listing contract
   C. option to purchase contract
   D. contract to pay $1,000 if someone will paint your house

20. Exclusive Right to Represent Buyer Agreements must have all of the following characteristics EXCEPT:
   A. be in writing
   B. have definite termination date
   C. specify provisions for an automatic renewal
   D. incorporate conspicuously the commission prescribed "Description of Agent Duties and Relationships"

21. What type of contract can be executed?
   A. valid
   B. voidable
   C. bilateral
   D. any of the above

22. What are the essential elements of a real estate listing contract?
   I. It must be written.
   II. There must be mutual assent.
   III. There must be consideration.
   A. I only
   B. II only
   C. II and III
   D. I, II, and III

23. A contract can be voidable if there is:
   A. duress
   B. mutual mistake
   C. willful misrepresentation
   D. all of the above

24. An Offer to Purchase and Contract is presented to the seller. The seller agrees to all terms and signs in front of his agent. Which type of agency allows the buyer in this scenario to withdraw the offer prior to communication of this acceptance to the buyer or buyer's agent?
   I. dual agency
   II. seller subagency
   III. exclusive buyer agency
   A. I and II
   B. II and III
   C. I and III
   D. I, II, and III

25. Earnest money is:
    A. synonymous with consideration
    B. typically held in a trust account
    C. a minimum of $250
    D. all of the above

26. Samuel Seller lists his property with Exclusive Realty. Eventually Samuel convinces a coworker, Wanda Wish, to purchase his home. In which situation would Samuel not owe a commission to Exclusive Realty?
    A. an open listing
    B. a percentage listing
    C. an exclusive right to sell listing
    D. a net listing

27. What type of real estate contract must be in writing per the Statute of Frauds?
    A. an Exclusive Right to Sell Listing agreement
    B. an Exclusive Right to Represent Buyer agreement
    C. an Offer to Purchase and Contract
    D. all of the above

28. Which of the real estate agency contracts contain a clause allowing the principal to fire the agent?
    A. an Exclusive Right to Sell Listing agreement
    B. an Exclusive Right to Represent Buyer agreement
    C. a Dual Agency agreement
    D. none of the above

29. Which of the following need to be listed as personal property on the Offer to Purchase and Contract?
    A. a basketball hoop
    B. a riding lawn mower
    C. custom-made plantation shutters
    D. all of the above

30. A buyer agent submits an offer on behalf of her principals to a seller's agent. The sellers like the offer but instruct their agent that they will pay only $1,500 in closing costs, instead of the $2,000 requested. The buyers tell their agent they will agree to the terms if the sellers include the refrigerator. Which of the following is correct in the last counteroffer?
    A. the seller is the offeror and the buyer is the offeree
    B. the buyer is the offeror and the seller is the offeree
    C. the sellers' agent needs to prepare a memo to buyer
    D. the buyers' agent needs to prepare a memo to seller

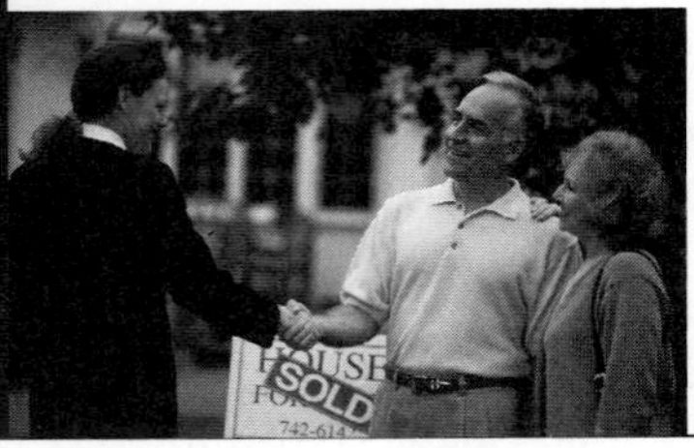


# Chapter 7

## KEY TERMS

acceleration clause
adjustable rate mortgage (ARM)
alienation clause
amortization
arrears
balloon payment
beneficiary
buydown loan
certificate of reasonable value (CRV)
conforming loans
conventional loan
deed in lieu of foreclosure
deed of trust
defaults
defeasance clause
deficiency judgment
disintermediation
due-on-sale clause
Equal Credit Opportunity Act (ECOA)
equity
equity of redemption
escrow account
Fannie Mae (FNMA)
Federal Housing Administration (FHA)
FHA-insured loan
foreclosure under power of sale
Freddie Mac (FHLMC)
Ginnie Mae (GNMA)
graduated payment mortgage (GPM)
hypothecation
interest
judicial foreclosure
lien theory
liquidity
loan assumption
loan origination fee
loan-to-value ratio
Maggie Mae (MGIC)
mortgage
mortgage banker
mortgage broker
mortgagee
mortgage insurance premium (MIP)
mortgagor
negative amortization
nonjudicial foreclosure
nonrecourse note
open-end mortgage
package mortgage
power of sale clause
prepaid items
prepayment penalty clause
principal
private mortgage insurance (PMI)
promissory note
purchase money mortgage
real estate investment trusts (REITs)
Regulation Z
release of liability
reverse mortgage
right of assignment
savings and loan associations (S&Ls)
secondary mortgage market
settlement
statutory redemption period
strict foreclosure
subject to a loan
substitution of entitlement
term loan
title theory
trustee
trustor
Truth-in-Lending Simplification and Reform Act (TILSRA)
up-front mortgage insurance premium (UFMIP)
usury
VA-guaranteed loan
wraparound mortgage

# Real Estate Finance

## LEARNING OBJECTIVES

At the conclusion of this chapter, you should be able to:

### Section 1: Operations of Real Estate Finance

1. Define the basic mortgage theories.
2. Define and describe the essential elements and common provisions of the mortgage note and the mortgage instrument (deed of trust).
3. Describe common note payment plans.
4. Describe the concepts of principal and interest, including calculations.
5. Define the rights of the parties in mortgage instruments.
6. Define three methods of sale of mortgaged property.
7. Describe the characteristics, major programs and payment plans, and qualification requirements of the following:
   a. Conventional mortgage loans
   b. FHA-insured loans
   c. VA-guaranteed loans
8. Describe the basic definitions, characteristics, and uses of other mortgage loans and payment methods.

### Section 2: Sources of Real Estate Finance

9. Describe common sources of financing.
10. Describe the major players in the secondary mortgage market.
11. Describe loan underwriting practices and procedures.
12. Define and describe mortgage legislation:
    a. Truth-in-Lending Simplification and Reform Act
    b. Equal Credit Opportunity Act

## IN THIS CHAPTER

Section 1 of this chapter, "Operations," outlines financing instruments such as mortgages, deeds of trust, and notes, and the various ways in which a real estate purchase can be financed. Knowledge of these financing methods is critical to real estate practitioners. Except in the unusual case of a cash sale, knowledge or lack of knowledge of the ways in which a sale can be financed may make the difference between a successful and an unsuccessful transaction. Section 2 of this chapter, "Sources," discusses major sources of real estate financing as well as the federal regulation of lending institutions and the secondary mortgage market.

# SECTION 1 OPERATIONS OF REAL ESTATE FINANCE

## PRINCIPAL, INTEREST, TAXES, AND INSURANCE

Understanding the terms *interest* and *principal* is essential to understanding notes, mortgages, deeds of trust, and all real estate financing methods. **Interest** is the *money paid for using someone else's money.* The **principal** is the *amount of money on which interest is either paid or received.* In the case of an interest-bearing note, principal is the amount of money the lender has lent the borrower and on which the borrower will pay interest to the lender.

Simple interest is usually used for mortgage loan interest. This means the annual rate of interest is used to calculate payments even though payments normally are made monthly. A payment plan in which payments are made every two weeks (biweekly) has become popular because it reduces the term of the loan and saves a significant amount of interest over the life of the loan. A current loan can sometimes be switched to this payment plan.

Mortgage loan interest almost always is calculated in **arrears;** that is, *a monthly payment due on the first of the month includes interest for using the money during the previous month.* Interest can also be calculated in advance; that is, a monthly payment due on the first of the month includes interest for the month in which the payment is due. When paying off or assuming a loan, one must know if the interest is paid in advance or in arrears to determine the amount of interest owed or to be prorated at closing. *Interest must be paid in arrears on all conforming loans, that is, loans sold in the secondary mortgage market.*

The P&I payment is the part of the payment covering the principal and interest. On a fixed-rate level payment loan, P&I stays constant for the life of the loan. In most cases, especially where the loan-to-value ratio is more than 80 percent, mortgage companies require taxes and insurance to be escrowed; that is, one-twelfth of the annual taxes and insurance (T&I) are paid each month with the P&I payment. This combined payment is called PITI (principal, interest, taxes, and insurance). Taxes and insurance can change over the life of the loan; therefore, mortgage companies perform an annual escrow analysis and adjust the T&I accordingly for the following year.

Mortgage companies have good reason for requiring the funds to be escrowed in order to pay the taxes and insurance themselves. A property tax lien takes precedence over all other liens, even the mortgage lien. If the property is foreclosed for back taxes, the taxes are paid first. The mortgage company will not get all of its money if the proceeds of the sale are not sufficient to cover expenses of sale, property tax, and loan balance. If the homeowner/mortgagor does not keep the insurance in force and the property is destroyed, the mortgage company's collateral is destroyed. By collecting one-twelfth of the taxes and insurance monthly and paying these bills themselves, mortgage companies ensure their liens' priority and protection of their collateral. In order for the mortgage company to always have enough money in the account to pay the taxes and insurance when they become due, extra taxes and insurance must be escrowed at closing and a one-year homeowner's insurance policy must be prepaid at closing (see Chapter 8, Closing Real Estate Transactions).

## AMORTIZATION AND DEBT SERVICE

**Amortization** is the gradual reduction of a mortgage loan amount from the original amount of the loan to a zero balance through periodic payments, which include both principal and interest. In the beginning, most of the payment goes toward interest (see Figure 7.3). As each successive payment is made, a little more goes toward principal and a little less toward interest (see Figure 7.5). Toward the end of the loan term, most of the payment goes toward principal and only a little toward interest.

Many institutions provide amortization schedules to borrowers. Agents or borrowers can quickly produce one on a personal computer via the Internet or an inexpensive software program. Any agent should be able to determine the P&I payment for any given loan amount at any interest rate for any period of time. In the past, agents relied on amortization tables, which list factors per $1,000 of the loan amount at any interest rate and any time period (see Figure 7.1). This is still a good method, and some agents carry a laminated pocket-sized table for quick reference. The agent only has to divide the loan amount by 1,000 to determine the number of units of $1,000 and multiply that number by the factor from the chart (see Figure 7.2). In this age of high technology, few agents use amortization tables.

**FIGURE 7.1**

An abbreviated amortization chart.

AMORTIZATION CHART (MONTHLY PAYMENTS PER $1,000 BORROWED)

| Annual interest rate | Years to fully amortize loan → 15 | 20 | 25 | 30 |
|---|---|---|---|---|
| 6.00 | 8.44 | 7.16 | 6.44 | 6.00 |
| 6.25 | 8.57 | 7.31 | 6.60 | 6.16 |
| 6.50 | 8.71 | 7.46 | 6.75 | 6.32 |
| 6.75 | 8.85 | 7.60 | 6.91 | 6.49 |
| 7.00 | 8.99 | 7.75 | 7.07 | 6.65 |
| 7.25 | 9.13 | 7.90 | 7.23 | 6.82 |
| 7.50 | 9.27 | 8.06 | 7.39 | 6.99 |
| 7.75 | 9.41 | 8.21 | 7.55 | 7.16 |
| 8.00 | 9.56 | 8.36 | 7.72 | 7.34 |
| 8.25 | 9.70 | 8.52 | 7.88 | 7.51 |
| 8.50 | 9.85 | 8.68 | 8.05 | 7.69 |
| 8.75 | 9.99 | 8.84 | 8.22 | 7.87 |
| 9.00 | 10.14 | 9.00 | 8.39 | 8.05 |
| 9.25 | 10.29 | 9.16 | 8.56 | 8.23 |
| 9.50 | 10.44 | 9.32 | 8.74 | 8.41 |
| 9.75 | 10.59 | 9.49 | 8.91 | 8.59 |
| 10.00 | 10.75 | 9.65 | 9.09 | 8.78 |

Note: This is an abbreviated amortization chart intended for example and learning purposes. Most real estate brokers find it easier to use a calculator to compute and compare payments and to solve other real estate math problems quickly.

**FIGURE 7.2**

Use of amortization chart.

*Example:* Assume a home purchase price of $87,500 with a conventional mortgage of 80% of the sales price at a rate of 8.5% for 30 years.

1. Amount of the loan: $87,500 × 80% = $70,000.
2. Figure 7.1 is given in a factor per $1,000; therefore, divide $70,000 by 1,000 = 70 units of 1,000.
3. Go to the 8.5% row. Read across to the 30-year column, and find the figure of $7.69. This is the payment per month per $1,000 of the loan.
4. Multiply 70 × $7.69 = $538.30. This is the monthly payment of principal and interest to amortize (kill, pay off) a loan of $70,000 at 8.5% for 30 years.

**FIGURE 7.3**
Interest paid per month.

*Example:* Use the data of Figure 7.2 to calculate how much of the payment (P&I) went to the interest portion (I) in the first month of the loan.

1. Interest (I) at any point is the principal (P) times the rate (R) times the period of time (T) you had the money, or:

   $I = P \times R \times T$

2. In the example,

   $I = \$70{,}000 \times 8.5\% \times 1/12$ of a year, or

   $$I = \frac{\$70{,}000 \times 0.085}{12} = \$495.83$$

3. Therefore, of the total payment of $538.30 in the first month, $495.83 went only to interest.

**FIGURE 7.4**
Principal reduction.

Using the above data, how much did the first payment reduce the principal?

| | |
|---|---|
| 1. Calculate the P & I. | $538.30 |
| 2. Subtract the amount that went to interest (I). | −495.83 |
| 3. The remainder went to principal (P). | $ 42.47 |

**FIGURE 7.5**
Loan balance after first and second payments.

Using the previous data, what is the loan balance after the first payment?

| | |
|---|---|
| 1. Calculate the amount that went to the principal (P). | $ 42.47 |
| 2. Subtract this amount from the previous balance. | $70,000.00 |
| 3. The remainder is the new balance on the loan. | $70,000.00 |
| | − 42.47 |
| | $69,957.53 |

To calculate the balance on the loan after the second payment, repeat the steps in Figure 7.3 and Figure 7.4 using the new balance of $69,957.53.

| | |
|---|---|
| 1. $I = \frac{\$69{,}957.53 \times .085}{12} =$ | $ 495.53 |
| 2. Monthly payment | $ 538.30 |
| 3. Subtract the amount that went to interest (I) | − 495.53 |
| 4. The remainder went to principal (P) | $ 42.77 |
| 5. Previous balance | $69,957.53 |
| 6. Subtract amount that went to principal | − 42.77 |
| 7. The remainder is the new balance on the loan | $69,914.76 |

Most use a real estate calculator, a laptop computer, or a personal computer that allows them to quickly calculate and compare payments on different loans and to store and print the results.

## EQUITY

**Equity** is the *difference between the market value of the property and what is owed on it.* If a homeowner pays $100,000 using a no-down-payment Department of Veterans Affairs (VA) loan for a property valued at $100,000, he has no equity. If he uses a loan with a 5 percent down payment, he begins with equity of $5,000. As payments are made, the part of the payment applied to the principal reduces the amount owed, producing equity. Adding improvements that increase the market value of the property (without borrowing the money to pay

**FIGURE 7.6**

Total interest paid over the life of the loan.

Continuing to use the data from Figure 7.5, how much interest is paid over the life of the loan?

1. Calculate the monthly payment: $538.30.
2. Calculate the total number of months to be paid: 30 years is 12 months × 30 = 360 payments.
3. Multiply the monthly payment by the total number of months to be paid to calculate the total of the payments:

   $538.30 × 360 payments = $193,788 total payback
4. Subtract the amount borrowed from the total of the payback to calculate the amount that went to interest:

   $193,788

   − 70,000

   $123,788 total interest paid

for them) also adds equity. Most properties appreciate in value over time, thereby increasing equity. As the market value of the property goes up and the amount owed on it decreases, equity increases. When the loan is completely paid, the owner then has 100 percent equity in the property.

## USURY

**Usury** is *interest charged in excess of the legal limit that is set by law*. When mortgage interest rates started to rise in the 1970, they hit usury limits in some states (which were as low as 10 percent). Had Congress not preempted state usury laws on first mortgage residential loans in 1980, the mortgage loan market would probably have come to a standstill. The rates on mortgages went up to 18 percent before gradually falling to the low rates of today. For a transaction to constitute usury, there must be a loan with an agreement to pay a higher interest rate than the law allows. Both lender and borrower must understand that the money is to be paid back, and there must be a corrupt intent to charge more than the law allows. Usury laws vary by state and are frequently revised. If a rate appears usurious, the agent should advise his client to seek competent legal advice.

## DISCOUNT POINTS AND YIELD

In making mortgage loans, lending institutions may charge *discount points* to increase the *yield* (profit) to the lender. Two aspects of discount points are important:

1. Each point charged by the lender costs somebody 1 percent of the loan amount and is paid at the time of loan closing.
2. The effect realized by the lender's charging points is to increase the effective interest rate. As a rule of thumb, each point charged will increase the loan's yield (effective interest rate) by 1/8 of a percentage point.

   The following chart is helpful in illustrating this concept:

   1 point = 1/8 of a percent increase in yield

   2 points = 2/8 = ¼ of a percent increase in yield

   3 points = 3/8 of a percent increase in yield

   4 points = 4/8 = ½ of a percent in yield

Lending institutions can charge discount points on conventional, Federal Housing Administration (FHA), or VA loans. Buyers or sellers can pay the points on all three types of loan, or they can choose a loan rate that requires no points. The buyer can negotiate with the lender any number of points to buy down the rate to a desirable rate, as long as she is paying the points. Each type of loan has limits on the amount of seller concessions; therefore, the total of points and other concessions paid by the seller for the buyer must not exceed those limits.

In the past, a buyer often paid points to buy down an interest rate. With the current low interest rates, many buyers opt for a "par" rate, the best rate they can get without discount points. Points are a "sunk cost." The borrower does not get them back when he sells or refinances. The borrower should look at the break-even point between a loan that has points and a par rate loan before making a choice. For example, the buyer could compare a $50,000 loan at 8.5 percent with no points and at 8 percent with 4 points. The following calculations show the effect to the borrower.

| | | |
|---|---|---|
| Points paid by borrower ($50,000 × .04) | = | $2,000.00 |
| Monthly principal and interest payment at 8.5% for 30 years | = | 384.46 |
| Monthly principal and interest payment at 8% for 30 years | = | 366.88 |
| Difference in payments | = | 17.58 per month |

Dividing the $2,000 paid in points by the monthly savings shows that it will take the borrower 113.76 months to save the $2,000 paid up front in points. That is approximately 9.5 years. Most loans are not held that long. Unless the borrower is reasonably sure of keeping the home that long or of selling it later under a loan assumption at the more advantageous 8 percent rate, the borrower may want to take the 8.5 percent loan with no points and invest the $2,000 elsewhere.

## LOAN FEES, LOAN VALUES, AND LOAN-TO-VALUE RATIO

Knowing the amount of PITI is an essential part of the prequalification process. If a buyer calls on a specific listing and absolutely wants only that property, then all the agent has to do is determine whether the prospective buyer qualifies (see Figure 7.10) for the PITI on that specific property. Most buyers, however, want to see a number of properties and need help in determining the amount of money a mortgage company is likely to lend them. If the agent determines the maximum amount of payment, including PITI, for which the client will qualify and the amount of money the client has for down payment and closing costs, he can calculate the maximum price the buyer can buy at the current interest rates (see Figure 7.11).

Shopping for the best loan is one of the agent's most important duties. This does not mean referring buyer clients to a friend at XYZ Mortgage Company, unless XYZ Mortgage Company has the best loan types, rates, and closing costs.

The best loan for any buyer depends on a number of factors, including the amount of money he has for down payment and closing costs, his income and debt load, the length of time he intends to occupy the property, his credit score, and/or qualifications for a first-time home buyer program or for a no-down-payment loan such as a VA or Rural Development loan.

Loan fees can vary greatly from one loan to another. The simple interest rate alone is not enough to determine the best loan. The annual percentage rate, a number that considers both the simple interest rate and closing costs, helps agents and clients compare loans more easily. A client planning to live in a property for 15 to 20 years or more may want to obtain the lowest interest rate possible even if he must pay more closing costs up front. A client knowing he is going to keep the property only two or three years may want to obtain a loan with a slightly higher interest rate with low or no closing costs. Some lenders offer loans with lender-funded closing costs, although at a slightly higher rate. An agent can calculate (or ask the mortgage banker to calculate) the break-even point between two loans.

| | |
|---|---|
| Monthly principal and interest payment at 6.5% for 30 years, $2,500 closing costs | $632.07 |
| Monthly principal and interest payment at 7% for 30 years, $0 closing costs | $665.30 |
| Difference in monthly payments | $33.23 |

It will take over 75 months before the borrower pays the extra $2,500 in closing costs. If he sells or refinances the property before 75 months, he will save with the higher interest loan.

Other factors can help determine which loan the client chooses. If the client does not have the $2,500, he may have no choice. At 6.5 to 7 percent, it is unlikely the rates will drop enough to make refinancing worthwhile. If the choice is between 9 and 9.5 percent, however, the borrower planning on keeping the property a long time may expect the interest rate to fall within a few years. He may want to go with the higher rate to avoid having "sunk costs" in his present loan when he refinances it.

Since a bank or other lending institution will not lend more than the appraised value of a property, the loan value is always the lesser of the sales price or appraised value. The loan amount is the loan value less the amount paid by the borrower as a down payment. Mortgage loans are generally classified according to their loan-to-value ratios (LTV). For example:

A buyer buys a home for $80,000. The appraised value of the home is also $80,000. If the buyer pays $16,000 as a down payment at closing, the LTV for this loan would be calculated as:

Loan Amount = $64,000 (80,000 − 16,000)

Loan Value = $80,000

LTV = 80% ($64,000/$80,000)

If the borrower has 20 percent for a down payment, she may choose a conventional loan. There is usually no private mortgage insurance with an 80 percent loan-to-value ratio. This avoids the Department of Veterans Affairs funding fee on VA loans and the mortgage insurance premium requirements of FHA. If she does not have 20 percent of the purchase price for a down payment, she can still go with a conventional loan. Most conventional loans require 5 percent down payment with that 5 percent coming from the borrower's own funds. Some conventional loans now require only 3 percent down payment with some flexibility as to the source of funds. Usually, credit and mortgage insurance premiums are higher on these loans.

Rural Development (RD) loans and VA loans are usually the only no-down-payment loans; however, down payment assistance is sometimes available for low- or moderate-income buyers, more often for first-time buyers. FHA loans are available with as little as 3 percent down payment and higher qualifying ratios than conventional loans.

## NOTES

In making a mortgage loan, the lender requires the borrower to sign a **promissory note,** or bond (see Figure 7.7). The note, which must be in writing, provides evidence that a valid debt exists. The note contains a *promise that the borrower will be personally liable for paying the amount of money set forth* in the note and specifies the manner in which the debt is to be paid. Payment is typically in monthly installments of a stated amount, commencing on a specified date. The note also states the annual rate of interest to be charged on the outstanding principal balance.

The note can be an interest-only note, on which interest is paid periodically until the note matures and the entire principal balance is paid at maturity. Construction notes are usually of this type. Or the note can be a single-payment loan that requires no payments on principal or interest until the note matures and the entire principal and interest is paid at maturity. This is seen more frequently in short-term notes. The note also can be an amortizing note, in which periodic payments are made on principal and interest until such time as the principal is completely paid. Most mortgage loans are of this type.

## THE MORTGAGE NOTE

A mortgage note is simply an IOU backed by a mortgage or deed of trust pledging the property as collateral for the loan. A valid mortgage note must contain a promise to pay a specified amount of money, must specify the terms of the repayment, and must be signed by the

**FIGURE 7.7**

A sample promissory note.

SATISFACTION: The debt evidenced by this Note has been satisfied in full this ______ day of __________, 19____

Signed: ______________________

# PROMISSORY NOTE

______________________, N.C.

$ ______________________ ______________________, 19______

FOR VALUE RECEIVED the undersigned, jointly and severally, promise to pay to ______________________________________________________________________________________________________________________________ or order,

the principal sum of ______________________________________________

DOLLARS ($ __________________), with interest from __________________, at the rate of __________________

per cent ( ______ %) per annum on the unpaid balance until paid or until default, both principal and interest payable in lawful money of the United States of America, at the office of ______________________________________________

or at such place as the legal holder hereof may designate in writing. It is understood and agreed that additional amounts may be advanced by the holder hereof as provided in the instruments, if any, securing this Note and such advances will be added to the principal of this Note and will accrue interest at the above specified rate of interest from the date of advance until paid. The principal and interest shall be due and payable as follows:



If not sooner paid, the entire remaining indebtedness shall be due and payable on ______________________.

If payable in installments, each such installment shall, unless otherwise provided, be applied first to payment of interest then accrued and due on the unpaid principal balance, with the remainder applied to the unpaid principal.

Unless otherwise provided, this Note may be prepaid in full or in part at any time without penalty or premium. Partial prepayments shall be applied to installments due in reverse order of their maturity.

In the event of (a) default in payment of any installment of principal or interest hereof as the same becomes due and such default is not cured within ten (10) days from the due date, or (b) default under the terms of any instrument securing this Note, and such default is not cured within fifteen (15) days after written notice to maker, then in either such event the holder may without further notice, declare the remainder of the principal sum, together with all interest accrued thereon and, the prepayment premium, if any, at once due and payable. Failure to exercise this option shall not constitute a wavier of the right to exercise the same at any other time. The unpaid principal of this Note and any part thereof, accrued interest and all other sums due under this Note and the Deed of Trust, if any, shall bear interest at the rate of ______________________ per cent ( ______ %) per annum after default until paid.

All parties to this Note, including maker and any sureties, endorsers, or guarantors hereby waive protest, presentment, notice of dishonor, and notice of acceleration of maturity and agree to continue to remain bound for the payment of principal, interest and all other sums due under this Note and the Deed of Trust notwithstanding any change or changes by way of release, surrender, exchange, modification or substitution of any security for this Note or by way of any extension or extensions of time for the payment of principal and interest; and all such parties waive all and every kind of notice of such change or changes and agree that the same may be made without notice or consent of any of them.

Upon default the holder of this Note may employ an attorney to enforce the holder's rights and remedies and the maker, principal, surety, guarantor and endorsers of this Note hereby agree to pay to the holder reasonable attorneys fees not exceeding a sum equal to fifteen percent (15%) of the outstanding balance owing on said Note, plus all other reasonable expenses incurred by the holder in exercising any of the holder's rights and remedies upon default. The rights and remedies of the holder as provided in this Note and any instrument securing this Note shall be cumulative and may be pursued singly, successively, or together against the property described in the Deed of Trust or any other funds, property or security held by the holder for payment or security, in the sole discretion of the holder. The failure to exercise any such right or remedy shall not be a waiver or release of such rights or remedies or the right to exercise any of them at another time.

This Note is to be governed and construed in accordance with the laws of the State of North Carolina.

This Note is given ______________________________________, and is secured by a ______________________________________________ ______________________________________ which is a __________ lien upon the property therein described.

IN TESTIMONY WHEREOF, each corporate maker has caused this instrument to be executed in its corporate name by its ______________________ President, attested by its ______________________ Secretary, and its corporate seal to be hereto affixed, all by order of its Board of Directors first duly given, the day and year first above written.

______________________________
(Corporate Name)

By: ______________________________

______________________ President

ATTEST:

______________________________

______________________ Secretary (Corporate Seal)

______________________________
(Corporate Name)

By: ______________________________

______________________ President

ATTEST:

______________________________

______________________ Secretary (Corporate Seal)

USE BLACK INK ONLY

IN TESTIMONY WHEREOF, each individual maker has hereunto set his hand and adopted as his seal the word "SEAL" appearing beside his name, the day and year first above written.

______________________________ (SEAL)

______________________________ (SEAL)

______________________________ (SEAL)

______________________________ (SEAL)

______________________________ (SEAL)

______________________________ (SEAL)

______________________________ (SEAL)

borrower. When the note is repaid, the mortgage or deed of trust is canceled. If the property is destroyed, condemned, or loses its value before the note is paid in full, the borrower is still responsible for paying the debt. If the lender forecloses on the property and the sale proceeds are insufficient to pay off the debt, the lender can get a deficiency judgment for the difference between the sale proceeds and what is actually owed (for exceptions, see sections "Deficiency Judgment" and "Nonrecourse Note"). This judgment would be a general lien allowing the lender to take action against other property belonging to the borrower.

Certain important items that are not essential to the validity of the note are often included in the note. These items are usually repeated in the mortgage or deed of trust. Nonessential items include acceleration clauses, prepayment penalty clauses, and due-on-sale clauses. An **acceleration clause** *provides the lender with the option of calling the entire loan due and payable at once if the buyer defaults or breaks the contract in any way.* Anything that violates the provisions of the note could trigger this clause. For example, the borrower could fail to make the payments or otherwise breach the contract by such actions as damaging the property, failing to make necessary repairs, or failing to maintain insurance.

A note may have a **prepayment penalty clause,** but mortgage loans for personal residences rarely include such a clause. "Government-related" loans (FHA, VA, and RD) and loans sold in the secondary mortgage market (conforming loans) do not allow prepayment penalties. North Carolina law prohibits prepayment penalties on first mortgage home loans with an original balance of $150,000 or less.

A lender frequently adds a **due-on-sale clause** (also called an **alienation clause**) to the note to prevent a future purchaser from assuming the loan without the lender's permission. A due-on-sale clause provides that if a buyer sells property to a new owner, the lender has the right to declare the entire note due and payable immediately or the lender may allow the new owner to assume the loan at current market interest rates.

## Negotiability of Note

Notes can either be negotiable or nonnegotiable. A **negotiable note** is a written promise to pay a specified sum of money according to specified terms to the *bearer or holder of the note.* The negotiable note will use such terms as "to bearer," "to holder," or "to a person or corporate or business entity, its heirs, successors, or assigns." It will not name an individual or entity as the payee but rather allows the payee to transfer its rights to receive payment to a third party. Most real estate notes are negotiable because mortgage lenders often sell their loans in the secondary mortgage markets. A **nonnegotiable note** is a written promise to pay a specified sum of money according to specified terms to a *particular individual or corporation.*

# MORTGAGE AND DEED OF TRUST

Typically, a borrower's personal promise to pay a debt is not enough security for the large amount of money involved in a mortgage loan. Therefore, the lender requires the additional security of the property itself as collateral for the loan. When a *borrower pledges property as security for the loan without surrendering possession,* it is called **hypothecation,** and this is accomplished through the mortgage or deed of trust instrument. Therefore, every mortgage loan has two instruments: (1) the note (a personal IOU) and (2) the mortgage or deed of trust (a pledge of real property). Pledging the property does not require the borrower to give up possession unless the borrower **defaults;** that is, the borrower fails to make payments as scheduled or fails to fulfill other obligations as set forth in the mortgage or deed of trust.

The two main lending practices, or theories of financing, are (1) lien theory and (2) title theory.

Lien Theory vs. Title Theory
(mortgage theory) vs. (granting theory)

## Lien Theory

In **lien theory** (mortgage theory), *the loan constitutes a lien against the real property.* The **mortgage** is a two-party instrument between the lender and the borrower. *The borrower gives a piece of paper (mortgage) to the lender in return for the borrowed funds.* The *borrower who gives the mortgage* is the **mortgagor.** The *lender who receives the mortgage* is the **mortgagee.** The borrower (mortgagor) retains title to the property, but this title is encumbered by the lien created by the mortgage in favor of the lender (mortgagee). If the lender is not paid according to terms of the mortgage and note, the lender can execute the lien or foreclose. States that use mortgage theories are called lien theory states. Most states are lien theory states.

## Title Theory

In **title theory** (granting theory), *a disinterested third party actually holds legal title to the property in security for the loan* through a **deed of trust** (see Figure 7.8). The deed of trust is the legal instrument through which the buyer/borrower conveys legal title in the property to a neutral third party called the trustee. The buyer/borrower retains equitable title in the property. This means that the buyer/borrower has the right to acquire legal title when the loan has been repaid. The **trustee,** who is usually an attorney, *holds the rights conveyed by the buyer/borrower in trust for the* **beneficiary,** who is the lender. The buyer/borrower, who is also called a **grantor** or **trustor,** signs a promissory note payable to the lender.

The lender then gives the buyer/borrower the money to buy the property (see Figure 7.9). If the buyer/borrower defaults on the promissory note, the beneficiary can ask the trustee who holds those rights conveyed by the buyer/borrower to begin foreclosure. *If the buyer/borrower lives up to the agreement he made with the beneficiary/lender, by repaying the loan in full, the trustee will return all the rights conveyed.* This obligation on the part of the trustee is contained in a clause called the **defeasance clause.** It is the **power of sale clause** that gives the trustee the right to sell the property if the buyer defaults. Since legal title is conveyed, states that use deeds of trust are called title theory states. North Carolina is a title theory state.

## Mortgage or Deed of Trust Requirements

For a mortgage or deed of trust to be legal and valid, it must contain the following essential elements:

1. The mortgage or deed of trust must be in writing, as required by the Statute of Frauds, because the mortgage or deed of trust pledges or conveys title to real property to secure payment of the note.
2. Because the mortgage or deed of trust is a contract, all parties must be identified and have contractual capacity.
3. There must be a valid debt to be secured by the mortgage or deed of trust. The existence of the valid debt is evidenced by the note.
4. To secure the debt in the mortgage or deed of trust, the mortgagor or trustor must have a valid interest in the property pledged or conveyed.
5. A legally acceptable description of the property must be included.
6. The mortgage or deed of trust must contain a mortgaging clause. In lien theory states, which use a mortgage form, the mortgaging clause is a statement demonstrating the mortgagor's intention to mortgage the property to the mortgagee. In title theory states, this clause takes the form of a deed of conveyance. The mortgaging clause in this case reads like the granting clause in a deed. This is not an absolute conveyance of title by the borrower; rather, it is a conditional conveyance made only to secure payment of the note.
7. The mortgage or deed of trust must contain a defeasance clause that defeats the lien and conveyance of title when the mortgage debt is fully satisfied.
8. The borrower must properly execute the mortgage or deed of trust. Only the borrower or grantor signs the document. The lender does not sign.
9. The mortgage or deed of trust must be delivered to and accepted by the mortgagee or trustee/beneficiary (lender).

**FIGURE 7.8** North Carolina deed of trust.

**NORTH CAROLINA DEED OF TRUST**

SATISFACTION: The debt secured by the within Deed of Trust together with the note(s) secured thereby has been satisfied in full.

This the ______________________ day of ______________________, 20___

Signed: ______________________

______________________

Parcel Identifier No. ____________ Verified by ____________ County or the ________ day of ____________, 20___

By: ______________________

Mail/Box to: ______________________

This instrument was prepared by: ______________________

Brief description for the Index: ______________________

THIS DEED of TRUST made this ________________ day of ________________, 20___, by and between:

| GRANTOR | TRUSTEE | BENEFICIARY |
|---|---|---|
| | | |

Enter in appropriate block for each party: name, address, and, if appropriate, character of entity, e.g. corporation or partnership

The designation Grantor, Trustee, and Beneficiary as used herein shall include said parties, their heirs, successors, and assigns, and shall include singular, plural, masculine, feminine or neuter as required by context.

WITNESSETH, That whereas the Grantor is indebted to the Beneficiary in the principal sum of ______________________ ______________________ Dollars ($____________),
as evidenced by a Promissory Note of even date herewith, the terms of which are incorporated herein by reference. The final due date for payments of said Promissory Note, if not sooner paid, is ________________, 20___.





(continued)

**FIGURE 7.8** Continued.

NOW, THEREFORE, as security for said indebtedness, advancements and other sums expended by Beneficiary pursuant to this Deed of Trust and costs of collection (including attorneys fees as provided in the Promissory Note) and other valuable consideration, the receipt of which is hereby acknowledged, the Grantor has bargained, sold, given and conveyed and does by these presents bargain, sell, give, grant and convey to said Trustee, his heirs, or successors, and assigns, the parcel(s) of land situated in the City of ____________________, ____________________ Township, ____________________ County, North Carolina, (the "Premises") and more particularly described as follows:

TO HAVE AND TO HOLD said Premises with all privileges and appurtenances thereunto belonging, to said Trustee, his heirs, successors, and assigns forever, upon the trusts, terms and conditions, and for the uses hereinafter set forth.

If the Grantor shall pay the Note secured hereby in accordance with its terms, together with interest thereon, and any renewals or extensions thereof in whole or in part, all other sums secured hereby and shall comply with all of the covenants, terms and conditions of this Deed of Trust, then this conveyance shall be null and void and may be canceled of record at the request and the expense of the Grantor.

If, however, there shall be any default (a) in the payment of any sums due under the Note, this Deed of Trust or any other instrument securing the Note and such default is not cured within ten (10) days from the due date, or (b) if there shall be default in any of the other covenants, terms or conditions of the Note secured hereby, or any failure or neglect to comply with the covenants, terms or conditions contained in this Deed of Trust or any other instrument securing the Note and such default is not cured within fifteen (15) days after written notice, then and in any of such events, without further notice, it shall be lawful for and the duty of the Trustee, upon request of the Beneficiary, to sell the land herein conveyed at public auction for cash, after having first giving such notice of hearing as to commencement of foreclosure proceedings and obtained such findings or leave of court as may then be required by law and giving such notice and advertising the time and place of such sale in such manner as may then be provided by law, and upon such and any resales and upon compliance with the law then relating to foreclosure proceedings under power of sale to convey title to the purchaser in as full and ample manner as the Trustee is empowered. The Trustee shall be authorized to retain an attorney to represent him in such proceedings.

The proceeds of the Sale shall after the Trustee retains his commission, together with reasonable attorneys fees incurred by the Trustee in such proceedings, be applied to the costs of sale, including, but not limited to, costs of collection, taxes, assessments, costs of recording, service fees and incidental expenditures, the amount due on the Note hereby secured and advancements and other sums expended by the Beneficiary according to the provisions hereof and otherwise as required by the then existing law relating to foreclosures. The Trustee's commission shall be five percent (5%) of the gross proceeds of the sale or the minimum sum of $ ____________ whichever is greater, for a completed foreclosure. In the event foreclosure is commenced, but not completed, the Grantor shall pay all expenses incurred by Trustee, including reasonable attorneys fees, and a partial commission computed on five per cent (5%) of the outstanding indebtedness or the above stated minimum sum, whichever is greater, in accordance with the following schedule, to-wit: one-fourth (1/4) thereof before the Trustee issues a notice of hearing on the right to foreclosure; one-half (1/2) thereof after issuance of said notice, three-fourths (3/4) thereof after such hearing; and the greater of the full commission or minimum sum after the initial sale.

And the said Grantor does hereby covenant and agree with the Trustee as follows:

1. INSURANCE. Grantor shall keep all improvements on said land, now or hereafter erected, constantly insured for the benefit of the Beneficiary against loss by fire, windstorm and such other casualties and contingencies, in such manner and in such companies and for such amounts, not less than that amount necessary to pay the sum secured by this Deed of Trust, and as may be satisfactory to the Beneficiary. Grantor shall purchase such insurance, pay all premiums therefor, and shall deliver to Beneficiary such policies along with evidence of premium payments as long as the Note secured hereby remains unpaid. If Grantor fails to purchase such insurance, pay premiums therefor or deliver said policies along with evidence of payment of premiums thereon, then Beneficiary, at his option, may purchase such insurance. Such amounts paid by Beneficiary shall be added to the principal of the Note secured by this Deed of Trust, and shall be due and payable upon demand of Beneficiary. All proceeds from any insurance so maintained shall at the option of Beneficiary be applied to the debt secured hereby and if payable in installments, applied in the inverse order of maturity of such installments or to the repair or reconstruction of any improvements located upon the Property.

2. TAXES, ASSESSMENTS, CHARGES. Grantor shall pay all taxes, assessments and charges as may be lawfully levied against said Premises within thirty (30) days after the same shall become due. In the event that Grantor fails to so pay all taxes, assessments and charges as herein required, then Beneficiary, at his option, may pay the same and the amounts so paid shall be added to the principal of the Note secured by this Deed of Trust, and shall be due and payable upon demand of Beneficiary.

3. ASSIGNMENTS OF RENTS AND PROFITS. Grantor assigns to Beneficiary, in the event of default, all rents and profits from the land and any improvements thereon, and authorizes Beneficiary to enter upon and take possession of such land and improvements, to rent same, at any reasonable rate of rent determined by Beneficiary, and after deducting from any such rents the cost of reletting and collection, to apply the remainder to the debt secured hereby.

4. PARTIAL RELEASE. Grantor shall not be entitled to the partial release of any of the above described property unless a specific provision providing therefor is included in this Deed of Trust. In the event a partial release provision is included in this Deed of Trust. Grantor must strictly comply with the terms thereof. Notwithstanding anything herein contained, Grantor shall not be



(continued)

**FIGURE 7.8** Continued.

entitled to any release of property unless Grantor is not in default and is in full compliance with all of the terms and provisions of the Note, this Deed of Trust, and any other instrument that may be securing said Note.

5. WASTE. The Grantor covenants that he will keep the Premises herein conveyed in as good order, repair and condition as they are now, reasonable wear and tear excepted, and will comply with all governmental requirements respecting the Premises or their use, and that he will not commit or permit any waste.

6. CONDEMNATION. In the event that any or all of the Premises shall be condemned and taken under the power of eminent domain, Grantor shall give immediate written notice to Beneficiary and Beneficiary shall have the right to receive and collect all damages awarded by reason of such taking, and the right to such damages hereby is assigned to Beneficiary who shall have the discretion to apply the amount so received, or any part thereof, to the indebtedness due hereunder and if payable in installments, applied in the inverse order of maturity of such installments, or to any alteration, repair or restoration of the Premises by Grantor.

7. WARRANTIES. Grantor covenants with Trustee and Beneficiary that he is seized of the Premises in fee simple, has the right to convey the same in fee simple, that title is marketable and free and clear of all encumbrances, and that he will warrant and defend the title against the lawful claims of all persons whomsoever, except for the exceptions hereinafter stated. Title to the property hereinabove described is subject to the following exceptions:

8. SUBSTITUTION OF TRUSTEE. Grantor and Trustee covenant and agree to and with Beneficiary that in case the said Trustee, or any successor trustee, shall die, become incapable of acting, renounce his trust, or for any reason the holder of the Note desires to replace said Trustee, then the holder may appoint, in writing, a trustee to take the place of the Trustee; and upon the probate and registration of the same, the trustee thus appointed shall succeed to all rights, powers and duties of the Trustee.

☐ **THE FOLLOWING PARAGRAPH, 9. SALE OF PREMISES, SHALL NOT APPLY UNLESS THE BLOCK TO THE LEFT MARGIN OF THIS SENTENCE IS MARKED AND/OR INITIALED.**

9. SALE OF PREMISES. Grantor agrees that if the Premises or any part thereof or interest therein is sold, assigned, transferred, conveyed or otherwise alienated by Grantor, whether voluntarily or involuntarily or by operation of law [other than: (i) the creation of a lien or other encumbrance subordinate to this Deed of Trust which does not relate to a transfer of rights of occupancy in the Premises; (ii) the creation of a purchase money security interest for household appliances; (iii) a transfer by devise, descent, or operation of law on the death of a joint tenant or tenant by the entirety; (iv) the grant of a leasehold interest of three (3) years or less not containing an option to purchase; (v) a transfer to a relative resulting from the death of a Grantor; (vi) a transfer where the spouse or children of the Grantor become the owner of the Premises; (vii) a transfer resulting from a decree of a dissolution of marriage, legal separation agreement, or from an incidental property settlement agreement, by which the spouse of the Grantor becomes an owner of the Premises; (viii) a transfer into an inter vivos trust in which the Grantor is and remains a beneficiary and which does not relate to a transfer of rights of occupancy in the Premises], without the prior written consent of Beneficiary, Beneficiary, at its own option, may declare the Note secured hereby and all other obligations hereunder to be forthwith due and payable. Any change in the legal or equitable title of the Premises or in the beneficial ownership of the Premises, including the sale, conveyance or disposition of a majority interest in the Grantor if a corporation or partnership, whether or not of record and whether or not for consideration, shall be deemed to be the transfer of an interest in the Premises.



10. ADVANCEMENTS. If Grantor shall fail to perform any of the covenants or obligations contained herein or in any other instrument given as additional security for the Note secured hereby, the Beneficiary may, but without obligation, make advances to perform such covenants or obligations, and all such sums so advanced shall be added to the principal sum, shall bear interest at the rate provided in the Note secured hereby for sums due after default and shall be due from Grantor on demand of the Beneficiary. No advancement or anything contained in this paragraph shall constitute a waiver by Beneficiary or prevent such failure to perform from constituting an event of default.

11. INDEMNITY. If any suit or proceeding be brought against the Trustee or Beneficiary or if any suit or proceeding be brought which may affect the value or title of the Premises, Grantor shall defend, indemnify and hold harmless and on demand reimburse Trustee or Beneficiary from any loss, cost, damage or expense and any sums expended by Trustee or Beneficiary shall bear interest as provided in the Note secured hereby for sums due after default and shall be due and payable on demand.

12. WAIVERS. Grantor waives all rights to require marshaling of assets by the Trustee or Beneficiary. No delay or omission of the Trustee or Beneficiary in the exercise of any right, power or remedy arising under the Note or this Deed of Trust shall be deemed a waiver of any default or acquiescence therein or shall impair or waive the exercise of such right, power or remedy by Trustee or Beneficiary at any other time.

13. CIVIL ACTION. In the event that the Trustee is named as a party to any civil action as Trustee in this Deed of Trust, the Trustee shall be entitled to employ an attorney at law, including himself if he is a licensed attorney, to represent him in said action and the reasonable attorney's fee of the Trustee in such action shall be paid by the Beneficiary and added to the principal of the Note secured by this Deed of Trust and bear interest at the rate provided in the Note for sums due after default.

14. PRIOR LIENS. Default under the terms of any instrument secured by a lien to which this Deed of Trust is subordinate shall constitute default hereunder.

15. OTHER TERMS.



(continued)

**FIGURE 7.8** Continued.

IN WITNESS WHEREOF, the Grantor has duly executed the foregoing as of the day and year first above written.

_______________________________ _______________________________ (SEAL)
(Entity Name)

By: _______________________________ _______________________________ (SEAL)
Title: _______________
By: _______________________________ _______________________________ (SEAL)
Title: _______________
By: _______________________________ _______________________________ (SEAL)
Title: _______________

USE BLACK INK ONLY

_______________________________ (SEAL)

_______________________________ (SEAL)

_______________________________ (SEAL)

---

SEAL-STAMP

USE BLACK INK ONLY

State of North Carolina - County of _______________
I, the undersigned Notary Public of the County and State aforesaid, certify that _______________ _______________ personally appeared before me this day and acknowledged the due execution of the foregoing instrument for the purposes therein expressed. Witness my hand and Notarial stamp or seal this _______ day of _______, 20__.
My Commission Expires: _______ _______________
Notary Public

---

SEAL-STAMP

USE BLACK INK ONLY

State of North Carolina - County of _______________
I, the undersigned Notary Public of the County and State aforesaid, certify that _______________ _______________ personally came before me this day and acknowledged that _he is the _______________ of _______________, a North Carolina or _______ corporation/limited liability company/general partnership/limited partnership (strike through the inapplicable), and that by authority duly given and as the act of each entity, _he signed the foregoing instrument in its name on its behalf as its act and deed. Witness my hand and Notarial stamp or seal, this _______ day of _______________, 20__.
My Commission Expires: _______ _______________
Notary Public

---

SEAL-STAMP

USE BLACK INK ONLY

State of North Carolina - County of _______________
I, the undersigned Notary Public of the County and State aforesaid, certify that _______________
_______________________________
_______________________________
Witness my hand and Notarial stamp or seal, this _______ day of _______, 20__.
My Commission Expires: _______ _______________
Notary Public

---

The foregoing Certificate(s) of _______________________________ is/are certified to be correct. This instrument and this certificate are duly registered at the date and time and in the Book and Page shown on the first page hereof.
_______________________ Register of Deeds for _______________ County
By: _______________________ Deputy/Assistant - Register of Deeds

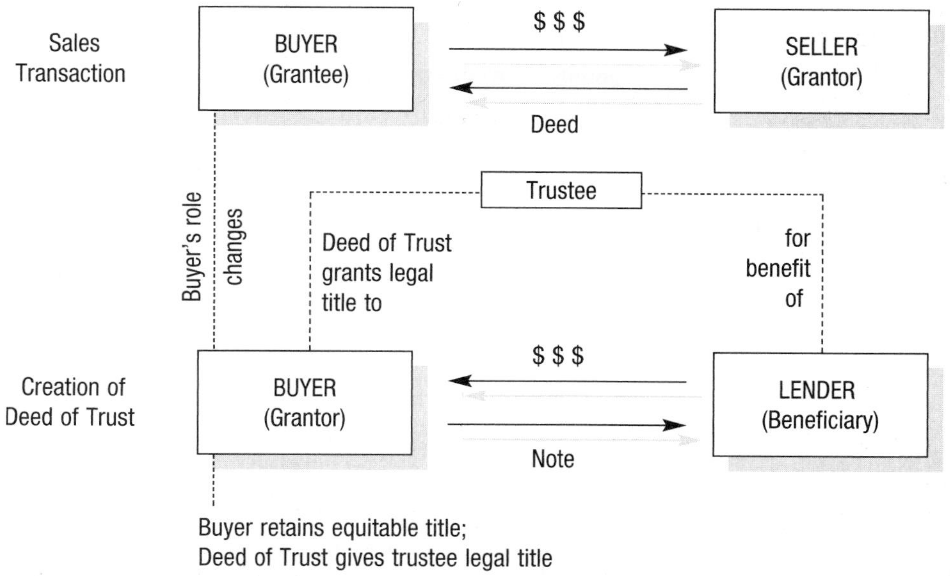


**FIGURE 7.9**
Relationships in a deed of trust transaction.

## CLAUSES AND COVENANTS

Examples of the various clauses and covenants included in a mortgage or deed of trust are presented below.

1. The note executed by the borrower, including acceleration, alienation, due-on-sale, and prepayment penalty clauses, is reproduced in the mortgage or deed of trust.
2. The mortgage and the deed of trust require the borrower to pay all real property taxes and assessments on a timely basis, keep the buildings in a proper state of repair and preservation, and protect the buildings against loss by fire or other casualty with an insurance policy written in an amount at least 80 percent of the value of the structures. Many lenders also require insurance for 100 percent of the loan value minus the lot value.
3. Both documents provide the right of foreclosure to the lender if the borrower defaults.
4. In the mortgage form and the deed of trust form, a covenant specifies that the borrower must have a good and marketable title to the property that is being pledged to secure payment of the note.
5. The mortgage or deed of trust may contain an alienation or due-on-sale clause entitling the lender to declare the principal balance immediately due and payable if the borrower sells the property during the loan term. The clause makes the loan unassumable without the lender's permission. Permission to assume the mortgage at an interest rate prevailing at the time of assumption can be given at the discretion of the lender. The alienation clause can provide for release of the original borrower from liability if an assumption is permitted. This release is sometimes referred to as a *novation.*
6. The mortgage or deed of trust always provides for execution by the borrower.
7. The mortgage or deed of trust provides for *acknowledgment* by the borrower to make the document eligible for recording on the public record for the lender's protection.

## RIGHTS OF BORROWER

In borrowing funds to finance a mortgage, the borrower has these legal rights:

1. The borrower has the right to possession of the property during the mortgage term as long as the borrower is not in default.

2. The defeasance clause gives the borrower the right to redeem the title or have the mortgage lien released at any time prior to default by paying the debt in full.
3. The borrower has the right of **equity of redemption.**

## Equity of Redemption

After default and up to the time a foreclosure sale is finalized, the borrower has an equitable right to redeem the property by paying the principal amount of the debt, accrued interest, and lender's costs incurred in initiating the foreclosure. The borrower's equity of redemption cannot be defeated by a clause in a mortgage or Deed of Trust and can be terminated only by the finalization of the foreclosure sale. After a property is sold on the courthouse steps, there is a ten-day "upset bid" period during which anyone can raise the bid by a stated margin and upset the previous bid. Another ten-day upset bid period then begins. This process continues until an upset bid period passes without another upset bid. At the end of the final ten-day period, the sale is finalized and the title passes to the new purchaser. Only then is the buyer's equitable right of redemption terminated. After this point, the buyer cannot get his property back by paying the entire debt and expenses.

Courts have recognized a borrower's equity of redemption for centuries, and the same protections have now been afforded the borrower through statutes in many states. North Carolina General Statutes 45-21.27 through 45-21.30 provide for a **statutory redemption period.** These statutes *allow a borrower to submit an upset bid during the ten-day upset period or periods following a foreclosure sale.* The borrower has a choice of redeeming his property by paying the debt owed the lender and costs of sale or bidding against others and reclaiming his property by outbidding them or forcing them to raise the bid closer to the fair market value. Finalization of the foreclosure sale after the end of the last ten-day upset period ends the statutory redemption period and the borrower's equity of redemption.

# RIGHTS OF LENDER

In lending funds to finance a mortgage, the lender has these rights:

1. The lender has the right to transfer or to assign the mortgage or deed of trust. This enables the lender to sell the loan, if he so desires, and thereby free up the money invested. The **right of assignment** provides liquidity to the loan because the *lender can sell the loan at any time and obtain the money invested rather than wait for payment of the loan over an extended time.*
2. The lender has the right to foreclose on the property, to take possession of the property (after foreclosure) if the borrower defaults on loan payments.

# FORECLOSURE

If the borrower does not make the payments as required or fails to fulfill other obligations as set forth in the mortgage or deed of trust, he or she is in default on the loan. The lender's ultimate power is to foreclose. **Foreclosure** is the *liquidation of title to the real property pledged to recover funds to pay off the debt.* The two types of foreclosure are *judicial* and *nonjudicial.*

## Judicial Foreclosure

**Judicial foreclosure,** common in lien theory states, *requires the lender to bring a lawsuit against the borrower and obtain a judgment for the amount of debt the borrower owes.* When the judgment is obtained, the lender requests the court to issue an execution instructing the sheriff to take possession of the mortgaged property and sell it for cash to the highest bidder at public auction. Title is conveyed to the purchaser by a sheriff's deed or a trustee's deed.

## Nonjudicial Foreclosure

**Nonjudicial foreclosure,** or **foreclosure under power of sale,** common in title theory states, *does not require the lender to bring a lawsuit against the defaulting borrower to obtain a judgment to foreclose.* It is, therefore, not court-ordered. The North Carolina deed of trust form (Figure 7.8) has a power of sale clause that gives the trustee the right to foreclose after complying with all legal requirements for foreclosure.

Nonjudicial foreclosure requires the mortgagee or trustee to file an abbreviated or summary court proceeding with a hearing before the clerk of the superior court. The sale of the property is advertised by posting a notice for a period of at least 15 days at the courthouse in the county where the property is located. The mortgagee or trustee must also advertise the sale in a newspaper published in the county in which the property is located at least once a week for a minimum of two consecutive weeks. The deed of trust may call for more stringent posting and advertising rules than required by state statutes. In both cases, the advertisement must describe the property and appoint a day and an hour for the sale to be held. Assuming the clerk of the court confirms the trustee's right to continue with the foreclosure, the sale is conducted by the trustee, who conveys the title to the new purchaser by a trustee's deed after the last ten day upset period ends without a bid.

## Strict Foreclosure

Under **strict foreclosure,** *the mortgage simply "cuts off" by court order.* The lender files a foreclosure petition with the court after the mortgagor is in default. The court then issues a decree requiring the borrower to satisfy the mortgage debt within a stated period of time or lose his equitable right to redeem the title. Once this right is lost, the borrower cannot assert rights in the title, which pass to the lender. The borrower forfeits all monies previously paid and has no right to surplus funds generated by the sale of the property. This type of foreclosure is not used in North Carolina, nor is it in favor in the United States.

## Deed in Lieu of Foreclosure

In a measure sometimes called a friendly foreclosure but more formally a **deed in lieu of foreclosure,** *a borrower in default simply conveys the title to the property to the lender to avoid record of foreclosure.* The disadvantage to the lender is that it does not eliminate other liens against the property. Furthermore, the lender loses the right to claim against mortgage insurance or guarantee programs such as FHA or VA.

## Distribution of Sale Proceeds

Proceeds of the mortgage foreclosure sale are distributed in the following order of priority:

1. All expenses of the sale are paid. These include court costs, trustee's fee, advertising fees, legal fees, accounting fees, and the like.
2. Any delinquent real or personal property tax liens and assessment liens are paid.
3. If there are no other lien holders with liens having priority over the lien of the mortgage or deed of trust, the lender is paid.
4. Any other creditors holding liens against the property are paid; however, creditors who are not secured by the foreclosed property are not paid from sale proceeds.
5. Any remaining monies (any surplus of equity) after items 1 through 4 have been satisfied are paid to the borrower.

## Deficiency Judgment

The borrower in a mortgage loan is personally liable for payment of the note. Therefore, if the proceeds of a foreclosure sale are not sufficient to satisfy the balance due the lender, the lender can sue for a **deficiency judgment** on the note. A deficiency judgment is *a court order stating that the borrower still owes the lender money.* (Note: North Carolina does not allow deficiency judgments when a seller forecloses on a purchase money mortgage, discussed later in this chapter.)

## Nonrecourse Note

One situation in which deficiency judgments are not available to the lender is in the case of a **nonrecourse note.** This type of note typically is used in mortgage loans secured by commercial property. Nonrecourse means *the borrower assumes no personal liability for paying the note;* therefore, the lender can look only to the property pledged in the mortgage to obtain the money owed in a case of default by the borrower.

# TYPES OF SALES TRANSACTION

Properties being sold often have loans secured by a mortgage or deed of trust. In order for the seller to give clear title to the buyer, these loans must be addressed. This can be done in several ways. The seller can pay off the existing loan with the proceeds from a cash sale. If the buyer has obtained new financing, the funds from the new loan provide cash to the seller to pay off the existing mortgage at closing. In both of these cases, the payoff of the loan cancels the mortgage or deed of trust and the seller has no further liability for the debt. Two other methods of addressing the existing loan are for the buyer to assume the loan or take title to the property "subject to" the lien of an existing loan.

## Cash Sales

Although cash sales are the exception in real estate, they are perhaps the simplest real estate transactions to process. They can be as simple as the seller providing a deed and the buyer providing the cash. Unfortunately, the simplicity of these cash transactions may cause an inexperienced real estate practitioner to make costly mistakes. No lender is involved in the transaction demanding an appraisal, a survey, a wood-destroying insect inspection, a structural inspection, deed recordation, payment of taxes or transfer fee, title search, and so on. Nonetheless, real estate practitioners have an obligation to make a reasonable effort to know and disclose to the buyer anything that might materially affect the value of the property and to safeguard the interests of their clients and be fair to the other party.

## Loan Assumption

Although most conventional fixed-rate real estate loans are not assumable, some are, along with FHA-insured and VA-guaranteed loans (discussed later in this chapter). When a purchaser assumes the seller's existing loan, the purchaser assumes liability for the loan and personal liability for payment of the note. Therefore, purchasers who default in loan payments can lose their property as a result of a foreclosure sale and may be subject to a deficiency judgment obtained by the lender.

In a **loan assumption,** the *seller whose loan was assumed remains liable for the loan and payment of the note unless specifically released from liability by the lender.* If the purchaser defaults and the proceeds of a foreclosure sale are insufficient to pay off the loan, the seller whose loan was assumed may be subject to a deficiency judgment by the lender. The lender can foreclose against the current title holder and can sue the original borrower (or anyone who assumed the loan from the original borrower before the current defaulting borrower assumed it) for a deficiency judgment if the proceeds of the foreclosure sale do not satisfy the loan debt. The seller's agent has a responsibility to inform the seller of a property sold under a loan assumption about potential future liability and the benefits of a release of liability from the lender at the time of sale; however, the agent should refer his client to an attorney for legal advice, if necessary. Most loans made since the late 1980s require a release of liability as a condition of assumability.

## Taking Title "Subject to" a Loan

If property is sold and title is conveyed subject to the lien of an existing loan (but that lien is not actually "assumed"), the lender can still foreclose against the property in the event of a default in loan payments. In taking title **subject to a loan,** *the new purchaser does not become liable for payment of the note.* Therefore, the lender cannot sue the purchaser for a deficiency judgment; but she can obtain a deficiency judgment only against the seller, who remains personally liable for paying the debt as evidenced by the note. When purchasing a property using a wraparound mortgage or a land sales contract, a purchaser can take title or some degree of title "subject to" a loan backed by a mortgage or deed of trust. A buyer cannot purchase a mortgaged property financed after the late 1980s "subject to" the mortgage loan since most loans since that time have a due-on-sale clause or require a loan assumption with release of liability.

## New Financing

Most real estate transactions require new financing. The savings and loan problems and mortgage foreclosures in many areas of the country prompted mortgage lenders, the FHA, the VA, and private mortgage insurance companies to tighten requirements for new financing. To help buyers choose the most advantageous method of new financing, today's real estate practitioner needs a thorough knowledge of real estate finance. Knowledge of down payments, closing cost regulations, amounts of allowable seller or third-party contributions, and methods of structuring the best possible payment plans is essential to a successful real estate transaction involving new financing. These aspects of finance and closing are discussed next.

# TYPES OF LOAN

This section discusses the various ways in which the purchase of real property is financed by the buyer. The various types of loan that an individual can obtain from lending institutions are divided into two groups: (1) Conventional loans are loans in which there is no participation by an agency of the federal government, and (2) government loans are those in which the federal government participates, either by insuring the loan to protect the lender (for example, FHA-insured loans) or by guaranteeing that the loan will be repaid (e.g., VA-guaranteed loans). The government also participates in loans through the Rural Development and Farm Service Agency, divisions of the U.S. Department of Agriculture (USDA). Rural Development loans can be direct or guaranteed loans. The Farm Service Agency makes direct loans.

## Conventional Loans

A **conventional loan,** *one that has no participation by an agency of the federal government,* can be uninsured or insured. In the uninsured conventional loan, the borrower's *equity* in the property provides sufficient security for the lender to make the loan; therefore, insurance to protect the lender in case of the borrower's default is not required. In these cases, the borrower obtains a loan that does not exceed 80 percent of the property value and thus has an equity of at least 20 percent. An insured conventional loan typically is a conventional loan in which the borrower has a down payment of only 5 percent or 10 percent and therefore borrows 90 to 95 percent of the property value. In these cases, *insuring repayment of the top portion of the loan to the lender is necessary in the event the borrower defaults.* The insurance is called **private mortgage insurance (PMI),** and private insurance companies issue the policies. Today private mortgage insurance companies insure more mortgage loans than the FHA does. The premiums and features of private mortgage insurance have grown more varied and complex in recent years.

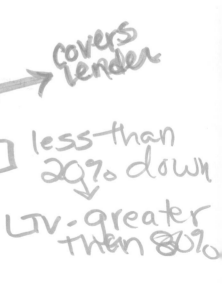

In the case of the 90 percent insured loan, repayment of the top 20 percent of the loan is insured. In the 95 percent insured loan, the top 25 percent of the loan is insured. This generally ensures that the lender will recoup the investment by means of the insurance proceeds and the foreclosure proceeds should the borrower default. The borrower pays the premium for the insurance. PMI is paid at closing, financed into the loan amount, or paid monthly. When the borrower's equity in the property reaches 20 percent of the original value on which the loan was based, the borrower may request the lender to discontinue the insurance requirement. The lender must automatically do so at 78%. See Figure 7.10 for an example of a qualifying worksheet for a conventional loan. Figure 7.11 shows an example of finding buyer's maximum loan amount and purchase price for a conventional loan.

**FIGURE 7.10**

Qualifying for a specific conventional loan.

Before approving a conventional mortgage loan, the lender must determine if the borrower will be able to meet the financial obligation of monthly house payments. Most often the lender requires that the monthly house payments not exceed 28% of the borrower's gross monthly income and that the total of all long-term obligations not exceed 36% of this income; this is referred to as the 28/36 rule.

For example, assume a sale price of $125,000, a loan amount of $100,000,* and an annual interest rate of 8.5% with a 30-year loan term. (Use the amortization chart on page 205 if you do not have a financial calculator.) Tax and insurance escrow numbers are given. In this case, the formula is applied as follows:

1. The lender calculates the total monthly payments:

| | |
|---|---|
| $768.91 | (P&I)** |
| 116.80 | for tax escrow (T) |
| 54.00 | for insurance escrow (I) |
| $939.71 | PITI (total monthly payment) |

2. Next, the borrower's gross monthly income is calculated by dividing the annual household salary by 12:

   $55,000 ÷ 12 = $4,583.33

3. The ratio of house payments to gross monthly income is determined by dividing the payment by monthly income:

   $939.71 ÷ $4,583.33 = 20.5%

   The first part of the 28/36 rule has been satisfied since this ratio is less than 28%.

4. All other long-term expense payments are added to determine the borrower's other long-term debt:

| | |
|---|---|
| $340.00 | car payments |
| 75.00 | credit card payments |
| 100.00 | personal loan |
| $515.00 | total monthly payment for long-term debt |

5. This total is added to the house payment:

| |
|---|
| $ 939.71 |
| 515.00 |
| $1,454.71 |

6. This total is divided by the monthly income to determine the ratio of long-term debt:

   $1,454.71 ÷ $4,583.33 = 31.7%

   The borrower qualifies for the loan since this ratio is less than 36%.

* This is an 80% loan-to-value ratio; therefore, it requires no private mortgage insurance (PMI). A higher loan-to-value ratio requires PMI to be included in payments.

** Amount determined by financial calculator. Using amortization chart, amount would be $769.

The loan industry has undergone some revolutionary changes within the past few years. Many new loan programs are driven primarily by the borrower's credit score, referred to as the FICO (Fair Isaac Scoring) by some credit reporting agencies. With a high enough FICO score, many borrowers can qualify for a variety of low or no-down-payment loans issued outside of the VA and FHA loan restrictions. These conventional loans often offer benefits such as competitive interest rates without the burden of funding fees or mortgage insurance premiums. As conventional loans, these products usually do not have the assumability with qualification feature of government loans.

## FHA-INSURED LOANS

Part of the mission of the **Federal Housing Administration (FHA),** created during the depression of the 1930s, was *to make home ownership available to more people, to improve housing construction standards, and to provide a more effective and stable method of financing homes.* It succeeded in this mission and provided the leadership to standardize procedures for qualifying buyers, appraising property, and evaluating construction. FHA has

**FIGURE 7.11**

Determining buyer's maximum payment loan amount and purchase price for a conventional loan.

Maximum loan amount and maximum purchase price calculations for 7% conventional loan with 20% down payment and no mortgage insurance premium.

1. $ 6,450 — borrower's gross monthly income
   × 28% — ratio for house payment
   $ 1,806 — maximum house payment under 28% ratio

2. $ 6,450 — borrower's gross monthly income
   × 36% — ratio for house payment and long-term debts
   $ 2,322 — maximum amount for house payment and long-term debt

3. Long-term expenses other than house payment:
   $ 400.00 — car payment
   200.00 — student loan payment
   100.00 — credit card payment
   $ 700.00 — total long-term debt

4. $ 2,322 — maximum house payment and long-term debt
   − 700 — long-term debt
   $ 1,622 — maximum house payment under 36% ratio

5. $ 1,622 — maximum house payment (PITI)—lesser of the two payments derived in steps 1 and 4
   − 300 — estimated taxes and insurance (T&I)
   $ 1,322 — maximum amount available for principal and interest payment (P&I)
   $\frac{\$1,322}{6.65} \times 1,000$ — maximum P&I payment / P&I factor/1,000 at 7% interest (from amortization chart, Figure 7.1)

   $198,800 borrower's maximum amount of loan at 7% for 30 years with a $1,322/per month payment

   $\frac{\text{loan amount}}{80\%} = \frac{\$198,800}{80\%} =$ Purchase price $248,500

   a. Since $6.65 is the payment on a $1,000 loan at 7% for 30 years, $1,322 is the payment on 198.8 units of $1,000 (198.8 × 6.65 × $1,322).

   b. Since borrower is making a down payment of 20%, the loan amount is 80% of purchase ($198,800 ÷ 80% = $248,500 maximum purchase price).

   $248,500 is the maximum purchase price buyer will qualify for with 20% down payment.

Notes:

- Less than 20% down payment would require private mortgage insurance (PMI).
- Some mortgage companies apply more liberal ratios with 20% down and other factors being good.
- Maximum purchase price can be increased by any down payment in addition to the 20%.
- Payment amount could increase to $1,806 by reducing debt load from $700 to $516.
- The figure derived from the 28% ratio is usually firm.
- The figure derived from the 36% ratio is somewhat flexible, provided credit, assets, and other factors are excellent.

been an agency of the U.S. Department of Housing and Urban Development (HUD) since 1968.

FHA does not make mortgage loans or supply the funds for FHA loans. Instead, the FHA insures loans on real property made by FHA approved lenders. An **FHA-insured loan** *protects lenders against financial loss.* The buyer pays for this insurance protection by paying an **up-front mortgage insurance premium (UFMIP)** at closing and an annual **mortgage insurance premium (MIP)** prorated monthly and paid with the monthly mortgage payment. This insurance enables the FHA-approved lenders to provide financing when the **loan-to-value ratio** is high. As explained earlier, loan-to-value ratio *compares the loan amount to the property value.* With a high ratio, the borrower has to make only a small down payment. The amount of insurance protection to the lender is sufficient to protect the lender from financial loss in the event of a foreclosure sale because these loans are insured for 100 percent of the loan amount.

The most popular FHA program is the FHA 203(b) loan, which allows an owner-occupant to purchase a one- to four-family dwelling with an FHA-insured loan. FHA now offers a reverse mortgage, FHA 255, which is designed for senior citizens, age 62 or older, who need to access the equity in their home while continuing to occupy it. The FHA 255 provides a monthly income for the mortgagor and sometimes also pays debts or the existing mortgage. The mortgage loan does not have to be paid as long as the mortgagors continue to occupy the home. When their occupancy terminates, the property is sold and the mortgage loan is paid out of the proceeds. The FHA 245 graduated payment loan, the FHA 203(k) purchase and rehabilitation loan, and the FHA 234(c) condominium loan are also available when circumstances warrant. The FHA 245 is also used to purchase a one- to four-family owner-occupied dwelling; however, the 203(k) and 234(c) is used only to purchase a single-family owner-occupied unit.

## FHA 203(b) Regular Loan Program

The FHA 203(b) regular loan program is the original and still the basic FHA program. It provides for insuring loans for the purchase or construction of one- to four-family dwellings. FHA does not set a maximum sales price, only a maximum loan amount. A buyer can purchase a home for more than the FHA maximum loan amount, but she must pay any amount above the maximum loan amount in cash. The maximum loan amount is based on *acquisition cost,* which is a combination of FHA-appraised value or sales price (whichever is lower) plus 100 percent of the buyer's closing costs the FHA will allow to be financed.

## FHA 245 Graduated Payment Loan

Under the graduated payment plan, payments are lower in the early years and increase at specified intervals until the payment reaches an amortizing basis. The monthly payment is kept lower in the early years of the mortgage term by not requiring the borrower to pay all of the interest due in those years. The unpaid interest, however, is added to the principal. As a result, the principal increases during those years (negative amortization).

The FHA graduated payment loan is available for purchasing or constructing a single-family dwelling to be occupied by the borrower. The original borrower and anyone assuming the borrower's loan during the graduated phase must sign a certification stating they are aware of the annual increases in monthly payments.

The borrower can refinance an FHA graduated payment loan at any time to a level-payment mortgage plan insured by the FHA; however, a borrower with a level payment FHA loan cannot refinance to a graduated payment FHA loan. The maximum loan amount is slightly lower under this program than for a regular FHA 203(b) loan to prevent the maximum principal balance from exceeding 97 percent of the appraised value or acquisition cost during the years of graduated payments. While this program is still authorized by FHA, the low interest rates of the last decade have diminished its usefulness. It is seldom used now.

## FHA Maximum Loan Amount

HUD/FHA sets basic loan limits for one- to four-family dwellings. Higher maximum loan limits are allowed in geographic regions designated as high-cost areas. See Figure 7.12 for the maximum FHA loan limits established for selected areas of North Carolina. The amounts shown are current as of January 2006. FHA guidelines require the purchaser to occupy a single-family dwelling or one unit of a two- to four-family dwelling.

**FIGURE 7.12**
FHA mortgage limits in selected areas of North Carolina.*

| AREA | SINGLE-FAMILY | FOUR-FAMILY |
|---|---|---|
| Asheville | $200,160 | $384,936 |
| Carteret County | 200,160 | 384,936 |
| Charlotte area | 200,160 | 384,936 |
| Greensboro, High Point, Winston-Salem area | 200,160 | 384,936 |
| Raleigh, Durham area | 200,160 | 384,936 |

*These amounts,which are updated periodically, are current as of January 2006. Thus,these figures are provided as examples only; check locally for most recent limits. The complete list can be found at https://entp.hud.gov/idapp/html/hicostlook.cfm.

## FHA Mortgage Insurance Premium

There are two phases of the FHA mortgage insurance premium: the up-front (or initial) premium (UFMIP) and the annual renewal premium (MIP). Currently the UFMIP is set at 1.50 percent of the loan amount and is not affected by the term of the loan or the loan-to-value ratio. Borrowers have a choice of paying the UFMIP in cash at closing or financing it into the loan. Most borrowers choose to finance it, and it is important to note that *the maximum loan amount for the area can be exceeded by the amount of the UFMIP if it is financed into the loan.*

While the up-front mortgage insurance premium charged on FHA loans is fixed at 1.50 percent for all FHA loans, the annual renewal premium varies based on the loan term and the loan-to-value ratio. The annual premium ranges from zero to one-half percent of the average unpaid principal balance.

## FHA Loan Qualification

Under current FHA loan qualification guidelines, the monthly housing expenses composed of principal, interest, taxes, homeowner's insurance, MIP paid monthly, and homeowner's association dues or assessments (if any) cannot exceed 29 percent of gross income.

The total housing expenses plus any of the borrower's recurring monthly debts that will extend for ten months or more cannot exceed 41 percent of monthly gross income (see Figures 7.13 and 7.14 for FHA loan qualification examples and 7.15 for maximum loan amount and cash to close). A borrower's total obligation and his ability to fulfill those obligations during the months after the loan closing remain a major consideration in underwriting the loan.

## FHA Loan Assumption Policies

In 1986, FHA began changing its policies toward assumptions of FHA-insured loans. Prior to December 1, 1986, FHA mortgages were freely assumable without qualification by buyers who want to occupy the property and even by investors. The Housing and Urban Development Reform Act of 1989 effectively stopped the making of new loans that allowed assumptions without a new buyer being able to give release of liability. A creditworthiness review is required for the assumption of all FHA loans that originated between December 1, 1986 and December 15, 1989. This requirement remains in effect throughout the life of a loan. For loans that originated after December 15, 1989, an assumption by a buyer wishing to occupy the property is allowed only after a complete buyer qualification. Furthermore, an assumption by a buyer looking to invest in the property is not allowed.

## FHA Changes

Significant changes have taken place in the FHA home loan program since its inception, but especially since 1983. Real estate agents should understand these changes when selling

**FIGURE 7.13**

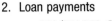

Qualifying buyer for a specific FHA loan payment (PITI and MIP).

1. Purchaser's monthly income = $3,000
2. Loan payments

| | |
|---|---|
| a. P&I $75,250 @ 9.5% for 30 years = 75.250 × 8.41 = | $ 632.85 |
| b. Tax and insurance escrow | $ 70.00 |
| c. Mortgage insurance premium (MIP) | $ 31.35 |
| d. Monthly PITI plus MIP | $ 734.20 |

3. Relation of housing expenses to gross income

$$\frac{\$734.20}{\$3{,}000} = 24.47\%$$

This is less than 29% and qualifies for the housing expense part of the formula.

4. Other long-term expenses

| | |
|---|---|
| a. Auto payment | $ 240.00 |
| b. Credit cards | 110.00 |
| c. Total | $ 350.00 |

5. Total long-term expenses

| | |
|---|---|
| a. Housing expense | $ 734.20 |
| b. Other payments | 350.00 |
| c. Total | $1,084.20 |

6. Relation of total long-term expenses to gross income

$$\frac{\$1{,}084.20}{\$3{,}000} = 36.14\%$$

This part of the formula also qualifies since it is less than 41%.

**FIGURE 7.14**

Qualification for maximum FHA mortgage loan payment (PITI and MIP).

1. Calculate borrower's gross monthly income by dividing annual household salary by 12.
   $48,000 ÷ 12 = $4,000
2. Multiply gross monthly income by 29%.
   $4,000 × 29% = $1,160
3. Multiply gross monthly income by 41%.
   $4,000 × 41% = $1,640 (amount available for housing expense under 28% ratio)
4. Add all other long-term debt of borrower.

| | |
|---|---|
| $300.00 | car payment |
| $175.00 | credit card payment |
| $100.00 | personal loan |
| $575.00 | total monthly payment for long-term debt |

5. Subtract total monthly payment from item 4 from 41% of monthly income from item 3.

| | |
|---|---|
| $1,640.00 | total housing expense and debt |
| $ 575.00 | total monthly payments on debt |
| $1,065.00 | total amount available for housing expense under 41% ratio |

The buyer qualifies for the lesser of amount determined by 29% and 41% ratios of $1,065.

| | |
|---|---|
| 1. Statutory Investment Requirement | |
| a. Contract sales price | $ 110,000 |
| b. Borrower-paid closing costs | $ 0 |
| c. Acquisition (before adjustments*)(1a + 1b) | $ 110,000 |
| d. Statutory investment requirement (1a × 0.03) | $ 3,300 |
| 2. Maximum Mortgage Calculation | |
| a. Lesser of sales price (1a) or value | $ 110,000 |
| b. Required adjustments | $ 0 |
| c. Mortgage basis (2a + 2b) | $ 110,000 |
| d. Maximum mortgage (2c × LTV factor) | $ 107,525 |
| (NC maximum LTV factor if 2a is $50,000 or less is 0.9875. If 2a is greater than $50,000, the maximum LTV factor is 0.9775.) | |
| 3. Actual Cash Investment Requirement | |
| a. Down payment (1c minus 2d) | $ 2,475 |
| b. Statutory investment requirement (1d) | $ 3,300 |
| c. Greater of 3a or 1d | $ 3,300 |
| d. Prepaid expenses | $ 0 |
| e. Discount points | $ 0 |
| f. Repairs/improvements (nonfinanceable) | $ 0 |
| g. MIP paid in cash | $ 0 |
| h. Nonrealty and other items | $ 0 |
| i. Total cash needed to close (sum of 3a–3f) | $ 3,300 |
| 4. Mortgage Reduction (if required per 3c) | |
| a. Acquisition (line 1c) | $ 110,000 |
| b. Total cash needed to close | $ 3,300 |
| c. Maximum loan amount | $ 106,700 |

**FIGURE 7.15**

Calculation of FHA maximum loan amount and cash required to close.

properties purchased with FHA loans that originated under rules different from those currently in effect. When such a property is listed, the agent should obtain copies of the documents relating to the original sale to determine what rules apply to the present sale in the case of a loan assumption or a loan payoff. Rules for loan assumption qualification, release of liability, notification and time of payoffs are important, and they differ according to when the loan was underwritten. Agents should remain current regarding FHA guidelines by looking to their broker-in-charge, the firm's training or loan processing department, a trade publication, or an FHA-approved lender.

## Contract Requirements

When a sales contract contingent upon the buyer's obtaining an FHA-insured loan is created prior to an FHA appraisal and commitment to insure, the FHA requires that the contract contain the following wording:

It is expressly agreed that, notwithstanding any other provisions of this contract, the purchaser shall not be obligated to complete the purchase of the property described herein or to incur any penalty by forfeiture of earnest money deposit or otherwise unless the seller has delivered to the purchaser a written statement issued by the Federal Housing Commissioner setting forth the appraised value of the property (exclusive of closing costs) of not less than $________, which statement seller hereby agrees to deliver to the purchaser promptly after such appraised value statement is made available to the seller. The purchaser shall, however, have the privilege and option of proceeding with the consummation of this contract without regard to the amount of the appraised valuation made by the Federal Housing Commissioner. The appraised valuation is arrived at to determine the maximum mortgage the Department will insure. HUD does not warrant the value or the condition of the property. The purchaser should satisfy himself/herself that the price and the condition of the property are acceptable.

FHA loans, as well as all other loans and sales of residential property built before 1978, require a lead-based paint disclosure to be signed on or before the date of the contract of sale. FHA required disclosure long before the newer federal law requiring disclosure was enacted (see Chapter 5 and Appendix C for additional information).

FHA requires all FHA buyers to sign the form "For Your Protection: Get a Home Inspection," HUD Form 92564-Cn, before signing the offer to purchase. Failure to do so will require the offer to Purchase and Contract to be reexecuted. This form informs the buyer what FHA does and does not do for her, defines the difference between appraisals and home inspections, and explains what a home inspection is and why a buyer needs one. FHA treats the home inspection as an allowable closing cost when determining maximum loan amount and cash required to close.

## DEPARTMENT OF VETERANS AFFAIRS GUARANTEED LOAN PROGRAM

Whereas the FHA programs insure loans, the Department of Veterans Affairs guarantees loans made through VA-approved lenders. Under a **VA-guaranteed loan**, the *VA guarantees repayment of the top portion of the loan to the lender* in the event the borrower defaults. Unlike the FHA, the VA does not set maximum loan amounts.

The VA-guaranteed loan can be a 100 percent loan, which requires no down payment. The loan amount can be 100 percent of the VA appraisal of the property set forth in the Department of Veterans Affairs **certificate of reasonable value (CRV)** or 100 percent of the sales price, whichever is less. The VA provides *this certificate, sometimes informally called the VA appraisal, to the lending institution as a basis for making the loan.* VA-guaranteed loans are available for the purchase or construction of one- to four-family dwellings. When obtaining the loan, the veteran must certify in writing that she will occupy the property being purchased. (If the veteran is on active duty, occupancy by the spouse will meet this requirement.) If the property is a multifamily dwelling (maximum of four units), the veteran must occupy one of the units.

### Eligibility

For the borrower to be eligible for a VA-guaranteed loan, he must qualify as a veteran under requirements of the Department of Veterans Affairs. If he is not on active duty, the veteran must have been discharged or released from duty under conditions other than dishonorable. The length of service required for eligibility depends on length and date of service and whether service was in war time or peace time. Members of the national guard and reservists are also eligible for VA guaranteed loans if they meet the time requirements. In some cases, veterans' widows and widowers who have not remarried are eligible for a VA-guaranteed loan. An eligible veteran with full entitlement may be able to obtain a VA loan with no down payment, the loan amount not to exceed the FNMA loan limit, which changes each year. That limit for 2006 was $417,000.

### Contract Requirements

If a contract of sale subject to the buyer's obtaining a VA-guaranteed loan is created prior to an appraisal and commitment by the VA, the Department of Veterans Affairs requires that the contract contain the following statement:

> It is expressly agreed that, notwithstanding any other provisions of this contract, the purchaser shall not incur any penalty by forfeiture of earnest money or otherwise be obligated to complete the purchase of the property described herein, if the contract purchase price or cost exceeds the reasonable value of the property established by the

**TABLE 7.1** VA funding fee schedule

| CATEGORY | REGULAR MILITARY | NAT'L GUARD & RESERVISTS |
|---|---|---|
| Initial Uses 0 to 4.99% down payment | 2.15% | 2.40% |
| Second and Subsequent Uses | | |
| 0 to 4.99% down payment | 3.35% | 3.35% |
| All Uses 5.0 to 9.9% down payment | 1.50% | 1.75% |
| All Uses 10% or more down payment | 1.50% | 1.50% |
| Assumptions | 0.50% | |
| Interest rate reduction refinance loan | 0.50% | |

Veterans Administration. The purchaser shall, however, have the privilege and option of proceeding with the consummation of this contract without regard to the amount of the reasonable value established by the Veterans Administration.

## VA Funding Fee

In order to guarantee a VA loan, the VA charges a funding fee on all VA loans except those to a veteran who is receiving compensation for service-connected disabilities, a veteran who is receiving retirement pay in lieu of disability compensation, and a spouse of a veteran who died in service or from a service-connected disability. The fee is paid in cash or financed into the loan amount. If the funding fee is financed, the loan may exceed the VA appraisal by the amount of the funding fee. The VA funding fee schedule is given in Table 7.1.

## Qualifying for VA Loans

The VA standards require the borrower to qualify under a net family support standard and a gross monthly income ratio (see Figure 7.16).

The VA Loan Analysis form is used to organize information on estimated home payments, long-term debt (six months or longer), and family dependents and to evaluate the reliability of monthly income. Net take-home pay is determined by taking the gross monthly income minus federal taxes, state taxes, Social Security tax, and other pension plans or deductions. This net income then is reduced by the amount of the estimated home payments, estimates for maintenance and utilities, and monthly payments on long-term debt to determine a residual balance available for family support.

This residual balance must meet regional standards established by the VA. For example, when the loan amount is less than $80,000, a family of four must currently have a monthly residual balance of $868 in the South, including North Carolina. If the loan exceeds $80,000 in this area, the residual is $1,003 (Figure 7.17).

The next step in the qualification is to compare the gross monthly income with the total of home payments, special assessments, homeowners' association dues, and debts that will extend for six months or longer or will have payments of more than $100 per month. This ratio is limited to 41 percent, although the ratio can sometimes be extended to 49.5 percent if the remaining residual balance exceeds the regional standard by 20 percent or more.

VA allows some exceptions in the qualification procedure. For example, the required residual is sometimes reduced for an active-duty or retired military person living near a military base. Although all members of the veteran's household are considered for the residual income calculation, an exclusion can be made for a household member with a verified source of income sufficient for his total support that is not included as effective income for loan qualification purposes.

If a VA applicant has an unusually large debt load, has no cash reserves, and is applying for a loan that will significantly increase his housing expenses, the loan may be disapproved regardless of a satisfactory residual.

**FIGURE 7.16**

VA qualification worksheet.

VA Qualification Wksheet

QUALIFICATION FOR SPECIFIC MORTGAGE LOAN PAYMENT

RATIO:

| | |
|---|---|
| A. Monthly income | $3,000.00 |
| B. PITI* | 950.00 |
| C. Recurring monthly payments | 350.00 |
| D. Total (B + C) | $1,300.00 |

D ÷ A: $1,300 ÷ $3,000 = 0.43 or 43% ratio

VA RESIDUAL INCOME:

| | |
|---|---|
| Gross monthly income | $ 3,000.00 |
| – taxes (federal, state, and Social Security) (see tax tables—not included) | 700.00 |
| – pension or retirement plan deductions | 150.00 |
| – long-term debts (monthly payments) | 350.00 |
| – maintenance and utilities (1321 sq. ft. of living area) 1321 x 0.14 = 184.94, rounded to $185 | 185.00 |
| – PITI for specific loan | 950.00 |
| Residual for family support | $ 665.00 |
| Required residual for family support (see table below) | $ 738.00 |

Difference between actual and required residual = –$73.00

Borrower will not qualify for this loan because residual family support is $73 below minimum required and ratio exceeds 41%. Borrower's residual must equal or exceed required residual. Borrower sometimes qualifies with a ratio up to 49.5% if his actual residual exceeds required residual by 20% or more.

DETERMINATION OF MAXIMUM AMOUNT OF MORTGAGE PAYMENT VA IS LIKELY TO APPROVE FOR BORROWER

RATIO:

| | | |
|---|---|---|
| Monthly income (A) × 41% (0.41) | $3,000.00 | (A) |
| | × 0.41 | |
| | $1,230.00 | (B) |
| Recurring monthly payment $ | 350.00 | (C) |

(B) − (C): 1,230 – 350 = $880 (amount remaining for PITI*)

VA RESIDUAL INCOME:

| | |
|---|---|
| Gross monthly income | $ 3,000.00 |
| – taxes (federal, state, and Social Security) (from tax tables—not included) | – 700.00 |
| – pension or retirement plan deductions | – 150.00 |
| – long-term debts (monthly payments) | – 350.00 |
| – maintenance and utilities (1321 sq. ft. of living area) 1321 x 0.14 = 184.94, rounded to $185 | 185.00 |
| – residual for family support | – 738.00 |
| Amount remaining for PITI* | $ 877.00 |

The borrower will qualify for a mortgage loan payment not to exceed $867, the lesser of these PITI amounts.

| | |
|---|---|
| Amount derived from debt-to-income ratio of 41% | = $880 |
| Amount derived from residual method | = $877 |

* Sometimes other housing expenses, such as homeowners' association dues or assessments paid on a monthly basis, must be added to the PITI before performing these calculations.

FIGURE 7.17
Residual income chart.

RESIDUAL INCOME CHART

| | Borrower | 2 | 3 | 4 | 5 | 6 | 7 |
|---|---|---|---|---|---|---|---|
| Under $80,000 | $382 | $641 | $772 | $ 868 | $ 902 | $ 977 | $1,052 |
| Over $80,000 | $441 | $738 | $889 | $1,003 | $1,039 | $1,119 | $1,199 |

MAINTENANCE AND UTILITIES

Living area of property in square feet x $0.14 = maintenance and utility costs.

Qualifying a veteran for a VA loan is not difficult; however, it requires consulting several tables to determine various taxes, maintenance costs, residual requirements, and child-care expenses. Military pay tables for active-duty veterans also are helpful. VA qualification can be time-consuming. Even though all practitioners should understand this qualification process, using a computer program to perform the qualification is highly recommended. Many inexpensive, easy-to-use programs incorporating these tables are available.

## Restoration of Entitlement

When a veteran is discharged from the service, he receives a "certificate of eligibility." This certificate states the maximum guarantee in effect at the time the veteran is discharged. The maximum mortgage amount available without a down payment is tied to the conforming loan limit which changes every year. If a veteran has used either full or partial entitlement in obtaining a VA loan, he can have that entitlement fully restored in one of the following ways:

1. The loan is paid in full and the veteran has disposed of the property. The VA now grants a *one-time* exception to this rule; that is, a veteran can pay the loan in full *without* disposing of the property and get his entitlement back. This returned entitlement can be used only once. Any subsequent use requires disposing of both properties and having entitlement restored on the last VA loan.
2. A veteran purchaser who has as much remaining entitlement as the original veteran used to obtain the original loan and also satisfies the VA requirements for income, credit, and occupancy assumes the VA loan from the original veteran borrower. The assuming veteran must meet the same requirements as an original VA loan applicant and must agree to substitute her entitlement for that of the original veteran purchaser.

A mere release of liability by the lender and the VA does not in itself restore entitlement. A **release of liability** is a *procedure by which a mortgage holder agrees not to hold a borrower responsible for a mortgage on a property when another has assumed that borrower's loan and responsibility for it.* Anyone, veteran or nonveteran, owner-occupant or investor, can assume a VA loan and give a release of liability; however, only a qualified veteran, who intends to occupy the property, can give a **substitution of entitlement.** Other than the one-time exception in item 1, *simply paying the loan in full is not sufficient to restore the entitlement; the veteran must no longer own the property.*

If a veteran has a partial entitlement remaining, he may be able to buy a second property using the remaining entitlement. Lenders will usually lend up to four times the amount of any remaining entitlement.

## History of Loan Guarantees

The loan guarantee the Department of Veterans Affairs gives to lenders who make VA loans has steadily increased over the years from the lesser of $2,000 or 50 percent of the loan amount, when the program was first initiated in 1944, to the present multilayered system.

### Negotiability of VA Interest Rate

The interest rate is negotiable between the veteran and the lender. The VA allows veterans to pay discount points to obtain a lower interest rate. Sellers may also agree to pay discount points for the buyers to obtain a lower rate, but they are not required to do so.

## OTHER ASPECTS OF FHA AND VA LOANS

### Escrow Account

Both FHA and VA loans require that the borrower maintain an **escrow account** (also called an impound account) with the lending institution. The *borrower must pay an impound into this account each month to accumulate money to pay the annual real property tax bill and the annual homeowner's insurance policy premium.* In addition, if the loan is used to purchase a condominium apartment or a townhouse, *escrow deposits may include an amount to pay the property owner's assessment.* At closing, the borrower must put money into the account to get it started and provide a head start for accumulating the necessary funds. This includes two months' payments toward the next hazard insurance premium; several months toward the payment of the real property tax bill; and, if the loan is insured by the FHA, the equivalent of one month's FHA mortgage insurance premium. The number of months of property tax placed in escrow usually is determined by the lender, depending on the length of time since the last payment of taxes. These *insurance and tax monies deposited at the time of closing* are called **prepaid items** and are not considered a part of the borrower's actual closing costs; they are in excess of the closing costs.

### Down Payment

If the VA certificate of reasonable value (CRV) is less than the price the veteran is willing to pay for a home, the veteran can still obtain the VA loan and make a down payment for the difference between the loan amount and the purchase price. The FHA maximum loan amount is based on the sales price, the appraisal price, or the maximum FHA loan available in the area, whichever is less. The borrower must pay anything over the maximum loan amount as a down payment. In the case of a VA or FHA loan, the borrower cannot finance the down payment unless the loan for the down payment is secured by collateral other than the property and that loan is disclosed to the lender. If the down payment is a gift, he must have a gift letter stating that he is under no obligation to repay the money.

### Miscellaneous

The maximum term of an FHA or VA loan is 30 years. Both types of loan are assumable, although with qualification after certain dates and at the interest rate at which the loan was originally created. Mortgages securing these loans cannot contain a due-on-sale or alienation clause as long as the purchaser meets the qualification requirements in effect at the time the loan was made and the loan is transferred in accordance with applicable regulations. In either an FHA or VA assumption, the difference between the loan amount assumed and the purchase price can be financed, although the loan payment on the amount financed must be considered in the qualification process on loan assumptions requiring release of liability. FHA and VA mortgages never require a **prepayment penalty,** *a charge for paying off the loan before the end of the mortgage term.*

## RURAL DEVELOPMENT AND FARM SERVICE AGENCY MORTGAGE LOANS

Whereas private mortgage lenders provide the funds for conventional, FHA, and VA loans, the government provides the funds for loans made through the USDA Rural Development (RD) direct program and Farm Service Agency (FSA). Through the Rural Housing Services

Agency, RD provides subsidized and nonsubsidized no-down-payment loans for low- to moderate-income individuals or families for the purchase of a home in rural areas. Rural areas include not only open country but also communities with 20,000 or fewer people. The Farm Service Agency, a separate USDA agency, makes loans to purchase and operate family-sized farms. The agent working in rural areas may want to contact RD and FSA for information packets that describe these and other programs, such as grants for repair and rehabilitation and technical assistance grants to aid nonprofit organizations in "self-help" housing projects.

The purpose of these programs is to provide financing in designated rural areas to improve rural housing, develop community facilities, and maintain and create rural employment. RD provides loans for the purchase, repair, and rehabilitation of single and multifamily residences. It also assists nonprofit groups in "self-help" housing projects. The RD direct loan is a 100 percent loan for a 33-year term with subsidized rates below other market loan rates.

In addition to the direct loan program, RD now has a nonsubsidized guaranteed program for borrowers who cannot qualify for any other loan. Rural development also has a hybrid loan which combines the direct and guaranteed loans. One-half of the loan amount is subsidized by RD and the other half is borrowed at the current rate from a lending institution. Designated lenders make 100 percent loans guaranteed by RD. These loans require no down payment and no private mortgage insurance and follow FHA guidelines for qualification ratios. There is no maximum loan amount; however, the income limits imposed by the program effectively limit the amount for which the borrower can qualify.

The FSA provides loans to purchase and operate family-sized farms. Some FSA loans can be amortized over 40 years. Upper limits for qualifying income are established for each local area, and the loan payments are based on the buyer's ability to pay.

## CLOSING OR SETTLEMENT COSTS

At the time of **settlement,** or *closing of a real estate transaction,* the buyer and the seller must satisfy the various expenses and obligations incurred in the transaction. If this is a new first mortgage from a lending institution, the buyer's cost typically is at least 3 percent of the loan amount plus any discount points charged. The seller's closing costs vary widely depending on the obligations that must be satisfied at the closing. One substantial obligation the seller may have is the requirement to satisfy an existing mortgage against the property. 3%

At various points in the process, the real estate agent provides the buyer or the seller or both with an estimate of closing costs. This typically occurs during the prequalification process and again as needed when offers or counteroffers are presented. At the time of listing the property and again when offers are presented, the agent usually gives the seller an estimate of net proceeds.

Typical buyer costs in closing a new loan and real estate transaction include the following:

1. Credit report charge.
2. The appraisal fee the lender charges to estimate the market value of the property to be pledged as security in the mortgage or deed of trust. (Appraisal is discussed in Chapter 9.)
3. The *financing charge required by the lender,* called the **loan origination fee** or loan service charge, usually ranges from 1 to 3 percent of the loan amount, although it cannot exceed 1 percent of the loan amount on a VA loan and 1 percent of the base loan amount on an FHA loan.
4. Attorney's fee for title examination and document preparation.
5. Title insurance premium.
6. Survey fee.
7. Cost of termite inspection and certification (seller's cost in a VA loan).
8. Mortgage guarantee insurance premium required in conventional insured loans when the loan-to-value ratio exceeds 80 percent.

9. Assumption fee charged by the lender if the buyer is assuming the seller's existing mortgage.
10. Discount points paid to obtain a loan or to buy down the interest rate.

Although buyers are responsible for their own closing costs and prepaid items, the VA, FHA, RD, and conventional lenders allow sellers, if they agree, to pay these items within specified limits. FHA takes into consideration closing costs and/or prepaids financed in the loan amount or paid by seller for the buyers when determining the maximum loan amount. The FHA allows the buyer to finance buyer's allowable closing costs, but the VA does not. Before preparing the offer, the agent should check with the lender regarding closing costs and prepaid items allowed by the loan program which need to be addressed in the offer to purchase and contract. The various closing or settlement costs that buyers and sellers incur in real estate transactions are discussed in detail in Chapter 8.

# TYPICAL LOAN REPAYMENT PLANS

## By Repayment Terms

In the early 1980s, there were more innovations in the types of loan than in the preceding 50 years. This was due to inflation and the accompanying increases in interest rates. Often these increases were radical and came about quickly. As a result, lending institutions, for their protection, shifted the burden resulting from rapid increases in interest rates from themselves to the borrowing public by making substantial innovations in mortgage loans. Various types of repayment plan are discussed here, some of which are available as conventional, FHA, VA, or RD loans.

### *Fixed Rate—Level-Payment Plan*

For this loan, the interest rate and the payment for principal and interest is fixed for the life of the loan. Although many other loan types became popular during the last twenty years and remain popular today, the Fixed Rate—Level-Payment Plan is the most widely used type of mortgage loan. * Taxes can go up.

### *Adjustable (Variable) Interest Rate* ARM

1yr. ARM - rate Adjusts every year ex. 3.25%

* Caps 1/6 * 6pts. over the life of the loan. can not go up more than 1pt.

CAPS = Best & worse case Scenario

The 1980s was a decade of turbulence in the real estate financing market. Interest rates soared from 9 percent to 18 percent and higher. In 1993 rates dropped to below 7 percent. In the last few years, rates again dropped to 5 percent or lower before starting to gradually rise again. Given these wide fluctuations, it is possible to understand the motivation of lending institutions to shift the burden of unpredictability from themselves to the borrower. Therefore, you can appreciate the development of the variable or the **adjustable rate mortgage (ARM)** from the lender's standpoint. Suppose you had $50,000 to commit to a 30-year fixed-rate loan. What interest rate would you accept?

The ARM entered as one solution to the problem of the uncertainty of future financial rates. In the ARM, *the parties agree to base mortgage rates on the fluctuations of a standard index.* Common indices include the cost of funds for savings and loan institutions, the national average mortgage rate, and the more popular one-year rate for the government's sale of treasury bills (T-Bills). An ARM designates an index and then adds a *margin* (measure of profit) above this index. For example, if the T-Bill index were 7 percent and the lender's margin were 2.5 percent, the ARM would call for an interest rate of 9.5 percent. (Margins are sometimes expressed as basis points, each basis point being 1/100 of a percent, or 250 basis points in the example.) ARM loans contain two limits that determine the maximum increase on the interest rate. The *cap,* or limit, is expressed as an adjustment cap (per adjustment period) or a lifetime cap (over the life of the loan). Typically, these caps are set at 2/6 for a conventional ARM loan and 1/5 for a government ARM loan. For example, the interest rate on a conventional ARM loan entered into at 7 percent could not

• Based on index & a margin
index + margin = New int. rate

adjust more than 2 percent per adjustment and during the entire loan life could not exceed 13 percent.

The ARM has definite advantages for the buyer, especially the short-term owner who expects to sell her home in the near future, perhaps because of a transfer of employment. The long-term owner, however, may fear the possibility of an ever-increasing mortgage rate. Such an apprehension should be moderated by the understanding that economic cycles rise and fall, and that, in the case of inflation, the value of the property would likely rise as well.

A significant concern in an ARM is the possibility of **negative amortization.** In this case, the index rises while the payment is fixed, causing *the payments to fall below the amount called for by the index. Such shortfall is added back to the principal, causing the principal to grow larger after the payment.* Loans with *payment caps* are often the loans that result in negative amortization.

## Graduated Payment Plan

GPM

In the **graduated payment mortgage (GPM)** the monthly payments are lower in the early years of the loan term. The *payments gradually increase at specified intervals until the payment amount is sufficient to amortize the loan over the remaining term.* The monthly payments are kept down in the early years by not requiring the borrower to pay all of the interest, the unpaid portion of which is added to the principal. This creates negative amortization. The purpose of this type of mortgage is to enable borrowers to achieve home ownership as a result of the lower initial monthly payments. An outstanding example of this type of mortgage loan is the FHA 245 graduated payment mortgage, which is discussed earlier in this chapter.

→ Risk of neg. Amortization

## Buydown Loan

– Someone temp. buys down int. rate → sounds like a discount point.

A **buydown loan** allows for either a *temporary or permanent* buydown of the interest rate. In the *temporary* version, the *lender allows the borrower to pay a lower interest rate in the early years of the loan.* The borrower must qualify at the note rate for FHA and VA loans. The lender agrees to this arrangement because the seller has agreed to pay the lender in advance for any shortfall that may result from the lower interest rate.

The seller, usually a builder, deposits the advance funds into a special escrow account with the lender. From this account, the lender withdraws the shortfall funds each month as the borrower makes the payments. A builder/seller may offer a 3/2/1 buydown plan to a buyer. Assume the current interest rate is 10 percent. A buyer/borrower would make payments based on 7 percent for the first year. The 3 percent shortfall is drawn from the account set up by the builder at the closing. The borrower makes payments at 8 percent the second year and 9 percent the third year. By the end of the third year, the account is depleted and the borrower then makes payments on the full 10 percent interest rate for the remaining life of the loan. There is no negative amortization.

→ Builders can offer lower monthly payments or "Free Upgrades"

The *permanent buydown* is used by borrowers in times of high interest rates. In return for paying discount points to the lender, *the borrower can permanently buy down the interest rate for the life of the loan.* Each discount point costs 1 percent of the loan amount and reduces the interest rate by 1/8 percent. For example, if the interest rate is 12 percent and a borrower pays 8 discount points, the interest rate will be 11 percent for the life of the loan. If the loan amount is \$50,000, the cost to the borrower is \$4,000 (\$50,000 × 8% = \$4,000).

* tax deductible for both buyer & seller

## Term Loan

= Int. only loan aka "Straight term loan"

The **term loan** requires *the borrower to make interest-only payments for a specified term.* At the end of the term, the borrower is required to pay the entire principal balance. This type of mortgage was generally in use at the time of the Depression in the 1930s. Many borrowers were unable to pay the principal when it came due, and lenders were unable to refinance the

* Int. only loans never get paid off. → Always attached to a balloon loan.

principal for the borrower, as had been the case in more prosperous times. As a result, many homeowners lost their property through foreclosure. Today this type of loan typically is used during the construction period of an improvement.

### Balloon Payment Plan

Any *final loan payment that is substantially larger than any previous payment in order to satisfy the remaining principal and interest* is called a **balloon payment.** A typical balloon payment loan occurs when the payments are amortized over a long time but the loan balance is due in full on a much sooner date. For example, a loan may have payments based on a 20-year amortization term but have a final due date in five years. If the balloon payment is to be a substantial amount, the note can provide for refinancing by the lender to provide the funds to the borrower in the event the borrower cannot otherwise make the payment.

*Last payment is bigger than other payments

## OTHER TYPES OF LOANS

### By Purpose or Special Feature

### Purchase Money Mortgage

• Seller-financing

Seller creates deed and conveys prop. to you. Acting like a bank
*puts a lien on title.

The **purchase money mortgage** is *a mortgage given by a buyer to the seller to cover part or all of the purchase price.* Here the seller becomes the lender and the buyer becomes the borrower. The seller conveys title to the buyer, who immediately reconveys or pledges it as security for the balance of the purchase price. The seller is financing the sale of his property for the buyer in the amount of the purchase money mortgage. The purchase money mortgage may be a first mortgage, a typical junior mortgage, or a junior mortgage in the form of a wraparound.

Ch. 6 - Seller financing - Installment land contract/contract for deed

### Construction Loan

A construction loan is a form of interim, or temporary, short-term financing used to obtain the funds needed to create improvements on land. The applicant for a construction loan submits, for the lender's appraisal, the plans and specifications for the structure to be built and the property on which the construction is to take place. The lender makes the construction loan based on the value resulting from an appraisal of the property and the construction plans and specifications. The loan contract states that disbursements will be made as specified stages of construction are completed. Interest is not charged until the money has been disbursed. Upon completion, the lender makes a final inspection and closes out the construction loan, which is paid off or converted to permanent, long-term financing.

*Most High Risk

Often the lender requires the builder to be bonded for completion of the property. The bond is made payable to the lender in the event the builder goes bankrupt and is unable to complete the structure. In this way, the lender has the funds to complete the construction so as to have a valuable asset to sell and to recover the monies extended under the construction loan.

• Builders or individual/Allow for small withdraws, usually int. only

### Takeout Loan

If the mortgage commitment during construction is strictly a short-term construction loan, it will be necessary to establish permanent financing (such as for 30 years) known as a *takeout loan.* Such a commitment is necessary to assure long-term financing within the means of the borrower.

↳ pay off the loan.

### Open-End Mortgage

An **open-end mortgage** is *one that can be refinanced without rewriting the mortgage* and incurring closing costs. A credit ceiling is established. When the original mortgage has been

HLOC - Home eq. line of Credit

paid down, the owner can draw additional funds up to the ceiling for purposes such as home improvements. This is not the typical residential mortgage. The currently popular home equity mortgages are considered to be in this category, however, since they are essentially an open-end line of credit secured by a second mortgage on the home.

### Blanket Mortgage

In this form of mortgage, two or more parcels of real estate are pledged as security for payment of a mortgage debt. The blanket mortgage usually contains release clauses that provide for the release of certain parcels of property from the mortgage lien as the loan balance is reduced by a specified amount. The mortgage should always provide that sufficient property value is subject to the mortgage lien to secure the remaining principal balance at any given time.

The blanket mortgage with release clauses is typically used by real estate developers. In this way, the mortgagor can obtain the release of certain parcels from the mortgage lien and convey a clear title to purchasers so as to generate a profit and provide the funds to make future mortgage payments.

### Package Mortgage

This is a mortgage in which *personal property, in addition to real property, is pledged to secure payment of the mortgage loan.* The **package mortgage** is used frequently in the sale of furnished condominium units and can include all furnishings in a unit.

### Reverse Mortgage

A **reverse mortgage** is essentially the opposite of the amortizing mortgage. To amortize is to reduce, or kill off, the balance of the loan with equal payments. In the reverse mortgage, *the homeowner does not pay the lender, but rather receives income payments from the lender.* The effect of this process is to build up, rather than liquidate, a mortgage. This may be useful to a retired homeowner who has a large equity in a property but relatively low income.

## By Mortgage Priority

### First Mortgage

A first mortgage may be the only mortgage or the mortgage that is higher in priority than all other mortgages on the same property. It gets its unique status from being the first mortgage to be recorded on a particular property.

### Junior Mortgage

A junior mortgage is any mortgage recorded after the first mortgage. A junior mortgage may be a second or third mortgage. It is important to note that a junior mortgage is always subordinate to a mortgage recorded before it.

In the event of a foreclosure sale, the holder of the first mortgage has the first claim against the sale proceeds, and the first mortgage debt must be satisfied before the holder of the second mortgage is entitled to any money from the sale. The holder of a third mortgage is not entitled to any of the sale proceeds until the second mortgage is satisfied, and so on down the line of priorities. The priority is established by the time (date and hour) the mortgage is recorded on the public record in the county where the property is located. The more junior the mortgage, the higher the risk. Junior mortgages are usually for a shorter term and higher interest rate because of the greater risk.

### Wraparound Mortgage

A **wraparound mortgage** is *a purchase money mortgage that includes but is subordinate to another mortgage on the same property.* It is, therefore, also a second or junior mortgage.

**FIGURE 7.18**

Example of benefits of the wraparound mortgage.

| | |
|---|---|
| $ 100,000 | Sale price |
| – $10,000 | Down payment |
| $ 90,000 | Wraparound mortgage given by buyer to seller |
| $ 40,000 | Balance remaining on seller's original mortgage, payments of $386.40, based on his original loan of $48,000 at 9% for 30 years |
| $ 90,000 | Wraparound mortgage to seller at 11% for the remaining 20 years of the original mortgage at monthly payments of $929.70 |

On a monthly basis, the seller collects $929.70 from the buyer, makes the payment of $386.40 to the original lender, and retains the difference of $543.30.

NR

The buyer makes payments to the seller on the wraparound. The seller is the mortgagor on the first mortgage and the mortgagee on the second or wraparound mortgage.

The seller makes payments on the existing (original) mortgage (which is thus being "wrapped around"), usually at a lower rate of interest than she is receiving from the buyer. The seller earns the difference between the payment she receives and the payment she makes, including the difference in interest received on the wraparound and the interest paid on the original mortgage (see Figure 7.18). Wraparounds work only if the existing first mortgage is assumable; that is, if the first mortgage does not contain a due-on-sale or alienation clause. As the number of loans without a due-on-sale or alienation clause declines, wraparound mortgages are becoming less common. The availability of low interest rates on first mortgages also dramatically reduces the need for wraparounds.

There are advantages and disadvantages to the buyer and the seller when using a wraparound mortgage. As in all other real estate transactions, all parties should seek competent legal and financial advice.

# MORTGAGE PRIORITIES

## Effect of Recordation

In North Carolina, to be effective against claims of third parties, all documents need to be recorded to establish a claim against a property. The Conner Act is discussed in Chapter 3, and the effect of the Pure Race System is discussed in Chapter 2. Although there are important exceptions, such as the real property tax lien, which always assumes the first priority (the tax collector has, in effect, already won the race to the courthouse), lenders are very careful to preserve their position in the claims against the property subject to the mortgage. As a rule, the lender will not only insist upon being in a first position but will also take care to assure that no other claims upset this priority. This is particularly true in the case of a construction loan, in which the borrower might have had some work started on the property before closing the loan. Since the mechanic's lien dates from the first day the work was provided, the lender will want to clear all such possibilities so as not to interfere with her claim to the first lien holder priority.

## Subordination of Mortgages

Mortgage priorities can be changed by agreement of the parties even after recording. For example, suppose a developer were to purchase land for the construction of new homes. The owner of the land may have taken a small down payment and agreed to release sections of the land as homes are built and sold. At this point, the landowner's mortgage on the sections is recorded in a first position priority. As discussed previously, no lender is going to agree to have her construction mortgage to the developer be placed secondary to the landowner or to anybody else. Therefore, as part of the land purchase negotiation, the developer can provide for the seller to move, or *subordinate* the original lien, and voluntarily place it behind the subsequent construction mortgage. Thus, the lender obtains the first position, and the landowner not only has a down payment but also has his land improved by the construction of the new home.

### Releases

Recording a release of a mortgage, note, claim, or deed of trust is just as important as recording the original document. Failure to do so may cloud the title to the property.

## THE ROLE OF THE FEDERAL RESERVE BANK

The Federal Reserve Bank (the Fed) is responsible for the nation's monetary policy. The President of the United States appoints a Federal Reserve Board of Governors who serve 14-year terms. The President appoints one of the members to serve a four-year term as chair. The chair of the Federal Reserve Board holds one of the most powerful positions in the country. The activities of the Federal Reserve Board have a powerful influence on the real estate market. Among its wide range of activities, the Fed enforces the Truth-in-Lending Simplification and Reform Act and Equal Credit Opportunity Act. Its most important influence derives from its control of monetary policy.

The Fed implements its monetary policies by controlling the money supply, influencing interest rates through its control of the discount rate, dictating cash reserve requirements for banks and other depository institutions, and controlling the amount of funds available in the banking system by its open market operations.

The Fed increases the money supply by creating money to buy U.S. Treasury Securities. It can move its large supplies of cash and government bonds in and out of the banking system at will. Buying government bonds for cash puts money into the banks, which then lend it to businesses, thereby stimulating a sluggish economy. Selling some of its supply of government bonds takes money from the banks in payment for the bonds, thereby reducing the amount the banks must lend and helping to slow an overheating economy. The Fed can also control the amount of money in circulation by increasing or decreasing the reserve requirements for depository institutions. These reserves consist of money each institution must keep on deposit with the Fed rather than lend to its customers. The higher the reserve requirement, the less money the bank has to lend. The lower the requirement, the more money the bank has to lend.

The Fed receives a lot of publicity when it raises or lowers the discount rate. Many real estate consumers thinks this automatically lowers mortgage interest rates. It does not. The discount rate is the rate the Fed charges its member institutions for money it lends them. It signals these institutions that an increase or decrease in interest rates is desired. The institutions are free to ignore the signal. They almost always heed the signal to increase their prime rate, the rate charged their best customers. Some may be a little slow to heed a signal to decrease their prime rate. Even if the prime rate decreases, long-term mortgage rates may not decrease accordingly. Short-term interest rates and long-term mortgage rates do not always increase or decrease in tandem.

A more detailed explanation of the use of these tools is beyond the scope of this text; however, agents should be aware of the effects the Fed's activities have on the real estate industry. The Fed has done an excellent job in the past few years of controlling inflation and keeping interest rates low and the economy sound. Those agents who have been in real estate for 20 years have seen firsthand that more people buy homes when wages and employment are high and interest rates are at 7 percent rather than at 15 to 18 percent.

# SECTION 2 SOURCES OF REAL ESTATE FINANCE

## PRIMARY SOURCES OF MORTGAGE FUNDS

### Savings and Loan Associations

**Savings and loan associations (S&Ls)** *lend money to construct housing, to purchase existing housing, and to effect improvements in existing housing.* As housing prices in some areas

NR

rose rapidly during the first five years of the twenty-first century, many buyers chose ARM's, interest only, or 100 percent LTV mortgages in expectation of continually rising prices. As the bubble burst, or at least deflated a little, and interest rates increased on ARM's, many recent buyers found themselves with increasing payments on ARM's. In the case of the interest only 100 percent LTV loans, owners not only had no equity in the beginning, but had a negative equity when the price of their home fell. The right loan for the right buyer partially depends upon how many risks that the buyer can handle without putting her in an untenable financial position. The agent should not give financial advice; however, she may point out the disadvantages of high risk loans and advise the buyer to seek financial advice from a competent financial advisor. Traditionally these organizations supplied more money for financing the purchase and construction of single-family dwellings than any other type of lending institution; they continue to invest a larger portion of their assets in residential real estate. Savings and loans are state chartered or federally chartered; however, the practical difference has been blurred by passage of the Financial Institutions Reform, Recovery, and Enforcement Act (FIRREA) in 1989. This Act, passed to curb the abuses and problems that led to the S&Ls' problems, affects all federally insured depository institutions. This legislation substituted (1) the Office of Thrift Supervision for the Federal Home Loan Bank Board and (2) the Savings Association Insurance Fund (SAIF) for the Federal Savings and Loan Insurance Corporation. The Federal Deposit Insurance Corporation (FDIC) now regulates banks and savings and loan associations; however, the insuring funds are maintained separately. The primary purposes for which S&Ls exist are (1) to encourage thrift (hence the term *thrifts*) and (2) to provide financing for residential properties.

## Savings Banks

Savings banks, formerly called mutual savings banks, are similar to savings and loan associations in that their main objectives are to encourage thrift and to provide financing for housing. These organizations exist primarily in the northeast portion of the United States and are chartered and regulated by the states in which they are located. Savings banks play a prominent role in financing housing in those states.

During the late 1970s and the 1980s, regulation changes allowed these institutions to branch out into other types of loan and to become more like commercial banks. These institutions currently differ from other depositor institutions primarily in form of ownership; they are depositor owned.

## Commercial Banks

Commercial banks can be federally or state chartered. In both cases, commercial banks are sources of mortgage money for construction, purchase of existing housing, and home improvements. Their loan policies are usually more conservative than those of other types of lending institution.

In the past, commercial banks favored short-term loans to avoid committing valuable assets for a long time. In recent years, commercial banks have steadily increased their mortgage holdings, and it has become easier for commercial banks to sell their loans in the secondary mortgage market. This enables the banks to recoup their cash in a few months, so commercial banks now make many more long-term loans.

Commercial banks also continue to be a source of short-term loans for construction and home improvement projects. Additionally, many offer warehouse lines of credit to mortgage companies to fund loans until the mortgage company can accumulate the loans in large blocks to sell to investors. This is called a *warehouse line of credit* because the funds are held "in warehouse" until the large loan blocks are sold.

## Mortgage Bankers and Mortgage Brokers

Mortgage bankers, also called mortgage companies, make mortgage loans for the construction of housing and the purchase of existing housing. They often specialize in FHA-insured loans and VA-guaranteed loans, although most also make conventional loans. A mortgage banker and a mortgage broker are quite different. A **mortgage banker** *makes and services mortgage loans.* A **mortgage broker** *brings together a lender and a borrower for a fee paid by the lending institution,* just as a real estate broker brings together a buyer and a seller of real property for a fee. Mortgage brokers generally work with and represent many lending institutions.

## Life Insurance Companies

At one time, a number of life insurance companies were active in making loans directly to individual mortgage borrowers. Today they provide funds to lending institutions to lend to individual borrowers and to provide funds for the purchase or construction of large real estate projects such as apartment complexes, office buildings, and shopping malls.

## Credit Unions

Credit unions are an excellent source of mortgage money for their members. Usually, credit unions offer mortgage loans to their membership at an interest rate below the commercial rate at any given time. To be financially able to make long-term mortgage loans, the credit union must be of substantial size. A federal employees credit union, a state employees credit union, and the credit union of a major industry are examples of large credit unions.

## Real Estate Investment Trusts

**Real estate investment trusts (REITs)** *make loans secured by real property.* REITs are owned by stockholders and enjoy certain federal income tax advantages. They provide financing for large commercial projects such as second-home developments, apartment complexes, shopping malls, and office buildings. REITs invest in properties as owners and managers, known as equity REITs, or they choose to lend money on projects owned by others, known as mortgage REITs.

## Individual Investors

Individuals also invest in mortgages. These individual investors usually are an excellent source for second mortgage loans. The seller of real property is definitely not to be overlooked as an individual investor. These sellers finance the sale of their properties by taking a regular second mortgage, taking a second mortgage in the form of a wraparound, taking a purchase money first mortgage, or financing by means of a contract for deed. In times of extremely high interest rates, a sale often cannot be made unless the seller provides a substantial part of the financing for the buyer.

## Government Agencies

Rural Development and the Farm Service Agency have already been mentioned as sources of mortgage funds for certain qualified buyers. Community development funds are sometimes available for down payments and closing cost assistance. North Carolina Housing Finance Agency sometimes provides down payment assistance and subsidized mortgage rates through local lenders and administers the Mortgage Credit Certificate Program, a federal program.

## Employers

Many employers provide closing cost assistance for transferees. Some provide down payment assistance. A few provide loan assistance, especially in the form of bridge loans, until the employee's former home sells. As its name implies, a bridge loan is a loan made to bridge the time gap between the purchase of a new home and the selling of the old one when the new buyer is unable to sell the old home before closing on the new one. Often the old home is used as collateral for the bridge loan, which is repaid when the old home sells.

# RESIDENTIAL LENDING PRACTICES AND PROCEDURES

## Loan Underwriting

Loan underwriting is the process by which an underwriter reviews loan documentation and evaluates a buyer's creditworthiness and the value of the property to be pledged as security for the payment of the note. The loan originator collects all the documentation and presents it to the underwriter, who may be an employee of the mortgage company, a private mortgage insurance company, or a government agency such as FHA, VA, RD, and FSA. These government agencies, except for RD and FSA, allow approved lenders to underwrite the government loans they process. The result of this evaluation is an approval or a disapproval of the loan.

## Property Analysis

The lender hires a state-licensed or state-certified appraiser to estimate the value of the property, that is, to appraise the property according to acceptable appraisal standards such as those developed by the Appraisal Institute. The primary purpose of the appraisal is to assure the lender that the value of the property is such that the property will sell for a price that will cover the loan amount and lender's costs should the borrower default and the lender need to foreclose.

The appraiser is not a home inspector; however, he does inspect and analyze the property, taking into account all factors that have a bearing on its value (see Chapter 9, Property Valuation, for details). The appraiser then submits a report of value, noting conditions that must be met. He will most likely require that rotten wood, peeling paint, broken glass, a worn-out roof, and safety hazards be corrected. Anything of this nature on the appraisal (and findings on the wood-destroying insect report) usually needs to be corrected and reinspected before closing the loan.

Note: A buyer should not rely on the appraisal as an inspection. He should be advised to inspect the property himself or hire a licensed home inspector.

The loan amount is based on the appraised value or sales price, whichever is lower. The lender determines the loan amount by multiplying the lesser of the sales or appraised value by the percentage indicated by the desired loan-to-value ratio. For example, if the contract sales price is $102,000, the appraised value is $100,000, and the LTV ratio is 95 percent, the lender will lend $95,000. The seller could reduce the sales price to the appraised value, the buyer could pay a $7,000 down payment, or the parties could cancel the contract, providing it was contingent upon a loan of 95 percent of contract sales price.

The lender wants to be assured of the property's value and condition; he also wants to be assured that the title to the property is clear when the loan is made and that his mortgage is the first mortgage. He gets this assurance by having an attorney search the title, give an attorney's opinion of title, and obtain a title insurance policy. The attorney does a preliminary search before closing and a final search just before recording the documents. This ensures that nothing happened to cloud the title between the initial search and closing and recording.

## Income, Credit, and Assets of the Loan Applicant

When evaluating the loan applicant, the lending institution requires the applicant to have a stable and effective income sufficient to enable the borrower to make the loan payments and to continue to meet other recurring financial obligations. The effective income may be a combination of an applicant's and a co-applicant's income (husband and wife, for example).

The applicant must also have a satisfactory credit history. The applicant is required to furnish credit information covering at least the two-year period immediately preceding the date of the application. If the applicant's credit history is unsatisfactory, the application may be denied regardless of the amount and quality of the applicant's income in relation to the loan payments.

The applicant's assets are also taken into consideration by the lending institution. If the applicant's income is borderline in relation to the mortgage payment required but the individual has sufficient good-quality assets, the existence of these assets may make the difference between approval and disapproval of the loan application.

## Prequalification of Buyer by Real Estate Agent

Although the real estate agent is not expected to perform the exact loan analysis completed by the mortgage loan officer, it is part of her professional duty to estimate the qualification limits for the home buyer. If a buyer were to come into an agent's office and ask to see a $450,000 property in an exclusive, high-value subdivision, it would be foolish and a violation of the agent's duty to the seller to make the appointment until she had some assurance the buyer could afford to purchase the home. Remember that as part of the agent's presentation to the seller to obtain the listing, she assured the seller she would present only qualified buyers rather than let the general public run through the home, as might happen if the seller were marketing the property. The manner in which the practitioner conducts the qualifying interview is a reflection of his communication and sales skills. Figure 7.2 illustrates the calculation of principal and interest payments using the amortization chart, and Figure 7.10 illustrates the data assembled to estimate the buyer's ability to qualify for the home.

# SECONDARY MORTGAGE MARKET

The primary mortgage market consists of lending institutions that make loans directly to borrowers. By contrast, the **secondary mortgage market** *buys and sometimes sells and services mortgages created in the primary mortgage market.* There must be an assignability feature, which allows the lender holding the mortgage to assign or sell the rights in the mortgage to another; thus, the money invested in the mortgage is freed without waiting for the borrower to repay the debt over the long mortgage term. Sale of the mortgage by the lender does not affect the borrower's rights or obligations. The mortgagor may not even be aware the mortgage has been sold; the original lending institution often continues to service the loan for the purchaser of the mortgage, and the mortgagor continues to make the necessary mortgage payments to the same lending institution that made the mortgage loan. If the purchaser of the mortgage prefers to service the mortgage, the original lender simply notifies the mortgagor to make payments to a different lender at a different address.

The secondary mortgage market benefits lending institutions and, in turn, the borrowing public by providing **liquidity** to mortgages. The mortgage is a liquid asset because *it can be readily converted to cash* by the lending institution selling the mortgage in the secondary market. Sale of the mortgage by the lender is especially beneficial in low-yield mortgages—those mortgages for which the lender receives a lesser return on her investment in terms of both discount and interest rate, expressed as an annual percentage rate. The lender gets the money out of these mortgages to reinvest in new mortgage loans at current higher yields. This provides stability in the supply of money for mortgage loans. Therefore, the secondary mortgage market benefits the borrowing public by enabling lending institutions to make money available for loans to qualified applicants.

Mortgage liquidity in the secondary market reduces the impact of disintermediation on lending institutions. **Disintermediation** is *the loss of funds available to lending institutions for making mortgage loans, caused by the withdrawal of funds by depositors for investment in higher-yield securities* in times of higher interest rates. Without the secondary mortgage market, disintermediation would result in funds available to lenders "drying up" to the extent that these loans would be practically unavailable. Some lending institutions limit their mortgage loans to their own assets rather than participate in the secondary mortgage market. For lenders that do participate in the secondary market, two types of markets are available: (1) the purchase and sale of mortgages between lending institutions and (2) the sale of mortgages by lending institutions to four organizations that provide a market for this purpose (FNMA, GNMA, FHLMC, and MGIC, discussed on the following pages).

## Activities among Lending Institutions

A major activity of the secondary mortgage market is the purchase and sale of mortgages by and among lending institutions. In this way, the market facilitates movement of capital from institutions that have funds to invest to lenders that do not have enough money for this purpose.

For example, at any time, the demand for mortgage loans may be low in a given locality. Institutions with funds available for making loans in those areas are unable to invest these funds in the local market by making primary mortgage loans. Their funds should be invested in mortgages where they can earn interest instead of being idle. At this same time, another part of the country may have a high demand for mortgage loans. A lender in that area may have a short supply of funds to lend to qualified loan applicants. The problems of both of these lending institutions can be solved if the institution whose funds are in short supply sells its mortgages on hand to a lender in another area that has a surplus of funds and a low demand for mortgage loans. As a result, the lender with otherwise idle funds has them invested in mortgages earning interest, as they should be, and the lender in short supply of money frees up capital invested in mortgages to meet the high demand for new mortgage loans in that area.

The direct sale of loans from investor to investor is legal and occurs relatively frequently, especially among small investors who sell to larger investors to make "pools." Much more likely are sales to organizations that buy and sell mortgages, as discussed in the following paragraphs.

## Sale to Organizations

The four organizations that actively participate in purchasing mortgages from financial institutions are the Federal National Mortgage Association (FNMA), the Government National Mortgage Association (GNMA), the Federal Home Loan Mortgage Corporation (FHLMC), and the Mortgage Guarantee Insurance Corporation (MGIC). See Figure 7.19 for a summary of allowable mortgage purchases by these organizations.

NR

### *Federal National Mortgage Association*

The Federal National Mortgage Association **(FNMA)** usually is referred to by its nickname, **Fannie Mae.** It is the oldest *secondary mortgage institution* and the largest holder of home mortgages. Fannie Mae was created in 1938 as a corporation completely owned by the federal government to provide a secondary market for residential mortgages. By 1968 it had evolved into a privately owned corporation. It is a profit-making organization, and its stock is listed on the New York Stock Exchange.

As a government-owned corporation, Fannie Mae was limited to purchasing FHA-insured mortgages and VA-guaranteed mortgages. As a privately owned corporation, it now also purchases conventional mortgages, which currently are a major portion of its business.

Fannie Mae buys mortgages regularly. Mortgage bankers are major sellers of mortgages to Fannie Mae. Savings and loan associations, savings banks, commercial banks,and life insurance companies also sell mortgages to Fannie Mae. Fannie Mae sells interest-bearing securities (bonds, notes, and debentures) to investors. These securities are backed by specific pools of mortgages purchased and held by Fannie Mae.

### *Government National Mortgage Association*

The popular name for the Government National Mortgage Association **(GNMA)** is taken from its acronym. **Ginnie Mae** was established in 1968, when Fannie Mae was fully

**FIGURE 7.19**
Allowable mortgage purchases.

ALLOWABLE MORTGAGE PURCHASES

| | VA | FHA | Conventional |
|---|---|---|---|
| FNMA | ✓ | ✓ | ✓ |
| GNMA | ✓ | ✓ | |
| FHLMC | | | ✓ |
| MGIC | | | ✓ |

converted to a private corporation. Ginnie Mae, an agency of the Department of Housing and Urban Development (HUD), *purchases mortgages to make capital available to lending institutions.* As a government agency, Ginnie Mae is limited to the purchase of VA-guaranteed and FHA-insured mortgages.

Ginnie Mae guarantees the "Ginnie Mae Pass-Through," a mortgage-backed security providing participation in a pool of FHA-insured or VA-guaranteed mortgages. The pass-throughs are originated by lending institutions, primarily mortgage bankers. Ginnie Mae guarantees these securities, making them highly secure investments for purchasers. The yield on each pass-through issue is guaranteed by the full faith and credit of the U.S. government; the pass-throughs are secured by the FHA-insured and VA-guaranteed loans; the lending institution originating the pass-through provides a guarantee as well. The government does not guarantee that investors in Ginnie Mae securities will make or not lose money on their investments. It only guarantees the loans backing the securities. When the interest rates change dramatically, the investor can make money or lose money.

## Federal Home Loan Mortgage Corporation

Like the other organizations, the Federal Home Loan Mortgage Corporation **(FHLMC),** has a nickname, **Freddie Mac,** and exists to increase the availability of mortgage credit and provide greater liquidity for savings associations. It achieves these objectives by purchasing mortgages. Congress created Freddie Mac in 1970 primarily to establish *a reliable market for the sale of conventional mortgages.* At that time, Fannie Mae purchased only a small number of conventional mortgages, although this number has increased, and Ginnie Mae cannot purchase conventional mortgages. Therefore, prior to Freddie Mac, lending institutions holding conventional mortgages were limited to the purchase and sale of these mortgages among themselves. Freddie Mac sells mortgage-participation certificates (PCs) and guaranteed-mortgage certificates (GMCs). These are securities that represent an undivided interest in specific pools of mortgages. Freddie Mac guarantees payment of principal and interest to purchasers of PCs and GMCs.

Freddie Mac was part of and was wholly owned by the Federal Home Loan Bank (FHLB) system. When Freddie Mac began, approximately 3,000 savings and loan associations held its stock. In 1988 these associations released the stock for sale, which provided another source of funds for Freddie Mac's operations. Any member of the system and any other financial institution whose deposits or accounts are insured by an agency of the federal government are eligible to sell mortgages to Freddie Mac. Although Freddie Mac purchases residential conventional mortgages primarily from savings and loan associations, it also purchases residential conventional mortgages from savings banks and commercial banks.

## Private Mortgage Insurers

Another participant in the secondary mortgage market is also an insurer of mortgage loans. The discussion on the conventional mortgage loan indicates that loans with an LTV above 80 require the participation of private mortgage insurance (PMI). One of the companies providing such insurance, Mortgage Guarantee Insurance Corporation (MGIC), entered the secondary mortgage market as a *purchaser of conventional loans.* This program is called **Maggie Mae.**

## Other Aspects of the Market

Primary lenders that wish to sell mortgages to Fannie Mae or Freddie Mac must use uniform loan documents that meet criteria established by FNMA and FHLMC. *Loans processed on uniform loan forms and according to FNMA/FHLMC guidelines* are called **conforming loans.** For example, these organizations do not purchase mortgages that contain a prepayment penalty, an extra charge for paying off a mortgage sooner than specified in its terms. This requirement is particularly advantageous to individual borrowers when they are required to pay off their mortgage as a condition of a contract of sale. In some cases, prepayment penalties on nonconforming loans are extremely high and, therefore, pose a real hardship to sellers.

In late 1980, Fannie Mae announced a new program that is highly beneficial to home sellers who are willing to finance the sale for a buyer by taking a purchase money first mortgage. Under the Fannie Mae program, the seller can have the mortgage prepared by a lending institution qualified to sell mortgages to Fannie Mae using uniform FNMA and FHLMC documents. The lending institution closes the transaction between seller and buyer and continues to service the loan for the seller for a fee. The institution collects the payments of principal and interest from the buyer and forwards them to the seller. In this way, sellers have an on-site expert to protect their interests and rights in the mortgage.

An important aspect of this Fannie Mae program is Fannie Mae's guarantee to purchase the mortgage if the sellers/mortgagees desire to sell and get their money out without waiting to complete a series of payments over the mortgage terms. Prior to this, sellers holding purchase money first mortgages had no reliable market for these mortgages if they wished to sell. This Fannie Mae program should provide additional incentive to home sellers to take purchase money first mortgages.

# FINANCING LEGISLATION

## Truth-in-Lending Simplification and Reform Act

The **Truth-in-Lending Simplification and Reform Act (TILSRA)** is a part of the Federal Consumer Credit Protection Act, which became effective July 1, 1969. It was subsequently amended to be known as the Truth-in-Lending Simplification and Reform Act (TILSRA) of 1980. The Truth-in-Lending Act empowered the Federal Reserve Board to implement the regulations in the act. TILSRA now *requires four chief disclosures: annual percentage rate, finance charge, amount financed, and total of payments. The Federal Reserve Board implemented these regulations by establishing Regulation Z.*

**Regulation Z** does not regulate interest rates but instead *provides specific consumer protections in mortgage loans for residential real estate.* All real estate loans for personal, family, household, or agricultural purposes are covered by Regulation Z. The regulation does not apply to commercial loans. Regulation Z also standardizes the procedures in residential loan transactions. It requires that the borrower be fully informed of all aspects of the loan transaction. In addition, the regulation applies to the advertisement of credit terms for residential real estate. The specific requirements of Regulation Z are discussed in the following paragraphs.

### *Disclosure*

At the time of application or within three days thereafter, the lender must provide the borrower with an estimated disclosure statement. If any terms change, and some usually do, the lender must provide an updated statement at or before closing. The disclosure must set forth the true, or effective, annual interest rate on a loan. This rate is called the *annual percentage rate (APR).* This rate may be higher than the interest expressed in the mortgage. For example, where certain fees and discount points charged by the lender are subtracted from the loan amount, the result is to increase the true rate of interest. This is because the borrower, as a result of the subtraction, has received a smaller loan amount and is paying interest on a larger amount. In addition to stating the true or effective annual interest rate on the loan, the disclosure statement must specify the finance charges, which include loan fees, interest, and discount points. The finance charge does not need to include such things as title examination, title insurance, escrow payments, document preparation fees, notary fees, or appraisal fees. The statement must also disclose the amount financed and the total of payments.

If the borrower is refinancing or obtaining a second mortgage loan and is pledging a principal residence already owned as security for such loan, the disclosure statement must

NR

provide for a right of rescission for the loan transaction. The right to rescind, or cancel, the loan must be exercised by the borrower prior to midnight of the third business day following the date the transaction was closed. The three-day right of rescission does not apply when the loan is to finance the purchase of a new home or the construction of a dwelling to be used as a principal residence.

### *Advertising*

Regulation Z also applies to advertising the credit terms available for the purchase of a home. The only specific thing that can be stated in the advertisement without making a full disclosure is the annual percentage rate spelled out in full, that is, not abbreviated as APR. If any other credit terms (trigger terms) are included in the advertisement, a full disclosure must be provided. For example, an advertisement mentioning a specific down payment *triggers* the requirement to make a complete disclosure of all of the following credit terms: the cash price of the property, the annual percentage rate, the amount of down payment, the amount of each payment, the date each payment is due, and the total number of payments over the mortgage term. If the annual percentage rate is not a fixed rate but is a variable rate, the ad must specify the rate to be a variable or adjustable rate. General statements regarding the financing can be made without a full disclosure. Such statements as "good financing available," "FHA financing available," and "loan assumption available" are satisfactory for this purpose. Real estate agents must take special care not to violate the advertising requirements of Regulation Z.

### *Penalties*

A violator of Regulation Z is subject to criminal liability and punishment by fine up to $5,000, imprisonment for up to one year, or both. In the event the borrower has suffered a financial loss as a result of the violation, the borrower can sue the violator under civil law in federal court for damages.

## Fair Credit Reporting Act

The purpose of the Fair Credit Reporting Act is to ensure that consumer credit reporting agencies use reasonable procedures to collect and evaluate relevant consumer credit information fairly and impartially and use this information properly and with respect for the consumer's privacy rights. The rationales underlying this Act are that fair and accurate credit reporting is essential to the banking system and that unfair methods of reporting credit erode public confidence essential to the operation of the banking system.

A consumer report is a credit reporting agency's communication of information (in any manner) about the consumer's credit, reputation, lifestyle, or personal characteristics for the actual or intended purpose of partially or completely determining a consumer's eligibility for employment, credit, insurance, or other purposes authorized by the Act.

Several items addressed by the Fair Credit Reporting Act are as follows:

1. Permissible uses of reports
2. Requirements pertaining to information in reports
3. Disclosure of information to consumers
4. Procedure for disputing report's accuracy
5. Consumer report user requirements
6. Civil liability for willful or negligent noncompliance with the Act
7. Penalties for unauthorized disclosure by consumer credit reporting agencies

People have the right to check their consumer reports and to force credit bureaus to correct mistakes in them. There is no charge for this check to the individual who has been denied credit based on information contained in the report. Credit reporting agencies must now provide one free credit report per year to anyone who requests his own report, even if the person requesting the report has not been denied credit. Otherwise, there is usually a service fee. Bankruptcies remain on a credit report for 10 years, but other information must be removed after 7 years. The FCRA is available at **http://www.ftc.gov/os/statutes/031224fcra.pdf.**

## The Equal Credit Opportunity Act

Congress enacted and amended **Equal Credit Opportunity Act (ECOA)** in the mid-1970s. Its purpose is to *prevent discrimination in the loan process* on the part of lending institutions. The Act requires financial institutions engaged in making loans to do so on an equal basis to all creditworthy customers without regard to discriminatory factors. The Equal Credit Opportunity Act is implemented by Regulation B of the Federal Reserve Board.

### *Requirements of ECOA*

This Act makes it unlawful for a creditor to discriminate against a loan applicant in any aspect of a credit transaction as follows:

1. On the basis of race, color, religion, sex, national origin, marital status, or age (unless the applicant is a minor because a minor does not have the capacity to contract)
2. Because part of the applicant's income is derived from a public assistance program
3. Because the applicant has, in good faith, exercised any right under the Federal Consumer Credit Protection Act, of which the Truth-in-Lending Law (Regulation Z) is a part

## SUMMARY OF IMPORTANT POINTS

contract

1. The purpose of a mortgage or deed of trust is to secure the payment of a promissory note.
2. Two legal theories regarding a mortgage or deed of trust are the lien theory and the title theory.
3. The requirements for a valid mortgage or deed of trust are (1) writing, (2) competent parties, (3) valid debt, (4) valid interest, (5) description, (6) mortgaging clause, (7) defeasance clause, (8) execution by borrower, and (9) delivery to and acceptance by lender or trustee.
4. The lender's rights are (1) possession upon default, (2) foreclosure, and (3) assignment of the finance instruments.
5. The borrower's rights are (1) possession prior to default, (2) to defeat lien by paying debt in full prior to default, and (3) right of equity of redemption.
6. The two types of foreclosure are judicial and nonjudicial. Foreclosure sale proceeds are distributed in a special order of priority. If the sale proceeds available to the lender are insufficient to satisfy the debt, the lender can sue for a deficiency judgment. Sellers who finance their own property with a purchase money deed of trust are not permitted a deficiency judgment in North Carolina.
7. A buyer assuming a seller's mortgage assumes liability on the mortgage and the note. The seller remains liable on the note unless specifically released by a mortgage clause or by the lender. A buyer taking title "subject to" an existing mortgage has no personal liability on the note to the lender.
8. A fully amortizing mortgage requires payments of principal and interest that will satisfy the debt completely over the mortgage term.

9. Various types of mortgage include balloon, open-end, graduated payment, adjustable rate, wraparound, package, blanket, construction, reverse, and junior.

10. The major sources of residential financing are savings and loan associations, savings banks, commercial banks, and mortgage bankers.

11. The methods of financing are insured and uninsured conventional mortgage loans, FHA-insured loans, VA-guaranteed loans, RD and FSA loans, and various types of seller financing.

12. Conventional loans are not required to be insured if the loan amount does not exceed 80 percent of the property value. Most conventional insured loans are 90 percent and 95 percent loans. The insurance is called private mortgage insurance (PMI). The premium is paid by the borrower.

13. FHA-insured and VA-guaranteed loans are made by qualified lending institutions to buyers who are going to occupy the property. Rates on both of these loans can be negotiated between lender and borrower. Either a borrower or a seller may pay the discount points, if any, on VA, FHA, or conventional loans.

14. The FHA programs include 203(b), 203(k), 245, and 234(c). The FHA insurance is called mortgage insurance premium (MIP) and protects the lender and the purchaser of the loan (that is, the secondary mortgage market) from a financial loss in the event of a foreclosure. The premium is paid by the borrower. The loan amount is a percentage of the acquisition cost as established by the FHA.

15. VA loans are guaranteed. VA loans can be made up to 100 percent of the property value established by a VA appraisal and stated in the certificate of reasonable value (CRV), which is issued by the VA.

16. FHA-insured and VA-guaranteed loans require escrow accounts, are for 30-year maximum terms, are assumable with qualification, and do not impose a prepayment penalty. VA-guaranteed loans made after March 1, 1988, require the assumptor to qualify, be approved by the VA, and pay a 1/2 percent assumption fee. The down payment can be borrowed if secured by other collateral. FHA-insured loans originated after December 15, 1989, require qualification to assume.

17. Real estate practitioners need to know the major sources of funding in their communities, as well as the qualification process for obtaining a loan. In offering her professional services to a seller, the agent has promised to present the property only to qualified purchasers. This duty can be performed properly only if the agent has a working understanding of the local financing programs that fit the buyer's needs and a reasonable idea of the potential buyer's ability to purchase the property.

18. Federal laws that regulate lending institutions in making consumer loans include Truth-in-Lending and ECOA.

19. The primary mortgage market is the activity of lending institutions making loans directly to individual borrowers. The secondary market is the activity of selling and buying mortgages that originated in the primary market. The secondary market consists of the purchase and sale of mortgages among lenders, as well as the sale of mortgages by lenders to Fannie Mae (FNMA), Ginnie Mae (GNMA), Freddie Mac (FHLMC), and Maggie Mae (MGIC). The market provides liquidity to mortgages, thereby reducing the effect of disintermediation for the benefit of lending institutions and borrowers as well.

20. Fannie Mae purchases VA, FHA, and conventional mortgages. Ginnie Mae purchases only government mortgages. Freddie Mac and Maggie Mae purchase only conventional mortgages.

## ITEMS TO CONSIDER FOR THE STATE EXAM

These areas represent questions frequently answered incorrectly by applicants for the North Carolina Real Estate License.

1. Mortgage instruments.
   a. The difference between the promissory note (I.O.U) and the deed of trust. (Instrument providing security for the note)
   b. Definition of the "power of sale" clause in the deed of trust. (Clause giving the trustee the power to sell the property without court action and to repay the debt from the proceeds.)
2. Characteristics of the adjustable rate mortgages (ARMs). One important characteristic is the possibility of a negative amortization.
3. Sales of mortgaged property.
   a. The effect of buying "subject to." (Buyer accepts no responsibility for the mortgage loans.)
   b. The effect of "assuming" a mortgage versus "subject to." (Buyer is responsible for loan. If buyer does not pay, the seller is responsible unless seller has received a release of liability from the mortgage company.)
4. How interest rates are set on FHA-insured loans and VA-guaranteed loans—by the local lender, not the government (not HUD, FHA, or VA).
5. The role of commercial banks and mortgage companies (mortgage brokers and mortgage bankers).
6. Characteristics of second mortgages; that is, they are usually for a shorter period at a higher rate.
7. FHA insurance protects the lender and the purchaser of the loan (secondary market).
8. Only the VA, not the local lender, can release the veteran from liability on the VA-guaranteed loan made before March 1, 1988. Under new rules for loans made after that date, the lender processes the release of liability paperwork for VA-guaranteed loans.
9. A due-on-sale clause, or an alienation clause, allows the lender to call the entire principal balance due and payable at once if the buyer sells the property.
10. Characteristics of construction loans.
    a. Shorter terms, therefore more attractive to a commercial bank.
    b. More risky than the typical mortgage loan.
    c. Usually secured by the construction site property.
11. A mortgage banker makes and services loans. A mortgage broker brings together a lender and borrower for a fee paid by the lending institution.
12. Underwriting is the loan review process that verifies all the loan documentation and evaluates the value of the property proposed to be pledged as security for the loan and the creditworthiness of the loan applicant in order to determine whether to approve a loan.

## REVIEW QUESTIONS

Answers to the review questions are in the Answer Key at the back of the book.

1. All of the following statements are applicable to real estate promissory notes EXCEPT:
   A. they must be written
   B. the borrower is personally liable for payment
   C. they must provide evidence of a valid debt
   D. they must be executed by the lender

2. Which of the following statements concerning a mortgage is correct?
   A. the purpose of a mortgage is to secure the payment of a promissory note
   B. the delivery of a mortgage is a conditional conveyance of title
   C. a mortgage is a three-party instrument
   D. the mortgage lender is called the mortgagor

3. Which of the following is not a right given to lenders by a deed of trust?
   A. assignment
   B. possession after default
   C. foreclosure
   D. equity of redemption

4. The clause that makes a mortgage unassumable is which of the following?
   A. defeasance
   B. alienation
   C. mortgaging
   D. prepayment

5. Which of the following gives a borrower the right to pay a debt in full and remove the mortgage lien at any time after default and prior to foreclosure?
   A. defeasance
   B. prepayment
   C. equity of redemption
   D. foreclosure

6. A deed in lieu of foreclosure conveys a title to which of the following?
   A. lender
   B. borrower
   C. trustee
   D. mortgagor

7. Which of the following is paid first from the proceeds of a foreclosure sale?
   A. mortgage debt
   B. real property taxes
   C. mortgagee's equity
   D. sale expenses

8. A deficiency judgment is available to which of the following?
   A. mortgagee
   B. mortgagor
   C. trustee
   D. trustor

9. A buyer assumed the seller's mortgage without the seller's obtaining release of liability. The buyer subsequently defaulted. Which of the following statements is correct?
   A. only the buyer is personally liable for payment of the note
   B. only the seller is personally liable for payment of the note
   C. both the buyer and the seller are personally responsible for payment of the note
   D. neither the buyer nor the seller is personally responsible

10. The type of mortgage requiring the borrower to pay only interest during the mortgage term is which of the following?
    A. balloon
    B. open-end
    C. term
    D. closed

11. The amount of interest paid on an amortizing mortgage at an annual rate of 12 percent for a month in which the principal balance is $73,000 is which of the following?
    A. $600
    B. $730
    C. $876
    D. $1,369

12. Which of the following is a mortgage that is not on a fully amortizing basis and therefore requires a larger final payment?
    A. graduated mortgage
    B. balloon mortgage
    C. open-end mortgage
    D. flexible mortgage

13. Which of the following statements regarding adjustable rate mortgages (ARMs) is correct?
    A. the interest rate changes according to changes in a selected index
    B. adjustable rate mortgages always contain a due-on-sale clause and a prepayment penalty
    C. all adjustable rate mortgages have a conversion feature that allows them to be converted to a fixed rate
    D. none of the above

14. Which of the following statements about wraparound mortgages is (are) true?
    A. the wraparound is a junior mortgage in an amount larger than the existing first mortgage
    B. it is not necessary that the existing first mortgage be assumable
    C. the interest rate on the first mortgage is usually higher than the rate on the wraparound mortgage
    D. all of the above

15. Which of the following is a mortgage in which two or more parcels of land are pledged?
    A. blanket
    B. package
    C. all-inclusive
    D. wraparound

16. Which of the following is a mortgage that is subordinate to another?
    A. leasehold
    B. blanket
    C. junior
    D. participation

17. The priority of mortgages in relation to one another is based on which of the following?
    A. time of execution
    B. time of recording
    C. time of delivery
    D. time of acknowledgment

18. Which of the following is a mortgage given by buyer to seller to secure payment of part of the purchase price?
    A. purchase money mortgage
    B. earnest money mortgage
    C. participation mortgage
    D. graduated payment mortgage

19. Insurance for the protection of lending institutions making conventional loans is:
    A. mutual mortgage insurance
    B. conventional mortgage insurance
    C. institutional insurance
    D. private mortgage insurance

20. The FHA programs are for which of the following purposes?
    A. making housing loans
    B. guaranteeing housing loans
    C. purchasing housing loans
    D. insuring housing loans

21. The FHA bases its commitment on a percentage of which of the following?
    A. certificate of reasonable value (CRV)
    B. purchase price
    C. selling price
    D. acquisition cost or appraisal value, whichever is less

22. Which of the following FHA programs provides for lower monthly payments in the early years of the mortgage term by not requiring the borrower to pay all of the interest at that time?
    A. 203(b)
    B. 203(k)
    C. 234(c)
    D. 245

23. The major benefit of the secondary mortgage market is to reduce the effect of which of the following?
    A. amortization
    B. liquidity
    C. disintermediation
    D. expensive settlement charges

24. Which of the following statements about VA loans is (are) correct?
    A. the repayment of a percentage of VA loans in the event of borrower default is guaranteed to the lender
    B. VA loans are for 100 percent of the lesser of property value established by the VA or the sales price
    C. a veteran can use his VA loan entitlement more than once under certain circumstances
    D. all of the above

25. All of the following statements about FHA and VA loans are correct EXCEPT:
    A. they are assumable
    B. they require a prepayment penalty
    C. the maximum term is 30 years
    D. they require an escrow account

26. Which of the following statements about discount points is (are) correct?
    A. each point charged increases the lender's yield on the loan by 1/8 percentage point
    B. each point charged by the lender costs 1 percent of the loan amount
    C. points may be paid by seller or buyer on VA, FHA, or conventional loans
    D. all of the above

27. All of the following statements about Regulation Z are correct EXCEPT:
    A. it applies to commercial mortgage loans
    B. it requires lenders to furnish a disclosure statement to the borrower
    C. it provides for a three-day right of rescission when a residence already owned is being pledged as security for a new mortgage
    D. it regulates the advertising of credit terms of property offered for sale

28. ECOA requires lenders to make consumer loans without regard to all of the following EXCEPT:
    A. age
    B. occupation
    C. sex
    D. marital status

29. The activity of lending institutions making mortgage loans directly to individual borrowers is:
    A. secondary mortgage market
    B. money market
    C. institutional market
    D. primary mortgage market

30. Which of the following is a government-owned corporation that purchases mortgages?
    A. Fannie Mae
    B. Ginnie Mae
    C. Freddie Mac
    D. Maggie Mae

# Chapter 8

## KEY TERMS

closing statement
credit
debit
double entry
good faith estimate
HUD Form No. 1
interim interest
jumbo loans
paid outside closing
prorating
Real Estate Settlement Procedures Act (RESPA)
*Settlement Cost: A HUD Guide*
single-entry
soil evaluation test

## LEARNING OBJECTIVES

At the conclusion of this chapter, you should be able to:

1. List the preliminaries to closing.
2. List the items required at closing.
3. Describe the process of the closing meeting.
4. Describe the placement of items as debits and credits in the closing statements.
5. Describe the provisions of the Real Estate Settlement Procedures Act (RESPA).
6. Calculate the balance due from the buyer or due to the seller in a closing statement.

# Closing Real Estate Transactions

## IN THIS CHAPTER

Closing is the consummation of the sales effort that began when the broker obtained a listing. This event is given different names in various parts of the country, such as settlement, passing of papers, and coming out of escrow. At the closing, the buyer receives a deed and the seller receives payment for the property. In some states, escrow companies do all the preparatory work necessary to close the transaction and actually do the final closing, but in North Carolina the predominant practice is to assemble the parties for a closing meeting.

## PRELIMINARIES TO CLOSING

The following is a list of the events that are a preliminary part of the closing process, along with an indication of which party is usually responsible for each according to the purchase contract. Of course, almost any of these items could have been provided for differently in the contract.

1. Arranging financing, buyer's responsibility.
2. Property survey, buyer's responsibility.
3. Termite or wood-destroying insect (WDI) inspection, buyer's responsibility. (Note: When property is purchased with a VA-guaranteed loan, the seller pays for the termite [WDI] report.) In North Carolina prior to 1988, the seller was ordinarily responsible for the termite (WDI) inspection. This situation provided a conflict for the inspector when the seller was his client and the buyer had the biggest stake in the outcome. According to current practice, as noted in the Offer to Purchase and Contract in Chapter 6, the buyer pays for the inspection, but the seller is expected to provide any needed treatment.
4. Title examination, buyer's responsibility.
5. Title insurance, buyer's responsibility.
6. Property inspection by the buyer. Whether the buyer chooses Alternative 1 or Alternative 2 in the Offer to Purchase and Contract, eligible repairs negotiated between the buyer and the seller are performed by the seller.

7. Clearing of title defects, seller's responsibility.
8. Insurance policy, buyer's responsibility.
9. Soil/site evaluation. A **soil evaluation test** is needed where a septic system is required for sewer facilities. The soil test, which replaced the old "perc test," is *an evaluation of the absorbency of the soil to bear the output of the septic system.* If the soil test indicates a septic system will not work, it may not be possible to establish a home on the property. Soil/site evaluation is negotiable between buyer and seller. The buyer usually pays, but when the property is purchased with a VA loan, the seller pays.
10. Drafting of closing documents:
    a. Deed preparation, seller's responsibility.
    b. Financing instruments (note and mortgage or deed of trust), buyer's responsibility.
    c. Bill of sale for personal property, seller's responsibility.
    d. Closing statements. The responsibility for these is examined in a later section.
11. Scheduling the closing, typically coordinated by the agent in coordination with the closing attorney.
12. Notifying buyer of certified funds needed to close, usually done by agent working with buyer after attorney has prepared a draft of the settlement statement.

# THE CLOSING MEETING

The closing meeting is usually conducted by the attorney who prepared the documents and who received appropriate funds into a trust account from which he makes the respective disbursements at the closing meeting, once everything is in order.

## Parties Present or Represented

The usual practice is to bring all the parties—buyers, sellers, closing attorney, selling agent, and listing agent—together at the closing. However, it is not necessary to have all of them physically present at the same time. For example, the seller may have moved out of town. In this case, the seller could have signed the deed in advance. Likewise, the buyer may have appointed another party power of attorney to execute all the closing documents on her behalf. The parties that need to be represented include the seller, to sign the closing statement, and the buyer, to sign the closing statement and financing instruments. Sometimes the loan officer of the bank is present as well.

## Location of Closing

There is no legal requirement concerning the location of closing. It is based on local custom, the type of transaction, or the convenience of the parties concerned. The most common practice in North Carolina is for the closing to take place in the office of the buyer's attorney. The buyer usually selects the closing attorney and designates the meeting's location; the lenders usually allow the buyer's attorney to conduct the closing. The closing attorney, therefore, usually works for the buyer and the lender. Although the attorney prepares the legal documents, the real estate agent has an important role in arranging the meeting and ensuring that all parties and documents are in place.

## Procedures at Closing

During the closing meeting, the attorney reviews the closing statement. All parties, including the real estate agents, must agree on the accuracy of the closing statement. Ideally, the closing attorney provided the agents a copy of the closing statement in advance of the closing. Once the accuracy of the statement is agreed upon, the buyer, seller, and attorney sign the closing statement.

The closing attorney conducts the closing meeting according to the terms of the contract and the instructions provided by the lender. After reviewing all documents with the parties, the attorney has them signed as appropriate. Many documents are typically involved in a real estate closing, but the most important are the deed transferring title of the property and the promissory note and deed of trust.

Before the closing, the closing attorney should have obtained a check for the earnest money deposit drawn on the trust account of the broker holding the earnest money. The closing attorney now collects a check for the amount due from the buyer (this needs to be a certified or comparably guaranteed check).

## Procedures after the Closing

Chapter 2 discusses the importance of the pure race system in recording documents. This has an important practical bearing on the closing meeting. The closing officer must be assured that all documents executed at closing can be recorded without problems. For example, a lien may have been filed against the property while the closing meeting was in progress. Therefore, the standard practice for attorneys is to adjourn the meeting after the process is completed, without the actual disbursement of funds. The attorney then proceeds to the courthouse to record the instruments. If there is no problem in this recording, she can make the appropriate disbursements, including paying the real estate fee to the broker. Finally, the attorney does the necessary income taxation reporting (see Chapter 13, Federal Income Taxation of Home Ownership).

# ITEMS REQUIRED AT CLOSING

A list of the documents involved in closing a real estate transaction follows. Not all of these are involved in all transactions, but all are possibilities.

1. Seller's responsibility
   a. Receipts for real estate taxes, assessments, and utilities
   b. Statement of the loan balance payoff
   c. Lien waivers
   d. Insurance policy, if it is to be assigned to the buyer
   e. Leases, if any
   f. Deed
   g. Bill of sale for any personal property
   h. Soil/site evaluation for septic system*
   i. Well/water certificate*
   j. Septic/sewer inspection*
   k. Termite report (Word Destroying Insect Report or WDIR)*
2. Buyer's responsibility
   a. Cash or certified check
   b. Financing documents
   c. Homeowner's insurance policy
   d. Title insurance policy
   e. Well/water certificate*
   f. Septic/sewer inspection*
   g. Termite report (WDIR)*

*(1) On new construction, seller usually pays for inspections and reports for well/water, septic/sewer, wood-destroying insects, and soil/site evaluations (these tests replace old "perc" tests) for septic systems. (2) On existing construction, buyer usually pays for inspections and reports for well/water, septic/sewer, and wood-destroying insects. (3) On VA-guaranteed loans, seller usually pays for inspections and reports on well/water, septic/sewer, and wood-destroying insects. VA did not change the regulation preventing buyer from paying these charges when the interest rate and points became negotiable.

In essence, a **closing statement** is simply *an accounting of the funds involved in a particular real estate transaction.* Each party to the transaction should receive copies. These parties include the selling and listing brokers, the buyer and seller, the lending institution, and the attorney. The broker must retain a copy of the closing statement in his file for 3 years.

A closing statement is a historical document prepared in advance; that is, the statement is prepared in advance of the closing, but it records what must happen at closing. The statement sets forth the distribution of monies involved in the transaction, that is, who is to pay a specific amount for each expense and who is to receive that amount.

The closing statement is usually prepared by the closing attorney. However, the North Carolina Real Estate License Law and the Real Estate Commission's Rules and Regulations require that the brokers involved in real estate sales transactions be responsible for delivering to the buyer and the seller a copy of the closing statement at closing or within five days after closing and be held responsible for the *accuracy* of the closing statement.

# PRORATIONS AT CLOSING

## Methods of Calculating Prorations

There are essentially four methods of **prorating,** or *dividing the settlement costs of items at closing.* Although choice of the method is guided by local custom in the real world, this book uses the first method exclusively for exam purposes, including the state exam.

1. The 360-day-year method. In this method, every month is presumed to have 30 days, including February. This is the simplest method to learn and has many practical applications. For example, whenever you are confronted with an annual cost, such as that for real property taxes or insurance, simply divide the annual amount by 360 to get a daily amount. Multiplying this daily amount by the number of days provides a quick and easy proration (see Figure 8.5). This is the method used on the state prelicensing exam.
2. The 365-day-year method, also known as the actual-days-in-the-year method. This is, of course, more exact and is the basis of the common prorations in the everyday world.
3. The actual-days-in-the-month method. In the event you were prorating interest on a mortgage for the month, the real-world (that is, the lender) parties would care if the month had 28 or 31 days.
4. Proration tables. Some closing officers like to refer to handbooks that convert each day in the month to a decimal figure. Once again, this book does not use this method but relies on the first method for the remaining discussion.

In calculating the exact days to be prorated, it is usually assumed that the day of closing is charged to the seller. Before beginning to prorate, think through the following steps:

1. Determine who has paid or is going to pay (see items with asterisk Figures 8.1 through 8.4).
2. If it is the seller, the seller is reimbursed for the buyer's portion; that is, credit seller and debit buyer for buyer's portion.

**FIGURE 8.1**
Debits to buyer's statement.

1. Purchase price
2. Hazard insurance
   (a) New Policy
   (b) Prorated assumed policy prepaid by seller*
3. Preparation of mortgage and note instruments
4. Survey
5. Title search
6. Title insurance
7. Credit report
8. Loan origination fee
9. Mortgage assumption fee
10. Mortgage interest
11. Mortgage insurance
12. Discount points
13. Recording of deed
14. Recording of mortgage instruments
15. Prorated real estate taxes prepaid by seller

*The following items may be debits to buyer's statement, depending on the contract and/or other agreements:*

16. Soil/site evaluation
17. Wood-destroying insect inspection
18. Well/water report
19. Sewer/septic inspection
20. Broker's fee

1. Earnest money deposit
2. Any mortgage money
3. Real property taxes in arrears, prorated*
4. Real property assessments in arrears
5. Mortgage interest on assumed loan*
6. Balance due from buyer

**FIGURE 8.2**

Credits to buyer's statement.

1. Real property taxes in arrears, prorated*
2. Delinquent real property taxes
3. Personal property taxes in arrears
4. Existing mortgage
5. Deed preparation
6. Unpaid utility bills
7. Mortgage interest on an assumed loan*
8. Balance due to the seller

*The following items may be debits to the seller's statement, depending on loan type and other agreements or regulations:*

9. Broker's fee
10. Soil/site evaluation
11. Wood-destroying insect inspection
12. Well/water report
13. Sewer/septic inspection

**FIGURE 8.3**

Debits to seller's statement.

1. Purchase price
2. Overpayments to be refunded
   a. Real estate taxes paid for the full year*
   b. Insurance policy paid in advance, if assumed*
3. Sale of personal property
4. Escrow account balance on assumed loan

**FIGURE 8.4**

Credits to seller's statement.

3. If it is the buyer, the buyer is reimbursed for the seller's portion; that is, credit buyer and debit seller for seller's portion.
4. The person (buyer or seller) who has paid or will pay the outside party (for example, tax collector, insurance company, mortgage company) is reimbursed or credited. The other person is debited.
5. The portion belonging to the person who has *not* paid or will *not* pay this outside party is always the person who is debited.
6. Draw a time line if you need help identifying the portion to be debited and credited.

## Prorated Entries on the Closing Statement

These items always require a **double-entry** format; that is, *an amount is collected from one party and given to the other.* In this case, it is a **debit,** or *charge to the first party,* and a **credit,** or *income to the other party,* in the same amount (see Figure 8.5).

Items commonly prorated are discussed on the following pages.

### *Real Property Tax*

If the tax is unpaid at the time of closing (that is, if it is in arrears), the sellers must pay their share of the tax year. In this case, the sellers' share of the unpaid taxes is debited to the sellers and this amount is given to the buyers. When the tax bill comes to the buyers at the end of the year, they have the sellers' share to put with their own share to pay the full bill. If, however, the sellers paid their tax bill for the entire year, they are due a refund for the portion of the tax year they paid for but did not use. In this case, the sellers would be getting a refund (credit) and the buyers would be purchasing this share from the sellers, a debit.

**FIGURE 8.5**
Rules for prorating.

1. *Never prorate personal property taxes.*
2. For real property, identify the period to be prorated:
   a. The calendar year; e.g., real property taxes
   b. The calendar month; e.g., mortgage interest
   c. The anniversary year; e.g., fire insurance
3. Reduce the pro rata period to an interval rate; e.g., divide the annual rate by the number of days in the year to get a daily rate.

   *Example:* Taxes of $630 per year are

   $\frac{\$630}{360} = \$1.75$ per day
4. Determine the number of days of the pro rata period that have been used.

   *Example:* Closing date July 23

   | | | |
   |---|---|---|
   | a. Full months used are Jan.–June | = | |
   | 6 × 30 | = | 180 |
   | b. Days in the month of settlement | = | +23 |
   | Total days used of the period | | 203 |
5. Multiply the daily rate by the number of days used; i.e.,

   $1.75 × 203 = $355.25 Amount used
6. Determine whether the cost is paid by seller in advance or is paid by buyer in arrears.
   a. If in arrears, debit (charge) seller and credit buyer $355.25.
   b. If the whole cost was paid in advance, calculate the overpayment to be refunded; i.e.,

   | | |
   |---|---|
   | Paid | $630.00 |
   | (−) Used | $355.25 |
   | Credit | $274.75 |

   c. Debit buyer and credit seller $274.75.

The date of closing is October 14. The real property tax for the year is $756; it is paid. Calculate the amount to be debited to the buyer.

1. Figure the daily rate of tax. $\frac{\$756}{360} = \$2.10/\text{day}$
2. Figure the number of days the buyer will own the property during the tax period.
3. Figure the buyer's share of the yearly tax by multiplying the number of days she will own the property by the daily tax rate.

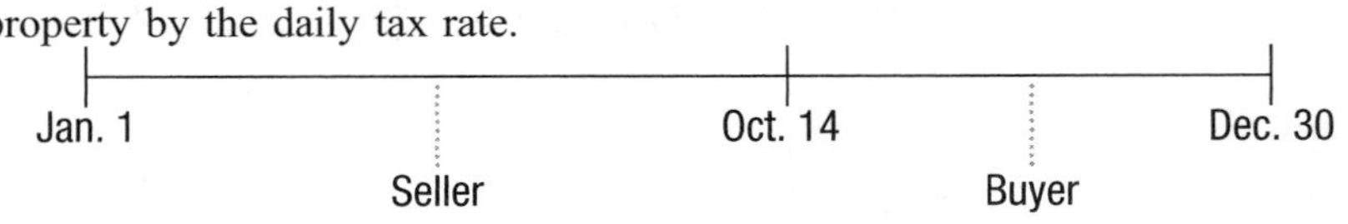

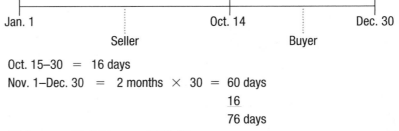

| | | | | |
|---|---|---|---|---|
| Oct. 15–30 | = | 16 days | | |
| Nov. 1–Dec. 30 | = | 2 months × 30 | = | 60 days |
| | | | | 16 |
| | | | | 76 days |

76 days × $2.10/day = $159.60

Debit buyer $159.60; credit seller $159.60.

A special case exists for closing after taxes are billed and have not been paid. Taxes are due September 1, but many people do not pay them until December. If a property closes during the period from September 1 to December 31 and taxes are unpaid, the taxes are paid at closing. The amount is prorated, and sellers and buyers are debited for their respective shares, which are paid by the closing attorney to the tax collector.

## Special Assessments

Typically, special assessments are not prorated and are paid by the seller. In some areas, this arrangement is altered by the contract, particularly in cash sales or loan assumptions. In these cases, the contract determines how special assessments are handled. If buyer and seller agree to prorate them, they are handled in the same way as other prorations. Most mortgage companies require them to be paid at closing if they have been billed. If the seller pays them at closing, they are a single-entry debit to the seller. If the buyer pays them at closing, they are a single-entry debit to the buyer.

## Assumed Insurance Policy

It is expected that the seller paid for the full insurance year and that there is the same type of entry as the real property taxes paid in advance.

***Example:*** The seller purchased an insurance policy for one year for \$540. The effective date was February 1 of the current year. This year she closed her house on May 15 and the buyer assumed the policy. Determine the amount to be credited to the seller.

1. Figure the daily rate. $\frac{\$540}{360} = \$1.50/\text{day}$

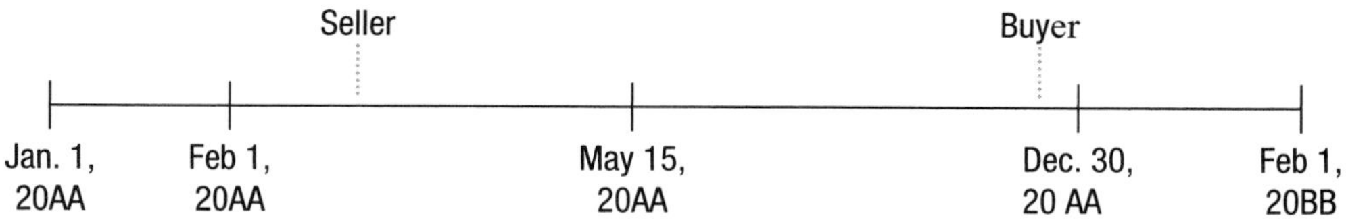


2. Calculate the number of days in 8 months. $8 \times 30 = 240$
   Add number of days in May. 15
   255

3. Multiply the number of days by the rate.
   $255 \times \$1.50 = \$382.50$ = total buyer's portion
   Debit buyer \$382.50; credit seller \$382.50.

## Homeowners' Association Dues

When homeowners' association dues apply to a real estate transaction, they appear as a prorated double-entry item on the closing statement. The payment schedule for homeowners' association dues varies from one association to another and may be due monthly, quarterly, or yearly. If the seller already paid for a time period that extends beyond closing, this item will appear as a credit to the seller and a debit to the buyer. If, however, dues have not been paid up to the date of closing, this item will appear as a debit to the seller and a credit to the buyer.

## Rents on Leased Property

In most cases, the seller-landlord would have collected the full month's rent at the beginning of the month and therefore owes a refund of the unearned days of the month to the buyer. There would be a debit to the seller and a credit to the buyer. Sometimes the rent has not been paid at closing, and the buyer must collect the rent later. The buyer owes the seller for the number of days in the month the seller owned the property. In such cases, the seller is credited and the buyer is debited.

## Interest on an Assumed Loan

Interest is always paid in arrears on a **conforming loan** (a loan that meets the guidelines of the secondary mortgage market). When interest is paid in arrears, the result is a debit to the seller and a credit to the buyer for the days of the month the seller used the existing loan. The interest paid in arrears accrues daily from when the interest was last paid until it is due again; therefore, the interest that has not been paid (accrued interest) is payable at the next payment date. The buyer is responsible for the portion of the interest due from the date of closing until the next payment date. The seller is responsible for the days from the last payment through the date of closing since he used the money for that period of time. The buyer will make that payment, including all the interest since the last payment. The buyer, therefore, must get the seller's portion of the interest at closing. When the next payment is due, the buyer adds the portion of the interest he got from the seller at closing to his own portion of the interest and makes the interest payment.

Interest on **jumbo loans** (those over the conforming loan limit) or on other nonconforming loans may have interest calculated in advance. If interest is paid in advance, the seller is credited and the buyer debited the unused portion of the month the seller paid for but did not use. This is because the seller paid interest for the month ahead when he made his last payment before closing. The buyer must reimburse the seller for the days the buyer will use during the closing month which already have been paid for by the seller.

The real estate agent should know how to figure interest in arrears or in advance; however, mortgage loans with interest paid in advance are rare.

***Example:*** The interest on an assumed mortgage is paid in arrears. The date of closing is August 16. The buyer is assuming a $58,000 mortgage with a 9 percent annual interest rate. Calculate the interest that will be credited to the buyer. (Remember, the same amount will be debited to the seller.)

1. Figure the interest to be paid in August.

$$\frac{\$58,000 \times 9\%}{12} = \$435.00$$

2. Figure the daily interest paid (30-day month).

$$\frac{\$435}{30} = \$14.50/\text{day}$$

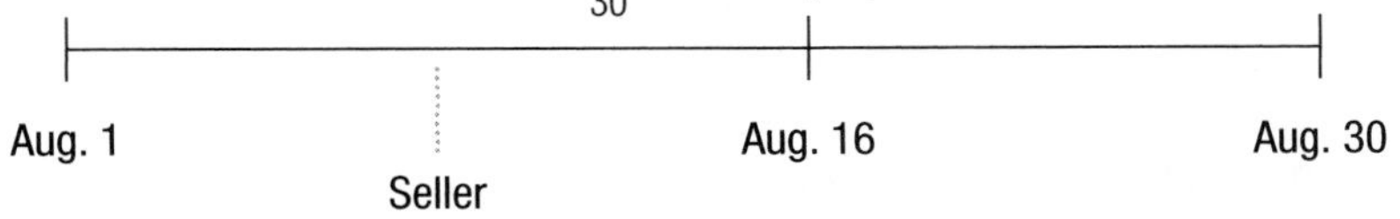


3. The buyer will pay interest for the entire month of August. The seller owes the buyer his "share" of the month's interest. The seller's share is calculated by multiplying the number of days the seller owes interest by the daily rate. Debit seller and credit buyer that amount.
   $16 \times \$14.50 = \$232$
4. Debit seller $232; credit buyer $232.

## Other Double-Entry Items, Not Prorated

The following items appear in their full amounts on both statements, as a debit to one party and a credit to the other.

1. Sale price
2. Assumed mortgage
3. Escrow account on an assumed mortgage
4. Unpaid personal property taxes
5. Purchase money mortgage, or second mortgage from buyer to seller
6. Tenant security deposit
7. Fuel oil and gas remaining in tank (if applicable)
8. Cost of separately sold personal property (if applicable)

## Single-Entry Items

One of the first common mistakes in learning how to do closing statements is to assume that every time something is entered in one statement, it must be entered in the other statement as well. This is not the case, however, as can be seen for **single-entry** items, *those charges paid by the buyer or the seller to a third party such as an appraiser, an attorney, a surveyor, or a lender.* The closing statement reflects not only the entries prorated between the buyer and the seller but also payments to third parties, such as the bank and surveyor, who receive payments that only show as disbursements (debits) from one of these two parties.

### *Single-Entry Items to the Seller*

1. Credits, typically none
2. Debits
   a. Existing mortgage
   b. Delinquent real estate taxes. These are taxes for a previous year and are only the seller's expense, as distinguished from unpaid taxes for the current year, which are a debit to the seller and a credit to the buyer.
   c. Personal property taxes, paid directly to tax collector
   d. Deed preparation
   e. Excise tax
   f. Discount points, if paid by seller*
   g. Broker's fee, when it is the seller's obligation
   h. Balance due to the seller

### *Single-Entry Items to the Buyer*

1. Credits
   a. Earnest money
   b. A new mortgage loan from anyone other than the seller. (Note: Remember, a purchase money mortgage or loan assumption is a double-entry non-pro-rated item.) Some people have trouble thinking of a mortgage as a credit, but at the time of closing, the lender gives (lends) the buyer money to give to the seller.
   c. Balance due from the buyer
2. Debits
   a. New insurance policy
   b. Loan origination fee
   c. Deed recording
   d. Mortgage recording
   e. Title insurance
   f. Discount points, if paid by buyer*
   g. Survey
   h. Appraisal fee
   i. Termite inspection/WDI
   j. Buyer's broker fees

*Conventional, FHA, and VA loans now allow the buyer or seller to pay points.

## Personal Property Taxes

Personal property taxes seldom appear on a closing statement now that taxes on motor vehicles no longer constitute a lien on real property. Taxes on licensed vehicles are now assessed when vehicles are licensed instead of coming due January 1 of each year. These taxes are not a lien against real property and are not reflected on the closing statement.

Unlicensed vehicles, boats, single-wide mobile homes, and farm equipment still are listed as personal property, and taxes on these items constitute liens against real property. Thus, taxes on these items sometimes appear on closing statements as "personal property tax." If the seller owns one or more of these items, on which taxes become due on January 1 of each year, personal property taxes may be included on the closing statement, depending on the date of closing and on agreement between buyer and seller. For example, if closing occurs before the tax bill is issued to the seller (approximately September 1), the personal property taxes may be entered as a debit to the seller and a credit to the buyer in an amount estimated from the previous year's taxes. The buyer is then responsible for paying the taxes when billed. If closing occurs after the tax statement has been issued but the personal property taxes have not been paid, they are likely to appear only as a debit to the seller and are to be paid to the tax collector from closing funds. In this case, the personal property taxes do not appear on the buyer's statement. Personal property taxes are never prorated. They are always the responsibility of the seller.

In some cases, personal property taxes are handled not on the closing statement but in some other manner agreed to by buyer and seller. Although not responsible for deciding how these taxes are handled, real estate licensees should be aware that personal property taxes may be due and, if due and not paid, constitute a lien on real property that must be considered at closing.

## PREPARATION OF CLOSING STATEMENTS

There are four types of closing statement: cash sale, purchase money mortgage, mortgage assumption, and new first mortgage given to a lending institution. All four of these are based on the same fundamental principles. The variation occurs because of the different manner in which the purchase price is paid by the buyer.

This chapter explains how to prepare debit- and credit-type closing statements. There are other formats for closing statements, but most are set up in this form. Additionally, the real estate examination requires that you have the ability to prepare debit and credit statements and to properly enter this information on the HUD-1 form.

The first step in preparing statements is to list all items in the transaction. Some of these items involve the buyer and the seller, other items are of concern only to the buyer, and a third category includes items of concern only to the seller. Entries that involve both parties appear in both statements, entries that involve only the buyer appear only in the buyer's statement, and entries that involve only the seller appear only in the seller's statement. The following are examples of these three categories.

The allocation of these items between the statements as well as the determination of whether an entry is a debit or a credit and to whom is mainly a matter of logic. *Debit* means the item is to be paid by the person in whose statement that item appears as a debit. In other words, it is an expense for that party. A debit can also mean a reduction in credits because of monies received to be applied toward the payment of a credit. *Credit* means the money is received by the person in whose statement it appears as a credit. A credit is also given for monies paid against an expense obligation in the transaction. These are discussed in the explanation of the illustrations that follow.

In the closing statement illustrations, each entry is based on the facts given for the particular statement. These are based, in most cases, on the typical allocations of the expense in a real estate transaction, and the usual rule is "He who benefits pays." You must realize, of course, that these typical or traditional allocations of expense items can be changed by the sales contract. In any given real estate transaction, the buyer or seller can agree in the sales contract to pay for various items normally paid by the other party.

Let's illustrate and analyze each of the four types of closing statement. For each type of statement, we provide a practice problem and solutions to the problem at the end of the chapter.

When preparing for real estate licensing examinations, practice is of extreme importance in the learning process. You've heard the old cliché "Practice makes perfect." It's true. To get the most benefit from the chapters in this book, including this one, you should do all the practice problems. If you have difficulty with a practice problem, go back and restudy the illustration for that type of problem.

## Cash Sale Statements

The cash statement is usually the least complex type because it contains fewer items. Following is a list of items involved in the transaction. The statement prepared from this list is a typical cash sale statement (see Figure 8.6). We also provide analysis of each entry. You should read and relate this analysis to each entry in the illustration of the completed closing statement.

Settlement Date: February 15, 20XX

Purchase Price: $95,000

Earnest Money: $3,000

Insurance Premium: $235 (paid by buyer)

Prorated Real Property Tax, Unpaid: $720

Deed Preparation: $25

Deed Recording: $3.50

Title Search: $315 (paid by buyer)

Termite/WDI Inspection: $75 (paid by buyer)

Excise Tax: $190

Broker's Fee at 7%: $6,650

**FIGURE 8.6** A cash sale closing statement.

| Settlement Date: February 15, 20XX | Seller's Statement | | Buyer's Statement | |
|---|---|---|---|---|
| | Debit | Credit | Debit | Credit |
| Purchase Price | $ | $95,000.00 | $95,000.00 | $ |
| Earnest Money | | | | 3,000.00 |
| Insurance Premium | | | 235.00 | |
| Prorated Real Property Tax | 90.00 | | | 90.00 |
| Deed Preparation | 25.00 | | | |
| Deed Recording | | | 3.50 | |
| Title Search | | | 315.00 | |
| Termite/WDI Inspection | | | 75.00 | |
| Excise Tax | 190.00 | | | |
| Broker's Fee | 6,650.00 | | | |
| **Total Debit/Credit** | **$6,955.00** | **$95,000.00** | **$95,628.50** | **$3,090.00** |
| Balance Due from Buyer | | | | 92,538.50 |
| Balance Due to Seller | 88,045.00 | | | |
| **Totals** | **$95,000.00** | **$95,000.00** | **$95,628.50** | **$95,628.50** |

## Analysis of the Cash Sale Statement

**Settlement date.** The settlement date for this transaction is February 15, 20XX. This is the date on which the closing took place. It is the calendar basis for all prorations in the closing statement. In making prorations, the day of closing or settlement date is always charged to the seller. The expenses for this date in a prorated item are to be paid by the seller. For the purposes of this text and the North Carolina licensing examination, all prorations are performed on a 30-day month; therefore, there are 360 days in a year.

**Purchase price.** Both buyer and seller are involved with the purchase price. The buyer is paying, and the seller is receiving. Since the buyer is paying, this is an expense and, therefore, appears as a debit in her statement. The seller is receiving, in gross, the corresponding amount; therefore, this is a credit to the seller in the amount of $95,000.

**Earnest money.** When the buyer entered into the contract of sale with the seller, she made a deposit of $3,000 in the form of earnest money, escrow money, or binder, as it is called. The buyer receives credit in the statement for having paid this $3,000. This money is usually held in the broker's trust or escrow account until closing. The broker brings a check for the $3,000 to the closing for the benefit of the buyer if he has not already transferred those funds to the attorney's trust account within the ten days prior to closing. This money is available at the closing to be applied to the buyer's obligations in the purchase.

**Insurance premium.** Every buyer wants to be protected against a financial loss resulting from a total or partial destruction of the property. Therefore, the buyer must have in force at closing a hazard insurance policy. This policy is for the buyer's benefit; therefore, it is an expense to the buyer—in this case, $235 appears as a debit to the buyer if it is paid by the closing attorney from buyer's funds as in this case. If the buyer has prepaid the policy premium before closing, it shows on the HUD-1 as **paid outside closing** (P.O.C.) and is not included in total debt.

**Prorated real property taxes.** The real property taxes are $720 for the calendar year starting January 1 and ending December 31. As the facts set forth, these taxes are not paid. At the end of the year, when the tax bill is due, the property will, of course, belong to the buyer. If the real property taxes are unpaid, they will constitute a tax lien against the property. To make an equitable distribution of these taxes as of the date of closing, the seller's share is collected at closing by debiting the seller the prorated amount of the tax bill and giving a corresponding credit to the buyer in the buyer's statement. The seller's share is for 45 days (January 1–February 15) of taxes at $2 per day, providing an entry of $90 debit to seller and credit to buyer.

**Deed preparation.** In the sales contract, the seller agreed to convey a marketable title to the buyer. To accomplish this conveyance, the seller must deliver a valid deed to the buyer and therefore retains an attorney to prepare this deed. Consequently, the cost of the deed preparation is an expense to the seller. In this illustration, there is an attorney's fee in the amount of $25 for this service. This $25 is entered as a debit (expense) to the seller in the seller's statement only.

**Deed recording.** The purpose of recording the deed is to protect the title for the buyer. Therefore, the buyer usually pays this recording fee. An expense to the buyer is entered as a debit in the amount of $3.50.

**Title search.** The data indicate that the buyer is to pay a fee to an attorney in the amount of $315 for a title search. The buyer has retained an attorney to perform this search to ensure that she is, in fact, receiving a marketable title from the seller. The attorney's fee for this service is an expense to the buyer; therefore, it is entered as a debit in the buyer's statement.

**Wood-destroying insect inspection.** When a new loan is involved, the lender usually requires an inspection for wood-destroying insects, commonly called a termite or WDI inspection or report, within 30 days before closing. It is for the buyer's benefit; therefore, the buyer usually pays. Because termites are endemic in North Carolina, this inspection should be performed even when not required by a lender. In our example, the buyer is debited $75. It is, however, an inspection for all wood-destroying insects including, but not limited to, termites, wood bores, and powder post beetles.

**Excise tax.** North Carolina requires that the seller pay an excise tax on the transfer of interests in real estate. To review the amount and calculation of this cost, as discussed in Chapter 3, recall that the tax is calculated as $1 for every $500 or fraction thereof of purchase price. The excise tax on the $95,000 sale price at $1 per 500 is $190, which appears as a debit to the seller.

**Broker's fee.** In the listing contract, the seller hired the broker to market the property. In this agreement, the seller agreed to pay the broker a commission of 7 percent of the property's final sales price of $95,000. Therefore, there is an entry of $6650 as a debit to the seller.

**Balance due from buyer.** This is the amount of money the buyer must pay at closing to satisfy her obligations in the transaction. The combination of the $3,000 earnest money, the prorated tax, and the $92,538.50 balance due from buyer will fulfill the financial responsibility.

The balance due from the buyer is obtained by totaling the buyer's debit column. This total shown on the statement is $95,628.50. The buyer's credits are subtracted from this total. These credits are $3,000 earnest money and $90 for the seller's share of the real property taxes. The total of these two credits is subtracted from the total of the buyer's debit column. The result is the difference between the buyer's debits and credits. The buyer has $92,538.50 less in credits than in debits. Therefore, the buyer must pay this amount at closing to satisfy her obligations. This amount is entered in the buyer's credit column because the buyer paid it at closing. Remember, this is a historical document prepared in advance. This is the amount the buyer must pay at closing or there will be no closing. The buyer's debit and credit columns are identical in total.

**Balance due to seller.** In this illustration, the seller has only one credit, which is the $95,000 purchase price. The seller's debits are subtracted from this credit. These debits are prorated real property taxes, deed preparation, excise tax, and broker's fee. Subtracting the total of these debits from the $95,000 credit establishes a difference of $88,045. The seller has $88,045 more in credits than in debits. Therefore, to satisfy the obligations due him at closing, the seller must receive a check in this amount. Since the seller received this check at closing, it is entered as a debit. Again, if the seller does not receive this amount, there will be no closing. With the entry of the amount due seller, the seller's debit and credit columns are equal.

**Other comments.** Notice that the totals of the buyer's statement and seller's statement are different. The reason for this is that the two statements are not completely related. The buyer has certain expenses and credits that are different from the seller's expenses and credits, therefore, the two statement totals are not the same.

Another entry sometimes seen in the seller's statement for a cash sale transaction is the satisfaction of the seller's existing mortgage. In the preceding illustration, if the seller had a mortgage on the property, he would need to pay this off to convey a clear title to the buyer. The cost of paying off such a mortgage by the seller would be an expense to the seller. Therefore, the cost of a seller's mortgage satisfaction would be a debit in the seller's statement and no corresponding credit in the buyer's statement because the buyer is not involved in this cost.

## Purchase Money Mortgage Closing Statement

This type of closing statement involves a mortgage given by the buyer to the seller for part of the purchase price. The seller is financing the sale of the property to the extent of the amount

**Practice—Practice—Practice**

As the old joke goes, a fellow stops another person on the street and asks him, "Hey, buddy. How do you get to Carnegie Hall?" to which, of course, the answer is "Practice!" How do you learn to do closing statements? There is only one way to learn, and that is to practice, practice, practice. You will learn how to complete closing statements once you put the pencil to the paper and do some yourself. There are four practice problems at the end of this chapter.

*(See Practice Problem 1: Cash Sale at the end of this chapter for an opportunity to apply the information covered in this section.)*

of the mortgage taken from the buyer; therefore, a purchase money mortgage is associated with owner financing. The discussion of this type of statement, as well as the next two, uses various terms to identify a mortgage. These terms are mortgage, deed of trust, and trust deed. For the purpose of closing statements, these terms are interchangeable.

Now look at a typical list of items to be accounted for by the statements for buyer and seller.

Settlement Date: September 27, 20XX

Purchase Price: $160,000

Earnest Money: $2,000

Insurance Policy: The seller paid $240 for a full year in advance; the effective date was February 1. At closing, the buyer is purchasing the remaining portion of the policy from the seller.

Real Property Tax: $536 (unpaid)

Personal Property Tax: $180

Purchase Money Mortgage: $95,000

Seller's Mortgage Satisfaction: $5,000

Termite/WDI Inspection: $75

Deed Preparation: $40

Mortgage and Note Preparation: $45

Deed Recording: $3.50

Mortgage Recording: $4.50

Title Search: $300

Excise Tax: $320

Broker's Fee: 6% of Purchase Price

Figure 8.7 shows closing statements for the buyer and seller that would result from this information.

## Analysis of the Purchase Money Mortgage Statement

In this analysis, we discuss only entries not covered in the analysis of the cash sale statement (see Figure 8.7).

**Insurance prorated.** This is the first time a prorated insurance premium has been introduced. In this example, the seller paid a full year's premium in advance, and the buyer is purchasing the unused portion of the policy for the remainder of the premium year. The seller paid $240 for a year (assume 360 days per year), and the effective date was February 1. The seller used only a portion of the year; the full months of February through August, which is $7 \times 30 = 210$ days, plus the 27 days of September, for a total of 237 days. Therefore, the dollar amount used is $158. When the amount used is subtracted from the full payment price of $240, you can see that the seller is due a refund of $82 (study Figure 8.8 for the calculations). Since the buyer is purchasing this remainder of the policy from the seller, the $82 is entered as a debit to the buyer and a corresponding credit to the seller.

**Personal property tax.** Closing is September 27, 20XX. Seller has received the tax bill but has not paid it. Personal property tax is paid directly to the tax collector; therefore, it is a debit to the seller and does not appear on the buyer's statement.

**Purchase money mortgage.** This is another new entry. The buyer is given credit for having given the seller a purchase money mortgage at closing. This is treated as though the buyer had given the seller $95,000 in cash toward the purchase price obligation of $160,000. A mortgage is an obligation to pay money, typically with interest, over a period

**FIGURE 8.7** Purchase money mortgage closing statement.

| Settlement Date: September 27, 20XX | Seller's Statement | | Buyer's Statement | |
|---|---|---|---|---|
| | Debit | Credit | Debit | Credit |
| Purchase Price | $ | $160,000.00 | $160,000.00 | $ |
| Earnest Money | | | | 2,000.00 |
| Insurance Prorated | | 82.00 | 82.00 | |
| Prorated Real Property Tax | 397.53 | | | 397.53 |
| Personal Property Tax | 180.00 | | | |
| Purchase Money Mortgage | 95,000.00 | | | 95,000.00 |
| Seller's Mortgage Satisfaction | 5,000.00 | | | |
| Termite/WDI Inspection | | | 75.00 | |
| Deed Preparation | 40.00 | | | |
| Mortgage and Note Preparation | | | 45.00 | |
| Deed Recording | | | 3.50 | |
| Mortgage Recording | | | 4.50 | |
| Title Search | | | 300.00 | |
| Excise Tax | 320.00 | | | |
| Broker's Fee | 9,600.00 | | | |
| **Total Debit/Credit** | **110,537.53** | **160,082.00** | **160,510.00** | **97,397.53** |
| Balance Due from Buyer | | | | 63,112.47 |
| Balance Due to Seller | 49,544.47 | | | |
| Totals | $160,082.00 | $160,082.00 | $160,510.00 | $160,510.00 |

of time. The fact that the seller received this mortgage from the buyer at closing results in an offsetting entry in the seller's debit column. So for a purchase money mortgage, there is a credit to the buyer and a corresponding debit to the seller.

**Seller's mortgage satisfaction.** Here is an example of the seller's having to pay off an existing mortgage, as discussed under "Other comments" following the analysis of the cash sale closing statement illustration. To create a new first mortgage to be given by the buyer to the seller, the seller's existing first mortgage must be paid off. Since this is a seller's expense, the payoff amount appears as a debit to the seller.

**Mortgage and note preparation.** The buyer must have a mortgage to deliver to the seller; therefore, the buyer pays an attorney to prepare these documents. This appears as a debit in the amount of $45 in this illustration in the buyer's statement. If you are not sure about the posting of these other entries, refer to Figure 8.6 and the analysis. *(See Practice Problem 2: Purchase Money Mortgage at the end of this chapter for an opportunity to apply the information studied in this section.)*

## Mortgage Assumption Statement

Now look at a statement in which the buyer is assuming the seller's existing mortgage. The buyer is paying part of the purchase price by the assumption of this mortgage.

**FIGURE 8.8**
To prorate an insurance policy.

1. Identify the appropriate time period (i.e., anniversary date; e.g., Feb.1 to Jan. 31 of the next year).
2. Calculate the number of days used; e.g., for closing Sept. 27:

| | |
|---|---|
| a. Full months used are Feb. through Aug. = $7 \times 30 = 210$ days | 210 |
| b. Days in settlement month | +27 |
| c. Total days used | 237 |

3. Calculate the daily rate; e.g.,

$$\frac{\$240}{360} = \$0.6666 \text{ (don't round off yet)}$$

4. Multiply days used times daily rate; e.g., $237 \times 0.6666 = \$158$.
5. If paid in advance, calculate the refund to be credited:

| | |
|---|---|
| a. Amount paid | $240 |
| b. Amount used | −158 |
| | $ 82 |

The seller's statement will show an $82 credit. The buyer's statement will show the same amount debited if he is assuming the policy from the seller.

In assuming the seller's mortgage, the buyer is agreeing to pay the principal and interest as well as assuming responsibility for the other conditions set forth in the mortgage contract. In this illustration, $49,000 of the $65,000 purchase price is being paid by the buyer in this fashion.

Settlement Date: November 13, 20XX

Purchase Price: $65,000

Earnest Money: $1,500

Annual Premium for New Insurance: $280

Real Property Taxes, Prepaid: $300

Seller's First Mortgage, to Be Assumed by Buyer: $49,000

Mortgage Interest: 9%

Termite/WDI Inspection: $70

Mortgage Assumption Fee: $135

Escrow Account: $300

Deed Recording: $3.50

Deed Preparation: $50

Excise Tax: $130

Broker's Fee: 6.5% of Purchase Price

Figure 8.9 shows closing statements for the buyer and seller that would result from this information.

## *Analysis of Mortgage Assumption Statement*

**Prorated real property taxes.** Notice that the closing date in this transaction is November 13, 20XX. With the closing so late in the year, the seller already paid real and personal property taxes. The seller is responsible for the real property taxes only for the portion of the year

**FIGURE 8.9** A mortgage assumption closing statement.

| Settlement Date: November 13, 20XX | Seller's Statement | | Buyer's Statement | |
|---|---|---|---|---|
| | Debit | Credit | Debit | Credit |
| Purchase Price | $ | $65,000.00 | $65,000.00 | $ |
| Earnest Money | | | | 1,500.00 |
| Insurance Premium | | | 280.00 | |
| Prorated Real Property Tax | | 39.17 | 39.17 | |
| Assumed Mortgage | 49,000.00 | | | 49,000.00 |
| Mortgage Interest Nov. 1–13 | 159.25 | | | 159.25 |
| Termite Inspection | | | 70.00 | |
| Mortgage Assumption Fee | | | 135.00 | |
| Escrow Account | | 300.00 | 300.00 | |
| Deed Recording | | | 3.50 | |
| Deed Preparation | 50.00 | | | |
| Excise Tax | 130.00 | | | |
| Broker's Fee | 4,225.00 | | | |
| **Total Debit/Credit** | **53,564.25** | **65,339.17** | **65,827.67** | **50,659.25** |
| Balance Due from Buyer | | | | 15,168.42 |
| Balance Due to Seller | 11,774.92 | | | |
| Totals | $65,339.17 | $65,339.17 | $65,827.67 | $65,827.67 |

during which he held title. Therefore, the seller is not responsible for the period from November 13 through the end of December. Since the seller paid the taxes for this period, he must be reimbursed by the buyer. This reimbursement for 1 month and 17 days of taxes is $39.17. The reimbursement is reflected in the closing statement by a credit to the seller and a corresponding debit to the buyer.

**Mortgage interest for November 1–13.** Transactions involving the assumption by the buyer of the seller's existing mortgage are concerned with the interest on that mortgage for the month of closing. Mortgage loans are set up so the interest is paid in arrears or in advance. In this illustrated transaction, the seller's mortgage interest was paid in arrears. In other words, the mortgage payment included a payment toward the reduction of principal and a payment of interest for the preceding month.

Payment on this mortgage is due on December 1, and with that payment, the buyer will be paying the interest for November as well as making a payment toward the reduction of principal. Since the buyer assumed the loan at closing, she is only responsible for 17 days of interest. When the buyer makes the first mortgage payment on December 1, however, she will be paying interest for the full month of November. Therefore, using the prorating technique, the buyer is credited with 13 days of the month's interest and a corresponding debit is entered to the seller. In this way, the seller is paying the interest for the first 13 days of November, while he was still responsible for the mortgage.

The mortgage assumed is $49,000 at 9 percent. Since the seller used this money for 13 days, the amount of interest he owes can be calculated by applying the Interest = Principal × Rate × Time (I = P × R × T) formula. The daily interest is calculated by multiplying the principal times the interest rate and dividing by 360 (days per year).

Multiplying by 13 days used:

$$I = \frac{\$49,000 \times 9\%}{360} \times 13 = \$159.25$$

**Mortgage assumption fee.** Lending institutions typically charge a small fee to transfer the mortgage record from the seller to the buyer who is assuming the seller's existing mortgage. The example shows a fee of $135. This is paid by the buyer who is assuming the mortgage; therefore, it appears as a debit to the buyer in the buyer's closing statement.

**Escrow account.** The seller has a mortgage escrow account with the lender for the purpose of accumulating the funds to pay the annual hazard insurance premium and annual tax bill when they come due. The NCAR Offer to Purchase and Contract (Loan Assumption Addendum) states that the buyer will buy the escrow account from the seller. The way to handle this on the closing statement is to have the buyer purchase this account from the seller on a dollar-for-dollar basis. The seller's escrow account balance is $300 at the date of closing. The seller will, therefore, receive a $300 credit for the amount of the account, with a corresponding debit in the buyer's statement to pay for the account.

*(See Practice Problem 3: Mortgage Assumption at the end of this chapter for an opportunity to apply the information in this section.)*

## New First Mortgage Statement

This is a transaction in which the purchaser is obtaining a loan from a lending institution. The security for this loan is a first mortgage given by the buyer to the lending institution.

Settlement Date: August 20, 20XX

Purchase Price: $194,000

Earnest Money: $2,500

Annual Premium for New Insurance: $382

Real Property Tax: $1,128 (unpaid)

First Mortgage: 80% of Purchase Price

Mortgage Preparation: $55

Title Insurance: $2.00 per thousand of Purchase Price

Survey: $175

Loan Origination: 1% of loan amount

Title Search: $360

Deed Recording: $7

Mortgage Recording: $10.50

Seller's Mortgage Satisfaction: $146,000

Deed Preparation: $60

Termite WDI Inspection: $50

Excise Tax: North Carolina rate

Broker's Fee: 7% of Purchase Price

Interim Interest at 8.5%: $403.09

The first entry in this closing statement that has not been discussed is the new first mortgage. The proceeds of this new first mortgage ($155,200) appear as a credit in the buyer's statement only. This money is available to the buyer to be applied to the satisfaction of his obligations in the transaction. Now three sources of funds are contributed to the payment of the buyer's cost instead of only two, as was seen previously. These are the buyer's earnest money deposit, the proceeds of the new first mortgage given to the lending institution, and the balance due from buyer that he is credited with paying at closing. Of course, the buyer has credits from the seller (in this case for the seller's share of the taxes), but these other three items are direct cash contributions by the buyer and available to the buyer to satisfy his obligations at closing.

Figure 8.10 shows closing statements for the buyer and seller that would result from this information.

## Other Costs to Buyer

The buyer's debit column lists a number of expense items associated with the new first mortgage. Two of these items require calculations. The loan origination fee and interim interest are based on the loan amount. In this case, the loan origination fee is 1 percent of the loan amount.

**FIGURE 8.10** A new first mortgage closing statement.

| Settlement Date: August 20, 20XX | Seller's Statement | | Buyer's Statement | |
|---|---|---|---|---|
| | Debit | Credit | Debit | Credit |
| Purchase Price | $ | $194,000.00 | $194,000.00 | $ |
| Earnest Money | | | | 2,500.00 |
| Insurance Premium | | | 382.00 | |
| Prorated Real Property Tax | 720.67 | | | 720.67 |
| First Mortgage | | | | 155,200.00 |
| Mortgage Preparation | | | 55.00 | |
| Title Insurance | | | 388.00 | |
| Survey | | | 175.00 | |
| Loan Origination | | | 1,552.00 | |
| Title Search | | | 360.00 | |
| Deed Recording | | | 7.00 | |
| Mortgage Recording | | | 10.50 | |
| Seller's Mortgage Satisfaction | 146,000.00 | | | |
| Deed Preparation | 60.00 | | | |
| Termite/WDI Inspection | | | 50.00 | |
| Excise Tax | 388.00 | | | |
| Broker's Fee | 13,580.00 | | | |
| Interim Interest | | | 403.09 | |
| **Total Debit/Credit** | **160,748.67** | **194,000.00** | **197,382.59** | **158,420.67** |
| Balance Due from Buyer | | | | 38,961.92 |
| Balance Due to Seller | 33,251.33 | | | |
| Totals | $194,000.00 | $194,000.00 | $197,382.59 | $197,382.59 |

Real estate agents should also know how to calculate **interim interest.** FHA, VA, RD, and conforming loans require payments on the first day of the month. (Interest must be paid for every day that money is used, however.) If a property closes on the first day of the month, the first payment will be due the first day of the following month. For example, if a property closes August 1, the first payment will be due September 1. If a property closes on any day other than the first of the month, the payment will not be due on the first of the following month, but on the first day of the second month after closing. In the above example, the property closes on August 20; therefore, the first payment is not due until October 1. The interest portion of the October 1 payment is for the use of the money during September (remember, interest is paid in arrears). The borrower has, however, used the money from August 20 through August 31 and must pay interest for that time (the *interim between closing and the end of the closing month;* hence, the term *interim interest*) at the rate of 8.5 percent.

To calculate the amount of interest per day, the formula is I = P × R × T.

Principal loan amount (80% of purchase price) = $155,200

Rate (percent) = 8.5%

Time = year

I = P × R × T

I = $155,200 × 8.5% × 1

I = $13,192 per year

I = 1 year's interest

I ÷ 12 = 1 month's interest

I ÷ 360 = 1 day's interest

Dividing by 360 provides the daily interest amount:

$13,192 ÷ 360 = $36.6444/day

*Note:* This could have been done in one step:

$155,200 × .085 ÷ 360 = $36.6444/day

In actual practice, the mortgage company will charge for every single day inclusive of the day of closing and the last day of the month; however, for test purposes, a 30-day month is used. If closing is on August 20, interest is due for every day from August 20 through August 30 inclusive; that is, 11 days. Remember, August 20 must be paid for, which means only 19 days were not used. Nineteen subtracted from 30 results in the 11 days used.

Multiplying the number of days by the interest per day provides total interim interest owed:

11 × $36.64 = $403.09

Many mortgage companies require this amount to be paid at closing. It is a single-entry item and shows on the buyer's closing statement as a debit.

*(See Practice Problem 4: New First Mortgage at the end of this chapter for an opportunity to apply the information in this section.)*

# THE REAL ESTATE SETTLEMENT PROCEDURES ACT

Congress enacted the **Real Estate Settlement Procedures Act (RESPA)** in 1974. It *regulates lending activities of lending institutions in making mortgage loans for housing.*

## Purpose of the Act

RESPA was enacted by Congress to:

1. Effect specific changes in the settlement process resulting in more effective advance disclosure of settlement costs to home buyers and sellers.

2. Protect borrowers from unnecessarily expensive settlement charges resulting from abusive practices.
3. Ensure that borrowers are provided with greater and more timely information about the nature and cost of the settlement process.
4. Eliminate referral fees or kickbacks that increase the cost of settlement services. In this regard, lenders are permitted to charge only for services that are actually provided to home buyers and sellers and in an amount the service actually costs the lender. Lenders are specifically prohibited from paying kickbacks for referrals.
5. Regulate reserve (also called impound or escrow) accounts for payment of property taxes and insurance premiums.

## RESPA Requirements

The following are required by the Act: * Also illegal to provide kickbacks to Mortg. Lenders.

1. *A good faith estimate.* At the time of loan application, the lender is required to provide the borrower with a **good faith estimate** of the *costs likely to be incurred at settlement* (see Figure 8.11).
2. *A home buyer's guide to settlement costs.* At the time of loan application, the lender must provide the borrower with a booklet currently entitled ***Settlement Cost: A HUD Guide.*** The guide includes the following information:
   a. Clear and concise language describing and explaining the nature and purpose of each settlement cost
   b. An explanation and a sample of the standard real estate settlement forms required by the Act

Lenders give GFE (Good faith estimate) in 3 days.

**FIGURE 8.11**

Lender's good faith estimate of closing costs.

| | |
|---|---|
| **ESTIMATED MONTHLY PAYMENTS** | |
| Principal and interest | ________ |
| Insurance escrow | ________ |
| Tax escrow | ________ |
| Mortgage insurance escrow | ________ |
| Other | ________ |
| TOTAL MONTHLY (PITI) | ________ |
| **CLOSING COSTS** | |
| 801 Loan origination fee | ________ |
| 802 Loan discount (points) | ________ |
| 803 Appraisal fee | ________ |
| 804 Credit report | ________ |
| 1107 Attorney's fee | ________ |
| 1108 Title insurance | ________ |
| 1201 Recording fees | ________ |
| 1301 Survey fees | ________ |
| TOTAL CLOSING COSTS | ________ |
| **PREPAID EXPENSES** | |
| 901 Interest to first payment | ________ |
| 902 Private mortgage insurance | ________ |
| 903 Insurance | ________ |
| 1002 City and county taxes | ________ |
| TOTAL PREPAID EXPENSES | ________ |

3 Laws for lenders:
1. GFE
2. HUD Guide

c. A description and an explanation of the nature and purpose of escrow accounts
d. An explanation of choices available to borrowers to avoid certain settlement charges
e. Examples and explanations of unfair practices and unreasonable or unnecessary settlement charges to be avoided

3. *HUD Form No. 1.* In making federally related residential mortgage loans, lenders are required to use a standard settlement *form that is designed to clearly itemize all charges to be paid by both borrower and seller as part of the final settlement.* The form has become known as **HUD Form No. 1,** or **HUD-1** (see Figure 8.12). This form must be available for inspection by the borrower 24 hours before final settlement if requested by buyer. In any case, it must be available at closing.

## The HUD-1 Settlement Statement

Real estate brokers are expected to be able to competently produce a HUD-1 settlement statement as a requirement of both the prelicensing and post-licensing brokers classes. Although this may seem a daunting task, the statement can be broken down into its respective parts with a great deal of ease. You will be expected to complete a HUD-1 on the course final and the state licensing examination.

The first thing to remember is that the HUD-1 is typically read from back to front; that is, the first page looked at is page 2. On page 2, there are eight sections. The first seven sections are where you place fees that involve the seller and a third party or the buyer and a third party. Generally, you do not see fees that are exchanged *between* the buyer and seller. Everything you see here is a debit to either the buyer or the seller. The eighth section is simply the subtotal of all of the fees on page 2. An important item to note is the position of the columns on the HUD-1. The buyer's column is on the left, and the seller's column is on the right. Remember this if you are transferring figures from your closing worksheet to the HUD-1.

The 700 section is probably the most interesting section to a new agent. This section deals with a well-earned commission. Most of the time, this is charged on the seller's side.

The 800 section deals with items payable in connection with the loan. These are the fees the lender charges to get the loan package prepared. Typical fees seen here are loan origination fees, discount points, credit reports, and appraisal fees. Unless otherwise stated or contraindicated by the type of loan, these fees are charged to the buyer. The rule of thumb, he who benefits pays, can be applied to this section. The loan is of benefit to the buyer, so he typically pays the fees.

The 900 section deals with items the lender requires to be paid in advance. These can include interim interest, a mortgage insurance premium, or hazard (homeowner's) insurance. These charges are also shown in the buyer's column.

The 1000 section is set aside for any monies that will be escrowed by the lender. An escrow account is established by the lender for the lender's protection. As discussed in Chapter 2, the lien with the highest priority is the property tax lien. When the lender ensures that the taxes are paid, he becomes the priority lien holder. Once again, the charges in this section are generally allocated to the buyer.

The 1100 section is a combination of two types of fee. The first type revolves around the attorney who is closing the loan. You will see fees related to her services, the title search, or document preparation, for example. The other type of fee that appears in this section deals with title insurance. The title insurance premium is shown on line 1108. Remember that title insurance may be obtained for the lender only or for the lender and purchaser. The buyer should be strongly encouraged to obtain a title policy covering her and the lender. Typical buyer charges in this section are attorney fees, title search (sometimes included within the attorney fees), and title insurance. A typical seller charge in this section includes deed preparation.

The 1200 section shows all transaction fees the city, county, and state government charge in connection with the closing. The fees include recording fees as well as excise tax (tax stamps). This may be the most confusing section when trying to determine whether the buyer or seller incurs a fee. Use this rule: He who benefits pays. Does the buyer or seller

**FIGURE 8.12** HUD Form No. 1.

OMB NO. 2502-0265

| A. U.S. DEPARTMENT OF HOUSING & URBAN DEVELOPMENT<br>**SETTLEMENT STATEMENT** | B. TYPE OF LOAN: |
|---|---|
| | 1.☐FHA 2.☐FmHA 3.☐CONV. UNINS. 4.☐VA 5.☐CONV. INS. |
| | 6. FILE NUMBER: TESTKECK / 7. LOAN NUMBER: |
| | 8. MORTGAGE INS CASE NUMBER: |

C. NOTE: *This form is furnished to give you a statement of actual settlement costs. Amounts paid to and by the settlement agent are shown. Items marked "[POC]" were paid outside the closing; they are shown here for informational purposes and are not included in the totals.*

1.0 3/98 Template File DEFAULT.PFT

| D. NAME AND ADDRESS OF BORROWER: | E. NAME AND ADDRESS OF SELLER: | F. NAME AND ADDRESS OF LENDER: |
|---|---|---|
| G. PROPERTY LOCATION: | H. SETTLEMENT AGENT:<br>PLACE OF SETTLEMENT | I. SETTLEMENT DATE: |

| J. SUMMARY OF BORROWER'S TRANSACTION | |
|---|---|
| **100. GROSS AMOUNT DUE FROM BORROWER:** | |
| 101. Contract Sales Price | |
| 102. Personal Property | |
| 103. Settlement Charges to Borrower (Line 1400) | |
| 104. | |
| 105. | |
| *Adjustments For Items Paid By Seller in advance* | |
| 106. City/Town Taxes to | |
| 107. County Taxes to | |
| 108. Assessments to | |
| 109. | |
| 110. | |
| 111. | |
| 112. | |
| *120. GROSS AMOUNT DUE FROM BORROWER* | |
| **200. AMOUNTS PAID BY OR IN BEHALF OF BORROWER:** | |
| 201. Deposit or earnest money | |
| 202. Principal Amount of New Loan(s) | |
| 203. Existing loan(s) taken subject to | |
| 204. | |
| 205. | |
| 206. | |
| 207. | |
| 208. | |
| 209. | |
| *Adjustments For Items Unpaid By Seller* | |
| 210. City/Town Taxes to | |
| 211. County Taxes to | |
| 212. Assessments to | |
| 213. | |
| 214. | |
| 215. | |
| 216. | |
| 217. | |
| 218. | |
| 219. | |
| *220. TOTAL PAID BY/FOR BORROWER* | |
| **300. CASH AT SETTLEMENT FROM/TO BORROWER:** | |
| 301. Gross Amount Due From Borrower (Line 120) | |
| 302. Less Amount Paid By/For Borrower (Line 220) | ( ) |
| *303. CASH ( FROM ) ( TO ) BORROWER* | 0.00 |

| K. SUMMARY OF SELLER'S TRANSACTION | |
|---|---|
| **400. GROSS AMOUNT DUE TO SELLER:** | |
| 401. Contract Sales Price | |
| 402. Personal Property | |
| 403. | |
| 404. | |
| 405. | |
| *Adjustments For Items Paid By Seller in advance* | |
| 406. City/Town Taxes to | |
| 407. County Taxes to | |
| 408. Assessments to | |
| 409. | |
| 410. | |
| 411. | |
| 412. | |
| *420. GROSS AMOUNT DUE TO SELLER* | |
| **500. REDUCTIONS IN AMOUNT DUE TO SELLER:** | |
| 501. Excess Deposit (See Instructions) | |
| 502. Settlement Charges to Seller (Line 1400) | |
| 503. Existing loan(s) taken subject to | |
| 504. Payoff of first Mortgage | |
| 505. Payoff of second Mortgage | |
| 506. | |
| 507. | |
| 508. | |
| 509. | |
| *Adjustments For Items Unpaid By Seller* | |
| 510. City/Town Taxes to | |
| 511. County Taxes to | |
| 512. Assessments to | |
| 513. | |
| 514. | |
| 515. | |
| 516. | |
| 517. | |
| 518. | |
| 519. | |
| *520. TOTAL REDUCTION AMOUNT DUE SELLER* | |
| **600. CASH AT SETTLEMENT TO/FROM SELLER:** | |
| 601. Gross Amount Due To Seller (Line 420) | |
| 602. Less Reductions Due Seller (Line 520) | ( ) |
| *603. CASH ( TO ) ( FROM ) SELLER* | 0.00 |

**FIGURE 8.12** Continued.

| L. SETTLEMENT CHARGES | | |
|---|---|---|
| **700. TOTAL COMMISSION Based on Price** $ @ 5.0000 % | PAID FROM BORROWER'S FUNDS AT SETTLEMENT | PAID FROM SELLER'S FUNDS AT SETTLEMENT |
| *Division of Commission (line 700) as Follows:* | | |
| 701. $ to | | |
| 702. $ to | | |
| 703. Commission Paid at Settlement | | |
| 704. to | | |
| **800. ITEMS PAYABLE IN CONNECTION WITH LOAN** | | |
| 801. Loan Origination Fee % to | | |
| 802. Loan Discount % to | | |
| 803. Appraisal Fee to | | |
| 804. Credit Report to | | |
| 805. Final Inspection Fee to | | |
| 806. Flood Life of Loan Fee to | | |
| 807. Tax Service Fee to | | |
| 808. VA/FHA Funding Fee | | |
| 809. Commitment Fee | | |
| 810. | | |
| 811. | | |
| **900. ITEMS REQUIRED BY LENDER TO BE PAID IN ADVANCE** | | |
| 901. Interest From to @ $ /day ( days %) | | |
| 902. MIP TotIns. for LifeOfLoan for months to | | |
| 903. Hazard Insurance Premium for 1.0 years to | | |
| 904. | | |
| 905. | | |
| **1000. RESERVES DEPOSITED WITH LENDER** | | |
| 1001. Hazard Insurance months @ $ per month | | |
| 1002. Mortgage Insurance months @ $ per month | | |
| 1003. City/Town Taxes months @ $ per month | | |
| 1004. County Taxes months @ $ per month | | |
| 1005. Assessments months @ $ per month | | |
| 1006. months @ $ per month | | |
| 1007. months @ $ per month | | |
| 1008. Aggregate Adjustment Fee months @ $ per month | | |
| **1100. TITLE CHARGES** | | |
| 1101. Settlement or Closing Fee to | | |
| 1102. Abstract or Title Search to | | |
| 1103. Title Examination to | | |
| 1104. Title Insurance Binder to | | |
| 1105. Document Preparation to | | |
| 1106. Notary Fees to | | |
| 1107. Attorney's Fees to | | |
| *(includes above item numbers:* ) | | |
| 1108. Title Insurance to | | |
| *(includes above item numbers:* ) | | |
| 1109. Lender's Coverage $ | | |
| 1110. Owner's Coverage $ | | |
| 1111. | | |
| 1112. | | |
| 1113. | | |
| **1200. GOVERNMENT RECORDING AND TRANSFER CHARGES** | | |
| 1201. Recording Fees: Deed $ ; Mortgage $ ; Releases $ | | |
| 1202. City/County Tax/Stamps: Deed ; Mortgage | | |
| 1203. State Tax/Stamps: Revenue Stamps ; Mortgage | | |
| 1204. | | |
| 1205. | | |
| **1300. ADDITIONAL SETTLEMENT CHARGES** | | |
| 1301. Survey to | | |
| 1302. Pest Inspection to | | |
| 1303. | | |
| 1304. | | |
| 1305. | | |
| **1400. TOTAL SETTLEMENT CHARGES (Enter on Lines 103, Section J and 502, Section K)** | 0.00 | |

Certified to be a true copy.

( TESTKECK / TESTKECK / )

benefit when there is a recording fee for a mortgage release? The seller benefits, as the lien no longer shows against him. Does the buyer or seller benefit when the deed is recorded? The buyer benefits, as the recording of the deed provides constructive notice that the buyer now owns the property.

The 1300 section is the catchall section. This section contains fees for the survey and Wood-Destroying Insect Inspection (also called termite inspection). It also denotes additional settlement charges, such as credit card payoffs, payment for repairs, and additional inspections.

The Offer to Purchase and Contract allows the buyer to request that the sellers pay some or all of the closing costs and prepaid items. This closing cost allowance is generally shown on page 2 of the HUD-1. Individual line items typically charged to the buyer are listed in the seller's column instead. This process is repeated until the total of the closing cost allowance is reached. You may also see the closing allowance on page 1 of the HUD-1 as a double-sided entry (credit buyer, debit seller) for the entire amount of the closing allowance.

The buyer's and seller's fees in Sections 700 through 1300 are totaled in the respective columns and placed on line 1400. These two totals are tested on the state exam. Now that page 2 is finished, look at page 1.

Sections A through I at the top of page 1 show the who, what, where, and when of the closing. These sections list the name and address of the buyer, seller, closing attorney, lender, the type of loan, loan number, location of property and date of the closing. The debits and credits are shown in the J (buyer's side) and K (seller's side) summaries using Sections 100 through 600.

The 100 section denotes all of the buyer's debits. They include the sales price, the total from line 1400 on page 2, and any other debits. The other debits generally arise from prorated taxes or assessments the seller already paid. Sometimes taxes paid at closing are shown in the 100 section as well. When taxes are paid at closing, they include the entire tax bill, which is paid to the taxing authority. Since the entire bill is paid, both parties need to be debited their share. You determine the share by prorating each party's portion. Remember that the figures recorded on the buyer's and seller's sides are not equal in this scenario because each one's share represents a different period of time. All of the debits listed in the 100 section are totaled and placed on lines 120 and 301.

The 200 section denotes all of the buyer's credits. The most difficult credit to comprehend is the loan amount credit. Many people view this as a very large debit. However, you should look at it from the standpoint that the lender is sending the loan amount to the attorney, not the other way around. The money is coming in to the closing table. Money in is a credit. The buyer also receives a credit in this section for taxes not yet paid. In most situations, the buyer is in possession of the property when the tax bill is due. The tax bill for the entire year is his responsibility, and he will be asked to pay it. The seller does not have a bill for just his portion. Since the buyer is required to pay both portions, the credit for the seller's portion needs to be given at closing. The other entries in this section include earnest money deposit, second loan amount, purchase money mortgage, and gift funds. The credits are totaled and placed on lines 220 and 302.

The difference between lines 301 and 302 is placed on line 303. Generally, this is a negative number representing the amount of money the buyer is required to bring to closing. A typical requirement is that this money be in certified funds. If 302 is larger than 301 due to a large earnest money deposit, for example, the difference is positive and the buyer will receive a refund at closing.

The 400 section denotes all of the seller's credits. Unfortunately for the seller, there is usually only one entry in this section, the sales price. There may be exceptions, such as the seller's prorated share of prepaid taxes, assumed prepaid insurance policy and payments for buyer's purchase of personal property or an escrow account in a loan assumption. The credits are totaled and entered on lines 420 and 601.

The 500 section denotes all of the seller's debits. In this section you enter items such as the seller's loan payoff, the total from the 1400 section, and prorated unpaid taxes and assessments. The debits are totaled and entered on lines 520 and 602.

The difference between line 601 and 602 is entered on line 603. This figure typically represents the amount of the check that will be disbursed to the seller. If you are dealing with a seller who has not owned the property for a very long time, you may encounter a situation in which 602 is greater than 601. In this case, the seller needs to bring certified funds to the closing table.

## SUMMARY OF IMPORTANT POINTS

1. The closing meeting is used in North Carolina to bring all parties together to execute the required documents transferring title to the buyer. Closing of the real estate transaction is the culmination of all of the agent's efforts. The buyer acquires title to a valuable asset, and the seller receives compensation out of which she pays her expenses of the sale.
2. The real estate broker is responsible for the accuracy of the closing statement, even though this document is usually prepared by another party, such as an attorney. The broker is also held accountable for the immediate delivery of the statement to all parties.
3. The real estate broker is responsible for the coordination of all details of the closing meeting, although an attorney usually conducts the meeting and prepares all of the documents.
4. Preliminaries to closing include property inspections, title examination, and drafting of documents, including the deed, financing instruments, and the closing statement.
5. The seller is responsible for preparing the deed, clearing any title defects, and providing receipts for the payment of taxes and utilities.
6. The buyer is responsible for title examination and insurance, hazard insurance, preparation of the financing instruments (promissory note and deed of trust), wood-destroying insect (termite) inspection (unless VA loan is used), and final inspection of the property.
7. The closing statement itemizes the expenses and credits for the buyer and the seller. A debit is a cost or expense to a party. A credit is income or something received by a party. Each party's total debits and credits must be identical, but the buyer's totals will be different from the seller's totals.
8. Prorating is the method of dividing expenses fairly between the buyer and the seller according to their respective responsibilities. The 360-day-year method is used for study and exam purposes. Annual expenses are divided by 360 and multiplied by the number of days used by a given party to calculate that person's expenses. All months are presumed to have 30 days for study and exam purposes.
9. Prorated entries include real property taxes (but not personal property taxes), an assumed insurance policy, and interest on an assumed loan. These items include a debit to one party and a corresponding credit to the other for their respective shares of the expense.
10. Not all double-entry items are prorated. Double-entry items not prorated include the purchase price, a purchase money mortgage, an assumed mortgage, tenant security deposits, and the escrow account on an assumed loan.
11. Not all items on the closing statement are double-entry. Single-entry debits to the buyer include cost of a new hazard insurance policy, title examination, title insurance, preparation of the financing instruments, recording fees, loan origination fees, credit report, and property survey. Termite/WDI inspections, well/water and septic/sewer reports, and discount points can be debits to the seller or the buyer, depending on the contract and other circumstances.

12. Single-entry credits to the buyer include earnest money, a new mortgage, and the balance due from the buyer.
13. There are no single-entry credits to the seller.
14. Single-entry debits to the seller include payoff of an existing mortgage, excise tax, preparation of the deed, any delinquent (versus arrears) property taxes, soil/site evaluation, utility bills, and the broker's fee. The final single-entry debit in the seller's statement is the balance due to the seller.
15. A useful check on the accuracy of the closing statement is to assume you are the attorney handling the collection and disbursement of funds from your trust account. You want to be certain the cash you take in is identical to the amount that is paid out. Funds received into your account include the buyer's earnest money, a new mortgage, and the balance due from the buyer. Funds disbursed include payments to third parties, such as insurance, inspections, loan fees, recording fees, credit report, survey, broker's fee, and balance due to the seller.
16. The four types of closing statement are (1) a cash sale, (2) a purchase money mortgage, (3) an assumed mortgage, and (4) a new first mortgage. Actual practice in preparing closing statements is the only way to learn how to do them correctly.

## ITEMS TO CONSIDER FOR THE STATE EXAM

1. *Double-entry items on the closing statement.* Students often do poorly when determining the proper entry of debits and credits. The best, if not only, way to work on this area is to make a list of debits and credits, single-entry versus double-entry, and double-entry prorated and double-entry not prorated for both parties.

   For example, how do the following items appear on the closing statement (consult the text to check your answers): buyer's earnest money deposit, a new first mortgage, unpaid real property taxes, prepaid personal property taxes, prepaid real property taxes, delinquent real property taxes, balance due to the seller, and balance due from the buyer? (Do the last two items need to be the same amount?)
2. *Closing statements.* The licensing exam requires the student to complete a HUD-1 form. The best way to prepare for this challenge is to study the four examples in the chapter and to do the practice problems on your own. Then transfer your answers to the HUD-1 form. Check your HUD-1 forms with completed HUD-1 forms provided by your instructor (or printed in this book).

## Practice Problem 1: Cash Sale

Use the following information to prepare statements on the worksheet. The solution to the problem is at the end of the chapter.

Settlement Date: May 4, 20XX

Purchase Price: $148,500

Earnest Money: $8,000

Insurance Premium: $294 (to be paid by buyer)

Real Property Taxes: $1,620 (unpaid)

Seller's Mortgage Satisfaction: $79,400

Termite Inspection: $50

Excise Tax: $297

Deed Recording: $5.50

Title Search: $485 (to be paid by buyer)

Deed Preparation: $35

Broker's Fee: 7.25%

*Note: No personal property taxes are allocated to the property.

PRACTICE PROBLEM 1 WORKSHEET

| Settlement Date: | Seller's Statement | | Buyer's Statement | |
|---|---|---|---|---|
| | Debit | Credit | Debit | Credit |
| | | | | |
| | | | | |
| | | | | |
| | | | | |
| | | | | |
| | | | | |
| | | | | |
| | | | | |
| | | | | |
| | | | | |
| | | | | |
| | | | | |
| | | | | |
| | | | | |
| Totals | | | | |

## Practice Problem 2: Purchase Money Mortgage

Use the following information to prepare statements on the worksheet. The solution to the problem is at the end of the chapter.

Settlement Date: March 15, 20XX

Purchase Price: $128,000

Earnest Money: $3,500

Insurance Policy: $540 (paid by seller for three years on November 30 in the year immediately preceding the closing; remaining policy value to be purchased by buyer)

Real Property Taxes: $1,440

Excise Tax: $1.00 per $500 of purchase price

Termite Inspection: $85

Purchase Money Mortgage, Given by Buyer to Seller: $100,000

Title Search: $415 (to be paid by buyer)

Seller's Mortgage Satisfaction: $4,400

Repairs: $300 (to be paid by seller)

Deed Preparation: $30

Mortgage Preparation: $35

Deed Recording Fee: $8

Broker's Fee: 7%

PRACTICE PROBLEM 2 WORKSHEET

| Settlement Date: | Seller's Statement | | Buyer's Statement | |
|---|---|---|---|---|
| | Debit | Credit | Debit | Credit |
| | | | | |
| | | | | |
| | | | | |
| | | | | |
| | | | | |
| | | | | |
| | | | | |
| | | | | |
| | | | | |
| | | | | |
| | | | | |
| | | | | |
| | | | | |
| | | | | |
| | | | | |
| | | | | |
| | | | | |
| | | | | |
| Totals | | | | |

## Practice Problem 3: Mortgage Assumption

Use the following information to prepare statements on the worksheet. The solution to the problem is at the end of the chapter.

Settlement Date: July 10, 20XX

Purchase Price: $99,500

Earnest Money: $4,500

Insurance Premium for New Policy: $278

Real Property Taxes: $900 (unpaid)

Assumed Mortgage: $72,000

Mortgage Interest for July: 9% (paid in arrears)

Mortgage Assumption Fee: $50

Purchase Money Second Mortgage from Buyer to Seller: $9,000

Seller's Escrow Account for Taxes and Insurance on Deposit with Mortgagee: $735 (to be purchased by buyer)

Deed Preparation: $30

Second Mortgage Preparation: $30

Deed and Second Mortgage Recording: $8

Title Search: $320

Seller gives buyer an allowance of $180 for light fixture being removed by seller.

Termite Inspection: $75

Excise Tax: $1.00 per $500

Broker's Fee: 7.5%

PRACTICE PROBLEM 3 WORKSHEET

| Settlement Date: | Seller's Statement | | Buyer's Statement | |
|---|---|---|---|---|
| | Debit | Credit | Debit | Credit |
| | | | | |
| | | | | |
| | | | | |
| | | | | |
| | | | | |
| | | | | |
| | | | | |
| | | | | |
| | | | | |
| | | | | |
| | | | | |
| | | | | |
| | | | | |
| | | | | |
| | | | | |
| | | | | |
| | | | | |
| | | | | |
| | | | | |
| | | | | |
| Totals | | | | |

## Practice Problem 4: New First Mortgage

Use the following information to prepare closing statements on the worksheet for a new first mortgage.

Settlement Date: July 18, 20XX

Purchase Price: $140,000 *

Earnest Money: $10,000 *Buyer credit

Insurance Premium for New Policy: $497 —Buyer debit

New 90% Conventional Loan: Calculate 4 discount points on the amount of the loan to be paid by the buyer.

*Real Property Taxes: $1,700 (unpaid) Debit Seller Buyer credit

Property Assessment: $1,540 for the year, unpaid, to be paid by seller

Seller's Existing Mortgage: $83,760

Private Mortgage Insurance (PMI): 1% of the loan amount

Deed of Trust Preparation: $50

Deed Preparation: $60

Credit Report: $50

Survey: $225

Termite Inspection: $125 – Seller debit

Loan Origination Fee: 1% of the loan amount

Title Search: $385

Termite Repairs: $650

Excise Tax: North Carolina rate

Recording Fees: $12

Broker's Fee: 6% of purchase price

Calculate Interim Interest at 8%

Discount PTS = Buyer debit

PRACTICE PROBLEM 4 WORKSHEET

| Settlement Date: | Seller's Statement | | Buyer's Statement | |
|---|---|---|---|---|
| | Debit | Credit | Debit | Credit |
| | | | | |
| | | | | |
| | | | | |
| | | | | |
| | | | | |
| | | | | |
| | | | | |
| | | | | |
| | | | | |
| | | | | |
| | | | | |
| | | | | |
| | | | | |
| | | | | |
| | | | | |
| | | | | |
| | | | | |
| | | | | |
| | | | | |
| | | | | |
| | | | | |
| | | | | |
| Totals | | | | |

### Solution to Practice Problem 1: Cash Sale

| Settlement Date: May 4, 20XX | Seller's Statement | | Buyer's Statement | |
|---|---|---|---|---|
| | Debit | Credit | Debit | Credit |
| Purchase Price | $ | $148,500.00 | $148,500.00 | $ |
| Earnest Money | | | | 8,000.00 |
| Insurance Premium | | | 294.00 | |
| Prorated Real Property Taxes | 558.00 | | | 558.00 |
| Seller's Mortgage Satisfaction | 79,400.00 | | | |
| Termite Inspection | | | 50.00 | |
| Excise Tax | 297.00 | | | |
| Deed Recording | | | 5.50 | |
| Title Search | | | 485.00 | |
| Deed Preparation | 35.00 | | | |
| Broker's Fee | 10,766.25 | | | |
| **Total Debit/Credit** | **91,056.25** | **148,500.00** | **149,334.50** | **8,558.00** |
| Balance Due from Buyer | | | | 140,776.50 |
| Balance Due to Seller | 57,443.75 | | | |
| Totals | $148,500.00 | $148,500.00 | $149,334.50 | $149,334.50 |

**Solution to Practice Problem 2: Purchase Money Mortgage**

| Settlement Date: March 15, 20XX | Seller's Statement | | Buyer's Statement | |
|---|---|---|---|---|
| | Debit | Credit | Debit | Credit |
| Purchase Price | $ | $128,000.00 | $128,000.00 | $ |
| Earnest Money | | | | 3,500.00 |
| Insurance, Prorated | | 487.00 | 487.00 | |
| Prorated Real Property Taxes | 300.00 | | | 300.00 |
| Excise Tax | 256.00 | | | |
| | | | | |
| Termite Inspection | | | 85.00 | |
| Purchase Money Mortgage | 100,000.00 | | | 100,000.00 |
| Title Search | | | 415.00 | |
| Seller's Mortgage Satisfaction | 4,400.00 | | | |
| Repairs | 300.00 | | | |
| Deed Preparation | 30.00 | | | |
| Mortgage Preparation | | | 35.00 | |
| Deed Recording | | | 8.00 | |
| Broker's Fee | 8,960.00 | | | |
| **Total Debit/Credit** | **114,246.00** | **128,487.00** | **129,030.00** | **103,800.00** |
| Balance Due from Buyer | | | | 25,230.00 |
| Balance Due to Seller | 14,241.00 | | | |
| Totals | $128,487.00 | $128,487.00 | $129,030.00 | $129,030.00 |

**Solution to Practice Problem 3: Mortgage Assumption**

| Settlement Date: July 10, 20XX | Seller's Statement | | Buyer's Statement | |
|---|---|---|---|---|
| | Debit | Credit | Debit | Credit |
| Purchase Price | $ | $99,500.00 | $99,500.00 | $ |
| Earnest Money | | | | 4,500.00 |
| Insurance Premium | | | 278.00 | |
| Prorated Real Property Taxes | 475.00 | | | 475.00 |
| Assumed Mortgage | 72,000.00 | | | 72,000.00 |
| Mortgage Interest for July | 180.00 | | | 180.00 |
| Mortgage Assumption Fee | | | 50.00 | |
| Purchase Money Second Mortgage | 9,000.00 | | | 9,000.00 |
| Escrow Account | | 735.00 | 735.00 | |
| Deed Preparation | 30.00 | | | |
| Second Mortgage Preparation | | | 30.00 | |
| Deed and Second Mortgage Recording | | | 8.00 | |
| Title Search | | | 320.00 | |
| Light Fixture Allowance | 180.00 | | | 180.00 |
| Termite Inspection | | | 75.00 | |
| Excise Tax | 199.00 | | | |
| Broker's Fee | 7,462.50 | | | |
| **Total Debit/Credit** | **89,526.50** | **100,235.00** | **100,996.00** | **86,335.00** |
| Balance Due from Buyer | | | | 14,661.00 |
| Balance Due to Seller | 10,708.50 | | | |
| Totals | $100,235.00 | $100,235.00 | $100,996.00 | $100,996.00 |

**Solution to Practice Problem 4: New First Mortgage**

| Settlement Date: July 18, 20XX | Seller's Statement | | Buyer's Statement | |
|---|---|---|---|---|
| | Debit | Credit | Debit | Credit |
| Purchase Price | $ | $140,000.00 | $140,000.00 | $ |
| Earnest Money | | | | 10,000.00 |
| Insurance Premium | | | 497.00 | |
| First Mortgage | | | | 126,000.00 |
| Discount Points | | | 5,040.00 | |
| Real Property Taxes | 935.00 | | | 935.00 |
| Property Assessment | 1,540.00 | | | |
| Seller's Mortgage Satisfaction | 83,760.00 | | | |
| PMI | | | 1,260.00 | |
| Deed of Trust Preparation | | | 50.00 | |
| Deed Preparation | 60.00 | | | |
| Credit Report | | | 50.00 | |
| Survey | | | 225.00 | |
| Termite Inspection | | | 125.00 | |
| Loan Origination Fee | | | 1,260.00 | |
| Title Search | | | 385.00 | |
| Termite Repairs | 650.00 | | | |
| Excise Tax | 280.00 | | | |
| Recording Fees | | | 12.00 | |
| Broker's Fee | 8,400.00 | | | |
| Interim Interest | | | 364.00 | |
| **Total Debit/Credit** | **95,625.00** | **140,000.00** | **149,268.00** | **136,935.00** |
| Balance Due from Buyer | | | | 12,333.00 |
| Balance Due to Seller | 44,375.00 | | | |
| Totals | $140,000.00 | $140,000.00 | $149,268.00 | $149,268.00 |

## REVIEW QUESTIONS

Answers to the review questions are in the Answer Key at the back of the book.

1. The amount of an assumed mortgage appears in:
   I. seller's closing statement.
   II. buyer's closing statement.
   A. I only
   B. II only
   C. both I and II
   D. neither I nor II

2. The amount of the earnest money deposit appears in:
   A. buyer's closing statement as a credit
   B. seller's closing statement as a debit
   C. buyer's closing statement as a debit
   D. seller's closing statement as a credit

3. If property were listed for sale at $130,000 and sold for $128,500, a 6 percent broker's fee would appear in the seller's statement as a:
   A. credit of $7,800
   B. debit of $7,710
   C. credit of $7,710
   D. debit of $7,800

4. The cost of preparing a deed appears as a:
   A. debit in the buyer's statement
   B. credit in the seller's statement
   C. credit in the buyer's statement
   D. debit in the seller's statement

5. If the closing date is June 30 and the seller's personal property taxes of $264 for the year are unpaid, the appropriate entry on the buyer's closing statement would be:
   I. a credit in the amount of $132.
   II. a debit in the amount of $264.
   A. I only
   B. II only
   C. both I and II
   D. neither I nor II

6. The proper entry on the closing statements for a transaction that closed on April 15 in which the buyer is purchasing the seller's insurance policy for which the seller paid an annual premium of $465 on November 30 would be a:
   A. credit to the seller in the amount of $290.63
   B. debit to the buyer in the amount of $174.37
   C. debit to the seller in the amount of $290.63
   D. credit to the buyer in the amount of $174.37

7. The day of closing is typically:
   A. charged to the seller
   B. charged to the buyer
   C. split equally between the buyer and seller
   D. it depends on the type of loan

8. In a real estate transaction, the buyer obtained a VA-guaranteed loan in the amount of $60,000. The lending institution charged 1 discount point, which the buyer agreed to pay. The cost of this point appears as a:
   A. credit to the buyer's statement of $600
   B. debit to the seller's statement of $600
   C. debit to the buyer's statement of $600
   D. credit to the seller's statement of $600

9. A buyer purchased a rental property and closed the transaction on July 20. The tenant had paid rent for the month of July in the amount of $600 on July 1. The rent should be shown as:
   I. a debit to the seller in the amount of $200.
   II. a credit to the buyer in the amount of $200.
   A. I only
   B. II only
   C. both I and II
   D. neither I nor II

10. The cost of an excise tax appears as a:
    A. credit to the seller
    B. debit to the buyer
    C. credit to the buyer
    D. debit to the seller

*For questions 11 and 12, use the following information:*
The contract purchase price for a home is $72,500, with a closing set for December 7. The seller will pay the excise tax, $50 deed preparation, and a 5 percent broker's fee. The balance on the seller's existing mortgage is $43,728.57. The buyer is obtaining an 80 percent conventional new first mortgage, with a loan origination fee of 1 percent of the loan, is paying $987 in miscellaneous costs, and has made a $2,500 earnest money deposit. The real property taxes are $900 per year, unpaid. Taxes will be paid at closing. The termite inspection costs $75.

11. What is the amount that will show on line 303?
    A. $12,574.50
    B. $12,649.50
    C. $13,699.50
    D. $13,799.50

12. What is the amount that will show on line 603?
A. $23,956.43
B. $23,958.93
C. $24,108.93
D. $24,951.43

13. A property sold for $151,050. The excise tax on the transaction is:
A. $151.50
B. $152.00
C. $302.00
D. $303.00

14. Provided nothing is written into the contract to the contrary in a loan assumption closing, a transferred escrow account will appear on the closing statement as a:
A. debit to buyer, credit to seller
B. credit to buyer, debit to seller
C. proration between buyer and seller
D. debit to buyer, does not appear on seller's statement

15. In a residential mortgage loan for the purchase of a property transaction, RESPA requires all of the following EXCEPT:
A. use of the HUD Form No. 1
B. a three-day right of rescission
C. a good faith estimate
D. the providing of *Settlement Cost: A HUD Guide*

16. Which expenses are typically prorated between the buyer and the seller on the closing statement?
A. private mortgage insurance
B. interim interest
C. commission to agent
D. real property taxes

17. Which item is ALWAYS a single-sided entry?
A. assumed mortgage
B. sales price
C. new first mortgage
D. rental income

18. In North Carolina, the closing meeting is typically held at the:
A. listing agent's office
B. selling agent's office
C. attorney's office
D. courthouse

# Chapter 9

## KEY TERMS

anticipation
appraisal
appraisal by capitalization
appraisal by summation
assessed value
book value
capitalization formula
cash flow
chronological age
comparable
comparative market analysis (CMA)
competition
condemnation value
conformity
contribution
cost
cost approach
debt service
depreciation
direct sales comparison approach
economic (external) obsolescence
effective age
effective demand
functional obsolescence
gross effective income
hazard insurance value
income approach
market value
mortgage loan value
net operating income
operating expenses
physical deterioration
plottage value
potential gross income
price
quantity survey method
replacement cost
replacement reserve
reproduction cost
residual income
square foot method
substitution
supply and demand
transferability
unit in place method
utility
value
value in use

# Property Valuation

## LEARNING OBJECTIVES

At the conclusion of this chapter, you should be able to:

1. Define the basic terminology of valuation.
2. Define the basic concepts of value, including appraisal, evaluation, valuation, value in use, and market value.
3. Describe the forces and factors that affect value.
4. Describe the economic principles of value.
5. Define the basic terminology of appraisal methodology.
6. Describe the general use and procedures of the direct sales comparison (market data) approach. Make simple adjustments to comparable properties to derive an indication of a subject property's value.
7. Describe the general use and procedures of the cost approach.
8. Describe the general use and procedures of the income approach.

## IN THIS CHAPTER

Real estate practitioners must have a good working knowledge of the principles of establishing the value of a given property. The Real Estate Commission holds an agent responsible for establishing an appropriate value for a listing and properly advising an owner of this value. If an agent recommends a value too low, the result will be a loss of money for the seller. In a like fashion, when an agent attempts to obtain a listing by telling the owner the property is worth far more than its true value, this is misrepresentation. In any event, the agent should be able to demonstrate the data and process by which she reached a conclusion of value. This chapter discusses the principle of valuation and demonstrates the three primary approaches to reaching a conclusion of property value. In addition to estimating property values for their sellers and buyers, real estate agents also need a good basic understanding of the process professional appraisers use in appraising real estate that is the subject of a sale or lease transaction.

## APPRAISER REGULATION

In 1989 in the aftermath of the savings and loan crisis, Congress passed the Financial Institutions Reform, Recovery, and Enforcement Act (FIRREA). One of the effects of this Act was to establish a regulatory system for real estate appraisers performing appraisals of property connected with federally related transactions. This includes the majority of real estate loans.

### Licensure and Certification

The North Carolina Appraisal Board operates a mandatory licensing and certification program, which enables real estate appraisers to become state licensed or state certified, enabling them to perform appraisals. An appraiser must be licensed to perform any appraisal.

### Comparative Market Analysis Exemption

Although not licensed or certified as appraisers, real estate agents are routinely involved in appraising real estate, usually to help a seller or buyer determine a property's estimated market value. Such an estimate of value is commonly referred to as a comparative market analysis (CMA). This is not considered a formal appraisal; therefore, it is not subject to the appraiser licensing regulations. However, the North Carolina Real Estate Commission holds the broker responsible for performing the CMA in a competent manner.

## BASIC APPRAISAL CONCEPTS

### Definition of Appraisal

An **appraisal** is, quite simply, *an estimate of value.* The term *appraisal* is also used to refer to the *act of estimating value.* While this term can apply to any estimate of value, in real estate, it is generally used only in reference to a formal, written estimate of value performed by a professional appraiser.

### Concepts of Value

#### *Value, Price, and Cost*

The terms *value, price,* and *cost* do not have the same meaning. **Value** results from *the anticipation of future benefits resulting from ownership of a particular property.* **Cost** is a *measure of expenditures of labor and materials made some time in the past*. Therefore, value is based on the future, whereas cost is based on the past.

**Price** is *the amount of money paid for a property.* Price may be more than or less than value or cost. Under normal market conditions, however, price is generally in line with value because the owner usually does not want to accept a price substantially less than value, nor does a purchaser want to pay an amount significantly in excess of value. The more knowledgeable buyers and sellers are about property value, the more closely related price and value will be.

Value is also referred to as *market value*. An appraiser estimates market value. *Price* and *market price* are used interchangeably.

#### *Market Value*

**Market value** is defined by federal regulations set forth in the FIRREA as follows:

The most probable price which a property should bring in a competitive and open market under all conditions requisite to a fair sale, the buyer and seller, each acting prudently, knowledgeably and assuming the price is not affected by undue stimulus.

Implicit in this definition is consummation of a sale as of a specified date and the passing of title from seller to buyer under all of the following conditions:

Buyer and seller are typically motivated.

Both parties are well informed or well advised and each is acting in what he considers his own best interest.

A reasonable time is allowed for exposure in the open market.

Payment is made in terms of cash in U.S. dollars or in terms of financial arrangements comparable thereto.

The price represents the normal consideration for the property sold unaffected by special or creative financing or sales concessions granted by anyone associated with the sale.

The Appraisal Institute, composed of the former American Institute of Real Estate Appraisers and the Society of Real Estate Appraisers, uses a definition that includes essentially the same factors.

### *Value in Use*

**Value in use** is *a special value to some person, usually the owner of a property. In this sense, the property takes on either a subjective or an objective value to the owner.* Subjective value may stem from pride of ownership and is probably not reflected by the general public. An owner often believes her property is worth more than its market value. The property's objective value to the owner may be an income from a use of the property for which there is little or no competitive market demand. In this case, the value in use may be greater than its value in exchange (the amount the owner could receive for it in money or other commodities).

## Valuation versus Evaluation

There is a significant difference between the concepts of valuation and evaluation. Valuation, or appraisal, is the subject of this section and is concerned with *estimating what the average buyer would pay for a property, or its fair market value.*

Evaluation is concerned with the economic feasibility of a project and can be considered in two areas: economic feasibility and land use.

An economic feasibility study might be concerned with the "workability" of a project, such as the development of a residential subdivision, office project, or shopping center. Before committing to the project, the developers would want to study the absorption rate of the market, that is, the effective demand by the public. Before financing a commercial project, a lender might require the developer to obtain a certain percentage of "rental achievements," that is, commitments for lease of a certain portion of the project.

A land utilization study evaluates what is the best current use of a given property. Often existing homes on a property could be best adapted to commercial uses. In the event of vacant land, one would want to determine if the land would best be developed for a residential subdivision or for commercial purposes.

## Types of Value

An appraisal is an estimate of value. Its usual purpose is to estimate the market value of a particular property. This is not always the case, however, as can be seen by the following discussion of assessed value, hazard insurance value, mortgage loan value, condemnation value, plottage value, and book value.

### *Assessed Value*

The **assessed value** of real property is *the value to which a local tax rate is applied to establish the amount of tax imposed on the property.* In North Carolina, the assessed value is supposed to be the same as the market value, but the reevaluation to accomplish this is required to be done only once every *eight years.* This eight-year reevaluation is called the octennial reappraisal and is mandatory. The county can appraise property more frequently than every eight years or can apply a horizontal adjustment to all or certain categories of property at the four-year point. This adjustment can be upward or downward to align the value to actual market value. A certain percentage adjustment is applied to all properties affected. The tax rate, however, can be changed *every year.* The tax rate is designated in dollars per $100 of assessed value. The assessed value, therefore, is divided by 100 and multiplied by the tax rate per 100 to calculate the annual tax bill.

## Hazard Insurance Value

In estimating the value of property as a basis for arriving at the amount of insurance that would adequately protect the structure against loss by fire or other casualty, an insurance company is concerned with *the cost of replacing or reproducing structures in the event of a total loss caused by an insured hazard.* This cost is calculated by multiplying a square foot replacement cost by the number of square feet in the structure. Land value is not included in calculating **hazard insurance value.**

## Mortgage Loan Value

In making a mortgage loan, a lender is interested in the value of the property pledged as security for the debt. In the event of a foreclosure, the lender must recover the debt from the sale of the property. Consequently, the **mortgage loan value,** *the value necessary to secure the repayment of the loan, is the dollar amount the lender believes the property will bring at a foreclosure sale.* Some lenders make a conservative value estimate, while others are more liberal; therefore, the mortgage loan value may be more or less than market value.

## Condemnation Value

When real property is condemned under the power of eminent domain, the property owner is entitled to receive *the fair market value of the property to compensate for the loss.* The fair market value is also known as the **condemnation value.** When an entire property is condemned, the condemnation value can easily be estimated. When only a part of a whole property is condemned, the problem is more complex. In such cases, the owner is entitled to compensation for the condemned property and for the loss of value to the remaining property. The amount for loss of value is typically greater than the value of the condemned property.

## Plottage Value

Plottage is based on the concept that the whole can be greater than the sum of its parts. **Plottage value** results from *the combination of two or more parcels of land into one tract with a total value that exceeds the value of the individual parts.*

## Book Value or Historic Value

This is *an artificial value used for accounting or tax purposes, in connection with establishing a depreciation schedule for a property.* Often this **book value** has nothing to do with the actual useful life of the property. For example, in 1980 the tax schedule assumed a property had a useful life of 40 years; in 1981 this became 15 years; then it was 18 years, then 19 years.

Assuming a residential property is assigned a tax life of 27.5 years, this would provide a straight line depreciation of 3.64 percent per year, or 29 percent for eight years.

| | |
|---|---|
| Original cost | $100,000 |
| 8 years' depreciation | −29,000 |
| Present book value | $71,000 |

## Additional Concepts of Value

For a property to have value, it must have certain legal and economic characteristics. The characteristics are (1) utility, (2) scarcity, (3) transferability, and (4) effective demand.

### *Utility*

**Utility** is *the ability to satisfy a need.* The property must be useful. It must be possible to use or adapt the property for some legal purpose. If the property cannot be put to some beneficial use and cannot fill a need of some kind, it does not have value.

### *Scarcity*

The degree of scarcity is based on the supply of the property in relation to the *effective demand* (see the section "Effective Demand") for the property. The more abundant the supply of property in comparison to the effective demand for property at any given time, the lower the value. Conversely, the fewer properties available on the market in comparison to the effective demand or bidding for these properties at any given time, the greater the value of the properties.

### *Transferability*

**Transferability** is a legal concept that must be present for a property to have value. Transferability is *what makes it possible for the owner to transfer the ownership interests to a prospective buyer.* These ownership interests include all of those expressed in the "bundle of rights" theory previously discussed.

### *Effective Demand*

**Effective demand** is *a desire or need for property that is coupled with the financial ability to satisfy the need.* In times of excessively high interest rates, many people with a strong desire and substantial need for housing are priced out of the mortgage market; therefore, the demand for property is not an effective demand because individuals who want to buy do not have the financial ability to satisfy the demand. In creating housing or other types of property, such as office buildings, shopping malls, and hotels, a developer must take into consideration not only the need for these types of property but also the financial ability of prospective tenants or purchasers to satisfy their need.

## Forces and Factors Influencing Value

The forces that affect real property value are (1) social, (2) economic, (3) governmental, and (4) physical.

### *Social Ideas and Standards*

Social forces include rates of marriage, birth, divorce, and death; the rate of population growth or decline; and public attitudes toward such things as education, cultural activities, and recreation.

### *Economic Forces*

Economic forces include employment levels, income levels, availability of credit, interest rates, price levels, and the amount of real property taxes.

### *Government Activities*

Governmental forces include regulations such as zoning laws, building codes, fire regulations, city or county planning, and regulations designed to promote or retard growth and development.

### Physical Forces

Physical forces are both natural and artificial. Natural forces include topography, soil conditions, mineral resources, size, shape, climate, and location. Artificial factors include utilities, proximity to streets and highways, availability of public transportation, and access.

## Basic Economic Principles of Value

### Supply and Demand

The economic principle of **supply and demand** is applicable to the real estate industry just as it is applicable to other economic activities in the free enterprise system. This principle states that *the greater the supply of any commodity in comparison with the demand for that commodity, the lower the value (high supply, low demand = lower value). Conversely, the smaller the supply and the greater the demand, the higher the value (low supply, high demand = higher value).* Therefore, factors that influence the demand and supply of real estate also affect property values—either beneficially or adversely.

### Anticipation

The principle of **anticipation** provides that *property value is based on the anticipation of the future benefits of ownership.* This is also stated as the present value of future income. Therefore, the future, not the past, is important in estimating the value of property. Changes in the expected demand for property can result from the creation of various improvements in an area, such as schools, shopping centers, and freeways. Therefore, real estate practitioners must be aware of plans for development in their local market area. There may be changes that will adversely affect the expected demand for property, resulting from such things as changes in surrounding land use patterns. Changes that cause an increase in demand will increase property values, whereas changes that cause a reduction in demand will cause depreciation.

### Substitution

The principle of **substitution** provides that *the highest value of a property has a tendency to be established by the cost of purchasing or constructing another property of equal utility and desirability, provided the substitution can be made without unusual delay.* Therefore, if two properties are on the market, each having the same degree of desirability and utility, and one is priced at $100,000 and the other is priced at $95,000, a buyer would substitute the $95,000 property instead of purchasing the $100,000 property. Simply put, buyers select the property that gives them the same amenities at the lower price. Substitution is the foundation of the **direct sales comparison approach** to valuation (see the section "Direct Sales Comparison Approach").

### Conformity

**Conformity** results from the *homogeneous or compatible uses of land within a given area. Adherence to the principle of conformity will result in maximizing property values.* Failure to adhere to the principle will result in inharmonious and incompatible uses of land within the area, with the consequence of depreciating property values. In residential subdivisions, conformity is achieved through the use of restrictive covenants. In other areas, conformity is accomplished through zoning laws and subdivision ordinances.

### Contribution

The principle of **contribution** states that *various elements of a property add value to the entire property.* For example, if a typical buyer would pay $5,500 more for a property with a garage than for the same property without a garage, the inference is that the element adds a value of $5,500 by itself.

This principle is used in the direct sales comparison approach to the value estimate in making adjustments to comparable properties in order to compare them to the subject property (the property that is the subject of the appraisal). For example, a subject property may have a fireplace, whereas a **comparable** does not. A comparable *is a recently sold property that is compared to the subject property (the property being valued) to determine the value of the subject property.* In making the appraisal, one must estimate the value increase resulting from the presence of the fireplace in the subject property compared with the loss in value resulting from the absence of the fireplace in the comparable.

The principle of contribution also applies to decisions regarding expenditures to modernize or improve a property. For example, will the addition of a garage or carport increase the value of a home sufficiently to cover the cost of constructing the improvement? This principle also applies to improving an investment property. For example, will the cost of improving the property by installing an elevator in a four-story office building be offset by the increase in rental income resulting from the installation of the elevator? In other words, does the elevator make a sufficient contribution to value in the form of additional property income to offset the cost associated with creating the improvement?

## Competition

The principle of **competition** states that *when the net profit generated by a property is excessive, the result is to create very strong competition.* For example, if a growth area contains only one or two properties of a certain type, such as one or two apartment complexes or office buildings, these properties will produce excess profits from rental income. The result is to attract a number of competitors eager to participate in the profits. Competition will cause a reduction in excess profits as the supply of competing services increases until excess profits are finally eliminated.

## Change

This principle states that change is continually affecting land use and, therefore, continually changing value. Every property and every area is constantly undergoing change; nothing remains the same. The only constant is that change will occur. Change causes an appreciation in value or a decrease in value. Change is constantly occurring, slowly or rapidly, in the physical and economic conditions of property. The appraisal is valid, therefore, only on the date of the appraisal. From a practical standpoint, lenders usually accept an appraisal for a reasonable length of time, barring dramatic change.

## Highest and Best Use

The principle of highest and best use is defined as "that possible and legal use or employment of land that will preserve its utility and yield a net income flow in the form of rent that when capitalized at the proper rate of interest, forms the highest present value of the land" (see Chapter 9 ). Land may be put to a variety of uses at any given time; however, there is only one highest and best use for a particular property at a particular time. The highest and best use of a property is different at different periods of time. For example, the highest and best use for land sometime in the past may have been for agricultural purposes, whereas the highest and best use at the present time may be for a shopping mall, an apartment complex, or an office building.

The highest and best use should be reasonable and probable and not speculative. It should be likely to occur soon, if not immediately. The highest and best use must be more than a dream. It must be physically possible, legally permissible, and financially feasible.

The principle of highest and best use can be illustrated by an example of the necessary activities and decisions to create an improvement on land to make the land productive. To accomplish the objective, there must be a coordinator who visualizes the investment opportunities and coordinates and employs capital and labor to create an improvement on land adhering to the principle of highest and best use. The coordinator or coordinators are typically specialists in one or more fields of real estate, such as a broker, builder, developer, or property manager. Assume the coordinators determine that the highest and best use of a particular parcel of land at the present time is to construct an apartment complex. The next decision is to determine the number of units to be constructed. Capital and labor are highly mobile, whereas land is immobile; therefore, capital and labor have the top priority on the income produced by the improvement. The remaining income is allocated to the land.

A coordinator's objective in adhering to the concept of highest and best use is to provide a **residual income** that, *when capitalized at the proper rate of interest, creates the highest present value of the land.* To accomplish this objective, care must be taken not to create an overimprovement or an underimprovement. If an overimprovement is created (too many apartment units are constructed), there will not be sufficient residual income for the land after the requirements of the coordinator, capital, and labor are satisfied. In other words, the investment in the improvement will exceed the ability of the improvement to provide sufficient net income to cover the priority demands and still provide a residual income that will result in the highest land value.

The same result will occur if an underimprovement is created (an insufficient number of apartment units are constructed). In this case, the improvement will not produce sufficient income to result in a residual income to create maximum land value.

The creation of an underimprovement or an overimprovement will result in depreciation of the property in the form of economic (external) obsolescence. Therefore, in adhering to the principle of highest and best use, the coordinator must establish not only the type of use but also the land's capacity to support a certain number of rental units.

The income allocated to the land as residual income under the principle of highest and best use is defined as *economic rent.* This is the rent the land is capable of producing when the most efficient use of the land is made to its optimum capacity. Rent that is agreed upon in a contract between landlord and tenant is called *contract rent.* The principle of highest and best use also applies to the construction of a single-family residence. For example, if it costs $125,000 to construct a home in a neighborhood of $75,000 houses, the result will be an overimprovement. Conversely, if a $50,000 house is constructed in an area of homes valued at $125,000 and up, an underimprovement will result. Consequently, the owner will have suffered a loss in value by not applying the land to its highest and best use in this location.

## THE VALUATION PROCESS

An appraisal is an estimate of property value based on factual data. In estimating property value, an organized and systematic program must be followed. The orderly progression of the appraisal process includes the following steps, listed in chronological order:

1. Define the appraisal problem. This includes the determination of the purpose of the appraisal and the type of value to be estimated.
2. Obtain a complete and accurate description of the property that is the subject of the appraisal. The appraisal report must contain a legal description of the property to locate and identify the property precisely. The identification must specify the limits of the area in the appraisal.
3. Inspect the surrounding area and the property to be appraised.
4. Determine the specific data required as the basis for the value estimate. Establish a separate estimate of land value, and perform a highest and best use analysis.
5. Analyze the data and arrive at a value estimate by three appraisal methods: market data, cost, and income.
6. Reconcile the results obtained by the three methods, thereby arriving at a value estimate.
7. Prepare the appraisal report.

1. The direct sales comparison approach
   *Compares subject property to similar properties sold recently*
2. The cost approach
   *Theoretically rebuilds the structure anew and then adjusts it to its present condition*
3. The income method
   *Applies the capitalization formula to the income (rent) produced*

**FIGURE 9.1**

Approaches to value (appraisal methods).

# APPROACHES TO VALUE

## Direct Sales Comparison (Market Data) Approach

This appraisal method is the primary approach for estimating the value of single-family owner-occupied dwellings and vacant land (see Figure 9.1). It involves a comparison of the property that is the subject of the appraisal with other properties that offer comparable utility and that have been sold recently. No two properties are exactly alike; however, many are comparable or similar in desirability and utility. In making the comparisons of the subject property and selected comparables, allowances are made for the differences by following the principle of contribution. A minimum of three comparables is absolutely necessary, and if available, as many as six comparables are appropriate.

Comparables should be as similar as possible in all respects to subject property. They may be found in real estate office files of closed sales, in the closed sales data of a multiple listing service, and from other appraisers. The more recent the date of sale of the comparable, the more valuable the comparable is to the appraisal process. Also of great importance is the degree of similarity of the physical characteristics of the comparable to the subject property and the location of the comparable.

### *Performing a Comparative Market Analysis*

Let's look at the sales comparisons approach portion of the appraisal process.

1. Collect all pertinent information for subject property by inspecting the property and acquiring necessary documents, such as deeds, surveys, and legal descriptions.
2. Enter information pertaining to subject property on CMA Worksheet (see Figure 9.2 for an example). An appraiser would enter the information into the Uniform Residential Appraisal Report (URAR) in the Sales Comparison Approach Section (see Figure 9.3). Enter the information obtained from your inspection with the homeowner, and proceed down the subject columns, entering all pertinent facts and amenities of the subject. No sales price or price per square foot can be entered at this time because that has not been determined.
3. Identify possible comparables from MLS data, real estate company files, or appraisers. Comparables must be closed sales.
4. Choose most suitable comparables by evaluating each possible comparable according to the following criteria:
   - Location
   - Size
   - Age
   - Lot/land value
   - Design
   - Type and quality of construction
   - Similarity of physical characteristics and amenities
   - Date of sale
   - Verified sales price
   - Seller concessions

**FIGURE 9.2** Sales comparison (market data) approach.

| Date: 12-9-CY | Subject Property | Comparable 1 | | Comparable 2 | | Comparable 3 | |
|---|---|---|---|---|---|---|---|
| Address | 524 Amortization Dr. | 602 Amortization Dr. | | 301 Acceleration Circle | | 12 Redemption Lane | |
| Sales Price | | | $192,000 | | $185,500 | | $182,500 |
| | | | Adjustment | | Adjustment | | Adjustment |
| Sale Date | | 11-10-CY | +$400 | 10-20-CY | + $800 | 6-11-CY | +$2,300 |
| Location | Good | Good | 0 | Good | 0 | Fair | + 1,000 |
| Lot Size | 150 × 175 (26,250 sq. ft.) | 140 × 170 (23,800) | + 500 | 150 × 170 (25,500) | 0 | 125 × 150 (18,750) | + 1,500 |
| Age | 5 | 6 | 0 | 7 | 0 | 8 | 0 |
| Condition | Good | Good | 0 | Fair | + 1,000 | Fair | + 1,000 |
| Square Footage | 1,800 | 1,900 | $-4,000 | 1,800 | 0 | 1,650 | +$6,000 |
| Bathrooms | 2½ | 3 | - 1,000 | 2½ | 0 | 2 | +1,000 |
| Style | Ranch | Ranch | 0 | Ranch | 0 | Ranch | 0 |
| Construction | Frame | Brick & Frame | 0 | Frame | 0 | Frame | 0 |
| Air Conditioning | Central | Central | 0 | Central | 0 | None | +$2,000 |
| Garage | Garage-2 Car | Garage-2 Car | 0 | Garage-2 Car | 0 | Carport-1 Car | + 3,500 |
| Driveway | Paved | Paved | 0 | Gravel | + 1,000 | Gravel | + 1,000 |
| TOTAL ADJUSTMENT | | | - 4,100 | | + 2,800 | | +19,300 |
| ADJUSTED PRICE | | | $187,900 | | $188,300 | | $201,800 |

Reconciliation Process

Comparable 1 $187,900 × 35% = $65,765
Comparable 2 $188,300 × 40% = $75,320
Comparable 3 $201,800 × 25% = $50,450

Weighted Average =$191,535 rounded to $191,600 indicated value of subject property

(Not all three properties are given the same importance. The appraiser has assigned the most weight to Comparable 2 since he believes it is most similar to the subject; Comparable 3, with the largest adjustment, is deemed to be at least similar and is assigned the least weight.)

**FIGURE 9.3** Uniform Residential Appraisal Report.

EDWARDS APPRAISAL SERVICE, INC.

# Uniform Residential Appraisal Report

File #

The purpose of this summary appraisal report is to provide the lender/client with an accurate, and adequately supported, opinion of the market value of the subject property.

**SUBJECT**

Property Address City State Zip Code
Borrower Owner of Public Record County
Legal Description
Assessor's Parcel # Tax Year R.E. Taxes $
Neighborhood Name Map Reference Census Tract
Occupant ☐ Owner ☐ Tenant ☐ Vacant Special Assessments $ ☐ PUD HOA $ ☐ per year ☐ per month
Property Rights Appraised ☐ Fee Simple ☐ Leasehold ☐ Other (describe)
Assignment Type ☐ Purchase Transaction ☐ Refinance Transaction ☐ Other (describe)
Lender/Client Address
Is the subject property currently offered for sale or has it been offered for sale in the twelve months prior to the effective date of this appraisal? ☐ Yes ☐ No
Report data source(s) used, offering price(s), and date(s).

**CONTRACT**

I ☐ did ☐ did not analyze the contract for sale for the subject purchase transaction. Explain the results of the analysis of the contract for sale or why the analysis was not performed.

Contract Price $ Date of Contract Is the property seller the owner of public record? ☐ Yes ☐ No Data Source(s)
Is there any financial assistance (loan charges, sale concessions, gift or downpayment assistance, etc.) to be paid by any party on behalf of the borrower? ☐ Yes ☐ No
If Yes, report the total dollar amount and describe the items to be paid.

**NEIGHBORHOOD**

**Note: Race and the racial composition of the neighborhood are not appraisal factors.**

| Neighborhood Characteristics | | | | One-Unit Housing Trends | | | | One-Unit Housing | | Present Land Use % | |
|---|---|---|---|---|---|---|---|---|---|---|---|
| Location | ☐ Urban | ☐ Suburban | ☐ Rural | Property Values | ☐ Increasing | ☐ Stable | ☐ Declining | PRICE | AGE | One-Unit | % |
| Built-Up | ☐ Over 75% | ☐ 25-75% | ☐ Under 25% | Demand/Supply | ☐ Shortage | ☐ In Balance | ☐ Over Supply | $ (000) | (yrs) | 2-4 Unit | % |
| Growth | ☐ Rapid | ☐ Stable | ☐ Slow | Marketing Time | ☐ Under 3 mths | ☐ 3-6 mths | ☐ Over 6 mths | Low | | Multi-Family | % |
| Neighborhood Boundaries | | | | | | | | High | | Commercial | % |
| | | | | | | | | Pred. | | Other | % |

Neighborhood Description

Market Conditions (including support for the above conclusions)

**SITE**

Dimensions Area Shape View
Specific Zoning Classification Zoning Description
Zoning Compliance ☐ Legal ☐ Legal Nonconforming (Grandfathered Use) ☐ No Zoning ☐ Illegal (describe)
Is the highest and best use of subject property as improved (or as proposed per plans and specifications) the present use? ☐ Yes ☐ No If No, describe

| Utilities | Public | Other (describe) | | Public | Other (describe) | Off-site Improvements - Type | Public | Private |
|---|---|---|---|---|---|---|---|---|
| Electricity | ☐ | ☐ | Water | ☐ | ☐ | Street | ☐ | ☐ |
| Gas | ☐ | ☐ | Sanitary Sewer | ☐ | ☐ | Alley | ☐ | ☐ |

FEMA Special Flood Hazard Area ☐ Yes ☐ No FEMA Flood Zone FEMA Map # FEMA Map Date
Are the utilities and off-site improvements typical for the market area? ☐ Yes ☐ No If No, describe
Are there any adverse site conditions or external factors (easements, encroachments, environmental conditions, land uses, etc.)? ☐ Yes ☐ No If Yes, describe

**IMPROVEMENTS**

| General Description | Foundation | Exterior Description materials/condition | Interior materials/condition |
|---|---|---|---|
| Units ☐ One ☐ One with Accessory Unit | ☐ Concrete Slab ☐ Crawl Space | Foundation Walls | Floors |
| # of Stories | ☐ Full Basement ☐ Partial Basement | Exterior Walls | Walls |
| Type ☐ Det. ☐ Att. ☐ S-Det./End Unit | Basement Area sq.ft. | Roof Surface | Trim/Finish |
| ☐ Existing ☐ Proposed ☐ Under Const. | Basement Finish % | Gutters & Downspouts | Bath Floor |
| Design (Style) | ☐ Outside Entry/Exit ☐ Sump Pump | Window Type | Bath Wainscot |
| Year Built | Evidence of ☐ Infestation | Storm Sash/Insulated | Car Storage ☐ None |
| Effective Age (Yrs) | ☐ Dampness ☐ Settlement | Screens | ☐ Driveway # of Cars |
| Attic ☐ None | Heating ☐ FWA ☐ HWBB ☐ Radiant | Amenities ☐ Woodstove(s) # | Driveway Surface |
| ☐ Drop Stair ☐ Stairs | ☐ Other Fuel | ☐ Fireplace(s) # ☐ Fence | ☐ Garage # of Cars |
| ☐ Floor ☐ Scuttle | Cooling ☐ Central Air Conditioning | ☐ Patio/Deck ☐ Porch | ☐ Carport # of Cars |
| ☐ Finished ☐ Heated | ☐ Individual ☐ Other | ☐ Pool ☐ Other | ☐ Att. ☐ Det. ☐ Built-in |

Appliances ☐ Refrigerator ☐ Range/Oven ☐ Dishwasher ☐ Disposal ☐ Microwave ☐ Washer/Dryer ☐ Other (describe)
Finished area **above** grade contains: Rooms Bedrooms Bath(s) Square Feet of Gross Living Area Above Grade
Additional features (special energy efficient items, etc.).

Describe the condition of the property (including needed repairs, deterioration, renovations, remodeling, etc.).

Are there any physical deficiencies or adverse conditions that affect the livability, soundness, or structural integrity of the property? ☐ Yes ☐ No If Yes, describe

Does the property generally conform to the neighborhood (functional utility, style, condition, use, construction, etc.)? ☐ Yes ☐ No If No, describe

Freddie Mac Form 70 March 2005 Page 1 of 6 Fannie Mae Form 1004 March 2005

Form 1004 — "WinTOTAL" appraisal software by a la mode, inc. — 1-800-ALAMODE

**FIGURE 9.3** Continued.

# Uniform Residential Appraisal Report

File #

**SALES COMPARISON APPROACH**

There are comparable properties currently offered for sale in the subject neighborhood ranging in price from $ to $ .

There are comparable sales in the subject neighborhood within the past twelve months ranging in sale price from $ to $ .

| FEATURE | SUBJECT | COMPARABLE SALE # 1 | | COMPARABLE SALE # 2 | | COMPARABLE SALE # 3 | |
|---|---|---|---|---|---|---|---|
| Address | | | | | | | |
| Proximity to Subject | | | | | | | |
| Sale Price | $ | | $ | | $ | | $ |
| Sale Price/Gross Liv. Area | $ sq.ft. | $ sq.ft. | | $ sq.ft. | | $ sq.ft. | |
| Data Source(s) | | | | | | | |
| Verification Source(s) | | | | | | | |
| VALUE ADJUSTMENTS | DESCRIPTION | DESCRIPTION | +(-) $ Adjustment | DESCRIPTION | +(-) $ Adjustment | DESCRIPTION | +(-) $ Adjustment |
| Sales or Financing Concessions | | | | | | | |
| Date of Sale/Time | | | | | | | |
| Location | | | | | | | |
| Leasehold/Fee Simple | | | | | | | |
| Site | | | | | | | |
| View | | | | | | | |
| Design (Style) | | | | | | | |
| Quality of Construction | | | | | | | |
| Actual Age | | | | | | | |
| Condition | | | | | | | |
| Above Grade Room Count | Total Bdrms. Baths | Total Bdrms. Baths | | Total Bdrms. Baths | | Total Bdrms. Baths | |
| Gross Living Area | sq.ft. | sq.ft. | | sq.ft. | | sq.ft. | |
| Basement & Finished Rooms Below Grade | | | | | | | |
| Functional Utility | | | | | | | |
| Heating/Cooling | | | | | | | |
| Energy Efficient Items | | | | | | | |
| Garage/Carport | | | | | | | |
| Porch/Patio/Deck | | | | | | | |
| | | | | | | | |
| | | | | | | | |
| | | | | | | | |
| Net Adjustment (Total) | | ☐ + ☐ - | $ | ☐ + ☐ - | $ | ☐ + ☐ - | $ |
| Adjusted Sale Price of Comparables | | Net Adj. % Gross Adj. % | $ | Net Adj. % Gross Adj. % | $ | Net Adj. % Gross Adj. % | $ |

I ☐ did ☐ did not research the sale or transfer history of the subject property and comparable sales. If not, explain

My research ☐ did ☐ did not reveal any prior sales or transfers of the subject property for the three years prior to the effective date of this appraisal.

Data Source(s)

My research ☐ did ☐ did not reveal any prior sales or transfers of the comparable sales for the year prior to the date of sale of the comparable sale.

Data Source(s)

Report the results of the research and analysis of the prior sale or transfer history of the subject property and comparable sales (report additional prior sales on page 3).

| ITEM | SUBJECT | COMPARABLE SALE #1 | COMPARABLE SALE #2 | COMPARABLE SALE #3 |
|---|---|---|---|---|
| Date of Prior Sale/Transfer | | | | |
| Price of Prior Sale/Transfer | | | | |
| Data Source(s) | | | | |
| Effective Date of Data Source(s) | | | | |

Analysis of prior sale or transfer history of the subject property and comparable sales

Summary of Sales Comparison Approach

Indicated Value by Sales Comparison Approach $

**RECONCILIATION**

**Indicated Value by: Sales Comparison Approach $ Cost Approach (if developed) $ Income Approach (if developed) $**

This appraisal is made ☐ "as is", ☐ subject to completion per plans and specifications on the basis of a hypothetical condition that the improvements have been completed, ☐ subject to the following repairs or alterations on the basis of a hypothetical condition that the repairs or alterations have been completed, or ☐ subject to the following required inspection based on the extraordinary assumption that the condition or deficiency does not require alteration or repair:

**Based on a complete visual inspection of the interior and exterior areas of the subject property, defined scope of work, statement of assumptions and limiting conditions, and appraiser's certification, my (our) opinion of the market value, as defined, of the real property that is the subject of this report is $ , as of , which is the date of inspection and the effective date of this appraisal.**

- Seller motivation
- Method of financing used by purchaser
- Terms and conditions of sale

*Location, size, and age:* These criteria can skew an appraisal if there are large differences. Location should be as close to the subject property as possible, preferably in the same subdivision and ideally on the same street. If no comparable exists in the subdivision or in the immediate vicinity of the subject, it is permissible to go to the closest subdivisions that are similar in price, style, amenity, and so on. It is preferable to compare county property to county property and city property to city property. Other factors that can be used to determine similar locations are school districts; proximity to shopping, churches, and other amenities; commuting distances to major employment areas; and so on.

*Large size differences can be especially problematic.* The smaller the size difference, the more accurate the results. The difference should be kept under 5 percent either way if possible. If size differences are small and there are no additional electrical, heating, and plumbing requirements necessary, the cost per square foot for the difference will probably be less than the total cost per square foot to build the entire structure. For example, if two nearly identical houses have a 50-square-foot difference and the smaller house sells for $100 per square foot, the extra 50 square feet in the larger house may be worth only $50 per square foot. The amount per square foot differs for location, age, quality, and presence or absence of amenities.

*Age:* Age difference, if significant, can affect the accuracy of an appraisal; therefore, it is best to compare properties of approximately the same age. Effective age, not actual age, is the standard used for determining value; however, chronological age is the proper one to enter on listings, MLS data, and so on. Both chronological age and effective age are noted on the appraisal. A 5-year-old home should not usually be compared to a 50-year-old home unless the 50-year-old home has been modernized to have a much younger effective age.

*Lot/land value:* Lots in different subdivisions can differ in price. Additional acreage, such as pastureland, may be of considerable value. Small differences in lot size in the same neighborhood usually require no adjustment.

*Design:* When possible, two-story homes should be compared to two-story homes, ranch homes to ranch homes, farmhouses to farmhouses, and contemporary homes to contemporary homes.

*Type and quality of construction:* Differences in types of construction vary from area to area. When possible, comparisons should be made between homes of like construction. A basic "spec" house built to minimum code is probably not worth as much as a custom-built house with hardwood floors, ceramic tile, an architectural roof, and upgraded appliances.

*Similarity of physical characteristics and amenities:* If one home has a pool, a hot tub, a large wired workshop, 10-foot ceilings, and a four-car garage, it may not be a good comparable for a similarly sized and aged home in the same neighborhood with a two-car garage, 8-foot ceilings, and none of the other amenities. The relatively recent increase in the demand for more and better car storage makes the number of garages, especially on higher-priced homes, an important amenity to consider. While an adjustment can easily be made for the difference between a one- and two-car garage, a home with a carport is not a good comparable for a house with a four-car garage.

*Date of sale:* In an appreciating market, the comparable's sold price must be adjusted upward since its value would have increased from the time of the sale until the present. In a depreciating market, the comparable's price would need to be adjusted downward (see Figure 9.4.).

Seller concessions: If a seller sells his property and pays $4,000 of the buyer's closing costs, the seller is actually receiving $4,000 less for his home, and the price must be adjusted accordingly. While appraisers were required to adjust for seller concessions in the past, they are no longer required to do so unless the concessions are excessive. In markets where seller concessions are the norm, they should be considered in the CMAand the listing process.

**FIGURE 9.4** When adjusting comparables to subject property, an appraiser must add to inferior properties and subtract from superior comparables to arrive at an adjusted comparison.

In this example, the inferior property has no garage, the subject property has a one-car garage, and the superior property has a two-car garage. The appraiser must adjust for these discrepancies.

*Seller motivation:* A distress sale may take place when a seller sells his home for significantly less than market value because he was facing foreclosure, bankruptcy, or divorce. This sale should not be used in a CMA/appraisal. If he sells for a reduced price to a relative or friend in a transaction that is not an arm's length transaction, that sale should not be used either.

*Method of financing used by purchaser:* The price may be affected positively or negatively by the type of financing. Properties sold with owner financing or as a loan assumption with a rate considerably below current market rates are sometimes sold at a premium price. Differences in financing between VA, FHA, and conventional loans are not as important now as in the past since government loans no longer require sellers to pay points and similar but not identical seller concessions are allowed on all types of loan.

5. On the CMA worksheet, enter data in the blanks one at a time for the three to six most comparable properties to subject.
6. Make the comparisons.

To understand the process of the direct sales comparison approach, refer to Figure 9.2. An important point to understand before using the chart is that the data values are the result of careful analysis of records maintained by the broker or appraiser. For example, a value of $3,500 for the difference between a two-car garage and a one-car carport is not an arbitrary number pulled from the air; rather, it is the result of carefully paired sales analysis data kept in the broker's files. Nor is the number the cost of building an element because, as explained earlier in the chapter, cost is not the same as value. To arrive at the proper value of an element, an agent must constantly abstract or reflect from the marketplace what the average buyer will pay for the element.

All of the data used in making the adjustments between the comparable properties and the subject property must be laid out in an orderly, detailed, and accurate manner, as illustrated in Figure 9.2. The comparison sets forth all of the property and nonproperty characteristics (such as location, physical characteristics, land or lot size, amenities, and condition) used in the value estimate.

Plus and minus adjustments are made to reconcile the differences and to arrive at a value estimate for the subject property on the basis of the price for which each comparable was sold. You always adjust the comparable, never the subject property (see Figure 9.4). Because you are trying to estimate the value of the subject property, it does not yet have a value to be adjusted.

First, an adjustment for the time of sale is made using an annual appreciation rate of 2½ percent, also derived from paired sales analysis data for the area. The sales price of the comparable is multiplied by the appreciation rate and divided by 12 to get a monthly appreciation, which is then multiplied by the number of months since the sale of that comparable.

Study the following example.

sales price $\times 2\frac{1}{2}\%$ = annual appreciation $\div$ 12 = monthly appreciation $\times$ number of months = appreciation adjustment

Comparable 1: $192,000 × 2½% = $4,800 ÷ 12 = $400 × 1 = $400

Comparable 2: $185,500 × 2½% = $4,637.50 ÷ 12 = $386.46 × 2 = $772.92 rounded to $800

Comparable 3: $182,500 × 2½% = $4,562.50 ÷ 12 = $380.21 × 6 = $2,281.25 rounded to $2,300

A plus adjustment to a comparable is made when the comparable is deficient in a particular respect when compared to the subject property. This is illustrated in Figure 9.2. The lot size adjustment of +$500 in Comparable 1 is made because of the smaller lot size of Comparable 1 in comparison to the lot size of the subject property. The adjustment indicates that Comparable 1 would have sold for $500 more had its lot size been as large as the subject property.

A minus adjustment to a comparable is made when it contains a specific feature that the subject property does not contain. For example, an adjustment of –$1,000 is made to Comparable 1 because it has three bathrooms instead of two-and-a-half, as does the subject property. Therefore, if Comparable 1 had the same number of bathrooms as the subject property, it would have sold for $1,000 less than it did.

Paired sales analysis data reveals that a gravel driveway is considered inferior to a paved driveway in the amount of $1,000. The subject has a paved driveway, as does Comparable 1; therefore, no adjustment is made to Comparable 1. Comparables 2 and 3 have gravel driveways that are inferior. If these comparable driveways were paved, the homes would have sold for $1,000 more than their actual sales price. Comparables 2 and 3 are inferior; therefore, $1,000 is added to their sales prices.

After all adjustments, the net adjustment amount for each comparable is calculated and the result applied to the price for which the comparable sold to arrive at an adjusted price. The adjusted price is an estimate of the price for which the comparable would have sold if all factors had been the same as the subject property. The adjusted prices of the comparables are reconciled to arrive at an indicated market value for the subject property. This reconciliation is a weighted average of the adjusted sales price of the comparable to determine a single reliable estimate of value for the property being appraised (the subject property). In 9.2, Comparable 2 is given the greatest weight (40%) because it requires the fewest adjustments and although this cannot be determined from the illustration it is located in the same subdivision as the subject property. Comparable #1 has slightly less similarity to the subject property than Comparable 2 and is only given a weight of 35%. Comparable 3 is given the least weight (25%) because it is located in a different subdivision and is least similar to the subject property. Note that the assigned percentage must equal 100% no matter how many comparables are used.

## Comparative Market Analysis

Part of the process of listing properties for sale by real estate agents is to recommend a market price that will be the listed price if agreed to by the owner. In arriving at this price, real estate agents perform a **comparative market analysis (CMA).** This procedure is *not an appraisal but is a presentation of the competition in the marketplace for this particular property.* The analysis takes into consideration properties that have been recently sold, as well as other properties currently on the market or sold, depending on the closing. The latter two should be used only if absolutely necessary and consideration is given to their diminished reliability. The client should be made aware of the reliability issues pertaining to the current listings and pending sales.

## The Cost Approach

The **cost approach,** or **appraisal by summation,** is the primary method for estimating the value of properties that are not single-family dwellings or vacant land and that are not properties that produce rental income; that is, they are unique properties. Examples include special-purpose buildings such as schools, factories, fire stations, hospitals, government office buildings, and libraries.

The first step in the cost approach is *to estimate the cost of reproducing or replacing the structure.* There is a definite difference between replacement cost and reproduction cost. **Reproduction cost** is *the cost of constructing an exact duplicate of the property when new.* **Replacement cost** is *based on constructing a building of comparable utility* using modern building techniques and materials. When a subject property was constructed many years ago, it is often impossible to estimate the cost of reproducing that property today. The materials and craftsmanship just may not be available. Therefore, the basis of the cost approach for older structures is replacement cost new. Reproduction cost new may be used for properties that have been constructed recently.

The procedure for estimating value by the cost approach is as follows:

1. Estimate construction costs to replace or reproduce the improvements.
2. Estimate total accrued depreciation of improvements.
3. Subtract depreciation of improvements from construction costs to determine value of improvements.
4. Estimate value of land using direct sales comparison approach.
5. Add the lot value to the value of the improvements to get the appraised value.

Methods of estimating reproduction or replacement costs include the quantity survey method, unit in place method, and the square foot method. Of these methods, the **quantity survey method** is the most accurate, but it is also the most complex and time-consuming. This is the method most builders use in calculating a cost estimate for a construction job. This method involves *the detailed determination of the exact quantity of each type of material to be used in the construction and the necessary material and labor costs applicable to each unit.* The final estimate includes a profit to the builder. The **unit in place method** is less detailed. The *cost of each component part of the structure is calculated, including material, labor, and overhead costs plus a profit to the builder.* The cost by the **square foot method** *is calculated by multiplying the number of square feet in the structure being appraised by the cost per square foot to construct the building using the current cost per square foot.* The estimated cost figures employed in any of these methods are available through construction cost services that publish construction cost estimates for various structures and structural components.

The next step in the cost approach is to deduct from the estimated cost of replacing or reproducing the property with new construction any depreciation resulting from any of the three forms of depreciation described next. The deduction of the dollar amount of depreciation provides the depreciated value of the structure as it exists at present. Next, the depreciated value of any other site improvement is added to the value of the structure to provide an estimate of the total depreciated value of all improvements.

## Depreciation Concepts and Definitions

**Depreciation** is defined as *a loss in value from any cause.* The loss in value is estimated by the difference between the present cost of constructing a new building of equal utility and design and the present market value of the depreciated property.

*Present* as used in this definition means on the day of the appraisal. Depreciation can be determined by three methods: age/life (straight line), market abstraction, and breakdown.

### *Age/Life (Straight Line) Method*

Several definitions are necessary to understand this concept.

The *economic life* of an improvement on a property is the period of time during which the improvement is beneficial to the owner. An improvement changes from totally useful to totally useless over its economic life, which is often more than 50 years.

The **chronological age** is *the actual age of a structure,* and the **effective age** is *the age the structure appears to be.* If a property is well maintained, it may appear to be younger than it is. Conversely, the apparent (effective) age may be greater than the actual age if adequate maintenance and modernization measures have not been taken.

An improvement's *remaining economic life* is the number of years it has left from the time of the appraisal to the end of its useful life. With these definitions in mind, the age/life, or straight line, method is easy to understand; however, it is not the most accurate. The subjectivity of this method makes it only as reliable as the judgment and experience of the appraiser using it.

Depreciation is defined by this method as a ratio between effective age and economic life. Suppose an improvement has a 50-year economic life. The structure's chronological age is 20 years, but because of superb care and timely maintenance, it is in the condition of a 15-year-old structure. Divide the effective age by the economic life to determine the depreciation. It has depreciated 30 percent, not 40 percent, as it would have if its chronological age were used. If it has an economic life of 50 years and its effective age is 15 years, it has 35 years of remaining economic life. Add its actual age (20 years) to the remaining 35 years (20 + 35 = 55), and note that the economic life has been extended for five years.

## Market Abstraction Method

The market abstraction method is a more objective and analytical method of determining depreciation than is the age/life (straight line) method. The market abstraction method assumes that replacement costs of comparable properties minus their sales prices approximate the cumulative depreciation. It applies the cost approach to comparable sales in an area by estimating the cost of improvements and adding that estimate to the values for the site and site improvements to arrive at the replacement cost of the comparable as if it were newly built at the time of the estimate. To use this method, subtract the sales price of the comparable from the above estimate to determine the cumulative depreciation. Divide the cumulative depreciation by the age in years of the comparable to find the annual depreciation rate. If this procedure is applied to several properties in the same neighborhood with similar results, it likely reflects the actual depreciation rate.

## Breakdown Method

Depreciation results from the following three causes: (1) physical deterioration, (2) functional obsolescence, and (3) economic obsolescence.

Depreciation in the form of physical deterioration and functional obsolescence results from forces within the property. These two forms of depreciation may be curable or incurable. It may be physically possible and economically practical to correct the causes of physical deterioration and functional obsolescence, or it may not be possible or economically practical to effect necessary changes. In cases where it is not physically possible or economically practical to cure the depreciation, the structure is typically torn down and replaced by a new structure (see Figure 9.5). Each of these three types of depreciation is caused by forces that have an adverse effect on the structure.

**Physical deterioration.** Depreciation can result from **physical deterioration,** such as:

1. Unrepaired damage to the structure caused by fire, explosion, vandalism, windstorm, or other action of the elements and damage caused by termites or other wood-boring insects.
2. Wear and tear resulting from normal use of the property when adequate maintenance measures are not taken to keep the property in good condition.
3. Wear and tear on short-lived items even when adequate maintenance is performed. For example, in a ten-year-old house with the original roof, carpet, appliances, and so on, these items serve their original purpose and it may not be practical to replace them. However, they are part of physical depreciation.

**FIGURE 9.5**

Three causes of depreciation.

| | |
|---|---|
| **Physical Deterioration** | |
| **Curable** | **Incurable*** |
| Roof leak | Severe foundation problems |
| Outdated paint | Deteriorated floor joists |
| **Functional Obsolescence** | |
| **Curable** | **Incurable*** |
| Outdated appliances | No interior plumbing |
| Exposed wiring | 7-foot-high ceilings |
| **Economic Obsolescence** | |
| **Curable**** | **Incurable** |
| | Four-lane highway in place of two-lane country road |
| | Zoning change from residential to commercial |

*These are listed as incurable based on the cost to correct the problem. All items listed can be cured, but the cost of repair may exceed the value of the home.

**Generally, economic obsolescence is seen as incurable only. Typically, it is beyond the homeowner's control to correct the problem.

**Functional obsolescence.** **Functional obsolescence** is a loss in value as a result of things such as:

1. Inadequacy or overadequacy of such things as wiring and plumbing and heating and cooling systems and insufficient or oversufficient number of bathrooms, closets, and other facilities.
2. Equipment that is out of date and not in keeping with current style and utility.
3. Exposed wiring or plumbing and lack of automatic controls for such things as furnaces and hot water heaters.
4. Faulty design resulting in inefficient use of floor space; poor location of rooms in relation to other rooms, such as location of bathrooms in relation to bedrooms; and such things as ceilings being too high or too low.

**Economic (external) obsolescence.** **Economic obsolescence** is *caused by forces outside the property and, therefore, is not curable by the property owner.* These changes can be locational or economic. Items 1 and 2 below are locational. Item 3 is economic. The owner has no control over the properties owned by others and is not able to take necessary corrective measures. Examples of this force include the following:

1. Changes in surrounding land use patterns; that is, forces outside the subject property resulting in increased vehicular traffic, air pollution, noise pollution, inharmonious land uses, and other hazards or nuisances adversely affecting the quality of the area.
2. Changes in zoning and building regulations that adversely affect the use of property.
3. A reduction in demand for property in the area caused by local economic factors, changes in growth patterns, population shifts, and other economic factors adversely affecting property value.

The last step in the cost approach is to estimate the value of the site as though it were vacant. The site value is estimated by the direct sales comparison approach, which employs the use of comparable parcels of land to arrive at the value estimate. The site is compared to comparable parcels of land that have been sold recently as a basis for the land value. The estimate of the land value by the direct sales comparison approach is added to the estimate of the total depreciated value of the improvements to provide a value estimate for the total property by the cost approach.

The various steps and calculations employed in the cost approach are illustrated by the example of the cost approach calculations in Figure 9.6.

**FIGURE 9.6**
Cost approach calculations.

| | | |
|---|---|---|
| Replacement or reproduction cost: | | |
| 21,000 sq. ft. @ $52.50 sq. ft. | | $1,102,500 |
| Less structure depreciation: | | |
| Physical deterioration | $33,075 | |
| Functional obsolescence | 44,100 | |
| Economic obsolescence | -0- | − 77,175 |
| Depreciated value of structure | | 1,025,325 |
| Depreciated value of other improvements: | | |
| Retaining walls | 10,000 | |
| Paved drive and parking | 15,000 | |
| Exterior lighting | 2,000 | |
| Fencing | 1,500 | 28,500 |
| Depreciated value of all improvements | | 1,053,825 |
| Land value by direct sales comparison | | 253,000 |
| Total property value | | $1,306,825 |

## The Income Approach

The **income approach,** or **appraisal by capitalization,** is *the primary method used to estimate the present value of properties that produce rental income.* Properties included in this category are apartment complexes, single-family rental houses, office buildings, shopping malls, parking garages, leased industrial plants, and individual properties occupied by commercial tenants.

The value of the property is estimated by capitalizing **net operating income (NOI)** into an indication of present value by the application of a capitalization rate. This procedure is illustrated in Figure 9.7. It shows an operating statement and the capitalization of the net annual income into an indication of value by applying the capitalization formula following the statement. A complete explanation of the income approach is presented by the analysis of the operating statement and the example of the application of the formula.

## *Analysis of Operating Statement*

**Income.** The apartment complex has a **potential gross income** of $1,350,000. This is *the income that would be produced if every apartment were rented 100 percent of the time* at $450/month *for 12 months.* It is not realistic to expect any rental property to be occupied 100 percent of the time on a continuing basis. Therefore, the potential gross income must be reduced by an allowance for vacancies (5 percent) that will inevitably occur and losses due to some tenants' failing to pay their rent or paying with checks that are not collectible (1 percent). In the example, it is anticipated that vacancy and credit losses will amount to 6 percent of gross potential income, or $81,000 per year.

This apartment complex has other income generated by vending machines and laundromat facilities used by the tenants. This income is projected to be $25,000 per year. With the addition of other income, the **gross effective income** equals *potential gross effective income minus vacancy and credit losses plus other income.* This gross effective income is the amount of money the apartment complex can realistically expect to generate in a 12-month period.

**Expenses.** To arrive at net income, which is the basis for calculating the value estimate in the income approach, various expenses must be subtracted from gross income. These expenses are divided into fixed expenses, operating expenses, and the expense of replacement reserve.

**FIGURE 9.7**
Operating statement.

| | | |
|---|---|---|
| 250-unit apartment complex with rent schedule of $450 per month per unit | | |
| Potential gross income: 250 × $450 × 12 | | $1,350,000 |
| Less vacancy and credit losses (6%) | | − 81,000 |
| Plus other income | | + 25,000 |
| Gross effective income | | $1,294,000 |
| Less expenses | | |
| Fixed expenses: | | |
| Property insurance | $ 24,500 | |
| Property taxes | 95,300 | |
| Licenses and permits | 1,200 | $ 121,000 |
| Operating expenses: | | |
| Maintenance | $106,000 | |
| Utilities | 103,200 | |
| Supplies | 16,000 | |
| Advertising | 7,500 | |
| Legal & accounting | 15,000 | |
| Wages & salaries | 90,000 | |
| Property management | 64,700 | $ 402,400 |
| Replacement reserve: | $ 25,000 | $ 25,000 |
| Total expenses | | $ (548,400) |
| Net operating income | | $ 745,600 |

**Fixed expenses.** These expenses do not fluctuate with the operating level of the complex. The fixed expenses remain essentially the same whether the occupancy rate is 95 percent or 75 percent and include the following: There is an expense of $24,500 in the form of an annual premium for a hazard insurance policy to protect against financial loss caused by fire or other casualty. Real property taxes are one of the largest expense items and amount to $95,300. The $1,200 cost for licenses and permits represents fees paid to local governments as required for the operation of vending machines and other income-producing facilities. The fixed expenses total $121,000 and are 9.27 percent of gross effective income.

**Operating expenses.** **Operating expenses,** or *the costs of operating a property held as an investment,* generally fluctuate with the operating level or occupancy level of the property. As in the case of the apartment complex, maintenance is a major operating expense, amounting to $106,000. This operating expense varies with the level of operation and is related, to a large degree, to the age and condition of the property when purchased. Older properties naturally require a higher level of expenditures for maintenance than newer properties. The maintenance covers not only the cost of repair and maintenance to the structures but also the maintenance of grounds and parking areas. The cost of utilities for the common areas and the cost of wages and salaries paid to employees follow maintenance costs as the next two largest expenses.

The property manager's fee of $64,700 is a percentage of the gross effective income. The property management fee in this example is 5 percent of gross effective income. The small expense items of legal and accounting fees, advertising, and supplies round out the operating expenses, which total $402,400, or 31.09 percent of gross effective income. Operating expenses represent the largest group in the three types of expense.

**Replacement reserve.** This expense item of $25,000 represents *an amount of money that is set aside each year to replace short-lived equipment* such as hot water heaters, ranges and ovens, dishwashers, and disposals. Setting aside an amount of money for this purpose each year enables the project to avoid the impact of a substantial expenditure in any given year when a number of short-lived items must be replaced.

**Total expenses and net income.** The total of the three types of expense amounts to $548,400, which represents 42.38 percent of gross effective income. **Debt service** *(mortgage*

$$I = R \times V \quad \text{Income} = \text{Rate} \times \text{Value} \qquad \text{Value} = \frac{\text{Income}}{\text{Rate}}$$

Given: Income = $745,600
Rate = 12%

$$\text{Value: } \frac{\$745{,}600}{12\%} = \text{Value} = \$6{,}213{,}333$$

**FIGURE 9.8**
Capitalization formula.

*principal and interest payments)* is not included in the list of expenses for appraisal purposes. For this purpose, debt service is considered a personal obligation of the property owner. In this way, the appraisal process puts all comparable properties on the same basis by eliminating an item that varies substantially from one property to another. Outside of the appraisal process, debt service would be deducted from gross effective income to arrive at cash flow. **Cash flow** is *the amount of money the owner actually receives in a given year prior to the subtraction of the income tax liability for the property.* When calculating net taxable income before depreciation, the payment of mortgage interest but not principal is deductible.

Higher Return → Buy cheaper

Net income is derived by subtracting total expenses from gross effective income. The net operating income of $745,600 represents a return of 12 percent on an investment of $6,213,333, as illustrated by the application of the **capitalization formula** in Figure 9.8.

The final step in estimating property value by the income approach is the application of the capitalization formula. This involves the simple process of dividing net operating income by a capitalization rate. The difficulty lies in arriving at the proper capitalization rate. A number of rather complex methods for establishing this rate are beyond the scope of this text and are not covered in prelicensing real estate examinations. In essence, however, the appropriate rate is that rate of return investors in comparable properties are achieving on investments in the same locality at the time of the appraisal. The rate of return on any investment includes a consideration of the risk factor. The greater the risk of loss taken by the investor, the higher potential rate of return the investor is entitled to expect.

In the application of the capitalization formula to the apartment complex, a rate of 12 percent was adopted as the appropriate rate for this investment in this area at this time. By dividing the net operating income of $745,600 by 0.12, a value estimate of $6,213,333 (typically rounded to $6,213,000) is indicated. In other words, if an investor paid this price for the apartment complex and continued to realize a net operating income of $745,600, the investor would realize a return of 12 percent before deductions for debt service and income tax. The investor's federal income tax may be reduced as a result of the deduction for depreciation, interest on debt services, property tax, and other expenses.

The importance of the selection of a proper capitalization rate cannot be overemphasized. Even a slight variation in this rate results in a substantial change in the value estimate. For example, if a 13 percent rate had been used in the foregoing example, the value estimate would be $5,735,384, which represents a reduction of indicated value of $477,949, or 7.69 percent of the original estimate. The higher the capitalization rate, the lower the value estimate; and, conversely, the lower the rate, the higher the resulting value estimate. Other examples of the application of the capitalization formula are found in Chapter 16, Real Estate Math.

## Gross Rent Multiplier

Gross rent multipliers are not a part of the income approach to the value estimate, but they may be used to estimate the value of property producing rental income. There is a degree of unreliability in the use of this method because calculations are based on gross income rather than net income. If the property has been managed efficiently, the gross income will provide a reliable basis for calculating an estimate of value. If expenses are out of line, however, gross income will not fairly reflect property value.

**FIGURE 9.9**
Calculating gross rent multipliers (GRMs).

| COMPARABLE | PRICE | MONTHLY GROSS | GRM | ANNUAL GROSS | GRM |
|---|---|---|---|---|---|
| No. 1 | $6,213,000 | $107,833 | 58 | $1,294,000 | 4.8 |
| No. 2 | 5,865,000 | 101,000 | 58 | 1,212,000 | 4.8 |
| No. 3 | 5,125,000 | 90,000 | 57 | 1,080,000 | 4.7 |
| No. 4 | 6,060,000 | 103,000 | 59 | 1,236,000 | 4.9 |
| No. 5 | 7,250,000 | 125,000 | 58 | 1,500,000 | 4.8 |
| No. 6 | 6,588,000 | 111,000 | 59 | 1,332,000 | 4.9 |
| Average GRM | | | 58 | | 4.8 |

**FIGURE 9.10**
Application of gross rent multiplier (GRM).

A. $\frac{\text{Comparable's Sales Price}}{\text{Rent}} = \text{GRM}$

B. Subject's Rent $\times$ GRM $=$ Estimate of Subject's Value

Gross rent multipliers are calculated by dividing the monthly or annual gross income of a property into the price for which it was sold. It does not matter whether gross annual or gross monthly income is used as long as one or the other is used consistently. The accompanying illustration (see Figure 9.9) provides examples of calculating gross income multipliers on a monthly and an annual basis. As you can see, a much lower multiplier results from the calculations based on annual income.

In estimating the value of an income property, gross rental incomes can be established for comparable income properties that have been sold recently. An average of the gross rent multipliers can be used as a multiplier for the gross monthly or annual income produced by a property under consideration to provide an indication of property value. For example, if the property being considered produced a gross monthly income of $99,000, this would be multiplied by the average gross rent multiplier of 58, as shown in the illustration. This multiplication ($99,000 × 58) provides a value indication of $5,742,000. This indicated value is as reliable as the gross monthly incomes and prices used in calculating the average gross rent multiplier (see Figure 9.10).

## RECONCILIATION AND APPRAISAL REPORT

When making an appraisal, a professional appraiser uses the most relevant approach to the value estimate as the primary appraisal method. Which method is most relevant depends on the type of property that is the subject of appraisal. For example, in estimating the value of a single-family owner-occupied dwelling, the most relevant method is the direct sales comparison, or market data approach. The qualified appraiser also estimates the value of the property by each of the other two methods. In the case of the single-family dwelling, the appraiser treats the property as though it were rental property and estimates the value using the income approach. Finally, the appraiser arrives at a value estimate by the cost approach.

As a practical matter, the results obtained by these three methods are not identical. There must be a reconciliation of the three approaches. In the reconciliation process, three factors are taken into consideration: the relevancy of each method to the subject property, the reliability of the data on which each estimate is based, and the strong and weak points of each method. After these considerations, the greatest weight should be given to the estimate resulting from the most appropriate or relevant method for the type of property that is the subject of the appraisal. For example, if the property is an office building, the most relevant approach and the one to receive the greatest weight would be the income approach. Even though the results obtained by the different approaches are not exactly the same, they should be reasonably close. Therefore, each approach provides a check on the other two. If the result by one method is considerably out of line with the others, this indicates some calculation error or some error in the data used as a basis.

The final step in the appraisal process is the preparation of the appraisal report. A sample uniform residential appraisal report form (URAR) is shown in Figure 9.3. The report contains the appraiser's opinion of value based on the observation of the results obtained by the three methods and the appraiser's reasons for adopting the final estimate of value. The appraisal report may be either a narrative or a form. The narrative report provides all factual data about the property and the elements of judgment used by the appraiser in arriving at the estimate of value. When a standard form is used to report the various property data and the appraisal method employed, it is called a form report. A form report does not contain narrative information, as the narrative report does, but simply sets forth various facts and figures used in the appraisal process and the reconciliation of the final estimate of market value.

## SUMMARY OF IMPORTANT POINTS

1. Value in exchange is the amount of money a typical buyer will give in exchange for a property. Value in exchange is market value.
2. For a property to have value, it must possess the characteristics of utility, scarcity, and transferability and there must be an effective demand.
3. Value, price, and cost are not the same.
4. The various types of value include market value, assessed value, hazard insurance value, mortgage loan value, condemnation value, book value, and plottage value.
5. The basic valuation principles are highest and best use, substitution, supply and demand, conformity, anticipation, contribution, competition, and change.
6. Depreciation is the loss in value from any cause. In structures (land does not depreciate), the causes of depreciation are physical deterioration, functional obsolescence, and economic obsolescence.
7. An appraisal is an estimate (not a determination) of value based on factual data. It is good for one day, that is, the day of the appraisal.
8. The direct sales comparison approach (market data approach) to value is the most relevant appraisal method for estimating the value of single-family owner-occupied dwellings and of vacant land. When one reconciles the three approaches on single-family owner-occupied dwellings, this approach should be heavily weighted.
9. The income approach, or appraisal by capitalization, is the most appropriate appraisal method for estimating the value of property that produces rental income. Net operating income (NOI) equals potential gross income minus vacancy and credit losses and expenses. Value is derived by dividing the NOI by the capitalization rate. The higher the capitalization rate, the lower the value estimate; the lower the rate, the higher the estimate.
10. The cost approach, or appraisal by summation, is the primary appraisal method for estimating the value of property that does not fall into the other categories.
11. A gross rent multiplier may be appropriate for estimating the value of rental property. The gross rent multiplier equals the selling price divided by the monthly or annual gross income. Conversely, the value of a property is derived by multiplying the gross rent by the gross rent multiplier.
12. An appraisal report provides a value estimate based on a reconciliation of the estimates obtained by all three approaches. Reconciliation is the process of weighted evaluation of the estimates derived from the three approaches to determine a single reliable estimate of value.

13. Real estate practitioners have a very important duty in the task of estimating the proper value of a property. Inherent in the practitioner's representation as an expert in the marketing of property is his duty to know the effect of the forces that affect value in his locality. When estimating a value, the practitioner, therefore, has a clear duty to be accurate and should be able to demonstrate sound data upon which his value estimate is based.

14. Contribution is the principle used in the direct sales comparison approach that states that various elements of a property add value to the entire property. In the direct sales comparison approach, one must estimate the value an element adds to the overall value.

15. In the direct sales comparison approach, always adjust the comparable. If the comparable is superior, subtract the amount from the sold price; if the comparable is inferior, add to the sold price.

16. The one and only use of land that will preserve its utility and yield the optimal income forms the highest and best *present* value of the land (may change over time).

## ITEMS TO CONSIDER FOR THE STATE EXAM

1. Definition of the concept of highest and best use and applications of the concept to common situations.
2. The process of reconciliation as opposed to averaging the various comparables.
3. How to use the direct sales comparison (market data) approach, including what types of property it applies to and how to select and adjust comparables. Remember: Always adjust the comparable. If the comparable is superior, subtract the amount from the comparable (two s's). If the comparable is inferior, add the amount to the comparable (two vowels). Study the adjustment process carefully from the chart in Figure 9.2 so you know how to make simple adjustments to the comparable sales.
4. Application of the cost approach, including how the value of the land is estimated and definition of effective age.
5. Application of the income approach, how to derive the net operating income, application of the capitalization formula (Figure 9.8), and the effects of using a higher or lower capitalization rate.

## REVIEW QUESTIONS

Answers to the review questions are in the Answer Key at the back of the book.

1. The basis of market value is most typically which of the following?
   A. value in use
   B. book value
   C. subjective value
   D. value in exchange

2. All of the following characteristics must be present for a property to have value EXCEPT:
   A. utility
   B. obsolescence
   C. transferability
   D. effective demand

3. Value is most closely related to which of the following?
   A. price
   B. competition
   C. cost
   D. supply

4. Adherence to the principle of conformity causes which of the following?
   A. depreciation
   B. minimizing value
   C. maximizing value
   D. competition

5. The first step in the appraisal process is to:
   A. define the appraisal problem
   B. obtain a complete and accurate description of subject property
   C. determine data required for estimate of value
   D. prepare the appraisal report

6. Physical deterioration is caused by:
   I. unrepaired damage.
   II. lack of adequate maintenance.
   A. I only
   B. II only
   C. both I and II
   D. neither I nor II

7. Functional obsolescence results from:
   I. faulty design and inefficient use of space.
   II. changes in surrounding land use patterns.
   A. I only
   B. II only
   C. both I and II
   D. neither I nor II

8. Which cause of depreciation is not curable by a property owner?
   A. economic obsolescence
   B. functional obsolescence
   C. competitive obsolescence
   D. physical deterioration

9. Which economic principle is used in making adjustments to comparables in an appraisal by the direct sales comparison approach?
   A. competition
   B. change
   C. contribution
   D. conformity

10. An appraisal is which of the following?
    A. estimate of value
    B. appropriation of value
    C. correlation of value
    D. determination of value

11. All of the following are approaches to value EXCEPT:
    A. cost approach
    B. contribution approach
    C. income approach
    D. direct sales comparison approach

12. The primary appraisal method for estimating the value of vacant land is which of the following?
    A. cost approach
    B. direct sales comparison approach
    C. income approach
    D. appraisal by capitalization

13. All of the following are important data in the selection of comparables for an owner-occupied single-family house EXCEPT:
    A. size
    B. income
    C. location
    D. condition

14. The income used as a basis for estimating value by the capitalization formula is which of the following?
    A. monthly net operating income
    B. annual gross effective income
    C. monthly gross effective income
    D. annual net operating income

15. If the potential gross income is $580,000, the net operating income is $480,000, and the capitalization rate is 11 percent, which of the following will be the estimate of property value?
A. $2,290,000
B. $2,990,000
C. $4,363,636
D. $5,280,000

16. All the following are deductible from gross effective income to arrive at net operating income for appraisal purposes EXCEPT:
A. maintenance
B. legal fees
C. replacement reserve
D. debt service

17. In the income approach, which of the following is deducted from gross potential income to calculate gross effective income?
A. fixed expenses
B. vacancy rate
C. other income
D. replacement reserve

18. The cost approach is the primary method for appraisal of a:
A. shopping mall
B. courthouse
C. parking lot
D. condominium

19. All the following are methods used for estimating replacement cost EXCEPT:
A. quantity survey
B. square foot
C. unit in place
D. quality survey

20. Which of the following is described as the cost of constructing a building of comparable utility using modern techniques and materials?
A. reproduction cost
B. operating cost
C. unit cost
D. replacement cost

21. An appraisal report may be a:
I. narrative report.
II. form report.
A. I only
B. II only
C. both I and II
D. neither I nor II

22. An appraisal is good for:
A. 1 day
B. 30 days
C. 90 days
D. 180 days

23. The foundation of the direct sales comparison approach is:
A. conformity
B. anticipation
C. contribution
D. substitution

24. The economic principle of supply and demand states that:
A. high supply and low demand = higher value
B. low supply and high demand = lower value
C. high supply and low demand = lower value
D. none of the above

25. All of the following are true about the principle of highest and best use EXCEPT:
A. it must be possible
B. it must be legal
C. there is only one highest and best use of a given property at a given time
D. it is highly speculative

26. Which is a curable form of obsolescence?
A. changes in zoning
B. unrepaired roof damage
C. population shifts
D. all of the above are curable by the property owner

27. Which economic principle results in maximizing property value?
A. supply and demand
B. substitution
C. conformity
D. competition

28. The principle of highest and best use for a property:
A. remains the same for the entire life of the property.
B. may change with time
C. requires that present use is the same as the future use
D. is used to calculate depreciation

29. The value of a half bath is $1,500. The comparable has a half bath, but the subject property does not. Which is correct?
A. subtract $1,500 from the subject
B. subtract $1,500 from the comparable
C. add $1,500 to the subject
D. add $1,500 to the comparable

30. An appraisal prepared by an appraiser is completed on which form?
A. a Competitive Market Analysis
B. a Uniform Residential Appraisal Report
C. a Comparative Market Analysis
D. any of the above

# Chapter 10

**KEY TERMS**

breach of condition
constructive eviction
escalated lease
estate at sufferance
estate at will
estate for years
estate from period to period
fit premises
full service leases
graduated lease
gross lease
ground lease
index lease
landlord
lease
lessee
lessor
net lease
North Carolina Residential Rental Agreements Act
North Carolina Tenant Security Deposit Act
peaceable self-help
percentage leases
periodic tenancy
privity of contract
privity of estate
reappraisal lease
residential eviction remedies
retaliatory eviction statute
sale and leaseback
sexual harassment
tenant

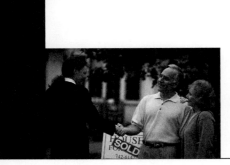

4pts.
Know lease terms/ lease types.

# Relationship of Landlord and Tenant

## LEARNING OBJECTIVES

At the conclusion of this chapter, you should be able to:

1. Describe the basic concepts and terminology of the relationship between landlord and tenant.
2. List and define the nonfreehold estates.
3. List the essential provisions of the North Carolina Residential Rental Agreements Act.
4. List the essential provisions of the North Carolina Tenant Security Deposit Act.
5. List the types and characteristics of leases.
6. Describe the essential and common provisions of leases.
7. Describe the application of the Statute of Frauds to leases.
8. Define the rights of the parties to a lease.
9. Describe the requirements for recording leases.

## DEFINITIONS

In the creation of the rental or leasehold estate, the roles of the two parties are defined in the **North Carolina Residential Rental Agreements Act.** As indicated by the word *residential,* the Act applies only to residential property. It does not regulate commercial property or transient-type quarters.

A **lease** is *a contract whereby a landlord gives a tenant the right to use and possess property for a specified period of time in exchange for rent.* The verbs *lease*, let, and *demise* all describe the conveyance of a possessory interest in property by a lease. Because a lease is both a contract and a conveyance, it creates two sets of rights and duties between the parties. The first, **privity of estate,** arises from traditional property law. The second, **privity of contract,** arises because of the express contractual promises of the lease. The *owner of the property* is the **landlord,** the *one who gives the lease*, who is also known as the **lessor.** The *one* *who receives the lease* is the **lessee,** or **tenant.** If the original tenant (lessee) subleases the property, she becomes the sublessor. The tenant to whom she subleases is the sublessee.

As introduced in Chapter 2, a leasehold estate is also known as a nonfreehold or less than freehold estate. The landlord, of course, retains title to the property and has a freehold estate. Therefore, in the creation of a lease, both freehold and nonfreehold estates exist at the same time. *The landlord owns the property but has handed over possession to the tenant.*

# ESTATES AND CONTRACTS

In the creation of a rental estate, two concepts are involved. The first, that of estates, is discussed above. As outlined in Chapter 2, estates can vary widely in the quantity and quality of interest in real property. The landlord maintains the highest quantity of interest by holding title to the land. He has, however, temporarily diminished his bundle of rights by giving the tenant the right of possession of the property, essentially to the landlord's exclusion. The right of possession reverts to the landlord/owner at the end of the lease; however, during the lease period, the tenant's right of possession creates an encumbrance.

The second concept is that of contract law, which establishes the rights and the duties of the parties. As we will see in the examination of the North Carolina Residential Rental Agreements Act, the duty of each party is related to the other party's performance.

# THE RESIDENTIAL RENTAL AGREEMENTS ACT

The real estate practitioner needs to be familiar with the important statutes of North Carolina that establish the duties of landlord and tenant. Additionally, the agent needs to understand that certain provisions of the statutes allow private (non–real estate agent) landlords certain options not available to the agents in their fiduciary duty to a landlord client.

## Obligations of Landlord and Tenant

An important statutory provision is that the duties of landlord and tenant are mutually dependent. If one party fails to fulfill her duties, the other party is excused from his respective responsibility. The concept of **constructive eviction** provides *a remedy for the tenant in the event the landlord fails to perform her duty,* such as that of maintaining the heating system. If the owner fails to do so, the tenant is excused from the lease, regardless of the remaining term. In a like manner, if the tenant fails to pay rent, the landlord is not required to allow the tenant to remain in the premises. The manner of eviction, however, is carefully regulated.

## Landlord's Statutory Duties

The landlord's major duty is to provide **fit premises,** that is, *fit for human habitation.* The landlord cannot waive this duty or excuse himself in any way. The landlord must comply with building codes; maintain and repair common areas; repair utilities such as heat, plumbing, and electrical; and repair appliances provided on the premises. Generally, the landlord must do whatever is needed to make and keep the unit habitable. These duties come under the "Warranty of Habitability."

Effective January 1, 1996, smoke detectors must be provided in all rental properties. New batteries are the landlord's responsibility when property is initially rented by a new tenant. Thereafter, batteries are the tenant's responsibility.

## Tenant's Statutory Duties

The tenant's primary duties are to maintain the individual living unit, including keeping the unit safe and clean; properly disposing of trash; keeping plumbing fixtures clean; and being financially responsible for any destruction, defacement, or damage.

### Tenant Remedies for Breach by Landlord

If a landlord fails to provide a habitable rental unit, a tenant can bring action against the landlord for damages, including the recovery of rent paid while the unit was uninhabitable. The courts can also require the landlord to correct defects in the property.

A tenant may not, however, remain in the property and unilaterally withhold rent without a court order. In the event of constructive eviction by the landlord, the tenant is excused from completing the lease term. *Constructive eviction* is deemed to have occurred if the landlord breaks his duty to provide fit and habitable premises and fails to remedy the problem within a reasonable length of time after being notified of the problem by the tenant.

### Application of the Law of Negligence

North Carolina law has traditionally applied the Law of Negligence differently to the occupied premises and common areas. The landlord is responsible for maintaining the common areas and is, therefore, potentially liable for injury occurring in these areas to a tenant, a tenant's family, and guests. The landlord's liability increases if it can be shown that he knew about the hazard that caused the injury and failed to correct it and if no negligence is shown on the part of the injured party.

In the past, the landlord was not usually held liable for injury occurring within the leased area itself because the tenant was responsible for that area. Since the North Carolina Residential Rental Agreements Act now holds the landlord responsible for keeping the premises safe and habitable, the landlord may face more liability in that area in the future. Although a violation of the Act does not create liability, it could possibly be used as evidence of liability, especially absent negligence on the part of the tenant.

## RETALIATORY EVICTION

The **retaliatory eviction statute** *protects tenants in asserting their rights,* such as requesting repairs or participating in a tenants union. The statute provides an *automatic defense* from eviction for up to one year from any such event.

## NORTH CAROLINA TENANT SECURITY DEPOSIT ACT

The **North Carolina Tenant Security Deposit Act** *sets limitations upon the holding of security deposits by the landlord.* Similar to the Residential Rental Agreements Act, this Act *applies only to residential property.* When collecting the money, the private landlord has two choices of what to do with the funds. The landlord can place the funds in a North Carolina bank trust account, in which case the landlord must notify the tenant of the bank's location. Alternatively, the landlord can guarantee the return of the funds with a performance bond and notify the tenant of the bonding company's name. (Note: Real estate agents can only use the trust account method. There are strict accounting rules [Rule A.0107] for the operation of trust accounts. Agents cannot use the bond option in their fiduciary capacity.)

Permitted uses of the deposit are limited to damage to the unit, nonfulfillment of the rental period, unpaid rent, court costs of eviction, and costs of rerental if the tenant breaches the lease. The landlord must account for and/or refund the funds within 30 days of the end of the lease.

Amounts that can be collected for security deposit are related to the period of the lease. If the tenancy is weekly, the maximum deposit is two weeks' rent; if the tenancy is monthly, a month and a half's rent; and if the tenancy is greater than a month, two months' rent. This Act also allows the landlord to require a *reasonable nonrefundable* pet deposit for pets kept on the premises by the tenant.

Frequent disputes arise over what is "normal" wear and tear and what is damage not due to "normal" wear and tear. Damage caused by everyday activities of reasonably careful people is probably normal wear and tear. Dirt and dust on walls and windows, worn or dirty carpet due to normal foot traffic or age, age-related repairs to appliances, and worn or frayed window treatments are examples of normal wear and tear. Examples of damage beyond ordinary wear and tear include anything broken by force; crayon, nail polish, motor oil, and so on, on carpets, walls, trim, or fixtures; burns or large holes on walls, carpets, countertops, and so on; extremely filthy premises or appliances; and fixtures requiring extraordinary cleaning.

Time spent with tenants upon renting, explaining what is expected of them, including a written explanation of expectations and a properly completed property condition report, greatly reduces the possibility of misunderstandings.

## RESIDENTIAL EVICTION REMEDIES

**Residential eviction** (or *judicial eviction*) **remedies** prohibit **peaceable self-help,** which *includes acts such as locking tenants out or shutting off their utilities.* Furthermore, the distress or distraint of chattel (personal property) is prohibited. Therefore, the landlord cannot seize the tenant's furniture, cut off the electricity, or put padlocks on the unit. His only remedy is to seek judicial eviction, which is also known as *summary ejectment* or *actual eviction.*

## DISCRIMINATION AND SEXUAL HARASSMENT

Federal and state laws prohibit discrimination against tenants based on race, color, religion, sex, handicap, familial status, or national origin. See Chapter 12, Fair Housing, for a detailed discussion on this topic.

North Carolina law also prohibits sexual harassment of a lessee or prospective tenant (N.C. General Statute 14-395) by a lessor or lessor's agent. **Sexual harassment** is defined as unsolicited overt requests or demands for sexual acts when submission to such conduct is made a term of execution or continuation of a lease agreement or submission or rejection of such conduct is used to determine whether rights under the lease are accorded.

## RIGHTS OF TENANTS IN PUBLIC HOUSING

Real estate practitioners are expected to have special expertise and training in all dealings with their clients and the general public. Therefore, agents need to know that North Carolina has legal precedent for establishing the concept that special rules or interpretations apply to tenants of public housing. In this type of housing, tenants are assumed to have a special entitlement to continued occupancy, which may not be suddenly terminated, especially if they have personal circumstances beyond their control. They are entitled to due process under federal and state constitutions.

## VACATION RENTAL ACT

The Vacation Rental Act became effective January 1, 2000. It applies to any landlord or agent who rents property used only for vacation, recreation, or leisure for time periods of fewer than 90 days, but specifically exempts hotels, motels, and certain other lodgings regulated by other North Carolina Statutes. The Act does not apply to rentals for business purposes or for short-term temporary residences for individuals with no other permanent resident to which they plan to return at some point after the rental.

The Act requires all vacation rental agreements to be in writing. Otherwise, such agreements are not enforceable. A tenant must accept a vacation rental agreement in one of the following ways:

1. By signing the agreement
2. By paying the landlord or broker a part of the consideration or security deposit AFTER the tenant receives a copy of the written agreement
3. By taking possession of the property AFTER receiving a copy of the agreement. As with most real estate—related issues, the general statutes put a greater burden on a broker

acting as agent for a principal than an owner or landlord acting for herself. A landlord renting his own property cannot enforce his contract with a tenant if the agreement is not in writing, but the landlord is not subject to the penalties of G.S. 75-1.1 for an unfair trade practice due to his failure to get the agreement in writing. However, the broker acting as a landlord's agent may be guilty of an unfair trade practice under G.S. 75-1.1 by failing to obtain a written agreement for a vacation rental. These penalties can be steep, including treble damages or a civil penalty, as well as attorney's fees.

The Vacation Rental Act requires tenant security deposits to be held in a trust account, mostly in accordance with the Tenant Security Deposit Act, but with minor modifications for the special circumstances of vacation rentals only. Under the Act, the landlord/agent may collect advance payments from the tenant and deposit such payments in a trust account. The landlord/agent may then withdraw/disburse from the trust account an amount not to exceed 50 percent of the gross rent prior to occupancy. This does not include 50 percent of other fees, such as security deposits.

The landlord does not have the option of having a bond rather than depositing monies into an escrow account. The landlord/agent has 45 rather than 30 days to account for deposit monies after the end of a vacation rental. In addition to permitted uses of the security deposit under the Tenant Security Deposit Act, the Vacation Rental Act specifically allows security deposits to be used to pay long-distance phone calls or cable charges that are a tenant's obligation.

Under the Act, a landlord/agent may charge reasonable fees to a tenant for making, transferring, or canceling the tenancy, provided such fees are included in the agreement and reasonably approximate the actual cost of such services. No other fees may be charged.

A landlord who cannot make the property available to a tenant in a fit and habitable condition must substitute a reasonably comparable property or refund the tenant's payment.

The Act provides some protection for tenants who have vacation rental agreements. Landlords voluntarily selling or transferring property covered under the Vacation Rental Act must disclose to purchasers or grantees the existence of any leases ending within 180 days after transfer of title to the grantee. The grantee takes the property subject to these rental agreements. After the sale, the landlords/sellers must also inform tenants of their rights under the Act. Tenants not protected by the Act, such as those whose tenancy ends beyond the 180-day period or those who tenancy is terminated by an involuntary transfer, are entitled to a refund of monies already paid minus some allowable deductions.

Within ten days after transfer of property covered by the Act, the buyer or his agent must notify each tenant of the property transfer in writing and inform each tenant as to whether he or she still has the right to occupy the property or to have any payments refunded. The new owner has no obligation to honor vacation rentals ending after 180 days of property transfer but may do so voluntarily. The Act provides for expedited eviction procedures for tenants in vacation rentals under tenancies for 30 days or less when such tenants have breached the agreement. Examples of breaches of the agreement include destroying property, exhibiting loud and disruptive behavior, and holding over beyond the end of the agreement. The landlord/agent must give the tenant a minimum of a four-hour notice to vacate the premise after a breach. Oral notice is allowed, but written notice is easier to document. The process moves rapidly. The case must be heard 12 to 48 hours after complaint is served and tenant is summoned. If the magistrate orders the tenant to vacate, the tenant must do so at the time set by court but no more than eight hours after the service of the order.

This expedited eviction procedure must not be abused. The Act imposes severe penalties for landlords/agents who act in bad faith without sufficient grounds or without a written agreement. Such penalties include civil penalties, treble damages, and possible criminal prosecution.

Landlord/tenant duties imposed by the Vacation Rental Act are essentially the same as landlord/tenant duties for other rental properties. The landlord must make a reasonable effort to provide safe, habitable, and fit premises and keep property repaired. The tenant must not do anything to purposely damage or destroy the property.

The Act entitles a tenant forced to evacuate a vacation rental by proper state or local authorities to a prorated refund unless the landlord/agent has offered the North Carolina

Department of Insurance approved "interruption insurance" covering this possible risk to the tenant at a cost of 8 percent or less of the total rental amount charged to the tenant. The Act also requires tenants to comply with a mandatory evacuation order by state and local government.

## NONFREEHOLD ESTATES

### Estate for Years

The *lease creating an* **estate for years** *must be for a definite period of time.* If there is any indefiniteness or vagueness regarding this matter, the contract will not create a lease in the form of an estate for years but will create a periodic tenancy or estate from year to year. A definite time period creates a lease in the form of an estate for years, even though the period may be for only six months, three months, or even less.

### Estate from Period to Period

An **estate from period to period** is commonly known as a **periodic tenancy** (and is also referred to as an *estate from year to year*). An example of an estate from period to period is the typical residential lease. Its key feature is that *it automatically renews itself at the end of the period unless one party gives notice to the other during a prescribed time at the end of the estate.* The statutory notice for an estate from year to year, if none is stated in the lease, is one month. For example, if the required notice period is one month and the parties entered the last 30 days of the lease without notifying the other of any change, a new lease would automatically be created for another period at the same terms. A lease can specify a longer notice.

The first two estates are essentially opposite in terms of what happens at the end of their original lease period. The estate for years terminates, and the estate from period to-period renews itself.

### Estate at Will

In the **estate at will,** the duration of the term is *completely unknown* at the time the estate is created. This is because the estate at will *may be terminated by either party at will, by simply giving the other party notice.* For example, the owners of a property in Asheville might allow some college students to occupy their home while they spend a portion of the winter in Florida. Both profit in that the owners have their home looked after in their absence, and the students have a place to stay for an indefinite period of time. Either party can terminate the arrangement, however, by simply providing notice to the other. The period of notice is instantaneous. In residential property, the notice need be only a few days; in vacation property, a few hours. If rent is paid and accepted, this type of tenancy is converted to a periodic tenancy.

Since the law provides that the land should be productive, the tenant at will does have some rights protected. If crops were planted, the tenant would still have the right to harvest the crops planted during the tenancy, even if the lease was terminated.

### Estate at Sufferance

An **estate at sufferance** is the lowest estate in real property. The term is simply used to describe *someone who had originally been in lawful possession of another's property but whose right to possession was terminated.* This could occur upon termination of any of the three previously discussed leasehold estates. The term is used to make a distinction between the tenant at sufferance who was originally in lawful possession of the property and someone who was on the property illegally from the beginning (trespasser). The estate at sufferance continues until such time that the property owner brings a legal action to evict the person wrongfully holding over or until the one holding over vacates voluntarily. During this period, the occupier is called a *tenant at sufferance.*

## TYPES OF LEASE

There are two primary classes of lease, based on the arrangement of paying the expenses of the rental property. A **gross lease** is one in which *the owner (lessor) pays all costs of operating and maintaining the property in addition to real property taxes and insurance.* A **net lease** means the *tenant (lessee) pays expenses such as taxes, assessments, maintenance, insurance, and utilities.* Some use terms such as *net, double net,* or even *triple net,* but the two major classifications, gross and net, are more appropriate. Most residential leases are gross leases, whereas a commercial lease is often a net lease.

### Fixed Rental (Flat or Gross)

← most common

A fixed rental lease, also known as a flat or gross lease, is one in which the rent does not change during the lease term.

Commercial leases:

### Net

- prorated share of expenses → TICAM - taxes, insurance, common area maintenance

In a net lease, the lessee agrees to pay, in addition to the fixed rental, all costs and expenses associated with the property. These costs and expenses include such things as real estate taxes and assessments, maintenance, insurance, and utilities. As a result of these payments by the lessee, the rental income is a net income to the lessor.

### Percentage

% - Retail / Restaurants → % of gross sales

Many commercial leases are **percentage leases.** The rent in a percentage lease includes a fairly low fixed amount of rent per month plus an additional monthly rent that is a percentage of the lessee's gross sales. The majority of commercial leases are percentage leases in cases where the lessee is using the property to conduct a retail business. This is especially true of shopping malls. The percentage lease *provides the lessor with a guaranteed monthly rental plus the opportunity to participate in the sales volume of the lessee on a percentage basis.* The disadvantage of this type of lease is that the landlord also shares the risk of loss with the tenant.

### Graduated

- Steps up.

A **graduated lease** is one in which *the rental amount changes from period to period over the lease term.* The change in rental amount is specified in the lease contract. For example, a lease may be at $300 per month for the first year, $350 per month the second year, and $400 per month the third year.

### Index

- i.e. ARM

An **index lease** is one in which *the rental amount is changed in proportion to changes in the Consumer Price Index*(CPI) published by the U.S. Department of Labor or other similar index. The lease specifies a percentage change in relation to the number of points the CPI changes annually.

### Full Service Lease

← Dry Ave. prop.

**Full service leases** are common in large office buildings and shopping centers. Under a full service lease, each tenant pays a portion of the overall operating expenses for the building and common areas in addition to a base rent.

### *Ground*

The **ground lease** is a *lease of unimproved land.* It normally contains a provision that a building will be constructed on the land by the lessee. The lease should always contain a provision as to the disposition of the improvements on the land constructed by the lessee at the end of the lease term. In the absence of a provision as to the disposition of the improvements at the end of the lease term, the improvements automatically belong to the lessor as owner of the land. The ground lease is a long-term lease because the lessee must have sufficient time to recoup costs and earn a profit during the term of the lease.

### *Mineral*

The lessee under a mineral lease has the right to search for and mine minerals during the lease period. Like other parts of the bundle of rights in real property, mineral rights can be severed from other rights in land. A mineral lease must be in writing, regardless of the duration, to comply with the North Carolina Statute of Frauds.

### *Reappraisal*

A **reappraisal lease** is one in which *changes in rental amount are based on changes in property value as demonstrated by periodic reappraisals of the property.* Such appraisals can occur at three- or five-year intervals in the case of a long-term lease. The rent changes a specified percentage of the previous year's rent as spelled out in the contract.

### *Escalated*

An **escalated lease** provides for *rental changes in proportion to the changes in the lessor's costs of ownership and operation of the property.* As changes occur in the lessor's obligations for real property taxes and operating expenses, the lease changes in specified proportions.

### *Sale and Leaseback*

A **sale and leaseback** is a transaction *wherein a property owner sells a property to an investor and the investor agrees to immediately lease the property back to the seller.* This type of transaction is usually used by an owner of business property who wishes to free up capital invested in the real estate while retaining possession of the property under a lease.

# COMMON LEASE PROVISIONS

## Essential Provisions

1. There must be mutual agreement to the terms of the contract by parties who have the legal capacity to contract.
2. The land must be identified clearly. A legal description is best, but usually a street address will suffice for a single-family dwelling.
3. All essential aspects of the agreement (rent, occupancy dates, terms, and so on) must be set forth.
4. All valid lease contracts must be supported by legal consideration.
5. The lease must contemplate a lawful objective.

## Other Provisions

In addition to the essential elements of a valid lease, many provisions are often found in lease contracts. The following is a discussion of some of the more common provisions.

- Tenants use. A lessor may wish to restrict the use of a rental unit (for example, residential use only), or a lessee may want to make a specific use a condition of the lease (for example, that a permit can be obtained to sell alcoholic beverages on the premises).

- Environmental matters. Provisions can prohibit the use, storage, or discharge of hazardous substances on the rented premises.
- Fixtures. If the lessee intends to add fixtures to the premises, a provision should address the issue of removal of these fixtures and the return of the premises to its original condition.
- Repairs (nonresidential property). Responsibility for repairs on commercial or industrial property depends on the type of property and specific lease provisions. Therefore, upkeep and repair responsibilities of the lessor and lessee should be carefully addressed in any such lease.
- Upfitting improvements. *Upfitting* involves improvements to a commercial property at the lessor's expense in order to obtain or retain a tenant.
- Assignments and subleases. A lease provision can restrict or prohibit a lessee's right to *assign* or *sublease* the premises. *Assignment* is the transfer of the lessee's entire remaining interest in the lease. *Subleasing* is essentially the making of a new lease in which the lessee also becomes a "sublessor" who has rented the premises to a "sublessee." A sublease does not relieve the original lessee of his liability under the terms of the original lease.
- Default. A well-drafted lease provides for remedies by the lessor and the lessee in the event of default.
- Renewal of lease. Unless there is an express provision for renewal of the lease, a lessee does not have an implied right to renew her lease.
- Option to purchase/right of first refusal. A lease provision giving the tenant an *option to purchase* should specify a purchase price, the type of conveyance to be made by the grantor/lessor, and the time and manner in which the lessee must exercise his option. A lease may also contain a provision for *right of first refusal,* whereby the tenant has the right to the first opportunity to purchase the property in the event the lessor decides to sell.
- Landlord's right to enter premises. Often provisions are used that give the landlord the right to enter the premises during the lease term in order to inspect the property, make necessary repairs, or show the premises to prospective buyers or tenants.

NR

Figure 10.1 reproduces pages 1 to 6 of NCAR's Residential Rental Contract. The following is a summary of some of the major aspects of this form. The names of the landlord (lessor) and tenant(s) (lessees) appear at the top of the form.

- The duration of the initial term of the contract is given. The period of the contract and specific starting and ending dates are given.
- The due dates of the first and subsequent rental payments are set forth.
- The amount of rent and the period for paying rent (yearly, monthly, weekly) are specified.
- Late payment fees are specified.
- The amount of security deposit and the name of the bank that will hold the deposit are specified.
- The tenant is also responsible for paying the returned check fees for each check of the tenant that is returned for insufficient funds.
- Number and type of pets, if allowed, and the non-refundable pet deposit is specified.
- Permitted occupants in addition to tenant are named.

1. This paragraph describes what is to happen at the end of this initial term. The lessor or lessee can give notice to terminate. If notice is not given, the initial term is then modified to a shorter period-to-period tenancy.
2. This paragraph informs the tenant when the first and subsequent rental payments will be due and that the tenant shall pay the rent on those dates without notice, demand, or deduction.

**FIGURE 10.1** Residential Rental Contact.

## RESIDENTIAL RENTAL CONTRACT

RESIDENT: ______________________________ ("Tenant")

OWNER: ______________________________ ("Landlord")

REAL ESTATE MANAGEMENT FIRM: ______________________________ ("Agent")

PREMISES: City: ______________ County: ______________ State of North Carolina
- ❑ Street Address: ______________________________
- ❑ Apartment Complex: ______________________ Apartment No. __________
- ❑ Other Description (Room, portion of above address, etc.): ______________________________

INITIAL TERM: Beginning Date of Lease: ____________ Ending Date of Lease: ____________

RENT: $ ____________ PAYMENT PERIOD: ❑ monthly ❑ weekly ❑ yearly ❑ other: ____________

LATE PAYMENT FEE: $ ____________ OR ________ % of rental payment, whichever is greater
*(State law provides that the late fee may not exceed $15.00 or five percent (5%) of the rental payment, whichever is greater.)*

SECURITY DEPOSIT: $ ______________________ to be deposited with: (check one) ❑ Landlord ❑ Agent
LOCATION OF DEPOSIT: (insert name of bank): ______________________________
BANK ADDRESS: ______________________________

RETURNED CHECK FEE: $ ____________ *(The maximum processing fee allowed under State law is $25.00.)*
SUMMARY EJECTMENT ADMINISTRATIVE FEE (see paragraph 17): $ ____________

PETS: ❑ PETS NOT ALLOWED ❑ PETS ALLOWED NONREFUNDABLE PET FEE (if pets allowed): $ ____________
TYPE OF PET PERMITTED (if pets allowed): ______________________________

PERMITTED OCCUPANTS (in addition to Tenant): ______________________________

IN CONSIDERATION of the promises contained in this Agreement, Landlord, by and through Agent, hereby agrees to lease the Premises to Tenant on the following terms and conditions:

1. **Termination and Renewal:** Either Landlord or Tenant may terminate the tenancy at the expiration of the Initial Term by giving written notice to the other at least ____________ days prior to the expiration date of the Initial Term. In the event such written notice is not given or if the Tenant holds over beyond the Initial Term, the tenancy shall automatically become a ______________ (period) to ______________ (period) tenancy upon the same terms and conditions contained herein and may thereafter be terminated by either Landlord or Tenant giving the other __________ days written notice prior to the last day of the then current period of the tenancy.

2. **Rent:** Tenant shall pay the Rent, without notice, demand or deduction, to Landlord or as Landlord directs. The first Rent payment, which shall be prorated if the Initial Term commences on a day other than the first day of the Payment Period, shall be due on ______________________ (date). Thereafter, all rentals shall be paid in advance on or before the **FIRST** day of each subsequent Payment Period for the duration of the tenancy.

3. **Late Payment Fees and Returned Check Fees:** Tenant shall pay the Late Payment Fee if any rental payment is not received by midnight on the fifth (5th) day after it is due. *This late payment fee shall be due immediately without demand therefor and shall be added to and paid with the late rental payment. Tenant also agrees to pay the Returned Check Fee for each check of Tenant that is returned by the financial institution because of insufficient funds or because the Tenant did not have an account at the financial institution.*

**FIGURE 10.1** Continued.

---

4. **Tenant Security Deposit:** The Security Deposit shall be administered in accordance with the North Carolina Tenant Security Deposit Act (N.C.G.S. § 42-50 et. seq.). IT MAY, IN THE DISCRETION OF EITHER THE LANDLORD OR THE AGENT, BE DEPOSITED IN AN INTEREST-BEARING ACCOUNT WITH THE BANK OR SAVINGS INSTITUTION NAMED ABOVE. ANY INTEREST EARNED UPON THE TENANT SECURITY DEPOSIT SHALL ACCRUE FOR THE BENEFIT OF, AND SHALL BE PAID TO, THE LANDLORD, OR AS THE LANDLORD DIRECTS. SUCH INTEREST, IF ANY, MAY BE WITHDRAWN BY LANDLORD OR AGENT FROM SUCH ACCOUNT AS IT ACCRUES AS OFTEN AS IS PERMITTED BY THE TERMS OF THE ACCOUNT.

Upon any termination of the tenancy herein created, the Landlord may deduct from the Tenant Security Deposit amounts sufficient to pay: (1) any damages sustained by the Landlord as a result of the Tenant's nonpayment of rent or nonfulfillment of the Initial Term or any renewal periods, including the Tenant's failure to enter into possession; (2) any damages to the Premises for which the Tenant is responsible; (3) any unpaid bills which become a lien against the Premises due to the Tenant's occupancy; (4) any costs of re-renting the Premises after a breach of this lease by the Tenant; (5) any court costs incurred by the Landlord in connection with terminating the tenancy; and (6) any other damages of the Landlord which may then be a permitted use of the Tenant Security Deposit under the laws of this State. No fees may be deducted from the Tenant Security Deposit until the termination of the tenancy. After having deducted the above amounts, the Landlord shall, if the Tenant's address is known to him, refund to the Tenant, within thirty (30) days after the termination of the tenancy and delivery of possession, the balance of the Tenant Security Deposit along with an itemized statement of any deductions. If there is more than one person listed above as Tenant, Agent may, in Agent's discretion, pay said balance to any such person, and the other person(s) agree to hold Agent harmless for such action. If the Tenant's address is unknown to the Landlord, the Landlord may deduct the above amounts and shall then hold the balance of the Tenant Security Deposit for the Tenant's collection for a six-month period beginning upon the termination of the tenancy and delivery of possession by the Tenant. If the Tenant fails to make demand for the balance of the Tenant Security Deposit within the six-month period, the Landlord shall not thereafter be liable to the Tenant for a refund of the Tenant Security Deposit or any part thereof.

If the Landlord removes Agent or Agent resigns, the Tenant agrees that Agent may transfer any Tenant Security Deposit held by Agent hereunder to the Landlord or the Landlord's designee and thereafter notify the Tenant by mail of such transfer and of the transferee's name and address. The Tenant agrees that such action by Agent shall relieve Agent of further liability with respect to the Tenant Security Deposit. If Landlord's interest in the Premises terminates (whether by sale, assignment, death, appointment of receiver or otherwise), Agent shall transfer the Tenant Security Deposit in accordance with the provisions of North Carolina General Statutes § 42-54.

5. **Tenant's Obligations:** Unless otherwise agreed upon, the Tenant shall:

(a) use the Premises for residential purposes only and in a manner so as not to disturb the other tenants;

(b) not use the Premises for any unlawful or immoral purposes or occupy them in such a way as to constitute a nuisance;

(c) keep the Premises, including but not limited to all plumbing fixtures, facilities and appliances, in a clean and safe condition;

(d) cause no unsafe or unsanitary condition in the common areas and remainder of the Premises used by him;

(e) comply with any and all obligations imposed upon tenants by applicable building and housing codes;

(f) dispose of all ashes, rubbish, garbage, and other waste in a clean and safe manner and comply with all applicable ordinances concerning garbage collection, waste and other refuse;

(g) use in a proper and reasonable manner all electrical, plumbing, sanitary, heating, ventilating, air conditioning, and other facilities and appliances, if any, furnished as a part of the Premises;

(h) not deliberately or negligently destroy, deface, damage or remove any part of the Premises (including all facilities, appliances and fixtures) or permit any person, known or unknown to the Tenant, to do so;

(i) pay the costs of all utility services to the Premises which are billed directly to the Tenant and not included as a part of the rentals, including, but not limited to, water, electric, telephone, and gas services;

(j) conduct himself and require all other persons on the Premises with his consent to conduct themselves in a reasonable manner and so as not to disturb other tenants' peaceful enjoyment of the Premises; and

(k) not abandon or vacate the Premises during the Initial Term or any renewals or extensions thereof. Tenant shall be deemed to have abandoned or vacated the Premises if Tenant removes substantially all of his possessions from the Premises.

(l) ____________________________________________
____________________________________________
____________________________________________

6. **Landlord's Obligations:** Unless otherwise agreed upon, the Landlord shall:

(a) comply with the applicable building and housing codes to the extent required by such building and housing codes;

(b) make all repairs to the Premises as may be necessary to keep the Premises in a fit and habitable condition; provided, however, in accordance with paragraph 10, the Tenant shall be liable to the Landlord for any repairs necessitated by the Tenant's intentional or negligent misuse of the Premises;





Tenant Initials ________ ________

**FIGURE 10.1** Continued.

(c) keep all common areas, if any, used in conjunction with the Premises in a clean and safe condition; and

(d) promptly repair all facilities and appliances, if any, as may be furnished by the Landlord as part of the Premises, including electrical, plumbing, sanitary, heating, ventilating, and air conditioning systems, provided that the Landlord, except in emergency situations, actually receives notification from the Tenant in writing of the needed repairs.

7. **Smoke Detectors:** Pursuant to North Carolina General Statutes § 42-42 and 42-43, the Landlord shall provide and install operable smoke detectors, either battery-operated or electrical, having an Underwriters' Laboratories, Inc., listing or other equivalent national testing laboratory approval. The Tenant shall notify the Landlord, in writing, of the need for replacement of or repairs to a smoke detector. The Landlord shall replace or repair the smoke detectors within 15 days of receipt of notification if the Landlord is notified of needed replacement or repairs in writing by the Tenant. The Landlord shall ensure that a smoke detector is operable and in good repair at the beginning of the Initial Term of the Tenancy. The Landlord shall place new batteries in any battery-operated smoke detectors at the beginning of the Initial Term of the tenancy; **the Tenant shall replace the batteries as needed during the tenancy.**

8. **Rules and Regulations:** The Tenant, his family, servants, guests and agents shall comply with and abide by all the Landlord's existing rules and regulations and such future reasonable rules and regulations as the Landlord may, at Landlord's discretion, from time to time, adopt governing the use and occupancy of the Premises and any common areas used in connection with them (the "Rules and Regulations"). Landlord reserves the right to make changes to the existing Rules and Regulations and to adopt additional reasonable rules and regulations from time to time; provided however, such changes and additions shall not alter the essential terms of this lease or any substantive rights granted hereunder and shall not become effective until thirty (30) days' written notice thereof shall have been furnished to Tenant. Tenant also agrees to abide by any applicable homeowners' association regulations as they now exist or may be amended. A copy of the existing Rules and Regulations, and any applicable homeowners' association regulations, are attached hereto and the Tenant acknowledges that he has read them. The Rules and Regulations shall be deemed to be a part of this lease giving to the Landlord all the rights and remedies herein provided.

9. **Right of Entry:** Landlord hereby reserves the right to enter the Premises during reasonable hours for the purpose of (1) inspecting the Premises and the Tenant's compliance with the terms of this lease; (2) making such repairs, alterations, improvements or additions thereto as the Landlord may deem appropriate; and (3) showing the Premises to prospective purchasers or tenants. Landlord shall also have the right to display "For Sale" or "For Rent" signs in a reasonable manner upon the Premises.

10. **Damages:** Tenant shall be responsible for and liable to the Landlord for all damage to, defacement of, or removal of property from the Premises whatever the cause, except such damage, defacement or removal caused by ordinary wear and tear, acts of the Landlord, his agent, or of third parties not invitees of the Tenant, and natural forces. Tenant agrees to pay Landlord for the cost of repairing any damage for which Tenant is responsible upon receipt of Landlord's demand therefor, and to pay the Rent during the period the Premises may not be habitable as a result of any such damage.

11. **Pets:** If pets are not allowed, Tenant agrees not to keep or allow anywhere on or about the Property any animals or pets of any kind, including but not limited to, dogs, cats, birds, rodents, reptiles or marine animals. If pets are allowed, Tenant acknowledges that the amount of the Pet Fee is reasonable and agrees that the Landlord shall not be required to refund the Pet Fee in whole or in part. If pets are allowed, Tenant agrees to reimburse Landlord for any primary or secondary damages caused thereby whether the damage is to the Premises or to any common areas used in conjunction with them, and to indemnify Landlord from any liability to third parties which may result from Tenant's keeping of such pet or pets.

The Tenant shall remove any pet previously permitted within ________ hours of written notification from the Landlord that the pet, in the Landlord's sole judgment, creates a nuisance or disturbance or is, in the Landlord's opinion, undesirable. If the pet is caused to be removed pursuant to this paragraph, the Landlord shall not be required to refund the Pet Fee; however, the Tenant shall be entitled to acquire and keep another pet of the type previously authorized.

12. **Alterations:** The Tenant shall not paint, mark, drive nails or screws into, or otherwise deface or alter walls, ceilings, floors, windows, cabinets, woodwork, stone, ironwork or any other part of the Premises or decorate the Premises or make any alterations, additions, or improvements in or to the Premises without the Landlord's prior written consent and then only in a workmanlike manner using materials and contractors approved by the Landlord. All such work shall be done at the Tenant's expense and at such times and in such manner as the Landlord may approve. All alterations, additions, and improvements upon the Premises, made by either the Landlord or Tenant, shall become the property of the Landlord and shall remain upon and become a part of the Premises at the end of the tenancy hereby created.

13. **Occupants:** The Tenant shall not allow or permit the Premises to be occupied or used as a residence by any person other than Tenant and the Permitted Occupants.

14. **Rental Application:** In the event the Tenant has submitted a Rental Application in connection with this lease, Tenant acknowledges that the Landlord has relied upon the Application as an inducement for entering into this Lease and Tenant warrants to Landlord that the facts stated in the Application are true to the best of Tenant's knowledge. If any facts stated in the Rental Application prove to be untrue, the Landlord shall have the right to terminate the tenancy and to collect from Tenant any damages resulting therefrom.

Page 3 of 6

Tenant Initials ________ ________

**STANDARD FORM 410 - T**
**© 7/2006**

**FIGURE 10.1** Continued.

15. **Tenant's Duties Upon Termination:** Upon any termination of the Tenancy created hereby, whether by the Landlord or the Tenant and whether for breach or otherwise, the Tenant shall: (1) pay all utility bills due for services to the Premises for which he is responsible and have all such utility services discontinued; (2) vacate the Premises removing therefrom all Tenant's personal property of whatever nature; (3) properly sweep and clean the Premises, including plumbing fixtures, refrigerators, stoves and sinks, removing therefrom all rubbish, trash, garbage and refuse; (4) make such repairs and perform such other acts as are necessary to return the Premises, and any appliances or fixtures furnished in connection therewith, in the same condition as when Tenant took possession of the Premises; provided, however, Tenant shall not be responsible for ordinary wear and tear or for repairs required by law or by paragraph 6 above to be performed by Landlord; (5) fasten and lock all doors and windows; (6) return to the Landlord all keys to the Premises; and (7) notify the Landlord of the address to which the balance of the Security Deposit may be returned. If the Tenant fails to sweep out and clean the Premises, appliances and fixtures as herein provided, Tenant shall become liable, without notice or demand, to the Landlord for the actual costs of cleaning (over and above ordinary wear and tear), which may be deducted from the Security Deposit as provided in paragraph 4 above.

16. **Tenant's Default:** In the event the Tenant shall fail to:

(a) pay the rentals herein reserved as and when they shall become due hereunder; or

(b) perform any other promise, duty or obligation herein agreed to by him or imposed upon him by law and such failure shall continue for a period of five (5) days from the date the Landlord provides Tenant with written notice of such failure, then in either of such events and as often as either of them may occur, the Landlord, in addition to all other rights and remedies provided by law, may, at its option and with or without notice to Tenant, either (i) terminate this lease or (ii) terminate the Tenant's right to possession of the Premises without terminating this lease. Regardless of whether Landlord terminates this lease or only terminates the Tenant's right of possession without terminating this lease, Landlord shall be immediately entitled to possession of the Premises and the Tenant shall peacefully surrender possession of the Premises to Landlord immediately upon Landlord's demand. In the event Tenant shall fail or refuse to surrender possession of the Premises, Landlord shall, in compliance with Article 2A of Chapter 42 of the General Statutes of North Carolina, reenter and retake possession of the Premises only through a summary ejectment proceeding. If a summary ejectment proceeding is instituted against Tenant, in addition to any court costs and past-due rent that may be awarded, Tenant shall be responsible for paying Landlord the Summary Ejectment Administrative Fee, the amount of which shall be reasonably related to the additional expense in filing the proceeding. In the event Landlord terminates this lease, all further rights and duties hereunder shall terminate and Landlord shall be entitled to collect from Tenant all accrued but unpaid rents and any damages resulting from the Tenant's breach. In the event Landlord terminates the Tenant's right of possession without terminating this lease, Tenant shall remain liable for the full performance of all the covenants hereof, and Landlord shall use reasonable efforts to re-let the Premises on Tenant's behalf. Any such rentals reserved from such re-letting shall be applied first to the costs of re-letting the Premises and then to the rentals due hereunder. In the event the rentals from such re-letting are insufficient to pay the rentals due hereunder in full, Tenant shall be liable to the Landlord for any deficiency. In the event Landlord institutes a legal action against the Tenant to enforce the lease or to recover any sums due hereunder, Tenant agrees to pay Landlord reasonable attorney's fees in addition to all other damages. No fees may be deducted from the Tenant Security Deposit until the termination of the tenancy.

17. **Landlord's Default; Limitation of Remedies and Damages:** Until the Tenant notifies the Landlord in writing of an alleged default and affords the Landlord a reasonable time within which to cure, no default by the Landlord in the performance of any of the promises or obligations herein agreed to by him or imposed upon him by law shall constitute a material breach of this lease and the Tenant shall have no right to terminate this lease for any such default or suspend his performance hereunder. In no event and regardless of their duration shall any defective condition of or failure to repair, maintain, or provide any area, fixture or facility used in connection with recreation or recreational activities, including but not limited to swimming pools, club houses, and tennis courts, constitute a material breach of this lease and the Tenant shall have no right to terminate this lease or to suspend his performance hereunder. In any legal action instituted by the Tenant against the Landlord, the Tenant's damages shall be limited to the difference, if any, between the rent reserved in this lease and the reasonable rental value of the Premises, taking into account the Landlord's breach or breaches, and in no event, except in the case of the Landlord's willful or wanton negligence, shall the Tenant collect any consequential or secondary damages resulting from the breach or breaches, including but not limited to the following items: damage or destruction of furniture or other personal property of any kind located in or about the Premises, moving expenses, storage expenses, alternative interim housing expenses, and expenses of locating and procuring alternative housing.

18. **Removal, Storage and Disposition of Tenant's Personal Property:**

(a) Ten days after being placed in lawful possession by execution of a writ of possession, the Landlord may throw away, dispose of, or sell all items of personal property remaining on the Premises. During the 10-day period after being placed in lawful possession by execution of a writ of possession, the Landlord may move for storage purposes, but shall not throw away, dispose of, or sell any items of personal property remaining on the Premises unless otherwise provided for in Chapter 42 of the North Carolina General Statutes. Upon the Tenant's request prior to the expiration of the 10-day period, the Landlord shall release possession of the property to the Tenant during regular business hours or at a time agreed upon. If the Landlord elects to sell the property at public or private sale, the Landlord shall give written notice to the Tenant by first-class mail to the Tenant's last known address at least seven

Must have repairs requests in writing

cannot sue over use of amenities — not constructive eviction

**FIGURE 10.1** Continued.

days prior to the day of the sale. The seven-day notice of sale may run concurrently with the 10-day period which allows the Tenant to request possession of the property. The written notice shall state the date, time, and place of the sale, and that any surplus of proceeds from the sale, after payment of unpaid rents, damages, storage fees, and sale costs, shall be disbursed to the Tenant, upon request, within 10 days after the sale, and will thereafter be delivered to the government of the county in which the rental property is located. Upon the Tenant's request prior to the day of sale, the Landlord shall release possession of the property to the Tenant during regular business hours or at a time agreed upon. The Landlord may apply the proceeds of the sale to the unpaid rents, damages, storage fees, and sale costs. Any surplus from the sale shall be disbursed to the Tenant, upon request, within 10 days of the sale and shall thereafter be delivered to the government of the county in which the rental property is located.

(b) If the total value of all property remaining on the Premises at the time of execution of a writ of possession in an action for summary ejectment is less than one hundred dollars ($100.00), then the property shall be deemed abandoned five days after the time of execution, and the Landlord may throw away or dispose of the property. Upon the Tenant's request prior to the expiration of the five-day period, the Landlord shall release possession of the property to the Tenant during regular business hours or at a time agreed upon.

19. **Bankruptcy:** If any bankruptcy or insolvency proceedings are filed by or against the Tenant or if the Tenant makes any assignment for the benefit of creditors, the Landlord may, at his option, immediately terminate this Tenancy, and reenter and repossess the Premises, subject to the provisions of the Bankruptcy Code (11 USC Section 101, et. seq.) and the order of any court having jurisdiction thereunder.

20. **Tenant's Insurance; Release and Indemnity Provisions:** The Tenant shall be solely responsible for insuring any of his personal property located or stored upon the Premises upon the risks of damage, destruction, or loss resulting from theft, fire, storm and all other hazards and casualties. Regardless of whether the Tenant secures such insurance, the Landlord and his agents shall not be liable for any damage to, or destruction or loss of, any of the Tenant's personal property located or stored upon the Premises regardless of the cause or causes of such damage, destruction, or loss, unless such loss or destruction is attributable to the intentional acts or willful or wanton negligence of the Landlord. The Tenant agrees to release and indemnify the Landlord and his agents from and against liability for injury to the person of the Tenant or to any members of his household resulting from any cause whatsoever except only such personal injury caused by the negligent, or intentional acts of the Landlord or his agents.

21. **Agent:** The Landlord and the Tenant acknowledge that the Landlord may, from time to time in his discretion, engage a third party ("the Agent") to manage, supervise and operate the Premises or the complex, if any, of which they are a part. If such an Agent is managing, supervising and operating the Premises at the time this lease is executed, his name will be shown as "Agent" on the first page hereof. With respect to any Agent engaged pursuant to this paragraph, the Landlord and the Tenant hereby agree that: (1) Agent acts for and represents Landlord in this transaction; (2) Agent shall have only such authority as provided in the management contract existing between the Landlord and Agent; (3) Agent may perform without objection from the Tenant, any obligation or exercise any right of the Landlord imposed or given herein or by law and such performance shall be valid and binding, if authorized by the Landlord, as if performed by the Landlord; (4) the Tenant shall pay all rentals to the Agent if directed to do so by the Landlord; (5) except as otherwise provided by law, the Agent shall not be liable to the Tenant for the nonperformance of the obligations or promises of the Landlord contained herein; (6) nothing contained herein shall modify the management contract existing between the Landlord and the Agent; however, the Landlord and the Agent may from time to time modify the management agreement in any manner which they deem appropriate; (7) the Landlord, may, in his discretion and in accordance with any management agreement, remove without replacing or remove and replace any agent engaged to manage, supervise and operate the Premises.

22. **Form:** The Landlord and Tenant hereby acknowledge that their agreement is evidenced by this form contract which may contain some minor inaccuracies when applied to the particular factual setting of the parties. The Landlord and Tenant agree that the courts shall liberally and broadly interpret this lease, ignoring minor inconsistencies and inaccuracies, and that the courts shall apply the lease to determine all disputes between the parties in the manner which most effectuates their intent as expressed herein. The following rules of construction shall apply: (1) handwritten and typed additions or alterations shall control over the preprinted language when there is an inconsistency between them; (2) the lease shall not be strictly construed against either the Landlord or the Tenant; (3) paragraph headings are used only for convenience of reference and shall not be considered as a substantive part of this lease; (4) words in the singular shall include the plural and the masculine shall include the feminine and neuter genders, as appropriate; and (5) the invalidity of one or more provisions of this lease shall not affect the validity of any other provisions hereof and this lease shall be construed and enforced as if such invalid provision(s) were not included.

23. **Amendment of Laws:** In the event that subsequent to the execution of this lease any state statute regulating or affecting any duty or obligation imposed upon the Landlord pursuant to this lease is enacted, amended, or repealed, the Landlord may, at his option, elect to perform in accordance with such statute, amendment, or act of repeal in lieu of complying with the analogous provision of this lease.

24. **Eminent Domain and Casualties:** The Landlord shall have the option to terminate this lease if the Premises, or any part thereof, are condemned or sold in lieu of condemnation or damaged by fire or other casualty.

25. **Assignment:** The Tenant shall not assign this lease or sublet the Premises in whole or part.

Tenant Initials ________ ________

Page 5 of 6

**STANDARD FORM 410 - T**
**© 7/2006**

**FIGURE 10.1** Continued.

26. **Waiver:** No waiver of any breach of any obligation or promise contained herein shall be regarded as a waiver of any future breach of the same or any other obligation or promise.

27. **Other Terms and Conditions:**

(a) ☐ (Check if applicable) The Premises were built prior to 1978. (Attach Standard Form # 430 - T, "Disclosure of Information on Lead-Based Paint and Lead-Based Paint Hazards.")

(b) If there is an Agent involved in this transaction, Agent hereby discloses to Tenant that Agent is acting for and represents Landlord.

(c) The following additional terms and conditions shall also be a part of this lease:

________________________________________

________________________________________

________________________________________

(d) Itemize all addenda to this Contract and attach hereto: ____________________

________________________________________

28. **Inspection of Premises:** Within ________ days of occupying the Premises, Tenant has the right to inspect the Premises and complete a Move-in Inspection Form.

29. **Notice:** Any notices required or authorized to be given hereunder or pursuant to applicable law shall be mailed or hand delivered to the following addresses:

Tenant: the address of the Premises

Landlord: the address of which rental payments are sent.

30. **Execution; Counterparts:** When Tenant signs this lease, he acknowledges he has read and agrees to the provisions of this lease. This lease is executed in ________ (number) counterparts with an executed counterpart being retained by each party.

31. **Entire Agreement:** This Agreement contains the entire agreement of the parties and there are no representations, inducements or other provisions other than those expressed in writing. All changes, additions or deletions hereto must be in writing and signed by all parties.

THE NORTH CAROLINA ASSOCIATION OF REALTORS®, INC. MAKES NO REPRESENTATION AS TO THE LEGAL VALIDITY OR ADEQUACY OF ANY PROVISION OF THIS FORM IN ANY SPECIFIC TRANSACTION.

| TENANT: | LANDLORD: |
| --- | --- |
| ____________________ (SEAL) | ____________________ (SEAL) |
| ____________________ (SEAL) | ____________________ (SEAL) |
| Date: ____________________ | By: ____________________, AGENT |
| | ____________________ (SEAL) |
| | Date: ____________________ |

3. This paragraph informs the tenant that a late payment fee will be due if rent is not paid by midnight on the fifth day after it is due. The tenant is also responsible for paying the returned check fees for each check of the tenant that is returned for insufficient funds.
4. The lease clearly explains how the tenant security deposit must be handled and how and when it may be used or disbursed as dictated by the North Carolina Tenant Security Deposit Act. The amount of the deposit must be within the statutory limits. A real estate agent must handle such funds through his or her agency trust account and inform the tenant of the location of the depository where the security deposit is held in trust. Accounting procedures are strictly regulated by Rule A.0107 of the Real Estate Commission. Although private (non–real estate agent) landlords have the option of guaranteeing the return of these funds with an insurance bond, the property management agent *cannot* use this option in his fiduciary capacity. In no case could a landlord simply place the funds in her own pocket without complying with one or the other of these alternatives, namely a trust or escrow account in an insured North Carolina bank or savings and loan or post a bond. An interest-bearing trust account is also provided for in compliance with the North Carolina Real Estate Commission Rules. Notice that this clause is set forth prominently in all capital letters, in compliance with Rule A.0107 requiring such terms to be "set forth in a conspicuous manner."
5. Then tenant's obligations include using the premises for lawful residential purposes, refraining from disturbing other tenants or creating a nuisance, keeping the premises clean, and safe and sanitary, disposing of all waste in compliance with all ordinances, using all systems and appliances properly and safely, avoiding defacing or destroying the property, paying all utility bills billed directly to him, and remaining in property for the lease term.
6. The landlord's obligations include complying with building and housing codes, providing and maintaining fit and habitable premises by making appropriate repairs, maintaining safe and clean premises, and promptly repairing all systems and appliances after receiving actual written notification from tenant.
7. The landlord will provide operable smoke detectors. It is the landlord's responsibility to install new batteries in the smoke detector at the beginning of the lease term. It is the tenant's responsibility to replace smoke detector batteries during the lease term.
8. The tenant agrees to comply with reasonable rules and regulations as established by the landlord through his agent.
9. The landlord may enter the property for the purpose of inspecting the premises and the tenant's compliance with the terms of the rental contract or for the purpose of making repairs or improvements to the property. The landlord must exercise this right at reasonable times. If this right were not given in the lease, the landlord would not have the right to enter. (Note: The Property Management Contract in Chapter 11 states that the landlord or agent will not enter property without making an appointment with the tenant.)
10. Tenant's responsibility for damages and restitution for damages beyond normal wear and tear are set forth.
11. Pets are generally not welcomed by landlords due to the increased risk of damage and cleaning costs. This paragraph provides that pets may be allowed, subject to an additional fee. This fee should not be confused with the security deposit. Since the fee is a nonrefundable cost to the tenant, it is paid directly to the landlord and not held in the trust account.
12. Alterations to the property are to be done only with the landlord's written consent and at tenant's expense.
13. Only the tenant and the named occupants can use the premises as a residence.
14. The tenant warrants the truth of facts provided on rental application.
15. Tenant's Duties Upon Termination: Tenant must leave property cleaned, swept, and in same condition as when he took possession. Tenant shall not be responsible for normal wear and tear. He must also remove all personal property, secure doors and windows,

disconnect utility service and pay utility bills. Finally, he must return keys and provide the landlord an address where the security deposit may be returned if there are no damages or other legitimate reasons for keeping the security deposit.

16. The landlord has the right to possess the rental property in the event of tenant default. However, the landlord may only do this through a summary ejectment proceeding if the tenant does not surrender possession voluntarily.
17. The tenant must notify the landlord in writing of alleged default by the landlord and give the landlord a reasonable time to correct default. Absent willful negligence, tenant is prohibited from collecting secondary or consequential damages.
18. The landlord can dispose of tenant's personal property ten days after lawful possession of the rental property, but only in accordance with state law. The value of the personal property may dictate the landlords options.
19. The landlord has the right to terminate the tenancy subject to provisions of the bankruptcy code.
20. It is the tenant's responsibility to insure his personal property, and the landlord is released of liability for injury of tenant and other occupants unless such injury is caused by landlord's or his agent's negligence.
21. The landlord can engage an agent to manage the property.
22. Both the landlord and the tenant acknowledge that their agreement is evidenced by the contract they are signing. They both also acknowledge that there may be minor inaccuracies in the form.
23. The landlord is given the authority to comply with changes in laws or statutes that occur after execution of the lease.
24. The landlord has the option to terminate the lease in the event of condemnation or damage by fire or other casualties.
25. This paragraph prevents assignment or subletting of the lease by the tenant. If the lessor does not want the lease to be assigned or sublet, both must be specified as they are in this lease form. If a lease is assigned, the remaining term of the lease is transferred without reversion of interest to the original lessee. If a lease is sublet, a part of the lease term is transferred, with a reversion of the remaining term to the original lessee.
26. A waiver of any breach of this contract cannot be construed as a waiver of any future breaches.
27. This paragraph itemizes addenda, any additional provisions, and provides for lead-based paint disclosure and disclosure that the agent represents the landlord.
28. The tenant acknowledges having inspected property or having the right to inspect before occupancy.
29. Required notices are to be sent to tenant at property address and to landlord at address where rental payment is delivered.
30. A counterpart is an original copy of the document. Typically, three originals are made—one for the tenant, another for the agent, and one for the landlord/owner. The tenants execute their signatures, and the agent can sign on behalf of the landlord under the authority granted her by the property management contract.
31. This document represents the entire agreement between the parties.

## Landlord's Implied Covenant of Quiet Enjoyment

In a lease, the covenant of quiet enjoyment is a promise that the lessee will not be disturbed in his use of the property because of a defect in the lessor's title. Every lease implies such a covenant, even if it is not directly expressed in the lease. This covenant protects the tenant only against claims arising from the landlord, the landlord's agents, and/or someone whose title is superior to that of the landlord. An actual or constructive eviction of the tenant by any of the above-named parties breaches this covenant.

## Termination of Leases

Leases are terminated in many ways. One primary consideration is that duties of landlord and tenant are mutually dependent. Thus, if one party fails his responsibility, the other party is relieved of her duty.

**Expiration of lease term.** As previously noted, a lease creating an estate for years automatically terminates upon the expiration of the lease term. No notice is required by the lessor to the lessee or vice versa.

**Agreement of the parties.** A lease, as other executory contracts, can be terminated by the mutual agreement of the parties. The release by each party of the other provides the consideration for the agreement to terminate.

**Breach of condition.** *If lessor or lessee fails to live up to his respective duties,* the lease can be terminated by **breach of condition.** The lessee has the primary duty to pay the rent promptly as well as maintain the individual unit and conform to the specified use. The lessor has the duty to maintain the utilities and common areas of the property. If the tenant fails to pay the rent or the landlord fails to provide heat, the rental contract is breached.

**Condemnation.** A lease can be terminated by condemnation under the power of eminent domain. If the entire property is condemned, the lessee is entitled to compensation from the lessor for the remaining value of her leasehold interest. If only a part of the leased property is condemned, the lease will provide a lessee with the option to terminate the lease or remain in possession of the remainder of the premises at a reduced rent.

**Judicial eviction (actual eviction, summary ejectment).** When the lessee fails to adhere to the conditions of the lease, the lessor has the right to evict the tenant. In the event the lessee fails to surrender possession upon demand, the lessor can resort to legal action to evict the tenant after giving the tenant sufficient notice before filing the suit. If the lessee does not surrender possession voluntarily after the court awarded the lessor a judgment for possession, the lessee can be forcibly removed by an officer of the court.

**Constructive eviction** Constructive eviction results from some action or inaction by the lessor that renders the premises unfit for habitation. The North Carolina Residential Rental Agreements Act obligates the lessor to provide heat, water, and electricity. If the lessor fails to do so through personal fault or negligence, the lessee is entitled to abandon the premises, terminate the lease, and sue for damages.

## Application of the Statute of Frauds

The North Carolina Statute of Frauds requires certain contracts to be in writing to be effective. The Statute of Frauds requires any lease contract with a duration of more than three years to be in writing.

## Recordation of Leases

In North Carolina, the Conner Act requires a lease that extends for a period of *more* than three years from the date of making to be recorded to be enforceable against third parties. When a lease required by the statute to be in writing is not recorded, a purchaser of the property is not required to honor the full term of the lease. However, if the lease is of short duration and, therefore, is not in writing, the fact that the lessee is in possession of the property at the time of a sale by the lessor will protect the lessee and thereby require the purchaser to honor the lease for the remainder of the term.

## SUMMARY OF IMPORTANT POINTS

1. A landlord is the lessor who retains a freehold estate (ownership) while conveying a nonfreehold estate (possession) to the tenant or lessee.
2. A rental interest involves the concepts of contracts and estates. Landlord and tenant statutes of the state clearly establish the duties and rights of both parties. A rental

interest is the conveyance of an estate (nonfreehold) by the landlord (lessor) to the tenant (lessee). The landlord retains title in the estate (freehold); thus, freehold and nonfreehold estates exist at the same time.

3. Landlords' and tenants' duties are mutually dependent; failure of one party to perform a duty excuses the other from his obligations. Failure of the landlord's duty constitutes constructive eviction. The tenant's failure to pay the rent is default and subjects the tenant to eviction (ejectment).

4. The North Carolina Residential Rental Agreements Act requires the landlord to maintain "fit premises" by maintaining the common areas, plumbing, heating and cooling systems, and any appliances provided.

   The landlord is required to provide a properly installed smoke detector. If it is battery-operated, the landlord must provide new batteries at the beginning of each tenancy.

   As of December 6, 1996, lead-based paint disclosure is required (see Chapter 4). The tenant must maintain the individual dwelling unit, complying with building codes, being responsible for damage, and properly disposing of trash.

5. The North Carolina Tenant Security Deposit Act requires landlords to account for tenants' funds by depositing the funds in an insured trust account or guaranteeing the return of the funds with an insurance bond. The tenant must be notified which of these mechanisms the landlord is using. Maximum limits for the amount of funds that can be held are set and are related to the rental period. Funds must be accounted for and/or returned within 30 days of the termination of the lease.

6. The retaliatory eviction doctrine protects the tenant from ejectment by the landlord if the tenant asserts her rights in good faith.

7. Residential eviction remedies prohibit the landlord from physically barring the tenant from the unit (peaceable self-help) as well as from seizing the tenant's personal property.

8. A tenant cannot unilaterally withhold rent but can seek court action for a refund or be excused from the lease if the landlord breaches his duty.

9. There are four primary types of lease: (1) An estate for years is for a fixed period of time, (2) an estate from period to period automatically renews itself in the absence of notice by either party within a prescribed period, (3) an estate at will is for an indefinite or undetermined period of time, and (4) an estate at sufferance arises when a tenant is still in possession of the premises after the legal rental period has expired.

10. The two primary classifications of leases are a gross lease, in which the owner pays all of the expenses of the property, and a net lease, in which the tenant pays some or all of the expenses. Types of lease based on the payment arrangement include percentage, flat, graduated, indexed, reappraisal, escalated, sale and leaseback, and mineral. A ground lease is for the rental of the land alone, which can be improved by the tenant.

11. Termination of leases can occur by (1) breach of condition, (2) expiration of the rental term, (3) mutual agreement, and (4) condemnation of the property.

12. Actual eviction (summary ejectment) occurs when the lessee fails to adhere to conditions of the lease. Constructive eviction results from action or inaction of the lessor that renders the premises uninhabitable.

13. A lease contract that extends for more than three years from the date of making is required to be in writing by the Statute of Frauds and to be recorded by the Conner Act in order to be enforceable.

14. The Vacation Rental Act provides for fees to be paid to travel agents by real estate agents under specific circumstances.

## ITEMS TO CONSIDER FOR THE STATE EXAM

1. *Gross versus net lease.* In a gross lease, typically residential, the landlord pays the expenses of the property. A net lease, in which the tenant pays some or all of the expenses, is more typical of commercial leases. (Think of gross income, from which you must pay expenses or deductions, versus net income, which is pure profit.)
2. *Lease terminology.* Refer to the text discussion of how leases are terminated. The lessor (landlord) is promising the sanctity of the tenant's use of the premises (covenant of quiet enjoyment). The concept of constructive eviction provides that when the lessor breaches this duty, the lessee (tenant) is excused from the lease, that is, fulfillment of the rental period.
3. The North Carolina Residential Rental Agreements Act does not protect transient occupancy or commercial quarters.

## REVIEW QUESTIONS

Answers to the review questions are found in the Answer Key at the back of the book.

1. In the creation of a nonfreehold estate:
   A. the landlord retains a freehold estate
   B. a freehold and nonfreehold estate exist at the same time
   C. the tenant has a nonfreehold estate
   D. all of the above

2. If the landlord fails to perform her duty, the tenant can do all of the following EXCEPT:
   A. abandon the premises
   B. decide by himself to refuse to pay rent
   C. terminate the lease
   D. sue for damages

3. All of the following are duties of the landlord EXCEPT:
   A. comply with building codes
   B. be responsible for destruction or defacement caused by the tenant
   C. repair utilities and appliances
   D. maintain the common areas

4. Jane Smith signed a lease for one year at a rent of $200 per month. She wanted to keep a small kitten in the apartment, but the landlord automatically assumed there would be some degree of damage by the pet for which he wanted to assess an additional fee of $100. What is the maximum security deposit he could collect from Jane?
   A. $200
   B. $300
   C. $400
   D. $500

5. Larry Landlord is a private citizen, non–real estate agent renting his own apartments without the help of a broker. He has received $1,000 in security deposits from his tenants. Which of the following is true?
   A. he must deposit these funds in a trust account
   B. he could spend $200 of the funds on a personal vacation after guaranteeing return of the money with a performance bond
   C. he can deposit these funds in his personal account without a bond
   D. he must provide a bond no matter where he deposits the money or what he does with it

6. Which of the following is (are) characteristics of leasehold estates?
   I. They are estates of unlimited duration.
   II. The holder of a leasehold estate has title to the property.
   A. I only
   B. II only
   C. both I and II
   D. neither I nor II

7. All of the following statements regarding an estate for years are correct EXCEPT:
   A. the duration of the estate must be definite
   B. the duration of the estate must be at least one year
   C. the estate automatically terminates without notice
   D. the contract creating an estate for years is, in some cases, required to be in writing in order to be valid

8. Which is an estate that automatically renews itself for consecutive periods?
   A. estate at will
   B. life estate
   C. estate from year to year
   D. estate for years

9. After the termination of a lease, a tenant continued in possession of the property without permission of the property owner. The tenant's status is:
   A. tenant at will
   B. lessee
   C. trespasser
   D. tenant at sufferance

10. All of the following are essential elements of a valid lease EXCEPT:
    A. the parties must have the legal capacity to contract
    B. the property must be clearly identified
    C. provision must be made for automatic renewal
    D. all essential aspects of the agreement (rent, occupancy dates, and so on) must be set forth

11. In which type of lease does the lessee agree to pay an increasing rental fee as sales in the demised property increase?
A. escalated
B. percentage
C. ground
D. none of the above

12. A lease contract provides for which of the following?
A. a freehold estate for the lessee
B. a nonfreehold estate for the lessor
C. a freehold estate for the tenant
D. a leasehold estate for the lessee

13. Which of the following is NOT a correct statement regarding the real property and contractual rights of the lessor and lessee as created by a residential lease contract?
A. the lessee has the exclusive right to possession and control of the leased premises during the term of the lease
B. the lessor retains the title to the leased premises during the term of the lease and has the right to regain possession upon the termination of the lease
C. the lessor has the right to enter the property at any time during the term of the lease
D. the landlord must provide premises fit for human habitation

14. All of the following are typical provisions of lease contracts for an estate for years EXCEPT:
A. provision for a term of indefinite duration
B. right of first refusal
C. right to make alterations
D. option to renew

15. Which of the following is a lease in which the rental amount is changed a specified percentage of the change in the Consumer Price Index?
A. percentage
B. index
C. escalated
D. graduated

16. A transaction in which a property owner sells the property and leases it from the purchaser is described as which of the following?
A. option to renew
B. sale and leaseback
C. ground lease
D. sublease

17. A lease is terminated by each of the following EXCEPT:
A. constructive eviction
B. condemnation
C. breach of condition
D. right of first refusal

18. Tina Tenant rents an apartment from Larry Landlord. Larry refuses to repair the heating and plumbing; therefore, Tina has no heat or water. Tina can legally:
A. remain in the apartment and refuse to pay rent
B. move out of the apartment and refuse to pay rent
C. either a or b
D. neither a nor b

19. If a tenant pays rent as well as maintenance, utilities, taxes, and insurance, the lease is a:
A. net lease
B. gross lease
C. ground lease
D. none of the above

20. Randy Renter starts a tenants' union to try to improve the maintenance of the apartment complex where he lives. Oscar Owner immediately gives Randy notice to move out. Randy has protection from eviction for one year under the doctrine of:
A. self-help
B. retaliatory eviction
C. constructive eviction
D. negligence

21. Oral agency is allowed when working with a:
A. licensee
B. lessor
C. lessee
D. lien holder

22. The Vacation Rental Act applies to consideration paid to:
A. tenants
B. property owners
C. real estate agents
D. travel agents

23. Which estate affords the tenant the most security?
A. estate at will
B. estate from year to year
C. estate at sufferance
D. freehold estate

# Chapter 11

## KEY TERMS

management plan
management proposal
operating budget
property management
property management agreement
property management report
property manager
resident manager
stabilized budget

## LEARNING OBJECTIVES

At the conclusion of this chapter, you should be able to:

1. Define the owner-property manager relationship.
2. Describe the principal functions of property managers.

# Real Estate Management

**IN THIS CHAPTER**

This chapter discusses the fiduciary duty of the real estate agent in the specialized field of property management and identifies his or her duty of agency in this area.

## THE OWNER-PROPERTY MANAGER RELATIONSHIP

### Purposes of Property Management

The basic purpose of **property management** is *to represent the owner or principal in much the same manner as the listing and selling agents represent the owner-seller of a property.* Inherent in this relationship is the fiduciary duty of agency that binds the agent to absolute fidelity to the owner's best interests. A **property manager** is usually *a special limited agent (broker);* however, a property manager of a large shopping center, office complex, or apartment building who has been given the authority to act in place of the owner and perform a wide variety of activities can be a general agent. In the owner-property manager relationship, the agent essentially stands in the place of the owners to perform the duties of an efficient business operation that the owners cannot or do not wish to perform for themselves. The owners may have many reasons for transferring their duties to the agent, such as that of owning multiple properties in various locations. Each property is a serious business investment that represents considerable potential advantages to the owners. It is often altogether fitting that the owners seek the skills of the real estate professional in order to gain the maximum advantage of their property. By virtue of her special training and experience, the agent offers the owners expertise that they may not possess.

### Types of Property Requiring Management

Many types of property can benefit from real estate management services of the broker. Residential property can include apartments, condominiums, single-family homes, and vacation property. Retail or commercial property can include offices, small retail stores, office condominiums, and large shopping malls. Industrial property is another specialization that can include industrial parks.

### Property Management Fee

All fees and rates of compensation between agents and principals are strictly negotiable between the parties. It is a violation of federal antitrust laws for competitors even to discuss such things as rates of compensation or the boycotting of another competitor based on a rate of compensation. Therefore, if any group of agents were to try to establish a "going rate" for property management (or anything else), they would be in serious trouble with the law. All agents who are parties to such conversations can be held liable.

Compensation negotiated between the principal and agent can take any number of forms. Often this form is that of a percentage of the rents actually collected, but the establishment of a flat fee or minimum fee is often added to the formula of compensation. Real estate agents should be able to calculate the total compensation due, given the formula or combination of formulas established by the parties. For example, Darby Apartments consists of eight units that rent for $325 per month and six units that rent for $275. The manager's fee is 10 percent of the gross monthly rents collected. During the month of March, two of the $325 units were vacant as was one of the $275 units. The manager's fee would be calculated as follows:

$$6 \times \$325 \times 10\% = \$195.00$$

$$5 \times \$275 \times 10\% = \frac{\$137.50}{\$332.50}$$

If a unit were rented for only a portion of the month, the rent and fee would be prorated according to the days actually used. For example, if one of the vacant $325 units were rented only for the last ten days of the month, this calculation would be:

$$\frac{\$325}{30} \times 10 \text{ days} \times 10\% = \$10.83 \text{ Manager's fee}$$

## Travel Agent Referral Fees in Vacation Rentals

A real estate agent may pay or promise to pay a travel agent a consideration under specific circumstances. According to Rule a.0109(e), this consideration may be made if the travel agent introduces the tenant to the agent in the normal course of the travel agent's business, if the travel agent has not engaged in an activity requiring a real estate license, and if the travel agent has not received money in connection with the vacation rental. This is a major revision in state law that in the past has only allowed the real estate agent to offer consideration or referral fees to other licensed real estate agents (in or out of North Carolina). The payment of any consideration or referral fee may be disbursed only after the conclusion of the rental period. The agent must also retain for three years records of these payments that include the details of the transaction such as the tenant's name, the travel agent's name, the amount paid to the travel agent, and the dates of tenancy.

# AGENCY RELATIONSHIP IN RENTALS

The point at which all agency agreements, including those with landlords and tenants, must be in writing depends on who the party is to the agreement. Agency agreements, with or without dual agency authorization, with property owners must be in writing from the beginning of any relationship between an agent and a property owner, whether the property owner's role is that of a seller or a lessor/landlord. Unlike an agency agreement with an owner/seller, which must be for a definite period and must expire on the stated date, agency agreements with lessors/landlords can contain an automatic renewal provided the landlord can end the agreement with notice at the end of the initial contract period or any subsequent renewal period.

If an agency relationship, with or without dual agency authorization, is to exist between an agent and a tenant, such agreement must be expressed from the beginning of the relationship and be committed to writing before the tenant makes an offer to rent or lease real estate to another. If the agreement seeks to bind the prospective tenant for a specific time period or restrict the tenant from working independently or with other agents, that fact must be in writing from the beginning of the relationship.

Undisclosed dual agency is prohibited in landlord–tenant transactions as well as sales transactions. If this permission is not given by either or both parties from the outset of the agency relationship and the need for dual agency later arises, permission must be obtained from both parties before dual agency can be initiated. Agents working with landlords or tenants are not required to provide the "Working With Real Estate Agents" brochure; however, it is a good practice to do so. While an agent is not required to give the tenant written notice that he is working as the landlord's agent, he should inform potential commercial and residential tenants that he represents the property owner and that the tenants should not tell the agent anything they do not want the property owner to know.

Rule A.0104(i) requires agents to disclose to all parties when they have entered a dual agency situation. This means that in the landlord–tenant situation, the dual agency must have been authorized in writing by the landlord and expressly authorized by the tenant, either orally or in writing. Such an express oral authorization by the tenant must be committed to writing before an offer to rent or lease is made.

## Property Management Contracts

The property manager's authority arises in basically the same way as the listing agent's authority, namely, through a clear employment agreement. Like the listing contract, the property management contract is with a broker or brokerage firm. Figure 11.1 illustrates the standard form adopted by the North Carolina Association of REALTORS®. This particular form is copyrighted for use by members only but serves as a good illustration of an appropriate form. The **property management agreement** should set out the following items, starting with the inception date and names of the parties:

1. The property location is identified. Note that an informal reference (street address) is usually sufficient for the property management agreement.
2. The duration of the agency agreement between the owner and real estate agent is defined.
3. The agent's fee is established.
4. The handling of other fees including processing tenant rental applications, late payment fees, and returned checks is discussed.
5. The agent's authority and responsibilities are spelled out in specific areas. Even though the agent is given more decision-making authority in this agreement than in the case of listing a property for sale, the agent is still considered a *special (limited) agent.* A property manager of a large complex who has vast authority to perform a wide variety of functions may be a general agent. Details of the agent's promises to the owner are identified. The Real Estate Commission holds that failure to perform the duties identified under this agreement constitutes *breach of agency,* a serious infraction of the license law.
6. Terms under which other agents may be compensated are authorized.
7. Methods of marketing are authorized.
8. The owner's covenants are defined, including the owner's agreement to pay for authorized services, to allow agent to offer property without discrimination, to maintain a specified amount of liability insurance, and to hold agent harmless if allowable by law from any claim resulting from managing property other than those claims resulting from agent's gross negligence or deliberate misconduct.
9. The handling of security deposits by the agent is specified in accordance with both license law and state law.
10. This paragraph authorizes the agent to put rental and tenant security deposits in an interest bearing trust account.
11. Reasonable notice must be provided to the tenant before the owner or agent may enter the premises.
12. If the property was built before 1978, the owner is required to disclose information about lead-based paint and lead-based paint hazards. It is the agent's responsibility to ensure the owner's compliance with this requirement.

**FIGURE 11.1** Exclusive Property Management Agreement.

## EXCLUSIVE PROPERTY MANAGEMENT AGREEMENT
### Long-term Rental Property

This Exclusive Property Management Agreement is entered into by and between ______________________________ ("Owner") and ______________________________ ("Agent").

IN CONSIDERATION of the mutual covenants and promises set forth herein, Owner hereby contracts with Agent, and Agent hereby contracts with Owner, to lease and manage the property described below, as well as any other property Owner and Agent may from time to time agree in writing will be subject to this Agreement (the "Property"), in accordance with all applicable laws and regulations, upon the terms and conditions contained herein.

1. **Property:** City:______________________ County: ______________________, NC
Street Address: ______________________
Other Description: ______________________

2. **Duration of Agreement:** This Agreement shall be binding when it has been signed and dated below by Owner and Agent. It shall become effective on ______________, ________, and shall be for an initial term of ______________. Not less than ________ days prior to the conclusion of the initial term, either party may notify the other party in writing of its desire to terminate this Agreement, in which case it shall terminate at the conclusion of the initial term. If not so terminated, this Agreement shall automatically renew for successive terms of ______________ each unless either party gives the other party written notice of its desire to terminate this Agreement at least ________ days prior to the conclusion of any such renewal term, in which case this Agreement shall terminate at the conclusion of such term. If Owner terminates this Agreement within ________ days of its effective date, Owner shall pay Agent a termination fee of ______________________________.

3. **Agent's Fee:** For services performed hereunder, Owner shall compensate Agent in the following manner:
❑ A fee equal to ______________________ percent ( __________ %) of gross rental income received on all rental agreements, or $ ______________ per month, whichever is greater.
❑ Other (*describe method of compensation*): ______________________________.

Agent may deduct Agent's Fee from gross receipts and collections received before remitting the balance of the receipts and collections to Owner. ***Note:*** No fees may be deducted from any tenant security deposit until the termination of the tenancy. Thereafter, any fees due Agent from Owner may be deducted from any portion of the security deposit due to Owner.

4. **Other Fees:** Agent may charge tenants reasonable administrative fees permitted by law and retain any such fees, including but not limited to, fees to cover the costs of processing tenant rental applications. If, in Agent's discretion, tenant leases provide for late payment fees and/or returned check fees, such fees, when collected by Agent, shall belong to ______________________ (Owner or Agent). Fees for purposes covered under the Tenant Security Deposit Act will be collected, held and disbursed in accordance with paragraphs 7 and 8 of this Agreement.

5. **Authority and Responsibilities of Agent:** During the time this Agreement is in effect, Agent shall:
   (a) Manage the Property to the best of Agent's ability, devoting thereto such time and attention as may be necessary;
   (b) OFFER THE PROPERTY TO THE PUBLIC FOR LEASING IN COMPLIANCE WITH ALL STATE AND FEDERAL HOUSING LAWS, INCLUDING BUT NOT LIMITED TO, ANY STATE AND FEDERAL LAWS PROHIBITING DISCRIMINATION ON THE BASIS OF RACE, COLOR, RELIGION, SEX, NATIONAL ORIGIN, HANDICAP OR FAMILIAL STATUS;
   (c) Use Agent's best efforts to solicit, secure and maintain tenants, including the authority to negotiate, execute, extend and renew leases in Owner's name for terms not in excess of ______________________;
   (d) Collect all rentals and other charges and amounts due under tenant leases and give receipts for amounts so collected;
   (e) Deliver to Owner within 45 days following the date of execution of any rental agreement an accounting which sets forth the name of the tenant, the rental rate and rents collected, and promptly provide a copy of any rental agreement to Owner upon reasonable request;

**FIGURE 11.1** Continued.

(f) Provide Owner monthly statements of all monies received and disbursed in connection with Agent's management of the Property, and remit to Owner rental proceeds collected, less any deductions authorized hereunder; provided: (1) this shall not constitute a guarantee by Agent for rental payments that Agent is unable to collect in the exercise of reasonable diligence; and (2) if, pursuant to this Agreement or required by law, Agent either has refunded or will refund in whole or in part any rental payments made by a tenant and previously remitted to Owner, Owner agrees to return same to Agent promptly upon Agent's demand;

(g) Make or cause to be made any repairs which, in Agent's opinion, may be necessary to preserve, maintain and protect the Property; provided, Agent may not make any repairs that exceed $ ______________________ without prior approval of Owner, except that in the case of an emergency, Agent may, without prior approval, make whatever expenditures on behalf of Owner that are reasonably necessary to preserve the Property or prevent further damage from occurring;

(h) Answer tenant requests and complaints and perform the duties imposed upon Owner by tenant leases or any local, state or federal law or regulations, including the authority to purchase such supplies and hire such labor as may be necessary in Agent's opinion to accomplish any necessary repairs;

(i) Retain such amounts from Owner's rental proceeds as may be necessary from time to time to establish and maintain a fund on behalf of Owner in the amount of $ ____________________ , from which Agent may pay expenses associated with the management and operation of the Property for which Owner is responsible hereunder;

(j) Negotiate partial refunds with tenants if, in Agent's reasonable opinion, the tenant's use and enjoyment of the Property has been or will be materially and adversely affected as a result of a defect in the condition of the Property (such as a repair to the electrical, plumbing, sanitary, heating or ventilating facilities or a major appliance that cannot be made reasonably and promptly);

(k) Institute and prosecute such proceedings in small claims court as may be necessary and advisable, in Agent's opinion, to recover rents and other sums due the Owner from tenants or to evict tenants and regain possession, including the authority, in Agent's discretion, to settle, compromise and release any and all such small claims proceedings; and

(l) ______________________________________________________________________________
______________________________________________________________________________
______________________________________________________________________________
______________________________________________________________________________
______________________________________________________________________________

**6. Cooperation With/Compensation To Other Agents:** Agent has advised Owner of Agent's company policies regarding cooperation and the amount(s) of any compensation, if any, that will be offered to subagents, tenant agents or both. Owner authorizes Agent to: (*Check ALL applicable authorizations*)

☐ Cooperate with subagents representing only the Owner and offer them the following compensation: ______________
______________________________________________________________________________

☐ Cooperate with tenant agents representing only the tenant and offer them the following compensation: ______________
______________________________________________________________________________

☐ Cooperate with and compensate agents from other firms according to the attached company policy.

Agent will promptly notify Owner if Agent offers compensation to a cooperating agent(s) that is different from that set forth above.

**7. Marketing:** Owner authorizes Agent to advertise the Property in such manner as may be appropriate in Agent's opinion, including the authority to: (*Check ALL applicable sections*)

☐ place "For Rent" signs on the Property (where permitted by law and relevant covenants) and to remove other such signs.

☐ place information about the Property on the Internet either directly or through a program of any listing service of which the Agent is a member or in which any of Agent's associates participates.

☐ permit other firms who belong to any listing service in which the Agent participates to advertise the Property on the Internet in accordance with the listing service rules and regulations.

☐ submit pertinent information concerning the Property to any listing service of which Agent is a member or in which any of Agent's associates participates and to furnish to such listing service notice of all changes of information concerning the Property authorized in writing by Owner. Owner authorizes Agent, upon execution of a rental contract for the Property, to notify the listing service of the rental, and to disseminate rental information, including rental price, to the listing service, appraisers and real estate brokers.

**8. Responsibilities of Owner:** During the time this Agreement is in effect, Owner shall:

(a) Be responsible for all costs and expenses associated with the maintenance and operation of the Property in accordance with the requirements of tenant leases or any local, state or federal law or regulations, including but not limited to NC General Statutes Section 42-42, and advance to Agent such sums as may be necessary from time to time to pay such costs and expenses;

Page 2 of 6

**STANDARD FORM 401**


Owner Initials __________ __________ Agent Initials __________

**FIGURE 11.1** Continued.

(b) Provide funds to Agent promptly upon Agent's request for any cost or expense for which Owner is responsible that Agent, in Agent's discretion, incurs on Owner's behalf, including but not limited to, the costs of advertising, emergency maintenance and repairs, utilities, property taxes, owners' association dues and assessments, court costs and attorney's fees; and further, pay interest at the rate of ______________________________ percent ( __________ %) per month on the amount of any outstanding balance thereof not paid to Agent within __________ days of Agent's written request therefor;

(c) NOT TAKE ANY ACTION OR ADOPT ANY POLICY THE EFFECT OF WHICH WOULD BE TO PREVENT AGENT FROM OFFERING THE PROPERTY FOR RENT IN COMPLIANCE WITH ALL APPLICABLE FEDERAL AND STATE LAWS AND REGULATIONS, INCLUDING BUT NOT LIMITED TO, THOSE LAWS AND REGULATIONS PROHIBITING DISCRIMINATION ON THE BASIS OF RACE, COLOR, RELIGION, SEX, NATIONAL ORIGIN, HANDICAP OR FAMILIAL STATUS IN THE LEASING OF THE PROPERTY;

(d) Carry, at Owner's expense, commercial general liability insurance (including products and completed operations coverage) against any and all claims or demands whatever arising out of, or in any way connected with, the operation, leasing and maintenance of the Property, which policies shall be written to the extent allowable so as to protect Agent in the same manner as Owner and which shall be in the minimum amounts of $ ____________________ for each injury or death of one person in each accident or occurrence, and $ ____________________ for property damage in each accident or occurrence; and provide at least annually a copy of such insurance policy or policies to Agent upon Agent's request; (Name of insurance agent: ______________________________ ; telephone no.: ____________________ )

(e) Indemnify and hold Agent harmless to the extent allowable by law from any and all costs, expenses, attorneys' fees, suits, liabilities, damages or claims for damages, including but not limited to, those arising out of any injury or death to any person or loss or damage to any property of any kind whatsoever and to whomsoever belonging, including Owner, in any way relating to the management of the Property by Agent or the performance or exercise of any duty, obligation or authority set forth herein or hereafter granted to Agent, except to the extent that such may be the result of gross negligence or willful or intentional misconduct by Agent; and

(f) ____________________________________________________________
____________________________________________________________
____________________________________________________________
____________________________________________________________
____________________________________________________________
____________________________________________________________
____________________________________________________________

**9. Tenant Security Deposits:** Agent may, in Agent's discretion, require tenants to make security deposits in an amount permitted by law to secure tenants' lease obligations (such security deposits shall hereinafter be referred to as "Tenant Security Deposits"). If the Agent requires Tenant Security Deposits, they shall be placed in a trust account in Agent's name in a North Carolina bank or savings and loan association. Upon the commencement of this Agreement, Owner shall deliver to Agent a list of any current tenants who previously made Tenant Security Deposits under existing leases and the amounts thereof. Simultaneously therewith, any such Tenant Security Deposits shall be placed in a trust account in Agent's name in a North Carolina bank or savings and loan association, and shall thereafter be administered in accordance with this Agreement.

**10. Trust Account Interest: Agent may, in Agent's discretion, place gross receipts and collections, including Tenant Security Deposits, in an interest bearing trust account in the name of Agent in an insured bank or savings and loan association in North Carolina. Interest on any such amounts shall belong to ______________________________ (Owner or Agent), except that with respect to any Tenant Security Deposits, tenant leases shall specify, in Agent's discretion, whether such interest shall be payable to Owner or to the tenant. If the lease provides that such interest is payable to the tenant, Agent shall account for the interest in the manner set forth in such lease. If the lease provides that such interest is payable to Owner or as Owner directs, then such interest shall be paid to Owner or Agent as set forth above. Agent may remove any interest payable to Agent from the account at all times and with such frequency as is permitted under the terms of the account and as the law may require.**

**11. Entry by Owner:** Owner agrees that neither Owner nor any third party acting at Owner's direction, shall enter the Property for any purpose whatsoever during any time that it is occupied by a tenant in the absence of reasonable notice to Agent or tenant and scheduling by Agent or tenant of an appropriate time for any such entry.

**12. Lead-Based Paint/Hazard Disclosure:** If the Property was built prior to 1978, Landlord understands that Landlord is required under 42 U.S.C. 4852(d) to disclose information about lead-based paint and lead-based paint hazards, and that Agent is required to ensure Landlord's compliance with said law. Landlord agrees to complete and sign a "Disclosure Of Information On Lead-Based Paint And Lead-Based Paint Hazards" form (NCAR form #430-T), photocopies of which will be provided by Agent to prospective tenants. In the alternative, Landlord authorizes Agent, in Agent's discretion, to fulfill Landlord's disclosure obligations by completing and signing said form on Landlord's behalf based on information provided by Landlord to Agent.

Page 3 of 6 **STANDARD FORM 401**

Owner Initials __________ __________ Agent Initials __________ **© 7/2006**

**FIGURE 11.1** Continued.

**13. Duties on Termination:** Upon termination of this Agreement by either party, each shall take such steps as are necessary to settle all accounts between them, including, but not limited to, the following:

(a) Agent shall promptly render to Owner all rents then on hand after having deducted therefrom any Agent's fees then due and amounts sufficient to cover all other outstanding expenditures of Agent incurred in connection with operating the Property;

(b) Agent shall transfer any security deposits held by Agent to Owner or such other person or entity as Owner may designate in writing; provided, Owner understands and acknowledges that the Tenant Security Deposit Act requires Owner to either deposit any such deposits in a trust account with a licensed and insured bank or savings institution located in North Carolina, or furnish a bond from an insurance company licensed to do business in North Carolina;

(c) Owner shall promptly pay to Agent any fees or amounts due the Agent under the Agreement and shall reimburse Agent for any expenditures made and outstanding at the time of termination;

(d) Agent shall deliver to Owner copies of all tenant leases and other instruments entered into on behalf of Owner (Agent may retain copies of such leases and instruments for Agent's records); and

(e) Owner shall notify all current tenants of the termination of this Agreement and transfer of any advance rents and security deposits to Owner.

**14. Sale of Property:** In the event Owner desires to sell the Property through Owner's own efforts or those of a firm other than Agent, Owner shall: (a) promptly notify Agent that the Property is for sale and, if applicable, disclose to Agent the name of the listing firm; and (b) promptly notify Agent if the Property goes under contract and disclose to Agent the agreed-upon closing date.

**15. Entire Agreement; Modification:** This Agreement contains the entire agreement of the parties and supercedes all prior written and oral proposals, understandings, agreements and representations, all of which are merged herein. No amendment or modification to this Agreement shall be effective unless it is in writing and executed by all parties hereto.

**16. Non-Waiver of Default:** The failure of either party to insist, in any one or more instances, on the performance of any term or condition of this Agreement shall not be construed as a waiver or relinquishment of any rights granted hereunder or of the future performance of any such term or condition, and the obligations of the non-performing party with respect thereto shall continue in full force and effect.

**17. Governing Law; Venue:** The parties agree that this Agreement shall be governed by and construed in accordance with the laws of the State of North Carolina, and that in the event of a dispute, any legal action may only be instituted in the county where the Property is located.

**18. Relationship of Parties:** Although Owner and Agent agree that they will actively and materially participate with each other on a regular basis in fulfilling their respective obligations hereunder, the parties intend for their relationship to be that of independent contractors, and nothing contained in this Agreement shall be construed to create a partnership or joint venture of any kind.

**19. Exclusivity:** Owner agrees that Agent shall be the exclusive rental agent for the Property, and that no other party, including Owner, shall offer the Property for rent during the time this Agreement is in effect. Any rent nevertheless received by Owner or any third party will be transferred to Agent and thereafter accounted for as if originally received by Agent, including the deduction therefrom of any fee due Agent hereunder.

**20. Default:** If either party defaults in the performance of any of its obligations hereunder, in addition to any other remedies provided herein or by applicable law, the non-defaulting party shall have the right to terminate this Agreement if, within thirty days after providing the defaulting party with written notice of the default and the intent to terminate, the default remains uncured.

**21. Costs in Event of Default:** If legal proceedings are brought by a party to enforce the terms, conditions or provisions of this Agreement, the prevailing party shall be entitled to recover all expenses (including, but not limited to, reasonable attorney fees, legal expenses and reasonable costs of collection) paid or incurred by such prevailing party in endeavoring to enforce the terms, conditions, or provisions of this Agreement and/or collect any amount owing in accordance with this Agreement.

**22. Authority to Enter into Agreement; Principal Contact:** Owner represents and warrants to Agent that Owner has full authority to enter into this Agreement, and that there is no other party with an interest in the Property whose joinder in this Agreement is necessary. Either ______________________________ or ______________________________ shall serve as Owner's principal contact for purposes of making all decisions and receiving all notices and rental payments contemplated by this Agreement, and all persons signing this Agreement as Owner hereby appoint either of said persons as Owner's agent and attorney-in-fact for the purposes set forth in this section.



Owner Initials __________ __________ Agent Initials __________

**FIGURE 11.1** Continued.

**23. Notices:** Any notices required or permitted to be given hereunder shall be in writing and mailed by certified mail to the appropriate party at the party's address set forth below.

**24. Binding Nature of Agreement:** This Agreement shall be binding upon and inure to the benefit of the heirs, legal and personal representatives, successors and permitted assigns of the parties.

**25. Assignments by Agent; Change of Ownership:** Owner agrees that at any time during the term of this Agreement, Agent may either assign Agent's rights and responsibilities hereunder to another real estate agency, or transfer to another person or entity all or part of the ownership of Agent's real estate agency, and that in the event of any such assignment or transfer, this Agreement shall continue in full force and effect; provided, that any assignee or transferee must be licensed to engage in the business of real estate brokerage in the State of North Carolina. In the event of any such assignment or transfer, Owner may, in addition to all other termination rights hereunder, terminate this Agreement without cause on sixty (60) days' prior written notice to the assignee or transferee of Owner's intent to terminate this Agreement.

**26. Other Professional Services:** Owner acknowledges that Agent is being retained solely as a real estate professional, and understands that other professional service providers are available to render advice or services to Owner at Owner's expense, including but not limited to an attorney, insurance agent, tax advisor, engineer, home inspector, environmental consultant, architect, or contractor. If Agent procures any such services at the request of Owner, Owner agrees that Agent shall incur no liability or responsibility in connection therewith.

**27. Addenda:** Any addenda to this Agreement are described in the following space and attached hereto: ____________________
______________________________________________________________________________
______________________________________________________________________________
______________________________________________________________________________.

The parties agree that any such addenda shall constitute an integral part of this Agreement. In the event of a conflict between this Agreement and any such addenda, the terms of such addenda shall control.

**THE AGENT SHALL CONDUCT ALL BROKERAGE ACTIVITIES IN REGARD TO THIS AGREEMENT WITHOUT RESPECT TO THE RACE, COLOR, RELIGION, SEX, NATIONAL ORIGIN, HANDICAP OR FAMILIAL STATUS OF ANY PARTY OR PROSPECTIVE PARTY TO THE AGREEMENT.**

THE NORTH CAROLINA ASSOCIATION OF REALTORS®, INC. MAKES NO REPRESENTATION AS TO THE LEGAL VALIDITY OR ADEQUACY OF ANY PROVISION OF THIS FORM IN ANY SPECIFIC TRANSACTION.

OWNER:

______________________________________________ (SEAL) DATE: ____________________

______________________________________________ (SEAL) DATE: ____________________

______________________________________________ (SEAL) DATE: ____________________

______________________________________________ (SEAL) DATE: ____________________

AGENT: ______________________________________________________________________
[Name of real estate firm]

By: ______________________________ Individual license # ________________ DATE: ____________________
[Authorized Representative]

Real Estate Agency: ______________________________________________________________
Address: ________________________________________________________________________
Telephone: ____________________ Fax: ______________ E-mail: ____________________________

**FIGURE 11.1** Continued.

**Owner:** ______________________________
Address: ______________________________
Telephone: ____________ Fax: ____________ E-mail: ____________
Social Security/Tax ID#: ____________

**Owner:** ______________________________
Address: ______________________________
Telephone: ____________ Fax: ____________ E-mail: ____________
Social Security/Tax ID#: ____________

**Owner:** ______________________________
Address: ______________________________
Telephone: ____________ Fax: ____________ E-mail: ____________
Social Security/Tax ID#: ____________

**Owner:** ______________________________
Address: ______________________________
Telephone: ____________ Fax: ____________ E-mail: ____________
Social Security/Tax ID#: ____________



STANDARD FORM 401

13. This paragraph provides for the agent's and the owner's duties to settle all accounts between them upon termination of the contract.
14. If the owner wishes to sell the property, the owner is required to notify the agent promptly of such intention. The owner is further required to notify the agent promptly if the property is put under contract.
15. The owner and the agent agree that the entire scope of their agreement has been defined as well as possible in this form as constructed and agree to standard rules of interpretation.
16. Non-waiver of default.
17. Any legal action instituted under the rental agreement will be heard only in the county in which the property is located.
18. The owner and agent agree to work with each other in an independent contractor relationship. Their relationship shall not be construed as a partnership or a joint venture.
19. The owner agrees that the agent will act as the exclusive rental agent for the property.
20. In the event of default by either party, in addition to other remedies available by law, the non-defaulting party may terminate the contract.
21. In the event of a default, all expenses related to the default shall be repaid to the prevailing party.
22. The owner warrants to the agent that he has the authority to enter into this property management contract. The owner also warrants that there is no other party with an interest in the property who would be required to sign the contract.
23. Any notices required by either party shall be in writing and shall be sent via certified mail.
24. The contract shall be binding upon heirs, legal and personal representatives, successors and permitted assigns of the parties.
25. Agent may assign his rights and responsibilities under the contract at any time to an entity licensed to engage in real estate brokerage in North Carolina. The owner may, however, terminate the contract without cause with 60 days written notice.
26. The owner acknowledges that the agent is being retained solely for real estate services and should not be relied upon for professional advice outside this area.
27. This paragraph lists any addenda attached to the contract.

## Duties of the Property Manager

Property management is one of a number of specializations within the real estate industry. A property manager is a licensed real estate broker or brokerage firm that manages properties for owners as an agent. In acting as an agent, the property manager is a fiduciary and, therefore, owes all of the obligations imposed by the law of agency to each owner-principal. Additionally, since the property manager acts as agent in renting, leasing, and perhaps selling the property, the property manager must have a real estate broker's license.

Any employee of the broker (property manager) who assists in any aspect of the property management process that requires negotiating rental or lease agreements or the amount of rents or security deposits must have a real estate broker's license, although the license may have provisional status attached to it. The property manager needs comprehensive specialized training to be able to satisfactorily perform the functions accepted under the typical contract with the property owner. One source for obtaining this training is by the Institute of Real Estate Management, an affiliate of the National Association of REALTORS®. Upon completion of this program, the individual receives a professional designation of Certified Property Manager (CPM). In contrast to a property manager, a **resident manager** is *a person living on the premises who is a salaried employee of the owner.* This person is required to have a real estate license unless he is employed by a corporation that owns the property or is a partner with an ownership interest in the entity that owns the property, if the owner is an entity other than a corporation.

According to NCGS 93A-2 (c) (6), there is an exception made for W-2 employees of licensed brokers (property managers) to do certain tasks associated with renting/leasing the unit. These tasks, however, do not include listing, buying, renting, leasing, or auctioning real estate or offering to list, sell, buy, rent, lease, or auction real estate for compensation for others. While a W-2 employee may not auction or offer to auction, he is not prohibited from being the crier at an auction. Only real estate licensees may auction or offer to auction and they must also be licensed as an auctioneer. Referring a potential client or customer to a licensee for compensation is also strictly prohibited.

The W-2 employee of a broker may perform certain ministerial tasks as outlined in NCGS 92-A-2 under the supervision of the employing broker. See Statues for details. Expert management is often necessary for income property to be a profitable investment. Competent management can provide a comprehensive, orderly program, on a continuing basis, of analyzing all of the investment aspects of a property to ensure a financially successful project.

# PRINCIPAL FUNCTIONS OF PROPERTY MANAGERS

Renting space, collecting rents, and paying expenses are important basic functions of property managers; however, their functions and responsibilities exceed these activities to a considerable extent. In essence, a property manager's basic responsibilities are to produce the best possible net operating income from the property and to maintain and increase the value of the principal's investment.

The property manager may perform all of these duties, but it is not uncommon for duties such as marketing, executing leases, collecting rents, maintaining property, enforcing rules, performing a landlord's legal duties, and instituting legal actions to be delegated to an affiliated leasing agent. Remember that any person engaged in negotiating terms of a rental agreement or lease must have a real estate license. Even when some duties are assigned to a leasing agent, the property manager normally does not delegate responsibility for the management plan, the preparation of income/expense reports, record maintenance, and the handling of monies collected.

## Preparing The Management Plan

Prior to entering into a management agreement with a property owner, the property manager must formulate a long-range plan to be followed in managing the property. The **management plan** is included in the **management proposal** submitted to the owner, along with a proposed management agreement. The formulation of the management plan includes the following steps:

1. *Analysis of the owner's objectives.* A determination of the owner's objective(s) in ownership of the property must be made. The property manager must be satisfied that these objectives are realistic. The owner's primary objective may be income, capital appreciation, or a tax shelter provided by depreciation. The Tax Reform Act of 1986 has limited the previous generous benefits in this area, but there are still significant tax advantages to the investor.
2. *Establishment of a rental schedule.* Several steps are involved in the formulation of a proper rental schedule that will provide the best income for the owner. First, one must evaluate the national, regional, and local trends for the particular type of property. For example, if one were to evaluate the market for office space, it would be important to note that there has been a general oversupply of such property on a national and regional scale. A careful local analysis is also essential to evaluate how this trend impacts the specific property and its unique location. Next, one needs to prepare an analysis of comparable properties that are currently for rent, just as one would identify comparable sales for listing a property. Finally, one should prepare an operating budget in advance, reflecting a realistic analysis of the projected income and expenses.

3. *Property analysis.* The property analysis covers a survey of the economic and physical aspects of the property. The economic aspects are data on previous duration of leases, vacancy and credit losses, rent schedules, and operating costs. The analysis of the physical aspects includes the determination of the condition of the property, necessary repairs, and necessary or appropriate capital expenditures.
4. *Preparation of budgets.* The last step in the formulation of a management plan is to establish an operating budget and a stabilized budget. The **operating budget** is *an annual budget and includes only those items of income and expense expected during a particular budget year.* The **stabilized budget** is *a forecast of income and expense as may be reasonably projected over a short term of years, typically five years.*

## Marketing and Renting the Property

The property manager needs to establish an effective advertising schedule to attract qualified tenants. This program must take into consideration many forms of advertising and other contacts to keep the recruitment of tenants as an ongoing process. In general, the manager strives to keep the vacancy rate low, since vacant property means loss of income not only to the owner but also to the manager if she is paid a percentage of the rents collected. A vacancy rate that is too low or nonexistent, however, may well be an indication of a rental schedule that is below market value. Therefore, a vacancy factor of about 3 percent is often taken as a favorable reflection of appropriate market rent as well as the marketing plan. A vacancy rate of 3 percent means the property is vacant 3 percent of the time. Conversely, an occupancy rate of 97 percent means the property is occupied 97 percent of the time. A property with a vacancy rate of 3 percent and an occupancy rate of 97 percent is vacant an average of 11 days per year and occupied an average of 354 days per year.

## Collecting Rents and Security Deposits

Perhaps the most important single function of the manager is the faithful accounting of all funds that come into her possession. North Carolina has three major statutes that impact the handling of funds of others in the agent's fiduciary role. The Real Estate License Law and the Rules and Regulations of the Real Estate Commission enforce strict duties of accounting under the operation of trust accounts. The North Carolina Residential Rental Agreements Act influences the relationship of the manager to tenants in residential property, such as that in the management of apartment buildings. The North Carolina Tenant Security Deposit Act specifically addresses the amounts, handling, accounting, and refund of funds belonging to tenants.

## Instituting Legal Actions

The real estate agent is not authorized to engage in actions that constitute the practice of law. Examples of such activities include giving legal advice or opinion, drafting contracts, and attempting to provide legal representation for another person. Just as the agent can institute legal action on his own behalf as a private citizen, however, the agent is authorized to file complaints and seek appropriate legal actions for the owner. These actions include the collection of rents and instituting proceedings for eviction.

## Maintaining the Property

The property manager is the trustee for the owner, who has placed a great deal of trust in and responsibility upon the agent to take proper care of a substantial financial asset. Upkeep of the property to maintain and increase its value is an ongoing task. The manager should have a schedule for daily routine attention as well as long-range plans for items such as painting and major repairs such as reroofing. If repairs and maintenance are not kept up appropriately, the attractiveness to tenants and subsequent rental income will suffer. Most property managers do not make debt service payments for the owner, since debt service is not considered an operating expense.

Property managers should consult the property owners to determine that the appropriate types and amount of insurance are maintained on the property. Insurance protects the property adequately from fire and other hazards and protects the owner and the agent from liability. The property management contract should designate the person responsible for maintaining the insurance coverage.

## Performing the Landlord's Duties

Upon signing the property management agreement, the landlord has essentially delegated her statutory duties to the real estate agent. Failure to perform these duties properly is a specific example of the breach of the duty of agency as defined by the Real Estate Commission, and it subjects the agent to serious penalties. In the case of residential property, the Residential Rental Agreements Act specifically requires the owner to maintain "fit premises." The owner and the agent are required to do all that is necessary to provide and maintain property so it is fit for human habitation. Individual leases may require other specific items of performance by the agent, such as certain services or maintenance. Failure to provide all such services as called for would breach the lease as well as the fiduciary agency duty.

A smoke detector law requires landlords and their agents to provide properly installed smoke detectors in all residential rental properties in North Carolina. Landlords and their agents are further required to install new batteries when a new tenant moves in and to repair inoperative smoke detectors when notified of the inoperative condition of the detector in writing by the tenant.

## Maintaining Records and Reporting to the Owner

Included in the agent's covenants is a requirement that the property manager provide a *periodic (monthly) accounting of all funds received and disbursed.* This accounting is called a **property management report.** It contains detailed information of all receipts and expenditures for the period covered (plus the year-to-date) and relates each item to the operating budget for the period.

Read and study the following examples. Apply the information given in the first problem to all of the problems.

1. John of AAA Realty manages Gail's property for an 8 percent monthly fee. In August, Units A and B were occupied. Each unit rents for \$570 per month. The rent for both units has been paid in full and on time. How much of the rent does Gail actually receive?
   a. Gross rent collected is the sum of the total rents:

$$\begin{array}{r} \$570 \\ +\ 570 \\ \hline \$1{,}140 \end{array}$$

   b. The property management fee is the gross rent collected times the monthly fee:

$$\$1{,}140 \times 8\% = \$91.20$$

   c. Gail's check equals the gross rent minus the fee:

$$\begin{array}{r} \$1{,}140.00 \\ -\ 91.20 \\ \hline \$1{,}048.80 \end{array}$$

2. In September, Unit A was rented for the entire month but Unit B was rented for only 14 days. How much does Gail receive this month?
   a. Prorate the amount collected for Unit B (base on 30-day month):

$$\frac{\$570}{30} \times 14 \text{ (occupied days)} = \$266$$

b. Gross rent collected:

$$\begin{array}{r} \$570 \\ +\,266 \\ \hline \$836 \end{array}$$

c. Gross rent times monthly fee:

$$\$836 \times 8\% = \$66.88$$

d. Gail's check equals the gross rent minus the fee:

$$\begin{array}{r} \$836.00 \\ -\ 66.88 \\ \hline \$769.12 \end{array}$$

3. In October, Gail's units were both rented. However, the plumbing in Unit A needed repair at a cost of $86, and Unit B was sprayed for insects at the normal rate of $25. These bills were deducted from the individual proceeds received from each unit. How much did she receive from Unit A? from Unit B? How much did she receive altogether?
   a. Determine the separate management fees for each unit:

| Unit A | Unit B |
|---|---|
| $570 × 8% = $45.60 | $570 × 8% = $45.60 |

   b. Determine the individual proceeds before the bills:

$$\begin{array}{r} \$570.00 \\ -\ 45.60 \\ \hline \$524.40 \end{array} \qquad \begin{array}{r} \$570.00 \\ -\ 45.60 \\ \hline \$524.40 \end{array}$$

   c. Subtract the individual expenses from each unit:

$$\begin{array}{r} \$524.40 \\ -\ 86.00 \\ \hline \$438.40 \end{array} \text{ from Unit A} \qquad \begin{array}{r} \$524.40 \\ -\ 25.00 \\ \hline \$499.40 \end{array} \text{ from Unit B}$$

   d. Add proceeds from Unit A and Unit B to find the total:

$$\begin{array}{r} \$438.40 \\ +\,499.40 \\ \hline \$937.80 \end{array}$$

## SUMMARY OF IMPORTANT POINTS

1. Property managers are agents entrusted with the fiduciary duty of managing property for others and, therefore, must have a real estate broker's license.
2. The property manager's basic responsibilities are to produce the best possible net operating income from the property and to maintain and increase the value of the principal's investment.
3. The property manager fulfills his basic responsibilities by formulating a management plan, soliciting tenants, leasing space, collecting rent, hiring and training employees, maintaining good tenant relations, providing for adequate maintenance, protecting

tenants, maintaining adequate insurance, keeping adequate records, and auditing and paying bills.

4. The management proposal contains performance commitments on the part of the property manager, if employed by the owner.

5. A primary function of the property manager is that of accounting for all funds received on behalf of the principal. Several state regulations, including the Residential Rental Agreements Act, the Tenant Security Deposit Act, and the North Carolina Real Estate License Law, govern this accounting process.

6. The management agreement is an employment contract in which a property manager is employed by a property owner to act as her agent. Like the listing agreement, it establishes the agency relationship. The property manager is responsible for fulfilling the owner's obligations, and failure to perform the duties properly is deemed a breach of the agency duty.

7. The property management report is a periodic accounting provided by a property manager to the property owner.

8. Properties that may require management are condominiums, cooperatives, apartments, single-family rental houses, mobile home parks, office buildings, shopping malls, and industrial property.

9. Agency agreements with owners/landlords must be in writing from the point of inception.

10. Agency agreements with tenants can be oral but must be converted to writing prior to making offer to rent or lease.

## REVIEW QUESTIONS

Answers to the review questions are in the Answer Key at the back of the book.

1. All of the following statements about property management are correct EXCEPT:
   A. property management is a specialized field within the real estate industry
   B. a property manager acts as an agent of the property owner
   C. the terms *property manager* and *resident manager* have the same meaning
   D. a property manager is a fiduciary

2. A property manager's basic responsibilities to the owner are to:
   I. produce the best possible net operating income from the property.
   II. maintain and increase the value of the owner's investment.
   A. I only
   B. II only
   C. both I and II
   D. neither I nor II

3. A budget based on forecast income and anticipated expenses over a period of years is called a(n):
   A. stabilized budget
   B. projected budget
   C. anticipated budget
   D. operating budget

4. Which of the following creates an agency relationship between a property manager and the property owner?
   A. management proposal
   B. management report
   C. management agreement
   D. management plan

5. A nonlicensed, salaried employee working for a licensed real estate broker who is contracted to manage property for a property owner can perform all of the following activities without a real estate license EXCEPT:
   A. marketing
   B. showing properties
   C. negotiating terms of a lease
   D. instituting legal actions

6. Failure of the broker to perform duties under the property management agreement:
   A. is a breach of the duty of agency
   B. would make the broker liable to the owner, but not to the Real Estate Commission
   C. would make the broker liable to the Real Estate Commission, but not to the owner
   D. none of the above

7. Amsley Arms Apartments consists of 13 units, 2 of which rent for $495 per month, 5 for $400 per month, and all the others for $350 per month. The broker's management fee is based on the gross monthly rents collected each month and is at the rate of 10 percent of all rents $400 or more and 7 percent of any rents less than $400. During the month of June, a check on one of the $495 units is returned unpaid, one of the $400 units is vacant, and one of the $350 units is rented for only seven days. What is the broker's management fee this month?
   A. $244.72
   B. $337.72
   C. $375.22
   D. $387.22

*Use the following information to solve questions 8–10.*
Management fee is 10%.
Units A and B rent for $500.
Units C–E rent for $600.
Owen Trent owns all units. JQP Properties manages the units.

8. During the month of September, all units were occupied. What was the total amount disbursed to the *owner?*
   A. $110
   B. $990
   C. $2,520
   D. $2,800

9. During October, Unit B was vacant but all the remaining units were occupied. What property management fee was collected by JQP Properties?
   A. $230
   B. $2,070
   C. $2,300
   D. none of the above

10. During November, all properties were rented for the entire month except Unit E. This unit was rented only from the first through the eighteenth. Which of the following is/are true?
    I. The gross rent collected was $2,560.
    II. JQP Properties earned $256.
    III. Mr. Trent earned $2,304.
    A. I only
    B. I and III only
    C. II and III only
    D. I, II, and III

11. Agency agreements must be in writing from the time of inception with a:
    A. licensee
    B. lessor
    C. lessee
    D. lien holder

12. With a tenant, oral agency must be converted to a written format prior to:
    A. the beginning of the lease term
    B. first substantial contact
    C. submitting an offer to purchase
    D. submitting an offer to lease or rent

# Chapter 12

## KEY TERMS

Americans with Disabilities Act
blockbusting
brokerage
Civil Rights Act of 1866
civil suit
disability
discriminatory advertising
Federal Fair Housing Act of 1968
Federal Fair Housing Amendments Act of 1988
North Carolina Fair Housing Act of 1983
North Carolina Human Relations Commission
redlining
steering

## LEARNING OBJECTIVES

At the conclusion of this chapter, you should be able to:

1. Describe the provisions of the Federal Fair Housing Act of 1968 as amended in 1988, including the criteria upon which discrimination is prohibited, definitions of terminology, exemptions, and provisions for enforcement.
2. Describe the provisions of the North Carolina Fair Housing Act of 1983,including unlawful discriminatory practices, exemptions, enforcement, and penalties.
3. Describe the provisions of the Civil Rights Act of 1866, including prohibitions and enforcement.

# Fair Housing

## IN THIS CHAPTER

This chapter discusses the federal laws that prohibit discrimination in housing, as well as the North Carolina Fair Housing Act of 1983. Of major importance is the Federal Fair Housing Act of 1968 (Title VIII of the 1968 Civil Rights Act), as amended. The other significant federal law is the Civil Rights Act of 1866. The 1968 Act applies specifically to housing, whereas the 1866 law prohibits all discrimination based on race in housing and in any other situation. The North Carolina Act is very similar to Title VIII of the 1968 Civil Rights Act but has significantly different exemptions.

## FEDERAL FAIR HOUSING ACT

Originally enacted by Congress as Title VIII of the Civil Rights Act of 1968, the **Federal Fair Housing Act of 1968** *prohibited discrimination in housing on the basis of race, color, religion, or national origin.* An amendment in the Housing and Community Development Act of 1974 added the prohibition against discrimination on the basis of sex. The **Federal Fair Housing Amendments Act of 1988** added *provisions to prevent discrimination based on both mental and physical handicaps or familial status.* The addition of the "handicapped" category requires landlords to allow persons with disabilities to make reasonable modifications to an apartment, at the tenant's expense, to accommodate their special needs. For example, a tenant must be allowed to install a ramp or widen doors to accommodate a wheelchair or install grab bars in a bathroom. At the end of the tenancy, the tenant must return the premises to their original condition, also at his own expense. The "familial status" category prevents landlords from recruiting for "Adults Only" in most circumstances. Provisions do exist, however, for elderly housing.

As the law presently exists, it is illegal to discriminate on the basis of race, color, religion, sex, national origin, handicap, or familial status in the sale or rental of housing or residential lots, in the advertising of the sale or rental of housing, in the financing of housing, and in the provision of real estate brokerage services.

### Definitions

The Act contains definitions of certain terms, as follows:

*Dwelling*—"Any building, structure, or portion thereof which is occupied as, or designed or intended for occupancy as, a residence by one or more families, and any vacant land which is offered for sale or lease for the construction or location thereon of any such building, structure or portion thereof."

*Elderly Housing*—Housing in which 80 percent of the units are occupied by at least one person aged 55 or older.

*Familial Status*—Includes children under age 18; pregnant women; or persons with, or in the process of obtaining, custody of children.

**FIGURE 12.1**

Poster for equal housing opportunity.

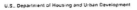

U.S. Department of Housing and Urban Development

EQUAL HOUSING
OPPORTUNITY

**We Do Business in Accordance With the Federal Fair Housing Law**

(The Fair Housing Amendments Act of 1988)

**It is Illegal to Discriminate Against Any Person Because of Race, Color, Religion, Sex, Handicap, Familial Status, or National Origin**

- In the sale or rental of housing or residential lots
- In advertising the sale or rental of housing
- In the financing of housing
- In the provision of real estate brokerage services
- In the appraisal of housing
- Blockbusting is also illegal

Anyone who feels he or she has been discriminated against may file a complaint of housing discrimination:
1-800-669-9777 (Toll Free)
1-800-927-9275 (TDD)

**U.S. Department of Housing and Urban Development**
**Assistant Secretary for Fair Housing and Equal Opportunity**
**Washington, D.C. 20410**

Previous editions are obsolete

form HUD-928.1 (8-93)

*Handicap*—Any physical or mental impairment that limits one or more of the essential functions of life.

*Person*—"Includes one or more individuals, corporations, partnerships, associations, labor organizations, legal representatives, mutual companies, joint stock companies, trusts, unincorporated organizations, trustees, trustees in bankruptcy, receivers, and fiduciaries."

*To Rent*—"Includes to lease, to sublease, to let, and otherwise to grant for a consideration the right to occupy premises not owned by the occupant."

The following discussion addresses specific acts prohibited in each category.

## Types of Discrimination

### Blockbusting

The Act specifically makes **blockbusting** (also known as panic peddling) illegal and defines the practice as *"for profit, to induce or attempt to induce any person to sell or rent any dwelling by representations regarding the entry or prospective entry into the neighborhood of a person or persons of a particular race, color, religion, sex, national origin, handicap, or familial status."* Blockbusting describes the practice of real estate agents attempting to induce owners to list property for sale or rent by telling them that persons of a particular race, color, religion, sex, national origin, handicap, or familial status are moving into the area.

### Steering

**Steering** is *the directing of prospective purchasers or tenants, especially minority purchasers or tenants, toward or away from specific neighborhoods because they belong to a* *protected class under the Fair Housing Act (i.e., because of their race, color, religion, sex, handicap, national origin, or familial status).* The prohibition against steering falls under the general prohibition of refusing to sell, rent, or negotiate the sale or rental of housing or residential lots. Examples of steering include a real estate agent (1) showing a white prospect properties located in areas populated only by white people, (2) showing black prospects properties only in integrated areas or areas populated only by blacks, (3) showing Polish prospects properties in areas populated only by Poles, and (4) showing tenants with disabilities only units in buildings already housing tenants with disabilities.

## Advertising

The Act specifies that it is illegal "to make, print, or publish, or cause to be made, printed, or published *any notice, statement, or advertisement, with respect to the sale or rental of a dwelling that indicates any preference, limitation, or discrimination based on race, color, religion, sex, national origin, handicap or familial status, or an intention to make any such preference, limitation, or discrimination.*" Examples of **discriminatory advertising** are (1) an advertisement for the sale of condominium units or rental apartments that contains pictures showing owners or tenants on the property who are of only one race, (2) an advertisement stating that the owner prefers tenants who are male college students, (3) a "For Sale" sign that specifies "No Puerto Ricans," and (4) an apartment advertisement stating "Adults Only."

## Sale or Rental of Housing

This category contains a limited number of exemptions for owners in renting or selling their own property. These exemptions are examined subsequently in the chapter. In the absence of an exemption, the following specific acts are prohibited:

1. Refusing to sell or rent housing or refusing to negotiate the sale or rental of residential lots on the basis of discrimination because of race, color, religion, sex, national origin, handicap, or familial status. This includes representing to any person on discriminatory grounds "that any dwelling is not available for inspection, sale, or rental when such dwelling is in fact available." Also, it is illegal "to refuse to sell or rent after the making of a bona fide offer, or to refuse to negotiate for the sale or rental of, or otherwise make unavailable or deny, a dwelling to a person" because of race, color, religion, sex, national origin, handicap, or familial status.

   Examples of violations of these prohibited acts are (1) advising a prospective buyer that a house has been sold when it has not, because of the prospect's national origin; (2) refusing to accept an offer to purchase because the offeror is a member of a particular religious faith; (3) telling a rental applicant that an apartment is not available for inspection because the applicant is a female (or male) when the apartment is actually vacant and available for inspection; (4) refusing to rent to a person confined to a wheelchair or refusing to make reasonable modifications (at the tenant's expense) to an apartment to accommodate the wheelchair; and (5) refusing to rent to a family with children.

2. The Act makes it illegal "to discriminate against any person in the terms, conditions, or privileges of sale or rental of a dwelling, or in the provision of services or facilities in connection therewith, because of race, color, religion, sex, national origin, handicap or familial status."

   Examples of prohibited acts in this category are as follows: (1) The manager of an apartment complex routinely requires tenants to have a security deposit in an amount equivalent to one month's rent unless the rental applicant is black, in which case a deposit equivalent to two months' rent is required. (2) The manager of an apartment complex restricts use of the complex swimming pool to white tenants only. (3) The owner of a condominium will include in the purchase of a condominium apartment a share of stock and membership in a nearby country club provided the purchaser is not from Israel. (4) A landlord charges a larger deposit to a couple with young children. (5) A landlord charges a higher rent to persons in wheelchairs.

## *Illegal Financing*

**Redlining** describes violations of the Fair Housing Act by lending institutions. The term is based on the theory that some lending institutions, prior to the enactment of the Fair Housing Act, may have circled certain areas on the map with a red line and refused to make loans to people who wanted to buy property in the areas circled.

The Act prohibits lending institutions from refusing to make loans to purchase, construct, or repair a dwelling by discriminating on the basis of race, color, religion, sex, national origin, handicap, or familial status. In the past, areas were redlined because they were highly integrated or populated by minorities. Today, however, the Fair Housing Act does not limit the prohibition against financial discrimination to the refusal to make loans because of the character of the neighborhood in which the property is located. The prohibition against discrimination also applies to individuals by making it illegal "to deny a loan or other financial assistance to a person applying therefore for the purpose of purchasing, constructing, improving, repairing, or maintaining a dwelling" or "to discriminate against him in fixing the amount, interest rate, duration, or other terms or conditions of such loan or other financial assistance."

## *Real Estate Brokerage Services*

The Act prohibits discrimination in the provision of **brokerage** services (designed to *bring buyers and sellers together to negotiate terms of a real estate sale*) and states that

> . . . it shall be unlawful to deny any person access to or membership or participation in any multiple listing service, real estate brokers' organization, or other service, organization, or facility relating to the business of selling or renting dwellings, or to discriminate against him in the terms or conditions of such access, membership or participation on account of race, color, religion, sex, national origin, handicap, or familial status.

This provision of the Fair Housing Law makes the denial of membership or the imposition of special terms or conditions of membership in any real estate organization on discriminatory grounds illegal. Additionally, the refusal of a multiple listing service to accept a property for inclusion in the service or the refusal of a member broker to place a listing in the service on discriminatory grounds is illegal. The Act requires real estate organizations and real estate agents to provide their services without discrimination.

## Exemptions

The Fair Housing Law provides exemptions to property owners under certain conditions. None of these exemptions is available, however, if either of the following has occurred:

1. Discriminatory advertising has been used.
2. The services of a real estate licensee or the services of any person in the business of selling or renting dwellings are used. (Additionally, North Carolina licensing provisions prohibit licensees from discriminatory practices in their personal dealings, even when they are acting for themselves and not as an agent for others.)

(For the purpose of the Act, a person is deemed to be in the business of selling or renting dwellings if the individual has, within the preceding 12 months, participated as principal in three or more transactions involving the sale or rental of any dwelling or any interest therein; the person has, within the preceding 12 months, participated as agent, other than in the sale of one's personal residence, in providing sales or rental facilities or sales or rental services in two or more transactions involving the sale or rental of any dwelling or any interest therein; or the individual is the owner of any dwelling designed or intended for occupancy by, or occupied by, five or more families.)

In the absence of either of the preceding, exemptions from the Fair Housing Act are available as follows:

1. An owner who does not own more than three single-family dwellings at one time is exempt. Unless the owner was living in or was the most recent occupant of the house sold, she is limited to only one exemption in any 24-month period.

2. An owner of an apartment building containing not more than four apartments is exempt in the rental of the apartments, provided the owner occupies one of the apartments as a personal residence.
3. Religious organizations are exempt as regards properties owned and operated for the benefit of their members only and not for commercial purposes, provided membership in the organization is not restricted on account of race, color, sex, national origin, handicap, or familial status.
4. A private club not open to the public is exempt as regards properties owned by the club to provide lodging for the benefit of the members and not for commercial purposes, provided membership in the organization is not restricted on account of race, color, religion, sex, national origin, handicap, or familial status.
5. In certain cases involving housing for the elderly, there is a limited exemption permitting discrimination based on familial status.

## Enforcement

The Fair Housing Act is enforced in three ways:

1. By administrative procedure through the Office of Equal Opportunity of the Department of Housing and Urban Development (HUD). HUD can act on its own information and initiative, and it must act in response to complaints filed up to one year after an alleged discrimination. If a state or local law where the property is located is substantially equivalent, HUD must refer the complaint to the state or to local authorities. In North Carolina, complaints are referred to the **North Carolina Human Relations Commission** unless there is a local equivalent fair housing agency. Complaints must be in writing and state the facts upon which an alleged violation is based. If HUD or the equivalent state or local organization is unable to obtain a voluntary conciliation and the appropriate one of these organizations determines that there are reasonable grounds for complaint, a charge will be filed and the case referred to an administrative law judge (ALJ), unless either party elects to have the case tried in a civil court. The ALJ may make a recommendation to the North Carolina Human Relations Commission. Three commissioners then determine whether to impose a civil penalty of up to $10,000 for a first offense, $25,000 if there has been another violation within five years, and $50,000 if there have been two or more violations in seven years. An individual can be fined $25,000 or $50,000 without limitation of time periods if he or she engages in multiple discriminatory practices.
2. The aggrieved party, with or without filing a complaint to HUD, can bring a **civil suit** in federal district court within two years of the alleged violation of the Act. A civil suit is *an action in a court of equity that seeks financial compensation for loss caused by another.* If the aggrieved party wins the case, the court can issue an injunction against the violator and award actual damages and punitive damages with no limitation by the statute.
3. The Department of Justice can file a civil suit in any appropriate U.S. District Court where the attorney general has reasonable cause to believe that any person or group is engaged in a pattern of violation of the Act and, as such, raises an issue of general public importance. The court can issue an injunction or a restraining order against the persons responsible and impose fines of up to $50,000 to "vindicate the public interest." A first-time fine of $50,000 may be imposed where a "pattern of practice" of discrimination is discovered.

# NORTH CAROLINA FAIR HOUSING ACT

## Unlawful Discrimination

The **North Carolina Fair Housing Act of 1983** is similar to the federal Fair Housing Act of 1968. The *prohibitions of discrimination in housing are virtually identical to those of the* *federal Act*. Therefore, any violation of these provisions subjects the individual to both state and federal penalties. The North Carolina Human Relations Commission and equivalent local agencies now handle fair housing complaints within North Carolina.

### Exemptions

Although the prohibited discrimination acts are essentially identical in the federal and state fair housing laws, the North Carolina Fair Housing Act has several very different exemptions.

1. Whereas the federal law provides an exemption for a private owner selling one's own home without the participation of a real estate broker, the state Act does not provide any such consideration. Therefore, the North Carolina law is more restrictive than the federal law on this point. In a FSBO (for sale by owner), the owner does *not* have the right to turn away a minority applicant. The state does, however, provide an exemption for the rental of rooms in a home (not a boarding house) occupied by the owner.
2. The federal Act provides exemptions for the owner of a rental unit of four families or fewer if the owner occupies one of the units. The state Act broadens this exemption to include the case in which the owner or a member of the owner's family occupies one of the units.
3. The state law also makes a provision for the rental of rooms in a single-sex dormitory, an issue that is not addressed in the federal law.

### Enforcement and Penalties

The North Carolina statute also makes different provisions for the enforcement of the law. The primary agency is the North Carolina Human Relations Commission. Any person who believes he has been discriminated against in a housing matter can file a complaint with this commission or an equivalent local enforcement agency. The commission or local agency must then investigate the situation and try to effect voluntary compliance with the law through negotiation and persuasion. If this action is not effective in gaining voluntary compliance, the commission/local agency must either initiate a lawsuit in a state court on behalf of the complainant or advise the aggrieved party of his right to start a private lawsuit. The individual has this latter right even if the commission/local agency does not find merit in the case through its own proceedings.

The North Carolina Human Relations Commission is certified as a "substantially equivalent agency" to HUD as defined in the federal statute. The commission enforces the 1968 Fair Housing Act and the 1988 amendments to it.

## CIVIL RIGHTS ACT

The first significant statute affecting equal housing opportunity was the **Civil Rights Act of 1866**. Far from being an obsolete law, this statute has had a major impact on fair housing concepts, interestingly through a landmark case in 1968, the same year the federal Fair Housing Act became law. In the case of *Jones* v. *Alfred H. Mayer Company,* the plaintiff was denied an apartment because of his race. The U.S. Supreme Court applied the Civil Rights Act of 1866 to prohibit racially based discrimination in housing, notwithstanding the exemptions written into the Fair Housing Act of 1968. The ruling provides an interesting interplay between the two acts. Although the 1968 statute has a number of exemptions, the 1866 law has no exemptions and, among other things, contains the blanket statement that all citizens have the same right to inherit, buy, sell, or lease all real and personal property. The basic interpretation of this statute is that *it prohibits all racial discrimination.* The exemptions provided for in the 1968 law *cannot* be used to enforce any racial discrimination.

## FAIR HOUSING IN NORTH CAROLINA

In addition to the two federal and one state Fair Housing Acts, real estate brokers have several other regulations to comply with in their brokerage practice:

1. Regulations of the North Carolina Real Estate Commission prohibit licensees from engaging in discriminatory practices in their personal transactions, that is, when not acting as an agent or a fiduciary. Even though a private individual (nonlicensee) still has a few limited exemptions to the laws, licensees are held to a higher standard of conduct. Thus, one who practices any form of discrimination on a personal level is disqualified from holding a certificate of public trust, in this case, a real estate license.
2. The following provision must be included in all written agency contracts, highlighted, as in boldface type:

   **The Broker Shall Conduct All his Brokerage Activities in Regard to this Agreement Without Respect to the Race, Color, Religion, Sex, National Origin, Handicap, or Familial Status of Any Buyer or Prospective Buyer, Seller or Prospective Seller, Tenant or Prospective Tenant, Landlord or Prospective Landlord.**
3. The Real Estate Commission's Rule A.1601 makes brokers who violate the state Fair Housing Act subject to disciplinary action by the commission.
4. Additionally, REALTORS® (remember, not all brokers are REALTORS®) are bound to a commitment to fair housing and equal opportunity through Article 10 of their Code of Ethics.

Thus, federal law, state law, and the Real Estate Licensing Commission require a real estate licensee practicing in North Carolina to practice fair housing. The REALTORS® Code of Ethics further requires REALTORS® to practice fair housing.

## EQUAL HOUSING OPPORTUNITY TODAY

When the concept of fair housing is discussed, many people have the idea that the issue has long been resolved through actions such as the civil rights movement of the 1960s. Despite the intention of the 1866 and the 1968 Civil Rights Acts to provide equal housing opportunity for all citizens, this goal has not been achieved in practice. Although the Fair Housing Act is more than 30 years old, a study by HUD a few years ago found that minorities are still confronted with a 48 percent chance of encountering discrimination in the purchase of a home and a 72 percent chance in leasing a rental unit.

Many proposals have been developed to correct this situation. One means of enforcing the law is through an organized program of testing by civil rights groups. In 1968 the Johnson administration supported a Fair Housing Initiatives Program (FHIP) to provide funding of testers. The National Association of REALTORS® (NAR) negotiated an agreement with HUD to ensure that funded testing is objective, reliable, and controlled and then provided its endorsement to the program. The program is ongoing.

## AMERICANS WITH DISABILITIES ACT

The **Americans with Disabilities Act,** which took effect on January 26, 1992, specifically *protects the rights of individuals with disabilities.* **Disability** is defined in USC 42, Sec. 12101, as a *physical or mental impairment that substantially limits one or more of the major life activities of a person.* Under this law, individuals with disabilities cannot be denied access to public transportation, any commercial facility, or public accommodation. This Act applies to all owners and operators of public accommodations and commercial facilities, regardless of the size or number of employees. It also applies to all local and state governments. Public accommodations are defined as private businesses that affect commerce and trade, such as inns, banks, places of education, and daycare centers. Commercial facilities are those intended for nonresidential use, such as factories.

To comply with this law, public accommodations and commercial facilities are to be designed, constructed, and altered to meet the accessibility standards of the new law if readily achievable. "Readily achievable" means able to be carried out without undue difficulty or expense. Examples of barriers to be removed or alterations to be made include placing ramps, lowering telephones, widening doors, installing grab bars in toilet stalls, and adding raised letters on elevator controls. Commercial facilities are not required to remove the barriers in existing facilities.

As of January 1993, all newly constructed public accommodations and commercial facilities must be readily accessible and usable by individuals with disabilities. The Americans with Disabilities Act is enforced by the U.S. attorney general. Punishment for violating this law includes injunctions against operation of a business, a fine up to $50,000 for the first offense, and a fine of $100,000 for subsequent offenses. Be aware that individuals with AIDS, alcoholism, or mental illness are included in the category of people with a mental or physical disability that impairs one or more of their life functions.

## SEXUAL HARASSMENT

It is a violation of North Carolina law for a lessor or his agent to sexually harass a tenant or prospective tenant. The landlord or his agent is prohibited from making unsolicited overt requests for sexual acts when submission to such conduct is a term of the execution or continuation of a lease or the according of tenant's rights under the lease.

## ITEMS TO CONSIDER FOR THE STATE EXAM

1. Be certain you can define the following types of discrimination:
   a. *Blockbusting* (also known as *panic peddling*)— for profit, inducing or attempting to induce any person to sell or rent any dwelling by representations regarding the entry or prospective entry into the neighborhood of a person or persons of a particular race, color, religion, sex, national origin, handicap, or familial status.
   b. *Steering*—directing prospective purchasers or tenants, especially minority purchasers or tenants, toward or away from specific neighborhoods because they belong to a protected class under the Fair Housing Act (i.e., because of their race, color, religion, sex, handicap, national origin, or familial status). The prohibition against steering falls under the general prohibition of refusing to sell, rent, or negotiate the sale or rental of housing or residential lots.
   c. *Redlining*—the practice of circling areas on a map with a red line and refusing to make loans to people who want to buy property in the areas circled.
2. The federal Fair Housing Act's prohibitions also apply to individuals. Therefore, it is illegal to deny a loan or other financial assistance to a person applying for the purpose of purchasing, constructing, improving, repairing, or maintaining a dwelling or to discriminate against a person in fixing the amount, interest rate, duration, or other terms or conditions of such a loan or other financial assistance by discriminating on the basis of race, color, religion, sex, national origin, handicap, or familial status.
3. The North Carolina Fair Housing Act contains discrimination prohibitions that are virtually identical to those of the federal Act. However, some of the exemptions are different:
   a. The state Act does not provide an exemption for a private owner selling her own home without the participation of a real estate broker, as in the federal law. In a North Carolina for sale by owner (FSBO), the owner does not have the right to turn away a minority applicant. (An exception is rental of rooms in a home occupied by the owner, but this exception does not include boarding houses.)
   b. The state Act broadens the federal exemption for owners of rental units of four families or fewer (if the owner occupies one of the units) to include the case in which a member of the owner's family is the occupant.
   c. The state Act also makes a provision for the rental of rooms in a single-sex dormitory, an issue that is not addressed in the federal law.

## SUMMARY OF IMPORTANT POINTS

1. The Federal Fair Housing Act of 1968, as amended, prohibits discrimination in housing because of race, color, religion, sex, national origin, mental or physical handicap, or familial status (family members under 18 years of age, pregnant women, or persons with or in the process of obtaining custody of children).
2. Discrimination is prohibited in the selling or renting of housing, in advertising the sale or rental of housing, in the financing of housing, and in providing real estate brokerage services. The Civil Rights Act also makes blockbusting illegal.
3. Four exemptions are provided to owners by the Federal Fair Housing Act in selling or renting housing: to owners who do not own more than three houses, owners of apartment buildings in which there are not more than four apartments where the owner occupies one of the apartments, religious organizations as regards properties used for the benefit of members only, and private clubs as regards lodging used for the benefit of members only.
4. The owners' exemptions are not available if the owner used discriminatory advertising or the services of a real estate broker. Additionally, North Carolina real estate licensees are prohibited from discriminatory practices in their personal affairs.
5. Title VIII of the 1968 Civil Rights Act, referred to as the Fair Housing Act, was amended significantly in 1988. It is now enforced through the office of Equal Opportunity of HUD by referring complaints to the North Carolina Human Relations Commission (NCHRC). The NCHRC first attempts voluntary conciliation and if necessary, refers the case to an administrative law judge, who can impose financial penalties of $10,000 to $50,000. Fair Housing violations may result in a civil suit in federal court or a lawsuit in federal court brought by the U.S. attorney general. Penalties of up to $50,000 may be imposed for the first offense if there is shown to be a pattern of discrimination.
6. North Carolina has its own Fair Housing Act, which is very similar to the federal act in its prohibitions of discrimination. The exemptions are different in that there is no exemption for the sale of a home by a private owner, and the exemption for an apartment building with four or fewer units is extended to include a unit occupied by an owner or a member of the owner's family.
7. North Carolina has its own Fair Housing Act enforcement agency, the North Carolina Human Relations Commission. This agency is recognized as being "substantially equivalent" to HUD and its federal enforcement procedures. The North Carolina Human Relations Commission is authorized to investigate complaints and initiate a lawsuit in a state court or advise the party of the right to do so alone. Several larger cities and counties also have local fair housing enforcement agencies recognized by HUD as "substantially equivalent."
8. The Civil Rights Act of 1866 prohibits discrimination only on the basis of race. The prohibition is not limited to housing but includes all real estate and personal property transactions. The Act can only be enforced by civil suit in federal court.
9. Real estate agents have additional restrictions imposed on them by the Real Estate Commission, as do REALTORS® by the REALTORS® Code of Ethics.

## REVIEW QUESTIONS

Answers to the review questions are in the Answer Key at the back of the book.

1. Sam Seller refused to accept an offer to purchase his home from Juan Alvarado because Sam considered the $50 deposit insufficient. As to Sam's refusal, which of the following is correct?
   A. Sam is in violation of the fair housing law because he discriminated on the basis of national origin
   B. since Sam refused the offer for financial reasons, he is not in violation of the 1968 Act
   C. Sam is in violation of the Civil Rights Act of 1866
   D. Sam is in violation of the North Carolina Fair Housing Act of 1983

2. Which of the following is not a basis of discrimination prohibited by the 1968 Federal Fair Housing Act and/or the 988 amendments?
   A. race
   B. sex
   C. occupation
   D. religion

3. Larry Landlord refused to rent one of five apartments in his building to Barbara Barrister, a black attorney. Which of the following statements about Larry's refusal is (are) correct?
   A. if Larry's refusal to rent to Barbara was because she is an attorney, he is not in violation of the 1968 Act
   B. if Larry's refusal to rent to Barbara was because she is female, Larry is in violation of the 1968 Act as amended in 1974
   C. if Larry's refusal to rent to Barbara was because she is black, he is in violation of the 1968 Act and the Civil Rights Act of 1866
   D. all of the above

4. Seller's Town Multiple Listing Service refuses to accept a listing of a property because the owner is from the former Soviet Union. Which of the following is correct?
   A. a multiple listing service (MLS) does not come under the Act because it is a private nonprofit organization
   B. the Act does not prohibit discrimination against Russians
   C. the listing broker's membership in the MLS may be terminated for taking the listing
   D. the MLS is in violation of the 1968 Act for denying access to the service because of the owner's national origin

5. A property manager refuses to rent an office because the rental applicant is black. The applicant has legal recourse under the:
   A. Civil Rights Act of 1968
   B. Civil Rights Act of 1866
   C. North Carolina Fair Housing Act of 1983
   D. North Carolina Residential Rental Agreements Act

6. In an advertisement offering her only house for sale, the owner states that she will give preference to cash buyers who are female and Roman Catholic. The owner subsequently refused a cash offer because the offeror was a male Presbyterian. Which of the following is (are) correct?
   I. Since the seller only owned only one house, she is exempt from the 1968 Act.
   II. Since the advertisement stated as a preference, it is not discriminatory.
   III. Since the North Carolina Fair Housing Act has no exemptions for an owner selling her own home, the seller has violated state law.
   IV. Since the advertisement was in fact discriminatory, the seller has violated the 1968 Act.
   A. I and II only
   B. II and III only
   C. I and III only
   D. III and IV only

7. A real estate agent showed white prospects houses in all-white areas only. This discriminatory practice is called:
   A. redlining
   B. blockbusting
   C. steering
   D. directing

8. Which of the following is exempt from the provisions of the 1968 Act?
   A. an owner of four houses
   B. an owner occupying one of four apartments in his or her building
   C. a religious organization renting 1 of 16 apartments it owns and operates for commercial purposes
   D. an owner listing a residential lot for sale with a real estate broker

9. A resident of Raleigh decided to sell her home by herself without listing it with a real estate company. There was no discriminatory advertising. When a black buyer asked to see the home, the owner refused. The owner:
   A. is in violation of the federal Fair Housing Act of 1968 FALSE
   B. is in violation of the North Carolina Fair Housing Act of 1983
   C. is not in violation of the Civil Rights Act of 1866
   D. all of the above

10. A resident of Asheville believed he was the victim of discrimination in the rental of an apartment and filed a complaint with the North Carolina Human Relations Commission. The possible solutions to his complaint include:
   A. persuasion and/or negotiation by the commission
   B. lawsuit by the commission in a state court
   C. private lawsuit in a state court
   D. all of the above

11. The Civil Rights Act of 1968 and the Fair Housing Amendments Act of 1988 (together called the Federal Fair Housing law) may be enforced by:
   I. a civil suit for damages in federal court.
   II. administrative procedures through HUD.
   III. action by the attorney general.
   A. I only
   B. II only
   C. I and II only
   D. I, II, and III

12. The owner of a FSBO (for sale by owner) availed herself of the exemption provided by the 1968 Act and refused to accept a purchase offer because the offeror was white. The offeror can do all of the following EXCEPT:
   A. pursue a lawsuit under the 1866 law
   B. seek legal action under the 1968 law
   C. seek legal action under the North Carolina Fair Housing Act
   D. file a complaint with the North Carolina Human Relations Commission

13. Jane Smith, a real estate broker, rented a room in her own private home but refused black tenants. Jane is in violation of:
   I. the Federal Fair Housing Act of 1968.
   II. the North Carolina Fair Housing Act of 1983.
   III. the Civil Rights Act of 1866.
   IV. North Carolina real estate licensing provisions.
   A. I and II only
   B. II and III only
   C. III and IV only
   D. I, II, III, and IV

14. An apartment manager refused to rent to a family with young children. How can the family seek relief?
   A. voluntary conciliation through arbitration with HUD, the North Carolina Human Relations Commission, or the equivalent
   B. have the case heard before an administrative law judge
   C. bring a civil suit in federal district court
   D. all of the above

15. A person confined to a wheelchair requested that an apartment be modified to meet his physical needs. Which of the following is true?
   A. the owner must make appropriate modifications at the owner's expense
   B. at the end of the tenancy, the disabled tenant must pay for returning the premises to their original condition
   C. the owner can refuse to rent to this tenant
   D. none of the above

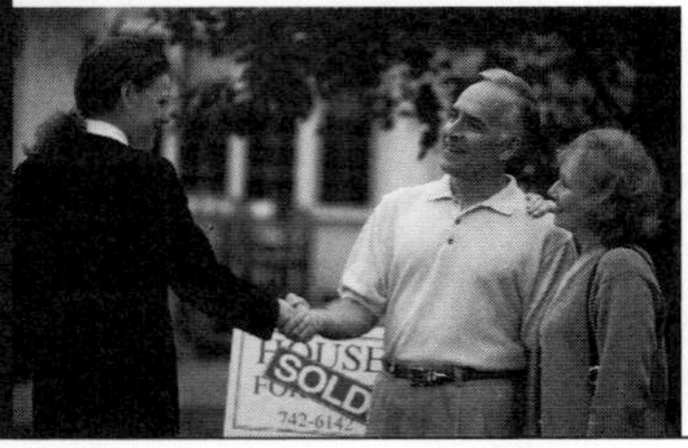


# Chapter 13

## KEY TERMS

acquisition debt
adjusted basis
basis
equity debt
inheritance basis
tax basis
tax-deductible expenses
Taxpayers Relief Act of 1997 (TRA 97)

## LEARNING OBJECTIVES

At the conclusion of this chapter, the student should be able to:

1. Define and list examples of income tax deduction benefits of home ownership.
2. Define basis, adjusted basis, amount realized, and gain realized in the sale of a personal residence.

# Federal Taxation of Home Ownership

**IN THIS CHAPTER**

Real estate licensees should have a basic understanding of the federal income tax laws that affect real property. Real estate brokers are not authorized to give tax advice to others, however, since each taxpayer's situation is different. Tax advice should only be given by competent professional tax counsel familiar with the taxpayer's position. Real estate brokers should recommend that buyers and sellers seek such counsel when appropriate. This chapter primarily discusses federal tax implications related to a principal residence.

## TAX DEDUCTIONS FOR HOMEOWNERS

Home ownership provides two **tax-deductible expenses:** *real property taxes paid to the local taxing authority* and *mortgage interest (not principal).* This includes discount points for obtaining a purchase or refinance loan (see page 376 for rules on discount point exemptions).

People who do not own real property often find it advantageous to use the allowable standard deduction when calculating taxes, especially since allowable deductions have decreased while the standard deduction has increased. Homeowners, however, may find that the allowable deductions for property taxes and mortgage interest, along with other deductible expenses, provide greater tax relief than does the standard deduction.

### Real Property Taxes

The taxes on real property are deductible for income tax purposes, but the deductions must be documented. They must be deducted from taxes for the year during which the homeowner or mortgage company actually paid them to the taxing authority. Assessments are not deductible when paid; however, they may be itemized to claim as additions to the **basis** *(the original cost of the property plus material improvements that increase its value)* when the property is sold.

### Mortgage Interest

The mortgage interest deduction for a personal residence is often a major advantage of home ownership. The tax savings depend on the amount of interest paid, the taxpayer's tax bracket, the amount of the minimum standard deduction, and the number of other itemized deductions the taxpayer claims. Recent trends toward lower interest rates and higher standard deductions have reduced or eliminated some tax savings, especially for owners of modestly priced homes financed at low interest rates.

Debt that generates "qualified residence interest" must be either acquisition debt or home equity debt. Both must be secured by the property. **Acquisition debt** is the debt incurred in the purchase of a personal residence. Interest generated by the first $1,000,000 of acquisition debt is deductible as mortgage interest. **Equity debt** is all debt secured by a qualified residence to the extent it does not exceed the fair market value of the residence reduced by the acquisition debt. Interest generated by the first $100,000 of home equity debt is deductible as mortgage interest. See page 377 for a discussion of deductibility of discount points for the purchase or refinance of a home.

# SALE OF A PERSONAL RESIDENCE BASIS

As mentioned previously, the basis is essentially the original cost of the property plus any capital improvements that increase its value. Certain costs of acquiring the property can be added to the basis. It is to the homeowner's advantage to have as large a basis as possible so as to minimize the tax gain realized when the property is eventually sold. Alternatively, the gain is minimized by deduction of certain items from the sales price. The application of these adjustments is discussed in the next section.

## Effect of Purchase and Sale

There are certain expenses for both buyer and seller in the purchase and sale of a personal residence. The following lists gives examples of these expenses and their application by the buyer or the seller in calculating taxable gain. You do not need to remember all of these examples. Rather, you should understand the principle that when the cost is paid by the owner in acquiring the property, the cost is included in the basis; when the cost is incurred in selling the property, the cost is deducted from the gross sales price.

1. The premium paid for a title insurance policy is subtracted from the selling price when paid by the seller. It is added to the buyer's basis when paid by the buyer.
2. Transfer taxes (ordinarily paid by the seller) are deducted by the seller from the selling price. When the tax is paid by the buyer, however, the amount is added to the buyer's basis.
3. The attorney's fees paid by the seller are deductible from the selling price. Attorney's fees paid by the buyer are added to the buyer's basis.
4. When the seller pays the attorney's fee for the preparation of a deed, this fee is deducted by the seller from the selling price. When the fee for drawing up the deed is paid by the buyer, it is added to the buyer's basis.
5. The buyer's closing costs that are allocable to purchasing the property are added to the buyer's basis, but expenses of borrowing the purchase price may not be added to the buyer's basis. Examples of expenses involved with obtaining the loan include appraisal fees, mortgage insurance premiums, charges by the lender's attorney, and credit report cost.
6. Discount points charged by lending institutions are deducted from the selling price when paid by the seller to enable the buyer to obtain a loan. These points are not deductible as interest by the seller.

   Until recently, if the property's seller paid the points for the buyer, the buyer could not deduct the points as interest because they were not paid directly by the buyer. The IRS has now stated that points paid by the seller for the buyer must be treated as paid directly by the buyer from funds not borrowed for this purpose. The buyer (taxpayer) will, however, reduce the basis of the new residence by an amount equal to points paid by the seller.

Discount points paid by the buyer to purchase a home are deductible as interest by the buyer for the year in which the points are paid. In 1986 the IRS ruled that discount points paid by the buyer to refinance an existing loan would need to be spread over the term of the loan. The essential difference is that if the buyer paid $2,000 in points for a new home, he could deduct all $2,000 in the year paid. If the buyer refinanced his present loan for 20 years, however, he could deduct only $100 per year. If the mortgage loan was not obtained to purchase or improve a principal residence, deduction of the discount points as interest must be spread over the life of the loan. For example, if a borrower paid $2,000 in discount points to obtain a 20-year conventional loan to purchase an apartment building, the discount points would be deductible at the rate of $100 per year for 20 years.

7. When the borrower pays a loan origination fee or loan processing fee, typically 1 percent of the amount of the loan, the fee is not deductible as interest since the fee is for loan services and not for the use of the money borrowed. Also, the borrower cannot add the cost of a loan origination or processing fee to the basis of the property because this is an expense of borrowing the purchase price rather than a cost of obtaining the property. Loan origination fees paid by the seller are a selling expense and are deducted from the sales price in arriving at the amount realized.
8. Other expense items such as surveys, escrow fees, title abstracts, recording fees, and advertising costs are added to the buyer's basis when paid by the buyer or subtracted from the selling price when paid by the seller.
9. The real estate commission paid by the seller is deducted from the selling price. The commission paid is not deductible from ordinary income by the seller.
10. Fix-up expenses, even if necessary for the sale, are no longer deductible.
11. The distance requirement for deduction of job-related moving expenses is that the new job location be 50 miles farther from the former residence than the old job location. For example, the distance from the transferee's former residence to his old job was 5 miles. The distance from his former residence to his new job must be at least 55 miles in order for him to be able to deduct job related moving expenses. Moving expenses are treated as income adjustments. Therefore, moving expenses that are not paid for or reimbursed by an employer are subtracted from income, a benefit for those who do not itemize deductions. In essence, only deductions for moving household and personal goods and traveling expenses, such as lodging during the trip from the old to the new location, are allowed.
12. A financial penalty (prepayment penalty) required by a lender for early payoff of a mortgage loan is deductible as interest by the borrower for the year in which the prepayment penalty is paid.
13. Most of the above expenses of the purchase of a residence are added to the basis of the new home. Most of the expenses of the sale of a residence are used to reduce the amount realized on the sale. Notable exceptions are costs associated with the mortgage loan, discount points paid by the buyer, pre-payment penalties, fix up expenses, and job related moving expenses. See items 5,6, 7, 10 and 11 from above for the tax treatment of these exceptions.

## *Computing Taxable Gain*

In computing the gain or loss in the sale of a principal residence, the first step is to establish the owner's **tax basis** in the property. The tax basis consists of *the price paid for the property plus any costs incurred in acquiring the property (other than those incurred in arranging financing) plus the costs of any capital improvements (not repairs) made during ownership.*

## Inheritance Basis

The *tax basis for all real property received by heirs is the market value of the property on the date of the death of the decedent* and not the market value at the time the decedent acquired the property. This provides a substantial benefit to heirs when they sell the property. As a result of this stepped-up **inheritance basis,** any tax on gains deferred under the old rollover rule during the lifetime of the decedent is eliminated.

# TAXPAYERS RELIEF ACT OF 1997 SECTION 121 EXCLUSION

## $250,000/$500,000 Home Sale Exclusion

The $250,000/$500,000 home sale exclusion in the Taxpayers Relief Act of 1997 (TRA 97) replaces both the over-55 rule and the rollover rule. Now anyone of any age who has owned and occupied a primary residence for two of the five years prior to selling it can exclude a gain up to $250,000. A married couple filing jointly can exclude up to $500,000. There is no limit to the number of times this exclusion can be used, provided the residence involved is a primary residence, the two-year ownership and occupancy requirement is met, and the exclusion has not been used during the preceding two years. Failing to meet the two-year requirement does not automatically disallow an exclusion, provided the failure is due to unforeseen circumstances such as a change in health or employment. In such cases, a prorated exclusion may be possible. A married couple using the $500,000 exclusion must both meet the two-year occupancy requirement, but only one of them must meet the two-year ownership requirement. Previous use of the $125,000 over-55 exclusion does not affect the use of the current $250,000/$500,000 exclusion.

Other important factors influence the amount of exclusion and/or taxes on the sale of a principal residence. In all of the following examples, assume all other conditions have been met. The basis of a primary residence can be adjusted upward by certain closing costs incurred when the residence is purchased and by the cost of certain improvements. The **adjusted basis** is, therefore, *the cost of the new home adjusted by closing costs ,and improvements.*

If one spouse dies, the other spouse can sell the property in the same year as the death and claim up to the $500,000 exclusion. However, the surviving spouse cannot file a joint return (unless he or she remarries) in future years, thereby limiting the exclusion to $250,000 in the years following the spouse's death.

Taxpayers who maintain an office in their homes cannot exclude that part of the gain attributable to the home office. They must pay capital gains tax on the part of the gain and recapture tax on any depreciation taken. If the taxpayer has ceased using the home office and returned the space to residential use two years prior to the date the property is sold, he can include the capital gain from the office portion in the exclusion. All of the gain except that resulting from depreciation after May 6, 1997, qualifies for the exclusion, provided the gain does not exceed the $250,000/$500,000 limit. Capital gain from the recapture of depreciation taken after May 6, 1997, is subject to a recapture tax not to exceed 25 percent. All other capital gain is taxed according to the taxpayers tax bracket not to exceed 15 percent.

The following examples illustrate the various options of two single taxpayers/homeowners who marry.

1. If neither has used the exclusion, each can exclude up to $250,000 from the sale of his or her respective house owned at the time of the marriage, providing the other requirements are met. If they qualify for these exclusions, they can use them whether filing a single or joint return. The provision of one sale every two years does not apply in this instance.
2. If one spouse has already used the $250,000 exclusion within the two years before the marriage, the other newly married taxpayer can still use his or her $250,000 exclusion.
3. After two years have passed since either used their exclusions, the couple can file a joint return and exclude the $500,000 gain on the property for which they both meet the use test.

This universal exclusion provides many opportunities for tax savings; however, the taxpayer should obtain competent tax advice on how the provision applies to her individual situation. For example, an owner may convert a vacation home or a single-family rental property to his primary residence for two years before selling it to get the exclusion. A contractor may build and occupy a house as his personal residence for two years before selling it, excluding the gain, and then repeat the process. While these transactions are apparently eligible for the exclusion, the real estate agent should refer her client to a tax expert rather than give tax advice.

Certain transactions other than the typical sale are considered sales under the universal exclusion provision. Exchange of a principal residence for another principal residence is considered a sale. Note that tax-free exchanges are available only for income-producing properties, not personal residences.

A foreclosure or repossession of a principal residence is considered a sale under the exclusion provision. Any gain from a foreclosure sale, exceeding the exclusion limits of $250,000/$500,000, is taxable and must be reported. If a debt is canceled through the foreclosure or repossession process, ordinary income may be created, which must be reported. The taxpayer in this situation should consult a tax adviser about bankruptcy and insolvency relief provisions that may apply. It is unlikely that a capital gain exceeding the exclusion limit would be realized from a foreclosure or bankruptcy; however, no bankruptcy or insolvency relief provisions apply against capital gain in this case. Lending institutions will notify the homeowner of the type and amount of income, that is, whether the income is ordinary income or income subject to capital gains tax.

The universal exclusion can be used when a personal residence is destroyed, stolen, seized, requisitioned, or condemned. The taxpayer can roll over any gain in excess of the exclusion amount into another personal residence using Section 1033, rollover of gain rules. The two-year rollover provision of this rule begins on the date condemnation was threatened or the date of property disposition, whichever is earlier. It ends two years after the close of the tax year in which the owner first realized any gain on the condemnation, destruction, theft, seizure, or requisition. The time period of ownership and use of the condemned, lost, or destroyed property rolls over into the new property.

Ownership in a cooperative is technically not ownership in real estate. It is ownership of stock in a corporation that owns the real estate in which each stockholder has a proprietary lease on an apartment. The stockholder/tenant can use the universal exclusion for the sale of his share of stock provided he meets the use requirement of the unit he is entitled to occupy and the two-year ownership requirement for the stock. Sometimes when planning an estate, a homeowner may choose to sell or transfer her primary residence while reserving the right of possession for her lifetime. The homeowner thus reserves a life estate and sells the remainder interest. At the death of the life estate holder, the remainderman will own the property, including the right of possession. The taxpayer selling or exchanging a remainder interest in a principal residence can use the universal exclusion, provided he does not sell it to a related party.

Gain on land that is part of the primary residence can be excluded. Gain on land used for investment or business purposes cannot be excluded. When a taxpayer has a single property with part of the land being associated with the home and part of the land used for business or income, he must be able to clearly differentiate which land is personal and which is business. There is seldom a problem with one acre or less. The courts have often allowed five or ten acres for personal use. When much larger amounts are involved, the taxpayer may need to provide credible evidence that he is using the property for personal use and not holding it for investment.

The universal exclusion simplifies but does not eliminate record keeping. It is still necessary to keep proof of the original cost of the residence and records and receipts of home improvements, especially if a future gain is likely to exceed the exclusion amount. Home buyers purchasing their first home since the end of the rollover rule need be concerned only with the records of one home at a time since they will not have rollover gains from a previous home. Once a homeowner has sold a home with an adjusted basis derived from rolling over gains from previous homes, she, too, can be concerned with the basis of each home individually. The homeowner should keep the records needed for her tax return.

The replacement of the rollover rule with the universal exclusion gives most homeowners/taxpayers the ability to downsize or rent without harmful tax consequences. Retirees, divorcees, empty nesters, and transferees relocating to a lower cost-of-living area are among those who benefit by not needing to reinvest their gains into a home equal to or more expensive than the adjusted sales price on their old home.

Occupancy requirements are not met by intent to occupy, moving in furniture, weekend or vacation use, or occupancy by a child or relative of a taxpayer.

Ownership and use period do not need to be simultaneous to qualify for the exclusion. For example, a tenant could rent a property as a tenant for 18 months, purchase it, live in it another 6 months, move out, rent it to someone else for 18 months, and then sell it and claim the exclusion. He has owned it for two years and lived in it for two years, but only six months were simultaneous. Or, as another example, he could have been a tenant for two years, bought the property, and leased it to someone for two years, in which case he would still qualify for the exemption as long as the two-year occupancy and the two-year ownership requirement were met within the five-year period before he sold it.

A partial exclusion, when permitted, is calculated by creating a fraction. The shorter of the use period or the time between the last sale and present sale, expressed in days, is the numerator and two years is the denominator. For example, a homeowner takes the exclusion on her home in Charlotte when she is transferred to Raleigh. She closes the sale on her home in Charlotte on September 15, 2001, and closes and moves into her new home in Raleigh on September 30, 2001. She is transferred to a new job out of state on September 30, 2002, and sells her home on December 15, 2002. It has been 15 months since she last used her exclusion. She owned her new home 14 1/2 months and occupied it for one year. One year is shorter than 15 months; therefore, 365 (days) is the numerator and 730 (days) is the denominator. The fraction of the exclusion she can claim is one-half.

When a taxpayer plans to close a transaction qualifying for an exclusion on or shortly after the two-year anniversary of her previous sale/exclusion, she should make certain she has accurate dates and accurate definitions of closing. While the sale date is usually the date of the closing statement, there are some circumstances in which the date the deed is signed or the date of recording is not the actual closing date. The date of sale is considered to be the earlier of two dates—date of delivery and acceptance of the deed or the time the buyer assumes possession and the burdens and benefits of ownership. The date that taxes and insurance are prorated indicates such a transfer on land sales contracts. Figure 13.1 shows examples of capital gain exclusions.

**FIGURE 13.1**

Calculation of realized gain and exclusion examples.

| | |
|---|---|
| Selling price of home | $750,000 |
| Less selling expenses | – 30,000 |
| Amount realized | $720,000 |
| Basis of home | $300,000 |
| Plus closing costs | + 5,000 |
| Plus improvements | + 20,000 |
| Adjusted basis of home | $325,000 |
| Amount realized | $720,000 |
| Minus adjusted basis | –325,000 |
| Gain realized | $395,000 |

Amount allowed by exclusion, assuming all conditions are met and taxpayers do not meet any partial exclusion rules:

| | |
|---|---|
| Single taxpayer | $250,000 |
| Married taxpayers filing jointly | $395,000 |
| Two unmarried taxpayers with equal interest and both meeting occupancy requirements | $197,500 each |
| Married taxpayers filing jointly with both meeting ownership and occupancy requirements and one meeting one-sale-in-two-years requirement | $250,000 |
| Newly married taxpayer filing jointly or singly selling the above home with the gain of $395,000 and another home with a gain of $105,000, each selling primary residences owned before marriage and each meeting ownership, use, and one-sale-in-two-years requirement | $250,000<br>+105,000<br>$355,000 |

## Reporting Features

Sale of a primary residence after May 6, 1997, at or below the exclusion amount does not require the real estate closing agent to notify the IRS using a Form 1099S. Revenue Procedure 98-20, however, requires the seller to provide the closing agent with certain assurances before January 31 of the year immediately following the year the property is sold or exchanged. The seller must certify that seller and spouse, if applicable, have met ownership, occupancy, and use requirements for the exclusion; that no part of the residence has been used for rental or business after May 6, 1997; and that the gain does not exceed the limit of $250,000/$500,000, whichever one applies. The certification must include a separate assurance for each requirement.

## SUMMARY OF IMPORTANT POINTS

1. There are definite tax advantages in the ownership of real property. A primary advantage is the deduction allowance for mortgage interest paid. Although the major portion of the payment on a mortgage loan in the early years goes to interest, the deductibility of this amount results in a lower effective interest rate than most people realize.
2. Real estate practitioners must refrain from giving tax advice.
3. A homeowner's real estate property taxes and mortgage interest are deductible expenses in calculating federal income tax liability.
4. Losses incurred in the sale of a home are not tax deductible.
5. The $250,000 exclusion for single taxpayers and the $500,000 exclusion for married taxpayers filing jointly is available to taxpayers of all ages. This exclusion can be used repeatedly as long as the ownership, use, and one-sale-in-two-years requirements are met.
6. Previous use of the over-55 exclusion does not affect the use of the new universal exclusion.
7. Fix-up expenses are no longer deductible under any circumstances.
8. A buyer's closing costs and improvements are allowable adjustments to the basis of a personal residence.
9. A seller's closing costs are subtracted from the sale price to obtain the adjusted sales price. Improvements are added to basis of old home to obtain the adjusted basis.
10. Gain equals the adjusted sales price minus the adjusted basis.

## REVIEW QUESTIONS

Answers to the review questions are in the Answer Key at the back of the book.

1. Which of the following is a tax-deductible expense resulting from home ownership?
   A. operating expenses
   B. depreciation
   C. mortgage interest
   D. energy usage

2. Discount points paid by a borrower to obtain a conventional mortgage loan to purchase a principal residence:
   A. do not increase the yield on the mortgage
   B. are not deductible by the borrower as interest
   C. are not deductible at all
   D. are deductible in the year paid

3. With regard to a real estate commission paid by a seller, which of the following is NOT correct?
   A. the commission can be deducted from the selling price as a selling expense in calculating the amount realized in the sale of a principal residence
   B. the commission paid can be deducted as a moving expense by the seller when itemizing tax-deductible expenses
   C. the commission is not deductible under any circumstance
   D. commission deducted as a moving expense is subject to a cap

*Questions 4 and 5 are based on the following information:*

Selling price of home $150,000
Selling expenses of home $10,000
Basis of home $80,000
Closing costs of home when it was purchased $5,000
Improvements to home $20,000

4. Adjusted basis of old home is:
   A. $75,000
   B. $85,000
   C. $100,000
   D. $105,000

5. Gain realized from old home is:
   A. $35,000
   B. $40,000
   C. $50,000
   D. $70,000

6. All of the following are considered sales under the universal exclusion provision EXCEPT:
   A. exchange of a principal residence for another principal residence
   B. foreclosure or repossession of a principal residence
   C. destruction or condemnation of a principal residence
   D. sale of a remainder interest to a related party while reserving a life estate for the grantor

7. All of the following are true of the universal exclusion EXCEPT:
   A. ownership and use period must be simultaneous
   B. a partial exclusion can sometimes be used if sale of residence results from a job transfer or health reasons
   C. a married couple can use the $500,000 joint exemption if only one of them owns the residence and both meet the occupancy requirement
   D. taxpayers who currently maintain an office in their home must pay capital gains tax on that part of the gain attributable to the office

8. The tax basis for inherited property is:
   A. the tax basis of the decedent
   B. the market value at the time of the decedent's death
   C. the purchase price the decedent paid for the property
   D. the market value at the time the heirs sell the property

9. For an interest on a debt to be considered "qualified residence interest" for tax deduction purposes, it can be all of the following EXCEPT:
   A. acquisition debt from the purchase of a personal residence
   B. equity debt secured by the property to the extent that the sum of acquisition and equity debt does not exceed fair market value of the property
   C. interest generated by the first $100,000 of equity debt
   D. interest generated by the first $2,000,000 of acquisition debt

10. Which of the following is NOT true about the universal exclusion in the sale of a primary residence?
    A. a married couple meeting the ownership, residency, and time requirements can exclude up to a $500,000 gain on a joint tax return
    B. a single individual meeting the ownership, residency, and time requirements can exclude up to a $250,000 gain on his individual tax return
    C. a husband and/or wife can use the exclusion only once in a lifetime; use by either husband or wife eliminates future exemptions
    D. a partial exclusion can sometimes be used if early sale of the residence is the result of a job transfer or is for health reasons

# Chapter 14

## KEY TERMS

co-insurance clause
condition
endorsement
exclusion
homeowner's policy
insurable interest
liability insurance
package policy
peril
property (or hazard) insurance

## LEARNING OBJECTIVES

At the conclusion of this chapter, you should be able to:

1. Define the basic concepts and terminology of insurance.
2. Describe the various types of homeowner's insurance policy.
3. Describe co-insurance.

# Property Insurance

## BASIC CONCEPTS AND TERMINOLOGY

Before reviewing different property insurance policies and clauses, it is important to define some basic terminology:

1. The insurer is the insurance company that provides the insurance coverage to the owner of the property or other parties who may have an insurable interest in the property.
2. The insured is the person who benefits from the insurance coverage provided by the insurer. The insured must have an insurable interest in the property.
3. Insurance that *provides coverage to the basic structure of the property* (that is, to the home itself or to other improvements) is called **property (or hazard) insurance.** The basic type of structural coverage begins with fire insurance protection.
4. An insurance **peril** is the *source of a loss.* The first peril insured against is that of fire.
5. In addition to insuring against the peril of fire, a property owner should consider purchasing **liability insurance,** which *provides coverage for the financial claims of others.*
6. A **package policy** *combines insurance coverage for the two major elements of property and liability.* Additionally, for an income-producing property such as an apartment building, a package policy can include coverage for loss of income in the event that a fire or another peril renders the property unfit to produce its normal rental income for a period of time.

## STANDARDIZED HOMEOWNER'S INSURANCE

Most fire insurance policies in the United States are based on the New York standard policy form as revised in 1943. The fire insurance policy indemnifies the insured against loss caused by fire. If the insured wishes to provide protection against losses resulting from other hazards, she must obtain an extended coverage endorsement to the fire policy. This endorsement, which is in the form of a rider attached to the fire policy, requires the payment of an additional premium. The extended coverage endorsement usually includes coverage from losses resulting from hail, explosion, windstorm, aircraft, civil commotion, vehicles, and smoke. A policy may have qualifications, exclusions, or conditions limiting coverage of some of these perils. One should check closely the details of the policy.

A package insurance policy is available to homeowners. This form of policy, called a **homeowner's policy,** *provides coverage for the structure and contents* (property insurance). A homeowner's tenants' policy for renters to cover their personal property is also available. The homeowner's policy also *provides coverage against a variety of hazards,* such as loss caused by fire, windstorm, hail, dust, waves, surface waters, freezing of plumbing, vandalism, and industrial smoke. Damage from dust or water are covered when either or both are forced in by wind or when the structure is damaged so that dust or water can enter through an opening caused by the damage and then damage the home's contents. The policy covers not only damage to the structure but also damage to the contents. Additionally, the homeowner's policy provides personal financial liability coverage to the policyholder. This protects the policyholder against liability for personal injury and property damage that he caused.

Homeowners' policies are identified as HO-2, -3, -4, and -6. HO-4 is the tenant's policy, and HO-6 is designed for condominiums and cooperatives. HO-2 and HO-3 cover owners of single-family dwellings. Few, if any, North Carolina insurance companies write HO-1 and HO-5 policies anymore. HO-3 with full replacement coverage is now used widely. HE-7 is an extended all-risk form that provides broad coverage for real and personal property. This coverage is usually marketed to owners of expensive properties.

Every hazard insurance policy must contain a description of the insured property. The street address is usually adequate; however, some insurers require a full legal description.

## Standard Form (HO-3) Policy

### *Agreement to Insure*

This introductory part of the policy establishes the contractual relationship between the insurer and the insured. In essence, the insurer agrees to provide financial reimbursement to the insured, provided the latter provides timely payments and acts in good faith with the insurance provider. The insurer sets forth restrictions in its part of the contract, and the insured agrees to abstain from deceptive practices.

### *Declaration Page*

The declaration page begins to spell out the details of the policy.

**Period of coverage.** The period of coverage is identified, usually starting at 12:01 a.m. Eastern Standard Time on a named date. Since this provision is an illustration of the specific nature of the policy, it is essential to pay close attention to detail. Obviously, no closing will proceed until verification that the policy is in effect. A related issue is the case in which a buyer wishes to take possession of the property before the sale is closed. One should pay close attention to the North Carolina Risk of Loss Statute, N.C.G.S. 39-39. Since the buyer can be held responsible for any loss before closing, he needs to make sure adequate insurance is in effect.

**Property description.** The type and construction of the property affects the insurance rating. Since the main peril is the risk of fire, the property structure and fire protection are primary considerations in establishing the rating.

**Coverage.** The coverage section describes the real property improvement that is insured. Coverage of the personal property contents is usually described as a percentage of the structure. Therefore, if the structure were insured at $100,000 with a 50 percent personal property coverage, the contents would be covered up to a value of $50,000; however, there are some personal property exceptions. Other aspects of coverage include outside living expenses if the structure is made uninhabitable. Loss of income is also covered in income-producing property. The total amount of the coverage is specified as the insurer's limit of liability. The standard deductible is $250; however, a $100 deductible is available with a higher premium.

**Endorsements.** Endorsements (additions to the general policy that increase the number of perils or items covered by the policy) are disclosed on the declaration page.

**Names.** The premium payment is specified in this section, as are the names of the insurance agent and the mortgagee (lender). The lender clearly has an interest in the property as collateral for the home mortgage. In the event of a loss, the lender would have a claim on the insurance policy along with the homeowner.

### *Standardized Policy Provisions*

This part of the policy contains all the details of the policy. If it is an HO-2 (that is, a "named peril" policy [also called broad form]), all of the covered perils insured against are itemized here. If the policy is an HO-3 (formerly called an "all-risk" form), those perils not covered are itemized. This policy is now referred to as "risk of direct physical loss," but it still functions the same way. It covers all perils except the itemized exclusions. The real and personal property covered, conditions, exclusions, and endorsements are also included here.

### *Definitions*

Other definitions that apply to insurance policies include the following:

1. A **condition** *limits the coverage of a specified property.* For example, if several persons have a financial interest in the property, a condition limits any one person's insurance claim to the amount of her financial interest in the property. Personal property such as boats, golf carts, and personal computers may be limited to a minimal value as a condition of the policy. Thus, certain items need additional special policies or riders to provide full insurance value.
2. An **exclusion** is *something that is not covered for loss.* A "risk of direct physical loss" policy clearly defines perils that are not insured. Examples include losses resulting from earthquake, nuclear hazard, flood, or acts of war.
3. An **endorsement** *adds coverage for specified items or perils that are not covered under other provisions of the policy.* For example, works of art, collectibles, and personal computers used in the home for business may have great value but are not insured under the basic policy. Therefore, it is important to add coverage for these items, with either a special policy or an endorsement to the master policy for the property. Insurance companies may require an appraisal before adding these items, depending on the value limits set by the individual company.

## SELECTED LEGAL ISSUES

### Insurable Interest

The insured must have a *legitimate financial interest,* known as an **insurable interest,** *in the property in order to be eligible for insurance coverage of any type.* In the absence of an insurable interest, the policy is void. Examples of persons having an insurable interest include owner, part owner, trustee, receiver, life tenant, mortgagor, and mortgagee.

### Co-Insurance

Insurance policies usually contain a **co-insurance clause.** This clause requires the *property owner to insure the property for at least 80 percent of its value.* Some policies require 90 percent or 100 percent, but 80 percent is the typical requirement in policies insuring an owner-occupied residence. If the coverage is for less than 80 percent of value, the policy will pay only a part of the loss in proportion to the percentage of value insured by the policy owner. For example, if a structure is worth $100,000, the co-insurance clause is 80 percent, and the insurance carried is $60,000, in the event of a partial loss ($30,000), the company's liability is only \$22,500. The amount of the insurance company's liability is calculated by using the following formula.

$$\frac{\text{Insurance carried}}{\text{Insurance required}} \times \text{Loss} = \text{Company's limit of liability}$$

$$\frac{\$60{,}000}{\$80{,}000} \times \$30{,}000 = \$22{,}500$$

If there is a loss of \$80,000 or more (insurance required), the insurance company's liability is the amount of insurance carried. This is illustrated by the following example.

| | |
|---|---|
| Value of structure | \$100,000 |
| Insurance required (80%) | \$80,000 |
| Insurance policy amount | \$60,000 |
| Loss | \$90,000 |

$$\frac{\text{Insurance carried}}{\text{Insurance required}} \times \text{Loss} = \text{Company's limit of liability}$$

$$\frac{\$60{,}000}{\$80{,}000} \times \$90{,}000 = \$67{,}500;$$

$$\text{Insurance company's liability} = \$60{,}000$$

Since the loss equals or exceeds the amount of insurance required by the co-insurance clause, the insurance company will pay the policy amount even though the requirement of the co-insurance clause is not met. However, in no event will the policy pay an amount in excess of the amount of coverage specified in the policy.

## Unoccupied Building Exclusion

A general concept of insurance risk is that a building left empty, without occupants to look after it, is at more risk than one that is constantly occupied. This is reflected in the fact that most policies lapse after a given period of time if the owners are not present. A building is considered *vacant* when the owners have moved out and have removed their personal property, such as furniture and household contents. Additionally, a property is considered *unoccupied* when the owner's property is still present but nobody has been physically present in the building for a stated period. Typically, when a building is vacant or unoccupied for the period specified by a policy, the policy ceases to cover all or certain perils.

The real estate practitioner should be aware of these limitations of policies, especially when taking a listing for an owner who is moving out of the home immediately. The listing agent should urge the owner to contact his insurance agent to be sure there is no lapse in coverage at this time.

## Interpretation of Policies

Although many policies now use plain language to assist the public in understanding the concepts contained in the policy, there is still room for misinterpretation based on certain blanket assumptions of the insured. Perhaps the best rule is not to make assumptions about areas that are not explained in detail by the insurer. A general rule of contracts is that the one who constructs the agreement (in this case, the insurer) has the burden in the event of an ambiguous phrase. Simple misunderstandings of clear terminology, however, will not work in favor of the insured. For example, not all kinds of personal property are covered under a homeowner's policy. A condition may limit the amount of coverage, such as by setting a low upper limit on a boat stored at the home. Additionally, there are exclusions for a number of items, such as currency, artwork, and collectibles. Of interest to real estate practitioners is the potential exclusion of any business activities that take place at a home residence, such as meeting customers, or the use of hardware, such as a personal computer for real estate work at home. Just as practitioners should not offer advice to others about insurance concerns, they should probably seek insurance advice to ensure that they are not exposed to uncovered liability in the use of their residence for business activities.

## Co-Owners

A hazard insurance policy covers only the person named as the insured in the policy and only to the extent of her interest. For example, if the title is held by two parties as tenants in common and the policy is in the name of only one of them and a loss occurs, the policy will pay only the person named as the insured. If the co-tenant named in the policy owned one-half interest in the property, the insurance company would pay up to one-half the face amount of the policy but no more than the loss sustained by the tenant in common owning the one-half interest. This is also important in the case of a married couple holding the title as joint tenants or by the entireties. If the policy names only one of them as the insured and that spouse dies, the surviving spouse receives title to the deceased spouse's half interest and becomes the sole owner of the entire property; but since the insurance policy did not include the surviving spouse's name as an insured, he or she would have no insurance protection in the event of a loss resulting from an insured hazard. Any time ownership in property is changed, the insurance coverage should also be changed to provide adequate protection for any owner or owners.

## Mortgagee's Insurable Interest

As previously stated, a mortgagee is an individual, a group of individuals, or an insurable organization that has an interest in a property. The mortgagee usually requires, in the mortgage, that the borrower maintain adequate hazard insurance coverage on the property. In this case, the policy is issued in the names of the mortgagee and the mortgagor. The policy protects the mortgagee up to the amount of principal balance owed within the coverage limits provided by the policy. In the event of a partial loss, the insurance company pays the mortgagor so she can make the appropriate repairs. In the event of a total loss, the mortgagee is paid first—up to the amount of the outstanding mortgage debt—with any surplus going to the mortgagor. Note: North Carolina uses a deed of trust rather than a mortgage. Therefore, mortgagor and mortgagee are not the precise terms for the borrower and lender. However, these are the terms commonly used in reference to insurance loss payee clauses.

## Assignment

Insurance policies are generally assignable with the written consent of the insurance company. A seller sometimes assigns her interest in a hazard insurance policy to a buyer of the property as of the date of closing, with the premium being prorated between buyer and seller. This is more likely to occur with purchases using loan assumptions than with purchases using new loans. The assignment is not valid, however, unless the written consent of the insurer is obtained. The insurance company typically provides evidence of consent by issuing an endorsement to the policy, changing the name of the insured.

## Flood Insurance

In areas designated as flood hazard areas by the Federal Emergency Management Agency (FEMA), flood insurance is required when financing is being provided by any federally regulated institution. Many property insurance agents offer this coverage, which can cost as much as or more than ordinary property insurance. One-twelfth of the annual flood insurance premium is included in the monthly payment considered by the mortgage company in the qualifying ratios for a loan. A purchaser, therefore, may not be able to buy as much house for the same payment in a flood area as he would elsewhere.

Land use restrictions specifying elevation, building materials, types of structures, and location and whether structures are permitted often apply to properties in flood areas. For example, an individual who is building a house on an oceanfront lot may need to build X number of feet from the ocean, may need to build on piers, and may need to locate the structure X number of feet above sea level. In certain wetlands, an individual may not be able to build at all.

## ITEMS TO CONSIDER FOR THE STATE EXAM

Be sure you can define the following terms:

1. *Endorsement.* An endorsement is something that is added to a basic policy; that is, another peril (source of loss) or item is covered. For example, the peril of earthquake is not covered by ordinary policies, but an endorsement to a policy can provide this protection. Likewise, valuable antiques not covered by an ordinary policy can be covered by an endorsement to the policy.
2. *Condition.* A condition limits the protection of a policy for special risk peril. Examples include the coverage of computer hardware used for business purposes at home or a boat on someone's property. Although one might be tempted to assume these items are covered as personal property, the condition might limit such coverage to a minimal amount, such as $100 to $500, that is far below the item's actual value.
3. *Co-insurance.* This is a concept greatly misunderstood by average clients. When they see a typical policy with an 80 percent co-insurance clause, they think they can recover 80 percent of a given loss. As you now know by studying the examples in this chapter, this is not correct. Co-insurance is simply a penalty clause requiring owners to carry a minimum amount, usually 80 percent, of the value and penalizing them proportionally if they do not. For example, since fire statistics indicate that the worst fire loss an average homeowner might expect is one-third of the structure's value, the owner might try to squeeze pennies by buying only 40 percent coverage. Referring to the formulas in the section "Co-Insurance," you see that if the home value was $100,000, the insurance purchased was $40,000, and the loss was for $20,000, the owner would be paid only $10,000. Even though the owner had $40,000 "coverage," the loss is only half covered.

What if the $100,000 home was covered with a $100,000 policy and an 80 percent co-insurance policy? In the event of a total loss, the owner would be paid the full $100,000 (not $80,000 or $125,000).

## SUMMARY OF IMPORTANT POINTS

1. The valuable asset of real property is subject to many risk factors and potential losses. A source of loss is called a peril. Homeowners' policies are package policies providing coverage for a number of perils to the structure, known as property insurance, as well as the financial claims of others, known as liability insurance.
2. A fire insurance policy indemnifies the insured against loss by fire. Protection from losses from other hazards are obtained by an extended coverage endorsement.
3. Package policies, or homeowners' policies, provide all usual protections in one policy. These policies are available to homeowners and renters.
4. To be eligible for insurance, an applicant must have an insurable interest in the property. Persons having an insurable interest include owner, part owner, trustee, receiver, life tenant, mortgagor, and mortgagee.
5. Every hazard insurance policy contains a co-insurance clause requiring the property owner to insure for at least 80 percent of the property value. In the event of a partial loss when the coverage is for less than 80 percent of value, the policy pays only part of the

loss. When the loss equals or exceeds the amount of coverage required by the co-insurance clause, however, the insurance company pays the policy amount even though the requirement of the co-insurance clause is not met.

6. Insurance policies are usually assignable with the written consent of the insurance company. The consent is evidenced by an endorsement to the policy.
7. Flood insurance is required in areas designated as flood hazard areas by FEMA. Other land use restrictions often apply in these areas.

## REVIEW QUESTIONS

Answers to the review questions are in the Answer Key at the back of the book.

1. A homeowner's insurance policy includes coverage for:
   I. structure and contents.
   II. personal liability.
   A. I only
   B. II only
   C. both I and II
   D. neither I nor II

2. Which of the following statements about hazard insurance policies is NOT correct?
   A. they are not assignable
   B. they contain a co-insurance clause
   C. there must be an insurable interest
   D. they protect only the person or persons named in the policy

3. If a home valued at $200,000 and insured for $120,000 by a policy with an 80 percent co-insurance clause suffers a loss of $175,000 from an insured hazard, what amount will the insurance company pay?
   A. $96,000
   B. $120,000
   C. $131,250
   D. $160,000

4. Those having an insurable interest in real property include all of the following EXCEPT:
   A. mortgagee
   B. life tenant
   C. trustee
   D. property manager

5. As tenants in common, James, Ann, and Meg own a property worth $100,000. Each has an equal interest. Meg insures the property in her name for $100,000. The property is completely destroyed. How much can Meg collect from the policy?
   A. $33,333
   B. $80,000
   C. $100,000
   D. nothing

# Chapter 15

## KEY TERMS

balloon framing
batter boards
bridging
Cape Cod style
casement window
certificate of occupancy
colonial style
contemporary style
contractor's license
double-hung windows
fascia
fixed window
flashing
footing
foundation vents
framing
French provincial style
frieze board
gable roof
girder
grade stakes
gypsum board (Sheetrock)
headers
hip roof
HVAC
insulation
joists
North Carolina Uniform Residential Building Code
on center
parging
piers
platform framing
post-and-beam framing
rafters
ranch style
reinforcement rods (rebar)
R-factor
ridge board
sheathing
sill
sliding window
soffit
studs
swinging window
trusses
Tudor style
2 x 4
vapor barrier
Victorian style
weather stripping
weepholes

# Basic House Construction

## LEARNING OBJECTIVES

At the conclusion of this chapter, you should be able to:

1. List the primary styles of residential architecture.
2. Describe the major components of residential construction, including foundation systems, framing, walls, ceiling and roof, windows, insulation, interior finishes, and heating/cooling systems.
3. Describe government regulation of residential construction.

## IN THIS CHAPTER

This chapter provides basic information about the principles, terminology, and methods of residential construction. The chapter is divided into 14 sections and gives an overview of the construction process from the foundation to the roof. Also included is common terminology used in residential construction. The material in this chapter is confined to wood-frame and masonry construction, the two most common types of residential construction in North Carolina.

## ARCHITECTURAL TYPES AND STYLES

The four basic types of home are one-story, one-and-a-half-story, two-story, and split-level. Homes of two-and-a-half and three stories can be found, but these homes typically are very large and expensive and thus are not as common as the others.

Although there are four basic types of home, there are many styles of residential construction. The most common styles are **ranch, contemporary, colonial, French provincial, Tudor, Cape Cod,** and **Victorian.** This list is certainly not all-encompassing, but it identifies the most common styles built in the 1900s. Figure 15.1 shows drawings of the various types and styles.

The popularity of a particular type and style of construction varies from person to person and region to region and ultimately is a matter of functionality, affordability, and taste. The ranch style tends to be of modest size and affordability, which contributes to its popularity. A one-and-a-half-story Cape Cod typically provides future expansion space on the upper level for a growing family. The traditional two-story is quite popular, as it can be

**FIGURE 15.1**
Architectural styles.

Copyright © 2003 by Home Planners, LLC, Tucson, Az.

built in a variety of styles to suit almost anyone's taste. Its extra space is perfect for a growing family or a family that needs extra room for any reason. The split-level, not as popular as the other types of construction, takes advantage of the terrain by having the lower level partially below ground, similar to a basement. One disadvantage to this type of construction is that stairs are required to get from one level to another. In some cases, as many as two or three sets of stairs are required. This typically is a disadvantage for older homeowners who do not desire to use stairs to access all areas of the house.

Many modern styles of housing take advantage of high and open ceilings, lofts, or balconies. A variety of styles exists in this category to suit modern tastes. A renaissance of Victorian architecture has occurred, and these new homes take advantage of factory-built molded trim and exterior detailing in an attempt to keep costs down and make the homes more affordable.

Of course, in any type or style of construction, the floor plan must provide functional utility. Good design increases the comfort and resale potential of any home. Good design includes a modern heating and cooling system, adequate closets and storage space, access to a bathroom for every bedroom, living and sleeping areas of sufficient size, and the proper placement and size of windows to provide adequate light and ventilation. The grouping of bedroom and bathroom areas so as to provide privacy is also important. The kitchen should be designed to provide an efficient, attractive work area, and it should be located near a utility, rear, or side entrance, for access to the outside. The traditional living room and living room/den arrangement is sometimes replaced by the "great room" (one large room that is used for both entertaining and daily family activities). Modern design may include an attached two-car garage, wood deck and/or patio, and a great room.

# LOCATION ON SITE

The location of the house on the building site can have a significant effect on value. Land use regulations and local covenants usually mandate a setback from the street and side and rear property lines. A location that takes advantage of views, privacy, terrain, and ease of access adds to the value and enjoyment of the home.

# FOUNDATIONS

## Footings

Arguably the most important foundation building block is the **footing.** The footing is *the concrete base below the frost line that supports the foundation of the structure.* To construct the footings, the building lines are laid out with **batter boards,** temporary wood members on posts that form an L shape outside the corners of the foundation. Strings are run from the batter boards to line up the placement of the foundation walls. Trenches are dug for the footings, which must rest on undisturbed soil. **Grade stakes** are then placed in the trenches to *measure and verify proper elevation and thickness of the footing* prior to pouring the concrete. Once this is complete, the footing can be poured. Footings are composed of cast-in-place concrete. When constructing footings, **reinforcement rods,** commonly known as **rebar,** should be *placed in the concrete to aid in temperature control and to strengthen the footing.* This is especially important in areas with unstable soil or a high water table and in coastal regions.

The width of the footing is twice the width of the foundation wall. The depth of the footing is usually a minimum of 8 inches (for one- and two-story homes); it should be the same thickness as the foundation wall. If the wall is thicker, the footing must be thicker. Footings for masonry fireplaces must be a minimum of 12 inches thick. The purpose of the footing is to support the foundation wall and, subsequently, the entire weight load of the structure. The footings must provide an adequate base for the structure to prevent settling of the house.

## Foundation Walls

Foundation walls in North Carolina generally are composed of poured concrete, masonry block, or brick. The most common type of foundation wall is made with masonry block and brick. The masonry block forms the back half of the wall and is covered with a brick veneer on the front. Vertical masonry **piers** are *built inside the foundation walls to provide additional support for the house.* If only masonry block is used in the foundation wall, the exterior portions of the blocks are faced with a smooth mortar finish known as **parging.** The parged walls are painted to improve the appearance of the foundation. In some instances, foundation walls are covered with stucco to improve the appearance and to hide the masonry block.

In level terrain, the foundation may be a concrete slab instead of a foundation wall. The concrete slab is poured directly on the ground and eliminates the crawl space or basement. The slab provides the floor of the dwelling and the support for the exterior and interior walls. The concrete slab method is less expensive than the foundation wall system or basement, but it is not practical in all building situations. This type of foundation falls into two categories. A *monolithic slab* is poured in one large section. The edges, which are thickened to a depth of 12 inches, serve as a footing to support the load of the exterior walls. A *floating slab* uses footings and a foundation wall to serve as the outside boundary inside of which the concrete slab is poured.

The foundation wall with crawl space is widely used throughout North Carolina. Basements, although popular, are expensive to construct and are seldom used in the eastern and coastal regions of the state due to a high water table. Moisture control is a serious problem that must be addressed in any foundation system. First, grading of the soil must assure that surface water is directed away from the foundation and that proper drainage is provided. Footing drain tile is used below grade around all concrete or masonry foundations enclosing habitable or usable space. Additionally, crawl spaces under homes must be properly graded to assure positive drainage.

Equally important, **foundation vents** must be installed in foundation walls to properly ventilate the crawl space underneath the house. Adequate vents and sometimes a **vapor barrier** are necessary to allow the crawl space and wood members of the floor system to remain dry and free from unnecessary moisture damage. Termite treatment is applied after the foundation is complete and prior to the vapor barrier installation. In the case of a concrete basement floor or slab, termite treatment and vapor barrier are applied prior to pouring the concrete. As additional termite preventive measures, all woody debris should be removed from under the foundation and all wood in direct contact with the ground or a concrete slab should be pressure-treated.

## FRAMING

**Framing** refers to the wooden skeleton of the home. Framing members are lumber with a nominal dimension of 2 inches thick. For example, a **2 × 4** is a piece of lumber theoretically 2 inches thick by 4 inches wide. It is actually slightly smaller. Wall **studs** are commonly 2 × 4s; 2 × 8s, 2 × 10s, or 2 × 12s are commonly used for **joists** for floor and ceiling framing. Usually, 2 × 6s or 2 × 8s are used as **rafters** in the roof system (see Figures 15.2 and 15.3).

### Flooring

The top of the foundation wall is finished off with a course of solid masonry. On top of this course of solid masonry rests the foundation **sill.** The sill is usually made up of pressure-treated 2 × 6s or 2 × 8s. In the event pressure-treated lumber is not used for the sill, metal **flashing** must be placed between the foundation wall and wooden member. The wooden sill is fastened to the foundation wall by anchor bolts or nails. The sill is the first wooden member of the house and is used as the nailing surface for the floor system.

The box sill, or banding, rests on the sill plate and is the same size wood member as the floor joists (2″ × 8″, 2″ × 10″, or 2″ × 12″). The banding runs around the top of the foundation wall, attached to the sill plate.

The floor joists span the distance between the foundation walls and the **girder** and provide support for the subfloor. The girder is either a steel beam or several wooden members fastened together (usually 2 × 10s, 2 × 12s, or larger) that spans the distance from one side of the foundation to the other. The joists rest on the girder for support. Typical framing places wooden members at 16 inches **on center.** The 16-inch spacing of framing members depends primarily on strength considerations for lumber sizing. Additionally, covering materials such as plywood, **sheathing,** and wallboard are made in 4-foot widths. The 16-inch spacing, therefore, provides a uniform nailing pattern of four rows for each piece of covering material.

Depending on the area to be spanned, the joists are doubled or even tripled to support the load. **Bridging** provides support and "stiffening" to the joists to prevent lateral movement of the joists. Bridging is usually constructed in one of two ways. One type of bridging is solid bridging, which uses the same size wooden member as the joists. This type of bridging forms a "solid" bridge between the joists. Cross-bridging uses 1 × 4s or 2 × 4s placed in an X pattern between the joists.

Some modern construction methods use wooden floor **trusses** in place of single floor joists. A truss is a support member constructed in a factory by nailing a number of smaller members (2 × 4s or 2 × 6s) together in a number of triangular patterns to provide maximum strength.

A plywood or particle board subflooring rests directly on top of the joists. Quality construction practice sees this subfloor glued and fastened with nails or shank screws to prevent nail popping and squeaky floors. Finish flooring rests on top of the subflooring. Typical finish flooring includes hardwood, tile, carpet, and vinyl.

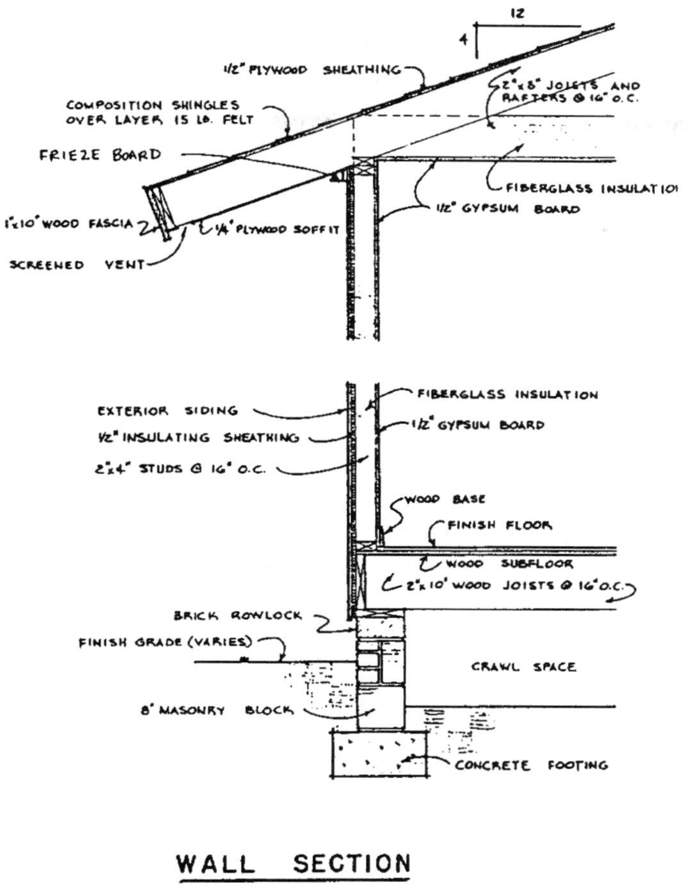


**FIGURE 15.2**

Typical wall section.

## Walls

The floor system usually serves as a stage or platform for the wall system. The walls are usually built of 2 × 4 studs, 16 inches on center. Less common is a wall system of 2 × 6s at 16 or 24 inches on center. A horizontal base plate, also called a sole plate, serves as the foundation for the wall system. A double top plate ties the walls together to provide additional support for the ceiling and roof system. Exterior and interior walls are framed in a rough carpentry skeleton. Openings in the wall for doors and windows must be reinforced to pick up the missing support for the vertical load. This is done with 2 × 8s, 2 × 10s, or 2 × 12s, known as **headers,** on end, over the top of the opening. Headers should form a solid wood bridge over the opening and extend to the bottom of the top plate. The type of framing described above is known as **platform framing** because the framing of the structure rests on a subfloor platform. Platform framing is the most common type of framing used in residential construction (see Figure 15.2).

An alternative to platform framing is **balloon framing.** This method uses a single system of wall studs that runs from the foundation through the first and second floors to the ceiling support. This method is rarely used in residential construction. A third type of framing is **post-and-beam framing.** These members are much larger than ordinary studs and may be 4 or 6 inches square. The larger posts can be placed several feet apart instead of 16 or 24 inches on center. Like balloon framing, this type of framing is seldom used in residential construction.

Plumbing, electrical, and heating and cooling systems are run through the walls, floors, and ceilings before they are covered up. Inspections by the local building inspector must be made before any of these systems can be covered with insulation and wallboard. A vapor barrier is applied to the warm (inside) wall on exterior walls. The vapor barrier is important

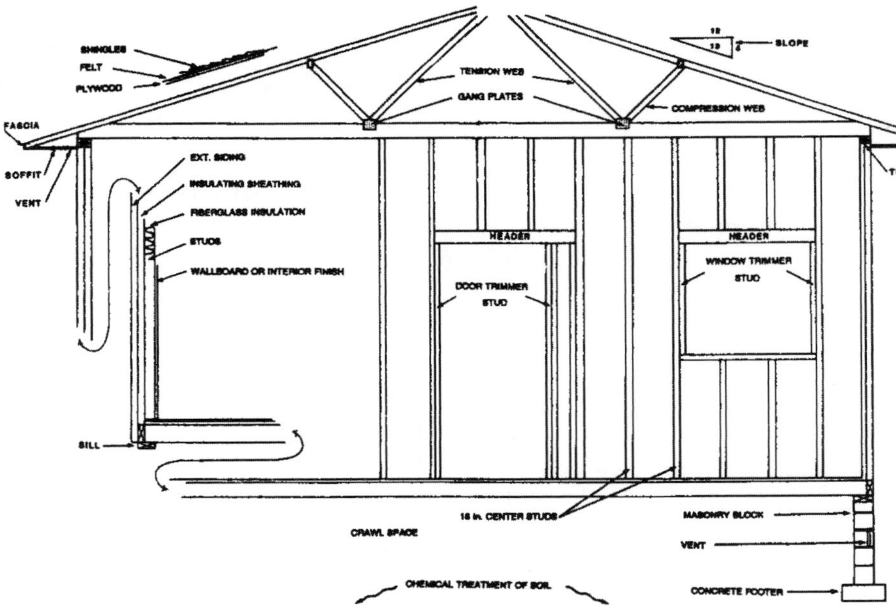


**FIGURE 15.3**
Roof section using truss system.

in preventing the warm interior air from mixing with the cold exterior air and forming condensation within the wall.

## Ceiling Framing and Roof

The ceiling joists rest on the top plate of the wall. These joists should be placed directly over the vertical studs for maximum bearing strength. The joists span the structure between the outer walls. In traditional framing, these joists are usually 2 × 8s, and the inner walls are important in helping to bear the load of the roof. This is different in the contemporary use of roof truss systems, in which the truss carries the load-bearing function to the outer walls. This feature provides freedom of placement of the inner walls. Since a roof truss is made up of a number of smaller members (usually 2 × 4s), the attic space is almost completely lost (see Figure 15.3).

The **ridge board** is the highest part of the framing and forms top line of the roof. Rafters are the long wooden members that are fastened to the ends of the ceiling joists; they form the gables of the roof. Rafters are usually 2 × 6s or 2 × 8s. The rafters are fastened to the ridge at the peak of the gable.

Contemporary residential construction sees roof styles in two varieties. These are the traditional **gable roof** and the **hip roof.** Some homes even employ both styles to create a distinctive roofline. The gable roof is the most popular roof style in North Carolina. In years past, the gambrel and mansard roof styles were sometimes used, but these styles were never as popular or as functional as the gable or hip. As a result, the mansard and gambrel are rarely used on houses, but they are sometimes found on barns, stables, and other types of nonresidential structure. (The gambrel roof actually resembles a barn.) Two other roof types—seldom found on homes but sometimes used on outbuildings or additions such as utility rooms or porches—are the *shed roof* (which resembles one side of a gable roof) and the *flat roof.* Figure 15.4 shows the four roof styles—gable, hip, gambrel, and mansard.

The part of the roof that extends beyond the exterior wall and forms the connection between the roof and the exterior walls is known as the *eave,* or overhang. The roof should extend at least 6 inches beyond the exterior of the structure. Common construction practices see a 12-inch overhang on the front and rear, with a 6-inch overhang on the side. The larger the overhang, the more protection there is from sun and rain for the exterior walls, windows, and doors.

The overhang is made up of three components: the soffit, the fascia, and the frieze board. The **soffit** is the area under the eave. This is made of wood, aluminum, or vinyl

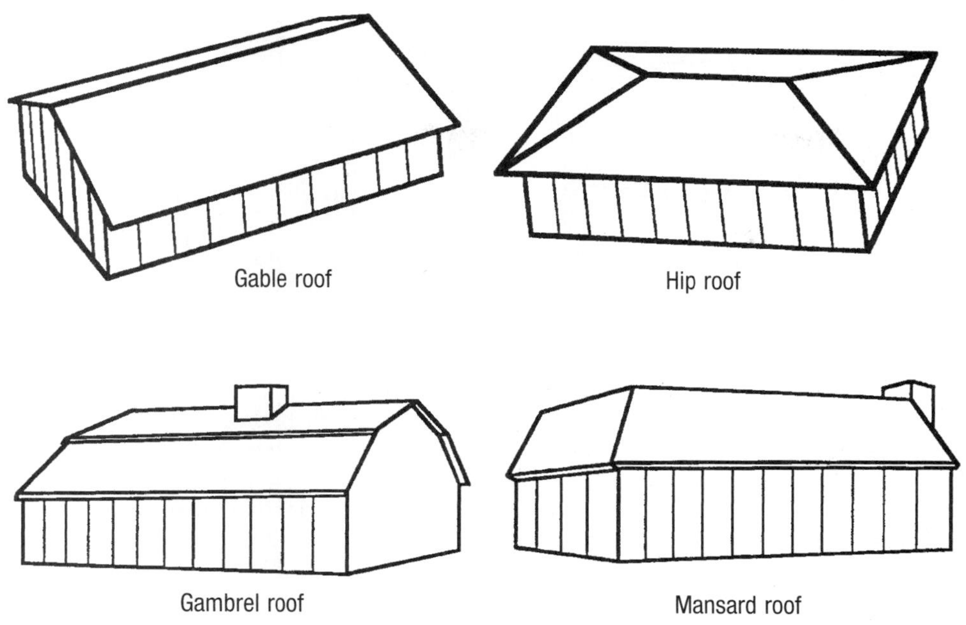


**FIGURE 15.4**
Roof styles.

(depending on the type of siding). The area of material facing the outer edge of the soffit is the **fascia.** The fascia is typically a 1 × 6 or 1 × 8. If guttering is installed on the roof, it is fastened to the fascia. The third component of the eave is the **frieze board.** This is a wooden member (usually a 2 × 4, 2 × 6, or 2 × 8) that is fastened directly under the soffit against the top of the wall. The function of the frieze board is both decorative and functional. The frieze board prevents wind and moisture from penetrating the junction of the soffit and sheathing. Depending on the style of the home, additional trim boards are sometimes fastened on and around the frieze board to give the house the desired look.

## EXTERIOR WALLS

The exterior wall of a house is covered with a sheathing material. This material is usually plywood or particleboard. The purpose of the sheathing is to strengthen the wall and add some insulation protection. An insulating "house wrap" is sometimes applied over this sheathing to increase the **R-factor** (resistance to heat transfer) of the walls. Upon this material, the exterior siding is applied.

There are several types of siding: aluminum, vinyl, masonite, fiber-cement board, and wood. Each type has advantages and disadvantages, and for every person who likes a particular type of siding, someone else doesn't. Regardless of the type, siding should be properly installed to prevent water damage to the house and to give the house a first-rate, professional appearance.

In brick construction, builders typically install sheathing paper or house wrap, which serves to seal the home from the intrusion of moisture through the brick. A small gap exists between the brick veneer walls and the interior sheathing. This is necessary to allow any moisture that seeps through the brick mortar to run down the back of the masonry wall and out through the **weepholes** at the bottom of the wall. Weepholes are small holes in the bottom course of brick that allow any moisture on the inside of the wall an avenue to the exterior and also allow ventilation into this area to keep the inside of the wall dry.

## WINDOWS

Windows fall into three general classes: **sliding, swinging,** and **fixed.** Although there are other classes, they are not as common. Windows manufactured today are made from wood, metals such as aluminum, and even some composite materials. Whereas older

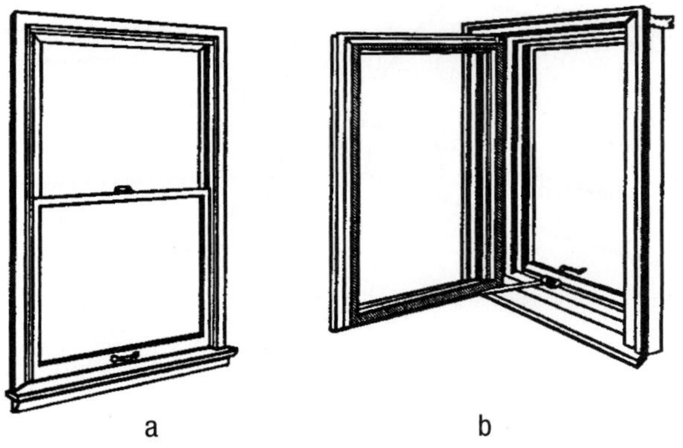


**FIGURE 15.5**
(a) Double-hung window and (b) casement window.

windows were a single pane of glass, contemporary windows are of a thermal insulating design with a double- or triple-glass pane. A small air space is sandwiched between the glass panes. This design provides excellent insulation and efficiency of heating and cooling, since windows make up a large portion of the wall and even roof surface area (in the case of skylights). Additionally, single-pane windows produce interior condensation in cold weather, which can damage woodwork and interior finishes. These antiquated single-pane windows require an exterior glass unit (storm window) to provide proper insulation in summer and winter.

The major parts of a window framework are labeled the same as the parts of a door opening. For example, the sill is the bottom or base part, the jamb is the side, and the header is the top of the opening.

The sash is the glass panel unit that slides up and down. In the past, glass manufacturers were only able to make small glass panes for windows. These windows were held together with wood strips known as mullions or grills. Today many windows have nonfunctional mullions or grills added as decorative strips to simulate a multiple pane appearance. The stile is the side part of the sash; the top and bottom portions of the sash are known as rails.

## Sliding Windows

### *Vertical Sliding (Double-Hung)*

The most common type of windows used in residential construction is vertical sliding, known as **double-hung windows** (see Figure 15.5). These windows are composed of two glass pane units, or sashes, that vertically slide by each other. In older construction, the weight of the heavy window unit was supported or balanced by a rope-(sash cord)-and-pulley system in the wall. Lighter modern systems are governed entirely by the friction of the unit sliding in its track.

### *Horizontal Sliding*

Horizontal sliding windows are often found in modern homes, sometimes in a bedroom. These units often have two sashes that slide by each other horizontally. In the case of a three-sash unit, the central portion is usually fixed, with only two sliding sashes. These windows are nearly identical in construction and composition to the double-hung vertical window described previously, except for the manner in which they open.

## Swinging Windows

The **casement window** has a sash hinged on one side, and it swings outward (see Figure 15.5). The swinging mechanism is usually a geared crank system with an operating handle on the interior sill. Latches are often used to lock this type of window for a weather-tight seal.

Older homes sometimes have jalousie, hopper, or awning windows. All of these windows swing inward or outward and, as a result, have limitations because they interfere with living space. Typically, these windows do not insulate well, and as technology and energy efficiency have improved window construction and insulating requirements, the jalousie, hopper, and awning windows have become a thing of the past. The only swinging window that seems to have improved and kept pace with technological and architectural improvements is the casement window.

### Fixed Windows

Fixed windows do not have movable sections. As air conditioning and ventilation systems have evolved, there is less need to have windows that can open. The common types of fixed window include picture, bay, bow, and Palladian. In some window assemblies, a fixed window may be a center section with some form of movable or openable window on either side. These windows are designed to allow maximum lighting and are strategically placed for maximum functionality and aesthetic appeal.

## DOORS

Doors, like windows, come in many shapes and styles. However, there are only two classes, interior and exterior. Doors can be made of wood, steel, aluminum, composite materials, and glass. Maximum insulation is desired in exterior doors, which are usually composed of solid wood or steel with a high-insulating core.

All doors and windows must be tightly sealed to prevent the movement of air around them. A high-quality door coupled with proper installation is essential for maintaining proper energy efficiency. External caulking around windows and doors helps complete the tight seal, as does **weather stripping** in the doorframes. When you consider the large area of walls that doors and windows occupy in a typical home, you can see why it is extremely important that they be properly installed; even tiny cracks and leaks can result in significant heating and cooling bills.

Common types of exterior door include the flush door, which is one continuous smooth unit, and the panel door, which is composed of several recessed or raised panels that may include glass. The sliding glass door unit is very popular and is used for access to patios, decks, and porches. The glass door often has one fixed panel and one panel that slides on a track or rollers. French doors have become popular high-style decorative units that open onto patios, decks, and porches.

Interior doors are usually made of wood. These doors differ from their exterior counterparts in that they usually do not have a solid core and are not designed for energy efficiency. Their main function is decoration and privacy. Interior doors can be flush, have panels, and even be glass (French doors).

## ROOFING

Once the structural skeleton of the roof system is in place, it is covered with plywood or particleboard *sheathing (decking)*. On top of this, roofing paper is applied to aid in weatherproofing the structure. On top of the roofing paper, shingles are applied. Most construction uses the fiberglass shingle, but tile and wood shingles are also used.

## INSULATION

The primary purpose of **insulation** is to resist the flow of heat from one area to another. It provides the double benefit of preventing heat loss in the winter and protecting against heat load in the summer. The areas of the home that must be insulated are the ceiling, walls, and floor. Insulation is rated in an R-factor. The larger the R-factor, the greater the degree of insulation. The North Carolina Residential Building Code requires installation of insulation with an R-factor of 13 in walls. R-30 is required in ceilings; R-19, in floors. Higher values are required in the colder northwestern portion of North Carolina (R-18 for walls and R-38 for ceilings). Homes built to superior energy efficient standards should exceed these minimum requirements. Local utility companies usually offer discount rates to homes meeting their energy efficient standards. Additionally, they sometimes offer low-cost loan programs to homeowners to improve the insulating value of their homes.

A common form of insulation is that of fiberglass sold in 15½" wide rolls, designed to fit in the space between framing members such as joists and studs. Unfaced rolls (without paper covering) and loose blown-in insulation can be added on top of existing attic insulation to improve the energy efficiency of homes. As previously discussed, exterior sheathings and house wrapping material can also provide a high degree of insulating value.

Insulation also provides a degree of soundproofing between adjacent floors and walls of town houses, condominiums, and apartments. Air leaking into or out of a home can significantly affect heat loss or gain. Therefore, careful attention should be paid to caulking around openings for plumbing and wiring and weather-stripping around windows and doors.

### Moisture Control

Normal household activities such as cooking, showering, and laundering create water vapor. Condensation from vapor that passes through interior wall surfaces can cause damage to the structure. For this reason, a vapor barrier (which may be made of plastic film, foil, or crafted paper) should be installed on the inside wall side of the insulation.

As in the crawl space below the house, proper ventilation of the attic space is important. This is accomplished through the use of vents to allow the free movement of air in the attic, which keeps moisture from forming, thereby rotting the wood. The ventilation also aids in removing unwanted heat from the attic, allowing air conditioners to work more efficiently in cooling the home. Roof vents come in many shapes and styles. Older homes usually have gable vents at the peak on each end of the house. Newer homes often use a single-piece ridge vent that is installed along the ridgeline. Intake vents are placed in the soffit or overhang of the roof. These vents allow air to travel from the outside, through the soffit vents, through the attic, and outside through the ridge vent.

## INTERIOR FINISHES

In most homes, the interior walls are finished with a wallboard material. This construction consists of **gypsum board,** or **Sheetrock**™**,** as it is commonly known. The panels essentially are a core of gypsum material covered with a treated paper. The careful placement of these sheets and the finishing of seams require a high degree of skill. Since this treatment acts as the interior finish and greatly affects the appearance of the home, it is usually done by a team of specialists. The panels are fastened with Sheetrock nails or screws or both, and the seams are bonded with a plasterlike drywall material. Once it dries, the seams are sanded and painted. Wallpaper also can be used in place of paint and is sometimes found in bathrooms and on accent walls.

A durable and popular finish in bathrooms, entryways, and kitchens is ceramic tile. This tile is used on floors and walls and comes in a wide variety of styles, sizes, textures, and colors. People often choose vinyl flooring instead of ceramic tile because of the cost savings. Like ceramic tile, vinyl comes in a wide variety of styles, sizes, textures, and colors.

Molded fiberglass tubs and showers have gained popularity in recent years. The relatively low cost of these fixtures often allows homeowners and builders to spend more for flooring and wall finishes. Prior to the use of these fiberglass fixtures, tubs and showers were either ceramic tile or a solid ceramic fixture. Both were more expensive than the newer fiberglass fixtures.

Such extras as hot tubs and saunas are gaining popularity among homeowners. Technology has made these once costly, hard-to-maintain systems very affordable to own and operate.

A good deal of attention should be given to the finished carpentry on the interior and exterior of the house. The quality of materials as well as the quality of work that goes into the construction of window and doorframes, baseboards, crown molding, trim, cabinets, and closets is a strong indication of the quality of the construction of the dwelling. Because a significant amount of money is spent to finish out the house, it only makes sense that it be done correctly and to the homeowner's quality standards.

## HEATING/AIR CONDITIONING SYSTEMS

**HVAC** is an acronym for heating, ventilation, and air conditioning. A wide variety of heating and cooling systems is available for residential construction. Older structures relied on heating systems such as fireplaces, electric baseboard heaters, and oil furnaces. Unfortunately, these systems were rather inefficient and costly to operate. In recent years, there has been interest in highly efficient fireplace inserts and freestanding wood stoves. Although picturesque, a modern masonry fireplace by itself is a very inefficient heating structure. It serves largely to exhaust air (and subsequently heat) from the house.

Despite America's love for wood stoves and the like, the only truly efficient heating system is a central unit. Older systems relied heavily on the convection of heated and cooled air to circulate and warm the house. This system required large ducts and vents to circulate the required volume of air throughout the house.

Today's heating and cooling systems use a central blower to distribute the heated or cooled air throughout the house. Each room is required to have an air duct, and return ducts to the main unit must be centrally located for maximum efficiency. These modern systems come in a variety of sizes and capabilities to suit a particular home and can be powered by gas or electricity.

The makeup of these systems is largely one of convenience, cost, and individual preference. Efficiency and operating costs should also be top priorities for builders and homeowners. Which system (gas or electric) is the most efficient and has the lowest installation and operating costs is an ongoing debate.

Gas forced-air furnaces are popular among many homeowners due to their relatively low cost; their high efficiency; and the warm, cozy environment they create when the heat comes on. Electric furnaces are popular for the same reasons, but rising utility costs over the past several years have made the electric furnace less economical than in the past.

Another popular heating and cooling system is the heat pump. The heat pump extracts heat from the outside, even in moderately cold weather, and transfers the heat into the home. The cycle is reversed in the summer to extract heat from the interior and produce air conditioning. A limitation of the heat pump is that it can only operate in moderate climates. In climates that have cold winters, a separate furnace, fireplace, or wood stove is necessary to provide the heat when the outside temperature drops. Another drawback to the heat pump is that the heat coming out of the vent feels cooler than that generated by a furnace. For this reason, homeowners often have a backup heating system to maintain a comfortable living environment.

Air conditioning systems usually are powered by electricity. As previously discussed, the heat pump is the only heating and cooling system that is built into the same unit. Furnaces typically are located in the utility room, basement, or garage, while the air conditioning unit is placed outside the house, which is necessary for proper operation and efficiency.

Advances in technology have integrated the heating, cooling, and ventilation controls into a central thermostat, eliminating the need for separate controls. A further advance is the development of "smart houses," which use a central computer to automate the entire operating infrastructure of the house. With these state-of-the-art systems, you can adjust the controls of the heating and cooling system, activate the lawn sprinkler, draw a bath, or program a security system—all by telephone or computer modem link. These systems are extremely expensive but offer tremendous savings in efficiency and productivity for homeowners.

Finally, when designing, replacing, or installing a new HVAC system, builders and homeowners should ensure that the system meets the requirements of the home. Modern practice often sees duplicate systems installed in homes of two or more stories. Although individual furnaces, heat pumps, and air conditioners are designed to adequately heat or cool a specific size home, many times these systems are underpowered or overworked in order to accomplish the task. The net result is a system that does not operate at peak efficiency and ultimately breaks down sooner than desired. With the installation of dual systems (one for the upstairs and one for the downstairs), the entire system can operate more efficiently, saving the homeowner considerable money in the long run. HVAC systems are very expensive, so it makes sense for homeowners to carefully research any such expenditure to ensure they are getting what they want and need in a heating and cooling system.

## Solar Heat

Much attention has been given to solar heat in recent years. Two main types of solar heating are passive and active.

Passive solar heating simply takes advantage of exposure to the sun. Direct exposure heats a given area during the day. Indirect exposure involves heating water units or masonry surfaces to "give off " heat during the night. In order to be able to incorporate passive solar heating, a home must be situated so the front or rear of the house faces south, and the southern exposure should incorporate sufficient windows to allow the sun's rays to penetrate the home.

Active solar heating involves a more sophisticated method of collecting, storing, and distributing heat. The system starts with a collection panel(s), with a glass front, water tubing, and black flat plates. The glass is useful in allowing the solar energy to enter, but preventing its escape. The black plates absorb the heat energy for transmission to the water tubing. The heated water is pumped to a storage tank for later distribution throughout the home. A heat exchange system provides for distribution of the heat from the circulated water.

Unfortunately, solar systems cannot provide more than 50 to 60 percent of the heating needed for a home. Thus, auxiliary systems (such as a furnace or heat pump) are needed.

# ELECTRICAL SYSTEMS

Like the HVAC system, the electrical system in a house serves a critical purpose. Care should be taken to ascertain the proper design, scope, and layout of electrical outlets and components and to ensure the system is adequate to handle the current and future requirements. Modern construction requires a 110/220 volt wiring system with a capacity of approximately 200 amps, fitted with circuit breakers. The electrical box/panel should be located in a utility room, basement, or garage for ease of access to reset circuit breakers and to perform maintenance.

The home should be wired with sufficient electrical wall receptacles for the use of the household. Utility areas such as garages and bathrooms require the installation of dedicated breakers to prevent accidental electrical shock. Additionally, the installation of smoke detectors outside sleeping areas is required to warn occupants of fire danger. These systems must be wired into the house's electrical current and have a battery backup. The smoke detector must have a visible warning light or be designed to give off a warning signal of 85 db at 10 feet. This is a requirement for all new residential construction, as outlined in the North Carolina residential building code.

# PLUMBING SYSTEMS

The adequacy and quality of the plumbing system are other important facets in the quality of residential construction. Common construction practice uses copper, brass, cast iron, galvanized steel, chlorinated polyvinyl chloride (CPVC), or polybutylene (PB) plastic pipe for water distribution systems. Each bathroom should be vented to the exterior by the use of a metal pipe that is run through the roof. The venting of sink traps is also required. All water fixtures should have separate cutoffs so a repair can be made without shutting down the entire system. Like the HVAC and electrical systems, the plumbing system should be designed for maximum efficiency and functional utility. Hot water heaters should be well insulated and large enough to accommodate the demands placed upon them. Typically, single-family homes require at least a 50-gallon water heater. A large home or a larger family may require a bigger water heater or multiple water heaters.

# GOVERNMENT REGULATION

## North Carolina Uniform Residential Building Code

North Carolina enforces a statewide residential building code that is designed to ensure uniformity, safety, sanitation, and high-quality construction of residential homes. The **North Carolina Uniform Residential Building Code** is based on the International Residential Code for One- and Two-Family Dwellings (as amended for North Carolina). The provisions of the International Code are compatible with the codes of the Building Officials Code Administrators International, Inc. (BOCA); the International Conference of Building Officials (ICBO); and the Southern Building Code Congress International, Inc. (SBCCI).

Each local government, county, or city has a building inspections department that enforces the local adaptations of the building code. Before any construction can begin, the builder must submit appropriate construction information in order to obtain a building permit. The inspection officer must then approve each stage of the construction before the next stage is allowed to begin. At the satisfactory completion of the construction and inspection process, a **certificate of occupancy** is issued. Typically, one cannot obtain permanent utility services for a home until the certificate of occupancy is issued.

## HUD/VA Minimum Standards

Homes built to be sold to buyers using an FHA-insured or VA-guaranteed loan do not need to be built under FHA or VA supervision or need a ten-year warranty. FHA requires a building certificate for any home under one year old. VA requires a builder to be on its approved builder's list before his or her new homes can be financed with a VA loan. All new construction requires a certificate of occupancy by the local building inspector. Such a certificate is issued only after all required inspections have been completed.

## Contractor Licensing

To obtain a **contractor's license,** an applicant must pass an examination. The examination tests state building codes, contract law, worker's compensation laws, blueprint reading/estimating, and Occupational Safety and Health Administration (OHSA) laws and regulations. In addition to passing an exam, an applicant must have a net worth of $17,000 to $150,000 depending on the classification of license requested. Property managers who oversee renovations and/or improvements to apartment complexes and/or commercial property which exceed $30,000, must also have a general contractor's license.

The Contractor's Licensing Board falls under the North Carolina Department of Insurance and is a separate entity not related to the Real Estate Commission.

# CONSTRUCTION FOR PRACTITIONERS

Real estate practitioners should learn to distinguish the features in a dwelling that show quality construction as well as those features that indicate construction of inferior quality. As a suggestion, those not familiar with construction techniques might spend time looking at homes in their area in various stages of construction. Additionally, agents can contact their local chapter of the National Association of Home Builders (NAHB) to get current information on building practices and trends in the industry. By doing either (or both), practitioners can gain a working knowledge of the construction process and an awareness of the quality of workmanship and materials in their area.

## TERMINOLOGY

**balloon framing** rarely used in residential construction. Balloon framing uses a single system of wall studs that runs from the foundation through the first and second floors to the ceiling support; it is an alternative to platform framing.

**batter boards** temporary wood members on posts that form an L shape outside the corners of the footing, which line up the placement of the foundation walls.

**bridging** wooden members (usually 1 × 4s or solid pieces the same size as the joists) that are placed between joists to hold them in place and prevent lateral movement.

**Cape Cod style** a one-and-a-half-story house that is characterized by a high-pitched roof with dormers. The Cape Cod style was first constructed in New England.

**casement window** a window that has a sash hinged on one side and that swings outward. The swinging mechanism is usually geared by a crank, with the operating handle on the interior sill.

**certificate of occupancy** a certificate issued by the local building inspector, stating that the construction project is complete, conforms to all state and local building codes, and is approved for occupancy.

**colonial style** a type of residential construction (usually two stories) that incorporates architectural features found in early American homes.

**contemporary style** a type of residential construction that incorporates modern designs and architectural features. A contemporary home can be in any configuration and have one, one-and-a-half, or two stories.

**contractor's license** a requirement for all builders in North Carolina if the project costs $30,000 or more. An applicant must have a net worth of at least $17,500 and pass a written examination. Projects that are under $30,000 do not require a contracts license.

**double-hung window** a window composed of two glass panes, or sashes, that slide vertically past each other. The sashes are governed by the friction of the units sliding in their tracks.

**fascia** the wood covering attached to the end of the roof rafters at the outer end. The fascia is one of three components of the eave.

**fixed windows** windows that do not have movable sections. Types of fixed window include bay, bow, picture, and Palladian.

**flashing** strips of metal or other waterproof material placed between the foundation and the first wooden member of the house or used to waterproof joints in other areas of construction.

**footing** the concrete base below the frost line that supports the foundation of a structure.

**foundation vents** small openable vents that are placed around the foundation of a house with a crawl space. The vents allow the free movement of air under the home, preventing the buildup of moisture, which can damage the wood subflooring.

**framing** the wooden skeleton of a home. The framing consists of the subfloor, walls, ceiling, and roof systems.

**French provincial style** a type of residential construction that incorporates a hip roof and French-influenced architectural features.

**frieze board** a wooden member (usually a 2″ × 4″, 2″ × 6″, or 2″ × 8″) that is fastened directly under the soffit against the sheathing. The frieze board is one of the three components of the roof overhang.

**gable roof** a roof consisting of two inclined planes joined over the center line of the house and resting on the two opposite roof plates on top of the studs. The triangular end walls are called gables.

**girder** a steel beam or several wooden members fastened together that span the foundation from one side to the other. The joists rest on the girder for support.

**grade stakes** small wooden stakes placed in the bottom of the footing trenches that are used to measure and verify the proper elevation and thickness of the footing.

**gypsum board (Sheetrock)** large panels of gypsum material covered in treated paper that are used as finish for interior walls. The gypsum board is fastened directly to the studs and ceiling joists.

**headers** wooden members used to support the free ends of joists, studs, or rafters over openings in the frame.

**hip roof** a roof consisting of four inclined planes joined together to form a rectangle.

**HVAC** an acronym for heating, ventilation, and air conditioning.

**insulation** material used in construction to prevent heat loss in the winter and to protect against heat load in the summer. Insulation is usually fiberglass material either in rolls or loose. The material is placed in the floor, exterior walls, and ceiling of homes.

**joist** a large wooden member (usually a $2'' \times 8''$, $2'' \times 10''$, $2'' \times 12''$, or larger) that is placed on edge horizontally to support a floor or ceiling.

**North Carolina Uniform Residential Building Code** rules, regulations, and procedures that ensure uniformity, safety, sanitation, and high-quality construction that must be followed by all builders and contractors. The building code is managed by the North Carolina Department of Insurance and the North Carolina Building Code Council.

**on center** refers to the placement of wooden members in the construction process. Usually, joists, studs, and rafters are placed at 16 or 24 inches on center to maximize strength and fastening of wallboard, plywood, and sheathing.

**parging** a smooth mortar-based finish used to cover exposed masonry blocks to hide mortar joints and seams.

**piers** vertical masonry structures (usually poured concrete, cement block, or brick) that are placed inside the foundation walls to support the subflooring. Piers are not used with concrete slabs or basements.

**platform framing** the most common type of framing used in residential construction. Platform framing is the construction of a floor system that serves as a stage, or platform, for the walls and the rest of the structure.

**post-and-beam framing** a type of framing in which large wooden members are placed several feet apart, instead of at 16 or 24 inches on center. Post-and-beam framing is rarely used in residential construction.

**rafter** the large, long wooden members that are fastened to the ends of the ceiling joists and ridge board. The rafters form the pitch of the roof. Plywood is fastened to the rafters to form the underlay of the roof covering.

**ranch style** a one-story home that is usually of modest size and affordability and that can be finished in siding, brick, or other types of exterior covering.

**reinforcement rods (rebar)** metal rods that can be placed in footings and poured concrete to aid in temperature control and strengthening of the concrete. They are highly recommended in areas with poor soil or a high water table.

**R-factor** stands for resistance to heat transfer. Insulation is rated in R-factors. The greater the R-factor, the greater the degree of insulation.

**ridge board** the long horizontal board at the highest part of the frame forming the top line of the roof. Rafters connect the ridge board to the ceiling joists.

**sheathing** wooden or composite material used to cover the exterior walls and roof of a house. Sheathing comes in various thicknesses and R-factors. The exterior siding and roof covering are fastened to the sheathing.

**sill** wooden member of the frame that is attached to the foundation. Sills must be flashed or be pressure-treated to aid in termite control.

**sliding window** one of the most common types of window used in residential construction. Sliding windows come in various sizes that slide vertically or horizontally to open.

**soffit** one of the three components of the overhang. The soffit is the area under the overhang extension that is composed of wood, aluminum, or vinyl. Usually, intake vents are installed in the soffit to aid in ventilation of the attic.

**stud** a vertical wooden member (2″ × 4″ or 2″ × 6″) that is used in the framing of a house. Studs are fastened between the sole and top plates and form the walls of a house.

**swinging window** a type of window that swings in or out to open. The most common type of swinging window used in residential construction is the casement window.

**truss** a framework of wooden members (usually 2 × 4s) that are nailed together in triangular patterns to provide support over a long span. The truss is used in subfloor and roof construction.

**Tudor style** a type of architecture that incorporates English designs and features. Tudor-style homes can be one story, two stories, or split-level.

**2 × 4** a piece of lumber theoretically 2 inches thick by 4 inches wide but actually slightly smaller.

**vapor barrier** heavy-duty plastic installed under concrete floor slabs, under homes with crawl spaces, and in exterior walls to prevent the intrusion of moisture into a structure.

**Victorian style** a type of architecture designed and built during the Victorian era. Victorian-style homes are characterized by large turrets, intricate detailing and trim work, and large porches. This type of architecture is once again popular in certain regions of the state and country.

**weather stripping** foam or metal insulating material that is placed around door and window frames to aid in preventing the intrusion of air into a home. Weather stripping comes in various thicknesses and sizes to meet many applications.

**weepholes** small holes in the bottom course of brick that allow any moisture on the inside of the wall an avenue to the exterior. The weepholes also allow ventilation of the interior wall to keep it dry.

## SUMMARY OF IMPORTANT POINTS

1. Wood-frame construction is the most popular method for residential building because it offers flexibility of design, is less expensive, is easy to insulate, and can be built relatively quickly.
2. A variety of styles are found in residential construction, including the single-story ranch, two-story contemporary, and one-and-a-half-story Cape Cod. Colonial, French provincial, Tudor, and Victorian styles are also found.

3. Foundation systems provide the proper support for a structure as well as control drainage and moisture.

4. The foundation footing must be carefully placed in firm, undisturbed soil or on solid rock. The footing must be below the frost line and should have a drainage system to carry groundwater away from the foundation.

5. Foundation walls are commonly made of poured concrete, masonry block, or brick. A smooth mortar exterior surfacing is known as parging.

6. The best protection against wood-destroying insects is chemical treatment of the soil. Termite treatment is applied after the foundation is complete and prior to the vapor barrier installation. In the case of a concrete slab, treatment and vapor barrier are applied prior to pouring the concrete.

7. The crawl space of a home must provide for adequate ventilation and waterproofing. Moisture buildup can cause major damage to wooden structural members. A vapor barrier can be installed in a crawl spaces and under concrete slabs.

8. Framing is the wooden skeleton of a structure. Framing is done with lumber of a nominal 4-inch width and 2-inch thickness based on the function of the component system. Framing is usually on 16-inch centers. This provides a uniform nailing pattern of four rows, since most structural covering materials are in 4-foot widths.

9. The floor system starts with a pressure-treated wood member, the sill plate (2″ × 6″), nailed to the foundation system, which is usually 8 inches wide. Wood joists (2″ × 8″, 2″ × 10″, or 2″ × 12″) support the subfloor material, which is commonly plywood sheets. Bridging is a system of bracing between the floor joists to add strength and prevent lateral movement of the floor support structure.

10. Finish floor systems consist of components such as hardwood, tile, linoleum, and carpet.

11. Wall framing is almost exclusively 2″ × 4″ studs placed 16 inches on center. Other methods include 2″ × 6″ studs 24 inches on center or larger post-and-beam framing of 4- or 6-inch square studs, which are spaced several feet apart.

12. The most common wall framing system is the platform method. This consists of a 2″ × 4″ base plate, an 8-foot 2″ × 4″ stud, and a double top plate. This system sits on top of the floor system, which serves as the platform for the wall. An alternative method is balloon framing, in which wall studs run from the foundation to the roof system of a two-story structure.

13. A truss is a number of wooden members nailed together into one framework. Trusses can be used for floor and roof framing.

14. A truss shifts the weight-bearing function to the outer walls. This provides freedom of placement of inner walls, which are usually non-weight-bearing since they are not required to support the roof.

15. The roof structural skeleton is usually built with 2″ × 8″ ceiling joists and 2″ × 6″ or 2″ × 8″ rafters. Contemporary roof construction can also use 2″ × 4″ trusses in place of conventional framing lumber.

16. The roof skeleton is usually covered with plywood, a felt paper underlayment, and shingles. Shingles are commonly made of asphalt or fiberglass.

17. Common roof types on residential property are gable, and hip. Mansard and gambrel are used much less frequently.

18. Exterior walls are usually covered with a sheathing material such as plywood, particleboard, or various brands of insulating sheathing. The final exterior siding or veneer is placed on top of the sheathing.

19. Insulation should be placed in floors, walls, and ceilings. The larger the R-factor number, the greater the resistance to heat flow and, therefore, the greater the insulating effect. A particularly effective place for insulation is the ceiling. This not only protects against heat loss in the winter but also insulates against heat load in the summer.
20. Windows fall into three general classes: sliding, swinging, and fixed. Windows are usually made of wood, metal, aluminum, or composite materials. Most construction uses double-pane glass windows to improve the energy efficiency of the home and to meet the state building code.
21. The interior finish is usually provided by gypsum board in the walls and the ceiling. Careful placement and finishing of this material is essential to the appearance of the home. Therefore, wallboard placement is usually done by a person who specializes in this job.
22. HVAC is an acronym for heating, ventilation, and air conditioning. Some systems use fuel oil or natural gas for energy, while heat pump systems use electricity.
23. Today's heating and cooling systems use a central blower to distribute the heated or cooled air throughout the house. Each room has an air duct, and return ducts are centrally located to maximize efficiency.
24. The heat pump is a modern system that cools in the summer as well as heats in the winter.
25. Air conditioning is typically a central forced-air system powered by electricity, but it can also be powered by gas or oil. Room air conditioning is often provided by window units.
26. A sill is a wooden member of the frame that is attached to the foundation.
27. Piers are vertical masonry structures placed inside foundation walls to support the subflooring.
28. Passive solar systems merely collect heat by placement of the building for the best exposure to the sun. Active systems are more complex in that they move the heat to other parts of the house.
29. Government regulation of home construction is evidenced in the residential building code, modified by city or county codes; minimum HUD standards for projects under their financing programs; and the licensing requirements of contractors.

## REVIEW QUESTIONS

Answers to the review questions are in the Answer Key at the back of the book.

1. The most common type of residential construction is which of the following?
   A. wood-frame
   B. solid brick
   C. prefabricated
   D. structural steel

2. The structure of a wood-frame home usually consists of:
   I. 8″ foundation walls on a concrete footing.
   II. 2″ × 10″ floor joists 16 inches on center.
   III. 2″ × 4″ wall studs 24 inches on center.
   A. I and II only
   B. II and III only
   C. I and III only
   D. I, II, and III

3. The supporting wall system members are which of the following?
   A. joists
   B. studs
   C. rafters
   D. wallboard

4. Soffit and fascia are found in which structural system?
   A. foundation
   B. wall
   C. floor
   D. roof

5. The best form of termite protection is:
   A. mechanical barriers
   B. chemical treatment
   C. concrete foundations
   D. slab construction

6. A soffit vent is found in the:
   A. crawl space
   B. roof overhang
   C. wall
   D. ceiling

7. A result of modern construction methods using truss systems is:
   A. greater attic space
   B. dependence on inner walls for load bearing
   C. less dependence on outer walls for load bearing
   D. freedom of inner wall placement

8. The structural member used to take up the support function over openings for windows or doors is a:
   A. header
   B. footing
   C. jamb
   D. joist

9. In reference to insulation:
   I. the greater the R-factor value, the lesser the insulation.
   II. insulation should be placed only in walls.
   A. I only
   B. II only
   C. both I and II
   D. neither I nor II

10. Members of the wall system include all of the following EXCEPT:
    A. sole plate
    B. joist
    C. stud
    D. double top plate

11. Piers are used to:
    A. form roof components
    B. support floor systems
    C. provide ventilation
    D. prevent erosion

12. Batter boards are used to:
    A. lay out building lines
    B. strengthen walls
    C. provide insulation
    D. increase ventilation

13. A gambrel roof is characterized by a:
    A. simple tentlike design
    B. nearly flat roof
    C. shedlike roof
    D. four-sided "barn" appearance

14. Exempt from the building contractor licensing requirement are:
    A. REALTORS®
    B. owner-developers
    C. projects of more than $125,000
    D. projects of less than $30,000

15. A wooden member of the frame that is attached to the foundation is a:
    A. stoop
    B. pier
    C. ridge board
    D. sill

16. Vertical masonry structures placed inside the foundation walls to support the subflooring are:
    A. headers
    B. sills
    C. piers
    D. joists

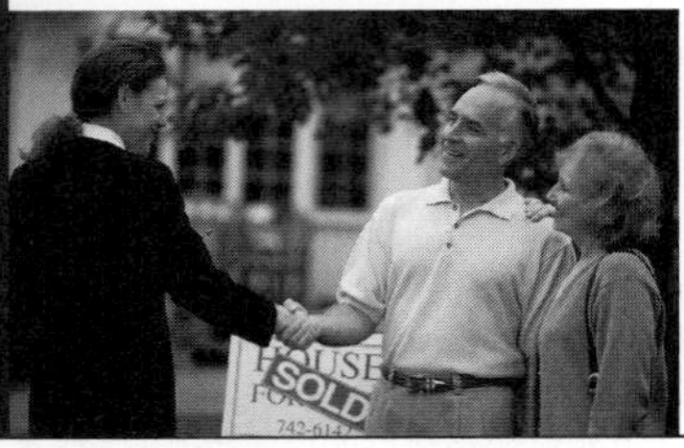

# Chapter 16

## LEARNING OBJECTIVES

At the conclusion of this chapter, you should be able to calculate:

1. Principal and simple interest.
2. Debt service and the reduction in the balance of a loan.
3. Loan origination and discount points.
4. Loan values and yields to the lender.
5. P&I factors.
6. Qualification of a buyer.
7. Applications of the market data (direct sales comparison) approach.
8. Real estate taxes and special assessments.
9. Hazard insurance premiums on an assumed policy.
10. Interest on an assumed mortgage.
11. Prorations at closing.
12. Multiple miscellaneous calculations in a closing statement to arrive at the bottom line for:
    a. balance of cash due from the buyer.
    b. balance of cash owed to the seller.
13. Brokerage commissions.
14. Sale price needed to provide specified net to seller.
15. Profit or loss on the sale of real estate.
16. Equity in a home and percent change in equity.
17. Area of irregularly shaped lots.
18. Federal income taxation of home ownership.
19. Excise tax.

# Real Estate Math

## IN THIS CHAPTER

When solving real estate math problems, it may be helpful to remember and use these hints:

1. *Memorize* the formulas.
2. Write them down before solving the problem.
3. Write out *all* important information as you are solving the problem.
4. Draw a diagram, if applicable.
5. Remember that the size of an acre is 43,560 square feet.
6. Check your answers for logic.

## SECTION 1 BASIC REAL ESTATE MATH

### FINANCE CALCULATIONS

#### Principal and Simple Interest

Chapter 7, Real Estate Finance, covers the important calculations of principal and interest and the related financial arithmetic. For review, the following is reproduced from Figure 7.2 in Chapter 7 to summarize the calculations discussed.

**Example:** Assume a home purchase price of $87,500 with a conventional mortgage of 80% of the sale price at a rate of 8.5% for 30 years.

1. Amount of the loan = $87,500 × 80% = $70,000.
2. Figure 7.1 is given in a factor per $1,000; therefore, divide $70,000 by 1,000 = 70 (the number of units of $1,000).
3. Go to the 8.5% row, read across to the 30-year column, and read the figure of $7.69. This is the payment per month per $1,000 of the loan.
4. Multiply 70 × $7.69 = $538.30. This is the monthly payment of principal and interest to amortize (kill, pay off) a loan of $70,000 at 8.5% for 30 years.

## Debt Service and the Reduction in the Balance of a Loan

Calculate how much of a payment goes to interest and what the balance will be on a loan after one payment is made.

**Solution:** Interest (I) is equal to principal (P) times interest rate (R) times the time period (T = 1 for annual interest; 1/12 for monthly interest)

or $I = P \times R \times T$

or loan balance × annual interest × 1/12 = monthly interest

$$\frac{\text{or loan balance} \times \text{annual interest}}{12} = \text{monthly interest}$$

If a loan balance was $70,000 at 8.5% interest for 30 years, using the chart in Figure 7.1, you retrieve the 8.5%, 30-year factor of $7.69.

Multiplying: 70 × $7.69 = $538.30 P&I

The interest portion is:

$$\frac{\$70,000 \times 8.5\%}{12} = \$495.83$$

Subtracting: $538.30 P&I

−495.83 I

$ 42.47 P

That is, of the total payment of $538.30, only $42.47 goes to reducing the principal in the first month.

Therefore: $70,000.00 Original principal

−42.47 Principal reduction

$69,957.53 New balance

To figure the new balance at the end of the second month, apply the same formulas as used above. This time use $69,957.53 as the loan balance.

The interest portion is:

$$\frac{\$69,957.73 \times 8.5\%}{12} = \$495.53$$

Subtracting: $538.30 P&I

−495.53 I (for second month)

$42.77 P

That is, of the total payment of $538.30, $42.77 is applied to the principal in the second month. Note that this is slightly more than the amount applied to the principal in the first month.

Therefore, subtracting

$69,957.53 Principal at end of first month

−42.77 Principal reduction in second month

$69,914.76 New balance at end of second month

Additionally, consider the following financial calculations.

**Example:** Calculate the interest paid over the life of a loan.

**Solution:** Take the monthly payment (P&I) times the number of months in the loan (years times 12). This will equal the total amount of payments (total P&I). Subtract the principal of the loan (P); the remainder is the amount that went to interest (I).

**Example:** A $70,000 loan at 8.5% for 30 years

From the amortization chart, find the factor $7.69 (per $1,000).

P&I = 70 × $7.69 = $538.30

Number of payments is 30 years × 12 = 360.

Total of payments is $538.30 × 360 = $193,788.

Subtract the principal (P) of $70,000.

Total interest paid over life of loan is $123,788.

## Loan Origination and Discount Points

Calculate the service charges to originate a loan.

**Solution:** Assume there will be two parts to the charges:

1. Origination fee 1%
2. Discount points, *each of which will also cost 1% of the loan*

**Example:** The costs to originate a $70,000 loan with 2.5 discount points would be:

1. Origination fee: 1% × $70,000 = $ 700
2. Discount points: 2.5% × $70,000 = $1,750

Total Costs $2,450

## Discount Points, Yields

Calculate (1) the cost of discount points and (2) the effect (yield) of points.

**Solution:** 1. Each point costs (somebody) 1% of the amount borrowed. Therefore, multiply the number of points times 1% times the loan amount.

**Example:** Sale price of $87,500 with an 80% loan and 2 1/2 discount points equals
Loan Amount = $87,500 × 80% = $70,000
Discount Points = $70,000 × 2.5 × .01 = $1,750

**Solution:** The effect or yield of discount points is calculated by the rule of thumb that each point raises the effective yield to the lender by 1/8 percent.

**Example:** An 8% loan with 3 points is a yield of 8% + 3/8% = 8 3/8%. Also, the cost to raise the yield of a $50,000 loan from 8% to 8 1/2% would be:
8% to 8 1/2% is 1/2%, or 4/8%, or 4 points (4%)
Thus, $50,000 times 4% = $2,000.

## Qualifying a Buyer

In Chapter 7, the following calculations were presented.

### *Example 1: Conventional Loan*

Before approving a conventional mortgage loan, the lender must determine if the borrower will be able to meet the financial obligation. Most often the lender requires that the monthly house payments not exceed 28% of the borrower's gross monthly income and that the total of all long-term obligations not exceed 36% of this income; this is referred to as the 28/36 rule. For example, assume a sale price of $125,000, a loan amount of $100,000,* and an annual interest rate of 8.5% with a 30-year loan term. (Use the amortization chart on page 205, Figure 7.1 if you do not have a financial calculator.) Tax and insurance escrow numbers are given. In this case, the formula is applied as follows:

1. The lender calculates the total monthly payments:

   $768.91 (PI)**
   116.80 for tax escrow (T)
   54.00 for insurance escrow (I)
   $939.71 PITI (total monthly payment)

2. Next, the borrower's gross monthly income is calculated by dividing the annual household salary by 12:

   $55.000 ÷ 12 = $4,583.33

3. The ratio of house payments to gross monthly income is determined by dividing the payment by monthly income:

   $939.71÷ $4,583.33 = 0.2050 or 20.5%

The first part of the 28/36 rule has been satisfied since this ratio is less than 28%.

4. All other long-term expense payments are added to determine the borrower's other long-term debt:

   $340.00 car payments
   75.00 credit card payments
   100.00 personal loan
   $515.00 total monthly payment for long-term debt

5. This total is added to the house payment:

   $ 939.71
   515.00
   $1,454.71

6. This total is divided by the monthly income to determine the ratio of housing payments and long-term debts:

   $1,454.71 ÷ $4,583.33 = 0.3174 or 31.7%

   The borrower qualifies for the loan since this ratio is less than 36%.

* This is an 80% loan-to-value ratio; therefore, it requires no private mortgage insurance (PMI). A higher loan-to-value ratio requires PMI to be included in payments.

** Amount determined by financial calculator. Using amortization chart, amount would be $769.

### *Example 2: Determining Buyer's Maximum Loan Amount and Purchase Price Paid for a Conventional Loan*

Maximum loan amount and maximum purchase price calculations for a 7% 30-year conventional loan with 20% down payment and no PMI. The Purchaser's gross monthly income is $6,450.

1. Borrower's gross monthly income times the ratio for housing payments equals the maximum house payment under 28% ratio:

   $6,450 × 28% = $1,806

2. Borrower's gross monthly income times the ratio for housing payments and long-term debts equals the maximum amount for house payments and long-term debt:

   $6,450 × 36% = $2,322

| | | |
|---|---|---|
| 3. | Long-term expenses other than house payment: | |
| | a. Auto payment | $400.00 |
| | b. Student loan payment | 200.00 |
| | c. Credit card payment | 100.00 |
| | d. Total long-term debt | $700.00 |
| 4. | a. Maximum amount for house payment (PITI) and long-term debt | $2,322 |
| | b. Long-term debt | − 700 |
| | c. Maximum house payment (PITI) under 36% ratio | $1,622 |
| 5. | a. Maximum house payment (PITI)—Lesser of the two payments derived in steps 1 and 4 | $1,622 |
| | b. Estimated taxes and insurance (T&I) | − 300 |
| | c. Maximum principal and interest payment (P&I) | $1,322 |

   d. Maximum P&I payment $\frac{\$1,322}{6.65} \times 1,000 = \$198,800$

   P&I factor × 1,000 at 7% interest
   (from amortization chart, Figure 7.1)

$198,800 amount of loan at 7% with a $1,322 per month payment

$$\frac{\text{loan amount}}{80\%} = \frac{\$198,800}{80\%} = \text{Purchase price } \$248,500$$

$248,500—Maximum purchase price with 20% down payment.

### *Example 3: Qualifying for an FHA Loan*

1. Purchaser's monthly income $3,000. Purchaser wants to borrow $75,250. FHA ratios are 29% and 41%.
2. Loan payments (housing expenses)
   a. Loan amount ÷ 1000 = # units of 1000
   Factor per unit of 1000 @ 9.5% interest for 30 years = $8.41
   $75,250 ÷ 1000 = 75.25 units of 1000
   # of units of 1000 × factor = P&I

| | |
|---|---|
| 75.25 × $8.41 = | $632.85 |
| b. Tax and insurance escrow | $ 70.00 |
| c. Mortgage insurance premium (MIP) | $ 31.35 |
| d. Monthly PITI plus MIP | $734.20 |

3. Relation of housing expense to gross income

$$\frac{\$734.20}{3,000\%} = 24.47\%$$

This is less than 29% and qualifies for the housing expense part of the formula.

4. Other long-term expenses

| | |
|---|---|
| a. Auto payment | $240.00 |
| b. Credit card payments | $110.00 |
| c. Total | $350.00 |

5. Total long-term housing payments and long-term debt

| | |
|---|---|
| a. Housing expense | $ 734.20 |
| b. Other payments | $ 350.00 |
| c. Total | $ 1,084.20 |

6. Relation of total long-term housing payments and long-term debt to gross income

$$\frac{\$1,084.20}{\$3,000} = 36.14\%$$

This part of the formula also qualifies since it is less than 41%.

### *Example 4: Qualification for Maximum FHA Mortgage Loan Payment*

1. Calculate borrower's gross monthly income by dividing annual household salary by 12.

$$\$48,000 \div 12 = \$4,000$$

2. Multiply gross monthly income by 29%.

$\$4,000 \times 29\% = \$1,160$. Amount available for PITI under the 29% ratio.

3. Multiply gross monthly income by 41%.
   $4,000 × 41% = $1,640 (amount available for monthly housing expense; which includes house payment (PITI) and long-term debt payments under 41% ratio)
4. Add all other long-term debt of borrower.

| | |
|---|---|
| $300.00 | car payment |
| $175.00 | credit card payment |
| $100.00 | personal loan |
| $575.00 | total monthly payment for long-term debt |

5. Subtract total other monthly long-term debt payments (item 4) from 41% of gross monthly income from item 3.

| | |
|---|---|
| $1,640.00 | total housing expense and debt |
| $ 575.00 | total monthly payment on debt |
| $1,065.00 | total amount available for housing expense (PITI) under 41% ratio |

The buyer qualifies for the lesser of the monthly housing payments (PITI) determined by the 29% and 41% ratios or $1,065. Note: You must reduce this number by the amount of taxes and insurance (T&I) to calculate principal and interest (P&I) before determining the loan amount using P&I. See example 2, #5 in Chapter 16, page 418. VA & FHA loans use same process as conventional loans for converting PITI to P&I and subsequently to a maximum loan amount.

### *Example 5: VA Qualification Worksheet*

QUALIFICATION FOR SPECIFIC MORTGAGE LOAN PAYMENT

RATIO:

| | |
|---|---|
| A. Monthly income | $3,000.00 |
| B. PITI* | 950.00 |
| C. Recurring monthly payments | 350.00 |
| D. Total (B + C) | $1,300.00 |

Total ÷ monthly Income or $\$1,300 \div \$3,000 =$ 0.43 or 43% ratio

VA RESIDUAL INCOME:

| | |
|---|---|
| Gross monthly income | $ 3,000.00 |
| – taxes (federal, state, and Social Security) (see tax tables—not included) | 700.00 |
| – pension or retirement plan deductions | 150.00 |
| – long-term debts (monthly payments) | 350.00 |
| – maintenance and utilities (1321 sq. ft. of living area) | 185.00 |
| $1321 \times 0.14 = 184.94$, rounded to $185 | |
| – PITI for specific loan | 950.00 |
| Residual for family support | $ 665.00 |
| Required residual for family support | $ 738.00 |

Difference between actual and required residual = −$73.00

Borrower will not qualify for this loan because residual family support is $73 below minimum required and ratio exceeds 41%. Borrower's residual must equal or exceed required residual. Borrower sometimes qualifies with a ratio up to 49.5% if his actual residual exceeds required residual by 20% or more.

DETERMINATION OF MAXIMUM AMOUNT OF MORTGAGE PAYMENT VA IS LIKELY TO APPROVE FOR BORROWER

RATIO:

| | |
|---|---|
| Monthly income (A) × 41% (0.41) | $3,000.00 (A) |
| | × 0.41 |
| | $1,230.00 (B) |
| Recurring monthly payment | $ 350.00 (C) |

(B) (C)
$\$1,230 - 350 = \$880$ (amount remaining for PITI*)

| VA RESIDUAL INCOME: | |
|---|---|
| Gross monthly income | $ 3,000.00 |
| – taxes (federal, state, and Social Security) (from tax tables—not included) | – 700.00 |
| – pension or retirement plan deductions | – 150.00 |
| – long-term debts (monthly payments) | – 350.00 |
| – maintenance and utilities (1321 sq. ft. of living area) 1321 × 0.14 = 184.94, rounded to $185 | – 185.00 |
| – residual for family support | – 738.00 |
| Amount remaining for PITI* | $ 877.00 |

The borrower will qualify for a mortgage loan payment not to exceed $877, the lesser of these PITI amounts.
Amount derived from debt-to-income ratio of 41% = $880
Amount derived from residual method = $877

# CLOSING STATEMENT PRORATIONS AND CALCULATIONS

## Proration of Real Estate Taxes

Prorating is the process of dividing something into appropriate shares. In the real estate brokerage, it involves dividing between the seller and the buyer the annual real property taxes, interest on an assumed loan, and rents as well as establishing the cost to the buyer of an insurance policy that is being purchased from the seller.

When prorating calculations, the best method is to determine the used portion. In the calculation of prorations for closing statements, the amount is figured to the day of closing. An example is prorating the real property tax for a closing to take place on May 30 where the annual real property tax is $240. The monthly tax rate is $20. Five months transpired in the tax year from January 1 through the end of May. Therefore, five months × $20 per month = $100 for the seller's share of the real property taxes. This amount appears in the closing statement as a debit to the seller and a credit to the buyer.

In prorating, every *month* is assumed to have *30 days.* Therefore, in problems that require the calculation of a daily rate, the monthly rate is divided by 30, even though the month may be February, to obtain the daily rate.

An even better way to approach proration is, as described in Chapter 8, to reduce all costs to a *daily basis.* Assuming 30 days in every month and 12 months per year, you can also assume there are *360 days per year* (for purposes of examples and the exam).

1. *Never prorate personal property taxes.*
2. For real property, identify the period to be prorated:
   a. The calendar year; e.g., real property taxes
   b. The calendar month; e.g., mortgage interest
   c. The anniversary year; e.g., fire insurance
3. Reduce the pro rata period to an interval rate; e.g., divide the annual rate by the number of days in the year to get a daily rate.

   *Example:* Taxes of $630 per year are

$$\frac{\$630}{360} = \$1.75 \text{ per day}$$

*Sometimes other housing expenses, such as homeowners' association dues or assessments paid on a monthly basis, must be added to the PITI before performing these calculations.

4. Determine the number of days of the pro rata period that have been used.
   *Example:* Closing date July 23
   a. Full months used are Jan.–June
   $$6 \times 30 = 180$$
   b. Days used in the month of settlement $= \underline{+23}$
   Total days used of the period 203
5. Multiply the daily rate by the number of days used; i.e.,
   $\$1.75 \times 203 = \$355.25$ Amount used
6. Determine whether the cost has been paid by seller in advance or will be paid by buyer in arrears.
   a. If in arrears, debit (charge) seller and credit buyer $355.25.
   b. If the whole cost was paid in advance, calculate the overpayment to be refunded; i.e.,

   Paid $630.00
   (−) Used <u>$355.25</u>
   Credit $274.75

   c. Debit buyer and credit seller $274.75.

One other rule to remember in prorating various costs for the closing statements is that the day of closing is charged to the seller.

### Examples

1. While preparing a closing statement for a closing to be held on August 14, a real estate broker determined that the annual real property taxes in the amount of $360 had not been paid. What will the broker put in the buyer's statement as the entry for real property taxes?

   **Solution:** $\dfrac{\$360}{12} = \$30$ per month

   $$\frac{\$30 \text{ per month}}{30 \text{ days}} = \$1 \text{ per day}$$

   $$7 \text{ months} \times \$30 = \$210$$
   $$14 \text{ days} \times \$1 = \$\ 14$$
   $$\$210 + \$14 = \$224$$

   **Answer:** Credit to buyer in the amount of $224. This is the seller's share of the real property taxes to cover the 7 months and 14 days of the tax year during which he owned the property. Note: Seller will be debited $224.

2. A sale is closed on September 15. The buyer is assuming the seller's mortgage, which has an outstanding balance of $32,000 as of the date of closing. The annual interest rate is 8%, and the interest is paid monthly, in arrears. What would be the interest proration on the closing statements prepared by the broker?

   **Solution:** $\$32,000 \times 8\% = \$2,560$ annual interest

   $$\frac{\$2,560}{12} = \$213.33 \text{ interest for September}$$

   $$\frac{\$213.33}{2} = \$106.66 \text{ interest for 1/2 month}$$

   $$\text{or } \frac{\$213.33}{30} = \$7.11 \text{ per day}$$

   $$\$7.11 \times 15 = \$106.66 \text{ interest for 15 days}$$

   **Answer:** Credit the buyer $106.66
   Debit the seller $106.66

   Since the interest is paid in arrears, the buyer is required to pay the interest for the full month of September when making the scheduled monthly payment on October 1. Therefore, the buyer is to be credited with the seller's share of one-half month's interest for September in the amount of \$106.66. The entry in the seller's closing statement would be a debit in this amount.

3. A house valued at \$80,000 was insured for 80% of value. The cost of the insurance was \$0.80 per \$100 of face amount. The homeowner paid the annual premium on February 1 for the year beginning February 1. On August 15, the homeowner closed on the sale. The buyers are having the seller's insurance policy endorsed to them. What will be the cost of this policy to the buyers in the year of the sale?

**Solution:** \$80,000 × 80% = \$64,000 face amount

$$\frac{\$64{,}000}{\$100} = 640 \text{ units of } \$100 \text{ of face amount}$$

\$0.80 (cost per \$100 of face amount) × 640 = \$512 annual premium

$$\frac{\$512}{12} = \$42.67 \text{ per month}$$

6.5 months \$42.67/month = \$277.36 used portion

\$512.00 − \$277.36 = \$234.64 unused portion

**Answer:** \$234.64. This will show on the closing statement as a credit to the seller and a debit to the buyer.

## Interest on an Assumed Mortgage

A loan is assumed. How will the interest appear on the closing statement? Calculate the interest through the day of closing.

**Solution:** Usually, this interest is paid in arrears; that is, it is currently unpaid. Therefore, the seller will be charged (debited) and the buyer will be credited the seller's portion of the month's interest that is unpaid.

For example, closing March 5, with the assumption of a \$42,137 loan at 12% annual interest,

Days = 5

Daily interest is $\frac{\$42{,}137 \times 12\%}{360} = \$14.05$

Multiply the days by the daily rate to calculate the dollar amount:

5 days × \$14.05 per day = \$70.25

For interest in arrears, this amount will be debited to the seller and credited to the buyer. If the seller paid a month's interest in advance, however, he would have already paid

30 days × \$14.05 = \$421.50

and is due a refund (credit) of the unused portion

\$421.50 − \$70.25 = \$321.25

which will be a credit to the seller and a debit to the buyer.

## Closing Statement Calculations

The information on the preparation of closing statements is discussed in detail in Chapter 8. Refer to the demonstration problems for the four types of closing statement. In the event you have not completed the practice problems by this time, do so now. The only way to learn how to prepare closing statements is to practice doing some on your own. Once you finish, you should check the calculations you entered to review the process and logic of the entries involved.

# APPRAISAL CALCULATIONS

The consideration of appraisal arithmetic is discussed in Chapter 9. Assuming a residential property is currently assigned a tax life of 27.5 years, this would provide a straight-line depreciation of 3.64 percent per year, or 29 percent for eight years.

| | |
|---|---|
| Original Cost | $100,000 |
| 8 years' depreciation | −$29,000 |
| Present book value | $ 71,000 |

One of the required calculations on the state exam is that of simple adjustments of comparable properties to derive an indication of the value of the subject property.

There are two basic steps to this process.

1. Determine the contribution of one element of the property in question. The strategy of this procedure, known as the paired sales analysis, is to locate two properties that are "identical" except for one feature. The difference between the prices paid for these two properties is then attributed to the feature in question. By comparing the two sales prices, one can reflect the value of the feature to buyers.

| | |
|---|---|
| a. Home 1: 1,500 sq. ft., 3 bedrooms, 2 baths, garage | $87,500 |
| b. Home 2: same features, no garage | −$82,000 |
| Garage value (to the buyer) | $ 5,500 |

2. These two properties have sold. You derive this information from several paired sales in the same way. The information is then used to do a CMA on another property which has not sold by adjusting the comparable to the subject. The rule here is that if the comparable is *better than* the subject, *subtract* the value of the element from the comparable. If the comparable is *inferior* to the subject, *add* the value of the element to the comparable sale price to bring it up to the estimated worth of the subject property.

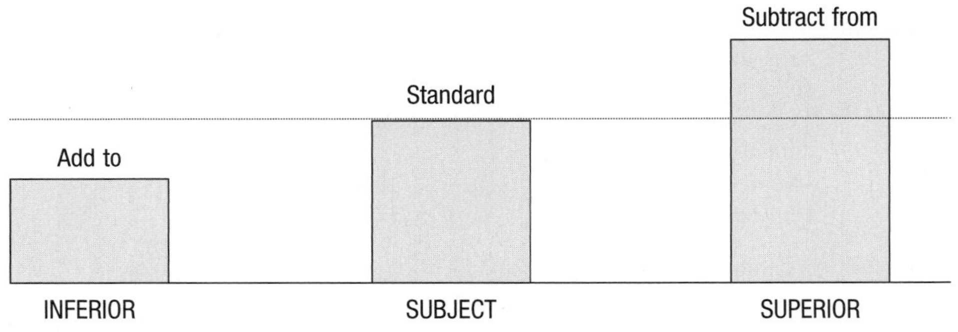


In this strategy, you are taking a known value (the price actually paid by a buyer or buyers) for a comparable property and adjusting this known to the unknown (subject property being appraised). Carefully examine Figure 16.1 to observe the following:

a. The adjustment for bedrooms
b. The adjustment for half baths
c. The adjustment for paving
d. The total net adjustment; that is, the sum of the plus and minus adjustments for each item
e. The final indication of value derived by adjusting the sales price of the comparables up or down by adding or subtracting net adjustments as required

## Capitalization Problems

As illustrated in Chapter 9, Property Valuation, the income approach derives an estimate of the value of the property by capitalizing the net income. Capitalization problems use rate, income, and value according to the formula, $I = R \times V$. This is the same formula used to calculate commission. Net operating income (NOI) is used to determine the capitalization rate.

**FIGURE 16.1** Direct sales (market data) comparison.

| Date: 12-9-CY | Subject Property | Comparable 1 | | Comparable 2 | | Comparable 3 | |
|---|---|---|---|---|---|---|---|
| Address | 524 Amortization Dr. | 602 Amortization Dr. | | 301 Acceleration Circle | | 12 Redemption Lane | |
| Sales Price | | | $192,000 | | $185,500 | | $182,500 |
| | | | Adjustment | | Adjustment | | Adjustment |
| Sale Date | | 11-10-CY | +$400 | 10-20-CY | + $800 | 6-11-CY | +$2,300 |
| Location | Good | Good | 0 | Good | 0 | Fair | + 1,000 |
| Lot Size | 150 × 175 (26,250 sq. ft.) | 140 × 170 (23,800) | + 500 | 150 × 170 (25,500) | 0 | 125 × 150 (18,750) | + 1,500 |
| Age | 5 | 6 | 0 | 7 | 0 | 8 | 0 |
| Condition | Good | Good | 0 | Fair | + 1,000 | Fair | + 1,000 |
| Square Footage | 1,800 | 1,900 | -$4,000 | 1,800 | 0 | 1,650 | +$6,000 |
| Bathrooms | 2½ | 3 | - 1,000 | 2½ | 0 | 2 | +1,000 |
| Style | Ranch | Ranch | 0 | Ranch | 0 | Ranch | 0 |
| Construction | Frame | Brick & Frame | 0 | Frame | 0 | Frame | 0 |
| Air Conditioning | Central | Central | 0 | Central | 0 | None | +$2,000 |
| Garage | Garage-2 Car | Garage-2 Car | 0 | Garage-2 Car | 0 | Carport-1 Car | + 3,500 |
| Driveway | Paved | Paved | 0 | Gravel | + 1,000 | Gravel | + 1,000 |
| TOTAL ADJUSTMENT | | | - 4,100 | | + 2,800 | | +19,300 |
| ADJUSTED PRICE | | | $187,900 | | $188,300 | | $201,800 |

Reconciliation Process

Comparable 1 $187,900 × 35% = $65,765

Comparable 2 $188,300 × 40% = $75,320

Comparable 3 $201,800 × 25% = $50,450

Weighted Average = $191,535 rounded to $191,600 indicated value of subject property

(All three properties are not given the same importance. The appraiser has assigned the most weight to Comparable 2 since he believes it is most similar to the subject; Comparable 3, with the largest adjustment, is deemed to be least similar and is assigned the least weight.)

1. An apartment building produces a net income of $4,320 per annum. The investor paid $36,000 for the apartment building. What is the owner's rate of return on investment?

   **Solution:** Income = $4,320, value = $36,000, rate is unknown

   $$I \div V = R$$

   $$\frac{\$4,320}{\$36,000} = 0.12 \text{ or } 12\%$$

   **Answer:** 12% annual rate of return on investment

2. An investor is considering the purchase of an office building for $75,000. The investor insists upon a 14% return on investment. What must be the amount of the annual net income from this investment to return a profit to the owner at a rate of 14%?

   **Solution:** Value = $75,000, rate = 14%, income is unknown

   $I = R \times V \quad 75{,}000 \times 14\% = \$10{,}500$

   **Answer:** $10,500 annual net income

3. In the appraisal of a shopping center, the appraiser established that the center produces a net income of $97,500. The appraiser developed the capitalization rate to be 13%. What should be the appraiser's estimate of market value for this shopping center?

   **Solution:** Income = $97,500, rate = 13%, value is unknown

   $$I \div R = V$$

   $$\frac{\$97,500}{13\%} = \$750,000$$

   **Answer:** $750,000 market value estimate

***Example 1:***

Replacement or reproduction cost:

| | | |
|---|---|---|
| 21,000 sq. ft. @ $52.50 sq. ft. | | $1,102,500 |
| Less structure depreciation: | | |
| Physical deterioration | $33,075 | |
| Functional obsolescence | 44,100 | |
| Economic obsolescence | -0- | 77,175 |
| Depreciated value of structure | | 1,025,325 |
| Depreciated value of other improvements: | | |
| Retaining walls | 10,000 | |
| Paved drive and parking | 15,000 | |
| Exterior lighting | 2,000 | |
| Fencing | 1,500 | 28,500 |
| Depreciated value of all improvements | | 1,053,825 |
| Land value by direct sales comparison | | 253,000 |
| Total property value | | $1,306,825 |

***Example 2:***

250-unit apartment complex with rent schedule of $450 per month per unit

| | |
|---|---|
| Potential gross income: 250 × $450 × 12 | $1,350,000 |
| Less vacancy and credit losses (6%) | – 81,000 |
| Plus other income | + 25,000 |
| Gross effective income | $1,294,000 |
| Less expenses | |

| | | |
|---|---|---|
| Fixed expenses: | | |
| Property insurance | $ 24,500 | |
| Property taxes | 95,300 | |
| Licenses and permits | 1,200 | $ 121,000 |
| Operating expenses: | | |
| Maintenance | $106,000 | |
| Utilities | 103,200 | |
| Supplies | 16,000 | |
| Advertising | 7,500 | |
| Legal & accounting | 15,000 | |
| Wages & salaries | 90,000 | |
| Property management | 64,700 | $ 402,400 |
| Replacement reserve: | $ 25,000 | $ 25,000 |
| Total expenses | | $ (548,400) |
| Net operating income | | $ 745,600 |

# MISCELLANEOUS CALCULATIONS

## Brokerage Commissions

Problems involving commissions are readily solved by a simple formula illustrated as follows:

$$\frac{I}{R \times V} \qquad \frac{\text{Income}}{\text{Rate} \times \text{Value}}$$

In this formula, I represents income, R represents rate, and V represents value. In these problems, one of the three elements is the unknown quantity that will be the answer to the problem. The other two elements are provided. When using the formula, simply cover the letter representing the unknown quantity and perform the calculation indicated. For example, if the unknown quantity or answer sought is income, covering the I in the formula reveals that rate is to be multiplied by value (R × V). The result of this multiplication will be the income. If the known quantities are income and rate and the unknown quantity is value, covering the V results in an indicated calculation of dividing rate into income. The result of this division will be the value.

To clarify the formula and its application in solving for any one of three possible unknowns, the following material is presented to demonstrate its use. The formula can also be written to solve for different unknowns, as follows:

$$\text{Rate} = \frac{\text{Income}}{\text{Value}}$$

$$\text{Value} = \frac{\text{Income}}{\text{Rate}}$$

Or, as discussed, the formula can be written and applied as follows: The horizontal line separating income from R × V indicates that in solving for rate, value is to be divided into income. When value is the unknown, rate is to be divided into income. The multiplication sign between R and V shows that rate is to be multiplied by value to solve for income when income is the unknown quantity. Simply cover the unknown item, and perform the indicated calculations.

### *Commission Problems*

1. A real estate broker sold a property for $80,000. Her rate of commission was 6%. What was the amount of commission in dollars?

   **Solution:** Commission value = $80,000, rate = 0.06, income is unknown
   $80,000 × 0.06 = $4,800

   **Answer:** $4,800 commission

2. A real estate broker earned a commission of \$3,000 in the sale of a residential property. His rate of commission was 6%. What was the selling price of the property?

   **Solution:** Income = \$3,000, rate = 0.06, value is unknown

$$\frac{\$3{,}000}{0.06} = \$50{,}000$$

   **Answer:** \$50,000 sales price

3. A real estate broker earned a commission of \$1,500 in the sale of a property for \$25,000. What was her rate of commission?

   **Solution:** Value = \$25,000, income = \$1,500, rate is unknown

$$\frac{\$1{,}500}{\$25{,}000} = 0.06$$

   **Answer:** 6% commission rate

4. A real estate agent sells a property for \$70,000. The commission on this sale to the real estate firm with whom the agent is associated is 6%. The selling agent receives 60% of the commission paid to the real estate firm. What is the firm's share of the commission in dollars?

   **Solution:** Value = \$70,000, rate = 0.06, income is unknown
   \$70,000 × 0.06 = \$4,200
   100% − 60% = 40% (firm's percentage of commission)
   \$4,200 × 0.40 = \$1,680
   **Answer:** \$1,680 firm's share of the commission

5. A broker's commission was 10% of the first \$50,000 of the sales price of a property and 8% on the amount of sales price over \$50,000. The broker received a total commission of \$7,000. What was the total selling price of the property?

   **Solution:**

   Step 1: Rate = 0.10, value = \$50,000, income is unknown \$50,000 × 0.10 = \$5,000 commission on first \$50,000 of sales price
   Step 2: Total commission minus commission on first \$50,000 = commission on amount over \$50,000
   \$7,000 − \$5,000 = \$2,000 commission on selling price over \$50,000
   Step 3: \$2,000 = income, 0.08 = rate, value is unknown

$$\frac{\text{Income}}{\text{Rate}} = \text{Value}$$

$$\frac{\$2,000}{0.08} = \$25,000$$

   Step 4: \$50,000 + \$25,000 = \$75,000
   **Answer:** \$75,000 total selling price

6. A seller advises a broker that he expects to net \$50,000 from the sale of his property after the broker's commission of 6% is deducted from the proceeds of the sale. For what price must the property be sold to provide a \$50,000 net return to the seller after paying the broker a 6% commission on the total sales price?
   **Solution:** 100% = gross sales price
   100% − 6% = 94%
   94% = net to owner
   \$50,000 = 94% × sales price
   Solving for the sales price
   $\frac{\$50{,}000}{94\%}$ = minimum sales price = \$53,191.48
   **Answer:** \$53,191.48 gross selling price

## Interest Problems

Interest problems also use the income, rate, value formula. The amount of interest is the income, the percent return on the money owed or invested is the rate, and the amount of money invested or borrowed is the value.

1. On October 1, a mortgagor made a $300 payment on her mortgage, which is at the rate of 10%. Of the $300 total payment for principal and interest, the mortgagee allocated $200 to the payment of interest. What is the principal balance due on the mortgage on the date of payment?

   **Solution:** $200 × 12 months = $2,400 annual interest income

   $$\frac{\text{Income}}{\text{Rate}} = \text{Value}$$

   $$\frac{\$\ 2{,}400}{10\%} = \$24,000$$

   **Answer:** $24,000 mortgage balance due

2. If an outstanding mortgage balance is $16,363.64 on the payment due date and the amount of the payment applied to interest is $150, what is the annual rate of interest charged on the loan?

   **Solution:** $150 × 12 months = $1,800 annual interest

   $$\frac{\text{Income}}{\text{Value}} = \text{Rate}$$

   $$\frac{\$1{,}800.00}{\$16{,}363.64} = 0.11 \text{ or } 11\%$$

   **Answer:** 11% interest rate

3. If $27,000 is invested at 8.25%, what will be the annual income resulting from the investment?

   **Solution:** Rate is 8.25%, value is $27,000, and income is unknown
   Value × Rate = Income
   $27,000 × 8.25% = $2,227.50

   **Answer:** $2,227.50 annual income

4. A mortgage loan of $50,000 at 11% interest requires monthly payments of principal and interest in the amount of $516.10 to fully amortize the loan for a term of 20 years. If the loan is paid over the 20-year term, how much interest does the borrower pay?

   **Solution:** 20 years × 12 months per year = 240 payments
   240 × $516.10 = $123,864 total amount paid (P & I)
   Total amount paid − principal borrowed = interest paid
   $123,864 − $50,000 = $73,864

   **Answer:** $73,864 interest paid

## Net Sales Price

A seller wants to net a certain amount after paying expenses on the sale of his property.

**Solution:**

Step 1: When the expenses are a fixed amount, such as painting or repairs, the first step is to add these to the desired after-expense amount.

Step 2: When paying a percent commission, such as 6% of the sales price, perform the following step:

100% − 6% = 94%

That is, the net price desired is 94% of the sales price needed. Therefore, if the seller wants to net $50,000 after paying $800 for repairs and a 7% commission:

$50,000 + $800 = $50,800 the net amount needed

100% − 7% = 93%
Therefore, $50,800 = 93% of the sale price needed.
Solving for the sales price:

$$\frac{\$50,800}{93\%} = \$54,624 \text{ minimum sale price}$$

## Equity Problems/Percent Change Problems

Calculate the percent change in an item, such as the percent increase in equity on a home.

**Solution:** Determine the dollar change or quantity change in the item in question. Then divide the *amount of change* by the *original value* of the item. Multiply your answer by 100 to convert it to a percentage.

1. A home was purchased for $38,000 with a $30,000 loan. Ten years later the home had a fair market value of $62,000 and the loan balance was amortized to $25,000. Calculate the percent change in equity.

   **Solution:** The dollar change in equity is calculated by subtracting all liens from the current fair market value.

   The original purchase price minus the original loan balance gives the original equity ($38,000 − $30,000 = $8,000).

   The current fair market value minus the current lien balance gives the current equity ($62,000 − $25,000 = $37,000).

   The current equity minus the original equity produces the *dollar change* in equity ($37,000 − $8,000 = $29,000).

   To calculate the *percent change in equity,* divide the *dollar change in equity* by the *original equity* and multiply by 100 (29,000 ÷ $8,000 × 100 = 362.50%).

2. A buyer purchased a home for $50,000 with an 80% loan. A few years later the home was worth $60,000 and the loan was paid down to $35,000. What was the percent change in equity?

   **Solution:** Step 1: Calculate the original equity.
   $50,000 value × 80% loan = $40,000
   $50,000 value − $40,000 loan = $10,000 equity

   Step 2: Calculate the new equity.
   $60,000 − $35,000 = $25,000 equity

   Step 3: Calculate the change in equity.
   $25,000 − $10,000 = $15,000 change in equity

   Step 4: Divide the amount of change by the original value.
   $$\frac{\$15,000}{\$10,000} = 1.50$$

   Step 5: Multiply 1.5 by 100% to change 1.50 to 150%.

   **Answer:** 150% increase in equity

## Area Problems

Problems involving the determination of the size of an area in square feet, cubic feet, number of acres, and so on, are frequent in the real estate brokerage business. When taking a listing, the broker should determine the number of square feet of heated area in the house. In establishing the lot size, the number of square feet should be determined so it can be translated into acreage, if desired. For measures and formulas to use in solving area problems, see Table 16.1.

### *Determining the Surface Area of a Rectangle or Square*

The surface area of a rectangle or square is determined by multiplying the width by the length. In a square, the width and length are the same. In terms of a simple formula,

AREA = LENGTH × WIDTH

**TABLE 16.1**
Measures and formulas

LINEAR MEASURE
12 inches = 1 ft
39.37 inches = 1 meter (metric system)
3 ft = 1 yd
16½ ft = 1 rod, 1 perch, or 1 pole
66 ft = 1 chain
5,280 ft = 1 mile

SQUARE MEASURE
144 sq inches = 1 sq ft
9 sq ft = 1 sq yd
30¼ sq yd = 1 sq rod
160 sq rods = 1 acre
2.47 acres = 1 hectare or 10,000 square meters (metric system)
43,560 sq ft = 1 acre
640 acres = 1 sq mile
1 sq mile = 1 section
36 sections = 1 township

CUBIC MEASURE
1,728 cubic inches = 1 cubic foot
27 cubic feet = 1 cubic yard
144 cubic inches = 1 board foot (12" × 12" × 1")

CIRCULAR MEASURE
360 degrees = circle
60 minutes = 1 degree
60 seconds = 1 minute

TAX VALUATION
*Per $100 of Assessed Value:* Divide the AV by 100; then multiply by tax rate.

$$\frac{\text{assessed value}}{100} \times \text{tax rate}$$

*Per Mill:* Divide the AV by 1,000; then multiply by tax rate.

$$\frac{\text{assessed value}}{1{,}000} \times \text{tax rate}$$

FORMULAS
1 side × 1 side = area of a square
width × length = area of a rectangle
½ base × height = area of a triangle
½ height × ($\text{base}_1$ + $\text{base}_2$) = area of a trapezoid
½ × sum of the bases = distance between the other two sides at the midpoint of the height of a trapezoid
length × width × depth = volume (cubic measure) of a cube or a rectangular solid

or

A = L × W (for a rectangle)

or

A = S × S (for a square)

1. A rectangular lot measures 90 feet by 185 feet. How many square feet does this lot contain?

 **Solution:** A = L × W
 = 90 × 185
 = 16,650 square feet (SF or sq. ft.)

 **Answer:** 16,650 SF

2. An acre of land has a width of 330 feet. If this acre of land were rectangular in shape, what would be its length?

 **Solution:** Since A = L × W, you can transpose this formula to solve for the length by applying the arithmetic operation of dividing both sides of the equation by WIDTH, or:

$$\frac{A}{W} = L$$

A number to learn at this time is that there are *43,560 square feet per acre.* Therefore, since you know the area in square feet and the width, you can solve for length.

43,560 = 330 × L

or $\frac{43{,}560}{330} = 132$

**Answer:** The lot is 132 feet deep.

3. If a parcel of land contained 32,670 square feet, what percent of an acre would it be?

**Solution:** $\frac{32{,}670}{43{,}560} = 0.75$

$0.75 = 75\%$

**Answer:** 75%

4. A room measures 15 feet by 21 feet. You want to install wall-to-wall carpet and need to calculate the exact amount of carpet required.

**Solution:** Since carpet is sold by the square yard, you need to convert square feet to square yards.

The number of square feet per square yard is $3 \times 3 = 9$ sq. ft. per square yard. Therefore, to convert size in square feet to size in square yards, you need to divide by 9.

Area $= 15 \times 21 = 315$ sq. ft.

**Answer:** $\frac{315}{9} = 35$ square yards of carpet

5. A property owner's lot is 80 feet wide and 120 feet deep (long). The lot is rectangular. The property owner plans to have a fence constructed along both sides and across the rear boundary of the lot. The fence is to be 5 feet high. The property owner has determined that the labor cost in constructing the fence will be $1.25 per linear foot. The material cost will be $3.00 per square yard. What is the total cost of constructing the fence?

**Solution:** Step 1: Determine the linear footage to establish the labor cost.

$2 \times 120$ feet $+ 80$ feet $= 320$ linear feet

320 feet $\times$ \$1.25 per linear foot $=$ \$400 labor cost

Step 2: Establish the number of square yards in the fence to determine material cost.

5 feet $\times$ 320 feet $=$ 1,600 square feet

1,600 sq. ft. $\div$ 9 (9 sq. ft. in 1 sq. yd.) $=$ 177.78 square yards

177.78 square yards $\times$ \$3/square yard $=$ \$533.34 material cost

\$533.34 + \$400 $=$ \$933.34 total cost

**Answer:** $933.34 total cost

6. The property owner in the above problem wants a fence post placed every 10 linear feet for the total length of the fence. How many fence posts are required?

**Solution:** $\frac{320 \text{ linear feet}}{10} = 32$

$32 + 1 = 33$

**Answer:** 33 posts

7. The property owner in the preceding two problems decides to enclose the property with a fence across the front of the property. How many fence posts will be required to enclose the entire property if the fence post interval is maintained at 10 feet?

**Solution:** $(2 \times 80 \text{ feet}) + (2 \times 120 \text{ feet}) = 400$ feet

$\frac{400}{10} = 40$

**Answer:** Total fence posts required for 400 linear feet is 40.

8. If a rectangular map measures 10 inches $\times$16 inches and 1 square inch of map surface represents an area of 20 square miles, how many square miles is represented by the map in total?

**Solution:** 10 inches $\times$ 16 inches = 160 square inches
160 $\times$ 20 sq. mi. = 3,200 sq. mi.
**Answer:** 3,200 square miles

9. A triangular lot measures 200 feet along the street and 500 feet in depth (length) on the side that is perpendicular to the front lot line. If the lot sold for 10 cents per square foot, what is the selling price?

**Solution:** Try to visualize a triangle as half a rectangle. Instead of measuring a triangle in length and width, label the dimensions as base and height. Therefore, you can visualize the formula for a triangle as half of the product of height times base, or:

$$A = \frac{h \times b}{2} =$$

$$\frac{500 \times 200}{2} = 50,000 \text{ square feet}$$

$$50,000 \text{ square feet} \times \$0.10 = \$5,000$$

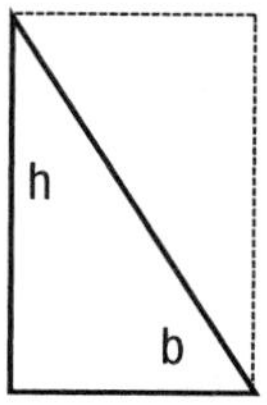


**Answer:** $5,000 sales price

10. A new 20′ $\times$ 25′ garage and a 20′ $\times$ 90′ driveway is to be installed. Both the garage floor and the driveway will be paved with concrete at a cost of $0.35 per square foot. What will be the minimum cost to pave the new garage and driveway?

**Solution:** Step 1: Area = length $\times$ width
Area of Garage 20 $\times$ 25
= 500
Area of Driveway 20 $\times$ 90
= 1,800
Total Area: 500 + 1,800
= 2,300 square feet
Step 2: Cost = 2,300 $\times$ $0.35
Cost = $805
**Answer:** $805 cost

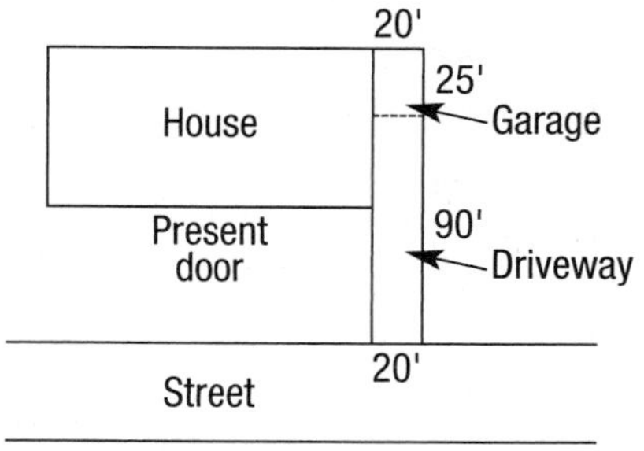


11. What percentage of the lot is occupied by the house shown in the diagram?

**Solution:** Step 1: Divide lot into one triangle and one rectangle.
Area of triangle = 1/2 base $\times$ height
A = 1/2 $\times$ 250 feet $\times$ 150 feet
A = 18,750 square feet
Area of rectangle = length $\times$ width
A = 400 feet $\times$ 150 feet
A = 60,000 square feet
Total lot area = 18,750 sq. ft.
+ 60,000 sq. ft.
Lot area = 78,750 square feet
Step 2: Divide house into two rectangles.
Area of small rectangle = L $\times$ W
A = 30 feet $\times$ 30 feet
A = 900 square feet
Area of large rectangle = L $\times$ W
A = 150 feet $\times$ 30 feet
A = 4,500 square feet
Total house area = 900 sq. ft. + 4,500 sq. ft.
A = 5,400 square feet

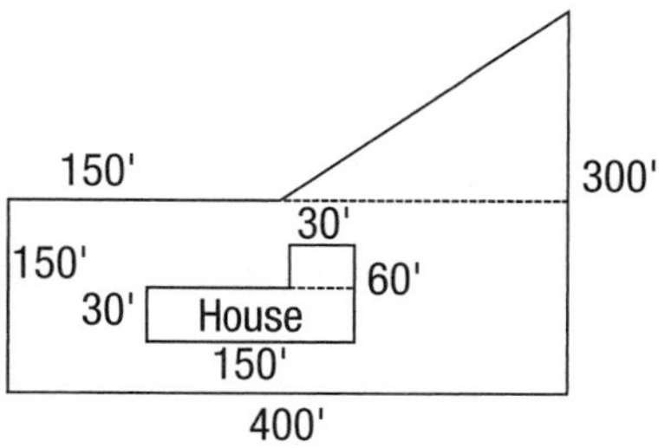

Step 3: Percentage of lot occupied by house = house footage ÷ lot footage

$$\frac{5{,}400}{78{,}750} = 0.0685$$

$0.0685 = 6.85\%$

**Answer:** 6.85% of lot occupied by house

12. How many square feet are in the following lot?

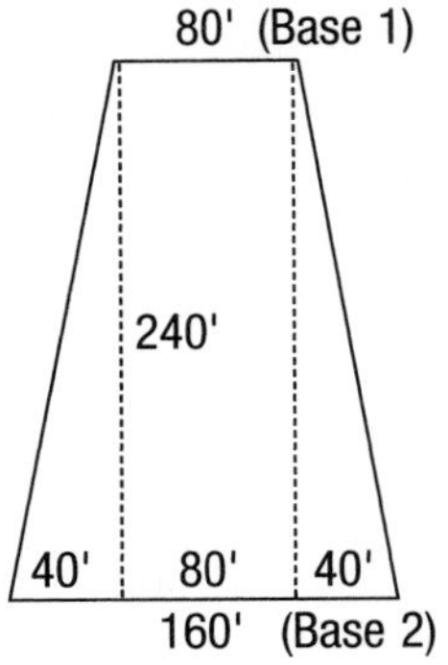


**Solution:** Divide the figure into common shapes you can work with, such as a rectangle and two triangles. By drawing two parallel lines, you carve the figure into a rectangle that measures 80 × 240 feet and two triangles that have a height of 240 feet. You can figure the base of each by subtracting the 80 feet of the rectangle from the total of 160 feet, which is a total of 80 feet for the two triangles, or 40 feet each.

Step 1: Area of the rectangle is
$A = 80 \times 240 = 19{,}200$ square feet

Step 2: Calculate the area of each triangle.

$A = \frac{1}{2}$ base × height

$$A = \frac{40 \times 240}{2} = 4,800$$

Since there are two triangles: 2 × 4,800 = 9,600 square feet.

**Answer:** Total area is, therefore,
19,200 sq. ft. + 9,600 sq. ft. = 28,800 square feet.

**Note:** This figure is a trapezoid, and its area can also be determined by using the formula for a trapezoid:
Area of trapezoid = 1/2 height × $(\text{base}_1 + \text{base}_2)$
$A = 120 \times (160 + 80)$
$A = 28{,}800$

13. A house measures 28 feet wide by 52 feet long and sells for $64,000. What is its price per square foot?

**Solution:** Step 1: Calculate the area.
$A = 28 \times 52 = 1{,}456$ square feet
Step 2: Divide the price by the area.

**Answer:** $\frac{\$64{,}000}{1{,}456} = \$43.96$ square feet

**Caution:** Since there is always a possibility of getting mixed up and dividing the wrong way, always check your answer before looking at the answer choices.

For example: $43.96 per square foot × 1,456 = $64,000
If you were to look at the answer choices before doing this check, you might find your answer even though it is *wrong;* the test often includes all likely wrong answers as distracter items.

14. A rectangular lot that measures 250 feet by 350 feet sells for $10,000. What is the price per square foot?

**Solution:** Step 1: $A = 250 \times 350 = 87{,}500$ square feet

Step 2: Divide the price by the size

$$\frac{\$10{,}000}{87{,}500} = \$0.114$$

**Caution:** As discussed in the problem above, check your answer before looking at the answer sheet. It is easy to come up with an answer of $8.75, which is, of course, wrong, but is guaranteed to be a choice in the answers.

15. The perimeter of a rectangular lot (see below) is 1,800 yards. The length is twice the width plus 6 yards. What is the length in feet?

**Solution:** Perimeter of a rectangle = (2 × width) + (2 × length)
Length = 2W + 6 yards
Width = W
Therefore:
$6 \times \text{width} + 12 \text{ yards} = \text{perimeter (1,800 yards)}$
$6 \times \text{width} = 1,800 - 12$
$6W = 1,788 \text{ yards}$
$W = \frac{1,788}{6}$
$W = 298 \text{ yards}$
$2 \times 298 + 6 = \text{length}$
$596 + 6 = 602 \text{ yards}$
$602 \times 3 = 1,806 \text{ (length in feet)}$

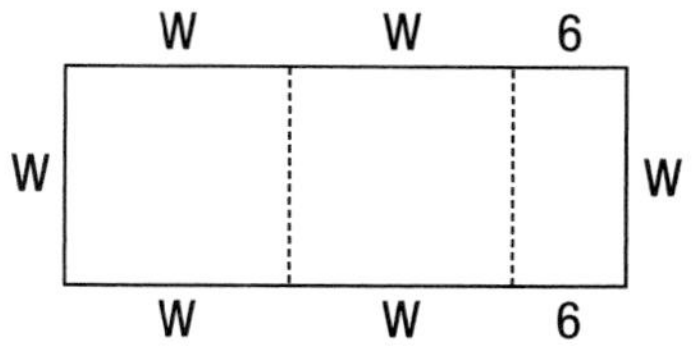


**Answer:** 1,806 feet

16. A house with the area shown originally cost $15 per square foot to build. If it were built today, it would cost $56,000. How much has the cost per square foot increased (in dollars)?

**Solution:** Divide the house into 3 triangles and 1 square.
Area of a triangle = 1/2 bh
A = 1/2 (40 × 20)
A = 400 sq. ft.
3×400 = 1200 sq. ft
Area of a square = 1 side × 1 side
A = 20 × 20
A = 400
Total area = 1,200 + 400
Total area = 1,600 square feet
$56,000 ÷ 1,600 = $35 cost per square foot today
$35 – $15 = $20 per square foot cost increase

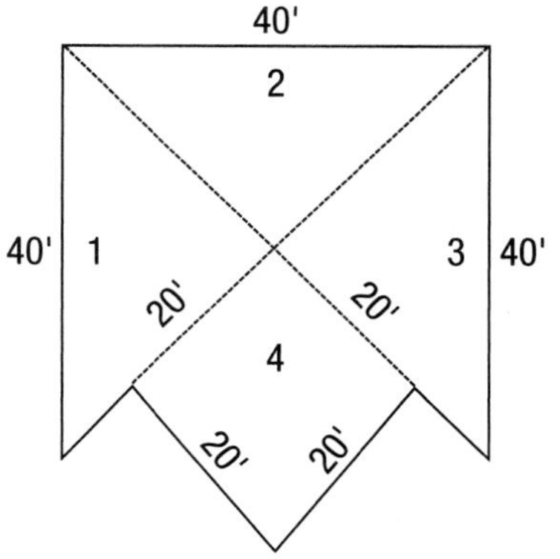


**Answer:** $20 per square foot

## *Cubic Area (Volume)*

The next type of area problem involves cubic area. Cubic area is three-dimensional. To determine the amount of cubic area or volume in a given space, multiply length × width × depth. Cubic area is not tested, but is useful to know.

17. A house under construction contains a rectangular basement that is 20 feet wide and 30 feet long. If the basement is excavated to a uniform depth of 12 feet, how many cubic yards of dirt must be removed?

**Solution:** Volume = Length × Width × Depth
Therefore, cubic feet per cubic yard is:
V = L × W × D or
cubic feet per cubic yard = 3 × 3 × 3 = 27
Therefore:
a. There are 27 cubic feet per cubic yard.
b. To change from cubic feet to cubic yards, you must divide by 27.

20 ft. × 30 ft. × 12 ft. = 7,200 cu. ft.
7,200 ÷ 27 (cu. ft. in 1 cu. yd.) = 266.67 cu. yd.

**Answer:** 266.67 cubic yards of dirt must be removed.

18. A home contains a triangular attic that is 15 feet wide, 30 feet long, and 6 feet high at the ridge beam of the roof. How many cubic feet of space are in the attic?

**Solution:** $\frac{15 \times 30 \times 6}{2} = 1,350$

**Answer:** 1,350 cubic feet

19. A homeowner obtains a quotation to have his driveway paved. The driveway is to be 9 feet wide, 30 yards long, and 4 inches thick. The quotation specifies that the labor cost will be $3 per square yard. The material cost is quoted at $4 per cubic foot. What will be the total cost of the driveway?

**Solution:** Labor cost
3 yd. × 30 yd. = 90 sq. yd.
90 sq. yd. × $3 = $270 labor cost
Material cost
9 ft. × 90 ft. × 1/3 ft. (or .333 ft) = 270 cu. ft.
270 cu. ft. × $4 per cu. ft. = $1,080 material cost
Total cost
$270 labor cost + $1,080 material cost = $1,350

**Answer:** $1,350 total cost of driveway construction

In the previous problems, the information was given in a mixture of feet, yards, and inches. In this type of problem, the dimensions must be converted to the same measurement to arrive at a correct answer. In calculating the labor cost, the dimensions to obtain the surface area were converted to yards because the labor cost was quoted at $3 per square yard. In calculating the material cost, the dimensions were converted to feet because the material cost was quoted at $4 per cubic foot. The 4 inches is 1/3 of a foot.

## *Property Management Fee Calculations*

Go over the following examples. Apply the information given in the first problem to all of the problems.

1. John of AAA Realty manages Gail's property for an 8 percent monthly fee. In August, Unit A and Unit B were occupied. Each unit rents for $570 per month. The rent for both units has been paid in full and on time. How much of the rent does Gail actually receive?
   a. Gross rent collected is the sum of the total rents:

   $$\begin{array}{r} \$\ \ 570 \\ \underline{+\ 570} \\ \$1,140 \end{array}$$

   b. The property management fee is the gross rent collected times the monthly fee:

   $$\$1,140 \times 8\% = \$91.20$$

   c. Gail's check equals the gross rent minus the fee:

   $$\begin{array}{r} \$1,140.00 \\ \underline{-\ 91.20} \\ \$1,048.80 \end{array}$$

2. In September, Unit A was rented for the entire month but Unit B was rented for only 14 days. How much does Gail receive this month?
   a. Prorate the amount collected for Unit B:

   $$\frac{\$570}{30\text{ (days in month)}} \times 14\text{ (occupied days)} = \$266$$

b. Gross rent collected:

$$\begin{array}{r} \$570 \\ +266 \\ \hline \$836 \end{array}$$

c. Gross rent times monthly fee:

$$\$836 \times 8\% = \$66.88$$

d. Gail's check equals the gross rent minus the fee:

$$\begin{array}{r} \$836.00 \\ -66.88 \\ \hline \$769.12 \end{array}$$

3. In October, Gail's units were both rented. However, the plumbing in Unit A needed repair at a cost of $86, and Unit B was sprayed for insects at the normal rate of $25. These bills were deducted from the individual proceeds received from each unit. How much did she receive from Unit A? From Unit B? How much did she receive altogether?

a. Determine the separate management fees for each unit:

| Unit A | Unit B |
|---|---|
| $570 × 8% = $45.60 | $570 × 8% = $45.60 |

b. Determine the individual proceeds before the bills:

| Unit A | Unit B |
|---|---|
| $570.00 | $570.00 |
| −45.60 | −45.60 |
| $524.40 | $524.40 |

c. Subtract the individual expenses from each unit:

| Unit A | Unit B |
|---|---|
| $524.40 | $524.40 |
| −86.00 | −25.00 |
| $438.40 from Unit A | $499.40 from Unit B |

d. Add proceeds from Unit A and Unit B to find the total:

$$\begin{array}{r} \$438.40 \\ +499.40 \\ \hline \$937.80 \end{array}$$

## Real Estate Taxation Problems

You need to understand certain terms to solve problems involving real property taxes. *Assessed value* (AV) is the value established by a tax assessor. The tax value or assessed value is usually a percentage of the estimated market value (MV) of the property and can be as much as 100 percent of market value. The amount of tax is calculated by multiplying the assessed value by the tax rate, which is expressed in dollars per $100 of assessed value in North Carolina.

1. If the market value of a property is $80,000 and the assessed value is 100% of the market value, what is the annual tax if the rate is $1.50 per $100 of tax value?

**Solution:** The assessed value is 100% of the market value, or $80,000 MV × 100% = $80,000 AV.
The tax rate is applied per $100 of the assessed value; therefore, divide the AV by 100 and multiply by the tax rate to calculate the annual taxes,

or

**Answer:** $\frac{\$80{,}000}{100} \times \$1.50 = \$1{,}200$

2. A property is sold at the market value. The annual real property tax is $588.80 at a tax rate of $1.15 per $100 of tax value. Assessed value is 80 percent of market value. What is the selling price?

**Solution:** Applying the $\frac{I}{R \times V}$ formula $V = \frac{I}{R}$,

we know the tax income = I = \$588.80;
the rate = R = \$1.15 ÷ 100, which is 1.15% or .0115; and V = assessed value.
Substituting these known items into the formula:

$$V = \frac{\$588.80}{.0115} = \$51,200$$

Since the assessed value is 80% of the market value:
\$51,200 = 80% × MV
Solving for MV:

$$MV = \frac{51,200}{80\%} = \$64,000$$

Market value = selling price = \$64,000

**Answer:** \$64,000 selling price

3. If the assessed value of a property is \$68,000, the annual tax paid is \$850, and the tax value is 100% of the assessed value, what is the tax rate?

**Solution:** $\frac{\$68,000}{100} = \$680$

$\frac{\$850}{680} = \$1.25$

**Answer:** Tax rate is \$1.25 per \$100 of tax value

4. The real property tax revenue required by a town is \$140,800. The assessed valuation of the taxable property is \$12,800,000. The tax value is 100% of the assessed value. What must the tax rate be per \$100 of assessed valuation to generate the necessary revenue?

**Solution:** $\frac{\text{Income}}{\text{Value}} = \text{Rate}$

$$\frac{\$140,800}{\$12,800,000} = \$0.011 \text{ (rate per \$1.00)}$$

$$\$0.011 \times 100 = \$1.10 \text{ per \$100}$$

**Answer:** Tax rate is \$1.10 per \$100 of assessed value

## Federal Taxation Problems

Chapter 13 noted that material improvements and certain closing costs can be added to the original cost of a property to increase the property's basis. The following formula illustrates the importance of a larger basis when calculating a gain. The example below illustrates the steps used to calculate the gain realized on the sale of a home.

| | |
|---|---|
| Selling price of home | \$750,000 |
| Less selling expenses | – 30,000 |
| Amount Realized | \$720,000 |
| Basis of home | \$300,000 |
| Plus closing costs | + 5,000 |
| Plus improvements | + 20,000 |
| Adjusted basis of home | \$325,000 |
| Amount realized | \$720,000 |
| Minus adjusted basis | –325,000 |
| Gain Realized | \$395,000 |

Amount allowed by exclusion, assuming all conditions are met and taxpayers do not meet any partial exclusion rules:

| | |
|---|---|
| Single taxpayer | \$250,000 |
| Married taxpayers filing jointly | \$395,000 |
| Two unmarried taxpayers with equal interest and both meeting occupancy requirements | \$197,500 each |
| Married taxpayers filing jointly with both meeting ownership and occupancy requirements and one meeting one-sale-in-two-years requirement | \$250,000 |
| Newly married taxpayer filing jointly or singly selling the above home with the gain of \$395,000 and another home with a gain of \$105,000, each selling primary residences owned before marriage and each meeting ownership, use, and one-sale-in-two-years requirement | \$250,000<br>+105,000<br>\$355,000 |

## Co-insurance Calculation

If a structure is worth \$100,000, the co-insurance clause is 80 percent, and the insurance carried is \$60,000, in the event of a partial loss (\$30,000), the company's liability is only \$22,500. The amount of the insurance company's liability is calculated by using the following formula.

$$\frac{\text{Insurance carried}}{\text{Insurance required}} \times \text{Loss} = \text{Company's limit of liability}$$

$$\frac{\$60{,}000}{\$80{,}000} \times \$30{,}000 = \$22{,}500$$

If there is a loss of \$80,000 or more (insurance required), the insurance company's liability is the amount of insurance carried. This is illustrated by the following example.

| | |
|---|---|
| Value of structure | \$100,000 |
| Insurance required (80%) | \$80,000 |
| Insurance policy amount | \$60,000 |
| Loss | \$90,000 |

$$\frac{\text{Insurance carried}}{\text{Insurance required}} \times \text{Loss} = \text{Company's limit of liability under this formula if the face amount of the policy equals or exceeds this amount}$$

$$\frac{\$60{,}000}{\$80{,}000} \times \$90{,}000 = \$67{,}500$$

Insurance company's liability = \$60,000

Since the loss equals or exceeds the amount of insurance required by the co-insurance clause, the insurance company will pay the policy amount even though the requirement of the co-insurance clause is not met. However, in no event will the policy pay an amount in excess of the amount of coverage specified in the policy.

# SECTION 2 PRACTICE WORKING IN REAL ESTATE MATH

This section is a "work-along" practice section that summarizes real estate math. The only way to assure yourself that you have mastered this area is to put the pencil to the paper, first verifying the examples presented and then doing the problems on your own. When you complete this section, you can be confident of successfully completing the math problems on the state exam and can look forward to treating these questions as easy bonus points toward your passing score.

Answers to the practice problems are provided in the Answer Key section at the back of the book.

## BROKERAGE COMMISSIONS

These problems can be seen as an application of the income, rate, value rule where

$$I = R \times V$$

That is, you solve for the missing element (in this case, the commission income) by multiplying rate times value.

1. On sales
   a. For example, $72,500 sale at 6% commission equals
      $72,500 × 6% = $4,350

**You try one:**

   b. A $45,900 sale at 3% commission equals

**Answer:**

2. On rentals
   a. For example, gross rent of $250 per unit with a total of 4 units at 10% commission equals
      4 × $250 × 10% = $100

**You try one:**

   b. A duplex rents for $295 per unit at 15% property management fee. What will the property management fee be?

**Answer:**

   c. On gross effective rentals, subtract for vacancy factor. For example, income of $2,500 per month, 7% vacancy, 10% commission =
      $2,500 − 7% (2500) × 10% = 232.50 commission

**You try one:**

   d. $4,300 full rent, 10% vacancy, 7% commission. What will the property management fee be?

**Answer:**

3. Commission splits
   a. For example, a sale of $72,500 with total commission of 6%, with 25% of the commission going to the listing agent. How much commission will the company receive? How much commission will the listing agent receive?
      $72,500 × 6% = $4,350
      $4,350 × 25% = $1,087.50

**You try one:**

   b. $54,000 sale with 7% commission to office, 15% of office income to agent. How much commission does the agent receive?

**Answer:**

## NET TO SELLER (NET LISTING)

1. If a seller wants to net $50,000 after paying a 6% commission, what is the minimum sales price she must receive? This is a percent relationship.
   100% minus 6% = 94%

Therefore, the \$50,000 the seller wants to net is 94% of the sale price.
$\$50{,}000 = 94\% \times \text{sale price}$
Solving for the sale price:

$$\text{Sale price} = \frac{\$50{,}000}{94\%} = \$53{,}191$$

**You try some:**

a. A seller wants to net \$65,000 after paying a 7% commission. What must the minimum sales price be?

**Answer:**

b. What would the minimum sales price need to be if the seller wanted to net \$75,000 after paying a 5% commission and \$800 for repairs?
Note: Add repairs to net price before dividing by 95%.

**Answer:**

# PROFIT/LOSS/EQUITY (INCLUDING PERCENT CHANGE)

*Rule:* Compare the amount of change in a factor to the beginning value of that factor.

1. For example, if you buy a property for \$38,000 and sell it for \$62,000, your amount of profit would be:

$$\begin{array}{r} \$62{,}000 \\ \underline{-38{,}000} \\ \$24{,}000 \end{array}$$

$$\text{The percent profit} = \frac{\text{amount of profit}}{\text{original value}} = \frac{\$24{,}000}{\$38{,}000} \times 100\% = .6316 \text{ or } 63.16\%$$

**You try one:**

2. You buy a property for \$72,000 and sell it for \$69,000. What is the loss and percent of loss?

**Answer:**

3. Equity and percent change in equity problems
   *Rules:*
   - Equity is the difference between value and obligations.
   - Compare the amount of the change (not the total new equity) to the starting amount.

   a. For example, if the value of the property is \$50,000 and the outstanding loan is \$40,000, the equity is \$10,000. Applying the percent change rule, if the value later is \$60,000 and the loan is paid down to \$30,000, the new equity is \$30,000. The percent change in equity is the amount of the change in equity (that is, \$30,000 [new] minus \$10,000 [old] = \$20,000) compared to the original, or:

$$\frac{\text{amount of change}}{\text{original}} = \frac{\$30{,}000 - \$10{,}000}{\$10{,}000} = \frac{20{,}000}{10{,}000} = 2$$

Note: Multiply 2 by 100% to change to a percent: $2 \times 100\% = 200\%$

**You try one:**

b. A property with an original value of \$38,000 with an 80% loan now has a value of \$72,000, and the loan is paid down to \$26,000. What is the percent change in equity?

**Answer:**

## Area Calculations

1. Convert acres to square feet and vice versa.
   a. For example, a lot measures 250 feet by 350 feet. How many square feet is it, and what portion of an acre is it?
   $250 \times 350 = 87{,}500$ square feet
   *Rule:* There are 43,560 square feet per acre. Divide this number into the total square feet to find the number of acres.

   $$\frac{87{,}500}{43{,}560} = 2.009 \text{ acres}$$

**You try one:**

   b. A lot measures 165 feet by 175 feet. How much of an acre is it? *Note:* An acre is approximately a square 208 feet on the side. This will help you "ballpark" an answer; that is, in the previous problem, you can see that the lot must be less than one acre, which helps you reconcile your answer.

**Answer:**

2. Formulas for calculating the area of various-shaped lots.
   a. Squares: Multiply the two sides

   $A = S \times S$

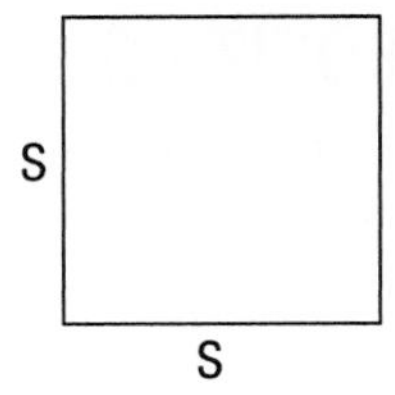


   b. Rectangles: Multiply the length by the width

   $A = L \times W$

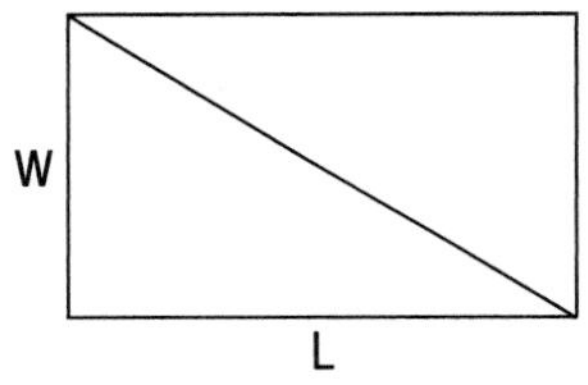


   c. Triangles: Visualize a triangle as half a rectangle

   $$A = \frac{\text{Base} \times \text{Height}}{2}$$

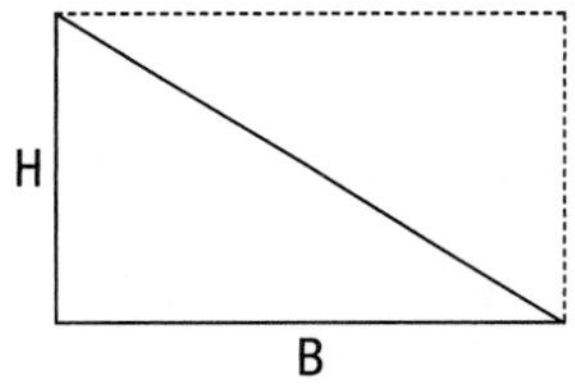


   d. Parallelograms: Ignore the width. You need to multiply the height by the base.
   $A = \text{Height} \times \text{Base}$

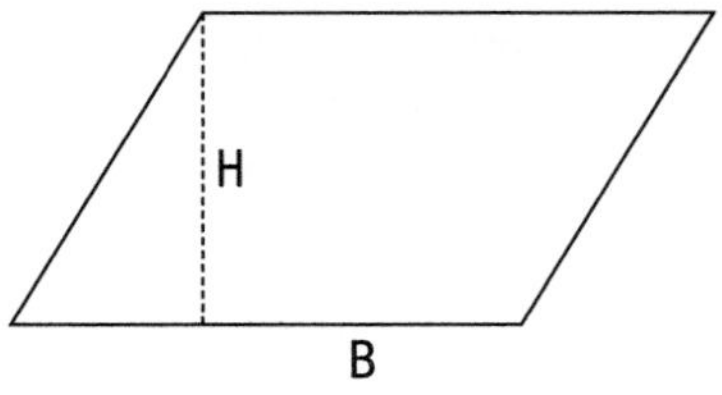


   e. Trapezoids: Multiply 1/2 the height by the sum of the bases.
   $A = 1/2 \text{ height} \times (\text{base}_1 + \text{base}_2)$

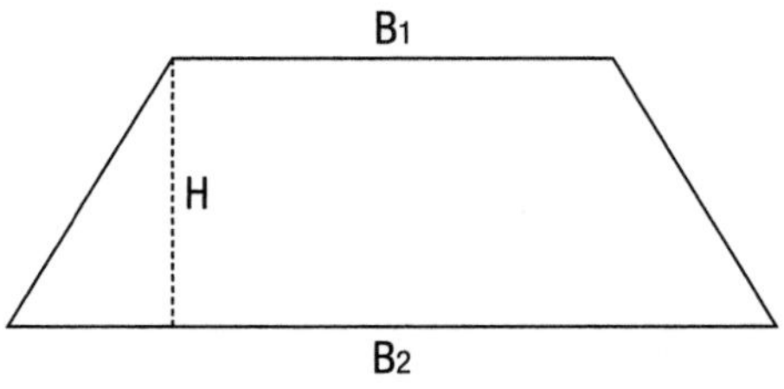

***Examples***

f. A square 20 feet each side
$= 20 \times 20 = 400$ square feet

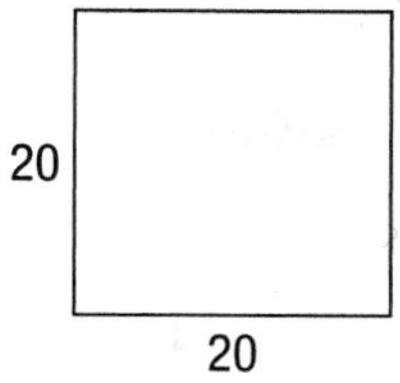


g. A rectangle 200 feet wide and 300 feet long
$= 200 \times 300 = 60{,}000$ square feet

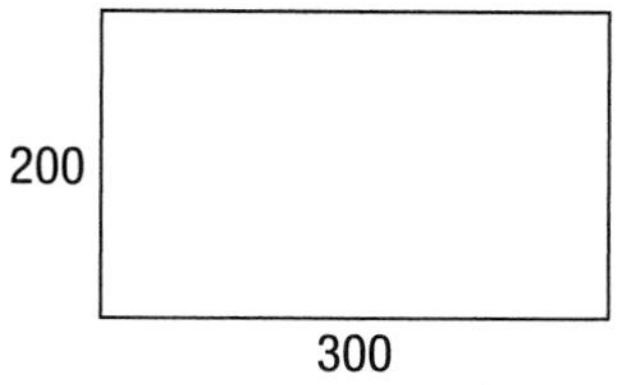


h. A triangle with a base of 30 feet and a height of 20 feet

$$\frac{20 \times 30}{2} = 300 \text{ square feet}$$

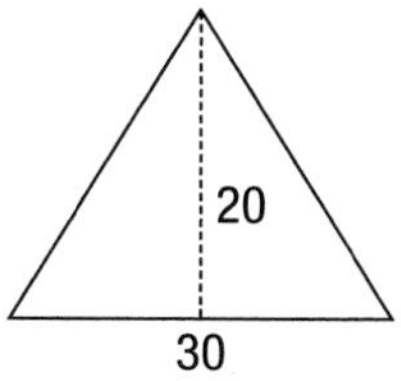


i. A parallelogram with a height of 50, a side of 60, and a base of 75
$= 50 \times 75 = 3{,}750$ (Ignore the side!)

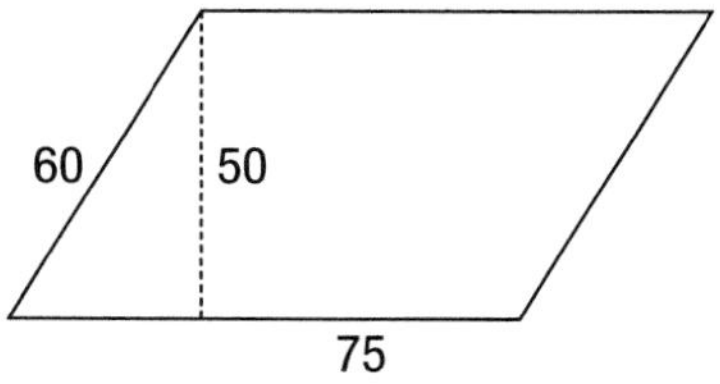


j. A trapezoid with one base 40, the other 80, and a height of 70

$$\frac{70}{2} \times (40 + 80) = 4{,}200$$

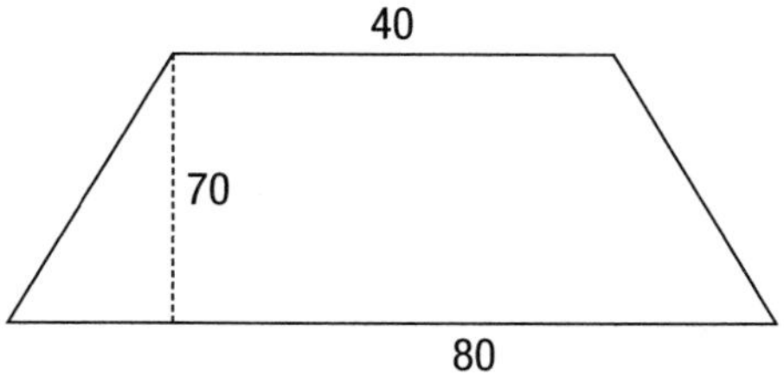


**You try some:**

k. A square 75 feet on the side =

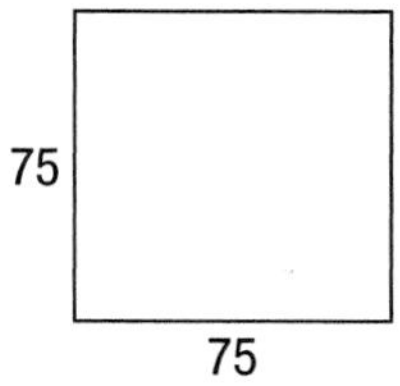


l. A rectangle 37 feet by 64 feet =

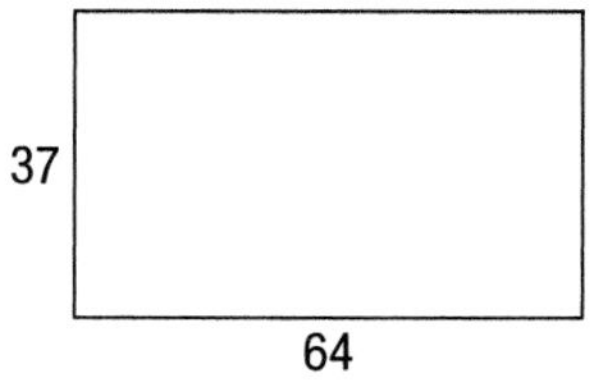

m. A triangle with a 50-foot base and a 75-foot height =

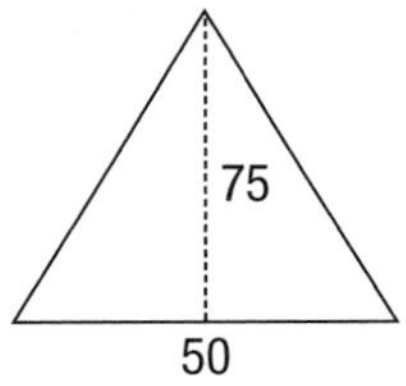


n. A parallelogram with a 180-foot height, a 200-foot side, and a 350-foot base =

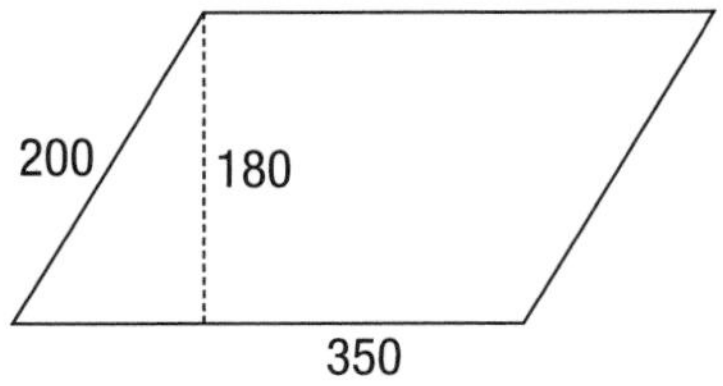


o. A trapezoidal lot with 275 feet on the front, 500 feet on the back, and 360 feet deep =

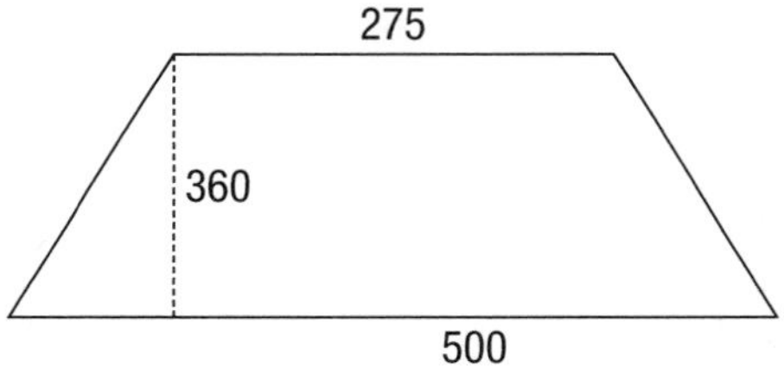


3. Cost/price per square foot, acre, or front foot
   *Rules:*
   - Divide price by size (think $ ÷ sq. ft.).
   - Check your work by reversing your calculations; that is, the Check/Step.

   a. A home with 1,600 square feet sells for $72,000. What is the price per square foot?

$$\frac{\text{Price}}{\text{Size}} = \frac{\$72{,}000}{1{,}600 \text{ square feet}} = \$45$$

**You try some:**

b. A 1,400-square foot home sells for $38,500. What is the price per square foot?

**Answer:**

c. A half-acre of land sells for $22,500. What is the cost per square foot?

**Answer:**

d. A lot with 360 front feet sells for $92,000. What is the cost per front foot?

**Answer:**

Don't forget the Check/Step in each example!

# AD VALOREM TAXES (GIVEN THE RATE AND THE ASSESSED VALUE)

*Rule:* Divide the assessed value (AV) by 100 and multiply by the tax rate.

1. If the assessed value is $62,500 and the tax rate is $0.75 per $100 of AV, what are the taxes per year?

$$\frac{\$\ 62{,}500}{100} \times \$0.75 = \$468.75$$

To calculate a monthly payment to tax escrow, simply divide the annual tax bill by 12.
**You try one:**

2. The AV is $69,000 and the rate is $1.25. What is the monthly payment to escrow?
**Answer:**

# EXCISE TAX

*Rule:* The rate is $1.00 per $500 or any fraction thereof of total purchase price. The loan amount or any assumed value does not affect excise tax.

1. A home sells for $96,000 cash. How much in excise tax must the seller pay?

$$\frac{\$96,000}{500} = \$192$$

**You try some:**

2. What is the excise tax on a $45,900 sale?
**Answer:**

3. What is the excise tax on a sale of $135,600 with the assumption of a $55,000 existing loan?
**Answer:**

4. What is the excise tax on a sale of $125,000 with a 90% new first mortgage?
**Answer:**

# FINANCIAL CALCULATIONS

1. Simple interest
*Rule:* I = P × R × T
Interest = principal × rate × time
   a. What is the interest for the month on a loan balance of $45,000 at 8.25% annual interest?

$$\frac{\$\ 45{,}000 \times 8.25\%}{12} = \$309.38 \text{ (a month is 1/12 of a year)}$$

**You try one:**
   b. What is the monthly interest on a loan of $28,700 at 9% interest?
**Answer:**

2. Total interest paid over the life of a loan
*Rule:* Calculate the total of the payments ($ per month × 12 months per year × number of years) minus the amount borrowed.
*Note:* This is not the I = P × R × T rule, which will, of course, be one of the wrong answer choices.

a. If the monthly payment of P&I is \$230.97 at 9% interest for 30 years on a loan of \$28,700, what is the total interest paid over the life of the loan?

$\$230.97 \times 12 \times 30 = \$83{,}149.20$ total paid

$\$83{,}149.20$ paid $-$ $\$28{,}700$ borrowed $= \$54{,}449.20$

**You try one:**

b. What is the interest paid on a loan of \$55,000 with payments of \$625 per month for 25 years?

**Answer:**

3. Use of an amortization chart

*Rule:* Divide the amount of the loan by 1,000, find the appropriate row and column in the chart (on page 206) (per thousands), and multiply the two numbers to find the monthly P&I.

a. A loan of \$45,000 at 9% for 15 years

$$= \frac{\$45,000}{1,000} = 45$$

$45 \times$ (factor from chart) $=$

$45 \times \$10.15 = \$456.75$

**You try one:**

What is the payment for a \$134,900 loan at 8.75% for 30 years?

**Answer:**

b. What is the total interest paid on the above loan?

**Answer:**

4. Debt service/mortgage reduction

*Rule:* Use the $I = P \times R \times T$ rule to calculate the monthly interest, and subtract this from the P&I. Subtract this principal amount from the previous balance.

a. What is the balance on a loan of \$28,700 at 9% after the first payment of \$231?

$I = P \times R \times T$

$$\frac{\$28{,}700 \times 9\%}{12} = \$215.25$$

$\$231.00$ P & I

$\underline{-215.25}$ I

$\$15.75$ P

$$\$28,700 - \$15.75 = \$28,684.25$$

**You try one:**

b. What is the balance after one payment on a loan of \$56,000 at 13.5% with payments of \$642?

**Answer:**

5. Origination fees and discount points

*Rule:* Each point costs 1% times the loan amount

a. A \$96,000 loan with 2.5 points

$= \$96.000 \times 2.5\% = \$2{,}400$

**You try one:**

b. A sale of \$117,500 with a 90% loan will cost how much for 4.5 points?

**Answer:**

6. Yield on a loan
   *Rule:* Each point is assumed to raise the effective yield to the lender of 1/8 of a percent.
   a. What is the effective yield to the lender of a 10% loan if he charges 6 points?
   6 points × 1/8 each = 6/8 = 3/4
   10 + 3/4 = 10.75

**You try one:**

b. What is the yield on a 9.75% loan with 4 points?

**Answer:**

c. What is the cost of points to raise the yield of a given loan to a certain effective rate?
   To raise a $50,000 loan from 9% to 93/8% would be 3 points times the loan amount = $50,000 × 3% = $1,500.

**You try one:**

d. What is the cost of points to raise a $65,000 loan at 10.50% to 11%?

**Answer:**

7. Qualifying the buyer
   *Rule:* Apply the given maximum expense/income ratios to the buyer's income. The buyer will qualify if her ratios do not exceed the guidelines.
   a. A lender's qualifying rule for a conventional loan is probably 28/36 for an 80% loan-to-value ratio, meaning the home payments cannot be more than 28% of a borrower's monthly income, nor can the borrower's total fixed expenses exceed 36%.
   If a buyer's income is $2,500 per month, the house payment cannot exceed:
   $2,500 × 28% = $700
   and the total house payment plus other debts cannot exceed:
   $2,500 × 36% = $900

**You try one:**

b. A buyer earns $36,000 per year. What are the buyer's maximum allowable house payment and house payment plus debt limits?

**Answer(s):**

# PRORATIONS AT CLOSING

1. Calculate the entry on a closing statement for real estate tax.
   **Solution:** For example, closing is on March 17 and real estate tax is $1,332 per year, unpaid.
   Step 1: Figure the days used.
   Jan.–Feb. = 2 × 30 = 60
   Plus 17 days of March +17
   77 days used

   Step 2: Figure the daily rate.

$$\frac{1,332}{360} = \$3.70$$

   Step 3: Figure the dollars used.
   $3.70 day × 77 days × $284.90 used

   Step 4: This entry will show as a $284.90 debit to the sellers since they owe this much for the tax year but have not paid. As a check on this figure, you could figure the buyer's portion of the year independently and ensure that the buyer's and seller's portions add up to the whole tax.

2. Prorate an insurance policy paid for by the seller and assumed by the buyer.

**Solution:** For example, closing is on April 27 and insurance of $500 per year was paid by the seller on October 1 of the previous year.

Step 1: Figure the used portion of the policy.

Oct.−Mar. = 6 months × 30 days = 180 days

plus the 27 days of April + 27

207 days

Step 2: Figure the daily rate.

$$\frac{\$500}{360} = \$1.3888 \text{ per day}$$

Step 3: Figure the dollar amount used.

207 days × $1.3888 per day = $287.50 used

Step 4: Now do NOT snatch defeat from the jaws of victory by searching the answer sheet for this number until you take a moment to THINK about what you are doing.

| | |
|---|---|
| the seller paid | $500.00 |
| but only used | −287.50 |
| therefore, is due a refund (credit) | $212.50 |

# PREPARATION OF CLOSING STATEMENTS

## Sample "Net Owed by Buyer" Closing Statement*

A buyer made a $5,000 earnest money deposit and contracted to purchase a house for $105,000. The buyer will be obtaining a $70,000 new first mortgage loan and paying the lender a l-point loan origination fee. The buyer also will be giving the seller a $20,000 second purchase money mortgage. The balance of the purchase price will be paid in cash at closing. Real estate taxes for the current year are estimated to be $1,440 and are unpaid. Additional closing expenses that must be paid by the buyer total $375. What is the net amount owed by the buyer at closing on April 15?

**Solution:** Step 1: Calculate loan origination fee:

1% (1 point) × $70,000 = $700

Step 2: Prorate real estate taxes:

$$\frac{\$1,440}{360} = \$4$$

$4 × 105 days (Jan. 1−Apr. 15) = $420 (seller's share)

Step 3: Make credit/debit adjustments to the purchase price:

| | |
|---|---|
| Purchase price | $105,000 |
| Deduct earnest money | − 5,000 |
| Deduct first mortgage | − 70,000 |
| Deduct second mortgage | − 20,000 |
| Deduct seller's share of RE taxes | − 420 |
| Add loan origination fee | + 700 |
| Add additional closing expenses | + 375 |
| Amount owed (cash needed) by buyer | $ 10,655 |

*Sample problems provided by the North Carolina Real Estate Commission, Education Department. Reproduced by permission.

## Sample "Net to Seller" Closing Statement*

A seller has contracted to sell his house for $95,000 and has agreed to pay a 7% brokerage fee to the listing broker. The buyer is obtaining a $75,000 new first mortgage loan. As of the day of closing, the outstanding principal balance on the seller's existing mortgage loan is $56,925 and accrued interest due for November is $545. Real estate taxes for the current year are $960 and have been paid by the seller. The seller must pay $90 in miscellaneous closing costs as well as the cost of excise tax at the cost of $1.00 per $500 or fraction thereof. How much will the seller net at closing on November 30?

**Solution:** Step 1: Calculate the brokerage fee

$7\% \times \$95{,}000 = \$6{,}650$

Step 2: Prorate the real estate (RE) taxes

$\frac{\$960}{12} = \$80$ (buyer's share)

Step 3: Calculate excise tax

$\frac{\$95{,}000}{500} = 190$

$190 \times \$1.00 = \$190$

Step 4: Make credit/debit adjustments to sales price

| | |
|---|---|
| Sales price | $95,000 |
| Add buyer's share of RE taxes | + 80 |
| Deduct principal balance of seller's mortgage | −56,925 |
| Deduct accrued interest on seller's mortgage | − 545 |
| Deduct brokerage fee | − 6,650 |
| Deduct miscellaneous closing costs | − 90 |
| Deduct cost of excise tax | − 190 |
| Net due to seller | $30,680 |

**You try some:**

**Practice Problem Number 1.** The closing date is March 3 for the sale of a $45,700 home. There is a $2,000 earnest money deposit, the real estate taxes are $300 per year and are not paid yet, and the personal property tax of $150 is also unpaid. The buyer is paying $225 for a new insurance policy, has miscellaneous expenses of $900, and will be obtaining a new mortgage for 95% of the sales price. The seller will pay excise tax (as discussed earlier in this chapter) as well as a real estate commission of 5%. Calculate the balance owed by the buyer and the balance due to the seller.

**Practice Problem Number 2.** The sale of a $60,000 home is closed July 17. The earnest money deposit is $5,000. The real property taxes of $575 and personal property taxes of $400 are unpaid. The seller's existing mortgage is $35,000, and he will pay excise tax and a 6% broker's fee. The buyer is paying $400 for a new insurance policy, is paying $1,400 in miscellaneous expenses, and is obtaining a loan for 90% of the sales price. Calculate the balance owed by the buyer and the balance due to the seller.

**Practice Problem Number 3.** On November 9, the sale of a $72,500 condominium is closed with the buyer assuming the seller's existing loan balance of $50,000, at an interest rate of 12%. The buyer made a deposit of $7,500. The seller already paid the full year's real property tax of $800 and the personal property tax of $275. The seller also paid a one-year insurance policy of $450 from February 1 of this year, and the buyer will be assuming the balance of this policy from the seller. The buyer's additional expenses are $1,750, and the seller will pay excise tax as well as a broker's fee of 7%. Calculate the bottom-line balances for the buyer and the seller.

*Sample problems provided by the North Carolina Real Estate Commission, Education Department. Reproduced by permission.

# SIMPLE APPRAISAL MATH

1. Simple adjustment of comparables to the subject property *Valuation Problem:* A 4-bedroom (BR) home sells for $85,000, and a similar 3-bedroom home sells for $81,000. A 2-bath home sells for $61,500; a 1-bath, for $58,000. A home with a paved drive sells for $55,000, and one with an unpaved drive sells for $52,700. You have a subject property in the same area of homes that has 3 bedrooms, 2 baths, and a gravel drive. Comparable sales include a $65,000 price with 4 BR, 2 baths, and paving; a sale of $51,200 with 2 BR, 1 bath, and gravel drive; and a third comparable at $64,500 with 3 BR, 3 baths, and paved drive.

*Calculate the listing value of the subject property.*

a. Abstract the value of the elements. Use the paired sales analysis technique to find two properties that are the same (identical) except for one element. Thus, the difference in price between those two properties is due to the contribution of that element. For example,

| | | Comp | minus | Comp | | equals |
|---|---|---|---|---|---|---|
| 1. Bedroom | = | 85,000 | – | 81,000 | = | $4,000 |
| 2. Bath | = | 61,500 | – | 58,000 | = | $3,500 |
| 3. Paving | = | 55,000 | – | 52,700 | = | $2,300 |

b. Construct an adjustment chart.

| Feature | Subject | Comp 1 | Adj | Comp 2 | Adj | Comp 3 | Adj |
|---|---|---|---|---|---|---|---|
| Price | ? | | $65,000 | | $51,200 | | $64,500 |
| Bedrooms | 3 | 4 | (–)4,000 | 2 | (+)4,000 | 3 | 0 |
| Baths | 2 | 2 | 0 | 1 | (+)3,500 | 3 | (–)3,500 |
| Paving | No | Yes | (–)2,300 | No | 0 | Yes | (–)2,300 |
| Total Adjustment | | | (–)6,300 | | (+)7,500 | | (–)5,800 |
| Indicated Price | | | $58,700 | | $58,700 | | $58,700 |

**You try one:**

2. A home sells for $72,500 with a carport and $70,000 without; one home with a deck sells for $50,000 and $48,500 without. One home sells for $58,700, and the identical home a block away, but with an interstate highway in its backyard, sells for $55,000. Your subject property has a carport, no deck, and no nearby interstate highway. Comparables are a $65,000 sale with deck and interstate highway but no carport, a $71,200 sale with carport and deck but no interstate highway, and a $66,000 sale with carport and interstate highway but no deck. Calculate the adjustments.

a. Abstract the value of each element:

| | | Comp | minus | Comp | equals |
|---|---|---|---|---|---|
| 1. Carport | = | | – | | = |
| 2. Deck | = | | – | | = |
| 3. Interstate | = | | – | | = |

b. Construct an adjustment chart:

| Feature | Subject | Comp 1 | Adj | Comp 2 | Adj | Comp 3 | Adj |
|---|---|---|---|---|---|---|---|
| Price | | | | | | | |
| Carport | | | | | | | |
| Deck | | | | | | | |
| Interstate | | | | | | | |
| Total Adjustment | | | | | | | |
| Indicated Price | | | | | | | |

## FEDERAL TAXATION

*Rule:* Deductions are subtracted from income for (a) mortgage interest, (b) real property tax, and (c) discount points (to originate a new loan but not to refinance an existing loan) in the year these expenses are paid.

1. Calculate the gain realized.
   *Rule:* Subtract the adjusted basis from the amount realized. The amount realized is the sales price minus the costs of the sale. Adjusted basis is the sum of (a) purchase price, (b) closing costs (except costs of loan), and (c) any capital improvements.
   a. A seller paid $90,000 for a home, $4,000 for allowable closing costs, and $8,000 for improvements; he sold it for $335,000 minus a 5% commission.

   His gain realized is calculated as follows:
   $ 90,000 Purchase
   4,000 Closing
   + 8,000 Improvements
   $102,000 **Adjusted basis**

   $335,000 Sales price
   16,750 Commission
   $318,250 **Amount realized**

   $318,250 Amount realized
   102,000 Adjusted basis
   $216,250 **Gain realized**

**You try one:**

   b. If you buy a house for $190,000 with $4,800 allowable closing costs, put in $10,000 of improvements, and sell it for $450,000 less a 4% commission, what is your gain realized? If you are a single taxpayer meeting all the conditions for the universal exclusion, how much of your gain is taxable?

**Answer:**

## SUMMARY

The practice problems in this chapter correspond directly to the calculations required on the state exam. Be sure to practice each problem so you have no surprises in the math section and can use it to boost your overall exam score, rather than burden it.

# Safety Issues for Real Estate Brokers

This text has focused on what you need to know to protect the interest of your clients and to help you avoid lawsuits and disciplinary action by the Real Estate Commission by providing you the knowledge to practice real estate in a professional and legally correct manner. An important aspect of the real estate business that still remains to discuss is the issue of personal safety while conducting business. Before you encounter your first potential client or customer, you should know how to protect yourself from those who seek to lure you into a dangerous situation on the pretext of buying or listing real estate.

Every year, too many real estate agents are assaulted, robbed, raped, or even murdered during or as a result of real estate activity. Most of these attacks can be prevented by using common sense and following proven safety practices. Agents frequently must talk to strangers and often are alone with people they barely know. The nature of the real estate business requires that agents exercise safety precautions by being aware of their surroundings, anticipating and avoiding danger, and by being prepared to escape a dangerous situation.

This discussion is not meant to be all encompassing and you may choose not to follow all of these suggestions. Adopt those pertinent to your situation, and continue to develop knowledge of safety procedures through your company's training program, seminars, and reading. Every company should have policies and procedures to ensure the safety of its employees and agents. Learn and follow these policies and build on that knowledge by accessing the wealth of additional information on safety including the "North Carolina Real Estate Agent Safety Guide," a joint publication of the NC Real Estate Commission and NCAR, continuing education courses and materials produced the National Association of REALTORS®.

Safety is important at the office, in advertising, between the office or property and your car, in your car, and in property being shown to an individual or at an open house. The following suggestions may help create a safer office environment.

1. An office location that is not isolated after normal business hours.
2. Well-lit parking lot and lights around perimeter of building, especially areas that would give a criminal an easy place to hide.
3. A security system to prevent unauthorized entry.
4. A personal security system that can be worn as a watch or pendant by agents when working alone at the office on evenings or weekends.
5. Security cameras, preferably with the images transmitted and stored off premises.
6. A single, monitored point of entry. Note: All doors must be able to be easily exited in case of fire.

7. An information center containing the following pertinent information about agents, clients, and customers which could help locate an agent in case of disappearance.
   - Information about clients and customers contain a picture ID, make and model of car, and license tag number, as well as other information as needed to verify identity.
   - An itinerary sheet showing routes, addresses, and call-in and return times.

   You should carefully establish and consistently apply criteria for this in order to avoid even the appearance of profiling members of a specific race, sex, national origin, or any other protected category.

Advertising often is overlooked as a hazard. Modify your advertising to protect your safety, beginning with these suggestions.

1. Consider not putting your picture on your cards or ads, especially if you are a woman. If you use a picture, avoid "glamour shots."
2. Use cell phone numbers, not home phone number on cards and ads.
3. Never advertise a house as vacant.
4. Do not include personal information in advertising.

An agent's vehicle is an essential tool for the practice of real estate. The following actions may help as you move to and from your vehicle, whether entering or leaving the office or a property alone or with customers or clients.

1. Observe activity around property before getting out of your car.
2. Check your car including the backseat before entering.
3. Lock doors while driving and when leaving car unattended.
4. Fill up your car with gas when it is half-full. Do not risk running out of gas.
5. Keep vehicle in good mechanical condition with routine maintenance and high quality puncture-resistant tires. Do not risk being stranded in a remote area.
6. Park your car on the street, if possible, when showing houses or sitting an open house. Position car for a fast get-away should it become necessary.
7. Keyless entry and automatic ignitions are great safety tools that you may want to consider on your next car if you do not presently have them. On-Star, a system using GPS tracking and telecommunications technology is also a great safety tool available on selected new cars. It tracks the location of the car and sends help when necessary. It also offers services such as unlocking car doors, alerting drivers to routine maintenance, and tracking and stopping the car if stolen.
8. An inexpensive portable GPS and a well-charged cell phone may provide a measure of safety. If you do not have a GPS, an On-Star, or equivalent system, have a good map and a cell phone with you and know your route before leaving the office.
9. Some guidelines suggest keeping an extra key in a hidden magnetized box on outside of car; however, a criminal may be able to easily locate it. It may be better to always have an extra key hidden in your clothes, but easily accessible.

Agents should always use common sense when showing property, including but not limited to the following practices.

1. Never meet a potential client, especially one you do not know, at a property, a hotel, or anywhere away from the office.
2. Always carry a well-charged cell phone. Keep the phone easily accessible, not in the bottom of a purse. Have your cell phone programmed to speed dial 911, the office, and home.
3. Always make sure someone else, co-worker, friend or family member, has seen your client or customer and that your client or customer knows he has been seen and can be identified. Even better, leave a client profile sheet and an itinerary sheet with the office staff or your family.

4. Avoid wearing expensive jewelry or carrying a large sum of money.
5. Check in with home or office periodically. Office and family should have an action plan for when they have not heard from you as scheduled and cannot reach you.
6. Have a code for when you are uncomfortable, but not so much so that you want to call 911. Some suggest calling the office and saying something similar to "Will you please locate the red file for 123 Happy Lane and tell me the dimensions of the lot?" That may be a little too obvious. Many people are accustomed to hearing Code Blue, Code Red, or Doctor White coming over hospital loudspeakers and may associate a color, especially red, with a distress call. No matter what the code is, it should be understood by everyone in your office or home.
7. Keep your keys readily available.
8. Wear comfortable shoes suitable for running. If you find yourself in danger while you are wearing shoes that would hamper running, kick them off and run barefoot.
9. Have your car parked for an easy getaway.
10. Always allow your client or customer to enter the home or room before you. Remain between the client and the exit.

An open house is potentially dangerous for the agent. Although agents and their seller-clients may never be willing to forego having an open house, agents may reduce the danger with the following precautions.

1. Never sit an open house alone in a remote area. Regardless of location, it is preferable to not sit any open house alone. Have your car parked for an easy escape.
2. Open only one entrance. Assure that open house guests do not leave another door unlocked through which they could later return and enter. You should be able to exit through any door, but only allow access through one entrance.
3. Take the same precautions as with showing houses.
4. Ask owners to secure valuables out of sight or off premises. Do the same for your own valuables.
5. Have specific times to check in with your family or the office.
6. Have someone call you periodically if you do not call them as scheduled.
7. Meet the neighbors when you are setting up for an open house. They may be able to provide assistance if needed.
8. Keep control. Do not allow groups to split up as you are showing the home, especially if it is occupied.

An open house is safest for the agent and the homeowner's possessions if there are two people to control traffic flow. A large group or two groups working together could out-maneuver the saviest agent working alone. It is sad to think you may need a bodyguard at an open house, but there are deceased agents who may still be alive if a trusted second person had been with them.

Perhaps the greatest danger an agent faces is being alone with clients and customers about whom he or she knows little or nothing. All is not always as it appears. Be alert and heed warning signs. If a customer's or client's strange behavior concerns you, pay attention to your instincts. Diplomatically end the relationship as soon as possible if you see signs of current drug or alcohol abuse, violent or irrational behavior toward his or her family, you, or others; or inappropriate remarks of a violent or sexual nature. If you sense immediate danger, forget the diplomacy and get out immediately. No commission is worth risking your life.

If someone wants to harm you, embarassment is irrelevant. You do not care what they think. Those who do not want to harm you will likely understand. Do not let the desire for a commission or the fear of embarassment prevent you from leaving a dangerous situation.

The most important key to your safety is to plan ahead. Knowing what you will do in the event of an emergency can help you retain your wits and survive. A self-defense course may give you more confidence, enabling you to remain calm and think clearly. Even if you are strong and proficient in self-defense, it is wiser to avoid or escape danger when possible. Fight only if you must. If you can neither run away nor fight, try talking with your assailant. You may be able to negotiate your release. Practicing safe habits every day and having the tools and skills at your disposal can help you practice real estate safely.

# Appendix A
# North Carolina Real Estate License Law, North Carolina Real Estate Commission Rules, Trust Account Guidelines, and License Law and Rule Comments

# NORTH CAROLINA REAL ESTATE LICENSE LAW

**Codified as Chapter 93A of the General Statutes of North Carolina**



**Please note: Certain "gender neutral" terms used in the Real Estate License Law as reprinted in this booklet are subject to final revision by the Revisor of Statutes.**

# Real Estate License Law

## [Codified as Chapter 93A of the General Statutes of North Carolina]

## ARTICLE 1. REAL ESTATE BROKERS.

**93A-1. License required of real estate brokers.**
From and after July 1, 1957, it shall be unlawful for any person, partnership, corporation, limited liability company, association, or other business entity in this State to act as a real estate broker, or directly or indirectly to engage or assume to engage in the business of real estate broker or to advertise or hold himself or herself or themselves out as engaging in or conducting such business without first obtaining a license issued by the North Carolina Real Estate Commission (hereinafter referred to as the Commission), under the provisions of this Chapter. A license shall be obtained from the Commission even if the person, partnership, corporation, limited liability company, association, or business entity is licensed in another state and is affiliated or otherwise associated with a licensed real estate broker in this State.

**93A-2. Definitions and exceptions.**

**(a)** A real estate broker within the meaning of this Chapter is any person, partnership, corporation, limited liability company, association, or other business entity who for a compensation or valuable consideration or promise thereof lists or offers to list, sells or offers to sell, buys or offers to buy, auctions or offers to auction (specifically not including a mere crier of sales), or negotiates the purchase or sale or exchange of real estate, or who leases or offers to lease, or who sells or offers to sell leases of whatever character, or rents or offers to rent any real estate or the improvement thereon, for others.

**(a1)** The term broker-in-charge within the meaning of this Chapter shall mean a real estate broker who has been designated as the broker having responsibility for the supervision of real estate salespersons engaged in real estate brokerage at a particular real estate office and for other administrative and supervisory duties as the Commission shall prescribe by rule.

**(a2)** The term provisional broker within the meaning of this Chapter means a real estate broker who, pending acquisition and documentation to the Commission of the education or experience prescribed by either G.S. 93A-4(a1) or G.S. 93A-4.3, must be supervised by a broker-in-charge when performing any act for which a real estate license is required.

**(b)** The term real estate salesperson within the meaning of this Chapter shall mean and include any person who was formerly licensed by the Commission as a real estate salesperson before April 1, 2006.

**(c)** The provisions of this Chapter shall not apply to and shall not include:

**(1)** Any person, partnership, corporation, limited liability company, association, or other business entity who, as owner or lessor, shall perform any of the acts aforesaid with reference to property owned or leased by them, where the acts are performed in the regular course of or as incident to the management of that property and the investment therein.

**(2)** Any person acting as an attorney-in-fact under a duly executed power of attorney from the owner authorizing the final consummation of performance of any contract for the sale, lease or exchange of real estate.

**(3)** The acts or services of an attorney-at-law.

**(4)** Any person, while acting as a receiver, trustee in bankruptcy, guardian, administrator or executor or any person acting under order of any court.

**(5)** Any person, while acting as a trustee under a trust agreement, deed of trust or will, or his or her regular salaried employees.

**(6)** Any salaried person employed by a licensed real estate broker, for and on behalf of the owner of any real estate or the improvements thereon, which the licensed broker has contracted to manage for the owner, if the salaried employee is limited in his or her employment to: exhibiting units on the real estate to prospective tenants; providing the prospective tenants with information about the lease of the units; accepting applications for lease of the units; completing and executing preprinted form leases; and accepting security deposits and rental payments for the units only when the deposits and rental payments are made payable to the owner or the broker employed by the owner. The salaried employee shall not negotiate the amount of security deposits or rental payments and shall not negotiate leases or any rental agreements on behalf of the owner or broker.

**(7)** Any owner who personally leases or sells his or her own property.

**(8)** Any housing authority organized in accordance with the provisions of Chapter 157 of the General Statutes and any regular salaried employees of the housing authority when performing acts authorized in this Chapter as to any property owned or leased by the housing authority. This exception shall not apply to any person, partnership, corporation, limited liability company, association, or other business entity that contracts with a housing authority to sell or manage property owned or leased by the housing authority.

**93A-3. Commission created; compensation; organization.**

**(a)** There is hereby created the North Carolina Real Estate Commission, hereinafter called the Commission. The Commission shall consist of nine members, seven members to be appointed by the Governor, one member to be appointed by the General Assembly upon the recommendation of the President Pro Tempore of the Senate in accordance with G.S. 120-121, and one member to be appointed by the General Assembly upon the recommendation of the Speaker of the House of Representatives in accordance with G.S. 120-121. At least three members of the Commission shall be licensed real estate brokers. At least two members of the Commission shall be persons who are not involved directly or indirectly in the real estate or real estate appraisal business. Members of the Commission shall serve three-year terms so staggered that the terms of three members expire in one year, the terms of three members expire in the next year, and the terms of three members expire in the third year of each three-year period. The members of the Commission shall elect one of their members to serve as chairman of the Commission for a term of one year. The Governor may remove any member of the Commission for misconduct, incompetency, or willful neglect of duty. The Governor shall have the power to fill all vacancies occurring on the Commission, except vacancies in legislative appointments shall be filled under G.S. 120-122.

**(b)** The provisions of G.S. 93B-5 notwithstanding, members of the Commission shall receive as compensation for each day spent on work for the Commission a per diem in an amount established by the Commission by rule, and mileage reimbursement for transportation by privately owned automobile at the business standard mileage rate set by the Internal Revenue Service per mile of travel along with actual cost of tolls paid. The total expense of the administration of this Chapter shall not exceed the total income therefrom; and none of the expenses of said Commission or the compensation or expenses of any office thereof or any employee shall ever be paid or payable out of the treasury of the State of North Carolina; and neither the Commission nor any officer or employee thereof shall have any power or authority to make or incur any expense, debt or other financial obligation binding upon the State of North Carolina. After all expenses of operation, the Commission may set aside an expense reserve each year not to exceed ten percent (10%) of the previous year's gross income; then any surplus shall go to the general fund of the State of North Carolina. The Commission may deposit moneys in accounts, certificates of deposit, or time deposits as the Commission may approve, in any bank, savings and loan association, or trust company. Moneys also may be invested in the same classes of securities referenced in G.S. 159-30(c).

**(c)** The Commission shall have power to make reasonable bylaws, rules and regulations that are not inconsistent with the provisions of this Chapter and the General Statutes; provided, however, the Commission shall not make rules or regulations regulating commissions, salaries, or fees to be charged by licensees under this Chapter.

**(c1)** The provisions of G.S. 93A-1 and G.S. 93A-2 notwithstanding, the Commission may adopt rules to permit a real estate broker to pay a fee or other valuable consideration to a travel agent for the introduction or procurement of tenants or potential tenants in vacation rentals as defined in G.S. 42A-4. Rules adopted pursuant to this subsection may include a definition of the term 'travel agent', may regulate the conduct of permitted transations, and may limit the amount of the fee or the value of the consideration that may be paid to the travel agent. However, the Commission may not authorize a person or entity not licensed as a broker to negotiate any real estate transaction on behalf of another.

**(c2)** The Commission shall adopt a seal for its use, which shall bear thereon the words "North Carolina Real Estate Commission." Copies of all records and papers in the office of the Commission duly certified and authenticated by the seal of the Commission shall be received in evidence in all courts and with like effect as the originals.

**(d)** The Commission may employ an Executive Director and professional and clerical staff as may be necessary to carry out the provisions of this Chapter and to put into effect the rules and regulations that the Commission may promulgate. The Commission shall fix salaries and shall require employees to make good and sufficient surety bond for the faithful performance of their duties. The Commission shall reimburse its employees for travel on official business. Mileage expenses for transportation by privately owned automobile shall be reimbursed at the business standard mileage set by the Internal Revenue Service per mile of travel along with the actual tolls paid. Other travel expenses shall be reimbursed in accordance with G.S. 138-6. The Commission may, when it deems it necessary or convenient, delegate to the Executive Director, legal counsel for the Commission, or other Commission staff, professional or clerical, the Commission's authority and duties under this Chapter, but the Commission may not delegate its authority to make rules or its duty to act as a hearing panel in accordance with the provisions of G.S. 150B-40(b).

**(e)** The Commission shall be entitled to the services of the Attorney General of North Carolina, in connection with the affairs of the Commission or may on approval of the Attorney General, employ an attorney to assist or represent it in the enforcement of this Chapter, as to specific matters, but the fee paid for such service shall be approved by the Attorney General. The Commission may prefer a complaint for violation of this Chapter before any court of competent jurisdiction, and it may take the necessary legal steps through the proper legal offices of the State to enforce the provisions of this Chapter and collect the penalties provided therein.

**(f)** The Commission is authorized to acquire, hold, convey, rent, encumber, alienate, and otherwise deal with real property in the same manner as a private person or corporation, subject only to the approval of the Governor and Council of State. The rents, proceeds, and other revenues and benefits of the ownership of real property shall inure to the Commission. Collateral pledged by the Commission for any encumbrance of real property shall be limited to the assets, income, and revenues of the Commission. Leases, deeds, and other instruments relating to the Commission's interest in real property shall be valid when executed by the executive director of the Commission. The Commission may create and conduct education and information programs relating to the real estate business for the information, education, guidance and protection of the general public, licensees, and applicants for license. The education and information programs may include preparation, printing and distribution of publications and articles and the conduct of conferences, seminars, and lectures. The Commission may claim the copyright to written materials it creates and may charge fees for publications and programs.

### 93A-4. Applications for licenses; fees; qualifications; examinations; privilege licenses; renewal or reinstatement of license; power to enforce provisions.

**(a)** Any person, partnership, corporation, limited liability company, association, or other business entity hereafter desiring to enter into business of and obtain a license as a real estate broker shall make written application for such license to the Commission in the form and manner prescribed by the Commission. Each applicant for a license as a real estate broker shall be at least 18 years of age. Each applicant for a license as a real estate broker shall, within three years preceding the date the application is made, have satisfactorily completed, at a school approved by the Commission, an education program consisting of at least 75 hours of classroom instruction in subjects determined by the Commission, or shall possess real estate education or experience in real estate transactions which the Commission shall find equivalent to the education program. Each applicant for a license as a real estate broker shall be required to pay a fee, fixed by the Commission but not to exceed thirty dollars ($30.00).

**(a1)** Each person who is issued a real estate broker license on or after April 1, 2006, shall initially be classified as a provisional broker and shall, within three years following initial licensure, satisfactorily complete, at a school approved by the Commission, a postlicensing education program consisting of 90 hours of classroom instruction in subjects determined by the Commission or shall possess real estate education or experience in real estate transactions which the Commission shall find equivalent to the education program. The Commission may, by rule, establish a schedule for completion of the prescribed postlicensing education that requires provisional brokers to complete portions of the 90-hour postlicensing education program in less than three years, and provisional brokers must comply with this schedule in order to be entitled to actively engage in real estate brokerage. Upon completion of the postlicensing education program, the provisional status of the broker's license shall be terminated. When a provisional broker fails to complete all 90 hours of required postlicensing education within three years following initial licensure, the broker's license shall be cancelled, and the Commission may, in its discretion, require the person whose license was cancelled to satisfy the postlicensing education program and the requirements for original licensure prescribed in this Chapter as a condition of license reinstatement, including the examination requirements and the license reinstatement fee prescribed by subsection (c) of this section.

**(a2)** An approved school shall pay a fee of ten dollars ($10.00) per licensee to the Commission for each licensee completing a postlicensing education course conducted by the school, provided that these fees shall not be charged to a community college, junior college, college, or university located in this State and accredited by the Southern Association of Colleges and Schools.

**(b)** Except as otherwise provided in this Chapter, any person who submits an application to the Commission in proper manner for a license as real estate broker shall be required to take an examination. The examination may be administered orally, by computer, or by any other method the Commission deems appropriate. The Commission may require the applicant to pay the Commission or a provider contracted by the Commission the actual cost of the examination and its administration. The cost of the examination and its administration shall be in addition to any other fees the applicant is required to pay under subsection (a) of this section. The examination shall determine the applicant's qualifications with due regard to the paramount interests of the public as to the applicant's competency. A person who fails the license examination shall be entitled to know the result and score. A person who passes the exam shall be notified only that the person passed the examination. Whether a person passed or failed the examination shall be a matter of public record; however, the scores for license examinations shall not be considered public records. Nothing in this subsection shall limit the rights granted to any person under G.S. 93B-8.

An applicant for licensure under this Chapter shall satisfy the Commission that he or she possesses the competency, honesty, truthfulness, integrity, and general moral character necessary to protect the public interest and promote public confidence in the real estate brokerage business. The Commission may investigate the moral character of each applicant for licensure and require an applicant to provide the Commission with a criminal record report. All applicants shall obtain criminal record reports from one or more reporting services designated by the Commission to provide criminal record reports. Applicants are required to pay the designated reporting service for the cost of these reports. If the results of any required competency examination and investigation of the applicant's moral character shall be satisfactory to the Commission, then the Commission shall issue to the applicant a license, authorizing the applicant to act as a real estate broker in the State of North Carolina, upon the payment of privilege taxes now required by law or that may hereafter be required by law.

**(b1)** The Department of Justice may provide a criminal record check to the Commission for a person who has applied for a license through the Commission. The Commission shall provide to the Department of Justice, along with the request, the fingerprints of the applicant, any additional information required by the Department of Justice, and a form signed by the applicant consenting to the check of the criminal record and to the use of the fingerprints and other identifying information required by the State or national repositories. The applicant's fingerprints shall be forwarded to the State Bureau of Investigation for a search of the State's criminal history record file, and the State Bureau of Investigation shall forward a set of the fingerprints to the Federal Bureau of Investigation for a national criminal history check. The Commission shall keep all information pursuant to this subsection privileged, in accordance with applicable State law and federal guidelines, and the information shall be confidential and shall not be a public record under Chapter 132 of the General Statutes.

The Department of Justice may charge each applicant a fee for conducting the checks of criminal history records authorized by this subsection.

**(c)** All licenses issued by the Commission under the provisions of this Chapter shall expire on the 30th day of June following issuance or on any other date that the Commission may determine and shall become invalid after that date unless reinstated. A license may be renewed 45 days prior to the expiration date by filing an application with and paying to the Executive Director of the Commission the license renewal fee. The license renewal fee is thirty dollars ($30.00) unless the Commission sets the fee at a higher amount. The Commission may set the license renewal fee at an amount that does not exceed fifty dollars ($50.00). The license renewal fee may not increase by more than five dollars ($5.00) during a 12-month period. The Commission may adopt rules establishing a system of license renewal in which the licenses expire annually with varying expiration dates. These rules shall provide for prorating the annual fee to cover the initial renewal period so that no licensee shall be charged an amount greater than the annual fee for any 12-month period. The fee for reinstatement of an expired license shall be fifty-five dollars ($55.00). In the event a licensee fails to obtain a reinstatement of such license within six months after the expiration date thereof, the Commission may, in its discretion, consider such person as not having been previously licensed, and thereby subject to the provisions of this Chapter relating to the issuance of an original license, including the examination requirements set forth herein. Duplicate licenses may be issued by the Commission upon payment of a fee of five dollars ($5.00) by the licensee. Commission certification of a licensee's license history shall be made only after the payment of a fee of ten dollars ($10.00).

**(d)** The Commission is expressly vested with the power and authority to make and enforce any and all reasonable rules and regulations connected with license application, examination, renewal, and reinstatement as shall be deemed necessary to administer and enforce the provisions of this Chapter. The Commission is further authorized to adopt reasonable rules and regulations necessary for the approval of real estate schools, instructors, and textbooks and rules that prescribe specific requirements pertaining to instruction, administration, and content of required education courses and programs.

**(e)** Nothing contained in this Chapter shall be construed as giving any authority to the Commission nor any licensee of the Commission as authorizing any licensee to engage in the practice of law or to render any legal service as specifically set out in G.S. 84-2.1 or any other legal service not specifically referred to in said section.

**93A-4.1. Continuing education.**

**(a)** The Commission shall establish a program of continuing education for real estate brokers. An individual licensed as a real estate broker is required to complete continuing education requirements in an amount not to exceed eight classroom hours of instruction a year during any license renewal period in subjects and at times the Commission deems appropriate. Any licensee who fails to complete continuing education requirements pursuant to this section shall not actively engage in the business of real estate broker.

**(a1)** The Commission may, as part of the broker continuing education requirements, require real estate brokers-in-charge to complete during each annual license period a special continuing education course consisting of not more than four classroom hours of instruction in subjects prescribed by the Commission.

**(b)** The Commission shall establish procedures allowing for a deferral of continuing education for brokers while they are not actively engaged in real estate brokerage.

**(c)** The Commission may adopt any reasonable rules not inconsistent with this Chapter to give purpose and effect to the continuing education requirement, including rules that govern:

**(1)** The content and subject matter of continuing education courses.

**(2)** The curriculum of courses required.

**(3)** The criteria, standards, and procedures for the approval of courses, course sponsors, and course instructors.

**(4)** The methods of instruction.

**(5)** The computation of course credit.

**(6)** The ability to carry forward course credit from one year to another.

**(7)** The deferral of continuing education for brokers and salespersons not engaged in brokerage.

**(8)** The waiver of or variance from the continuing education requirement for hardship or other reasons.

**(9)** The procedures for compliance and sanctions for noncompliance.

**(d)** The Commission may establish a nonrefundable course application fee to be charged to a course sponsor for the review and approval of a proposed continuing education course. The fee shall not exceed one hundred twenty-five dollars ($125.00) per course. The Commission may charge the sponsor of an approved course a nonrefundable fee not to exceed seventy-five dollars ($75.00) for the annual renewal of course approval.

An approved course sponsor shall pay a fee of ten dollars ($10.00) per licensee to the Commission for each licensee completing an approved continuing education course conducted by the sponsor.

The Commission shall not charge a course application fee, a course renewal fee, or any other fee for a continuing education course sponsored by a community college, junior college, college, or university located in this State and accredited by the Southern Association of Colleges and Schools.

**(e)** The Commission may award continuing education credit for an unapproved course or related educational activity. The Commission may prescribe procedures for a licensee to submit information on an unapproved course or related educational activity for continuing education credit. The Commission may charge a fee to the licensee for each course or activity submitted. The fee shall not exceed fifty dollars ($50.00).

**93A-4.2. Broker-in-charge qualification.**

To be qualified to serve as a broker-in-charge of a real estate office, a real estate broker shall possess at least two years of full-time real estate brokerage experience or equivalent part-time real estate brokerage experience within the previous five years or real estate education or experience in real estate transactions that the Commission finds equivalent to such experience and shall complete, within a time prescribed by the Commission, a course of study prescribed by the Commission for brokers-in-charge not to exceed 12 classroom hours of instruction. A provisional broker may not be designated as a broker-in-charge.

**93A-4.3. Elimination of salesperson license; conversion of salesperson licenses to broker licenses.**

**(a)** Effective April 1, 2006, the Commission shall discontinue issuing real estate salesperson licenses. Also effective April 1, 2006, all salesperson licenses shall become broker licenses, and each person holding a broker license that was changed from salesperson to broker on that date shall be classified as a provisional broker as defined in G.S. 93A-2(a2).

**(b)** A provisional broker as contemplated in subsection (a) of this section who was issued a salesperson license prior to October 1, 2005, shall, not later than April 1, 2008, complete a broker transition course prescribed by the Commission, not to exceed 24 classroom hours of instruction, or shall demonstrate to the Commission that he or she possesses four years' full-time real estate brokerage experience or equivalent part-time real estate brokerage experience within the previous six years. If the provisional broker satisfies this requirement by April 1, 2008, the provisional status of his or her broker license will be terminated, and the broker will not be required to complete the 90-classroom-hour broker postlicensing education program prescribed by G.S. 93A-4(a1). If the provisional broker fails to satisfy this requirement by April 1, 2008, his or her license will be placed on inactive status, if not already on inactive status, and he or she must complete the 90-classroom-hour broker postlicensing education program prescribed by G.S. 93A-4(a1) in order to terminate the provisional status of the broker license and to be eligible to return his or her license to active status.

**(c)** An approved school or sponsor shall pay a fee of ten dollars ($10.00) per licensee to the Commission for each licensee completing a broker transition course conducted by the school or sponsor, provided that these fees shall not be charged to a community college, junior college, college, or university located in this State and accredited by the Southern Association of Colleges and Schools.

**(d)** A provisional broker as contemplated in subsection (a) of this section, who was issued a salesperson license between October 1, 2005, and March 31, 2006, shall,

15 punishments!

not later than April 1, 2009, satisfy the requirements of G.S. 93A-4(a1). Upon satisfaction of the requirements of G.S. 93A-4(a1), the provisional status of the broker's license will be terminated. If the provisional broker fails to satisfy the requirements of G.S. 93A-4(a1) by April 1, 2009, the broker's license shall be cancelled, and the person will be subject to the requirements for licensure reinstatement prescribed by G.S. 93A-4(a1).

**(e)** A broker who was issued a broker license prior to April 1, 2006, shall not be required to complete either the 90-classroom-hour broker postlicensing education program prescribed by G.S. 93A-4(a1) or the broker transition course prescribed by subsection (b) of this section.

**(f)** For the purpose of determining a licensee's status, rights, and obligations under this section, the Commission may treat a person who is issued a license on or after the October 1, 2005, or April 1, 2006, dates cited in subsections (a), (b), (d), or (e) of this section as though the person had been issued a license prior to those dates if the only reason the person's license was not issued prior to those dates was that the person's application was pending a determination by the Commission as to whether the applicant possessed the requisite moral character for licensure. If a license application is pending on April 1, 2006, for any reason other than a determination by the Commission as to the applicant's moral character for licensure, and if the applicant has not satisfied all education and examination requirements for licensing in effect on April 1, 2006, the applicant's application shall be cancelled and the application fee refunded.

**(g)** No applications for a real estate salesperson license shall be accepted by the Commission between September 1, 2005, and September 30, 2005.

### 93A-5. Register of applicants; roster of brokers; financial report to Secretary of State.

**(a)** The Executive Director of the Commission shall keep a register of all applicants for license, showing for each the date of application, name, place of residence, and whether the license was granted or refused. Said register shall be prima facie evidence of all matters recorded therein.

**(b)** The Executive Director of the Commission shall also keep a current roster showing the names and places of business of all licensed real estate brokers, which roster shall be kept on file in the office of the Commission and be open to public inspection.

**(c)** On or before the first day of September of each year, the Commission shall file with the Secretary of State a copy of the roster of real estate brokers holding certificates of license, and at the same time shall also file with the Secretary of State a report containing a complete statement of receipts and disbursements of the Commission for the preceding fiscal year ending June 30 attested by the affidavit of the Executive Director of the Commission.

### 93A-6. Disciplinary action by Commission.

**(a)** The Commission has the power to take disciplinary action. Upon its own initiative, or on the complaint of any person, the Commission may investigate the actions of any person or entity licensed under this Chapter, or any other person or entity who shall assume to act in such capacity. If the Commission finds probable cause that a licensee has violated any of the provisions of this Chapter, the Commission may hold a hearing on the allegations of misconduct.

The Commission has the power to suspend or revoke at any time a license issued under the provisions of this Chapter, or to reprimand or censure any licensee, if, following a hearing, the Commission adjudges the licensee to be guilty of:

**(1)** Making any willful or negligent misrepresentation or any willful or negligent omission of material fact.

**(2)** Making any false promises of a character likely to influence, persuade, or induce.

**(3)** Pursuing a course of misrepresentation or making of false promises through agents, advertising or otherwise.

**(4)** Acting for more than one party in a transaction without the knowledge of all parties for whom he or she acts.

**(5)** Accepting a commission or valuable consideration as a real estate salesperson for the performance of any of the acts specified in this Article or Article 4 of this Chapter, from any person except his or her broker-in-charge or licensed broker by whom he or she is employed.

**(6)** Representing or attempting to represent a real estate broker other than the broker by whom he or she is engaged or associated, without the express knowledge and consent of the broker with whom he or she is associated.

**(7)** Failing, within a reasonable time, to account for or to remit any moneys coming into his or her possession which belong to others.

**(8)** Being unworthy or incompetent to act as a real estate broker in a manner as to endanger the interest of the public.

**(9)** Paying a commission or valuable consideration to any person for acts or services performed in violation of this Chapter.

**(10)** Any other conduct which constitutes improper, fraudulent or dishonest dealing.

**(11)** Performing or undertaking to perform any legal service, as set forth in G.S. 84-2.1, or any other acts constituting the practice of law.

**(12)** Commingling the money or other property of his or her principals with his or her own or failure to maintain and deposit in a trust or escrow account in an insured bank or savings and loan association in North Carolina all money received by

*Commingling + Separate trust accounts

him or her as a real estate licensee acting in that capacity, or an escrow agent, or the custodian or manager of the funds of another person or entity which relate to or concern that person's or entity's interest or investment in real property, provided, these accounts shall not bear interest unless the principals authorize in writing the deposit be made in an interest bearing account and also provide for the disbursement of the interest accrued.

(13) Failing to deliver, within a reasonable time, a completed copy of any purchase agreement or offer to buy and sell real estate to the buyer and to the seller.

(14) Failing, at the time the transaction is consummated, to deliver to the seller in every real estate transaction, a complete detailed closing statement showing all of the receipts and disbursements handled by him or her for the seller or failing to deliver to the buyer a complete statement showing all money received in the transaction from the buyer and how and for what it was disbursed.

(15) Violating any rule or regulation promulgated by the Commission.

The Executive Director shall transmit a certified copy of all final orders of the Commission suspending or revoking licenses issued under this Chapter to the clerk of superior court of the county in which the licensee maintains his or her principal place of business. The clerk shall enter these orders upon the judgment docket of the county.

**(b)** Following a hearing, the Commission shall also have power to suspend or revoke any license issued under the provisions of this Chapter or to reprimand or censure any licensee when:

(1) The licensee has obtained a license by false or fraudulent representation;

(2) The licensee has been convicted or has entered a plea of guilty or no contest upon which final judgment is entered by a court of competent jurisdiction in this State, or any other state, of the criminal offenses of: embezzlement, obtaining money under false pretense, fraud, forgery, conspiracy to defraud, or any other offense involving moral turpitude which would reasonably affect the licensee's performance in the real estate business;

(3) The licensee has violated any of the provisions of G.S. 93A-6(a) when selling, leasing, or buying his or her own property;

(4) The broker's unlicensed employee, who is exempt from the provisions of this Chapter under G.S. 93A-2(c)(6), has committed, in the regular course of business, any act which, if committed by the broker, would constitute a violation of G.S. 93A-6(a) for which the broker could be disciplined; or

(5) The licensee, who is also a State-licensed or State-certified real estate appraiser pursuant to Chapter 93E of the General Statutes, has violated any provisions of Chapter 93E of the General Statutes and has been reprimanded or has had his or her appraiser license or certificate suspended or revoked by the Appraisal Board.

**(c)** The Commission may appear in its own name in superior court in actions for injunctive relief to prevent any person from violating the provisions of this Chapter or rules promulgated by the Commission. The superior court shall have the power to grant these injunctions even if criminal prosecution has been or may be instituted as a result of the violations, or whether the person is a licensee of the Commission.

**(d)** Each broker shall maintain complete records showing the deposit, maintenance, and withdrawal of money or other property owned by his or her principals or held in escrow or in trust for his or her principals. The Commission may inspect these records periodically, without prior notice and may also inspect these records whenever the Commission determines that they are pertinent to an investigation of any specific complaint against a licensee.

**(e)** When a person or entity licensed under this Chapter is accused of any act, omission, or misconduct which would subject the licensee to disciplinary action, the licensee, with the consent and approval of the Commission, may surrender his or her or its license and all the rights and privileges pertaining to it for a period of time established by the Commission. A person or entity who surrenders his or her or its license shall not thereafter be eligible for or submit any application for licensure as a real estate broker or salesperson during the period of license surrender.

**(f)** In any contested case in which the Commission takes disciplinary action authorized by any provision of this Chapter, the Commission may also impose reasonable conditions, restrictions, and limitations upon the license, registration, or approval issued to the disciplined person or entity. In any contested case concerning an application for licensure, time share project registration, or school, sponsor, instructor, or course approval, the Commission may impose reasonable conditions, restrictions, and limitations on any license, registration, or approval it may issue as a part of its final decision.

**93A-6.1. Commission may subpoena witnesses, records, documents, or other materials.**

**(a)** The Commission, Executive Director, or other representative designated by the Commission may issue a subpoena for the appearance of witnesses deemed necessary to testify concerning any matter to be heard before or investigated by the Commission. The Commission may issue a subpoena ordering any person in possession of records, documents, or other materials, however maintained, that concern any matter to be heard before or investigated by the Commission to produce the records, documents, or other materials for inspection or deliver the same into the custody of the Commission's authorized representatives. Upon written request, the Commission shall revoke a subpoena if it finds that the evidence, the production of which is required, does not relate to a matter in issue, or if the subpoena does not describe with sufficient particularity the evidence, the production of which is required, or if for any other reason in law the subpoena is invalid. If any person shall fail to fully and promptly comply with a subpoena issued under this section, the Commission may apply to any judge of the superior court resident in any county where the person to whom the subpoena is issued maintains a residence or place of business for an order compelling the person to show cause why he or she should not be held in contempt of the Commission and its processes. The court shall have the power to impose punishment for acts that would constitute direct or indirect contempt if the acts occurred in an action pending in superior court.

**(b)** The Commission shall be exempt from the requirements of Chapter 53B of the General Statutes with regard to subpoenas issued to compel the production of a licensee's trust account records held by any financial institution. Notwithstanding that exemption, the Commission shall serve, pursuant to G.S. 1A-1, Rule 4(j) of the N.C. Rules of Civil Procedure or by certified mail to the licensee's last known address, a copy of the subpoena and notice that the subpoena has been served upon the financial institution. Service of the subpoena and notice on the licensee shall be made within 10 days following service of the subpoena on the financial institution holding the trust account records.

**93A-7. Power of courts to revoke.**

Whenever any person, partnership, association or corporation claiming to have been injured or damaged by the gross negligence, incompetency, fraud, dishonesty or misconduct on the part of any licensee following the calling or engaging in the business herein described and shall file suit upon such claim against such licensee in any court of record in this State and shall recover judgment thereon, such court may as part of its judgment or decree in such case, if it deem it a proper case in which so to do, order a written copy of the transcript of record in said case to be forwarded by the clerk of court to the chairman of the said Commission with a recommendation that the licensee's certificate of license be revoked.

**93A-8. Penalty for violation of Chapter.**

Any person violating the provisions of this Chapter shall upon conviction thereof be deemed guilty of a Class 1 misdemeanor.

**93A-9. Licensing nonresidents.**

(a) An applicant from another state, which offers licensing privileges to residents of North Carolina, may be licensed by conforming to all the provisions of this Chapter and, in the discretion of the Commission, such other terms and conditions as are required of North Carolina residents applying for license in such other state; provided that the Commission may exempt from the examination prescribed in G.S. 93A-4 a broker or salesperson duly licensed in another state if a similar exemption is extended to licensed brokers from North Carolina. A license applicant who has been a resident of North Carolina for not more than 90 days may be considered by the Commission as a nonresident for the purposes of this subsection.

(b) The Commission may issue a limited broker's license to a person or an entity from another state or territory of the United States without regard to whether that state or territory offers similar licensing privileges to residents in North Carolina if the person or entity satisfies all of the following:

**(1)** Is of good moral character and licensed as a real estate broker or salesperson in good standing in another state or territory of the United States.

**(2)** Only engages in business as a real estate broker in North Carolina in transactions involving commercial real estate and while the person or entity is affiliated with a resident North Carolina real estate broker.

**(3)** Complies with the laws of this State regulating real estate brokers and rules adopted by the Commission.

The Commission may require an applicant for licensure under this subsection to pay a fee not to exceed three hundred dollars ($300.00). All licenses issued under this subsection shall expire on June 30 of each year following issuance or on a date that the Commission deems appropriate unless the license is renewed pursuant to the requirements of G.S. 93A-4. A person or entity licensed under this subsection may be disciplined by the Commission for violations of this Chapter as provided in G.S. 93A-6 and G.S. 93A-54.

Any person or entity licensed under this subsection shall be affiliated with a resident North Carolina real estate broker, and the resident North Carolina real estate broker shall actively and personally supervise the licensee in a manner that reasonably assures that the licensee complies with the requirements of this Chapter and rules adopted by the Commission. A person or entity licensed under this subsection shall not, however, be affiliated with a resident North Carolina real estate provisional broker. The Commission may exempt applicants for licensure under this subsection from examination and the other licensing requirements under

G.S. 93A-4. The Commission may adopt rules as it deems necessary to give effect to this subsection, including rules establishing: (i) qualifications for licensure; (ii) licensure and renewal procedures; (iii) requirements for continuing education; (iv) conduct of persons and entities licensed under this subsection and their affiliated resident real estate brokers; (v) a definition of commercial real estate; and (vi) any requirements or limitations on affiliation between resident real estate brokers and persons or entities seeking licensure under this subsection.

**93A-10. Nonresident licensees; filing of consent as to service of process and pleadings.**

Every nonresident applicant shall file an irrevocable consent that suits and actions may be commenced against such applicant in any of the courts of record of this State, by the service of any process or pleading authorized by the laws of this State in any county in which the plaintiff may reside, by serving the same on the Executive Director of the Commission, said consent stipulating and agreeing that such service of such process or pleadings on said Executive Director shall be taken and held in all courts to be valid and binding as if due service had been made personally upon the applicant in this State. This consent shall be duly acknowledged, and, if made by a corporation, shall be executed by an officer of the corporation. The signature of the officer on the consent to service instrument shall be sufficient to bind the corporation and no further authentication is necessary. An application from a corporation or other business entity shall be signed by an officer of the corporation or entity or by an individual designated by the Commission.

In all cases where process or pleadings shall be served, under the provisions of this Chapter, upon the Executive Director of the Commission, such process or pleadings shall be served in duplicate, one of which shall be filed in the office of the Commission and the other shall be forwarded immediately by the Executive Director of the Commission, by registered mail, to the last known business address of the nonresident licensee against which such process or pleadings are directed.

**93A-11. Reimbursement by real estate independent contractor of brokers' workers' compensation.**

**(a)** Notwithstanding the provisions of G.S. 97-21 or any other provision of law, a real estate broker may include in the governing contract with a real estate salesperson whose nonemployee status is recognized pursuant to section 3508 of the United States Internal Revenue Code, 26 U.S.C. § 3508, an agreement for the salesperson to reimburse the broker for the cost of covering that salesperson under the broker's workers' compensation coverage of the broker's business.

**(b)** Nothing in this section shall affect a requirement under any other law to provide workers' compensation coverage or in any manner exclude from coverage any person, firm, or corporation otherwise subject to the provisions of Article 1 of Chapter 97 of the General Statutes.

**93A-12. Disputed monies.**

**(a)** A real estate broker licensed under this Chapter may deposit with the clerk of court in accordance with this section monies, other than a residential security deposit, the ownership of which are in dispute and that the real estate broker received while acting in a fiduciary capacity.

**(b)** The disputed monies shall be deposited with the clerk of court in the county in which the property for which the disputed monies are being held is located. At the time of depositing the disputed monies, the real estate broker shall certify to the clerk of court that the persons who are claiming ownership of the disputed monies have been notified in accordance with subsection (c) of this section that the disputed monies are to be deposited with the clerk of court and that the persons may initiate a special proceeding with the clerk of court to recover the disputed monies.

**(c)** Notice to the persons who are claiming ownership to the disputed monies required under subsection (b) of this section shall be provided by delivering a copy of the notice to the person or by mailing it to the person by first-class mail, postpaid, properly addressed to the person at the person's last known address.

**(d)** A real estate broker shall not deposit disputed monies with the clerk of court until 90 days following notification of the persons claiming ownership of the disputed monies.

**(e)** Upon the filing of a special proceeding to recover the disputed monies, the clerk shall determine the rightful ownership of the monies and distribute the disputed monies accordingly. If no special proceeding is filed with the clerk of court within one year of the disputed monies being deposited with the clerk of court, the disputed monies shall be deemed unclaimed and shall be delivered by the clerk of court to the State Treasurer in accordance with the provisions of Article 4 of Chapter 116B of the General Statutes.

**Sections 93A-13 through 93A-15:** Reserved for future codification purposes.

## ARTICLE 2.
## REAL ESTATE RECOVERY FUND.

**93A-16. Real Estate Recovery Fund created; payment to fund; management.**

**(a)** There is hereby created a special fund to be known as the "Real Estate Recovery Fund" which shall be set aside and maintained by the North Carolina Real Estate Commission. Said fund shall be used in the manner provided under this Article for the payment of unsatisfied judgments where the aggrieved person has suffered a direct monetary loss by reason of certain acts committed by any real estate salesperson licensed before April 1, 2006, or by any real estate broker.

**(b)** On September 1, 1979, the Commission shall transfer the sum of one hundred thousand dollars ($100,000) from its expense reserve fund to the Real Estate Recovery Fund. Thereafter, the Commission may transfer to the Real Estate Recovery Fund additional sums of money from whatever funds the Commission may have, provided that, if on December 31 of any year the amount remaining in the fund is less than fifty thousand dollars ($50,000), the Commission may determine that each person or entity licensed under this Chapter, when renewing his or her or its license, shall pay in addition to his or her license renewal fee, a fee not to exceed ten dollars ($10.00) per broker and five dollars ($5.00) per salesperson as shall be determined by the Commission for the purpose of replenishing the fund.

**(c)** The Commission shall invest and reinvest the moneys in the Real Estate Recovery Fund in the same manner as provided by law for the investment of funds by the clerk of superior court. The proceeds from such investments shall be deposited to the credit of the fund.

**(d)** The Commission shall have the authority to adopt reasonable rules and procedures not inconsistent with the provisions of this Article, to provide for the orderly, fair and efficient administration and payment of monies held in the Real Estate Recovery Fund.

### 93A-17. Grounds for payment; notice and application to Commission.

**(a)** An aggrieved person who has suffered a direct monetary loss by reason of the conversion of trust funds by a real estate salesperson licensed before April 1, 2006, or by any licensed real estate broker shall be eligible to recover, subject to the limitations of this Article, the amount of trust funds converted and which is otherwise unrecoverable provided that:

- **(1)** The act or acts of conversion which form the basis of the claim for recovery occurred on or after September 1, 1979;
- **(2)** The aggrieved person has sued the real estate broker or salesperson in a court of competent jurisdiction and has filed with the Commission written notice of such lawsuit within 60 days after its commencement unless the claim against the Real Estate Recovery Fund is for an amount less than three thousand dollars ($3,000), excluding attorneys fees, in which case the notice may be filed within 60 days after the termination of all judicial proceedings including appeals;
- **(3)** The aggrieved person has obtained final judgment in a court of competent jurisdiction against the real estate broker or salesperson on grounds of conversion of trust funds arising out of a transaction which occurred when such broker or salesperson was licensed and acting in a capacity for which a license is required; and
- **(4)** Execution of the judgment has been attempted and has been returned unsatisfied in whole or in part.

Upon the termination of all judicial proceedings including appeals, and for a period of one year thereafter, a person eligible for recovery may file a verified application with the Commission for payment out of the Real Estate Recovery Fund of the amount remaining unpaid upon the judgment which represents the actual and direct loss sustained by reason of conversion of trust funds. A copy of the judgment and return of execution shall be attached to the application and filed with the Commission. The applicant shall serve upon the judgment debtor a copy of the application and shall file with the Commission an affidavit or certificate of such service.

**(b)** For the purposes of this Article, the term "trust funds" shall include all earnest money deposits, down payments, sales proceeds, tenant security deposits, undisbursed rents and other such monies which belong to another or others and are held by a real estate broker or salesperson acting in that capacity. Trust funds shall also include all time share purchase monies which are required to be held in trust by G.S. 93A-45(c) during the time they are, in fact, so held. Trust funds shall not include, however, any funds held by an independent escrow agent under G.S. 93A-42 or any funds which the court may find to be subject to an implied, constructive or resulting trust.

**(c)** For the purposes of this Article, the terms "licensee", "broker", and "salesperson" shall include only individual persons licensed under this Chapter as brokers or individual persons who were licensed under this Chapter as salespersons prior to April 1, 2006. The terms "licensee", "broker", and "salesperson" shall not include a time share developer, time share project, independent escrow agent, corporation or other entity licensed under this Chapter.

### 93A-18. Hearing; required showing.

Upon such application by an aggrieved person, the Commission shall conduct a hearing and the aggrieved person shall be required to show:

- **(1)** He or she is not a spouse of the judgment debtor or a person representing such spouse; and
- **(2)** He or she is making application not more than one year after termination of all judicial proceedings, including appeals, in connection with the judgment;
- **(3)** He or she has complied with all requirements of this Article;
- **(4)** He or she has obtained a judgment as described in G.S. 93A-17, stating the amount owing thereon at the date of application;

(5) He or she has made all reasonable searches and inquiries to ascertain whether the judgment debtor is possessed of real or personal property or other assets liable to be sold or applied in satisfaction of the judgment;

(6) That by such search he or she has discovered no real or personal property or other assets liable to be sold or applied, or that he or she has discovered certain of them, describing them, but that the amount so realized was insufficient to satisfy the judgment, stating the amount realized and the balance remaining due on the judgment after application of the amount realized; and

(7) He or she has diligently pursued his or her remedies including attempted execution on the judgment against all the judgment debtors which execution has been returned unsatisfied. In addition to that, he or she knows of no assets of the judgment debtor and that he or she has attempted collection from all other persons who may be liable to him or her in the transaction for which he or she seeks payment from the Real Estate Recovery Fund if there be any such other persons.

**93A-19. Response and defense by Commission and judgment debtor; proof of conversion.**

**(a)** Whenever the Commission proceeds upon an application as set forth in this Article, counsel for the Commission may defend such action on behalf of the fund and shall have recourse to all appropriate means of defense, including the examination of witnesses. The judgment debtor may defend such action on his or her own behalf and shall have recourse to all appropriate means of defense, including the examination of witnesses. Counsel for the Commission and the judgment debtor may file responses to the application, setting forth answers and defenses. Responses shall be filed with the Commission and copies shall be served upon every party by the filing party. If at any time it appears there are no triable issues of fact and the application for payment from the fund is without merit, the Commission shall dismiss the application. A motion to dismiss may be supported by affidavit of any person or persons having knowledge of the facts and may be made on the basis that the application or the judgment referred to therein do not form a basis for meritorious recovery within the purview of G.S. 93A-17, that the applicant has not complied with the provisions of this Article, or that the liability of the fund with regard to the particular licensee or transaction has been exhausted; provided, however, notice of such motion shall be given at least 10 days prior to the time fixed for hearing. If the applicant or judgment debtor fails to appear at the hearing after receiving notice of the hearing, the applicant or judgment debtor shall waive his or her rights unless the absence is excused by the Commission.

**(b)** Whenever the judgment obtained by an applicant is by default, stipulation, or consent, or whenever the action against the licensee was defended by a trustee in bankruptcy, the applicant, for purposes of this Article, shall have the burden of proving his or her cause of action for conversion of trust funds. Otherwise, the judgment shall create a rebuttable presumption of the conversion of trust funds. This presumption is a presumption affecting the burden of producing evidence.

**93A-20. Order directing payment out of fund; compromise of claims.**

Applications for payment from the Real Estate Recovery Fund shall be heard and decided by a majority of the members of the Commission. If, after a hearing, the Commission finds the claim should be paid from the fund, the Commission shall enter an order requiring payment from the fund of whatever sum the Commission shall find to be payable upon the claim in accordance with the limitations contained in this Article.

Subject to Commission approval, a claim based upon the application of an aggrieved person may be compromised; however, the Commission shall not be bound in any way by any compromise or stipulation of the judgment debtor. If a claim appears to be otherwise meritorious, the Commission may waive procedural defects in the application for payment.

**93A-21. Limitations; pro rata distribution; attorney fees.**

**(a)** Payments from the Real Estate Recovery Fund shall be subject to the following limitations:

**(1)** The right to recovery under this Article shall be forever barred unless application is made within one year after termination of all proceedings including appeals, in connection with the judgment;

**(2)** The fund shall not be liable for more than twenty-five thousand dollars ($25,000) per transaction regardless of the number of persons aggrieved or parcels of real estate involved in such transaction; and

**(3)** The liability of the fund shall not exceed in the aggregate twenty-five thousand dollars ($25,000) for any one licensee within a single calendar year, and in no event shall it exceed in the aggregate fifty thousand dollars ($50,000) for any one licensee.

**(4)** The fund shall not be liable for payment of any judgment awards of consequential damages, multiple or punitive damages, civil penalties, incidental damages, special damages, interest, costs of court or action or other similar awards.

**(b)** If the maximum liability of the fund is insufficient to pay in full the valid claims of all aggrieved persons whose claims relate to the same transaction or to the same licensee, the amount for which the fund is liable shall be distributed among the claimants in a ratio that their respective claims bear to the total of such valid claims or in such manner as the Commission, in its discretion, deems equitable. Upon petition of counsel for the Commission, the Commission may require all claimants and prospective claimants to be joined in one proceeding to the end that the respective rights of all such claimants to the Real Estate Recovery Fund may be equitably resolved. A person who files an application for payment after the maximum liability of the fund for the licensee or transaction has been exhausted shall not be entitled to payment and may not seek judicial review of the Commission's award of payment to any party except upon a showing that the Commission abused its discretion.

**(c)** In the event an aggrieved person is entitled to payment from the fund in an amount of one thousand five hundred dollars ($1,500) or less, the Commission may allow such person to recover from the fund reasonable attorney's fees incurred in effecting such recovery. Reimbursement for attorney's fees shall be limited to those fees incurred in effecting recovery from the fund and shall not include any fee incurred in obtaining judgment against the licensee.

**93A-22. Repayment to fund; automatic suspension of license.**
Should the Commission pay from the Real Estate Recovery Fund any amount in settlement of a claim or toward satisfaction of a judgment against a licensed real estate broker or salesperson, any license issued to the broker or salesperson shall be automatically suspended upon the effective date of the order authorizing payment from the fund. No such broker or salesperson shall be granted a reinstatement until the fund has been repaid in full, including interest at the legal rate as provided for in G.S. 24-1.

**93A-23. Subrogation of rights.**
When the Commission has paid from the Real Estate Recovery Fund any sum to the judgment creditor, the Commission shall be subrogated to all of the rights of the judgment creditor to the extent of the amount so paid and the judgment creditor shall assign all his or her right, title, and interest in the judgment to the extent of the amount so paid to the Commission and any amount and interest so recovered by the Commission on the judgment shall be deposited in the Real Estate Recovery Fund.

**93A-24. Waiver of rights.**
The failure of an aggrieved person to comply with this Article shall constitute a waiver of any rights hereunder.

**93A-25. Persons ineligible to recover from fund.**
No real estate broker or real estate salesperson who suffers the loss of any commission from any transaction in which he or she was acting in the capacity of a real estate broker or real estate salesperson shall be entitled to make application for payment from the Real Estate Recovery Fund for such loss.

**93A-26. Disciplinary action against licensee.**
Nothing contained in this Article shall limit the authority of the Commission to take disciplinary action against any licensee under this Chapter, nor shall the repayment in full of all obligations to the fund by any licensee nullify or modify the effect of any other disciplinary proceeding brought under this Chapter.

**Sections 93A-27 through 93A-31:** Reserved for future codification purposes.

## ARTICLE 3.
## PRIVATE REAL ESTATE SCHOOLS.

**Interested persons may obtain a copy of Article 3 by making written request to the North Carolina Real Estate Commission.**

## ARTICLE 4.
## TIME SHARES.

**93A-39. Title.**
This Article shall be known and may be cited as the "North Carolina Time Share Act."

**93A-40. Registration required of time share projects; real estate license required.**

**(a)** It shall be unlawful for any person in this State to engage or assume to engage in the business of a time share salesperson without first obtaining a real estate broker license issued by the North Carolina Real Estate Commission under the provisions of Article I of this Chapter, and it shall be unlawful for a time share developer to sell or offer to sell a time share located in this State without first obtaining a certificate of registration for the time share project to be offered for sale issued by the North Carolina Real Estate Commission under the provisions of this Article.

**(b)** A person responsible as general partner, corporate officer, joint venturer or sole proprietor who intentionally acts as a time share developer, allowing the offering of sale or the sale of time shares to a purchaser, without first obtaining registration of the time share project under this Article shall be guilty of a Class I felony.

**93A-41. Definitions.**
When used in this Article, unless the context otherwise requires, the term:

**(1)** "Commission" means the North Carolina Real Estate Commission;

**(2)** "Developer" means any person or entity which creates a time share or a time share project or program, purchases a time share for purpose of resale, or is engaged in the business of selling its own time shares and shall include any person or entity who controls, is controlled by, or is in common control with the developer which is engaged in creating or selling time shares for the developer, but a person who purchases a time share for his or her occupancy, use, and enjoyment shall not be deemed a developer;

**(3)** "Enrolled" means paid membership in exchange programs or membership in an exchange program evidenced by written acceptance or confirmation of membership;

**(4)** "Exchange company" means any person operating an exchange program;

**(5)** "Exchange program" means any opportunity or procedure for the assignment or exchange of time shares among purchasers in the same or other time share project;

**(5a)** "Independent escrow agent" means a licensed attorney located in this State or a financial institution located in this State;

**(6)** "Managing agent" means a person who undertakes the duties, responsibilities, and obligations of the management of a time share program;

**(7)** Person" means one or more natural persons, corporations, partnerships, associations, trusts, other entities, or any combination thereof;

**(7a)** "Project broker" means a natural person licensed as a real estate broker and designated by the developer to supervise brokers at the time share project;

**(8)** "Purchaser" means any person other than a developer or lender who owns or acquires an interest or proposes to acquire an interest in a time share;

**(9)** "Time share" means a right to occupy a unit or any of several units during five or more separated time periods over a period of at least five years, including renewal options, whether or not coupled with a freehold estate or an estate for years in a time share project or a specified portion thereof, including, but not limited to, a vacation license, prepaid hotel reservation, club membership, limited partnership, vacation bond, or a plan or system where the right to use is awarded or apportioned on the basis of points, vouchers, split, divided, or floating use;

**(9a)** "Time share instrument" means an instrument transferring a time share or any interest, legal or beneficial, in a time share to a purchaser, including a contract, installment contract, lease, deed, or other instrument;

**(10)** "Time share program" means any arrangement for time shares whereby real property has been made subject to a time share;

**(11)** "Time share project" means any real property that is subject to a time share program;

**(11a)** "Time share registrar" means a natural person who is designated by the developer to record or cause time share instruments and lien releases to be recorded and to fulfill the other duties imposed by this Article;

**(12)** "Time share salesperson" means a person who sells or offers to sell on behalf of a developer a time share to a purchaser; and

**(13)** "Time share unit" or "unit" means the real property or real property improvement in a project which is divided into time shares and designated for separate occupancy and use.

**93A-42. Time shares deemed real estate.**

**(a)** A time share is deemed to be an interest in real estate, and shall be governed by the law of this State relating to real estate.

**(b)** A purchaser of a time share may in accordance with G.S. 47-18 register the time share instrument by which he or she acquired his or her interest and upon such registration shall be entitled to the protection provided by Chapter 47 of the General Statutes for the recordation of other real property instruments. A time share instrument transferring or encumbering a time share shall not be rejected for recordation because of the nature or duration of that estate, provided all other requirements necessary to make an instrument recordable are complied with.

**(c)** The developer shall record or cause to be recorded a time share instrument:

**(1)** Not less than six days nor more than 45 days following the execution of the contract of sale by the purchaser; or

**(2)** Not later than 180 days following the execution of the contract of sale by the purchaser, provided that all payments made by the purchaser shall be placed by the developer with an independent escrow agent upon the expiration of the 10-day escrow period provided by G.S. 93A-45(c).

**(d)** The independent escrow agent provided by G.S. 93A-42(c)(2) shall deposit and maintain the purchaser's payments in an insured trust or escrow account in a bank or savings and loan association located in this State. The trust or escrow account may be interest-bearing and the interest earned shall belong to the developer, if agreed upon in writing by the purchaser; provided, however, if the time share instrument is not recorded within the time periods specified in this section, then the interest earned shall belong to the purchaser. The independent escrow agent shall return all payments to the purchaser at the expiration of 180 days following the execution of the contract of sale by the purchaser, unless prior to that time the time share instrument has been recorded. However, if prior to the expiration of 180 days following the execution of the contract of sale, the developer and the purchaser provide their written consent to the independent escrow agent, the developer's obligation to record the time share instrument and the escrow period may be extended for an additional period of 120 days. Upon recordation of the time share instrument, the independent escrow agent shall pay the purchaser's funds to the developer. Upon request by the Commission, the independent escrow agent shall promptly make available to the Commission inspection of records of money held by him or her.

**(e)** In no event shall the developer be required to record a time share instrument if the purchaser is in default of his or her obligations.

**(f)** Recordation under the provisions of this section of the time share instrument shall constitute delivery of that instrument from the developer to the purchaser.

**93A-43. Partition.**

When a time share is owned by two or more persons as tenants in common or as joint tenants either may seek a partition by sale of that interest but no purchaser of a time share may maintain an action for partition by sale or in kind of the unit in which such time share is held.

**93A-44. Public offering statement.**

Each developer shall fully and conspicuously disclose in a public offering statement:

**(1)** The total financial obligation of the purchaser, which shall include the initial purchase price and any additional charges to which the purchaser may be subject;

**(2)** Any person who has or may have the right to alter, amend or add to charges to which the purchaser may be subject and the terms and conditions under which such charges may be imposed;

**(3)** The nature and duration of each agreement between the developer and the person managing the time share program or its facilities;

**(4)** The date of availability of each amenity and facility of the time share program when they are not completed at the time of sale of a time share;

**(5)** The specific term of the time share;

**(6)** The purchaser's right to cancel within five days of execution of the contract and how that right may be exercised under G.S. 93A-45;

**(7)** A statement that under North Carolina law an instrument conveying a time share must be recorded in the Register of Deeds Office to protect that interest; and

**(8)** Any other information which the Commission may by rule require.

The public offering statement shall also contain a one page cover containing a summary of the text of the statement.

**93A-45. Purchaser's right to cancel; escrow; violation.**

**(a)** A developer shall, before transfer of a time share and no later than the date of any contract of sale, provide a prospective purchaser with a copy of a public offering statement containing the information required by G.S. 93A-44. The contract of sale is voidable by the purchaser for five days after the execution of the contract. The contract shall conspicuously disclose the purchaser's right to cancel under this subsection and how that right may be exercised. The purchaser may not waive this right of cancellation. Any oral or written declaration or instrument that purports to waive this right of cancellation is void.

**(b)** A purchaser may elect to cancel within the time period set out in subsection (a) by hand delivering or by mailing notice to the developer or the time share salesperson. Cancellation under this section is without penalty and upon receipt of the notice all payments made prior to cancellation must be refunded immediately.

**(c)** Any payments received by a time share developer or time share salesperson in connection with the sale of the time share shall be immediately deposited by such developer or salesperson in a trust or escrow account in an insured bank or savings and loan association in North Carolina and shall remain in such account for 10 days or cancellation by the purchaser, whichever occurs first. Payments held in such trust or escrow accounts shall be deemed to belong to the purchaser and not the developer. In lieu of such escrow requirements, the Commission shall have the authority to accept, in its discretion, alternative financial assurances adequate to protect the purchaser's interest during the contract cancellation period, including but not limited to a surety bond, corporate bond, cash deposit or irrevocable letter of credit in an amount equal to the escrow requirements.

**(d)** If a developer fails to provide a purchaser to whom a time share is transferred with the statement as required by subsection (a), the purchaser, in addition to any rights to damages or other relief, is entitled to receive from the developer an amount equal to ten percent (10%) of the sales price of the time share not to exceed three thousand dollars ($3,000). A receipt signed by the purchaser stating that he or she has received the statement required by subsection (a) is prima facie evidence of delivery of such statement.

**93A-46. Prizes.**

An advertisement of a time share which includes the offer of a prize or other inducement shall fully comply with the provisions of Chapter 75 of the General Statutes.

**93A-47. Time shares proxies.**

No proxy, power of attorney or similar device given by the purchaser of a time share regarding the management of the time share program or its facilities shall exceed one year in duration, but the same may be renewed from year to year.

**93A-48. Exchange programs.**

**(a)** If a purchaser is offered the opportunity to subscribe to any exchange program, the developer shall, except as provided in subsection (b), deliver to the purchaser, prior to the execution of (i) any contract between the purchaser and the exchange company, and (ii) the sales contract, at least the following information regarding such exchange program:

**(1)** The name and address of the exchange company;

**(2)** The names of all officers, directors, and shareholders owning five percent (5%) or more of the outstanding stock of the exchange company;

**(3)** Whether the exchange company or any of its officers or directors has any legal or beneficial interest in any developer or managing agent for any time share project participating in the exchange program and, if so, the name and location of the time share project and the nature of the interest;

**(4)** Unless the exchange company is also the developer a statement that the purchaser's contract with the exchange company is a contract separate and distinct from the sales contract;

**(5)** Whether the purchaser's participation in the exchange program is dependent upon the continued affiliation of the time share project with the exchange program;

**(6)** Whether the purchaser's membership or participation, or both, in the exchange program is voluntary or mandatory;

**(7)** A complete and accurate description of the terms and conditions of the purchaser's contractual relationship with the exchange company and the procedure by which changes thereto may be made;

**(8)** A complete and accurate description of the procedure to qualify for and effectuate exchanges;

**(9)** A complete and accurate description of all limitations, restrictions, or priorities employed in the operation of the exchange program, including, but not limited to, limitations on exchanges based on seasonality, unit size, or levels of occupancy, expressed in boldfaced type, and, in the event that such limitations, restrictions, or priorities are not uniformly applied by the exchange program, a clear description of the manner in which they are applied;

**(10)** Whether exchanges are arranged on a space available basis and whether any guarantees of fulfillment of specific requests for exchanges are made by the exchange program;

**(11)** Whether and under what circumstances an owner, in dealing with the exchange company, may lose the use and occupancy of his or her time share in any properly applied for exchange without his or her being provided with substitute accommodations by the exchange company;

**(12)** The expenses, fees or range of fees for participation by owners in the exchange program, a statement whether any such fees may be altered by the exchange company, and the circumstances under which alterations may be made;

**(13)** The name and address of the site of each time share project or other property which is participating in the exchange program;

**(14)** The number of units in each project or other property participating in the exchange program which are available for occupancy and which qualify for participation in the exchange program, expressed within the following numerical groupings, 1-5, 6-10, 11-20, 21-50 and 51, and over;

**(15)** The number of owners with respect to each time share project or other property which are eligible to participate in the exchange program expressed within the following numerical groupings, 1-100, 101-249, 250-499, 500-999, and 1,000 and over, and a statement of the criteria used to determine those owners who are currently eligible to participate in the exchange program;

**(16)** The disposition made by the exchange company of time shares deposited with the exchange program by owners eligible to participate in the exchange program and not used by the exchange company in effecting exchanges;

**(17)** The following information which, except as provided in subsection (b) below, shall be independently audited by a certified public accountant in accordance with the standards of the Accounting Standards Board of the American Institute of Certified Public Accountants and reported for each year no later than July 1, of the succeeding year:

**a.** The number of owners enrolled in the exchange program and such numbers shall disclose the relationship between the exchange company and owners as being either fee paying or gratuitous in nature;

**b.** The number of time share projects or other properties eligible to participate in the exchange program categorized by those having a contractual relationship between the developer or the association and the exchange company and those having solely a contractual relationship between the exchange company and owners directly;

**c.** The percentage of confirmed exchanges, which shall be the number of exchanges confirmed by the exchange company divided by the number of exchanges properly applied for, together with a complete and accurate statement of the criteria used to determine whether an exchange requested was properly applied for;

**d.** The number of time shares or other intervals for which the exchange company has an outstanding obligation to provide an exchange to an owner who relinquished a time share or interval during the year in exchange for a time share or interval in any future year; and

**e.** The number of exchanges confirmed by the exchange company during the year; and

**(18)** A statement in boldfaced type to the effect that the percentage described in subparagraph (17)c. of subsection (a) is a summary of the exchange requests entered with the exchange company in the period reported and that the percentage does not indicate a purchaser's/owner's probabilities of being confirmed to any specific choice or range of choices, since availability at individual locations may vary.

The purchaser shall certify in writing to the receipt of the information required by this subsection and any other information which the Commissioners may by rule require.

**(b)** The information required by subdivisions (a), (2), (3), (13), (14), (15), and (17) shall be accurate as of December 31 of the year preceding the year in which the information is delivered, except for information delivered within the first 180 days of any calendar year which shall be accurate as of December 31 of the year two years preceding the year in which the information is delivered to the purchaser. The remaining information required by subsection (a) shall be accurate as of a date which is no more than 30 days prior to the date on which the information is delivered to the purchaser.

**(c)** In the event an exchange company offers an exchange program directly to the purchaser or owner, the exchange company shall deliver to each purchaser or owner, concurrently with the offering and prior to the execution of any contract between the purchaser or owner and the exchange company the information set forth in subsection (a) above. The requirements of this paragraph shall not apply to any renewal of a contract between an owner and an exchange company.

**(d)** All promotional brochures, pamphlets, advertisements, or other materials disseminated by the exchange company to purchasers in this State which contain the percentage of confirmed exchanges described in (a)(17)c. must include the statement set forth in (a)(18).

### 93A-49. Service of process on exchange company.

Any exchange company offering an exchange program to a purchaser shall be deemed to have made an irrevocable appointment of the Commission to receive service of lawful process in any proceeding against the exchange company arising under this Article.

### 93A-50. Securities laws apply.

The North Carolina Securities Act, Chapter 78A, shall also apply, in addition to the laws relating to real estate, to time shares deemed to be investment contracts or to other securities offered with or incident to a time share; provided, in the event of such applicability of the North Carolina Securities Act, any offer or sale of time shares registered under this Article shall not be subject to the provisions of G.S. 78A-24 and any real estate broker registered under Article 1 of this Chapter shall not be subject to the provisions of G.S. 78A-36.

### 93A-51. Rule-making authority.

The Commission shall have the authority to adopt rules and regulations that are not inconsistent with the provisions of this Article and the General Statutes of North Carolina. The Commission may prescribe forms and procedures for submitting information to the Commission.

### 93A-52. Application for registration of time share project; denial of registration; renewal; reinstatement; and termination of developer's interest.

**(a)** Prior to the offering in this State of any time share located in this State, the developer of the time share project shall make written application to the Commission for the registration of the project. The application shall be accompanied by a fee in an amount fixed by the Commission but not to exceed one thousand five hundred dollars ($1,500), and shall include a description of the project, copies of proposed time share instruments including public offering statements, sale contracts, deeds, and other documents referred to therein, information pertaining to any marketing or managing entity to be employed by the developer for the sale of time shares in a time share project or the management of the project, information regarding any exchange program available to the purchaser, an irrevocable appointment of the Commission to receive service of any lawful process in any proceeding against the developer or the developer's time share salespersons arising under this Article, and such other information as the Commission may by rule require.

Upon receipt of a properly completed application and fee and upon a determination by the Commission that the sale and management of the time shares in the time share project will be directed and conducted by persons of good moral character, the Commission shall issue to the developer a certificate of registration authorizing the developer to offer time shares in the project for sale. The Commission shall within 15 days after receipt of an incomplete application, notify the developer by mail that the Commission has found specified deficiencies, and shall, within 45 days after the receipt of a properly completed application, either issue the certificate of registration or notify the developer by mail of any specific objections to the registration of the project. The certificate shall be prominently displayed in the office of the developer on the site of the project.

The developer shall promptly report to the Commission any and all changes in the information required to be submitted for the purpose of the registration. The developer shall also immediately furnish the Commission complete information regarding any change in its interest in a registered time share project. In the event a developer disposes of, or otherwise terminates its interest in a time share project, the developer shall certify to the Commission in writing that its interest in the time share project is terminated and shall return to the Commission for cancellation the certificate of registration.

**(b)** In the event the Commission finds that there is substantial reason to deny the application for registration as a time share project, the Commission shall notify the applicant that such application has been denied and shall afford the applicant an opportunity for a hearing before the Commission to show cause why the application should not be denied. In all proceedings to deny a certificate of registration, the provisions of Chapter 150B of the General Statutes shall be applicable.

**(c)** The acceptance by the Commission of an application for registration shall not constitute the approval of its contents or waive the authority of the Commission to take disciplinary action as provided by this Article.

**(d)** All certificates of registration granted and issued by the Commission under the provisions of this Article shall expire on the 30th day of June following issuance thereof, and shall become invalid after such date unless reinstated. Renewal of such certificate may be effected at any time during the month of June preceding the date of expiration of such registration upon proper application to the Commission and by the payment of a renewal fee fixed by the Commission but not to exceed one thousand five hundred dollars ($1,500) for each time share project. The developer shall, when making application for renewal, also provide a copy of the report required in G.S. 93A-48. Each certificate reinstated after the expiration date thereof shall be subject to a fee of fifty dollars ($50.00) in addition to the required renewal fee. In the event a time share developer fails to reinstate the registration within 12 months after the expiration date thereof, the Commission may, in its discretion, consider the time share project as not having been previously registered, and thereby subject to the provisions of this Article relating to the issuance of an original certificate. Duplicate certificates may be issued by the Commission upon payment of a fee of one dollar ($1.00) by the registrant developer. Except as prescribed by Commission rules, all fees paid pursuant to this Article shall be nonrefundable.

### 93A-53. Register of applicants; roster of registrants; registered projects; financial report to Secretary of State.

**(a)** The Executive Director of the Commission shall keep a register of all applicants for certificates of registration, showing for each the date of application, name, business address, and whether the certificate was granted or refused.

**(b)** The Executive Director of the Commission shall also keep a current roster showing the name and address of all time share projects registered with the Commission. The roster shall be kept on file in the office of the Commission and be open to public inspection.

**(c)** On or before the first day of September of each year, the Commission shall file with the Secretary of State a copy of the roster of time share projects registered with the Commission and a report containing a complete statement of income received by the Commission in connection with the registration of time share projects for the preceding fiscal year ending June 30th attested by the affidavit of the Executive Director of the Commission. The report shall be made a part of those annual reports required under the provisions of G.S. 93A- 5.

### 93A-54. Disciplinary action by Commission.

**(a)** The Commission shall have power to take disciplinary action. Upon its own motion, or on the verified complaint of any person, the Commission may investigate the actions of any time share salesperson, developer, or project broker of a time share project registered under this Article, or any other person or entity who shall assume to act in such capacity. If the Commission finds probable cause that a time share salesperson, developer, or project broker has violated any of the provisions of this Article, the Commission may hold a hearing on the allegations of misconduct.

The Commission shall have the power to suspend or revoke at any time a real estate license issued to a time share salesperson or project broker, or a certificate of registration of a time share project issued to a developer; or to reprimand or censure such salesperson, developer, or project broker; or to fine such developer in the amount of five hundred dollars ($500.00) for each violation of this Article, if, after a hearing, the Commission adjudges either the salesperson, developer, or project broker to be guilty of:

**(1)** Making any willful or negligent misrepresentation or any willful or negligent omission of material fact about any time share or time share project;

**(2)** Making any false promises of a character likely to influence, persuade, or induce;

**(3)** Pursuing a course of misrepresentation or making

of false promises through agents, salespersons, advertising or otherwise;

(4) Failing, within a reasonable time, to account for all money received from others in a time share transaction, and failing to remit such monies as may be required in G.S. 93A- 45 of this Article;

(5) Acting as a time share salesperson or time share developer in a manner as to endanger the interest of the public;

(6) Paying a commission, salary, or other valuable consideration to any person for acts or services performed in violation of this Article;

(7) Any other conduct which constitutes improper, fraudulent, or dishonest dealing;

(8) Performing or undertaking to perform any legal service as set forth in G.S. 84-2.1, or any other acts not specifically set forth in that section;

(9) Failing to deposit and maintain in a trust or escrow account in an insured bank or savings and loan association in North Carolina all money received from others in a time share transaction as may be required in G.S. 93A-45 of this Article or failing to place with an independent escrow agent the funds of a time share purchaser when required by G.S. 93A-42(c);

(10) Failing to deliver to a purchaser a public offering statement containing the information required by G.S. 93A-44 and any other disclosures that the Commission may by regulation require;

(11) Failing to comply with the provisions of Chapter 75 of the General Statutes in the advertising or promotion of time shares for sale, or failing to assure such compliance by persons engaged on behalf of a developer;

(12) Failing to comply with the provisions of G.S. 93A-48 in furnishing complete and accurate information to purchasers concerning any exchange program which may be offered to such purchaser;

(13) Making any false or fraudulent representation on an application for registration;

(14) Violating any rule or regulation promulgated by the Commission;

(15) Failing to record or cause to be recorded a time share instrument as required by G.S. 93A-42(c), or failing to provide a purchaser the protection against liens required by G.S. 93A-57(a); or

(16) Failing as a time share project broker to exercise reasonable and adequate supervision of the conduct of sales at his or her project or location by the brokers and salespersons under his or her control.

**(a1)** The clear proceeds of fines collected pursuant to subsection (a) of this section shall be remitted to the Civil Penalty and Forfeiture Fund in accordance with G.S. 115C-457.2.

**(b)** Following a hearing, the Commission shall also have power to suspend or revoke any certificate of registration issued under the provisions of this Article or to reprimand or censure any developer when the registrant has been convicted or has entered a plea of guilty or no contest upon which final judgment is entered by a court of competent jurisdiction in this State, or any other state, of the criminal offenses of: embezzlement, obtaining money under false pretense, fraud, forgery, conspiracy to defraud, or any other offense involving moral turpitude which would reasonably affect the developer's performance in the time share business.

**(c)** The Commission may appear in its own name in superior court in actions for injunctive relief to prevent any person or entity from violating the provisions of this Article or rules promulgated by the Commission. The superior court shall have the power to grant these injunctions even if criminal prosecution has been or may be instituted as a result of the violations, or regardless of whether the person or entity has been registered by the Commission.

**(d)** Each developer shall maintain or cause to be maintained complete records of every time share transaction including records pertaining to the deposit, maintenance, and withdrawal of money required to be held in a trust or escrow account, or as otherwise required by the Commission, under G.S. 93A-45 of this Article. The Commission may inspect these records periodically without prior notice and may also inspect these records whenever the Commission determines that they are pertinent to an investigation of any specific complaint against a registrant.

**(e)** When a licensee is accused of any act, omission, or misconduct under this Article which would subject the licensee to disciplinary action, the licensee may, with the consent and approval of the Commission, surrender his or her or its license and all the rights and privileges pertaining to it for a period of time to be established by the Commission. A licensee who surrenders his or her or its license shall not be eligible for, or submit any application for, licensure as a real estate broker or registration of a time share project during the period of license surrender. For the purposes of this section, the term licensee shall include a time share developer.

**93A-55. Private enforcement.**

The provisions of the Article shall not be construed to limit in any manner the right of a purchaser or other person injured by a violation of this Article to bring a private action.

**93A-56. Penalty for violation of Article.**

Except as provided in G.S. 93A-40(b) and G.S. 93A-58, any person violating the provisions of this Article shall be guilty of a Class 1 misdemeanor.

**93A-57. Release of liens.**

**(a)** Prior to any recordation of the instrument transferring a time share, the developer shall record and furnish notice to the purchaser of a release or subordination of all liens affecting that time share, or shall provide a surety bond or insurance against the lien from a company acceptable to the Commission as provided for liens on real estate in this State, or such underlying lien document shall contain a provision wherein the lienholder subordinates its rights to that of a time share purchaser who fully complies with all of the provisions and terms of the contract of sale.

**(b)** Unless a time share owner or a time share owner who is his or her predecessor in title agree otherwise with the lienor, if a lien other than a mortgage or deed of trust becomes effective against more than one time share in a time share project, any time share owner is entitled to a release of his or her time share from a lien upon payment of the amount of the lien attributable to his or her time share. The amount of the payment must be proportionate to the ratio that the time share owner's liability bears to the liabilities of all time share owners whose interests are subject to the lien. Upon receipt of payment, the lien holder shall promptly deliver to the time share owner a release of the lien covering that time share. After payment, the managing agent may not assess or have a lien against that time share for any portion of the expenses incurred in connection with that lien.

**93A-58. Registrar required; criminal penalties; project broker.**

**(a)** Every developer of a registered project shall, by affidavit filed with the Commission, designate a natural person to serve as time share registrar for its registered projects. The registrar shall be responsible for the recordation of time share instruments and the release of liens required by G.S. 93A-42(c) and G.S. 93A-57(a). A developer may, from time to time, change the designated time share registrar by proper filing with the Commission and by otherwise complying with this subsection. No sales or offers to sell shall be made until the registrar is designated for a time share project.

The registrar has the duty to ensure that the provisions of this Article are complied with in a time share project for which he or she is registrar. No registrar shall record a time share instrument except as provided by this Article.

**(b)** A time share registrar shall be guilty of a Class I felony if he or she knowingly or recklessly fails to record or cause to be recorded a time share instrument as required by this Article.

A person responsible as general partner, corporate officer, joint venturer or sole proprietor of the developer of a time share project shall be guilty of a Class I felony if he or she intentionally allows the offering for sale or the sale of time share to purchasers without first designating a time share registrar.

**(c)** The developer shall designate for each project and other locations where time shares are sold or offered for sale a project broker. The project broker shall act as supervising broker for all time share salespersons at the project or other location and shall directly, personally, and actively supervise all such persons at the project or other location in a manner to reasonably ensure that the sale of time shares will be conducted in accordance with the provisions of this Chapter.

**93A-59. Preservation of time share purchaser's claims and defenses.**

**(a)** For one year following the execution of an instrument of indebtedness for the purchase of a time share, the purchaser of a time share may assert against the seller, assignee of the seller, or other holder of the instrument of indebtedness, any claims or defenses available against the developer or the original seller, and the purchaser may not waive the right to assert these claims or defenses in connection with a time share purchase. Any recovery by the purchaser on a claim asserted against an assignee of the seller or other holder of the instrument of indebtedness shall not exceed the amount paid by the purchaser under the instrument. A holder shall be the person or entity with the rights of a holder as set forth in G.S. 25-3-301.

**(b)** Every instrument of indebtedness for the purchase of a time share shall set forth the following provision in a clear and conspicuous manner:

**"NOTICE: FOR A PERIOD OF ONE YEAR FOLLOWING THE EXECUTION OF THIS INSTRUMENT OF INDEBTEDNESS, ANY HOLDER OF THIS INSTRUMENT OF INDEBTEDNESS IS SUBJECT TO ALL CLAIMS AND DEFENSES WHICH THE PURCHASER COULD ASSERT AGAINST THE SELLER OF THE TIME SHARE. RECOVERY BY THE PURCHASER SHALL NOT EXCEED AMOUNTS PAID BY THE PURCHASER UNDER THIS INSTRUMENT."**

**Sections 93A-60 through 93A-69:** Reserved for future codification purposes.

## Article 5.
## Real Estate Appraisers.
## [Repealed]

# NORTH CAROLINA REAL ESTATE COMMISSION RULES

## CHAPTER 93A

**Statutory Authority: Sections 93A-3(c), 93A-4(d), 93A-33, and 93A-51 of the North Carolina Real Estate License Law; and the North Carolina Administrative Procedures Act.**

## NORTH CAROLINA ADMINISTRATIVE CODE
## TITLE 21
## OCCUPATIONAL LICENSING BOARDS
## CHAPTER 58
## REAL ESTATE COMMISSION

### Subchapter 58A
### Real Estate Brokers

#### Section A.0100 General Brokerage



#### Section A.0200 General Provisions (Repealed)

#### Section A.0300 Application for License



#### Section A.0400 Examinations



#### Section A.0500 Licensing



#### Section A.0600 Real Estate Commission Hearings



#### Section A.0700 Petitions for Rules

#### Section A.0800 Rule Making

#### Section A.0900 Declaratory Rulings

#### Section A.1000 Schools (Transferred to 21 NCAC 58C .0100)

#### Section A.1100 Real Estate Pre-Licensing Courses (Transferred/Repealed. Transfers are at 21 NCAC 58C .0300)

#### Section A.1200 Certification of Real Estate Instructors (Repealed)

#### Section A.1300 Private Real Estate Schools (Transferred/Repealed. Transfers are at 21 NCAC 58C .0200)

#### Section A.1400 Real Estate Recovery Fund

### Section A.1500 Forms (Repealed)

### Section A.1600 Discriminatory Practices Prohibited

A.1601 Fair Housing

### Section A.1700 Mandatory Continuing Education

Rule
A.1701 Purpose and Applicability
A.1702 Continuing Education Requirement
A.1703 Continuing Education for License Activation
A.1704 No Credit for Pre-Licensing Courses
A.1705 Attendance and Participation Requirements
A.1706 Repetition of Courses
A.1707 Elective Course Carry-Over Credit
A.1708 Equivalent Credit
A.1709 Extensions of Time to Complete
A.1710 Denial or Withdrawal of Continuing Education Credit
A.1711 Continuing Education Required of Nonresident Licensees

### Section A .1800 Limited Nonresident Commercial Licensing

Rule
A.1801 General Provisions
A.1802 Definitions
A.1803 Requirements for Licensure; Application and Fee
A.1804 Active Status
A.1805 Renewal
A.1806 Limitations
A.1807 Affiliation with Resident Broker
A.1808 Trust Monies
A.1809 Advertising
A.1810 Payment of Fees

### Section A .1900 Postlicensing Education

Rule
A.1901 Purpose and Applicability
A.1902 Postlicensing Education Requirement
A.1903 Extensions of Time to Complete Postlicensing Education
A.1904 Denial or Withdrawal of Postlicensing Education Credit

## Subchapter 58B Time Shares

### Section B.0100 Time Share Registration

Rule
B.0101 Application for Registration
B.0102 Registration Fee
B.0103 Renewal of Time Share Project Registration
B.0104 Amendments to Time Share Project Registration
B.0105 Notice of Termination

### Section B.0200 Public Offering Statement

Rule
B.0201 General Provisions
B.0202 Public Offering Statement Summary
B.0203 Receipt for Public Offering Statement

### Section B.0300 Cancellation

Rule
B.0301 Proof of Cancellation

### Section B.0400 Time Share Sales Operations

Rule
B.0401 Retention of Time Share Records
B.0402 Time Share Agency Agreements and Disclosure

### Section B.0500 Handling and Accounting of Funds

Rule
B.0501 Time Share Trust Funds

### Section B.0600 Project Broker

Rule
B.0601 Designation of Project Broker
B.0602 Duties of the Project Broker

### Section B.0700 Time Share Forms

Rule
B.0701 Forms for Time Share Projects

## Subchapter 58C Real Estate Prelicensing Education

## Subchapter 58D Real Estate Appraisers (Repealed)

## Subchapter 58E Real Estate Continuing Education

## Subchapter 58F Brokerage Transition Course

# CHAPTER 58
# REAL ESTATE COMMISSION
## Subchapter 58A
## Real Estate Brokers

### SECTION A.0100
### GENERAL BROKERAGE

#### A.0101 Proof of Licensure

(a) The annual license renewal pocket card issued by the Commission to each licensee shall be retained by the licensee as evidence of licensure. Each licensee shall carry his or her pocket card on his or her person at all times while engaging in real estate brokerage and shall produce the card as proof of licensure whenever requested.

(b) The qualifying broker of a firm shall retain the firm's renewal pocket card at the firm and shall produce it upon request as proof of firm licensure as required by Rule .0502.

(c) Every licensed real estate business entity or firm shall prominently display its license certificate or facsimile thereof in each office maintained by the entity or firm. A broker-in-charge shall also prominently display his or her license certificate in the office where he or she is broker-in-charge.

(d) Every licensee shall include his or her license number in agency contracts and disclosures as provided in Rule .0104 of this subchapter.

#### A.0102 Branch Office (Repealed)

#### A.0103 Licensee Name and Address

Upon initial licensure and at all times thereafter, every licensee shall assure that the Commission has on record the licensee's current personal name, firm name, trade name, residence address and firm address. Every licensee shall notify the Commission in writing of each change of personal name, firm name, trade name, residence address and firm address within ten days of said change. All addresses shall be sufficiently descriptive to enable the Commission to correspond with and locate the licensee.

#### A.0104 Agency Agreements and Disclosure

(a) Every agreement for brokerage services in a real estate transaction and every agreement for services connected with the management of a property owners association shall be in writing. Every agreement for brokerage services between a broker and an owner of the property to be the subject of a transaction must be in writing from the time of its formation. Every agreement for brokerage services between a broker and a buyer or tenant shall be express and shall be reduced to writing not later than the time one of the parties makes an offer to purchase, sell, rent, lease, or exchange real estate to another. However, every agreement between a broker and a buyer or tenant which seeks to bind the buyer or tenant for a period of time or to restrict the buyer's or tenant's right to work with other agents or without an agent shall be in writing from its formation. A broker shall not continue to represent a buyer or tenant without a written agreement when such agreement is required by this rule. Every written agreement for brokerage services of any kind in a real estate transaction shall provide for its existence for a definite period of time, shall include the licensee's license number, and shall provide for its termination without prior notice at the expiration of that period, except that an agency agreement between a landlord and broker to procure tenants or receive rents for the landlord's property may allow for automatic renewal so long as the landlord may terminate with notice at the end of any contract period and any subsequent renewals. For the purposes of this rule, an agreement between licensees to cooperate or share compensation shall not be considered an agreement for brokerage services and, except as required by Rule .1807 of this Subchapter, need not be memorialized in writing.

(b) Every listing agreement, written buyer agency agreement or other written agreement for brokerage services in a real estate transaction shall contain the following provision: The broker shall conduct all his brokerage activities in regard to this agreement without respect to the race, color, religion, sex, national origin, handicap or familial status of any party or prospective party to the agreement. The provision shall be set forth in a clear and conspicuous manner which shall distinguish it from other provisions of the agreement. For the purposes of this Rule, the term, familial status, shall be defined as it is in G.S. 41A-3(1b).

(c) In every real estate sales transaction, a broker shall, at first substantial contact directly with a prospective buyer or seller, provide the prospective buyer or seller with a copy of the publication "Working with Real Estate Agents," set forth the broker's name and license number thereon, review the publication with the buyer or seller, and determine whether the agent will act as the agent of the buyer or seller in the transaction. If the first substantial contact with a prospective buyer or seller occurs by telephone or other electronic means of communication where it is not practical to provide the "Working with Real Estate Agents" publication, the broker shall at the earliest opportunity thereafter, but in no event later than three days from the date of first substantial contact, mail or otherwise transmit a copy of the publication to the prospective buyer or seller and review it with him or her at the earliest practicable opportunity thereafter. For the purposes of this rule, "first substantial contact" shall include contacts between a broker and a consumer where the consumer or broker begins to act as though an agency relationship exists and the consumer begins to disclose to the broker personal or confidential information.

(d) A real estate broker representing one party in a transaction shall not undertake to represent another party in the transaction without the written authority of each party. Such written authority must be obtained upon the formation of the relationship except when a buyer or tenant is represented by a broker without a written agreement in conformity with the requirements of paragraph (a) of this rule. Under such circumstances, the written authority for dual agency must be reduced to writing not later than the time that one of the parties represented by the broker makes an offer to purchase, sell, rent, lease, or exchange real estate to another party.

(e) In every real estate sales transaction, a broker working directly with a prospective buyer as a seller's agent or subagent shall disclose in writing to the prospective buyer at the first substantial contact with the prospective buyer that the broker represents the interests of the seller. The written disclosure shall include the broker's license number. If the first substantial contact occurs by telephone or by means of other electronic communication where it is not practical to provide written disclosure, the broker shall immediately disclose by similar means whom he represents and shall immediately mail or otherwise transmit a copy of the written disclosure to the buyer. In no event shall the broker mail or transmit a copy of the written disclosure to the buyer later than three days from the date of first substantial contact with the buyer.

(f) In every real estate sales transaction, a broker representing a buyer shall, at the initial contact with the seller or seller's agent, disclose to the seller or seller's agent that the broker represents the buyer's interests. In addition, in every real estate sales transaction other than auctions, the broker shall, no later than the time of delivery of an offer to the seller or seller's agent, provide the seller or seller's agent with a written confirmation disclosing that he represents the interests of the buyer. The written confirmation may be made in the buyer's offer to purchase and shall include the broker's license number.

(g) The provisions of Paragraphs (c), (d) and (e) of this Rule shall not apply to real estate licensees representing sellers in auction sales transactions.

(h) A broker representing a buyer in an auction sale transaction shall, no later than the time of execution of a written agreement memorializing the buyer's contract to purchase, provide the seller or seller's agent with a written confirmation disclosing that he represents the interests of the buyer. The written confirmation may be made in the written agreement.

(i) A firm which represents more than one party in the same real estate transaction is a dual agent and, through the brokers associated with the firm, shall disclose its dual agency to the parties.

(j) When a firm represents both the buyer and seller in the same real estate sales transaction, the firm may, with the prior express approval of its buyer and seller clients, designate one or more individual brokers associated with the firm to represent only the interests of the seller and one or more other individual brokers associated with the firm to represent only the interests of the buyer in the transaction. The authority for designated agency must be reduced to writing not later than the time that the parties are required to reduce their dual agency agreement to writing in accordance with subsection (d) of this rule. An individual broker shall not be so designated and shall not undertake to represent only the interests of one party if the broker has actually received confidential information concerning the other party in connection with the transaction. A broker-in-charge shall not act as a designated broker for a party in a real estate sales transaction when a provisional broker under his or her supervision will act as a designated broker for another party with a competing interest.

(k) When a firm acting as a dual agent designates an individual broker to represent the seller, the broker so designated shall represent only the interest of the seller and shall not, without the seller's permission, disclose to the buyer or a broker designated to represent the buyer:

(1) that the seller may agree to a price, terms, or any conditions of sale other than those established by the seller;

(2) the seller's motivation for engaging in the transaction unless disclosure is otherwise required by statute or rule; and

(3) any information about the seller which the seller has identified as confidential unless disclosure of the information is otherwise required by statute or rule.

(l) When a firm acting as a dual agent designates an individual broker to represent the buyer, the broker so designated shall represent only the interest of the buyer and shall not, without the buyer's permission, disclose to the seller or a broker designated to represent the seller:

(1) that the buyer may agree to a price, terms, or any conditions of sale other than those offered by the buyer;

(2) the buyer's motivation for engaging in the transaction unless disclosure is otherwise required by statute or rule; and

(3) any information about the buyer which the buyer has identified as confidential unless disclosure of the information is otherwise required by statute or rule.

(m) A broker designated to represent a buyer or seller in accordance with Paragraph (j) of this Rule shall disclose the identity of all of the brokers so designated to both the buyer and the seller. The disclosure shall take place no later than the presentation of the first offer to purchase or sell.

(n) When an individual broker represents both the buyer and seller in the same real estate sales transaction pursuant to a written agreement authorizing dual agency, the parties may provide in the written agreement that the broker shall not disclose the following information about one party to the other without permission from the party about whom the information pertains:

(1) that a party may agree to a price, terms or any conditions of sale other than those offered;

(2) the motivation of a party for engaging in the transaction, unless disclosure is otherwise required by statute or rule; and

(3) any information about a party which that party has identified as confidential, unless disclosure is otherwise required by statute or rule.

### A.0105 Advertising

(a) Blind Ads. A licensee shall not advertise the sale, purchase, exchange, rent or lease of real estate, for another or others, in a manner indicating the offer to sell, purchase, exchange, rent, or lease is being made by the licensee's principal only. Every such advertisement shall conspicuously indicate that it is the advertisement of a broker or brokerage firm and shall not be confined to publication of only a post office box number, telephone number, or street address.

(b) Registration of Assumed Name. In the event that any licensee shall advertise in any manner using a firm name or an assumed name which does not set forth the surname of the licensee, the licensee shall first file the appropriate certificate with the office of the county register of deeds in compliance with G.S. 66-68 and notify the Commission in writing of the use of such a firm name or assumed name.

(c) Authority to Advertise.

(1) A provisional broker shall not advertise the sale, purchase, exchange, rent or lease of real estate for another or others without his or her broker's consent and without including in the advertisement the name of the broker or firm with whom the provisional broker is associated.

(2) A licensee shall not advertise or display a "for sale" or "for rent" sign on any real estate without the consent of the owner or his or her authorized agent.

(d) Business names. A licensee shall not include the name of a provisional broker or an unlicensed person in the name of a sole proprietorship, partnership or non-corporate business formed for the purpose of real estate brokerage.

(e) A person licensed as a limited nonresident commercial broker shall comply with the provisions of Rule .1809 of this Subchapter in connection with all advertising concerning or relating to his or her status as a North Carolina licensee.

### A.0106 Delivery of Instruments

(a) Except as provided in Paragraph (b) of this Rule, every broker shall immediately, but in no event later than five days from the date of execution, deliver to the parties thereto copies of any required written agency agreement, contract, offer, lease, or option affecting real property.

(b) A broker may be relieved of his or her duty under Paragraph (a) of this Rule to deliver copies of leases or rental agreements to the property owner, if the broker:

(1) obtains the express written authority of the property owner to enter into and retain copies of leases or rental agreements on behalf of the property owner;

(2) executes the lease or rental agreement on a pre-printed form, the material terms of which may not be changed by the broker without prior approval by the property owner except as may be required by law;

(3) promptly provides a copy of the lease or rental agreement to the property owner upon reasonable request; and

(4) delivers to the property owner within 45 days following the date of execution of the lease or rental agreement, an accounting which identifies the leased property and which sets forth the names of the tenants, the rental rates and rents collected.

### A.0107 Handling and Accounting of Funds

(a) Except as provided herein, all monies received by a licensee acting in his or her fiduciary capacity shall be deposited in a trust or escrow account maintained by a broker not later than three banking days following receipt of such monies except that earnest money deposits paid by means other than currency which are received on offers to purchase real estate and tenant security deposits paid by means other than currency which are received in connection with real estate leases shall be deposited in a trust or escrow account not later than three banking days following acceptance of such offer to purchase or lease; the date of acceptance of such offer to purchase or lease shall be set forth in the purchase or lease agreement. All monies received by a provisional broker shall be delivered immediately to the broker by whom he or she is employed, except that all monies received by nonresident commercial licensees shall be delivered as required by Rule .1808 of this Subchapter. A licensee may accept custody of a check or other negotiable instrument made payable to the seller of real property as option money only for the purpose of delivering the instrument to the optionor-seller. While the instrument is in the custody of the licensee, the licensee shall, according to the instructions of the buyer-optionee, either deliver it to the seller-optionor or return it to the buyer-optionee. The licensee shall safeguard the instrument and shall be responsible to the parties on the instrument for its prompt and safe delivery. In no event shall a licensee retain such an instrument for more than three business days after the acceptance of the option contract.

(b) In the event monies received by a licensee while acting in a fiduciary capacity are deposited in a trust or escrow account which bears interest, the licensee having custody over such monies shall first secure from all parties having an interest in the monies written authorization for the deposit of the monies in an interest-bearing account. Such authorization shall specify how and to whom the interest will be disbursed, and, if contained in an offer, contract, lease, or other transaction instrument, such authorization shall be set forth in a conspicuous manner which shall distinguish it from other provisions of the instrument.

(c) Closing statements shall be furnished to the buyer and the seller in the transaction not more than five days after closing.

(d) Trust or escrow accounts shall be so designated by the bank or savings and loan association in which the account is located, and all deposit tickets and checks drawn on said account as well as the monthly bank statement for the account shall bear the words "Trust Account" or "Escrow Account."

(e) A licensee shall maintain and retain records sufficient to identify the ownership of all funds belonging to others. Such records shall be sufficient to show proper deposit of such funds in a trust or escrow account and to verify the accuracy and proper use of the trust or escrow account. The required records shall include:

(1) bank statements.

(2) canceled checks which shall be referenced to the corresponding journal entry or check stub entries and to the corresponding sales transaction ledger sheets or for rental transactions, the corresponding property or owner ledger sheets. Checks shall conspicuously identify the payee and shall bear a notation identifying the purpose of the disbursement. When a check is used to disburse funds for more than one sales transaction, owner, or property, the check shall bear a notation identifying each sales transaction, owner, or property for which disbursement is made, including the amount disbursed for each, and the corresponding sales transaction, property, or owner ledger entries. When necessary, the check notation may refer to the required information recorded on a supplemental disbursement worksheet which shall be cross-referenced to the corresponding check. In lieu of retaining canceled checks, a licensee may retain digitally imaged copies of the canceled checks or substitute checks provided that such images are legible reproductions of the front and back of such instruments with no smaller images than 1.1875 x 3.0 inches and provided that the licensee's bank retains for a period of at least six years the original checks, "substitute checks" as described in 12 C.F.R. 229.51 or the capacity to provide substitute checks as described in 12 C.F.R. 229.51 and makes the original or substitute checks available to the licensee and the Commission upon request.

(3) deposit tickets. For a sales transaction, the deposit ticket shall identify the purpose and remitter of the funds deposited, the property, the parties involved, and a reference to the corresponding sales transaction ledger entry. For a rental transaction, the deposit ticket shall identify the purpose and remitter of the funds deposited, the tenant, and the corresponding property or owner ledger entry. For deposits of funds belonging to or collected on behalf of a property owner association, the deposit ticket shall identify the property or property interest for which the payment is made, the property or interest owner, the remitter, and the purpose of the payment. When a single deposit ticket is used to deposit funds collected for more than one sales transaction, property owner, or property, the required information shall be recorded on the ticket for each sales transaction, owner, or property, or the ticket may refer to the same information recorded on a supplemental deposit worksheet which shall be cross-referenced to the corresponding deposit ticket.

(4) a payment record sheet for each property or interest for which funds are collected and deposited into a property owner association trust account as required by Subsection (i) of this Rule. Payment record sheets shall identify the amount, date, remitter, and purpose of payments received, the amount and nature of the obligation for which payments are made, and the amount of any balance due or delinquency.

(5) a separate ledger sheet for each sales transaction and for each property or owner of property managed by the licensee identifying the property, the parties to the transaction, the amount, date, and purpose of the deposits and from whom received, the amount, date, check number, and purpose of disbursements and to whom paid, and the running balance of funds on deposit for the particular sales transaction or, in a rental transaction, the particular property or owner of property. Monies held as tenant security deposits in connection with rental transactions may be accounted for on a separate tenant security deposit ledger for each property or owner of property managed by the licensee. For each security deposit the tenant security deposit ledger shall identify the remitter, the date the deposit was paid, the amount, the tenant, landlord, and subject property. For each disbursement of tenant security deposit monies, the ledger shall identify the check number, amount, payee, date, and purpose of the disbursement. The ledger shall also show a running balance. When tenant security deposit monies are accounted for on a separate ledger as provided herein, deposit tickets, canceled checks and supplemental worksheets shall reference the corresponding tenant security deposit ledger entries when appropriate.

(6) a journal or check stubs identifying in chronological sequence each bank deposit and disbursement of monies to and from the trust or escrow account, including the amount and date of each deposit and a reference to the corresponding deposit ticket and any supplemental deposit worksheet, and the amount, date, check number, and purpose of disbursements and to whom paid. The journal or check stubs shall also show a running balance for all funds in the account.

(7) copies of contracts, leases and management agreements.

(8) closing statements and property management statements.

(9) covenants, bylaws, minutes, management agreements and periodic statements relating to the management of a property owner association.

(10) invoices, bills, and contracts paid from the trust account, and any documents not otherwise described herein necessary and sufficient to verify and explain record entries.

Records of all receipts and disbursements of trust or escrow monies shall be maintained in such a manner as to create an audit trail from deposit tickets and canceled checks to check stubs or journals and to the ledger sheets. Ledger sheets and journals or check stubs must be reconciled to the trust or escrow account bank statements on a monthly basis. To be sufficient, records of trust or escrow monies must include a worksheet for each such monthly reconciliation showing the ledger sheets, journals or check stubs, and bank statements to be in agreement and balance.

(f) All trust or escrow account records shall be made available for inspection by the Commission or its authorized representatives in accordance with Rule 58A .0108.

(g) In the event of a dispute between the seller and buyer or landlord and tenant over the return or forfeiture of any deposit other than a residential tenant security deposit held by a licensee, the licensee shall retain said deposit in a trust or escrow account until the licensee has obtained a written release from the parties consenting to its disposition or until disbursement is ordered by a court of competent jurisdiction. Alternatively, the licensee may deposit the disputed monies with the appropriate clerk of court in accordance with the provision of G.S. 93A-12. If it appears to a licensee holding a disputed deposit that a party has abandoned his or her claim, the licensee may disburse the money to the other claiming parties according to their written agreement provided that the licensee first makes a reasonable effort to notify the party who has apparently abandoned his or her claim and provides that party with an opportunity to renew his or her claim to the disputed funds. Tenant security deposit monies shall be disposed of in accordance with the requirements of N.C.G.S. 42-50 through 56 and N.C.G.S. 42A-18.

(h) A licensee may transfer earnest money deposits in his or her possession collected in connection with a sales transaction from his or her trust account to the closing attorney or other settlement agent not more than ten days prior to the anticipated settlement date. A licensee shall not disburse prior to settlement any earnest money in his or her possession for any other purpose without the written consent of the parties.

(i) The funds of a property owner association, when collected, maintained, disbursed or otherwise controlled by a licensee, are trust monies and shall be treated as such in the manner required by this Rule. Such funds must be deposited into and maintained in a trust or escrow account dedicated exclusively for funds belonging to a single property owners association and may not be commingled with funds belonging to other property owner associations or other persons or parties. A licensee who undertakes to act as manager of a property owner association or as the custodian of funds belonging to a property owner association shall provide the association with periodic statements which report the balance of association funds in the licensee's possession or control and which account for the funds the licensee has received and disbursed on behalf of the association. Such statements must be made in accordance with the licensee's agreement with the association, but in no event shall the statements be made less frequently than every 90 days.

(j) Every licensee shall safeguard the money or property of others coming into his or her possession in a manner consistent with the requirements of the Real Estate License Law and the rules adopted by the Commission. A licensee shall not convert the money or property of others to his or her own use, apply such money or property to a purpose other than that for which it was paid or entrusted to him or her, or permit or assist any other person in the conversion or misapplication of such money or property.

(k) In addition to the records required by paragraph (e) of this rule, a licensee acting as agent for the landlord of a residential property used for vacation rentals shall create and maintain a subsidiary ledger sheet for each property or owner of such properties onto which all funds collected and disbursed are identified in categories by purpose. On a monthly basis, the licensee shall reconcile the subsidiary ledger sheets to the corresponding property or property owner ledger sheet.

(l) In lieu of maintaining a subsidiary ledger sheet, the licensee may maintain an accounts payable ledger sheet for each owner or property and each vendor to whom trust monies are due for monies collected on behalf of the owner or property identifying the date of receipt of the trust monies, from whom the monies were received, rental dates, and the corresponding property or owner ledger sheet entry including the amount to be disbursed for each and the purpose of the disbursement. The licensee may also maintain an accounts payable ledger sheet in the format described in paragraph (k) above for vacation rental tenant security deposit monies and vacation rental advance payments.

### A.0108 Retention of Records

Licensees shall retain records of all sales, rental, and other transactions conducted in such capacity, whether the transaction is pending, completed or terminated prior to its successful conclusion. The licensee shall retain such records for three years after all funds held by the licensee in connection with the transaction have been disbursed to the proper party or parties or until the successful or unsuccessful conclusion of the transaction, whichever occurs later. Such records shall include contracts of sale, written leases, agency contracts, options, offers to purchase, trust or escrow records, earnest money receipts, disclosure documents, closing statements, brokerage cooperation agreements, declarations of affiliation, and any other records pertaining to real estate transactions. All such records shall be made available for inspection and reproduction by the Commission or its authorized representatives without prior notice.

### A.0109 Brokerage Fees and Compensation

(a) A licensee shall not receive, either directly or indirectly, any commission, rebate or other valuable consideration of more than nominal value from a vendor or a supplier of goods and services for an expenditure made on behalf of the licensee's principal in a real estate transaction without the written consent of the licensee's principal.

(b) A licensee shall not receive, either directly or indirectly, any commission, rebate or other valuable consideration of more than nominal value for services which the licensee recommends, procures, or arranges relating to a real estate transaction for any party, without full disclosure to such party; provided, however, that nothing in this Rule shall be construed to permit a licensee to accept any fee, kickback or other valuable consideration that is prohibited by the Real Estate Settlement Procedures Act of 1974 (12 USC 2601 et. seq.) or any rules and regulations promulgated by the United States Department of Housing and Urban Development pursuant to such Act.

(c) The Commission shall not act as a board of arbitration and shall not compel parties to settle disputes concerning such matters as the rate of commissions, the division of commissions, pay of brokers, and similar matters.

(d) Except as provided in (e) of this rule, a licensee shall not undertake in any manner, any arrangement, contract, plan or other course of conduct, to compensate or share compensation with unlicensed persons or entities for any acts performed in North Carolina for which licensure by the Commission is required.

(e) A broker may pay or promise to pay consideration to a travel agent in return for procuring a tenant for a vacation rental as defined by the Vacation Rental Act if:

(1) the travel agent only introduces the tenant to the broker, but does not otherwise engage in any activity which would require a real estate license;

(2) the introduction by the travel agent is made in the regular course of the travel agent's business; and

(3) the travel agent has not solicited, handled or received any monies in connection with the vacation rental.

For the purpose of this rule, a travel agent is any person or entity who is primarily engaged in the business of acting as an intermediary between persons who purchase air, land, and ocean travel services and the providers of such services. A travel agent is also any other person or entity who is permitted to handle and sell tickets for air travel by the Airlines Reporting Corporation (ARC). Payments authorized hereunder shall be made only after the conclusion of the vacation rental tenancy. Prior to the creation of a binding vacation rental agreement, the broker shall provide a tenant introduced by a travel agent a written statement advising him or her to rely only upon the agreement and the broker's representations about the transaction. The broker shall keep for a period of three years records of a payment made to a travel agent including records identifying the tenant, the travel agent and their addresses, the property and dates of the tenancy, and the amount paid.

### A.0110 Broker-in-Charge

(a) Every real estate firm shall designate a broker to serve as the broker-in-charge at its principal office and a broker to serve as broker-in-charge at any branch office. No broker shall be broker-in-charge of more than one office at a time. If a firm shares office space with one or more other firms, one broker may serve as broker-in-charge of each firm at that location. No office or branch office of a firm shall have more than one designated broker-in-charge. A broker who is a sole proprietor shall designate himself or herself as a broker-in-charge if the broker engages in any transaction where the broker is required to deposit and maintain monies belonging to others in a trust account, engages in advertising or promoting his or her services as a broker in any manner, or has one or more other brokers affiliated with him or her in the real estate business. Each broker-in-charge shall declare in writing his or her status as broker-in-charge to the Commission on a form prescribed by the Commission within 10 days following the broker's designation as broker-in-charge. The broker-in-charge shall assume the responsibility at his or her office for:

(1) the retention and display of current license renewal pocket cards by all brokers employed at the office for which he or she is broker-in-charge; the proper display of licenses at such office in accordance with Rule .0101 of this Section; and assuring that each licensee employed at the office has complied with Rules .0503, .0504 and .0506 of this Subchapter;

(2) the proper notification to the Commission of any change of business address or trade name of the firm and the registration of any assumed business name adopted by the firm for its use;

(3) the proper conduct of advertising by or in the name of the firm at such office;

(4) the proper maintenance at such office of the trust or escrow account of the firm and the records pertaining thereto;

(5) the proper retention and maintenance of records relating to transactions conducted by or on behalf of the firm at such office, including those required to be retained pursuant to Rule .0108 of this Section;

(6) the proper supervision of provisional brokers associated with or engaged on behalf of the firm at such office in accordance with the requirements of Rule .0506 of this Subchapter;

(7) the proper supervision of all licensees employed at the office for which he or she is broker-in-charge with respect to adherence to agency agreement and disclosure requirements.

(b) When used in this Rule, the term:

(1) "Branch Office" means any office in addition to the principal office of a broker which is operated in connection with the broker's real estate business; and

(2) "Office" means any place of business where acts are performed for which a real estate license is required.

(c) To qualify to serve as a broker-in-charge, a broker shall not be a provisional broker and shall:

(1) possess at least two years of full-time real estate brokerage experience or equivalent part-time real estate brokerage experience within the previous five

years or real estate education or experience in real estate transactions that the Commission finds equivalent to such experience; and

(2) complete the Commission's 12 classroom hour broker-in-charge course either within three years prior to designation as a broker-in-charge or within 120 days following designation as a broker-in-charge.

A broker-in-charge shall certify his or her experience qualifications in the written broker-in-charge declaration he or she submits to the Commission and shall provide to the Commission upon request evidence that he or she possesses the required experience. Status as a broker-in-charge shall be immediately terminated if a broker-in-charge fails to complete the broker-in-charge course during the required time period or if the Commission finds the broker-in-charge does not possess the required experience. A broker-in-charge, upon written request of the Commission or a broker who has been affiliated with the broker-in-charge within the previous five years, shall provide the Commission or broker, on a form prescribed by the Commission, an accurate written statement regarding the broker's work at the office of the broker-in-charge, including the dates of affiliation, average number of hours worked per week, and the number and type of properties listed, sold, bought, leased, or rented for others by the broker during his or her affiliation with the broker-in-charge.

(d) A broker who was the broker-in-charge of a real estate office on April 1, 2006, whose broker-in-charge declaration was received by the Commission prior to that date, and who has completed the Commission's broker-in-charge course within five years prior to April 1, 2006 or within 120 days following designation as a broker-in-charge, may continue to serve as a broker-in-charge thereafter until his or her status is terminated as provided in paragraph (e) of this Rule.

(e) A broker's status as a broker-in-charge shall be terminated upon the occurrence of any of the following events:

(1) The broker's license expires or the broker's right to engage in real estate brokerage is suspended, revoked or surrendered;

(2) the broker's license is made inactive for any reason, including failure to satisfy the continuing education requirements described in Rule .1702 of this Subchapter or paragraph (f) of this Rule;

(3) the license of the broker's firm expires or the firm's right to engage in real estate brokerage is suspended, revoked, or surrendered;

(4) the broker's firm is dissolved or otherwise ceases to be lawfully entitled to engage in business in North Carolina; or

(5) the broker ceases to act as the broker-in-charge of the office for which he or she was designated as broker-in-charge.

When a broker's status as a broker-in-charge is terminated and the broker subsequently seeks to again serve as broker-in-charge of the same or a different office, the broker must fully satisfy all the current broker-in-charge experience and education qualification requirements stated in this Rule, and a broker-in-charge course taken by such broker prior to April 1, 2006 shall not be recognized toward the current education requirement. However, when a broker terminates his or her broker-in-charge status with one office and contemporaneously declares himself or herself broker-in-charge of a different office with the same or a different firm, this change shall be considered a transfer rather than a termination and the broker shall not be required to satisfy the current broker-in-charge experience and education qualification requirements.

(f) To continue to serve as a broker-in-charge, a broker shall complete during each license period a special four classroom hour continuing education course prescribed by the Commission for brokers-in-charge. This course must first be taken during the first full license period following designation as a broker-in-charge and must subsequently be taken each license period. The course shall satisfy the broker's general continuing education elective course requirement, but the broker must continue to take the continuing education update course each license period. When a broker-in-charge fails to take the special continuing education course for brokers-in-charge during any license period, his or her broker-in-charge status will be terminated at the end of that license period.

(g) Each broker-in-charge shall notify the Commission in writing of any change in his or her status as broker-in-charge within 10 days following the change.

(h) A licensed real estate firm shall not be required to designate a broker-in-charge if it:

(1) has been organized for the sole purpose of receiving compensation for brokerage services furnished by its qualifying broker through another firm or broker;

(2) is designated a Subchapter S corporation by the United States Internal Revenue Service;

(3) has no branch office; and

(4) has no person associated with it other than its qualifying broker.

(i) A broker-in-charge residing outside of North Carolina who is the broker-in-charge of a principal or branch office not located in North Carolina shall not be required to complete the broker-in-charge course or the special continuing education course prescribed for brokers-in-charge under paragraph (f) of this Rule..

(j) A nonresident commercial real estate broker licensed under the provisions of Section .1800 of this Subchapter shall not act as or serve in the capacity of a broker-in-charge of a firm or office in North Carolina.

### A.0111 Drafting Legal Instruments

(a) A broker acting as an agent in a real estate transaction shall not draft offers, sales contracts, options, leases, promissory notes, deeds, deeds of trust or other legal instruments by which the rights of others are secured; however, a broker may complete preprinted offer, option contract, sales contract and lease forms in real estate transactions when authorized or directed to do so by the parties.

(b) A broker may use electronic, computer, or word processing equipment to store preprinted offer and sales contract forms which comply with Rule .0112, as well as preprinted option and lease forms, and may use such equipment to complete and print offer, contract and lease documents. Provided, however, a broker may not alter the form before it is presented to the parties. If the parties propose to delete or change any word or provision in the form, the form must be marked to indicate the change or deletion made. The language of the form shall not be modified, rewritten, or changed by the broker or their clerical employees unless directed to do so by the parties.

(c) Nothing contained in this rule shall be construed to prohibit a broker from making written notes, memoranda or correspondence recording the negotiations of the parties to a real estate transaction when such notes, memoranda or correspondence do not themselves constitute binding agreements or other legal instruments.

### A.0112 Offers and Sales Contracts

(a) A broker acting as an agent in a real estate transaction shall not use a preprinted offer or sales contract form unless the form describes or specifically requires the entry of the following information:

(1) the names of the buyer and seller;

(2) a legal description of the real property sufficient to identify and distinguish it from all other property;

(3) an itemization of any personal property to be included in the transaction;

(4) the purchase price and manner of payment;

(5) any portion of the purchase price that is to be paid by a promissory note, including the amount, interest rate, payment terms, whether or not the note is to be secured, and other material terms;

(6) any portion of the purchase price that is to be paid by the assumption of an existing loan, including the amount of such loan, costs to be paid by the buyer or seller, the interest rate and number of discount points and a condition that the buyer must be able to qualify for the assumption of the loan and must make every reasonable effort to quality for the assumption of the loan;

(7) the amount of earnest money, if any, the method of payment, the name of the broker or firm that will serve as escrow agent, an acknowledgment of earnest money receipt by the escrow agent, and the criteria for determining disposition of the earnest money, including disputed earnest money, consistent with Commission Rule .0107 of this Subchapter;

(8) any loan that must be obtained by the buyer as a condition of the contract, including the amount and type of loan, interest rate and number of discount points, loan term, loan commitment date, and who shall pay loan closing costs; and a condition that the buyer shall make every reasonable effort to obtain the loan;

(9) a general statement of the buyer's intended use of the property and a condition that such use must not be prohibited by private restriction or governmental regulation;

(10) the amount and purpose of any special assessment to which the property is subject and the responsibility of the parties for any unpaid charges;

(11) the date for closing and transfer of possession;

(12) the signatures of the buyer and seller;

(13) the date of offer and acceptance;

(14) a provision that title to the property must be delivered at closing by general warranty deed and must be fee simple marketable title, free of all encumbrances except ad valorem taxes for the current year, utility easements, and any other encumbrances specifically approved by the buyer, or a provision otherwise describing the estate to be conveyed, and encumbrances, and the form of conveyance;

(15) the items to be prorated or adjusted at closing;

(16) who shall pay closing expenses;

(17) the buyer's right to inspect the property prior to closing and who shall pay for repairs and improvements, if any;

(18) a provision that the property shall at closing be in substantially the same condition as on the date of the offer (reasonable wear and tear excepted), or a descdription of the required property condition at closing: and

(19) a provision setting forth the identity of each real estate agent and firm involved in the transaction and disclosing the party each agent and firm represents.

The provisions of this rule shall apply only to preprinted offer and sales contract forms which a broker acting as an agent in a real estate transaction proposes for use by the buyer and seller. Nothing contained in this Rule shall be construed to prohibit the buyer and seller in a real estate transaction from altering, amending or deleting any provision in a form offer to purchase or contract; nor shall this Rule be construed to limit the rights of the buyer and seller to draft their own offers or contracts or to have the same drafted by an attorney at law.

(b) A broker acting as an agent in a real estate transaction shall not use a preprinted offer or sales contract form containing the provisions or terms listed in Subparagraphs (b)(1) and (2) of this Rule. A broker or anyone acting for or at the direction of the broker shall not insert or cause such provisions or terms to be inserted into any such preprinted form, even at the direction of the parties or their attorneys:

(1) any provision concerning the payment of a commission or compensation, including the forfeiture of earnest money, to any broker or firm; or

(2) any provision that attempts to disclaim the liability of a broker for his or her representations in connection with the transaction.

# STATE OF NORTH CAROLINA
# RESIDENTIAL PROPERTY DISCLOSURE STATEMENT

## INSTRUCTIONS TO PROPERTY OWNERS

1. G.S. 47E requires owners of residential real estate (single-family homes and buildings with up to four dwelling units) to furnish purchasers a property disclosure statement. This form is the only one approved for this purpose. A disclosure statement must be furnished in connection with the sale, exchange, option and sale under a lease with option to purchase (unless the tenant is already occupying or intends to occupy the dwelling). A disclosure statement is not required for some transactions, including the first sale of a dwelling which has never been inhabited and transactions of residential property made pursuant to a lease with option to purchase where the lessee occupies or intends to occupy the dwelling. For a complete list of exemptions, see G.S. 47E-2.
2. You must check one of the boxes for each of the 20 questions on the reverse side of this form.
   a. If you check "Yes" for any question, you must describe the problem or attach a report from an engineer, contractor, pest control operator or other expert or public agency describing it. If you attach a report, you will not be liable for any inaccurate or incomplete information contained in it so long as you were not grossly negligent in obtaining or transmitting the information.
   b. If you check "No", you are stating that you have no actual knowledge of any problem. If you check "No" and you know there is a problem, you may be liable for making an intentional misstatement.
   c. If you check "No Representation", you have no duty to disclose the conditions or characteristics of the property, even if you should have known of them.
   * If you check "Yes" or "No" and something happens to the property to make your Statement incorrect or inaccurate (for example, the roof begins to leak), you must promptly give the purchaser a corrected Statement or correct the problem.
3. If you are assisted in the sale of your property by a licensed real estate broker, you are still responsible for completing and delivering the Statement to the purchasers; and the broker must disclose any material facts about your property which they know or reasonably should know, regardless of your responses on the Statement.
4. You must give the completed Statement to the purchaser no later than the time the purchaser makes an offer to purchase your property. If you do not, the purchaser can, under certain conditions, cancel any resulting contract (See **"Note to Purchasers"** below). You should give the purchaser a copy of the Statement containing your signature and keep a copy signed by the purchaser for your records.

---

**Note to Purchasers: If the owner does not give you a Residential Property Disclosure Statement by the time you make your offer to purchase the property, you may under certain conditions cancel any resulting contract and be entitled to a refund of any deposit monies you may have paid. To cancel the contract, you must personally deliver or mail written notice of your decision to cancel to the owner or the owner's agent within three calendar days following your receipt of the Statement, or three calendar days following the date of the contract, whichever occurs first. However, in no event does the Disclosure Act permit you to cancel a contract after settlement of the transaction or (in the case of a sale or exchange) after you have occupied the property, whichever occurs first.**

---

5. In the space below, type or print in ink the address of the property (sufficient to identify it) and your name. Then sign and date.

Property Address: ____________________

Owner's Name(s): ____________________

*Owner(s) acknowledge having examined this Statement before signing and that all information is true and correct as of the date signed.*

Owner Signature: ____________________ Date ________

Owner Signature: ____________________ Date ________

*Purchaser(s) acknowledge receipt of a copy of this disclosure statement; that they have examined it before signing; that they understand that this is not a warranty by owner or owner's agent; that it is not a substitute for any inspections they may wish to obtain; and that the representations are made by the owner and not the owner's agent(s) or subagent(s). Purchaser(s) are encouraged to obtain their own inspection from a licensed home inspector or other professional.*

Purchaser Signature: ____________________ Date ________

Purchaser Signature: ____________________ Date ________

(OVER)

Property Address/Description: ______________________________

*[Note: In this form, "property" refers only to dwelling unit(s) and not sheds, detached garages or other buildings.]*

**Regarding the property identified above, do you know of any problem (malfunction or defect) with any of the following:**

| | Yes* | No | No Representation |
|---|---|---|---|
| 1. FOUNDATION, SLAB, FIREPLACES/CHIMNEYS, FLOORS, WINDOWS (INCLUDING STORM WINDOWS AND SCREENS), DOORS, CEILINGS, INTERIOR AND EXTERIOR WALLS, ATTACHED GARAGE, PATIO, DECK OR OTHER STRUCTURAL COMPONENTS including any modifications to them? | ☐ | ☐ | ☐ |
| a. Siding is ☐ Masonry ☐ Wood ☐ Composition/Hardboard ☐ Vinyl ☐ Synthetic Stucco ☐ Other ________ | | | ☐ |
| b. Approximate age of structure? ________ | | | ☐ |
| 2. ROOF (leakage or other problem)? | ☐ | ☐ | ☐ |
| a. Approximate age of roof covering? ________ | | | ☐ |
| 3. WATER SEEPAGE, LEAKAGE, DAMPNESS OR STANDING WATER in the basement, crawl space or slab? | ☐ | ☐ | ☐ |
| 4. ELECTRICAL SYSTEM (outlets, wiring, panel, switches, fixtures etc.)? | ☐ | ☐ | ☐ |
| 5. PLUMBING SYSTEM (pipes, fixtures, water heater, etc.)? | ☐ | ☐ | ☐ |
| 6. HEATING AND/OR AIR CONDITIONING? | ☐ | ☐ | ☐ |
| a. Heat Source is: ☐ Furnace ☐ Heat Pump ☐ Baseboard ☐ Other________ | | | ☐ |
| b. Cooling Source is: ☐ Central Forced Air ☐ Wall/Window Unit(s) ☐ Other________ | | | ☐ |
| c. Fuel Source is: ☐ Electricity ☐ Natural Gas ☐ Propane ☐ Oil ☐ Other ________ | | | ☐ |
| 7. WATER SUPPLY (including water quality, quantity and water pressure)? | ☐ | ☐ | ☐ |
| a. Water supply is: ☐ City/County ☐ Community System ☐ Private Well ☐ Other ________ | | | ☐ |
| b. Water pipes are: ☐ Copper ☐ Galvanized ☐ Plastic ☐ Other ________ ☐ Unknown | | | ☐ |
| 8. SEWER AND/OR SEPTIC SYSTEM? | ☐ | ☐ | ☐ |
| a. Sewage disposal system is: ☐ Septic Tank ☐ Septic Tank with Pump ☐ Community System ☐ Connected to City/County System ☐ City/County System available ☐ Straight pipe (wastewater does not go into a septic or other sewer system [note: use of this type of system violates state law]) ☐ Other ________ | | | ☐ |
| 9. BUILT-IN APPLIANCES (RANGE/OVEN, ATTACHED MICROWAVE, HOOD/FAN, DISHWASHER, DISPOSAL, etc.)? | ☐ | ☐ | ☐ |

**Also regarding the property identified above, including the lot, other improvements, and fixtures located thereon, do you know of any:**

| | Yes* | No | No Representation |
|---|---|---|---|
| 10. PROBLEMS WITH PRESENT INFESTATION, OR DAMAGE FROM PAST INFESTATION OF WOOD DESTROYING INSECTS OR ORGANISMS which has not been repaired? | ☐ | ☐ | ☐ |
| 11. PROBLEMS WITH DRAINAGE, GRADING OR SOIL STABILITY OF LOT? | ☐ | ☐ | ☐ |
| 12. PROBLEMS WITH OTHER SYSTEMS AND FIXTURES: CENTRAL VACUUM, POOL, HOT TUB, SPA, ATTIC FAN, EXHAUST FAN, CEILING FAN, SUMP PUMP, IRRIGATION SYSTEM, TV CABLE WIRING OR SATELLITE DISH, OR OTHER SYSTEMS? | ☐ | ☐ | ☐ |
| 13. ROOM ADDITIONS OR OTHER STRUCTURAL CHANGES ? | ☐ | ☐ | ☐ |
| 14. ENVIRONMENTAL HAZARDS (substances, materials or products) including asbestos, formaldehyde, radon gas, methane gas, lead-based paint, underground storage tank, or other hazardous or toxic material (whether buried or covered), contaminated soil or water, or other environmental contamination)? | ☐ | ☐ | ☐ |
| 15. COMMERCIAL OR INDUSTRIAL NUISANCES (noise, odor, smoke, etc.) affecting the property? | ☐ | ☐ | ☐ |
| 16. VIOLATIONS OF BUILDING CODES, ZONING ORDINANCES, RESTRICTIVE COVENANTS OR OTHER LAND-USE RESTRICTIONS? | ☐ | ☐ | ☐ |
| 17. UTILITY OR OTHER EASEMENTS, SHARED DRIVEWAYS, PARTY WALLS OR ENCROACHMENTS FROM OR ON ADJACENT PROPERTY? | ☐ | ☐ | ☐ |
| 18. LAWSUITS, FORECLOSURES, BANKRUPTCY, TENANCIES, JUDGMENTS, TAX LIENS, PROPOSED ASSESSMENTS, MECHANICS' LIENS, MATERIALMENS' LIENS, OR NOTICE FROM ANY GOVERNMENTAL AGENCY that could affect title to the property? | ☐ | ☐ | ☐ |
| 19. OWNERS' ASSOCIATION OR "COMMON AREA" EXPENSES OR ASSESSMENTS? | ☐ | ☐ | ☐ |
| 20. FLOOD HAZARD or that the property is in a FEDERALLY-DESIGNATED FLOOD PLAIN? | ☐ | ☐ | ☐ |

* **If you answered "Yes" to any of the above questions, please explain (Attach additional sheets, if necessary):** ______________________________

______________________________

| | |
|---|---|
| Owner Initials and Date | Owner Initials and Date |
| Purchaser Initials and Date | Purchaser Initials and Date |

### A.0113 Reporting Criminal Convictions and Disciplinary Actions

Any broker who is convicted of any felony or misdemeanor or who has disciplinary action taken against him or her by any governmental agency in connection with any other occupational license shall file with the Commission a written report of such conviction or disciplinary action within 60 days of the final judgment or final order in the case. A form for this report is available from the Commission.

### A.0114 Residential Property Disclosure Statement

(a) Every owner of real property subject to a transfer of the type contemplated by G.S. 47E-1, 47E-2, and 47E-3, shall complete the ... residential property disclosure statement and furnish a copy of the complete statement to a purchaser in accordance with the requirements of G.S. 47E-4. The form shall bear the seal of the North Carolina Real Estate Commission and shall read as follows:

(b) The form described in Paragraph (a) of this Rule may be reproduced, but the form shall not be altered or amended in any way.

## SECTION A.0200<br>GENERAL PROVISIONS<br>(Repealed)

## SECTION A.0300<br>APPLICATION FOR LICENSE

### A.0301 Form

An individual or business entity who wishes to file an application for a broker license shall make application on a form prescribed by the Commission and can obtain the required form upon request to the Commission. In general, the application form for an individual calls for information such as the applicant's name and address, the applicant's social security number, satisfactory proof of the applicant's identity, places of residence, education, prior real estate licenses, and such other information necessary to identify the applicant and determine the applicant's qualifications and fitness for licensure. The application form for a business entity is described in Rule .0502 of this Section.

### A.0302 Filing and Fees

(a) Applications for a real estate license shall be complete and, except as provided by Rule .0403 of this Subchapter, shall be submitted to the Commission's office accompanied by the application fee. Examination scheduling of applicants who are required to pass the real estate licensing examination shall be accomplished in accordance with Rule .0401 of this Subchapter.

(b) Except for persons applying for licensure under the provisions of Section .1800 of this Subchapter, the license application fee shall be $30.00. In addition to the license application fee, applicants for licensure who are required to take the license examination must pay the examination fee charged by the Commission's authorized testing service in the form and manner acceptable to the testing service. Persons applying for licensure under Section .1800 of this Subchapter shall pay the application fee set forth in Rule .1803 of this Subchapter.

(c) An applicant shall update information provided in connection with an application or submit a newly completed application form without request by the Commission to assure that the information provided in the application is current and accurate. Failure to submit updated information prior to the issuance of a license may result in disciplinary action against a licensee in accordance with G.S. §93A-6(b)(1). In the event that the Commission requests an applicant to submit updated information or to provide additional information necessary to complete the application and the applicant fails to submit such information within 90 days following the Commission's request, the Commission shall cancel the applicant's application. The license application of an individual found by the Commission to be qualified for the licensing examination shall be immediately canceled if the applicant fails to pass a scheduled licensing examination, fails to appear for and take any examination for which the applicant has been scheduled without having the applicant's examination postponed or absence excused in accordance with Rule .0401(b) and (c) of this Section, or fails to take and pass the examination within 180 days of filing a complete application as described in Rule .0301 of this Section and having the application entered into the Commission's examination applicant file. Except as permitted otherwise in Rule .0403 of this Subchapter, an applicant whose license application has been canceled and who wishes to obtain a real estate license must start the licensing process over by filing a complete application to the Commission and paying all required fees.

### A.0303 Payment of Application Fees

Payment of application fees shall be made to the Commission by bank check, certified check, money order, debit card, or credit card. Once an application has been filed and processed, the application fee may not be refunded.

### A.0304 Equivalent Experience Qualifications for Applicants

Experience obtained by a broker applicant in violation of law or rule may not be recognized by the Commission as fulfilling the requirements for licensure when the applicant is requesting the Commission to waive the prescribed education requirement based wholly or in part on equivalent experience obtained by the applicant.

## SECTION A.0400 EXAMINATIONS

### A.0401 Scheduling Examinations

(a) An applicant who is required and qualified to take the licensing examination shall be provided a notice of examination eligibility that shall be valid for a period of 180 days and for a single administration of the licensing examination. Upon receipt of the notice of examination eligibility, the applicant shall contact the Commission's authorized testing service to pay for and schedule the examinations in accordance with procedures established by the testing service. The testing service will schedule applicants for examination by computer at their choice of one of the testing locations and will notify applicants of the time and place of their examinations.

(b) An applicant may postpone a scheduled examination provided the applicant makes the request for postponement directly to the Commission's authorized testing service in accordance with procedures established by the testing service. An applicant's examination shall not be postponed beyond the 180 day period allowed for taking the examination without first refiling another complete application with the Commission.

A request to postpone a scheduled licensing examination without complying with the procedures for re-applying for examination described in Rule .0403 of this Subchapter shall be granted only once unless the applicant satisfies the requirements for obtaining an excused absence stated in Paragraph (c) of this Rule.

(c) An applicant may be granted an excused absence from a scheduled examination if the applicant provides evidence that the absence was the direct result of an emergency situation or condition which was beyond the applicant's control and which could not have been reasonably foreseen by the applicant. A request for an excused absence must be promptly made in writing and must be supported by documentation verifying the reason for the absence.

The request must be submitted directly to the testing service in accordance with procedures established by the testing service. A request for an excused absence from an examination shall be denied if the applicant cannot be rescheduled and examined prior to expiration of the 180 day period allowed for taking the examination without first refiling another complete application with the Commission.

### A.0402 Subject Matter and Passing Scores

(a) The real estate licensing examination shall test applicants on the following general subject areas:

(1) real estate law;
(2) real estate brokerage law and practices;
(3) the Real Estate License Law, rules of the Commission, and the Commission's trust account guidelines;
(4) real estate finance;
(5) real estate valuation (appraisal);
(6) real estate mathematics; and
(7) related subject areas.

(b) In order to pass the real estate licensing examination, an applicant must attain a score at least equal to the passing score established by the Commission in compliance with psychometric standards for establishing passing scores for occupational licensing examinations as set forth in the "Standards for Educational and Psychological Testing" jointly promulgated by the American Educational Research Association, the American Psychological Association, and the National Council on Measurement in Education. Passing applicants will receive only a score of "pass"; however, failing applicants will be informed of their actual score. A passing examination score obtained by a license applicant shall be recognized as valid for a period of one year from the date of examination, during which time the applicant must fully satisfy any remaining requirements for licensure that were pending at the time of examination; provided that the running of the one-year period shall be tolled upon mailing the applicant the letter contemplated in 21 NCAC 58A .0616(b) informing the applicant that his or her moral character is in question, and shall resume running when the applicant's application is either approved for license issuance, denied or withdrawn. The application of an applicant with a passing examination score who fails to satisfy all remaining requirements for licensure within one year shall be canceled and the applicant shall be required to reapply and satisfy all requirements for licensure, including retaking and passing the license examination, in order to be eligible for licensure.

### A.0403 Re-applying for Examination

(a) An individual whose license application has been canceled and whose 180 day examination eligibility period has expired who wishes to be rescheduled for the real estate license examination must re-apply to the Commission by filing a complete license application as described in Rule .0301 of this Subchapter and paying the prescribed application fee. Subsequent examinations shall be scheduled in accordance with Rule .0401 of this Section.

(b) An individual whose license application has been canceled who wishes to be rescheduled for the license examination before the expiration of his or her 180 day examination eligibility period may utilize an abbreviated electronic license application and examination rescheduling procedure by directly contacting the Commission's authorized testing service, paying both the license application fee and the examination fee to the testing service, and following the testing service's established procedures.

(c) An applicant who fails the license examination shall not be allowed to retake the examination for at least 10 calendar days.

### A.0404 Cheating and Related Misconduct

Applicants shall not cheat or attempt to cheat on an examination by any means, including both giving and receiving assistance, and shall not communicate in any manner for any purpose with any person other than an examination supervisor during an examination. Applicants shall not disrupt the quiet and orderly administration of an examination in any manner. Violation of this Rule shall be grounds for dismissal from an examination, invalidation of examination scores, and denial of a real estate license, as well as for disciplinary action if the applicant has been issued a license.

### A.0405 Confidentiality of Examinations

Licensing examinations are the exclusive property of the Commission and are confidential. No applicant or licensee shall obtain, attempt to obtain, receive or communicate to other persons examination questions. Violation of this Rule shall be grounds for denial of a real estate license if the violator is an applicant and disciplinary action if the violator is a licensee.

### A.0406 Examination Review

An applicant who fails the license examination may review the examination at the testing center immediately following completion of the examination and receipt of the applicant's examination results but prior to leaving the testing center. An applicant who fails the examination and who declines the opportunity to immediately review the examination prior to leaving the testing center will be deemed to have waived the right to review the examination. An applicant who is reviewing his or her failed examination may not have any other person present during his or her review, nor may any other person review an examination on behalf of an applicant. An applicant who passes the license examination may not review the examination.

## SECTION A.0500 LICENSING

### A.0501 Character (Repealed)

### A.0502 Business Entities

(a) Every business entity other than a sole proprietorship shall apply for and obtain from the Commission a firm license prior to engaging in business as a real estate broker. An entity that changes its business form shall be required to submit a new application immediately upon making the change and to obtain a new license. Incomplete applications shall not be acted upon by the Commission. Application forms for partnerships, corporations, limited liability companies, associations and other business entities required to be licensed as brokers shall be available upon request to the Commission and shall require the applicant to set forth:

(1) the name of the entity;
(2) the name under which the entity will do business;
(3) the type of business entity;
(4) the address of its principal office;
(5) the entity's North Carolina Secretary of State Identification Number if required to be registered with the Office of the North Carolina Secretary of State;
(6) the name, real estate license number and signature of the proposed principal broker for the proposed firm;
(7) the address of and name of the proposed broker-in-charge for each office where brokerage activities will be conducted, along with a completed broker-in-charge declaration form for each proposed broker-in-charge;
(8) any past criminal conviction of and any pending criminal charge against any principal in the company or any proposed broker-in-charge;
(9) any past revocation, suspension or denial of a business or professional license of any principal in the company or any proposed broker-in-charge;
(10) if a general partnership, a full description of the applicant entity, including a copy of its written partnership agreement or if no written agreement exists, a written description of the rights and duties of the several partners;
(11) if a business entity other than a corporation, limited liability company or partnership, a full description of the organization of the applicant entity, including a copy of its organizational documents evidencing its authority to engage in real estate brokerage;
(12) if a foreign business entity, a certificate of authority to transact business in North Carolina and an executed consent to service of process and pleadings; and
(13) any other information required by this rule.

The Commission also may require the applicant to declare in the license application that the applicant's organizational documents authorize the firm to engage in the real estate business and to submit organizational documents, addresses of affiliated persons and similar information. For purposes of this Paragraph, the term principal shall mean any person or entity owning ten percent or more of the business entity, or who is an officer, director, manager, member, partner or who holds any other comparable position.

(b) After filing a written application with the Commission and upon a showing that at least one principal of said business entity holds a broker license on active status and in good standing and will serve as qualifying broker of the entity, the entity shall be licensed provided it appears that the applicant entity employs and is directed by personnel possessed of the requisite truthfulness, honesty, and integrity. The qualifying broker of a partnership of any kind must be a general partner of the partnership; the qualifying broker of a limited liability company must be a manager of the company; and the qualifying broker of a corporation must be an officer of the corporation. A licensed business entity may serve as the qualifying broker of another licensed business entity if the qualifying broker-entity has as its qualifying broker a natural person who is licensed as a broker. The natural person who is qualifying broker shall assure the performance of the qualifying broker's duties with regard to both entities. A provisional broker may not serve as a qualifying broker.

(c) The licensing of a business entity shall not be construed to extend to the licensing of its partners, managers, members, directors, officers, employees or other persons acting for the entity in their individual capacities regardless of whether they are engaged in furthering the business of the licensed entity.

(d) The qualifying broker of a business entity shall assume responsibility for:

(1) designating and assuring that there is at all times a broker-in-charge for each office and branch office of the entity at which real estate brokerage activities are conducted;

(2) renewing the real estate broker license of the entity;

(3) retaining the firm's renewal pocket card at the firm and producing it as proof of firm licensure upon request and maintaining a photocopy of the firm license certificate and pocket card at each branch office thereof;

(4) notifying the Commission of any change of business address or trade name of the entity and the registration of any assumed business name adopted by the entity for its use;

(5) notifying the Commission in writing of any change of his or her status as qualifying broker within ten days following the change;

(6) securing and preserving the transaction and trust account records of the firm whenever there is a change of broker-in-charge at the firm or any office thereof and notifying the Commission if the trust account records are out of balance or have not been reconciled as required by rule .0107 of this chapter;

(7) retaining and preserving the transaction and trust account records of the firm upon termination of his or her status as qualifying broker until a new qualifying broker has been designated with the Commission or, if no new qualifying broker is designated, for the period of time for which said records are required to be retained by Rule .0108 of this chapter; and

(8) notifying the Commission if, upon the termination of his or her status as qualifying broker, the firm's transaction and trust account records cannot be retained or preserved or if the trust account records are out of balance or have not been reconciled as required by Rule .0107(e) of this chapter.

(e) Every licensed business entity and every entity applying for licensure shall conform to all the requirements imposed upon it by the North Carolina General Statutes for its continued existence and authority to do business in North Carolina. Failure to conform to such requirements shall be grounds for disciplinary action or denial of the entity's application for licensure. Upon receipt of notice from an entity or agency of this state that a licensed entity has ceased to exist or that its authority to engage in business in this state has been terminated by operation of law, the Commission shall cancel the license of the entity.

### A.0503 License Renewal; Penalty for Operating While License Expired

(a) All real estate licenses issued by the Commission under G.S. 93A, Article 1 shall expire on the 30th day of June following issuance. Any licensee desiring renewal of a license shall apply for renewal within 45 days prior to license expiration by submitting a renewal application on a form provided by the Commission and submitting with the application the required renewal fee of forty dollars ($40.00).

(b) Any person desiring to renew his or her license on active status shall, upon the second renewal of such license following initial licensure, and upon each subsequent renewal, have obtained all continuing education required by G.S. 93A-4A and Rule .1702 of the Subchapter.

(c) A person renewing a license on inactive status shall not be required to have obtained any continuing education in order to renew such license; however, in order to subsequently change his or her license from inactive status to active status, the licensee must satisfy the continuing education requirement prescribed in Rule .1703 or Rule .1711 of the Subchapter.

(d) Any person or firm which engages in the business of a real estate broker while his, her, or its license is expired is subject to the penalties prescribed in G.S. 93A-6.

### A.0504 Active and Inactive License Status

(a) Except for licenses that have expired or that have been canceled, revoked, suspended or surrendered, all licenses issued by the Commission shall be designated as being either on active status or inactive status. The holder of a license on active status may engage in any activity requiring a real estate license and may be compensated for the provision of any lawful real estate brokerage service. The holder of a license on inactive status may not engage in any activity requiring a real estate license, including the referral for compensation of a prospective seller, buyer, landlord or tenant to another real estate licensee or any other party. A licensee holding a license on inactive status must renew such license and pay the prescribed license renewal fee in order to continue to hold such license. The Commission may take disciplinary action against a licensee holding a license on inactive status for any violation of G.S. 93A or any rule promulgated by the Commission, including the offense of engaging in an activity for which a license is required while a license is on inactive status.

(b) A license issued to a provisional broker shall, upon initial licensure, be assigned to inactive status, except that a license issued to a provisional broker based on reciprocity with another licensing jurisdiction shall be assigned to active status. A license issued to a firm or a broker other than a provisional broker shall be assigned to active status. Except for persons licensed under the provisions of Section .1800 of this Subchapter, a broker may change the status of his or her license from active to inactive status by submitting a written request to the Commission. A provisional broker's license shall be assigned by the Commission to inactive status when the provisional broker is not under the active, direct supervision of a broker-in-charge. A firm's license shall be assigned by the Commission to inactive status when the firm does not have a qualifying broker with an active license in good standing. Except for persons licensed under the provisions of Section .1800 of this Subchapter, a broker shall also be assigned to inactive status if, upon the second renewal of his or her license following initial licensure, or upon any subsequent renewal, he or she has not satisfied the continuing education requirement described in Rule .1702 of this Subchapter.

(c) A provisional broker with an inactive license who desires to have such license placed on active status must comply with the procedures prescribed in Rule .0506 of this Section.

(d) A broker, other than a provisional broker, with an inactive license who desires to have such license placed on active status shall file with the Commission a request for license activation on a form provided by the Commission containing identifying information about the broker, a statement that the broker has satisfied the continuing education requirements provided by Rule .1703 of this Subchapter, the date of the request, and the signature of the broker. Upon the mailing or delivery of this form, the broker may engage in real estate brokerage activities requiring a license; however, if the broker does not receive from the Commission a written acknowledgment of the license activation within 30 days of the date shown on the form, the broker shall immediately terminate his or her real estate brokerage activities pending receipt of the written acknowledgment from the Commission. If the broker is notified that he or she is not eligible for license activation due to a continuing education deficiency, the broker must terminate all real estate brokerage activities until such time as the continuing education deficiency is satisfied and a new request for license activation is submitted to the Commission.

(e) A firm with an inactive license which desires to have its license placed on active status shall file with the Commission a request for license activation on a form provided by the Commission containing identifying information about the firm and its qualifying broker. If the qualifying broker has an inactive license, he or she must satisfy the requirements of Paragraph (d) of this Rule. Upon the mailing or delivery of the completed form by the qualifying broker, the firm may engage in real estate brokerage activities requiring a license; however, if the firm's qualifying broker does not receive from the Commission a written acknowledgment of the license activation within 30 days of the date shown on the form, the firm shall immediately terminate its real estate brokerage activities pending receipt of the written acknowledgment from the Commission. If the qualifying broker is notified that the firm is not eligible for license activation due to a continuing education deficiency on the part of the qualifying broker, the firm must terminate all real estate brokerage activities until` such time as the continuing education deficiency is satisfied and a new request for license activation is submitted to the Commission.

(f) A person licensed as a broker under Section .1800 of this Subchapter shall maintain his or her license on active status at all times as required by Rule .1804 of this Subchapter.

### A.0505 Reinstatement of Expired License, Revoked, Surrendered or Suspended License

(a) Licenses expired for not more than six (6) months may be reinstated upon the submission of a complete and accurate application and payment of a fifty-five dollar ($55.00) reinstatement fee. In order to reinstate such license on active status, the applicant shall also present clear and convincing evidence of having obtained such continuing education as is required by Rule .1703 of this Subchapter to change an inactive license to active status. A person reinstating such a license on inactive status shall not be required to have obtained any continuing education in order to reinstate such license; however, in order to subsequently change his or her reinstated license from inactive status to active status, the licensee must satisfy the continuing education requirement prescribed in Rule .1703 of this Subchapter, and be supervised by a broker-in-charge in compliance with the requirements of Rule .0506 of this Section.

(b) Reinstatement of licenses expired for more than 6 (six) months may be considered upon the submission of a complete and accurate application and payment of a fifty-five dollar ($55.00) fee. Applicants must satisfy the Commission that they possess the current knowledge, skills and competence, as well as the truthfulness, honesty and integrity, necessary to function in the real estate business in a manner that protects and serves the public interest. To demonstrate current knowledge, skills and competence, the Commission may require such applicants to complete real estate education or pass the license examination or both.

(c) Reinstatement of a revoked license may be considered upon the submission of a complete and accurate application and payment of a thirty dollar ($30.00) fee. Applicants must satisfy the same requirements as those prescribed in Paragraph (b) of this Rule for reinstatement of licenses expired for more than six (6) months.

(d) Reinstatement of a license surrendered under the provisions of G.S. 93A-6(e) may be considered upon termination of the period of surrender specified in the order approving the surrender and upon the submission of a complete and accurate application and payment of a thirty dollar ($30.00) fee. Applicants must satisfy the same requirements as those prescribed in Paragraph (b) of this Rule for reinstatement of licenses expired for more than six (6) months.

(e) When a license is suspended by the Commission, the suspended license shall be restored at the end of the period of active suspension provided that any applicable license renewal fees that accrued during the time of the suspension are paid by the licensee. In order for the license to be restored on active status, the licensee shall be required to also demonstrate that the licensee has satisfied the continuing education requirement for license activation prescribed by Rule .1703 of this Subchapter and that the licensee is supervised by a broker-in-charge in compliance with the requirements of Rule .0506 of this Section, if applicable.

### A.0506 Provisional Broker to be Supervised by Broker

(a) This Rule shall apply to all real estate provisional brokers.

(b) A provisional broker may engage in or hold himself or herself out as engaging in activities requiring a real estate license only while his or her license is on active status and he or she is supervised by the broker-in-charge of the real estate firm or office where the provisional broker is associated. A provisional broker may be supervised by only one broker-in-charge at a time.

(c) Upon a provisional broker's association with a real estate broker or brokerage firm, the provisional broker and the broker-in-charge of the office where the provisional broker will be engaged in the real estate business shall immediately file with the Commission a provisional broker supervision notification on a form provided by the Commission containing identifying information about the provisional broker and the broker-in-charge, a statement from the broker-in-charge certifying that he or she will supervise the provisional broker in the performance of all acts for which a license is required, the date that the broker-in-charge assumes responsibility for such supervision, and the signatures of the provisional broker and broker-in-charge. If the provisional broker is on inactive status at the time of associating with a broker or brokerage firm, the provisional broker and broker-in-charge shall also file, along with the provisional broker supervision notification, the provisional broker's request for license activation on a form provided by the Commission containing identifying information about the provisional broker, the provisional broker's statement that he or she has satisfied the continuing education requirements prescribed by Rule .1703 of this Subchapter, the provisional broker's statement that he or she has satisfied the postlicensing education requirements, if applicable, prescribed by Rule .1902 of this Subchapter, the date of the request, and the signatures of the provisional broker and the provisional broker's proposed broker-in-charge. Upon the mailing or delivery of the required form(s), the provisional broker may engage in real estate brokerage activities requiring a license under the supervision of the broker-in-charge; however, if the provisional broker and broker-in-charge do not receive from the Commission a written acknowledgment of the provisional broker supervision notification and, if appropriate, the request for license activation, within 30 days of the date shown on the form, the broker-in-charge shall immediately terminate the provisional broker's real estate brokerage activities pending receipt of the written acknowledgment from the Commission. If the provisional broker and broker-in-charge are notified that the provisional broker is not eligible for license activation due to a continuing education deficiency, the broker-in-charge shall cause the provisional broker to immediately cease all activities requiring a real estate license until such time as the continuing education deficiency is satisfied and a new provisional broker supervision notification and request for license activation is submitted to the Commission.

(d) A broker-in-charge who certifies to the Commission that he or she will supervise a provisional broker shall actively and directly supervise the provisional broker in a manner which reasonably assures that the provisional broker performs all acts for which a real estate license is required in accordance with the Real Estate License Law and Commission rules. A supervising broker who fails to supervise a provisional broker as prescribed in this Rule may be subject to disciplinary action by the Commission.

(e) Upon the termination of the supervisory relationship between a provisional broker and his or her broker-in-charge, the provisional broker and the broker-in-charge shall provide written notification of the date of termination to the Commission not later than 10 days following said termination.

### A.0507 Payment of License Fees

Checks, credit cards, and other forms of payment given the Commission for fees due which are returned unpaid shall be considered cause for license denial, suspension, or revocation.

### A.0508 Duplicate License Fee (Repealed)

### A.0509 Duplicate License Fee

A licensee may, by filing a prescribed form and paying a five dollar ($5.00) fee to the Commission, obtain a duplicate real estate license or pocket card to replace an original license or pocket card which has been lost, damaged or destroyed or if the name of the licensee has been lawfully changed.

## SECTION A.0600
## REAL ESTATE COMMISSION HEARINGS

### A.0601 Complaints/Inquiries/Motions/Other Pleadings

(a) There shall be no specific form required for complaints. To be sufficient, a complaint shall be in writing, identify the respondent licensee and shall reasonably apprise the Commission of the facts which form the basis of the complaint.

(b) When investigating a complaint, the scope of the Commission's investigation shall not be limited only to matters alleged in the complaint. In addition, a person making a complaint to the Commission may change his or her complaint by submitting the changes to the Commission in writing.

(c) When a complaint has not been submitted in conformity with this rule, the Commission's legal counsel may initiate an investigation if the available information is sufficient to create a reasonable suspicion that any licensee or other person or entity may have committed a violation of the provisions of the Real Estate License Law or the rules adopted by the Commission.

(d) There shall be no specific forms required for answers, motions, or other pleadings relating to contested cases before the Commission, except they shall be in writing. To be sufficient, the document must reasonably apprise the Commission of the matters it alleges or answers. To be considered by the Commission, every answer, motion, request or other pleading must be submitted to the Commission in writing or made during the hearing as a matter of record.

(e) During the course of an investigation of a licensee, the Commission, through its legal counsel or other staff, may send the licensee a Letter of Inquiry requesting the licensee to respond. The Letter of Inquiry, or attachments thereto, shall set forth the subject matter being investigated. Upon receipt of the Letter of Inquiry, the licensee shall respond within 14 calendar days. Such response shall include a full and fair disclosure of all information requested. Licensees shall include with their written response copies of all documents requested in the Letter of Inquiry.

(f) Hearings in contested cases before the Commission shall be conducted according to the provisions of Article 3A of Chapter 150B of the General Statutes of North Carolina.

(g) Persons who make complaints are not parties to contested cases, but may be witnesses.

### A.0616 Procedures For Requesting Hearings When Applicant's Character Is In Question

(a) When the moral character of an applicant for licensure or approval is in question, the applicant shall not be licensed or approved until the applicant has affirmatively demonstrated that the applicant possesses the requisite truthfulness, honesty and integrity. For the purposes of this rule, applicant means any person or entity making application for licensure as a real estate broker or for licensure or approval as a prelicensing or continuing education instructor, director, coordinator, school, or sponsor. When the applicant is an entity, it shall be directed and controlled by persons who are truthful and honest and who possess integrity.

(b) When the character of an applicant is in question, the Commission shall defer action upon the application until the applicant is notified by letter. The letter informing the applicant that his or her moral character is in question shall be sent by certified mail, return receipt requested, to the address shown upon the application. The applicant shall have 60 days from the date of receipt of this letter to request a hearing before the Commission. If the applicant fails to request a hearing within this time or if a properly addressed letter is returned to the Commission undelivered, applicant⊠s right to a hearing shall be considered waived and the application shall be deemed denied. If the applicant makes a timely request for a hearing in accordance with the provisions of this rule, the Commission shall provide the applicant with a Notice of Hearing and hearing as required by Article 3A of Chapter 150B of the North Carolina General Statutes.

(c) Nothing in this Rule shall be interpreted to prevent an unsuccessful applicant from reapplying for licensure or approval if such application is otherwise permitted by law.

## SECTION A.0700
## PETITIONS FOR RULES

## SECTION A.0800
## RULE MAKING

## SECTION A.0900
## DECLARATORY RULINGS

## SECTION A.1000
## SCHOOLS
## (Transferred to C.0100)

## SECTION A.1100
## REAL ESTATE PRE-LICENSING COURSES

**(Transferred/Repealed.Transfers are at C.0300 Prelicensing and Pre-certification Courses)**

## SECTION A.1200
## CERTIFICATION OF REAL ESTATE INSTRUCTORS
## (Repealed)

## SECTION A.1300
## PRIVATE REAL ESTATE SCHOOLS
## (Transferred/Repealed. Transfers are at C.0200)

## SECTION A.1400
## REAL ESTATE RECOVERY FUND

## SECTION A.1500 FORMS (Repealed)

***Interested persons may obtain a copy of Sections A.0600 through A.1500 by making written request to the North Carolina Real Estate Commission.***

## SECTION A.1600
## DISCRIMINATORY PRACTICES PROHIBITED

### A.1601 Fair Housing

Conduct by a licensee which violates the provisions of the State Fair Housing Act constitutes improper conduct in violation of G.S. 93A-6(a)(10).

## SECTION A.1700
## MANDATORY CONTINUING EDUCATION

### A.1701 Purpose and Applicability

This Section describes the continuing education requirement for real estate brokers authorized by G.S. 93A-4A, establishes the continuing education requirement to change a license from inactive status to active status, establishes attendance requirements for continuing education courses, establishes the criteria and procedures relating to obtaining an extension of time to complete the continuing education requirement, establishes the criteria for obtaining continuing education credit for an unapproved course or related educational activity, and addresses other similar matters.

### A.1702 Continuing Education Requirement

(a) Except as provided in 21 NCAC 58A.1708 and A.1711, in order to renew a broker license on active status, the person requesting renewal of a license shall, upon the second renewal of such license following initial licensure, and upon each subsequent annual renewal, have completed, within one year preceding license expiration, eight classroom hours of real estate continuing education in courses approved by the Commission as provided in Subchapter 58E. Four of the required eight classroom hours must be obtained each license period by completing a mandatory update course developed annually by the Commission. The remaining four hours must be obtained by completing one or more Commission-approved elective courses described in Rule .0305 of Subchapter 58E. The licensee bears the responsibility for providing, upon request of the Commission, evidence of continuing education course completion satisfactory to the Commission.

(b) No continuing education shall be required to renew a broker license on inactive status; however, to change a license from inactive status to active status, the licensee must satisfy the continuing education requirement described in Rule .1703 of this Section.

(c) No continuing education shall be required for a licensee who is a member of the U. S. Congress or North Carolina General Assembly in order to renew his or her license on active status.

(d) The terms "active status" and "inactive status" are defined in Rule .0504 of this Subchapter. For continuing education purposes, the term "initial licensure" shall include the first time that a license of a particular type is issued to a person, the reinstatement of a canceled, revoked or surrendered license and any license expired for more than six months. The issuance, pursuant to G.S. 93A-4.3, of a broker license on provisional status on April 1, 2006 to licensees who held a salesperson license as of that date shall not be considered to constitute initial licensure for continuing education purposes.

### A.1703 Continuing Education for License Activation

(a) A broker requesting to change an inactive license to active status on or after the licensee's second license renewal following his or her initial licensure shall be required to demonstrate completion of continuing education as described in Paragraph (b) or (c) of this Rule, whichever is appropriate.

(b) If the inactive licensee's license has properly been on active status at any time since the preceding July 1, the licensee is considered to be current with regard to continuing education and no additional continuing education is required to activate the license.

(c) If the inactive licensee's license has not properly been on active status since the preceding July 1 and the licensee has a deficiency in his or her continuing education record for the previous license period, the licensee must make up the deficiency and fully satisfy the continuing education requirement for the current license period in order to activate the license. Any deficiency may be made up by completing, during the current license period or previous license period, approved continuing education elective courses; however, such courses will not be credited toward the continuing education requirement for the current license period. When crediting elective courses for purposes of making up a continuing education deficiency, the maximum number of credit hours that will be awarded for any course is four hours. When evaluating the continuing education record of a licensee with a deficiency for the previous license period to determine the licensee's eligibility for active status, the licensee shall be deemed eligible for active status if the licensee has fully satisfied the continuing education requirement for the current license period and has taken any two additional continuing education courses since the beginning of the previous license period, even if the licensee had a continuing education deficiency prior to the beginning of the previous license period.

### A.1704 No Credit for Prelicensing or Postlicensing Courses

No credit toward the continuing education requirement shall be awarded for completing a real estate prelicensing or postlicensing course.

### A.1705 Attendance and Participation Requirements

In order to receive any credit for satisfactorily completing an approved continuing education course, a licensee must attend at least 90 percent of the scheduled classroom hours for the course, regardless of the length of the course, and must comply with student participation standards described in Rule .0511 of Subchapter 58E. No credit shall be awarded for attending less than 90 percent of the scheduled classroom hours.

### A.1706 Repetition of Courses

A continuing education course may be taken only once for continuing education credit within a single license period.

### A.1707 Elective Course Carry-Over Credit

A maximum of four hours of continuing education credit for an approved elective course taken during the current license period may be carried over to satisfy the continuing education elective requirement for the next following license period if the licensee receives no continuing education elective credit for the course toward the elective requirement for the current license period or the previous license period. However, if a continuing education elective course is used to wholly or partially satisfy the elective requirement for the current or previous license period, then any excess hours completed in such course which are not needed to satisfy the four-hour elective requirement for that license period may not be carried forward and applied toward the elective requirement for the next following license period.

### A.1708 Equivalent Credit

(a) A licensee may request that the Commission award continuing education credit for a course taken by the licensee that is not approved by the Commission, or for some other real estate education activity, by making such request on a form prescribed by the Commission and submitting a nonrefundable evaluation fee of thirty dollars ($30.00) for each request for evaluation of a course or real estate education activity. In order for requests for equivalent credit to be considered and credits to be entered into a licensee's continuing education record prior to the June 30 license expiration date, such requests and all supporting documents must be received by the Commission on or before June 10 preceding expiration of the licensee's current license, with the exception that requests from instructors desiring equivalent credit for teaching Commission-approved continuing education courses must be received by June 30. Any equivalent continuing education credit awarded under this Rule shall be applied first to make up any continuing education deficiency for the previous license period and then to satisfy the continuing education requirement for the current license period; however, credit for an unapproved course or educational activity, other than teaching an approved elective course, that was completed during a previous license period may not be applied to a subsequent license period.

(b) The Commission may award continuing education elective credit for completion of an unapproved course which the Commission finds equivalent to the elective course component of the continuing education requirement set forth in Section .0300 of Subchapter 58E. Completion of an unapproved course may serve only to satisfy the elective requirement and cannot be substituted for completion of the mandatory update course.

(c) Real estate education activities, other than teaching a Commission-approved course, which may be eligible for credit include, but are not limited to: developing a Commission-approved elective continuing education course, authorship of a published real estate textbook; and authorship of a scholarly article, on a topic acceptable for continuing education purposes, which has been published in a professional journal such as a law journal or professional college or university journal or periodical. The Commission may award continuing education elective credit for activities which the Commission finds equivalent to the elective course component of the continuing education requirement set forth in Section .0300 of Subchapter 58E. No activity other than teaching a Commission-developed mandatory update course shall be considered equivalent to completing the mandatory update course.

(d) The Commission may award credit for teaching the Commission-developed mandatory update course and for teaching an approved elective course. Credit for teaching an approved elective course shall be awarded only for teaching a course for the first time. Credit for teaching a Commission-developed mandatory update course may be awarded for each licensing period in which the instructor teaches the course. The amount of credit awarded to the instructor of an approved continuing education course shall be the same as the amount of credit earned by a licensee who completes the course. Licensees who are instructors of continuing education courses approved by the Commission shall not be subject to the thirty dollar ($30.00) evaluation fee when applying for continuing education credit for teaching an approved course. No credit toward the continuing education requirement shall be awarded for teaching a real estate prelicensing or postlicensing course.

(e) A licensee completing a real estate appraisal prelicensing, precertification or continuing education course approved by the North Carolina Appraisal Board may obtain real estate continuing education elective credit for such course by submitting to the Commission a written request for equivalent continuing education elective credit accompanied by a nonrefundable processing fee of twenty dollars ($20.00) and a copy of the certificate of course completion issued by the course sponsor for submission to the North Carolina Appraisal Board.

### A.1709 Extensions of Time to Complete Continuing Education

A licensee on active status may request and be granted an extension of time to satisfy the continuing education requirement for a particular license period if the licensee provides evidence satisfactory to the Commission that he or she was unable to obtain the necessary education due to an incapacitating illness or other circumstance which existed for a substantial portion of the license period and which constituted a severe and verifiable hardship such that to comply with the continuing education requirement would have been impossible or unreasonably burdensome. The Commission shall in no case grant an extension of time to satisfy the continuing education requirement for reasons of business or personal conflicts. The Commission also shall not grant such an extension of time when, in the opinion of the Commission, the principal reason for the licensee's inability to obtain the required education in a timely manner was unreasonable delay on the part of the licensee in obtaining such education. If an extension of time is granted, the licensee shall be permitted to renew his or her license on active status but the license shall be automatically changed to inactive status at the end of the extension period unless the licensee satisfies the continuing education requirement prior to that time. If an extension of time is not granted, the licensee may either satisfy the continuing education requirement prior to expiration of the license period or renew his or her license on inactive status. The length of any extension of time granted and the determination of the specific courses which shall be accepted by the Commission as equivalent to the continuing education the licensee would have been required to have completed had the licensee not been granted the extension is wholly discretionary on the part of the Commission. The licensee's request for an extension of time must be submitted on a form prescribed by the Commission.

### A.1710 Denial or Withdrawal of Continuing Education Credit

(a) The Commission may deny continuing education credit claimed by a licensee or reported by a course sponsor for a licensee, and may withdraw continuing education credit previously awarded by the Commission to a licensee upon finding that:

(1) The licensee or course sponsor provided incorrect or incomplete information to the Commission concerning continuing education completed by the licensee;

(2) The licensee failed to comply with either the attendance requirement established by Rule .1705 of this Section or the student participation standards set forth in Rule .0511 of Subchapter 58E; or

(3) The licensee was mistakenly awarded continuing education credit due to an administrative error.

(b) When continuing education credit is denied or withdrawn by the Commission under Paragraph (a) of this Rule, the licensee remains responsible for satisfying the continuing education requirement. However, when an administrative error or an incorrect report by a course sponsor results in the denial or withdrawal of continuing education credit for a licensee, the Commission may, upon request of the licensee, grant the licensee an extension of time to satisfy the continuing education requirement.

(c) A licensee who obtains or attempts to obtain continuing education credit through misrepresentation of fact, dishonesty or other improper conduct shall be subject to disciplinary action pursuant to G.S. 93A-6.

### A.1711 Continuing Education Required of Nonresident Licensees

(a) Real estate brokers licensed in North Carolina but residing in another state at the time they apply for license renewal who wish to renew their licenses on active status may fully satisfy the continuing education requirement by any one of the following means:

(1) A nonresident licensee may, at the time of license renewal, hold a real estate license on active status in another state and certify on a form prescribed by the Commission that the licensee holds such license.

(2) A nonresident licensee may, within one year preceding license expiration, complete the Commission-prescribed Update course plus one Commission-approved continuing education elective course, or complete two Commission-approved continuing education elective courses.

(3) A nonresident licensee may, within one year preceding license expiration, complete eight classroom hours in courses approved for continuing education credit by the real estate licensing agency in the licensee's state of residence or in the state where the course was taken. To obtain credit for a continuing education course completed in another state and not approved by the Commission, the licensee must submit a written request for continuing education credit accompanied by a nonrefundable processing fee of twenty dollars ($20.00) per request and evidence satisfactory to the Commission that the course was completed and that the course was approved for continuing education credit by the real estate licensing agency in the licensee's state of residence or in the state where the course was taken.

(4) A nonresident licensee may obtain eight hours equivalent credit for a course or courses not approved by the Commission or for related educational activities as provided in Rule .1708 of this Section. The maximum amount of continuing education credit the Commission will award a nonresident licensee for an unapproved course or educational activity is eight hours.

(b) When requesting to change an inactive license to active status, or when applying for reinstatement of a license expired for not more than six months, a nonresident broker may fully satisfy the continuing education requirements described in Rules .0505 and .1703 of this Subchapter by complying with any of the options described in Paragraph (a) of this Rule, except that the requirements in (a)(2) and (a)(3) restricting the taking of courses to one year preceding license expiration shall not be applicable.

(c) No carry-over credit to a subsequent license period shall be awarded for a course taken in another state that has not been approved by the North Carolina Real Estate Commission as an elective course.

## SECTION A .1800 LIMITED NONRESIDENT COMMERCIAL LICENSING

### A.1801 General Provisions

(a) Any person resident in a state or territory of the United States other than North Carolina may perform the acts or services of a real estate broker in North Carolina in transactions involving commercial real estate if said person first applies for and obtains a limited nonresident commercial real estate broker license as provided in this Section.

(b) Corporations, business associations and entities shall be ineligible for licensure under this Section.

(c) Nothing in this Section shall be construed to limit the rights of any person duly licensed as a real estate broker in North Carolina under the provisions of N.C.G.S.§§ 93A-4 or 93A-9(a).

### A.1802 Definitions

For the purposes of this Section:

(1) "Commercial Real Estate" means any real property or interest therein, whether freehold or non-freehold, which at the time the property or interest is made the subject of an agreement for brokerage services:

(a) is lawfully used primarily for sales, office, research, institutional, warehouse, manufacturing, industrial or mining purposes or for multifamily residential purposes involving five or more dwelling units;

(b) may lawfully be used for any of the purposes listed in (1) above by a zoning ordinance adopted pursuant to the provisions of Article 18 of Chapter 153A or Article 19 of Chapter 160A of the General Statutes or which is the subject of an official application or petition to amend the applicable zoning ordinance to permit any of the uses listed in (1) above which is under consideration by the government agency with authority to approve the amendment; or

(c) is in good faith intended to be immediately used for any of the purposes listed in (1) above by the parties to any contract, lease, option, or offer to make any contract, lease, or option.

(2) "Qualifying state" means the state or territory of the United States where an applicant for, and the holder of, a limited nonresident commercial license issued under this Section is licensed in good standing as a real estate broker or salesperson. The qualifying state must be the state or territory where the applicant or limited nonresident commercial licensee maintains his or her primary place of business as a real estate broker or salesperson. Under no circumstances may North Carolina be a qualifying state.

### A.1803 Requirements For Licensure; Application And Fee

(a) A person desiring to obtain a broker license under this Section shall demonstrate to the Real Estate Commission that:

(1) he or she is a resident of a state or territory of the United States other than North Carolina;

(2) he or she is licensed as a real estate broker in a qualifying state and that said license is on active status and not in abeyance for any reason. If licensed as a salesperson, he or she shall also demonstrate that he or she is acting under the supervision of a broker in accordance with the applicable governing statutes or regulations in the qualifying state; and

(3) he or she possesses the requisite honesty, truthfulness, integrity, and moral character for licensure as a broker in North Carolina.

A person applying for licensure under this Section shall not be required to show that the state or territory where he or she is currently licensed offers reciprocal licensing privileges to North Carolina brokers.

(b) A person desiring to be licensed under this Section shall submit an application on a form prescribed by the Commission and shall show the Commission that he or she has satisfied the requirements set forth in (a) of this rule. In connection with his or her application a person applying for licensure under this rule shall provide the Commission with a certification of license history from the qualifying state where he or she is licensed. He or she shall also provide the Commission with a report of his or her criminal history from the service designated by the Commission. An applicant for licensure under this Section shall be required to update his or her application as required by Rule .0302(c) of this Subchapter.

(c) The fee for persons applying for licensure under this Section shall be $100 and shall be paid in the form of a certified check, bank check, cashier's check, money order, or by credit card. Once paid, the application fee shall be non-refundable.

(d) If the Commission has received a complete application and the required application fee and if the Commission is satisfied that the applicant possesses the moral character necessary for licensure, the Commission shall issue to the applicant a limited nonresident commercial real estate broker license.

### A.1804 Active Status

Broker licenses issued under this Section shall be issued on active status and shall remain valid only so long as the licensee's license in the qualifying state remains valid and on active status. In addition, a license issued to a salesperson under this Section shall remain valid only while the salesperson is acting under the supervision of a real estate broker in accordance with the applicable laws and rules in the qualifying state. Individuals licensed under this Section shall immediately notify the Commission if his or her license in the qualifying state lapses or expires, is suspended or revoked, made inactive, or is placed in abeyance for any reason.

### A.1805 Renewal

(a) A license issued under this Section shall expire on June 30 following issuance unless it is renewed in accordance with the provisions of Rule .0503 and Rule .1711 of this Subchapter.

(b) The Commission shall not renew a license issued under this Section unless the licensee has demonstrated that he or she has complied with the requirements of paragraph (a) of this rule and that his or her license in the qualifying state is on active status in good standing and is not lapsed, expired, suspended, revoked, or in abeyance for any reason.

### A.1806 Limitations

(a) A person licensed under this Section may act as a real estate broker in this state only if:

(1) he or she does not reside in North Carolina;

(2) the real property interest which is the subject of any transaction in connection with which he or she acts as a broker in this state is commercial real estate as that term is defined in Rule .1802 of this Section; and

(3) he or she is affiliated with a resident North Carolina real estate broker as required in rule .1807 of this Section.

(b) A nonresident commercial real estate broker licensed under the provisions of Section .1800 of this Subchapter shall not act as or serve in the capacity of a broker-in-charge of a firm or office in North Carolina.

### A.1807 Affiliation With Resident Broker

(a) No person licensed under N.C.G.S. 93A-9(b) shall enter North Carolina to perform any act or service for which licensure as a real broker is required unless he or she has first entered into a brokerage cooperation agreement and declaration of affiliation with an individual who is a resident in North Carolina licensed as a North Carolina real estate broker.

(b) A brokerage cooperation agreement as contemplated by this rule shall be in writing and signed by the resident North Carolina broker and the non-resident commercial licensee. It shall contain:

(1) the material terms of the agreement between the signatory licenses;

(2) a description of the agency relationships, if any, which are created by the agreement among the nonresident commercial licensee, the resident North Carolina broker, and the parties each represents;

(3) a description of the property or the identity of the parties and other information sufficient to identify the transaction which is the subject of the affiliation agreement; and

(4) a definite expiration date.

(c) A declaration of affiliation shall be written and on the form provided by the Commission and shall identify the nonresident commercial licensee and the affiliated resident North Carolina licensee. It shall also contain a description of the duties and obligations of each as required by the North Carolina Real Estate License Law and rules duly adopted by the Commission. The declaration of affiliation may be a part of the brokerage cooperation agreement or separate from it.

(d) A nonresident commercial licensee may affiliate with more than one resident North Carolina broker at any time. However, a nonresident commercial licensee may be affiliated with only one resident North Carolina broker in a single transaction.

(e) A resident North Carolina broker who enters into a brokerage cooperation agreement and declaration of affiliation with a nonresident commercial licensee shall:

(1) verify that the nonresident commercial licensee is licensed in North Carolina;

(2) actively and directly supervise the nonresident commercial licensee in a manner which reasonably insures that the nonresident commercial licensee complies with the North Carolina Real Estate License Law and rules adopted by the Commission; and

(3) promptly notify the Commission if the nonresident commercial licensee violates the Real Estate License Law or rules adopted by the Commission; and

(4) insure that records are retained in accordance with the requirements of the Real Estate License Law and rules adopted by the Commission; and

(5) maintain his or her license on active status continuously for the duration of the brokerage cooperation agreement and the declaration of affiliation.

(f) The nonresident commercial licensee and the affiliated resident North Carolina broker shall each retain in his or her records a copy of brokerage cooperation agreements and declarations of affiliation from the time of their creation and for at least three years following their expiration. Such records shall be made available for inspection and reproduction by the Commission or its authorized representatives without prior notice.

### A.1808 Trust Monies

A nonresident commercial licensee acting as real estate broker in North Carolina shall immediately deliver to the North Carolina resident broker with whom he or she is affiliated all money belonging to others received in connection with the nonresident commercial licensee's acts or services as a broker. Upon receipt of said money, the resident North Carolina broker shall cause said money to be deposited in a trust account in accordance with the provisions of Rule .0107 of this Subchapter.

### A.1809 Advertising

In all advertising involving a nonresident commercial licensee's conduct as a North Carolina real estate broker and in any representation of such person's licensure in North Carolina, the advertising or representation shall conspicuously identify the nonresident commercial licensee as a "Limited Nonresident Commercial Real Estate Broker.

### A.1810 Payment Of Fees

Commissions, fees, or other compensation earned by a nonresident commercial licensee shall not be paid directly to the licensee if said licensee is employed by or working for a real estate broker or firm. Instead, such fees or compensation shall be paid to the licensee's employing broker or firm.

## SECTION A .1900 POSTLICENSING EDUCATION

### A.1901 Purpose and Applicability

This section prescribes specific procedures relating to the postlicensing education requirement for real estate brokers as prescribed by G.S. 93A-4(a1).

### A.1902 Postlicensing Education Requirement

(a) The 90 classroom hour postlicensing education program shall consist of three 30 classroom hour courses prescribed by the Commission which may be taken in any sequence. A provisional broker as described in G.S. 93A-4(a1) or G.S. 93A-4.3(d) must satisfactorily complete at least one of the 30-hour courses during each of the first three years following the date of his or her initial licensure as a broker in order to retain his or her eligibility to actively engage in real estate brokerage. Upon completion of all three courses by a provisional broker, the provisional status of the broker's licenseshall be terminated by the Commission. The three courses shall be devoted to:

(1) real estate brokerage relationships and responsibilities;

(2) real estate contracts and transactions; and

(3) specialized topics, including commercial real estate, rental management, real estate finance, real estate appraisal, real estate development, and real estate regulation.

(b) If a provisional broker as described in G.S. 93A-4(a1) or G.S. 93A-4.3(d) fails to complete the required postlicensing education described in paragraph (a) of this Rule by the end of either the first or second year following the date of his or her initial licensure as a broker, his or her license shall be placed on inactive status. Between the end of the first year after initial licensure and the end of the third year after initial licensure, a provisional broker who is subject to the postlicensing education requirement and who desires to activate a license that is on inactive status shall make up any postlicensing education deficiency as well as satisfy the continuing education requirements for license activation described in Rule .1703 of this Subchapter, satisfy the requirement for supervision by a broker-in-charge described in Rule .0506 of this Subchapter and file with the Commission a request for license activation as described in Rule .0504 of this Subchapter.

(c) If a provisional broker as described in G.S. 93A-4(a1) or G.S. 93A-4.3(d) fails to complete all three postlicensing courses within three years following the date of his or her initial licensure, his or her license shall be cancelled and, in order to reinstate such license, the former broker must satisfy the requirements described in G.S. 93A-4(a1) and Rule .0505 of this Subchapter.

### A.1903 Extensions Of Time To Complete Postlicensing Education

A provisional broker as described in G.S. 93A-4(a1) or G.S. 93A-4.3(d) may request and be granted an extension of time to satisfy the postlicensing education requirement for the first and second years following the date of his or her initial licensure as a broker if the licensee provides evidence satisfactory to the Commission that he or she was unable to obtain the necessary education due to an incapacitating illness or other circumstance which existed for a substantial portion of the year in question and which constituted a severe and verifiable hardship such that to comply with the education requirement would have been impossible or unreasonably burdensome. The Commission shall in no case grant an extension of time to satisfy the postlicensing education requirement that extends beyond the end of the third year after initial licensure as a broker. The Commission also shall not grant an extension of time when the reason for the request is a business or personal conflict or when, in the opinion of the Commission, the principal reason for the provisional broker's failure to obtain the required education in a timely manner was unreasonable delay on the part of the provisional broker in obtaining such education. If an extension of time is granted, the provisional broker may retain his or her license on active status until expiration of the extension period, but the license shall be automatically changed to inactive status at the end of the extension period unless the licensee obtains the required postlicensing education prior to that time. If an extension of time is not granted, the provisional broker's license shall be treated as described in Rule .1902(b) of this Section. A request for an extension of time must be submitted on a form prescribed by the Commission.

### A .1904 Denial Or Withdrawal Of Postlicensing Education Credit

(a) The Commission may deny postlicensing education credit claimed by a provisional broker or reported by a school for a provisional broker, and may withdraw postlicensing education credit previously awarded by the Commission to a provisional broker and make appropriate license status changes for that licensee upon finding that:

(1) The provisional broker or school provided incorrect or incomplete information to the Commission concerning postlicensing education completed by the provisional broker; or

(2) The provisional broker was mistakenly awarded postlicensing education credit due to an administrative error.

(b) When postlicensing education credit is denied or withdrawn by the Commission under Paragraph (a) of this Rule, the provisional broker remains responsible for satisfying the postlicensing education requirement in a timely manner.

(c) A licensee who obtains or attempts to obtain postlicensing education credit through misrepresentation of fact, dishonesty or other improper conduct shall be subject to disciplinary action pursuant to G.S. 93A-6.

# Subchapter 58B
# Time Shares

## SECTION B.0100
## TIME SHARE PROJECT REGISTRATION

### B.0101 Application for Registration

(a) Every application for time share project registration shall be filed at the Commission's office upon a form prescribed by the Commission. Every such application shall contain or have appended thereto:

(1) information concerning the developer's title or right to use the real property on which the project is located, including a title opinion provided by an independent attorney performed within 30 days preceding the date of application;

(2) information concerning owners of time shares at the project other than the developer;

(3) a description of the improvements and amenities located at the project, including a description of the number and type of time share units;

(4) a description of the time share estate to be sold or conveyed to purchasers;

(5) information concerning the developer and his or her financial ability to develop the project (including the developer's most recent audited financial statement, any loan commitments for completion of the proposed time share project, a projected budget for the construction, marketing and operation of the time share project until control by purchasers is asserted, and details of any source of funding for the time share project other than consumer sales proceeds), and information concerning the marketing and managing entities and their relationship to the developer;

(6) the developer's name and address, past real estate development experience and such other information necessary to determine the moral character of those selling and managing the project;

(7) copies of all documents to be distributed to time share purchasers at the point of sale or immediately thereafter; and

(8) such information as may be required by G.S. 93A-52.

The form shall also describe the standards for its proper completion and submission.

(b) In accordance with G.S. 93A-52, an application for time share registration shall be considered to be properly completed when it is wholly and accurately filled out and when all required documents are appended to it and appear to be in compliance with the provisions of the Time Share Act, and, where the project is a condominium, the Condominium Act or Unit Ownership Act.

(c) An entity which owns time shares at a time share project where there are one or more existing registered developers may also apply to the Commission for registration of its time shares, provided that the entity does not control a registered developer, is not controlled by a registered developer, and is not in common control of the project with a registered developer.

### B.0102 Registration Fee

(a) Every application for time share project registration must be accompanied by a certified check made payable to the North Carolina Real Estate Commission. For the initial registration of any time share project, or for a subsequent registration of a time share project by a developer proposing to sell or develop time shares equivalent to at least 20 per cent of the original time share project, the fee is $1,000.00. For a subsequent registration of a previously or presently registered time share project by a developer proposing to sell or develop time shares equivalent to less than 20 per cent of the original time share project, the fee is $800.00. For an initial or subsequent time share project consisting of a single family dwelling unit or a single dwelling unit in a multiple dwelling unit property and in which 10 or less time shares will be or have been created, the fee is $600.00. For any time share registration by a homeowner association for the purpose of re-selling time shares in its own project which it has acquired in satisfaction of unpaid assessments by prior owners, the fee is $400.00.

(b) Applications for registration not accompanied by the appropriate fee shall not be considered by the Commission.

(c) In the event a properly completed application filed with the Commission is denied for any reason, or if an incomplete application is denied by the Commission or abandoned by the developer prior to a final decision by the Commission, the amount of two hundred fifty dollars ($250.00) shall be retained by the Commission from the application fee and the balance refunded to the applicant developer.

### B.0103 Renewal of Time Share Project Registration

(a) Every developer desiring the renewal of a time share project registration shall apply for the same in writing upon a form prescribed by the Commission during the month of June. Every such renewal application shall be accompanied by a certified check made payable to the North Carolina Real Estate Commission in the amount of seven hundred fifty dollars ($750.00). To renew the time share project registration, the properly completed renewal application accompanied by the prescribed fee must be received at the Commission's office prior to the expiration of the certificate of registration.

(b) Applications for the renewal of a time share project registration shall be signed by the developer, by two executive officers of the developer, or by the developer's attorney at law and shall certify that the information contained in the registration filed with the Commission is accurate and current on the date of the renewal application. Making a false certification on a time share project registration renewal application shall be grounds for disciplinary action by the Commission.

### B.0104 Amendments to Time Share Project Registration

(a) A developer shall notify the Commission immediately, but in no event later than 15 days, after any material change in the information contained in the time share project registration.

(b) A material change shall be any change which reflects a difference in:

(1) the nature, quality or availability of the purchaser's ownership or right to use the time share;

(2) the nature, quality or availability of any amenity at the project;

(3) the developer's title, control or right to use the real property on which the project is located;

(4) the information concerning the developer, the managing or marketing entities, or persons connected therewith, previously filed with the Commission;

(5) the purchaser's right to exchange his or her unit; however, a change in the information required to be disclosed to a purchaser by G.S. 93A-48 shall not be a material change; or

(6) the project or time share as originally registered which would be significant to a reasonable purchaser.

(c) Amendments to time share project registrations shall be submitted in the form of substitute pages for material previously filed with the Commission. New or changed information shall be conspicuously indicated by underlining in red ink. Every amendment submitted shall be accompanied by a cover letter signed by the developer or the developer's attorney containing a summary of the amendment and a statement of reasons for which the amendment has been made. The cover letter shall state:

(1) the name and address of the project and its registration number;

(2) the name and address of the developer;

(3) the document or documents to which the amendment applies;

(4) whether or not the changes represented by the amendment required the assent of the time share owners and, if so, how the assent of the time share owners was obtained; and

(5) the recording reference in the office of the register of deeds for the changes, if applicable.

Developers of multiple projects must submit separate amendments and cover letters for each project for which amendments are submitted.

(d) The Commission may, in its discretion, require the developer to file a new time share project registration application in the place of an amendment form. Such refiling shall be without fee.

### B.0105 Notice of Termination

(a) A developer of a registered time share project which, for any reason, terminates its interest, rights, ownership or control of the project or any significant part thereof shall immediately notify the Commission in writing on a form prescribed by the Commission for that purpose. Notice of termination to the Commission shall include the date of termination, the reasons therefor, the identity of the developer's successor, if any, and a report on the status of time share sales to purchasers on the date of termination.

(b) Upon receipt of a properly executed notice of termination of the developer's interest in a time share project, the Commission shall enter a notation of cancellation of registration in the file of the project, and shall notify the developer of cancellation. A developer's failure to give notice of termination as provided herein shall not prevent cancellation of the project's registration under G.S. 93A-52

## SECTION B.0200
## PUBLIC OFFERING STATEMENT

### B.0201 General Provisions

(a) Information contained in a public offering statement shall be accurate on the day it is supplied to a purchaser. Before any public offering statement is supplied to a purchaser, the developer shall file a copy of the statement with the Commission.

(b) In addition to the information required to be contained in a public offering statement by G.S. 93A-44, every public offering statement shall disclose to the purchaser of a time share complete and accurate information concerning:

(1) the real property type of the time share program, whether tenancy-in-common, condominium or other, and a description of the estate the purchaser will own, the term of that estate and the remainder interest, if any, once the term has expired;

(2) the document creating the time share program, a statement that it is the document which governs the program and a reference to the location where the purchaser may obtain or examine a copy of the document;

(3) whether or not the property is being converted to a time share from some other use and, if so, a statement to that effect and disclosure of the prior use of the property;

(4) the maximum number of time shares in the project, each recreational and other commonly used facility offered, and who or what will own each facility, if the project is to be completed in one development or construction phase;

(5) if the project is planned in phased construction or development, the complete plan of phased offerings, including the maximum number of time shares which may be in the project, each recreational and other commonly used facility, who or what will own each facility, and the developer's representations regarding his or her commitment to build out the project;
(6) the association of owners or other entity which will ultimately be responsible for managing the time share program, the first date or event when the entity will convene or commence to conduct business, each owner's voting right, if any, and whether and for how long the developer, as time share owner, will control the entity;
(7) the location where owners may inspect the articles and bylaws of the owners association, or other organizational documents of the entity and the books and records it produces;
(8) whether the entity has lien rights against time share owners for failure to pay assessments;
(9) whether or not the developer has entered into a management contract on behalf of the managing entity, the extent to which the managing entity's powers are delegated to the manager and the location where a copy of the management contract may be examined;
(10) whether or not the developer will pay assessments for time shares which it owns and a statement that the amount of assessments due the managing entity from owners will change over time, as circumstances may change;
(11) whether or not the developer sponsors or will sponsor a rental or resale program and, if so, a summary of the program or programs; and
(12) the developer's role at the project, if the developer is a separate entity from any other registered developer of the time share project.

(c) The inclusion of false or misleading statements in a public offering statement shall be grounds for disciplinary action by the Commission.

### B.0202 Public Offering Statement Summary

Every public offering statement shall contain a one page cover prescribed by the Commission and completed by the developer entitled Public Offering Statement Summary. The Public Offering Statement Summary shall read as follows:

**PUBLIC OFFERING STATEMENT SUMMARY**

**NAME OF PROJECT:**
**NAME AND REAL ESTATE LICENSE NUMBER OF BROKER:**

This Public Offering Statement contains information which deserves your careful study, as you decide whether or not to purchase a time share.

The Public Offering Statement includes general information about the real estate type, the term, and the size of this time share project. It also includes a general description of the recreational and other facilities existing now, or to be provided in the future. The Public Offering Statement will tell you how maintenance and management of the project will be provided and how the costs of these services will be charged to purchasers. From the Public Offering Statement, you will also learn how the project will be governed and whether purchasers will have a voice in that government. You will also learn that a time share instrument will be recorded to protect your real estate interest in your time share.

The Public Offering Statement contains important information, but is not a substitute for the detailed information contained in the contract of purchase and the legal documents which create and affect the time share program at this project.

Please study this Public Offering Statement carefully. Satisfy yourself that any questions you may have are answered before you decide to purchase. If a salesperson or other representative of the developer has made a representation which concerns you, and you cannot find that representation in writing, ask that it be pointed out to you.

**NOTICE**

**UNDER NORTH CAROLINA LAW, YOU MAY CANCEL YOUR TIME SHARE PURCHASE WITHOUT PENALTY WITHIN FIVE DAYS AFTER SIGNING YOUR CONTRACT. TO CANCEL YOUR TIME SHARE PURCHASE, YOU MUST MAIL OR HAND DELIVER WRITTEN NOTICE OF YOUR DESIRE TO CANCEL YOUR PURCHASE TO (name and address of project). IF YOU CHOOSE TO MAIL YOUR CANCELLATION NOTICE, THE NORTH CAROLINA REAL ESTATE COMMISSION RECOMMENDS THAT YOU USE REGISTERED OR CERTIFIED MAIL AND THAT YOU RETAIN YOUR POSTAL RECEIPT AS PROOF OF THE DATE YOUR NOTICE WAS MAILED. UPON CANCELLATION, ALL PAYMENTS WILL BE REFUNDED TO YOU.**

### B.0203 Receipt for Public Offering Statement

(a) Prior to the execution of any contract to purchase a time share, a time share developer or a time share salesperson shall obtain from the purchaser a written receipt for the public offering statement, which shall display, directly over the buyer signature line in type in all capital letters, no smaller than the largest type on the page on which it appears, the following statement: DO NOT SIGN THIS RECEIPT UNLESS YOU HAVE RECEIVED A COMPLETE COPY OF THE PUBLIC OFFERING STATEMENT TO TAKE WITH YOU.

(b) Receipts for public offering statements shall be maintained as part of the records of the sales transaction.

## SECTION B.0300 CANCELLATION

### B.0301 Proof of Cancellation

(a) The postmark date affixed to any written notice of a purchaser's intent to cancel his or her time share purchase shall be presumed by the Commission to be the date the notice was mailed to the developer. Evidence tending to rebut this presumption shall be admissible at a hearing before the Commission.

(b) Upon receipt of a purchaser's written notice of his or her intent to cancel his or her time share purchase, the developer, or his or her agent or representative, shall retain the notice and any enclosure, envelope or other cover in the developer's files at the project, and shall produce the file upon the Commission's request.

(c) When there is more than one registered developer at a time share project and a purchaser gives written notice of his or her intent to cancel his or her time share purchase that is received by a developer or sales staff other than the one from whom his or her time share was purchased, the developer or sales staff receiving such notice shall promptly deliver it to the proper developer who shall then honor the notice if it was timely sent by the purchaser.

## SECTION B.0400 TIME SHARE SALES OPERATIONS

### B.0401 Retention of Time Share Records

A time share developer and a time share salesperson shall retain or cause to be retained for a period of three years complete records of every time share sale, rental, or exchange transaction made by or on behalf of the developer. Records required to be retained shall include but not be limited to offers, applications and contracts to purchase, rent or exchange time shares; records of the deposit, maintenance and disbursement of funds required to be held in trust; receipts; notices of cancellation and their covers if mailed; records regarding compensation of salespersons; public offering statements; and any other records pertaining to time share transactions. Such records shall be made available to the Commission and its representatives upon request.

### B.0402 Time Share Agency Agreements and Disclosure

Time share sales transactions conducted by licensees on behalf of a time share developer are subject to 21 NCAC 58A .0104.

## SECTION B.0500 HANDLING AND ACCOUNTING OF FUNDS

### B.0501 Time Share Trust Funds

(a) Except as otherwise permitted by G.S. 93A-45(c), all monies received by a time share developer or a time share broker in connection with a time share sales transaction shall be deposited into a trust or escrow account not later than three banking days following receipt and shall remain in such account for ten days from the date of sale or until cancellation by the purchaser, whichever first occurs.

(b) All monies received by a person licensed as a broker in connection with a time share transaction shall be delivered immediately to his or her project broker.

(c) When a time share purchaser timely cancels his or her time share purchase, the developer shall refund to the purchaser all monies paid by the purchaser in connection with the purchase. The refund shall be made no later than 30 days following the date of execution of the contract. Amounts paid by the purchaser with a bank card or a credit card shall be refunded by a cash payment or by issuing a credit voucher to the purchaser within the 30-day period.

(d) Every project broker shall obtain and keep a written representation from the developer as to whether or not lien-free or lien-subordinated time share instruments can be recorded within 45 days of the purchaser's execution of the time share purchase agreement. When a lien-free or lien-subordinated instrument cannot be recorded within said time period, on the business day following the expiration of the ten day time share payment escrow period, a project broker shall transfer from his or her trust account all purchase deposit funds or other payments received from a purchaser who has not canceled his or her purchase agreement, to the independent escrow agent in a check made payable to the independent escrow agent. Alternatively, the check may be made payable to the developer with a restrictive endorsement placed on the back of the check providing "For deposit to the account of the independent escrow agent for the (name of time share project) only."

## SECTION B.0600 PROJECT BROKER

### B.0601 Designation of Project Broker

The developer of a registered time share project shall designate for each project subject to the developer's control a project broker by filing with the Commission an affidavit on the form prescribed. The developer may from time to time change the designated project broker by filing a new designation form with the Commission within ten days following the change. A broker licensed under the provisions of Section .1800 of Subchapter 58A shall not be designated as a project broker. Provisional brokers shall not be designated as a project broker.

### B.0602 Duties of the Project Broker

(a) The broker designated by the developer of a time share project to be project broker shall assume responsibility for:

(1) The display of the time share project certificate registration and the license certificates of the real estate brokers associated with or engaged on behalf of the developer at the project;
(2) The determination of whether each licensee employed has complied with Rules .0503 and .0506 of Subchapter 58A;
(3) The notification to the Commission of any change in the identity or address of the project or in the identity or address of the developer or marketing or managing entities at the project;
(4) The deposit and maintenance of time share purchase or rental monies in a trust or escrow account until proper disbursement is made; and
(5) The proper maintenance of accurate records at the project including all records relating to the handling of trust monies at the project, records relating to time share sales and rental transactions and the project registration and renewal.

(b) The project broker shall review all contracts, public offering statements and other documents distributed to the purchasers of time shares at the project to ensure that the documents comport with the requirements of the Time Share Act and the rules adopted by the Commission, and to ensure that true and accurate documents have been given to the purchasers.

(c) The project broker shall not permit time share sales to be conducted by any person not licensed as a broker, and shall not delegate or assign his or her supervisory responsibilities to any other person, nor accept control of his or her supervisory responsibilities by any other person.

(d) The project broker shall notify the Commission in writing of any change in his or her status as project broker within ten days following the change.

### SECTION B.0700— TIME SHARE FORMS

#### B.0701 Forms for Time Share Projects

B.0701 is not reprinted in this booklet but is available upon written request to the North Carolina Real Estate Commission.

## Subchapter 58C Real Estate Prelicensing Education

Rules for Subchapter 58C are not reprinted in this booklet but are available upon written request to the North Carolina Real Estate Commission.

## Subchapter 58D Real Estate Appraisers (Repealed)

## Subchapter 58E Real Estate Continuing Education

Rules for Subchapter 58E are not reprinted in this booklet but are available upon written request to the North Carolina Real Estate Commission.

## Subchapter 58F Broker Transition Course

### SECTION .0100 – REQUIREMENTS

#### F .0101 Basic Requirement

A provisional broker who was issued a real estate salesperson license prior to October 1, 2005 that was changed to a broker license on provisional status on April 1, 2006 in accordance with G.S. 93A-4.3(a), shall, as prescribed in G.S. 93A-4.3(b), complete a broker transition course consisting of 24 classroom hours of instruction prescribed by the Commission not later than April 1, 2008, unless the provisional broker can demonstrate to the Commission not later than April 1, 2008 that he or she possesses four years' full-time real estate brokerage experience or equivalent part-time real estate brokerage experience within the previous six years.

The remaining rules in this section are not reprinted, but are available upon written request to the NCREC.

# TRUST ACCOUNT GUIDELINES

## I. INTRODUCTION

"Trust" is perhaps the one word which best describes the relationship of the real estate licensee to his or her clients and customers. The seller trusts the licensee to promote his or her best interests in the sale of the property. The investor trusts the licensee/rental manager to manage his or her property and protect the investment. The buyer trusts the licensee to provide complete and accurate information concerning the property which he or she is considering buying. But perhaps nowhere is the licensee's position of trust more clearly illustrated than in his or her role as custodian of the funds of others; i.e., "trust money."

The following information is provided for the purpose of assisting North Carolina real estate licensees in understanding and carrying out their duties and responsibilities as trustees for the funds of others. It is important that both licensees and persons studying for real estate licenses carefully study this material, and that practicing licensees review and evaluate their current procedures in light of this information.

While no single treatment of this subject can possibly answer all questions or address all situations that the licensee may encounter, nevertheless, an attempt has been made to deal with those questions that arise most frequently and to address those situations most often encountered during the course of "typical" real estate transactions. In addition, the specialized areas of property owner association management and rental management have been given separate treatment where it was deemed necessary.

Licensees are reminded that questions or problems involving the handling or accounting of trust money should be directed to the Real Estate Commission office in Raleigh.

## II. LEGAL REQUIREMENTS

For most people, a home represents the largest single investment (the most expensive purchase) they will ever make. Rental payments and security deposits represent a substantial financial investment on the part of tenants. Consequently, during the course of real estate transactions, sizable sums of money change hands, a great deal of which passes through the hands of the real estate licensee. Recognizing the very serious consequences of the licensee's actions as a trustee for these funds, the Real Estate License Law (N.C.G.S. 93A) includes a number of provisions designed to govern the activities of real estate licensees acting in the capacity of trustee.

In general, these provisions require licensees to deposit trust monies in an escrow or trust account maintained by a broker (separate from the broker's general or operating account); to maintain complete records of deposits and withdrawals; and to make a final accounting to the persons for whom the broker is holding the funds. G.S. 93A-6(a) grants the Real Estate Commission authority to suspend or revoke any real estate license or to reprimand or censure any licensee where the licensee is deemed to be guilty of:

**(7)** Failing, within a reasonable time, to account for or to remit any moneys coming into his or her possession which belong to others.

**(12)** Commingling the money or other property of his or her principals with his or her own or failure to maintain and deposit in a trust or escrow account in an insured bank or savings and loan association in North Carolina all money received by him or her as a real estate licensee acting in that capacity, or an escrow agent, or the temporary custodian of the funds of others, in a real estate transaction; provided, these accounts shall not bear interest unless the principals authorize in writing the deposit be made in an interest bearing account and also provide for the disbursement of the interest accrued.

**(14)** Failing, at the time the transaction is consummated, to deliver to the seller in every real estate transaction, a complete detailed closing statement showing all of the receipts and disbursements handled by him or her for the seller or failing to deliver to the buyer a complete statement showing all money received in the transaction from the buyer and how and for what it was disbursed.

Also,

**(d)** Each broker shall maintain complete records showing the deposit, maintenance, and withdrawal of money or other property owned by his principals or held in escrow or in trust for his principals. The Commission may inspect these records periodically, without prior notice and may also inspect these records whenever the Commission determines that they are pertinent to an investigation of any specific complaint against a licensee.

With regard to monies received in time share sales transactions, G.S. 93A-45 requires that:

**(c)** Any payments received by a time share developer or time share salesperson in connection with the sale of the time share shall be immediately deposited by such developer or salesperson in a trust or escrow account in an insured bank or savings and loan association in North Carolina and shall remain in such account for 10 days or cancellation by the purchaser, whichever occurs first. Payments held in such trust or escrow accounts shall be deemed to belong to the purchaser and not the developer.

In addition, the Real Estate Commission has adopted rules to enable it to administer the statutes. Specifically, these rules are:

### A. 0107 Handling and Accounting of Funds

(a) Except as provided herein, all monies received by a licensee acting in his or her fiduciary capacity shall be deposited in a trust or escrow account maintained by a broker not later than three banking days following receipt of such monies except that earnest money deposits paid by means other than currency which are received on offers to purchase real estate and tenant security deposits paid by means other than currency which are received in connection with real estate leases shall be deposited in a trust or escrow account not later than three banking days following acceptance of such offer to purchase or lease; the date of acceptance of such offer to purchase or lease shall be set forth in the purchase or lease agreement. All monies received by a provisional broker shall be delivered immediately to the broker by whom he or she is employed, except that all monies received by nonresident commercial licensees shall be delivered as required by Rule .1808 of this Subchapter. A licensee may accept custody of a check or other negotiable instrument made payable to the seller of real property as option money only for the purpose of delivering the instrument to the optionor-seller. While the instrument is in the custody of the licensee, the licensee shall, according to the instructions of the buyer-optionee, either deliver it to the seller-optionor or return it to the buyer-optionee. The licensee shall safeguard the instrument and shall be responsible to the parties on the instrument for its prompt and safe delivery. In no event shall a licensee retain such an instrument for more than three business days after the acceptance of the option contract.

(b) In the event monies received by a licensee while acting in a fiduciary capacity are deposited in a trust or escrow account which bears interest, the licensee having custody over such monies shall first secure from all parties having an interest in the monies written authorization for the deposit of the monies in an interest-bearing account. Such authorization shall specify how and to whom the interest will be disbursed, and, if contained in an offer, contract, lease, or other transaction instrument, such authorization shall be set forth in a conspicuous manner which shall distinguish it from other provisions of the instrument.

(c) Closing statements shall be furnished to the buyer and the seller in the transaction not more than five days after closing.

(d) Trust or escrow accounts shall be so designated by the bank or savings and loan association in which the account is located, and all deposit tickets and checks drawn on said account as well as the monthly bank statement for the account shall bear the words "Trust Account" or "Escrow Account."

(e) A licensee shall maintain and retain records sufficient to identify the ownership of all funds belonging to others. Such records shall be sufficient to show proper deposit of such funds in a trust or escrow account and to verify the accuracy and proper use of the trust or escrow account. The required records shall include:

(1) bank statements.

(2) canceled checks which shall be referenced to the corresponding journal entry or check stub entries and to the corresponding sales transaction ledger sheets or for rental transactions, the corresponding property or owner ledger sheets. Checks shall conspicuously identify the payee and shall bear a notation identifying the purpose of the disbursement. When a check is used to disburse funds for more than one sales transaction, owner, or property, the check shall bear a notation identifying each sales transaction, owner, or property for which disbursement is made, including the amount disbursed for each, and the corresponding sales transaction, property, or owner ledger entries. When necessary, the check notation may refer to the required information recorded on a supplemental disbursement worksheet which shall be cross-referenced to the corresponding check. In lieu of retaining canceled checks, a licensee may retain digitally imaged copies of the canceled checks or substitute checks provided that such images are legible reproductions of the front and back of such instruments with no smaller images than 1.1875 x 3.0 inches and provided that the licensee's bank retains for a period of at least six years the original checks, "substitute checks" as described in 12 C.F.R. 229.51 or the capacity to provide substitute checks as described in 12 C.F.R. 229.51 and makes the original or substitute checks available to the licensee and the Commission upon request.

(3) deposit tickets. For a sales transaction, the deposit ticket shall identify the purpose and remitter of the funds deposited, the property, the parties involved, and a reference to the corresponding sales transaction ledger entry. For a rental transaction, the deposit ticket shall identify the purpose and remitter of the funds deposited, the tenant, and the corresponding property or owner ledger entry. For deposits of funds belonging to or collected on behalf of a property owner association, the deposit ticket shall identify the property or property interest for which the payment is made, the property or interest owner, the remitter, and the purpose of the payment. When a single deposit ticket is used to deposit funds collected for more than one sales transaction, property owner, or property, the required information shall be recorded on the ticket for each sales transaction, owner, or property, or the ticket may refer to the same information recorded on a supplemental deposit worksheet which shall be cross-referenced to the corresponding deposit ticket.

(4) a payment record sheet for each property or interest for which funds are collected and deposited into a property owner association trust account as required by Subsection (i) of this Rule. Payment record sheets shall identify the amount, date, remitter, and purpose of payments received, the amount and nature of the obligation for which payments are made, and the amount of any balance due or delinquency.

(5) a separate ledger sheet for each sales transaction and for each property or owner of property managed by the

licensee identifying the property, the parties to the transaction, the amount, date, and purpose of the deposits and from whom received, the amount, date, check number, and purpose of disbursements and to whom paid, and the running balance of funds on deposit for the particular sales transaction or, in a rental transaction, the particular property or owner of property. Monies held as tenant security deposits in connection with rental transactions may be accounted for on a separate tenant security deposit ledger for each property or owner of property managed by the licensee. For each security deposit the tenant security deposit ledger shall identify the remitter, the date the deposit was paid, the amount, the tenant, landlord, and subject property. For each disbursement of tenant security deposit monies, the ledger shall identify the check number, amount, payee, date, and purpose of the disbursement. The ledger shall also show a running balance. When tenant security deposit monies are accounted for on a separate ledger as provided herein, deposit tickets, canceled checks and supplemental worksheets shall reference the corresponding tenant security deposit ledger entries when appropriate.

(6) a journal or check stubs identifying in chronological sequence each bank deposit and disbursement of monies to and from the trust or escrow account, including the amount and date of each deposit and a reference to the corresponding deposit ticket and any supplemental deposit worksheet, and the amount, date, check number, and purpose of disbursements and to whom paid. The journal or check stubs shall also show a running balance for all funds in the account.

(7) copies of contracts, leases and management agreements.

(8) closing statements and property management statements.

(9) covenants, bylaws, minutes, management agreements and periodic statements relating to the management of a property owner association.

(10) invoices, bills, and contracts paid from the trust account, and any documents not otherwise described herein necessary and sufficient to verify and explain record entries.

Records of all receipts and disbursements of trust or escrow monies shall be maintained in such a manner as to create an audit trail from deposit tickets and canceled checks to check stubs or journals and to the ledger sheets. Ledger sheets and journals or check stubs must be reconciled to the trust or escrow account bank statements on a monthly basis. To be sufficient, records of trust or escrow monies must include a worksheet for each such monthly reconciliation showing the ledger sheets, journals or check stubs, and bank statements to be in agreement and balance.

(f) All trust or escrow account records shall be made available for inspection by the Commission or its authorized representatives in accordance with Rule 58A .0108.

(g) In the event of a dispute between the seller and buyer or landlord and tenant over the return or forfeiture of any deposit other than a residential tenant security deposit held by a licensee, the licensee shall retain said deposit in a trust or escrow account until the licensee has obtained a written release from the parties consenting to its disposition or until disbursement is ordered by a court of competent jurisdiction. Alternatively, the licensee may deposit the disputed monies with the appropriate clerk of court in accordance with the provision of G.S. 93A-12. If it appears to a licensee holding a disputed deposit that a party has abandoned his or her claim, the licensee may disburse the money to the other claiming parties according to their written agreement provided that the licensee first makes a reasonable effort to notify the party who has apparently abandoned his or her claim and provides that party with an opportunity to renew his or her claim to the disputed funds. Tenant security deposit monies shall be disposed of in accordance with the requirements of N.C.G.S. 42-50 through 56 and N.C.G.S. 42A-18.

(h) A licensee may transfer earnest money deposits in his or her possession collected in connection with a sales transaction from his or her trust account to the closing attorney or other settlement agent not more than ten days prior to the anticipated settlement date. A licensee shall not disburse prior to settlement any earnest money in his or her possession for any other purpose without the written consent of the parties.

(i) The funds of a property owner association, when collected, maintained, disbursed or otherwise controlled by a licensee, are trust monies and shall be treated as such in the manner required by this Rule. Such funds must be deposited into and maintained in a trust or escrow account dedicated exclusively for funds belonging to a single property owners association and may not be commingled with funds belonging to other property owner associations or other persons or parties. A licensee who undertakes to act as manager of a property owner association or as the custodian of funds belonging to a property owner association shall provide the association with periodic statements which report the balance of association funds in the licensee's possession or control and which account for the funds the licensee has received and disbursed on behalf of the association. Such statements must be made in accordance with the licensee's agreement with the association, but in no event shall the statements be made less frequently than every 90 days.

(j) Every licensee shall safeguard the money or property of others coming into his or her possession in a manner consistent with the requirements of the Real Estate License Law and the rules adopted by the Commission. A licensee shall not convert the money or property of others to his or her own use, apply such money or property to a purpose other than that for which it was paid or entrusted to him or her, or permit or assist any other person in the conversion or misapplication of such money or property.

(k) In addition to the records required by paragraph (e) of this rule, a licensee acting as agent for the landlord of a residential property used for vacation rentals shall create and maintain a subsidiary ledger sheet for each property or owner of such properties onto which all funds collected and disbursed are identified in categories by purpose. On a monthly basis, the licensee shall reconcile the subsidiary ledger sheets to the corresponding property or property owner ledger sheet.

(l) In lieu of maintaining a subsidiary ledger sheet, the licensee may maintain an accounts payable ledger sheet for each owner or property and each vendor to whom trust monies are due for monies collected on behalf of the owner or property identifying the date of receipt of the trust monies, from whom the monies were received, rental dates, and the corresponding property or owner ledger sheet entry including the amount to be disbursed for each and the purpose of the disbursement. The licensee may also maintain an accounts payable ledger sheet in the format described in paragraph (k) above for vacation rental tenant security deposit monies and vacation rental advance payments.

### B. 0501 Time Share Trust Funds

(a) Except as otherwise permitted by G.S. 93A-45(c), all monies received by a time share developer or a time share broker in connection with a time share sales transaction shall be deposited into a trust or escrow account not later than three banking days following receipt and shall remain in such account for ten days from the date of sale or until cancellation by the purchaser, whichever first occurs.

(b) All monies received by a person licensed as a broker in connection with a time share transaction shall be delivered immediately to his or her project broker.

(c) When a time share purchaser timely cancels his or her time share purchase, the developer shall refund to the purchaser all monies paid by the purchaser in connection with the purchase. The refund shall be made no later than 30 days following the date of execution of the contract. Amounts paid by the purchaser with a bank card or a credit card shall be refunded by a cash payment or by issuing a credit voucher to the purchaser within the 30-day period.

(d) Every project broker shall obtain and keep a written representation from the developer as to whether or not lien-free or lien-subordinated time share instruments can be recorded within 45 days of the purchaser's execution of the time share purchase agreement. When a lien-free or lien-subordinated instrument cannot be recorded within said time period, on the business day following the expiration of the ten day time share payment escrow period, a project broker shall transfer from his or her trust account all purchase deposit funds or other payments received from a purchaser who has not canceled his or her purchase agreement, to the independent escrow agent in a check made payable to the independent escrow agent. Alternatively, the check may be made payable to the developer with a restrictive endorsement placed on the back of the check providing "For deposit to the account of the independent escrow agent for the (name of time share project) only."

The Commission considers violations of these laws and rules to be a particularly serious matter. In fact, more licensees are disciplined for trust money or trust account violations than for any other single type of offense.

## III. TRUST MONEY

### Definition

In the context of real estate transactions, "trust money" is most commonly money belonging to others received by a real estate licensee who is acting as an agent in a real estate transaction. Certain monies, such as tenant security deposits and time share down payment monies are trust money simply because the law declares them to be. Also, a licensee who acts as the temporary custodian of money belonging to others must hold that money in trust even if the circumstances are only collateral to the licensee's role as an agent in a real estate related matter, e.g., a listing agent receives money from his out-of-town seller to use to maintain the property. A licensee who collects money on behalf of a property owner association for a fee must deposit that money into a properly designated trust or escrow account.

The most common examples of trust money are earnest money deposits, down payments, tenant security deposits, rents, homeowner association dues and assessments, and money received from final settlements. In the case of resort and other short-term rentals, trust money would also include advance reservation deposits and the state (and local, if applicable) sales taxes on the gross receipts from such rentals.

Except for depositing and maintaining in a trust account $100 (or such other amount as may be required) to cover bank charges, it is inappropriate for a licensee to mix trust money held for others with the licensee's own money. This impermissible mixing of trust money and licensee money is referred to as commingling. For example, it would be commingling if a licensee were to deposit commissions earned on a real estate sales transaction into the licensee's trust account. It would also be commingling if a licensee were to deposit $1,000 of the licensee's own money into the licensee's trust account in order to maintain a daily bank balance that would avoid bank service charges.

When a licensee commingles the money he or she holds for others with his or her own in the same bank account, he or she creates doubt whether the account is, in fact, a trust account. These doubts may deprive the account of the special status given to trust accounts and may place money belonging to the licensee's customers and clients in jeopardy.

## IV. TRUST ACCOUNTS

### Definition/Purpose

A "trust account" (or "escrow account") is simply a bank account into which trust money (and only trust money) is deposited. It must be a *separate custodial account* which provides for *withdrawal of funds on demand* (without prior notice).

By depositing trust money in a trust account and keeping accurate records that identify each depositor (buyer, seller, landlord, tenant, etc.), the depositors are protected from the funds being "frozen" (attached) should the broker/trustee become involved in legal action or become incapacitated or die. Also, deposits are insured by the Federal Deposit Insurance Corporation (FDIC), up to $100,000 per each individual for whom funds are deposited. For example, if a broker is holding $60,000 in his or her trust account for one client, and $50,000 for another, both clients' deposits will be fully insured, assuming neither has other money on deposit in personal accounts in the same bank which would raise the total of his or her money in the bank over $100,000. (Funds in excess of $100,000 for one individual at the same bank are not insured, whether the funds are in one account or spread among several accounts.) Furthermore, by placing these funds in a separate account, brokers are less likely to confuse the trust money with their personal or business funds and inadvertently use trust money (which belongs to others) for personal or business purposes.

### Opening the Account

Trust accounts must be opened and maintained in either an insured bank or savings and loan association in North Carolina. A broker who is not using his or her real estate license is not required to open or maintain a trust account. Likewise, if a practicing broker does not collect or otherwise handle the funds of others, no trust account is required. Only when the broker or a licensee associated with the broker or under the broker's supervision takes possession of trust money must the broker open and properly maintain a trust account.

When a broker holds trust money in sales or rental transactions, only one trust account is required, and all earnest money deposits, tenant security deposits, rents, and other trust money can be deposited into this one common account. However, brokers who are active in both sales and rental management often find it helpful to use more than one trust account. For example, they may wish to keep a "general sales trust account" for earnest money deposits, settlement proceeds, etc., and a "rental trust account" for tenant security deposits, rents, and related receipts. Although it is not required, many brokers involved in rental management elect to maintain an additional "security deposit trust account" for the purpose of separating tenant security deposits from rents and other related receipts.

Brokers who manage a property owner association must deposit and maintain that association's trust funds in a trust or escrow account dedicated exclusively for funds of that association. A property owner association's trust funds must not be commingled with the funds belonging to another property owner association or with the funds belonging to third parties (earnest money deposits, security deposits, rents, etc. belonging to third parties). Brokers may open more than one trust account for a property owner association. A provisional broker coming into control of the trust funds of an association must deposit and maintain that association's trust funds in a trust account maintained by a broker.

### Broker-Owner Trust Monies

Brokers who sell or lease their own property must not commingle funds received in connection with these properties with funds they hold in trust for others. Earnest money, tenant security deposits and other funds required to be held in trust in connection with broker-owned property must be held in a separate trust account.

For example, if a broker does business as a sole proprietorship, and also owns several rental houses, the broker must not deposit either the rents or the tenant security deposits for the rental properties he or she owns into his or her sole proprietorship trust account since it contains other clients' funds. This would constitute commingling. Instead, because the Tenant Security Deposit Act requires all residential landlords to keep the tenant's security deposit in a trust account, the broker should set up a separate trust account for the security deposits from his or her own tenants.

Only when the owner of the rental property and the owner of the real estate company are separate legal identities may the broker deposit trust monies from the rental property into the real estate company trust account. Thus, for example, if the broker's real estate company is a corporation and the rental property is owned by the broker individually, then the corporation may manage the individual broker's rental property and may deposit both rental receipts and tenant security deposits into the corporate trust account(s) established for third party clients of the corporation.

A broker who is uncertain whether money from personally-owned rental properties can be deposited into his or her trust account should maintain a separate trust account in order to assure compliance and avoid commingling.

A trust account must be designated as a "Trust Account" or "Escrow Account" by the bank (or savings and loan association) in which the account is located, and all bank statements, deposit tickets and checks drawn on the account must bear the words, "Trust Account" or "Escrow Account."

Trust accounts are subject to the same service charges as regular checking accounts. Whenever possible, brokers should arrange for the depository to either bill them for these expenses or charge these expenses to the broker's personal or general operating account. However, if such arrangements cannot be made, the broker may deposit and maintain in his or her trust account a maximum of $100.00 of his or her personal funds (or such other amount as may be required) to cover such charges. A broker who keeps $100 of his or her own money in the trust account must be careful to properly enter and identify personal funds on the deposit ticket and on a personal funds ledger sheet in his or her trust account records. Thereafter, the broker must record any bank charges as they occur in his or her trust account journal or check stub running balance and post the bank charges on the personal funds ledger sheet.

### Interest-Bearing Trust Accounts

Trust money may be deposited in an interest-bearing trust account ONLY under the following conditions: (1) the broker must obtain from the persons for whom he or she is holding the funds written authorization to deposit the funds into an interest-bearing account; (2) the authorization must clearly specify how and to whom the interest will be disbursed; and (3) if the authorization is contained in an offer, contract, lease or other transaction instrument, it must be set forth in a manner which shall draw attention to the authorization and distinguish it from other provisions of the instrument (for example, italics, boldface type, underlining, a blank __________ to be filled in with the name of the party to whom the interest will be paid, or some similar means).

Inasmuch as trust money must be deposited in a demand account in an insured bank or savings and loan association, the investment of such funds in any type of security, including government bonds, would be prohibited. The investment of trust money in most certificates of deposit is also prohibited. Trust money may be maintained in a certificate of deposit with an insured bank or savings and loan association only if the certificate of deposit is insured and the terms governing it permit withdrawal of the trust money on demand and without any penalty that would reduce the principal amount of the trust money invested in this manner. Trust monies may not be deposited in sweep accounts or invested in repurchase agreements.

## V. DEPOSITING TRUST MONEY

### Who Should Deposit?

When listing property for sale or lease, a provision should be included in the listing or rental management agreement naming the broker as trustee or escrow agent for the purpose of receiving and holding trust money. Likewise, offers to purchase, sales agreements, leases, etc. should specify in whose account the trust money will be held so that all persons who have an interest in the funds will know whom to hold responsible for their safekeeping.

Unless the parties have agreed otherwise, trust money received by a licensee working with a buyer in a co-brokered sales transaction should be immediately delivered to the listing broker for deposit into the listing broker's trust account. In general, all trust money received by an individual licensee who is associated with or employed by a broker or brokerage firm should, of course, be deposited in the trust account of the employing broker or firm. All trust money received by a provisional broker must be immediately delivered to the provisional broker's supervising broker.

A broker may transfer possession of trust money to a bookkeeper, secretary, or some other clerical employee for that person to deposit the funds in a trust account; however, the broker will still be held responsible for the care and custody of such funds. Brokers should closely and diligently supervise the acts of these persons. Periodic audits and bonding of such persons is recommended.

### When to Deposit?

Earnest money received on offers to purchase and tenant security deposits received in connection with leases must be deposited in a trust account not later than three banking days following acceptance of the offer to purchase or lease; however, cash deposits must be deposited not later than three banking days following receipt of such deposits. The date of acceptance must be shown in the purchase or lease agreement. Rents, settlement proceeds, and other trust money must be deposited in a trust account not later than three banking days following receipt of the funds.

A licensee who accepts custody of a check or other negotiable instrument made payable to the seller of real property as option money is not required to deposit the money in a trust or escrow account. The licensee shall handle the check according to the instructions of the buyer-optionee and either deliver the check to the seller-optionor or return it to the buyer-optionee. After acceptance of the option contract, the licensee has three business days to deliver the check.

In the event of a dispute between the seller-optionor and buyer-optionee over option money in the form of a check or other negotiable instrument made payable to the seller of the property, the licensee shall handle the money according to the instructions of the buyer-optionee.

Option money received by a licensee in the form of cash must be deposited into a trust or escrow account within three banking days of receipt.

## VI. DISBURSING TRUST MONEY

### Permitted Uses/Access

The instrument creating the trust (sales contract, rental management agreement, lease, etc.) should clearly state to whom and under what conditions the trust money will be disbursed (especially in the event the transaction is not consummated). Brokers may disburse trust money only for the purpose(s) set forth in this instrument; for example, brokers may not use trust money to pay for credit reports, surveys, appraisal fees, or other transaction expenses without the consent of both the buyer and the seller, or the landlord and tenant.

Access to trust money should be limited and carefully controlled. Although a broker may authorize a secretary, a bookkeeper, or some other person who is not a party to the transaction to sign checks withdrawing trust money, the broker will not escape liability and responsibility for the misuse of the funds by such persons. Again, brokers are advised to closely supervise these persons, and periodic audits and bonding of such persons are recommended.

### When to Disburse?

**Sales Transactions:**

In "sales transactions," brokers will normally disburse trust money upon the happening of one of the following events:

(1) Upon revocation or rejection of an offer. A buyer (offeror) may revoke an offer to purchase at any time prior to being notified of the acceptance of the offer. If the buyer revokes his or her offer or if the offer is rejected by the seller (offeree), then the broker should return the earnest money to the buyer. However, if the earnest money is in the form of a personal check which has already been deposited by the broker, the broker should not refund the deposit until the check has cleared.

(2) Upon termination of a transaction. If, for some reason, a transaction is not consummated and there is no dispute between the parties as to the disposition of the trust money, then the broker should disburse the money according to the provisions of the sales agreement. However, in the event of a dispute between the buyer and seller over the funds (or if the broker has reason to believe that such a dispute may arise), then the broker must attempt to obtain a written release from the parties consenting to its disposition. Failing this, the broker must retain the funds in his or her trust account until the dispute is litigated by the parties and disbursement is ordered by a court of competent jurisdiction or the broker utilizes the new G.S. 93A-12 procedure.

(3) Upon closing of a transaction. At the successful conclusion of a real estate transaction, any funds pertaining to the transaction which are on deposit in the broker's trust account should be paid to and subsequently disbursed by the person designated to close the transaction (usually an attorney or lending officer).

Occasionally, however, the broker will actually conduct the closing and disburse the funds. In such cases, brokers should not transfer trust money from their trust account to their general business account for final disbursement, because this would result in a commingling of trust money and non-trust money during that period of time in which the trust money is in the business account. Trust money should be disbursed directly from the trust account to the persons entitled to such funds.

Furthermore, brokerage fees, including interest earned on interest-bearing accounts, or commissions (when earned), should be disbursed promptly (within 30 days) from the trust account to the broker's general business account, with each check clearly indicating the specific transaction to which it applies. When a broker retains deposit money in his or her trust account in order to pay all or a part of the commission or fees owed to him or other licensees involved, he or she should pay the money from his or her trust account into his or her general business account and make further payments from that account. Brokers should not, of course, withdraw from the trust account any portion of their earned commissions prior to closing without the express consent of all parties to the transaction.

### Option Transactions:

Option money in the form of cash that has been deposited into the trust or escrow account must be disbursed not more than three business days following the acceptance of the option contract. However, in the event of a dispute between the seller-optionor and buyer-optionee over the funds (or if the broker has reason to believe that such a dispute may arise), then the broker must attempt to obtain a written release from the parties consenting to its disposition, and failing this, the broker must retain the funds in his or her trust account until the dispute is litigated by the parties and disbursement is ordered by a court of competent jurisdiction.

### Lease Transactions:

In "lease transactions," that is, transactions involving the leasing or renting of real estate for others, the leasing agent or rental manager must deposit all rental income and tenant security deposits in his or her trust account; likewise, all disbursements required in connection with the property must be made directly from the trust account to the person(s) entitled to such funds. In general, disbursements of rental income are made to pay the operating expenses of the leased property (utilities, maintenance, mortgage payments, administrative costs, etc.) with the balance being remitted to the property owner. The scope and extent of the rental manager's authority to expend funds on behalf of the owner should be expressly stated in the Rental Management Agreement.

The rental manager must pay these operating expenses in a timely manner; however, disbursements must not at any time exceed the amount of funds on hand for that particular property owner. For example, if the manager has collected only $300 in rent from property owned by Mr. A, he or she cannot disburse $400 from his or her trust account to repair Mr. A's roof. Although the total of all funds in the trust account may be sufficient to cover the $400 expenditure, such payment would, of course, result in the disbursement of funds belonging to other persons to pay for Mr. A's roof.

The Rental Management Agreement should specify the procedure to follow in situations where expenses exceed receipts for a particular owner. For example, the agreement may authorize the broker to hold a certain sum of money in reserve, or the manager may agree to pay such expenses from his or her general operating account and then be reimbursed as rents are collected. The rental manager should not, however, place any of his or her own funds into his or her trust account to offset such "deficit spending," because this would, of course, constitute a commingling of the rental manager's funds with funds which he or she is holding for others.

Regarding the disposition of tenant security deposits, the rental manager or leasing agent should be aware that such deposits may be used only for certain specified purposes, and if not used, the deposit must be promptly refunded to the tenant (certainly within 30 days after termination of the tenancy). Chapter 42, Article 6 of the North Carolina General Statutes, entitled "Tenant Security Deposit Act," with which brokers acting in the capacity of rental managers, leasing agents, etc. should be thoroughly familiar, sets forth the permitted uses of the deposit. These permitted uses are nonpayment of rent, actual damage to the premises, excluding ordinary wear and tear, nonfulfillment of the rental period, unpaid bills which become a lien on the property, the reasonable costs of re-renting the premises after breach of the lease by the tenant, costs of removal and storage of tenant's property after a summary ejectment proceeding and court costs in connection with terminating the tenancy. Brokers must remain aware that security deposits are the property of the tenants, not the owners, during the duration of the tenancy.

Rental management fees, including interest earned by the broker, should be disbursed promptly (within 30 days) from the trust account to the broker's general business account, and division of earned fees among the broker's agents should be handled through the general business account.

### Disputed Funds

**Rule A.0107(g)** dictates what licensees must do with funds they are holding in trust if the parties to the transaction disagree as to who is entitled to the funds. Note, that if there is no dispute, the licensee is free to release the monies to the party entitled to receive same under the parties' contract. However, if the parties do not agree on the distribution of the trust monies, then a licensee is not authorized to release the monies, but must continue to hold them in his/her trust account until one of the following occurs, either: 1) the parties agree in writing how the funds should be disbursed, **or** 2) one of the parties sues the other and obtains a court order, **or** 3) the broker utilizes a new procedure which became available October 1, 2005 which allows the broker, following written notice to the parties, to pay the disputed funds to the Clerk of Court and remove him/herself from the situation. Note that *residential tenant security deposits* generally are not subject to A.0107(g) because State law requires that all such deposits be disbursed either to the property owner or to the tenant, as appropriate, within 30 or 45 days (long term rental versus vacation rental) of the termination of the tenancy.

The new law is **G.S. 93A-12**, which now provides an avenue for brokers to lawfully rid their trust accounts of disputed monies where the parties to the dispute refuse to come to an agreement or refuse to initiate a legal action to determine who is entitled to the monies. In short, it allows a broker to deposit disputed trust monies, *other than residential tenant security deposits*, received as a licensee acting in a fiduciary capacity with the Clerk of Court in the county where the property is located. The broker first must *notify* all parties claiming ownership of or entitlement to the monies *in writing* that the broker intends to pay the monies to the Clerk of Court 90 days following the notice and that the parties may initiate a special proceeding with the Clerk to recover the disputed funds within one year following the deposit. Notice must either be delivered to the person or sent "... by first class mail, postpaid, properly addressed to the person at the person's last known address." When the broker deposits the disputed funds with the Clerk of Court, s/he must "certify" to the Clerk that notice was given to all parties at least 90 days prior to depositing the funds with the Clerk.

Once the broker gives the required notice to all parties and properly follows the procedure to deposit the funds with the Clerk of Court, the broker's responsibility is over. If any party files a special proceeding with the Clerk within one year of the funds being deposited, then the Clerk will proceed to hear the case, determine "rightful ownership" and disburse the funds. If no party initiates a special proceeding with the Clerk within one year of the monies being deposited with the Clerk, then the Clerk is to escheat the funds to the State Treasurer. Escheat is also available to licensees for unclaimed residential tenant security deposits, for example. Licensees may find more information concerning escheat at *www.treasurer.state.nc.us*

### Abandonment of Claim

Occasionally, because of the passage of time, it appears that a party who disputed disbursement of an earnest money deposit or other funds has abandoned his/her claim. In that event, **Rule A.0107(g)** provides yet another option to those discussed above, namely:

> ... If it appears to a licensee holding a disputed deposit that a party has abandoned his or her claim, the licensee may disburse the money to the other claiming parties according to their written agreement *provided that the licensee first makes a reasonable effort to notify the party* who has apparently abandoned his or her claim *and provides that party with an opportunity to renew his or her claim* to the disputed funds....

The Commission recommends that licensees notify the party who has apparently abandoned his/her claim by certified mail, return receipt requested, in order to document the broker's effort and to aid in knowing if and when the notification was received. Include in the notice a statement that the licensee intends to disburse the funds to a named person unless the party to whom notice is sent renews his/her claim within a reasonable time frame from receipt of the notice, such as two (2) weeks.

## VII. RECORDKEEPING AND ACCOUNTING

### Retention of Records

Licensees are required to maintain complete records of all trust account receipts and disbursements, including bank statements, canceled checks (or imaged copies of canceled checks), deposit tickets, closing statements, rental management reports and agreements, copies of offers (both accepted and rejected), copies of contracts, leases, rental management agreements, property owner association management agreements, covenants, bylaws, minutes, periodic statements, brokerage cooperation agreements, declarations of affiliation and other transaction records. The licensee shall retain such records for three years after all funds held by the licensee in connection with the transaction have been disbursed to the proper party or parties or until the successful or unsuccessful conclusion of the transaction, whichever occurs later as promulgated by Rule A.0108. Rule A.0107(e) requires licensees to maintain copies of these documents as well as other detailed books and records. The use and maintenance of separate ledger sheets comparable to those illustrated in the "Guidelines" is required. In the event a branch office maintains a separate trust account, a separate bookkeeping system should be maintained in such office.

### Trust Account Journal

Pursuant to Rule A.0107(e)(6), the broker's trust account records must include a journal or check stubs. The journal records in chronological sequence trust money received and disbursed by the broker on behalf of all parties. The bookkeeping entries recorded in the journal must include the following information: 1) the amount and date of each bank deposit and an appropriate reference to the corresponding deposit ticket and any supplemental deposit worksheet (the Commission recommends sequentially numbering deposit tickets and noting the number on the journal and the supplemental deposit worksheet); 2) the amount, date, check number and purpose of disbursements and to whom paid; and 3) a running balance for all funds in the trust account (the running balances must be recorded after each deposit and disbursement entry).

### Trust Account Ledgers

In a real estate sales transaction where a broker receives trust funds, ledger sheets record in chronological sequence trust money received (earnest money deposits, closing proceeds, etc.) and disbursed by the broker for each sales transaction. In the case of rental management, ledger sheets record in chronological sequence trust money received (rents, security deposits, etc.) and disbursed by the broker for a particular property or property owner. Each ledger sheet must identify the seller or landlord's name, the buyer or tenant's name and the property address of the property sold or managed by the broker. The bookkeeping entries to each ledger sheet must include: 1) the amount, date, and purpose of the bank deposits and from whom received; 2) the amount, date, check number and purpose of disbursements and to whom paid; and 3) a running balance of funds on deposit for the particular sales transaction or, in a rental transaction, the particular property or property owner.

### Security Deposit Ledgers

The receipt of a tenant security deposit and any corresponding disbursement of the security deposit for a property managed by a broker may be recorded on a separate ledger sheet apart from the ledger sheet that records the income and expenses on behalf of the property or property owner. This ledger sheet must identify the property owner's name, the tenant's name, and the property address. The bookkeeping entries posted to this security deposit ledger sheet must include the same information as described above under "Trust Account Ledgers."

### Payment Record Sheets

In a property owner association transaction where a broker receives trust funds, a payment record sheet for each property or property interest records in chronological sequence the accrual of assessments or monies due and any corresponding receipt of monies. Each payment record sheet must identify 1) the amount, date, remitter and purpose of payments received, 2) the amount and nature of the obligation, and 3) the amount of balance due or delinquency. Essentially, a payment record sheet is an accounts receivable ledger maintained on an accrual account basis and maintained by property or property interest.

### Timeliness

It must be emphasized that ***all receipts and disbursements must be recorded in the journal and posted to the applicable ledger sheet in a timely manner.*** Also, reconciliation worksheets should be prepared within a reasonable time frame after receipt of the trust account bank statement. A broker's failure to follow these accounting and bookkeeping principles increases the risk of errors and the misapplication of trust money.

### Trust Account Deposit Tickets

A broker should maintain as part of his or her trust account records a bank-validated deposit ticket for each bank deposit. This bank-validated deposit ticket is the broker's record evidencing deposit of trust funds into the trust account. In a sales transaction, the bank-validated deposit ticket must identify 1) the purpose (earnest money deposit) and the remitter of funds deposited; 2) the property; 3) the parties involved (buyer and seller); and 4) a reference to the corresponding sales transaction ledger sheet. If the remitter and the buyer are the same, then only one name would be required to identify both the remitter and buyer.

In a rental transaction, the bank-validated deposit ticket must identify 1) the purpose (rent, security deposit, etc.) and the remitter of funds deposited; 2) the tenant; and 3) the corresponding property or owner ledger sheet. If the remitter and the tenant are the same, then only one name would be required to identify both the remitter and the tenant.

In a property owner association transaction, the bank-validated deposit ticket must identify 1) the property or property interest (example: time share interest) for which the payment is deposited, 2) the property or interest owner, 3) the remitter, and 4) the purpose of the payment.

### Trust Account Checks

Original canceled checks must be obtained from the bank for all broker trust accounts. They must be retained as part of the broker's trust account records. In lieu of canceled checks, a broker may retain digitally imaged copies of the canceled checks or substitute checks. The front and back of the digitally imaged copies must be legible. The image of each check must be no smaller than 1.1875 x 3.0 inches. Also, the bank must retain the original canceled checks or substitute checks for a period of at least 6 years and provide the checks upon request. Canceled checks can be retained on a computer CD ROM (produced by the bank) as long as the checks can be reproduced as described above.

When preparing a check disbursing trust monies from a trust account, the broker must include on the face of the check a reference to the corresponding journal entry or check stub entry. The check number and date on the check are sufficient to reference the corresponding journal entry as long as the check is easily traceable to the entry recording the check in the journal.

Also, the check must reference the corresponding sales transaction ledger sheets or for rental transactions, the corresponding property or owner ledger sheets. In a sales transaction, identifying the buyer, seller and property address on the check is sufficient to reference a check to the sales transaction ledger. For a rental transaction, identifying the property address on the check is sufficient to reference a check to a property ledger sheet or an owner's name is sufficient to reference a check to an owner ledger sheet.

The purpose of the disbursement must be identified on the face of the check or on the corresponding supplemental disbursement worksheet.

### Supplemental Worksheets

A bank deposit ticket may include monies from more than one real estate transaction and it may be impractical to identify on it all the monies deposited into the trust account on a deposit ticket. When a single deposit ticket is used for multiple transactions, the broker may create a supplemental deposit worksheet and record on it the information necessary to properly trace the deposited monies. For example, rents collected in cash from various tenants could be recorded on a single deposit ticket as currency and deposited in a lump sum amount. The required identifying information must then be recorded on a supplemental deposit worksheet referencing the deposit ticket. To reference the worksheet to the deposit ticket, the broker must at least record the date and the total amount of the deposit on the worksheet. The Commission recommends sequentially numbering the deposit tickets and recording that number on the worksheet, journal, and ledger sheets as well as the date and the amount.

Likewise, a check may represent disbursements applicable to more than one sales transaction, property, or property owner ledger sheet and it may be impractical to identify all the corresponding ledger sheets on the check itself. For example, one check may be written to disburse rental management fees applicable to various properties. In such an instance, a supplemental disbursement worksheet referencing the corresponding check (date, check number, payee and amount) must be prepared for the check showing the identity of the monies disbursed out of the trust account as outlined above under "Trust Account Checks".

### Reconciliation/Trial Balance

Rule A.0107(e) further requires that brokers report all receipts and disbursements of trust monies in such a manner as to create a clear audit trail from deposit tickets and canceled checks to check stubs or journals and to the ledger sheets. A broker must reconcile ledger sheets and his or her journal or check stubs to the trust account bank statements on a monthly basis. The broker must create a worksheet (Trial Balance) for each such monthly reconciliation and must retain the worksheet (Trial Balance) as part of his or her trust account records.

The trial balance must identify each ledger (e.g. buyer and seller, property address, tenant, etc.) and show the ledger balances as of the date of the trial balance. A trial balance is simply a list of all funds in the trust or escrow account and the identification of the owners of those funds. The month-end bank statement balance must be reconciled to the checkbook and/or journal balance (i.e. running balance of funds on deposit) taking into consideration outstanding checks and deposits. The checkbook and/or journal balance should equal (be balanced with) the total outstanding liability as shown on the ledgers (individual transaction ledgers).

Trust account records must be retained by brokers for at least three years after all the funds held by the licensee in connection with the transaction have been disbursed or until the successful or unsuccessful conclusion of the transaction, whichever occurs later. The trust account records must be made available for inspection by the Commission or its authorized representatives without prior notice. [NOTE: The Real Estate Commission employs Trust Account Auditors to make "spot inspections" of trust accounts and to assist in the investigation of complaints alleging improper handling of trust money.]

### Computers

The Commission receives numerous inquiries concerning the format of bookkeeping systems, especially computerized bookkeeping systems. The Commission cannot endorse or recommend a specific computer product for brokers to use. The basic requirements for the computerized bookkeeping system are the same as those requirements for a manual system. The broker-in-charge is encouraged to review these requirements prior to investing in a computerized bookkeeping system that may not comply with Commission guidelines.

Certain software vendors have submitted to the Commission their bookkeeping software systems for evaluation of compliance with the Commission's Rules and Trust Account Guidelines. A list of the softwares evaluated and found to substantially comply can be found on the Commission's web site at ncrec.state.nc.us.

### Accounting to Principals

Brokers must account for all trust money which they receive and disburse during the course of a real estate transaction. In the rental management area, this accounting would be in the form of a "rental management report", in sales transactions, a "closing statement" and in property owner association management, a "periodic statement" is used.

Although no specific form or format is required, the rental management report, the closing statement and the periodic statement must set forth in a clear and concise fashion a complete accounting of all funds received and disbursed by the broker.

### Rental Management Reports:

The "rental management report" is simply a periodic accounting to the owner of all funds received and paid out in connection with the owner's property. The major item of income is, of course, rent, and the major expense items include utilities, maintenance expenses, and administrative costs. It is the responsibility of the broker/rental manager to see that the property owner receives this income and expense report at such times as are required by the management agreement (usually monthly) and that the report covers all receipts and disbursements handled by the rental manager on behalf of the owner. The broker/rental manager must also make a full accounting to the tenant, within 30 days of the termination of the tenancy, regarding the tenant's security deposit (See G.S. 42-52).

**Closing Statements:**

The "closing statement" is used in sales transactions to show all receipts and disbursements that the broker has handled for the seller, and all money that the broker has received from the buyer and how much money was disbursed. While it is the broker's responsibility to see that the buyer and seller receive a copy of this statement(s) at the closing of the transaction (or not more than five days after closing), the broker is not required to personally prepare the closing statements. He or she may instead elect to adopt the statements prepared by the person who closed the transaction (usually an attorney or lending officer) provided such statements account for all funds received and disbursed in the transaction; however, the broker will be held responsible for the accuracy of closing statements he or she provides to the parties, regardless of who prepares such closing statements.

**Periodic Statements:**

Licensees who manage a property owner association or who are the custodian of funds of an association must provide to that association periodic statements of not only the balance of the trust funds in the licensee's control but also an accounting of the trust funds received and disbursed on behalf of the association. The periodic statements must be provided by the licensee to the property owner association in accordance with the property management agreement, but in no event less frequently than every 90 days. The property owner association balance sheet and income statement of the funds in the licensee's control is sufficient to account to the association as periodic statements.

YOUR REALTY COMPANY, INC.

TRUST ACCOUNT JOURNAL

NC Insured Bank A/C# 123-456-7890

| DATE | DESCRIPTION | NUM | | DEPOSITS | CHECKS | BALANCE |
|---|---|---|---|---|---|---|
| | | | | | | |
| 1/03/0X | DEPOSIT | 0X-1 (A) | √ | $3,600.00 | | $3,600.00 |
| 1/04/0X | DEPOSIT | 0X-2 | √ | $2,300.00 | | $5,900.00 |
| 1/11/0X | Ajax-Plumbing - 143 N. Blvd - Repairs | 101 | √ | | $75.00 | $5,825.00 |
| 1/20/0X | Gerald Howard - 143 N. Blvd Net Jan Rent to Owner | 102 | | | $465.00 | $5,360.00 |
| 1/21/0X | Your Realty Company, Inc. 1/0X Mgt Fees | 103 | √ | | $115.00 | $5,245.00 |
| 1/22/0X | Jack Thomas - NSF - 1362 Main St | DM (B) | √ | | $2,500.00 | $2,745.00 |
| 1/30/0X | Perry Mason, Attorney 119 Maple Closing | 104 | | | $1,000.00 | $1,745.00 |
| 1/31/0X | DEPOSIT | 0X-3 | | $2,500.00 | | $4,245.00 |
| 1/31/0X | NC Insured Bank Check Printing Charges | DM | √ | | $25.00 | $4,220.00 |
| | | | | | | |

(A) - Referenced to sequentially numbered deposit tickets
(B) - Debit Memo
√ - Cleared Bank

**DEPOSIT TICKET**

YOUR REALTY COMPANY, INC.
TRUST ACCOUNT
DATE 1/3/0X

**# 0X-1**

| | DOLLARS | CENTS |
|---|---|---|
| CURRENCY | | |
| COINS | | |
| CHECKS | | |
| 1. Your Realty Co, Inc. | $100 | 00 |
| 2. Personal Funds | | |
| 3. | | |
| 4. Jones to Wood - EMD | $1,000 | 00 |
| 5. 119 Maple St | | |
| 6. | | |
| 7. Clay to Thomas | $2,500 | 00 |
| 8. EMD - 1362 Main | | |
| 9. Street | | |
| TOTAL | $3,600 | 00 |

**DEPOSIT TICKET**

YOUR REALTY COMPANY, INC.
TRUST ACCOUNT
DATE 1/31/0X

**# 0X-3**

| | DOLLARS | CENTS |
|---|---|---|
| CURRENCY | | |
| COINS | | |
| CHECKS | | |
| 1. Thomas - 1362 Main | $2,500 | 00 |
| 2. Street - Redeposit | | |
| 3. EMD - NSF Check | | |
| 4. Clay, Seller | | |
| 5. | | |
| 6. | | |
| 7. | | |
| 8. | | |
| 9. | | |
| TOTAL | $2,500 | 00 |

## DEPOSIT TICKET

YOUR REALTY COMPANY, INC.
TRUST ACCOUNT
DATE 1/4/0X
(C) # 0X-2

| | DOLLARS | CENTS |
|---|---|---|
| CURRENCY SDW (C) | $2,300 | 00 |
| COINS | | |
| CHECKS | | |
| 1. | | |
| 2. | | |
| 3. | | |
| 4. | | |
| TOTAL | $2,300 | 00 |

**(C) - Referenced to supplemental deposit worksheet for deposit ticket #2.**

SUPPLEMENTAL DEPOSIT WORKSHEET
Deposit Ticket #2 (D)
1/4/0X

| REMITTER/BUYER/TENANT | PROPERTY | PURPOSE | AMOUNT |
|---|---|---|---|
| Clark | 143 North Boulevard | Security Deposit | $600.00 |
| Clark | 143 North Boulevard | Jan Rent | $600.00 |
| Stephens | 2500 Johnson Street | Security Deposit | $550.00 |
| Stephens | 2500 Johnson Street | Jan Rent | $550.00 |
| | TOTAL | | $2,300.00 |

**(D)-Supplemental deposit worksheet cross-referenced back to deposit ticket #2.**

# LEDGERS

NAME: *Your Realty Company, Inc. - Personal Funds* ACCOUNT NO.

ADDRESS: SHEET NO.

| DATE | | ITEMS | | DEPOSITS | CHECKS | BALANCE |
|---|---|---|---|---|---|---|
| 1/03 | 0X | Your Realty Company Inc. Personal Funds | 0X-1 | $100.00 | | $100.00 |
| 1/31 | 0X | NC Insured Bank Check Printing Charges | DM | | $25.00 | $75.00 |
| | | | | | | |

NAME: *Jones (Seller) to Wood (Buyer)* ACCOUNT NO.

ADDRESS: *119 Maple St* SHEET NO.

| DATE | | ITEMS | | DEPOSITS | CHECKS | BALANCE |
|---|---|---|---|---|---|---|
| 1/03 | 0X | John Wood EMD | 0X-1 | $1,000.00 | | $1,000.00 |
| 1/30 | 0X | Perry Mason, Attorney Closing | 104 | | $1,000.00 | $0.00 |
| | | | | | | |

NAME: *Clay (Seller) to Thomas (Buyer)* ACCOUNT NO.

ADDRESS: *1362 Main Street* SHEET NO.

| DATE | | ITEMS | | DEPOSITS | CHECKS | BALANCE |
|---|---|---|---|---|---|---|
| 1/03 | 0X | Jack Thomas EMD | 0X-1 | $2,500.00 | | $2,500.00 |
| 1/22 | 0X | Jack Thomas NSF | DM | | $2500.00 | $0.00 |
| 1/31 | 0X | Jack Thomas Redeposit NSF EMD Check | 0X-3 | $2,500.00 | | $2,500.00 |
| | | | | | | |

# LEDGERS

| NAME: Gerald Howard, Owner - - Clark, Tenant | | | | | | ACCOUNT NO. |
|---|---|---|---|---|---|---|
| ADDRESS: 143 North Boulevard | | | | | | SHEET NO. |
| DATE | | ITEMS | | DEPOSITS | CHECKS | BALANCE |
| 1/04 | 0X | Charles Clark<br>Security Deposit | 0X-2 | $600.00 | | $600.00 |
| 1/04 | 0X | Charles Clark<br>Jan Rent | 0X-2 | $600.00 | | $1,200.00 |
| 1/11 | 0X | Ajax Plumbing Repairs | 101 | | $75.00 | $1,125.00 |
| 1/20 | 0X | Gerald Howard<br>Net Jan Rent To Owner | 102 | | $465.00 | $660.00 |
| 1/21 | 0X | Your Realty Co., Inc.<br>Jan Management Fee | 103 | | $60.00 | $600.00 |
| | | | | | | |

| NAME: Allan Ward, Owner - - Stephens, Tenant | | | | | | ACCOUNT NO. |
|---|---|---|---|---|---|---|
| ADDRESS: 2500 Johnson Street | | | | | | SHEET NO. |
| DATE | | ITEMS | | DEPOSITS | CHECKS | BALANCE |
| 1/04 | 0X | Blake Stephens<br>Security Deposit | 0X-2 | $550.00 | | $550.00 |
| 1/04 | 0X | Blake Stephens<br>Jan Rent | 0X-2 | $550.00 | | $1,100.00 |
| 1/21 | 0X | Your Realty Co., Inc.<br>Jan Management Fee | 103 | | $55.00 | $1,045.00 |
| | | | | | | |
| | | | | | | |

**Your Realty Company**
**Trust Account**
**Anytown, NC 12345** **103**

1/21/0X

Your Realty Company, Inc. $ 115.00

One hundred fifteen and 00/100 ---------------------------Dollars

1/0X Mgt Fees - SCW John Broker

SUPPLEMENTAL CHECK WORKSHEET
1/21/0X - CHECK #103 - YOUR REALTY CO., INC. (E)

| PROPERTY | PURPOSE | AMOUNT |
|---|---|---|
| 143 North Boulevard | 1/0X Management Fees | $60.00 |
| 2500 Johnson Street | 1/0X Management Fees | $55.00 |
| | | $115.00 |

(E) - Date and check number provide cross-reference to corresponding check.

Bank Account Reconciliation
Your Realty Company, Inc.

Period Ending 1/31/0X

Ending Balance from Bank Statement A. $ 3,185.00

List Deposits in Transit $ 2,500.00
(Deposits posted to the journal that have not cleared the bank)

Total Deposits in Transit + B. $ 2,500.00

List Outstanding Checks
(Checks posted to the journal that have not cleared the bank)

| Check | Date | Amount |
|---|---|---|
| 102 | 1/20/0X | $ 465.00 |
| 104 | 1/30/0X | $ 1,000.00 |
| | | $ |

Total Outstanding Checks - C. $ 1,465.00

Reconciled Bank Balance D. $ 4,220.00

# YOUR REALTY COMPANY, INC.
# TRIAL BALANCE

NC INSURED BANK A/C# 123-456-789

DATE: 1/31/0X

| OWNER | PROPERTY | AMOUNT |
|---|---|---|
| Your Realty Company, Inc. | | $75.00 |
| Clay | 1362 Main Street | $2,500.00 |
| Howard | 143 North Boulevard | $600.00 |
| Ward | 2500 Johnson Street | $1,045.00 |
| | | |
| | | |
| TOTAL | | $4,220.00 |

**NOTE**

**The total on the trial balance equals the reconciled bank balance on the bank reconciliation and the journal running balance as of 1/31/0X.**

# LICENSE LAW AND RULE COMMENTS

### Comments on Selected Provisions of the North Carolina Real Estate License Law and Real Estate Commission Rules

## INTRODUCTION

These comments on selected North Carolina Real Estate License Law and Real Estate Commission Rules provisions are intended to assist real estate licensees, prelicensing course students and others in understanding the License Law and Commission rules. The comments are organized in a topic format that often differs from the sequence in which the topics are addressed in the License Law and Commission rules. The topics selected for comment here are of particular importance and/or are likely to be frequently encountered in the usual course of real estate practice. The appropriate references to the License Law and Commission rules are provided beside each listed topic.

## LICENSE REQUIREMENT

### General [G.S. 93A-1 and 93A-2]

Anyone who for compensation transacts real estate business in this state as an agent for another must have a North Carolina real estate broker license. This requirement applies to any person or entity who directly or indirectly engages in the business of a real estate broker while physically in the state of North Carolina. A real estate licensee is commonly referred to as a real estate "agent," although the latter does not actually appear in the License Law.

Most individual broker licenses are issued on "provisional" status. The primary difference between a provisional broker and a broker not on provisional status is that the latter may operate as an unsupervised independent agent while a provisional broker must work under the supervision of a broker who has been designated with the Real Estate Commission as "broker-in-charge" of a real estate office.

A broker-in-charge is a broker who has been designated with the Commission as the broker having responsibility for the supervision of provisional brokers engaged in real estate brokerage at a particular real estate office and for other administrative and supervisory duties prescribed by Commission rule.

Note that a real estate "licensee" is NOT automatically a "REALTOR®." A licensed real estate agent is a REALTOR® only if he/she belongs to the National Association of REALTORS®, a private trade association.

### Licensing of Business Entities [G.S. 93A-1 and 93A-4; Rule A.0502]

In addition to individuals (persons), "business entities" also must be licensed in order to engage in the real estate business. Any corporation, partnership, limited liability company, association or other business entity (other than a sole proprietorship) must obtain a separate real estate firm broker license.

### Activities Requiring a License [G.S. 93A-2]

Persons and business entities who for compensation perform the activities listed below as an agent for others are considered to be performing brokerage activities and must have a North Carolina real estate license. There is no exemption for engaging in a limited number of transactions. A person or entity who performs a brokerage service in even one transaction must be licensed. Similarly, no fee or other compensation is so small as to exempt one from the application of the statute when acting for another in a real estate transaction. Brokerage activities include:

1. Listing (or offering to list) real estate for sale or rent, including any act performed by a real estate licensee in connection with obtaining and servicing a listing agreement. Examples of such acts include, but are not limited to, soliciting listings, providing information to the property owner, and preparing listing agreements or property management agreements.
2. Selling or buying (or offering to sell or buy) real estate, including any act performed by a real estate licensee in connection with assisting others in selling or buying real estate. Examples of such acts include, but are not limited to, advertising listed property for sale, "showing" listed property to prospective buyers, providing information about listed property to prospective buyers, negotiating a sale or purchase of real estate, and assisting with the completion of contract offers and counteroffers using preprinted forms and communication of offers and acceptances.
3. Leasing or renting (or offering to lease or rent) real estate, including any act performed by real estate licensees in connection with assisting others in leasing or renting real estate. Examples of such acts include, but are not limited to, advertising listed property for rent, "showing" listed rental property to prospective tenants, providing information about listed rental property to prospective tenants, negotiating lease terms, and assisting with the completion of lease offers and counteroffers using preprinted forms and communication of offers and acceptances.
4. Conducting (or offering to conduct) a real estate auction. (Mere criers of sale are excluded.) NOTE: An auctioneer's license is also required to auction real estate.
5. Selling, buying, leasing, assigning or exchanging any

interest in real estate, including a leasehold interest, in connection with the sale or purchase of a business.

6. Referring a party to a real estate licensee, if done for compensation. Any arrangement or agreement between a licensee and an unlicensed person that calls for the licensee to compensate the unlicensed person in any way for finding, introducing or referring a party to the licensee has been determined by North Carolina's courts to be prohibited under the License Law. Therefore, no licensee may pay a finder's fee, referral fee, "bird dog" fee or similar compensation to an unlicensed person.

### Unlicensed Employees — Permitted Activities

The use of unlicensed assistants and other unlicensed office personnel in the real estate industry is very widespread and the Commission is frequently asked by licensees what acts such persons may lawfully perform. To provide guidance to licensees regarding this matter, the Commission has prepared the following list of acts that an unlicensed assistant or employee may lawfully perform so long as the assistant or employee is salaried or hourly paid and is not paid on a per-transaction basis.

An unlicensed, salaried (i.e., W-2) employee MAY:

1. Receive and forward phone calls and electronic messages to licensees.
2. Submit listings and changes to a multiple listing service, but only if the listing data or changes are compiled and provided by a licensee.
3. Secure copies of public records from public repositories (i.e., register of deeds office, county tax office, etc.).
4. Place "for sale" or "for rent" signs and lock boxes on property at the direction of a licensee.
5. Order and supervise routine and minor repairs to listed property at the direction of a licensee.
6. Act as a courier to deliver or pick up documents.
7. Schedule appointments for showing property listed for sale or rent.
8. Communicate with licensees, property owners, prospects, inspectors, etc. to coordinate or confirm appointments.
9. Show rental properties managed by the employee's employing broker to prospective tenants and complete and execute preprinted form leases for the rental of such properties.
10. Type offers, contracts and leases from drafts of preprinted forms completed by a licensee.
11. Record and deposit earnest money deposits, tenant security deposits and other trust monies, and otherwise maintain records of trust account receipts and disbursements, under the close supervision of the office broker-in-charge, who is legally responsible for handling trust funds and maintaining trust accounts.
12. Assist a licensee in assembling documents for closing.
13. Compute commission checks for licensees affiliated with a broker or firm and act as bookkeeper for the firm's bank operating accounts.

### Exemptions [G.S. 93A-2]

The following persons and organizations are specifically exempted from the requirement for real estate licensure:

1. **Property owners** when selling or leasing their own property. This includes both individual property owners personally selling or leasing their property and business entities selling or leasing real estate owned by the business entity. To qualify under this exemption, the person or entity must be the actual title holder or share title with an undivided interest.

[Note: The Commission takes the position that the *bona fide* officers and employees of a **corporation** need not be licensed to sell or lease real estate belonging to the corporation. This is because corporations have a separate legal identity and can only function through its officers and employees, thus such officers and employees must be exempt when selling or leasing the corporation's property in order to give effect to the corporation exemption. However, the officers and employees of other business entities are considered to be exempt only if they personally are title owners of the property to be sold or leased. Thus, a partner in a general partnership is exempt as an owner when selling or leasing partnership-owned real estate, but an officer or employee of the partnership who is not also a partner is not exempt.]

2. Persons acting as **attorneys-in-fact** under a power of attorney in *consummating performance* under a contract for the sale, lease or exchange of real estate. (Note: This limited exemption applies only to the final completion of a transaction already commenced. The licensing requirement may not be circumvented by obtaining a power of attorney.)
3. **Attorneys-at-law** when performing real estate activities in the normal course of providing legal services to their clients, such as when administering an estate or trust. Attorneys may NOT otherwise engage in real estate brokerage practice without a real estate license.
4. **Persons acting under court order** (e.g., receivers, trustees in bankruptcy, guardians or personal representatives)
5. **Trustees** acting under a trust agreement, deed of trust or will.
6. Certain **salaried employees of broker-property managers.** (See G.S. 93A-2(c)(6) for details.)

**NOTE:** Although there is no specific statutory exemption for real estate **appraisers**, persons who appraise real estate for compensation are not required to have a real estate license to conduct such appraisals. However, such persons are required to be licensed or certified as a real estate appraiser by the North Carolina Appraisal Board.

## THE REAL ESTATE COMMISSION

### Composition [G.S. 93A-3(a)]

The Real Estate Commission consists of nine (9) members who serve three-year terms. Seven members are appointed by the Governor and two are appointed by the General Assembly upon the recommendations of the Speaker of the House of Representatives and the President Pro Tempore of the Senate. At least three (3) members must be licensed brokers. At least two (2) members must be "public members" who are NOT involved directly or indirectly in the real estate brokerage or appraisal businesses.

### Purpose and Powers [G.S. 93A-3(a), (c) and (f); G.S. 93A-6(a) and (b);G.S. 93A-4(d) and 93A-4A]

The principal purpose of the Real Estate Commission is to protect the interests of members of the general public in their dealings with real estate brokers. This is accomplished through the exercise of the following statutory powers granted to the Commission:

1. Licensing real estate brokers and brokerage firms, and registering time share projects.
2. Establishing and administering a prelicensing and postlicensing education program for prospective licensees as well as a continuing education program for licensees.
3. Providing education and information relating to the real estate brokerage business for licensees and the general public.
4. Regulating the business activities of brokers and brokerage firms, including disciplining licensees who violate the License Law or Commission rules.

It should be noted that the Commission is specifically prohibited, however, from regulating commissions, salaries or fees charged by real estate licensees and from arbitrating disputes between parties regarding matters of contract such as the rate and/or division of commissions, pay of agents or similar matters. [See G.S. 93A-3(c) and Rule A.0109.]

### Disciplinary Authority [G.S. 93A-6(a)-(c)]

The Real Estate Commission is authorized to take a variety of disciplinary actions against licensees who the Commission finds guilty of violating the License Law or Commission rules while acting as real estate licensees. These are: reprimand, censure, license suspension and license revocation. The License Law also permits a licensee under certain circumstances to surrender his/her license with the consent of the Commission. Disciplinary actions taken against licensees are regularly reported in the Commission's newsletter which is distributed to all licensees and also may be reported in local and regional newspapers.

It should be noted that licensees may be disciplined by the Commission for committing acts prohibited by the License Law when selling, leasing, or buying real estate for themselves, as well as for committing such acts in transactions handled as agents for others. [G.S. 93A-6(b)(3)]

The Commission also has the power to seek in its own name injunctive relief in superior court to prevent any person (licensees and others) from violating the License Law or Commission rules. A typical example of where the Commission might pursue injunctive relief in the courts is where a person engages in real estate activity without a license or during a period when the person's license is suspended, revoked or expired. [G.S. 93A-6(c)]

Any violation of the License Law or Commission rules is a criminal offense (misdemeanor) and may be prosecuted in a court of law. However, a finding by the Commission that a licensee has violated the License Law or Commission rules does not constitute a criminal conviction. [G.S. 93-8]

## PROHIBITED ACTS BY LICENSEES

G.S. 93A-6 provides a list of prohibited acts which may result in disciplinary action against licensees. Discussed below are the various prohibited acts, except for those related to handling and accounting for trust funds, which are discussed in the Commission's "Trust Account Guidelines," and the failure to deliver certain instruments to parties in a transaction, which is discussed in the subsequent section on "General Brokerage Provisions."

**Important Note**

The provisions of the License Law relating to misrepresentation or omission of a material fact, conflict of interest, licensee competence, handling of trust funds, and improper, fraudulent or dishonest dealing generally apply independently of other statutory law or case law such as the law of agency. Nevertheless, another law may have an effect on the application of a License Law provision. For example, the requirements of the N.C. Tenant Security Deposit Act relating to the accounting to a tenant for a residential security deposit within 30 days after termination of a tenancy amplify the general License Law provisions (and Commission rules) requiring licensees to account for such funds within a reasonable time. Thus, in this instance, a violation of the Tenant Security Deposit Act's provisions would also be considered by the Commission to be a violation of the License Law.

Similarly, the law of agency and the law of contracts, which are derived from case law, may be taken into consideration when applying the provisions of the License Law. Thus, a licensee's agency status and role in a transaction might affect the licensee's duties under the license law. Examples of how an agent's duties under the License Law may be affected by the application of other laws are included at various points in this section on "Prohibited Acts by Licensees."

### Misrepresentation or Omission [G.S. 93A-6(a)(1)]

Misrepresentation or omission of a material fact by brokers is prohibited, and this prohibition includes both "willful" and "negligent" acts. A "willful" act is one that is done intentionally and deliberately, while a "negligent" act is one that is done unintentionally. A "misrepresentation" is communicating false information, while an "omission" is failing to provide or disclose information where there is a duty to provide or disclose such information.

For purposes of applying G.S. 93A-6(a)(1), whether a fact is "material" depends on the facts and circumstances of a particular transaction and the application of statutory and/or case law. The Commission has historically interpreted "material facts" under the Real Estate License Law to at least include:

**Facts about the property itself** (such as a structural defect or defective mechanical systems);

**Facts relating directly to the property** (such as a pending zoning change or planned highway construction in the immediate vicinity); and

**Facts relating directly to the ability of the agent's principal to complete the transaction** (such as a pending foreclosure sale).

Regardless of whom the agent represents, these "material" facts must be disclosed to both the agent's principal and to third parties the agent deals with on the principal's behalf. In addition, an agent has a duty to disclose to his principal any information that may affect the principal's rights and interests or influence the principal's decision in the transaction.

Note, however, that G.S. 39-50 and 42-14.2 specifically provide that the fact that a property was occupied by a person who died or had a serious illness while occupying the property is NOT a material fact. Thus, agents do not need to voluntarily disclose such a fact. If a prospective buyer or tenant specifically asks about such a matter, the agent may either decline to answer or respond honestly. If, however, a prospective buyer or tenant inquires as to whether a previous owner or occupant had AIDS, the agent is prohibited by fair housing laws from answering such an inquiry because persons with AIDS are considered to be "handicapped" under such laws.

This introductory information should assist in understanding G.S. 93A-6(a)(1), which establishes four separate (although closely related) categories of conduct which are prohibited. These are discussed below, and a few examples of prohibited conduct are provided for each category.

**Willful Misrepresentation** — Where an agent who has "actual knowledge" of a material fact deliberately misinforms a buyer, seller, tenant or landlord concerning such fact. Also, where an agent who does NOT have actual knowledge of a matter material to the transaction provides incorrect information concerning such matter to a buyer, seller, tenant or landlord without regard for the actual truth of the matter (i.e., where an agent intentionally provides information without knowing whether it is true and the information provided is in fact not true).

**Note**: The following examples of willful misrepresentation apply regardless of the agent's status (seller's agent or buyer's agent) or role (listing agent or selling agent).

**Example:** An agent knows that a listed house has a severe flooding problem during heavy rains. In response to a question from a prospective buyer who is being shown the house during dry weather, the agent states that there is no flooding problem.

**Example:** An agent knows that the heat pump at a listed house is inoperative, but tells a prospective buyer that all mechanical systems and appliances are in good condition.

**Example:** An agent knows that the approximate market value of a house is $80,000, but tells the property owner that the house is worth $90,000 in order to obtain a listing.

**Example:** An agent is completely unfamiliar with the features or condition of a listed property; however, the agent informs a prospective buyer that the plumbing is in good working order without first checking with the owner. (The agent in such instance is acting without regard for the truth of the matter being represented. If the plumbing in fact needs significant repair, then the agent may be guilty of willful misrepresentation.)

**Example:** Without checking with the owner, an agent tells a prospective buyer of a listed house that heating and cooling costs are "very reasonable." (Because the agent acted without regard for the truth of the matter, he may be guilty of willful misrepresentation if heating and cooling costs are in fact extraordinarily high.)

**Negligent Misrepresentation** — Where an agent unintentionally misinforms a buyer, seller, tenant or landlord concerning a material fact either because he does not have actual knowledge of the fact, because he has incorrect information, or because of a mistake by the agent. If the agent "should reasonably have known" the truth of the matter that was misrepresented, then the agent may be guilty of "negligent misrepresentation" even though he was acting in good faith.

Negligent misrepresentation by real estate agents occurs frequently in real estate transactions. The most common situation results from the recording of incorrect information in an MLS® computer or book due to the negligence of the listing agent. When a prospective buyer is subsequently provided the incorrect information from the MLS® by the agent working with the buyer, a negligent misrepresentation occurs.

A listing agent is generally held to a higher standard with regard to negligent misrepresentation of material facts about a listed property to a buyer than is a selling agent who is acting as a seller's subagent. This is because (1) The listing agent is in the best position to ascertain facts about the property, (2) the listing agent is expected to take reasonable steps to assure that property data included with the listing is correct and (3) it is considered reasonable for a selling agent to rely on the accuracy of the listing data in most instances. However, a buyer's agent may in some cases be held to a higher standard than a seller's subagent because of the buyer's agent's duties to the buyer under the law of agency and the buyer's agent's special knowledge of the buyer's particular situation and needs.

**Example:** An agent has previously sold several lots in a subdivision under development and all those lots passed a soil suitability test for an on-site septic system. The agent then sells Lot 35 without checking as to whether this lot satisfies the soil test; however, the agent informs the buyer that Lot 35 will support an on-site septic system when in fact the contrary is true. (The agent was at least negligent in not checking the soil test result on Lot 35 and guilty of negligent misrepresentation. This result is not affected by the agent's agency status or role in the transaction.)

**Example:** An owner tells a listing agent with ABC Realty that his house has 1850 heated square feet. Without personally verifying the square footage, the agent records 1850 square feet on the listing form. The listing is placed in the local MLS and the MLS book is distributed showing the house as having 1850 square feet. The house is subsequently sold by a sales agent with XYZ Realty who tells the buyer that according to the MLS data, the house has 1850 square feet. The buyer later discovers that the house actually has only 1750 square feet. (In this situation, the listing agent did not make a direct misrepresentation to the buyer; however, he initiated the chain of communication which led to the buyer being misinformed, and thus indirectly misrepresented a material fact. Further, his failure to verify the square footage constituted negligence. Therefore, the listing agent is guilty of a negligent misrepresentation. Although the selling agent directly communicated the incorrect information to the buyer, he probably acted reasonably in relying on the data in the MLS book. In this case, if the selling agent had no reason to doubt the MLS data, the selling agent is not guilty of a negligent misrepresentation. Note, however, that if the square footage discrepancy had been sufficiently large that a reasonably prudent selling agent should have known the listed data was incorrect, then the selling agent would also have been guilty of negligent misrepresentation. The result in this particular example is not affected by the selling agent's agency status (seller's subagent or buyer's agent), although this might be a factor in other situations.

**Willful Omission** — Where the agent has "actual knowledge" of a material fact and a duty to disclose such fact to a buyer, seller, tenant, or landlord, but he deliberately fails to disclose such fact.

**Example:** An agent knows that a zoning change is pending which would adversely affect the value of a listed property, but fails to disclose such information to a prospective buyer. The agent has committed a willful omission and this result is not affected by the agent's agency status or role in the transaction.

[**Note:** Information about a pending zoning change (or planned highway) that would enhance the value of a seller's property must also be disclosed to the seller, even if the agent is a buyer's agent.]

**Example:** An agent knows that the city has just decided to extend water and sewer lines to a subdivision that has been plagued for years by serious water quality and sewage disposal problems. This will result in a substantial increase in the value of homes in the subdivision. The agent, who is working with a buyer to purchase a house in the subdivision, does not inform the seller of the city's recent decision. The agent has committed a willful omission and this result is not affected by the agent's agency status or role in the transaction.

**Example:** An agent knows that a listed house has a major defect (e.g., crumbling foundation, no insulation, malfunctioning septic tank, leaking roof, termite infestation, etc.) but fails to disclose such information to a prospective buyer. The agent has committed a willful omission and this result is not affected by the agent's agency status or role in the transaction.

**Example:** A selling agent working with a buyer as a subagent of the seller learns that the buyer is willing to pay more than the price in the buyer's offer, but fails to disclose this information to the seller (or listing agent) when presenting the offer. The selling agent has committed a willful omission. If, however, the selling agent were acting as a buyer's agent, then the result would be different because the agent does not represent the seller.

**Example:** A buyer's agent becomes aware that the seller with whom his buyer is negotiating is under pressure to sell quickly and may accept much less than the listing price. Believing such information should always be kept confidential, the buyer's agent does not provide the buyer with this information. The buyer's agent is guilty of a willful omission. An agent must disclose to his principal any information that might affect the principal's decision in the transaction.

**Example:** Suppose in the immediately preceding example that the seller's property is listed with the firm of the buyer's agent and the firm's policy is to practice dual agency in in-house sales situations where it represents both the seller and the buyer. In this situation, the buyer's agent would not be considered to have committed a willful omission under the License Law by not disclosing the information about the seller's personal situation to the buyer. Note: This assumes however that the buyer's agent properly disclosed his status as a buyer's agent to the seller or seller's agent upon "initial contact," that dual agency was properly authorized in writing by both the seller and buyer preferably prior to showing the seller's property to the buyer, but no later than presentment of any offer, and that the dual agency agreement provided for this limitation on disclosure. This position on the application of the License Law has been adopted by the Real Estate Commission to promote fairness and equity in transactions involving dual agency.

**Negligent Omission** — Where an agent does NOT have actual knowledge of a material fact, but he "should reasonably have known" of such fact, then he may be guilty of "negligent omission" if he fails to disclose this fact to a buyer, seller, tenant or landlord, even though he acted in good faith in the transaction.

The prohibition against negligent omission creates a "duty to discover and disclose" material facts which a reasonably prudent agent would typically have discovered in the course of the transaction. A listing agent is typically in a much better position than a selling agent to discover material facts relating to a listed property and thus, will be held to a higher standard than will a selling agent acting as a seller's subagent. On the other hand, a buyer's agent in some circumstances may be held to a higher standard than a seller's subagent because of the buyer's agent's duties to the buyer under the law of agency, particularly if the buyer's agent is aware of a buyer's special needs with regard to a property. Again we see how the agency relationships between agents and principals to a transaction and the agent's role in the transaction can affect a licensee's duties and responsibilities under the License Law.

Instances of negligent omission occur much less frequently than instances of negligent misrepresentation. This is because most facts about a listed property are recorded on a detailed property data sheet from which information is taken for inclusion in MLS computers/books. If incorrect information taken from an MLS computer/book is passed on to a prospective purchaser, then a "misrepresentation," rather than an "omission," has occurred. Nevertheless, there are examples of negligent omission which can be cited.

**Example:** A listing agent lists for sale a house located adjacent to a street that is about to be widened into a major thoroughfare. The thoroughfare project has been very controversial and highly publicized. The city recently finalized its decision to proceed with the project and the plans for the street widening are recorded in the city planner's office. A buyer, working with a selling agent, makes an offer to buy the house. The listing agent does not disclose the street widening plans to the buyer or selling agent and claims later that he was not aware of the plans. In this situation, both the listing and selling agents are probably guilty of a negligent omission because each "should reasonably have known" of the street widening plans, clearly a material fact, and should have disclosed this fact to the buyer. This result is not affected by whether the selling agent is a buyer agent or seller's subagent.

**Example:** A seller has a 30,000 square foot commercial property for sale which cannot be expanded under local zoning laws. The buyer is looking for property in the 25,000 - 30,000 square foot range, but has told his buyer's agent that he needs a property where he can expand to 50,000 square feet or more in the future. The seller does not think to advise the buyer's agent that the property cannot be expanded, and the buyer's agent makes no inquiry about it although he is aware of the buyer's special needs. The buyer's agent is guilty of a negligent omission for failing to discover and disclose a special circumstance that he knew was important to his client.

**Example:** When listing a house, a listing agent is told by the seller that one area of the roof leaks badly when it rains, but the moisture so far is being contained in the attic. The listing agent forgets to note this on the MLS data sheet and forgets to disclose the leaking roof problem to prospective buyers and selling agents. The listing agent is guilty of a negligent omission. Because his failure to disclose the leaking roof problem was unintentional, the listing agent is not guilty of a willful omission; however, his forgetfulness resulting in his failure to disclose the defect constitutes a negligent omission.

### Making False Promises [G.S. 93A-6(a)(2)]

Real estate brokers are prohibited from "making any false promises of a character likely to influence, persuade or induce." It is unimportant whether the broker originally intended to honor his promise; failure to honor a promise is sufficient to constitute a violation of this provision. The promise may relate to any matter which might influence, persuade or induce a person to perform some act which he might not otherwise perform.

**Example:** An agent promises a prospective apartment tenant that the apartment he is considering renting will be repainted before the tenant moves in. The agent then fails to have the work done after the lease is signed.

**Example:** An agent promises a property owner that if he lists his house for sale with the agent's firm, then the firm will steam-clean all the carpets and wash all the windows. The firm then fails to have the work done after the listing contract is signed.

### Other Misrepresentations [G.S. 93A-6(a)(3)]

Real estate brokers are prohibited from pursuing a course of misrepresentation (or making of false promises) through other agents or through advertising or other means.

**Example:** In marketing subdivision lots for a developer, a broker regularly advertises that the lots for sale are suitable for residential use when in fact the lots will not pass a soil suitability test for on-site sewage systems.

**Example:** A broker is marketing a new condominium complex which is under construction. Acting with the full knowledge and consent of the broker, the broker's agents regularly inform prospective buyers that units will be available for occupancy on June 1, when in fact the units won't be available until at least September 1.

### Conflict of Interest [G.S. 93A-6(a)(4) and (6); Rule A.0104(d)]

G.S. 93A-6(a)(4) prohibits a real estate agent from "acting for more than one party in a transaction without the knowledge of all parties for whom he or she acts." Commission Rule A.0104(d) takes this a step further by providing that a broker or brokerage firm representing one party in a transaction shall not undertake to represent another party in the transaction without the express written authority (i.e., authorization of dual agency) of each party (subject to one exception, explained in the dual agency section). A typical violation of this provision occurs when the agent has only one principal in a transaction but acts in a manner which benefits another party without the principal's knowledge. In such a situation, the agent violates the duty of loyalty and consent owed to his principal.

**Example:** A house is listed with Firm X. When showing the house to a prospective buyer not represented by Firm X, an agent of Firm X advises the buyer to offer substantially less than the listing price because the seller must move soon and is very anxious to sell the property fast. The agent and Firm X are contractually obligated to represent only the seller. By advising the prospective buyer as indicated in this example, the agent is acting to benefit the buyer without the seller's knowledge and consent. This act violates both the License Law and the Law of Agency.

**Example:** An agent with Firm Y assists her sister in purchasing a house listed with Firm X without advising Firm X or the seller of her relationship with the buyer. The agent is "officially" acting as a subagent of the seller in the transaction. In this situation, there is an inherent conflict of interest on the part of the agent. If the agent does not disclose her relationships to both parties, then the agent violates both the License Law and Law of Agency. In fact, since her allegiance lies with her sister, the agent should instead act as a buyer's agent from the outset. The same would be true if the buyer were a close friend or business associate of the agent, or in any way enjoyed a special relationship to the agent which would clearly influence the agent to act in behalf of the buyer rather than the seller.

G.S. 93A-6(a)(4) also prohibits any "self-dealing" on the part of an agent. For example, if an agent attempts to make a secret profit in a transaction where he is supposed to be representing a principal, then the agent violates this "conflict of interest" provision.

**Example:** An agent lists a parcel of undeveloped property which is zoned for single-family residential use. The agent knows that this property is about to be rezoned for multi-family residential use, which will greatly increase the property's value. Rather than informing the seller of this fact, the agent offers to buy the property at the listed price, telling the seller that he wants to acquire the property as a long-term investment. The deal closes. Several months later, after the rezoning has been accomplished, the agent sells the property at a substantial profit.

G.S. 93A-6(a)(6) prohibits a licensee from "representing or attempting to represent a real estate broker other than the broker by whom he or she is engaged or associated, without the express knowledge and consent of the broker with whom he or she is associated." Brokers may work for or be associated with more than one real estate company, so long as they have the express consent of all brokers-in-charge. Provisional brokers may never engage in brokerage activities for more than one company at a time.

### Improper Brokerage Commission [G.S. 93A-6(a)(5) and (9)]

No person may pay a commission or valuable consideration to any other person for acts or services performed in violation of the License Law. [G.S. 93A-6(a)(9)] This provision flatly prohibits anyone from paying an unlicensed person for acts which require a real estate license. Following are examples of prohibited payments:

**Example:** The payment by brokers of commissions to previously licensed sales associates who failed to properly renew their licenses (for any acts performed after their licenses had expired). [Note that payment *could* properly be made for commissions earned while the license was on active status, even if the license is inactive or expired at time of payment. The key is, was the license on active status at the time all services were rendered which generated the commission?]

**Example:** The payment of a commission, salary or fee by brokers to unlicensed employees or independent contractors (e.g., secretaries, "trainees" who haven't passed the license examination, etc.) for performing acts or services requiring a real estate license.

**Example:** The payment by brokers of a "finder's fee," "referral fee," "bird dog fee," or any other valuable consideration to unlicensed persons who find, introduce, or bring together parties to a real estate transaction. This is true even if the ultimate consummation of the transaction is accomplished by a licensed broker and even if the act is performed without expectation of compensation. Thus, a broker may NOT compensate a friend, relative, former client or any other unlicensed person for "referring" a prospective buyer, seller, landlord or tenant to such broker. This prohibition extends to "owner referral" programs at condominium or time share complexes and "tenant referral" programs at apartment complexes.

In addition, a licensed "provisional" broker may NOT accept any compensation for brokerage services from anyone other than his employing broker or brokerage firm. Consequently, a broker may not pay a commission or fee directly to a provisional broker of another broker or firm. Any such payment, as well as bonuses, must be made through the provisional broker's employing broker or firm. [G.S. 93A-6(a)(5)]

### Unworthiness and Incompetence [G.S. 93A-6(a)(8)]

This broad provision authorizes the Real Estate Commission to discipline any broker who, based on the agent's conduct and consideration of the public interest, is found to be unworthy or incompetent to work in the real estate business. A wide range of conduct may serve as the basis for a finding of unworthiness or incompetence, including conduct which violates other specific provisions of the License Law or Commission rules. Here are a few examples of improper conduct which do not specifically violate another License Law provision but which might support a finding of unworthiness or incompetence.

1. Failure to properly complete (fill in) real estate contracts or to use contract forms which are legally adequate.
2. Failure to diligently perform the services required under listing contracts or property management contracts.
3. Failure to provide accurate closing statements to sellers and buyers or accurate income/expense reports to property owners.

### Improper Dealing [G.S. 93A-6(a)(10)]

This broad provision prohibits a real estate agent from engaging in "any other conduct [not specifically prohibited elsewhere in the License Law] which constitutes improper, fraudulent or dishonest dealing." The determination as to whether particular conduct constitutes "improper, fraudulent or dishonest dealing" is made by the Real Estate Commission on a case-by-case basis. Therefore, a broad range of conduct might be found objectionable under this provision, depending on the facts in a case.

One category of conduct which violates this provision is any breach of the duty to exercise skill, care, and diligence in behalf of a client under the Law of Agency. (Note that other breaches of Agency Law duties constituting either a "misrepresentation or omission," a "conflict of interest" or a "failure to properly account for trust funds" are covered by other specific statutory provisions.)

Another category of conduct which violates this provision is any violation of the State Fair Housing Act. This is mentioned separately under the "Discriminatory Practices" heading.

**Example:** A broker is personally conducting the closing of a real estate sale he has negotiated. The seller does not show up for the closing. In order to avoid a delay in closing the transaction, the broker forges the seller's signature on a deed to the property and proceeds with the closing in the seller's absence.

**Example:** An agent assists a prospective buyer in perpetrating a fraud in connection with a mortgage loan application by preparing two contracts — one with false information for submission to the lending institution, and another which represents the actual agreement between seller and buyer. (This practice is commonly referred to as "dual contracting" or "contract kiting.")

**Example:** A broker lists a property for sale and agrees in the listing contract to place the listing in the local MLS, to advertise the property for sale, and to use his best efforts in good faith to find a buyer. The broker places a "For Sale" sign on the property, but fails to place the property in the MLS for more than 30 days and fails to otherwise advertise the property during the listing period. (The broker has failed to exercise reasonable skill, care and diligence in behalf of his client as required by the listing contract and the Law of Agency.)

**Example:** An agent is aware that the owners of a house listed with his company are out of town for the weekend, yet the agent gives a prospective buyer the house keys and allows such prospect to look at the listed house without accompanying the prospect. (The agent has failed to exercise reasonable skill, care and diligence in behalf of his client.)

### Discriminatory Practices [G.S. 93A-6(a)(10); Rule A.1601]

Any conduct by a broker which violates the provisions of the State Fair Housing Act is considered by the Commission to constitute "improper conduct" and to be a violation of the License Law.

### Practice of Law [G.S. 93A-4(e); G.S. 93A-6(a)(11); Rule A.0111]

Brokers may not perform for others any legal service described in G.S. 84-2.1 or any other legal service. Following are several examples of real estate-related legal services which brokers may NOT provide.

1. Drafting legal documents such as deeds, deeds of trust, leases and real estate sales contracts for others. Although brokers may "fill in" or "complete" preprinted real estate contract forms which have been drafted by an attorney, they may NOT under any circumstances complete or fill in deed or deed of trust forms.
2. Abstracting or rendering an opinion on legal title to real property.
3. Providing "legal advice" of any nature to clients and customers, including advice concerning the nature of any interest in real estate or the means of holding title to real estate. (Note: Although providing advice concerning the legal ramifications of a real estate sales contract is prohibited, merely "explaining" the provisions of such a contract is not only acceptable, but highly recommended.)

### Other Prohibited Acts [G.S. 93A-6(b)]

In addition to those prohibited acts previously discussed, G.S. 93A-6(b) prescribes several other specific grounds for disciplinary action by the Commission, including:

1. Where a licensee has obtained a license by false or fraudulent representation (e.g., falsifying documentation of prelicensing education, failing to disclose prior criminal convictions, etc.).
2. Where a licensee has been convicted of, or pled guilty or no contest to, certain types of criminal offenses.
3. Where a broker's unlicensed employee, who is exempt from licensing under G.S. 93A-2(c)(6) (property management exception), has committed an act which, if committed by the broker, would have constituted a violation of the License Law.
4. Where a licensee who is also a State-licensed or State-certified real estate appraiser has violated any of the provisions of the North Carolina Real Estate Appraisers Act and been disciplined by the N.C. Appraisal Board.

Lastly, be aware that under (b)(3), licensees may be disciplined for violating any of the 15 provisions under subsection (a) when selling, buying, or leasing their own property.

## GENERAL BROKERAGE PROVISIONS

Discussed below are selected Commission rules related to general brokerage.

### Agency Agreements and Disclosure [Rule A.0104]

Provided below is a brief summary of the various provisions of the Commission's rule regarding agency agreements and disclosure. For a much more in-depth discussion of this rule and its application, the reader is referred to the Commission's *North Carolina Real Estate Manual*.

**Agency Agreements:** Rule A.0104(a) requires all agency agreements for brokerage services (in both sales and lease transactions) to be in writing. Paragraph (a):

- Requires written agreements with property owners (whether sellers or lessors, commercial or residential) from the inception of the relationship;
- Allows express **oral** buyer/tenant agency agreement from the outset of the relationship which must be reduced to *writing no later than the time any party to the transaction wants to extend an offer.* As a practical matter, this oral agreement needs to address all key aspects of the relationship, including agent compensation, authorization for dual agency, etc.

(**Note:** Agreement must be in writing from the outset if it seeks to limit the buyer/tenant's right to work with other agents or binds the client to the agent for any definite time period. In other words, an oral buyer/tenant agency agreement is non-exclusive and must be terminable by the client at any time.)

Further, every written agency agreement of any kind must also:

- Provide for its existence for a definite period of time and terminate without prior notice at the expiration of that period. [Exception: an agency agreement between a broker and a landlord to procure tenants for the landlord's property may allow for automatic renewal so long as the landlord may terminate with notice at the end of any contract or renewal period.]
- Contain the Rule A.0104(b) non-discrimination (fair housing) provision, namely: "The broker shall conduct all brokerage activities in regard to this agreement without respect to the race, color, religion, sex, national origin, handicap or familial status of any party or prospective party to the agreement." This provision must be set forth in a clear and conspicuous manner which shall distinguish it from other provisions of the agency agreement.
- Include the license number of the individual licensee who signs the agreement.

Allowing an agent to to work with a buyer under an express oral buyer agency agreement is intended to address the problem of buyers being reluctant to sign a written buyer agency agreement at the outset of their relationship with a buyer agent. The idea underlying this approach is to allow an agent to work *temporarily* with a prospective buyer as a buyer's agent under an *oral agreement* while the agent establishes a rapport with the buyer that makes the buyer feel more comfortable with signing a written buyer agency agreement.

Although the rule allows oral buyer/tenant agency agreements until the point in time when any party is ready to present an offer, it nevertheless is highly advisable that agents have such agreements reduced to writing and signed by the buyer/tenant at the earliest possible time in order to avoid misunderstanding and conflict between the buyer/tenant and agent. Recall also that the agent must obtain a written buyer/tenant agency agreement from the buyer/tenant not later than the time any party to the transaction extends an offer to any other. If the buyer/tenant will not sign a written buyer/tenant agency agreement prior to an offer being presented, then the agent may not continue to work with the buyer/tenant as a buyer/tenant's agent. Moreover, the agent may not begin at this point to work with the buyer/tenant as a seller's subagent unless the agent (1) fully advises the buyer/tenant of the consequences of the agent switching from buyer/tenant's agent to seller's agent (including the fact that the agent would have to disclose to the seller/lessor any information, including "confidential" information about the buyer/tenant, that might influence the property owner's decision in the transaction), (2) obtains the buyer/tenant's consent, and (3) obtains the consent of the property owner and listing firm, which is the property owner's agent.

**Agency Disclosure Requirement:** While Rule A.0104(a) now requires all agency agreements, whether for lease or sales transactions or association management, to be in writing, the Rule A.0104(c) *disclosure* requirement still applies only to sales transactions. It requires licensees to provide prospective buyers and sellers, at first substantial contact, with a copy of the *Working with Real Estate Agents* brochure, to review the brochure with them and then reach an agreement regarding their agency relationship. The licensee providing the brochure should also include his/her name and license number on the brochure. Note that the obligation under this rule is not satisfied merely by handing the prospective seller or buyer the brochure to read. The agent is required to review the contents of the brochure with the prospective buyer or seller and then reach agreement with the prospective buyer or seller as to whether the agent will work with the buyer or seller as his/her agent or as the agent of the other party. In the case of a prospective **seller**, the agent may either (1) act as the seller's agent, which is the typical situation and which requires a written agreement from the outset of their relationship, or (2) work with the seller as a buyer's agent if the agent already represents a prospective buyer. In the case of a prospective **buyer**, the agent may either (1) act as the buyer's agent under either an oral or written agreement as addressed in Rule A.0104(a), or (2) work with the buyer as a seller's agent, disclosure of which must be in writing from the outset.

**Disclosure of Agency Status by Sellers' Agents and Subagents to Prospective Buyers:** Paragraph (e) of Rule A.0104, like (c), requires a seller's agent or subagent in sales transactions to disclose his/her agency status in writing to a prospective buyer at the "first substantial contact" with the buyer. It is recommended that sellers' agents make this required written disclosure using the form provided for this purpose in the *Working with Real Estate Agents* brochure that must be provided to buyers (as well as to sellers) at first substantial contact. This form has a place for the buyer to acknowledge receipt of the brochure and disclosure of agency status, thereby providing the agent with written evidence of having provided the brochure and disclosure. The disclosure may, however, be made using a different form — the most important point is that the disclosure of seller agency be made in writing in a timely manner. The reason for this requirement is that buyers tend to assume that an agent they contact to work with them in locating a property to purchase is "their" agent and is working primarily in their interest. This may or may not be the case in reality. The purpose of the disclosure requirement is to place prospective buyers on notice that the agent they are dealing with is NOT "their" agent before the prospective buyer discloses to the agent information which the buyer would not want a seller to know because it might compromise the buyer's bargaining position.

Most frequently, **"first substantial contact"** will occur at the first "face-to-face" meeting with a prospective buyer. However, the point in time that "first substantial contact" with a prospective buyer occurs will vary depending on the particular situation and may or may not be at the time of the first or initial contact with the prospective buyer. Many first contacts are by telephone and do not involve discussions which reach the level that would require disclosure, although some initial phone contacts, especially those with out-of-town buyers, could reach this level. *"First substantial contact"* occurs at the point in time when a discussion with a prospective buyer begins to focus on the buyer's specific property needs and desires or on the buyer's financial situation. Typically, that point in time is reached when the agent is ready to solicit information from the prospective buyer that is needed to identify prospective properties to show the buyer. Therefore, *an agent planning to work with a prospective buyer as a seller's agent or subagent should assure that disclosure of his/her agency status is made in writing to the prospective buyer prior to obtaining from the prospective buyer any personal or confidential information* that the buyer would not want a seller to know. A few examples of such personal or confidential information include: The maximum price a buyer is willing to pay for a property; the buyer's ability to pay more than the price offered by the buyer; or the fact that a buyer has a special interest in purchasing the seller's property rather than some other similar property. In any event, the disclosure must be made prior to discussing with the prospective buyer his/her specific needs or desires regarding the purchase of a property. As a practical matter, this means the *disclosure will always need to be made prior to showing a property to a prospective buyer.* The best policy is to simply make the disclosure at the earliest possible time.

If first substantial contact occurs by telephone or by means of other electronic communication where it is not practical to provide written disclosure, the agent shall immediately disclose by similar means whom he/she represents and shall immediately, but in no event later than three days from the date of first substantial contact, mail or otherwise transmit a copy of the written disclosure to the buyer.

**Disclosure of Agency Status by Buyers' Agents to Sellers or Sellers' Agents:** Paragraph (f) of Rule A.0104 requires a buyer's agent to disclose his/her agency status to a seller or seller's agent at the "initial contact" with the seller or seller's agent. "Initial contact" will typically occur when a buyer's agent telephones or otherwise contacts the listing firm to schedule a showing. The initial disclosure may be oral, but a written confirmation of the previous oral disclosure must be made (except in auction sale transactions) no later than the time of delivery of an offer to purchase. The written confirmation may be (and usually is) included in the offer to purchase. In fact, Commission Rule A.0112(a)(19) requires that any preprinted offer to purchase and contract form used by an agent include a provision providing for confirmation of agency status by each real estate agent (and firm) involved in the transaction.

**Consent to Dual Agency:** Paragraph (d) of Rule A.0104 requires generally that an agent must obtain the written authority of all parties prior to undertaking to represent those parties as a dual agent. It is important to note that this requirement applies to *all real estate transactions* (sales and lease/rentals), not just to sales transactions. [In sales transactions, this written authority to act as a dual agent is usually limited to "in-house" sales transactions and is usually included in the listing and buyer agency contracts. If those contracts do not grant such authority, then the agent must have both the seller and buyer consent to the dual agency prior to beginning to act as a dual agent for both parties.]

Paragraph (d) of Rule A.0104 currently requires written authority for dual agency from the formation of the relationship except situations where a buyer/tenant is represented by an agent working under an oral agency agreement as permitted by A.0104(a), in which case written authority for dual agency must be obtained no later than the time one of the parties represented by the agent working as a dual agent makes an offer to purchase, sell, rent, lease, or exchange real estate to the other party. Thus, it is permissible for the agent to operate for a limited period of time under an oral dual agency agreement. It is very important to remember that G.S. 93A-6(a)(4) still requires agents to obtain the consent of all parties prior to beginning to act as a dual agent for those parties. Therefore, it is essential that agents electing to operate as a dual agent for a limited period of time without obtaining this authority in writing still explain fully the consequences of their acting as a dual agent and obtain the parties' oral consent.

As a practical matter in sales transactions, agents will frequently have already obtained written authority to act as a dual agent for in-house sales transactions at the time the initial written listing or buyer agency agreement is executed. However, under Paragraph (a) of Rule A.0104, many buyer's agents may elect to work with their buyer clients for a period of time under an oral buyer agency agreement. Paragraph (d) permits such buyer's agents to also operate for a limited period of time as a dual agent in order to deal with situations where a buyer client is interested in a property listed with the agent's firm. Note that, although an oral dual agency agreement for a limited period of time is permitted by Commission rules, it is strongly recommended that agents have any dual agency agreement in writing from the outset of the dual agency arrangement. This will provide the agent with some evidence that the matter of dual agency was discussed with the parties and that they consented to it. Such evidence could prove quite useful if a party later asserts that the agent did not obtain their consent for dual agency in a timely manner.

**Auction Sales:** Paragraph (g) of Rule A.0104 provides that the provisions of Paragraphs (c), (d) and (e) of the Rule shall not apply to real estate licensees representing sellers in auction sales transactions. Note that in auction sales, the real estate agents involved almost invariably work only as seller's agents and this fact is considered to be self-evident. Thus, there is no need for agents to distribute and review the *Working with Real Estate Agents* brochure, no need for disclosure of agency status by the seller's agents, and no dual agency. For the unusual situation where a buyer may be represented by an agent in an auction sale transaction, Paragraph (h) of Rule A.0104 provides that such a buyer's agent shall, no later than the time of execution of a written agreement memorializing the buyer's contract to purchase, provide the seller or seller's agent with a written confirmation that he/she represents the buyer.

**Dual Agency Status of Firm:** Paragraph (i) of Rule A.0104 codifies in the Commission's rules the common law rule that a firm which represents more than one party in the same real estate transaction is a dual agent, and further states that the firm, through the brokers affiliated with the firm, shall disclose its dual agency to the parties. This rule provision does not establish any additional requirement for licensees and is intended merely to clarify that the Commission follows the common law rule. In other words, dual agency is not limited to those situations where an individual agent is working with both a buyer client and seller client (or lessor and commercial tenant) in the same transaction. If one agent of a firm is working with a buyer client of the firm and another agent of the same firm is working with a seller client of the firm in a transaction involving the sale of the seller client's property to the buyer client, then the firm is a dual agent (as it also holds both agency agreements). However, a firm functions through its employees, namely, its associated agents; thus, under the common law, whenever the firm is a dual agent of certain parties in a transaction, all licensees affiliated with that firm are also dual agents of those parties in that transaction.

**Designated Agency:** Paragraphs (j) - (m) of Rule A.0104 authorize real estate firms to engage in a form of dual agency practice referred to in the rule as "designated agency" in certain sales transactions involving in-house dual agency. "Designated agency" is an optional method of practicing dual agency that may be adopted by a real estate firm if the firm establishes a policy consistent with the Commission's designated agency rules. Designated agency involves appointing or "designating" an individual agent(s) in a firm to represent only the interests of the seller and another individual agent(s) to represent only the interests of the buyer when a firm has an in-house dual agency situation.

The principal advantage of the designated agency approach over the "standard" dual agency approach is that each of a firm's clients (seller and buyer) receive fuller representation by their designated agent. In the typical dual agency situation, client advocacy is essentially lost because the dual agent may not seek an advantage for (i.e, "advocate" for) one client to the detriment of the other client. The dual agent must remain completely neutral and impartial at all times. Designated agency returns "advocacy" to the services provided by the respective designated agents and allows them to more fully represent their respective clients.

Authority to practice designated agency must be in writing no later than the time a written dual agency agreement is required under A.0104(d). Additional required procedures for practicing designated agency are clearly spelled out in Paragraphs (j) - (m) and are not discussed further here. For more detailed coverage of dual and designated agency, the reader is once again referred to the Commission's *North Carolina Real Estate Manual.*

**Dual Agency by Individual Agent:** Paragraph (n) of Rule A.0104 authorizes individual brokers representing both the buyer and seller in the same real estate transaction pursuant to a written dual agency agreement to include in the agreement a provision authorizing the broker not to disclose certain "confidential" information about one party to the other party without permission from the party about whom the information pertains. This provision is intended to allow individual dual agents to treat confidential information about their clients in a manner similar to that allowed for firms practicing designated agency.

### Advertising [Rule A.0105]

The rule prohibits "blind ads;" rather, all advertising must indicate that it is the advertisement of a broker or brokerage firm. Be aware that A.0105(c)(1) prohibits "provisional" brokers from advertising "without his or her broker's consent" and must include the broker's name in the advertising. Lastly, licensees may not advertise under an assumed name without registering the assumed name with the applicable County Register of Deeds office and no business entity (other than a corporation) may include in its name the name of an unlicensed person or salesperson. [See A.0105(b) and (d)]. [See also 2005-2006 Real Estate Update materials, Advertising.]

### Delivery of Instruments [G.S. 93A-6(a)(13) and (14); Rules A.0106 and A.0107(c)]

Among other things, Rule A.0106 requires agents to "immediately, but in no event later than five days from the date of execution, deliver to the parties thereto copies of any ... offer..." This does NOT mean that agents may in every case wait up to five days to present an offer to a seller. Rather, it means that an agent must immediately, as soon as possible, present to the seller any offer received by the agent. If the agent is the "selling agent," then the offer should be immediately presented to the "listing agent" who should, in turn, immediately present the offer to the seller. The "five day" provision is included only to allow for situations where the seller is not immediately available (e.g., seller is out of town), and represents an outside time limit within which offers must always be presented. In all cases where the seller is available, the offer should be presented as soon as possible.

The same rule also means that a prospective buyer who signs an offer must immediately be provided a copy of such offer. (A photocopy is acceptable for this purpose.) Do NOT wait until after the offer is accepted (or rejected) by the seller.

In addition, this rule means that an offer must be immediately presented to a seller *even if there is a contract pending on the property.* Of course, in this instance, it is essential that the agent also advise the seller that serious legal problems could result from the seller's acceptance of such offer and that the seller should contact an attorney if he is interested in treating the offer as a "back-up" offer or in attempting to be released from the previously signed contract.

### Retention of Records [Rule A.0108]

Note that as of September 1, 2002, licensees are required to maintain and retain various documents pertaining to their brokerage transactions for three years from the successful or unsuccessful conclusion of the transaction or the disbursement of all trust monies pertaining to that transaction, whichever occurs later. Thus, a licensee holding a disputed earnest money deposit which isn't finally disbursed until July, 2004 from a transaction that terminated without closing in September, 2002, would be required to retain the A.0108 transaction file documents until July, 2007.

### Brokerage Fees and Compensation [Rule A.0109]

This rule prohibits a broker from receiving any form of valuable consideration from a vendor or supplier of goods or services in connection with an expenditure made on behalf of his principal in a real estate transaction without first obtaining the written consent of the principal.

**Example:** A broker manages several rental units for various owners and routinely employs Ajax Cleaning Service to clean the units after the tenants leave. The broker pays Ajax a $50 per unit fee for its services out of rental proceeds received and deposited in his trust account. Ajax then "refunds" to the broker $10 for each $50 fee it receives, but the property owners are not aware that the broker receives this payment from Ajax in addition to his regular brokerage fee. The broker in this situation is making a secret profit without the property owners' knowledge and is violating the rule.

This rule also prohibits a broker from receiving any form of valuable consideration for recommending, procuring, or arranging services for a party to a real estate transaction without full disclosure to such party. The party for whom the services are recommended, procured, or arranged does not have to be the agent's principal.

**Example**: An agent sells a listed lot to a buyer who wants to build a house on the lot. Without the buyer's knowledge, the agent arranges with ABC Homebuilders for ABC to pay the agent a 3% referral fee if the agent recommends ABC to the buyer and the buyer employs ABC to build his house. The agent then recommends ABC to the buyer, ABC builds the buyer's house for $100,000 and ABC secretly pays the agent $3,000 for his referral of the buyer. The agent has violated this rule. (Note that the buyer in this situation likely paid $3,000 more for his house than was necessary because it is very likely the builder added the agent's referral fee to the price he charged the buyer for building the house. The main point here is that the buyer had the right to know that the agent was not providing disinterested advice when recommending the builder.)

**Example:** A selling agent in a real estate transaction, while acting as a subagent of the seller, recommends to a buyer who has submitted an offer that the buyer apply to Ready Cash Mortgage Company for his mortgage loan. The agent knows that Ready Cash will pay him a "referral fee" of $100 for sending him the buyer's business if the loan is made to the buyer, but the agent does not disclose this fact to the buyer. If the agent subsequently accepts the referral fee from the lender, he will have violated this rule. (The buyer has the right to know that the agent's recommendation is not a disinterested one.)

While A.0109(d) continues to absolutely prohibit licensees from sharing compensation with any unlicensed person for acts which require a real estate license, paragraph (e), which was added to Rule A.0109 effective September 1, 2002, allows one narrow, limited exception, namely: licensees may pay referral fees to travel agents who contact them to book *vacation rentals only*, so long as well-defined procedures are followed.

### Broker-in-Charge [Rule A.0110]

Every firm is required to designate a broker to serve as broker-in-charge at each office. The broker-in-charge is the person the Commission will hold responsible for the supervision and management of an office. The seven specific responsibilities of a broker-in-charge are enumerated in Paragraph (a). Brokers designated as a broker-in-charge on or after April 1, 2006 must have the equivalent of two years full-time brokerage experience within the preceding five years and must take the Commission's broker-in-charge course within 120 days of being designated, unless they already have taken the 12-hour course within the preceding three years.

The only people who might be designated broker-in-charge after April 1, 2006 who may not be required to take the 12-hour broker-in-charge course are those who already are designated as brokers-in-charge before March 31, 2006, who are transferrring from office A to office B *with no lapse in their status as a broker-in-charge.* To remain a broker-in-charge, all brokers-in-charge will be required to take special annual broker-in-charge electives written by the Commission but taught by approved Update instructors as part of the broker's 8-hours of continuing education each year. Any broker-in-charge who suffers any break or lapse in their status as broker-in-charge for any reason will be required to satisfy the two-year experience requirement and take the 12-hour broker-in-charge course to be redesignated as a broker-in-charge after April 1, 2006, unless they have had the 12-hour course within the preceding three years.

### Drafting Legal Instruments [Rule A.0111]

This rule prohibits licensees from drafting legal instruments, e.g., contracts, deeds, deeds of trust, etc., but does allow them to fill in the blanks on preprinted sales contract and lease forms, which is not construed to be the unauthorized practice of law.

### Offers and Sales Contracts [Rule A.0112]

This rule specifies what minimum terms must be contained in any preprinted offer or sales contract form a licensee, acting as an agent, proposes for use by a party in a real estate transaction.

### Reporting Criminal Convictions [Rule A.0113]

Licensees are required to report to the Commission any criminal convictions or any disciplinary action taken against them by any other professional board within sixty (60) days of the final judgment or order in the case. This reporting requirement is ongoing in nature.

### Residential Property Disclosure Statement [Rule A.0114]

State law requires that most residential property owners complete a disclosure form to give to prospective purchasers. The form seeks to elicit information about the condition of the property by asking various questions, to which owners may answer "yes," "no," or "no representation." Failure to provide a buyer with this form may allow the buyer to cancel the contract by notifying the seller in writing within three calendar days of contract acceptance.

## HANDLING TRUST FUNDS

See the "Trust Account Guidelines" contained in this booklet for complete coverage of this important topic. Licensees and applicants should have a thorough knowledge and understanding of the "Trust Account Guidelines."

# Appendix B
## Residential Square Footage Guidelines

## INTRODUCTION

It is often said that the three most important factors in making a homebuying decision are "location," "location," and "location." Other than "location," the single most-important factor is probably the size or "square footage" of the home. Not only is it an indicator of whether a particular home will meet a homebuyer's space needs, but it also affords a convenient (though not always accurate) method for the buyer to estimate the value of the home and compare it with other properties.

Although real estate agents are not required by the Real Estate License Law or Real Estate Commission rules to report the square footage of properties offered for sale (or rent), when they do report square footage, it is essential that the information they give prospective purchasers be accurate. At a minimum, information concerning square footage should include the amount of *living area* in the dwelling. The following guidelines and accompanying illustrations are designed to assist real estate brokers and salespersons in measuring, calculating and reporting (both orally and in writing) the *living area* contained in detached and attached single-family residential buildings. When reporting square footage, real estate agents should carefully follow these *Guidelines* or any other standards that are comparable to them, including those approved by the American National Standards Institute, Inc. (ANSI) which are recognized by the North Carolina Real Estate Commission as comparable standards.* Agents should be prepared to identify, when requested, the standard used.

*The following materials were consulted in the development of these *Guidelines:*
The *American National Standard for Single-Family Residential Buildings: Square Footage-Method for Calculating* approved by the American National Standards Institute, Inc.
*House Measuring & Square Footage* published by the Carolina Multiple Listing Services. Inc.;
Materials compiled by Bart T. Bryson, MAI, SRA, and Mary L. D'Angelo.

Real estate appraisers and lenders generally adhere to more detailed criteria in arriving at the *living area* or "gross living area" of residential dwellings. This normally includes distinguishing "above-grade" from "below-grade" area, which is also required by many multiple listing services. "Above-Grade" is defined as space on any level of a dwelling which has *living area* and no earth adjacent to any exterior wall on that level. "Below-Grade" is space on any level which has *living area,* is accessible by interior stairs, and has earth adjacent to any exterior wall on that level. If earth is adjacent to any portion of a wall, the entire level is considered "below-grade." Space that is "at" or "on grade" is considered "above-grade."

While real estate agents are encouraged to provide the most complete information available about properties offered for sale, the *Guidelines* recognize that the separate reporting of "above-grade" and "below-grade" area can be impractical in the advertising and marketing of homes. For this reason, *real estate agents are permitted under these Guidelines to report square footage of the dwelling as the total "living area"* without a separate distinction between "above-grade" and "below-grade" areas. However, to help avoid confusion and concern, agents should alert purchasers and sellers that the appraisal report may reflect differences in the way *living area* is defined and described by the lender, appraiser, and the *North Carolina Building Code* which could affect the amount of *living area* reported.

## Living Area Criteria

*Living area* (sometimes referred to as "heated living area" or "heated square footage") is space that is intended for human occupancy and is:

1. *Heated* by a conventional heating system or systems (forced air, radiant, solar, etc.) that are permanently installed in the dwelling - not a portable heater - which generates heat sufficient to make the space suitable for year-round occupancy;
2. *Finished,* with walls, floors and ceilings of materials generally accepted for interior construction (e.g., painted drywall/sheet rock or panelled walls, carpeted or hardwood flooring, etc.) and with a ceiling height of at least seven feet, except under beams, ducts, etc. where the height must be at least six feet four inches *[Note: In rooms with sloped ceilings (e.g., finished attics, bonus rooms, etc.) you may also include as living area the portion of the room with a ceiling height of at least five feet if at least one-half of the finished area of the room has a ceiling height of at least seven feet.];* and
3. *Directly accessible from other living area* (through a door or by a heated hallway or stairway).

Determining whether an area is considered *living area* can sometimes be confusing. Finished rooms used for general living (living room, dining room, kitchen, den, bedrooms, etc.) are normally included in *living area.* For other areas in the dwelling, the determination may not be so easy. *For example, the following areas are considered* ***living area*** *if they meet the criteria (i.e., heated, finished, directly accessible from living area):*

- **Attic,** but note in the listing data that the space is located in an attic (Fig. 2). *[Note: If the ceiling is sloped, remember to apply the "ceiling height" criteria.]*
- **Basement (or "Below-Grade"),** but note in the listing data that the space is located in a basement or "below-grade" (Fig. 1). *[Note: For reporting purposes, a "basement" is defined as an area below the entry level of the dwelling which is accessible by a* ***full*** *flight of stairs and has earth adjacent to some portion of at least one wall above the floor level.]*
- **Bay Window,** if it has a floor, a ceiling height of at least seven feet, and otherwise meets the criteria for living area (Fig. 2).
- **Bonus Room (e.g., Finished Room over Garage)** (Fig. 3). *[Note: If the ceiling is sloped, remember to apply the "ceiling height" criteria.]*
- **Breezeway** (enclosed).
- **Chimney** if the chimney base is inside *living area.* If the chimney base is outside the *living area* but the

hearth is in the *living area,* include the hearth in the *living area* but not the chimney base (Fig. 1).

- **Closets,** if they are a functional part of the *living area*.
- **Dormers** (Fig. 6).
- **Furnace (Mechanical) Room** Also, in order to avoid excessive detail, if the furnace, water heater, etc. is located in a small closet in the *living area,* include it in *living area* even if it does not meet other *living area* criteria (Fig. 4).
- **Hallways,** if they are a functional part of the *living area*.
- **Laundry Room/Area** (Fig. 6).
- **Office** (Fig. 1).
- **Stairs,** if they meet the criteria and connect to *living area* (Fig. 1, 2, 3, 4, 5, 6). Include the stairway with the area from which it descends, **not to exceed the area of the opening in the floor.** If the opening for the stairway exceeds the length and width of the stairway, deduct the excess open space from the upper level area. Include as part of the lower level area the space beneath the stairway, regardless of its ceiling height.
- **Storage Room** (Fig. 6).

Note in the listing data and advise purchasers of any space that does not meet the criteria for *living area* but which contributes to the value of the dwelling; for example, unfinished basements, unfinished attics (with permanent stairs), unfinished bonus rooms, shops, decks, balconies, porches, garages and carports.

## Helpful Hints

Concealed in the walls of nearly all residential construction are pipes, ducts, chases, returns, etc. necessary to support the structure's mechanical systems. Although they may occupy *living area,* to avoid excessive detail, do **not** deduct the space from the living area.

When measuring and reporting the *living area* of homes, be alert to any remodel-ing, room additions (e.g., an enclosed porch) or other structural modifications to assure that the space meets all the criteria for *living area*. **Pay particular attention to the heating criteria, because the heating system for the original structure may not be adequate for the increased square footage.** Although agents are not required to determine the adequacy of heating systems, they should at least note whether there are heat vents, radiators or other heat outlets in the room before deciding whether to include space as *living area*.

When an area that is not part of the *living area* (e.g., a garage) shares a common wall with the *living area,* treat the common wall as the exterior wall for the *living area*; therefore, the measurements for the *living area* will include the thickness of the common wall, and the measurements for the other area will not.

Interior space that is open from the floor of one level to the ceiling of the next higher level is included in the square footage for the lower level only. However, any area occupied by interior balconies, lofts, etc. on the upper level or stairs that extend to the upper level is included in the square footage for the upper level.

## Measurements

The amount of *living area* and "other area" in dwellings is based upon **exterior measurements.** A one hundred-foot-long tape measure is recommended for use in measuring the exterior of dwellings, and a thirty-foot retractable tape for measuring interior and hard-to-reach spaces. A tape measure that indicates linear footage in "tenths of a foot" will greatly simplify your calculations. For best results, take a partner to assist you in measuring. But if you do not have someone to assist you, a screwdriver or other sharp tool can be used to secure the tape measure to the ground.

Begin at one corner of the dwelling and proceed with measuring each exterior wall. **Round off your measurements to the nearest inch** (or tenth-of-a-foot if your tape indicates footage in that manner). Make a sketch of the structure. Write down each measurement as you go, and record it on your sketch. A clipboard and graph paper are helpful in sketching the dwelling and recording the measurements. Measure *living area* and "other area," but identify them separately on your sketch. Look for offsets (portions of walls that "jut out"), and adjust for any "overlap" of exterior walls (Fig. 3) or "overhang" in upper levels ( Fig. 5).

When you cannot measure an exterior surface (such as in the case of attics and below-grade areas), measure the perimeter walls of the area from the inside of the dwelling. Remember to add **six inches** for each exterior wall and interior wall that you encounter in order to arrive at the exterior dimensions (Fig. 2, 3, 4, 6).

Measure all sides of the dwelling, making sure that the overall lengths of the front and rear sides are equal, as well as the ends. Then inspect the interior of the dwelling to identify spaces which cannot be included in *living area*. You may also find it helpful to take several photographs of the dwelling for later use when you return to your office.

## Calculating Square Footage

From your sketch of the dwelling, identify and separate *living area* from "other area." If your measurements are in inches (rather than tenths-of-a-foot), convert your figures to a decimal as follows:

| | |
|---|---|
| 1" = .10 ft. | 7" = .60 ft. |
| 2" = .20 ft. | 8" = .70 ft. |
| 3" = .25 ft. | 9" = .75 ft. |
| 4" = .30 ft | 10" = .80 ft. |
| 5" = .40 ft. | 11" = .90 ft. |
| 6" = .50 ft. | 12" = 1.00 ft. |

Calculate the *living area* (and other area) by multiplying the length times the width of each rectangular space. Then add your subtotals and round off your figure for total square footage to the nearest **square foot.** Double-check your calculations. When in doubt, recheck them and, if necessary, re-measure the house.

## Attached Dwellings

When measuring an "attached" single-family home (e.g., townhouse, duplex, condominium, etc.), use the same techniques just described. If there is a common wall, measure to the inside surface of the wall and add **six inches.** [*Note: In the case of* condominiums, *do not include the thickness of exterior or common walls.*] Do not include any "common areas" (exterior hallways, stairways, etc.) in your calculations.

## Proposed Construction

For proposed construction, your square footage calculations will be based upon dimensions described in blueprints and building plans. When reporting the projected square footage, be careful to disclose that you have calculated the square footage based upon plan dimensions. Therefore, the square footage may differ in the completed structure. Do not rely on any calculations printed on the plans.

## Agents' Responsibilities

**(Effective May 9, 2001)**

Real estate agents are expected to be able to accurately calculate the square footage of most dwellings. When reporting square footage, whether to a party to a real estate transaction, another real estate agent, or others, a real estate agent is expected to provide accurate square footage information that was compiled using these *Guidelines* or comparable standards. While an agent is expected to use reasonable skill, care and diligence when calculating square footage, it should be noted that the Commission does not expect absolute perfection. Because all properties are unique and no guidelines can anticipate every possibility, minor discrepancies in deriving square footage are not considered by the Commission to constitute negligence on the part of the agent. Minor variations in tape readings and small differences in rounding off or conversion from inches to decimals, when multiplied over distances, will cause reasonable discrepancies between two competent measurements of the same dwelling. In addition to differences due to minor variations in measurement and calculation, discrepancies between measurements may also be attributable to reasonable differences in interpretation. For instance, two agents might reasonably differ about whether an addition to a dwelling is sufficiently finished under these *Guidelines* to be included within the measured living area. Differences which are based upon an agent's thoughtful judgment reasonably founded on these or other similar guidelines will not be considered by the Commission to constitute error on the agent's part. Deviations in calculated square footage of less than five percent will seldom be cause for concern.

As a general rule, the most reliable way for an agent to obtain accurate square footage data is by personally measuring the dwelling unit and calculating the square footage. It is especially recommended that *listing agents* use this approach for dwellings that are not particularly unusual or complex in their design.

As an alternative to personally measuring a dwelling and calculating its square footage, an agent may rely on the square footage reported by other persons when it is reasonable under the circumstances to do so. Generally speaking, an agent working with a buyer (either as a buyer's agent or as a seller's agent) may rely on the listing agent's square footage representations except in those unusual instances when there is an error in the reported square footage that should be obvious to a reasonably prudent agent. For example, a buyer's agent would not be expected to notice that a house advertised as containing 2200 square feet of living area in fact contained only 2000 square feet. On the other hand, that same agent, under most circumstances, would be expected to realize that a house described as containing 3200 square feet really contained only 2300 square feet of living area. If there is such a "red flag" regarding the reported square footage, the agent working with the buyer should promptly point out the suspected error to the buyer and the listing agent. The listing agent should then verify the square footage and correct any error in the information reported.

It is also appropriate for an agent to rely upon measurements and calculations performed by other professionals with greater expertise in determining square footage. A new agent who may be unsure of his or her own calculations should seek guidance from a more experienced agent. As the new agent gains experience and confidence, he or she will become less reliant on the assistance of others. In order to ensure accuracy of the square footage they report, even experienced agents may wish to rely upon a competent state-licensed or state-certified appraiser or another agent with greater expertise in determining square footage. For example, an agent might be confronted with an unusual measurement problem or a dwelling of complex design. The house described in Figure 8 in these *Guidelines* is such a property. When an agent relies upon measurements and calculations personally performed by a competent appraiser or a more expert agent, the appraiser or agent must use these *Guidelines* or other comparable standards and the square footage reported must be specifically determined in connection with the current transaction. An agent who relies on another's measurement would still be expected to recognize an obvious error in the reported square footage and to alert any interested parties.

Some sources of square footage information are by their very nature unreliable. For example, an agent should **not** rely on square footage information determined by the property owner or included in property tax records. An agent should also **not** rely on square footage information included in a listing, appraisal report or survey prepared in connection with an earlier transaction.

In areas where the prevailing practice is to report square footage in the advertising and marketing of homes, agents whose policy is **not** to calculate and report square footage must disclose this fact to prospective buyer and seller clients before entering into agency agreements with them.

## ILLUSTRATIONS

For assistance in calculating and reporting the area of homes, refer to the following illustrations showing the *living area* shaded. To test your knowledge, an illustration and blank "Worksheet" for a home with a more challenging floor plan has also been included. (There is also a completed "Worksheet" for the Practice Floor Plan.) In reviewing the illustrations, assume that for those homes with basements, attics, etc., the exterior measurements shown have been derived from interior measurements taking into account walls and partitions. Where there is a common wall between *living area* and other area, the measurements shown in the illustrations include the thickness of the common wall in *living area* except in the condominium example where wall thickness is not included.

## One Story With Basement And Carport

(Figure 1)

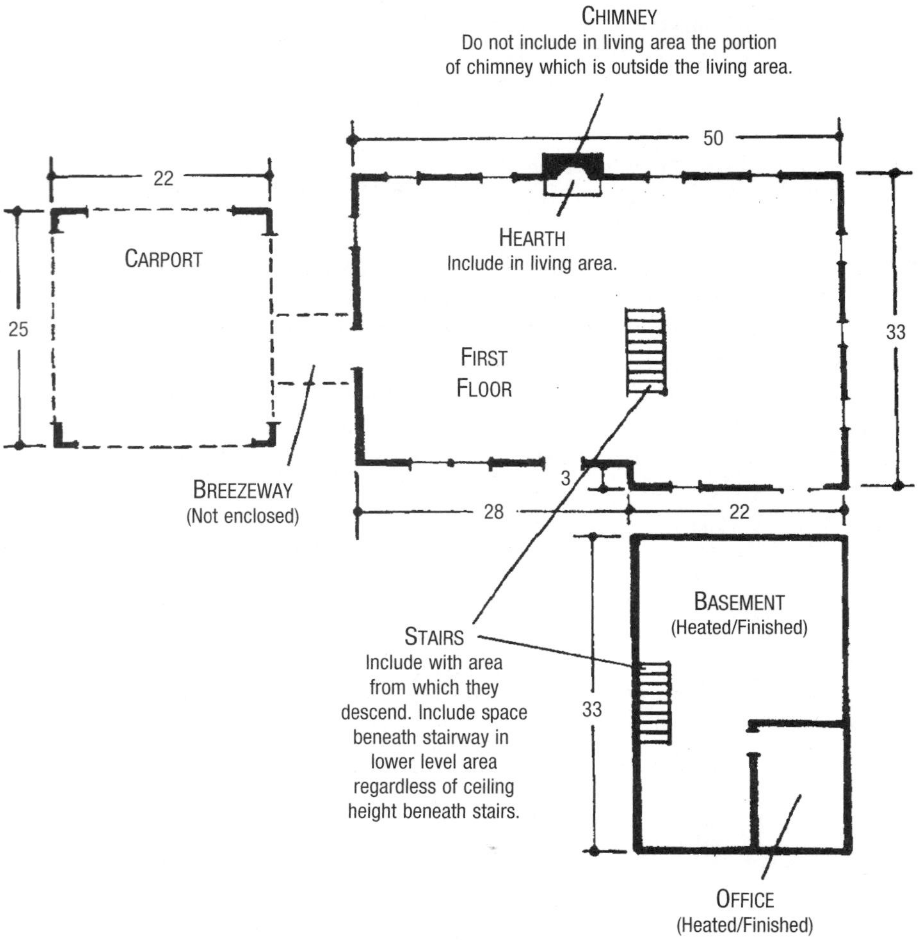
CHIMNEY
Do not include in living area the portion of chimney which is outside the living area.
50
22
HEARTH
Include in living area.
CARPORT
25
FIRST FLOOR
33
3
BREEZEWAY
(Not enclosed)
28
22
BASEMENT
(Heated/Finished)
STAIRS
Include with area from which they descend. Include space beneath stairway in lower level area regardless of ceiling height beneath stairs.
33
OFFICE
(Heated/Finished)

## One Story With Basement And Carport Worksheet

| Living Area | | | |
|---|---|---|---|
| Area | Dimensions | Subtotal | Total |
| 1st Floor | 50 x 30 | 1,500 | |
| | 3 x 22 | + 66 | 1,566 |
| Basement | 22 x 33 | | 726 |
| Total | | | 2,292 |
| | | | |
| | | | |
| | | | |

| Other Area | | | |
|---|---|---|---|
| Area | Dimensions | Subtotal | Total |
| Carport | 22 x 25 | | 550 |
| | | | |
| | | | |
| | | | |
| | | | |
| | | | |
| | | | |

Report: One-story detached house with 2,292 square feet of living area of which 726 square feet are in a finished basement, plus a 550-square-foot carport.

## Two Story With Open Foyer And Finished Attic

(Figure 2)

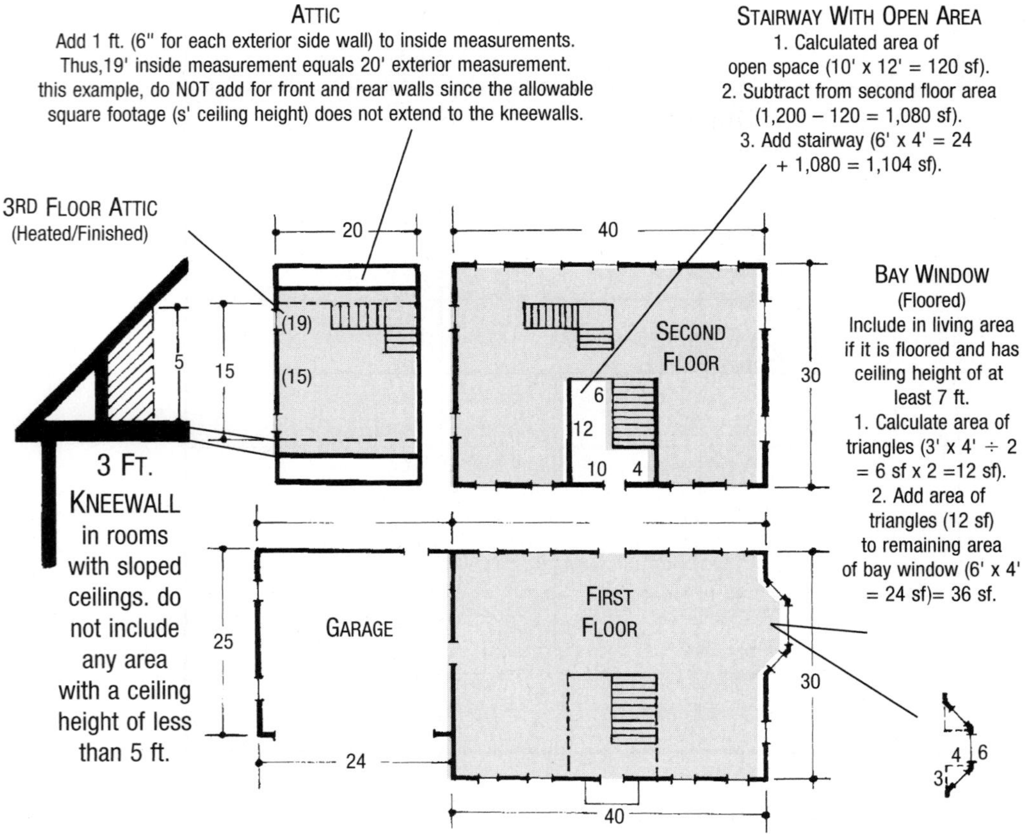

Attic
Add 1 ft. (6" for each exterior side wall) to inside measurements. Thus,19' inside measurement equals 20' exterior measurement. this example, do NOT add for front and rear walls since the allowable square footage (s' ceiling height) does not extend to the kneewalls.
Stairway With Open Area
1. Calculated area of open space (10' x 12' = 120 sf).
2. Subtract from second floor area (1,200 – 120 = 1,080 sf).
3. Add stairway (6' x 4' = 24 + 1,080 = 1,104 sf).
3rd Floor Attic
(Heated/Finished)
20
40
(19)
(15)
5
15
Second Floor
6
12
10
4
30
Bay Window
(Floored)
Include in living area if it is floored and has ceiling height of at least 7 ft.
1. Calculate area of triangles (3' x 4' ÷ 2 = 6 sf x 2 =12 sf).
2. Add area of triangles (12 sf) to remaining area of bay window (6' x 4' = 24 sf)= 36 sf.
3 Ft. Kneewall in rooms with sloped ceilings. do not include any area with a ceiling height of less than 5 ft.
25
Garage
First Floor
30
24
40
4
6
3

## Two Story With Open Foyer and Finished Attic Worksheet

| Living Area | | | |
|---|---|---|---|
| Area | Dimensions | Subtotal | Total |
| 1st Floor | 40 x 30 | 1,200 | |
| Bay Window | | 36 | 1,236 |
| 2nd Floor | 40 x 30 | 1,200 | |
| | 10 x 12 | –120 | |
| | 4 x 6 | +24 | 1,104 |
| Fin. Attic | 20 x 15 | | 300 |
| Total | | | 2,640 |
| **Other Area** | | | |
| Area | Dimensions | Subtotal | Total |
| Garage | 25 x 24 | | 600 |
| | | | |
| | | | |
| | | | |
| | | | |
| | | | |
| | | | |

Report: Two-story detached house with 2,640 square feet of living area of which 300 square feet are in a finished attic, plus a 600-square-foot garage.

## Two Story With "Bonus Room" Over Garage

(Figure 3)

### Bonus Room

If the "Bonus Room" is accessible from living area through a door, hallway or stairway, Include in living area; otherwise, report as other area.

Add 6" to inside measurements for each exterior wall. Thus, 14' x 23.5' inside measurement equals 15' x 24' exterior measurements. In rooms with sloped ceilings, add 6" for each kneewall at least 5' in height.

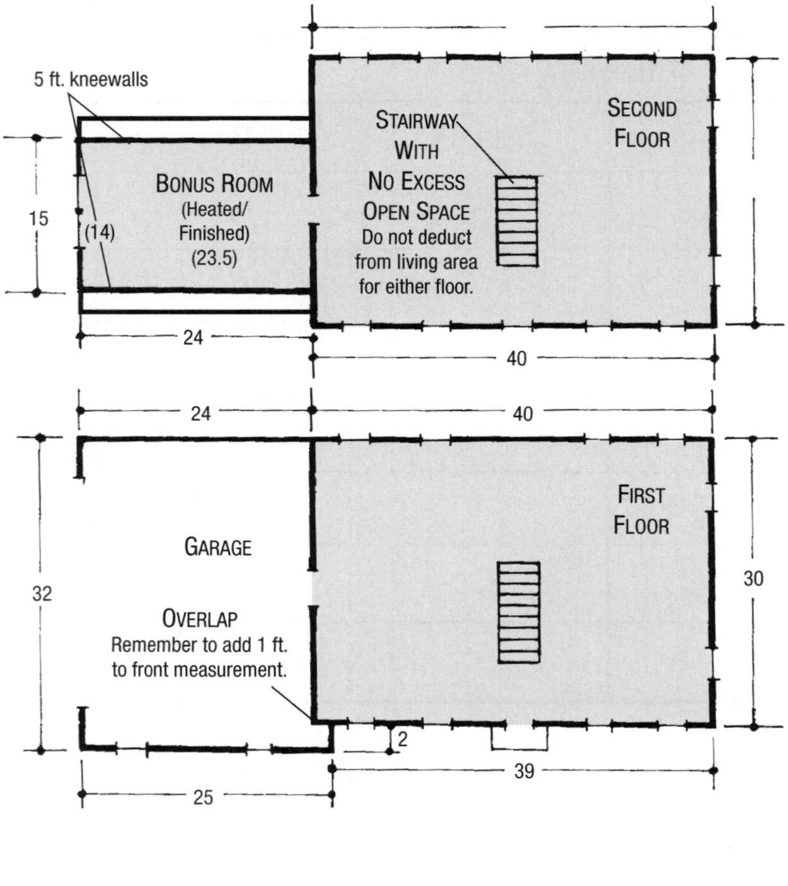

## TWO STORY WITH "BONUS ROOM" OVER GARAGE WORKSHEET

| LIVING AREA | | | |
|---|---|---|---|
| AREA | DIMENSIONS | SUBTOTAL | TOTAL |
| 1st Floor | 40 x 30 | | 1,200 |
| 2nd Floor | 40 x 30 | | 1,200 |
| Bonus Room | 15 x 24 | | 360 |
| Total | | | 2,760 |
| | | | |
| | | | |
| | | | |

| OTHER AREA | | | |
|---|---|---|---|
| AREA | DIMENSIONS | SUBTOTAL | TOTAL |
| Garage | 24 x 32 | 768 | |
| | 1 x 2 | +2 | 770 |
| | | | |
| | | | |
| | | | |
| | | | |
| | | | |

REPORT: TWO-STORY DETACHED HOUSE WITH 2,760 SQUARE FEET OF LIVING AREA OF WHICH 360 SQUARE FEET ARE IN A "BONUS ROOM" OVER THE GARAGE, PLUS A 770-SQARE-FOOT GARAGE.

## Split Foyer

(Figure 4)

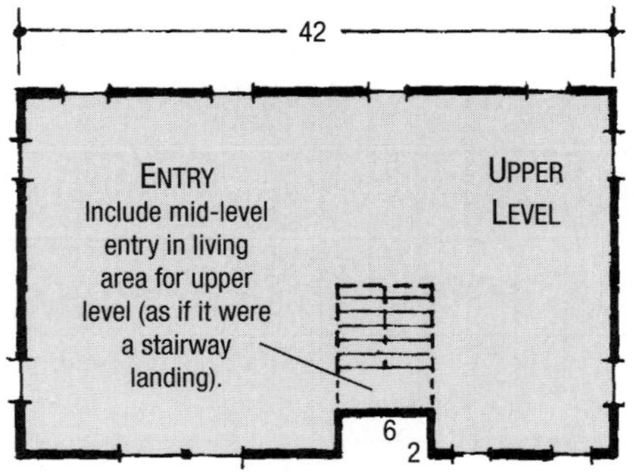
42
Entry
Include mid-level entry in living area for upper level (as if it were a stairway landing).
Upper Level
6
2

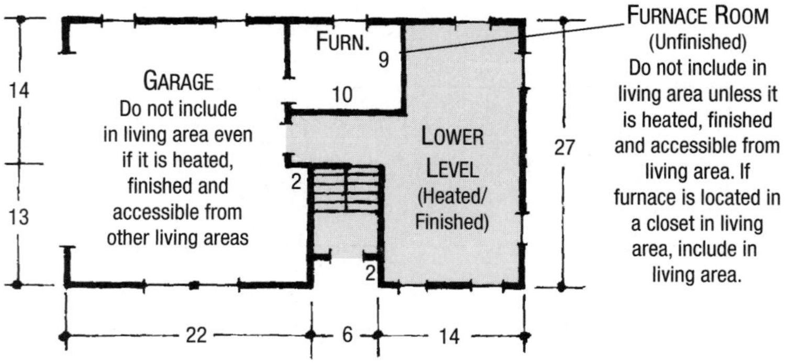
Furn.
9
10
Garage
Do not include in living area even if it is heated, finished and accessible from other living areas
Lower Level
(Heated/ Finished)
14
13
27
2
2
22
6
14
Furnace Room
(Unfinished)
Do not include in living area unless it is heated, finished and accessible from living area. If furnace is located in a closet in living area, include in living area.

## Split Foyer Worksheet

| Living Area | | | |
|---|---|---|---|
| **Area** | **Dimensions** | **Subtotal** | **Total** |
| Upper Level | 27 x 42 | 1,134 | |
| | 6 x 2 | –12 | 1,122 |
| Lower Level | 22 x 27 | 594 | |
| | 6 x 2 | –12 | |
| | 13 x 2 | –26 | |
| | 9 x 10 | –90 | 466 |
| Total | | | 1,588 |

| Other Area | | | |
|---|---|---|---|
| **Area** | **Dimensions** | **Subtotal** | **Total** |
| Garage | 27 x 20 | 540 | |
| | 2 x 13 | +26 | 566 |
| Furnace Room | 9 x 10 | | 90 |
| | | | |
| | | | |
| | | | |
| | | | |

REPORT: SPLIT-FOYER DETACHED HOUSE WITH 1,588 SQUARE FEET OF LIVING AREA, PLUS A 566 SQUARE-FOOT GARAGE AND 90-SQUARE-FOOT FURNACE ROOM.

## Split (Tri-) Level With Overhang

(Figure 5)

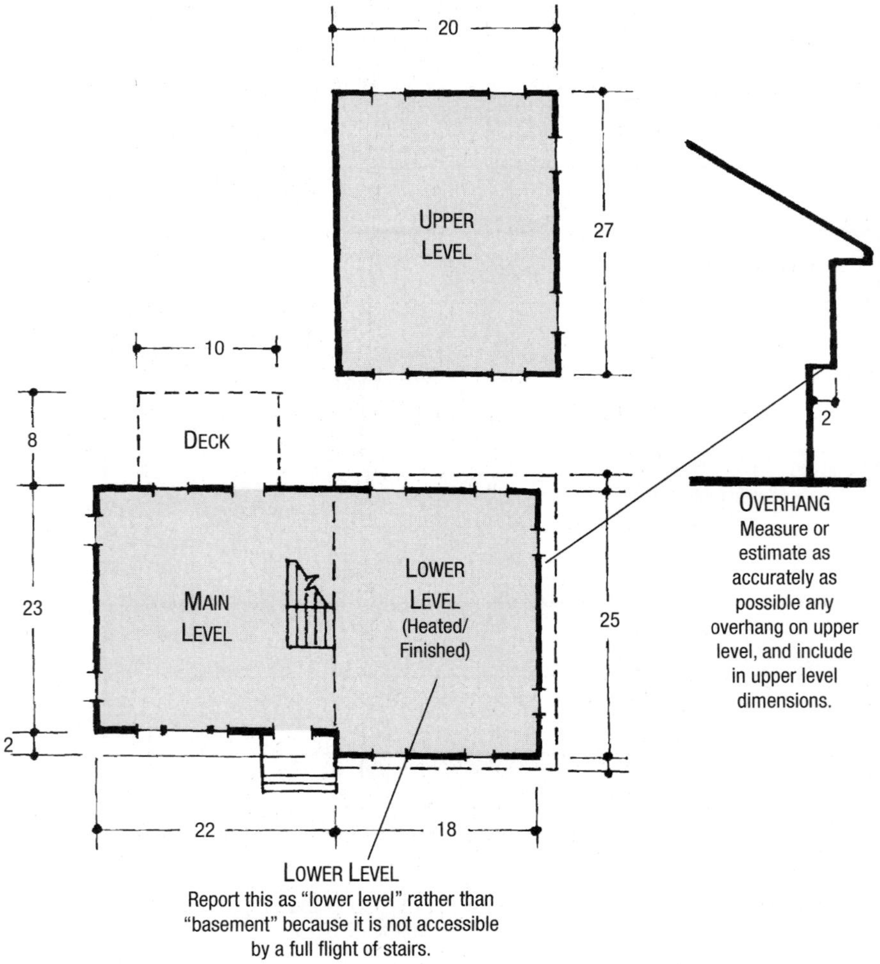
20
Upper Level
27
10
Deck
8
Main Level
23
2
Lower Level (Heated/ Finished)
25
22
18
2
Overhang
Measure or estimate as accurately as possible any overhang on upper level, and include in upper level dimensions.
Lower Level
Report this as "lower level" rather than "basement" because it is not accessible by a full flight of stairs.

## Split (Tri-) Level With Overhang Worksheet

| Living Area | | | |
|---|---|---|---|
| Area | Dimensions | Subtotal | Total |
| Main Level | 22 x 23 | | 506 |
| Lower Level | 18 x 25 | | 450 |
| Upper Level | 27 x 20 | | 540 |
| Total | | | 1,496 |
| | | | |
| | | | |
| | | | |

| Area | Dimensions | Subtotal | Total |
|---|---|---|---|
| Deck | 8 x 10 | | 80 |
| | | | |
| | | | |
| | | | |
| | | | |
| | | | |
| | | | |

Report: Split-level detached house with 1,496 square feet of living area, plus an 80-square-foot deck.

## ONE AND ONE-HALF STORY

(Figure 6)

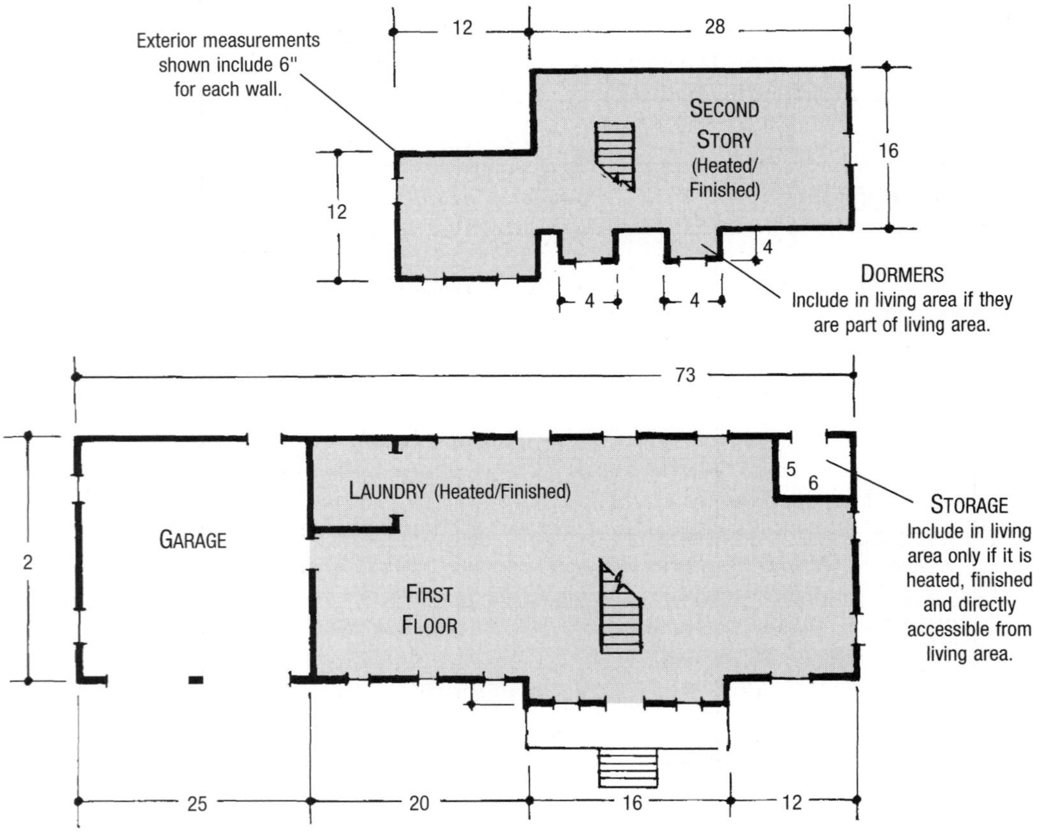
Exterior measurements shown include 6" for each wall.
12
28
SECOND STORY (Heated/ Finished)
16
12
4
4
4
DORMERS Include in living area if they are part of living area.
73
LAUNDRY (Heated/Finished)
5
6
STORAGE Include in living area only if it is heated, finished and directly accessible from living area.
GARAGE
2
FIRST FLOOR
25
20
16
12

## One And One-Half Story Worksheet

| Living Area | | | |
|---|---|---|---|
| **Area** | **Dimensions** | **Subtotal** | **Total** |
| 1st Floor | 48 x 22 | 1,056 | |
| | 16 x 2 | +32 | |
| | 5 x 6 | –30 | 1,058 |
| 2nd Floor | 16 x 28 | 448 | |
| | 4 x 4 | +16 | |
| | 4 x 4 | +16 | |
| | 12 x 12 | +144 | 624 |
| Total | | | 1,682 |
| **Other Area** | | | |
| **Area** | **Dimensions** | **Subtotal** | **Total** |
| Garage | 22 x 25 | | 550 |
| Storage | 5 x 6 | | 30 |
| | | | |
| | | | |
| | | | |
| | | | |

Report: One and one-half story detached house with 1,682 square feet of living area, plus a 550-square-foot garage.

## CONDOMINIUM

(Figure 7)

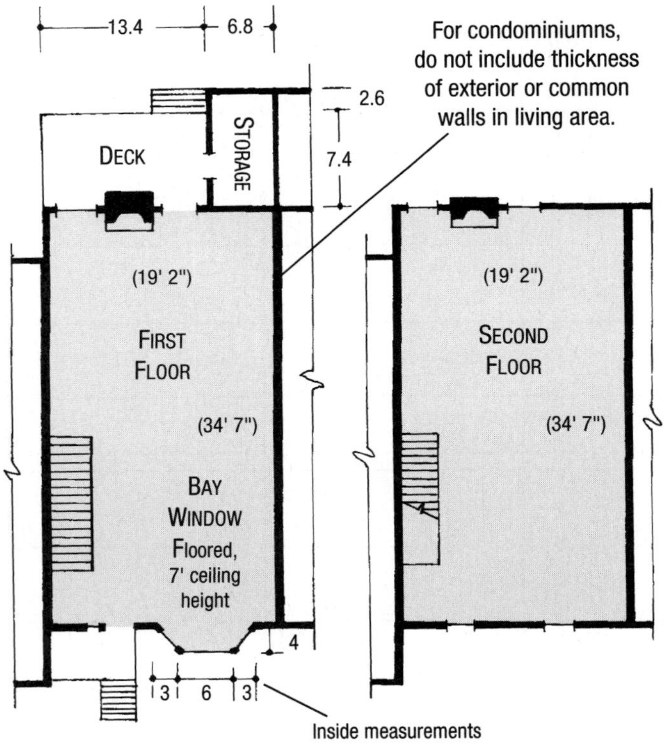
13.4
6.8
2.6
7.4
For condominiumns, do not include thickness of exterior or common walls in living area.
DECK
STORAGE
(19' 2")
FIRST FLOOR
(34' 7")
BAY WINDOW
Floored, 7' ceiling height
4
3
6
3
Inside measurements
(19' 2")
SECOND FLOOR
(34' 7")

## CONDOMINIUM WORKSHEET

| LIVING AREA | | | |
|---|---|---|---|
| AREA | DIMENSIONS | SUBTOTAL | TOTAL |
| 1st Floor | 34.6 x 19.2 | 664.3 | |
| Bay Window | | 36.0 | 700 |
| 2nd Floor | 34.6 x 19.2 | 664.3 | 664 |
| Total | | | 1,364 |
| | | | |
| | | | |
| | | | |

| OTHER AREA | | | |
|---|---|---|---|
| AREA | DIMENSIONS | SUBTOTAL | TOTAL |
| Deck | 13.4 x 7.4 | 99.2 | 99 |
| Storage | 10 x 6.8 | | 68 |
| | | | |
| | | | |
| | | | |
| | | | |
| | | | |

REPORT: TWO-STORY CONDOMINIUM WITH 1,364 SQUARE FEET OF LIVING AREA, PLUS A 99 SQUARE FOOT DECK.

## PRACTICE FLOOR PLAN

(Figure 8)

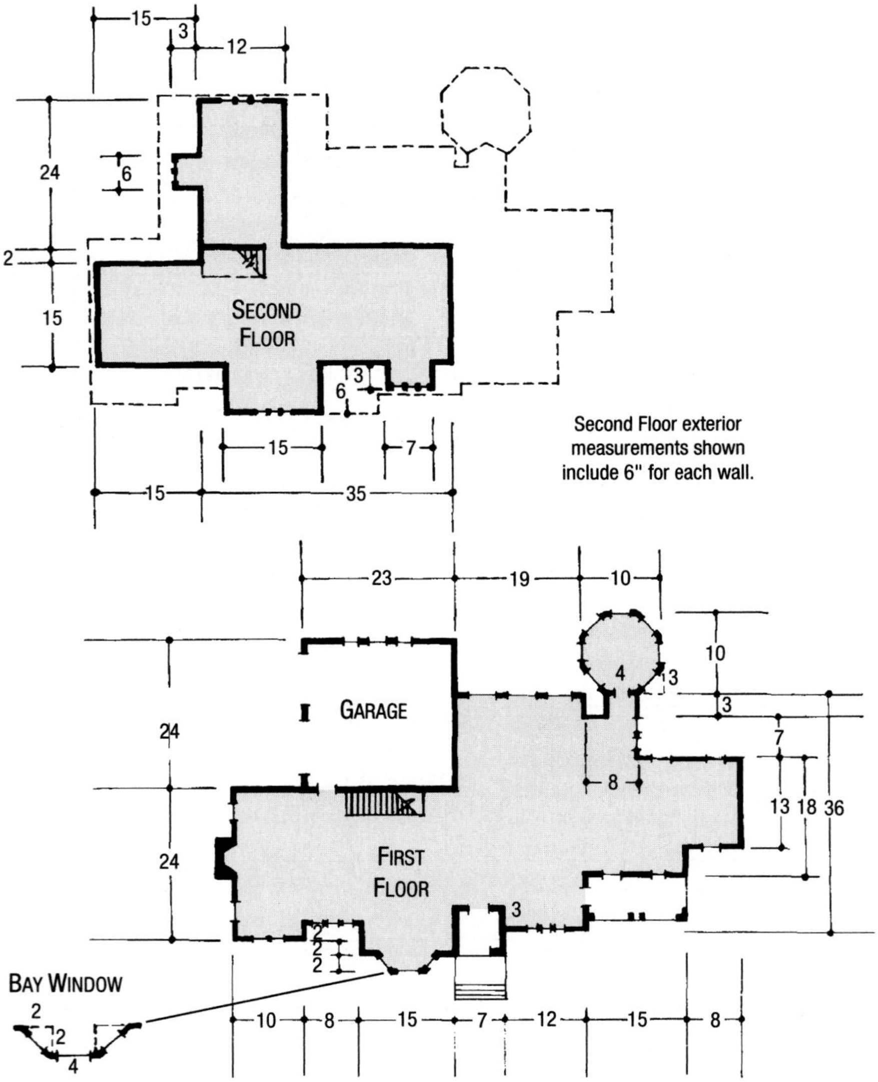

## PRACTICE FLOOR PLAN WORKSHEET

| LIVING AREA | | | |
|---|---|---|---|
| AREA | DIMENSIONS | SUBTOTAL | TOTAL |
| | | | |
| | | | |
| | | | |
| | | | |
| | | | |
| | | | |
| | | | |
| | | | |
| | | | |
| | | | |

| OTHER AREA | | | |
|---|---|---|---|
| AREA | DIMENSIONS | SUBTOTAL | TOTAL |
| | | | |
| | | | |
| | | | |
| | | | |

REPORT:

# Appendix C
# A Guide to Common Real Estate Environmental Hazards*

## INTRODUCTION

*Does this home fit my needs and those of my family? Is this a safe, secure home, free from potential hazards? Is this home a good investment and will it retain and increase its value in the years ahead?*

These are among the hundreds of questions that home buyers ask themselves as part of the home-buying thought process. It is a good policy, this questioning, a means of gathering hard facts that can be used to balance the emotional feelings that are so much a part of buying a home.

In ever-increasing numbers, home buyers today find it necessary to add new kinds of questions to their quest for information. Environmental concerns are becoming an element of the home-buying thought process.

Although it is unrealistic to expect that any home will be free of all forms of environmental influences, most homes (and the areas surrounding most homes) in the United States generally do not contain materials and substances that pose a health threat. However, in recent years, new concerns have been raised as our understanding of the natural environment has increased. Substances such as radon gas and asbestos have provoked new questions about how and where we build homes and manage their upkeep.

## HOME-BUYING CONSIDERATIONS

For the majority of Americans, the purchase of a home is the single greatest investment of a lifetime. Will the presence of an undetected environmental hazard have a long-term negative impact on that investment? Does the presence of a hazard have the potential to affect the health of the occupants? If hazards can be safely removed or mitigated, will the process alter the homeowner's lifestyle? These questions—and others like them—are, and should be, part of the home buyer's thought process today.

As our knowledge of the natural environment evolves, the body of law governing potentially harmful environmental hazards and their effect on real estate transactions also is evolving. The rights and responsibilities of buyers and sellers are determined by state and local laws or terms negotiated into the sales contract between buyer and seller.

Thus, before buying a home, prudent home buyers may want to obtain information about the potential impact of environmental hazards. Local, county, or state health or environmental departments are sources of such information. And while builders, real estate appraisers, real estate sales licensees, and lenders are not experts about the environment, these individuals may be of assistance in locating additional sources of information regarding environmental matters. Private home inspectors also may be useful in detecting the existence of potentially hazardous conditions if the sales contract provides for such an inspection.

The pages that follow provide general information about some of the environmental hazards that have the potential to affect the home environment. While this information is believed to be accurate, it is not meant to be comprehensive or authoritative. This publication provides introductory information to help home buyers understand the possible risk of exposure to potentially harmful environmental hazards in and around the home.

The agencies and individuals contributing to or assisting in the preparation of this booklet—or any individual acting on behalf of any of these parties—do not make any warranty, guarantee, or representation (express or implied) with respect to the usefulness or effectiveness of any information, method, or process disclosed in this material or assume any liability for the use of (or for damages arising from the use of) any information, method, or process disclosed in this material.

## RADON

### What is radon and where is it found?

Radon is a colorless, odorless, tasteless gas that occurs worldwide in the environment as a byproduct of the natural decay of uranium present in the earth. Radon

*Compiled by National Council of Savings Institutions, Office of Thrift Supervision, Society of Real Estate Appraisers, The Appraisal Foundation, U.S. Environmental Protection Agency, and U.S. League of Savings Institutions. This document is in the public domain.

is present in varying quantities in the atmosphere and in soils around the world.

**How does radon enter a home?**

Radon that is present in surrounding soil or in well water can be a source of radon in a home. Radon from surrounding soil enters a home through small spaces and openings, such as cracks in concrete, floor drains, sump pump openings, wall/floor joints in basements, and the pores in hollow block walls. It also can seep into ground water and remain entrapped there. Therefore, if a home is supplied with water taken from a ground water source (such as a well), there is greater potential for a radon problem. The likelihood of radon in the water supply is greatly reduced for homes supplied with water from a municipal water supply.

**Is radon found throughout a home, or just in certain rooms or areas?**

Radon generally concentrates most efficiently in the areas of a home closest to the ground. Radon levels generally decrease as one moves higher up in the structure.

**How can I tell if a home has a radon problem?**

The only way to know whether or not a home has a radon problem is to test it. Radon levels vary from house to house depending on the construction of the house and the soil surrounding it. There are several ways to make a preliminary screening test for radon. Preliminary screening test kits can be bought over the counter in many hardware, grocery, and convenience stores. Tests that measure the amount of radon in water normally require you to send a sample of tap water to a laboratory for analysis. State agencies should be consulted if the home water supply is suspected as a source of radon.

When purchasing a radon detection kit, you should examine the package for indications that the kit has been approved by federal or state health, environmental protection, or consumer protection agencies. Directions should be followed carefully when using a radon detection kit to assure that proper measurements are obtained. Short-term testing (ranging from a few days to several months) is one way to determine if a potential problem exists. Long-term testing (lasting for up to one year) is a more accurate way to determine if radon is present. Both short- and long-term testing devices are easy to use and relatively inexpensive.

**Why is radon harmful?**

Radon gas breaks down into radioactive particles (called decay products) that remain in the air. As you breathe these particles, they can become trapped in your lungs. As these particles continue to break down, they release bursts of energy (radiation) that can damage lung tissue. This damage can cause lung cancer. When radon gas and its decay products enter your home, they remain in circulation in the enclosed air. Out of doors, radon is not a problem for human beings because the surrounding air allows the gas to diffuse in the atmosphere.

**What health risks are associated with radon?**

The health risk associated with prolonged inhalation of radon decay products is an increased risk of developing lung cancer. There are indications that risk increases as the level of radon concentration and duration of exposure increase. The U.S. Environmental Protection Agency (EPA) has determined that short term exposure to a high concentration of radon is not as severe a risk as long-term exposure to a lower level of the gas.

**What is an acceptable level of indoor radon?**

The concentration of radon in air is measured in units of picocuries per liter of air (pCi/L). Estimates suggest that most homes will contain from one to two picocuries of radon per liter of air. If preliminary tests indicate radon levels greater than four picocuries per liter of air in livable areas of the home, the EPA recommends that a follow-up test be conducted. No level of radon is considered safe; there are risks even at very low levels. To put this into perspective, the EPA estimates that the risk of dying from lung cancer as the result of an annual radon level of four picocuries is equivalent to the risk from smoking ten cigarettes a day or having 200 chest xrays a year. A picocurie level of 40 equates to smoking two packs of cigarettes a day, while a level of 100 equates to 2,000 chest x-rays a year.

**How are radon risk levels calculated?**

The EPA's risk assessments assume an individual is exposed to a given concentration of radon over a lifetime of roughly 70 years, and spends 75 percent of his or her time in the home.

**Can the level of radon in a home be reduced?**

Yes, there are many effective and relatively inexpensive methods of reducing radon levels in a home. The method used will vary from house to house and from region to region. The techniques used will depend on the source of the gas, the ways in which it enters the home, and the kind of construction used in the home. If radon is present in water supplies, it can be removed altogether or reduced by the installation of special filter systems.

**What will it cost to reduce the level of radon in a home?**

The costs for radon reduction will depend on the number of sources, the amount of radon in the surrounding land or in the water supply, and the kind of construction used in the home. Normally, the costs of installing radon reduction equipment range from several hundred dollars to several thousand dollars. If the system chosen involves fans, pumps, or other appliances, operating costs for these devices may cause increases in monthly utility bills.

### Is radon removal a "do-it-yourself project"?

Not usually. In some cases, homeowners should be able to treat the problem themselves; however, it is not always possible for homeowners to diagnose the source of radon or to install systems that will reduce the level. Radon source diagnosis and mitigation normally require skills, experience, and tools not available to the average homeowner; therefore, it is always prudent to consider the use of trained personnel. When seeking a contractor to assist with a radon problem, you should first consult local, county, or state government agencies for recommendations of qualified radon-reduction contractors.

### What is the government doing about radon?

The federal government has undertaken an extensive public outreach effort to encourage individuals to test their homes. This effort includes a national hotline, 1-800-SOS-RADON, for obtaining further information on radon testing. EPA also is working closely with state and local governments and the private sector to research and demonstrate cost-effective methods for reducing indoor radon levels and with builders to develop radon-resistant new construction techniques.

## ASBESTOS

### What is asbestos and where is it found?

Asbestos is a fibrous mineral found in rocks and soil throughout the world. Asbestos has been used in architectural and construction applications because it is strong, durable, fire retardant, and an efficient insulator. Alone or in combination with other materials, asbestos can be fashioned into a variety of products that have numerous applications within the building industry—such as flooring, walls, ceiling tiles, exterior housing shingles, insulation or fire retardant for heating and electrical systems, etc.

### Is asbestos dangerous?

Asbestos has been identified as a carcinogen. Once ingested, asbestos fibers lodge in the lungs. Because the material is durable, it persists in tissue and concentrates as repeated exposures occur over time. It can cause cancer of the lungs and stomach among workers and others who have experienced prolonged work-related exposure to it. The health effects of lower exposures in the home are less certain; however, experts are unable to provide assurance that any level of exposure to asbestos fibers is completely safe.

### Under what circumstances do asbestos-containing products in the home become a health risk?

Home health risks arise when age, accidental damage, or normal cleaning, construction, or remodeling activities cause the asbestos-containing materials to crumble, flake, or deteriorate. When this happens, minute asbestos fibers are released into the air and can be inhaled through the nose and mouth. The fibers can cling to clothing, tools, and exposed flesh; cleanup operations can then dislodge the fibers and free them to circulate in the air.

### Can I expect to find asbestos in newer homes, and where in the home should I look for asbestos?

According to the EPA, many homes constructed in the United States during the past 20 years probably do not contain asbestos products. Places where asbestos sometimes can be found in the home include: around pipes and furnaces in older homes as insulating jackets and sheathing; in some vinyl flooring materials; in ceiling tiles; in exterior roofing, shingles, and siding; in some wallboards; mixed with other materials and troweled or sprayed around pipes, ducts, and beams; in patching compounds or textured paints; and in door gaskets on stoves, furnaces, and ovens.

### How can I identify asbestos in the home?

You may hire a qualified professional who is trained and experienced in working with asbestos to survey the home. A professional knows where to look for asbestos, how to take samples properly, and what corrective actions will be the most effective. EPA regional asbestos coordinators can provide information on qualified asbestos contractors and laboratories. In addition, the manufacturer of a product may be able to tell you, based on the model number and age of the product, whether or not the product contains asbestos.

### What should I do if I think there is asbestos in a home I have purchased?

Generally, if the material is in good condition and is in an area where it is not likely to be disturbed, leave the asbestos-containing material in place. Extreme care should be exercised in handling, cleaning, or working with material suspected of containing asbestos. If the material is likely to be banged, rubbed, handled, or taken apart—especially during remodeling—you should hire a trained contractor and reduce your exposure as much as possible. Common construction and remodeling operations can release varying amounts of asbestos fibers if the material being worked on contains asbestos. These operations include hammering, drilling, sawing, sanding, cutting, and otherwise shaping or molding the material. Routine cleaning operations (such as brushing, dusting, vacuum cleaning, scraping, and scrubbing) can also release hazardous fibers from asbestos-containing materials. Vinyl flooring products that contain asbestos can be cleaned in a conventional manner, but these products can release some asbestos fibers if they are vigorously sanded, ground, drilled, filed, or scraped.

The repair or removal of asbestos-containing products from a home is generally a complicated process. It depends on the amount of these products present, the percentage of asbestos they contain, and the manner in which asbestos is incorporated into the product. Total removal of even small amounts of asbestos-containing material is usually the last alternative. You should contact local, state, or federal health or consumer product agencies before deciding on a course of action. To ensure safety and elimination of health hazards, asbestos repair or removal should be performed only by properly trained contractors.

Many home repair or remodeling contractors do not yet have the requisite tools, training, experience, or equipment to work safely with asbestos or to remove it from a home. Furthermore, asbestos removal workers are protected under federal regulations that specify special training, protective clothing, and special respirators for these workers.

### Are exterior asbestos shingles a health risk?

When properly installed on the exterior of a home, asbestos-containing products present little risk to human health. However, if siding is worn or damaged, spray painting it will help seal-in the fibers.

### What is being done about the potential problem of exposure to asbestos in the home?

Over the years, the U.S. Environmental Protection Agency (EPA) and the Consumer Product Safety Commission (CPSC) have taken several steps to reduce the consumer's exposure to asbestos. Most recently these steps include requiring labeling of products containing asbestos and announcing a phased-in ban of most asbestos products by 1996.

# LEAD

### What is lead, and why is it hazardous to our health?

Lead is a metallic element found worldwide in rocks and soils. The toxic effects of lead have been known since ancient times. Recent research has shown that lead represents a greater hazard at lower levels of concentration than had been thought. Airborne lead enters the body when an individual breathes lead particles or swallows lead dust. Until recently, the most important source of airborne dust was automobile exhaust.

When ingested, lead accumulates in the blood, bones, and soft tissue of the body. High concentrations of lead in the body can cause death or permanent damage to the central nervous system, the brain, the kidneys, and red blood cells. Even low levels of lead may increase high blood pressure in adults.

Infants, children, pregnant women, and fetuses are more vulnerable to lead exposure than others because the lead is more easily absorbed into growing bodies and their tissues are more sensitive to the damaging effects of the lead. Because of a child's smaller body weight, an equal concentration of lead is more damaging to a child than it would be to an adult.

### What are the sources of lead in and around the home?

Lead can be present in drinking water, in paint used to decorate the interior or exterior of a home, in the dust within a home, and in soil around the home.

## Lead in Drinking Water

### Are there acceptable levels of lead in drinking water?

The EPA Office of Drinking Water has proposed regulations under the Safe Drinking Water Act (SDWA) that establish a maximum contaminant level for lead in drinking water of five micrograms per liter and a maximum contaminant level goal of zero. [Note: One microgram per liter is equal to one part per billion (ppb).] These levels or goals are set by EPA to control contamination that may have an adverse effect on human health. Non enforceable health-based goals are intended to protect against known or anticipated adverse health effects with an adequate margin of safety. Both the current maximum contamination level and goal are 50 micrograms per liter. Although the Public Health Service first set these levels in the 1960s before much of the current knowledge about the harmful effects of lead at low levels was gained, the EPA included them unchanged in the Safe Drinking Water Act of 1985. EPA, however, is now revising these standards to reflect its increased concern.

### I have heard that materials containing lead have been banned from use in public water supplies. If this is true, how does lead enter drinking water in the home?

In 1986, amendments to the Safe Drinking Water Act banned any further use of materials containing lead in public water supplies and in residences connected to public water supplies. In 1988, the U.S. Congress banned the use of lead-based solder in plumbing applications within homes and buildings. However, many homes built prior to 1988 contain plumbing systems that use lead-based solder in pipe connections. In such systems, lead can enter drinking water as a corrosion byproduct when plumbing fixtures, pipes, and solder are corroded by drinking water. In these instances, lead levels in water at the kitchen tap can be far higher than those found in water at treatment plants.

The combination of copper pipes connected with lead-based solder is found in many homes and can result in high levels of lead in water. In these circumstances, galvanic corrosion between the two metals releases relatively large amounts of lead into the water. The amount of lead in this kind of home water system will be higher when water has been at rest in the pipes for a period of time.

The EPA has determined that newly installed solder is most easily dissolved. As the home ages, mineral deposits build up on the inner walls of water pipes and act as an insulating barrier between the water and the solder. Data compiled by the EPA indicates that during the first five years following home construction, water in the home may have high levels of lead, with the highest levels recorded during the first 24 months.

### Can I tell by looking at pipes and plumbing fixtures whether or not water in the home will contain harmful levels of lead?

No. Visual inspection of pipe joints and solder lines is not an accurate means of determining whether or not decaying solder is a source of lead. A simple chemical test can determine whether the solder used in a home is lead-containing or not. Many jurisdictions make use of this test as a regular procedure in plumbing inspections. And while many newer homes rely on nonmetallic plumbing lines, the majority of faucets and plumbing fixtures used today can contribute some lead to home water supplies. However, these contributions can be eliminated effectively by running the faucet for 15 seconds before drawing drinking water.

### How can I tell if a home has a problem with lead in the water?

The only way to determine lead levels in water is to test a sample of the water. Should you suspect that lead is present in drinking water, or if you wish to have water tested, contact local, county, or state health or environmental departments for information about qualified testing laboratories.

### Is lead in water a concern in newly renovated older homes?

If the renovation included replacement of aging water pipes with copper or other metal piping, you should check with the renovating contractor to ensure that lead solder was not used in pipe joints. Further, some old homes contain water systems made of pipes that can contain high levels of lead. If the original water lines remain in the house, you should question the renovating contractor regarding his or her knowledge of pipe composition.

## Lead-Based Paint

### How prevalent is lead-based paint?

According to the EPA, it is estimated that leadbased paint was applied to approximately two-thirds of the houses built in the U.S. before 1940; onethird of the houses built from 1940 to 1960; and to an indeterminate (but smaller) portion of U.S. houses since 1960.

### How can I tell whether the paint in a home contains lead?

The only accurate way to determine if paint in a home contains lead is to remove a sample of the paint and have it tested in a qualified laboratory. Should you suspect that lead is present in paint, or if you wish to have paint tested, contact local, county, or state health or environmental departments for information about qualified testing laboratories.

### I have heard about problems when children eat chips of lead-based paint, but are there any other ways that lead-based paint can be harmful?

While the health hazards to children from eating lead-based paint chips have been known for some time, other sources of exposure to lead in household air and dust have been documented only recently. Lead can enter the air within a home when surfaces covered with lead-based paint are scraped, sanded, or heated with an open flame in paint-stripping procedures. Once released into the home atmosphere, lead particles circulate in the air and can be inhaled or ingested through the mouth and nose. Lead particles freed in fine dust or vapors settle into carpet fibers and fabric and can be recirculated in the air by normal household cleaning (such as sweeping and dusting) and through the normal hand to-mouth behavior of young children, which results in the ingestion of potentially harmful amounts of any lead present in household dust. Fine lead particles penetrate the filter systems of home vacuum cleaners and are recirculated in the exhaust air streams of such appliances. Lead also can enter household air from outdoor sources (such as contaminated soil) and from recreational activities that require the use of solder or materials containing lead.

### How can I get rid of lead-based paint safely?

It is best to leave lead-based paint undisturbed if it is in good condition and there is little possibility that it will be eaten by children. Other procedures include covering the paint with wallpaper or some other building material, or completely replacing the painted surface. Pregnant women and women who plan to become pregnant should not do this work. Professional paint removal is costly, time consuming, and requires everyone not involved in the procedure to leave the premises during removal and subsequent clean-up operations. In addition, if the house was built prior to 1950, there is a good chance that lead from exterior surface paint has accumulated in surrounding soils. Keep the yard well vegetated to minimize the likelihood of children being exposed to contaminated dust. Clean the floors, windowsills, and other surfaces regularly, preferably with wet rags and mops. Practice good hygiene with your children, especially frequent hand washing.

# HAZARDOUS WASTES

### What are hazardous wastes?

Hazardous wastes are those waste products that could pose short- or long-term danger to personal health or the environment if they are not properly disposed of or managed. These wastes can be produced by large business and industries (such as chemical and manufacturing plants), by some small businesses (such as drycleaners and printing plants), and by individuals who improperly apply, store, or dispose of compounds that contain potentially toxic ingredients (which can be found in chemical fertilizers, pesticides, and household products).

Concentrations of hazardous wastes occur in the environment when these wastes are handled, managed, or disposed of in a careless or unregulated manner. For many decades, hazardous industrial wastes were improperly disposed of on land, and their toxic components remained in the earth or seeped into ground water and drinking water supplies. The widespread use of pesticides and other agricultural chemicals also has resulted in the seepage and run-off of toxic compounds into land and water supplies. In addition, EPA estimates that as many as 2 million of the more than 5 million underground storage tanks in the United States may be leaking—discharging gasoline, petroleum products, and other hazardous liquids into the soil and, potentially, into ground water sources.

### What is being done to locate and clean up hazardous waste sites?

During the past 20 years, the U.S. Congress has enacted a body of interlocking laws and regulatory procedures aimed at the abatement of environmental hazards. The Superfund Act was enacted in 1980 (and amended in 1986) to provide more than $10 billion for the detection and clean-up of sites where hazardous waste is a problem. The revenue for Superfund is raised through taxes on petrochemical companies and other manufacturers. Under the law, the EPA, other federal agencies, and individual states may draw the necessary funds to allow them to react in hazardous waste emergency situations and to conduct long-term, permanent clean-ups of hazardous waste sites.

### How can I determine if a home is affected by a hazardous waste site?

Generally, testing for hazardous waste involves skills and technology not available to the average homeowner or home remodeling contractor.

The EPA has identified more than 30,000 potentially contaminated waste sites nationwide and has completed a preliminary assessment of more than 27,000 of these sites. The Agency publishes a National Priorities List of sites that will require action through the Superfund. Sites suspected of containing hazardous wastes are mapped at the time of the EPA preliminary assessment and communities likely to be affected by the site are notified. Thus, the nearest regional office of the EPA should have information on the location and status of local hazardous waste sites. The addresses and telephone numbers of these regional offices are listed in the back of this publication.

Furthermore, local and state governments maintain offices and agencies for locating and managing hazardous waste sites. These offices often are good sources for current information about the location and possible effects of these sites.

### What are the primary health hazards associated with hazardous wastes?

The specific health hazards in homes contaminated by hazardous wastes are determined by the kinds and amounts of toxic substances present. Some hazardous wastes can cause death even when ingested in small amounts. Other hazardous wastes have been linked to elevated risks of cancer, permanent damage to internal body organs, respiratory difficulties, skin rashes, birth defects, and diseases that attack the central nervous system.

### Can hazardous waste concentrations be removed from my property or reduced to non-hazardous levels?

The ability to remove or mitigate hazardous wastes will depend on the kinds, amounts, and sources of the wastes that are present. Generally, the removal of hazardous wastes from a property is beyond the capability of an individual homeowner.

# GROUND WATER CONTAMINATION

### What causes ground water contamination?

Ground water contamination occurs when hazardous chemical wastes, pesticides, or other agricultural chemicals (such as fertilizer) seep down through the soil into underground water supplies. Faulty private septic systems, improperly managed municipal sewer systems, and leaking industrial injection wells can also contribute to ground water contamination. In recent years, leaking underground storage tanks also have posed a threat to ground water. Half of all Americans and 95 percent of rural Americans use ground water for drinking water.

### Is ground water contamination harmful?

The U.S. Center for Disease Control reports an average of approximately 7,500 cases of illness linked to drinking water in the United States each year. This estimate generally is thought to be considerably lower than the actual figures because drinking water contaminants are not always considered in the diagnoses of illnesses.

### How can I tell if the water in a home is contaminated?

The only way to know whether or not the water in a home is contaminated is to test it. Since 1977, federal law has required water suppliers to periodically sample and test the water supplied to homes. If tests reveal that a national drinking water standard has been violated, the supplier must move to correct the situation and must also notify the appropriate state agency of the violation. Customers must be notified also, usually by a notice in a newspaper, an announcement on radio or television, or a letter from the health department that supervises the water supplier. If the home is supplied with water from its own private well, laboratory testing of a water sample is the only way to determine if the water supply is contaminated. Should you suspect that water is contaminated, or if you wish to have water tested, contact local, county, or state health or environmental departments for information about qualified testing laboratories.

### What can be done to decontaminate a home water supply?

If the home is supplied by an outside water supply source, federal law requires the provider to correct any contamination problems. When homes are supplied by private wells, analysis and treatment of the contaminated water may solve the problem.

### What will it cost to decontaminate a home water supply?

Normally, consumers bear no direct financial responsibility for eliminating contamination from water supplied by an outside source (if the water was contaminated when it was delivered); the supplier bears the primary responsibility for correcting contamination problems. In the case of contaminated water supplied from a private well (or water from an outside source that becomes contaminated after it is received from the supplier), the cost of decontamination will depend on the kinds and amounts of contaminants present.

In the majority of cases, decontamination of a private water source involves technology and knowledge beyond the scope of the average homeowner. State and local environmental and water quality officials may be able to provide additional information and assistance for decontamination of private water sources.

### What is being done about ground water contamination?

The U.S. Environmental Protection Agency has the lead responsibility for assuring the quality and safety of the nation's ground water supply. The EPA's approach is focused in two areas: minimizing the contamination of ground water and surface waters needed for human consumption and monitoring and treating drinking water before it is consumed. In 1986, the U.S. Congress passed a set of amendments that expanded the protection provided by the Safe Drinking Water Act of 1974. These amendments streamlined the EPA's regulation of contaminants, banned all future use of lead pipe and lead solder in public drinking water systems, mandated greater protection of ground water sources, and authorized EPA to file civil suits or issue administrative orders against public water systems that are in violation of the Act.

Working with the states, EPA has set national standards for minimum levels of a number of contaminants and is mandated to set such standards for additional contaminants by 1991. In addition, EPA and the states are working to devise a national strategy for the monitoring and management of ground water supplies.

## FORMALDEHYDE

### What is formaldehyde?

Formaldehyde is a colorless, gaseous chemical compound that is generally present at low, variable concentrations in both indoor and outdoor air. It is emitted by many construction materials and consumer products that contain formaldehyde-based glues, resins, preservatives, and bonding agents. Formaldehyde also is an ingredient in foam that was used for home insulating until the early 1980s.

### Where is formaldehyde found in the home?

Sources of formaldehyde in the home include smoke, household products, and unvented fuelburning appliances (like gas stoves or kerosene space heaters). Formaldehyde, by itself or in combination with other chemicals, serves a number of purposes in manufactured products. For example, it is used to add permanent press qualities to clothing and draperies, as a component of glues and adhesives, and as a preservative in some paints and coating products.

In homes, the most significant sources of formaldehyde are likely to be in the adhesives used to bond pressed wood building materials and in plywood used for interior or exterior construction. Urea-formaldehyde (UF) resins are found in wood products that are intended for indoor use. Phenolformaldehyde (PF) resins are used in products intended for exterior uses. UF resins emit significantly more formaldehyde gas than PF resins.

Certain foam insulating materials once widely used in housing construction (urea-formaldehyde foam or UFFI) also contain large amounts of formaldehyde. While contractors have voluntarily stopped using UFFI foam insulation, the material is present in many homes that were originally insulated with UFFI.

### What health risks are associated with formaldehyde?

Formaldehyde has been shown to cause cancer in animals, but there is no definitive evidence linking the chemical to cancer in humans. Higher-than-normal levels of formaldehyde in the home atmosphere can trigger asthma attacks in individuals who have this condition. Other health hazards attributed to formaldehyde include skin rashes; watery eyes, burning sensations in the eyes, throat, and nasal passages; and breathing difficulties. Most persons will first react to formaldehyde when the levels are in the range of 0.1 to 1.1 parts per million. Some individuals acquire a reduced tolerance to formaldehyde following their initial exposure to the gas. In these instances, subsequent exposures to even small amounts of formaldehyde will cause reactions.

### Do some kinds of homes carry a greater formaldehyde health risk than others?

Yes, materials containing formaldehyde were used extensively in the construction of certain prefabricated and manufactured homes. Since 1985, the federal government, through the U.S. Department of Housing and Urban Development, has enforced regulations that sharply curtail the use of materials containing formaldehyde in these types of housing to the lower-emitting products. However, use of formaldehyde compounds is still widespread in the manufacture of furniture, cabinets, and other building materials.

### What can be done to reduce formaldehyde levels in a home?

Reducing formaldehyde levels in the home can be a simple or complex task depending on the source of the gas. Initial procedures often include steps to increase ventilation and improve circulation of outside air through the home. If new furniture, drapery, or other sources are contributing to higher-than-normal levels of formaldehyde, removal of these items (or limiting the number of new items introduced into the home) may be all that is needed.

In some instances, home subflooring or walls may be the source of formaldehyde, or foam insulation between inner and outer walls may be emitting the gas. If increased ventilation does not produce acceptable results in these instances, homeowners may be required to remove the formaldehyde-bearing material. Such procedures will be costly, time-consuming, and temporarily disruptive of life in the home.

### How can I tell if the home I wish to buy contains formaldehyde-bearing materials?

In the case of a new home, you should consult with the builder before you purchase the house if you suspect the presence of materials that emit high levels of formaldehyde. Most builders will be able to tell you if construction materials contain ureaformaldehyde or they may direct you to manufacturers who can provide information about specific products. In the case of an older home, formaldehyde-emitting materials may not be visually evident and the current owners may not have specific product information. Because formaldehyde emissions from building materials decrease as the materials age (particularly over the first two or three years), older urea-formaldehyde building materials most probably will not be a significant source of formaldehyde emissions.

If you suspect the presence of formaldehyde, you may wish to hire a qualified building inspector to examine the home for the presence of formaldehydeemitting materials. In addition, home monitoring kits are currently available for testing formaldehyde levels in the home. Be sure that the testing device will monitor for a minimum of 24 hours to assure that the sampling period is truly representative.

## SOURCES OF ADDITIONAL INFORMATION

Additional information on radon air quality and environmental hazards may be obtained from the United States Environmental Protection Agency, the North Carolina Department of Environment, Health and Natural Resources, the North Carolina Cooperative Extension Services, North Carolina State University, College of Agriculture & Life Sciences.

*This information may be obtained on the internet or from the numerous brochures published by these and other federal, state and local agencies

# Appendix D
# Diagnostic Practice Test

## Chapter 1 Basic Real Estate Concepts

1. The characteristic of land that specifies that it is a unique commodity is which of the following?
   A. nonhomogeneity
   B. availability
   C. situs
   D. indestructibility
2. Ownership of land includes all of the following EXCEPT:
   A. surface of the land
   B. area below surface of the land
   C. personal property on the land
   D. area above the surface of the land
3. The characteristic of land that has the greatest effect on land value is:
   A. nonhomogeneity
   B. location (situs)
   C. indestructibility
   D. immobility
4. Such things as wage and employment levels, interest rates, and real property tax rates are described as:
   A. physical factors affecting land use
   B. artificial factors affecting land use
   C. natural factors affecting land use
   D. economic factors affecting land use
5. The real estate market is:
   I. local in character.
   II. a free market.
   A. I only
   B. II only
   C. both I and II
   D. neither I nor II
6. A listing contract authorizes a real estate agent to act as a:
   A. principal
   B. fiduciary
   C. legal adviser
   D. settlement agent
7. All of the following factors affect supply and demand in the real estate market EXCEPT:
   A. population migrations
   B. interest rates
   C. availability of construction materials
   D. brokerage specializations
8. All of the following are examples of public land use controls EXCEPT:
   A. deed restrictions
   B. building codes
   C. zoning
   D. environmental control laws
9. The real estate market is:
   I. subject to recurring economic cycles.
   II. slow to react to changes in supply and demand.
   A. I only
   B. II only
   C. both I and II
   D. neither I nor II

## Chapter 2 Property Ownership and Interests

1. Annual crops such as wheat and corn are:
   A. easements
   B. emblements
   C. encroachments
   D. encumbrances
2. Which of the following is a right in the land of another requiring ownership of adjoining land?
   A. profit
   B. appurtenant easement
   C. license
   D. easement in gross
3. Prescription is a method of creating which of the following?
   A. license
   B. encroachment
   C. lien
   D. easement

4. An estate created for the life of a person other than the life tenant is called a life estate:
   A. purautre vie
   B. in remainder
   C. by dower
   D. in reversion

5. A title in fee simple absolute provides all of the following rights EXCEPT:
   A. possession
   B. condemnation
   C. control
   D. quiet enjoyment

6. All of the following are powers of government EXCEPT:
   A. police power
   B. escheat
   C. estovers
   D. taxation

7. Freehold estates that are not inheritable are called:
   A. life estates
   B. leasehold estates
   C. defeasible estates
   D. fee simple estates

8. The owner of a condominium apartment holds title to the common areas as a:
   A. joint tenant
   B. community property
   C. tenant in common
   D. tenant by the entirety

9. A trespass on another's land as a result of an intrusion by some structure or other object is an:
   A. encroachment
   B. easement
   C. estate
   D. emblement

10. An estate created by a demise is called:
    A. fee simple
    B. community property
    C. freehold
    D. leasehold

11. The right to take minerals, soil, or timber from another's land is called:
    A. periodic tenancy
    B. trust
    C. lien
    D. profit à prendre

12. Easements are created in all of the following ways EXCEPT:
    A. prescription
    B. lis pendens
    C. condemnation
    D. dedication

13. Liens that are given the highest priority are:
    A. income tax liens
    B. judgment liens
    C. real property tax liens
    D. mortgage liens

14. Estates of limited duration are:
    A. freehold estates
    B. licenses
    C. easements
    D. leasehold estates

15. Emblements are also referred to as:
    A. fruits of industry
    B. fruits of nature
    C. real property
    D. easements

## Chapter 3 Transfer of Title to Real Property

1. A gift of real property by will is which of the following?
   A. testate
   B. bequest
   C. escheat
   D. devise

2. Of the following types of deed, which provides the grantee with the least assurance of title?
   A. quitclaim
   B. executor's
   C. grant
   D. special warranty

3. All of the following are required to effect voluntary alienation of title during life EXCEPT:
   A. recording of deed
   B. delivery of a valid deed to the grantee
   C. voluntary acceptance of delivery by the grantee
   D. grantor's signature

4. Placing a deed on the public record provides which of the following?
   A. public notice
   B. constructive notice
   C. actual notice
   D. effective notice

5. Recording protects the grantee against:
   I. subsequent purchasers from the grantor.
   II. creditors of the grantor.
   A. I only
   B. II only
   C. both I and II
   D. neither I nor II

6. The wording "seised of said premise in fee" means:
   A. the grantor has a fee simple title to the property
   B. the title is free from encumbrances
   C. the grantor has only an easement to convey
   D. the occupant has possession of premises only as long as he pays the monthly fee

7. The statement made by a grantor to a qualified public official that the signing of a deed (or another instrument) was done by him and was a voluntary act is called a(n):
   A. abstract
   B. conveyance
   C. covenant
   D. acknowledgment

8. All of the following statements about title insurance policies are correct EXCEPT:
   A. a title acceptable to a title insurance company is called an insurable title
   B. a title insurance premium is paid only once
   C. a title insurance policy protects the mortgagee against title defects existing both before and after the time the loan is made
   D. a title insurance policy protects the grantee against title defects existing before the time she receives title

9. Which of the following may lawfully give an opinion as to the quality of a title?
   A. attorney-in-fact
   B. escrow agent
   C. real estate broker
   D. attorney-at-law

10. The term *intestate* means that:
   A. a person has died and all of her property is located in the state in which the decedent resided
   B. a person has died with no valid will
   C. a deceased person has insufficient assets to require a probate
   D. a deceased person's assets will pass to the state

## Chapter 4 Land Use Controls

1. Deed restrictions that provide for a reversion of title are called:
   A. certificates
   B. conditions
   C. clusters
   D. covenants

2. Which of the following about a nonconforming use is (are) correct?
   A. if abandoned, it cannot be reinstated
   B. if destroyed, it can be replaced with a different nonconforming use
   C. the use was begun after the zoning ordinance was in place
   D. all of the above

3. A property owner subject to a special hardship by strict compliance with a zoning standard may apply for:
   A. spot zoning
   B. variance
   C. nonconforming use
   D. cumulative zoning

4. Zoning laws are enforced by which of the following?
   A. escheat
   B. conditions
   C. police power
   D. exclusive use

5. Cluster zoning provides for which of the following?
   A. deed restrictions
   B. HUDs
   C. PUDs
   D. interstate land sales

6. The Interstate Land Sales Full Disclosure Act requires which of the following?
   A. property report
   B. enabling act
   C. zoning
   D. cumulative use

7. Zoning ordinances regulate all of the following EXCEPT:
   A. setbacks
   B. lot size for construction
   C. construction cost
   D. building height

## Chapter 5 Laws and Regulations Governing Brokerage Relationships

1. An agent is a:
   A. principal
   B. fiduciary
   C. trustor
   D. client

2. A listing contract creates an agency relationship in which:
   A. the broker is a general agent
   B. the seller is principal
   C. the seller is a special agent
   D. the broker is a universal agent

3. As a result of a provisional broker's negligence in filling in the provisions in a contract of sale, the seller incurred a financial loss. Liability for this loss may be imposed upon:
   A. the agent only
   B. the agent employing broker only
   C. both the agent and the employing broker
   D. neither the agent nor the employing broker

4. A seller tells his broker that he is very anxious to sell and will accept $5,000 less than the listed price. The broker may share this information with:
   A. sales agents in her office
   B. a cooperating MLS agent acting as a buyer's agent
   C. the buyer
   D. anyone interested in the property

5. Bill Broker obtains a listing from Oliver Owner and publishes the information in the MLS. Agent Sam Smith, from another office acting as a subagent, finds a prospective purchaser, Bob Buyer. Fiduciary relationships exist between all of the following EXCEPT:
   A. Oliver and Bill
   B. Bill and Sam
   C. Sam and Bob
   D. Sam and Oliver

Bill Broker
Sam B Bob
Sam - Subagent

## Chapter 6 Real Estate Contracts

1. A contract in which one party makes a promise of compensation if another party renders a service in return is which of the following?
   A. unilateral
   B. multilateral
   C. trilateral
   D. bilateral

2. Mutual promises supply which of the following?
   A. competency
   B. consideration
   C. contingency
   D. collateral

3. Which of the following statements about offers is correct?
   A. they must not be illusory
   B. they may not be revoked
   C. they must be accompanied by earnest money
   D. they must be notarized

4. An owner listed her property with three brokerage firms. In each case, she retained the right to sell the property herself without being obligated to pay a commission to any of the brokers. The type of listing contract given to each broker is called:
   A. exclusive
   B. net
   C. multiple
   D. open

5. Which of the following statements is (are) true concerning contract for deed or installment land contract?
   A. it is a financing statement
   B. it is a contract of sale
   C. it must be in writing
   D. all of the above

6. An oral option is which of the following?
   A. void
   B. valid
   C. enforceable
   D. voidable

7. A party to a contract to buy and sell real property may pursue which of the following legal remedies against the other party in breach of contract?
   A. action for breach of contract and specific performance
   B. action for breach of contract or specific performance
   C. breach of contract only
   D. specific performance only

## Chapter 7 Real Estate Finance

1. All of the following are requirements for mortgage validity EXCEPT:
   A. granting clause
   B. mortgaging clause
   C. execution by mortgagor
   D. valid debt

2. All of the following are rights of a mortgagor EXCEPT:
   A. defeasance
   B. foreclosure
   C. equity of redemption
   D. possession

3. Which of the following gives the mortgagee the right to declare the entire principal balance immediately due and payable if the mortgagor is in default?
   A. acceleration clause
   B. alienation clause
   C. statutory foreclosure clause
   D. assignment clause

4. Which of the following enables the mortgagee to sell the mortgage in the secondary mortgage market?
   A. assignment clause
   B. due-on-sale clause
   C. mortgaging clause
   D. power of sale clause

5. Friendly foreclosure is also called:
   A. beneficial foreclosure
   B. statutory foreclosure
   C. strict foreclosure
   D. deed in lieu of foreclosure

6. The process of liquidating a financial obligation by installment payments of principal and interest is described as:
   A. amortization
   B. acceleration
   C. alienation
   D. acquisition

7. Using the amortization schedule in Chapter 7, Figure 7.1, determine which of the following is the monthly payment of principal and interest required to fully amortize a $50,000, 20-year mortgage loan at 7% interest.
   A. $332.50
   B. $357.14
   C. $387.50
   D. $449.40

PI = ?

20 yrs = 240 months

8. A lending institution making an FHA-insured loan at 7% interest increases the yield to 7 1/4% by charging which of the following number of discount points?
   A. 1
   B. 2
   C. 4
   D. 6

.25%

1 Discount point = what percent?

9. Which of the following provides the highest loan-to-value ratio?
   A. conventional
   B. FHA 245
   C. 95 percent insured conventional
   D. FHA 203(b)

10. An investor using leverage to maximize his return on investment would likely prefer which of the following loan-to-value ratios?
   A. 80%
   B. 97%
   C. 100%
   D. 95 %

11. Which of the following regulates a maximum loan amount based on purchase price or acquisition costs and area of country where property is located?
   A. RESPA
   B. VA
   C. FHA
   D. Regulation Z

12. Which of the following provides for a three-day right of rescission to refinance a loan on a primary residence?
   A. RESPA
   B. VA
   C. FHA
   D. Regulation Z

13. Which of the following purchases only conventional mortgages?
   A. Ginnie Mae
   B. Fannie Mae
   C. Freddie Mac
   D. none of the above

14. The loss of funds available to lending institutions for making mortgage loans because of depositor withdrawals is called:
   A. disintermediation
   B. liquidation
   C. discrimination
   D. amortization

15. Brantley Buyer obtained an FHA-insured loan to purchase a home. The difference between the purchase price and the loan amount was $3,100. Which of the following statements about the $3,100 is correct?
    A. Brantley can pay this amount from his existing assets or borrow on the security of another asset such as his stocks
    B. Brantley can satisfy this amount by giving the seller a purchase money second mortgage
    C. Brantley can borrow the $3,100 from a relative at 6 percent interest
    D. Brantley can obtain the money by giving a lending institution a second mortgage

## Chapter 8 Closing Real Estate Transactions

1. On June 16, 2000, a seller closed the sale of her home. The annual taxes of $775 and the water bill of $86 for the current year had been paid in full by the seller prior to the sale. If these payments are prorated, which of the following amounts would be returned to the seller? (Answers are rounded.)
   A. $357
   B. $397
   C. $430
   D. $464

2. The tax year in sellerstown begins each January 1. Charles Conveyor paid $1080 to satisfy his tax bill through the end of current year. On February 1 of the same year, Charles paid a one-year fire insurance premium of $626 for a policy effective that date, which was transferred to buyer at closing. What was the prorated amount returned to Charles when he closed the sale of his home on October 28? (Answers are rounded.)
   A. $1412
   B. $1316
   C. $626
   D. $346

3. On April 1, Chuck and Sara Vollaro made the mortgage payment of principal and interest for April on their home in the amount of $402.50. (Interest is paid in arrears.) On April 20, the Vollaros closed on the sale of their home to Harry and Helen Hudson. The Hudsons assumed the Vollaros's mortgage with a principal balance of $42,000 and an interest rate of 9 percent. Which of the following is the correct closing statement entry for interest?
   A. seller's credit—$210
   B. buyer's credit—$105
   C. buyer's credit—$210
   D. seller's debit—$315

Arrears
Why not Seller credit!?

4. The sale of a rental property was closed on December 12. On December 1, the tenant had paid December rent in the amount of $510. A correct closing statement entry for this transaction would be:
   A. seller's debit—$204
   B. buyer's credit—$306
   C. seller's credit—$204
   D. buyer's credit—$204

Why is this $ going to the buyer when the Seller Paid in Advance!?

## Chapter 9 Property Valuation

1. The type of demand that has an effect on market value is which of the following?
   A. urgent
   B. unlimited
   C. restrictive
   D. effective

2. In arriving at a price for listing purposes, real estate agents perform which of the following?
   A. a competitive market analysis
   B. market surveys
   C. appraisals
   D. assessments

3. Which of the following statements about the principle of highest and best use is (are) correct?
   I. It applies to the construction of a single-family dwelling.
   II. It applies to the construction of a shopping mall.
   A. I only
   B. II only
   C. both I and II
   D. neither I nor II

4. An owner whose property is condemned is entitled to be compensated for which of the following?
   A. book value
   B. assessed value
   C. market value
   D. mortgage value

5. The age of a property based on the remaining years of useful life is described as:
   A. economic
   B. useful
   C. chronological
   D. physical

6. Historic value is the same as which of the following?
   A. book value
   B. condemnation value
   C. assessed value
   D. reproduction cost

7. An appraisal by summation is based on which of the following?
   A. replacement cost
   B. comparables
   C. annual income
   D. rate of return

8. The unit in place method is used in which of the following?
   A. cost approach
   B. income approach
   C. comparable approach
   D. direct sales comparison approach

9. Which of the following is (are) correct?
   A. land does not depreciate
   B. structures depreciate
   C. depreciation results from physical deterioration, functional obsolescence, and/or economic obsolescence
   D. all of the above

## Chapter 10 Relationship of Landlord and Tenant

1. A residential lease provides the lessee with which of the following?
   A. exclusive right to possession and control of the property during the term of the lease
   B. title to the property for the duration of the term of the lease
   C. the right to harvest timber
   D. the right to use the property for any use, whether personal, business, legal, or illegal

2. Which of the following is NOT true concerning a leasehold estate for ten years?
   A. the contract must be in writing
   B. the contract must be executed by the lessor and delivered to and accepted by the lessee
   C. the contract must be notarized
   D. the contract must be recorded to be effective against third parties

3. An action or inaction by the lessor that results in the property being unusable is which of the following?
   A. actual eviction
   B. constructive eviction
   C. sandwich lease
   D. assignment

4. A lease is which of the following?
   I. a contract
   II. an estate
   A. I only
   B. II only
   C. both I and II
   D. neither I nor II

5. A leasehold that automatically renews unless proper notice is given is an:
   A. estate for years
   B. estate from period to period
   C. estate at will
   D. estate at sufferance

## Chapter 11 Real Estate Management

1. The first step in creating an owner-manager relationship is which of the following?
   A. management proposal
   B. management report
   C. management agreement
   D. management fee

2. All of the following titles apply to property managers EXCEPT:
   A. fiduciary
   B. agent
   C. licensee
   D. resident

3. A property manager's fee is often a combination of a base fee and a percentage of which of the following?
   A. gross potential income
   B. gross operating income
   C. gross effective income
   D. net operating income

4. Periodic financial reports provided to the owner are called:
   A. stabilized budgets
   B. operating reports
   C. management statements
   D. property management reports

## Chapter 12 Fair Housing

1. An owner's exemptions from the Fair Housing Act of 1968 are lost if:
   I. the owner uses discriminatory advertising.
   II. the owner lists the property with a real estate broker.
   A. I only
   B. II only
   C. both I and II
   D. neither I nor II

2. The term *redlining* applies to which of the following?
   A. brokers
   B. developers
   C. landlords
   D. lenders

3. The act of real estate agents to induce property owners to enter listing contracts by telling them that persons of a particular race, color, religion, sex, handicap, familial status, or national origin are moving into their neighborhood, thereby causing property values to depreciate, is called:
   A. blockbusting
   B. steering
   C. redlining
   D. integration

4. The act of real estate agents directing prospective purchasers to integrated areas to avoid integration of nonintegrated areas is called:
   A. redlining
   B. blockbusting
   C. steering
   D. directing

5. The Civil Rights Act of 1968 applies to all of the following EXCEPT:
   A. residential lots
   B. office space
   C. apartments
   D. residential condominium units

## Chapter 13 Federal Taxation of Home Ownership

1. Which of the following statements regarding points paid by the buyer on the purchase of his primary residence to obtain a loan is true?
   A. points are not deductible
   B. points are added to the costs basis of the home
   C. points may be deducted as interest in the year of the purchase
   D. a prorated portion of the total points paid may be deducted each year over the life of the loan

2. The calculation of realized gain on the sale of a personal residence is determined by
   A. selling price minus selling expenses
   B. sales price minus basis
   C. amount realized from sale minus adjusted basis of home
   D. sales price minus adjusted basis of home

3. Which of the following is a deductible expense for homeowners?
   A. real property taxes
   B. maintenance
   C. mortgage principal payments
   D. energy usage

4. Regarding tax information, a real estate agent should:
   A. be skilled at providing tax advice to his clients
   B. never discuss tax matters with a client
   C. be aware of tax information and able to discuss taxes with clients in a general manner without giving tax advice
   D. never charge a separate fee for tax consultations and advice since this is part of the service an agent should provide for her real estate commission

5. Fix-up expenses incurred to prepare a home for sale are:
   A. deductible if bills are incurred within 90 days of closing on the sale of a home
   B. deductible only if required by an appraiser
   C. deductible only if required in the offer to purchase as condition of sale
   D. not deductible under any circumstances

## Chapter 14 Property Insurance

1. The clause in a fire insurance policy requiring the property owner to insure for a stated minimum percentage of property value is called:
   A. fire clause
   B. co-insurance clause
   C. extended coverage clause
   D. insurable interest clause

2. Which is likely to have the least insurable interest?
   A. mortgagee
   B. mortgagor
   C. spouse
   D. nephew

3. Which is correct of insurance terminology?
   A. casualty provides protection from financial claims of others
   B. liability protects the physical structure
   C. an endorsement deletes coverage for specified items that would otherwise be covered by the policy
   D. a peril is a source of loss Consider the following information for questions 4 and 5: Betty's house structure is valued at $100,000 with an 80 percent co-insurance clause. She has a $100,000 insurance policy and the house is completely destroyed by fire.

4. In this situation, Betty will collect:
   A. $64,000
   B. $80,000
   C. $100,000
   D. $125,000

5. If Betty had only purchased $60,000 insurance and suffered a $40,000 loss, she would have collected:
   A. $20,000
   B. $30,000
   C. $40,000
   D. $60,000

## Chapter 15 Basic House Construction

1. Insulation should be placed where in a home?
   A. floors
   B. walls
   C. ceilings
   D. all of the above

2. Foundation and flooring systems typically include which of the following?
   A. concrete footing and joist
   B. sole and top plates
   C. studs and headers
   D. rafters and collar beams

3. Studs and sheathing are found in the:
   A. foundation
   B. floor
   C. wall
   D. ceiling

4. Typical framing includes:
   A. 2″ × 4″ floors, 16″ OC
   B. 2″ × 10″ floors, 24″ OC
   C. 2″ × 4″ walls, 16″ OC
   D. 2″ 8″ roofs, 36″ OC

5. Which is correct regarding window styles?
   A. double-hung are vertical sliding
   B. jalousie are horizontal sliding
   C. casement windows slide up and down
   D. hopper windows open like an awning

## Chapter 16 Real Estate Math

1. What does the selling price of a property need to be to net the owner $68,000 after paying a 6% broker's fee and satisfying a mortgage of $16,000?
   A. $72,080
   B. $88,080
   C. $89,040
   D. $89,362

2. A broker with The Action Company sold a property for $125,000. The owner paid The Action Company 6%, which The Action Company shared with the broker on a 4:3 ratio. If the broker share was 4 and Action's share was 3, how much money did the broker receive?
   A. $3,214
   B. $4,285
   C. $4,343
   D. $7,142

3. An investor purchased property for 11% below market value. Four months later he sold the property for 5% above market value. What was his percent of profit?
   A. 15%
   B. 16%
   C. 17%
   D. 18%

4. An 18-year-old building has an economic life of 40 years. If the original value of the building was $275,000, what is the value today?
   A. $50,000
   B. $61,111
   C. $123,750
   D. $151,250

5. An apartment building produces a monthly net income of $3,600. If the owner paid $440,000 for the building, what is the annual rate of return?
   A. 8.18%
   B. 9.8%
   C. 10.18%
   D. 11.8

6. An investor purchased an office building for $750,000. What is the net annual income necessary to provide a 14% return on this investment?
   A. $64,500
   B. $105,000
   C. $122,340
   D. $186,666

7. What amount of interest will the mortgagor pay on a 20-year mortgage loan of $55,000 at 13 1/2% interest with monthly payments of $664.40 if he pays off the loan over the full term?
   A. $74,250
   B. $104,456
   C. $148,500
   D. $184,184

8. A broker received a commission of 11% in the sale of a tract of land 900 feet square. (This tract measures 900 feet on each side.) If the property sold for $2,300 per acre, what was the commission amount?
   A. $4,517
   B. $4,704
   C. $9,034
   D. $9,409

9. A house had an assessed value of $45,000, and the lot had an assessed value of $9,000. The property was taxed at 80% of assessed value at a rate of $3.10 per $100. If the assessed valuation is to be increased by 20%, what is the amount of taxes to be paid on the property?
   A. $518.40
   B. $1,607.04
   C. $1,674.00
   D. $2,008.80

10. A house valued at $180,000 was insured for 85% of value. The annual premium was 60 cents per $100 of the face amount of the policy. The homeowner paid a one-year premium in February. On July 20 the following year, he closed the sale of his home. The buyer is having this policy endorsed to him. What will be the cost to the buyer?
    A. 549.50
    B. 570.00
    C. 433.50
    D. 484.50

11. A percentage lease stipulates a minimum rent of $1,000 per month and 2% of the annual gross sales of the lessee over $440,000. The total rent paid by the end of the year was $24,000. What was the lessee's gross business income for the year?
    A. $464,000
    B. $600,000
    C. $1,040,000
    D. $1,640,000

# Appendix E
# Practice Exam

*The following practice questions will provide valuable experience in working with the format of the licensing exam as you make final preparations for your exam.*

## Real Estate Law

1. Which of the following statements about zoning is correct?
   A. in exclusive-use zoning, property may be used only as specified for that particular zoning area
   B. if a nonconforming structure is destroyed, it may be replaced by a different type of non-conforming structure
   C. spot zoning is legal in all circumstances
   D. a variance can be obtained to permit a substantial deviation from the zoning ordinances

2. Which of the following statements about real property taxes is (are) correct?
   A. the tax rate is applied to assessed value to calculate the tax bill
   B. real property taxes are the largest source of revenue for local governments
   C. real property taxes attach to the land as of January 1
   D. all of the above

3. A gift of real property by will is a:
   A. remise
   B. demise
   C. devise
   D. bequest

4. Which of the following provides the grantee with the greatest assurance of title?
   A. special warranty
   B. deed of gift
   C. general warranty
   D. grant deed

5. Which of the following is (are) benefit(s) of recording a deed?
   A. it protects the grantee against future conveyances by the grantor
   B. it protects the grantee against the grantor's creditors
   C. it provides constructive notice to all that title is now vested in the grantee
   D. all of the above

6. Which of the following requires the grantor to execute a deed of correction if necessary?
   A. covenant of seisin
   B. covenant for further assurances
   C. covenant against encumbrances
   D. covenant of right to convey

7. All of the following are rights of a life tenant who holds the title pur autre vie EXCEPT:
   A. encumber
   B. devise
   C. alienation
   D. waste

8. Leasehold estates are created by which of the following?
   A. remise
   B. deed
   C. demise
   D. devise

9. The owner(s) of the real property may hold title in all of the following ways EXCEPT:
   A. tenants in common
   B. lessees
   C. severalty
   D. joint tenants

10. A claim, lien, charge, or liability attached to and binding upon real property is a(n):
    A. encumbrance
    B. community property
    C. license
    D. syndication

11. A cooperative is managed by which of the following?
    A. board of directors
    B. association
    C. partnership
    D. tenants

12. An owner of a condominium office:
    I. may pledge her property as security for a mortgage loan.
    II. is assessed by the property owners' association.
    A. I only
    B. II only
    C. both I and II
    D. neither I nor II

13. Time-sharing is associated with which of the following?
    A. cooperatives
    B. profits
    C. joint ventures
    D. condominiums
14. Which of the following is a deductible expense for homeowners when calculating federal income tax liability on their principal residence?
    A. mortgage principal
    B. real property taxes
    C. energy credits
    D. repairs
15. Which of the following deeds gives the grantor the greatest degree of liability?
    A. special warranty
    B. gift
    C. grant
    D. general warranty
16. Restrictive/protective covenants are which of the following?
    A. conditions
    B. encumbrances
    C. public land use controls
    D. zoning classifications
17. Which of the following statements is correct?
    A. spot zoning is legal in all cases
    B. restrictive/protective covenants are enforced by court injunction
    C. restrictive/protective covenants are government restrictions
    D. all nonconforming uses are illegal
18. Deed restrictions that are enforced by a suit for damages or by an injunction are:
    A. conditions
    B. conveyances
    C. covenants
    D. considerations
19. Public land use controls in the form of subdivision ordinances are an exercise of:
    A. power of eminent domain
    B. general plan for development
    C. police power
    D. Interstate Land Sales Full Disclosure Act
20. A property owner in a recently zoned area was permitted to continue to use his property in a manner that did not comply with the zoning requirements. This use is described as which of the following?
    A. exclusive-use zoning
    B. deviation
    C. nonconforming use
    D. private control of land use

## Real Estate Brokerage

21. An agent associated with Lighthouse Realty effects a sale of property listed by Point Hazard Realty. In this transaction, the agent is an agent of which of the following?
    I. seller
    II. Lighthouse Realty
    A. I only
    B. II only
    C. both I and II
    D. neither I nor II
22. Which of the following statements is NOT correct?
    A. a principal is responsible for acts of his agent while engaged in activities concerning the agency
    B. an agent is in a fiduciary relationship to her principal
    C. the agent has no duties to third parties in a transaction
    D. the principal owes cooperation to the agent
23. A person living on the managed premises as a salaried employee engaged to rent and lease apartments is called a(n):
    A. property manager
    B. rental agent
    C. employee manager
    D. resident manager
24. The monthly accounting by the property manager is called:
    A. stabilized budget
    B. property management report
    C. management budget
    D. financial report
25. All of the following are required of property managers EXCEPT:
    A. showing and leasing property
    B. deciding owner's objectives
    C. collecting rent
    D. providing for the protection of tenants
26. Which of the following types of listing contracts give Sthe broker commission entitlement if the listed property is sold by anyone during the listing term?
    A. net
    B. open
    C. exclusive
    D. exclusive right to sell
27. The amount of earnest money appears on closing statements as a:
    A. credit to buyer
    B. debit to seller
    C. credit to seller
    D. debit to buyer

28. Sara Seller was satisfied with all of the terms of an offer to purchase her property from Bill Buyer except the date of possession, which she changed from April 9 to April 10. Which of the following is correct?
    A. Sara's acceptance created a valid contract
    B. Sara did not accept Bill's offer
    C. Sara made a counteroffer, which Bill must accept since the change was so minor
    D. none of the above

29. A sandwich lease is created by:
    A. devise
    B. subletting
    C. surrender
    D. recording

30. When an option is exercised, it becomes which of the following?
    A. lease
    B. offer
    C. multiple listing
    D. contract of sale

31. An agreement that is a financing instrument and a contract of sale is called a(n):
    A. option
    B. lease
    C. contract for deed
    D. exclusive agency

32. An agreement (compromise) in which one party to a previous agreement agrees to receive something different and the other party agrees to do something different from that agreed to in a previous contract is:
    A. novation
    B. assignment
    C. accord and satisfaction
    D. carry-over contract

33. Which of the following is a test to determine whether a real estate broker is legally entitled to a commission?
    A. acceptance
    B. accountability
    C. assignment
    D. assumption

34. A buyer made an offer to purchase a seller's land if the buyer decided to buy a tract adjoining the seller's land. Which of the following describes this offer?
    A. indefinite
    B. illusory
    C. unilateral
    D. fraudulent

35. Failure to comply with the terms of an offer as to the manner of communicating acceptance may result in which of the following?
    A. termination of offer
    B. extension of offer
    C. acceptance of offer
    D. duress

36. The Fair Housing Act of 1968 prohibits discrimination in the rental of all of the following EXCEPT:
    A. offices
    B. apartments
    C. houses
    D. residential lots

37. The Fair Housing Act of 1968 prohibits all of the following EXCEPT:
    A. discriminatory advertising
    B. use of brokerage services
    C. steering
    D. redlining

38. Inducing an owner to list property by telling the owner that persons of a particular national origin are moving into the neighborhood is called:
    A. steering
    B. redlining
    C. blockbusting
    D. profiteering

39. Exemptions to the Fair Housing Act of 1968 are lost if:
    I. discriminatory advertising is used.
    II. real estate brokerage services are used.
    A. I only
    B. II only
    C. both I and II
    D. neither I nor II

40. A property manager's fee may consist of a base fee plus which of the following?
    A. a percentage of the rental income received
    B. a percentage of the gross potential income
    C. a percentage of the net income
    D. a percentage of the stabilized budget

41. Which of the following statements about property managers is (are) correct?
    A. property managers are in a fiduciary relationship to property owners
    B. property managers must have a real estate license in North Carolina
    C. property managers must account for all funds received in the course of their property management duties
    D. all of the above

42. The sales associates of Excellent Realty, Ltd., obtained several excellent listings in Exclusive Estates by advising homeowners that a number of Asian families were moving into Exclusive Estates and, therefore, their property values would be substantially depressed. This activity is most accurately described as which of the following?
    A. steering
    B. blockbusting
    C. soliciting
    D. redlining

43. The type of listing contract that is most beneficial to the broker and the seller is which of the following?
    A. exclusive right to sell
    B. net
    C. open
    D. exclusive agency

44. When listing a home for sale, the broker advised the seller that since he owned only one house, the listing was exempt from the prohibitions of the Fair Housing Act of 1968. Which of the following statements about the broker's advice is correct?
    A. the broker acted correctly in advising the seller about the exemption
    B. the broker should give good legal advice to sellers and buyers
    C. the broker should give legal advice only when asked by sellers or buyers
    D. none of the above

45. An agent associated with Metro Realty, Inc., obtained an offer for a property listed by Preferred Real Estate Company that she gave to Sam Slicker, the listing agent with Preferred, for presentation to the property owner. Realizing the amount of the offer was such that it would probably not be accepted, Sam increased the amount by $3,000 prior to presentation. Which of the following statements correctly characterizes Sam's actions?
    A. Sam should have obtained the approval of Metro Realty before changing the offer
    B. Sam's action was in violation of his fiduciary obligations and was completely improper
    C. while Sam's action was improper, it did not violate the licensing law
    D. Sam's action required the approval of his broker-in-charge

46. In the process of preparing an offer for commercial property, the broker was asked by two purchasers to recommend the most beneficial way for them to take title to the property. Which of the following should be the broker's recommendation?
    A. tenants in common
    B. in severalty
    C. ask an attorney
    D. ask the listing agent

47. On the broker's recommendation, a seller accepted an offer that was 8% below the listed price. The broker did not disclose to the listing seller that the buyer was the broker's brother-in-law. Which of the following is (are) correct?
    I. The broker violated his obligations as agent of the seller.
    II. The fact that the buyer is related to the broker does not need to be divulged to the seller.

    A. I only
    B. II only
    C. both I and II
    D. neither I nor II

## NC Real Estate License Law, Commission Rules, and Trust Account Guidelines

48. An agent received two offers for a listed property within ten minutes. One offer was 2% less than the listed price, and the other was 6% less than the listed price. The agent should present to the seller:
    A. neither offer
    B. both offers
    C. the highest offer
    D. the lowest offer

49. A real estate agent must provide:
    A. copies of agency contracts to principals
    B. copies of offers and contracts of sale to buyers and sellers
    C. copies of closing statements to buyers and sellers
    D. all of the above

50. A real estate agent advised a prospective buyer that the property the buyer was considering was scheduled for annexation into the city limits. This disclosure constituted which of the following?
    A. disloyalty to principal
    B. misrepresentation
    C. required disclosure to buyer
    D. violation of disclosure of information by agent

51. After inspecting a property, the prospective buyer told the selling agent, who was also the listing agent, that she liked the property but would not pay the listed price of $75,000. Knowing the owner was very anxious to sell, the agent suggested that the prospective buyer make an offer of $70,000. Which of the following statements about this situation is NOT correct?
    A. since the agent knew the owner was anxious to sell, he acted correctly
    B. the agent violated his obligations as an agent
    C. the agent should not make the suggestion without the express permission of the seller
    D. the agent's violation of the law of agency is also a violation of the licensing law

52. Mary Barker, an agent associated with Lasting Homes Realty, advised a seller that his property would sell for at least $150,000. Relying on this price quotation, the seller listed the property at a price of $150,000. Comparable sales and listings of competitive properties at the time were in the range of $105,000 to $110,000. The seller refused several offers between $106,000 and $112,000 during the 120-day term of the listing contract. The seller eventually sold his property for $98,000 due to depressed economic conditions since the expiration of the listing with Lasting Homes. Which of the following statements about these events is (are) correct?
    I. Mary Barker committed an act of misrepresentation and may be liable for the resulting financial loss incurred by the seller.
    II. Since Mary is an agent of Lasting Homes Realty, Lasting Homes may be held liable for the seller's damages.

    A. I only
    B. II only
    C. both I and II
    D. neither I nor II

53. While a broker was inspecting a property for listing, the property owner told the broker the house contained 2,400 square feet of heated living area. Relying on this information, the broker listed the property and represented it to prospective buyers as containing 2,400 square feet. After purchasing the property, the buyer accurately determined that there were only 1,850 square feet and sued for damages for the difference in value between 2,400 square feet and 1,850 square feet. Which of the following is correct?
    A. the broker is not liable because he relied on the seller's positive statement as to the square footage
    B. the seller is not liable because the broker, not the seller, represented the property to the buyer as containing 2,400 square feet
    C. neither the broker nor the seller is liable since it is the buyer's responsibility to check the square footage
    D. both the broker and the seller are liable

54. A real estate broker is responsible for all of the following EXCEPT:
    A. acts of sales associates while engaged in the brokerage activities
    B. maintaining a trust, or escrow, account
    C. adhering to commission schedule recommended by the local Board of REALTORS®
    D. representing property honestly, fairly, and accurately to prospective buyers

55. A broker deposited a buyer's check for $6,000 earnest money in her escrow account. Prior to the closing and at the seller's requestr, the broker paid $1,200 from the escrow account for repairs for damage caused by termites in the house. This expense was necessary so the seller could provide the required repairs for the buyer. Which of the following statements about this transaction is correct?
    A. since the $1,200 disbursement from the broker's escrow account was made at the seller's request and benefited both buyer and seller, the broker acted properly
    B. the broker's action constituted an act of commingling and was improper
    C. the broker properly disbursed the funds since he did not need permission from either buyer or seller to disburse funds for this purpose
    D. the broker acted improperly since both buyer's and seller's consent is needed to disburse any escrow funds before the transaction is closed

56. A real estate broker may do all of the following EXCEPT:
   A. have a buyer's deed recorded
   B. make a title examination
   C. act as agent of the grantee to accept deed delivery
   D. execute a certificate of title opinion

57. Which statement is NOT correct regarding time-share licensing and registration?
   A. a broker must be in charge of the premises
   B. the developer must have a broker license
   C. all salespeople must have a real estate license
   D. the time-share project must be registered with the Real Estate Commission

58. The time-share public offering statement must include all of the following EXCEPT:
   A. the total financial obligation of purchaser
   B. disclosure of who can make or change rules
   C. date that any amenities will be available
   D. names of all other owners of time-shares in the project

59. Funds paid to a time-share developer:
   A. belong to the seller immediately
   B. belong to the buyer for ten days
   C. must be immediately placed within an independent escrow agent
   D. must be returned to the buyer if a time-share instrument has not been recorded in 90 days

60. A seller was so happy with the sale of her property that she offered a $500 bonus. This payment can be given directly to which of the following?
   A. the broker in charge of listing company
   B. the listing broker
   C. the selling broker
   D. any of the above

61. Betty Broker owns three real estate offices in town. Which of the following is correct?
   A. she can be the broker-in-charge of all three offices
   B. she can designate a provisional broker to manage one of the offices under her supervision
   C. she can be broker-in-charge of two or more offices if they are within 5 miles of each other
   D. each office must have its own broker-in charge

62. Broker Larry Listing estimated a house to be 1,800 square feet and published this information in the MLS, when in fact the house is only 1,750 square feet. Cooperating broker (subagent) Carla represented the home as published in the MLS to a buyer. The commission is likely to find which broker at fault?
   A. Larry
   B. Carla
   C. both Larry and Carla
   D. neither Larry nor Carla

## Real Estate Finance

63. An alienation clause makes a mortgage:
   A. defeasible
   B. unassumable
   C. incontestable
   D. adjustable

64. Pledging real property to secure payment of a mortgage debt is described as:
   A. hypothecating
   B. amortizing
   C. liquidating
   D. participating

65. At loan closing, the lender may require the borrower to prepay into an escrow account a specified amount of money to be used for future payments of all of the following EXCEPT:
   A. real property taxes
   B. hazard insurance
   C. property owner's assessment
   D. broker's commission

66. Which of the following FHA programs is (are) used to insure loans for the purchase or construction of one- to four-family dwellings if one unit is occupied by the owner?
   A. 234(c)
   B. FHA 245
   C. 203(b)
   D. all of the above

67. Which of the following is (are) ways that a veteran borrower can have eligibility fully restored?
   I. dispose of the property and pay off the VA guaranteed loan
   II. sell the property to a qualified veteran who assumes the VA-guaranteed loan and substitutes his entitlement for that of the original borrower

   A. I only
   B. II only
   C. both I and II
   D. neither I nor II

68. All of the following are financing instruments EXCEPT:
A. deed in trust
B. note
C. junior mortgage
D. contract for deed

69. Nonjudicial foreclosure is also called:
A. friendly foreclosure
B. foreclosure by action
C. strict foreclosure
D. foreclosure under power of sale

70. A mortgage providing that the lender makes payments to the homeowners is called:
A. reverse annuity mortgage
B. package mortgage
C. adjustable mortgage
D. wraparound mortgage

71. A blanket mortgage usually contains which of the following?
A. closed-end clause
B. release clauses
C. good-faith estimate
D. due-on-sale clause

72. Which of the following regulates the advertisement of credit terms available for a house offered for sale?
A. RESPA
B. Fannie Mae
C. Equal Credit Opportunity Act
D. Regulation Z

73. Which of the following is limited to purchasing FHA-insured and VA-guaranteed mortgages?
A. Fannie Mae
B. Freddie Mac
C. Maggie Mae
D. Ginnie Mae

74. What is the purpose of a deed of trust?
A. secure the payment of a note
B. provide protection for the mortgagor
C. create personal liability of the buyer
D. prevent assumption

75. Which lien has priority to mortgage foreclosure sale proceeds?
A. mortgage lien
B. income tax lien
C. real property tax lien
D. mechanic's lien

76. Which of the following requires immediate payment of the principal balance when the borrower is in default on a loan?
A. equity of redemption
B. prepayment penalty
C. right of lender to possession
D. acceleration

## Real Estate Valuation

77. Adherence to which of the following maximizes land value?
A. principle of contribution
B. principle of change
C. principle of anticipation
D. principle of highest and best use

78. In estimating the value of an office building containing 22,400 square feet, an appraiser established the annual rental income to be $400,000. The appraiser also learned that monthly expenses averaged $16,700. If the average investor in this property was realizing a net return of 13.5%, what would be the appraiser's estimate of the value of the property?
A. $1,478,518
B. $1,484,444
C. $2,962,962
D. $2,964,600

79. A competitive market analysis is performed when:
A. assessing property
B. pricing property
C. appraising property
D. condemning property

80. For which type of property would the direct sales comparison be the most relevant appraisal method?
A. farmland
B. library
C. office complex
D. mobile home park

81. The principle providing that the highest value of a property has a tendency to be established by the cost of purchasing or constructing a building of equal utility and desirability is the principle of:
A. highest and best use
B. competition
C. supply and demand
D. substitution

82. A property with road frontage adjoining Dick and Jane's land, which had no road frontage, was offered for sale. The value of the available property to Dick and Jane is most accurately described as:
A. market value
B. objective value
C. appraised value
D. subjective value

83. Which of the following is (are) included in a competitive or comparative market analysis?
   I. properties that have sold recently
   II. properties currently on the market
   A. I only
   B. II only
   C. both I and II
   D. neither I nor II

84. An appraiser who was estimating the value of a four-story government building determined that each floor measured 90 feet by 80 feet with a replacement cost of $60 per square foot. She also observed that the building had depreciated 25% as the result of physical and functional obsolescence. Other site improvements were estimated to have depreciated 20% from a new value of $160,000. The appraiser also estimated the land associated with the building to be worth $362,000. What is the correct value estimate of the property value by the cost approach?
   A. $814,000
   B. $846,000
   C. $1,786,000
   D. $1,818,000

*Use the following answers for questions 85–87.*

A. direct sales comparison (market data) approach
B. cost approach
C. income approach
D. none of the above

85. Which appraisal method is most appropriate to a unique property such as a church or post office?

86. Which appraisal method is most appropriate to residential property?

87. Which appraisal method is most appropriate to vacant land?

88. The direct sales comparison approach takes into consideration all of the following factors EXCEPT:
   A. comparable properties sold within the last six months
   B. the method of financing of comparable sales
   C. the price the seller thinks the property is worth
   D. age and condition of comparable properties

*Use the following data for questions 89–92.*

A developer builds four houses in one area at the same time. The following data are specifications of each house and its respective sales price:

1. 1,500 sq ft, 3 bedrooms, 2 baths, carport: $87,500
2. 1,600 sq ft, 3 bedrooms, 2 baths, no carport: $91,000
3. 1,500 sq ft, 3 bedrooms, 2 baths, no carport: $85,000
4. 1,600 sq ft, 3 bedrooms, 2 baths, basement, no carport: $95,000

89. What is the value of a carport?
   A. $1,500
   B. $2,500
   C. $4,000
   D. $6,000

90. What is the value of a basement?
   A. $1,500
   B. $2,500
   C. $4,000
   D. $6,000

91. A 1500-square-foot, three-bedroom, two-bath house with a basement and carport in the same area by the same builder is offered for resale by the owner. What should the listing price be?
   A. $85,000
   B. $87,500
   C. $91,500
   D. $95,000

92. A 1600-square-foot, three-bedroom, two-bath house with no basement and no carport in the same area by the same builder is offered for resale by its owner. What should the listing price be?
   A. $85,000
   B. $87,000
   C. $91,000
   D. $95,000

## Real Estate Math

93. The closing of the purchase of a commercial property was on April 8. The real property taxes of $5,760 have not been paid by the seller. Which of the following is a correct closing statement entry for taxes?
   A. $4,192 buyer's credit
   B. $1,568 seller's debit
   C. $1,568 seller's credit
   D. $4,192 buyer's debit

94. A buyer assumed a seller's existing 11%, $80,000 first deed of trust on the settlement date of June 12. The seller made the monthly payment on June 1 with interest in arrears. Which of the following is a correct settlement statement entry for the interest?
 A. $293.28 buyer's credit
 B. $439.92 seller's credit
 C. $439.92 seller's debit
 D. $293.28 seller's credit

95. All of the following items will be listed on page 2 of the HUD-1 form EXCEPT:
 A. government recording fees
 B. sales price
 C. loan origination fee
 D. commission

96. A seller had paid an annual hazard insurance premium of $540 for a policy effective on February 12. At settlement on April 16 of the same year, the buyer purchased the policy from the seller. This transaction is correctly entered on the settlement statements as:
 A. $96 seller's credit
 B. $444 buyer's credit
 C. $96 buyer's credit
 D. $444 seller's credit

97. If a real estate agent listed and sold a property for $90,000 and received 60% of the 7% commission paid to her employing broker, how much did the agent receive?
 A. $2,520
 B. $2,646
 C. $3,780
 D. $5,400

98. A real estate broker sold a 6.61-acre tract of land for $1,600 per acre and earned a 9% commission. How much did the broker receive? (Answers are rounded.)
 A. $661
 B. $952
 C. $992
 D. $1,983

99. If the monthly payment on a $60,000 fully amortizing mortgage loan at 12% APR for a 20-year term is $661.20, how much is the principal reduced by the first monthly payment?
 A. $61.20
 B. $72.00
 C. $600.00
 D. $612.20

100. In making an FHA-insured loan of $45,000, a lending institution charged sufficient discount points to increase the yield on the loan from 8% to 8 1/8%. The cost of the points was:
 A. $45
 B. $225
 C. $450
 D. $900

101. A triangular tract of land is 8,000 feet deep and has highway frontage of 4,000 yards. If Ajax Realty Company listed this property at 9% commission and sold it for $1,600 per acre, what was Ajax's commission?
 A. $105,785
 B. $158,678
 C. $218,160
 D. $317,355

102. A property with a market value of $80,000 is assessed at 75% of the market value. What is the tax rate per $100 if the tax bill is $900?
 A. $1.125
 B. $1.50
 C. $11.25
 D. $15.00

103. If the closing date is November 10 and the seller has paid the real property taxes of $2,880 for the current tax year of January 1 through December 31, which of the following is the correct closing statement entry for taxes?
 A. seller's debit $2,480
 B. seller's credit $400
 C. buyer's credit $400
 D. buyer's debit $2,480

104. The buyer assumed a seller's 11%, $74,000 mortgage at closing on July 12. The seller had made the mortgage payment of $773.34, including principal and interest, on July 1. Interest is paid in arrears. Which of the following is the correct closing statement entry for interest?
 A. buyer's credit $406.98
 B. seller's credit $271.32
 C. buyer's debit $406.98
 D. seller's debit $271.32

105. A sales contract provided that the buyer was to pay $65,000 for a seller's property by giving a purchase money mortgage for $30,000 and the balance in cash at closing. The buyer made a good faith deposit of $6,500 when he made the offer. The seller's share of the real property taxes credited to the buyer was $850. The buyer's other closing costs totaled $900. What amount must the buyer pay at closing?
A. $27,650
B. $27,700
C. $28,550
D. $35,050

106. What net annual operating income must a property manager produce from a property to provide an 8% return to the owner who paid $763,000 for the property?
A. $9,538
B. $61,040
C. $95,375
D. $104,849

107. An owner's office building was producing a net annual operating income of $140,000. If the owner paid $1,166,666 for the property, what rate of return was she receiving on her investment?
A. 8.3%
B. 12%
C. 14%
D. 16.3%

# Answer Key

## End-of-Chapter Review Questions

### Chapter 1 Basic Real Estate Concepts

| | | | | |
|---|---|---|---|---|
| 1. C | 7. B | 13. C | 19. C | 25. C |
| 2. B | 8. C | 14. C | 20. B | 26. D |
| 3. D | 9. C | 15. C | 21. C | 27. A |
| 4. D | 10. C | 16. A | 22. C | 28. D |
| 5. D | 11. B | 17. B | 23. A | 29. D |
| 6. D | 12. D | 18. B | 24. B | 30. B |

### Chapter 2 Property Ownership and Interests

| | | | | |
|---|---|---|---|---|
| 1. C | 8. B | 15. B | 22. A | 29. D |
| 2. B | 9. B | 16. A | 23. D | 30. C |
| 3. A | 10. D | 17. D | 24. C | 31. D |
| 4. D | 11. D | 18. A | 25. D | 32. C |
| 5. D | 12. A | 19. B | 26. B | 33. C |
| 6. A | 13. C | 20. B | 27. C | 34. A |
| 7. B | 14. B | 21. A | 28. B | 35. D |

### Chapter 3 Transfer of Title to Real Property

| | | | | |
|---|---|---|---|---|
| 1. A | 7. B | 13. A | 19. D | 25. D |
| 2. C | 8. A | 14. B | 20. C | 26. C |
| 3. A | 9. D | 15. C | 21. B | 27. D |
| 4. C | 10. D | 16. C | 22. D | 28. B |
| 5. D | 11. C | 17. B | 23. D | 29. D |
| 6. D | 12. A | 18. A | 24. B | 30. B |

## Chapter 4 Land Use Controls

| | | | | |
|---|---|---|---|---|
| 1. C | 6. B | 11. B | 16. B | 21. D |
| 2. D | 7. D | 12. C | 17. D | 22. D |
| 3. B | 8. A | 13. C | 18. B | 23. D |
| 4. D | 9. C | 14. D | 19. A | 24. D |
| 5. B | 10. A | 15. B | 20. D | 25. A |

## Chapter 5 Laws and Regulations Governing Brokerage Relationships

| | | | | |
|---|---|---|---|---|
| 1. A | 6. C | 11. D | 16. B | 21. D |
| 2. D | 7. A | 12. D | 17. A | 22. D |
| 3. C | 8. A | 13. B | 18. D | 23. C |
| 4. D | 9. D | 14. A | 19. C | 24. D |
| 5. C | 10. D | 15. D | 20. B | 25. C |

## Chapter 6 Real Estate Contracts

| | | | | |
|---|---|---|---|---|
| 1. C | 7. B | 13. D | 19. A | 25. B |
| 2. C | 8. B | 14. A | 20. C | 26. A |
| 3. D | 9. D | 15. D | 21. D | 27. C |
| 4. C | 10. C | 16. C | 22. D | 28. D |
| 5. A | 11. D | 17. D | 23. D | 29. B |
| 6. D | 12. D | 18. B | 24. B | 30. B |

## Chapter 7 Real Estate Finance

| | | | | |
|---|---|---|---|---|
| 1. D | 7. D | 13. A | 19. D | 25. B |
| 2. A | 8. A | 14. A | 20. D | 26. D |
| 3. D | 9. C | 15. A | 21. D | 27. A |
| 4. B | 10. C | 16. C | 22. D | 28. B |
| 5. C | 11. B | 17. B | 23. C | 29. D |
| 6. A | 12. B | 18. A | 24. D | 30. B |

## Chapter 8 Closing Real Estate Transactions

| | | | | |
|---|---|---|---|---|
| 1. C | 5. D | 9. C | 13. D | 17. C |
| 2. A | 6. A | 10. D | 14. A | 18. C |
| 3. B | 7. A | 11. C | 15. B | |
| 4. D | 8. C | 12. C | 16. D | |

## Solution to Chapter 8 Questions 11–12

| Item | Seller Debit | Seller Credit | Buyer Debit | Buyer Credit |
|---|---|---|---|---|
| Price | $ | $72,500.00 | $72,500.00 | $ |
| Loan | | | | 58,000.00 |
| Origination Fee | | | 580.00 | |
| Misc | | | 987.00 | |
| E/M | | | | 2,500.00 |
| RE Tax | 842.50 | | 57.50 | |
| Termite | | | 75.00 | |
| Deed | 50.00 | | | |
| Fee | 3,625.00 | | | |
| Excise Tax | 145.00 | | | |
| Mortgage | 43,728.57 | | | |
| BALANCE | | | | |
| –Buyer owes | | | | 13,699.50 |
| –Seller gets | 24,108.93 | | | |
| TOTALS | $72,500.00 | $72,500.00 | $74,199.50 | $74,199.50 |

## Chapter 9 Property Valuation

1. D
2. B
3. A
4. C
5. A
6. C
7. A
8. A
9. C
10. A
11. B
12. B
13. B
14. D
15. C
16. D
17. B
18. B
19. D
20. D
21. C
22. A
23. D
24. C
25. D
26. B
27. C
28. B
29. B
30. B

## Chapter 10 Relationship of Landlord and Tenant

1. D
2. B
3. B
4. C
5. B
6. D
7. B
8. C
9. D
10. C
11. B
12. D
13. C
14. A
15. B
16. B
17. D
18. B
19. A
20. B
21. C
22. D
23. B

## Chapter 11 Real Estate Management

1. C
2. C
3. A
4. C
5. C
6. A
7. B
8. C
9. A
10. D
11. B
12. D

## Chapter 12 Fair Housing

1. B
2. C
3. D
4. D
5. B
6. D
7. C
8. B
9. B
10. D
11. D
12. B
13. C
14. D
15. B

## Chapter 13 Federal Taxation of Home Ownership

1. C
2. D
3. C
4. D
5. A
6. D
7. A
8. B
9. D
10. C

## Chapter 14 Property Insurance

1. C
2. A
3. B
4. D
5. A

## Chapter 15 Basic House Construction

1. A
2. A
3. B
4. D
5. B
6. B
7. D
8. A
9. D
10. B
11. B
12. A
13. D
14. D
15. D
16. C

## Chapter 16 Real Estate Math

### *Brokerage Commissions*

1. b. $1,377
2. b. $88.50
2. d. $270.90
3. b. $567.00

### *Net to Seller*

1. a. $69,892.47
   b. $79,789.47

### *Profit/Loss/Equity*

2. $3,000, 4.167%
3. b. 505.26%

### *Area*

1. b. 0.66 acres
2. k. 5,625 sq. ft.
   l. 2,368 sq. ft.
   m. 1,875 sq. ft.
   n. 63,000 sq. ft.
   o. 139,500 sq. ft.
3. b. $27.50/sq. ft.
   c. $ 1.03/sq. ft.
   d. $ 255.56/front ft.

### *Taxes*

2. $71.88

### *Excise Tax*

2. $92
3. $272
4. $250

### *Finance*

1. b. $215.25
2. b. $132,500
3. b. $1,285.60
3. c. $327,914.92
4. b. $55,988
5. b. $4,758.75
6. b. 10.25
6. d. $2,600
7. b. $840, $1,080

## *Closing Statements*

**Problem No. 1**

| Balance owed by Buyer | | Balance due to Seller | |
|---|---|---|---|
| Sales Price | $ 45,700 | Sales Price | $ 45,700 |
| Insurance | 225 | RE Tax | −52.50 |
| Misc | 900 | Pers Tax | −150 |
| E/M | −2,000 | Excise Tax | −92 |
| RE Tax | −52.50 | Broker's Fee | −2,285 |
| Mortgage | −43,415 | Balance Due | $ 43,120.50 |
| Balance Owed | $ 1,357.50 | | |

**Problem No. 2**

| Balance owed by Buyer | | Balance due to Seller | |
|---|---|---|---|
| Sales Price | $ 60,000 | Sales Price | $ 60,000 |
| Insurance | 400 | RE Tax | −314.65 |
| Misc | 1,400 | Pers Tax | −400 |
| E/M | −5,000 | Mortgage | −35,000 |
| RE Tax | −314.65 | Excise Tax | −120 |
| Mortgage | −54,000 | Broker's Fee | −3,600 |
| Balance Owed | $ 2,485.35 | Balance Due | $ 20,565.35 |

**Problem No. 3**

| Balance owed by Buyer | | Balance due to Seller | |
|---|---|---|---|
| Sales Price | $ 72,500 | Sales Price | $ 72,500 |
| Insurance | 101.25 | RE Tax | 113.33 |
| Misc | 1,750 | Insurance | 101.25 |
| RE Tax | 113.33 | Mortgage | −50,000 |
| E/M | −7,500 | Mortgage Interest | −150 |
| Mortgage | −50,000 | Stamps | 145 |
| Mortgage Interest | −150 | Broker's Fee | −5,075 |
| Balance Owed | $ 16,814.33 | Balance Due | $ 17,344.58 |

*Valuation*

**Step No. 1**

Use a paired sales analysis to define the value of the elements:

1. Carport $72,500 – $70,000 = – $2,500
2. Deck $50,000 – $48,500 = – $1,500
3. Interstate highway $55,000 – $58,700 = – $3,700

**Step No. 2**

| Feature | Subject | Comp 1 | Adj | Comp 2 | Adj | Comp 3 | Adj |
|---|---|---|---|---|---|---|---|
| Price | | | $65,000 | | $71,200 | | $66,000 |
| Carport | Yes | No | +2,500 | Yes | 0 | Yes | 0 |
| Deck | No | Yes | −1,500 | Yes | −1,500 | No | 0 |
| Interstate Highway | No | Yes* | +3,700 | No | 0 | Yes* | +3,700 |
| Total Adjustment | | | +4,700 | | −1,500 | | 3,700 |
| Indicated Price | | | $69,700 | | $69,700 | | $69,700 |

*Because a location on an interstate highway is a negative factor that reduces the value of the property, it is treated as an increase in value when comparing a comparable home on a highway to a subject home that is not located on an interstate highway. Remember that the cost of the comparable is always adjusted to arrive at a probable sale price if the comparable were just like the subject home. Therefore, Comparables 1 and 3 would have sold for $3,700 more if they were not located on a highway.

*Federal Taxation*

2. b. $227,200, $0

# Appendix D: Diagnostic Test

## Chapter 1

1. A
2. C
3. B
4. D
5. C
6. B
7. D
8. A
9. C

## Chapter 2

1. B
2. B
3. D
4. A
5. B
6. C
7. A
8. C
9. A
10. D
11. D
12. B
13. C
14. D
15. A

## Chapter 3

1. D
2. A
3. A
4. B
5. C
6. A
7. D
8. C
9. D
10. B

## Chapter 4

1. B
2. A
3. B
4. C
5. C
6. A
7. C

## Chapter 5

1. B
2. B
3. C
4. A
5. C

## Chapter 6

1. A
2. B
3. A
4. D
5. D
6. A
7. B

## Chapter 7

1. A
2. B
3. A
4. A
5. D
6. A
7. C
8. B
9. D
10. C
11. C
12. D
13. C
14. A
15. A

## Chapter 8

1. D
2. D
3. C
4. B

## Chapter 9

1. D
2. A
3. C
4. C
5. A
6. A
7. A
8. A
9. D

## Chapter 10

1. A
2. C
3. B
4. C
5. B

## Chapter 11

1. A
2. D
3. C
4. D

## Chapter 12

1. C
2. D
3. A
4. C
5. B

## Chapter 13

1. C
2. C
3. A
4. C
5. D

## Chapter 14

1. B
2. D
3. D
4. C
5. B

## Chapter 15

1. D
2. A
3. C
4. C
5. A

## Chapter 16

1. D
2. B
3. D
4. D
5. B
6. B
7. B
8. B
9. B
10. D
11. C

# Appendix E: Practice Exam
## Real Estate Law

| | | | |
|---|---|---|---|
| 1. A | 6. B | 11. A | 16. B |
| 2. D | 7. D | 12. C | 17. B |
| 3. C | 8. C | 13. D | 18. C |
| 4. C | 9. B | 14. B | 19. C |
| 5. D | 10. A | 15. D | 20. C |

## Real Estate Brokerage

| | | | |
|---|---|---|---|
| 21. C | 28. B | 35. A | 42. B |
| 22. C | 29. B | 36. A | 43. A |
| 23. D | 30. D | 37. B | 44. D |
| 24. B | 31. C | 38. C | 45. B |
| 25. B | 32. C | 39. C | 46. C |
| 26. D | 33. A | 40. A | 47. A |
| 27. A | 34. B | 41. D | |

## North Carolina Real Estate License Law

| | | | |
|---|---|---|---|
| 48. B | 52. C | 56. D | 60. A |
| 49. D | 53. D | 57. B | 61. D |
| 50. C | 54. C | 58. D | 62. A |
| 51. A | 55. D | 59. B | |

## Real Estate Finance

| | | | |
|---|---|---|---|
| 63. B | 67. C | 71. B | 75. C |
| 64. A | 68. A | 72. D | 76. D |
| 65. D | 69. D | 73. D | |
| 66. C | 70. A | 74. A | |

## Real Estate Valuation

| | | | |
|---|---|---|---|
| 77. D | 81. D | 85. B | 89. B |
| 78. A | 82. D | 86. A | 90. C |
| 79. B | 83. A | 87. A | 91. C |
| 80. A | 84. C | 88. C | 92. C |

## Real Estate Math

| | | | |
|---|---|---|---|
| 93. B | 97. C | 101. B | 105. C |
| 94. A | 98. B | 102. B | 106. B |
| 95. B | 99. A | 103. B | 107. B |
| 96. D | 100. C | 104. D | |

# Glossary

This glossary presents definitions of real estate terms that appear in the text. Many of these terms have other meanings in other contexts; all definitions here refer to real estate. Numbers in parentheses indicate the chapters in which the terms are discussed. We also include definitions of terms that are not specifically discussed in this text but may be included in the license examinations.

**abandonment** The surrender or release of a right, a claim, or an interest in real property. **(2)**

**acceleration clause** A provision in a mortgage or deed of trust that permits the lender to declare the entire principal balance of the debt immediately due and payable if the borrower is in default. **(7)**

**access** A way of approach or entrance onto a property. **(2)**

**accord and satisfaction** A new agreement by contracting parties that is satisfied by full performance, thereby terminating a prior contract. **(6)**

**acknowledgment** A formal statement before an authorized official (e.g., notary public) by a person who executed a deed, contract, or other document that it was (is) his or her free act. **(3)**

**acquisition cost** The basis used by the FHA in calculating the loan amount. **(7)**

**acquisition debt** The debt incurred in the purchase of a personal residence.

**acre** A land area of 43,560 square feet. **(16)**

**actual age** Chronological age. **(9)**

**actual eviction** The removal of a tenant by the landlord because the tenant breached a condition of a lease or other rental contract. **(10)**

**actual notice** The knowledge that a person has of a fact. **(3)**

**adjoining lands** Lands that share a boundary line. **(2)**

**adjustable rate mortgage (ARM)** One in which the interest rate changes according to changes in a predetermined index. **(7)**

**adjusted basis** The value of property used to determine the amount of gain or loss realized by the owner upon sale of the property; equals acquisition cost plus capital improvements minus depreciation taken. **(13)**

**adjusted sales price** Sales price minus selling expenses. Also called amount realized. **(13)**

**adjustments** In the sales comparison approach to value, additions or subtractions to sales prices of comparable properties to make comparables like the subject property. **(9)**

**administrator** A man appointed by a court to administer the estate of one who has died intestate. **(3)**

**administrator's deed** One executed by an administrator to convey title to estate property. **(3)**

**administratrix** A woman appointed by a court to administer the estate of one who has died intestate. **(3)**

**ad valorem** Latin meaning "according to value"; the basis for taxes on real property. **(2)**

**adverse possession** A method of acquiring title to real property by conforming to statutory requirement. A form of involuntary alienation of title. **(3)**

**agency** The fiduciary relationship between a principal and an agent. **(5)**

**agency agreement** An employment contract between principal and agent that sets forth all the terms and conditions of employment including specifying the authority given to the agent and the compensation of the agent. **(5)**

**agent** A person authorized by another to act on his or her behalf. **(5)**

**agreement** A contract. Mutual assent between two or more parties. **(6)**

**air rights** Rights in the air space above the surface of land. **(2)**

**alienation** Transfer of title to real property. **(2)**

**alienation clause** A clause in a mortgage or deed of trust that entitles the lender to declare the entire principal balance of the debt immediately due and payable if the borrower sells the property during the mortgage term. **(6, 7)**

**allodial system** A type of land ownership in the United States whereby title to real property may be held absolutely by individuals. **(2)**

**amendment** A change or modification of a zoning ordinance by the local legislative authority. **(4)**

**amenities** Benefits resulting from the ownership of a particular property. **(9)**

**Americans with Disabilities Act** A federal law protecting the rights of individuals with physical or mental impairments. **(12)**

**amortization** The gradual reduction of a mortgage loan through periodic payments of principal and interest over a specific term to satisfy a mortgage loan. **(7)**

**amortization schedule** A printed list of periodic payments of principal and interest over a specific term to satisfy a mortgage loan. Usually shows total payment, amount going to principal and interest and the loan balance after each payment, as well as total principal and interest paid to date. **(7)**

**annual** Yearly.

**annual percentage rate (APR)** The actual effective rate of interest charged on a loan expressed on an annual basis; not the same as the simple interest rate. It takes into account certain closing costs and discount points charged by the lender; therefore, it may be higher than simple interest. **(7)**

**anticipation** In valuing property, value based on the present value of anticipated future benefits of ownership. **(9)**

**apparent authority** A fact situation that creates the appearance of an agent's authority. **(5)**

**appraisal** An estimate of property value based on factual data. **(9)**

**appraisal by capitalization** Also called income approach; an approach to the appraisal of income-producing real estate that estimates the property's value based on the amount of net income the property will produce over its life. **(9)**

**appraisal by summation** *See* **cost approach. (5)**

**appraisal process** An organized and systematic program for estimating real property value. **(9)**

**appraisal report** A report containing an estimate of property value and the data on which the estimate is based. **(9)**

**appreciation** An increase in property value. **(9)**

**approaches to value** Methods of estimating real property value. **(9)**

**appurtenance** All rights or privileges that result from ownership of a particular property and that move with the title. **(2)**

**appurtenant easement** A right of use in the adjoining land of another that moves with the title to the property benefiting from the easement. **(2)**

**arrears** Delinquent in meeting an obligation. The payment of interest for a prior period as scheduled. **(7)**

**asking price** The price specified in a listing contract. **(6)**

**assessed value** The value to which a local tax rate is applied to calculate the amount of real property tax. **(9)**

**assessment** A levy against property. **(2)**

**assessor** An local government official who has the responsibility for establishing the value of property for tax purposes. **(2)**

**assignee** One to whom contractual rights are transferred. **(6)**

**assignment** A transfer of legal rights and obligations by one party to another. **(6)**

**assignment of a lease** The transfer by a lessee of the remaining term of a lease without reversion of interest to the lessee. **(10)**

**assignor** One transferring contractual rights to another. **(6)**

**assumable mortgage** One that does not contain an alienation clause. **(7)**

**attorney-in-fact** A person appointed to perform legal acts for another under a power-of-attorney. **(6)**

**auction** A form of property sale in which people bid against one another. **(6)**

**availability (also called scarcity)** An economic characteristic of land describing that land as a commodity having a fixed supply base. **(1)**

**balloon payment** One in which the scheduled payment will not fully amortize the loan over the term. Therefore, it requires a final payment called a balloon payment, larger than the uniform payments, to satisfy the debt fully. **(7)**

**base lines** East-west lines in the rectangular method of property description (not used in North Carolina). **(3)**

**base rent** The fixed or minimum rent portion in a percentage lease. **(10)**

**basis** The value of property for income tax purposes. Adjusted basis is original acquisition cost (purchase price plus allowable closing costs) plus capital improvements less accrued depreciation. **(13)**

**beneficiary** The recipient of a gift of personal property by will. **(3, 7)**

**bequest** A gift of personal property by will. **(3)**

**bilateral contract** An agreement based on mutual promises of specified consideration. **(6)**

**bill of sale** An instrument transferring ownership of personal property. **(1)**

**blanket mortgage** One in which two or more parcels of real property are pledged to secure the payment of the note. **(7)**

**blockbusting** For profit, to induce or attempt to induce any person to sell or rent any dwelling by representations regarding the entry or prospective entry into the neighborhood of a person or persons of a particular race, color, religion, sex, familial status, handicap, or national origin. **(12)**

**bona fide** Latin meaning "in good faith." **(12)**

**book value** The value as it appears on the books of the owner, usually for tax purposes. **(9)**

**breach of condition** Failure of landlord or tenant to perform his or her respective duties under the terms of the lease, thereby giving the other party grounds for terminating the lease agreement. **(10)**

**breach of contract** Failure without legal excuse to perform a promise that forms the whole or part of a contract. **(6)**

**breach of duty** The failure to fulfill an agent's duty to his or her principal. This includes disloyalty; disobedience; lack of skill, care, and diligence; and failure to either properly disclose information or to accurately account for funds. **(5)**

**broker** A person or an organization acting as agent for others in negotiating the purchase and sale of real property or other commodities for a fee. **(1, 5)**

**brokerage** The business of bringing buyers and sellers together and assisting in negotiations for the terms of sale of real estate. **(12)**

**building codes** Public controls regulating construction. **(4)**

**bundle of rights** The rights of an owner of a freehold estate to possession, enjoyment, control, and disposition of real property. **(2)**

**buydown loan** A loan with a reduced interest rate that a seller, developer, or buyer has obtained by paying money up front. **(7)**

**buyer agency agreement** A contract in which a buyer engages an agent to act on the buyer's behalf in purchasing a property. **(5)**

**buyer's agent** A real estate agent who acts solely on behalf of the buyer and owes all fiduciary duties of agency to the buyer. **(5)**

**capacity of parties** The ability of parties to perceive and understand what they are contracting to do. All parties to a contract must be mentally competent and must have reached the age of majority. **(6)**

**capital improvement** An item that adds value to the property, adapts the property to new uses, or prolongs the life of property. Maintenance is not a capital improvement. **(13)**

**capitalization** The process of converting future income into an indication of the present value of a property by applying a capitalization rate to net annual income. **(9)**

**capitalization formula** Investment or value of real estate times the capitalization rate equals the annual net income of the real estate. **(9)**

**capitalization rate** The rate of interest appropriate to the investment risk as a return on and return of the investment. **(9)**

**carry-over clause** A clause in a listing contract protecting the broker's commission entitlement for a specified time after expiration of the contract. Also called extender clause. **(6)**

**cash flow** Regular income produced by a rental property after deducting operating expenses and debt service. **(9)**

**casualty insurance** Protects against damage to the physical structure of an insured property. **(14)**

**caveat emptor** Literally "let the buyer beware." **Does not relieve agent's obligation of disclosing material facts. (5)**

**certificate of eligibility** A statement provided to veterans of military service setting forth the amount of loan guarantee to which they are entitled at that time. **(7)**

**Certificate of Occupancy** A document issued by a local government agency after a satisfactory inspection of a structure, authorizing the occupancy of the structure. **(4)**

**certificate of reasonable value (CRV)** A document establishing the value of a property as the basis for the loan guarantee by the Department of Veterans Affairs to the lender. **(7)**

**chain of title** The successive conveyances of title to a particular parcel of land. **(3)**

**change** The principle stating that change is continually affecting land use and therefore continually altering value. **(9)**

**chattel** Personal property. **(1)**

**chronological age** Actual age of a structure. **(9)**

**civil penalty** Payment or redress for a private civil wrong imposed by a civil, not a criminal, proceeding. **(5)**

**Civil Rights Act of 1866** A federal law that prohibits all discrimination on the basis of race. **(12)**

**Civil Rights Act of 1968** Title VIII, commonly known as the Fair Housing Act, as amended in 1974 and 1988, prohibits discrimination in housing on the basis of race, color, national origin, religion, sex, handicap, or familial status (children). **(12)**

**civil suit** An action in a court of equity that seeks financial compensation for loss caused by another. **(12)**

**client** The principal, to whom the agent owes fiduciary duties. **(5)**

**closing** The consummation of a real estate contract. Also called settlement. **(1)**

**closing costs** Expenses incurred in the purchase and sale of real property paid at the time of settlement or closing. **(8)**

**closing statement** An accounting of the funds received and disbursed in a real estate transaction. **(8)**

**cloud on a title** A claim against a title to real property. **(3)**

**cluster zoning** A form of zoning providing for several types of land use within a zoned area. **(4)**

**Code of Ethics** A standard of conduct required by license laws and by the National Association of REALTORS®. **(1, 12)**

**co-insurance clause** A requirement of hazard insurance policies that property be insured for a certain percentage of value to obtain the full amount of a partial loss. **(14)**

**collateral** Property pledged as security for the payment of a debt. **(7)**

**color of title** A defective claim to a title. **(3)**

**commercial property** Property producing rental income or used in business. **(11)**

**commingle** To mix the money or property of others by an agent with the agent's personal or business funds or other property. **(5)**

**commission** A fee paid for the performance of services, such as a broker's commission. **(1)**

**commissioner's deed** A form of judicial deed executed by a commissioner. **(3)**

**commitment** A promise, such as a promise by a lending institution to make a certain mortgage loan. **(7)**

**common areas** Property to which title is held by co-owners as a result of ownership of a condominium unit. **(2)**

**common law** By judicial precedent or tradition as opposed to a written statute. **(2)**

**community-based planning** A form of land use control originating in the grassroots of a community. **(4)**

**community planning** A plan for the orderly growth of a city or a county to result in the greatest social and economic benefits to the people. **(4)**

**community property** A form of co-ownership limited to husband and wife. Does not include the right of survivorship. North Carolina is not a community property state. **(2)**

**comparable** A property that is similar to a property being appraised by the direct sales comparison approach. **(9)**

**comparative market analysis (CMA)** Presentation and analysis of the competition in the marketplace for a particular property for the purpose of arriving at a market price or listing price. **(9)**

**competent parties** Persons and organizations legally qualified to manage their own affairs, including entering into contracts. **(6)**

**competition** The principle stating that when the net profit generated by a property is excessive, the result will be to create very strong competition. **(9)**

**complete performance** Execution of a contract by virtue of all parties having fully performed all terms. **(6)**

**condemnation** The exercise of the power of eminent domain. The taking of private property for public use by paying just compensation. **(2)**

**condemnation value** The market value of property condemned. **(9)**

**conditions** (a) Facts or events that, if they occur or fail to occur, automatically create or extinguish a legal obligation. **(4)** (b) A term for certain limits in the insurance coverage of a specified property. **(14)**

**condominium** A form of ownership of real property recognized in all states that consists of individual ownership of some aspects and co-ownership of other aspects of the property. **(2)**

**conforming loans** Those processed on uniform loan forms and according to FNMA/FHLMC guidelines. **(7)**

**conformity** The homogeneous uses of land within a given area, which results in maximizing land value. **(9)**

**Conner Act** Requires certain documents (e.g., deeds, purchase contracts, and leases over three years) to be recorded to be enforceable against third parties. **(3)**

**consideration** Anything of value as recognized by law offered as an inducement to contract such as money, action, or forbearance, or a promise to act or a promise to forbear. **(6)**

**construction loan** A short-term loan, secured by a mortgage, to obtain the funds to construct an improvement on land. **(7)**

**construction mortgage** A temporary mortgage used to borrow the money to construct an improvement on land. **(7)**

**constructive eviction** The right of a tenant to move out and stop paying rent resulting from some action or inaction by the landlord that renders the premises unsuitable for the use agreed to in a lease or another rental contract. **(10)**

**constructive notice** Notice of a fact on the public record that is considered to be known to everyone, even though he or she has not actually been notified of such fact. Everyone is bound by this knowledge. **(3)**

**Consumer Price Index (CPI)** An index of the change in prices of various commodities and services that provides a measure of the rate of inflation. **(10)**

**contingency** A condition in a contract relieving a party of liability if a certain event occurs. **(6)**

**contract** An agreement between competent parties upon legal consideration to do or abstain from doing some legal act. **(6)**

**contract for deed** A contract of sale and a financing instrument wherein the seller agrees to convey title when the buyer completes the purchase price installment payments. Also called installment land contract, land contract, and conditional sales contract. **(6)**

**contract rent** The amount of rent agreed to in a lease. **(9)**

**contractual capacity** Having the ability to understand the terms of a contract and the consequences of nonperformance. **(6)**

**contribution** The principle that for any given part of a property, its value is the result of the contribution that part makes to the total value by being present or the amount that it subtracts from total value as a result of its absence. **(9)**

**conventional life estates** Those created by intentional act of the parties. **(2)**

**conventional loan** One in which the federal government does not insure or guarantee the payment to the lender. **(7)**

**conveyance** Transfer of title to real property. **(2)**

**cooperating broker** One who participates in the sale of a property through the listing broker. **(5)**

**cooperative** A form of ownership in which stockholders in a corporation occupy property owned by the corporation under a lease. **(2)**

**co-owners** *See* co-ownership.

**co-ownership** Title to real property held by two or more persons (co-owners) at the same time. There are many forms of co-ownership, including tenancy in common, tenancy by the entirety, and joint tenancy. Also called concurrent ownership. **(2)**

**corporation** A form of organization existing as a legal entity. An artificial person. **(2)**

**corporeal** Tangible things. **(2)**

**cost** A measure of expenditure of labor and material made sometime in the past. **(9)**

**cost approach** An appraisal method whereby the cost of constructing a substitute structure is calculated, depreciation is deducted, and land value is added. **(9)**

**counteroffer** A promise or a request by an offeree that terminates the original offer from an offeror by rejecting it and substituting a new offer in its place. **(6)**

**covenant** A promise in writing. **(4)**

**covenant against encumbrances** A promise in a deed that there are no encumbrances against the title except those set forth in the deed. **(3)**

**covenant of quiet enjoyment** A promise in a deed (or lease) that the grantee (or lessee) will not be disturbed in his or her use of the property because of a defect in the grantor's (or lessor's) title. **(3)**

**covenant of right to convey** A promise in a deed that the grantor has the legal capacity to convey the title. **(3)**

**covenant of seisin** A promise in a deed assuring the grantee that the grantor has the title being conveyed. **(3)**

**covenant of warranty** A promise in a deed that the grantor will guarantee and defend the title against lawful claimants. **(3)**

**credit** In a closing statement, money to be received or credit given for money or a stated obligation. **(8)**

**creditor** One to whom a debt is owed. **(2)**

**cul-de-sac** A dead-end street with a circular turnaround at the dead end. **(3)**

**cumulative-use zoning** A type of zoning permitting a higher priority use even though different from the type of use designated for the area. **(4)**

**curable depreciation** A condition of property that exists when correction is physically possible and the cost of correction is less than the value increase. **(9)**

**curtesy** A husband's interest in the real property of his wife. **(2)**

**customer** The "third party" in a transaction; the agent works *with* the customer but not *for* him. **(5)**

**damages** The amount of financial loss as a result of the action of another. **(6)**

**debit** In a closing statement, an expense, money, or charge against the seller or buyer. **(8)**

**debt service** Principal and interest payments on a debt. **(9)**

**decedent** A dead person. **(3)**

**declaration of restrictions** The instrument used to record restrictive covenants on the public record. **(2)**

**decree** An order of a court. **(2)**

**dedication** An appropriation of land or an easement therein by the owner to the public. **(2)**

**deed** A written instrument that transfers an interest in real property when signed by grantor and delivered to the grantee. **(3)**

**deed in lieu of foreclosure** A conveyance of title to the lender by a borrower in default to avoid a record of foreclosure. Also called friendly foreclosure. **(7)**

**deed of correction** A deed executed to correct an error in a prior deed. Also called a deed of confirmation. **(3)**

**deed of gift** A warranty or quitclaim deed conveying title as a gift to the grantee. **(3)**

**deed of release** A deed executed by a mortgage lender to release a title from the lien of a mortgage when the debt has been satisfied. Also used to release a dower right. **(3)**

**deed of surrender** A deed executed by a life tenant to convey his or her estate to the remainder or reversionary interest. **(3)**

**deed of trust** A form of security instrument pledging real property as security for the loan by conveying legal title to a third party, who is called a trustee until the loan is paid in full. **(7)**

**deed restrictions** Limitations on land use appearing in deeds. **(4)**

**default** Failure to perform an obligation. **(6, 7)**

**defeasance clause** The clause in a mortgage or a deed of trust giving the borrower the right to redeem the title and have the mortgage lien released at any time prior to default by paying the debt in full. **(7)**

**defeasible** Subject to being defeated by the occurrence of a certain event. **(2)**

**defeasible fee** A title that is subject to being lost if certain conditions occur. **(2)**

**deficiency judgment** A judgment obtained by a lender for the difference between the amount of foreclosure sale proceeds and the amount needed to satisfy the mortgage debt. **(7)**

**demise** To convey an estate for years. Synonymous with lease or let. **(10)**

**density** The number of persons or structures per acre. **(4)**

**Department of Housing and Urban Development (HUD)** A federal agency involved with housing. **(12)**

**depreciated value** The original basis of a property less the amount of depreciation taken at any point in time. **(9)**

**depreciation** Loss in value from any cause. **(9)**

**descent** The distribution of property of one who has died intestate to legally qualified heirs. **(3)**

**Description by reference** A valid legal description that refers to a recorded plat or other publicly recorded document.

**devise** A gift of real property by will. **(3)**

**devisee** The recipient of a gift of real property by will. **(3)**

**direct sales comparison approach** The primary approach in estimating the value of vacant land and single-family owner-occupied dwellings. Also called market data approach. **(9)**

**disability** A physical or mental impairment that substantially limits one or more of a person's major life activities. **(12)**

**disclosure of information** The prompt and total communication to the principal by the agent of any information that is material to the transaction for which the agency was created. **(5)**

**disclosure statement** An accounting of all financial aspects of a mortgage loan required of lenders to borrowers in residential mortgage loans by Regulation Z of the Federal Reserve Board. **(7)**

**discount points** A percentage of the loan amount required by the lender for making a mortgage loan. **(7)**

**discriminatory advertising** Any advertising that states or indicates a preference, limitation, or discrimination on the basis of race, color, religion, sex, familial status, handicap, or national origin in offering housing for sale or rent. **(12)**

**disintermediation** The loss of funds available to lending institutions for making mortgage loans caused by the withdrawal of funds by depositors for making investments that provide greater yields. **(7)**

**dominant tenement** Land benefiting from an appurtenant easement. **(2)**

**double entry** An amount of money showing on the closing statement for both buyer and seller. It is an amount collected from one party and given to the other party, therefore, a debit to the first party and a credit to the other party. **(8)**

**dower** A wife's interest in the real property of her husband. **(2)**

**dual agency** Representing two parties at the same time or in the same transaction. This practice is illegal unless all parties are properly informed and consent to the agency. **(6)**

**due-on-sale clause** *See* alienation clause. **(6, 7)**

**duress** The inability of a party to exercise his or her free will because of fear of another party. **(6)**

**earnest money** A deposit of money made by a buyer at the time of making an offer to demonstrate the earnest intent to purchase. Also called binder, good faith deposit, or escrow deposit. **(6)**

**easement** A nonpossessory right of use in the land of another. **(2)**

**Easement by necessity** Created by operation of law to allow access to land locked property.

**Easement by dedication** A portion of property set aside for use by the public (e.g. roadways, parks).

**easement in gross** A personal right of use in the land of another without the requirement that the holder of the right own adjoining land. **(2)**

**economic (external) obsolescence** A loss in value caused by such things as changes in surrounding land use patterns and failure to adhere to the principle of highest and best use. **(9)**

**economic life** The period of time during which a property is economically beneficial to the owner. **(9)**

**economic rent** The amount of rent an owner could receive for a property; established by the property's market. **(9)**

**effective age** The age of a property based on its remaining economic life. **(9)**

**effective demand** A desire for property accompanied by the financial ability to satisfy the desire by purchasing the property. **(9)**

**effective interest rate** The actual rate of interest being paid. **(7)**

**ejectment** A legal action to evict a tenant from property. **(10)**

**emblements** Personal property growing in the soil that requires planting and cultivation. Annual crops. Also, the right of former owners to reenter property to cultivate and harvest annual crops that were planted by them. **(2)**

**eminent domain** The power of government to take private property for public use. **(2)**

**employment authority** A document or contract giving a real estate agent the right to act for a principal with certain specific guidelines in a real estate contract (i.e., a listing contract or a buyer's agency contract). **(5)**

**enabling acts** Laws passed by state legislatures authorizing cities and counties to regulate land use within their jurisdictions. **(4)**

**encroachment** A trespass on the land of another as a result of an intrusion by some structure or other object. **(2)**

**encumbrance** A claim, lien, charge, or liability attached to and binding upon real property. **(2)**

**endorsement** An addition to an insurance policy to add coverage of some property or against some peril that is not in the basic policy. **(14)**

**enforceable** A contract in which the parties may be required legally to perform. **(6)**

**environmental impact statement** A statement required by the national Environmental Policy Act that must be submitted before initiating or changing a land use that may adversely affect the environment. **(4)**

**Environmental Policy Act** A federal law that requires filing an environmental impact statement with the EPA prior to changing or initiating a land use or development. **(4)**

**Environmental Protection Agency (EPA)** A federal agency that oversees land, air and water through development and enforcement of regulations use. **(4)**

**Equal Credit Opportunity Act (ECOA)** A federal law prohibiting discrimination in consumer loans. **(7)**

**equitable title** An interest in real estate such that a court will take notice and protect the owner's rights. **(6)**

**equity debt** All debt secured by a qualified residence to the extent it does not exceed the fair market value of the residence reduced by the acquisition debt.

**equity of redemption** The borrower's right to redeem the title pledged or conveyed in a mortgage or deed of trust after default and prior to a foreclosure sale by paying the debt in full, accrued interest, and lender's costs. **(7)**

**escalated lease** One in which the rental amount changes in proportion to the lessor's costs of ownership and operation of the property. **(10)**

**escheat** The power of government to take title to property left by a person who has died without leaving a will or qualified heirs. **(2)**

**escrow account** (a) An account maintained by a real estate broker in an insured bank for the deposit of other people's money; also called trust account. **(2, 5)** (b) An account maintained by the borrower with the lender in certain mortgage loans, also known as an impound account or reserve account, to accumulate the funds to pay an annual insurance premium, a real property tax, and/or a homeowner's association assessment. **(7)**

**estate** An interest in real property sufficient to give the owner of the estate the right to possession of real property. **(2)**

**estate at sufferance** Describes the situation of someone continuing to occupy property after lawful authorization has expired. A form of leasehold estate. **(10)**

**estate at will** A leasehold estate that may be terminated at the will of either party. **(10)**

**estate for years** A leasehold estate of definite duration. **(10)**

**estate from period to period** A leasehold estate that automatically renews itself for consecutive periods until terminated by notice given by either party. Also called estate from year to year and periodic tenancy. **(10)**

**estate in real property** An interest sufficient to provide the right to use, possession, and control of land and establishes the degree and duration of ownership. **(2)**

**estoppel** The prevention of a person from making a statement contrary to a previous statement. **(5)**

**estovers** The right of a life tenant or lessee to cut timber on the property for fuel or to use in making repairs. **(2)**

**et al.** Latin for "and others."

**et ux.** Latin for "and wife."

**eviction** A landlord's action that interferes with the tenant's use or possession of the property. Eviction may be actual or constructive. **(10)**

**excise tax** A state tax that a grantor must affix to a deed. It provides a rough indication of purchase price and is a valuable data source for the broker's records. **(3)**

**exclusion** Something not covered for loss by an insurance policy. **(14)**

**exclusive agency** A listing given to one broker only (exclusive), who is entitled to the commission if the broker or any agent of the listing broker effects a sale, but it imposes no commission obligation on the owner who sells the property to a person who was not interested in the property by efforts of the listing broker or an agent of the listing broker. **(6)**

**exclusive right to sell** A listing given to one broker only who is entitled to the commission if anyone sells the property during the term of the listing contract. **(6)**

**exclusive-use zoning** A type of zoning in which only the specified use may be made of property within the zoned district. **(4)**

**executed contract** An agreement that has been fully performed. **(6)**

**execution** The signing of a contract or another legal document. **(3)**

**executor** A man appointed in a will to see that the terms of the will are carried out. **(3)**

**executory contract** An agreement that has not been fully performed. **(6)**

**executrix** A woman appointed in a will to see that the terms of the will are carried out. **(3)**

**express agency** Any oral or written agreement establishing a trust relationship between a principal and agent. **(5)**

**express authority** That authority specifically granted in a contract. **(5)**

**express contract** One created verbally or in writing by the parties. **(6)**

**extender clause** *See* **carry-over clause. (6)**

**Fair Housing Act of 1968 (as amended)** A federal prohibition of discrimination in the sale, rental, or financing of housing on the basis of race, color, religion, sex, national origin, handicap, or familial status. **(12)**

**fair market value** A price for property agreed upon between buyer and seller in a competitive market with neither party being under undue pressure. **(9)**

**Fannie Mae (FNMA)** The shortened name for the Federal National Mortgage Association. **(7)**

**Federal Home Loan Mortgage Corporation (Freddie Mac)** A secondary mortgage market institution (corporation) that only purchases conventional loans. **(7)**

**Federal Housing Administration (FHA)** The federal agency that insures mortgage loans to protect lending institutions. **(7)**

**Federal National Mortgage Association (Fannie Mae)** A privately owned corporation that purchases FHA, VA, and conventional mortgages. **(7)**

**Federal Reserve Bank** Regulates monetary policy by controlling the money supply and the discount rate. **(7)**

**fee simple absolute** An inheritable freehold estate in land that is the greatest form of real property ownership. **(2)**

**fee simple determinable** A defeasible fee (title) that terminates automatically if conditions of the title are violated. **(2)**

**fee simple subject to a condition subsequent** A defeasible fee (title) by which the grantor or his heirs may reenter the property and bring legal action to terminate the grantee's estate and regain title and possession if conditions of title are violated. **(2)**

**feudal system** A type of land ownership previously existing in England whereby only the king could hold absolute title to real property. **(2)**

**FHA-insured loan** A mortgage loan in which the payments are insured by the Federal Housing Administration. **(7)**

**fiduciary** A person, such as an agent, who is placed in a position of trust in relation to the person for whose benefit the relationship is created. Essentially the same as a trustee. **(5)**

**final settlement** Consummation of a contract to buy and sell real property. **(6)**

**first mortgage** One that is superior to later recorded mortgages. **(7)**

**first substantial contact** A flexible standard that typically occurs when an agent and a prospective buyer discuss in any detail the buyer's interest in purchasing property. **(5)**

**fit premises** Residential property that is in fit condition for human habitation. In North Carolina a landlord is required to do whatever is necessary to put and maintain fit premises. **(10)**

**fixed-rate loan** One in which the interest does not change. **(7)**

**fixture** Personal property that has become real property by having been permanently attached to real property. **(2)**

**fix-up expenses** Costs incurred by the seller of a principal residence in preparing it for sale. **(13)**

**flat fee** Commission arrangement in which the broker takes a listing based on a specified payment of money by the seller to the broker at time of listing. **(6)**

**foreclosure** The legal procedure by which a loan or real property secured by either a mortgage or deed of trust by selling the property in accordance with applicable legal requirements and apply the proceeds to the loan if the borrower breaches the contract by failing to make payments, maintain the property, and/or keep the property insured. **(3)**

**foreclosure under power of sale** *See* **nonjudicial foreclosure. (7)**

**foreshore** The land between high and low watermarks. **(2)**

**fraud** An intentional false statement of a material fact. **(6)**

**Freddie Mac (FHLMC)** The shortened name for the Federal Home Loan Mortgage Corporation, an agency that purchases mortgages, especially conventional mortgages, in the secondary mortgage market. **(7)**

**Freehold** An interest in land of at least a lifetime and is therefore generally identified with the concept of title or ownership

**freehold estate** A right of title to land. **(2)**

**free market** An economic condition in which buyer and seller are able to negotiate a purchase and sale without undue pressure, urgency, or outside influences other than the law of supply and demand. **(1)**

**friendly foreclosure** An absolute conveyance of title to the lender by the mortgagor in default to avoid a record of foreclosure. Also called a deed in lieu of foreclosure. **(7)**

**front foot** A linear foot of property frontage on a street or highway. **(16)**

**fruits of industry (fructus industriales)** Growing things on real estate that require planting each season and cultivation (e.g., crops). These are typically considered personal property and not real property. **(2)**

**fruits of the soil (fructus naturales)** Growing things that do not require planting or cultivation but grow naturally and are perennial (e.g., forest trees and native shrubs). They are designated in law as real property as long as they are attached to the soil. **(2)**

**full performance** The usual manner of terminating contracts. **(6)**

**full-service leases** A lease requiring each tenant to pay a portion of the overall operating expenses for the building and common areas in addition to a base rent; common in large office buildings and shopping centers. **(10)**

**functional obsolescence** A loss in value resulting from such things as faulty design, inadequacies, overadequacies, and out-of-date equipment. **(9)**

**future interest (also called future estate)** The right in real property of a person holding a remainder or reversionary interest who will vest at some time in the future in a property during the tenancy of a life tenant. **(2)**

**gain realized** The excess of the amount realized over the adjusted basis. **(13)**

**general agency** Full authority over one particular field of business or aspect of personal affairs of the principal (e.g., a property manager managing an apartment complex for the owner). **(5)**

**general agent** One who is authorized to conduct a broad scope of business for his or her principal but whose authority is limited in some way (e.g., one who is authorized to manage another's business). **(5)**

**general lien** One that attaches to all property of the debtor within the jurisdiction of the court. **(2)**

**general warranty deed** A deed in which there is an unlimited warranty of title. **(3)**

**Ginnie Mae (GNMA)** A nickname for Government National Mortgage Association, a U.S. government agency that purchases FHA and VA mortgages. **(7)**

**good faith estimate** The lender's estimate of a borrower's settlement costs that is required by RESPA to be furnished to borrowers at time of loan application. **(8)**

**Government National Mortgage Association (Ginnie Mae)** A government agency that purchases FHA and VA mortgages. **(7)**

**government rectangular survey system** A type of land description by townships and sections. **(3)**

**graduated lease** One in which the rental amount changes in specified amounts over the lease term. **(10)**

**graduated payment mortgage (GPM)** One in which the payments are lower in the early years but increase on a scheduled basis until they reach an amortizing level. **(7)**

**grantee** One who receives title to real property by deed. **(3)**

**granting clause** The clause in a deed containing words of conveyance. **(3)**

**grantor** One who conveys title to real property by deed. **(3)**

**gross effective income** Gross potential income less deductions for vacancy and credit losses plus other income. **(9)**

**gross income** Income received without the subtraction of expenses. **(7)**

**gross lease** One in which the lessor pays all costs of operating and maintaining the property and real property taxes. **(10)**

**gross rent multiplier** A number used to estimate the value of income property. Also called gross income multiplier. **(9)**

**ground lease** A lease of unimproved land. **(10)**

**habitable** Suitable for the type of occupancy intended. **(10)**

**handicap** A mental or physical impairment that limits at least one major human activity that qualifies the person with the impairment to protection under the Fair Housing Act. **(12)**

**hazard insurance value** The cost of replacing a structure completely destroyed by an insured hazard. **(9)**

**heir** A person legally eligible to receive property of a decedent. **(3)**

**hereditaments** All the corporeal and incorporeal attributes of real estate that can be inherited. **(2)**

**highest and best use** The use of land that will preserve its utility and yield a net income in the form of rent that forms, when capitalized at the proper rate of interest, the highest present value of the land. **(1)**

**highway access controls** Limitations on connections between a property and a highway acquired for public safety through the condemnation process. **(4)**

**holding over** The act of a tenant remaining in possession of property after the termination of a lease. **(10)**

**homeowner's policy** An insurance policy that covers the property's structure and contents (property insurance) and protects the policyholder against personal injury and property damage caused by the policyholder. **(14)**

**homogeneous** Similar and compatible land uses. **(4)**

**Housing and Urban Development (HUD)** An agency of the federal government concerned with housing programs and laws. **(12)**

**HUD Form No. 1** A standard settlement form required by RESPA. **(8)**

**Human Relations Commission** *See* **North Carolina Humans Relations Commission.**

**hypothecation** Pledging property as security for the payment of a debt without giving up possession. **(7)**

**illusory offer** One that does not obligate the offeror. **(6)**

**immobility** A physical characteristic of land describing the impossibility of relocating land from one place to another. **(1)**

**implied authority** Authority that arises from custom. **(5)**

**implied contract** One created by deduction from the conduct of the parties rather than from the direct words of the parties. Opposite of an express contract. **(6)**

**implied warranty** One presumed by law to exist in a deed though not expressly stated. **(2)**

**improved land** Land on which structures or roads exist. **(2)**

**improvements** Structures, walls, roads, and so on. **(1)**

**income approach** The primary method of estimating the value of properties that produce rental income. Also called appraisal by capitalization. **(9)**

**income property** One that produces rental income. **(9)**

**incompetent** A person who is not capable of managing his or her own affairs. **(6)**

**incorporeal** Intangible things such as rights. **(2)**

**incurable depreciation** That which is not physically correctable or not economically practical to correct. **(9)**

**indestructibility** A physical characteristic of land meaning that land is a permanent commodity and cannot be destroyed. **(1)**

**index lease** One in which the rental amount is changed in proportion to changes in a measure such as the Consumer Price Index. **(10)**

**ingress and egress** The right to enter (ingress) and to exit (egress) from a parcel of land. **(2)**

**inheritance basis** The market value of property at date of decedent's death, for tax purposes. **(13)**

**injunction** An instruction of a court to discontinue a specified activity. **(4)**

**installment land contract** *See* **contract for deed.**

**instrument** A written legal document such as a contract, note, and mortgage. **(7)**

**insurable interest** The financial interest that one must have in a property in order to obtain insurance on the property. **(14)**

**insured conventional loan** One in which the loan payment is insured by private mortgage insurance to protect the lender. **(7)**

**interest** Money paid for the use of money. **(7)** Also an ownership or right. **(2)**

**interim financing** Short-term or temporary financing, such as a construction loan. **(7)**

**interim interest** Interest paid on the loan amount from the date of closing through the end of the closing month inclusive. It can be collected at closing, on the first day of the month following closing, or with the first regular payment. No interim interest is due if closing occurs on the first day of the month. **(8)**

**Interstate Land Sales Full Disclosure Act** A federal law regulating the interstate sale of land under certain conditions. **(4)**

**intestate** A person who has died without leaving a valid will. **(3)**

**intestate succession** Distribution of property by descent as provided by statute. **(2)**

**invalid** Not legally enforceable. **(4)**

**irrevocable** That which cannot be changed or canceled.

**joint tenancy** A form of co-ownership that includes the right of survivorship. **(2)**

**judgment** A court determination that one party is indebted to another. When properly filed, it creates a lien on the debtor's property. **(2)**

**judgment lien** A general lien resulting from a court decree. **(2)**

**judicial deed** One executed by an official with court authorization. **(3)**

**judicial foreclosure** A court proceeding to require that property be sold to satisfy a mortgage lien. **(7)**

**jumbo loans** When a loan amount is higher than the conforming limit.

**junior mortgage** One that is subordinate to a prior mortgage. **(7)**

**jurisdiction** The extent of the authority of a court. **(2)**

**laches** The loss of legal rights because of failure to assert them on a timely basis.

**land** The surface of the earth, the area above and below the surface, and everything attached naturally (trees, crops) thereto. **(2)**

**land contract** *See* **contract for deed. (6)**

**land grant** The conveyance of land as a gift for the benefit of the public.

**landlocked** With regard to property, without access to a public road. **(2)**

**landlord** One who owns real property and leases it to another. Also referred to as lessor. **(10)**

**land use controls** Governmental controls (e.g., zoning laws, building codes) or private controls (e.g., deed restrictions, subdivision covenants) that dictate how the land can be used. **(1)**

**lateral support** The right of land to be supported in its natural state by adjacent land. **(2)**

**lawful** Legal, not prohibited by law. **(4)**

**lease** A contract wherein a landlord gives a tenant the right of use and possession of property for a limited time in return for rent. **(10)**

**leasehold estate** Nonfreehold estate. A leasehold estate is of limited duration and provides the right to possession and control, but not title. **(2)**

**leasehold policy** A policy insuring a lessee against defects in the lessor's title. **(3)**

**legal capacity** The ability to contract. **(3)**

**legal description** A description of land recognized by law. **(3)**

**legal entity** A person or organization with legal standing or capacity. **(5)**

**legal rate of interest** The maximum rate permitted by law.

**Less-than-freehold estate** Nonfreehold estates.

**lessee** A tenant under a lease. **(10)**

**lessor** A landlord under a lease. **(10)**

**leverage** The use of borrowed funds, which allows an owner to control an investment greater than the owner's equity in the investment. The larger the percentage of borrowed money, the greater the leverage. **(1)**

**levy** Imposition of a tax executing a lien. **(2)**

**liability insurance** Protects a property owner against the financial claims of others. **(14)**

**license** A personal privilege to do a particular act or series of acts on the land of another. **(5)**

**licensee** One who holds a license, e.g., a person granted a real estate license by the North Carolina Real Estate Commission. **(5)**

**lien** A claim that one person has against the property of another for some debt or charge which entitles the lien holder to have the claim satisfied from the property of the debtor. **(2)**

**lien foreclosure sale** A sale of real property at public auction to satisfy a specific or general lien against the property. These sales do not have the consent of the owner/debtor, and title is typically conveyed by trustee's deed. **(3)**

**lien theory** The legal theory that a mortgage creates a lien against the real property pledged in the mortgage to secure the payment of a debt. **(7)**

**life estate** A freehold estate created for the duration of the life or lives of certain named person or persons. A noninheritable estate. **(2)**

**life estate in remainder** A form of life estate in which certain persons called remaindermen are designated to receive the title upon termination of the life tenancy. **(2)**

**life estate in reversion** A form of life estate that reverts to the creator of the estate in fee simple upon termination. **(2)**

**life estate pur autre vie** An estate in which the duration is measured by the life of someone other than the life tenant. **(2)**

**life tenant** One holding a life estate. **(2)**

**liquidated damages** An amount of money to be paid and received as compensation for a breach of contract. **(6)**

**liquidity** The fact that an asset can be converted to cash. **(7)**

**lis pendens** Literally "a lawsuit pending." Notice of pending litigation whose outcome potentially will affect title to all or part of a new owner's property. **(2)**

**listing contract** An agreement whereby a property owner employs a real estate broker to look for a buyer for the property described in the contract and promises to compensate the agent. **(1, 5)**

**litigation** A lawsuit.

**littoral rights** The rights of owners bordering large bodies of water such as oceans to access of that water body. **(2)**

**loan assumption** The transfer of loan obligations to a purchaser of the mortgaged property. **(7)**

**loan commitment** The obligation of a lending institution to make a certain mortgage loan. **(6)**

**loan origination fee** The financing charge required by the lender. **(7)**

**loan-to-value ratio** The relationship between the amount of a mortgage loan or the sales price, whichever is lower and the lender's opinion of the value of the property pledged to secure the payment of the loan. **(7)**

**location (situs)** An economic characteristic of land having the greatest effect on value of any other characteristic. **(1)**

**loyalty** An absolute duty of an agent to a principal to serve the best interest of the principal. **(5)**

**Maggie Mae (MGIC)** A secondary mortgage market corporation of the Mortgage Guaranty Insurance Corporation. **(7)**

**management agreement** A contract wherein an owner employs a property manager. **(11)**

**management plan** A long-range program prepared by a property manager for the management of a property. **(11)**

**management proposal** A program for operating a property submitted to the owner by a property manager. **(11)**

**marital life estates** Those created by the exercise of the right of dower, curtesy, or a statutory substitute. **(2)**

**marketable title** One that is free from reasonable doubt and that a court would require a purchaser to accept. **(3)**

**Marketable Title Act** North Carolina legislation designed to extinguish old defects in the title by providing that when a chain of title can be established for 30 years without conflicts, claims outside this chain are extinguished. This Act has exceptions. **(3)**

**market value** The value in terms of money agreed upon by a willing buyer and seller, neither being under undue pressure and each being knowledgeable of market conditions at the time. **(9)**

**master plan** Created for the purpose of providing for the orderly growth of a community that will result in the greatest social and economic benefits to the people in the community. **(4)**

**material fact** An important fact that may affect a person's judgment. **(6)**

**mechanics' liens** Statutory liens available to persons supplying labor (mechanic) or material (materialmen) to the construction of an improvement on land if they are not paid. **(2)**

**metes and bounds** A system of land description by distances and directions. **(3)**

**mineral lease** A nonfreehold (leasehold) estate in the area below the surface of land. **(2)**

**mineral rights** The right to take minerals from the earth; the landowner holds these rights or can sell or lease them to others. **(2)**

**minor** A person who has not attained the statutory age of majority. **(6)**

**misdemeanor** A criminal violation punishable by a fine and/or imprisonment. It is not considered as severe an offense as a felony. **(5)**

**modification by improvement** An economic characteristic of land providing that the economic supply of land is increased by improvements made to land and on land. **(1)**

**mortgage** A written instrument used to pledge a title to real property to secure the payment of a promissory note. **(7)**

**mortgage banker** A form of organization that makes and services mortgage loans. **(7)**

**mortgage broker** One who arranges a mortgage loan between a lender and borrower for a fee. **(7)**

**mortgagee** The lender in a mortgage loan receiving a mortgage from the borrower/mortgagor. **(7)**

**mortgagee's policy** A policy that insures a mortgagee against defects in a title pledged by a mortgagor to secure payment of a mortgage loan. **(3)**

**mortgage insurance premium (MIP)** A fee charged by the Federal Housing Administration (FHA) to insure FHA loans. There is both an upfront fee, which can be added to the loan amount or paid in cash at closing, and an annual fee, which can be paid with the monthly payments. **(7)**

**mortgage loan value** The value sufficient to secure the payment of a mortgage loan. **(9)**

**mortgage satisfaction** Full payment of a mortgage loan. **(8)**

**mortgaging clause** The clause in a mortgage or deed of trust that demonstrates the intention of the mortgagor to mortgage the property to the mortgagee. **(7)**

**mortgagor** The borrower in a mortgage loan who executes and delivers a mortgage to the lender. **(7)**

**multiple listing** A type of listing by an organized method of sharing or pooling listings by member brokers. **(6)**

**multiple listing service (MLS)** An organized method of sharing or pooling listings by member brokers. **(5, 6)**

**mutual assent** The voluntary agreement of all parties to a contract as evidenced by an offer and acceptance. **(6)**

**mutual savings banks** Similar to savings and loan associations. These banks provide a substantial source of financing for housing. **(7)**

**narrative appraisal report** A statement of an opinion of value containing the elements of judgment as well as the data used in arriving at the value estimate. **(9)**

**National Association of REALTORS®** The largest and most prominent trade organization of real estate licensees. **(1)**

**negative amortization** When the loan payment amount is not sufficient to cover interest due, the shortfall is added back into principal, causing principal to grow larger after payment is made. **(7)**

**negative covenants** *See* **restrictive covenants.**

**negligent misrepresentation** An unintended misrepresentation of a material fact that the party did not make knowingly but should have known the truth by exercising due skill, care, and diligence. **(5, 6)**

**negligent omission** An unintended failure to communicate a known material fact. An unintended failure to communicate unknown material fact by a person responsible for disclosing it because this person did not exercise the due skill, care, and diligence that would have revealed the fact. **(5)**

**net income** Gross income less operating expenses. Also called net operating income. **(9)**

**net lease** One in which the lessee pays a fixed amount of rent plus the costs of operation of the property. **(10)**

**net listing** Not a type of listing but a method of establishing the listing broker's commission as all money above a specified net amount to the seller. **(6)**

**net operating income** Gross operating income minus operating expenses. **(9)**

**nonconforming use** A use of land that does not conform to the use permitted by a zoning ordinance for the area but is allowed to continue because it preceded the zoning ordinance. **(4)**

**nonfreehold estate** An estate (interest in land) of less than freehold (lifetime, ownership), i.e., rental property. **(2, 10)**

**nonhomogeneity** A physical characteristic of land describing that land as a unique commodity. **(1)**

**nonjudicial foreclosure** A form of foreclosure that does not require court action to conduct a foreclosure sale. Also called foreclosure under power of sale. **(7)**

**nonrecourse note** A note in which the borrower has no personal liability for payment. **(7)**

**North Carolina Condominium Act** Legislation passed in 1986 that set requirements for the sale or resale of condominiums. Requirements include disclosure, right to rescind contract for seven days, special escrow rules, and timely provision of required documents. **(2)**

**North Carolina Fair Housing Act of 1983** State fair housing law that is almost identical to the federal fair housing laws; however, it provides no exemptions for owners selling their own property, and it broadens rental exemption slightly. **(12)**

**North Carolina Human Relations Commission** A state agency that, as a substantially equivalent agency to HUD, is currently enforcing the 1968 Fair Housing Act and its 1988 amendments. **(12)**

**North Carolina Residential Rental Agreements Act** A North Carolina statute that affects residential rentals in North Carolina by setting forth the mutually dependent obligations and duties of landlords and tenants, as well as the remedies available for breach of contract by the landlord. **(10)**

**North Carolina Tenant Security Deposit Act** A North Carolina statute that requires a landlord or his or her agent to ensure that residential rental deposits are placed in a trust account or guaranteed with a bond and specifies the amount and permitted use of such deposits. The tenant must be notified of the disposition of such deposits. **(10)**

**notary public** A person authorized by a state to take oaths and acknowledgments. **(3)**

**notice of lis pendens** A notice on the public record warning all persons that a title to real property is the subject of a lawsuit and any lien resulting from the suit will attach to the title held by a purchaser from the defendant. **(2)**

**novation** The substitution of a new contract for a prior contract. **(6)**

**null and void** Invalid, without legal force or effect. **(6)**

**obsolescence** A loss in property value caused by external or functional factors. **(9)**

**occupancy** Physical possession of property. **(2)**

**offer** A promise made to another conditional upon acceptance by a promise or an act made in return. **(6)**

**offer and acceptance** Necessary elements for the creation of a contract. **(6)**

**offeree** One to whom an offer is made. **(6)**

**offeror** One making an offer. **(6)**

**offer to purchase and contract** A bilateral enforceable contract for the sale of real property. **(1, 7)**

**omission** The failure to disclose information. **(5)**

**open-end mortgage** One that may be refinanced without rewriting the mortgage. **(7)**

**open listing** A listing given to one or more brokers wherein the broker procuring a sale is entitled to the commission but imposes no commission obligation on the owner in the event the owner sells the property to a person who was not interested in the property by one of the listing brokers. **(6)**

**operating budget** A yearly budget of income and expense for a particular property prepared by a property manager. **(11)**

**operating expenses** The costs of operating a property held as an investment. **(9)**

**operating statement** A report of receipts and disbursements in evidence of net income of rental property. **(9)**

**operation of law** The manner in which the rights and/or liabilities of parties may be changed by the application of law without the act or cooperation of the parties. **(2)**

**opinion of title** An attorney's report based on a title examination, setting forth the examiner's opinion of the quality of a title to real property. **(3)**

**option** A contract giving one (optionee) the exclusive right to buy a property from the owner (optionor) at a specified price for a specified time. **(6)**

**optionee** One who receives an option. **(6)**

**optionor** One who gives an option. **(6)**

**option to purchase** A contract whereby a property owner (optionor) sells a right to purchase his or her property to a prospective buyer (optionee). **(6)**

**ordinance** A law enacted by a local government. **(4)**

**origination fee** A service charge made by a lending institution for making a mortgage loan. **(7)**

**overlay district** A zoning device that superimposes a particular zoning over one or more zoning areas. Examples are flood zones and historic preservation districts. **(4)**

**override clause** Also called extender, or carry-over, clause. It provides for seller to pay the full commission to broker for any sale to registered prospects within the specified period after the termination of the contract. **(6)**

**ownership** The right to use, control, possess, and dispose of property. **(2)**

**ownership in severalty** Title to real property held in the name of one person only. **(2)**

**owner's association** The organization of owners having the responsibility of providing for the operation and maintenance of the common areas of a condominium or residential subdivision. Also called property owner's association. **(2)**

**package mortgage** One in which personal property as well as real property is pledged to secure payment of the note. **(7)**

**package policy** A type of insurance policy that combines the elements of property and liability. **(14)**

**paid outside closing (P.O.C)** Items paid by the buyer or seller before closing, which appear on the closing statement, but are not included in totals.

**parol** An oral statement. **(6)**

**Parol Evidence Rule** Rule of evidence and law that states the written words contain all of the agreement and that oral statements not agreeing with the written word are to be disregarded. **(6)**

**partition** A legal proceeding dividing property of co-owners so that each holds title in severalty to a specific portion of the property. **(2)**

**party wall** A common wall used by two adjoining structures. **(2)**

**peaceable self-help** The illegal activity of landlords to bar tenants from a premise, e.g., locking out. **(10)**

**percentage lease** One in which the rental amount is a combination of a fixed amount plus a percentage of the lessee's gross sales. **(10)**

**peril** The source of a loss, e.g., fire is the major peril to a home. **(14)**

**periodic tenancy** A lease that automatically renews for successive periods unless terminated by either party. Also called an estate from year to year. **(10)**

**permanence** A physical characteristic of land referring to its indestructibility.

**personal property** All property that is not land and is not permanently attached to land. Everything that is movable. **(1, 2)**

**personalty** Personal property or chattels. **(1)**

**physical deterioration** A loss in value caused by unrepaired damage or inadequate maintenance. **(9)**

**PITI** Letters following the amount of a mortgage payment designating that the payment includes principal, interest, taxes, and insurance. **(7)**

**planned unit development (PUD)** A type of zoning ordinance which permits a special use; thereby enabling a designated area or subdivision to have a combination of property types, such as, residential housing, recreation facilities, and business establishments. **(4)**

**planning** A program for the development of a city or a county designed to provide for orderly growth. **(4)**

**plat** A property map. **(3)**

**plat books** Books wherein plats are recorded on the public record. **(3)**

**pledge** To provide property as security for the payment of a debt or for the performance of a promise. **(7)**

**plottage value** Increment of value resulting from combining two or more parcels of land into one tract having a value exceeding the total value of the individual parcels. **(9)**

**point of beginning** A reasonably easy-to-locate point tied to a well-established reference point from which a surveyor begins the metes and bounds description. After sighting all distances and directions of the perimeter of the property, the description must close, that is, return to the point of beginning. **(3)**

**points** *See* **discount points.**

**police power** The power of government to regulate the use of real property for the benefit of the public interest. **(2)**

**population density** The relationship of the number of people to a given land area. **(4)**

**potential gross income** The amount of rental income that would be received if all units were rented 100 percent of the time and there were no credit losses. **(9)**

**power of attorney** An instrument appointing an attorney-in-fact. **(5)**

**power of sale clause** Gives the trustee the right to sell the property if the buyer defaults. **(7)**

**prepaid items** Funds paid at closing to start an escrow account required in certain mortgage loans. Also called prepaids. **(7)**

**prepayment penalty clause** States that a financial penalty is imposed on a borrower for paying a mortgage loan prior to the expiration of the full mortgage term or before a time specified in the loan. **(7)**

**prescription** A method of acquiring an easement by continuous and uninterrupted use without permission. **(2)**

**prescriptive easement** One obtained by open, continued, and uninterrupted use without the owner's permission. **(2)**

**price** The amount of money paid for a property. **(9)**

**prima facie** Latin meaning "on the fact of it." A fact presumed to be true unless disproved by contrary evidence.

**primary mortgage market** The activity of lenders making mortgage loans to individual borrowers. **(7)**

**prime rate** The interest rate a lender charges the most creditworthy customers. **(7)**

**principal** (a) In the law of agency, one who appoints an agent to represent him or her. **(5)** (b) The amount of money on which interest is either owed or received. **(7)**

**principal residence** The home the owner or renter occupies most of the time. **(13)**

**private land use controls** The regulations of land use by individuals or nongovernment organizations in the form of deed restrictions and restrictive covenants. **(4)**

**private mortgage insurance (PMI)** A form of insurance required in high loan-to-value ratio conventional loans to protect the lender in case of borrower default in loan payment. **(7)**

**private property** That which is not owned by government. **(2)**

**privity of contract** One of two sets of rights and duties between parties in a lease; arises from contractual promises expressed in the lease. **(10)**

**privity of estate** One of two sets of rights and duties between parties in a lease; arises from traditional property law. **(10)**

**probate** The procedure for proving a will's validity. **(3)**

**profit,** or **profit à prendre** The right to participate in the profits of the land of another. **(2)**

**promissory note** A written promise to pay a debt as set forth in the writing. **(7)**

**promulgate** To put in effect by public announcement.

**Property,** or **hazard, insurance** Insurance that provides coverage to the basic structure of the property. **(14)**

**property management** Comprehensive, orderly, continuing program analyzing all investment aspects of a property and coordinating the leasing and maintenance of the property to ensure a financially successful project. **(11)**

**property management agreement** An employment contract setting up the agency relationship between the property owner and the real estate agent that gives the agent the responsibility of managing the property, including such responsibilities as negotiating, leasing, repairing and maintaining the property, collecting rents, and accounting for funds. **(6, 11)**

**property management report** A periodic financial report prepared by a property manager for the owner. **(11)**

**property manager** One who manages properties for an owner(s) as the owner's agent. **(11)**

**property report** Disclosure required under Interstate Land Sales Disclosure Act. **(4)**

**proprietary lease** A lease for an apartment unit in a development owned by a corporation in which the lessee owns stock entitling him to lease a unit. **(2)**

**prorating** Dividing certain settlement costs between buyer and seller. **(8)**

**provisional broker** In real estate in North Carolina, a person licensed as a broker with a provisional status attached to the license, who can perform the same real estate functions as a broker who does not have a provisional status, but under the supervision of a broker-in-charge (BIC).

**public land use controls** The regulation of land use by government organizations in the form of zoning laws, building codes, subdivision ordinances, and environmental protection laws. **(4)**

**public offering statement** A statement disclosing all material facts about a property. State and federal laws require a developer to provide prospective purchasers such a statement in certain circumstances. **(2)**

**public record** A record providing constructive notice of real property conveyances and other matters. **(2, 3)**

**pur autre vie** French meaning "for the life of another." A life estate measured by the life of someone other than the life tenant. **(2)**

**purchase money mortgage** A mortgage given by a buyer to a seller to secure the payment of all or part of the purchase price. **(7)**

**quantity survey method** A method for estimating replacement or reproduction cost. **(9)**

**quiet enjoyment** The use or possession of property that is undisturbed by an enforceable claim of superior title. **(3)**

**quitclaim** To relinquish or release a claim to real property. **(3)**

**quitclaim deed** A deed that contains no warranty of title. It is used to remove a cloud on a title. It conveys whatever interest, if any, the grantor has. **(3)**

**range** An area of land defined by the rectangular survey system of land description. **(3)**

**rate of return** The percentage of the net income produced by a property or another investment. **(9)**

**ready, willing, and able** Describes a buyer who is ready to buy, willing to buy, and financially able to pay the asking price. **(6)**

**real estate** Land and everything that is permanently attached to land. Interchangeable with the terms *real property* and *realty.* **(1)**

**real estate broker** A person or organization who negotiates real estate sales, exchanges, or rentals for others for compensation or a promise of compensation. **(1)**

**Real Estate Commission** The state agency responsible for the administration and enforcement of real estate license laws. **(1)**

**real estate investment trust (REIT)** A form of business trust owned by shareholders who make mortgage loans. **(7)**

**real estate market** A local activity in which real property is sold, exchanged, leased, or rented at prices set by competing forces. **(1)**

**Real Estate Settlement Procedures Act (RESPA)** Law requiring advance disclosure of settlement costs and other specified information mandating specific closing statement forms and prohibiting kickbacks. **(8)**

**realized gain** Actual profit resulting in a sale. **(13)**

**real property** Land and everything permanently attached to land, including all rights and interests in the land. **(1)**

**REALTOR®** A registered trademark of the National Association of REALTORS®. Its use is limited to members only. **(1)**

**realty** Land and everything permanently attached to land. **(1)**

**reappraisal lease** One in which changes in rental amount are based on changes in property value as demonstrated by periodic reappraisals of the property. **(10)**

**reconciliation** The process of weighted evaluation of the estimate derived from the three approaches to determine a single reliable estimate of value. **(9)**

**recording** The registration of a document on the public record. **(3)**

**rectangular survey** *See* **government survey system.**

**redemption** *See* **equity of redemption.**

**redlining** The refusal of lending institutions to make loans for the purchase, construction, or repair of a dwelling because the area in which the dwelling is located is integrated or populated by minorities. **(12)**

**referral fee** A percentage of a broker's commission paid to another broker for referring a buyer or a seller. **(6)**

**refinancing** Obtaining a new mortgage loan to pay and replace an existing mortgage. **(7)**

**registration certificate** Document from Real Estate Commission showing a time-share is properly registered. It must be obtained before marketing the property. **(16)**

**Reg B** Regulation through which the Federal Reserve Board implements the Equal Credit Opportunity Act.

**Regulation Z** Requirements issued by the Federal Reserve Board in implementing the Truth-in-Lending Law, which is a part of the Federal Consumer Credit Protection Act. **(7)**

**reject** To refuse to accept an offer; to kill the offer. **(6)**

**release clause** A provision in a mortgage to release certain properties from the mortgage lien when the principal is reduced by a specified amount. **(7)**

**release of liability** The procedure by which a mortgage holder agrees not to hold a borrower responsible for a mortgage on a property when that property has been bought by someone else who has assumed the seller's loan and the responsibility for it. **(7)**

**remainder** A future interest in a life estate. **(2)**

**remainderman** One having a future interest in a life estate. **(2)**

**remise** To release or give up. **(3)**

**replacement cost** The amount of money required to replace a structure with another structure of comparable utility. **(9)**

**replacement reserve** A fund to replace assets when they wear out. **(9)**

**repossession** Regaining possession of property as a result of a breach of contract by another. **(13)**

**reproduction cost** The amount of money required to build an exact duplicate of a structure. **(9)**

**rescission** Cancellation of a contract when another party is in default. **(6)**

**residential eviction remedies** Judicial eviction, also known as summary ejectment, is the only legal residential eviction remedy in North Carolina. **(10)**

**resident manager** A person employed to manage a building who lives on the premises. **(11)**

**residual income** The income allocated to the land under the principle of highest and best use. **(9)**

**residual method** A method used by the U.S. Department of Veteran Affairs to determine the veteran's ability to meet the financial obligations of his or her house payment. It is the residual income remaining after taxes, debts, and housing expenses are subtracted from gross income. **(7)**

**RESPA** *See* **Real Estate Settlement Procedures Act.**

**restrictive/protective covenants** Limitations on land use binding on all property owners. A form of private land use control. **(4)**

**retainer fee** A small monetary compensation paid by the buyer up front for an agent's services. **(6)**

**retaliatory eviction statute** The doctrine protecting a tenant from eviction for having asserted his or her rights. Provides an automatic defense for up to one year after such an event. **(10)**

**reverse mortgage** Mortgage allowing elderly homeowners to borrow against the equity in their homes to help meet living expenses while continuing to occupy their home. **(7)**

**reversionary interest** A return of title to the holder of a future interest, such as the grantor in a life estate not in remainder. **(2)**

**revocation** The withdrawal of an offer. **(6)**

**right of assignment** Allows lender to sell a loan at any time and obtain money invested rather than wait for completion of the loan term. **(7)**

**right of first refusal** A written agreement that provides for a potential buyer to have the first opportunity to purchase a property before it is offered to anyone else or to purchase the property on the same terms as an offer received from another offeror. This agreement may appear in a lease or in articles of association. It does not have to be in another document. It can stand on its own. The seller is not obligated to sell, but if he does, he must give the holder of this right, the first opportunity to purchase the property before it is offered to anyone else. **(6)**

**right of survivorship** The right of an owner to receive the title to a co-owner's share upon death of the co-owner, as in the case of joint tenancy and tenancy by the entirety. **(2)**

**riparian rights** The rights of an owner of property adjoining a watercourse such as a river, including access to and use of the water. **(2)**

**run with the land** Rights that move from grantor to grantee along with a title. **(4)**

**sale and leaseback** A transaction whereby an owner sells his or her property to an investor who immediately leases the property to the seller as agreed in the sales contract. **(10)**

**sales contract** An agreement between buyer and seller on the price and other terms and conditions of the sale of property. **(6)**

**savings and loan associations (S&Ls)** A major source of funds for financing residential real estate. **(7)**

**scarcity** In short supply in comparison with demand. **(1, 9)**

**secondary mortgage market** The market in which mortgages are sold by lenders. **(7)**

**second mortgage** One next in priority after a first mortgage. **(7)**

**section** An area of land described by the rectangular survey system consisting of 640 acres and being 1 mile square. **(3)**

**seisin** Possession of a freehold estate in land. **(3)**

**seizin** An alternative spelling of *seisin.* **(3)**

**separate ownership** Ownership in severalty by one spouse. **(2)**

**servient tenement** Land encumbered by an easement. **(2)**

**setback** The distance from a front or interior property line to the point where a structure can be located. **(4)**

**settlement** The consummation of a real estate contract. Also called closing. **(7)**

**Settlement Cost: A HUD Guide** A booklet explaining aspects of loan settlement required by RESPA. **(8)**

**settlement costs** Expenses paid by buyers and sellers at the time of consummation of a real estate sales contract. Also called closing costs. **(8)**

**severalty** A type of ownership or estate in which only one person holds title to a piece of real property. **(2)**

**sexual harassment** A unsolicited overt request or demand for sexual acts when submission to such conduct is a condition of the execution or continuation of a lease or the according of tenant's rights under a lease.

**Sherman Antitrust Act** A federal law that prohibits price fixing; in the case of real estate, it prohibits brokers to agree to charge certain rates of commission to listing sellers. **(6)**

**single entry** An item that appears as a debit or credit on either the buyer's or seller's closing statement, but not on both. **(8)**

**situs** Location of land. **(1)**

**soil evaluation test** An analysis of the absorbency of the soil to bear the output of a septic tank. **(8)**

**special agency** Limited authority to act on behalf of the principal, such as created by a listing. **(5)**

**special agent** One who is limited to a very narrow duty on behalf of his or her principal, e.g., as a real estate agent to find a buyer. **(6)**

**special assessment** A levy by a local government against real property for part of the cost of making an improvement to the property, such as paving streets, installing water lines, and making sidewalks. **(2)**

**special use** An exception, or special use, built into a zoning ordinance that must be granted if the criteria for the exception are met. **(4)**

**special warranty deed** A deed containing a limited warranty of title limited to the time the seller owned the property. **(3)**

**specific lien** One that attaches to one particular property only. **(2)**

**specific performance** An instruction of a court requiring a defaulting party to a contract to buy and sell real property to carry out his or her obligations under the contract. **(1)**

**spot zoning** The rezoning of a particular property in a zoned area to permit a use different from that authorized for the rest of the area. It is illegal unless there is a clearly established, reasonable basis for it. **(4)**

**square foot method** A technique to estimate the total cost of construction in which the total number of square feet to be constructed is multiplied by a cost per square foot to derive total cost. **(9)**

**stabilized budget** A forecast of income and expense as may be reasonably projected over a period of several years, prepared by a property manager. **(11)**

**statement of record** A document disclosing specific information that the developer must file with HUD before offering unimproved lots in interstate commerce by telephone or through the mail. **(4)**

**Statute of Frauds** A law in effect in all states requiring certain contracts to be in writing to be valid. **(3, 7)**

**statute of limitations** State laws establishing the time period within which certain lawsuits may be brought. **(2)**

**statutory redemption period** A statutory time period after a foreclosure sale during which the borrower may still redeem the title. **(7)**

**steering** The practice of directing prospective purchasers or tenants toward or away from specific neighborhoods because they belong to a protected class under the Fair Housing Act. **(12)**

**straight-line depreciation** A depreciation method whereby the property is depreciated in equal annual installments over the years of useful life. **(9)**

**strict foreclosure** A proceeding in which a court gives a borrower in default a specified time period to satisfy the debt to prevent transfer of the title to the mortgaged property to the lender. Illegal in North Carolina. **(7)**

**subagent** A person appointed by an agent to assist in performing some or all of the tasks of the agency. **(5)**

**subdivision regulation (ordinance)** Public control of the development of residential subdivisions. **(4)**

**subjacent support** The right to have one's land supported from below. **(2)**

**subject to a loan** A method of taking title to a property with a mortgage on it without becoming liable for the note payments. **(7)**

**sublet** The transfer of only part of a lease term with reversion to the lessee. **(10)**

**subordinate** Lower in priority. **(7)**

**substitution** The principle providing that the highest value of a property has a tendency to be established by the cost of purchasing or constructing another property of equal utility and desirability, provided the substitution could be made without unusual delay. **(9)**

**substitution of entitlement** The process by which one veteran pledges entitlement for a VA loan he or she is assuming in order to free up the entitlement of the original veteran/borrower. **(7)**

**success fee** Buyer's agent's compensation that may be received from the seller if the seller or seller's agent has offered compensation to the buyer's agent. **(6)**

**suit to quiet title** A suit brought before the court to eliminate a cloud on a title or to establish title (i.e., in an adverse possession claim). **(3)**

**supply and demand** The principle stating that the greater the supply of any commodity in comparison to demand, the lower the value. Conversely, the smaller the supply and the greater the demand, the higher the value. **(9)**

**survivorship** The right of the surviving co-owner(s) to receive automatically a deceased co-owner's title of property immediately without probate. **(2)**

**taking title subject to a mortgage** Accepting a title pledged to secure a mortgage and with no personal liability for the payment of the note. **(7)**

**taxable gain** The amount of profit or gain subject to tax (recognized gain minus applicable exclusion amount if any). **(13)**

**taxation** One of the four powers of government. The power of government to tax, among other things, real property. **(2)**

**tax basis** The value of property for income tax purposes; consists of original cost plus capital improvements less accrued depreciation. **(13)**

**tax-free exchange** Trading of like-kind properties held as an investment or for use in business. **(13)**

**Taxpayers Relief Act of 1997 (TRA 97)** Legislation that exempts from taxation profits on the sale of a personal residence of up to $500,000 for married couples filing jointly and $250,000 for singles. To qualify, sellers must have owned and used the home as their principal residence for at least two of the five years before the sale. **(13)**

**tax shelter** A method of tax avoidance such as protecting income from taxation by allowable depreciation. **(11)**

**tenancy by the entirety** A form of co-ownership limited to husband and wife with the right of survivorship. **(2)**

**tenancy in common** A form of co-ownership that does not include the right of survivorship. **(2)**

**tenant** Lessee. A person possessing real property with the owner's permission. **(10)**

**tenement** Land and all corporeal and incorporeal rights in land. **(2)**

**term loan** One that requires the borrower to pay interest only during the mortgage term with the principal due at the end of the term. **(7)**

**testate** To have died leaving a valid will. **(3)**

**testator** A man who has died and left a valid will. **(3)**

**testatrix** A woman who has died and left a valid will. **(3)**

**third party** The person or party in a transaction other than the principal and his or her agent. In a subagency relationship, the buyer is a third party; in a buyer's agency relationship, the seller is the third party. **(5)**

**time share** As defined by Article IV of the North Carolina Real Estate Law, a time share is the right to occupy one unit or one of several units, for at least five nonconsecutive periods, over a span of at least 5 years, whether it is deemed a freehold or leasehold estate. No matter what terminology is used to describe the arrangement, if it meets this definition, it is a time share. **(2)**

**title** Total body of facts or evidence on which ownership is based or approved. **(2)**

**title examination** A search of the public record to determine the quality of a title to real property. **(3)**

**title insurance** An insurance policy protecting the insured from a financial loss caused by a defect in a title to real property. **(3)**

**title theory** The legal theory followed in some states that a mortgage conveys a title to real property to secure the payment of a debt. **(7)**

**title transfer tax** A tax imposed on the conveyance of title to real property by deed. **(3)**

**Torrens System** A system of title recordation. **(3)**

**tort** A civil wrong by an agent for which the principal can be held accountable, i.e., negligence, misrepresentation, or fraud. **(5)**

**town house** A dwelling unit in a housing complex in which the owner or owners of an individual unit own the unit and land under the unit, and the homeowner's association owns and maintains the common areas. **(2)**

**tract** An area of land.

**trade fixtures** Items installed by a commercial tenant that are removable upon termination of the tenancy. **(2)**

**transferability** The ability to transfer property ownership from seller to buyer. **(9)**

**trapezoid** An area with two parallel sides and two nonparallel sides. **(16)**

**trespass** Unlawful entry on the land of another. **(2)**

**trust account** An account maintained by a real estate broker in an insured bank for the deposit of other people's money. Also called escrow account. **(5)**

**trust deed** *See* **deed of trust.**

**trustee** (a) One who holds title to property for the benefit of another called a beneficiary. **(7)** (b) Another name for an agent. **(5)**

**trustor** One who conveys title to a trustee. **(7)**

**Truth-in-Lending Law** *See* **Regulation Z. (7)**

**Truth-in-Lending Simplification and Reform Act (TILSRA)** Part of the Federal Consumer Credit Protection Act. It requires four chief disclosures: annual percentage rate, finance charge, amount financed, and total of payments. **(7)**

**undivided interest** Ownership of fractional parts not physically divided. **(2)**

**undue influence** Improper or wrongful influence by one party over another whereby the will of a person is overpowered so that he or she is induced to act or prevented from acting on free will. **(6)**

**Uniform Commercial Code (UCC)** A standardized and comprehensive set of commercial laws regulating security interests in personal property. **(2)**

**unilateral contract** An agreement wherein one party makes a promise of compensation to the other party and the second party returns an action in response to the promise, although he is not legally obligated to do so. **(6)**

**uninsured conventional loan** One in which the loan payment is not insured to protect the lender. **(7)**

**unintentional misrepresentation** An innocent false statement of a material fact. **(6)**

**unit in place method** The technique used in appraising real estate under the cost approach, in which the cost of replacement or reproduction is grouped by stages of construction. **(9)**

**universal agency** Complete authority over all activity of the principal. May be created by an unlimited power of attorney. **(5)**

**up-front mortgage insurance premium (UFMIP)** An insurance premium charged at the time an FHA loan is closed to insure the mortgage lender against default by the borrowers on an FHA loan. **(7)**

**useful life** The period of time that a property is expected to be economically useful. **(9)**

**usury** Charging a rate of interest higher than the rate allowed by law.

**utility** Capable of serving a useful purpose. **(9)**

**vacancy rate** A projected rate of the percentage of rental unit vacancies that will occur in a given year. **(11)**

**VA-guaranteed loan** A mortgage loan in which the loan payment is guaranteed to the lender by the Department of Veterans Affairs. **(7)**

**valid contract** An agreement that is legally binding and enforceable. **(6)**

**value** The amount of money (or goods) considered of equal worth to the subject property. There are many types of value, e.g., market value, book value, assessed value, and so on. **(9)**

**value in exchange** The amount of money a property may command for its exchange. This is the market value and is a negotiated value. **(9)**

**value in use** A subjective value that is not market value, derived from the usefulness of the property. **(9)**

**variance** A permitted deviation from specific requirements of a zoning ordinance because of the special hardship to a particular property owner. **(4)**

**vendee** Purchaser.

**vendor** Seller.

**void contract** An agreement that is absolutely unenforceable and has no legal force or effect. **(6)**

**voidable contract** One which appears valid, but may be avoided by one of the parties without legal consequences because it contains a defect. If the party who may avoid the contract based on the defect, does not identify the defect and takes action to avoid the contract, the contract is valid and enforceable. **(6)**

**voluntary alienation** The transfer of title freely by the owner. **(3)**

**waste** A violation of the right of estovers. **(2)**

**weighted average** In the direct sales comparison method of appraisal, reconciliation by giving more weight to comparables most similar to subject property. **(9)**

**will** The legal instrument to dispose of a decedent's property according to his or her instructions. *See* **devise, bequest. (3)**

**willful misrepresentation** A deliberate false statement concerning a material fact by one who knows the true fact and is responsible for disclosing it. **(5)**

**willful omission** A deliberate failure to inform a party of a known material fact when one has an obligation to that party to relay all material facts. **(5)**

**words of conveyance** Wording in a deed demonstrating the definite intention to convey a particular title to real property to a named grantee. **(3)**

**wraparound mortgage** A junior mortgage in an amount exceeding a first mortgage against the property and that encompasses that mortgage. **(7)**

**yield** The return on an investment. **(7)**

**zoning** A public law regulating land use. **(4)**

**zoning ordinance** A statement setting forth the type of use permitted under each zoning classification and specific requirements for compliance. **(4)**

# Index